Theory and Applications of Computability

In cooperation with the association Computability in Europe

Books published in this series will be of interest to the research community and graduate students, with a unique focus on issues of computability. The perspective of the series is multidisciplinary, recapturing the spirit of Turing by linking theoretical and real-world concerns from computer science, mathematics, biology, physics, and the philosophy of science.The series includes research monographs, advanced and graduate texts, and books that offer an original and informative view of computability and computational paradigms.

Friedrich Otto

Restarting Automata

The Standard Type of Restarting Automaton and Its Variants

Springer

Friedrich Otto
Computer Science
University of Kassel
Kassel, Germany

ISSN 2190-619X ISSN 2190-6203 (electronic)
Theory and Applications of Computability
ISBN 978-3-031-70093-4 ISBN 978-3-031-70094-1 (eBook)
https://doi.org/10.1007/978-3-031-70094-1

This Springer imprint is published by the registered company Springer Nature Switzerland AG
The registered company address is: Gewerbestrasse 11, 6330 Cham, Switzerland

Preface

The subject of this monograph are restarting automata. Motivated by the linguistic technique of 'analysis by reduction,' *Petr Jančar*, *František Mráz*, *Martin Plátek*, and *Jörg Vogel* presented the first type of the restarting automaton at the conference FCT 1995 in Dresden [85]. Similar to a Turing machine, a restarting automaton has a finite-state control, a tape that initially contains the input, and a read/write head that works on that tape. However, as for a linear bounded automaton (see, e.g., [81]), the length of the tape of a restarting automaton is bounded by the length of the input, where two particular letters called *sentinels* are used to mark the beginning and the end of the tape. In addition, a look-ahead of finite size $k-1$ is attached to the read/write head, which means that, at any moment, the restarting automaton sees a factor of length k of the current contents of its tape. Finally, and most importantly, a restarting automaton, as defined in [85], restarts as soon as it executes a rewrite operation, that is, the head jumps back to the left sentinel and the finite-state control is reset to the initial state. Moreover, each rewrite operation simply deletes one or more letters, that is, the factor of length k under the read/write head and inside the look-ahead is reduced to a word which is of length at most $k-1$, and the length of the tape is shortened correspondingly. Thus, the tape can either be viewed as being flexible, or it can be interpreted as a doubly linked list of letters.

Subsequently, many variants of the restarting automaton have been defined and studied. In particular, proper length-reducing rewrite operations have replaced the original delete steps, additional non-input letters, called *auxiliary letters*, have been added to the alphabet, and the original combined rewrite/restart operation has been split into a rewrite operation and a separate restart operation. The first comprehensive presentation of this early development can be found in František Mráz's PhD thesis [156].

As explained in the first papers on this topic (see, e.g., [85, 86, 87]), the definition of the restarting automaton was motivated by the linguistic technique of *analysis by reduction*. This technique, which can be used to analyze sentences in natural languages with a rather free word order like Czech (or Latin or German), consists of a sequence of step-by-step simplifications of a given sentence. Each of these simplifications is realized by a single reduction operation, which consists of either the deletion of one or several words from that sentence or the replacement of a (possibly discontinuous) substring of that sentence by a shorter substring. It is required that each application of such a reduction operation must preserve the syntactical correctness of the sentence. In Section 1.8, a detailed example is given, although for a sentence in English.

From the motivation through the analysis by reduction, it follows that the restarting automaton is not a specific type of automaton, but that it is rather a family of various types of automata that are specified through several parameters (see Definition 1.9.18). In Chapter 2, the influence of the various parameters on the expressive capacity of the resulting types of restarting automata is studied in detail. It has been a significant objective for this monograph to collect all these results in one place and to present them in a uniform way. Other topics presented include the descriptional complexity of restarting automata, which is discussed in Chapter 3, and the inductive inference of restarting automata (Chapter 4). Advanced notions and extensions of the standard type of the restarting automaton like cooperating distributed and parallel communicating systems of restarting automata, restarting automata that produce output, and restarting automata for picture languages and for tree languages are the topics for the second volume of this monograph.

The author became interested in restarting automata in 1999, when, in cooperation with his doctoral student Gundula Niemann, he succeeded in characterizing the Church-Rosser languages through a particular type of deterministic restarting automaton [183]. Then, at the conference DLT 2001 in Vienna, he met František Mráz. This meeting instigated a very fruitful cooperation that is still ongoing. In fact, in 2005, František Mráz spent four months at the University of Kassel, supported by a grant from the Deutsche Forschungsgemeinschaft, and the author has been visiting the Faculty of Mathematics and Physics of Charles University in Prague on numerous occasions.

This monograph would not have been possible without all those colleagues and students of mine who have worked on restarting automata and who have most willingly shared their results and insights with me. Foremost, I have to thank my colleagues from Charles University in Prague, Iveta Mrázová, František Mráz, and Martin Plátek and their students, Peter Černo and Petr Hoffmann, for their hospitality and their willingness to discuss their work with me. Moreover, I'm indebted to Tomasz Jurdziński from the University of Wrocław, Daniel Průša from the Czech Technical University in Prague, to Martin Kutrib, Markus Holzer, Andreas Malcher, Jens Reimann, and Matthias Wendlandt from the University of Giessen, to Peter Leupold, now living in Tarragona, to Benedek Nagy, now at the Eastern Mediterranean University at Famagusta, North Cyprus, and to my doctoral students at the University of Kassel, Norbert Hundeshagen, Kent Kwee, Hartmut Messerschmidt, Gundula Niemann, Heiko Stamer, Marcel Vollweiler, and Qichao Wang. Last, but not least, I'm most thankful to my wife, Donata Golla, and my daughter Laura and my son René-Pascal for their patience with me while I was working on this monograph and for their emotional support.

Friedrich Otto
Kaufungen

Contents

Introduction

Modern *Formal Language and Automata Theory* has many sources in Mathematics, Biology, and Linguistics. In response to David Hilbert's famous list of mathematical problems [69], Kurt Gödel established the incompleteness of arithmetic [53] and Alan Turing, formalizing the notions of algorithm and computation, proved that there are functions that are not computable [251]. This means, in particular, that there are sets of words (that is, languages) for which membership cannot be decided algorithmically. As a consequence, much work concentrated since then on identifying means to define and to characterize classes of functions that are computable and classes of languages that are decidable. In 1936, Stephen Kleene presented the general recursive functions [108], and later he characterized the class of languages that can be presented by so-called regular expressions through finite-state acceptors [109] (see [110]).

Concerning the influence of biology on Formal Language Theory, at least three sources should be mentioned. First of all, Aristid Lindenmayer introduced formal systems to describe the growth of filamentous organisms [141, 142, 143]. As the growth of such organisms is a dynamic process that is highly parallel, these formal systems, nowadays known as *L-systems*, specify the development of (formalized) organisms through concurrent and repeated applications of a group of morphisms to all letters of a given word. In this way, a set of words, that is, a language, is generated from an initial word. For a survey on the theory of L-systems, we refer to the article [105] by Lila Kari, Grzegorz Rozenberg, and Arto Salomaa. Secondly, by modelling double-stranded DNA molecules as words on a four-letter alphabet and activities on these molecules that are induced by certain enzymes through an operation called *splicing*, Tom Head introduced the so-called *splicing systems* [65]. Such a system describes a language through a multi-set of words that develops dynamically through repeated applications of the operation of splicing (see also [216]). This initiated what is now known as *DNA computing* [26]. Thirdly, Gheorghe Păun established the field of *membrane computing* [215]. Here a finite hierarchical system of areas called *membranes* that each contain a multi-set of elements (that is, numbers or words) is used to generate a set of numbers or words. With each membrane in a membrane system (or *P-system*), a set of rules is associated that describe how the elements in that membrane develop and/or pass into an inner or outer membrane. In addition, membranes may be newly generated inside a given membrane, or a membrane may dissolve, which means that not only the sets of objects inside the structure but also the structure itself develops dynamically (see [26]).

In this monograph, however, we focus on the influence of linguistics on the development of Formal Language Theory. In [27], Noam Chomsky studied several formal methods for describing linguistic structures in order to determine whether they can provide simple and revealing grammars for English. One of these methods is the so-called *phrase-structure grammar*, which is motivated by the syntactic description of the sentences of a language in terms of 'immediate constituent analysis.' In such a description, the words of a given sentence are grouped into phrases, which are then repeatedly grouped into smaller constituent phrases until finally the ultimate constituents are reached. These phrases are then classified as noun phrases (NP), verb phrases (VP), etc., in this way providing information on the structure of the sentence in terms of these constituents. As it turned out, the general phrase-structure grammars (or phrase-structure grammars of type 0) lead to the class of recursively enumerable languages, that is, those languages for which there exist Turing machines that, starting from an initial configuration corresponding to an input word w, will eventually halt if and only if the word w belongs to the language considered. By placing stronger and stronger restrictions on the productions of a phrase-structure grammar, the grammars of types 1, 2, and 3 are obtained that generate the context-sensitive languages, the context-free languages, and the regular languages, respectively. These classes of languages, which constitute the famous *Chomsky hierarchy*, have also been characterized by various restricted variants of the Turing machine, where the access of the machine to its tape is limited in various ways. In addition, numerous results on closure and non-closure under various operations have been established for the classes of the Chomsky hierarchy. In order to establish notation and to collect the relevant results, we present the Chomsky hierarchy in Section 1.2 together with a number of closely related language classes.

The decidability or undecidability of basic decision problems like the membership problem, the emptiness problem, the finiteness problem, or the equivalence problem have been established for the classes of the Chomsky hierarchy (see, e.g., [81]). Also, initiated by the seminal paper [63] of Juris Hartmanis and Richard E. Stearns, the computational complexity of these problems has been studied in detail. While the membership problem for context-free languages is decidable in polynomial time, it turned out that there are already context-sensitive languages for which this problem is intractable. Accordingly, the context-free languages and the regular languages have found numerous applications in various areas of computer science due to their many nice properties. In Section 1.4, we restate some of these results in short.

While Noam Chomsky's phrase-structure grammars had (and still have) a large impact on the development of (theoretical) computer science, the original goal of describing linguistic structures in order to provide simple and revealing grammars for English was not achieved. In fact, as argued by Stuart M. Shieber in [245], natural languages are not context-free. In Section 1.5, some arguments supporting this view are summarized. As a consequence, many other devices for generating (or accepting) languages have been developed.

In 1969, Solomon Marcus introduced the so-called *contextual grammars*, which exploit the fundamental concepts of simple sentences and contexts from linguistics [147] (see, also, [214]). The basic idea is the following. A (natural) language L contains certain simple sentences that are generally accepted by any native speaker of that language as being correct sentences. Accordingly, one can assume that there is a finite set L_0 of such simple sentences which can then be taken as a starting point for L. Next, one may choose a set C of pairs of words (u, v), called *contexts*, and rules of how to extend sentences from L_0 by adjoining contexts, that is, if the sentence w from L_0 can be factored as $w = xyz$ and if (u, v) is a fitting context, then the word $xuyvz$ is another (more complicated) sentence from L. In this way, the basic set L_0 is extended to a larger subset L_1 of the language L. By iterating this process, a set $\hat{L}$ is obtained, which is characterized by the conditions that every sentence from L_0 belongs to $\hat{L}$, and for every sentence $w = xyz \in \hat{L}$ and every applicable context (u, v), also the sentence $xuyvz$ belongs to $\hat{L}$. By choosing the basic set L_0 and the set of contexts C in an appropriate way, the resulting language $\hat{L}$ coincides with (or is a close approximation of) the language L.

By putting restrictions on the set of contexts admitted and on the way in which contexts are adjoined, different types of contextual grammars and languages are obtained. Based on the survey paper by Andrzej Ehrenfeucht, Gheorghe Păun, and Grzegorz Rozenberg [43], we describe contextual grammars and languages in Section 1.3 and outline some fundamental results on them. In particular, we shall see that most classes of contextual languages considered are incomparable to the class of context-free languages with respect to inclusion.

Abstracting from a particular way of generating languages, the notion of a mildly context-sensitive family of languages has been coined by Aravind K. Joshi in [90]. In short, a class $\mathcal{L}$ of languages is called *mildly context-sensitive* if it contains all context-free languages, if it contains certain non-context-free languages, if the membership problem for each language in $\mathcal{L}$ is decidable in polynomial time, and if the languages in $\mathcal{L}$ satisfy a certain growth property (see Definition 1.5.3 for details). Many formalisms have been presented that define families of mildly context-sensitive languages. The first one is the notion of *tree adjoining grammars*, introduced in [91]. A derivation in a context-free grammar can be depicted in the form of a *syntax tree*, where each derivational step corresponds to the replacement of a leaf of that tree which is labeled with a nonterminal X by a tree that corresponds to the right-hand side of a production with left-hand side X. Now the tree adjoining grammars generalize this process by allowing the replacement of inner (non-leaf) nodes by trees. In Section 1.5, we describe the tree adjoining grammars in short.

Similar to syntactic structures based on constituents, syntactic descriptions based on the notion of *dependency* have a long tradition in linguistics, particularly in Eastern Europe (see, e.g., the survey by Alexander Dikovsky and Larissa Modina [41]). Dependencies are expressed explicitly as binary relations between word forms. Essentially, a sentence is represented by a *dependency tree*, in which the word forms occur as (labels of) nodes and the various dependency relations are expressed by edges. In comparison to syntax trees or constituent trees, dependency trees have the advantage of being more succinct, explicit, and expressive. In addition, they are also invariant with respect to the word order, which is important for languages with a rather 'free word order' like Czech, Russian, or Latin. We consider dependency structures in Section 1.6 and address free word order languages in Section 1.7.

A particular technique for analyzing a given sentence of a natural language is the so-called *analysis by reduction*, which, by performing a step-by-step simplification of the sentence, discovers dependencies and independencies between the various word forms and constructs a dependency tree for that sentence [243] (see also [145]). An analysis by reduction of a given sentence consists of a sequence of step-by-step simplifications of that sentence. Each simplification is realized by a single *reduction operation*, which consists of either the deletion of one or several word forms from the given sentence or the replacement of a (possibly discontinuous) substring of the given sentence by a shorter substring. Each application of such a reduction preserves the syntactical correctness of the sentence.

By looking at all possible sequences of reductions, a *reduction scheme* is obtained. From such a reduction scheme, a dependency tree for the corresponding sentence can be derived, where a word form u *depends on* a word form v, if along each path in the reduction scheme, u is deleted *before* v, and two word forms u and v are *mutually independent* if there are paths in the reduction scheme such that along one of them, u is removed before v, while along the other one, v is removed before u. Finally, if the given sentence is not syntactically correct, the step-by-step simplification continues until the core of an error is detected eventually.

In order to perform the simplifications of an analysis by reduction on a given sentence of a natural language, one must be able to understand the meaning of that sentence. This prerequisite, which is easily fulfilled by a native speaker of the corresponding language, cannot be satisfied by an automated system for language analysis or translation. In fact, for such a system, the syntactic analysis of a given sentence, as realized by the analysis by reduction, constitutes the first part of its sentence analysis. Therefore, such a system requires additional morphological, syntactical, and semantical information on the word forms of the given sentence (see, e.g., [145]). Such information can be provided by tagging the word forms of the sentence, that is, to each word form, a finite sequence of *tags* is added that give morphological, syntactical, or semantical information on that word form, producing a fully disambiguated form of the given sentence. We illustrate the technique of analysis by reduction using several simple examples in Section 1.8.

To model the analysis by reduction, Petr Jančar, František Mráz, Martin Plátek, and Jörg Vogel presented a new type of automaton, which they called *restarting automaton*, at the conference FCT 1995 in Dresden [85]. As defined in that paper, a restarting automaton consists of a finite-state control, a finite tape that initially contains the input and which is bordered on the left by the sentinel $\rhd$ and on the right by the sentinel $\lhd$, and a read/write window of a fixed finite size $k \geq 1$. This type of automaton differs from the Turing machine (or, rather, the *linear-bounded automaton*) in three important aspects:

- A restarting automaton works in *cycles*, where in each cycle, it scans the tape from left to right until it detects a position at which it is to apply a delete/restart operation. A delete/restart operation removes one or more letters from the contents of the window and restarts the automaton, which means that the window is repositioned at the left end of the tape.

- The tape of a restarting automaton is *flexible*, that is, it adjusts to the length of the tape inscription. Thus, whenever one or more letters are removed during a delete/restart step, then the tape is shortened accordingly.

- By a delete/restart step, the finite-state control is reset to the initial state, that is, all the information that the restarting automaton may have collected in its finite-state control while scanning the tape from left to right is forgotten during a delete/restart step.

Despite these limitations, the deterministic variant of the (above type of) restarting automaton, which is called an R-*automaton*, accepts a proper superset of the deterministic context-free languages, while the nondeterministic variant is even more expressive. However, the latter is not sufficient to accept all context-free languages. Therefore, in subsequent papers, Petr Jančar, František Mráz, Martin Plátek, and Jörg Vogel extended the restarting automaton in several ways:

- The delete/restart operation was generalized to a rewrite/restart operation in that, instead of simply deleting one or more letters, the contents of the window is rewritten into a shorter word [86].

- In addition to the input alphabet, a finite set of so-called *auxiliary letters* was introduced that can be used in rewrite steps [87].

- The combined rewrite/restart operation was split into a rewrite operation and a separate restart operation. Thus, after executing a rewrite step, such an automaton can still keep on reading its tape until it finally executes a restart step.

Through these generalizations, a type of restarting automaton, called RRWW-*automaton*, was obtained that accepts a superclass of the context-free languages [87]. Observe that the auxiliary letters provide a means to model the operation of tagging an input sentence. Furthermore, in addition to the input language of an RRWW-automaton, we can also consider its *characteristic language*. The characteristic language consists of all words over the tape alphabet (that is, input letters and auxiliary letters) that are accepted by the automaton. Subsequently, many additional variants and extensions of the restarting automaton were introduced and studied (see, e.g., [192, 193]). In fact, the restarting automaton has also been extended to models that process rectangular arrays of letters, that is, picture languages [196], and to models that process ranked trees, that is, tree languages [247].

In this monograph, we present most of the various types of restarting automata from the literature in a uniform way and relate them to each other and to the types of automata and languages traditionally studied in Formal Language Theory. In order to achieve a uniform presentation of the various types of restarting automata, we regard the restarting automaton as a family of automata that are specified through several parameters (see Definition 1.9.18):

- the size of the read/write window,

- the number of states,

- the number of auxiliary letters,

- the set of admitted operations,

- the number of rewrite steps that may be executed within a cycle (that is, between two subsequent restart steps).

By varying the values of these parameters, we obtain a rich collection of types of restarting automata and of the corresponding classes of languages.

Without further restrictions, the restarting automaton is a universal computing device (see Theorem 1.9.11). In order to limit the expressive capacity of the restarting automaton, we place a general restriction on the rewrite operations that are allowed for any type of restarting automaton in that we require that each rewrite operation must be *weight-reducing*, that is, for each restarting automaton, there exists a weight function such that each rewrite operation replaces the window contents with a word of strictly smaller weight (see Definition 1.9.12). This restriction implies that the overall number of rewrite steps in any computation is bounded linearly in the length of the input. In addition, it guarantees that the class of languages that are accepted by any given type of restarting automaton is a subclass of the class CSL of context-sensitive languages.

In Section 1.9, we provide a detailed definition of the restarting automaton, explain its workings, and present some examples. In particular, we introduce the *Error Preserving Property* and the *Correctness Preserving Property* for restarting automata. The former expresses the fact that a restarting automaton always transforms a syntactically incorrect sentence into a syntactically incorrect sentence (Proposition 1.9.6), while the latter says that a deterministic restarting automaton always transforms a syntactically correct sentence into a syntactically correct sentence (Proposition 1.9.8). Moreover, this section contains an overview of the major characterizations of the classes of an extended Chomsky hierarchy through various types of restarting automata (see Figure 1.12). These results are presented without proofs, but references to the original papers are provided. In addition, detailed outlines of most proofs can be found in Chapter 2.

The main part of volume I of this monograph, which comprises three chapters, is structured as follows.

Chapter 2 is devoted to the influence of the various parameters mentioned above on the expressive capacity of the restarting automaton. As such, it constitutes the central part of the monograph. In Section 2.1, we consider those types of restarting automata that were initially defined by Petr Jančar, František Mráz, Martin Plátek, and Jörg Vogel. All these types have in common that they execute exactly one rewrite step in each cycle, and that this rewrite step must be length-reducing. They differ in the type of move operations allowed and with respect to the use of auxiliary letters. Moreover, we also consider the extension to the corresponding types of weight-reducing restarting automata, admitting rewrite steps that are not necessarily length-reducing, but that are weight-reducing with respect to some weight function.

Interestingly, for nondeterministic types of restarting automata, the option of being able to use move-left steps does not increase the expressive capacity (Corollaries 2.1.3 and 2.1.4), while for deterministic types of restarting automata, this option is important (see Theorems 1.9.24 and 1.9.25). Moreover, the use of auxiliary letters by a type of restarting automaton corresponds to the closure of the corresponding class of languages under the operation of intersection with regular languages (Theorem 2.1.11). Furthermore, we study restarting automata that are *weakly monotone* or even *monotone*. These notions of monotonicity place restrictions on the form of the computations that a restarting automaton may execute, in this way restricting its expressive capacity. Various types of weakly monotone restarting automata characterize the class GCSL of growing context-sensitive languages (Corollary 2.1.33), whereas the corresponding types of monotone restarting automata characterize the class CFL of context-free languages (Corollary 2.1.41). An overview of the various characterizations of the lower classes of an extended Chomsky hierarchy by certain types of weight-reducing restarting automata is provided in Figure 2.3.

In Section 2.2, we study the influence of the number of auxiliary letters on the expressive capacity of a restarting automaton. First, in Subsection 2.2.1, we consider various types of restarting automata that have no auxiliary letters at all. For certain deterministic types of restarting automata that are monotone (or *left-monotone*), it turns out that the same language classes are obtained no matter whether auxiliary letters are available or not. We then concentrate on nondeterministic types of restarting automata and on deterministic non-monotone types. By providing a sequence of particular example languages, we prove that, for these types of restarting automata, the absence of auxiliary letters restricts their expressive capacity considerably. In fact, we present detailed hierarchies of language classes that are obtained from the various types of restarting automata without auxiliary letters. The complete taxonomy of restarting automata without auxiliary letters is presented in Figure 2.8.

At the end of Subsection 2.2.1, we also discuss the so-called *clearing restarting automaton*, which is a type of restarting automaton without auxiliary letters and without states that is specified through a finite set of so-called *rewrite instructions*. Such a rewrite instruction provides a delete operation that is controlled by a context of limited size. This type of restarting automaton was introduced by Peter Černo and František Mráz in [257, 258] in connection with a study on inductive inference ('automated learning') of restarting automata, a topic that we address in Chapter 4. These clearing restarting automata induce an infinite strictly ascending hierarchy of language classes based on the size of the contexts admitted in their rewrite instructions (Theorem 2.2.36). They accept all regular languages and even some languages that are not context-free, but they do not even accept all deterministic context-free languages.

Then, in Subsection 2.2.2, we look at restarting automata with just a single auxiliary letter, where we first consider the so-called *Δ-clearing restarting automaton* and the *Δ^*-clearing restarting automaton*. These types of restarting automata are obtained from the clearing restarting automaton by admitting a single auxiliary letter Δ and instructions that rewrite input letters into occurrences of this auxiliary letter. They are sufficiently expressive to accept all context-free languages (Theorem 2.2.45). The taxonomy of the various types of clearing restarting automata is depicted in Figure 2.9.

Finally, in Subsection 2.2.3, we present some results on restarting automata that make very efficient use of their auxiliary letters. Actually, we consider two types of restrictions simultaneously: the number of auxiliary letters in the tape alphabet, which can be viewed as a measure of the *descriptional complexity* of a restarting automaton, and the number of occurrences of auxiliary letters on the tape during a computation, which can be viewed as a *dynamic* complexity measure. It is shown that each *k-linear language* is accepted by a restarting automaton that uses at most two occurrences of a single auxiliary letter during a computation (Theorem 2.2.65). On the other hand, to accept all context-free languages, a non-constant sublinear number of occurrences of auxiliary letters in computations is required (Corollary 2.2.60). The inclusion relations concerning the utilization of auxiliary letters are summarized in Figure 2.10.

In Section 2.3, we study the influence that the size of the read/write window has on the expressive capacity of the various types of restarting automata. First, we consider the case of restarting automata without auxiliary letters. Here it is rather easy to see that, for each type of restarting automaton, the window size induces an infinite strictly ascending hierarchy of language classes (Corollary 2.3.3). Then we explore the expressive capacity of those restarting automata without auxiliary letters that have a fixed window size $k \geq 1$. As it turns out, several rather restricted types of restarting automata with window size one accept just the regular languages, that is, they are equivalent to finite-state acceptors. The taxonomy of restarting automata without auxiliary letters and window size one or two is depicted in Figure 2.11 and, for $k \geq 5$, the taxonomy of restarting automata without auxiliary letters and window size k is depicted in Figure 2.14. For the intermediate cases of window size $k = 3$ and $k = 4$, the known results are summarized in Figure 2.12, but here several inclusion relations are still open.

Next, in Subsection 2.3.2, we investigate the influence that the window size has on the expressive capacity of certain types of length-reducing restarting automata with auxiliary letters. Here it turns out that window size two is sufficient for monotone types of restarting automata, both in the nondeterministic case (Corollary 2.3.42) as well as in the deterministic case (Corollary 2.3.46). For weight-reducing restarting automata with separate rewrite and restart instructions (that is, restarting automata of type sRRWW), even window size one suffices (Subsection 2.3.3), as this type of restarting automaton is equivalent to the so-called *finite-change automaton* that was introduced by Burchard von Braunmühl and Rutger Verbeek in [262]. In the special case of (weakly) monotone and/or deterministic automata, window size two again yields the full expressive capacity of the corresponding type of restarting automaton.

Then, in Subsection 2.3.4, we consider some types of restarting automata that are known as 'ordered restarting automata.' These types of restarting automata, which have been studied in detail by Kent Kwee in his doctoral dissertation [129], are particular weight-reducing restarting automata with a window of size three that, however, in each rewrite step, just replace the letter in the middle of the window with another, smaller letter (that is, a letter with less weight). This means, in particular, that the length of the tape remains fixed during a computation. The deterministic ordered restarting automaton yields another characterization for the regular languages, while the nondeterministic variant accepts a class of languages that is incomparable to the classes of (deterministic) context-free and growing context-sensitive languages with respect to inclusion. By introducing an additional delete operation that simply removes the letter in the middle of the window, we obtain the so-called 'ordered restart-delete automaton.' The deterministic variant of this type of restarting automaton has a much larger expressive capacity than the ordered restarting automaton as it accepts a proper superclass of the deterministic context-free languages. Finally, in Subsection 2.3.5, various restricted types of weight-reducing restarting automata of window size one are studied. The taxonomy of (weight-reducing) restarting automata with small window size, including the various types of ordered restarting automata, is depicted in Figure 2.15.

In Section 2.4, we investigate the expressive capacity of restarting automata that have a single state only. As such an automaton cannot change its state, we can ignore the state altogether and speak of *stateless* restarting automata. In Subsection 2.4.1, we consider the stateless variants of those types of restarting automata with a combined rewrite/restart step (that is, sRWW-automata). Not surprisingly, the stateless variants are, in general, less expressive than the corresponding variants with states. However, this only holds for most of those types of restarting automata that do not admit auxiliary letters. The characterizations of the classes of (deterministic) context-free languages, Church-Rosser languages, and growing context-sensitive languages through certain restricted types of sRWW-automata with auxiliary letters, as described in Section 1.9, carry over to the stateless variants of the corresponding types of restarting automata. In these cases, the option of using auxiliary letters in rewrite steps makes up for the absence of states. The inclusion relations between the language classes that are defined by the various types of stateless sRWW-automata are summarized in Figure 2.16.

Next, we concentrate on one of the most restricted types of restarting automaton, the *stateless deterministic R-automaton.* With window size one, these automata just accept a very simple proper subclass of the regular languages, but the window size induces a strictly ascending infinite hierarchy of language classes within the Church-Rosser languages that is incomparable to the class of regular languages with respect to inclusion (Figure 2.17). Then, in Subsection 2.4.2, we study the effect of the restriction to a single state on restarting automata that, after executing a rewrite step, may continue to read their tape before performing a restart. These are the so-called *stateless sRRWW-automata* and their variants. Thus, even after executing a rewrite operation, such an automaton still has the option of accepting or rejecting instead of performing a restart. As also such an automaton must only execute a single rewrite step in each cycle, we assume that it can distinguish between the part of a cycle *before* a rewrite step and the part *after* a rewrite step. It turns out that, in the presence of auxiliary letters, the stateless restarting automata of this form that are deterministic and/or monotone have the same expressive capacity as the corresponding types of restarting automata with states.

In Section 2.5, we study the influence of the number of rewrite steps executed within a single cycle on the expressive capacity of the various types of restarting automata. For each type of restarting automaton without auxiliary letters, the number of allowed rewrites per cycle induces an infinite strictly ascending hierarchy of language classes (Proposition 2.5.3). However, for weight-reducing restarting automata with auxiliary letters, the number of allowed rewrites per cycle does not influence the expressive capacity at all. For these automata, even admitting an unbounded number of rewrites per cycle does not increase their expressive capacity (Corollary 2.5.7).

Then we focus on *constrained computations* of restarting automata. In natural languages with a high degree of word order freedom, syntactic phenomena like dependencies (subordinations) or valences do not depend on the word order (that is, on the individual positions of the individual words). This means that some permutations of sentences from these languages are in some (important) sense syntactically equivalent. Here we consider this phenomenon in a formal way. Various types of j-monotonicity for restarting automata can serve as parameters for the degree of word order freedom and for the complexity of the word order in sentences (languages). We combine the degree of j-monotonicity and the number of rewrites per cycle, which leads to the notion of *j-constrained computations.* By studying this notion formally, we obtain an adequate tool for modelling and comparing formal descriptions of (natural) languages with different degrees of word order freedom and word order complexity. Actually, we concentrate on characteristic languages (that is, on types of restarting automata without auxiliary letters) as the full analysis by reduction is applied to tagged sentences.

Then, in Subsection 2.5.3, we relate restarting automata of type RR (that is, automata that can only delete letters but that have separate rewrite (that is, delete) and restart steps), which may execute up to t delete steps per cycle, to t-contextual languages with regular selection (see Section 1.3). We introduce an additional locality restriction for the latter, which yields a correspondence to RR-automata that execute a single delete step of *cut-index* t within each cycle. Such a delete step removes exactly t factors from the current contents of the window. As it turns out, the cut-index induces strictly ascending infinite hierarchies of language classes for deterministic and nondeterministic R- and RR-automata.

In the fourth subsection of Section 2.5, we finally turn to a restricted class of restarting automata that have two windows. This model is motivated by the phenomenon of *long-distance scrambling*, which induces a dependency between items across a large distance. Certainly, two independent heads or windows can help in this matter. In fact, in [55], an ad-hoc variant of the restarting automaton is defined that has two windows: one window can only delete a single letter in a rewrite step, while the other window may rewrite a non-empty word into a word of length at most one. It is shown in [55] that a certain restricted type of these restarting automata corresponds to *sorted dependency insertion grammars with regular selectors* that work in a top-down derivation style. Here we present a rather restricted type of restarting automaton with two windows, called *det-2-RR-automaton*. Such an automaton is deterministic, and the rewrite operations that it can perform are only deletions. In addition, we require that within a cycle, each of the two windows executes at most one such operation. It is shown that the window size induces an infinite strictly ascending hierarchy of language classes for det-2-RR-automata. The relations between the classes of this hierarchy and the classes of the Chomsky hierarchy are depicted in Figure 2.19.

Chapter 2 is completed by Section 2.6. So far, we have used auxiliary letters quite freely to encode information about computations of restarting automata without much regard for their linguistic motivation. Here we study two extensions of the restarting automaton that yield a closer relationship between auxiliary letters and characteristic languages on the one hand and input letters and languages on the other hand. In Subsection 2.6.1, we formalize the analysis by reduction by using deterministic restarting automata for *proper languages*. These automata work on *characteristic languages*, that is, on languages that include auxiliary letters (categories) in addition to the input letters. The *proper language* is obtained from a characteristic language by removing all auxiliary letters from its words (sentences). By requiring that the automata considered are *lexicalized*, we then restrict the lengths of the blocks of auxiliary letters that are allowed on the tape by a constant. This restriction is quite natural from a linguistic point of view, as these blocks of auxiliary letters model the meta-language categories from individual linguistic layers with which an input word is being enriched when its disambiguated form is being produced. We use deterministic restarting automata in order to ensure the *correctness preserving property* for the analysis. In fact, we also concentrate on *strongly lexicalized* restarting automata. This additional restriction requires that all rewrite operations must be deletions. Observe that a proper language is much more closely related to the characteristic language of a restarting automaton than the input language, as it contains the projections of all words from the characteristic language, that is, each word from the characteristic language contributes to the proper language. In Figures 2.20 and 2.21, we depict the inclusion relations that we obtain between the classes of proper languages that are defined by various types of lexicalized length-reducing restarting automata.

In Subsection 2.6.2, we study *h-lexicalized* restarting automata. For an h-lexicalized restarting automaton, each auxiliary letter is closely connected to an input letter by a morphism that maps each auxiliary letter to an input letter. In this way, each auxiliary letter can be interpreted as a pair that consists of an input letter and some additional information (tags). Now the *h-proper language* of an h-lexicalized restarting automaton is obtained from the characteristic language of that automaton by replacing each occurrence of an auxiliary letter with an occurrence of its associated input letter. This implies that all words from the characteristic language that occur within an accepting computation of an h-lexicalized restarting automaton contribute to the h-proper language of that automaton.

Additionally, the constraint of *strong cyclic form* is considered for h-lexicalized restarting automata. The strong cyclic form requires that acceptance and rejection are only possible for short words, that is, a restarting automaton must first reduce a given word into a short word by executing a sequence of cycles before it can accept or reject. We also introduce a constraint that bounds the number of cycles in accepting computations of restarting automata. Based on this constraint and the strong cyclic form, it is possible to extend the complexity results that are obtained for classes of infinite languages even to classes of finite languages. This is quite useful for the formulation of techniques for the localization of syntactic errors. Recall that in Formal Language Theory, one is mainly concerned with the structure of infinite languages. In fact, finite languages are mainly considered to be trivial in Formal Language Theory, as they can simply be described by enumerating their elements. In fact, the class of finite languages is already a proper subclass of the regular languages. In traditional and corpus linguistics, however, only finite language phenomena can be directly observed. Accordingly, it is quite difficult to directly apply techniques and results from Formal Language Theory in a linguistic setting. Now in combination with the strong cyclic form, the restriction on the number of allowed cycles in accepting computations allows us to carry results on restarting automata over to classes of finite languages. Figure 2.22 depicts the resulting two-dimensional hierarchy of language classes. By requiring that the RLWWC-automata considered are only allowed to execute a bounded number of cycles in each accepting computation, corresponding two-dimensional hierarchies are obtained for the resulting classes of h-proper languages and lexicalized analyses. It follows from Lemma 2.6.42 that the h-proper languages of the latter automata are finite. Thus, the characteristic and the h-proper languages of hRLWWC-automata in strong cyclic form allow common classifications of finite phenomena as well as classifications of their infinite relaxations. As for restarting automata, monotonicity is a synonym for context-freeness, we are also able to distinguish degrees of monotonicity not only for infinite languages, but also for finite languages.

Finally, as pointed out in Section 1.5, context-free languages are neither sufficient nor adequate for modelling natural languages. Therefore, other, more expressive formalizations have been proposed in the literature. Among these are the so-called 'mildly context-sensitive languages' (see Definition 1.5.3) that have received much attention. In Theorem 2.6.53, we relate a class of h-proper languages of rather restricted restarting automata in the strong cyclic form to the concept of mildly context-sensitive languages.

In summary, Chapter 2 shows that, through the process of varying the miscellaneous parameters of the restarting automaton, we obtain a rather rich universe of types of automata and the corresponding classes of languages. Some of these types of restarting automata nicely correspond to certain important classes of the (extended) Chomsky hierarchy, while others are well adopted to model the linguistic technique of analysis by reduction.

In the remaining chapters of the present monograph, several other important aspects of the work on restarting automata are presented.

In Chapter 3, we discuss the *descriptional complexity* of various types of restarting automata, both in relation to finite-state acceptors and in relation to other types of restarting automata. First, we investigate this topic for some types of restarting automata that characterize the class of regular languages. In Section 3.1, nondeterministic R-automata and deterministic RR-automata with window size one are considered, which both are known to characterize the regular languages. Accordingly, we compare the size of a description of an R- or a deterministic RR-automaton of window size one to the size of a description of a finite-state acceptor of minimal size that accepts the same (regular) language. For a finite-state acceptor, the number of states is usually taken as the measure for its size (see, e.g., [75]). As R- and deterministic RR-automata do not have any auxiliary letters, the number of states is also a reasonable measure for their sizes. Following Martin Kutrib's and Jens Reimann's studies in [126, 127, 128], we show that there is an exponential trade-off when converting an R- or a deterministic RR-automaton of window size one into a (nondeterministic or deterministic) finite-state acceptor for the same language. In fact, rather exact upper and lower bounds have been obtained for these conversions (see Figure 3.1).

In Section 3.2, we turn to stateless ordered restarting automata. As the stateless (deterministic and nondeterministic) ordered restarting automaton characterizes the class of regular languages, each stateless ordered restarting automaton is equivalent to a finite-state acceptor. Obviously, for a stateless type of automaton, we need a different measure for the size. Following [195, 205], we use the cardinality of the tape alphabet as a measure for the size of a stateless ordered restarting automaton. This is reasonable as, because of its window of size three, a stateless ordered restarting automaton with a tape alphabet of cardinality n can have up to $O(n^4)$ transitions, while a deterministic finite-state acceptor with k states over an alphabet of size n has at most $k \cdot n$ transitions and a nondeterministic finite-state acceptor with k states over an alphabet of size n has at most $n \cdot k^2$ transitions. Thus, for all these types of automata, the size of an encoding of the transition relation is polynomially related to the respective measure. We shall see that stateless deterministic ordered restarting automata are exponentially more succinct than nondeterministic finite-state acceptors (Corollary 3.2.14) and doubly exponentially more succinct than deterministic finite-state acceptors (Corollary 3.2.15). Actually, this fact remains valid even for stateless deterministic ordered restarting automata that are reversible (Subsection 3.2.1). We also take a look at the descriptional complexity of stateless ordered restart-delete automata. As they accept a class of languages that includes the context-free languages, it is not surprising that the trade-off for turning a stateless ordered restart-delete automaton accepting a regular language into an equivalent stateless ordered restarting automaton is non-recursive, that is, it cannot be limited from above by any recursive function (Subsection 3.2.2).

Then, in Section 3.3, we study the trade-offs for the conversion of a restarting automaton of window size k into an equivalent automaton of the same type with only window size $k-1$. For deterministic and nondeterministic restarting automata of type RW and of type RRW, we prove that the corresponding trade-offs are non-recursive for all $k \geq 3$. Here the main idea consists in constructing a deterministic RW-automaton of window size k that accepts a language that encodes the computation of a given deterministic Turing machine on empty input. This language is accepted by an RW-automaton of window size $k-1$ if and only if it is finite. Hence, the halting problem for Turing machines on empty input, which is known to be undecidable, is reduced to the problem considered. By following the same strategy, but using a technically somewhat more involved construction, corresponding non-recursive trade-offs are also obtained for deterministic and nondeterministic restarting automata of type R and of type RR and for all $k \geq 5$.

Finally, in Section 3.4, we consider trade-offs between monotone RWW- and RRWW-automata on the one hand and deterministic RWW- and RRWW-automata and some of their subclasses on the other hand. Following [77, 228], we show that many trade-offs for the conversions between these types of restarting automata are non-recursive, too. These results emphasize the incomparability results from Subsection 2.2.1, which show that the language classes accepted by the various types of nondeterministic monotone restarting automata are incomparable under inclusion to those language classes that are accepted by the various types of non-monotone deterministic restarting automata (see Figure 2.8).

As the restarting automaton is a formal model for the linguistic technique of 'analysis by reduction,' it can be used to study the language-theoretical foundations of this linguistic technique, establishing theoretical results or refuting conjectures. However, it is quite difficult to design a restarting automaton for a comprehensive language like, e.g., a substantial subset of a natural language. Accordingly, several methods have been proposed in the literature for learning restarting automata (that is, analysis by reduction) from positive (and negative) samples of reductions. In Chapter 4, we consider these methods. As a restarting automaton realizes the process of analysis by reduction, one does not simply want to learn the language that is accepted by this restarting automaton, but, in addition, one wants to learn the reduction relation that this automaton induces on the corresponding set of characteristic words. Hence, this task is similar to the task of learning a rewriting system (see, e.g., [45, 176]).

In Sections 4.1 and 4.2, we describe some results that have been obtained on learning certain restricted types of restarting automata from positive data. Here the task of learning a restarting automaton is subdivided into the task of learning the single-step reduction relation $\vdash_M^{c}$ of a restarting automaton M and of learning the set of simple sentential forms $S_C(M)$, that is, those words from the characteristic language of M that are accepted without executing any rewrite operations. In Section 4.1, restarting automata are considered that are defined by meta-instructions for which the (regular) context conditions are strictly j-testable languages. In this setting, the learner is given a sequence of individual reductions and positive samples of simple words. The task of learning a restarting automaton that is compatible with the given positive data is split into the task of learning individual meta-instructions by a helpful teacher, who, in addition, also provides information on the rewrite steps of the reductions given.

In Section 4.2, we then present Petr Hoffmann's Omega* method of inferring a restarting automaton from full samples of successful sequences of analysis by reduction [71]. These samples are complete sequences of reductions that transform a given word into a simple word. Here no helpful teacher is assumed, but the rewrite steps are extracted from the given reductions using a simple heuristic. For this approach to succeed, the restarting automata considered are fairly restricted. First of all, the context conditions of all meta-instructions are restricted to be k-reversible languages (see, e.g., [2]), and it is required that the restarting automata considered are single automata, that is, they have only a single accepting meta-instruction and, for each rewrite step $l \to r$, there is only a single rewriting meta-instruction containing this rewrite step (see Section 4.2 for the definition). In addition to presenting the Omega* method, we also restate the results from [73] on the expressive capacity of these types of restarting automata.

Finally, in Section 4.3, we concentrate on the problem of learning clearing (and subword clearing) restarting automata from an informant, that is, we are given positive and negative samples. These results, which are taken from [254, 256], extend to all types of limited context restarting automata. Unfortunately, the problem of deciding whether there exists a clearing restarting automaton M that is consistent with a given finite set S^+ of positive samples and a given finite set S^- of negative samples such that the width of each instruction of M is bounded by a given constant l is already intractable (see Theorems 4.3.16 and 4.3.17).

In the second volume of this monograph, we present several proper extensions of the restarting automaton as defined in Section 1.9. These include *nonforgetting* types of restarting automata as introduced by Hartmut Messerschmidt and Heiko Stamer in [153], *cooperating distributed systems* (*CD-systems*) of restarting automata, and *parallel communicating systems* (*PC-systems*) of restarting automata.

In addition, we present types of restarting automata that produce output. As defined in Section 1.9, the restarting automaton is a *language-accepting device.* This observation also applies to the CD-systems and to the PC-systems of restarting automata. However, the goal of performing analysis by reduction on a given input sentence is not simply to accept or reject that sentence, but to extract syntactical and semantical information from that sentence and, therewith, to transform it into another form, that is, into a corresponding formal representation (see, e.g., [145]). Hence, it appears reasonable to model analysis by reduction through binary relations on words. Accordingly, we consider various types of *restarting transducers* and *weighted restarting automata.*

Moreover, extensions of the restarting automaton are studied that process more general inputs than just words. In particular, various types of restarting automata are discussed that process two-dimensional rectangular arrays of letters, that is, *pictures.*

Finally, the restarting automaton, as defined in Section 1.9, works on linear text, that is, words, despite the fact that in linguistics (as well as in Formal Language Theory and its applications), trees are often used to describe sentences of a language together with some structural information on these sentences. Here we just mention the well-known *syntax* or *derivation trees* (see Section 1.2) and the *dependency trees* (see Section 1.6). Therefore, it is only natural to extend the notion of a restarting automaton from words to trees. Following [247], a corresponding generalization will be presented in the last chapter of Volume 2.

All (or almost all) results presented in this monograph have already been published in conference proceedings, journal papers, or doctoral dissertations. Also, in the survey papers [192, 193], the relations between certain types of restarting automata and the classes of the Chomsky hierarchy have been described. However, the many different types of restarting automata that have been studied and the many results that have been obtained on them have not yet been presented together in a uniform way, and no guide to the literature on restarting automata is currently available. This monograph has been written to fill these gaps. In order to not overburden the text with too many technical details, and as the complete proofs have already appeared elsewhere, we present the definitions and results in full details, illustrate them with examples, but mostly only provide outlines of proofs. These outlines show the proof techniques used, but for the full details, the interested reader is pointed to the original publications.

Each volume of the monograph closes with two appendices. In the first appendix, all the open problems encountered in the corresponding volume are collected and, in the second appendix, a list of those example languages is given that are used repeatedly throughout the text. For each example language, the results obtained are given together with references to the corresponding points in the text.

Chapter 1

Analysis by Reduction

After presenting some basic notions on alphabets, words, languages, and operations on words and languages in Section 1.1, we restate Noam Chomsky's phrase structure grammars and their restricted variants in Section 1.2. In particular, we present an extended version of the Chomsky hierarchy together with the well-known characterizations of the classes of this hierarchy by classical models of automata. Then, in Section 1.3, we consider various classes of contextual languages. These languages are generated by contextual grammars, which were introduced by Solomon Marcus in [147], exploiting two fundamental concepts from linguistics: the notion of a word (or string) over a given finite non-empty alphabet, and the notion of a context. Naturally, we look at the relationship between the classes of contextual languages on the one hand and the classes of the Chomsky hierarchy on the other hand. In the next section, we are concerned with the complexity of the membership problem for the languages from the Chomsky hierarchy, introducing the corresponding complexity classes. In Section 1.5, we take a short look at *mildly context-sensitive languages*, a concept relating formal languages to linguistics. Then, in Section 1.6, we define dependency trees and dependency grammars, and in Section 1.7, we consider languages with a free word order. Finally, in Section 1.8, we come to the *analysis by reduction*, a technique from linguistics for analyzing sentences of natural languages with a free word order. From the analysis by reduction, we extract the basic steps that are then used in Section 1.9 to define a general model of the *restarting automaton*. This model has a number of parameters that can be used to specify particular types of restarting automata. This chapter closes with a short survey on the types of restarting automata that were studied in the first papers on this topic, relating them to some of the classes of the extended Chomsky hierarchy mentioned above.

F. Otto, *Restarting Automata*, Theory and Applications of Computability,
https://doi.org/10.1007/978-3-031-70094-1_1

1.1 Preliminaries: Words, Languages, and Operations

Here we introduce most of the basic notions we shall use throughout this monograph in order to establish notation. We use $\mathbb{N}$ to denote the set of all non-negative integers, that is, $\mathbb{N} = \{0, 1, 2, 3, \ldots\}$, while $\mathbb{N}_+$ denotes the set of all positive integers, that is, $\mathbb{N}_+ = \mathbb{N} \setminus \{0\}$. For a set S, the notation $\mathcal{P}(S)$ is used to denote the *power set* of S, that is, the set of all subsets of S, and $\mathcal{P}_{\text{fin}}(S)$ denotes the set of all finite subsets of S. As we shall mainly be concerned with languages and methods for describing them through finite means, we first need to make clear what we understand by the word 'language.' Informally, a language is a collection (or set) of elements called 'sentences' or 'words.' These are finite sequences constructed from a finite 'vocabulary' or 'alphabet.' Accordingly, we must first fix the meaning of the word 'alphabet.'

Definition 1.1.1 *An* alphabet Σ *is a finite set of elements that are called* letters (*or* symbols). *These letters are considered as atomic items that cannot be split into smaller parts and that are pairwise distinct and easily distinguishable. We use* $|\Sigma|$ *to denote the* cardinality *of the alphabet* Σ, *that is, the number of letters in* Σ.

For example, $\Sigma_1 = \{a, b, \ldots, z, A, B, \ldots, Z, \text{␣}\}$ is an alphabet of cardinality $|\Sigma_1| = 53$. In many cases, one restricts one's attention to the binary alphabet $\Sigma_2 = \{0, 1\}$ or even to a unary alphabet of the form $\Sigma_3 = \{a\}$. On the other hand, in a linguistic application, we may take the set of all English phonemes as our alphabet (see, e.g., [27]). Another possibility is to take a subset of all English words as our alphabet, e.g., $\Sigma_4 = \{\text{THE}, \text{A}, \text{BLACK}, \text{LITTLE}, \text{DOG}, \text{CAT}, \text{CHASES}\}$.

Next we consider the operation of forming 'sentences' or 'words' over an alphabet.

Definition 1.1.2 *Let* $\Sigma = \{a_1, a_2, \ldots, a_k\}$ *be an alphabet of cardinality* $k \geq 1$.

(a) *For each positive integer* $n \geq 1$, *a* word *of length* n *is a sequence* $(a_{i_1}, a_{i_2}, \ldots, a_{i_n})$ *of letters* $a_{i_1}, a_{i_2}, \ldots, a_{i_n}$ *taken from* Σ. *To simplify the notation, this word is written as* $a_{i_1} a_{i_2} \cdots a_{i_n}$. *The set of all words of length* n *over* Σ *is denoted by* Σ^n.

(b) *For denotational convenience, we also introduce a word of length 0, which is written as* λ. *It is called the* empty word *over* Σ. *Then* Σ^0 *denotes the set* $\Sigma^0 = \{\lambda\}$.

(c) *The* set of all non-empty words *over* Σ *is denoted by* Σ^+, *that is,* $\Sigma^+ = \bigcup_{n \geq 1} \Sigma^n$.

(d) *The* set of all words *over* Σ *is denoted by* Σ^*, *that is,* $\Sigma^* = \Sigma^+ \cup \{\lambda\} = \bigcup_{n \geq 0} \Sigma^n$.

(e) *For each word* $w \in \Sigma^*$, $|w|$ *is used to denote the length of* w. *The corresponding function* $|\cdot| : \Sigma^* \to \mathbb{N}$ *is called the* length function.

(f) *For each positive integer* $n \geq 1$, *we use* $\Sigma^{\leq n}$ *to denote the set of all words of length at most* n, *that is,* $\Sigma^{\leq n} = \bigcup_{k=0}^{n} \Sigma^k$, *and* $\Sigma^{<n} = \Sigma^{\leq n-1}$.

In what follows, we identify the set Σ^1 of words of length one over Σ with the set Σ of letters, that is, we do not distinguish between a word of length one and the corresponding letter. Furthermore, as the underlying alphabet does not really influence the empty word λ, we use λ to denote the empty word for any alphabet.

Example 1.1.3 *For the alphabet* $\Sigma_1 = \{a, b, \ldots, z, A, B, \ldots, Z, \text{␣}\}$, *Age* $\in \Sigma_1^3$, *language* $\in \Sigma_1^8$, *and Jim␣has␣a␣headache* $\in \Sigma_1^{18}$. *For* $\Sigma_2 = \{0, 1\}$, *we have* $\Sigma_2^2 = \{00, 01, 10, 11\}$, *and for* $\Sigma_3 = \{a\}$, *we have* $\Sigma_3^4 = \{aaaa\}$. ■

By putting a word v of length n right behind another word u of length m, we obtain the word uv of length $m + n$. Mathematically, this is formulated through the following function.

Definition 1.1.4 *Let* Σ *be an alphabet. The function* $\cdot : \Sigma^* \times \Sigma^* \to \Sigma^*$ *of* concatenation (*or* product *or* juxtaposition) *is defined by taking* $u \cdot v = uv$ *for all* $u, v \in \Sigma^*$.

Obviously, $|u \cdot v| = |u| + |v|$ for all words $u, v \in \Sigma^*$. The operation of concatenation has the following important properties.

Lemma 1.1.5 *Let Σ be an alphabet.*

(a) *The operation of concatenation is* associative, *that is, for all $u, v, w \in \Sigma^*$, $(u \cdot v) \cdot w = u \cdot (v \cdot w)$.*

(b) *For all $u \in \Sigma^*$, $u \cdot \lambda = \lambda \cdot u = u$.*

(c) *If $u \cdot v = u \cdot w$, then $v = w$* (Left cancellability).

(d) *If $u \cdot w = v \cdot w$, then $u = v$* (Right cancellability).

(e) *If $u \cdot v = x \cdot y$, then exactly one of the following cases holds:*

(1) *$|u| = |x|$, $u = x$, and $v = y$.*

(2) *$|u| > |x|$, and there exists a word $z \in \Sigma^+$ such that $u = x \cdot z$ and $y = z \cdot v$.*

(3) *$|u| < |x|$, and there exists a word $z \in \Sigma^+$ such that $x = u \cdot z$ and $v = z \cdot y$.*

Parts (a) and (b) show that the set Σ^*, together with the binary operation of concatenation, has the algebraic structure of a *monoid* with the identity λ. In fact, $(\Sigma^*, \cdot, \lambda)$ is the *free monoid* generated by Σ, which means that each word $w \in \Sigma^*$ has a unique representation as a product (concatenation) of letters from Σ. For more information on free monoids, see, e.g., the monograph by Gerard Lallement [135].

To simplify the notation, we often use exponents to write words in a shorter and better readable form, where we take $w^0 = \lambda$, $w^1 = w$, and $w^{n+1} = w^n \cdot w$ for all $w \in \Sigma^*$ and all $n \in \mathbb{N}$. So a^3 denotes the word aaa, and $a(ba)^3b^4a$ denotes the word $abababab bbba$.

Definition 1.1.6 *Let Σ be an alphabet, and let $w = a_1a_2\cdots a_n \in \Sigma^n$, where $n \geq 1$ and $a_i \in \Sigma$ for all $i = 1, 2, \ldots, n$.*

(a) *If $w = xyz$ for some $x, y, z \in \Sigma^*$, then x is a* prefix, *y is a* factor, *and z is a* suffix *of w.*

(b) *For $1 \leq i \leq n$ and $1 \leq k \leq n - i + 1$, we use $w[i, k]$ to denote the factor of length k of w that starts at position i, that is, $w[i, k] = a_ia_{i+1}\cdots a_{i+k-1}$. To simplify the notation, $w[i, 1]$ is just denoted by $w[i]$.*

(c) *Each word of the form $w[1, k]$, $1 \leq k < n$, is called a* proper prefix *of w, each word of the form $w[i, k]$, $i \geq 2$ and $k \leq n - i$, is called an* inner factor *of w, and each word of the form $w[i, n - i + 1]$, $i \geq 2$, is called a* proper suffix *of w.*

(d) *We use $^R : \Sigma^* \to \Sigma^*$ to denote the* mirror function *that maps the word $w = a_1a_2\cdots a_{n-1}a_n$ to its mirror image or* reversal *$w^R = a_na_{n-1}\cdots a_2a_1$.*

Now we come to the main notion of this monograph which is that of a 'language.' As we are mainly concerned with the syntactic structure of a language and not the semantics (or meaning) of its sentences (or words), we take the following simple definition.

Definition 1.1.7 *Let Σ be an alphabet. A* language *on Σ is any subset L of the set Σ^* of all words over Σ.*

For example, $L_1 = \{ 0^n1^n \mid n \geq 0 \}$ is a language on $\Sigma_2 = \{0, 1\}$, and $L_{\text{exp}} = \{ a^{2^n} \mid n \geq 0 \}$ is a language on $\Sigma_3 = \{a\}$. Furthermore, the set of all English sentences without punctuation marks is a language on $\Sigma_1 = \{a, b, \ldots, z, A, B, \ldots, Z, \llcorner\!\lrcorner\}$. Obviously, all these languages are of infinite cardinality. On the other hand, $L = \Sigma_2^5$ is a language on Σ_2 of cardinality $|L| = 2^5 = 32$.

Below we need certain operations on languages, which we now define.

Definition 1.1.8 *Let L_1 and L_2 be two languages on an alphabet Σ.*

(a) *The* union *of* L_1 *and* L_2 *is the language* $L_1 \cup L_2 = \{ w \in \Sigma^* \mid w \in L_1 \text{ or } w \in L_2 \}$.

(b) *The* intersection *of* L_1 *and* L_2 *is the language* $L_1 \cap L_2 = \{ w \in \Sigma^* \mid w \in L_1 \text{ and } w \in L_2 \}$.

(c) *The* complement *of* L_1 *is the language* $L_1^c = \{ w \in \Sigma^* \mid w \notin L_1 \}$.

(d) *The* product *(or* concatenation*) of* L_1 *and* L_2 *is the language*

$$L_1 \cdot L_2 = \{ uv \in \Sigma^* \mid u \in L_1 \text{ and } v \in L_2 \}.$$

(e) *For each* $n \geq 2$*, the* n-th power *of* L_1 *is the language*

$$L_1^n = \{ u_1 u_2 \cdots u_n \mid u_1, u_2, \ldots, u_n \in L_1 \}.$$

Furthermore, $L_1^1 = L$ *and* $L_1^0 = \{\lambda\}$.

(f) *The* Kleene plus *of* L_1 *is the language* $L_1^+ = \bigcup_{n \geq 1} L_1^n$.

(g) *The* Kleene star *of* L_1 *is the language* $L_1^* = \bigcup_{n \geq 0} L_1^n = L_1^+ \cup \{\lambda\}$.

(h) *The* mirror image *(or* reversal*) of* L_1 *is the language* $L_1^R = \{ w^R \mid w \in L_1 \}$.

(i) *The* shuffle *of* L_1 *and* L_2 *is the language* $\mathrm{sh}(L_1, L_2) = \bigcup_{u \in L_1, v \in L_2} \mathrm{sh}(u, v)$*, where*

$$\begin{aligned} \mathrm{sh}(u, v) = \{ u_1 v_1 u_2 v_2 \cdots u_m v_m \mid\, & m \geq 0, u_1, u_2, \ldots, u_m, v_1, v_2, \ldots, v_m \in \Sigma^*, \\ & u = u_1 u_2 \cdots u_m, \text{ and } v = v_1 v_2 \cdots v_m \}. \end{aligned}$$

For example, if $L_1 = \{ ab^i \mid i \geq 1 \}$ and $L_2 = L_1^R = \{ b^j a \mid j \geq 1 \}$, then

$$L_1 \cdot L_2 = \{ ab^{i+j} a \mid i, j \geq 1 \} = \{ ab^n a \mid n \geq 2 \} \text{ and } L_2 \cdot L_1 = \{ b^j aab^i \mid i, j \geq 1 \}.$$

Furthermore, for all $n \geq 2$,

$$\begin{aligned} L_1^n &= \{ ab^{i_1} ab^{i_2} \cdots ab^{i_n} \mid i_1, i_2, \ldots, i_n \geq 1 \}, \\ L_1^+ &= \{ ab^{i_1} ab^{i_2} \cdots ab^{i_n} \mid n \geq 1, i_1, i_2, \ldots, i_n \geq 1 \}, \text{ and} \\ L_1^* &= \{\lambda\} \cup \{ ab^{i_1} ab^{i_2} \cdots ab^{i_n} \mid n \geq 1, i_1, i_2, \ldots, i_n \geq 1 \}. \end{aligned}$$

Finally, $\mathrm{sh}(L_1, L_2) = \{ b^i ab^j ab^k \mid i, j, k \geq 0, i + j \geq 1, j + k \geq 1, \text{ and } i + j + k \geq 2 \}$.

Let Σ and Γ be two (not necessarily distinct) alphabets. A *morphism* from Σ^* to Γ^* is a mapping $h : \Sigma^* \to \Gamma^*$ that satisfies the condition $h(uv) = h(u)h(v)$ for all words $u, v \in \Sigma^*$. It is easily seen that $h(\lambda) = \lambda$. Furthermore, as each word w from Σ^* has a unique factorization as a sequence of letters, we see that the morphism h is unambiguously described by the mapping $h : \Sigma \to \Gamma^*$ that yields the word $h(a) \in \Gamma^*$ for each letter $a \in \Sigma$. A morphism $h : \Sigma^* \to \Gamma^*$ is called *non-erasing* (or λ*-free*) if $h(a) \neq \lambda$ for all $a \in \Sigma$. Finally, if $\Gamma \subseteq \Sigma$, then the morphism π_Γ that is defined through

$$\pi_\Gamma(a) = \begin{cases} a, & \text{if } a \in \Gamma \\ \lambda, & \text{if } a \in \Sigma \setminus \Gamma \end{cases}$$

is called the *projection* from Σ^* onto Γ^*.

Definition 1.1.9 *Let* Σ *and* Γ *be two alphabets, let* $L_1 \subseteq \Sigma^*$*,* $L_2 \subseteq \Gamma^*$*, and let* $h : \Sigma^* \to \Gamma^*$ *be a morphism.*

(a) *The* image *of* L_1 *under* h *is the language* $h(L_1) = \{ h(w) \mid w \in L_1 \} \subseteq \Gamma^*$.

(b) *The* pre-image *of* L_2 *with respect to* h *is the language* $h^{-1}(L_2) = \{ w \in \Sigma^* \mid h(w) \in L_2 \}$.

For example, let $\Sigma = \{a, b\}$ and $\Gamma = \{c\}$, and let $h : \Sigma^* \to \Gamma^*$ be the morphism that is defined by taking $h(a) = c$ and $h(b) = c$. Then $h(w) = c^{|w|}$ for each word $w \in \Sigma^*$. For $L_1 = \{ ab^i \mid i \geq 1 \}$, $h(L_1) = \{ c^j \mid j \geq 2 \}$, and $h^{-1}(cc) = \{aa, ab, ba, bb\}$. Furthermore, $\pi_{\{a\}}(L_1) = \{a\}$ and $\pi_{\{b\}}(L_1) = \{ b^i \mid i \geq 1 \}$, while $\pi_{\{a\}}^{-1}(a) = \{ b^i a b^j \mid i, j \geq 0 \}$.

Finally, for $a \in \Sigma$, $|w|_a$ denotes the *a-length* of w, which is the number of occurrences of the letter a in w. Thus, we see that $\pi_{\{a\}}^{-1}(a) = \{w \in \{a, b\}^* \mid |w|_a = 1\}$. For a subset Γ of Σ, $|w|_\Gamma = \sum_{a \in \Gamma} |w|_a$ is the *Γ-length* of w. Obviously, $|w| = |w|_\Sigma$.

Next we present a syntactically defined class of languages that has found many applications in the design of editors and parsers due to its nice closure and algorithmic properties. The languages of this class are specified through so-called regular expressions that are defined recursively, but they can actually be characterized in many different ways (see Section 1.2). Below we provide the definition of these expressions together with the description of the languages they specify.

Definition 1.1.10 *Let Σ be an alphabet, and let Γ be the following extended alphabet:*

$$\Gamma = \Sigma \cup \{\emptyset, \lambda, +, *, (,)\}.$$

The regular expressions $\mathsf{RA}(\Sigma)$ on Σ are defined as follows, where a language $L(r) \subseteq \Sigma^*$ is associated to each expression r:

(1)	$\emptyset \in \mathsf{RA}(\Sigma)$	$: L(\emptyset) = \emptyset,$
(2)	$\lambda \in \mathsf{RA}(\Sigma)$	$: L(\lambda) = \{\lambda\},$
(3)	*For all* $a \in \Sigma : a \in \mathsf{RA}(\Sigma)$	$: L(a) = \{a\}.$
(4)	*For all* $r, s \in \mathsf{RA}(\Sigma), (r + s) \in \mathsf{RA}(\Sigma)$	$: L(r + s) = L(r) \cup L(s).$
(5)	*For all* $r, s \in \mathsf{RA}(\Sigma), (rs) \in \mathsf{RA}(\Sigma)$	$: L(rs) = L(r) \cdot L(s).$
(6)	*For all* $r \in \mathsf{RA}(\Sigma), (r^*) \in \mathsf{RA}(\Sigma)$	$: L(r^*) = (L(r))^*.$

We illustrate this definition by presenting a few simple examples.

Example 1.1.11 (a) *Let r be the expression $(((0 + 1)^*)((00)((0 + 1)^*)))$. Then r is built from the simple expressions 0 and 1 as illustrated by the following tree:*

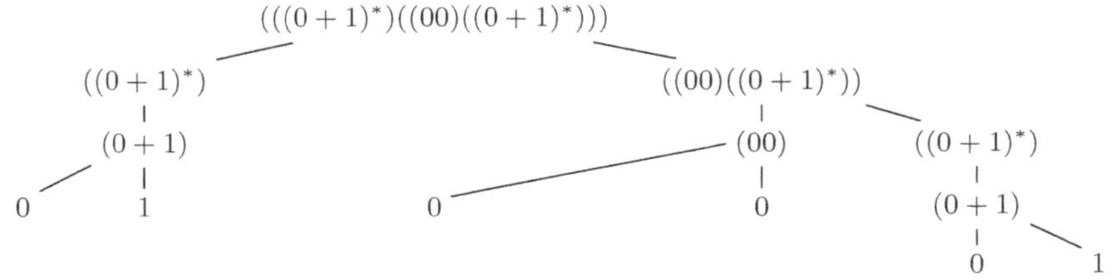

A word $w \in \{0, 1\}^*$ belongs to the language $L(r)$ iff it contains the word 00 as a factor, that is, $L(r) = \{ w \in \{0, 1\}^* \mid \exists u, v \in \{0, 1\}^* : w = u00v \}$.

(b) *Let $s = ((0 + \lambda)((1 + 10)^*))$. Then $L(s) = \{0, 1\}^* \smallsetminus L(r) = (L(r))^c$.*

(c) *Let $t = ((a + b)(((a + b)(a + b))^*))$. Then $L(t) = \{ u \in \{a, b\}^* \mid |u| \equiv 1 \mod 2 \}$.*

(d) *As the operations of union and product are associative, we can save some brackets in expressions of the form $((rs)t)$ or $(r + (s + t))$, writing them simply as rst or $r + s + t$. If L is a finite language $L = \{x_{1,1}x_{1,2} \cdots x_{1,n_1}, x_{2,1}x_{2,2} \cdots x_{2,n_2}, \ldots, x_{m,1}x_{m,2} \cdots x_{m,n_m}\}$, where $m \geq 1$, $x_{i,j} \in \Sigma$, and $n_1, n_2, \ldots, n_m \geq 0$, then L is described by the regular expression $r = (x_{1,1}x_{1,2} \cdots x_{1,n_1}) + (x_{2,1}x_{2,2} \cdots x_{2,n_2}) + \cdots + (x_{m,1}x_{m,2} \cdots x_{m,n_m})$.* ■

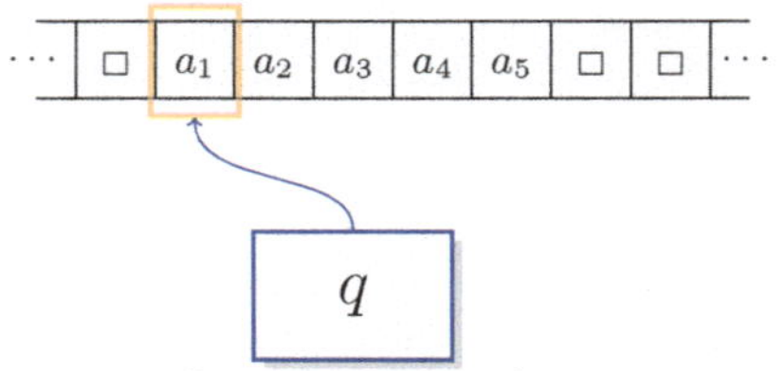

Figure 1.1: A Turing machine

The expression REG(Σ) denotes the class of all languages over Σ that can be described by regular expressions on Σ, and REG denotes the class of all languages that can be specified by regular expressions. REG coincides with the *class of regular languages* that we shall encounter in the next section. From Example 1.1.11 (d), we see that REG contains all finite languages, and from Example 1.1.11 (a), we see that it also contains certain infinite languages. It follows immediately from the definition that the class REG is closed under the operations of union, product, and Kleene star, and it is also easily seen that it is also closed under the application of a morphism and under the operation of reversal. Further closure properties will follow easily from other characterizations of this class (see below).

Finally, we restate in short the definition of the fundamental type of computing device that is the basis for many other types of automata and transducers considered below: the Turing machine. The Turing machine was first presented in a landmark paper by Alan Turing in 1936 [251] in an attempt to formalize the notion of *computation*. Such a machine consists of a *finite-state control*, which can be in any of a finite number of (internal) states, an unbounded *tape* that is divided into *squares* or *cells* that each contain a single letter from a finite tape alphabet, and a *read/write head* that can move along the tape, reading and writing. A Turing machine can be depicted as shown in Figure 1.1. Formally, the Turing machine is defined as follows.

Definition 1.1.12 *A* Turing machine M *is defined by a 7-tuple* $M = (Q, \Sigma, \Gamma, \delta, q_0, \square, F)$, *where* Q *is a finite set of (internal)* states, Σ *is a finite* input alphabet, Γ *is a finite* tape alphabet *containing the input alphabet as well as the* blank symbol $\square$, $\delta : ((Q \smallsetminus F) \times \Gamma) \to (Q \times \Gamma \times \{\mathrm{L}, \mathrm{R}, \mathrm{N}\})$ *is the* transition function, $q_0 \in Q$ *is the* initial state, *and* $F \subseteq Q$ *is the set of* final *or* halting states.

A computation of a Turing Machine M starts with an input word $w \in \Sigma^*$ on the tape, while the head is on the left-most letter of that word, and the finite-state control is in the initial state q_0. Based on the current state, say q, and the letter under its head, say a, the Turing machine executes the operation described by $\delta(q, a)$. If $\delta(q, a) = (q', b, \mathrm{L})$, then the internal state is changed from q to q', the letter a under the head is replaced with the letter b, and the head is moved one position to the left. Analogously, if $\delta(q, a) = (q', b, \mathrm{R})$, then the internal state is changed from q to q', the letter a under the head is replaced with the letter b, and the head is moved one position to the right, and finally, if $\delta(q, a) = (q', b, \mathrm{N})$, then the internal state is changed from q to q', the letter a under the head is replaced with the letter b, and the head stays at the current position. This continues until a final state $q \in F$ is reached. As $\delta(q, a)$ is not defined for $q \in F$, M halts in this situation. Since during the course of a computation, the head of M may leave the part of the tape that originally contained the input, it is assumed that at the start all other tape squares contain the blank symbol $\square$.

To describe the computations of a Turing machine, we need a compact way for presenting its overall situation at any moment of time. For doing so, the notion of configuration has been coined.

Definition 1.1.13 *Let* $M = (Q, \Sigma, \Gamma, \delta, q_0, \square, F)$ *be a Turing machine.*

(a) *A* configuration *of* M *is a word of the form* $uqv \in \Gamma^* \cdot Q \cdot \Gamma^+$. *Here* $q \in Q$ *is the current state of* M, *the tape contains the word* uv *that is preceded and followed only by occurrences* *of the blank symbol* $\square$*, and the head is currently on the first letter of* v*. A configuration of the form* q_0w *with* $w \in \Sigma^*$ *is called an* initial configuration *and a configuration of the form* uqv *with* $q \in F$ *is called a* final *(or* halting*)* configuration.

(b) *The* single-step computation relation *that the transition function* δ *induces on the set of configurations of* M *is denoted by* $\vdash_M$*. The* computation relation $\vdash_M^*$ *is the reflexive and transitive closure of the single-step computation relation.*

(c) *An input word* $w \in \Sigma^*$ *is said to be* accepted *by* M *if the computation of* M *that begins with the initial configuration* q_0w *ends with a final configuration, that is,* $q_0w \vdash_M^* uqv$ *holds for some* $u, v \in \Gamma^*$ *and a final state* $q \in F$*.*

(d) *The language* $L(M)$ accepted by M *is the set* $L(M) = \{ w \in \Sigma^* \mid w \text{ is accepted by } M \}$.

The following simple example illustrates this definition.

Example 1.1.14 *Let* $M = (Q, \Sigma, \Gamma, \delta, q_0, \square, F)$ *be defined by taking* $Q = \{q_0, q_1, q_2, q_3, q_a, q_b, q_a', q_b'\}$, $\Sigma = \{a, b\}$, $\Gamma = \{a, b, 0, 1, \square\}$, $F = \{q_3\}$*, and the transition function* δ *is defined by the following table:*

δ	q_0	q_1	q_2	q_a	q_b	q_a'	q_b'
a	$(q_a, \square, \text{R})$	(q_1, a, L)	$(q_2, \square, \text{L})$	(q_a, a, R)	(q_b, a, R)	$(q_1, \square, \text{L})$	$(q_2, \square, \text{L})$
b	$(q_b, \square, \text{R})$	(q_1, b, L)	$(q_2, \square, \text{L})$	(q_a, b, R)	(q_b, b, R)	$(q_2, \square, \text{L})$	$(q_1, \square, \text{L})$
$\square$	$(q_3, 1, \text{N})$	$(q_0, \square, \text{R})$	$(q_0, 0, \text{N})$	$(q_a', \square, \text{L})$	$(q_b', \square, \text{L})$	$(q_3, 1, \text{N})$	$(q_3, 1, \text{N})$
0	$(q_0, 0, \text{N})$	$(q_0, 0, \text{N})$	$(q_0, 0, \text{N})$	$(q_0, 0, \text{N})$	$(q_0, 0, \text{N})$	$(q_0, 0, \text{N})$	$(q_0, 0, \text{N})$
1	$(q_0, 1, \text{N})$	$(q_0, 1, \text{N})$	$(q_0, 1, \text{N})$	$(q_0, 1, \text{N})$	$(q_0, 1, \text{N})$	$(q_0, 1, \text{N})$	$(q_0, 1, \text{N})$

We claim that $L(M) = \{ w \in \{a, b\}^* \mid w = w^R \}$*, the language of palindromes over* Σ*. Indeed, if* $w = aua$ *for some word* $u \in \Sigma^*$*, then the computation of* M *on input* w *begins with*

$$q_0w = q_0aua \vdash_M q_aua \vdash_M^{|u|+1} uaq_a\square \vdash_M uq_a'a \vdash_M u'q_1c \vdash_M^{|u|} q_1\square u \vdash_M q_0u,$$

where $u = u'c$ *for some* $c \in \Sigma$*, and* $q_0\square \vdash_M q_31$*. It now follows easily that* M *accepts all palindromes. On the other hand, if* $z = aub$*, then*

$$q_0z = q_0aub \vdash_M q_aub \vdash_M^{|u|+1} ubq_a\square \vdash_M uq_a'b \vdash_M u'q_2c \vdash_M^{|u|} q_2\square \vdash_M q_00 \vdash_M q_00 \vdash_M \cdots,$$

that is, M *does not halt on input* z*. Thus, it follows that* $L(M) = \{ w \in \{a, b\}^* \mid w = w^R \}$*.* ■

A language L is called *recursively enumerable* if there exists a Turing machine M such that $L = L(M)$. The class of all recursively enumerable languages is denoted by RE.

If the transition function δ of the Turing machine M from Example 1.1.14 is changed by taking $\delta(q_2, \square) = (q_3, 0, \text{N})$, then the new machine M' shows the following behavior given a word $w \in \Sigma^*$ as input:

$$q_0w \vdash_{M'}^* \begin{cases} q_31, & \text{if } w = w^R, \\ q_30, & \text{otherwise.} \end{cases}$$

Hence, $L(M') = \Sigma^*$, but M' can be seen as computing the characteristic function of the language of palindromes. Actually, if L is a language on Σ, then the *characteristic function* χ_L of L is defined as

$$\chi_L(w) = \begin{cases} 1, & \text{if } w \in L, \\ 0, & \text{if } w \notin L. \end{cases}$$

A language L is called *recursive* if there exists a Turing machine that computes its characteristic function χ_L. Thus, the above example shows that the language of palindromes over $\{a, b\}$ is recursive.

It is easily seen that the complement of a recursive language is also recursive. Furthermore, from a Turing machine for computing the characteristic function χ_L, one can easily obtain a Turing machine that accepts the language L. Hence, if L is recursive, then L and its complement are both recursively enumerable. Interestingly, also the converse holds. Thus, we have the following equivalence (see, e.g., [79]).

Theorem 1.1.15 *A language L is recursive iff L and its complement L^c are both recursively enumerable.*

This result implies, in particular, that the complement L^c of a language L that is recursively enumerable, but not recursive, is not even recursively enumerable.

The Turing machine is a very robust model of a computing device, as it has been shown that its computational capacity is not influenced by many extensions or variations of the above definition (see, e.g., [79]). For example,

- instead of a set F of final states, a Turing Machine may just have a unique final state.
- A Turing Machine can be constructed in such a way that it never returns to its initial state q_0 during a computation.
- Every computation can be done without writing anything to the left of the input word, that is, the tape can be seen as being unbounded only to the right.
- Every accepting computation can be made to stop with the head on the left-most non-blank symbol on the tape.
- During each step of a computation, a Turing machine may be required to write a non-blank symbol, which implies that all tape squares visited contain non-blank symbols at the end of a computation.
- Instead of a single tape, a Turing machine may have a fixed positive number of tapes.
- Finally, the transition function δ can be extended to allow nondeterminism.

All these types and variants of Turing machines characterize the same class of languages, the class RE of recursively enumerable languages.

1.2 Phrase Structure Grammars

First, we recall Noam Chomsky's phrase-structure grammars and their most important restricted variants, the context-sensitive grammars, the context-free grammars, and the regular grammars. From these grammars, we obtain the famous Chomsky hierarchy of classes of (formal) languages, of which we then consider an extended version (see the diagram in Figure 1.8).

In [27], Noam Chomsky studies formal methods for describing linguistic structures in order to determine whether they can provide simple and revealing grammars for English. One of these methods are the so-called phrase-structure grammars, which are motivated by the syntactic description of a sentence of a natural language in terms of its 'immediate constituents.' In such a description, the words of a given sentence are grouped into phrases, which are then repeatedly grouped into smaller constituent phrases until, finally, the ultimate constituents are reached. These phrases are then classified as noun phrases (NP), verb phrases (VP), etc., in this way providing information on the structure of the sentence in terms of these constituents.

Example 1.2.1 *Consider the sentence* 'The black dog chases a little cat.' *This sentence can be deconstructed as follows:*

<table>
<tr><td>The</td><td>black</td><td>dog</td><td>chases</td><td>a</td><td>little</td><td>cat</td><td>.</td></tr>
<tr><td rowspan="2">Article</td><td rowspan="2">Adjective</td><td rowspan="2">Noun</td><td rowspan="2">Verb</td><td>Article</td><td>Adjective</td><td>Noun</td><td rowspan="3">Punct. Mark</td></tr>
<tr><td colspan="3">NP</td></tr>
<tr><td colspan="3">NP</td><td colspan="4">VP</td></tr>
<tr><td colspan="8">Sentence</td></tr>
</table>

■

To describe the structure of a sentence in this way, we need additional letters that denote the various categories or types of constituents. These additional letters will be called 'nonterminals.' We now present the definition of the (general) phrase-structure grammar. However, we slightly deviate from the original definition of Noam Chomsky [27, 29] in that we require that the left-hand side of any production of any grammar must contain at least one occurrence of a nonterminal.

Definition 1.2.2 *A* phrase-structure grammar *G is specified through a four-tuple $G = (N, T, S, P)$, where*

- *N is a finite alphabet of* nonterminals *(or* variables*),*
- *T is a finite alphabet of* terminals *(or* terminal symbols*), where T is disjoint from N,*
- *$S \in N$ is the* start symbol, *and*
- *$P \subseteq (N \cup T)^* \times (N \cup T)^*$ is a finite set of* productions *(or* rules*), which are written in the form $(\ell \to r)$. For each production $(\ell \to r) \in P$, it is required that $|\ell|_N \geq 1$, that is, the left-hand side of each production contains at least one occurrence of a nonterminal.*

A phrase-structure grammar $G = (N, T, S, P)$ is used to generate the sentences (or words) of a language as follows.

Definition 1.2.3 *Let $G = (N, T, S, P)$ be a phrase-structure grammar.*

(a) *If $x = u\ell v$ and $z = urv$ for some words $u, v \in (N \cup T)^*$ and a production $(\ell \to r) \in P$, then y can be* derived *from x* in a single step, *which is expressed as $x \Rightarrow_G y$.*

(b) *If $x = z_0 \Rightarrow_G z_1 \Rightarrow_G z_2 \Rightarrow_G \cdots \Rightarrow_G z_n = y$, where $n \geq 0$, then y is* derivable *from x* in n steps. *This is expressed as $x \Rightarrow_G^n y$.*

(c) *If $x \Rightarrow_G^n y$ for some $n \geq 0$, then y is* derivable *from x, which is written as $x \Rightarrow_G^* y$. The (binary) relation $\Rightarrow_G^*$ on $(N \cup T)^*$ is called the* derivation relation *of G.*

(d) *For $A \in N$, $\hat{L}_A(G) = \{y \in (N \cup T)^* \mid A \Rightarrow_G^* y\}$ is the set of A-*sentential forms *of G, and $\hat{L}(G) = \hat{L}_S(G)$ is the set of* sentential forms *of G.*

(e) *For* $A \in N$, $L_A(G) = \{ x \in T^* \mid A \Rightarrow_G^* x \}$ *is the* A-language *of* G, *and* $L(G) = L_S(G)$ *is the* language *generated by* G. *Obviously,* $L_A(G) = \hat{L}_A(G) \cap T^*$ *for all* $A \in N$, *and* $L(G) = \hat{L}(G) \cap T^*$.

For deriving the sentence in Example 1.2.1, the following simple grammar can be used.

Example 1.2.1 (cont.)

$$\begin{array}{lrcl} \text{Let} & N & = & \{\langle Sentence\rangle, \langle NP\rangle, \langle VP\rangle, \langle Article\rangle, \langle Adjective\rangle, \langle Noun\rangle, \langle Verb\rangle, \langle Punct.\ Mark\rangle\}, \\ & T & = & \{\text{The}, \text{a}, \text{black}, \text{little}, \text{dog}, \text{cat}, \text{chases}, .\}, \end{array}$$

and

$$\begin{array}{rcl} P & = & \{(\langle Sentence\rangle \to \langle NP\rangle\ \langle VP\rangle\ \langle Punct.\ Mark\rangle), \\ & & (\langle NP\rangle \to \langle Article\rangle\ \langle Adjective\rangle\ \langle Noun\rangle), \\ & & (\langle VP\rangle \to \langle Verb\rangle\ \langle NP\rangle), \\ & & (\langle Article\rangle \to \text{The}), (\langle Article\rangle \to \text{a}), \\ & & (\langle Adjective\rangle \to \text{black}), (\langle Adjective\rangle \to \text{little}), \\ & & (\langle Verb\rangle \to \text{chases}), (\langle Noun\rangle \to \text{dog}), (\langle Noun\rangle \to \text{cat}), \\ & & (\langle Punct.\ Mark\rangle \to .)\}. \end{array}$$

Using the grammar $G = (N, T, \langle Sentence\rangle, P)$, the example sentence 'The black dog chases a little cat.' can be derived as follows:

$$\begin{array}{rcl} \langle Sentence\rangle & \Rightarrow_G & \langle NP\rangle\ \langle VP\rangle\ \langle Punct.\ Mark\rangle \\ & \Rightarrow_G & \langle Article\rangle\ \langle Adjective\rangle\ \langle Noun\rangle\ \langle VP\rangle\ \langle Punct.\ Mark\rangle \\ & \Rightarrow_G & \text{The}\ \langle Adjective\rangle\ \langle Noun\rangle\ \langle VP\rangle\ \langle Punct.\ Mark\rangle \\ & \Rightarrow_G & \text{The black}\ \langle Noun\rangle\ \langle VP\rangle\ \langle Punct.\ Mark\rangle \\ & \Rightarrow_G & \text{The black dog}\ \langle VP\rangle\ \langle Punct.\ Mark\rangle \\ & \Rightarrow_G & \text{The black dog}\ \langle Verb\rangle\ \langle NP\rangle\ \langle Punct.\ Mark\rangle \\ & \Rightarrow_G & \text{The black dog chases}\ \langle NP\rangle\ \langle Punct.\ Mark\rangle \\ & \Rightarrow_G & \text{The black dog chases}\ \langle Article\rangle\ \langle Adjective\rangle\ \langle Noun\rangle\ \langle Punct.\ Mark\rangle \\ & \Rightarrow_G & \text{The black dog chases a}\ \langle Adjective\rangle\ \langle Noun\rangle\ \langle Punct.\ Mark\rangle \\ & \Rightarrow_G & \text{The black dog chases a little}\ \langle Noun\rangle\ \langle Punct.\ Mark\rangle \\ & \Rightarrow_G & \text{The black dog chases a little cat}\ \langle Punct.\ Mark\rangle \\ & \Rightarrow_G & \text{The black dog chases a little cat .} \end{array}$$

This derivation can be displayed graphically by the following *syntax tree*:

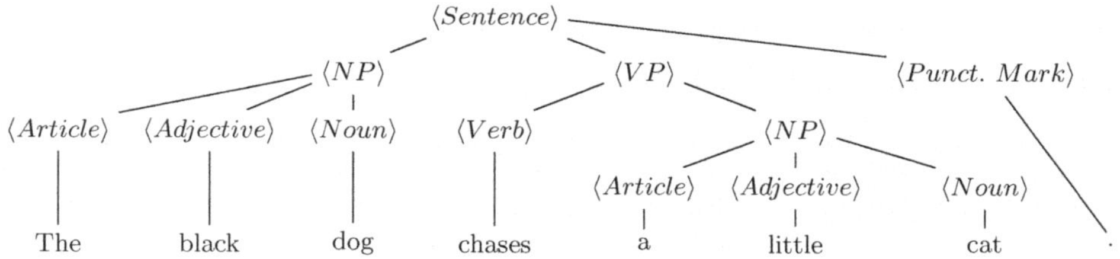

■

It is easily seen that the grammar G of Example 1.2.1 generates a finite language only:

$$L(G) = \left\{ \begin{array}{c} \text{The} \\ \text{a} \end{array} \right\} \left\{ \begin{array}{c} \text{black} \\ \text{little} \end{array} \right\} \left\{ \begin{array}{c} \text{dog} \\ \text{cat} \end{array} \right\} \text{chases} \left\{ \begin{array}{c} \text{The} \\ \text{a} \end{array} \right\} \left\{ \begin{array}{c} \text{black} \\ \text{little} \end{array} \right\} \left\{ \begin{array}{c} \text{dog} \\ \text{cat} \end{array} \right\} \{\ .\ \},$$

where one alternative is chosen from each of the curly brackets. Here is another example grammar that, however, generates an infinite language.

Example 1.2.4 *Let* $N = \{S, A, B\}$, $T = \{a, b, c\}$, *and*

$$P = \{(S \to AcB), (S \to SS), (A \to a), (B \to b), (BA \to \lambda)\}.$$

Recall that λ *denotes the empty word. Then* $G = (N, T, S, P)$ *generates the language*

$$L(G) = \{ ac^{n_1}bac^{n_2}b \cdots ac^{n_{k-1}}bac^{n_k}b \mid k \geq 1, n_1, n_2, \ldots, n_k \geq 1 \}.$$

To see this, let us consider a derivation in G. As we must eventually rewrite all occurrences of the start symbol S, such a derivation is either of the form

$$S \Rightarrow_G AcB \Rightarrow_G^2 acb,$$

or it begins as follows, where $n \geq 2$:

$$S \Rightarrow_G SS \Rightarrow_G^* S^n \Rightarrow_G^n (AcB)^n = AcBAcB \cdots AcBAcB.$$

To some of the factors BA, we can now apply the production $(BA \to \lambda)$, which yields a sentential form $Ac^{n_1}BAc^{n_2}B \cdots Ac^{n_k}B$. Here $k \geq 1$ and $n_1 + n_2 + \cdots + n_k = n$. Finally, by rewriting the remaining nonterminals A and B into terminals, we obtain the word $ac^{n_1}bac^{n_2}b \cdots ac^{n_k}b$, which is an element of the language given above. Conversely, it is easily seen that each element of the given language can be generated in this way. ■

Definition 1.2.5 $\mathcal{L}_0$ *denotes the class of all languages that are generated by phrase-structure grammars.*

As shown by Noam Chomsky in [27, 29], the language class $\mathcal{L}_0$ coincides with the class RE of recursively enumerable languages. Recall that a language $L \subseteq T^*$ is *recursively enumerable* if there exists a Turing machine M such that, starting from its initial configuration on input $w \in T^*$, M will eventually halt if and only if w belongs to the language L.

Theorem 1.2.6 ([27]) $\mathcal{L}_0 = \mathsf{RE}$.

If $L = L(G)$ for a phrase-structure grammar $G = (N, T, S, P)$, then a nondeterministic Turing machine can be constructed that, given a word $w \in T^*$ as input, simply guesses a derivation $S \Rightarrow_G^* w$, if $w \in L$. On the other hand, if $w \notin L$, then no such derivation can be found, and therefore, the Turing machine cannot succeed. This shows that L is indeed recursively enumerable. For the converse implication, one constructs a phrase-structure grammar G from a given Turing machine M such that a terminal derivation of G consists of three parts:

1. first, an encoding of a word $w \in T^*$ is generated;
2. then a computation of M on input w is simulated;
3. and finally, if this computation halts, then the word w is regenerated from the encoding of the halting configuration of M.

A detailed proof can be found, e.g., in [81].

The language class $\mathcal{L}_0$ is closed under many operations like, e.g., union, intersection, product, Kleene star, morphisms, and inverse morphisms, but it is not closed under complementation (see, e.g., [81]). However, it has poor algorithmic properties as, in general, not even the membership problem is decidable for a language from this class. Here, the *membership problem* for a language $L \subseteq T^*$ is defined as follows:

INSTANCE:	A word $w \in T^*$.
QUESTION:	Is w an element of the language L?

The membership problem for L is called *decidable* if there exists an algorithm (a Turing machine) that computes the characteristic function χ_L of L. Hence, we see that the membership problem for a language L is decidable if and only if L is recursive. Therefore, recursive languages are often simply called *decidable* languages. Accordingly, Noam Chomsky concentrated on certain restrictions for phrase-structure grammars that lead to less expressive types of grammars. Actually, he formulated three restrictions that are increasingly serious. These restrictions yield the grammars of type 1, type 2, and type 3, while the unrestricted phrase-structure grammars are refered to as *grammars of type 0*. Here is the first of Noah Chomsky's restrictions.

Definition 1.2.7 *Let $G = (N, T, S, P)$ be a phrase-structure grammar. Without loss of generality we assume that the start symbol S does not occur on the right-hand side of any production.*

(a) *The grammar G is a* context-sensitive grammar *if each production $(\ell \to r) \in P$ has the form $\ell = \alpha A \beta$ and $r = \alpha x \beta$, where $A \in N$, $x \in (N \cup T)^+$, and $\alpha, \beta \in (N \cup T)^*$. In addition, P may contain the production $(S \to \lambda)$. Following Noam Chomsky's notation, context-sensitive grammars are also called* grammars of type 1.

(b) *A language $L \subseteq T^*$ is* context-sensitive *or* of type 1 *if there exists a context-sensitive grammar G such that $L = L(G)$. The* class of context-sensitive languages *is denoted by CSL. It is also denoted by $\mathcal{L}_1$.*

(c) *The grammar G is called* monotone *if $|\ell| \leq |r|$ holds for each production $(\ell \to r) \in P$ satisfying $\ell \neq S$.*

From the above definition, it follows immediately that each context-sensitive grammar is monotone. On the other hand, it has already been pointed out in [29] that each monotone grammar can be converted into a context-sensitive grammar that generates the same language. Here is a simple example that illustrates this conversion.

Example 1.2.8 *Let G be the monotone grammar*

$$G = (\{S, B\}, \{a, b, c\}, S, \{S \to aSBc, S \to abc, cB \to Bc, bB \to bb\}).$$

We claim that $L(G)$ coincides with the language $L = \{\, a^n b^n c^n \mid n \geq 1 \,\}$.

First, proceeding by induction on n, we show that $a^n b^n c^n \in L(G)$ for all $n \geq 1$. For $n = 1$, we have $S \Rightarrow_G abc$. Now, assuming that $S \Rightarrow_G^* a^n b^n c^n$ has been shown for some $n \geq 1$, we consider the following derivation:

$$S \Rightarrow_G aSBc \Rightarrow_G^* a \cdot a^n b^n c^n \cdot Bc \Rightarrow_G^n a^{n+1} b^n B c^{n+1} \Rightarrow_G a^{n+1} b^{n+1} c^{n+1},$$

which shows that $a^{n+1} b^{n+1} c^{n+1} \in L(G)$, too. Hence, $L \subseteq L(G)$ follows.

Conversely, let $w \in L(G)$, that is, there exists a derivation $S \Rightarrow_G^m w$ for some $m \geq 1$. If $m = 1$, then $w = abc$; otherwise, this derivation starts with an application of the production $(S \to aSBc)$. By applying this production n times, we obtain the sentential form $a^n S (Bc)^n$, which can be rewritten into a sentential form $a^n S \alpha$ by applying the production $(cB \to Bc)$ a number of times, where $\alpha \in \{B, c\}^+$ and $|\alpha|_B = |\alpha|_c = n$. In order to get rid of the occurrence of the start symbol S, the production $(S \to abc)$ must be used eventually, that is, we have $a^n S \alpha \Rightarrow_G a^{n+1} bc\alpha$. The only way to rewrite the occurrences of the nonterminal B in α into terminal words is provided by the production $(bB \to bb)$, which means that all occurrences of the letter c must be moved to the right across all occurrences of the nonterminal B using the production $(cB \to Bc)$. Thus, we see that the above derivation continues as follows:

$$a^{n+1} bc\alpha \Rightarrow_G^* a^{n+1} b B^n c^{n+1} \Rightarrow_G^* a^{n+1} b^{n+1} c^{n+1}.$$

Thus, it follows that $L(G) = L$.

The grammar G is not context-sensitive because of the production $(cB \to Bc)$. To turn G into an equivalent context-sensitive grammar G', we first introduce a new nonterminal C together with the production $(C \to c)$, and we replace the production $(cB \to Bc)$ with the production $(CB \to BC)$. Then we introduce another two new nonterminals Z_1 and Z_2, and we replace the production $(CB \to BC)$ with the context-sensitive productions

$$(CB \to Z_1 B), (Z_1 B \to Z_1 Z_2), (Z_1 Z_2 \to B Z_2), \text{ and } (B Z_2 \to BC).$$

Thus, we obtain the context-sensitive grammar $G' = (\{S, B, C, Z_1, Z_2\}, \{a, b, c\}, S, P')$, where P' is defined as follows:

$$\begin{aligned} P' \;=\; & \{(S \to aSBc), (S \to abc), (bB \to bb), (C \to c), \\ & (CB \to Z_1 B), (Z_1 B \to Z_1 Z_2), (Z_1 Z_2 \to B Z_2), (B Z_2 \to BC)\}. \end{aligned}$$

■

If G is a monotone grammar, and if $S \Rightarrow_G \alpha_1 \Rightarrow_G \alpha_2 \Rightarrow_G \cdots \Rightarrow_G \alpha_n = w$ is a derivation in G, then $|\alpha_i| \leq |w|$ for all $1 \leq i \leq n$. Hence, in order to decide whether a word $w \in T^n$ belongs to the language $L(G)$, it suffices to inspect all sentential forms $\alpha \in (N \cup T)^*$ of length $|\alpha| \leq n$ that can be derived from S and to check whether the word w is among them. It follows that the membership problem for the language $L(G)$ is decidable (in exponential time). In particular, this implies that CSL is a proper subclass of the class $\mathcal{L}_0$. Actually, the language class CSL has been characterized as a space complexity class, as a language is context-sensitive if and only if it it accepted by a so-called linear-bounded automaton. Such an automaton can be depicted as shown in the diagram in Figure 1.2.

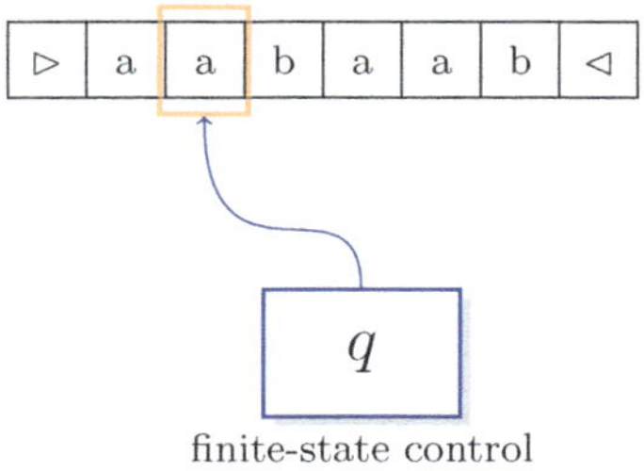

Figure 1.2: A linear-bounded automaton

Definition 1.2.9 (a) *A* linear-bounded automaton *(an LBA) is a nondeterministic Turing machine* $M = (Q, \Sigma, \Gamma, \delta, q_0, \Box, \{q_1\})$ *with a single tape and two end-of-tape markers* $\rhd, \lhd \in (\Gamma \smallsetminus \Sigma)$. *Here* Q *is a finite set of internal states,* $q_0 \in Q$ *is the* initial state, $q_1 \in Q$ *is the* halting state, Σ *is a finite input alphabet,* Γ *is a finite tape alphabet that contains* Σ, *the blank symbol* $\Box$, *and the end-of-tape markers* $\rhd$ *and* $\lhd$, *and*

$$\delta : (Q \smallsetminus \{q_1\}) \times \Gamma \to P_{\text{fin}}(Q \times \Gamma \times \{\text{L}, \text{N}, \text{R}\})$$

is the transition relation. A transition $(q', b, \text{L}) \in \delta(q, a)$ *means that* M, *being in state* q *with the letter* $a \in \Gamma$ *under its head, can replace* a *with the letter* b, *move its head one step to the left, and change to state* q'. *Analogously,* $(q', b, \text{N}) \in \delta(q, a)$ *means that* M, *being in state* q *with the letter* $a \in \Gamma$ *under its head, can replace* a *with the letter* b *and change to state* q' *without moving its head, and finally,* $(q', b, \text{R}) \in \delta(q, a)$ *means that* M, *being in state* q *with the letter* $a \in \Gamma$ *under its head, can replace* a *with the letter* b, *move its head one step to the right, and change to state* q'. *Here it is required that* $\delta(q, \rhd) \subseteq \{\, (q', \rhd, \text{R}) \mid q' \in Q \,\}$ *and that* $\delta(q', \lhd) \subseteq \{\, (q', \lhd, \text{L}) \mid q' \in Q \,\}$ *for each state* $q \in Q$, *that is, on seeing the end-of-tape marker* $\rhd$ *(or* $\lhd$*) under its head, the automaton* M *can just change its state and move to the right (left) without doing any rewriting. In addition,* M *cannot replace any letter from* $\Gamma \smallsetminus \{\rhd, \lhd\}$ *with one of the symbols* $\rhd$ *or* $\lhd$.

(b) *A* configuration *of* M *is a word of the form* $q \rhd u \lhd$ *or* $\rhd u_1 q u_2 \lhd$, *where* $q \in Q$ *and* $u, u_1, u_2 \in (\Gamma \smallsetminus \{\rhd, \lhd\})^*$. *It describes the situation that* M *is in state* q *with the inscription* $\rhd u \lhd$ *or* $\rhd u_1 u_2 \lhd$ *on its tape and its head on the left end-of-tape marker* $\rhd$ *or on the first symbol of* $u_2 \lhd$, *respectively. The transition function* δ *of* M *induces a* single-step computation relation $\vdash_M$ *on the set of configurations of* M, *and* $\vdash_M^*$ *denotes the* computation relation *of* M, *which is the reflexive and transitive closure of the relation* $\vdash_M$.

(c) *For* $w \in \Sigma^*$, $q_0 \rhd w \lhd$ *is the* initial configuration *of* M *on input* w, *that is,* M *starts in its initial state* q_0 *with the inscription* $\rhd w \lhd$ *on its tape and its head on the left end-of-tape marker* $\rhd$.

(d) *A configuration* $q \rhd u \lhd$ *or* $\rhd u_1 q u_2 \lhd$ *is called a* final configuration *if* q *is the halting state* q_1.

(e) *A word* $w \in \Sigma^*$ *is* accepted *by* M *if there exists a computation of* M *that starts from the initial configuration on input* w *and that reaches a* final configuration *of* M. *The language* $L(M) = \{ w \in \Sigma^* \mid w \text{ is accepted by } M \}$ *is the set of all input words that are accepted by* M, *and* $\mathcal{L}(\mathsf{LBA})$ *denotes the class of all languages that are accepted by LBAs.*

Obviously, an LBA M that processes an input $w \in \Sigma^n$ cannot leave the part of its tape that contains the input w, apart from the end-of-tape markers $\rhd$ and $\lhd$, which it can only visit without being able to change them. Instead of using these end-of-tape markers, we could just mark the first and the last letter of w in a special way. This shows that each computation of M on input w just needs n tape squares, that is, the space used is just $|w|$. On the other hand, it can be shown that each nondeterministic Turing machine that only needs space $|w|$ for each input w can be simulated by an LBA. Turing machines of this form are said to be *linear space-bounded.* If we use the notation $\mathsf{NSPACE}(n)$ to denote all those languages that are accepted by nondeterministic Turing machines that are linear space-bounded, then we can formulate the following characterization, which was established by Shigeyuki Kuroda.

Theorem 1.2.10 ([116]) $\mathcal{L}_1 = \mathsf{CSL} = \mathcal{L}(\mathsf{LBA}) = \mathsf{NSPACE}(n)$.

The proof of this result is essentially the same as the one for Theorem 1.2.6. If $L = L(G)$ for a monotone grammar $G = (N, T, S, P)$, then on input w, an LBA can simply guess a derivation $S \Rightarrow_G^* w$, if $w \in L$. On the other hand, if $w \notin L$, then no such derivation can be found, and therefore, the LBA cannot succeed. This shows that L is indeed accepted by an LBA. To prove the converse implication, one constructs a monotone grammar G from a given LBA M such that a terminal derivation of G consists of three parts:

1. first, an encoding of a word $w \in T^*$ is generated;
2. then a computation of M on input w is simulated;
3. and finally, if this computation halts, then the word w is regenerated from the encoding of the halting configuration of M.

A detailed proof can be found, e.g., in [81].

Based on the above characterization, it is easily seen that the language class CSL is closed under the operations of union, intersection, product, Kleene star, non-erasing morphisms, and inverse morphisms (see, e.g., [81]). In addition, as it is a space complexity class, it is also closed under the operation of complementation [82, 250]. On the other hand, while the membership problem is decidable (in exponential time) for each context-sensitive grammar, *emptiness* and *finiteness* are undecidable for these grammars (see, e.g., [81]), that is, there does not exist an algorithm (a Turing machine) that, given a context-sensitive grammar G as input, can decide in a finite number of steps whether or not the language $L(G)$ is empty (finite).

The LBA considered above is a restricted variant of the nondeterministic Turing machine. Obviously, one can also define the corresponding type of deterministic automaton, the *deterministic linear-bounded automaton* or DLBA. We use DCSL to denote the class of all languages that are accepted by DLBAs. Then DCSL coincides with the deterministic space complexity class $\mathsf{DSPACE}(n)$. Of course, $\mathsf{DCSL} \subseteq \mathsf{CSL}$, but it is still an unsolved problem whether this is a proper inclusion. This is the famous *LBA problem* [62].

Corollary 1.2.11 $\mathsf{DCSL} = \mathcal{L}(\mathsf{DLBA}) = \mathsf{DSPACE}(n) \subseteq \mathsf{CSL}$.

Now, deviating from Noam Chomsky's restrictions, we consider an intermediate class of grammars that was introduced by Elias Dahlhaus and Manfred K. Warmuth in [39] and that has received much attention in the literature since.

Definition 1.2.12 *Let* $G = (N, T, S, P)$ *be a phrase-structure grammar. Without loss of generality, we assume that the start symbol* S *does not occur on the right-hand side of any production.*

(a) *The grammar G is called* strictly monotone *if $|\ell| < |r|$ holds for each production $(\ell \to r) \in P$ satisfying $\ell \neq S$. In [39], these grammars have been called* growing.

(b) *A language $L \subseteq T^*$ is* growing context-sensitive *if there exists a strictly monotone grammar G such that $L = L(G)$, and GCSL denotes the* class of growing context-sensitive languages.

(c) *The grammar G is called* quasi-growing [24] *if there exists a* weight function $\omega : (N \cup T) \to \mathbb{N}_+$ *such that $\omega(\ell) < \omega(r)$ holds for each production $(\ell \to r) \in P$ satisfying $\ell \neq S$. Here the function ω is extended to a morphism $\omega : (N \to T)^* \to \mathbb{N}$ by taking $\omega(\lambda) = 0$ and $\omega(\alpha x) = \omega(\alpha) + \omega(x)$ for each sentential form $\alpha \in (N \cup T)^*$ and each letter $x \in N \cup T$.*

Before studying the growing context-sensitive languages in some detail, we consider a simple example.

Example 1.2.13 *Let $G = (N, T, S, P)$ be the grammar that is given through $N = \{S, A, B, C, D\}$, $T = \{a\}$, and*

$$\begin{aligned} P \;=\; & \{(S \to a), (S \to aa), (S \to AC), (A \to AD), (A \to aa), \\ & (DB \to BBD), (DC \to BBC), (C \to aa), (B \to aa)\}. \end{aligned}$$

Obviously, G is strictly monotone, and hence, $L(G)$ is a growing context-sensitive language. We claim that $L(G)$ coincides with the language $L_{\text{exp}} = \{ a^{2^n} \mid n \geq 0 \}$. For proving this, we establish the following technical result, from which the above claim follows as $(S \to a), (S \to aa) \in P$ and $AB^{2^i-2}C \Rightarrow_G^{2^i} a^{2^{i+1}}$ by the productions $(A \to aa)$, $(B \to aa)$, and $(C \to aa)$.

Claim. $\hat{L}(G) \cap \{A, B, C\}^* = \{ AB^{2^i-2}C \mid i \geq 1 \}$.

Proof. *As $S \Rightarrow_G AC = AB^{2^1-2}C$ and $AB^{2^i-2}C \Rightarrow_G ADB^{2^i-2}C \Rightarrow_G^{2^i-2} AB^{2^{i+1}-4}DC \Rightarrow_G AB^{2^{i+1}-2}C$, we see that each word of the form $AB^{2^i-2}C$ can be generated in G.*

Conversely, let $\alpha \in \{A, B, C, D\}^*$ be a sentential form of G, that is, $S \Rightarrow_G^* \alpha$. From the form of the productions in P, we see that $\alpha = A\gamma C$ for some $\gamma \in \{B, D\}^*$. If γ is to contain no occurrence of the nonterminal D, then we see again from the form of the productions in P that $\gamma = B^{2^i-2}$ for some $i \geq 1$. ■

It has been shown by Gerhard Buntrock and Krzysztof Loryś in [24] that the class GCSL coincides with the class of languages that are generated by quasi-growing grammars, and that it also coincides with the class of languages that are generated by quasi-growing monotone grammars. Furthermore, it has been observed by Gundula Niemann and Jens Woinowski in [187] that each growing context-sensitive language is generated by a grammar that is context-sensitive and at the same time quasi-growing. In addition, it is shown in [24] that GCSL is an *abstract family of languages* (that is, an AFL), which means that this class is closed under the operations of union, product, Kleene plus (or iteration), intersection with regular languages, non-erasing morphisms, and inverse morphisms. Finally, Elias Dahlhaus and Manfred Warmuth proved that the membership problem for any growing context-sensitive language is decidable in polynomial time [39], where, however, the degree of the polynomial run time depends on the grammar considered. And indeed, Gerhard Buntrock and Krzysztof Loryś complemented this result in [24] by establishing that the *uniform membership problem* for growing context-sensitive languages is NP-complete with respect to log-space (one-way) reductions. Here the uniform membership problem takes as input a strictly monotone grammar G and a terminal word w and asks whether $w \in L(G)$ holds.

The class GCSL has also been characterized by a special type of two-pushdown automaton [25, 186], which is a two-tape Turing machine both tapes of which are used as pushdowns or first-in last-out storage devices. A two-pushdown automaton can be depicted as shown in the diagram in Figure 1.3. Formally, it is defined as follows.

Definition 1.2.14 *A* two-pushdown automaton (TPDA) *with* pushdown windows of size k *is a nondeterministic automaton $P = (Q, \Sigma, \Gamma, \delta, k, q_0, \perp, t_1, t_2, F)$, where Q is a finite set of states, Σ is*

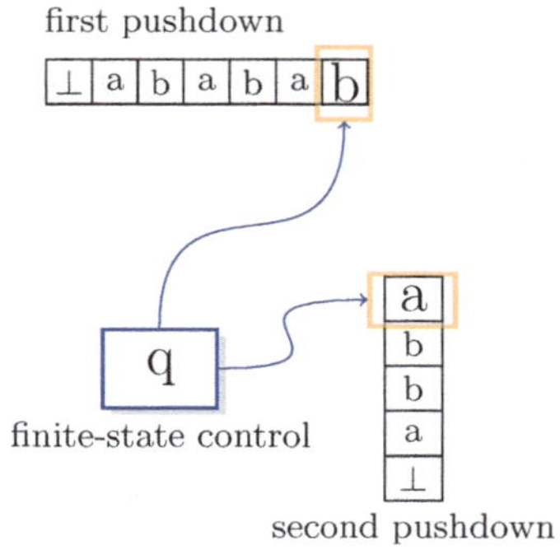

Figure 1.3: A two-pushdown automaton with pushdown windows of size 1

a finite input alphabet, Γ is a finite tape alphabet containing Σ, $q_0 \in Q$ is the initial state, $\bot \in \Gamma \smallsetminus \Sigma$ is the bottom marker of the pushdown stores, $t_1, t_2 \in (\Gamma \smallsetminus \Sigma)^*$ is the preassigned contents of the first and second pushdown store, respectively, $F \subseteq Q$ is the set of final (or halting) states, and δ is the transition relation. To each triple (q, u, v), where $q \in Q$ is a state, $u \in \Gamma^k \cup \{\bot\} \cdot \Gamma^{<k}$ is the contents of the topmost part of the first pushdown store, and $v \in \Gamma^k \cup \Gamma^{<k} \cdot \{\bot\}$ is the contents of the topmost part of the second pushdown store, it associates a finite set of triples from $Q \times \Gamma^* \times \Gamma^*$. The automaton P is a deterministic two-pushdown automaton *(DTPDA), if δ is a (partial) function.*

If P is in state q seeing the suffix u of the contents of the first pushdown and the prefix v of the contents of the second pushdown in its windows, and if $(q', u', v') \in \delta(q, u, v)$, then by applying this transition, P changes to state q', the suffix u of the first pushdown is replaced with the word u', and the prefix v of the second pushdown is replaced with the word v'.

A *configuration* of a (D)TPDA is written as xqy, where $q \in Q$ is the current state, $x \in \Gamma^*$ is the contents of the first pushdown store with the first letter of x at the bottom and the last letter of x at the top, and $y \in \Gamma^*$ is the contents of the second pushdown store with the last letter of y at the bottom and the first letter of y at the top. Thus, the above step will transform a configuration of the form $\bot xuqvy\bot$ into the configuration $\bot xu'q'v'y\bot$, and the configuration of the TPDA depicted in the diagram in Figure 1.3 is $\bot abababqabba\bot$. For an input word $w \in \Sigma^*$, the corresponding initial configuration is $\bot t_1 q_0 w t_2 \bot$. The computation relation that a (D)TPDA P induces on its set of configurations is denoted by $\vdash_P^*$. The (D)TPDA P accepts with empty pushdown stores, that is,

$$L(P) = \{ w \in \Sigma^* \mid \bot t_1 q_0 w t_2 \bot \vdash_P^* q \text{ for some } q \in F \}$$

is the *language accepted by P*. Observe that the input is provided to a TPDA as (a part of) the initial contents of its second pushdown store, and that in order to accept, a TPDA is required to empty its pushdown stores. Thus, it is forced to consume its input completely.

It can easily be seen that each Turing machine can be simulated by a DTPDA, and conversely, a TPDA can be simulated by a (nondeterministic) Turing machine (see, e.g., [79]). Hence, the class of languages that are accepted by (D)TPDAs coincides with the class RE of recursively enumerable languages. Here, however, we are interested in certain restricted variants of the TPDA.

Definition 1.2.15 ([25, 186]) *Let $P = (Q, \Sigma, \Gamma, \delta, k, q_0, \bot, t_1, t_2, F)$ be a (D)TPDA.*

(a) *The (D)TPDA is called* shrinking *if there exists a* weight function *$\varphi : Q \cup \Gamma \to \mathbb{N}_+$ such that, for all transitions $(p, u', v') \in \delta(q, u, v)$, $\varphi(u'pv') < \varphi(uqv)$. Here φ is extended to a morphism $\varphi : (Q \cup \Gamma)^* \to \mathbb{N}$ in the obvious way.*

(b) *The (D)TPDA is called* length-reducing *if $|u'v'| < |uv|$ holds for all transitions $(p, u', v') \in \delta(q, u, v)$.*

Thus, if P is a shrinking TPDA with weight function φ, then $\varphi(C) > \varphi(C')$ whenever $C \vdash_P C'$, and if P is a length-reducing TPDA, then $|C| > |C'|$ whenever $C \vdash_P C'$. Obviously, each length-reducing TPDA is shrinking with weight function $\varphi(a) = 1$ for all $a \in Q \cup \Gamma$.

We illustrate the way in which a TPDA works with a simple example.

Example 1.2.16 *We present a length-reducing DTPDA for the language* $L_{\text{exp}} = \{\, a^{2^n} \mid n \geq 0 \,\}$. *Let* $P_{\text{exp}} = (\{q_0, q_1, q_+\}, \{a\}, \{a, \bot\}, \delta, 2, q_0, \bot, \lambda, \lambda, \{q_+\})$, *where the transition function* δ *is defined as follows:*

$$\begin{array}{llcllll}
(1) & \delta(q_0, \bot, a\bot) & = & (q_+, \lambda, \lambda), & (6) & \delta(q_0, aa, \bot) & = & (q_1, \lambda, a\bot),\\
(2) & \delta(q_0, \bot, aa) & = & (q_0, \bot a, \lambda), & (7) & \delta(q_1, aa, a\bot) & = & (q_1, \lambda, aa\bot),\\
(3) & \delta(q_0, \bot a, aa) & = & (q_0, \bot aa, \lambda), & (8) & \delta(q_1, aa, aa) & = & (q_1, \lambda, aaa),\\
(4) & \delta(q_0, \bot a, \bot) & = & (q_+, \lambda, \lambda), & (9) & \delta(q_1, \bot, aa) & = & (q_0, \bot a, \lambda),\\
(5) & \delta(q_0, aa, aa) & = & (q_0, aaa, \lambda), & (10) & \delta(q_1, \bot, a\bot) & = & (q_+, \lambda, \lambda).
\end{array}$$

Let $w = a^{2^n}$. *Given* w *as input,* P_{exp} *proceeds as follows:*

$$\begin{array}{lllll}
\bot q_0 w \bot = \bot q_0 a^{2^n} \bot & \vdash_{P_{\text{exp}}}^{2^{n-1}} & \bot a^{2^{n-1}} q_0 \bot & \vdash_{P_{\text{exp}}} & \bot a^{2^{n-1}-2} q_1 a \bot \\
& \vdash_{P_{\text{exp}}}^{2^{n-2}-1} & \bot q_1 a^{2^{n-2}} \bot & \vdash_{P_{\text{exp}}} & \bot a q_0 a^{2^{n-2}-2} \bot,
\end{array}$$

that is, it first checks whether the number of a's is even, shifting all a's from the second pushdown to the first pushdown, thereby dividing the number of a's by two, and then it checks whether the number of a's on the first pushdown is even, shifting all a's from the first pushdown back to the second pushdown, again dividing the number of a's by two. This continues until either a single a is obtained, and then P_{exp} *enters state* q_+ *and accepts, or until an uneven number of a's larger than two is detected on one of the pushdowns, and then* P *gets stuck without accepting. Thus, we see that indeed* $L(P_{\text{exp}}) = L_{\text{exp}}$. ■

The main result of [25] states that a language is growing context-sensitive iff it is accepted by a shrinking TPDA. In [186], this result is strengthened to length-reducing TPDAs.

Theorem 1.2.17 ([25, 186]) *For a language* $L \subseteq \Sigma^*$, *the following three conditions are equivalent:*

(a) *L is a growing context-sensitive language.*

(b) *There exists a shrinking TPDA P such that $L(P) = L$.*

(c) *There exists a length-reducing TPDA P such that $L(P) = L$.*

From a shrinking TPDA M that accepts a language $L \subseteq \Sigma^*$, one can construct a quasi-growing gammar G such that the derivations of G simulate the computations of M in reverse order. Conversely, let $G' = (N, \Sigma, S, P)$ be a quasi-growing monotone grammar. We can associate a set of rules R_G with G by taking $R_G = \{\, u \to v \mid (v \to u) \in P \,\}$. Then, for each word $w \in \Sigma^*$, $w \Rightarrow_{R_G}^* S$ iff $w \in L(G)$. In fact, if $w \in L(G)$, then there is an *ordered derivation* [59] from w to S with respect to R_G, which means that, in such a derivation, no step is performed entirely to the left of the previous step. Now one can design a shrinking TPDA M' that simulates the ordered derivations with respect to R_G, which shows that $L(M') = L(G')$. Finally, if M_s is a shrinking TPDA with weight function φ, then we can define a morphism $h : \Gamma^* \to (\Gamma \cup \{\#\})^*$ by taking $h(a) = a\#^{\varphi(a)-1}$ for all $a \in \Gamma$. Then $|h(w)| = \varphi(w)$ for each word $w \in \Gamma^*$. It is now easy to design a length-reducing TPDA M_s' such that, given the word $h(w)$ as input, M_s' simulates the computations of M_s on input w. By using an encoding and a technically involved compression technique (see [186]), a length-reducing TPDA M_l can be obtained that, given a word $w \in \Sigma^*$ as input, simulates the computations of M_s' on input $h(w)$, which implies that $L(M_l) = L(M_s)$.

From results presented by A.V. Gladkij [52] (see also Ronald V. Book's PhD thesis [16]), it follows that the so-called *Gladkij language*

$$L_{\text{Glad}} = \{\, wcw^Rcw \mid w \in \{a, b\}^* \,\}$$

is not growing context-sensitive. Also it is shown in [25] that the *copy language*

$$L_{\text{copy}} = \{ ww \mid w \in \{a,b\}^* \}$$

and the *marked copy language*

$$L'_{\text{copy}} = \{ wcw \mid w \in \{a,b\}^* \}$$

are not growing context-sensitive. On the other hand, the complements of these languages are growing context-sensitive (in fact, they are even context-free, see below). Furthermore, L_{Glad} is the intersection of the two languages

$$L_1 = \{ wcw^R cz \mid w,z \in \{a,b\}^* \} \text{ and } L_2 = \{ wcz^R cz \mid w,z \in \{a,b\}^* \},$$

which are growing context-sensitive (in fact, context-free). Thus, we see that the class GCSL is neither closed under complementation nor under intersection. In addition, it can be shown that this class is not closed under arbitrary morphisms [23]. Finally, the languages above are all accepted by DLBAs. In fact, we have the following proper inclusion.

Corollary 1.2.18 $\mathsf{GCSL} \subsetneq \mathsf{DCSL}$.

In [150], Robert McNaughton reviews the above results on growing context-sensitive languages and asks whether GCSL should be inserted as a new class into the Chomsky hierarchy.

The growing context-sensitive languages are characterized by the nondeterministic shrinking TPDAs. What about the deterministic shrinking TPDAs? In [151], Robert McNaughton and Paliath Narendran, together with the author, introduced a class of languages based not on grammars or automata but on a special class of string-rewriting systems: the class CRL of *Church-Rosser languages*. A detailed study of these languages can be found in Gundula Niemann's doctoral dissertation [181], which contains the following characterization of the class of Church-Rosser languages.

Theorem 1.2.19 ([181, 186]) *For a language $L \subseteq \Sigma^*$, the following three conditions are equivalent:*

(a) *L is a Church-Rosser language.*

(b) *There exists a shrinking DTPDA P such that $L(P) = L$.*

(c) *There exists a length-reducing DTPDA P such that $L(P) = L$.*

Hence, the Church-Rosser languages can be interpreted as the deterministic variants of the growing context-sensitive languages. Example 1.2.16 above shows that $L_{\text{exp}} = \{ a^{2^n} \mid n \geq 0 \}$ is a Church-Rosser language. On the other hand, based on the characterization through length-reducing DTPDAs, Tomasz Jurdziński and Krzysztof Loryś proved that the language of palindromes of even length $L_{\text{pal}} = \{ ww^R \mid w \in \{a,b\}^* \}$ is not Church-Rosser [93] (see also [188]). As the latter is clearly growing context-sensitive, this yields the following proper inclusion.

Corollary 1.2.20 $\mathsf{CRL} \subsetneq \mathsf{GCSL}$.

The class CRL is closed under the operations of complementation, intersection with regular sets, reversal, and inverse morphisms, but it is not closed under intersection, union, product, Kleene star, and non-erasing morphisms [181, 186].

Furthermore, the membership problem for a Church-Rosser language is decidable in linear time, as a length-reducing DTPDA can easily be simulated by a two-tape Turing machine that runs in linear time. Unfortunately, the following problems are undecidable for Church-Rosser languages [151] and, therewith, also for growing context-sensitive languages:

The Emptiness Problem:
INSTANCE: A Church-Rosser language L given through a length-reducing DTPDA.
QUESTION: Is L empty?

The Finiteness Problem:
INSTANCE: A Church-Rosser language L given through a length-reducing DTPDA.
QUESTION: Is L finite?

After this excursion, we now return to Noam Chomsky's original classes of grammars and the corresponding classes of languages by studying the second of his restrictions for phrase-structure grammars.

Definition 1.2.21 *Let $G = (N, T, S, P)$ be a phrase-structure grammar. Without loss of generality, we assume that the start symbol S does not occur on the right-hand side of any production.*

(a) *The grammar G is a* context-free grammar *if each production $(\ell \to r) \in P$ has the form $\ell = A$ and $r = x$, where $A \in N$ and $x \in (N \cup T)^*$. Following Noam Chomsky's notation, context-free grammars are also called* grammars of type 2.

(b) *A language $L \subseteq T^*$ is* context-free *or* of type 2 *if there exists a context-free grammar G such that $L = L(G)$, and CFL denotes the* class of context-free languages. *This class is also denoted by $\mathcal{L}_2$.*

(c) *A context-free grammar $G = (N, T, S, P)$ is in* Chomsky normal form *(CNF) if each production $(A \to x) \in P$ satisfies the condition that $x \in T$ or $x \in N^2$. In addition, P may contain the production $(S \to \lambda)$.*

We see that the phrase-structure grammar given in Example 1.2.1 is actually of type two. As shown there, each derivation in a grammar of this type can be displayed in the form of a syntax tree. Furthermore, each context-free grammar can be turned into a context-free grammar in CNF for the same language [29]. As each context-free grammar in CNF is obviously context-sensitive and easily shown to be also quasi-growing, this shows that the context-free languages are contained in the growing context-sensitive languages. We illustrate the definitions above by presenting some simple, but important examples.

Example 1.2.22 *Let $n \geq 1$, $\Sigma_n = \{a_1, a_2, \ldots, a_n\} \cup \{b_1, b_2, \ldots, b_n\}$, and let $G_n = (\{S\}, \Sigma_n, S, P_n)$ with*

$$P_n = \{(S \to \lambda), (S \to SS)\} \cup \{\, (S \to a_i S b_i) \mid 1 \leq i \leq n \,\}.$$

Then $L(G_n)$ is the semi-Dyck language *D_n (see, e.g., [60]). Here each letter a_i can be seen as an opening bracket, and the letter b_i is the corresponding closing bracket. Then $D_n = L(G_n)$ consists of all correctly bracketed expressions over Σ_n. For example, the word $a_1a_2b_2a_3b_3b_1$ belongs to D_3, but the word $a_1a_3b_2a_2b_3b_1$ does not.*

By taking $G'_n = (\{S\}, \Sigma_n, S, P'_n)$ with

$$P'_n = \{(S \to \lambda), (S \to SS)\} \cup \{\, (S \to a_i S b_i), (S \to b_i S a_i) \mid 1 \leq i \leq n \,\},$$

we obtain $L(G'_n) = D'_n$, the Dyck language *over Σ_n (again, see [60]). In this case, the letter b_i is interpreted as a left inverse and a right inverse of the letter a_i. For example, the word $a_1a_3b_2a_2b_3b_1$ belongs to D'_3.* ∎

Finally, we demonstrate the conversion of a context-free grammer into CNF.

Example 1.2.23 *Let $G_1 = (\{S\}, \{a, b\}, S, P_1)$ with $P_1 = \{(S \to \lambda), (S \to aSa), (S \to bSb)\}$. Then G_1 is a context-free grammar that generates the language $L_{\text{pal}} = \{\, ww^R \mid w \in \{a, b\}^* \,\}$. Of course, G_1 is not in CNF as the right-hand side of the second and third productions are not of the correct form, and as the start symbol occurs on the right-hand side of these productions.*

In order to eliminate the latter problem, we introduce a new nonterminal A and replace P_1 with the following set of productions:

$$P_2 = \{(S \to \lambda), (S \to aAa), (S \to bAb), (A \to \lambda), (A \to aAa), (A \to bAb)\}.$$

Next we eliminate the λ-production $(A \to \lambda)$ by replacing it with the productions $(S \to aa)$, $(S \to bb)$, $(A \to aa)$, and $(A \to bb)$.

Finally, we introduce four new nonterminals X_a, X_b, Y, Z and replace the above productions with the following set of productions:

$$\begin{aligned} P_3 = \{ & (S \to \lambda), (S \to X_aX_a), (S \to X_bX_b), (S \to X_aY), (S \to X_bZ), \\ & (A \to X_aX_a), (A \to X_bX_b), (A \to X_aY), (A \to X_bZ), \\ & (X_a \to a), (X_b \to b), (Y \to AX_a), (Z \to AX_b)\}. \end{aligned}$$

Then the grammar $G_3 = (\{S, A, X_a, X_b, Y, Z\}, \{a, b\}, S, P_3)$ is in CNF, and it can be checked quite easily that it generates the language L_{pal}. ■

As the language L_{pal} is not Church-Rosser (see above), we conclude that the class CFL of context-free languages is not contained in the class CRL of Church-Rosser languages. On the other hand, the Church-Rosser language $L_{\text{exp}} = \{ a^{2^n} \mid n \geq 0 \}$ is not context-free. This is an easy consequence of the following lemma.

Lemma 1.2.24 (Pumping Lemma for Context-Free Languages [6])
Let L be a context-free language over Σ. Then there exists a positive constant k_L such that each word $w \in L$ of length $|w| \geq k_L$ has a factorization of the form $w = uvxyz$ that satisfies the following three conditions:

$$(1)\ |vxy| \leq k_L,\ (2)\ |vy| > 0,\ \textit{and}\ (3)\ uv^ixy^iz \in L \textit{ for all } i \in \mathbb{N}.$$

Assume that L_{exp} were context-free, and let $k \geq 1$ denote the corresponding constant from the Pumping Lemma. Consider the word $w = a^{2^k}$. Then $w \in L_{\text{exp}}$ and $|w| = 2^k > k$. Hence, w has a factorization $w = uvxyz$ that satisfies the three conditions of the Pumping Lemma. This means that $u = a^i$, $v = a^j$, $x = a^r$, $y = a^s$, and $z = a^{2^k-i-j-r-s}$, where $j + r + s \leq k$ and $j + s > 0$. Then $uv^2xy^2z = a^ia^{2j}x^ra^{2s}a^{2^k-i-j-r-s} = a^{2^k+j+s}$, and as $0 < j + s \leq j + r + s \leq k$, we see that $2^k < 2^k + j + s \leq 2^k + k < 2^{k+1}$, which shows that $2^k + j + s$ is not a power of two. Thus, the word uv^2xy^2z is not an element of the language L_{exp}, a contradiction! This means that the language L_{pal} is actually not context-free. Hence, we have the following results.

Corollary 1.2.25 $\mathsf{CFL} \subsetneq \mathsf{GCSL}$, *while* CFL *is incomparable to* CRL *with respect to inclusion.*

By applying the Pumping Lemma, it can easily be shown that the following languages are not context-free, either:

- the language of *multiple agreements*: $L_{\text{mul}} = \{ a^nb^nc^n \mid n \geq 0 \}$, and
- the language of *cross-serial dependencies*: $L_{\text{cd}} = \{ a^mb^na^mb^n \mid m, n \geq 0 \}$.

These languages embody certain phenomena that occur in some natural languages (see, e.g., [245]), supporting the argument that natural languages are not context-free. Observe, however, that both these languages are accepted by shrinking DTPDAs, and so they are Church-Rosser.

From given context-free grammars G_1 and G_2, one can construct context-free grammars for the languages $L(G_1) \cup L(G_2)$, $L(G_1) \cdot L(G_2)$, $(L(G_1))^*$, $(L(G_1))^R$, and $h(L(G_1))$, where h is a morphism. On the other hand, the intersection of the two context-free languages

$$L_1 = \{ a^mb^mc^n \mid m, n \geq 0 \} \text{ and } L_2 = \{ a^mb^nc^n \mid m, n \geq 0 \}$$

yields the language of multiple agreements L_{mul}, which is not context-free. Thus, we have the following closure and non-closure properties for the class CFL of context-free languages.

Corollary 1.2.26 *The class* CFL *of context-free languages is closed under the operations of union, product, Kleene star, reversal, and the application of a morphism, but it is not closed under intersection and complementation.*

The Chomsky normal form guarantees that each inner node (that is, each non-leaf) of a syntax tree has two children and that each derivation of a word of length $n > 0$ comprises $n-1$ applications of productions of the form $(A \to BC)$, where A, B, C are nonterminals, and n applications of terminal productions (that is, productions of the form $(A \to a)$, where A is a nonterminal and a is a terminal). These properties are quite handy in certain constructions or proofs. For example, the proof of the Pumping Lemma is quite easy if the underlying grammar is assumed to be in CNF (see, e.g., [79]). However, for some applications, another form of the productions of a context-free grammar are more advantageous.

Definition 1.2.27 *Let $G = (N, T, S, P)$ be a context-free grammar such that the start symbol S does not occur on the right-hand side of any production.*

(a) *The grammar G is in* Greibach normal form *if each production $(A \to x)$ satisfies the condition that $x \in T \cdot N^*$. In addition, P may contain the production $(S \to \lambda)$.*

(b) *The grammar G is in* quadratic Greibach normal form *if each production $(A \to x)$ satisfies the condition that $x \in T \cdot N^{\leq 2}$. In addition, P may contain the production $(S \to \lambda)$.*

For example, the grammar $G = (\{S, A, B\}, \{a, b\}, S, P)$, where

$$P = \{(S \to \lambda), (S \to aAB), (S \to aB), (A \to aAB), (A \to aB), (B \to b)\},$$

is in quadratic Greibach normal form. It generates the language $L(G) = \{\, a^n b^n \mid n \geq 0 \,\}$.

Theorem 1.2.28 ([56, 230]) *From a given context-free grammar G, one can effectively construct an equivalent context-free grammar G' in (quadratic) Greibach normal form.*

The Greibach normal form guarantees that each derivation of a word of length $n > 0$ consists of exactly n steps. In fact, in each left-most derivation, the i-th letter of w is generated by the i-th step of this derivation. This simplifies the process of parsing significantly.

Next we turn to the pushdown automaton, which is a model of automaton that corresponds to the context-free languages. A pushdown automaton consists of a finite-state control, an input tape with a read-only head, and a pushdown, which is an auxiliary tape that is only used as a last-in first-out storage. A pushdown automaton can be depicted as shown in the diagram in Figure 1.4. Formally, it is defined as follows.

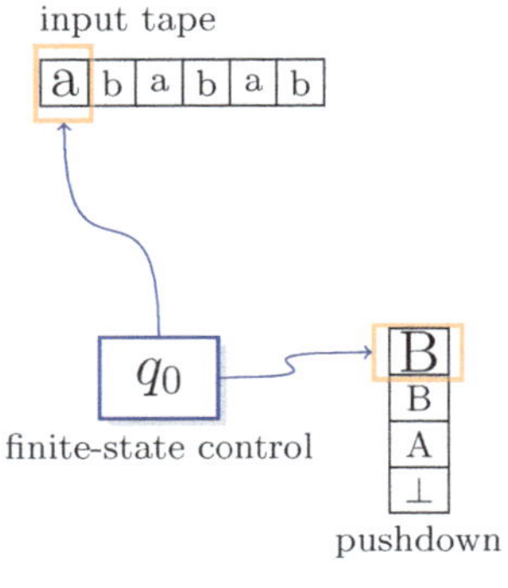

Figure 1.4: A pushdown automaton

Definition 1.2.29 *A* pushdown automaton, *or a* PDA, *is a nondeterministic automaton that is defined by a 7-tuple* $P = (Q, \Sigma, \Gamma, \delta, q_0, \bot, F)$, *where* Q *is a finite set of states,* Σ *is a finite input alphabet,* Γ *is a finite pushdown alphabet containing the* bottom marker $\bot$ *of the pushdown store,* $q_0 \in Q$ *is the initial state,* $F \subseteq Q$ *is the set of accepting states, and* δ *is the transition relation. To each triple* (q, a, B), *where* $q \in Q$ *is a state,* $a \in \Sigma \cup \{\lambda\}$, *and* $B \in \Gamma$ *is the topmost letter on the pushdown store, it associates a finite set of pairs from* $Q \times \Gamma^*$.

If P is in state q seeing the letter $a \in \Sigma$ on the input tape and the letter $B \in \Gamma$ as the topmost letter on its pushdown, and if $(q', v') \in \delta(q, a, B)$, then by applying this transition, P changes to state q', the letter a is consumed from the input tape, and the letter B on top of the pushdown is replaced with the word v'. Furthermore, if P is in state q with the letter $B \in \Gamma$ as the topmost letter on its pushdown, and if $(q', u') \in \delta(q, \lambda, B)$, then by applying this transition, P changes to state q' and replaces the letter B on the top of its pushdown with the word u' without taking the current input letter into account.

A *configuration* of a PDA is described by a triple (q, x, y), where $q \in Q$ is the current state, $x \in \Gamma^*$ is the still unread part of the input, and $y \in \Gamma^*$ is the contents of the pushdown store with the first letter of y at the bottom and the last letter of y at the top. Thus, the above step will transform a configuration of the form $(q, ax, \bot yB)$ into the configuration $(q', x, \bot yv')$, and the configuration of the PDA depicted in the diagram in Figure 1.4 is $(q_0, ababab, \bot ABB)$. For an input word $w \in \Sigma^*$, the corresponding initial configuration is $(q_0, w, \bot)$. The computation relation that a PDA P induces on its set of configurations is denoted by $\vdash_P^*$. The PDA P accepts either by final state or by empty pushdown, that is,

$$L(P) = \{\, w \in \Sigma^* \mid \exists q \in F\, \exists \alpha \in \Gamma^* : (q_0, w, \bot) \vdash_P^* (q, \lambda, \alpha) \,\}$$

is the *language accepted by* P *by final state*, and

$$N(P) = \{\, w \in \Sigma^* \mid \exists q \in Q : (q_0, w, \bot) \vdash_P^* (q, \lambda, \lambda) \,\}$$

is the *language accepted by* P *by empty pushdown.*

We illustrate this definition by presenting a PDA for the language $L_{\text{pal}} = \{\, ww^R \mid w \in \{a, b\}^* \,\}$.

Example 1.2.30 *Let* $P_1 = (Q, \Sigma, \Gamma, \delta, q_0, \bot, F)$ *be the PDA that is defined by* $Q = \{q_0, q_1, q_2, q_3\}$, $F = \{q_3\}$, $\Sigma = \{a, b\}$, *and* $\Gamma = \{A, B, \bot\}$, *where* δ *is given by the following table:*

Current State	*Input Letter*	*Pushdown Symbol*	*Transition*
q_0	a	$\bot$	$\{(q_1, \bot A)\}$
q_0	b	$\bot$	$\{(q_1, \bot B)\}$
q_0	λ	$\bot$	$\{(q_3, \lambda)\}$
q_1	a	A	$\{(q_1, AA)\}$
q_1	a	B	$\{(q_1, BA)\}$
q_1	b	A	$\{(q_1, AB)\}$
q_1	b	B	$\{(q_1, BB)\}$
q_1	λ	A	$\{(q_2, A)\}$
q_1	λ	B	$\{(q_2, B)\}$
q_2	a	A	$\{(q_2, \lambda)\}$
q_2	b	B	$\{(q_2, \lambda)\}$
q_2	λ	$\bot$	$\{(q_3, \lambda)\}$

Given the word abba as input, the PDA P_1 *can execute the following computation (among others):*

$$\begin{aligned} (q_0, abba, \bot) &\vdash_{P_1} (q_1, bba, \bot A) \vdash_{P_1} (q_1, ba, \bot AB) \vdash_{P_1} (q_2, ba, \bot AB) \\ &\vdash_{P_1} (q_2, a, \bot A) \vdash_{P_1} (q_2, \lambda, \bot) \vdash_{P_1} (q_3, \lambda, \lambda), \end{aligned}$$

that is, P_1 *accepts the word abba by final state as well as by empty pushdown. In fact, it is not hard to see that* $L(P_1) = N(P_1) = \{\, ww^R \mid w \in \{a, b\}^* \,\}$. ■

While for the above PDA P_1, the two languages $L(P_1)$ and $N(P_1)$ coincide, this is not true in general. We illustrate this fact with the following simple example.

Example 1.2.31 *Let $P_2 = (Q, \Sigma, \Gamma, \delta, q_0, \bot, F)$ be the PDA that is defined by $Q = \{q_0, q_1\}$, $F = \{q_0\}$, $\Sigma = \{a, b\}$, and $\Gamma = \{\bot\}$, where δ is given by the following table:*

Current State	*Input Symbol*	*Pushdown Symbol*	*Transition*
q_0	a	$\bot$	$\{(q_1, \bot)\}$
q_1	b	$\bot$	$\{(q_0, \bot)\}$

On input abab, the PDA P_2 can execute the following computation:

$$(q_0, abab, \bot) \vdash_{P_2} (q_1, bab, \bot) \vdash_{P_2} (q_0, ab, \bot) \vdash_{P_2} (q_1, b, \bot) \vdash_{P_2} (q_0, \lambda, \bot),$$

that is, P_2 accepts the word abab by final state. In fact, it is not hard to see that $L(P_2) = \{ab\}^*$. On the other hand, P_2 cannot possibly empty its pushdown, which shows that $N(P_2) = \emptyset$. ■

While for a given PDA P, the languages $L(P)$ and $N(P)$ may differ, it can be shown that the resulting classes of languages coincide (see, e.g., [79]).

Proposition 1.2.32

(a) *From a PDA P_1, one can effectively construct a PDA P_2 such that $N(P_2) = L(P_1)$.*

(b) *From a PDA P_1, one can effectively construct a PDA P_2 such that $L(P_2) = N(P_1)$.*

This means that, in what follows, we can always use the acceptance mode that suits our purpose best. Concerning the expressive capacity of pushdown automata, the following characterization has been obtained.

Theorem 1.2.33 ([30, 237])
A language $L \subseteq \Sigma^*$ is accepted by a PDA if and only if it is context-free.

Let $L \subseteq \Sigma^*$ be a context-free language. By Theorem 1.2.28, there exists a context-free grammar $G = (V, \Sigma, S, P)$ in (quadratic) Greibach normal form for L. From G, we obtain a PDA $P_G = (Q, \Sigma, \Gamma, \delta, q_0, \bot, \emptyset)$ for L by taking $Q = \{q_0\}$, $\Gamma = V$, $\bot = S$, and by defining the transition relation δ as follows:

$$\begin{array}{rcll} \delta(q_0, a, A) & = & \{\,(q_0, \alpha^R) \mid (A \to a\alpha) \in P\,\} & \text{for all } a \in \Sigma \text{ and } A \in V, \\ \delta(q_0, \lambda, S) & = & \{(q_0, \lambda)\}, & \text{if } (S \to \lambda) \in P. \end{array}$$

Then the accepting computations of P_G correspond exactly to the left-most derivations in G, showing that $N(P_G) = L(G) = L$. We illustrate this construction with another simple example.

Example 1.2.34 *Let $G = (V, \Sigma, S, P)$ be given by $V = \{S, A, B, C\}$, $\Sigma = \{a, b\}$, and*

$$\begin{array}{rcl} P & = & \{S \to \lambda, S \to aA, S \to bB, S \to aCA, S \to bCB, \\ & & \;A \to a, B \to b, C \to aA, C \to bB, C \to aCA, C \to bCB\}. \end{array}$$

Then G is in quadratic Greibach normal form, and it can be seen quite easily that $L(G) = L_{\text{pal}}$. From G, the above construction yields the PDA $P_G = (\{q_0\}, \{a, b\}, \{S, A, B, C\}, \delta, q_0, S, \emptyset)$, where the transition relation δ is defined as follows:

$$\begin{array}{rclrcl} \delta(q_0, a, S) & = & \{(q_0, A), (q_0, AC)\}, & \delta(q_0, a, A) & = & \{(q_0, \lambda)\}, \\ \delta(q_0, b, S) & = & \{(q_0, B), (q_0, BC)\}, & \delta(q_0, b, B) & = & \{(q_0, \lambda)\}, \\ \delta(q_0, a, C) & = & \{(q_0, A), (q_0, AC)\}, & \delta(q_0, \lambda, S) & = & \{(q_0, \lambda)\}. \\ \delta(q_0, b, C) & = & \{(q_0, B), (q_0, BC)\}, & & & \end{array}$$

Now the (left-most) derivation

$$S \Rightarrow_G aCA \Rightarrow_G abCBA \Rightarrow_G abbBBA \Rightarrow_G abbbBA \Rightarrow_G abbbbA \Rightarrow_G abbbba$$

is reflected by the following computation of P_G:

$$\begin{array}{llllll} (q_0, abbbba, S) & \vdash_{P_G} & (q_0, bbbba, AC) & \vdash_{P_G} & (q_0, bbba, ABC) & \vdash_{P_G} & (q_0, bba, ABB) \\ & \vdash_{P_G} & (q_0, ba, AB) & \vdash_{P_G} & (q_0, a, A) & \vdash_{P_G} & (q_0, \lambda, \lambda). \end{array}$$

Conversely, every accepting computation of P_G *corresponds to a left-most derivation by* G. *It follows that* $N(P_G) = L(G) = L_{\mathrm{pal}}$. ■

On the other hand, a context-free grammar G_P can be constructed from a given PDA P such that $L(G) = N(P_G)$. However, this construction is more involved, as it has to cover all possible cases that may occur in the definition of P, that is, a finite number of states and all possible forms of transitions (see, e.g., the construction given in [79]). Together these constructions show the following result.

Corollary 1.2.35 *For each PDA* P_1 *that does not accept on empty input, there exists a PDA* P_2 *such that* $L(P_2) = L(P_1)$, P_2 *has only a single state, it does not perform any* λ*-steps, and the size of its pushdown can increase by at most one in any step.*

In addition to its accepted language, there is another language that we can associate with a PDA: the language of possible pushdown contents. Let $P = (Q, \Sigma, \Gamma, \delta, q_0, \perp, F)$ be a PDA. Without loss of generality we may assume that during any computation of P, its pushdown contents is always a word from the set $\perp \cdot (\Gamma \smallsetminus \{\perp\})^*$. Thus, P does not empty its pushdown, the symbol at the bottom of the pushdown is always the bottom marker $\perp$, and this symbol cannot occur anywhere else in the pushdown. For an input word $w \in \Sigma^*$, let

$$\mathrm{SC}_P(w) = \{\, \alpha \in (\Gamma \smallsetminus \{\perp\})^* \mid \exists q \in F : (q_0, w, \perp) \vdash_P^* (q, \lambda, \perp\alpha) \,\}$$

be the set of *possible pushdown contents of* P *on input* w. For a language $H \subseteq \Sigma^*$,

$$\mathrm{SC}_P(H) = \bigcup_{w \in H} \mathrm{SC}_P(w).$$

Thus, P can be seen as realizing a transformation $\mathrm{SC}_P : \mathcal{P}(\Sigma^*) \to \mathcal{P}((\Gamma \smallsetminus \{\perp\})^*)$. Concerning this transformation, the following result is known.

Theorem 1.2.36 ([57]) *Let* $P = (Q, \Sigma, \Gamma, \delta, q_0, \perp, F)$ *be a PDA with input alphabet* Σ, *and let* H *be a regular language over* Σ. *Then* $\mathrm{SC}_P(H)$ *is a regular language over* $\Gamma \smallsetminus \{\perp\}$.

If $L \subseteq \Delta^*$ is a context-free language, and if $h : \Sigma^* \to \Delta^*$ is a morphism, then

$$h^{-1}(L) = \{\, w \in \Sigma^* \mid h(w) \in L \,\}$$

is the pre-image of L under h. As L is context-free, there exists a PDA P_L such that $L(P_L) = L$. From P_L and the morphism h, one can now construct a PDA P_h such that $L(P_h) = h^{-1}(L)$ (see, e.g., [79]). Also from P_L and a regular expression r, one can construct a PDA $P_\cap$ such that $L(P_\cap) = L \cap L(r)$. Thus, we have the following additional closure properties for the class CFL of context-free languages.

Corollary 1.2.37 *The class* CFL *of context-free languages is closed under the operations of applying an inverse morphism and of taking the intersection with a regular language.*

To complete our introduction to context-free languages, it should be mentioned that the membership problem ('Does a given word belong to the context-free language considered?'), the emptiness problem ('Is the language generated by a given context-free grammar empty?'), and the finiteness problem ('Is the language generated by a given context-free grammar finite?') are decidable (see, e.g., [79]), while the universality problem ('Does the language generated by a given context-free grammar contain all words over the terminal alphabet?'), the regularity problem ('Is the language generated by a given context-free grammar a regular language?'), and the equivalence problem ('Do two given context-free grammars generate the same language?') are undecidable.

The PDA as defined in Definition 1.2.29 is a nondeterministic machine model. In Example 1.2.30, the PDA P_1 uses nondeterminism to guess the middle of a given input in order to switch from pushing letters onto its pushdown to comparing pushdown symbols to input letters and popping. Here we turn to a restricted type of PDA, the deterministic pushdown automaton.

Definition 1.2.38 *A PDA $P = (Q, \Sigma, \Gamma, \delta, q_0, \bot, F)$ is a* deterministic pushdown automaton, *or a* DPDA, *if $|\delta(q, a, B)| + |\delta(q, \lambda, B)| \leq 1$ for all states $q \in Q$, all input letters $a \in \Sigma$, and all pushdown symbols $B \in \Gamma$.*

Thus, if $\delta(q, \lambda, B)$ is defined for a state $q \in Q$ and a pushdown symbol $B \in \Gamma$, then $\delta(q, a, B)$ is undefined for all input letters $a \in \Sigma$, that is, whenever a λ-step is possible, then no reading step is. Accordingly, the single-step computation relation $\vdash_P$ of P is deterministic, as each configuration of P has at most a single immediate successor configuration. We illustrate this definition by presenting a DPDA for the language $L'_{\text{pal}} = \{\, wcw^R \mid w \in \{a, b\}^* \,\}$.

Example 1.2.39 *Let $P'_1 = (Q, \Sigma, \Gamma, \delta, q_0, \bot, F)$ be the DPDA that is defined by $Q = \{q_0, q_1, q_2\}$, $F = \{q_2\}$, $\Sigma = \{a, b, c\}$, and $\Gamma = \{A, B, \bot\}$, where δ is given by the following table:*

Current State	*Input Symbol*	*Pushdown Symbol*	*Transition*
q_0	a	$\bot$	$(q_1, \bot A)$
q_0	b	$\bot$	$(q_1, \bot B)$
q_0	c	$\bot$	$(q_2, \bot)$
q_1	a	A	(q_1, AA)
q_1	a	B	(q_1, BA)
q_1	b	A	(q_1, AB)
q_1	b	B	(q_1, BB)
q_1	c	A	(q_2, A)
q_1	c	B	(q_2, B)
q_2	a	A	(q_2, λ)
q_2	b	B	(q_2, λ)

On input abcba, the DPDA P'_1 executes the following computation:

$$\begin{aligned}(q_0, abcba, \bot) &\vdash_{P'_1} (q_1, bcba, \bot A) \vdash_{P'_1} (q_1, cba, \bot AB) \vdash_{P'_1} (q_2, ba, \bot AB)\\ &\vdash_{P'_1} (q_2, a, \bot A) \quad\;\; \vdash_{P'_1} (q_2, \lambda, \bot),\end{aligned}$$

that is, P'_1 accepts the word abcba by final state. In fact, $L(P_1) = \{\, wcw^R \mid w \in \{a, b\}^* \,\}$. ∎

Concerning DPDAs, the following 'normal form' has been established (see, e.g., [3]).

Proposition 1.2.40 *For each DPDA $P_1 = (Q_1, \Sigma, \Gamma_1, \delta_1, q_0, \bot, F_1)$, there exists a DPDA $P_2 = (Q_2, \Sigma, \Gamma_2, \delta_2, p_0, \bot, F_2)$ such that the following conditions are satisfied:*

(a) *P_1 and P_2 accept the same language by final state, that is, $L(P_1) = L(P_2)$,*

(b) *during each λ-transition, P_2 pops from its pushdown, that is, if $\delta_2(p, \lambda, B) = (p', \alpha)$, then $\alpha = \lambda$, and*

(c) *during each reading transition, P_2 increases the height of its pushdown by at most one letter, that is, if $\delta_2(p, a, B) = (p', \alpha)$ for some $a \in \Sigma$, then $|\alpha| \leq 2$.*

Based on this 'normal form,' constructions and proofs concerning DPDAs and their computations can often be simplified significantly.

For each DPDA P, the language $N(P)$ of words that are accepted by P by empty pushdown is *prefix-free*, which means that no proper prefix of any word $w \in N(P)$ belongs to $N(P)$. Indeed, if $w = uv$ for some $v \neq \lambda$, then the computation of P on input w begins by processing the prefix u of w. Now, if $u \in N(P)$, then the computation of P on input u has the form $(q_0, u, \perp) \vdash_P^* (q, \lambda, \lambda)$, where $q \in Q$. Thus, as P is deterministic, the computation of P on input w looks as follows:

$$(q_0, w, \perp) = (q_0, uv, \perp) \vdash_P^* (q, v, \lambda),$$

and as P cannot proceed with an empty pushdown, it gets stuck without being able to process the remaining input v. This shows that $w = uv \notin N(P)$, a contradiction. Hence, we see that Proposition 1.2.32 (a) does not holds for DPDAs. Accordingly, below we just consider acceptance by final state for DPDAs.

Definition 1.2.41 *A language $L \subseteq \Sigma^*$ is called* deterministic context-free *if there exists a DPDA P such that $L = L(P)$, and* DCFL *denotes the class of deterministic context-free languages.*

From Example 1.2.39, we see that $L'_{\text{pal}} = \{ wcw^R \mid w \in \{a, b\}^* \}$ is a deterministic context-free language. Furthermore, $L_1 = \{ ca^nb^n \mid n \geq 0 \}$ and $L_2 = \{ da^{2n}b^n \mid n \geq 0 \}$ are deterministic context-free, too. In fact, also the language $L_1 \cup L_2 = \{ ca^nb^n, da^{2n}b^n \mid n \geq 0 \}$ is deterministic context-free, while it can be shown that $(L_1 \cup L_2)^R = \{ b^na^nc, b^na^{2n}d \mid n \geq 0 \}$ is not deterministic context-free by applying the following technical result (see, e.g., [60]).

Theorem 1.2.42 (Iteration Theorem for DCFL [60]) *Let L be a deterministic context-free language over Σ. Then there exists a constant c that depends on L such that each word $z \in L$ containing at least c marked positions admits a factorization of the form $z = uvwxy$ that satisfies all of the following conditions:*

(1) $v \neq \lambda$,

(2) $uv^iwx^iy \in L$ *for all* $i \geq 0$,

(3) u, v *and* w *or* w, x *and* y *contain marked positions,*

(4) *the number of marked position in* vwx *is at most* c,

(5) *and finally, if* $y \neq \lambda$, *then for each* $m, n \geq 0$ *and each* $\alpha \in \Sigma^*$:
$uv^{m+n}wx^n\alpha \in L$ *iff* $uv^mw\alpha \in L$.

Obviously, DCFL is a proper subclass of CFL. Using DPDAs, it can be shown that the class DCFL is closed under the operation of complementation (see, e.g., [81]). Furthermore, it is closed under inverse morphisms. On the other hand, $\{ a^mb^mc^n \mid m, n \geq 0 \}$ and $\{ a^mb^nc^n \mid m, n \geq 0 \}$ are deterministic context-free, while their intersection is the language $\{ a^mb^mc^m \mid m \geq 0 \}$, which is not context-free. Thus, we see that the class DCFL is neither closed under intersection nor under union. Also it is not closed under reversal (as seen from the example language $L_1 \cup L_2$ above) nor under non-erasing morphisms. Finally, it is not closed under the operations of product and iteration, either (see, e.g., [60]).

From Proposition 1.2.40, we see that the membership problem for each deterministic context-free language can be solved in linear time. Furthermore, emptiness and finiteness are decidable for DPDAs, as they are decidable for context-free languages. On the other hand, while it is undecidable, in general, whether a given context-free grammar generates a regular language, it is decidable whether the language $L(P)$ accepted by a given DPDA P is regular [248]. Finally, given two DPDAs P_1 and P_2, it is, in general, undecidable whether $L(P_1)$ is contained in $L(P_2)$, but as shown by Géraud Sénizergues in [239] (see also [240, 241, 242]), it is decidable whether two DPDAs accept the same language.

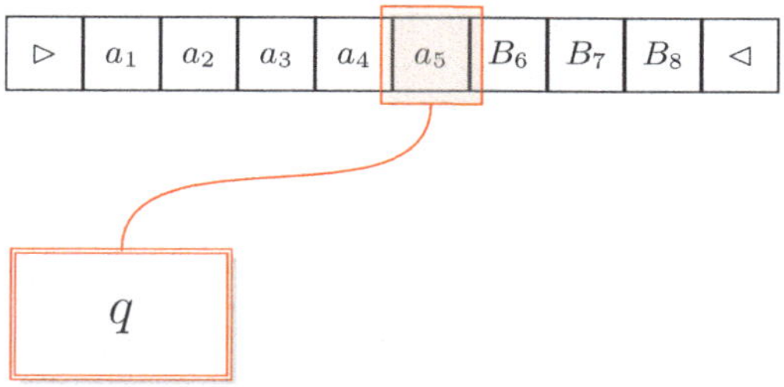

Figure 1.5: A deterministic right-to-left sequential transducer

Next we consider a generalization of the class of deterministic context-free languages, the class LRR of *left-to-right regular languages* of Karel Čulik II and Rina Cohen [37]. These languages are defined through an extension of Donald E. Knuth's LR(k) grammars [111] by admitting an arbitrarily long look-ahead of a restricted form. However, they can also be characterized through a combination of a DPDA and a special type of transducer.

Definition 1.2.43 *A* deterministic right-to-left sequential transducer (*DRLST*) *is a one-tape machine with a finite-state control that can be depicted as shown in Figure 1.5. It is defined by a 7-tuple* $G = (Q, \Sigma, \Delta, \triangleright, \triangleleft, q_0, \delta)$, *where* Q *is a finite set of states,* Σ *is a finite input alphabet,* Δ *is a finite output alphabet,* $\triangleright$ *and* $\triangleleft$ *are markers for the left and right end of the tape,* $q_0 \in Q$ *is the initial state, and* $\delta : Q \times \Sigma \to Q \times \Delta$ *is a partial transition function. If* $\delta(q, a) = (q', B)$, *then on seeing the input letter* a, G *changes from state* q *to state* q', *it replaces the letter* a *with the output letter* B, *and it moves its read/write head one step to the left.*

For $w \in \Sigma^*$, *the corresponding initial configuration of* G *is* $\triangleright w q_0 \triangleleft$, *that is, the tape contains the word* w *enclosed by the sentinels* $\triangleright$ *and* $\triangleleft$, G *is in its initial state, and its head is placed on the right sentinel* $\triangleleft$. *The computation of* G *on input* w *is called* successful *if it reaches a configuration of the form* $q \triangleright U \triangleleft$, *where* $q \in Q$ *and* $U \in \Delta^*$. *The word* U *is called the* output *that is produced by this computation. Thus,* G *induces a partial mapping from* Σ^* *to* Δ^*, *which we also denote by* G. *So* $G(w)$ *will denote the word* $U \in \Delta^*$ *that* G *produces from* w *by processing it from right to left.*

We also illustrate this definition with a simple example.

Example 1.2.44 *Let* $G = (Q, \Sigma, \Delta, \triangleright, \triangleleft, q_0, \delta)$ *be the DRLST that is defined by taking* $Q = \{q_0, q_1, q_2, q_3, q_4\}$, $\Sigma = \{a, b, c, d\}$, $\Gamma = \{a_1, a_2, b_1, b_2, c, d\}$ *and by defining the transition function* δ *as follows:*

$$\begin{array}{llcllllcl}
(1) & \delta(q_0, \triangleleft) & = & (q_0, \triangleleft), & & & & & \\
(2) & \delta(q_0, c) & = & (q_1, c), & (6) & \delta(q_0, d) & = & (q_2, d), \\
(3) & \delta(q_1, a) & = & (q_1, a_1), & (7) & \delta(q_2, a) & = & (q_2, a_2), \\
(4) & \delta(q_1, b) & = & (q_3, b_1), & (8) & \delta(q_2, b) & = & (q_4, b_2), \\
(5) & \delta(q_3, b) & = & (q_3, b_1), & (9) & \delta(q_4, b) & = & (q_4, b_2).
\end{array}$$

It is easily seen that G *has successful computations only for words from the set* $b^* \cdot a^* \cdot \{c, d\}$, *and that* $G(b^m a^n c) = b_1^m a_1^n c$ *and* $G(b^m a^n d) = b_2^m a_2^n d$ *for all* $m, n \geq 0$. ■

Next we present the left-to-right regular grammars and languages from [37].

Definition 1.2.45 *Let* $G = (N, T, S, P)$ *be a context-free grammar, where we assume without loss of generality that* S *does not occur on the right-hand side of any production. Then* $\Rightarrow_{R,G}^*$ *denotes the right-most derivation relation induced by* G. *A* right sentential form *is any word* $\alpha \in (N \cup T)^*$ *such that* $S \Rightarrow_{R,G}^* \alpha$ *holds.*

(a) *Let* $\pi = \{E_1, E_2, \ldots, E_n\}$ *be a partition of* T^* *into* n *disjoint regular sets. Then* $x \equiv y \bmod(\pi)$ *denotes the fact that* x *and* y *belong to the same subset* E_i*. The context-free grammar* $G = (N, T, S, P)$ *is called* $\mathrm{LR}(\pi)$*, if, for any right-most derivations of the form*

$$S \Rightarrow^*_{R,G} \alpha_1 A_1 y_1 \Rightarrow_{R,G} \alpha_1 \gamma y_1 \quad \textit{and} \quad S \Rightarrow^*_{R,G} \alpha_2 A_2 y_3 \Rightarrow_{R,G} \alpha_1 \gamma y_2,$$

where $A_1, A_2 \in N$*,* $\alpha_1, \alpha_2, \gamma \in (N \cup T)^*$*, and* $y_1, y_2, y_3 \in T^*$*,* $y_1 \equiv y_2 \bmod(\pi)$ *implies that* $A_1 = A_2$*,* $\alpha_1 = \alpha_2$*, and* $y_2 = y_3$*.*

(b) *A context-free grammar is called* left-to-right regular (LR-regular) *if it is* $LR(\pi)$ *for some regular partition* π *of* Σ^**. A language* L *is* left-to-right regular *(or an LRR-language) if* $L = L(G)$ *for some LR-regular grammar* G*, and* LRR *denotes the class of all left-to-right regular languages.*

Let $L \subseteq \Sigma^*$ be an LRR-language. According to the proof of Theorem 2.1 of [37], there exists a DRLST G such that $L_1 = G(L)$ is a deterministic context-free language. In fact, proceeding from right to left, G outputs a pair of the form (a, p_a) for each letter a read, where p_a is some additional information that depends on the suffix already read by G. Thus, the languages from the class LRR admit a restricted form of two-phase processing: an input word w is first scanned from right to left using a DRLST G, and then the result of that scan (the word $G(w)$) is processed from left to right by a DPDA, which then either accepts or rejects. Obviously, the language

$$L' = \{\, b_1^n a_1^n c, b_2^n a_2^{2n} d \mid n \geq 0 \,\}$$

is accepted by a DPDA. In combination with the DRLST G from Example 1.2.44, this shows that the language

$$(L_1 \cup L_2)^R = \{\, b^n a^n c, b^n a^{2n} d \mid n \geq 0 \,\}$$

considered above is in LRR. As each deterministic context-free language belongs to LRR, we have the following proper inclusion.

Corollary 1.2.46 $\mathsf{DCFL} \subsetneq \mathsf{LRR}$.

As the class CFL is closed under reversal, it can be shown that $G(L)$ is a context-free language for each context-free language L and each DRLST G. Thus, we see that the class LRR is contained in CFL. On the other hand, the language

$$L = \{\, a^m b^{2m} a^n b^n, a^m b^m a^{n+k} b^n \mid k, m, n \geq 1 \,\}$$

is clearly context-free, but, as shown in [37], it is not an LRR-language. Furthermore, using Proposition 1.2.40, it can be shown that each LRR-language is accepted by a shrinking DTPDA, which means that it is Church-Rosser by Theorem 1.2.19. In fact, we have the following proper inclusion.

Corollary 1.2.47 $\mathsf{LRR} \subsetneq \mathsf{CFL} \cap \mathsf{CRL}$.

Actually, LRR is even contained in the class UCFL of *unambiguous context-free languages* [37]. Karel Čulik II and Rina Cohen also considered closure properties and decision problems for the class LRR.

Theorem 1.2.48 ([37])

(a) *The class* LRR *is incomparable under inclusion to the class* $\mathsf{DCFL}^R = \{\, L^R \mid L \in \mathsf{DCFL} \,\}$.

(b) *The class* LRR *is an* abstract family of deterministic languages, *that is, it is closed under marked union, marked Kleene star, and inverse marked GSM mappings.*

(c) *It is decidable whether a given left-to-right regular language is regular.*

Finally, we consider still another subclass of the context-free languages that is obtained by placing a restriction on the productions of context-free grammars.

Definition 1.2.49 *Let $G = (N, T, S, P)$ be a context-free grammar such that the start symbol S does not occur on the right-hand side of any production.*

(a) *The grammar G is a* linear grammar *if each production $(A \to r) \in P$ satisfies the condition that $r \in (T^* \cdot N \cdot T^*) \cup T^*$.*

(b) *A language $L \subseteq T^*$ is* linear context-free *if there exists a linear grammar G such that $L = L(G)$, and* LIN *denotes the* class of linear context-free languages.

(c) *A linear grammar $G = (N, T, S, P)$ is in* normal form *if each production $(A \to x) \in P$ satisfies the condition that $x \in T$, or $x \in T \cdot N$, or $x \in N \cdot T$. In addition, P may contain the production $(S \to \lambda)$.*

As shown by Arnold L. Rosenberg in [229], each linear grammar can be converted into an equivalent linear grammar that is in normal form. We illustrate this conversion with a simple example.

Example 1.2.50 *In Example 1.2.23, we considered the context-free grammar*

$$G_2 = (\{S, A\}, \{a, b\}, S, \{(S \to \lambda), (S \to aAa), (S \to bAb), (A \to \lambda), (A \to aAa), (A \to bAb)\}.$$

Obviously, this grammar, which generates the language $L_{\text{pal}} = \{ ww^R \mid w \in \{a, b\}^* \}$, is linear. In order to convert this grammar into a linear grammar in normal form, we proceed as follows. First, we eliminate the λ-production $(A \to \lambda)$ by replacing it with the productions $(S \to aa)$, $(S \to bb)$, $(A \to aa)$, and $(A \to bb)$. Next, we introduce four new nonterminals X_a, X_b, B_a, B_b and replace the above productions with the following set of productions:

$$\begin{aligned} P_3 \quad = \quad & \{(S \to \lambda), (S \to aX_a), (S \to bX_b), (S \to aB_a), (S \to bB_b), \\ & (A \to aX_a), (A \to bX_b), (A \to aB_a), (A \to bB_b), \\ & (X_a \to a), (X_b \to b), (B_a \to Aa), (B_b \to Ab)\}. \end{aligned}$$

Then the grammar $G_3 = (\{S, A, X_a, X_b, B_a, B_b\}, \{a, b\}, S, P_3)$ is a linear grammar in normal form, and it can be checked easily that it generates the language L_{pal}. ■

In order to illustrate the expressive capacity of linear grammars, we consider still another example.

Example 1.2.51 *Let $G = (\{S, A, B\}, \{a, b, c, d\}, S, P)$ be the linear grammar that contains the following set of productions:*

$$P = \{(S \to c), (S \to d), (S \to Ac), (S \to Bd), (A \to bAa), (A \to ba), (B \to bBaa), (B \to baa)\}.$$

Then G generates the language $L(G) = \{ b^n a^n c, b^n a^{2n} d \mid n \geq 0\}$, which is not deterministic context-free. ■

Thus, we see that the linear context-free languages are not a subclass of the deterministic context-free languages. Actually, we can do even better. It is easily seen that the language

$$L_\vee = \{ a^m b^m c^n \mid m, n \geq 0\} \cup \{ a^m b^n c^n \mid m, n \geq 0 \}$$

is linear context-free. On the other hand, $L_\vee$ is inherently ambiguous [60], and hence, it is not an LRR-language [37]. Hence, the linear languages are not even contained in the class of left-to-right regular languages.

To prove that a given language is not linear context-free, the following 'Pumping Lemma' is very useful (see, e.g., [3]).

Lemma 1.2.52 (Pumping Lemma for Linear Context-Free Languages)
Let L be a linear context-free language over Σ. Then there exists a positive constant k_L such that each word $w \in L$ of length $|w| \geq k_L$ has a factorization of the form $w = uvxyz$ that satisfies the following three conditions:

$$(1)\ |vy| > 0, (2)\ |uvyz| \leq k_L, \text{ and } (3)\ uv^ixy^iz \in L \text{ for all } i \in \mathbb{N}.$$

Using this lemma, it can be shown easily that the deterministic context-free language $L = \{ a^m b^m c^n d^n \mid n \geq 0 \}$ is not linear context-free. Indeed, assume to the contrary that L is linear context-free, and let $k = k_L$ be the corresponding constant for L from the Pumping Lemma above. Consider the word $w = a^k b^k c^k d^k$, which belongs to L and which has length $4k$. Then w admits a factorization $w = uvxyz$ that satisfies the three conditions given above. As $|uvyz| \leq k$, we see that $u = a^i$, $v = a^{i'}$, $y = d^j$, $z = d^{j'}$ for some integers $i, i', j, j' \geq 0$ satisfying $i' + j \geq 1$ and $i + i' + j + j' \leq k$, and $x = a^{k-i-i'} b^k c^k d^{k-j-j'}$. But then

$$w_0 = uv^0xy^0z = a^i a^{k-i-i'} b^k c^k d^{k-j-j'} d^{j'} = a^{k-i'} b^k c^k d^{k-j},$$

which does not belong to L as $k - i' < k$ or $k - j < k$. This yields a contradiction, showing that L does not satisfy Lemma 1.2.52, that is, L is not linear context-free. Thus, we obtain the following inclusion and non-inclusion results.

Corollary 1.2.53 $\mathsf{LIN} \subsetneq \mathsf{CFL}$, *but the class* LIN *of linear languages is incomparable under inclusion to the classes* DCFL *of deterministic context-free languages and* LRR *of left-to-right regular languages.*

From the fact that $L = \{ a^m b^m c^n d^n \mid n \geq 0 \}$ is not linear context-free, we see that the class LIN is not closed under the operation of product, and it is not closed under Kleene star, either. On the other hand, it is easily seen that LIN is closed under the operations of union, reversal, and intersection with regular sets. Furthermore, it is closed under morphisms and inverse morphisms. However, as the languages $\{ a^m b^m c^n \mid m, n \geq 0 \}$ and $\{ a^m b^n c^n \mid m, n \geq 0 \}$ are linear context-free, while their intersection $\{ a^n b^n c^n \mid n \geq 0 \}$ is not even context-free, we see that LIN is not closed under the operations of intersection and complementation.

As LIN is a (proper) subclass of CFL, emptiness and finiteness are obviously decidable for linear context-free languages. However, universality, regularity, and equivalence are still undecidable for them.

We see from Theorem 1.2.33 that, for each linear context-free language L, there exists a PDA P such that $L(P) = L$. In fact, from the form of the productions of a linear grammar for L, we can conclude that each accepting computation of P can be split into two parts:

- while a prefix of the input is being read, a word is pushed onto the pushdown of P, that is, during this phase, the size of the pushdown contents does not decrease from any configuration to the next,
- then, while the corresponding suffix of the input is being read, symbols are popped from the pushdown, that is, during this phase, the size of the pushdown contents does not increase from any configuration to the next.

A PDA that shows this behavior is called a *one-turn* PDA. The following characterization has been established for the class LIN.

Theorem 1.2.54 ([51]) *A language L is linear context-free iff there exists a one-turn PDA P such that $L = L(P)$.*

Finally, we consider one-turn PDAs that are deterministic, that is, one-turn DPDAs.

Definition 1.2.55 *A language L is called* deterministic linear *if there exists a 1-turn DPDA P such that $L = L(P)$. The class of deterministic linear languages is denoted by* DLIN.

The DPDA constructed in Example 1.2.39 is actually one-turn. This means that the language L'_{pal} belongs to the class DLIN. Obviously, DLIN is contained in the intersection of DCFL and LIN. However, the language $L = \{ a^n b^m a^p b^q \mid n = m \text{ or } p = q \}$ is linear context-free and deterministic context-free, but it is not accepted by any one-turn DPDA [3]. Thus, we have the following proper inclusions, where the latter follows from the fact that LIN and DCFL are incomparable under inclusion.

Corollary 1.2.56 $\mathsf{DLIN} \subsetneq \mathsf{LIN} \cap \mathsf{DCFL} \subsetneq \mathsf{DCFL}$.

Finally, we come to the last of Noam Chomsky's classes of grammars.

Definition 1.2.57 *Let $G = (N, T, S, P)$ be a phrase-structure grammar. Without loss of generality we assume that the start symbol S does not occur on the right-hand side of any production.*

(a) *The grammar G is* left regular *if each production $(\ell \to r) \in P$ has the form $\ell = A$ and $r = x$, where $A \in N$ and $x \in (N \cdot T^*) \cup T^*$.*

(b) *The grammar G is* right regular *if each production $(\ell \to r) \in P$ has the form $\ell = A$ and $r = x$, where $A \in N$ and $x \in (T^* \cdot N) \cup T^*$.*

(c) *The grammar G is called* regular *if it is left or right regular. Following Noam Chomsky's notation, regular grammars are also called* grammars of type 3.

(d) *A language $L \subseteq T^*$ is* regular *or* of type 3 *if there exists a regular grammar G such that $L = L(G)$, and $\mathcal{L}_3$ is used to denote the* class of regular languages, *that is, the class of languages that are generated by regular grammars.*

(e) *A left regular grammar $G = (N, T, S, P)$ is in* normal form *if each production $(A \to x) \in P$ satisfies the condition that $x \in T$ or $x \in N \cdot T$. In addition, P may contain the production $(S \to \lambda)$.*

(f) *A right regular grammar $G = (N, T, S, P)$ is in* normal form *if each production $(A \to x) \in P$ satisfies the condition that $x \in T$ or $x \in T \cdot N$. In addition, P may contain the production $(S \to \lambda)$.*

We also illustrate this definition with some simple examples.

Example 1.2.58 (a) *Let $G_1 = (\{S, A\}, \{a, b\}, S, \{(S \to aA), (A \to baA), (A \to \lambda)\})$. Then G_1 is right regular, and $L(G_1) = \{ a(ba)^n \mid n \geq 0 \} = a(ba)^*$.*

(b) *Let $G_2 = (\{S, A\}, \{a, b\}, S, \{(S \to a), (S \to Aba), (A \to Aba), (A \to a)\})$. Then G_2 is left regular, and $L(G_2) = L(G_1)$.* ■

It is easily seen from the definition that $\mathcal{L}_3$ contains all finite languages, that it is closed under the operations of reversal, union, product and Kleene star, and that it is closed under morphisms. In particular, it follows that REG, the class of languages defined by regular expressions (see Definition 1.1.10), is contained in $\mathcal{L}_3$. Actually, we shall see below that these two classes coincide.

It should be noted that each left regular (right regular) grammar can be converted into a left regular (right regular) grammar that is in normal form. We illustrate this process for the right regular grammar G_1 from the above example.

Example 1.2.59 *Let $G_1 = (\{S, A\}, \{a, b\}, S, \{(S \to aA), (A \to baA), (A \to \lambda)\})$. First, we replace the λ-production $(A \to \lambda)$ with the productions $(S \to a)$ and $(A \to ba)$. Next, we introduce new nonterminals B and C and replace the productions $(A \to baA)$ and $(A \to ba)$ with the productions $(A \to bB), (B \to aA), (A \to bC), (C \to a)$. This yields the right regular grammar $G'_1 = (\{S, A, B, C\}, \{a, b\}, S, P'_1)$, where*

$$P'_1 = \{(S \to a), (S \to aA), (A \to bB), (A \to bC), (B \to aA), (C \to a)\},$$

which is in normal form. ■

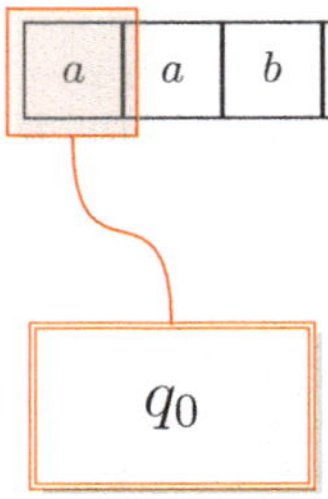

Figure 1.6: A deterministic finite-state acceptor

The machine model for characterizing the regular languages is the finite-state acceptor. It is defined as follows.

Definition 1.2.60 *A* deterministic finite-state acceptor (DFA) *is a one-tape machine with a finite-state control that can be depicted as shown in Figure 1.6. Formally, it is defined by a 5-tuple $A = (Q, \Sigma, q_0, \delta, F)$, where Q is a finite set of states, Σ is a finite input alphabet, $q_0 \in Q$ is the initial state, $\delta : Q \times \Sigma \to Q$ is a partial transition function, and $F \subseteq Q$ is a set of final states. If $\delta(q, a) = q'$, then, on seeing the input letter a, A changes from state q to state q' and moves its head one step to the right.*

The DFA A is called complete *if δ is a total function, that is, it is defined for all pairs $(q, a) \in Q \times \Sigma$.*

For $w \in \Sigma^*$, the corresponding initial configuration of A is $q_0 w$, that is, the tape contains the word w, A is in its initial state, and its head is placed on the first letter of w. The computation of A on input w is called successful *if it reaches a configuration of the form wq, where $q \in F$. The language accepted by A, which consists of all words $w \in \Sigma^*$ for which the computation of A on w is successful, is denoted by $L(A)$.*

Again we illustrate this definition with a simple example.

Example 1.2.61 *Let $A = (\{q_0, q_1, q_2\}, \{a, b\}, q_0, \delta, \{q_1\})$, where the transition function δ is given by the folloing table:*

δ	q_0	q_1	q_2
a	q_1	q_2	q_1
b	q_0	q_1	q_2

Given the word $w = aabaabab$ as input, A executes the following computation:

$$\begin{array}{llllllll} q_0aabaabab & \vdash_A & aq_1abaabab & \vdash_A & aaq_2baabab & \vdash_A & aabq_2aabab \\ & \vdash_A & aabaq_1abab & \vdash_A & aabaaq_2bab & \vdash_A & aabaabq_2ab \\ & \vdash_A & aabaabaq_1b & \vdash_A & aabaababq_1, & & \end{array}$$

which is successful, as q_1 is a final state. In fact, $L(A) = \{ w \in \{a, b\}^* \mid |w|_a \equiv 1 \bmod 2 \}$. ■

The DFA in the above example is complete. In fact, if $A = (Q, \Sigma, q_0, \delta, F)$ is an incomplete DFA, then one can construct a complete DFA $A' = (Q \cup \{q_\perp\}, \Sigma, q_0, \delta', F)$, where $q_\perp$ is a new state, by defining the transition function δ' as follows:

$$\begin{array}{lcl} \delta'(q, a) & = & \begin{cases} \delta(q, a), & \text{if } \delta(q, a) \text{ is defined,} \\ q_\perp, & \text{otherwise,} \end{cases} \\ \delta'(q_\perp, a) & = & q_\perp \text{ for all } a \in \Sigma. \end{array}$$

From a given DFA A, one can easily construct a right regular grammar G in normal form such that $L(G) = L(A)$. Also, one can construct a regular expression r such that $L(r) = L(A)$ [152] (see, e.g., [79]). This means that $L(A)$ belongs to the class REG. To derive the converse implication, a generalized version of the DFA is used, the nondeterministic finite-state acceptor.

Definition 1.2.62 *A* nondeterministic finite-state acceptor (NFA) *is defined by a 5-tuple* $A = (Q, \Sigma, S, \delta, F)$, *where* Q, Σ, *and* F *are defined as for a DFA, but* $S \subseteq Q$ *is a set of initial states, and* $\delta : Q \times \Sigma \to \mathcal{P}(Q)$ *is a transition relation, that is, for each* $q \in Q$ *and* $a \in \Sigma$, $\delta(q, a)$ *is a subset of* Q. *If* $\delta(q, a) = \{q_1, q_2, \ldots, q_m\}$, *then, on seeing the input letter* a, A *changes from state* q *to some state* q_i *chosen nondeterministically from* $\delta(q, a)$ *and moves its head one step to the right.*

For $w \in \Sigma^*$, *an initial configuration of* A *on input* w *is* qw *for any* $q \in S$, *that is, the tape contains the word* w, A *is in one of its initial states, and its head is placed on the first letter of* w. *In general,* A *has many computations for a given input word. A computation of* A *on input* w *is called* successful *if, starting from one of the initial configurations on input* w, *it reaches a configuration of the form* wq_f *for some* $q_f \in F$. *The language accepted by* A, *which consists of all words* $w \in \Sigma^*$ *for which* A *has a successful computation, is denoted by* $L(A)$.

Here is an example of an NFA.

Example 1.2.63 *Let* $A = (\{q_0, q_1, q_2, q_3\}, \{a, b\}, \{q_0\}, \delta, \{q_3\})$ *be the NFA that is defined by the following transition relation:*

δ	q_0	q_1	q_2	q_3
a	$\{q_0\}$	$\{q_2\}$	$\emptyset$	$\emptyset$
b	$\{q_0, q_1\}$	$\emptyset$	$\{q_3\}$	$\emptyset$

On input $w = ababab$, A *can execute the following four computations:*

(1) $q_0ababab \vdash_A aq_0babab \vdash_A abq_1abab \vdash_A abaq_2bab \vdash_A ababq_3ab,$

(2) $q_0ababab \vdash_A aq_0babab \vdash_A abq_0abab \vdash_A abaq_0bab \vdash_A ababq_0ab \vdash_A ababaq_0b \vdash_A abababq_0,$

(3) $q_0ababab \vdash_A aq_0babab \vdash_A abq_0abab \vdash_A abaq_0bab \vdash_A ababq_0ab \vdash_A ababaq_0b \vdash_A abababq_1,$

(4) $q_0ababab \vdash_A aq_0babab \vdash_A abq_0abab \vdash_A abaq_0bab \vdash_A ababq_1ab \vdash_A ababaq_2b \vdash_A abababq_3,$

but only the last one is successful. It follows that $w \in L(A)$, *in fact, it can be shown that* $L(A) = \{\, w \in \{a, b\}^* \mid w$ *has the suffix* $bab \,\}$. ■

From a right regular grammar G that is in normal form, one can easily construct an NFA A such that $L(A) = L(G)$. Thus, we see that $\mathcal{L}_3$ is contained in $\mathcal{L}(\mathsf{NFA})$. However, also the converse inclusion holds. This can be shown by the following *power set construction*.

Proposition 1.2.64 ([226]) *From a given NFA* A *with* n *states, one can effectively construct a DFA* B *with at most* 2^n *states such that* $L(B) = L(A)$.

Proof. Let $A = (Q, \Sigma, S, \delta, F)$ be an NFA with $|Q| = n$. The DFA $B = (Q_B, \Sigma, p_0, \delta_B, F_B)$ is obtained by taking $Q_B = \mathcal{P}(Q)$, the power set of Q, $p_0 = S$ is the initial state,

$$F_B = \{\, H \subseteq Q \mid H \cap F \neq \emptyset \,\}$$

is the set of final states, and the transition function δ_B is defined by taking

$$\delta_B(H, a) = \bigcup_{q \in H} \delta(q, a)$$

for all $H \subseteq Q$ and $a \in \Sigma$. Then $|Q_B| = 2^n$, and it can be verified that $L(B) = L(A)$ holds. □

In summary, the above considerations yield the following characterization.

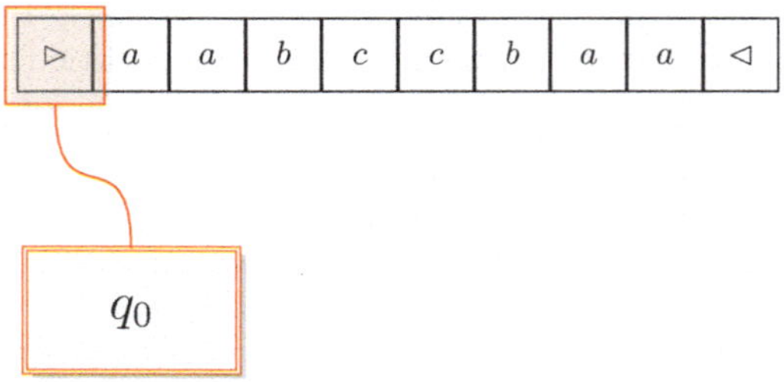

Figure 1.7: A deterministic two-way finite-state acceptor

Corollary 1.2.65 ([29, 109, 226]) *For a language $L \subseteq \Sigma^*$, the following conditions are equivalent:*

(a) *There exists regular grammar G such that $L(G) = L$.*

(b) *There exists a regular expression r such that $L(r) = L$.*

(c) *There exists a DFA A such that $L(A) = L$.*

(d) *There exists an NFA B such that $L(B) = L$.*

In addition, there are some important extensions of the DFA and the NFA.

Definition 1.2.66 *A* nondeterministic finite-state acceptor with λ-transitions (λ-*NFA*) *is defined by a 5-tuple $A = (Q, \Sigma, S, \delta, F)$, where Q, Σ, S and F are defined as for an NFA, but the transition relation δ is defined as $\delta : Q \times (\Sigma \cup \{\lambda\}) \to \mathcal{P}(Q)$, that is, for all $q \in Q$, it contains the λ-transitions $\delta(q, \lambda)$. If $\delta(q, \lambda) = \{q_1, q_2, \ldots, q_m\}$, then A can change from state q to some state q_i chosen nondeterministically from $\delta(q, \lambda)$ without reading any letter.*

The following simple example illustrates the way in which a λ-NFA works.

Example 1.2.67 *Let $A = (\{q_0, q_1, q_2\}, \{a, b, c\}, \{q_0\}, \delta, \{q_2\})$, where the transition relation δ is defined as follows:*

δ	q_0	q_1	q_2
a	$\{q_0\}$	$\emptyset$	$\emptyset$
b	$\emptyset$	$\{q_1\}$	$\emptyset$
c	$\emptyset$	$\emptyset$	$\{q_2\}$
λ	$\{q_1\}$	$\{q_2\}$	$\{q_2\}$

Then A can execute the following computation:

$$\begin{array}{lllllllll} q_0aabbcc & \vdash_A & aq_0abbcc & \vdash_A & aaq_0bbcc & \vdash_A & aaq_1bbcc & \vdash_A & aabq_1bcc \\ & \vdash_A & aabbq_1cc & \vdash_A & aabbq_2cc & \vdash_A & aabbcq_2c & \vdash_A & aabbccq_2, \end{array}$$

that is, $aabbcc \in L(A)$. In fact, $L(A) = \{\, a^i b^j c^k \mid i, j, k \geq 0 \,\}$. ■

However, the λ-NFA is not more expressive than the NFA (or the DFA), which can be shown by using a modified power set construction (see, e.g., [79]).

Proposition 1.2.68 *From a given λ-NFA A with n states, one can effectively construct a DFA B with at most 2^n states such that $L(B) = L(A)$.*

Another extension of the DFA is the deterministic two-way finite-state acceptor, which can read its input not just once, but several times.

Definition 1.2.69 *A* deterministic two-way finite-state acceptor (2DFA) *is a one-tape machine with a finite-state control that can be depicted as shown in Figure 1.7. A 2DFA is defined by a 7-tuple* $A = (Q, \Sigma, \triangleright, \triangleleft, q_0, \delta, F)$*, where* Q *is a finite set of states,* Σ *is a finite input alphabet,* $\triangleright, \triangleleft \notin \Sigma$ *are special symbols, called* sentinels*, that are used to mark the left and the right end of the tape,* $q_0 \in Q$ *is the initial state,* $F \subseteq Q$ *is a set of final states, and*

$$\delta : (Q \times (\Sigma \cup \{\triangleright, \triangleleft\})) \to (Q \times \{L, R\})$$

is a partial transition function. If $\delta(q, a) = (q', L)$*, then on seeing the input letter* a*,* A *changes from state* q *to state* q' *and moves its head one step to the left, and if* $\delta(q, a) = (q', R)$*, then on seeing the input letter* a*,* A *changes from state* q *to state* q' *and moves its head one step to the right. In addition, it is required that* δ *satisfies the following restrictions:*

$$\forall q, q' \in Q : \delta(q, \triangleright) \neq (q', L) \text{ and } \delta(q, \triangleleft) \neq (q', R),$$

that is, when scanning the left (right) sentinel, then A *cannot perform a move-left (move-right) step.*

For $w \in \Sigma^*$*, the corresponding initial configuration of* A *is* $q_0 \triangleright w \triangleleft$*, that is, the tape contains the word* w *surrounded by the sentinels* $\triangleright$ *and* $\triangleleft$*,* A *is in its initial state, and its head is placed on the left sentinel* $\triangleright$*. The computation of* A *on input* w *is called* successful *if it reaches a configuration of the form* $\triangleright w q \triangleleft$*, where* $q \in F$*. The language accepted by* A*, which consists of all words* $w \in \Sigma^*$ *for which the computation of* A *on* w *is successful, is denoted by* $L(A)$*.*

Again we illustrate this definition by providing a simple example.

Example 1.2.70 *Let* $A = (\{q_0, q_1, q_2, q_3, q_4, q_+\}, \{a, b\}, \triangleright, \triangleleft, q_0, \delta, \{q_+\})$ *be the 2DFA that is defined by the following transition function:*

δ	q_0	q_1	q_2	q_3	q_4	q_+
$\triangleright$	(q_0, R)	$-$	$-$	$-$	$-$	$-$
a	(q_0, R)	(q_2, L)	(q_3, L)	(q_4, L)	(q_+, R)	(q_+, R)
b	(q_0, R)	(q_2, L)	(q_3, L)	(q_4, L)	$-$	(q_+, R)
$\triangleleft$	(q_1, L)	$-$	$-$	$-$	$-$	$-$

On input $w = ababba$*,* A *executes the following computation:*

$$\begin{array}{llllll} q_0 \triangleright ababba \triangleleft & \vdash_A & \triangleright q_0 ababba \triangleleft & \vdash_A^6 & \triangleright ababbaq_0 \triangleleft & \vdash_A & \triangleright ababbq_1 a \triangleleft \\ & \vdash_A & \triangleright ababq_2 ba \triangleleft & \vdash_A & \triangleright abaq_3 bba \triangleleft & \vdash_A & \triangleright abq_4 abba \triangleleft \\ & \vdash_A & \triangleright abaq_+ bba \triangleleft & \vdash_A^3 & \triangleright ababbaq_+ \triangleleft, & & \end{array}$$

that is, A *accepts on input ababba. It can be checked that*

$$L(A) = \{ w \in \{a, b\}^* \mid |w| \geq 4 \text{ and the 4th letter from the right of } w \text{ is an } a \}. \qquad \blacksquare$$

Actually, 2DFAs can be used to reverse computations of DFAs. The following result, which is taken from [1], pages 212–213 (see also Lemma 3 of [80]), will be of use to us later.

Lemma 1.2.71 *Let* A *be a DFA. For each word* x *and each integer* i*,* $1 \leq i \leq |x|$*, let* $q_A(x, i)$ *be the state of* A *after processing the prefix of length* i *of* x*. Then there exists a 2DFA* A' *such that, for each input* x *and each* $i \in \{2, 3, \ldots, |x|\}$*, the following condition is satisfied:*

- *if* A' *starts its computation on* x *in state* $q_A(x, i)$ *with its head on* $x[i]$*, then* A' *finishes its computation in state* $q_A(x, i-1)$ *with its head on* $x[i-1]$*.*

Thus, a 2DFA exists that, knowing the state of a DFA at a position i, computes the state of that DFA at the previous position. Also a nondeterministic version of the 2DFA, the *nondeterministic two-way finite-state acceptor (2NFA)* can be defined. However, the following result holds.

Proposition 1.2.72 ([226, 244]) *From a given 2DFA (2NFA) A, one can effectively construct an NFA B such that $L(B) = L(A)$.*

The proof uses the notion of *crossing sequence*. During a computation, a 2DFA A may visit a tape cell several times by entering it either from its left-hand neighbour or from its right-hand neighbour. So we can keep a list to which we append the current state each time A enters the current tape cell from the left and another list to which we append the current state each time A enters the current tape cell from the right. These lists are called crossing sequences. Thus, for an input of length n, we obtain $2n$ crossing sequences. It can be proved that, within an accepting computation of A, no crossing sequence can contain multiple occurrences of any state. This implies that there are only finitely many possible crossing sequences. Now an NFA can be designed that, while reading the given input w from left to right, guesses the crossing sequences of the computation of A on input w and verifies that these crossing sequences do indeed describe an accepting computation of A. The details can be found, e.g., in [81].

Because of Proposition 1.2.68 and Proposition 1.2.72, we can extend Corollary 1.2.65 as follows.

Corollary 1.2.73 *For a language $L \subseteq \Sigma^*$, the following conditions are equivalent:*

(a) *There exists regular grammar G such that $L(G) = L$.*

(b) *There exists λ-NFA A such that $L(A) = L$.*

(c) *There exists a 2DFA B such that $L(B) = L$.*

(d) *There exists a 2NFA C such that $L(C) = L$.*

From the many characterizations of the regular languages, one can easily derive the following closure properties for the class REG.

Corollary 1.2.74 *The class REG is closed under the operations of union, intersection, complementation, product, Kleene plus and Kleene star, reversal, the application of a morphism, and inverse morphisms.*

For later reference, we also introduce the following technical notions (see [81]).

Definition 1.2.75 *A* generalized sequential machine *(or a* GSM*) is an NFA with output. Formally, it is defined by a 6-tuple $G = (Q, \Sigma, \Delta, q_0, E, F)$, where Q is a finite set of states, $q_0 \in Q$ is the initial state, $F \subseteq Q$ is the set of final states, Σ is a finite* input alphabet, *Δ is a finite* output alphabet, *and $E \subset Q \times \Sigma \times Q \times \Delta^*$ is a finite set of transitions. If G is in state q scanning the input letter a, and if $(q, a, q', v) \in E$, then G can enter state q', move its input head one step to the right, and emit (output) the word v. With the GSM G, we associate the language $L(G)$, which consists of all input words $x \in \Sigma^*$ such that, starting from the intial configuration q_0x, G can execute a computation that consumes x completely and that ends in a final state. Furthermore, we define the binary relation $R(G) \subseteq \Sigma^* \times \Delta^*$ as follows. Let $x \in \Sigma^*$ be an input word. If $x \in L(G)$ and if $q_0x \vdash_G q_1x_1 \vdash_G \cdots \vdash_G q_f$ is an accepting computation of G, then during this computation, G generates a word $z \in \Delta^*$ that is obtained as the concatenation of all consecutive words that G outputs during this computation. Then*

$$R(G) = \{ (x, z) \mid x \in L(G) \text{ and } z \in \Delta^* \text{ such that there exists an accepting computation of } G \text{ on input } x \text{ that outputs } z \}.$$

Observe that a GSM is not allowed to perform λ-steps, and that $L(G) \in \mathsf{REG}(\Sigma)$.

Definition 1.2.76 *A* deterministic generalized sequential machine *(or a* DGSM*) G is a DFA with output. Formally, it is specified by a 6-tuple $G = (Q, \Sigma, \Delta, q_0, \delta, F)$, where Q, Σ, and Δ are a finite set of states, an input alphabet, and an output alphabet, respectively, $q_0 \in Q$ is the initial state, $\delta : Q \times \Sigma \to Q \times \Delta^*$ is a (partial) transition function, and $F \subseteq Q$ is a set of final states. If G is in state q scanning the input letter a, and if $\delta(q, a) = (p, w)$, then in the next step, G will enter state p, move its head one step to the right, and emit (output) the word w. With this DGSM, we associate the language $L(G)$, which consists of all input word $x \in \Sigma^*$ such that, starting from the intial configuration q_0x, G executes a computation that consumes x completely and that ends in a final state. Furthermore, we define the partial mapping $G : \Sigma^* \to \Delta^*$ as follows. Let $x \in \Sigma^*$ be an input word. If $x \in L(G)$, that is, if G ends up in a final state when processing the input x starting from its initial state q_0, then $G(x) \in \Delta^*$ denotes the concatenation of all consecutive words that G outputs while processing the word x. Obviously, G is a mapping from $L(G)$ into Δ^*.*

A DGSM $G = (Q, \Sigma, \Delta, q_0, \delta, F)$ is a uniform DGSM *(or a* UDGSM*) if it outputs a single letter for each input letter, that is, for all $q \in Q$ and all $a \in \Sigma$, if $\delta(q, a) = (p, w)$, then $w \in \Delta$.*

If G is a uniform DGSM, then $|G(x)| = |x|$ for each word $x \in L(G)$. Concerning DGSMs, the following result is easily proved.

Proposition 1.2.77 *The class* REG *is closed under DGSM-mappings, that is, if G is a DGSM with input alphabet Σ and output alphabet Δ, and if $L \in \mathsf{REG}(\Sigma)$, then $G(L) = \{ G(x) \mid x \in L \} \in \mathsf{REG}(\Delta)$.*

For proving that a given language L is not regular, one can use the following Pumping Lemma, which is a variant of a result by Yehoshua Bar-Hillel, Micha A. Perles, and Eli Shamir [6].

Lemma 1.2.78 (Pumping Lemma for Regular Languages)
Let L be a regular language over Σ. Then there exists a positive constant k_L such that, for each word $z \in L$ of length $|z| \geq k_L$ and each factorization $z = gwh$, where $|w| = k_L$, there exists a factorization of the form $w = uxv$ that satisfies the following three conditions:

$$(1)\ |x| > 0, (2)\ |ux| \leq k_L, \text{ and } (3)\ gux^ivh \in L \text{ for all } i \in \mathbb{N}.$$

By applying this Pumping Lemma, it is easily verified that the deterministic linear language $L = \{ a^m b^m \mid m \geq 0 \}$ is not regular. Thus, we get the following proper inclusion.

Corollary 1.2.79 *The class* REG *of regular languages is a proper subclass of the class* DLIN *of deterministic linear languages.*

We complete this overview by taking a short look at decision problems for regular languages. Obviously, the membership problem is decidable for each regular language. Indeed, a DFA can be used that scans a given input w from left to right and that accepts if and only if w belongs to the language considered.

Furthermore, the proofs for the equivalence of the various characterizations of REG listed in Corollaries 1.2.65 and 1.2.73 are all constructive, that is, from a specification of type $\mathcal{A}$ of a regular language L, e.g., a 2DFA, one can construct a specification of type $\mathcal{B}$ of L, e.g., a right regular grammar. Also the closure of REG under the operations union, intersection, complementation, etc., is constructive. For example, from specifications of regular languages L_1 and L_2, one can effectively construct a specification of the language $L_1 \cup L_2$. Based on these constructions, it is easily seen that emptiness, finiteness, universality, containment, and equivalence are decidable for regular languages. For example, let L_1 and L_2 be two regular languages given by DFAs A_1 and A_2. Then $L_1 \subseteq L_2$ iff $L_1 \cap L_2^c = \emptyset$. From A_1 and A_2, we can construct a DFA B for the language $L_1 \cap L_2^c$. Hence, $L_1 \subseteq L_2$ iff $L(B) = \emptyset$, which in turn holds iff no final state of B is reachable from its initial state.

To complete this section, we recall the various language classes and types of automata that we have encountered. Based on Noam Chomsky's phrase-structure grammars and their restrictions,

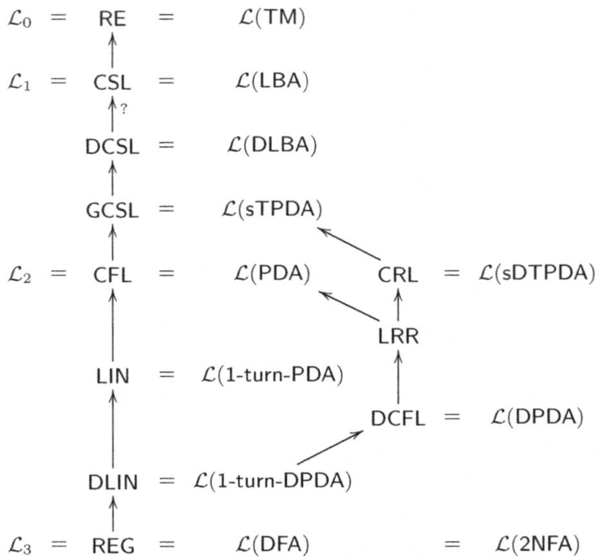

Figure 1.8: The extended Chomsky hierarchy.

we obtained the classes $\mathcal{L}_0$, $\mathcal{L}_1$, $\mathcal{L}_2$, and $\mathcal{L}_3$ that constitute the so-called Chomsky hierarchy. In addition, by taking variants of those types of automata that characterize these language classes, we obtained further classes like, e.g., GCSL, CRL, DCFL, LIN, and DLIN. The diagram in Figure 1.8 shows all these language classes, it gives some of their characterizations by automata, and it displays the inclusion relations between them. In that diagram, an arrow $\mathcal{C}_1 \rightarrow \mathcal{C}_2$ denotes the proper inclusion $\mathcal{C}_1 \subsetneq \mathcal{C}_2$, while the arrow $\mathsf{DCSL} \rightarrow_? \mathsf{CSL}$ denotes the inclusion $\mathsf{DCSL} \subseteq \mathsf{CSL}$ for which it is open whether it is proper or not. Moreover, language classes that are not connected by a sequence of arrows are incomparable under inclusion. Furthermore, s(D)TPDA denotes the class of shrinking (D)TPDAs. Finally, we have seen some of the closure and non-closure properties and learnt about the solvability and insolvability of decision problems for these language classes.

1.3 Contextual Grammars

In 1969, Solomon Marcus introduced the so-called *contextual grammars*, which exploit two fundamental concepts from linguistics: the notion of a word (or string) over a given finite non-empty alphabet and the notion of a context [147]. The basic idea is the following. Let L be a (natural) language. Certain simple sentences of that language are generally accepted as correct sentences by any native speaker of that language. Accordingly, one can assume that there is a finite set L_0 of such simple sentences. These can now be taken as a starting point for L. Next, one may choose a set C of pairs (u, v) of words, called *contexts*, and rules of how to extend sentences from L_0 by adjoining contexts, that is, if $w = xyz \in L_0$ and (u, v) is a fitting context, then $xuyvz$ is another (more complicated) sentence from L. In this way, the basic set L_0 is extended to a larger subset L_1 of the language L. By iterating this process, a set $\hat{L}$ is obtained, which is characterized by the following conditions: every sentence from L_0 belongs to $\hat{L}$, and for every sentence $w = xyz \in \hat{L}$ and every applicable context (u, v), also the sentence $xuyvz$ belongs to $\hat{L}$. By choosing the basic set L_0 and the set of contexts C in an appropriate way, the resulting language $\hat{L}$ coincides with (or is a close approximation of) the language L. For a detailed account on the motivation behind contextual grammars, we refer to Solomon Marcus's paper [148]. Here, however, we are more concerned with those aspects of contextual grammars that relate them to formal language theory, where the survey paper by Andrzej Ehrenfeucht, Gheorghe Păun, and Grzegorz Rozenberg [43] serves as our main reference.

Definition 1.3.1

(a) *A* total contextual grammar *is given through a four-tuple* $G = (\Sigma, A, C, \varphi)$, *where*

- Σ *is a finite non-empty alphabet,*
- $A \subseteq \Sigma^*$ *is a finite language over* Σ,
- $C \subseteq \Sigma^* \times \Sigma^*$ *is a finite set of pairs of words over* Σ, *and*
- $\varphi : \Sigma^* \times \Sigma^* \times \Sigma^* \to \mathcal{P}(C)$ *is a mapping.*

The words in A *are called* axioms, *the pairs in* C *are called* contexts, *and the mapping* φ *is a* choice mapping.

(b) *With* G, *we associate the derivation relation* $\Rightarrow_G^*$ *on* Σ^*. *It is the reflexive and transitive closure of the following relation, where* $x, y \in \Sigma^*$:

$$x \Rightarrow_G y \text{ if } \exists x_1, x_2, x_3 \in \Sigma^* \exists (u, v) \in \varphi(x_1, x_2, x_3) : x = x_1x_2x_3 \text{ and } y = x_1ux_2vx_3.$$

(c) *The language* $L(G)$ *generated by* G *is defined as*

$$L(G) = \{\, x \in \Sigma^* \mid \exists w \in A : w \Rightarrow_G^* x \,\}.$$

Thus, a total contextual grammar G generates a language $L(G)$ without using any nonterminals. The derivation process defined by G is very simple indeed: A word x is split into three factors $x = x_1x_2x_3$, then a context $(u, v) \in C$ is chosen such that $(u, v) \in \varphi(x_1, x_2, x_3)$, and, finally, the context is inserted around the inner factor x_2, which yields the word $y = x_1ux_2vx_3$. It is easily verified that $L(G)$ is the smallest subset of Σ^* that contains the set A of axioms and that is closed under the derivation relation $\Rightarrow_G$.

We now illustrate the above definition with a few simple examples.

Example 1.3.2 *Let* L *be a finite subset of* Σ^*, *and let* $G = (\Sigma, L, \emptyset, \emptyset)$. *Then* $L(G) = L$. ■

Example 1.3.3 *Let* $G = (\Sigma, \{\lambda\}, \{\lambda\} \times \Sigma, \varphi)$, *where* $\varphi(\lambda, x, \lambda) = \{\, (\lambda, a) \mid a \in \Sigma \,\}$ *for all words* $x \in \Sigma^*$ *and* $\varphi(x_1, x_2, x_3) = \emptyset$, *whenever* $x_1 \neq \lambda$ *or* $x_3 \neq \lambda$. *Then* $L(G) = \Sigma^*$. ■

Next, we define two special cases of contextual grammars, for which the operation of adjoining a context is restricted in a natural way.

Definition 1.3.4 *Let $G = (\Sigma, A, C, \varphi)$ be a total contextual grammar.*

(a) *The grammar G is called an* external *contextual grammar if $\varphi(x_1, x_2, x_3) = \emptyset$ whenever $x_1 \neq \lambda$ or $x_3 \neq \lambda$.*

(b) *The grammar G is called an* internal *contextual grammar if $\varphi(x_1, x_2, x_3) = \varphi(x_1', x_2, x_3')$ for all $x_1, x_1', x_2, x_3, x_3' \in \Sigma^*$.*

If G is an external contextual grammar, then $x_2 \Rightarrow_G ux_2v$, if $(u, v) \in \varphi(\lambda, x_2, \lambda)$, and if G is an internal contextual grammar, then $x = x_1'x_2x_3' \Rightarrow_G x_1'ux_2vx_3'$, whenever there exist words $x_1, x_3 \in \Sigma^*$ such that $(u, v) \in \varphi(x_1, x_2, x_3)$. Thus, in both cases, the context adjoined depends only on the (inner) factor x_2. Accordingly, we can simplify the choice mapping for external and internal contextual grammars to be of the form $\varphi : \Sigma^* \to \mathcal{P}(C)$. Obviously, a contextual grammar of this form can be interpreted as both, an external and an internal contextual grammar. Consequently, we introduce the following notation for the corresponding derivation relations:

(Ex) $x \Rightarrow_{\text{ex}} y$ if $y = uxv$ for some $(u, v) \in \varphi(x)$;
(In) $x \Rightarrow_{\text{in}} y$ if $x = x_1x_2x_3, y = x_1ux_2vx_3$ for some $x_1, x_2, x_3 \in \Sigma^*$ and $(u, v) \in \varphi(x_2)$.

We speak about *external derivations* and *internal derivations*. Hence, with a contextual grammar G of the form above, we can associate two languages, an *external contextual language*

$$L_{\text{ex}}(G) = \{\, x \in \Sigma^* \mid \exists\, w \in A : w \Rightarrow_{\text{ex}}^* x \,\}$$

and an *internal contextual language*

$$L_{\text{in}}(G) = \{\, x \in \Sigma^* \mid \exists\, w \in A : w \Rightarrow_{\text{in}}^* x \,\}.$$

We continue with some more examples.

Example 1.3.5 *Let $G = (\Sigma, A, C, \varphi)$ be a contextual grammar, where $\Sigma = \{a, b\}$, $A = \{\lambda\}$, $C = \{(a, b)\}$, and $\varphi(x) = C$ for all words $x \in \Sigma^*$. Then $L_{\text{ex}}(G) = \{\, a^nb^n \mid n \geq 0\}$, as in each derivational step, an occurrence of the letter a is attached at the left end of the current word and an occurrence of the letter b is attached at the right end of the current word. On the other hand, $L_{\text{in}}(G)$ is the semi-Dyck language D_1 (see Example 1.2.22), as in each derivational step, an occurrence of the letter a and an occurrence of the letter b are inserted in the current word, where the letter b is somewhere to the right of the letter a. Observe that D_1 can be characterized by the following condition:*

$$w \in D_1 \text{ iff } |w|_a = |w|_b \text{ and } \forall w = uv : |u|_a \geq |u|_b.$$ ■

The choice function φ in the above example is particularly simple as it assigns the set C of all possible contexts to each and every word from Σ^*.

Definition 1.3.6 *A contextual grammar $G = (\Sigma, A, C, \varphi)$ is called a contextual grammar* without choice *if $\varphi(w) = C$ holds for all words $w \in \Sigma^*$.*

We write such a contextual grammar simply as $G = (\Sigma, A, C)$.

Example 1.3.7 *Let $G = (\Sigma, A, C)$ be the contextual grammar without choice that is specified through $\Sigma = \{a, b, c\}$, $A = \{\lambda\}$, and*

$$C = \{(ab, c), (a, bc), (bc, a), (b, ca), (ac, b), (a, cb), (ba, c), (b, ac), (ca, b), (c, ab), (cb, a), (c, ba)\}).$$

We claim that $L_{\text{in}}(G) = \{w \in \Sigma^* \mid |w|_a = |w|_b = |w|_c\}$. Indeed, if $\lambda \Rightarrow_{\text{in}}^* w$, then $|w|_a = |w|_b = |w|_c$, as $|uv|_a = |uv|_b = |uv|_c = 1$ for each context $(u, v) \in C$. Conversely, let $w \in \Sigma^+$ such that $|w|_a = |w|_b = |w|_c = n$. We proceed by induction on n. If $n = 1$, then $w \in \{abc, acb, bac, bca, cab, cba\}$ and $\lambda \Rightarrow_{\text{in}} w$ follows. Furthermore, if $n > 1$, then w admits a factorization of the form $w = x^mxyuzv$ such that $\{x, y, z\} = \{a, b, c\}$. Let $w' = x^muv$. Then $|w'|_a = |w'|_b = |w'|_c = n - 1$. Hence, by the induction hypothesis, $\lambda \Rightarrow_{\text{in}}^* w' = x^muv \Rightarrow_{\text{in}} x^mxyuzv = w$, as (xy, z) belongs to C. This completes the proof of the above claim. ■

Observe that the language $\{ w \in \{a,b,c\}^* \mid |w|_a = |w|_b = |w|_c \}$ is not context-free.

Example 1.3.8 *Let $G = (\Sigma, A, C, \varphi)$ be the contextual grammar that is specified through $\Sigma = \{a\}$, $A = \{\lambda, a^3\}$, $C = \{(\lambda, a), (\lambda, a^2)\}$, and the choice mapping φ which is defined as follows:*

$$\varphi(a^i) = \begin{cases} (\lambda, a), & \text{if } i \geq 1 \text{ and } i+1 \neq 2^k \text{ for all } k \geq 0, \\ (\lambda, a^2), & \text{if } i \geq 1 \text{ and } i+1 = 2^k \text{ for some } k \geq 0, \\ \emptyset, & \text{if } i = 0. \end{cases}$$

Then $L_{\text{ex}}(G) = \{ a^n \mid n \geq 0, n \neq 2^k \text{ for all } k \geq 0 \}$ and $L_{\text{in}}(G) = \{a\}^* \setminus \{a, a^2\}$. ■

Example 1.3.9 *Let $L \subseteq \Sigma^*$ be a language, and let $c \notin \Sigma$ be an additional letter. We define a contextual grammar $G_L = (\Sigma \cup \{c\}, \{\lambda\}, \{ (\lambda, a) \mid a \in \Sigma \cup \{c\} \}, \varphi)$ by taking*

$$\varphi(x) = \begin{cases} \{ (\lambda, a) \mid a \in \Sigma \}, & \text{if } x \in \Sigma^* \setminus L, \\ \{ (\lambda, a) \mid a \in \Sigma \} \cup \{(\lambda, c)\}, & \text{if } x \in L, \\ \emptyset, & \text{if } |x|_c \geq 1. \end{cases}$$

Then $L_{\text{ex}}(G_L) = \Sigma^* \cup L \cdot \{c\}$. ■

Observe that the choice mapping φ in Example 1.3.9 is not computable, if the language L happens to be non-recursive. In this situation, the language $L_{\text{ex}}(G_L)$ is non-recursive, too.

Example 1.3.10 *Let $G = (\Sigma, A, C, \varphi)$ be the contextual grammar that is defined through $\Sigma = \{a, b, c\}$, $A = \{b\}$, $C = \{(a, a), (\lambda, b), (c, c)\}$, and the choice mapping*

$$\varphi(x) = \begin{cases} \{(a, a), (\lambda, b)\}, & \text{if } x \in a^* \cdot b \cdot a^*, \\ \{(\lambda, b)\}, & \text{if } x = a^m b a^n b^k \text{ for some } m, n \geq 0 \text{ and } k \geq 1, k \neq n, \\ \{(\lambda, b), (c, c)\}, & \text{if } x = a^m b a^n b^n \text{ for some } m, n \geq 1, \\ \emptyset, & \text{otherwise.} \end{cases}$$

Then $L_{\text{ex}}(G) = \{ a^n b a^n \mid n \geq 0 \} \cup \{ a^m b a^m b^n \mid m \geq 0, n \geq 1 \} \cup \{ c a^n b a^n b^n c \mid n \geq 1 \}$. Observe that this language is not context-free. ■

Example 1.3.11 *Let $G = (\Sigma, A, C, \varphi)$ be specified through $\Sigma = \{a, b, c, d\}$, $A = \{abcd\}$, $C = \{(a, c), (b, d)\}$, and*

$$\varphi(w) = \begin{cases} \{(a, c)\}, & \text{if } w = ab^i c \text{ for some } i \geq 1, \\ \{(b, d)\}, & \text{if } w = bc^i d \text{ for some } i \geq 1, \\ \emptyset, & \text{otherwise.} \end{cases}$$

Then it can be checked quite easily that $L_{\text{in}}(G) = \{ a^m b^n c^m d^n \mid m, n \geq 1 \}$, which is another well-known example of a non-context-free language. ■

Below, we consider the following classes of contextual grammars and the corresponding classes of languages generated by them.

Definition 1.3.12 (a) TC *denotes the class of all total contextual grammars.*

(b) ECC *denotes the class of all external contextual grammars.*

(c) ICC *denotes the class of all internal contextual grammars.*

(d) EC *denotes the class of all external contextual grammars without choice.*

(e) IC *denotes the class of all internal contextual grammars without choice.*

(f) *By requiring that the choice mapping φ used must be recursive, we obtain the subclasses TC_c, ECC_c, and ICC_c.*

(g) *For each type* T *of contextual grammars,* $\mathcal{L}(\mathsf{T})$ *is used to denote the corresponding class of contextual languages.*

In order to show that a language belongs to a given class of contextual languages, it suffices to provide a contextual grammar of the corresponding form that generates that language. From Example 1.3.5, we have $\{a^n b^n \mid n \geq 0\} \in \mathcal{L}(\mathsf{EC})$ and $D_1 \in \mathcal{L}(\mathsf{IC})$. By Example 1.3.7, $\{w \in \Sigma^* \mid |w|_a = |w|_b = |w|_c\} \in \mathcal{L}(\mathsf{IC})$, by Example 1.3.8, $\{a^n \mid n \geq 0, n \neq 2^k \text{ for all } k \geq 0\} \in \mathcal{L}(\mathsf{ECC}_c)$, by Example 1.3.9, $\Sigma^* \cup L \cdot \{c\} \in \mathcal{L}(\mathsf{ECC})$ for each language $L \subseteq \Sigma^*$, and by Example 1.3.11, $\{a^m b^n c^m d^n \mid m, n \geq 1\} \in \mathcal{L}(\mathsf{ICC}_c)$.

On the other hand, it is much more difficult to prove that a language does not belong to a given class of contextual languages. For the corresponding task for the class of context-free languages, we have the 'Pumping Lemma' (Lemma 1.2.24), which provides a necessary combinatorial condition that is satisfied by each context-free language. For some classes of contextual languages, similar combinatorial conditions have been established.

Definition 1.3.13 *Let* $L \subseteq \Sigma^*$ *be a language.*

(a) *The language* L *is said to satisfy the* external bounded step (EBS) property, *if there is a constant* $p \in \mathbb{N}_+$ *such that, for each* $x \in L$, $|x| > p$, *there exists an element* $y \in L$ *such that* $x = uyv$ *and* $0 < |uv| \leq p$.

(b) *The language* L *is said to satisfy the* internal bounded step (IBS) property, *if there is a constant* $p \in \mathbb{N}_+$ *such that, for each* $x \in L$, $|x| > p$, *there exists an element* $y \in L$ *such that* $x = x_1 u x_2 v x_3$, $y = x_1 x_2 x_3$, *and* $0 < |uv| \leq p$.

(c) *The language* L *is said to satisfy the* bounded length increase (BLI) property, *if there is a constant* $p \in \mathbb{N}_+$ *such that, for each* $x \in L$, $|x| > p$, *there exists an element* $y \in L$ *such that* $0 < |x| - |y| \leq p$.

It is easily seen that the EBS property and the IBS property subsume the BLI property. However, the converse does not hold. For example, the language $L = \{a^n b^n c^n d^n e^n \mid n \geq 1\}$ satisfies the BLI property for the constant $p = 5$, but from a word $a^n b^n c^n d^n e^n$ $(n \geq 2)$, one does not get another element of L by removing any context of the form (u, v). Accordingly, L neither satisfies the EBS property nor the IBS property.

For the following considerations, we assume that each context (u, v) considered satisfies the condition $|uv| > 0$, that is, we exclude the trivial context (λ, λ). Actually, for the types of contextual grammars introduced above, the empty context (λ, λ) is of no use, as a word is not changed by the operation of adjoining the empty context. The following theorem relates the EBS property to the external contextual languages.

Theorem 1.3.14 *A language* $L \subseteq \Sigma^*$ *is generated by an external contextual grammar if and only if it satisfies the EBS property.*

Proof. Let $G = (\Sigma, A, C, \varphi)$ be an external contextual grammar such that $L_{\text{ex}}(G) = L$. We want to show that the language L satisfies the EBS property. Accordingly, let

$$p_1 = \max\{\,|x| \mid x \in A\,\},\ p_2 = \max\{\,|uv| \mid (u, v) \in C\,\},\ \text{and } p = \max\{p_1, p_2\}.$$

Let $x \in L$ such that $|x| > p$. Then $x \in L_{\text{ex}}(G) \smallsetminus A$. Hence, there exists an element $y \in L$ such that $y \Rightarrow_{\text{ex}} x$, which means that $x = uyv$ for a context $(u, v) \in \varphi(y)$. This implies that $0 < |uv| \leq p$.

Conversely, let $p \in \mathbb{N}_+$ be a constant such that $L \subseteq \Sigma^*$ satisfies the EBS property for this constant. We define an external contextual grammar $G = (\Sigma, A, C, \varphi)$ by taking

$$\begin{aligned} A &= \{\,x \in L \mid |x| \leq p\,\}, \\ C &= \{\,(u, v) \mid u, v \in \Sigma^* \text{ such that } 0 < |uv| \leq p\,\}, \\ \varphi(x) &= \{\,(u, v) \in C \mid uxv \in L\,\} \text{ for all } x \in \Sigma^*. \end{aligned}$$

$$\begin{aligned} \text{Then } L_{\text{ex}}(G) &= A \cup \{ u_n \cdots u_2 u_1 w v_1 v_2 \cdots v_n \mid n \geq 1, w \in A, (u_1, v_1) \in \varphi(w), \\ &\qquad (u_i, v_i) \in \varphi(u_{i-1} \cdots u_1 w v_1 \cdots v_{i-1}), i = 2, 3, \ldots, n \} \\ &= L. \end{aligned}$$

□

The next theorem relates the IBS property to the total contextual languages.

Theorem 1.3.15 *A language $L \subseteq \Sigma^*$ is generated by a total contextual grammar if and only if it satisfies the IBS property.*

Proof. Let $G = (\Sigma, A, C, \varphi)$ be a total contextual grammar such that $L(G) = L$. We claim that L satisfies the IBS property. Accordingly, let

$$p_1 = \max\{ |x| \mid x \in A \}, \ p_2 = \max\{ |uv| \mid (u, v) \in C \}, \text{ and } p = \max\{p_1, p_2\}.$$

Let $x \in L$ such that $|x| > p$. Then $x \in L(G) \setminus A$. Hence, there is a factorization $x = x_1 u x_2 v x_3$ such that $y = x_1 x_2 x_3 \in L$ and $(u, v) \in \varphi(x_1, x_2, x_3)$. It follows that $0 < |uv| \leq p$.

Conversely, let be $p \in \mathbb{N}_+$ be a constant such that $L \subseteq \Sigma^*$ satisfies the IBS property for this constant. We define a total contextual grammar $G = (V, A, C, \varphi)$ by taking

$$\begin{aligned} A &= \{ x \in L \mid |x| \leq p \}, \\ C &= \{ (u, v) \mid u, v \in \Sigma^*, 0 < |uv| \leq p \}, \\ \varphi(x_1, x_2, x_3) &= \{ (u, v) \in C \mid x_1 u x_2 v x_3 \in L \} \text{ for all } x_1, x_2, x_3 \in \Sigma^*. \end{aligned}$$

Then $L(G) = L$ follows. □

As an immediate consequence, we obtain the following implications.

Corollary 1.3.16

(a) *All contextual languages satisfy the BLI property.*

(b) *All internal contextual languages satisfy the IBS property.*

We can use these results to show that certain languages do not belong to a given class of contextual languages. For example, $L_{\text{exp}} = \{ a^{2^n} \mid n \geq 0 \} \notin \mathcal{L}(\mathsf{TC})$, as L_{exp} does not satisfy the BLI property, and $a \cdot b^+ \cdot a \notin \mathcal{L}(\mathsf{ECC})$, as this language does not satisfy the EBS property. Moreover, $L_{c,3} = \{ a^n b a^n b a^n \mid n \geq 0 \} \notin \mathcal{L}(\mathsf{TC})$ and $L_{c,5} = \{ a^n b^n c^n d^n e^n \mid n \geq 0 \} \notin \mathcal{L}(\mathsf{TC})$, as neither of these languages satisfies the IBS property. Observe that the latter two languages do, however, satisfy the BLI property. Finally, the language $L_{c,4} = \{ a^n b^n c^n d^n \mid n \geq 0 \} \in \mathcal{L}(\mathsf{TC})$, as this language satisfies the IBS property for the constant $p = 4$. Comparing $L_{c,4}$ to $L_{c,5}$, we see that total contextual grammars can count up to four, but not up to five.

Next, we present some combinatorial conditions that are necessarily satisfied by languages that are generated by external or internal contextual grammars without choice.

Definition 1.3.17 *Let Σ be a finite alphabet of cardinality $|\Sigma| \geq 2$.*

(a) *A language $L \subseteq \Sigma^*$ is said to have the* mix property 1, *if there is a constant $p \in \mathbb{N}_+$ such that the following condition is satisfied:*

(Mix1) *Whenever $a, b \in \Sigma$ are two different letters and $x, y \in L$ are two words such that $|x|_a > p$ and $|y|_b > p$, then, for each $n \geq 1$, there exists a word $z_n \in L$ such that $|z_n|_a \geq n$ and $|z_n|_b \geq n$.*

(b) *A language $L \subseteq \Sigma^*$ is said to have the* mix property 2, *if there is a constant $p \in \mathbb{N}_+$ such that the following condition is satisfied:*

(Mix2) *Whenever $a, b \in \Sigma$ are two different letters and $x, y \in L$ are two words such that $|x|_a > p$ and $|y|_b > p$, then, for each $n \geq 1$, there exists a word $z_n \in L$ such that $z_n = x_1 x_2 \cdots x_n$, where x_i has the form $x_i = x_{i,1} a x_{i,2} b x_{i,3}$ $(1 \leq i \leq n)$.*

Obviously, the property (Mix2) implies the property (Mix1). The next result shows that the property (Mix1), respectively (Mix2), is necessarily satisfied by any language that is generated by an external, respectively an internal, contextual grammar without choice.

Theorem 1.3.18

(a) *Each language in the class* $\mathcal{L}(\mathsf{EC})$ *satisfies the property (Mix1).*

(b) *Each language in the class* $\mathcal{L}(\mathsf{IC})$ *satisfies the property (Mix2).*

Proof. Let $G = (\Sigma, A, C)$ be a contextual grammar without choice, that is, $\varphi(x) = C$ for all $x \in \Sigma^*$, and assume that $|\Sigma| \geq 2$. We choose the constant $p = \max\{\, |w| \mid w \in A\,\}$.

(a) Let $x, y \in L_{\text{ex}}(G)$ such that $|x|_a > p$ und $|y|_b > p$, where $a, b \in \Sigma$, $a \neq b$. Then $x, y \notin A$, and hence, there exist contexts $(u, v), (u', v') \in C$ such that $|uv|_a > 0$ and $|u'v'|_b > 0$. Notice that (u, v) and (u', v') could be the same context. By adjoining these contexts repeatedly to a word from the set A, we can generate words $z_n \in L_{\text{ex}}(G)$ that satisfy the properties $|z_n|_a \geq n$ and $|z_n|_b \geq n$.

(b) As in (a), there exist contexts $(u, v), (u', v') \in C$ such that $|uv|_a > 0$ und $|u'v'|_b > 0$. Based on the internal derivation mode, these contexts can now be adjoined to a word from the set A such that the resulting words $z_n \in L_{\text{in}}(G)$ contain n subsequent factors in which an occurrence of the letter b is preceded by an occurrence of the letter a. □

Using these necessary conditions, we obtain the following negative results.

Corollary 1.3.19 (a) $L_{c,6} = \{a\}^+ \cup \{b\}^+ \notin \mathcal{L}(\mathsf{EC}) \cup \mathcal{L}(\mathsf{IC})$.

(b) $L_{c,7} = \{a\}^+ \cdot \{b\}^+ \notin \mathcal{L}(\mathsf{IC})$.

(c) $L_{c,8} = \{\, a^n b^n \mid n \geq 1\,\} \notin \mathcal{L}(\mathsf{IC})$.

Proof. The language $L_{c,6} = \{a\}^+ \cup \{b\}^+$ does not have the property (Mix1), and hence, it does not have the property (Mix2), either. Hence, it is neither generated by an external nor by an internal contextual grammar without choice.

The language $L_{c,7} = \{a\}^+ \cdot \{b\}^+$ has the property (Mix1), but not the property (Mix2). Furthermore, the language $L_{c,8} = \{\, a^n b^n \mid n \geq 1\,\}$ does not have the property (Mix2), either. Thus, these languages are not generated by internal contextual grammars without choice. □

Observe, however, that the languages $L_{c,6}$, $L_{c,7}$, and $L_{c,8}$ satisfy the EBS property, which means that $L_{c,6}, L_{c,7}, L_{c,8} \in \mathcal{L}(\mathsf{ECC})$ by Theorem 1.3.14.

Taking $L = \{\, a^{2^n} \mid n \geq 0\,\}$, Example 1.3.9 shows that the language $L' = \{a\}^* \cup \{\, a^{2^n} c \mid n \geq 0\,\}$ is in the class $\mathcal{L}(\mathsf{ECC})$. This observation implies that there is no pumping lemma for this class of contextual languages. However, in contrast to the situation for external contextual languages, we have the following result for internal contextual languages.

Theorem 1.3.20 *Let* $L \subseteq \Sigma^*$ *be a language from the class* $\mathcal{L}(\mathsf{ICC})$. *Then there are two constants* $p, q \in \mathbb{N}_+$ *such that the following condition is satisfied: Each word* $z \in L$ *of length* $|z| > p$ *admits a factorization of the form* $z = uvwxy$, *where* $u, v, w, x, y \in \Sigma^*$ *and* $0 < |vx| \leq q$, *such that* $uv^iwx^iy \in L$ *for all* $i \geq 0$.

Proof. Let $G = (\Sigma, A, C, \varphi)$ be an internal contextual grammar such that $L_{\text{in}}(G) = L$. We take $p = \max\{\, |w| \mid w \in A\,\}$ and $q = \max\{\, |uv| \mid (u, v) \in C\,\}$. Let $z \in L$ be a word such that $|z| > p$. Then $z \notin A$, and hence, there is a word $y \in L$ such that $y \Rightarrow_{\text{in}} z$, that is, $y = x_1x_2x_3$ and $z = x_1ux_2vx_3$ for some context $(u, v) \in \varphi(x_2)$. Thus, $y = x_1u^0x_2v^0x_3 \Rightarrow_{\text{in}} z = x_1ux_2vx_3 \Rightarrow_{\text{in}} x_1u^2x_2v^2x_3 \Rightarrow_{\text{in}} \cdots \Rightarrow_{\text{in}} x_1u^jx_2v^jx_3$ for all $j \geq 2$, that is, $x_1u^ix_2v^ix_3 \in L$ for all $i \geq 0$. □

As the language $L_{c,9} = \{\, a^n b^n c^n \mid n \geq 0\,\}$ does not satisfy this pumping lemma, we see that $L_{c,9} \notin \mathcal{L}(\mathsf{ICC})$. The above pumping lemma implies that the languages from $\mathcal{L}(\mathsf{ICC})$ satisfy the IBS property. On the other hand, the language $L_{c,10} = \{a\}^+ \cup \{ a^n b a^m b a^p \mid n+m+p = 2^k, k \geq 1 \}$ satisfies the IBS property, but it does not satisfy the condition of the pumping lemma. Thus, the condition of the pumping lemma is strictly stronger than the IBS property.

In analogy to the proof of Theorem 1.3.20, the following pumping lemma can be established for external contextual grammars without choice.

Theorem 1.3.21 *Let $L \subseteq \Sigma^*$ be a language from the class $\mathcal{L}(\mathsf{EC})$. Then there are two constants $p, q \in \mathbb{N}_+$ such that the following condition is satisfied: Each word $z \in L$ of length $|z| > p$ admits a factorization of the form $z = uyv$, where $u, y, v \in \Sigma^*$ and $0 < |uv| \leq q$, such that $u^i y v^i \in L$ for all $i \geq 0$.*

From the above pumping lemmas, we immediately obtain the following result.

Corollary 1.3.22 *For each language $L \in \mathcal{L}(\mathsf{ICC}) \cup \mathcal{L}(\mathsf{EC})$, there are integers $c, d \in \mathbb{N}_+$ such that, for each $n \in \mathbb{N}$, L contains a word w_n satisfying the condition $|w_n| = c + n \cdot d$.*

The next condition is related to the EBS property.

Definition 1.3.23 *For a language $L \subseteq \Sigma^*$, the sets $\mathrm{Min}_i(L)$, $i \geq 0$, are defined recursively as follows:*

$$\begin{aligned} \mathrm{Min}_0(L) &= \{ x \in L \mid \text{No proper factor of } x \text{ is an element of } L \}, \\ \mathrm{Min}_{i+1}(L) &= \mathrm{Min}_i(L) \cup \mathrm{Min}_0(L \smallsetminus \mathrm{Min}_i(L)) \textit{ for all } i \geq 0. \end{aligned}$$

From this definition we see that

$$\begin{aligned} \mathrm{Min}_1(L) &= \mathrm{Min}_0(L) \cup \mathrm{Min}_0(L \smallsetminus \mathrm{Min}_0(L)) \\ &= \{ x \in L \mid \text{No proper factor of } x \text{ is an element of } L \} \\ &\quad \cup \{ x \in L \mid \text{If } y \text{ is a proper factor of } x \text{ such that } y \in L, \text{ then } y \in \mathrm{Min}_0(L) \}. \end{aligned}$$

For example, for $L_{c,11} = a^* \cdot b \cdot a^* \cdot b \cdot a^*$, we have $\mathrm{Min}_0(L_{c,11}) = b \cdot a^* \cdot b$, and

$$\begin{aligned} \mathrm{Min}_1(L_{c,11}) &= b \cdot a^* \cdot b \cup \mathrm{Min}_0(a^+ \cdot b \cdot a^* \cdot b \cdot a^* \cup a^* \cdot b \cdot a^* \cdot b \cdot a^+) \\ &= b \cdot a^* \cdot b \cup ab \cdot a^* \cdot b \cup b \cdot a^* \cdot b \cdot a. \end{aligned}$$

In fact, it follows inductively that $\mathrm{Min}_i(L_{c,11}) = \{ a^r \cdot b \cdot a^* \cdot b \cdot a^s \mid 0 \leq r+s \leq i \}$ for all $i \geq 0$. The following theorem establishes a serious restriction for the sets $\mathrm{Min}_i(L)$ of an external contextual language L.

Theorem 1.3.24 *If $L \in \mathcal{L}(\mathsf{ECC})$, then $\mathrm{Min}_i(L)$ is necessarily a finite set for each $i \geq 0$.*

For the proof, which proceeds by induction on i, we refer to [43]. It follows that the language $L_{c,11}$ is not generated by any external contextual grammar, as the set $\mathrm{Min}_0(L_{c,11})$ is infinite. Analogously, the language $L_{c,9} = \{ a^n b^n c^n \mid n \geq 0 \}$ is not an external contextual language, either, as $\mathrm{Min}_0(L_{c,9}) = L_{c,9}$ is also infinite.

Definition 1.3.25 *Let Σ be a finite alphabet, and let $L \subseteq \Sigma^*$ be a language over Σ.*

(a) *The* density function $\rho_L : \mathbb{N} \to \mathbb{N}$ *of L is defined through $\rho_L(n) = |L \cap \Sigma^n|$ for all $n \geq 0$, that is, $\rho_L(n)$ is the number of words of length n in L.*

(b) *A language $L \subseteq \Sigma^*$ is called* k-slender *for an integer $k \geq 1$, if $\rho_L(n) \leq k$ holds for all $n \geq 0$, and it is called* slender, *if it is k-slender for some $k \geq 1$.*

(c) *A language $L \subseteq \Sigma^*$ is called* thin, *if it is 1-slender, that is, for each $n \geq 0$, L contains at most one word of length n.*

Obviously, a unary language, that is, a language $L \subseteq \{a\}^*$, is necessarily thin, as there is only a single word of each length. If, however, the alphabet Σ has cardinality r for some $r \geq 2$, then there are r^n words of length n for all $n \geq 0$. The next result shows that languages generated by internal contextual grammars without choice are almost never slender.

Theorem 1.3.26 ([43]) *If $L \in \mathcal{L}(\mathsf{IC})$ is an infinite language that contains occurrences of at least two different letters, then L is not slender.*

From this result, we see that the languages $L_{c,12} = \{a\} \cup \{b\}^*$ and $L_{c,13} = \{a\} \cdot \{b\}^*$ are not generated by any internal contextual grammars without choice, as both these languages are slender. Observe, however, that $L_{c,13} \in \mathcal{L}(\mathsf{EC})$, as it is generated by the external contextual grammar without choice $G = (\{a,b\}, \{a\}, \{(\lambda, b)\})$. Moreover, $L_{c,13} = L_{\text{in}}(G')$ for the internal contextual grammar $G' = (\{a,b\}, \{a\}, \{(\lambda, b)\}, \varphi)$, where $\varphi(a) = \{(\lambda, b)\}$ and $\varphi(x) = \emptyset$ for all other words x.

Finally, we establish the following negative result.

Lemma 1.3.27 $L_{\text{pal}} = \{\, ww^R \mid w \in \{a,b\}^+ \,\} \notin \mathcal{L}(\mathsf{ICC})$.

Proof. Assume to the contrary that $L_{\text{pal}} = L_{\text{in}}(G)$ for a contextual grammar $G = (\{a,b\}, A, C, \varphi)$. As L_{pal} is infinite, there are a factor x of a word of L_{pal} and a context $(u,v) \in \varphi(x)$ such that $|uv| > 0$. Assume that $|v|_a > 0$. We consider the word $w = xb^kb^kx^R \in L_{\text{pal}}$, where $k > 2 \cdot |uv|$. Then $w = xb^kb^kx^R \Rightarrow_{\text{in}}^* uuxvvb^kb^kx^R = w'$, which implies that $w' \in L_{\text{in}}(G)$. Hence, $w' = yy^R$ for some word y, which implies that $y = uuxvvb^{k-|uv|}$ and $y^R = b^{|uv|}b^kx^R$. This in turn yields $xb^{k+|uv|} = y = uuxvvb^{k-|uv|}$, which shows that $v \in \{b\}^*$, a contradiction.

The case $|v|_b > 0$ is dealt with in the same manner. Thus, it follows that $v = \lambda$, which implies that $|u|_a > 0$ or $|u|_b > 0$.

Assume that $|u|_a > 0$, the other case is completely analogous. We consider the word $w = x^Rb^kb^kx \in L_{\text{pal}}$, where $k > 2 \cdot |u|$. We obtain $w = x^Rb^kb^kx \Rightarrow_{\text{in}}^* x^Rb^kb^kuux = w' \in L_{\text{in}}(G)$. Hence, there exists a word y such that $w' = yy^R$. This yields $y = x^Rb^k \cdot b^{|u|}$ and $y^R = b^{k-|u|}uux$, which shows that $y = x^Rb^{|u|+k} = x^Ru^Ru^Rb^{k-|u|}$. Thus, $u \in \{b\}^*$, again a contradiction.

It follows that $L_{\text{pal}} \neq L_{\text{in}}(G)$, that is, $L_{\text{pal}} \notin \mathcal{L}(\mathsf{ICC})$. □

The language L_{pal} satisfies the IBS property and the property (Mix1). Moreover, this language fulfills the properties of Theorem 1.3.20. Thus, not even all these properties together are sufficient to guarantee that a language is generated by an internal contextual grammar. The following theorem describes the inclusions between the various classes of contextual languages.

Theorem 1.3.28
(a) $\mathcal{L}(\mathsf{IC}) \subsetneq \mathcal{L}(\mathsf{ICC}_c) \subsetneq \mathcal{L}(\mathsf{ICC})$.
(b) $\mathcal{L}(\mathsf{EC}) \subsetneq \mathcal{L}(\mathsf{ECC}_c) \subsetneq \mathcal{L}(\mathsf{ECC})$.
(c) $\mathcal{L}(\mathsf{TC}_c) \subsetneq \mathcal{L}(\mathsf{TC})$.
(d) $\mathcal{L}(\mathsf{ICC}_c) \subsetneq \mathcal{L}(\mathsf{TC}_c)$.
(e) $\mathcal{L}(\mathsf{ECC}_c) \subsetneq \mathcal{L}(\mathsf{TC}_c)$.
(f) $\mathcal{L}(\mathsf{ICC}) \subsetneq \mathcal{L}(\mathsf{TC})$.
(g) $\mathcal{L}(\mathsf{ECC}) \subsetneq \mathcal{L}(\mathsf{TC})$.

Proof. All these inclusions are immediate consequences of the definitions of the various types of contextual grammars. Thus, it remains to prove that they all are proper inclusions.

By Corollary 1.3.19 (a), $L_{c,6} = \{a\}^+ \cup \{b\}^+ \notin \mathcal{L}(\mathsf{EC}) \cup \mathcal{L}(\mathsf{IC})$. However, it is easily checked that $L_{c,6} \in \mathcal{L}(\mathsf{ECC}_c) \cap \mathcal{L}(\mathsf{ICC}_c)$. Hence, the inclusions $\mathcal{L}(\mathsf{IC}) \subseteq \mathcal{L}(\mathsf{ICC}_c)$ and $\mathcal{L}(\mathsf{EC}) \subseteq \mathcal{L}(\mathsf{ECC}_c)$ are proper.

By Theorem 1.3.14, $\{a\} \cdot \{b\}^+ \cdot \{a\} \notin \mathcal{L}(\mathsf{ECC})$, as this language does not satisfy the EBS property. On the other hand, it is easily seen that $\{a\} \cdot \{b\}^+ \cdot \{a\} \in \mathcal{L}(\mathsf{ICC}_c)$. Moreover, the language $L_{c,9} = \{\, a^nb^nc^n \mid n \geq 0 \,\}$ does not satisfy Theorem 1.3.20, which implies that $L_{c,9} \notin \mathcal{L}(\mathsf{ICC})$. However, $L_{c,9} \in \mathcal{L}(\mathsf{TC}_c)$, as it is generated by the total contextual grammar $G_9 = (\{a,b,c\}, \{\lambda, abc\}, \{(a,bc)\}, \varphi)$, where φ is the recursive function that is defined through $\varphi(a^n, b^n, c^n) = \{(a,bc)\}$ for all $n \geq 1$ and $\varphi(x) = \emptyset$ for all other words $x \in \{a,b,c\}^*$. Together these observations imply that the inclusions $\mathcal{L}(\mathsf{ECC}_c) \subseteq \mathcal{L}(\mathsf{TC}_c)$, $\mathcal{L}(\mathsf{ECC}) \subseteq \mathcal{L}(\mathsf{TC})$, $\mathcal{L}(\mathsf{ICC}_c) \subseteq \mathcal{L}(\mathsf{TC}_c)$, and $\mathcal{L}(\mathsf{ICC}) \subseteq \mathcal{L}(\mathsf{TC})$ are proper.

Next, let $\mathsf{X} \in \{\mathsf{ICC}, \mathsf{ECC}, \mathsf{TC}\}$. It remains to prove that the inclusion $\mathcal{L}(\mathsf{X}_c) \subseteq \mathcal{L}(\mathsf{X})$ is proper. From the definition of TC_c, we see that all languages in the class $\mathcal{L}(\mathsf{TC}_c)$ are recursively enumerable. Now let $L \subseteq \Sigma^*$ be a language that is not recursively enumerable (see Section 1.2), and let $c \notin \Sigma$ be an additional letter. Then, by Example 1.3.9, the language $\Sigma^* \cup L \cdot \{c\}$ is generated by an external contextual grammar. However, with L, also the language $\Sigma^* \cup L \cdot \{c\}$ is not recursively enumerable. Hence, it is not in $\mathcal{L}(\mathsf{TC}_c)$, that is, the inclusions $\mathcal{L}(\mathsf{ECC}_c) \subseteq \mathcal{L}(\mathsf{ECC})$ and $\mathcal{L}(\mathsf{TC}_c) \subseteq \mathcal{L}(\mathsf{TC})$ are proper.

Finally, let $d \notin \Sigma \cup \{c\}$ be another new letter. We construct an internal contextual grammar $G_L = (\Sigma \cup \{c, d\}, \{cc\}, \{ (\lambda, a) \mid a \in \Sigma \} \cup \{(d, d)\}, \varphi)$, where φ is defined through $\varphi(cc) = \{ (\lambda, a) \mid a \in \Sigma \}$ and $\varphi(cx) = \{(d, d)\}$ for all $x \in L$. Then

$$L_{\text{in}}(G_L) = \{cc\} \cdot \Sigma^* \cup \{ cd^n cx_1 dx_2 d \cdots x_n dx_{n+1} \mid n \geq 1, x_1, x_2, \ldots, x_{n+1} \in \Sigma^*, \text{ and } x_1 x_2 \cdots x_i \in L, 1 \leq i \leq n \}.$$

Thus, we have the following equivalence: $w \in L$ iff $cdcwd \in L_{\text{in}}(G_L)$. This, however, implies that the language $L_{\text{in}}(G_L)$ is not recursively enumerable, either. It follows that the inclusion $\mathcal{L}(\mathsf{ICC}_c) \subseteq \mathcal{L}(\mathsf{ICC})$ is also proper. This completes the proof of Theorem 1.3.28. □

Moreover, we have the following incomparability results.

Proposition 1.3.29 *For all* $\mathsf{X} \in \{\mathsf{IC}, \mathsf{ICC}_c, \mathsf{ICC}\}$ *and* $\mathsf{Y} \in \{\mathsf{EC}, \mathsf{ECC}_c, \mathsf{ECC}\}$, *the language classes* $\mathcal{L}(\mathsf{X})$ *and* $\mathcal{L}(\mathsf{Y})$ *are incomparable under inclusion.*

Proof. By Theorem 1.3.24, $L_{c,11} = a^* \cdot b \cdot a^* \cdot b \cdot a^* \notin \mathcal{L}(\mathsf{ECC})$. However, $L_{c,11} = L_{\text{in}}(G)$ for the internal contextual grammar without choice $G = (\{a, b\}, \{bb\}, \{(\lambda, a)\})$, that is, $L_{c,11} \in \mathcal{L}(\mathsf{IC})$. On the other hand, by Lemma 1.3.27, $L_{\text{pal}} \notin \mathcal{L}(\mathsf{ICC})$, while $L_{\text{pal}} = L_{\text{ex}}(G')$ for the external contextual grammar without choice $G' = (\{a, b\}, \{\lambda\}, \{(a, a), (b, b)\})$, that is, $L_{\text{pal}} \in \mathcal{L}(\mathsf{EC})$. These two examples yield all the above incomparability results. □

Next, we relate the various classes of contextual languages to the classes of the (extended) Chomsky hierarchy (see Figure 1.8). Let FIN denote the class of all finite languages. As observed in Section 1.2, FIN is a proper subset of the class REG of regular languages. In fact, FIN is also properly contained in $\mathcal{L}(\mathsf{IC})$ and in $\mathcal{L}(\mathsf{EC})$.

Lemma 1.3.30 $\mathsf{FIN} \subsetneq \mathcal{L}(\mathsf{IC}) \cap \mathcal{L}(\mathsf{EC})$.

Proof. Example 1.3.2 shows the inclusion, which is obviously proper, as also the infinite language $\{a, b\}^*$ is contained in $\mathcal{L}(\mathsf{IC}) \cap \mathcal{L}(\mathsf{EC})$. □

Recall from Definition 1.2.49 that a linear grammar $G = (N, T, S, P)$ is a context-free grammar for which each production $(A \to r) \in P$ satisfies the condition that $r \in (T^* \cdot N \cdot T^*) \cup T^*$. The class of languages that are generated by linear grammars is the class LIN of linear languages. Here we need a subclass of the linear languages, the class LIN_1 of linear languages that are generated by linear grammars that have only a single nonterminal. Obviously, $\{ a^n b^n \mid n \geq 0 \}$ is generated by the linear grammar $(\{S\}, \{a, b\}, S, \{(S \to aSb), (S \to \lambda)\})$. On the other hand, $L = \{ a^n b^n, a^n c^{2n} \mid n \geq 0 \} \in \mathsf{LIN}$ is not generated by any linear grammar that has only a single nonterminal, that is, $L \in \mathsf{LIN} \setminus \mathsf{LIN}_1$. Thus, LIN_1 is indeed a proper subclass of the linear languages. Here we obtain the following characterization for this class.

Theorem 1.3.31 $\mathcal{L}(\mathsf{EC}) = \mathsf{LIN}_1$.

Proof. Let $G = (\Sigma, A, C)$ be a contextual grammar without choice, that is, $\varphi(x) = C$ for all $x \in \Sigma^*$. Then

$$L_{\text{ex}}(G) = A \cup \{ u_n \cdots u_2 u_1 w v_1 v_2 \cdots v_n \mid n \geq 1, w \in A, (u_i, v_i) \in C \text{ for all } i = 1, 2, \ldots, n \}.$$

It is easily seen that this language is also generated by the linear grammar $G' = (\{S\}, \Sigma, S, P)$, where

$$P = \{ (S \to w) \mid w \in A \} \cup \{ (S \to uSv) \mid (u, v) \in C \}.$$

Thus, $\mathcal{L}(\mathsf{EC}) \subseteq \mathsf{LIN}_1$.

Conversely, let $G = (\{S\}, \Sigma, S, P)$ be a linear grammar with only a single nonterminal. We define an external contextual grammar without choice $G' = (\Sigma, A, C)$ as follows:

$$\begin{array}{rcl} A & = & \{ w \in \Sigma^* \mid (S \to w) \in P \}, \\ C & = & \{ (u, v) \in \Sigma^* \times \Sigma^* \mid (S \to uSv) \in P \}. \end{array}$$

Then it is easily checked that $L_{\text{ex}}(G') = L(G)$. Thus, $\mathsf{LIN}_1 = \mathcal{L}(\mathsf{EC})$ follows. □

The next result shows that the derivation relation of a regular grammar can be simulated by the process of adjoining contexts. For the proof, we refer to [43].

Theorem 1.3.32 $\mathsf{REG} \subsetneq \mathcal{L}(\mathsf{ICC}_c)$.

We recall from Example 1.3.11 that $\{ a^m b^n c^m d^n \mid m, n \geq 1 \} \in \mathcal{L}(\mathsf{ICC}_c)$, although this language is not even context-free. This shows, in particular, that the inclusion in Theorem 1.3.32 is proper. Total contextual grammars are even sufficient to generate all context-free languages.

Theorem 1.3.33 $\mathsf{CFL} \subsetneq \mathcal{L}(\mathsf{TC}_c)$.

Proof. From the Pumping Lemma for context-free languages (Lemma 1.2.24), we see that each context-free language satisfies the IBS property. Thus, Theorem 1.3.15 implies that each context-free language is generated by a total contextual grammar, that is, $\mathsf{CFL} \subseteq \mathcal{L}(\mathsf{TC})$. As each context-free language is recursive, we see from the proof of Theorem 1.3.15 that each context-free language is even generated by a total contextual grammar with a recursive choice function. This yields the intended inclusion. Now the above language $\{ a^m b^n c^m d^n \mid m, n \geq 1 \} \in \mathcal{L}(\mathsf{ICC}_c)$ shows that CFL is just a proper subclass of $\mathcal{L}(\mathsf{TC}_c)$. □

Finally, we have the following inclusion.

Theorem 1.3.34 $\mathcal{L}(\mathsf{IC}) \subsetneq \mathsf{CSL}$.

Proof. Let $G = (\Sigma, A, C)$ be an internal contextual grammar without choice. Assume that $C = \{(u_1, v_1), (u_2, v_2), \ldots, (u_m, v_m)\}$, where, for all $1 \leq i \leq m$, $u_i \neq \lambda$ or $v_i \neq \lambda$. We define a monotone grammar (see Definition 1.2.7) $G' = (N, \Sigma, S, P)$ by taking

$$N = \{S, T_1, T_2\} \cup \{ L_i \mid 1 \leq i \leq m, u_i \neq \lambda \}$$

and

$$\begin{array}{rcl} P & = & \{ (S \to w) \mid w \in A \} \\ & & \cup \{ (S \to wT_1) \mid w \in A \} \\ & & \cup \{ (T_1 \to T_2T_1), (T_1 \to T_2) \} \\ & & \cup \{ (aT_2 \to T_2a) \mid a \in \Sigma \} \\ & & \cup \{ (T_2 \to L_iv_i) \mid 1 \leq i \leq m, u_i \neq \lambda \} \\ & & \cup \{ (T_2 \to v_i) \mid 1 \leq i \leq m, u_i = \lambda \} \\ & & \cup \{ (aL_i \to L_ia) \mid a \in \Sigma, 1 \leq i \leq m, u_i \neq \lambda \} \\ & & \cup \{ (L_i \to u_i) \mid 1 \leq i \leq m, u_i \neq \lambda \}. \end{array}$$

We claim that $L(G') = L_{\text{in}}(G)$. Let $x \in L_{\text{in}}(G)$, that is, there are $w \in A$ and an integer $k \geq 0$ such that

$$w \Rightarrow_{\text{in}} w_1 \Rightarrow_{\text{in}} \ldots \Rightarrow_{\text{in}} w_{k-1} \Rightarrow_{\text{in}} w_k = x.$$

Proceeding by induktion on k, we show that $S \Rightarrow^*_{G'} xT_1$ and $S \Rightarrow^*_{G'} x$, which yields $x \in L(G')$.

If $k = 0$, then $x = w \in A$, and we have the derivations $S \Rightarrow_{G'} wT_1$ and $S \Rightarrow_{G'} w$. Now assume that $S \Rightarrow^*_{G'} w_{k-1}T_1$ and $S \Rightarrow^*_{G'} w_{k-1}$ have already been proved. As $w_{k-1} \Rightarrow_{\text{in}} w_k = x$, there are a factorization $w_{k-1} = x_1x_2x_3$ and a context $(u_i, v_i) \in C$ such that $w_k = x_1u_ix_2v_ix_3$. Obviously, we

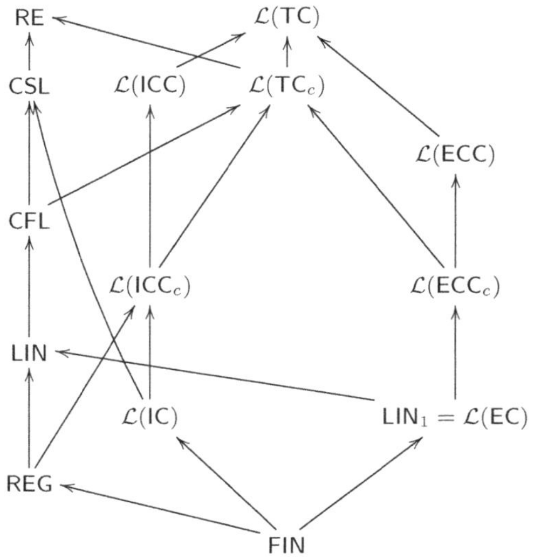

Figure 1.9: The inclusion relations between the various types of contextual languages and the classes of the Chomsky hierarchy. Each arrow denotes a proper inclusion, and classes that are not connected by a sequence of arrows are incomparable with respect to inclusion.

have $w_{k-1}T_1 \Rightarrow_{G'} w_{k-1}T_2T_1$ and $w_{k-1}T_1 \Rightarrow_{G'} w_{k-1}T_2$. If $u_i \neq \lambda$, we can construct the following derivations in G':

$$\begin{aligned} S &\Rightarrow_{G'}^* w_{k-1}T_1 \Rightarrow_{G'} w_{k-1}T_2 \Rightarrow_{G'}^* x_1x_2T_2x_3 \\ &\Rightarrow_{G'} x_1x_2L_iv_ix_3 \Rightarrow_{G'}^* x_1L_ix_2v_ix_3 \Rightarrow_{G'} x_1u_ix_2v_ix_3 = w_k, \end{aligned}$$

and, analogously,

$$S \Rightarrow_{G'}^* w_{k-1}T_1 \Rightarrow_{G'} w_{k-1}T_2T_1 \Rightarrow_{G'}^* x_1u_ix_2v_ix_3T_1 = w_kT_1.$$

If $u_i = \lambda$, then $v_i \neq \lambda$, and we obtain corresponding derivations. Thus, $L_{\text{in}}(G) \subseteq L(G')$.

To prove the converse inclusion, let $x \in L(G')$. Then there exists a derivation $S \Rightarrow_{G'} \alpha_1 \Rightarrow_{G'} \cdots \Rightarrow_{G'} \alpha_k = x$. By induction on k, it can be verified that $x \in L_{\text{in}}(G)$. Hence, we obtain $L(G') = L_{\text{in}}(G)$.

It follows that $\mathcal{L}(\mathsf{IC}) \subseteq \mathsf{CSL}$. By Theorem 1.3.15, the context-sensitive language $L_{c,3} = \{ a^nba^nba^n \mid n \geq 1 \}$ is not generated by any contextual grammar. Hence, $\mathcal{L}(\mathsf{IC}) \subseteq \mathsf{CSL}$ is in fact a proper inclusion. □

In addition, we have the following incomparability results between the classes of the Chomsky hierarchy and the various classes of contextual languages.

Theorem 1.3.35 (a) *The class* REG *of regular languages is incomparable to the classes* $\mathcal{L}(\mathsf{IC})$, $\mathcal{L}(\mathsf{EC})$, $\mathcal{L}(\mathsf{ECC}_c)$, *and* $\mathcal{L}(\mathsf{ECC})$ *with respect to inclusion.*

(b) *The classes* LIN *and* CFL *are incomparable to the classes* $\mathcal{L}(\mathsf{IC})$, $\mathcal{L}(\mathsf{ICC}_c)$, $\mathcal{L}(\mathsf{ICC})$, $\mathcal{L}(\mathsf{ECC}_c)$, *and* $\mathcal{L}(\mathsf{ECC})$ *with respect to inclusion.*

(c) *The class* CSL *of context-sensitive languages is incomparable to the classes* $\mathcal{L}(\mathsf{ICC}_c)$, $\mathcal{L}(\mathsf{ICC})$, $\mathcal{L}(\mathsf{ECC}_c)$, $\mathcal{L}(\mathsf{ECC})$, $\mathcal{L}(\mathsf{TC}_c)$, *and* $\mathcal{L}(\mathsf{TC})$ *with respect to inclusion.*

(d) *The class* RE *of recursively enumerable languages is incomparable to the classes* $\mathcal{L}(\mathsf{ICC})$, $\mathcal{L}(\mathsf{ECC})$, *and* $\mathcal{L}(\mathsf{TC})$ *with respect to inclusion.*

Operation	$\mathcal{L}(\mathsf{IC})$	$\mathcal{L}(\mathsf{EC})$	$\mathcal{L}(\mathsf{ICC})$	$\mathcal{L}(\mathsf{ECC})$	$\mathcal{L}(\mathsf{TC})$
Union	-	-	-	+	+
Intersection	-	-	-	-	-
Complementation	-	-	-	-	-
Product	-	-	-	-	+
Kleene plus	-	-	-	-	+
Non-erasing morphism	-	+	-	+	+
Finite substitution	-	+	-	+	+
Substitution	-	-	-	-	+
Intersection with regular sets	-	-	-	-	-
Inverse morphism	-	-	-	-	-
Reversal	+	+	+	+	+

Figure 1.10: Closure and non-closure properties of the various classes of contextual languages, where + indicates that a class is closed under the corresponding operation, while – expresses the fact that a class is not closed under the corresponding operation.

Proof. (a) As the regular language $L_{c,2} = \{a\} \cdot \{b\}^+ \cdot \{a\}$ does not satisfy the EBS property, it does not belong to $\mathcal{L}(\mathsf{ECC})$ by Theorem 1.3.14. On the other hand, $L_{c,8} = \{\, a^n b^n \mid n \geq 1 \,\} \in \mathcal{L}(\mathsf{EC}) \smallsetminus \mathsf{REG}$. Moreover, $L_{c,6} = \{a\}^+ \cup \{b\}^+ \in \mathsf{REG} \smallsetminus \mathcal{L}(\mathsf{IC})$ by Corollary 1.3.19(a), and the semi-Dyck language D_1 is contained in $\mathcal{L}(\mathsf{IC}) \smallsetminus \mathsf{REG}$ (see Example 1.3.5).

(b) By Lemma 1.3.27, the linear language L_{pal} is not contained in $\mathcal{L}(\mathsf{ICC})$. On the other hand, the non-context-free language $\{\, w \in \{a,b,c\}^* \mid |w|_a = |w|_b = |w|_c \,\}$ is in $\mathcal{L}(\mathsf{IC})$ by Example 1.3.7. Furthermore, as noted in (a), the language $L_{c,2} = \{a\} \cdot \{b\}^+ \cdot \{a\}$ is not generated by any external contextual grammar, that is, $L_{c,2} \in \mathsf{LIN} \smallsetminus \mathcal{L}(\mathsf{ECC})$, and, in Example 1.3.10, we encountered a non-context-free language L that belongs to the class $\mathcal{L}(\mathsf{ECC}_c)$.

(c) If $L \subseteq \Sigma^*$ is a recursive language that is not context-sensitive, then the construction from Example 1.3.9 yields a recursive external contextual grammar for a language that is not context-sensitive, either. For internal contextual grammars, an analogous result is obtained by using the technique from the corresponding part of the proof of Theorem 1.3.28. On the other hand, the language $L_{\exp} \notin \mathcal{L}(\mathsf{TC})$ by Corollary 1.3.16(a), but $L_{\exp}$ is context-sensitive.

(d) Finally, the classes $\mathcal{L}(\mathsf{ICC})$ and $\mathcal{L}(\mathsf{ECC})$ contain languages that are not recursively enumerable (see Example 1.3.9 and the proof of Theorem 1.3.28). Together with the results on the language $L_{\exp}$ in (c), this yields the incomparability results concerning the class RE. □

The diagram in Figure 1.9 summarizes the relations between the various types of contextual languages and the classes of the Chomsky hierarchy.

It is easily seen that each of the above classes of contextual languages is closed under the operation of reversal, that is, if $L \in \mathcal{L}(\mathsf{IC})$, then $L^R = \{\, w^R \mid w \in L \,\} \in \mathcal{L}(\mathsf{IC})$, and analogously for the other classes. On the other hand, none of the above classes of contextual languages is closed under the operation of intersection with a regular language. In fact, we have the closure and non-closure properties that are summarized in the table in Figure 1.10 (see [43]). For example, the language $\{a\}^* \cdot \{b\} \cdot \{a\}^*$ is generated by the internal contextual grammar without choice $G = (\{a,b\}, \{b\}, \{(\lambda, a), (a, \lambda)\})$. Now let $h : \{a,b\}^* \to \{a,b\}^*$ be the morphism that is defined through $a \mapsto a$ and $b \mapsto bb$. Then $h(a^* \cdot b \cdot a^*) = \{a\}^* \cdot \{bb\} \cdot \{a\}^*$. However, it is easily seen that this language is not generated by any internal contextual grammar without choice. It follows that the class $\mathcal{L}(\mathsf{IC})$ is not closed under non-erasing morphisms, and hence, it is not closed under finite substitutions, either. In fact, the language classes $\mathcal{L}(\mathsf{IC})$ and $\mathcal{L}(\mathsf{ICC})$ are *anti-AFLs*, that is, they are not closed under any of the six AFL operations.

Finally, we turn to a generalization of the contextual grammars, the so-called *t-contextual gram-*

mars, where $t \geq 2$ is a positive integer [214]. In each derivational step of such a grammar, t factors (contexts) are inserted at t places into a word. Obviously, for these grammars, the corresponding selection mappings are more complicated than for the standard contextual grammars.

Definition 1.3.36 ([214]) *For $t \in \mathbb{N}_+$, a* t-contextual grammar *is a system $G = (\Sigma, A, C, f)$, where Σ is a finite alphabet, A is a finite language over Σ, $C \subseteq (\Sigma^*)^t$ is a finite set of* t-contexts *over Σ, and $f : (\Sigma^*)^{t+1} \to \mathcal{P}(C)$ is the* selection mapping.

The derivation relation $\Rightarrow_G^*$ *that is induced by G is the reflexive and transition closure of the single-step derivation relation $\Rightarrow_G$ that is defined as follows:*

$$\begin{aligned} x \Rightarrow_G y \quad \text{if} \quad & \exists x_1, x_2, \ldots, x_{t+1}, u_1, u_2, \ldots, u_t \in \Sigma^* : \\ & x = x_1 x_2 x_3 \cdots x_t x_{t+1} \text{ and } y = x_1 u_1 x_2 u_2 x_3 \cdots x_t u_t x_{t+1} \\ & \text{such that } (u_1, u_2, \ldots, u_t) \in f(x_1, x_2, \ldots, x_{t+1}). \end{aligned}$$

The language generated by G is the set $L(G) = \{ v \mid \exists u \in A : u \Rightarrow_G^* v \}$.

As defined above, t-contextual grammars are very general in that they may use selection mappings of arbitrary complexity. Accordingly, various restrictions have been considered to reduce the generality of the selection mapping [214]. Of particular interest are those types of contextual grammars for which the selection mapping can be described through regular expressions as in the case of contextual grammars with regular selection introduced in [174]. Analogously, we obtain t-contextual grammars with regular selection.

Definition 1.3.37 ([101, 170]) *Let t be a positive integer. A* t-contextual grammar with regular selection *is a $(t+5)$-tuple*

$$G = (\Sigma, A, C, \mathcal{L}_1, \mathcal{L}_2, \ldots, \mathcal{L}_{t+1}, f),$$

where Σ, A, and C are defined as above, $\mathcal{L}_1, \mathcal{L}_2, \ldots, \mathcal{L}_{t+1}$ are finite sets of regular languages over Σ, and

$$f : \mathcal{L}_1 \times \mathcal{L}_2 \times \cdots \times \mathcal{L}_{t+1} \to \mathcal{P}(C)$$

is the (regular) t-selection mapping.

Now $x \Rightarrow_G y$ holds if there exist sets $P_1 \in \mathcal{L}_1, P_2 \in \mathcal{L}_2, \ldots, P_{t+1} \in \mathcal{L}_{t+1}$ and words $x_1 \in P_1$, $x_2 \in P_2, \ldots, x_{t+1} \in P_{t+1}$ such that

$$x = x_1 x_2 x_3 \cdots x_t x_{t+1} \text{ and } y = x_1 u_1 x_2 u_2 x_3 \cdots x_t u_t x_{t+1}$$

for some context $(u_1, u_2, \ldots, u_t) \in f(P_1, P_2, \ldots, P_{t+1})$. As before, the language generated by G is the set $L(G) = \{ v \mid \exists u \in A : u \Rightarrow_G^* v \}$.

It is easily verified that this definition is equivalent to the definition of t-contextual grammars with selection of type REG of [214]. Thus, the expressive capacity of t-contextual grammars with regular selection strictly increases with the value of the parameter t.

We use the notation CGR[t] to denote the class of all t-contextual grammars with regular selection. Apparently, CGR[2] coincides with the class of contextual grammars with regular selection from [174]. Restrictions that are imposed on the sets of words describing the places of insertion will be put in parentheses after CGR[t]. Thus, CGR[t]($\mathcal{C}_1, \mathcal{C}_2, \ldots, \mathcal{C}_{t+1}$), where $\mathcal{C}_1, \mathcal{C}_2, \ldots, \mathcal{C}_{t+1}$ are sets of regular languages, denotes the class of t-contextual grammars of the form

$$G = (\Sigma, A, C, \mathcal{L}_1, \mathcal{L}_2, \ldots, \mathcal{L}_{t+1}, f),$$

where $\mathcal{L}_i$ is a finite subset of $\mathcal{C}_i$, $i = 1, 2, \ldots, t+1$. Among the possible restrictions are the following:

- REG, which means that any regular language is admitted at this point,
- FIN, which means that any finite language is admitted at this point.

For example, $\mathsf{CGR}[2](\{\Sigma^*\}, \mathsf{FIN}, \{\Sigma^*\})$ denotes the class of 2-contextual grammars with regular selection which can insert contexts around a finite set of possible infixes for arbitrary prefixes and suffixes. This class corresponds obviously to the class of internal contextual grammars with finite choice (see [214] for the definition).

We also illustrate these definitions by providing a simple example. Recall from the remarks following Corollary 1.3.16 that $L_{c,5} = \{ a^n b^n c^n d^n e^n \mid n \geq 0 \} \notin \mathcal{L}(\mathsf{TC})$.

Example 1.3.38 *Let $G_{c,5}$ be the 3-contextual grammar that is defined through*

$$G = (\Sigma, A, C, \mathcal{L}_1, \mathcal{L}_2, \mathcal{L}_3, \mathcal{L}_4, f),$$

where $\Sigma = \{a, b, c, d, e\}$, $A = \{\lambda, abcde\}$, $C = \{(ab, cd, e)\}$, $\mathcal{L}_1 = \{a^+\}$, $\mathcal{L}_2 = \{b^+ \cdot c^+\}$, $\mathcal{L}_3 = \{d^+\}$, $\mathcal{L}_4 = \{e^+\}$, and $f(x_1, x_2, x_3, x_4) = C$, if $(x_1, x_2, x_3, x_4) \in \{a^+\} \times \{b^+ \cdot c^+\} \times \{d^+\} \times \{e^+\}$ and $f(x_1, x_2, x_3, x_4) = \emptyset$, otherwise. Then

$$abcde = a \cdot bc \cdot d \cdot e \Rightarrow_{G_{c,5}} a \cdot ab \cdot bc \cdot cd \cdot d \cdot e \cdot e = a^2b^2c^2d^2e^2,$$

and it is easily seen that $L(G_{c,5}) = L_{c,5}$. Thus, $L_{c,5} \in \mathcal{L}(\mathsf{CGR}[3])$. ■

By using analogous example languages, the proper inclusion of $\mathcal{L}(\mathsf{CGR}[t])$ in $\mathcal{L}(\mathsf{CGR}[t+1])$ can be established for all $t \geq 1$. Thus, we have the following result.

Corollary 1.3.39 ([214]) *The classes of t-contextual languages $(\mathcal{L}(\mathsf{CGR}[t]))_{t \geq 1}$ form an infinite strictly ascending hierarchy.*

1.4 On the Complexity of the Membership Problem

The membership problem is clearly the most fundamental decision problem for languages:

INSTANCE: A word w.
QUESTION: Is w an element of the language L considered?

A language L is called decidable (or recursive) if it has a decidable membership problem, that is, there exists an algorithm (e.g., a Turing machine) that decides membership in L by computing the characteristic function χ_L of L. From Theorem 1.2.6, we know that the language class $\mathcal{L}_0$ coincides with the class RE of recursively enumerable languages. As there exist recursively enumerable languages that are not recursive, we see that Noam Chomsky's class $\mathcal{L}_0$ contains languages for which the membership problem is not decidable. Therefore, this class is way too large to be of practical importance. Accordingly, we concentrate on some of its proper subclasses.

Let L be a context-sensitive language. Then there exists a monotone grammar $G = (N, T, S, P)$ that generates L, which means that $|\ell| \leq |r|$ for each production $(\ell \to r) \in P$ (see Definition 1.2.7). Thus, if $w \in T^*$ belongs to L, then there exists a derivation

$$S \Rightarrow_G \alpha_1 \Rightarrow_G \alpha_2 \Rightarrow_G \cdots \Rightarrow_G \alpha_n = w$$

for w in G, and it follows that $|\alpha_i| \leq |w|$ for all $i = 1, 2, \ldots, n$. Hence, starting from the start symbol S, one can simply enumerate all sentential forms of G up to length $|w|$, and check whether the word w is encountered in this process. In the affirmative, we know that w is an element of the language L, while in the negative, we can conclude that w is not an element of L. This shows that for Noam Chomsky's class $\mathcal{L}_1$, and therewith for all classes contained in $\mathcal{L}_1$, the membership problem is decidable.

Actually, the same approach works for contextual grammars. Let $G = (\Sigma, A, C, f)$ be a contextual grammar with a recursive choice mapping f. Then a word $w \in \Sigma^*$ belongs to the language $L(G)$ if and only if it can be derived in at most $|w|$ many steps from an element of the set A. Thus, taking

$$H_0(G) = A \text{ and } H_{i+1}(G) = H_i(G) \cup \{\, w \in \Sigma^* \mid \exists x \in H_i(G) : x \Rightarrow_G w \,\} \text{ for all } i \geq 0,$$

we see that $w \in L(G)$ iff $w \in H_{|w|}(G)$. As the choice function f is recursive, the sets $H_i(G)$, $i \geq 1$, are computable, that is, the membership problem for the contextual grammars from the class TC_c is decidable.

However, knowing that the membership problem for a given language is decidable is usually not good enough. In fact, one would often like to know the *complexity* of this problem, that is, the amount of resources required to solve it. In order to discuss this topic, we introduce a few basic concepts from complexity theory, where the monograph [5] serves as our main reference. Accordingly, we take the following variant of the Turing machine as our basic computing device. This model has $k \geq 1$ semi-infinite tapes which are only infinite to the right, and each of these tapes has a separate read/write head.

Definition 1.4.1 *A* Turing machine with k semi-infinite tapes *is defined by an 8-tuple* $M = (Q, \Sigma, \Gamma, \delta, q_0, \Box, F, k)$, *where* Q *is a finite set of (internal)* states, Σ *is a finite* input alphabet, Γ *is a finite* tape alphabet *containing the input alphabet as well as the* blank symbol $\Box$,

$$\delta : ((Q \smallsetminus F) \times \Gamma^k) \to Q \times (\Gamma \times \{\mathrm{L}, \mathrm{R}, \mathrm{N}\})^k$$

is the transition function, $q_0 \in Q$ *is the* initial state, *and* $F \subseteq Q$ *is the set of* final *or* accepting states.

A computation of a Turing Machine M with k tapes (or a TM_k-machine, for short) starts with an input word $w \in \Sigma^*$ on the first tape and only blank symbols on the other tapes, while all heads are on the first cells of their tapes, and the finite-state control is in the initial state q_0. If M is in state q with the letter a_i under the head on tape i, $1 \leq i \leq k$, then it executes the operation described by $\delta(q, a_1, a_2, \ldots, a_k)$. If

$$\delta(q, a_1, a_2, \ldots, a_k) = (q', b_1, o_1, b_2, o_2, \ldots, b_k, o_k),$$

where $q' \in Q$, $b_1, b_2, \ldots, b_k \in \Gamma$, and $o_1, o_2, \ldots, o_k \in \{\mathrm{L}, \mathrm{R}, \mathrm{N}\}$, then the internal state is changed from q to q', the letter a_i is replaced with the letter b_i, and the head on tape i is moved according to the operation o_i for all $1 \leq i \leq k$. This continues until a final state $q \in F$ is reached. If $\delta(q, a_1, a_2, \ldots, a_k)$ is undefined, then M gets stuck. Since, during the course of a computation, the head on the first tape may leave the part of the tape that originally contained the input, it is assumed that all other tape squares of tape 1 initially contain the blank symbol.

To describe computations of a k-tape Turing machine, we need a compact way for presenting its overall situation at any moment of time.

Definition 1.4.2 *Let $M = (Q, \Sigma, \Gamma, \delta, q_0, \Box, F, k)$ be a k-tape Turing machine.*

(a) *A* configuration *of M is a k-tuple of words of the form*

$$(u_1 q v_1, u_2 q v_2, \ldots, u_k q v_k) \in (\Gamma^* \cdot Q \cdot \Gamma^*)^k.$$

Here $q \in Q$ is the current state of M, the i-th tape contains the word $u_i v_i$ that is followed only by occurrences of the blank symbol, and the i-th head is currently on the first letter of v_i (or on the first blank symbol following $u_i v_i$ if $v_i = \lambda$). A configuration of the form $(q_0 w, q_0, \ldots, q_0)$ with $w \in \Sigma^*$ is called an initial configuration *and a configuration of the form $(u_1 q v_1, u_2 q v_2, \ldots, u_k q v_k)$ with $q \in F$ is called a* final configuration.

(b) *The* single-step computation relation *that the transition function δ induces on the set of configurations of M is denoted by $\vdash_M$. The* computation relation *$\vdash_M^*$ is the reflexive and transitive closure of the single-step computation relation.*

(c) *An input word $w \in \Sigma^*$ is said to be* accepted *by M if the computation of M that begins with the initial configuration $(q_0 w, q_0, \ldots, q_0)$ ends with a final configuration, that is,*

$$(q_0 w, q_0, \ldots, q_0) \vdash_M^* (u_1 q v_1, u_2 q v_2, \ldots, u_k q v_k)$$

holds for some $u_1, u_2, \ldots, u_k, v_1, v_2, \ldots, v_k \in \Gamma^*$ and a final state $q \in F$.

(d) *The language* accepted by *M is the set $L(M) = \{ w \in \Sigma^* \mid w \text{ is accepted by } M \}$.*

Even though the k-tape Turing machine is a generalization of the model of the Turing machine that we considered in Section 1.1, it can be shown that it accepts exactly the same class of languages. Actually, we still need a further generalization.

Definition 1.4.3 *A* nondeterministic Turing machine with k semi-infinite tapes *M is defined by an 8-tuple $M = (Q, \Sigma, \Gamma, \delta, q_0, \Box, F, k)$, where Q, Σ, Γ, q_0, $\Box$, and F are defined as for a k-tape Turing machine, but δ is defined as*

$$\delta : (Q \setminus F) \times \Gamma^k \to \mathcal{P}(Q \times (\Gamma \times \{\mathrm{L}, \mathrm{R}, \mathrm{N}\})^k),$$

that is, δ assigns a finite set of $(2k+1)$-tuples $(q', b_1, o_1, b_2, o_2, \ldots, b_k, o_k) \in Q \times (\Gamma \times \{\mathrm{L}, \mathrm{R}, \mathrm{N}\})^k$ to each $(k+1)$-tuple $(q, a_1, a_2, \ldots, a_k) \in (Q \setminus F) \times \Gamma^k$.

If a nondeterministic k-tape Turing machine (an NTM_k-machine, for short) M is in state q with the letter a_i under the head on tape i, $1 \leq i \leq k$, then it executes one of the operations described by $\delta(q, a_1, a_2, \ldots, a_k)$. If

$$\delta(q, a_1, a_2, \ldots, a_k) = \{ (q'_j, b_{j,1}, o_{j,1}, b_{j,2}, o_{j,2}, \ldots, b_{j,k}, o_{j,k}) \mid j = 1, 2, \ldots, m \},$$

then one of these $(2k+1)$-tuples is chosen nondeterministically from this set and the corresponding actions are executed. The configurations are described just as for k-tape Turing machines, and also the computation relation that M induces on its set of configurations is denoted by $\vdash_M^*$. Now the language $L(M)$ is the set of all words $w \in \Sigma^*$ such that a final configuration can be reached by M starting from the initial configuration $(q_0 w, q_0, \ldots, q_0)$.

Despite the fact that k-tape nondeterministic Turing machines are much more general than k-tape Turing machines, it can be shown that they just accept the same languages. In fact, the following result holds.

Theorem 1.4.4 $\mathcal{L}_0 = \mathcal{L}(\mathsf{TM}_k) = \mathcal{L}(\mathsf{NTM}_k)$ *for all* $k \geq 1$.

Based on the above models of the Turing machine, we now introduce so-called complexity classes. As a first step, we associate the notions of running time and work space to Turing machines.

Definition 1.4.5 *Let M be a k-tape Turing machine.*

(a) *The* computation time *of M on input w is the number of computational steps that M executes until it halts on input w, if $w \in L(M)$; otherwise, we say that the computation time of M on w is undefined. It is denoted as* $\mathrm{t}_M(w)$.

(b) *The* running time *of M, denoted as* time_M, *is the (partial) function from $\mathbb{N}$ to $\mathbb{N}$ that is defined as follows:*

$$\mathrm{time}_M(n) = \begin{cases} \max\{\, \mathrm{t}_M(w) \mid w \in \Sigma^n \,\}, & \text{if } \mathrm{t}_M(w) \text{ is defined for all } w \in \Sigma^n, \\ \text{undefined}, & \text{otherwise.} \end{cases}$$

(c) *The* computation space *of M on input w is the maximal number of tape cells that M visits during its computation on input w, if this number is finite; otherwise, we say that the computation space of M on w is undefined. It is denoted as* $\mathrm{s}_M(w)$.

(d) *The* work space *of M, denoted as* space_M, *is the (partial) function from $\mathbb{N}$ to $\mathbb{N}$ that is defined as follows:*

$$\mathrm{space}_M(n) = \begin{cases} \max\{\, \mathrm{s}_M(w) \mid w \in \Sigma^n \,\}, & \text{if } \mathrm{s}_M(w) \text{ is defined for all } w \in \Sigma^n, \\ \text{undefined}, & \text{otherwise.} \end{cases}$$

For nondeterministic Turing machines, the corresponding definitions are not as straightforward, since such a machine may have many different computations for the same input, some of them possibly accepting, others non-accepting. In the following definition, the best possible case is always chosen, that is, the shortest computation is considered or the one with the least computation space. In addition, non-accepting computations are simply ignored.

Definition 1.4.6 *Let M be a nondeterministic k-tape Turing machine.*

(a) *The* computation time *of M on input w is the number of computational steps that M executes in the shortest accepting computation on input w, if $w \in L(M)$; otherwise, it is simply taken as 1. It is denoted as* $\mathrm{t}_M(w)$.

(b) *The* running time *of M, denoted as* time_M, *is the function from $\mathbb{N}$ to $\mathbb{N}$ that is defined as follows:*

$$\mathrm{time}_M(n) = \max\{\, \mathrm{t}_M(w) \mid w \in \Sigma^n \,\}.$$

(c) *The space required by a given computation of M on input w is the maximal number of cells that M visits during this computation. The* computation space *of M on input w is the minimum space required by any accepting computation of M on input w, if $w \in L(M)$; otherwise, the computation space of M on w is set to 1. It is denoted as* $\mathrm{s}_M(w)$.

(d) *The* work space *of M, denoted as* space_M, *is the function from $\mathbb{N}$ to $\mathbb{N}$ that is defined as follows:*

$$\text{space}_M(n) = \max\{\, s_M(w) \mid w \in \Sigma^n \,\}.$$

We say that a language L is accepted by a (deterministic or nondeterministic) multitape Turing machine M within *time* (or *space*) $f(n)$ if and only if the running time (work space) of M is bounded from above by the function f, that is, for all $n \in \mathbb{N}$, $\text{time}_M(n) \leq f(n)$ (or $\text{space}_M(n) \leq f(n)$).

Based on the running time (or the work space), we can compare two Turing machines that accept the same language. If one of them has a smaller running time (work space) than the other, then we can say that this one is more *efficient* with respect to time (or space). In addition, one can try to develop lower bounds for decision problems by showing that no Turing machine for solving a given problem has running time (or work space) below a certain bound.

Finally, we introduce those complexity classes that we shall need to classify membership problems.

Definition 1.4.7 (a) *Let $f : \mathbb{N}_+ \to \mathbb{N}_+$ be a function such that $f(n) \geq n+1$ for all $n \geq 1$. Then* $\text{DTIME}(f)$ *denotes the class of languages that are accepted by deterministic multitape Turing machines within time $f(n)$, and* $\text{NTIME}(f)$ *denotes the class of languages that are accepted by nondeterministic multitape Turing machines within time $f(n)$.*

(b) *Let $s : \mathbb{N}_+ \to N_+$ be a function such that $s(n) \geq n$ for all $n \geq 1$. Then* $\text{DSPACE}(s)$ *denotes the class of languages that are accepted by deterministic multitape Turing machines within space $s(n)$, and* $\text{NSPACE}(s)$ *denotes the class of languages that are accepted by nondeterministic multitape Turing machines within space $s(n)$.*

Obviously, $\text{DTIME}(f) \subseteq \text{NTIME}(f)$ and $\text{DSPACE}(s) \subseteq \text{NSPACE}(s)$ for all bounds f and s. It is also easily seen that $\text{DTIME}(f) \subseteq \text{DSPACE}(f)$ and $\text{NTIME}(f) \subseteq \text{NSPACE}(f)$. Furthermore, if the function f is well-behaved with respect to work space, that is, if it is *space-constructible* (see, e.g. [5]), then $\text{NSPACE}(s) \subseteq \text{DTIME}(2^{\mathcal{O}(s)})$, where

$$\mathcal{O}(s) = \{\, f : \mathbb{N}_+ \to \mathbb{N}_+ \mid \exists r > 0\, \exists n \geq 1\, \forall m \geq n : f(m) \leq r \cdot s(m) \,\}.$$

Here $\text{DTIME}(2^{\mathcal{O}(s)})$ is simply a shorthand for the expression $\bigcup_{f \in \mathcal{O}(s)} \text{DTIME}(2^f)$.

Let L be a context-sensitive language. Then L is accepted by an LBA, which is essentially a nondeterministic (single-tape) Turing machine with work space $f(n) = n$. This yields the following statement.

Corollary 1.4.8 $\mathsf{DCSL} = \text{DSPACE}(n) \subseteq \mathsf{CSL} = \text{NSPACE}(n) \subseteq \text{DTIME}(2^{\mathcal{O}(n)})$.

Of course, the above time bound of $2^{\mathcal{O}(n)}$ is just an upper bound. However, there is a strong indication that the membership problem for context-sensitive languages really needs exponential running time.

Definition 1.4.9 (a) *Let* EXPTIME *be the class of all languages that are accepted by a deterministic multitape Turing machine in running time 2^p, where p is a polynomial.*

(b) *Let* PSPACE *be the class of all languages that are accepted by deterministic multitape Turing machines with polynomially bounded work space, that is, if $L \in$ PSPACE, then there are a Turing machine M and a polynomial p such that M accepts L within work space p.*

(c) *The class of all languages that are accepted by nondeterministic multitape Turing machines with polynomially bounded running time is denoted by* NP.

(d) *The class of all languages that are accepted by deterministic multitape Turing machines with polynomially bounded running time is denoted by* P.

Obviously, P $\subseteq$ NP $\subseteq$ PSPACE $\subseteq$ EXPTIME, and it can be shown that P is a proper subclass of EXPTIME (see, e.g., [5]), but it is still open which of the above inclusions is proper. In particular, the question of whether P is a proper subclass of NP is the famous *P versus NP problem*.

A language L is called *PSPACE-complete* (*NP-complete*) if it belongs to PSPACE (NP) and if each other language from PSPACE (from NP) can be reduced to L through a reduction that is computable in polynomial time. If L is PSPACE-complete (NP-complete) and if the membership problem for L could be solved deterministically in polynomial time, then by combining the corresponding polynomial time reduction with the algorithm for solving the membership problem for L, we would obtain an algorithm for solving the membership problem for any language from PSPACE (from NP) in polynomial time. This would mean that PSPACE = P (NP = P), which would be a surprising result. Therefore, it is rather unlikely that the membership problem for any PSPACE-complete (or NP-complete) language can be solved deterministically in polynomial time. In this sense, PSPACE-complete languages are seen as the hardest languages in PSPACE, and analogously, NP-complete languages are seen as the hardest languages in NP. The following result shows that there are context-sensitive languages for which the membership problem is most probably not solvable in polynomial time.

Theorem 1.4.10 ([106]) *There exists a deterministic context-sensitive language that is PSPACE-complete.*

Thus, there are (deterministic) context-sensitive languages for which the membership problems cannot be solved in polynomial time unless the complexity class PSPACE equals the class P. It follows that the class of context-sensitive languages is too expressive to allow efficient algorithms for the membership problem. Accordingly, we must turn to classes in the Chomsky hierarchy that are properly below the context-sensitive languages.

In [39], it is shown that the membership problem for any growing context-sensitive language is solvable in polynomial time. However, the degree of the polynomial time bound for this problem depends on the language considered. In fact, the *uniform membership problem* for growing context-sensitive languages, which takes as input a strictly monotone grammar G and a word w, asking whether w is generated by G, is NP-complete [24]. Hence, for efficiency reasons, also the class of growing context-sensitive languages is still too large.

However, the situation is much better for context-free languages (see, e.g., [79]).

Theorem 1.4.11 *The membership problem for any context-free language can be solved deterministically in time $\mathcal{O}(n^3)$.*

The CYK-algorithm, discovered independently by John Cocke [35], Tadao Kasami [107], and Daniel H. Young [272], works as follows. Let $G = (V, \Sigma, S, P)$ be a context-free grammar in Chomsky normal form, and let $w = a_1a_2 \cdots a_n$ be a given terminal word, where $a_1, a_2, \ldots, a_n \in \Sigma$ and $n \geq 1$. For each $i = 1, 2, \ldots, n$ and each $j = 0, 1, 2, \ldots, n-i$, the set $T[i, j]$ is defined by taking

$$T[i,j] = \{ X \in V \mid X \Rightarrow_G^* a_i a_{i+1} \ldots a_{i+j} \}.$$

These sets can be determined by computing a corresponding table T using the technique of 'dynamic programming,' which takes time $\mathcal{O}(n^3)$. In fact, it was already observed in [272] that this algorithm only has running time $\mathcal{O}(n^2)$ for linear grammars. Now w belongs to the language $L(G)$ if and only if the start symbol S is an element of the set $T[1, n-1]$.

Another algorithm with the same worst-case time complexity was developed by Jay Earley [42]. It has the advantage of running in just quadratic time for all unambiguous context-free grammars. On the other hand, it has been shown that the membership problem for context-free languages can be reduced to the problem of multiplying boolean matrices [252], which yields a time bound of $\mathcal{O}(n^{2.81})$ for the membership problem. Thus, we see that the context-free languages admit efficient algorithms for solving their membership problems.

For a Church-Rosser language, the membership problem is even decidable in linear time, that is, if L is a Church-Rosser language and w an input word, then there exists an algorithm that decides the membership of w in L in time $c \cdot |w|$ for a constant $c \geq 1$ that depends on L. This follows immediately from the characterization of the class CRL by the length-reducing DTPDA (see Theorem 1.2.19). As $\mathsf{DCFL} \subseteq \mathsf{LRR} \subseteq \mathsf{CRL}$, the membership problems for left-to-right regular languages and for deterministic context-free languages are also decidable in linear time. Finally, from the characterization of the regular languages by the DFA (see Corollary 1.2.65), we see that the membership problem for a regular language is even decidable in realtime, that is, it just takes $|w|$ steps to decide whether the word w belongs to a given regular language. Thus, within the class of Church-Rosser languages, the membership problem can be solved very efficiently.

1.5 On Mildly Context-Sensitive Languages

Due to their efficiency with respect to parsing and translation, the regular and the context-free languages have found many applications. In particular, regular and context-free grammars have been (and are still being) used to describe the syntax of programming languages. The first programming language, the syntax of which was completely described by a context-free grammar (in Backus-Naur form), was ALGOL 60 (see, e.g., [4]). Another popular example is the language PASCAL [266], which we consider in the following two examples.

Example 1.5.1 *In the programming language PASCAL, the unsigned constants of type* real *are defined through the following diagram (see, e.g., [67]):*

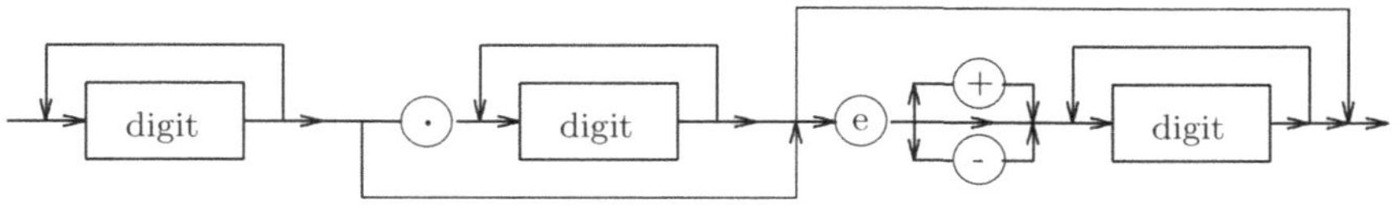

From this diagram, we can easily construct a right regular grammar $G_{\text{real}} = (N, T, S, P)$ *for the set of real constants of PASCAL. We take*

- N = $\{\langle$*unsigned number*$\rangle$, $\langle$*remainder*$\rangle$, $\langle$*decimal*$\rangle$, $\langle$*decimal remainder*$\rangle$, $\langle$*exponent*$\rangle$, $\langle$*digit*$\rangle$, $\langle$*sequence of digits*$\rangle\}$,
- $T = \{0, 1, \ldots, 9, ., e, +, -\}$,
- S = $\langle$*unsigned number*$\rangle$,

and let P contain the following productions:

$\langle$*unsigned number*$\rangle \to 0\langle$*remainder*$\rangle \mid 1\langle$*remainder*$\rangle \mid \ldots \mid 9\langle$*remainder*$\rangle$
$\langle$*remainder*$\rangle \to 0\langle$*remainder*$\rangle \mid 1\langle$*remainder*$\rangle \mid \ldots \mid 9\langle$*remainder*$\rangle \mid .\langle$*decimal*$\rangle \mid e\langle$*exponent*$\rangle \mid \lambda$
$\langle$*decimal*$\rangle \to 0\langle$*decimal remainder*$\rangle \mid \ldots \mid 9\langle$*decimal remainder*$\rangle$
$\langle$*decimal remainder*$\rangle \to 0\langle$*decimal remainder*$\rangle \mid \ldots \mid 9\langle$*decimal remainder*$\rangle \mid e\langle$*exponent*$\rangle \mid \lambda$
$\langle$*exponent*$\rangle \to +\langle$*sequence of digits*$\rangle \mid -\langle$*sequence of digits*$\rangle \mid \langle$*sequence of digits*$\rangle$
$\langle$*sequence of digits*$\rangle \to 0\langle$*sequence of digits*$\rangle \mid \ldots \mid 9\langle$*sequence of digits*$\rangle \mid \langle$*digit*$\rangle$
$\langle$*digit*$\rangle \to 0 \mid 1 \mid \cdots \mid 9$

It is easily checked that $L(G_{\text{real}})$ *is the set of words from* T^* *that represent an unsigned constant of type* real *in PASCAL.* ■

However, the set of expressions in PASCAL is not a regular language anymore, in fact, it is not even a linear language. Hence, to define this set, we need a context-free grammar that is not linear.

Example 1.5.2 *The following context-free grammar* $G_{\text{expr}} = (N, T, S, P)$ *defines a subset of the expressions in PASCAL. Here we take*

- N = $\{\langle$*expression*$\rangle$, $\langle$*simple expr*$\rangle$, $\langle$*term*$\rangle$, $\langle$*factor*$\rangle$, $\langle$*variable*$\rangle$, $\langle$*variable id*$\rangle$, $\langle$*sign*$\rangle$, $\langle$*unsigned constant*$\rangle$, $\langle$*constant id*$\rangle$, $\langle$*comparative op*$\rangle$, $\langle$*add op*$\rangle$, $\langle$*mul op*$\rangle$, $\langle$*unsigned number*$\rangle$, $\langle$*letter*$\rangle$, $\langle$*digit*$\rangle\}$,
- $T = \{0, 1, \ldots, 9, A, B, \ldots, Z, a, b, \ldots, z, +, -, *, /, \text{DIV}, \text{MOD}, (,), ., <, \leq, >, \geq, =, \neq\}$,
- S = $\langle$*expression*$\rangle$,

and let P contain the following productions:

$\langle$*expression*$\rangle \to \langle$*simple expr*$\rangle \mid \langle$*simple expr*$\rangle\langle$*comparative op*$\rangle\langle$*simple expr*$\rangle$
$\langle$*simple expr*$\rangle \to \langle$*sign*$\rangle\langle$*term*$\rangle \mid \langle$*sign*$\rangle\langle$*term*$\rangle\langle$*add op*$\rangle\langle$*term*$\rangle$
$\langle$*term*$\rangle \to \langle$*factor*$\rangle \mid \langle$*factor*$\rangle\langle$*mul op*$\rangle\langle$*factor*$\rangle$

$$\begin{array}{ll}
\langle factor \rangle & \rightarrow \langle variable \rangle \mid \langle unsigned\ constant \rangle \mid (\langle expression \rangle) \\
\langle unsigned\ constant \rangle & \rightarrow \langle constant\ id \rangle \mid \langle unsigned\ number \rangle \\
\langle constant\ id \rangle & \rightarrow \langle letter \rangle \mid \langle constant\ id \rangle \langle letter \rangle \mid \langle constant\ id \rangle \langle digit \rangle \\
\langle variable \rangle & \rightarrow \langle variable\ id \rangle \\
\langle variable\ id \rangle & \rightarrow \langle letter \rangle \mid \langle variable\ id \rangle \langle letter \rangle \mid \langle variable\ id \rangle \langle digit \rangle \\
\langle comparative\ op \rangle & \rightarrow < \mid \leq \mid > \mid \geq \mid = \mid \neq \\
\langle add\ op \rangle & \rightarrow + \mid - \\
\langle mul\ op \rangle & \rightarrow * \mid / \mid \mathrm{DIV} \mid \mathrm{MOD} \\
\langle sign \rangle & \rightarrow + \mid - \mid \lambda \\
\langle letter \rangle & \rightarrow A \mid B \mid \cdots \mid Z \mid a \mid b \mid \cdots \mid z \\
\langle digit \rangle & \rightarrow 0 \mid 1 \mid \cdots \mid 9 \\
\langle unsigned\ number \rangle & \rightarrow \cdots \ (\textit{see Example 1.5.1}).
\end{array}$$

For example, the expressions

$$a1 + (a2 - 3.14) * (17 * a3) \ \textit{and}\ (3.14 * a_1)\mathrm{DIV}(a_2/(a_3 + (-a_4)))$$

can be derived by this grammar. ■

Although the syntax of PASCAL is described by a context-free grammar, there is additional information, in particular, about context conditions, that is described more informally through text accompanying the productions of the context-free grammar. These context conditions include, e.g., the requirement that a variable must be declared before it is being used or that the type of a variable used within an expression must fit the type required by the operations used. And indeed, as first stated by Robert W. Floyd in [46], ALGOL 60 is not a context-free language due to these context conditions. This argument carries over to PASCAL (and many other imperative languages), as shown by Stefan Sokolowski [246]. Thus, in order to define a programming language like PASCAL in a completely formal way, formalisms must be used that are more expressive than context-free grammars, for example, *attribute grammars*, as introduced by Donald E. Knuth in [112]. See, e.g., [212] for a survey on attribute grammars.

Now we turn to the question of whether context-free grammars are an adequate tool to describe natural languages. Although Noam Chomsky introduced the phrase-structure grammars as a means to describe natural languages [27], he already states in [28] that 'there appears to be good evidence that devices of the kinds studied here (that is, phrase-structure grammars) are not adequate for the formulation of a full grammar for a natural language.' In particular, this applies to context-free grammars.

A serious problem one has to deal with when describing natural languages by context-free grammars is the word order. The complexity of the word order of natural languages can be illustrated by several constructions that are found in various languages. The following example shows a non-context-free construction in Dutch, which is considered to be a language with fixed word order. It is taken from [21]:

> (dat) Jan Piet Marie de kinderen zag helpen laten zwemmen.
> [*(that)-Jan-Piet-Marie-the-children-saw-help-make-swim.*]
> [*(that) Jan saw Piet help Marie make the children swim.*]

When denoting the nouns with the letters a, b, c, and d and the corresponding verb phrases with the letters $\bar{a}$, $\bar{b}$, $\bar{c}$, and $\bar{d}$, then we see that the structure of this sentence is of the form $abcd\bar{a}\bar{b}\bar{c}\bar{d}$. Thus, this example shows a duplication-like structure of the form $w\overline{w}$, where $\overline{w}$ is the word obtained from w by replacing each letter with its barred copy. This structure is not even growing context-sensitive, as the copy language $L_{\mathrm{copy}} = \{ ww \mid w \in \{a,b\}^* \}$ is not a growing context-sensitive language [25].

Similar constructions can be found in many other languages. Stuart M. Shieber found the following construction in Swiss German [245]:

Jan säit das mer d'chind em Hans es huus haend wele laa hälfe aastrüche.
[*Jan-said-that-we-the-children-Hans-the-house-wanted-to-let-help-paint.*]
[*Jan said that we wanted to let the children help Hans paint the house.*]

It has the structure $xwa^m b^n yc^m d^n z$, where a and b stand for dative and accusative noun phrases, respectively, while c and d represent the corresponding dative and accusative verb phrases, respectively. Based on such observations, Stuart M. Shieber concludes that Swiss German is not a context-free language.

Our final example is from Czech, a language with a considerable degree of word order freedom. In Czech, the syntactic relations between the words in a sentence are not specified by their relative positions, but by a rich inflexion. Often all permutations of the words in a clause are possible. For example, all the following sentences are correct in Czech:

- Všichni prošli kursem. [*All-passed-the-course.*]
- Kursem všichni prošli.
- Kursem prošli všichni.
- Prošli všichni kursem.
- Prošli kursem všichni.
- Všichni kursem prošli.

A context-free grammar for dealing with cases like this would be very large and cumbersome.

In summary, it follows that context-free grammars are neither sufficient nor well suited to model natural languages in general. Hence, other, more expressive, formalisms have been proposed. In [90], Aravind K. Joshi coined the notion of 'mildly context-sensitive languages' to describe classes of grammars and languages that are slightly more powerful than context-free grammars and that are suitable to express natural languages. According to [104], this notion can be defined as follows.

Definition 1.5.3 (a) *A family $\mathcal{L}$ of languages is called* mildly context-sensitive *if it satisfies the following four conditions:*

(1) *$\mathcal{L}$ contains all context-free languages,*

(2) *$\mathcal{L}$ can describe cross-serial dependencies, that is, for some $n \geq 2$, $\mathcal{L}$ contains the language $\{ w^k \mid w \in \Sigma^* \}$ for each $k \leq n$ and each terminal alphabet Σ,*

(3) *the membership problem for each language in $\mathcal{L}$ is decidable in polynomial time, and*

(4) *all languages in $\mathcal{L}$ have the* constant growth property.

(b) *A language $L \subseteq \Sigma^*$ satisfies the* constant growth property *if there are a constant $c_0 > 0$ and a finite set of constants $C \subset \mathbb{N}_+$ such that, for all $w \in L$, if $|w| > c_0$, then there exists a word $w' \in L$ such that $|w| = |w'| + c$ for some $c \in C$.*

(c) *A formalism $\mathcal{F}$ (e.g., a class of grammars) is called* mildly context-sensitive *if the family of languages $\mathcal{L}_{\mathcal{F}} = \{ L \mid \exists G \in \mathcal{F} : L = L(G) \}$ is mildly context-sensitive.*

If a language L has the constant growth property, then the maximal distance in length between a word from L and its nearest neighbour in L is bound from above by a constant that depends on L. This condition is similar to the BLI property of Definition 1.3.13. Recall from Corollary 1.3.16 that all contextual languages satisfy the BLI property, and hence, they all have the constant growth property. On the other hand, the Church-Rosser language $L_{\text{exp}} = \{ a^{2^n} \mid n \geq 0 \}$ (see Example 1.2.16) does not have this property. In fact, the constant growth property can be seen as a generalization of the notion of semi-linearity.

Definition 1.5.4 *Let $\Sigma = \{a_1, a_2, \ldots, a_n\}$ be an alphabet, and let*

$$\mathbb{N}^n = \{ (m_1, m_2, \ldots, m_n) \mid m_1, m_2, \ldots, m_n \in \mathbb{N} \}$$

be the set of n-tuples of natural numbers. With respect to componentwise addition, $\mathbb{N}^n$ *is a commutative monoid. Furthermore, let* $\pi : \Sigma^* \to \mathbb{N}^n$ *be the morphism that is defined by mapping* a_i *to* $(0, \ldots, 0, 1, 0, \ldots, 0)$*, where the* 1 *is in the i-th position,* $1 \le i \le n$*. Then*

$$\pi(w) = (|w|_{a_1}, |w|_{a_2}, \ldots, |w|_{a_n})$$

for all words $w \in \Sigma^*$*. The morphism* π *is called* Parikh mapping.

(a) *A subset* $M \subseteq \mathbb{N}^n$ *is called* linear, *if there are elements* $\alpha_0, \alpha_1, \ldots, \alpha_m \in \mathbb{N}^n$ $(m \ge 0)$ *such that* $M = \{\, \alpha_0 + i_1 \cdot \alpha_1 + i_2 \cdot \alpha_2 + \cdots + i_m \cdot \alpha_m \mid i_1, i_2, \ldots, i_m \in \mathbb{N} \,\}$.

(b) *A subset of* $\mathbb{N}^n$ *is called* semi-linear, *if it can be written as the union of finitely many linear subsets of* $\mathbb{N}^n$.

(c) *A language* $L \subseteq \Sigma^*$ *is* semi-linear, *if* $\pi(L)$ *is a semi-linear subset of* $\mathbb{N}^n$.

(d) *Two languages* $L_1 \subseteq \Sigma^*$ *und* $L_2 \subseteq \Sigma^*$ *are called* letter-equivalent, *if* $\pi(L_1) = \pi(L_2)$.

It is easily seen that each semi-linear language has the constant growth property. In [213], Rohit J. Parikh proved that a language is semi-linear if and only if it is letter-equivalent to a regular language and that each context-free language is semi-linear. In particular, this means that all context-free languages have the constant growth property.

As the copy language $L_{\text{copy}} = \{\, ww \mid w \in \{a,b\}^* \,\}$ is not growing context-sensitive, we see that the class GCSL of growing context-sensitive languages, which contains the Church-Rosser languages, does neither satisfy condition (2) nor condition (4) of Definition 1.5.3, that is, GCSL is not a family of mildly context-sensitive languages.

The first formalism defining a family of mildly context-sensitive languages are the *tree adjoining grammars* (TAG) that were introduced in [91]. When looking at syntax trees, a derivational step of a context-free grammar corresponds to replacing a leaf labeled with a nonterminal X by a tree that corresponds to the right-hand side of a production with left-hand side X. Now the TAGs generalize this process by allowing the replacement of inner (non-leaf) nodes by new trees.

A TAG consists of a finite set of *initial trees*, which are elementary syntax trees with root label S (the start symbol), and a finite set of *auxiliary trees*. Each auxiliary tree has exactly one leaf that has the same label as its root. Starting from an elementary tree T_0, a new tree can be obtained by adjoining an auxiliary tree T with root label X to a node n of T_0 with label X, that is, the subtree T/n of T_0, which is rooted at node n, is replaced with a copy of the tree T, and the subtree T/n is attached at the leaf of T with label X. To get a better control over this process of adjoining trees, the internal nodes of the initial and auxiliary trees can be marked as OA (*obligatory adjunction*, that is, an adjunction must be performed at this node) or NA (*null adjunction*, that is, no adjunction is allowed at this node). Furthermore, for each node that is not marked by NA, one can specify a subset of the auxiliary trees that can be adjoined at this node. Now this process is iterated until a tree is obtained that does not contain any nodes marked by OA and all leaves of which are labeled with terminal symbols or λ. The following example, which is taken from [104], illustrates this process.

Example 1.5.5 *The following TAG generates the language* $L_{\text{copy}} = \{\, ww \mid w \in \{a,b\}^* \,\}$:

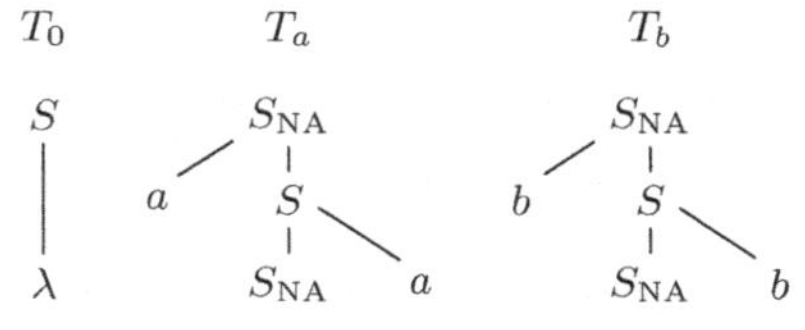

A syntax tree for the word abab is obtained as follows:

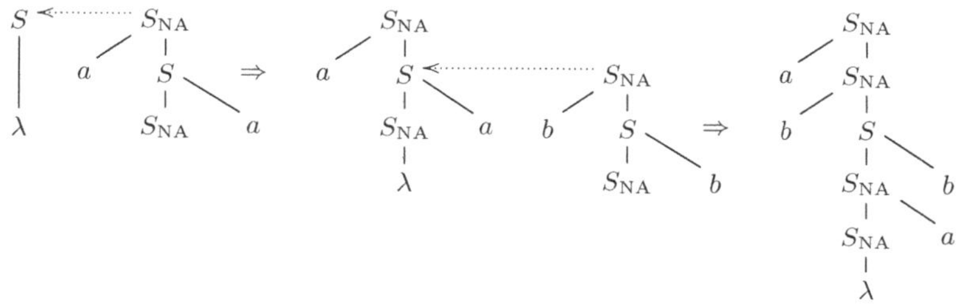

■

In [92], it is shown that the tree adjoining grammars are weakly equivalent to *head grammars*, *combinatory categorial grammars*, and *linear indexed grammars*, which means that all these formalisms generate the same class of languages.

The *linear context-free rewriting systems* of [261] and the *multiple context-free grammars* studied in [238] are two further formalisms that generate families of weakly context-sensitive languages. They are weakly equivalent, but they are more expressive than TAGs. Finally, *range concatenation grammars* are still more expressive. In fact, as shown in [12], they generate all languages that are parsable in polynomial time. This, however, means that not all the languages generated by range concatenation grammars satisfy the constant growth property. For a detailed study on parsing methods for these weakly context-sensitive formalisms, see [104].

Of course, further formalisms for describing mildly context-sensitive families of languages have been defined and investigated. Here we just mention the *buffer augmented pregroup grammars* of [50], the input-reversal pushdown automata with unlimited number of reversals of [20], and the two-head pushdown automata of [177].

1.6 Dependency Structures

Let $G = (N, \Sigma, S, P)$ be a context-free grammar. For each word $w \in \Sigma^*$ that belongs to the language $L(G)$ generated by G, the grammar G provides one or more derivations of the form

$$S \Rightarrow_G \alpha_1 \Rightarrow_G \alpha_2 \Rightarrow_G \cdots \Rightarrow_G \alpha_{n-1} \Rightarrow_G \alpha_n = w.$$

As seen in Section 1.2, this derivation can be depicted as a syntax tree T of the form

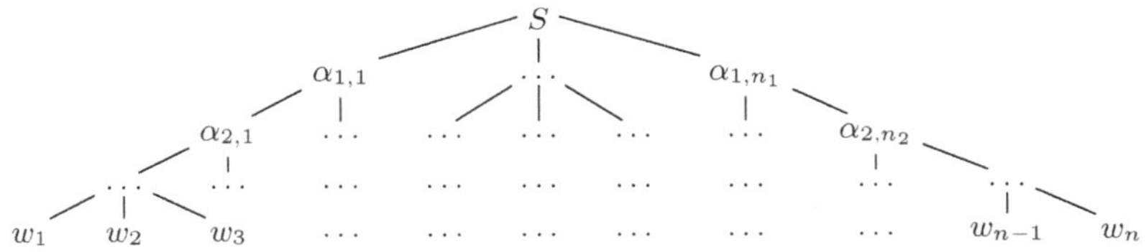

where $\alpha_i = \alpha_{i,1}\alpha_{i,2}\cdots\alpha_{i,n_i}$, $i = 1, 2, \ldots, n-1$, and $w = w_1 w_2 \cdots w_n$. The root of this syntax tree is labelled with the start symbol S, and its leaves, when read from left to right, are labelled with the letters of w. We use the notation $\mathrm{gr}(T) = w$ to express this fact.

Each nonterminal of G denotes a syntactic category. If $(A \to B_1 B_2)$ is a production of G, where A, B_1, B_2 are nonterminals, then this says that a phrase-structure γ of type B_1 followed by a phrase-structure δ of type B_2 yields the phrase-structure $\gamma\delta$ of type A. Furthermore, a production of the form $(A \to x)$, where $x \in \Sigma^*$, tells us that the word x is a phrase-structure of type A. Hence, the productions of the grammar G establish a relationship between the various types of phrase-structures, and, in addition to the (word) language $L(G)$ that consists of all words that can be generated by G, we can also consider the set $L_{\mathrm{Tree}}(G)$ of all syntax trees that can be obtained using the grammar G. Obviously, a word $w \in \Sigma^*$ belongs to the language $L(G)$ if and only if there exists a syntax tree $T \in L_{\mathrm{Tree}}(G)$ such that $\mathrm{gr}(T) = w$.

Let T be a syntax tree over G such that $\mathrm{gr}(T) = w = w_1 w_2 \cdots w_n \in \Sigma^n$, and let v be a node of T. The subtree of T that is rooted at node v is denoted by T/v. If this node is labelled with the nonterminal A, then the subtree T/v can be seen as a syntax tree (of category A) that describes a derivation of a subword $\mathrm{gr}(T/v) = u$ of w from the nonterminal A. This subword is a phrase-structure belonging to the category A. Obviously, the subword u is a continuous subword (that is, a factor) of w, that is, there are indices $1 \le i \le j \le n$ such that $u = w_i w_{i+1} \cdots w_j$. This shows that, for each node occuring in the syntax tree T, the terminal word that is derived in T from this node is a factor of w.

In the literature, other ways of representing the words of a (formal) language are also used. Here we are specifically interested in the so-called dependency trees.

Definition 1.6.1 ([41]) *A* dependency tree *is a finite directed tree $T = (V, E)$ the nodes of which are labelled with lexical units (terminals) and the directed edges of which are labelled with names of structural relations. For a dependency tree $T = (V, E)$, a node v_2 is said to* r-depend *on a node v_1, if $(v_1, v_2) \in E$ is an edge of T that is labelled by r. This is expressed as* $\mathrm{DEP}(v_1, v_2, r)$ *or as* $\mathrm{dep}(v_1, v_2)$*, when the name of the relation is of no concern. We use* DOM *to denote the* dominance relation*, which is the reflexive and transitive closure of the relation* dep*. Thus,* $\mathrm{DOM}(v_1, v_2)$ *holds if v_1 is an ancestor of v_2 (or v_2 is a descendant of v_1) in T.*

Example 1.6.2 (a) *A dependency tree T_1 on the word aaacbbb:*

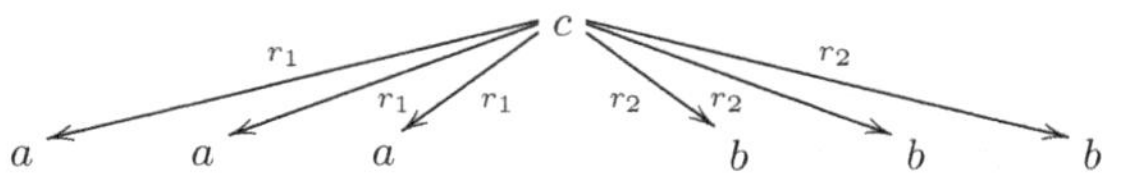

Here all vertices with label a r_1-depend on the vertex with label c, and all vertices with label b r_2-depend on the vertex with label c.

(b) *Another dependency tree T_2 on the word aaacbbb:*

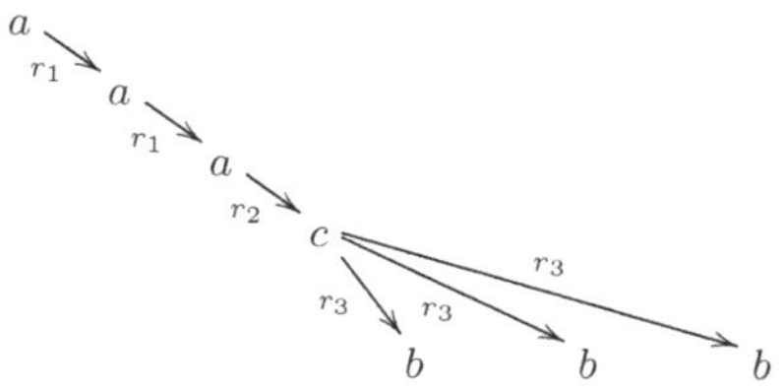

(c) *A dependence tree T_3 on the sentence* 'That man ate an apple.' *(from [269]), where the verb* ate *is the predicate of this sentence with two dependents, the nouns* man *and* apple, *which are the subject and the direct object of this verb. The nouns are preceded by the determiners* that *and* an*:*

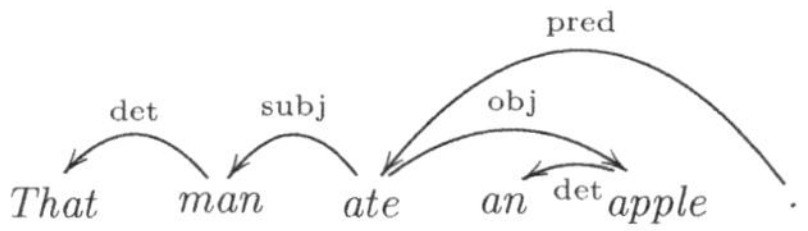

(d) *A dependency tree T_4 on the sentence* 'He called a friend of mine.'*, where the nodes are labelled by the letters a to g and the corresponding lexical units are written below the tree. In addition, the edge labels are omitted and the edges are oriented downwards:*

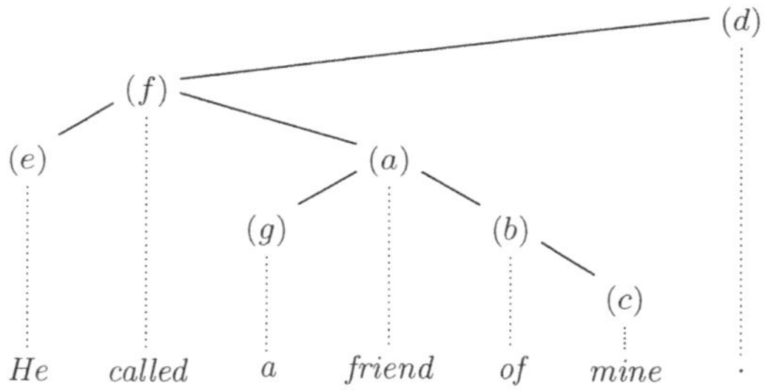

Here vertex e depends on vertex f, which in turn depends on vertex d.

(e) *A dependency tree T_5 on the phrase* 'les fleurs que j'ai offertes' *(from [41]):*

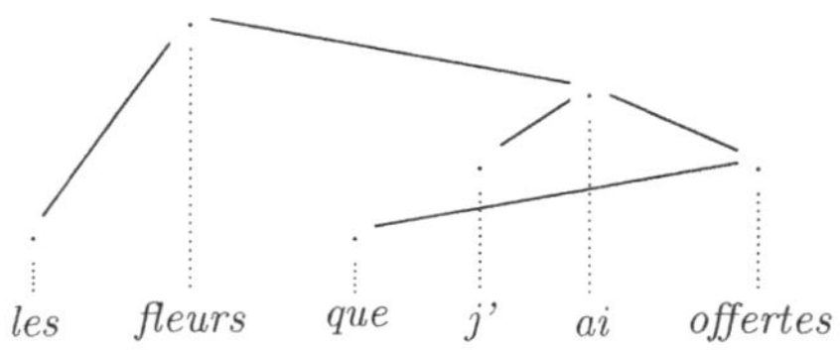

■

In addition to the dependency relations expressed by their edges, the trees in Example 1.6.2 also describe a linear order on their nodes, the *word order*, which is obtained by reading the lexical units from left to right. While syntax trees are inseparable from word order, dependency trees can be considered with or without word order.

Dependency trees are used to represent sentences of natural languages that are possibly augmented by morphological and/or semantical information together with dependency relations between their words. For example, in [115], Jürgen Kunze describes in detail how to construct dependency trees for German sentences. Actually, dependency trees can be generated by so-called dependency grammars.

Definition 1.6.3 ([47, 64]) *Let Σ be an alphabet of terminal symbols, and let X be an auxiliary alphabet of names or symbols for types of occurrences of terminal symbols, where $\Sigma \cap X = \emptyset$. Furthermore, let $\psi : \Sigma \to \mathcal{P}(X)$ be an* assignment function *that assigns a set of possible types to each terminal symbol.*

A dependency grammar *$D = (X, \Sigma, \psi, R)$ consists of two disjoint alphabets X and Σ, an assignment function ψ, and a finite set of rules of the following three types:*

(1) *A* dependency rule *is a statement about the valence of one kind of unit, written as*

$$X_i(X_{j_1}, X_{j_2}, \ldots, X_{j_{r-1}}, *, X_{j_{r+1}}, \ldots, X_{j_n}).$$

It consists of one auxiliary character as governing *element (here X_i) and a number of auxiliary characters as* dependent *elements (here X_{j_1} to X_{j_n}); all these elements are auxiliary symbols.*

This rule implicitly orders all elements in it by the order of the elements within the parentheses. The asterisk marks the position of the governor among its dependents. The valence of X_i given by this rule is just the given set of dependent elements, where the order is given by the relative order in the sequence X_{j_1} to X_{j_n}.

(2) *A* terminal rule *$X_i(*)$ states that a terminal corresponding to type X_i can occur without dependents.*

(3) *An* initial rule *$*(X_i)$ states that a unit of type X_i can occur without being governed. The corresponding unit X_i is called a* main *or* central *unit of the grammar D.*

The dependency trees generated by the dependency grammar D are obtained as follows. First, an initial rule $*(X_i)$ is chosen, which tells us that a dependency tree for a sentence of type X_i is to be generated. Next, a dependency rule $X_i(X_{j_1}, X_{j_2}, \ldots, X_{j_{r-1}}, *, X_{j_{r+1}}, \ldots, X_{j_n})$ with governing element X_i is chosen. This rule is applied to $*(X_i)$ by replacing X_i by the string $X_i(X_{j_1}, X_{j_2}, \ldots, X_{j_{r-1}}, *, X_{j_{r+1}}, \ldots, X_{j_n})$, which yields an expression of the form

$$*(X_i(X_{j_1}, X_{j_2}, \ldots, X_{j_{r-1}}, *, X_{j_{r+1}}, \ldots, X_{j_n})).$$

Then we choose a dependency rule $X_{j_1}(X_{h_1}, *, X_{h_2})$ with governing element X_{j_1} and replace the occurrence of X_{j_1} using that rule, obtaining

$$*(X_i(X_{j_1}(X_{h_1}, *, X_{h_2}), X_{j_2}, \ldots, X_{j_{r-1}}, *, X_{j_{r+1}}, \ldots, X_{j_n})).$$

This process continues using dependency and terminal rules until an expression is obtained in which each occurrence of an auxiliary symbol is immediately followed by a sequence in brackets that contains an asterisk, that is, an expression of the following form:

$$*(X_i(X_{j_1}(X_{h_1}(*), *, X_{h_2}(*)), X_{j_2}(*), \ldots, X_{j_{r-1}}(*), *, X_{j_{r+1}}(*), \ldots, X_{j_n}(*))).$$

At that stage each occurrence of an asterisk, but the outermost, is replaced with a terminal symbol a_r of the type X_r that corresponds to the governing element of the rule that was used to introduce that asterisk, that is, a terminal symbol a_r such that $X_r \in \psi(a_r)$.

Finally, from the resulting expression of the form

$$*(X_i(X_{j_1}(X_{h_1}(a_{h_1}), a_{j_1}, X_{h_2}(a_{h_2})), X_{j_2}(a_{j_2}), \ldots, X_{j_{r-1}}(a_{j_{r-1}}), a_i, X_{j_{r+1}}(a_{j_{r+1}}), \ldots, X_{j_n}(a_{j_n}))),$$

a dependency tree is constructed by analyzing this expression, drawing directed edges from each governing element to all its dependent elements.

The set of all dependency trees that can be derived from the dependency grammar D is denoted by $L_{\mathrm{DTree}}(D)$, and $L(D)$ denotes the set of all words $w \in \Sigma^*$ that are obtained by reading the labels of the nodes of the dependency trees from $L_{\mathrm{DTree}}(D)$ from left to right.

We illustrate this definition by providing some examples.

Example 1.6.4 *Let* $X = \{A, B, C\}$ *and* $\Sigma = \{a, b, c\}$, *let* $\psi(a) = \{A\}$, $\psi(b) = \{B\}$, $\psi(c) = \{C\}$, *and let* D_1 *be the dependency grammar that is given by the following rules:*

$$(1)\ *(A),\ (2)\ A(*, A, B),\ (3)\ A(*, C, B),\ (4)\ B(*),\ (5)\ C(*).$$

Using these rules, we can derive an expression as follows:

$$\begin{array}{lll} *(A) & \vdash & *(A(*, A, B))\ \text{(by rule (2))} \\ & \vdash & *(A(*, A(*, A, B), B))\ \text{(again by rule (2))} \\ & \vdash & *(A(*, A(*, A(*, C, B), B), B))\ \text{(by rule (3))} \\ & \vdash^* & *(A(*, A(*, A(*, C(*), B(*)), B(*)), B(*)))\ \text{(by rules (4) and (5)).} \end{array}$$

Replacing each occurrence of an asterisk (but the outermost) by a corresponding terminal element yields the expression $*(A(a, A(a, A(a, C(c), B(b)), B(b)), B(b)))$, *which is an encoding of the following dependency graph:*

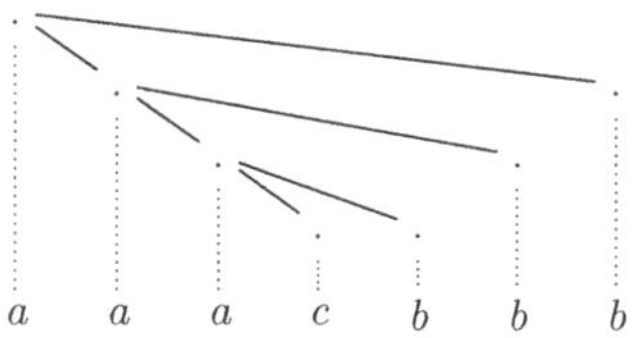

It is easily seen that the language of terminal words generated by the dependency grammar D_1 *is the context-free language* $L(D_1) = \{ a^n cb^n \mid n \geq 1 \}$. ∎

Example 1.6.5 *This example is taken from [64]. We want to analyze the sentence '*Children eat candy neatly*'. Accordingly, the terminal symbols contain the morphemes* child, -ren, eat, neat, *and* -ly, *the auxiliary alphabet contains the categories* V_α *of verb morphemes,* N *of nouns,* N_{pl} *of plural nouns,* D_β *of adverbs, and* L *and* S *of certain endings with the associating mapping* ψ *that maps* child *to* N_{pl}, -ren *to* S, eat *to* V_α, candy *to* N, neat *to* D_β, *and* -ly *to* L. *We assume that the dependency grammar* D_2 *contains the following rules:*

$$(1)\ *(V_\alpha),\ (2)\ V_\alpha(N_{pl}, *, N, D_\beta),\ (3)\ N_{pl}(*, S), (4)\ D_\beta(*, L),\ (5)\ S(*),\ (6)\ L(*),\ (7)\ N(*).$$

Then we can derive the following expression:

$$\begin{array}{lll} *(V_\alpha) & \vdash & *(V_\alpha(N_{pl}, *, N, D_\beta))\ \text{by rule (2)} \\ & \vdash & *(V_\alpha(N_{pl}(*, S), *, N, D_\beta))\ \text{by rule (3)} \\ & \vdash & *(V_\alpha(N_{pl}(*, S), *, N, D_\beta(*, L)))\ \text{by rule (4)} \\ & \vdash^* & *(V_\alpha(N_{pl}(*, S(*)), *, N(*), D_\beta(*, L(*))))\ \text{by rules (5) to (7).} \end{array}$$

Replacing the asterisks, we obtain the expression

$$*(V_\alpha(N_{pl}(\textit{child}, S(\textit{-ren})), \textit{eat}, N(\textit{candy}), D_\beta(\textit{neat}, L(\textit{-ly})))),$$

which yields the following dependency tree:

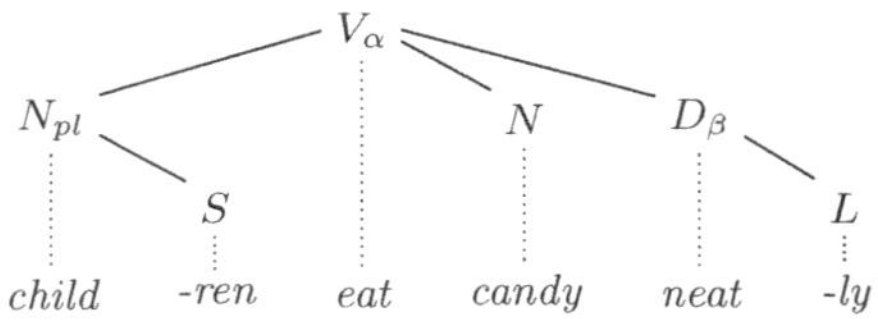

It follows that the sentence child-ren eat candy neat-ly *belongs to the language* $L(D_2)$. ∎

Definition 1.6.6 *Let* $T = (V, E)$ *be a dependency tree, let* $w = a_1a_2 \cdots a_n$ *be the corresponding word from* Σ^+ *that is obtained by reading the terminal node labels from left to right, and let* $1 \leq i \leq j \leq n$. *Then the* closed interval $[a_i, a_j]$ *is the factor* $a_ia_{i+1} \cdots a_j$. *A closed interval* $[a_i, a_j]$ *is called an* arrow interval *if* $\text{dep}(a_i, a_j)$ *or* $\text{dep}(a_j, a_i)$, *that is, one of the border elements governs the other one. The governing element is called the* head *of the arrow interval. Finally, an arrow interval* $[a_i, a_j]$ *is called* complete *if all its elements are dominated by its head.*

Example 1.6.2 (cont.)

(a) The interval $[a, b] = acbb$ is not an array interval, as a is not dependent on b nor is b dependent on a. However, $[a, c] = aac$ is an array interval that is complete, as both occurrences of a are dependent on c.

(c) The interval [*ate*, *apple*] = *ate an apple* is a complete array interval.

(d) [*called*, *of*] = *called a friend of* is also a complete array interval.

(e) [*que*, *offertes*] = *que j' ai offertes* is an array interval, as *que* depends on *offertes*, but it is not complete, as *j'* and *ai* are not dominated by *offertes*. ∎

Definition 1.6.7 *A dependency tree $T = (V, E)$ is called* projective *if all its arrow intervals are complete.*

It is easily seen that the dependency trees T_1 to T_4 in Example 1.6.2 (a) to (d) are projective, while the dependency tree T_5 in Example 1.6.2 (e) is not.

Let $T = (V, E)$ be a dependency tree. For a node $v \in V$, the subtree T/v of T with the node v as root is called the *maximal projection* of v, and $\mathrm{gr}(v)$ denotes the word that is obtained by reading the labels of the nodes of the subtree T/v from left to right. Using this notion, the projectivity of dependency trees can be characterized as follows (see [41]).

Theorem 1.6.8 *A dependency tree T is projective if and only if the maximal projections of all its nodes yield closed intervals.*

Observe that the maximal projection T_5/*offertes* of the dependency tree T_5 in Example 1.6.2 (e) just contains the single edge (*offertes*, *que*), while the interval [*que*, *offertes*] of T_5 also contains the vertices *j'* and *ai*. Hence, T_5 is not projective.

Let $D = (X, \Sigma, \psi, R)$ be a dependency grammar and let

$$\begin{array}{lll} *(X_i) & \vdash & *(X_i(X_{j_1}, X_{j_2}, \ldots, X_{j_{r-1}}, *, X_{j_{r+1}}, \ldots, X_{j_n})) \\ & \vdash & *(X_i(X_{j_1}(X_{h_1}, *, X_{h_2}), X_{j_2}, \ldots, X_{j_{r-1}}, *, X_{j_{r+1}}, \ldots, X_{j_n})) \\ & \vdash^* & *(X_i(X_{j_1}(X_{h_1}(*), *, X_{h_2}(*)), X_{j_2}(*), \ldots, X_{j_{r-1}}(*), *, X_{j_{r+1}}(*), \ldots, X_{j_n}(*))) \end{array}$$

be a derivation in D, from which we obtain the derivation tree

$$*(X_i(X_{j_1}(X_{h_1}(a_{h_1}), a_{j_1}, X_{h_2}(a_{h_2})), X_{j_2}(a_{j_2}), \ldots, X_{j_{r-1}}(a_{j_{r-1}}), a_i, X_{j_{r+1}}(a_{j_{r+1}}), \ldots, X_{j_n}(a_{j_n})))$$

by applying the assignment function ψ. It can easily be shown by induction on the length of this derivation that the maximal projections of all the nodes of this derivation tree yield closed intervals. This implies the following result.

Theorem 1.6.9 *For each dependency grammar D, all dependency trees in the set $L_{\mathrm{DTree}}(D)$ are projective.*

Actually, for each dependency grammar D, there is a natural number k such that the degree of the nodes of all dependency trees in the set $L_{\mathrm{DTree}}(D)$ is bounded from above by k. Furthermore, there is a close correspondence between dependency grammars and context-free (phrase-structure) grammars.

Definition 1.6.10 ([41]) *Let T be a syntax tree of a context-free grammar $G = (V, \Sigma, S, P)$ such that $\mathrm{gr}(T) = w \in \Sigma^*$, and let $T_D = (V, E)$ be a dependency tree on w. The syntax tree T is said to* conform *to the dependency tree T_D if the following two conditions are met:*

(1) *for each node v of T_D, there exists a node v' of T such that $\mathrm{gr}(v) = \mathrm{gr}(T/v')$, and*

(2) *for each node v' of T, $\mathrm{gr}(T/v')$ is the maximal projection of a node v of T_D.*

Example 1.6.11 *Let*

$$G = (\{A, B, C, D\}, \{a, b, c\}, A, \{A \to DAB, A \to DCB, B \to b, C \to c, D \to a\}),$$

let

$$A \Rightarrow DAB \Rightarrow DDABB \Rightarrow DDDCBBB \Rightarrow^7 aaacbbb$$

be a derivation, and let T be the corresponding syntax tree:

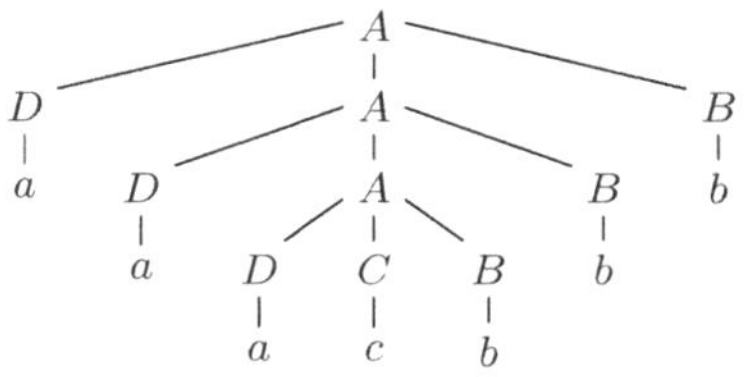

It is easily seen that this syntax tree conforms to the dependency tree generated by the dependency grammar in Example 1.6.4. ■

Let $D = (X, \Sigma, \psi, R)$ be a dependency grammar. From D, we construct a context-free grammar $G = (V, \Sigma, S, P)$ by taking $V = X \cup \{ X_{i,0} \mid X_i \in X \} \cup \{S\}$ and

$$\begin{aligned} P \;=\; & \{ S \to X_i \mid *(X_i) \in R \} \cup \\ & \{ X_i \to X_{j_1} \cdots X_{j_{r-1}} X_{i,0} X_{j_{r+1}} \cdots X_{j_n} \mid X_i(X_{j_1}, \ldots, X_{j_{r-1}}, *, X_{j_{r+1}}, \ldots, X_{j_n}) \in R \} \cup \\ & \{ X_i \to a \mid a \in \Sigma, X_i \in \psi(a), X_i(*) \in R \} \cup \\ & \{ X_{i,0} \to a \mid a \in \Sigma, X_i \in \psi(a) \}. \end{aligned}$$

Example 1.6.12 *Let $D_1 = (X, \Sigma, \psi, R)$ be the dependency grammar from Example 1.6.4, that is, $X = \{A, B, C\}$, $\Sigma = \{a, b, c\}$, $\psi(a) = \{A\}$, $\psi(b) = \{B\}$, $\psi(c) = \{C\}$, and R consists of the following rules:*

$$(1)\ *(A),\ (2)\ A(*, A, B),\ (3)\ A(*, C, B),\ (4)\ B(*),\ (5)\ C(*).$$

From the above construction, we obtain the context-free grammar $G = (V, \Sigma, S, P)$, where $V = \{S, A, B, C, A_0, B_0, C_0\}$ and P is defined as follows:

$$P = \{S \to A, A \to A_0AB, A \to A_0CB, B \to b, C \to c, A_0 \to a, B_0 \to b, C_0 \to c\}.$$

Actually, we can simplify this grammar by deleting the nonterminals S, B_0, and C_0 and the corresponding productions and by taking A as the start symbol. The resulting grammar is essentially the grammar from Example 1.6.11 with A_0 playing the role of the nonterminal D. ■

It can now be shown that, for each dependency grammar D, the above construction yields a context-free grammar G such that not only $L(D) = L(G)$, but in addition, for each dependency tree $T_D \in L_{\text{DTree}}(D)$, there exists a syntax tree $T \in L_{\text{Tree}}(G)$ that conforms to T_D, and conversely, for each syntax tree $T \in L_{\text{Tree}}(G)$, there exists a dependency tree $T_D \in L_{\text{DTree}}(D)$ such that T conforms to T_D. This means that each dependency grammar is *strongly equivalent* to some context-free grammar.

However, also a converse result holds. Let $G = (V, \Sigma, S, P)$ be a context-free grammar in quadratic Greibach normal form (see Definition 1.2.27). For each nonterminal $A \in V$, let

$$\Sigma_A = \{ b \in \Sigma \mid \exists \alpha \in V^* : (A \to b\alpha) \in P \},$$

that is, Σ_A is the set of terminal symbols that occur on the right-hand sides of A-productions. From G, we now construct a dependency grammar $D = (X, \Sigma, \psi, R)$ by taking

$$X = \{ A_b \mid A \in V \text{ and } b \in \Sigma_A \},$$

by defining $\psi : \Sigma \to \mathcal{P}(X)$ through $\psi(b) = \{ A_b \mid A \in V \text{ and } b \in \Sigma_A \}$, and by taking the following set of rules:

$$\begin{aligned} R \;=\; & \{ *(S_b) \mid b \in \Sigma_S \} \cup \\ & \{ A_b(*, B_c) \mid (A \to bB) \in P \text{ and } c \in \Sigma_B \} \cup \\ & \{ A_b(*, B_c, C_d) \mid (A \to bBC) \in P, c \in \Sigma_B, \text{ and } d \in \Sigma_C \} \cup \\ & \{ A_b(*) \mid A \in V \text{ and } b \in \Sigma_A \}. \end{aligned}$$

Example 1.6.13 *Let G be the context-free grammar $G = (\{S, A, B, C\}, \{a, b, c\}, S, P)$, where*

$$P = \{(S \to c), (S \to aAB), (S \to aCB), (A \to aAB), (A \to aCB), (B \to b), (C \to c)\},$$

which is in quadratic Greibach normal form generating the language $L(G) = \{ a^n cb^n \mid n \geq 0 \}$. Then $\Sigma_S = \{a, c\}$, $\Sigma_A = \{a\}$, $\Sigma_B = \{b\}$, and $\Sigma_C = \{c\}$. The above construction yields the dependency grammar $D = (X, \{a, b, c\}, \psi, R)$, where $X = \{S_a, S_c, A_a, B_b, C_c\}$, $\psi(a) = \{S_a, A_a\}$, $\psi(b) = \{B_b\}$, $\psi(c) = \{S_c, C_c\}$, and R contains the following rules:

$$\begin{array}{llllll} (1) & *(S_a), & (5) & A_a(*, A_a, B_b), & (9) & A_a(*), \\ (2) & *(S_c), & (6) & A_a(*, C_c, B_b), & (10) & B_b(*), \\ (3) & S_a(*, A_a, B_b), & (7) & S_a(*), & (11) & C_c(*). \\ (4) & S_a(*, C_c, B_b), & (8) & S_c(*), & & \end{array}$$

From G, we can derive the following syntax tree T:

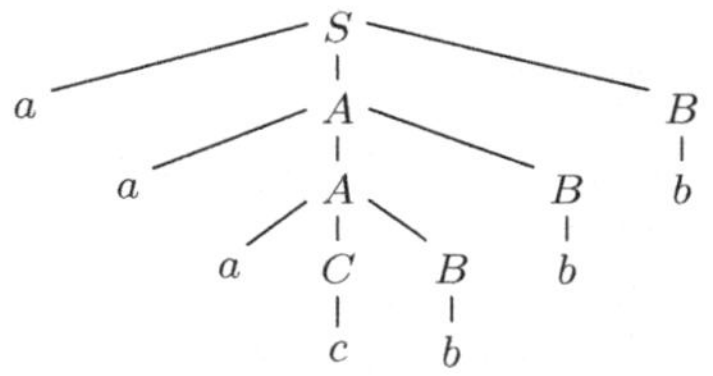

Using the dependency grammar D, we obtain the sequence

$$\begin{aligned} *(S_a) & \vdash *(S_a(*, A_a, B_b)) \\ & \vdash^2 *(S_a(*, A_a(*, A_a, B_b), B_b(*))) \\ & \vdash^2 *(S_a(*, A_a(*, A_a(*, C_c, B_b), B_b(*)), B_b(*))) \\ & \vdash^2 *(S_a(*, A_a(*, A_a(*, C_c(*), B_b(*)), B_b(*)), B_b(*))), \end{aligned}$$

from which we get the following dependency tree T_D:

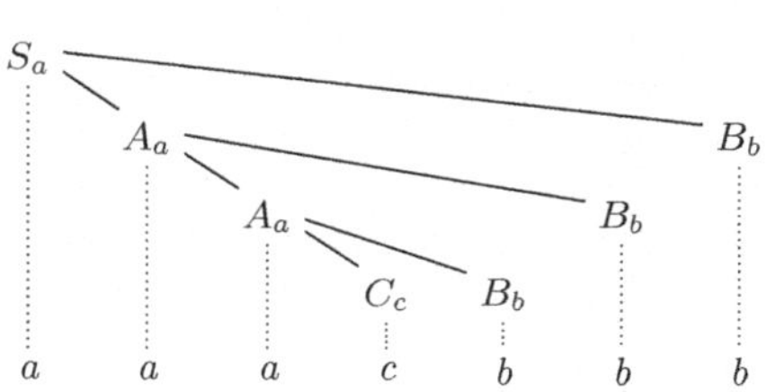

Obviously, the syntax tree T conforms to the dependency tree T_D. ■

Thus, for each context-free grammar G in (quadratic) Greibach normal form, there exists a dependency grammar D such that $L(D) = L(G)$, and, in addition, for each dependency tree $T_D \in L_{\text{DTree}}(D)$, there exists a syntax tree $T \in L_{\text{Tree}}(G)$ that conforms to T_D, and conversely, for each syntax tree $T \in L_{\text{Tree}}(G)$, there exists a dependency tree $T_D \in L_{\text{DTree}}(D)$ such that T conforms to T_D. This means that each context-free grammar in Greibach normal form is *strongly equivalent* to some dependency grammar. Thus, we have the following result.

Theorem 1.6.14 ([41]) *The dependency grammars are strongly equivalent to context-free grammars, that is, for each dependency grammar, there exists a context-free grammar that is strongly equivalent to it, and conversely, for each context-free grammar (in Greibach normal form), there exists a dependency grammar that is strongly equivalent to it.*

Essentially, syntax trees of context-free grammars correspond to projective dependency trees. In the literature, many other types of dependency grammars have also been studied (see, e.g., [41]). Here we just present the so-called dependency tree grammars.

Definition 1.6.15 *A* dependency tree grammar *(DTG) is given by a 5-tuple $G = \langle W, C, N, I, R\rangle$, where W is a set of word-forms (terminals), C is a set of categories (nonterminals), N is a set of dependency names, $I \in C$ is the main category (start symbol), and R is a set of composition rules of the form $A \to d$, where $A \in C$ and $d \in \Delta(W, C, N)$ is a dependency tree, that is, d is a dependency tree the nodes of which are labelled by word-forms from W and categories from C and the edges of which are labelled by dependency names from N.*

Let d_1, d_2 be two dependency trees from $\Delta(W, C, N)$. The tree d_2 is immediately derivable *from d_1, written as $d_1 \Rightarrow_G d_2$, if $\text{gr}(d_1) = u_1 A u_2$ for some $A \in C$, and there is a rule $A \to d$ in R such that $d_2 = d_1[A\backslash d]$, that is, d_2 is obtained from d_1 by replacing the leaf of d_1 that is labelled by the distinguished occurrence of the category A by the tree d. The class of dependency trees generated by G is then $L_{\text{DTree}}(G) = \{\, d \in \Delta(W, N) \mid I \Rightarrow_G^* d \,\}$.*

We illustrate this definition by presenting two simple examples.

Example 1.6.16 (a) *Let $G_1 = \langle\{a, b, c\}, \{A\}, \{l, r\}, A, R\rangle$, where R contains the rules $A \to c$ and $A \to$* 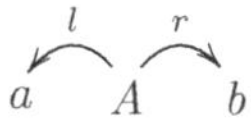

. In this DTG we get the following derivation:

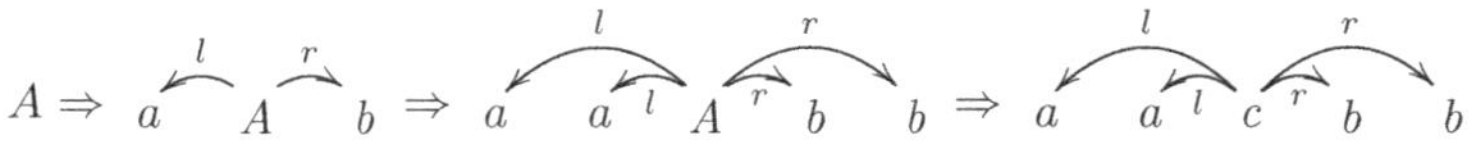

(b) *Let $G_2 = \langle\{a, b, c\}, \{A\}, \{l, r\}, A, R\rangle$, where R contains the rules $A \to a$ and $A \to$* 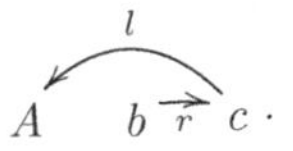

. In this DTG we get the following derivation:

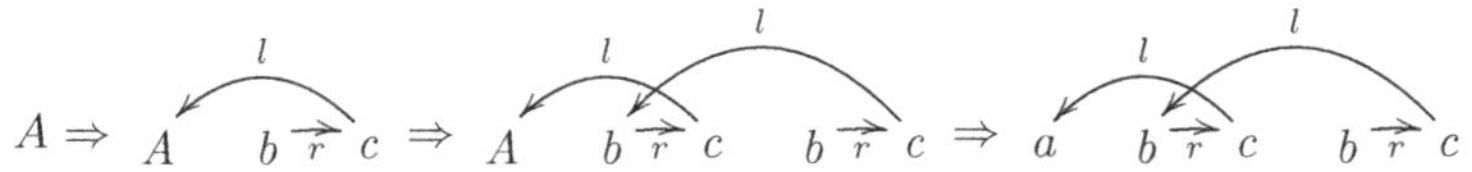

■

Observe that the dependency trees generated by the DTG G_1 are projective, but that there is no upper bound for the degree of their nodes, while $L_{\text{DTree}}(G_2)$ contains non-projective dependency trees. From Theorem 1.6.9, we see thus that dependency tree grammars are more expressive than the dependency grammars from Definition 1.6.3. For more information on the various types of dependency grammars and their relationship to each other see, e.g., the survey by Alexander Dikovsky and Larissa Modina [41]. Let us note that for modeling the syntax of European natural languages, one actually needs to work with dependency trees that have no bound for the degree of their nodes, and one also needs to work with non-projective dependency trees.

1.7 Free Word Order Languages

In a programming language like PASCAL, the order of the words (that is, symbols) in a valid sentence (that is, a syntactically correct program) is fixed by the rules of the underlying (context-free) grammar. Also in some natural languages like English, the word order of sentences is essentially fixed by the syntactic structure. Accordingly, large parts of such languages can be described adequately through phrase-structure grammars. On the other hand, for the description of the syntactic structure of a language like Latin, Dutch, Italian, German, Czech or Russian that has a high degree of word order freedom, it appears that approaches based on dependency are better suited. However, is there a way to formally define the notion of word order freedom and measure its degree for a given language? The following definitions and discussion follow [189].

Definition 1.7.1 *Let $T = (V, E)$ be a dependency tree for a word $w = a_1a_2\cdots a_n$, let v be a vertex of T, and let T/v be the subtree of T with root v. Then* $\mathrm{gr}(v) = a_{i_1}a_{i_2}\cdots a_{i_m}$ *for some indices satisfying $1 \leq i_1 \leq i_2 \leq \cdots \leq i_m \leq n$. For $j \in \{1, 2, \ldots, m-1\}$, if $i_{j+1} - i_j > 1$, then we say that the pair (i_j, i_{j+1}) creates a* hole *in* $\mathrm{gr}(v)$.

Example 1.7.2 *We consider the Czech sentence*

Bohatou rodiče našli synovi nevěstu.
[Rich$_{acc}$ parents$_{nom}$ *found* son$_{dat}$ bride$_{acc}$.]
[*Rich is the bride which the parents found for their son.*]

and the following dependency tree T_1 for it:

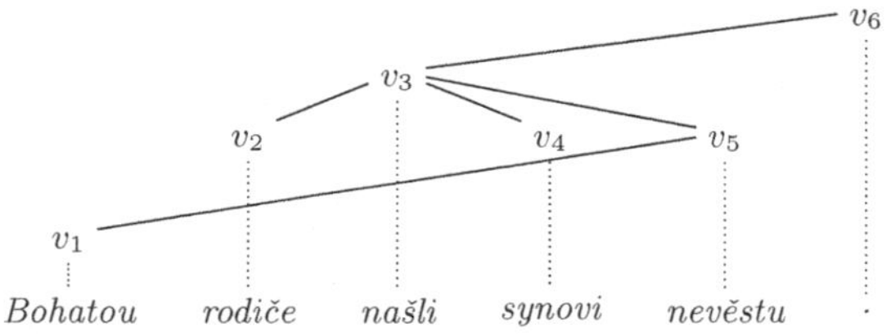

Obviously, $\mathrm{gr}(v_5) =$ Bohatou nevěstu *contains a hole.* ■

We see from Theorem 1.6.8 that a dependency tree $T = (V, E)$ is projective if and only if, for none of its vertices $v \in V$, $\mathrm{gr}(v)$ contains a hole.

Definition 1.7.3 *Let $T = (V, E)$ be a dependency tree for a word $w = a_1a_2\cdots a_n$, and let v be a vertex of T. The* number of holes *in* $\mathrm{gr}(v)$, *that is, the number of holes in the subtree T/v, is denoted by* $\mathrm{dNh}(v, T)$, *and* $\mathrm{dNh}(T) = \max\{\, \mathrm{dNh}(v, T) \mid v \in V \,\}$.

It is easily seen that $\mathrm{dNh}(T_1) = 1$ for the dependency tree T_1 from Example 1.7.2.

Example 1.7.4 *We consider the Czech sentence*

Co se Petr komu rozhodl koupit k Vánocům ?
[*What - Petr to whom decided to buy for Christmas ?*]
[*What did Peter decide to buy to whom for Christmas?*]

and the following dependency tree T_2 for it:

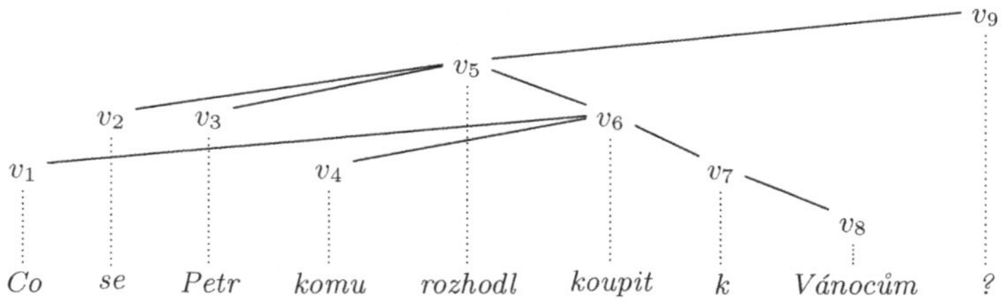

Then $\mathrm{gr}(v_6) =$ Co komu koupit k Vánocům *contains two holes, and* $\mathrm{dNh}(T_2) = 2$. ■

The number $\mathrm{dNh}(T)$ is a complexity measure for dependency trees. This measure can be generalized to (terminal) words as follows.

Definition 1.7.5 *Let Σ be a finite alphabet, and let T_D be a set of dependency trees for words over Σ. A function $D : \Sigma^* \to \mathcal{P}(T_D)$ that assigns a set of dependency trees to words over Σ such that, for each $w \in \Sigma^*$ and each $T \in D(w)$, T is a dependency tree for the word w (that is, $\mathrm{gr}(T) = w$), is called a* dependency analysis *over Σ.*

Let $L \subseteq \Sigma^*$ be a language. A dependency analysis $D : \Sigma^* \to \mathcal{P}(T_D)$ is called a dependency analysis of the language *L if $L = \{ w \in \Sigma^* \mid D(w) \neq \emptyset \}$, that is, the language L consists of those words for which the dependency analysis D yields dependency trees.*

Based on this notion, we can define a measure for the non-projectivity of a language.

Definition 1.7.6 *Let L be a language over Σ, let $w \in L$, and let D be a dependency analysis of L. Then $\mathrm{dNh}(w, D) = \max_{T \in D(w)} \mathrm{dNh}(T)$ is the* magnitude of non-projectivity *of the sentence w with respect to the dependency analysis D.*

The measure $\mathrm{dNh}(L, D) = \sup_{w \in L} \mathrm{dNh}(w, D)$ is called the magnitude of non-projectivity *of the language L with respect to the dependency analysis D.*

The magnitude of non-projectivity is a measure of the word order complexity of dependency-based languages. In fact, the word order complexity of these languages has two sources: the word order freedom and word order constraints. The magnitude of non-projectivity can also be seen as a measure for the word order freedom of a dependency-based language, for example, it is connected with the notion of Free-Order Dependency Grammars (FODG's) (see, e.g., [219]). Based on examples, Karel Oliva and Martin Plátek argue in [189] that, in Czech, the number of holes in a dependency (sub)tree might not have an upper bound. This indicates that Czech has indeed a word order of a high degree.

1.8 Analysis by Reduction

Following Noam Chomsky's work, the syntactic structure of sentences in English (or any other language with a fixed word order) is usually described by phrase structure grammars (see Section 1.2). In such a description, the words of a given sentence are grouped into phrases, which are then repeatedly grouped into smaller constituent phrases until the ultimate constituents are finally reached. In this way, information on the structure of the sentence is provided in terms of these constituents. Observe that, in such a description, each phrase corresponds to a continuous subsequence of the given sentence.

On the other hand, the syntactic structure of sentences in Czech (or Latin, German, or any other language with a rather free word order) is more often described through dependencies. By performing a step-by-step simplification of a given sentence, called *analysis by reduction*, dependencies and independencies between the various words of the sentence can be determined and a dependency tree (see Section 1.6) can be constructed for the sentence considered. Here we describe the analysis by reduction in some detail following [144], [145], and [87].

An analysis by reduction of a given sentence consists of a sequence of step-by-step simplifications of that sentence. Each simplification during an analysis by reduction is realized by a single *reduction operation*, which consists of either

(i) the deletion of one or several words from the given sentence or

(ii) the replacement of a (possibly discontinuous) substring of the given sentence with a shorter substring.

Each application of such a reduction operation must preserve the syntactical correctness of the sentence, that is, the new sentence obtained by applying a reduction operation must be syntactically correct if and only if the sentence to which the reduction operation is applied is syntactically correct.

Example 1.8.1 *We consider the following sentence in English:*

(S1) They mean that the means she means are very mean.

By applying local transformations, this sentence can be simplified in three different ways while preserving the syntactical correctness: either we delete the word that *from the sentence, which yields the new sentence*

(S2) They mean the means she means are very mean.

or we delete the words she means *from the sentence, which yields the new sentence*

(S3) They mean that the means are very mean.

or we delete the word very *from the sentence, which yields the new sentence*

(S4) They mean that the means she means are mean.

By applying one of the latter two transformations to the sentence (S2)*, we obtain the sentences*

(S5) They mean the means are very mean.

and

(S6) They mean the means she means are mean.

In addition, we can delete the words They mean *from the sentence* (S2)*, which yields the sentence*

(S7) The means she means are very mean.

From the sentence (S3)*, we obtain the sentences*

(S5) They mean the means are very mean.

and

(S8) They mean that the means are mean.

Finally, from the sentence (S4)*, we can derive the sentences*

(S6) They mean the means she means are mean.

and

(S8) They mean that the means are mean.

From each of the sentences (S5), (S6), *and* (S8) *we obtain the sentence*

(S9) They mean the means are mean.

from which we finally get the syntactically correct simple sentence

(S10) The means are mean.

Also from the sentence (S7) *we can derive the sentences*

(S11) The means she means are mean.

and

(S12) The means are very mean.

which both lead to the sentence (S10)*. Finally, we can delete the words* They mean *from the sentence* (S6)*, which again leads to the sentence* (S11)*. These reductions can be illustrated by the following* reduction scheme*, in which each arrow is indexed by the word(s) that is (are) deleted by the corresponding transformation:*

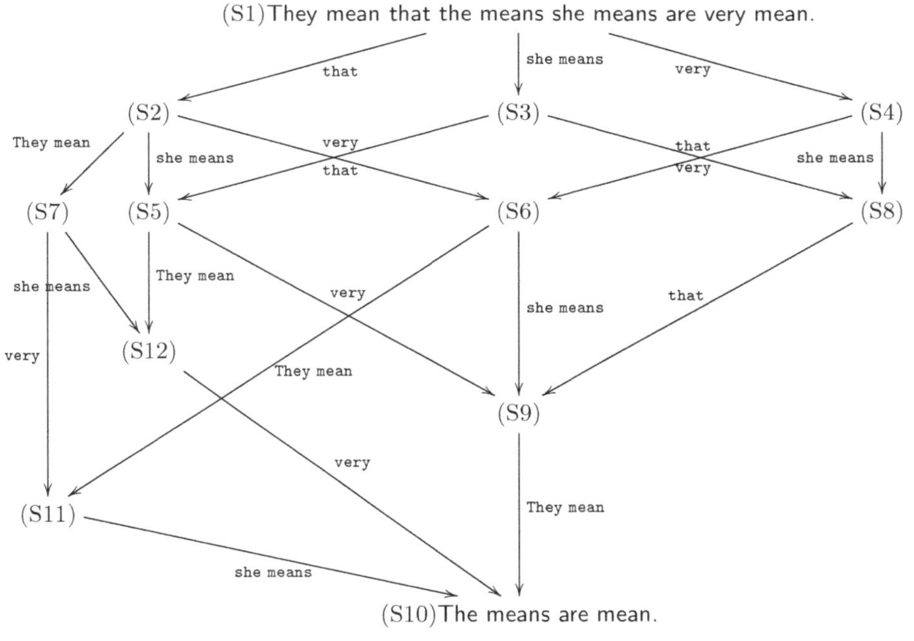

■

From such a reduction scheme, one can derive a dependency tree for the corresponding sentence, where

1. a word u *depends on* a word v, if along each path in the reduction scheme, the word u is deleted *before* the word v, and

2. two words u and v are *mutually independent* if there are paths in the reduction scheme such that along one of them, u is removed before v, while along the other one, v is removed before u.

From the analysis of the sentence (S1) in Example 1.8.1, we obtain the following dependencies and independencies between the words of this sentence.

Example 1.8.1 (cont.) *In the above reduction scheme for the sentence* (S1), *we see that the word* that *is always deleted before the phrase* They mean, *that is, the word* that *depends on the latter phrase, and the phrase* she means *depends on the phrase* the means. *On the other hand, the phrase* she means *and the word* very *are mutually independent, since on the path* $(S1) \to (S3) \to (S8)$, *the phrase* she means *is removed before the word* very, *while on the path* $(S1) \to (S4) \to (S8)$, *the word* very *is removed before the phrase* she means. *The resulting* dependency tree *looks as follows:*

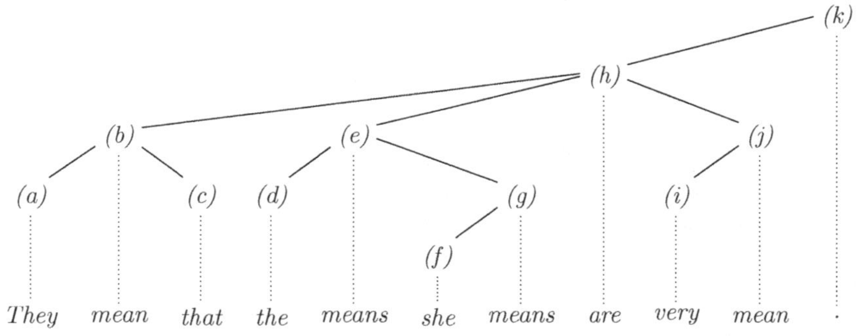

■

In the example above, all reduction operations applied during the analysis by reduction presented are deletions. In the next example from [87], some reduction operations are also used that replace substrings.

Example 1.8.2 *Here we consider the following sentence in English:*

(T1) Peter and Jane work very slowly.

Here the substring Peter and Jane work *can be replaced with the shorter substring* Jane works, *which yields the sentence*

(T2) Jane works very slowly.

Another possible reduction step consists in replacing the substring Peter and Jane work *by the substring* Peter works, *resulting in the sentence*

(T3) Peter works very slowly.

Obviously, we can delete the word very *from each of these sentences, which yields the sentence*

(T4) Peter and Jane work slowly.

from (T1),

(T5) Jane works slowly.

from (T2), *and*

(T6) Peter works slowly.

from (T3). *Finally, the word* slowly *can be removed from these sentences. In fact, we obtain the following reduction scheme for the sentence* (T1):

Word	Tags
They	⟨Pronoun⟩ ⟨Plural⟩
mean	⟨Verb⟩ ⟨Present Tense⟩ ⟨Plural⟩
that	⟨Conjunction⟩
the	⟨Article⟩
means	⟨Noun⟩ ⟨Plural⟩
she	⟨Pronoun⟩ ⟨Singular⟩
means	⟨Verb⟩ ⟨Present Tense⟩ ⟨Singular⟩
are	⟨Verb⟩ ⟨Present Tense⟩ ⟨Plural⟩
very	⟨Adverb⟩
mean	⟨Adjective⟩
.	⟨End of Sentence⟩

Table 1.1: Tagging the sentence of Example 1.8.1

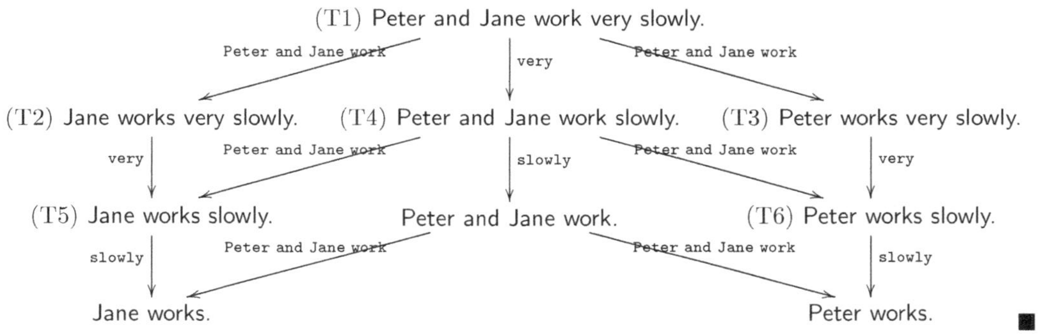

■

Finally, if the given sentence is not syntactically correct, then the step-by-step simplification of the analysis by reduction of this sentence continues until the core of an error is detected. This is shown in the following example, which is also taken from [87].

Example 1.8.3 *Here we consider the following syntactically incorrect sentence in English:*

(E1) Martin, Peter, and Jane works slowly.

Here the word Martin *can be deleted, which yields the sentence*

(E2) Peter and Jane works slowly.

From this sentence we can delete the word slowly, *thus obtaining the sentence*

(E3) Peter and Jane works.

The sentence (E3) *cannot be reduced any further. It constitutes the core of an error.* ■

In order to be able to perform the simplifications of an analysis by reduction of a given sentence of a natural language as shown above, one must be able to understand the meaning of that sentence. This prerequisite, which is easily fulfilled by a native speaker of the corresponding language, can in general not be satisfied by an automated system for language analysis or translation. In fact, for such a system, the syntactic analysis of a given sentence, as realized by the analysis by reduction, constitutes the first part of its sentence analysis. Therefore, such a system requires additional morphological, syntactical, and semantical information on the words of the given sentence (see, e.g., [145]). Such information can be provided by tagging the words of the sentence, that is, a finite sequence of *tags* that encode morphological, syntactical, or semantical information is added to each word.

Example 1.8.1 (cont.) *We first recall the sentence* (S1)*:*

They mean that the means the means are very mean.

To the words of this sentence, we may add tags providing syntactical information, as shown in Table 1.1. Now the corresponding input for the analysis by reduction consists of the words of the sentence (S1) *together with the added tags:*

They ⟨*Pronoun*⟩ ⟨*Plural*⟩ mean ⟨*Verb*⟩ ⟨*Present Tense*⟩ ⟨*Plural*⟩ that ⟨*Conjunction*⟩ the ⟨*Article*⟩ means ⟨*Noun*⟩ ⟨*Plural*⟩ she ⟨*Pronoun*⟩ ⟨*Singular*⟩ means ⟨*Verb*⟩ ⟨*Present Tense*⟩ ⟨*Singular*⟩ are ⟨*Verb*⟩ ⟨*Present Tense*⟩ ⟨*Plural*⟩ very ⟨*Adverb*⟩ mean ⟨*Adjective*⟩ . ⟨*End of Sentence*⟩

During the analysis by reduction, each word is processed together with its tags. ■

In summary, for the analysis by reduction, we consider an extended input sentence, which is a finite sequence of words from a natural language that are annotated by tags. This sentence is then simplified step-by-step by executing local transformations that preserve the syntactical correctness of the sentence. This process continues until either a correct simple sentence is obtained or until the core of an error is detected. In the former case, the input sentence is accepted as being syntactically correct, while in the latter case, it is rejected as being syntactically incorrect. For performing these local transformations, the following basic operations are used:

- the current sentence is scanned from left to right (or from right to left),
- a small part of the current sentence is simplified by deleting or replacing some words,
- and finally, a restart is executed so that the process can continue with the new sentence obtained by the above simplification.

1.9 Restarting Automata: The General Model

Motivated by the analysis by reduction, *Petr Jančar*, *František Mráz*, *Martin Plátek*, and *Jörg Vogel* presented the first type of the *restarting automaton* at the international conference FCT 1995 in Dresden [85]. An automaton of this type scans a given input sentence from left to right, it executes a single delete operation, and then it restarts to continue its computation on the now shortened sentence. Later, this model was extended several times by admitting non-input letters in the working alphabet of the automaton and by introducing more general types of rewrite steps (see, e.g., the survey papers [192] and [193]). Here, however, instead of following the historical development, we first present a general version of the restarting automaton, from which we then obtain the various types that have been studied in the literature by restricting some of its parameters.

In order to design a model of an automaton that imitates the analysis by reduction, the following ingredients are needed:

- The input sentence, which is a sequence of word forms, must be represented in some way. Following the usage in classical automata theory, we take a (finite) *input alphabet* Σ, where each letter of Σ represents a word form. Then an input sentence is represented by a finite sequence of letters over Σ, that is, by a word $w \in \Sigma^*$.

- To encode additional information (tags), we use *auxiliary letters*, that is, we take a (finite) *working alphabet* Γ that extends the input alphabet Σ.

- To mark the beginning and the end of the current sentence, we take special symbols $\rhd$ and $\lhd$, called *sentinels*.

- As the sentence to be analyzed will be changed by local transformations that may extend or shorten the sentence, the current word must be stored in a dynamic data structure that supports such changes. For example, a *doubly linked list of cells* or a *flexible tape* can be used, where each cell of the list or the tape stores a single letter of the current sentence (word).

- As a local transformation may affect several letters of the current word, we take a *read/write window* of a fixed finite size for scanning the list or tape.

- To process the information that is obtained by scanning the current word, we employ a *finite-state control*.

- Finally, for executing the analysis, we must provide a *program* that determines the sequence of elementary operations. This program will be provided in the form of a *transition function*.

Based on these considerations, the *hardware* of the restarting automaton can be depicted as illustrated in the diagram in Figure 1.11, where lower-case letters represent input letters, upper-case letters represent auxiliary letters, and q denotes a state. Formally, the general model of the restarting automaton is defined as follows.

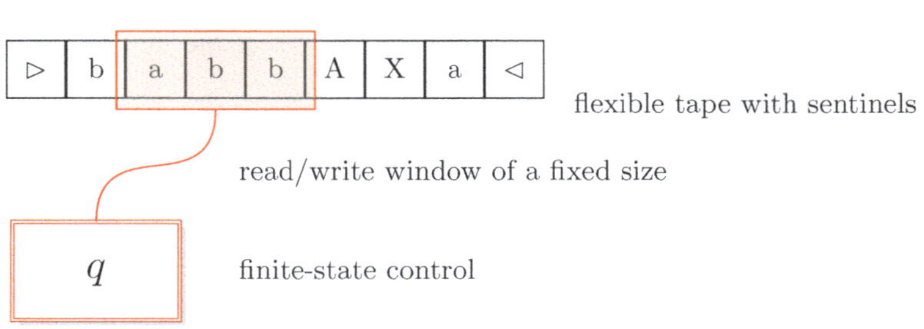

Figure 1.11: The hardware of the restarting automaton

Definition 1.9.1 *A* restarting automaton *is defined by an 8-tuple* $M = (Q, \Sigma, \Gamma, \triangleright, \triangleleft, q_0, k, \delta)$, *where*

- Q *is a finite set of states,*
- Σ *is a finite input alphabet,*
- Γ *is a finite working alphabet such that* $\Sigma \subseteq \Gamma$, *where the letters in* $\Gamma \setminus \Sigma$ *are called* auxiliary letters,
- $\triangleright, \triangleleft \notin \Gamma$ *are the markers for the left and right ends of the tape, called* sentinels,
- $q_0 \in Q$ *is the* restart state, *which also serves as* initial state,
- $k \geq 1$ *is the size of the read/write window, and*
- $\delta : Q \times \mathcal{PC}^{(k)} \to \mathcal{P}((Q \times (\{\text{MVR}, \text{MVL}\} \cup \Gamma^*)) \cup \{\text{Restart}, \text{Accept}, \text{Reject}\})$ *is the transition relation.*

Here $\mathcal{PC}^{(k)}$ *is the set of* possible contents *of the read/write window of* M, *where*

$$\begin{array}{lcl} \mathcal{PC}^{(0)} & = & \emptyset, \quad \mathcal{PC}^{(1)} \;=\; \Gamma \cup \{\triangleright, \triangleleft\}, \text{ and} \\ \mathcal{PC}^{(n)} & = & (\triangleright \cdot \Gamma^{n-1}) \cup \Gamma^n \cup (\Gamma^{\leq n-1} \cdot \triangleleft) \cup (\triangleright \cdot \Gamma^{\leq n-2} \cdot \triangleleft) \text{ for all } n \geq 2. \end{array}$$

The transition relation δ *may contain up to six different types of transition steps that are defined as follows:*

(1) *A* move-right step *(MVR) has the form* $(q', \mathsf{MVR}) \in \delta(q, u)$, *where* $q, q' \in Q$ *and* $u \in \mathcal{PC}^{(k)}$ *such that* $u \neq \triangleleft$. *If* M *is in state* q *and sees the word* u *in its read/write window, then this move-right step causes* M *to shift the read/write window one position to the right and to enter state* q'. *However, if the contents of the read/write window is only the right sentinel* $\triangleleft$, *then no shift to the right is possible.*

(2) *A* move-left step *(MVL) is of the form* $(q', \mathsf{MVL}) \in \delta(q, u)$, *where* $q, q' \in Q$ *and* $u \in \mathcal{PC}^{(k)}$ *such that* $u \notin \triangleright \cdot \Gamma^*$. *It causes* M *to shift the read/write window one position to the left and to enter state* q'. *This, however, is only possible if the window is not already at the left end of the tape.*

(3) *A* rewrite step *is of the form* $(q', v) \in \delta(q, u)$, *where* $q, q' \in Q$, $u \in \mathcal{PC}^{(k)}$, $\triangleright \neq u \neq \triangleleft$, *and* $v \in \mathcal{PC}^{(n)}$ *for some* $n \geq 0$. *It causes* M *to replace the contents* u *of the read/write window with the word* v *and to enter state* q'. *In addition, the read/write window is placed immediately to the right of the word* v *written. However, some additional restrictions apply in that the sentinels* $\triangleright$ *and* $\triangleleft$ *must not disappear from the tape nor that new occurrences of these sentinels are created. Furthermore, the read/write window must not move across the right sentinel* $\triangleleft$, *that is, if the word* u *ends in* $\triangleleft$, *then so does the word* v, *and after performing the rewrite operation, the read/write window is placed on the right sentinel* $\triangleleft$.

(4) *A* restart step *is of the form* $\mathsf{Restart} \in \delta(q, u)$, *where* $q \in Q$ *and* $u \in \mathcal{PC}^{(k)}$. *It causes* M *to move its read/write window to the left end of the tape, so that the first letter it contains is the left sentinel* $\triangleright$, *and to re-enter the restart state* q_0.

(5) *An* accept step *is of the form* $\mathsf{Accept} \in \delta(q, u)$, *where* $q \in Q$ *and* $u \in \mathcal{PC}^{(k)}$. *It causes* M *to halt and accept.*

(6) *A* reject step *is of the form* $\mathsf{Reject} \in \delta(q, u)$, *where* $q \in Q$ *and* $u \in \mathcal{PC}^{(k)}$. *It causes* M *to halt and reject.*

In general, the automaton M *is* nondeterministic, *that is, there can be two or more instructions in the set* $\delta(q, u)$ *for some state* $q \in Q$ *and some window contents* $u \in \mathcal{PC}^{(k)}$. *If this is not the case, then the automaton is* deterministic. *We use the prefix det- to denote deterministic types of restarting automata.*

In order to illustrate this definition and the following ones, we provide a simple example.

Example 1.9.2 *Let* $M_1 = (Q, \Sigma, \Gamma, \triangleright, \triangleleft, q_0, 3, \delta)$ *be the restarting automaton that is defined by taking* $Q = \{q_0, q_c, q_d, q_r\}$, $\Sigma = \Gamma = \{a, b, c, d\}$, *and* δ *as given by the following table:*

(1)	$\delta(q_0, x)$	$=$	$\{(q_0, \mathsf{MVR})\}$	*for all* $x \in \{\triangleright aa, \triangleright ab, aaa, aab\}$,
(2)	$\delta(q_0, \triangleright x \triangleleft)$	$=$	$\{\mathsf{Accept}\}$	*for all* $x \in \{c, d\}$,
(3)	$\delta(q_0, abb)$	$=$	$\{(q_c, b), (q_d, \lambda)\}$,	
(4)	$\delta(q_0, abc)$	$=$	$\{(q_r, c)\}$,	
(5)	$\delta(q_c, bbb)$	$=$	$\{(q_c, \mathsf{MVR})\}$,	
(6)	$\delta(q_d, bbb)$	$=$	$\{(q_d, \mathsf{MVR})\}$,	
(7)	$\delta(q_c, bbc)$	$=$	$\{(q_c, \mathsf{MVR})\}$,	
(8)	$\delta(q_d, bbd)$	$=$	$\{(q_d, \mathsf{MVR})\}$,	
(9)	$\delta(q_c, x\triangleleft)$	$=$	$\{\mathsf{Restart}\}$	*for all* $x \in \{bc, c\}$,
(10)	$\delta(q_d, x\triangleleft)$	$=$	$\{\mathsf{Restart}\}$	*for all* $x \in \{bd, d\}$,
(11)	$\delta(q_r, \triangleleft)$	$=$	$\{\mathsf{Restart}\}$,	
(12)	$\delta(q, x)$	$=$	$\{\mathsf{Reject}\}$	*for all other pairs* $(q, x) \in Q \times \mathcal{PC}^{(3)}$. ■

Observe that the restarting automaton M_1 has no auxiliary letters and that it is not deterministic, as $\delta(q_0, abb)$ contains the two rewrite transitions (q_c, b), which deletes the prefix ab of the window contents abb, and (q_d, λ), which deletes the complete window contents abb.

To describe the overall situation of a restarting automaton, we now introduce the notion of a configuration.

Definition 1.9.3 *A* configuration *of a restarting automaton* $M = (Q, \Sigma, \Gamma, \triangleright, \triangleleft, q_0, k, \delta)$ *is a word* $\alpha q \beta$, *where* $q \in Q$, *and either* $\alpha = \lambda$ *and* $\beta \in \{\triangleright\} \cdot \Gamma^* \cdot \{\triangleleft\}$ *or* $\alpha \in \{\triangleright\} \cdot \Gamma^*$ *and* $\beta \in \Gamma^* \cdot \{\triangleleft\}$. *Here* $q \in Q$ *represents the current state,* $\alpha\beta$ *is the current contents of the tape, and it is understood that the read/write window contains the first* k *letters of* β *(or all of* β *if* $|\beta| \leq k$*).*

A restart configuration *of* M *is of the form* $q_0 \triangleright w \triangleleft$, *where* $w \in \Gamma^*$; *if* $w \in \Sigma^*$, *then* $q_0 \triangleright w \triangleleft$ *is also called an* initial configuration *of* M.

Finally, we use Accept *to denote the* accept configurations *of* M, *which are those configurations that* M *reaches by executing an accept step, and* Reject *to denote the* reject configurations *of* M, *which are those configurations that* M *reaches by executing a reject step. Also a configuration of the form* $\alpha q \beta$ *such that* $\delta(q, \beta_1) = \emptyset$, *where* β_1 *is the current contents of the read/write window, is a* reject configuration. *A* halting configuration *of* M *is either an accept or a reject configuration.*

The transition relation δ *induces a* computation relation $\vdash_M^*$ *on the set of configurations of* M, *which is the reflexive and transitive closure of the* single-step computation relation $\vdash_M$. *Here* $C_1 \vdash_M C_2$ *holds for two configurations* C_1 *and* C_2 *of* M *if* C_2 *can be obtained from* C_1 *by an application of a single transition.*

A word $x \in \Gamma^*$ *is* accepted *by* M, *if there exists a computation of* M *which starts with the restart configuration* $q_0 \triangleright x \triangleleft$ *and which finally reaches an accept configuration. The* characteristic *(or* basic*) language accepted by* M *is defined by*

$$L_C(M) = \{\, x \in \Gamma^* \mid q_0 \triangleright x \triangleleft \vdash_M^* \mathsf{Accept} \,\}.$$

Moreover, $L(M)$ *is the* input language *accepted by* M, *which is defined by*

$$L(M) = \{\, w \in \Sigma^* \mid q_0 \triangleright w \triangleleft \vdash_M^* \mathsf{Accept} \,\}.$$

The input language $L(M)$ is obviously just the intersection $L_C(M) \cap \Sigma^*$.

Example 1.9.2 (cont.) *The configurations* $q_0 \triangleright aab \triangleleft$, $q_0 \triangleright abc \triangleleft$, *and* $q_0 \triangleright abbd \triangleleft$ *are initial configurations of the restarting automaton* M_1. *From the configuration* $q_0 \triangleright abbd \triangleleft$, M_1 *reaches the* *configuration* $\rhd q_0 abbd\lhd$ *by executing a MVR transition of type* (1)*, and from this configuration, it obtains the configurations* $\rhd bq_c d\lhd$ *and* $\rhd q_d d\lhd$ *by the rewrite transitions* (3)*. From the former of these,* M_1 *rejects, while from the latter, it reaches the restart configuration* $q_0\rhd d\lhd$ *by a transition of type* (10)*, which yields the configuration* Accept *by a transition of type* (2)*. Thus, we have the accepting computation*

$$q_0\rhd abbd\lhd \vdash_{M_1} \rhd q_0 abbd\lhd \vdash_{M_1} \rhd q_d d\lhd \vdash_{M_1} q_0\rhd d\lhd \vdash_{M_1} \mathsf{Accept}.$$

Actually, it is easily seen that

$$L(M_1) = L_{\mathrm{C}}(M_1) = \{\, a^n b^n c, a^n b^{2n} d \mid n \geq 0 \,\},$$

which is a well-known example of a context-free language that is not deterministic context-free. ■

Definition 1.9.4 *Any finite computation of a restarting automaton* M *consists of certain phases. A phase, called a* cycle*, starts in a restarting configuration, the window is moved along the tape by executing MVR, MVL, and rewrite operations until a restart operation is performed and thus, a new restarting configuration is reached. If no further restart operation is performed, any finite computation necessarily finishes in a halting configuration – such a phase is called a* tail*. We require that* M *performs* at least one *rewrite operation in each cycle. During a tail, rewrite operations may or may not occur. The execution of a complete cycle is denoted by* $\vdash^{c}_{M}$*, and* $\vdash^{c^*}_{M}$ *is the reflexive transitive closure of this relation. It can be seen as the* rewrite relation *that* M *realizes on its set of restarting configurations.*

Example 1.9.2 (cont.) *The restarting automaton* M_1 *executes* exactly one *rewrite transition in each cycle. For each* $n \geq 1$*, it can execute the cycles*

$$q_0\rhd a^n b^n c \lhd \vdash^{c}_{M_1} q_0\rhd a^{n-1} b^{n-1} c\lhd$$

and

$$q_0\rhd a^n b^{2n} d\lhd \vdash^{c}_{M_1} q_0\rhd a^{n-1} b^{2n-2} d \lhd .$$

■

The transformations applied during an analysis by reduction of a given sentence are required to preserve the syntactical correctness of the sentence, that is, if a sentence S_1 is transformed into a sentence S_2, then S_2 is syntactically correct if and only if S_1 is. For restarting automata, this condition can be formalized by the following two properties.

Definition 1.9.5 (Error Preserving Property).
Let $M = (Q, \Sigma, \Gamma, \rhd, \lhd, q_0, k, \delta)$ *be a restarting automaton. This automaton is said to satisfy the* Error Preserving Property (EPP) for its characteristic (input) language, *if, for all words* u, v *over its working (input) alphabet,*

$$q_0\rhd u\lhd \vdash^{c^*}_{M} q_0\rhd v \lhd \quad \text{and } u \notin L_{\mathrm{C}}(M)\ (u \notin L(M))$$

imply that $v \notin L_{\mathrm{C}}(M)$ $(v \notin L(M))$*, either.*

If $v \in L_{\mathrm{C}}(M)$ for a restarting automaton M, then M has an accepting computation of the form $q_0\rhd v\lhd \vdash^{c^*}_{M}$ Accept. Hence, from $q_0\rhd u\lhd \vdash^{c^*}_{M} q_0\rhd v\lhd$, it follows immediately that

$$q_0\rhd u\lhd \vdash^{c^*}_{M} q_0\rhd v\lhd \vdash^{c^*}_{M} \mathsf{Accept}$$

is an accepting computation, that is, $u \in L_{\mathrm{C}}(M)$, too. This yields the following observation.

Proposition 1.9.6 *Each restarting automaton satisfies the Error Preserving Property for its characteristic language and for its input language.*

Definition 1.9.7 (Correctness Preserving Property).
Let $M = (Q, \Sigma, \Gamma, \rhd, \lhd, q_0, k, \delta)$ be a restarting automaton. This automaton is said to satisfy the Correctness Preserving Property (CPP) for its characteristic (input) language, *if, for all words u, v over its working (input) alphabet,*

$$q_0 \rhd u \lhd \vdash_M^{c^*} q_0 \rhd v \lhd \quad \textit{and } u \in L_C(M) \ (u \in L(M))$$

imply that $v \in L_C(M)$ ($v \in L(M)$), too.

If M is a deterministic restarting automaton and $u \in \Gamma^*$, then M has a unique computation for the restart configuration $q_0 \rhd u \lhd$. If $u \in L_C(M)$, then this computation is accepting. Now, if $q_0 \rhd u \lhd \vdash_M^{c^*} q_0 \rhd v \lhd$, then the cycles transforming $q_0 \rhd u \lhd$ into $q_0 \rhd v \lhd$ necessarily constitute an initial segment of this accepting computation, which implies that the corresponding final segment of this computation has the form $q_0 \rhd v \lhd \vdash_M^* \mathsf{Accept}$. Thus, $v \in L_C(M)$ follows.

Proposition 1.9.8 *Each deterministic restarting automaton satisfies the Correctness Preserving Property for its characteristic language and for its input language.*

Consider the restarting automaton M_1 from Example 1.9.2. This automaton is nondeterministic, but it can be checked easily that it satisfies the CPP. In fact, its only nondeterministic transition is (3), where it chooses between deleting a factor ab or a factor abb. In the former case, it enters state q_c, while in the latter, it enters state q_d. Now the restart transitions (9), (10), and (11) guarantee that in the former case, M_1 can restart only if the tape contents ends with the letter c, while in the latter case, M_1 can restart only if the tape contents ends with the letter d. This shows that an incorrect guess in (3) will prevent a successful completion of the current cycle, just leading to a rejecting tail.

To further illustrate the CPP for restarting automata, we consider another example.

Example 1.9.9 *Let $M_2 = (Q, \Sigma, \Gamma, \rhd, \lhd, q_0, 3, \delta)$ be the deterministic restarting automaton that is defined by taking $Q = \{q_0, q_r\}$, $\Sigma = \{a, b, c, d\}$, $\Gamma = \Sigma \cup \{C, D\}$, and δ as given by the following table:*

(1)	$\delta(q_0, x)$	=	(q_0, MVR)	*for all* $x \in \{\rhd aa, aaa, aab, \rhd ab, abb, abc, bbb, bbc, bbd\}$,			
(2)	$\delta(q_0, \rhd x \lhd)$	=	Accept	*for all* $x \in \{c, d, C, D\}$,			
(3)	$\delta(q_0, bc\lhd)$	=	$(q_r, bC\lhd)$,	(7)	$\delta(q_0, abC)$	=	(q_r, aCC),
(4)	$\delta(q_0, bd\lhd)$	=	$(q_r, bD\lhd)$,	(8)	$\delta(q_0, abD)$	=	(q_r, aDD),
(5)	$\delta(q_0, bbC)$	=	(q_r, bCC),	(9)	$\delta(q_0, aCC)$	=	(q_r, C),
(6)	$\delta(q_0, bbD)$	=	(q_r, bDD),	(10)	$\delta(q_0, aDD)$	=	(q_r, λ),
(11)	$\delta(q_0, x)$	=	Reject	*for all other* $x \in \mathcal{PC}^{(3)}$,			
(12)	$\delta(q_r, x)$	=	$\mathsf{Restart}$	*for all* $x \in \mathcal{PC}^{(3)}$.			

Obviously, M_2 accepts the words c and d immediately. So let $w \in \Sigma^+ \smallsetminus \{c, d\}$. Starting from the initial configuration $q_0 \rhd w \lhd$, M will reject while scanning w from left to right unless w is of the form $w = a^m b^n c$ or $w = a^m b^n d$ for some positive integers m and n. In these cases, the configuration $\rhd a^m b^{n-1} q_0 bc \lhd$ or $\rhd a^m b^{n-1} q_0 bd \lhd$ is reached by repeatedly performing the transition steps (1), and then either the letter c is rewritten into the letter C by (3) or the letter d is rewritten into the letter D by (4), and M_2 restarts. In the following cycles, all occurrences of the letter b are replaced with C or D, proceeding from right to left, using transitions (5) to (8), which yields the restarting configuration $q_0 \rhd a^m C^{n+1} \lhd$ or $q_0 \rhd a^m D^{n+1} \lhd$. Finally, the factor aC or the factor aDD is repeatedly deleted by transitions (9) or (10). It follows that

$$L(M_2) = \{\, a^n b^n c, a^n b^{2n} d \mid n \geq 0 \,\} = L(M_1).$$

■

By Proposition 1.9.8, M_2 satisfies the CPP for its characteristic language and its input language. However, observe that $q_0 \rhd a^n b^n c \lhd \vdash^c_{M_2} q_0 \rhd a^n b^n C \lhd$ is the first cycle of the accepting computation of M_2 on input $a^n b^n c$, and that, while $a^n b^n c \in L(M_2)$, $a^n b^n C \notin L(M_2)$. In fact, for each restarting configuration $q_0 \rhd y \lhd$ in any accepting computation of M_2 with the exception of the corresponding initial configuration, the tape contents y is not an element of the language $L(M_2)$, as it contains at least one occurrence of an auxiliary letter. Thus, for the input language of M_2, the CPP is completely trivial.

The next example illustrates the fact that the CPP does not hold, in general, for the characteristic language of a nondeterministic restarting automaton.

Example 1.9.10 *Let $M_3 = (Q, \Sigma, \Gamma, \rhd, \lhd, q_0, 4, \delta)$ be the nondeterministic restarting automaton that is defined by taking $Q = \{q_0, q_r\}$, $\Sigma = \{a, b, c, d\}$, $\Gamma = \Sigma \cup \{C, D\}$, and δ as given by the following table:*

$$\begin{array}{rlcll}
(1) & \delta(q_0, x) & = & \{(q_0, \mathsf{MVR})\} & \textit{for all } x \in \{\rhd a^3, a^4, a^3b, a^2b^2, \rhd a^2b, \rhd ab^2, \rhd abc\} \cup \\
 & & & & \{\rhd a^2C, \rhd a^2D, \rhd aCb, \rhd aDb, a^3C, a^3D, a^2Cb, a^2Db\}, \\
(2) & \delta(q_0, \rhd x \lhd) & = & \{\mathsf{Accept}\} & \textit{for all } x \in \{c, d, Cc, Dd\}, \\
(3) & \delta(q_0, ab^3) & = & \{(q_r, Cb^2), (q_r, Db)\}, & \\
(4) & \delta(q_0, ab^2c) & = & \{(q_r, Cbc)\}, & (7)\ \ \delta(q_0, aCb^2) = \{(q_r, Cb)\}, \\
(5) & \delta(q_0, ab^2d) & = & \{(q_r, Dd)\}, & (8)\ \ \delta(q_0, aCbc) = \{(q_r, Cc)\}, \\
(6) & \delta(q_0, abc\lhd) & = & \{(q_r, Cc\lhd)\}, & (9)\ \ \delta(q_0, aDb^2) = \{(q_r, D)\}, \\
(10) & \delta(q_0, x) & = & \{\mathsf{Reject}\} & \textit{for all other } x \in \mathcal{PC}^{(4)}, \\
(11) & \delta(q_r, x) & = & \{\mathsf{Restart}\} & \textit{for all } x \in \mathcal{PC}^{(4)}.
\end{array}$$

Given an input of the form $a^m b^n z$ for some $z \in \{c, d\}$ and $m, n \geq 3$, M_3 moves its window to the factor ab^3, which it then replaces with either Cb^2 or with Db (see (3)), in this way guessing whether $z = c$ or $z = d$. In the following cycles, it replaces the factor aCb^2 with Cb in (7), the factor $aCbc$ with Cc in (8), or the factor aDb^2 with D in (9), and it accepts on reaching the tape contents Cc or Dd (see (2)). It follows that

$$L(M_3) = \{\, a^n b^n c, a^n b^{2n} d \mid n \geq 0 \,\} = L(M_1).$$

For the restarting (initial) configuration $q_0 \rhd a^3 b^6 d \lhd$, the tape contents $a^3 b^6 d$ belongs to the language $L(M_3)$, and therewith, it is an element of the characteristic language $L_C(M_3)$. However, $q_0 \rhd a^3 b^3 d \lhd \vdash^c_{M_3} q_0 \rhd a^2 C b^2 d \lhd$, and the tape contents $a^2 C b^2 d$ of the latter restart configuration is not an element of the language $L_C(M_3)$. This shows that the restarting automaton M_3 does not satisfy the CPP for its characteristic language. However, as each of the rewrite transitions of M_3 has an occurrence of an auxiliary letter on its right-hand side, we see that M_3 trivially satisfies the CPP for its input language. ■

We now turn to the expressive capacity of the restarting automaton. The following result shows that without further restrictions, the restarting automaton is a universal computing device.

Theorem 1.9.11 *Each recursively enumerable language is accepted by a deterministic restarting automaton that executes exactly one rewrite step in each cycle.*

Proof. Let $T = (Q_T, \Sigma, \Gamma, \delta_T, p_0, \Box, F_T)$ be a deterministic Turing machine (see Section 1.1). We define a restarting automaton $M = (Q, \Sigma, \Delta, \rhd, \lhd, q_0, 2, \delta)$ by taking $\Delta = \Gamma \cup (Q_T \times \Gamma)$, where each letter of the form $(p, A) \in Q_T \times \Gamma$ will be used to encode the state of the Turing machine together with the contents of the tape cell that the head currently scans. Thus, a configuration of the form $upAv$ of the Turing machine T is encoded by the restarting configuration $q_0 \rhd u(p, A)v \lhd$ of M. From the letter (p, A), the restarting automaton M can determine the next step of T, and it can then replace the letter (p, A) together with its neighbour on the left or on the right. For example, if $\delta_T(p, A) = (p', B, L)$, and if the cell to the left of the letter (p, A) contains the letter C from Γ, then M simply replaces the factor $C(p, A)$ with the word $(p', C)B$. It follows that M can simulate each computational step of T by executing a complete cycle. Finally, M accepts if and when T accepts. It follows that $L(M) = L(T)$, which completes the proof, as a language is recursively enumerable if and only if there is a Turing machine that accepts it. □

In order to limit the expressive capacity of the restarting automaton, we introduce the following serious restrictions. For the notion of a weight function, we refer to Definition 1.2.12.

Definition 1.9.12 *Let* $M = (Q, \Sigma, \Gamma, \rhd, \lhd, q_0, k, \delta)$ *be a restarting automaton.*

(a) M *is called* length-reducing *if* $|v| < |u|$ *for each rewrite transition* $(q', v) \in \delta(q, u)$.

(b) M *is called* weight-reducing (*or* shrinking) *if there exists a weight function* $\omega : \Gamma \to \mathbb{N}_+$ *such that* $\omega(v) < \omega(u)$ *holds for each rewrite transition* $(q', v) \in \delta(q, u)$.

For weight-reducing restarting automata, we obtain the following upper bound for the number of cycles in a computation.

Proposition 1.9.13 *If* M *is a weight-reducing restarting automaton, then each computation that begins with a tape contents of length* n *consists of at most* $c \cdot n$ *cycles and a tail, where* $c \geq 1$ *is a constant that depends on the underlying weight function.*

Proof. Let $M = (Q, \Sigma, \Gamma, \rhd, \lhd, q_0, k, \delta)$ be a restarting automaton and let $\omega : \Gamma \to \mathbb{N}_+$ be a weight function such that $\omega(v) < \omega(u)$ holds for each rewrite transition $(q', v) \in \delta(q, u)$. For a word $u \in \Gamma^n$, the maximal possible weight is $c \cdot |u| = c \cdot n$, where $c = \max\{\, \omega(a) \mid a \in \Gamma \,\}$ is the maximal weight of a single letter. As within each cycle of each computation, M executes at least one rewrite step, we see that $\omega(x_1) > \omega(x_2)$ for each cycle $q_0 \rhd x_1 \lhd \vdash_M^c q_0 \rhd x_2 \lhd$. Thus, each computation starting from the restart configuration $q_0 \rhd u \lhd$ consists of at most $c \cdot n$ cycles and a tail. □

Actually, the above proof shows that each computation of a weight-reducing restarting automaton that begins with a tape contents of length n contains at most $c \cdot n$ rewrite steps. This upper bound now yields the following simulation result for weight-reducing restarting automata.

Proposition 1.9.14 *Each weight-reducing restarting automaton can be simulated by a nondeterministic two-tape Turing machine that is simultaneously quadratically time-bounded and linearly space-bounded.*

Proof. Let $M = (Q, \Sigma, \Gamma, \rhd, \lhd, q_0, k, \delta)$ be a weight-reducing restarting automaton and let ω be a corresponding weight function. From the above remark, we see that each accepting computation of M for a word $u \in \Gamma^n$ contains at most $c \cdot n$ rewrite steps and $c \cdot n$ restart steps, where $c = \max\{\, \omega(a) \mid a \in \Gamma \,\}$.

We consider a shortest accepting computation of M for some input $u \in \Sigma^n$. If

$$q_0 \rhd u \lhd \vdash_M^c q_0 \rhd u_1 \lhd \vdash_M^c q_0 \rhd u_2 \lhd \vdash_M^{c^{m-2}} q_0 \rhd u_m \lhd$$

is an initial part of this computation, where $m \geq 0$, then $|u_i| \leq \omega(u_i) \leq c \cdot n$ for all $1 \leq i \leq m$. Now let $q_0 \rhd u_i \lhd \vdash_M^c q_0 \rhd u_{i+1} \lhd$ be a cycle within this computation. This cycle begins with a sequence of move operations. Then a rewrite step is executed that is followed by another sequence of move operations, and further rewrite steps followed by sequences of move operations may follow until finally a restart step completes the cycle. As the tape contents has length at most $c \cdot n$, there are at most $|Q| \cdot (c \cdot n + 2)$ many different configurations that can be encountered during a sequence of move operations. If during such a sequence, the same configuration is encountered more than once, then this sequence contains a cyclic subsequence. This subsequence can then be cut out, leading to an accepting computation of M on input u that has shorter length. By our choice of the accepting computation considered, this is not possible, which implies that each of the above sequences of move operations is of length at most $|Q| \cdot (c \cdot n + 2)$. This means that the above computation contains at most $((|Q| \cdot (c \cdot n + 2)) + 1) \cdot (2 \cdot (c \cdot n) + 1)$ many steps: at most $c \cdot n$ many rewrite steps, at most $c \cdot n$ many restart steps, one accept step, and at most $|Q| \cdot (c \cdot n + 2)$ many move operations before any of the other steps.

We now simulate M by a nondeterministic two-tape Turing machine T. A configuration $\triangleright uqvw \triangleleft$ of M, where $u, v, w \in \Gamma^*$ and $|v| = k$ is the current window contents, will be encoded by a configuration of T of the form $(p[q, v], w\triangleleft, \triangleright u)$, where $p[q, v]$ is a state of T that stores the state q of M and that contains a buffer of length k that stores the current window contents v. The first tape contains the suffix $w\triangleleft$ of the tape contents of M, and the second tape contains the corresponding prefix $\triangleright u$. Furthermore, the head of the first tape is on the first letter of $w\triangleleft$, while the head of the second tape is on the last letter of $\triangleright u$. In particular, a restart configuration $q_0 \triangleright x_1 x_2 \triangleleft$ of M is encoded by a configuration of the form $(p[q_0, \triangleright x_1], x_2\triangleleft, \lambda)$, where $|x_1| = k - 1$.

Now a MVR transition of M is simulated by a single step of T that moves the first letter of v from the buffer to tape 2 and that shifts the first letter of w to the end of the buffer. In a symmetric way, a MVL transition is simulated. Furthermore, a rewrite transition $(q', z) \in \delta(q, v)$ is simulated by attaching z to the inscription of tape 2, by shifting the prefix of length k of $w\triangleleft$ from tape 1 into the buffer, and by replacing the state q of M stored within the finite-state control of T by q'. This simulation takes at most $\max\{k, |z|\} \leq c \cdot k$ many steps, as $|z| \leq \omega(z) < \omega(v) \leq c \cdot k$. Finally, a restart transition Restart $\in \delta(q, v)$ is simulated by first shifting the word v from the buffer to tape 1, by then shifting the word $\triangleright u$ from tape 2 to tape 1, and by finally reading the prefix of length k from tape 1 into the buffer. This simulation takes $2k + |u| + 1$ many steps.

As seen above, an accepting computation of M of minimal length on an input of length n contains at most $c \cdot n$ many rewrite steps, at most $c \cdot n$ many restart steps, one accept step, and at most $(|Q| \cdot (c \cdot n + 2)) \cdot (2 \cdot (c \cdot n) + 1)$ many move operations. As the tape contents is bounded in length from above by $c \cdot n$, the simulation of each of the restart transitions within this computation takes at most $2k + c \cdot n + 1$ many steps. It follows that the above computation can be simulated by T taking $\mathcal{O}(n^2)$ steps and using $\mathcal{O}(n)$ tape cells, that is, we obtain the time-bound $\mathcal{O}(n^2)$ and the space-bound $\mathcal{O}(n)$. □

Thus, we have the following complexity result, where NTIMESPACE(n^2, n) denotes the class of languages accepted by nondeterministic Turing machines having a quadratic time-bound and a linear space-bound.

Corollary 1.9.15 *For each weight-reducing restarting automaton M,*

$$L_C(M), L(M) \in \text{NTIMESPACE}(n^2, n).$$

For weight-reducing deterministic restarting automata, the proof above yields the corresponding result, where DTIMESPACE(n^2, n) denotes the class of languages accepted by deterministic Turing machines having a quadratic time-bound and a linear space-bound.

Corollary 1.9.16 *For each weight-reducing deterministic restarting automaton M,*

$$L_C(M), L(M) \in \text{DTIMESPACE}(n^2, n).$$

For the rest of this monograph, we require the following general restriction.

Fact 1.9.17 *In what follows, all restarting automata considered will be required to be* weight-reducing (*or even* length-reducing)*!*

The definition of the restarting automaton (Definition 1.9.1) is quite general, as there are several parameters the values of which can be chosen to specify a particular type of restarting automaton.

Definition 1.9.18 *A* type of restarting automaton *is defined by choosing particular values (or ranges) for the following* parameters:

- *the number $|Q| \geq 1$ of states,*
- *the number $|\Gamma \smallsetminus \Sigma| \geq 0$ of auxiliary letters,*

- *the size $k \geq 1$ of the read/write window,*
- *the type of move transitions allowed,*
- *the type of rewrite transitions allowed,*
- *the number $j \geq 1$ of allowed rewrite steps per cycle, and*
- *the positions at which rewrite transitions are applied.*

For example, the *type of move transitions* refers to the option of using MVL steps as well as MVR steps, and the *type of rewrite transitions* refers to the option of, e.g., using only length-reducing rewrite transitions or using just deletions. Furthermore, concerning the *positions* at which rewrite transitions are applied, we may require that they are only allowed at the right end of the tape. Another restriction is imposed by the notion of monotonicity.

Definition 1.9.19 *Let $M = (Q, \Sigma, \Gamma, \rhd, \lhd, q_0, k, \delta)$ be a restarting automaton.*

(a) *For a configuration $\rhd uqvw\lhd$ of M, the number*

$$D_r(\rhd uqvw\lhd) = |vw\lhd| = k + |w| + 1$$

is the right distance *of this configuration. It is the length of the suffix of the tape contents that begins with the factor that is currently inside the window of M, that is, it is the distance from the left end of the window to the right end of the tape.*

(b) *Let $\rhd uqvw\lhd \vdash_M \rhd uzq'w\lhd$ be a rewrite step within a computation of M in which a rewrite transition $(q', z) \in \delta(q, v)$ is applied. Then $D_r(\rhd uqvw\lhd)$ is also called the* right distance of this rewrite step.

(c) *A computation of M is called* monotone *if the sequence of right distances of the rewrite steps within this computation is non-increasing, that is, whenever*

$$\rhd uqvw\lhd \vdash_M \rhd uzq'w\lhd \vdash_M^* \rhd u_1q_1v_1w_1\lhd \vdash_M \rhd u_1z_1q_1'w_1\lhd$$

is part of this computation, where $(q', z) \in \delta(q, v)$ and $(q_1', z_1) \in \delta(q_1, v_1)$ are rewrite transitions, then

$$D_r(\rhd uqvw\lhd) \geq D_r(\rhd u_1q_1v_1w_1\lhd).$$

(d) *The restarting automaton M is called* monotone *if each of its computations that begins with an initial configuration is monotone.*

The restarting automaton M_1 in Example 1.9.2 has 4 states only, it has no auxiliary letters, it has window size 3, it is nondeterministic, it does not use MVL transitions, all its rewrite transitions are deletions, and it is monotone. In fact, starting from a configuration of the form $q_0\rhd a^m b^n x\lhd$, where $m \geq 1$, $n \geq 2$, and $x \in \{c, d\}$, M_1 rewrites the inner factor abb into either b or λ. Thus, the corresponding rewrite step has right distance $n + 3$, and as the exponent n is reduced in each cycle, we see that M_1 is indeed monotone. Furthermore, M_1 executes exactly one rewrite step in each cycle.

The restarting automaton M_2 in Example 1.9.9 has 2 states only, it has 2 auxiliary letters, it has window size 3, and it is deterministic and weight-reducing. In fact, we can choose the weight function $\omega(a) = \omega(C) = \omega(D) = 1$ and $\omega(b) = \omega(c) = \omega(d) = 2$. Furthermore, M_2 does not use MVL transitions, and it is non-monotone, as starting from a configuration of the form $q_0\rhd a^m b^n x\lhd$, where $m \geq 1$, $n \geq 2$, and $x \in \{c, d\}$, the suffix $b^n x$ is rewritten letter by letter, from right to left, into the word C^{n+1} or D^{n+1}. Also M_2 just executes a single rewrite step in each cycle.

Finally, the restarting automaton M_3 in Example 1.9.10 has 2 states only, it has 2 auxiliary letters, it has window size 4, it is nondeterministic and length-reducing, it does not use MVL transitions, it is monotone, and it executes a single rewrite step in each cycle, too.

Definition 1.9.20 *Let* RS *be a type of restarting automata. Then* $\mathcal{L}_C(\mathsf{RS})$ *denotes the* class of characteristic languages *of restarting automata of type* RS, *and* $\mathcal{L}(\mathsf{RS})$ *denotes the* class of input languages *of restarting automata of type* RS.

We conclude this section with a short survey on the types of restarting automata that were introduced and studied in the first papers on this topic. In particular, we present the characterizations of several classes of the extended Chomsky hierarchy depicted in the diagram in Figure 1.8 by various rather restricted types of restarting automata that were derived in those papers.

The type of restarting automaton that was first introduced by Petr Jančar, František Mráz, Martin Plátek, and Jörg Vogel at the international conference FCT 1995 in Dresden [85] is the so-called *R-automaton*. An R-automaton has a finite number of states and a finite window size, it has no auxiliary letters, it executes exactly one rewrite step in each cycle, which is just a deletion that is immediately followed by a restart step, and it does not use any MVL steps. The main result of [85] states the following characterization, where the prefix det- is used to denote deterministic types of restarting automata and the prefix mon- is used to denote monotone types of restarting automata.

Theorem 1.9.21 ([85]) $\mathcal{L}(\mathsf{det\text{-}mon\text{-}R}) = \mathsf{DCFL}$.

The inclusion from left to right follows from the observation that the monotone computations of a deterministic R-automaton can be simulated quite easily by a DPDA. Just notice that, within a monotone computation, the tape contents is essentially processed (rewritten) from left to right. Accordingly, a DPDA can store the prefix of the tape contents of the R-automaton being simulated that has already been processed on its pushdown store, while the suffix of the tape contents that is still to be processed is the remaining input. For the converse inclusion, recall that, if L is a deterministic context-free language on Σ, then the product $L \cdot \{\lhd\}$ is a prefix-free deterministic context-free language. Hence, it can be parsed by an LR(0)-parser (see, e.g., [81]). From such a parser, a monotone deterministic R-automaton can be derived for the language L.

In [175] (and also in [86]), the R-automaton is extended to the so-called *RW-automaton*, which, in addition to deletions, also admits length-reducing rewrite transitions that replace a non-empty word with another word. As the aforementioned simulation of the monotone computations of a deterministic R-automaton by a DPDA extends to RW-automata, the following generalization of the above characterization is obtained.

Theorem 1.9.22 ([86]) $\mathcal{L}(\mathsf{det\text{-}mon\text{-}RW}) = \mathsf{DCFL}$.

Finally, in [87], the authors introduce the so-called *RWW-automaton*, which is obtained from the RW-automaton by admitting auxiliary letters. Thus, a rewrite transition of an RWW-automaton may replace a word over the input alphabet with a shorter word possibly containing auxiliary letters. As the above simulation of the monotone computations of a deterministic R-automaton by a DPDA even generalizes to RWW-automata and to the nondeterministic case, the following characterizations are obtained.

Theorem 1.9.23 ([87]) (a) $\mathcal{L}(\mathsf{det\text{-}mon\text{-}RWW}) = \mathsf{DCFL}$.
(b) $\mathcal{L}(\mathsf{mon\text{-}RWW}) = \mathsf{CFL}$.

Here the containment of CFL in $\mathcal{L}(\mathsf{mon\text{-}RWW})$ is derived from the observation that a monotone RWW-automaton can simulate the right-most derivations of a context-free grammar in Chomsky normal form in reverse order. For this simulation, auxiliary letters are needed, that is, the characterization of the context-free languages by monotone RWW-automata does not carry over to RW-automata (see [87]).

Also in [87], Petr Jančar, František Mráz, Martin Plátek, and Jörg Vogel study the *RRWW-automaton*, which is obtained from the RWW-automaton by abandoning the requirement that an automaton must restart immediately after executing a rewrite step. Thus, in each cycle, an

RRWW-automaton can scan the suffix of the tape contents that is to the right of the place where the rewrite transition of that cycle is executed. For these automata, they establish the following extension of Theorem 1.9.23, which is obtained by a non-trivial generalization of the aforementioned simulation of a monotone (deterministic) RWW-automaton by a (D)PDA.

Theorem 1.9.24 ([87]) (a) $\mathcal{L}(\mathsf{det\text{-}mon\text{-}RRWW}) = \mathsf{DCFL}$.
(b) $\mathcal{L}(\mathsf{mon\text{-}RRWW}) = \mathsf{CFL}$.

In [194], the deterministic monotone RL- and RLWW-automata are studied. These automata are obtained from the deterministic monotone RR- and RRWW-automata by admitting the use of MVL transitions. An automaton of this type can first scan its tape completely from left to right and then, by applying MVL steps, it can move its window back to a position at which it executes a rewrite transition. Using quite sophisticated simulation techniques, the following characterization is derived, where LRR is the class of left-to-right regular languages from Definition 1.2.45.

Theorem 1.9.25 ([194]) $\mathcal{L}(\mathsf{det\text{-}mon\text{-}RL}) = \mathcal{L}(\mathsf{det\text{-}mon\text{-}RLWW}) = \mathsf{LRR}$.

Up to here, we have only looked at various types of monotone restarting automata. In [183, 185], the non-monotone variants of the deterministic RWW- and RRWW-automata are studied, leading to the following characterization.

Theorem 1.9.26 ([181, 183, 185]) $\mathcal{L}(\mathsf{det\text{-}RWW}) = \mathcal{L}(\mathsf{det\text{-}RRWW}) = \mathsf{CRL}$.

This result is again proved by simulation. On the one hand, the accepting computations of a deterministic RRWW-automaton can be simulated quite easily by a length-reducing DTPDA (see Definition 1.2.15 and Theorem 1.2.19). Here a key observation is the fact that a deterministic RRWW-automaton with a window of size k is necessarily weakly monotone of degree $k-1$ (see below). Conversely, it can be shown that the accepting computations of a DTPDA can be simulated by a deterministic RWW-automaton. Here the use of auxiliary letters is unavoidable, that is, deterministic RW- and RRW-automata are strictly less expressive.

The notion of weak monotonicity was introduced in [94] as a generalization of the notion of monotonicity.

Definition 1.9.27 *Let* $M = (Q, \Sigma, \Gamma, \rhd, \lhd, q_0, k, \delta)$ *be a restarting automaton and let* $c \geq 0$ *be an integer.*

(a) *A computation of* M *is called* weakly monotone of degree c *if, from one rewrite step to the next within this computation, the right distance increases by at most* c*, that is, whenever*

$$\rhd uqvw \lhd \vdash_M \rhd uzq'w \lhd \vdash_M^* \rhd u_1q_1v_1w_1 \lhd \vdash_M \rhd u_1z_1q_1'w_1 \lhd$$

is a part of this computation, where $(q', z) \in \delta(q, v)$ *and* $(q_1', z_1) \in \delta(q_1, v_1)$ *are rewrite transitions and the sub-computation* $\rhd uzq'w \lhd \vdash_M^* \rhd u_1q_1v_1w_1 \lhd$ *does not contain a rewrite step, then*

$$D_r(\rhd u_1q_1v_1w_1 \lhd) \leq D_r(\rhd uqvw \lhd) + c.$$

(b) *The restarting automaton* M *is called* weakly monotone *if there exists an integer* $c \geq 0$ *such that each of its computations that begins with an initial configuration is weakly monotone of degree* c.

The prefix wmon- will be used to denote weakly monotone types of restarting automata. Obviously, monotonicity is just weak monotonicity of degree 0. The simulation of a length-reducing DTPDA by a deterministic RWW-automaton carries over to the nondeterministic case. Also the simulation of a deterministic RRWW-automaton by a length-reducing DTPDA generalizes to nondeterministic RRWW-automata that are weakly monotone. As the length-reducing nondeterministic TPDA characterizes the class GCSL of growing context-sensitive languages (see Theorem 1.2.17), the weakly monotone restarting automata yield a characterization for the growing context-sensitive languages.

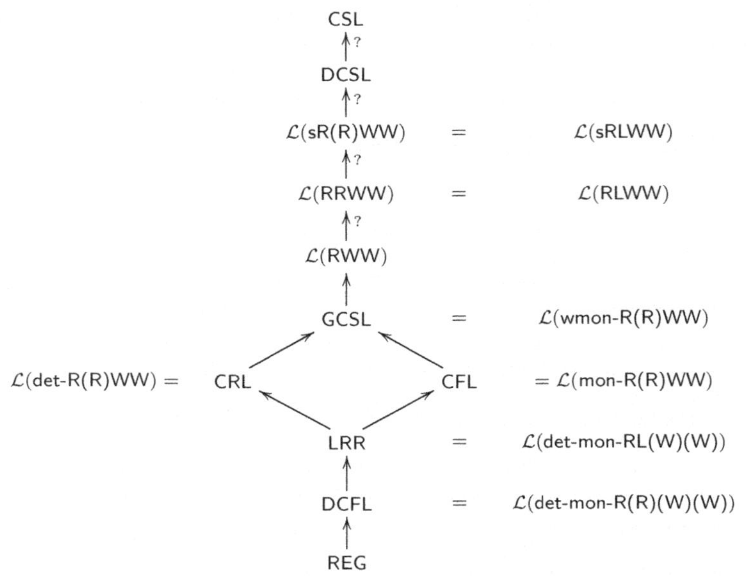

Figure 1.12: A characterization of the lower part of an extended Chomsky hierarchy by various subtypes of sRLWW-automata. An arrow indicates a proper inclusion, while an arrow indexed by a question mark indicates an inclusion that is not known to be proper.

Theorem 1.9.28 ([94, 184])

$$\mathcal{L}(\mathsf{wmon\text{-}RWW}) = \mathcal{L}(\mathsf{wmon\text{-}RRWW}) = \mathcal{L}(\mathsf{wmon\text{-}RLWW}) = \mathsf{GCSL} \subsetneq \mathcal{L}(\mathsf{RWW}).$$

Finally, in [99], the RWW-, the RRWW-, and the RLWW-automata are further extended by admitting weight-reducing instead of just length-reducing rewrite transitions. Restarting automata of this form are also called *shrinking*. Accordingly, we use the prefix s to denote types of restarting automata that are weight-reducing. For the above types of weight-reducing restarting automata, the following results are known.

Theorem 1.9.29 ([99]) $\mathcal{L}(\mathsf{sRWW}) = \mathcal{L}(\mathsf{sRRWW}) = \mathcal{L}(\mathsf{sRLWW}) \subseteq \mathsf{DCSL}$.

The above results are summarized in the diagram in Figure 1.12. In Chapter 2, all these types of restarting automata, and many others, will be studied systematically by taking a close look at the various parameters that are used to define types of restarting automata (see Definition 1.9.18).

Chapter 2

The Restarting Automaton and Its Parameters

The general model of the restarting automaton, as defined in Definition 1.9.1, has a number of parameters that can be used to specify particular types of restarting automata (see Definition 1.9.18). Here we look at each of these parameters in turn. For each of them, we study its influence on the expressive capacity of the resulting types of restarting automata.

In Section 2.1, we start with the various types of restarting automata that were initially defined by Petr Jančar, František Mráz, Martin Plátek, and Jörg Vogel. All these types have in common that they execute exactly one rewrite step in each cycle, and that this rewrite step must be length-reducing. They differ in the type of move operations and with respect to the use of auxiliary letters. However, we also include the extensions to the corresponding types of weight-reducing restarting automata, admitting rewrite transitions that are not necessarily length-reducing, but that are weight-reducing with respect to some weight function.

In Section 2.2, we concentrate on restarting automata without auxiliary letters, comparing the expressive capabilities of the various types. In addition, we also consider restarting automata that have only a single auxiliary letter.

Then, in Section 2.3, we consider the most obvious numerical parameter: the size of the read/write window. We shall see that, for certain types of restarting automata, the window size can be limited to two without restricting the expressive capacity of these types of restarting automata, while for other types, the window size induces infinite ascending hierarchies of language classes. Finally, in Section 2.4, we study restarting automata with only a single state (so-called *stateless* restarting automata).

While all types of restarting automata considered up to this point execute only a single rewrite step in each cycle, in Section 2.5, we look at what happens when we increase this number. Finally, we study proper languages of lexicalized and h-lexicalized restarting automata in Section 2.6. The latter are restarting automata for which the auxiliary letters are related to the input letters via an alphabetic morphism, which is motivated by the requirement that auxiliary letters (like, e.g., tags) should have a linguistically meaningful interpretation.

F. Otto, *Restarting Automata*, Theory and Applications of Computability,
https://doi.org/10.1007/978-3-031-70094-1_2

2.1 Restricting the Operations

In their first papers on restarting automata, Petr Jančar, František Mráz, Martin Plátek, and Jörg Vogel introduced a number of types of restarting automata. These restarting automata have an arbitrary finite number of states, an arbitrary finite number of auxiliary letters, and an arbitrary finite positive window size. However, for all these types, it is required that an automaton executes exactly one length-reducing rewrite step in each cycle. The authors established a particular notation for the various types of these automata. Here we summarize these definitions and restate the corresponding notation.

Definition 2.1.1 ([85, 86, 87]) *Let $M = (Q, \Sigma, \Gamma, \rhd, \lhd, q_0, k, \delta)$ be a restarting automaton, where Q is a finite set of states, Σ is a finite input alphabet, Γ is a finite working alphabet such that $\Sigma \subseteq \Gamma$, $\rhd, \lhd \notin \Gamma$ are the markers for the left and right ends of the tape, called* sentinels, *$q_0 \in Q$ is the* restart state, *which also serves as* initial state, *$k \geq 1$ is the size of the read/write window, and*

$$\delta : Q \times \mathcal{PC}^{(k)} \to \mathcal{P}((Q \times (\{\mathrm{MVR}, \mathrm{MVL}\} \cup \Gamma^*)) \cup \{\mathrm{Restart}, \mathrm{Accept}, \mathrm{Reject}\})$$

is the transition relation (see Definition 1.9.1 for details). This restarting automaton is called an RLWW-automaton *if it may use MVR, MVL, length-reducing rewrite, restart, accept, and reject transitions, but it is required to execute exactly one rewrite step in each cycle.*

By restricting the set of allowed transitions, the following subtypes are obtained:

- *an* RRWW-automaton *is an RLWW-automaton that does not use any MVL transitions;*
- *an* RWW-automaton *is an RRWW-automaton that restarts immediately after executing a rewrite transition, that is, for this type of restarting automaton, the rewrite and restart transitions can be combined into a single transition;*
- *an* RLW-automaton *is an RLWW-automaton that does not have any auxiliary letters, that is, for this automaton, $\Gamma = \Sigma$;*
- *an* RRW-automaton *is an RRWW-automaton that does not have any auxiliary letters;*
- *an* RW-automaton *is an RWW-automaton without auxiliary letters;*
- *an* RL-automaton *is an RLW-automaton for which each rewrite transition simply deletes some letters, that is, if $(q', v) \in \delta(q, u)$ is a rewrite transition of this automaton, then v is a proper scattered subword of u;*
- *an* RR-automaton *is an RRW-automaton for which each rewrite transition simply deletes some letters; and finally,*
- *an* R-automaton *is an RW-automaton for which each rewrite transition deletes some letters.*

Observe that the prefixes RL-, RR-, and R- express a restriction on the move operations, while the suffixes -WW, -W, and -λ express a restriction on the rewrite transitions. The table in Figure 2.1 summarizes these restrictions.

For example, the restarting automaton M_1 of Example 1.9.2 is an RR-automaton, and the automaton M_3 of Example 1.9.10 is an RWW-automaton.

The definition above gives nine different types of restarting automata. However, a general result of Martin Plátek shows that, with respect to the classes of languages accepted, the three types that include MVL transitions are not needed (in the case of nondeterminism).

Theorem 2.1.2 ([218]) *For each RLWW-automaton $M = (Q, \Sigma, \Gamma, \rhd, \lhd, q_0, k, \delta)$, there exists an RRWW-automaton $M' = (Q', \Sigma, \Gamma, \rhd, \lhd, q_0', k, \delta')$ such that M' has exactly the same rewrite transitions as M and $L_C(M') = L_C(M)$. In addition, if M is monotone or weakly monotone, then so is M'. In fact, M' can be constructed effectively from M.*

	with auxiliary letters (-WW)	without auxiliary letters (-W)	deletions only (-λ)
MVL steps (RL-)	RLWW	RLW	RL
no MVL steps (RR-)	RRWW	RRW	RR
no MVL steps and combined rewrite and restart steps (R-)	RWW	RW	R

Table 2.1: Various types of restarting automata obtained by restricting the move and rewrite transitions

As M' has the same input and working alphabets as M, it follows from the equality $L_C(M') = L_C(M)$ that also $L(M') = L(M)$. Furthermore, if M is a restarting automaton of type RLW (or RL), then M' is a restarting automaton of type RRW (or RR).

Proof outline for Theorem 2.1.2. Let $M = (Q, \Sigma, \Gamma, \rhd, \lhd, q_0, k, \delta)$ be an RLWW-automaton. Each cycle of each computation of M consists of two phases:

(1) First, M scans its tape by using MVR and MVL steps. This phase ends when M executes a rewrite step.

(2) After executing a rewrite step, M scans its tape again using MVR and MVL steps. This phase ends with a restart step.

The situation for the tail of a computation is similar. Here, however, the tail can end in either phase (1) or phase (2) with an accept or a reject transition.

During each of these phases, M behaves essentially like a nondeterministic two-way finite-state acceptor (a 2NFA, see Section 1.2). According to Proposition 1.2.72, a nondeterministic one-way finite-state acceptor can be constructed that simulates this 2NFA by guessing corresponding crossing sequences and verifying that these sequences are compatible with each other and with the tape contents. Thus, in order to simulate a cycle of M, the RRWW-automaton M' must simulate the two phases of this cycle in parallel by guessing corresponding crossing sequences. In addition, it must determine (or guess) the rewrite transition that is executed by M and the position at which it is executed. Of course, it must take the result of this rewrite transition into account when checking the correctness of the crossing sequences that it chooses for the second phase of the cycle of M. In this way, M' can simulate a computation of M cycle by cycle. Analogously, it can simulate the tail of a computation of M. It follows that $L_C(M') = L_C(M)$. As M' executes exactly the same rewrite transitions as M, it follows that M' is monotone (or weakly monotone), if M is. □

Thus, we obtain the following equalities, where for any type RS of restarting automata, $\mathcal{L}(\text{RS})$ denotes the class of input languages that are accepted by automata of type RS, and $\mathcal{L}_C(\text{RS})$ denotes the class of basic (characteristic) languages of automata of type RS.

Corollary 2.1.3 *For each prefix* $\mu \in \{\mathsf{mon}\text{-}, \mathsf{wmon}\text{-}, \lambda\}$,

(a) $\mathcal{L}_C(\mu\text{-}\mathsf{RLWW}) = \mathcal{L}_C(\mu\text{-}\mathsf{RRWW})$ *and* $\mathcal{L}(\mu\text{-}\mathsf{RLWW}) = \mathcal{L}(\mu\text{-}\mathsf{RRWW})$.

(b) $\mathcal{L}_C(\mu\text{-}\mathsf{RLW}) = \mathcal{L}_C(\mu\text{-}\mathsf{RRW})$ *and* $\mathcal{L}(\mu\text{-}\mathsf{RLW}) = \mathcal{L}(\mu\text{-}\mathsf{RRW})$.

(c) $\mathcal{L}_C(\mu\text{-}\mathsf{RL}) = \mathcal{L}_C(\mu\text{-}\mathsf{RR})$ *and* $\mathcal{L}(\mu\text{-}\mathsf{RL}) = \mathcal{L}(\mu\text{-}\mathsf{RR})$.

From Theorems 1.9.24 and 1.9.25, we see that a corresponding result does not hold for deterministic RLWW-automata.

In [99], the weight-reducing (or shrinking) variants of the above types of restarting automata are introduced and studied. Here an RLWW-automaton M is called *weight-reducing* (or *shrinking*) if there is a weight function ω such that $\omega(v) < \omega(u)$ holds for each rewrite transition $(q', v) \in \delta(q, u)$ of M (see Definition 1.9.12 (b)). Using the prefix s to denote weight-reducing types of restarting automata, we thus get the sRLWW-, the sRLW-, the sRRWW-, the sRRW-, the sRWW-, and the sRW-automaton. For example, the automaton M_2 of Example 1.9.9 is an sRWW-automaton. As all rewrite transitions of RL-, RR-, and R-automata are simply deletions, there is no difference between the length-reducing and the weight-reducing variants for these types of restarting automata.

From the arguments given in the proof outline above, it immediately follows that Theorem 2.1.2 extends to weight-reducing RLWW-automata. Hence, we also have the following equalities.

Corollary 2.1.4 *For each prefix* $\mu \in \{\mathsf{mon}\text{-}, \mathsf{wmon}\text{-}, \lambda\}$,

(a) $\mathcal{L}_C(\mu\text{-}\mathsf{sRLWW}) = \mathcal{L}_C(\mu\text{-}\mathsf{sRRWW})$ *and* $\mathcal{L}(\mu\text{-}\mathsf{sRLWW}) = \mathcal{L}(\mu\text{-}\mathsf{sRRWW})$.

(b) $\mathcal{L}_C(\mu\text{-}\mathsf{sRLW}) = \mathcal{L}_C(\mu\text{-}\mathsf{sRRW})$ *and* $\mathcal{L}(\mu\text{-}\mathsf{sRLW}) = \mathcal{L}(\mu\text{-}\mathsf{sRRW})$.

For RRWW-automata, the following normalization result is easily derived by using standard techniques from automata theory.

Lemma 2.1.5 *From an RRWW-automaton M, one can effectively construct an RRWW-automaton M' that satisfies the following conditions:*

(a) $L_C(M') = L_C(M)$ *and* $L(M') = L(M)$,

(b) *M' can execute an accept or a restart transition only when the right sentinel $\lhd$ is inside its read/write window.*

Thus, for an RRWW-automaton, we may assume that, in each cycle of each computation and also during the tail of each accepting computation, the read/write window moves all the way to the right end of the tape before a restart is made, respectively, before the automaton halts and accepts.

Based on this observation, each cycle (and also each accepting tail) of a computation of an RRWW-automaton can be split into three phases:

(1) First, the window is moved from left to right by a sequence of MVR steps.

(2) Next, a rewrite step is executed.

(3) Finally, another sequence of MVR steps carries the window to the right end of the tape, where a restart (or an accept) step completes the cycle (the accepting tail).

Accordingly, the transition relation of an RRWW-automaton can be described through a sequence of so-called *meta-instructions* [184] of the form

$$(R_1, u \to v, R_2) \text{ and } (\rhd \cdot R \cdot \lhd, \mathsf{Accept})$$

where R_1, R_2, and R are regular expressions, called the *regular constraints* of these instructions, and u and v are words. Here the rule $u \to v$ embodies a rewrite transition of the RRWW-automaton M considered. On trying to execute the meta-instruction $(R_1, u \to v, R_2)$, M will get stuck (and so reject) starting from a restarting configuration $q_0 \rhd w \lhd$, if w does not admit a factorization of the form $w = w_1 u w_2$ such that $\rhd w_1 \in L(R_1)$ and $w_2 \lhd \in L(R_2)$. On the other hand, if w does have a factorization of this form, then one such factorization is chosen nondeterministically, and $q_0 \rhd w \lhd$ is transformed into the restarting configuration $q_0 \rhd w_1 v w_2 \lhd$. In order to describe the tails of accepting computations, meta-instructions of the form

$$(\rhd \cdot R \cdot \lhd, \mathsf{Accept})$$

are used, where the words from the regular language $L(R)$ are accepted by M in tail computations.

We illustrate this concept by describing the RR-automaton M_1 of Example 1.9.2 by meta-instructions.

Example 2.1.6 *The RR-automaton M_1 can be defined by the following meta-instructions:*

$$\begin{array}{llll} (1) & (\rhd \cdot a^*, \quad abb \to b, \quad b^* \cdot c\lhd), & (4) & (\rhd c \lhd, \quad \mathsf{Accept}), \\ (2) & (\rhd \cdot a^*, \quad abc \to c, \quad \lhd), & (5) & (\rhd d \lhd, \quad \mathsf{Accept}). \\ (3) & (\rhd \cdot a^*, \quad abb \to \lambda, \quad b^* \cdot d\lhd), & & \end{array}$$

■

As an RWW-automaton restarts immediately after executing a rewrite step, each cycle of a computation of an RWW-automaton M consists of two phases only. Accordingly, the transition relation of an RWW-automaton can be described by a finite sequence of *meta-instructions* of the form

$$(R, u \to v) \text{ and } (\rhd \cdot R \cdot \lhd, \mathsf{Accept}),$$

where R is a regular expression, and u and v are words. On trying to execute the meta-instruction $(R, u \to v)$, M will get stuck (and so reject) starting from a restarting configuration $q_0 \rhd w \lhd$, if the word w does not admit a factorization of the form $w = w_1 u w_2$ such that $\rhd w_1 \in L(R)$. On the other hand, if the word w does have a factorization of this form, then one such factorization is chosen nondeterministically, and $q_0 \rhd w \lhd$ is transformed into the restarting configuration $q_0 \rhd w_1 v w_2 \lhd$. For describing tails of accepting computations, meta-instructions of the form

$$(\rhd \cdot R \cdot \lhd, \mathsf{Accept})$$

are used, where the words from the regular language $L(R)$ are accepted by M in tail computations.

We illustrate this concept by describing the sRWW-automaton M_2 of Example 1.9.9 by meta-instructions.

Example 2.1.7 *The sRWW-automaton M_2 can be defined by the following meta-instructions:*

$$\begin{array}{llll}
(1) & (\rhd \cdot a^* \cdot b^*, \quad bc\lhd \to bC\lhd), & (6) & (\rhd \cdot a^*, \quad abD \to aDD),\\
(2) & (\rhd \cdot a^* \cdot b^*, \quad bd\lhd \to bD\lhd), & (7) & (\rhd \cdot a^*, \quad aCC \to C),\\
(3) & (\rhd \cdot a^* \cdot b^*, \quad bbC \to bCC), & (8) & (\rhd \cdot a^*, \quad aDD \to \lambda),\\
(4) & (\rhd \cdot a^* \cdot b^*, \quad bbD \to bDD), & (9) & (\rhd \cdot \{c, d, C, D\} \cdot \lhd, \mathsf{Accept}).\\
(5) & (\rhd \cdot a^*, \quad abC \to aCC), & &
\end{array}$$

■

Motivated by the above way of presenting restarting automata by meta-instructions, the following result from [218] can be established. Just recall that during the first and the third phase of a cycle, an RRWW-automaton essentially behaves like an NFA, which means that the arguments from the proof of the Pumping Lemma for regular languages can be used.

Proposition 2.1.8 (Pumping Lemma)
For any RLWW-automaton $M = (Q, \Sigma, \Gamma, \rhd, \lhd, q_0, k, \delta)$, there exists a constant p such that the following holds. Assume that $q_0 \rhd uvw \lhd \vdash^c_M q_0 \rhd uv'w \lhd$, where $u = u_1 u_2 u_3$ and $|u_2| = p$. Then there exists a factorization $u_2 = z_1 z_2 z_3$ such that z_2 is non-empty and

$$q_0 \rhd u_1 z_1 (z_2)^i z_3 u_3 v w \lhd \vdash^c_M q_0 \rhd u_1 z_1 (z_2)^i z_3 u_3 v' w \lhd$$

holds for all $i \geq 0$, that is, z_2 is a 'pumping factor' in the above cycle. Similarly, such a pumping factor can be found in any factor of length p of w. Such a pumping factor can also be found in any factor of length p of a word accepted in a tail computation.

As we shall see later, this proposition is quite useful for proving that some languages cannot be accepted by certain types of restarting automata. Obviously, it also applies to shrinking RLWW-automata.

From Section 1.2, we recall that the marked copy language $L'_{\text{copy}} = \{ w\#w \mid w \in \{a,b\}^* \}$ is not growing context-sensitive. The following example, however, shows that this language is accepted by an RWW-automaton.

Example 2.1.9 *Let $M' = (Q, \Sigma, \Gamma, \rhd, \lhd, q_0, 4, \delta)$ be the RWW-automaton on $\Sigma = \{a, b, \#\}$ and $\Gamma = \Sigma \cup \{\#'\} \cup \Gamma'$, where $\Gamma' = \{ [c, d, S] \mid c, d \in \{a, b\}, S \in \{0, 1\} \}$, that is given through the* *following sequence of meta-instructions. Here* $c, d, e, f \in \{a, b\}$, $S, S' \in \{0, 1\}$, *and* $\bar{S} = 1 - S$:

(1) $(\triangleright, cd \to [c, d, 0])$,
(2) $(\triangleright \cdot \Gamma'^* \cdot [e, f, S], cd \to [c, d, \bar{S}])$,
(3) $(\triangleright [c, d, 0] \cdot \{a, b\}^* \cdot \#, cd \to [c, d, 0])$,
(4) $(\triangleright \cdot \Gamma'^* \cdot [c, d, S] \cdot \{a, b\}^* \cdot \# \cdot \Gamma'^* \cdot [e, f, \bar{S}], cd \to [c, d, S])$,
(5) $(\triangleright \cdot \Gamma'^*, [c, d, S] \cdot X \cdot [e, f, S'] \to \#')$ *for all* $X \in \{\#, \#'\}$,
(6) $(\triangleright \cdot \Gamma'^*, [c, d, S] \cdot g \cdot X \cdot [e, f, S'] \to g\#')$ *for all* $g \in \{a, b\}, X \in \{\#, \#'\}$,
(7) $(\triangleright \cdot X \cdot \triangleleft, \mathsf{Accept})$ *for all* $X \in \{\#, \#'\}$,
(8) $(\triangleright \cdot gXg \cdot \triangleleft, \mathsf{Accept})$ *for all* $g \in \{a, b\}, X \in \{\#, \#'\}$.

Let the word abaab#abaab be given as input. Then M' *can execute the following computation, where, in each restarting configuration, we underline the factor that is rewritten in the next cycle:*

$$
\begin{array}{lll}
q_0 \triangleright \underline{ab}aab\#abaab\triangleleft & \vdash^c_{(1)} & q_0 \triangleright [a, b, 0]aab\#\underline{ab}aab\triangleleft \\
& \vdash^c_{(3)} & q_0 \triangleright [a, b, 0]\underline{aa}b\#[a, b, 0]aab\triangleleft \\
& \vdash^c_{(2)} & q_0 \triangleright [a, b, 0][a, a, 1]b\#[a, b, 0]\underline{aa}b\triangleleft \\
& \vdash^c_{(4)} & q_0 \triangleright [a, b, 0]\underline{[a, a, 1]b\#[a, b, 0]}[a, a, 1]b\triangleleft \\
& \vdash^c_{(6)} & q_0 \triangleright \underline{[a, b, 0]b\#'[a, a, 1]}b\triangleleft \\
& \vdash^c_{(6)} & q_0 \triangleright b\#'b\triangleleft \\
& \vdash_{(8)} & \mathsf{Accept}.
\end{array}
$$

We see that the meta-instructions (1) and (2) compress the first $\{a, b\}$*-factor* $a_1a_2a_3a_4a_5a_6\cdots$ *of a given input into a word of the form* $[a_1, a_2, 0][a_3, a_4, 1][a_5, a_6, 0]\cdots$. *The meta-instructions (3) and (4) compress the second* $\{a, b\}$*-factor in the same way. The alternating values in the third components of the* Γ'*-symbols guarantee that, between any two applications of meta-instructions (3) or (4), at least one application of meta-instruction (2) takes place. It follows that the meta-instructions (1) to (4) can compress the first two* $\{a, b\}$*-factors completely only if the second factor is a scattered subword of the first factor. Now the meta-instructions (5) and (6) delete the compressed factors in a synchronous manner, and* M' *accepts if and only if the two factors have the same length. Together these observations imply that* M' *accepts an input* w *if and only if* w *has the form* $w = u\#u$ *for some word* $u \in \{a, b\}^*$, *that is, we see that* $L(M') = L'_{\text{copy}}$. ∎

In fact, also the following result has been established on the expressive capacity of RWW-automata.

Theorem 2.1.10 ([94]) *There exists an RWW-automaton which accepts a language that is NP-complete with respect to log-space reductions.*

Thus, RWW-automata are already quite expressive. From the definitions above, it is easily seen that the various types of restarting automata yield the hierarchy of language classes that is illustrated in the diagram in Figure 2.1. Of course, it remains to determine which of the inclusions displayed in this diagram are proper. In Section 2.2, we shall study those language classes that are defined by the various types of restarting automata without auxiliary letters. Here we concentrate on those language classes that are defined by restarting automata that may use auxiliary letters. The next result illustrates the general role that auxiliary letters play for restarting automata. It is a slight generalization of a result that has been presented in [185] for RWW- and RRWW-automata.

Theorem 2.1.11 *A language* L *is accepted by a (deterministic) RLWW-automaton if and only if there are a (deterministic) RLW-automaton* M_1 *and a regular language* R *such that* $L = L(M_1) \cap R$.

Proof outline. Let $M = (Q, \Sigma, \Gamma, \triangleright, \triangleleft, q_0, k, \delta)$ be a (deterministic) RLWW-automaton accepting a language $L = L(M) \subseteq \Sigma^*$. By choosing $M_1 = (Q, \Gamma, \Gamma, \triangleright, \triangleleft, q_0, k, \delta)$ and $R = \Sigma^*$, we obtain a (deterministic) RLW-automaton M_1 and a regular language R such that

$$L = L(M) = L_C(M) \cap \Sigma^* = L_C(M_1) \cap \Sigma^* = L(M_1) \cap R.$$

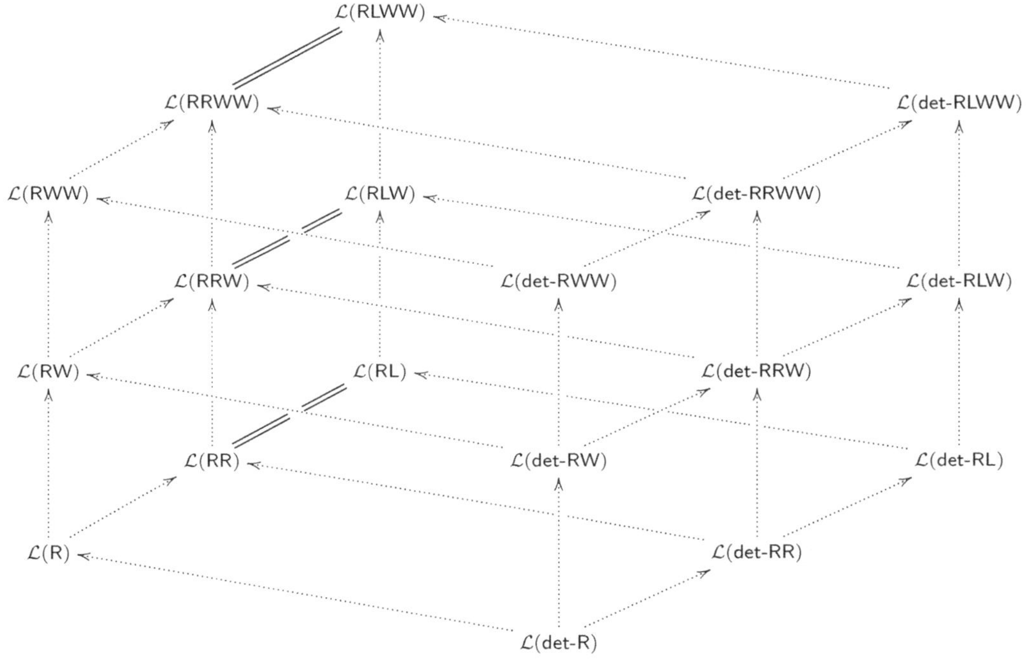

Figure 2.1: Inclusions between the language classes defined by the basic types of restarting automata. The equalities, expressed by =, follow from Theorem 2.1.2, while dotted arrows denote (not necessarily proper) inclusions.

Conversely, let $M_1 = (Q_1, \Gamma, \Gamma, \triangleright, \triangleleft, q_0, k_1, \delta_1)$ be a (deterministic) RLW-automaton, let R be a regular language, and let $L = L(M_1) \cap R$. From M_1 and R, we now construct a (deterministic) RLWW-automaton $M = (Q, \Gamma, \Delta, \triangleright, \triangleleft, q_0, k, \delta)$ such that $L(M) = L$. We take $\Delta = \Gamma \cup \Gamma'$, where $\Gamma' = \{ a' \mid a \in \Gamma \}$ contains marked copies of the letters from Γ, $k = k_1 + 1$, and, for each rewrite transition $(q', v) \in \delta_1(q, u)$ of M_1, M will have rewrite transitions of the form $(q', va') \in \delta(q, ua)$ for all $a \in \Gamma$. Thus, M has essentially the same rewrite transitions as M_1, but, during each rewrite step, the next letter to the right of the rewritten factor is replaced with its marked copy. Actually, also rewrite transitions must be added to M that have marked letters inside u. Then each accepting computation of M corresponds to an accepting computation of M_1, and vice versa. Finally, M is extended in that, in each cycle, it first scans its tape contents, looking for occurrences of marked letters. If there is none, then it realizes that no rewrite step has yet been executed. Accordingly, it checks whether the current tape contents is an element of the regular language R. In the negative, it halts and rejects, while in the affirmative, it executes a cycle of M_1. Since after the simulation of the first cycle of M_1, the tape will contain marked letters, it follows that the membership test for the language R is only executed once in each computation, that is, before the first rewrite step is executed. Hence, it follows that $L(M) = L(M_1) \cap R$. □

Together with the corresponding results from [185], this characterization yields the following closure properties.

Corollary 2.1.12 *The language classes $\mathcal{L}(\mathsf{RLWW})$, $\mathcal{L}(\mathsf{RRWW})$, and $\mathcal{L}(\mathsf{RWW})$ and their deterministic counterparts are closed under the operation of intersection with regular languages.*

Actually, the proof of Theorem 2.1.11, as well as the proofs of the corresponding results for RWW- and RRWW-automata from [185], carry over to weight-reducing restarting automata. Hence, we also have the following results.

Theorem 2.1.13 *A language L is accepted by a (deterministic) sRLWW-automaton (sRRWW-automaton or sRWW-automaton) if and only if there are a (deterministic) sRLW-automaton (sRRW-automaton or sRW-automaton) M_1 and a regular language R such that $L = L(M_1) \cap R$.*

Corollary 2.1.14 *The language classes $\mathcal{L}(\mathsf{sRLWW})$, $\mathcal{L}(\mathsf{sRRWW})$, and $\mathcal{L}(\mathsf{sRWW})$ and their deterministic counterparts are closed under the operation of intersection with regular languages.*

In fact, the nondeterministic language classes above are also closed under some other important operations.

Proposition 2.1.15 ([94]) *The language classes $\mathcal{L}((\mathsf{s})\mathsf{RWW})$, $\mathcal{L}((\mathsf{s})\mathsf{RRWW})$, and $\mathcal{L}((\mathsf{s})\mathsf{RLWW})$ are closed under union and product.*

Proof outline. *Closure under union*: Let M_i $(i = 1, 2)$ be (s)RWW-automata accepting the languages $L_1 \subseteq \Sigma^*$ and $L_2 \subseteq \Sigma^*$, respectively. An RWW-automaton M for the language $L = L_1 \cup L_2$ proceeds as follows. In its first step, M guesses whether to simulate M_1 or M_2. In order to fix this guess for later cycles, M replaces the prefix a_1a_2 of length 2 of its input with an auxiliary letter of the form $[a_1, a_2, 1]$ or $[a_1, a_2, 2]$. In subsequent steps, the indicator $i \in \{1, 2\}$ is preserved, and on seeing i, M simulates the automaton M_i. Hence, M accepts the language L. The same construction works for (s)RRWW- and (s)RLWW-automata.

Closure under product: Let M_i $(i = 1, 2)$ be (s)RRWW-automata accepting the languages L_1 and L_2, respectively. An (s)RRWW-automaton M for the language $L = L_1 \cdot L_2$ is obtained as follows.

First, starting from the initial configuration $q_0 \triangleright w \triangleleft$, M guesses a factorization $w = uv$. In order to fix this guess, M combines the last letter a of u and the first letter b of v into a special auxiliary letter $[a, b]$. As M can scan its tape completely in each cycle, it can ensure that w does not already contain a letter of this form. Then, in subsequent cycles, M simulates M_1 on u, and if M_1 accepts, then M continues with simulating M_2 on v. Thus, M accepts the product $L_1 \cdot L_2$. Obviously, the same idea works for (s)RLWW-automata.

For (s)RWW-automata, the situation is slightly more complicated, as an (s)RWW-automaton does not see the suffix of its tape contents that is to the right of the position of a rewrite step. Hence, M may execute several cycles in which factorizations are guessed and marked by auxiliary letters, proceeding from right to left. However, as we can assume that an (s)RWW-automaton always accepts at the right end of its tape, it can determine whether two or more factorization steps have been performed, in which case M would reject. Hence, we see that, from (s)RWW-automata for L_1 and L_2, an (s)RWW-automaton M for $L_1 \cdot L_2$ can be obtained. □

Recall from [186] that the class CRL of Church-Rosser languages, which coincides with the deterministic classes $\mathcal{L}(\mathsf{det\text{-}(s)RWW})$ and $\mathcal{L}(\mathsf{det\text{-}(s)RRWW})$ (see Theorem 1.9.26 and Corollary 2.1.34), is not closed under union or product.

Proposition 2.1.16 ([94]) *The language classes $\mathcal{L}(\mathsf{(s)RRWW})$ and $\mathcal{L}(\mathsf{(s)RLWW})$ are closed under the operation of reversal.*

Proof outline. As an (s)RLWW-automaton can simply move its window to the right end of the tape and then read the tape contents from right to left, the result is obvious for (s)RLWW-automata.

For (s)RRWW-automata, we observe the following. Let M be an (s)RRWW-automaton accepting the language L. The transition relation of M can be described by a finite sequence of meta-instructions of the form $(\rhd \cdot R_1, u \to v, R_2 \cdot \lhd)$, where R_1 and R_2 are regular languages, and u and v are words that describe a rewrite transition of M. By replacing each meta-instruction of this form by the meta-instruction $(\rhd \cdot R_2^R, u^R \to v^R, R_1^R \cdot \lhd)$, where $R_i^R = \{ w^R \mid w \in R_i \}$, $i = 1, 2$, we obtain an (s)RRWW-automaton that accepts the language L^R. □

It is currently open whether the language class $\mathcal{L}(\mathsf{(s)RWW})$ is closed under reversal, too. Also it remains open whether the language classes $\mathcal{L}(\mathsf{(s)RWW})$ and $\mathcal{L}(\mathsf{(s)RRWW})$ are closed under complementation or intersection.

Problem 2.1.17 (a) *Is the language class $\mathcal{L}(\mathsf{(s)RWW})$ closed under the operation of reversal, that is, for $L \in \mathcal{L}(\mathsf{(s)RWW})$, is the language L^R necessarily in $\mathcal{L}(\mathsf{(s)RWW})$, too?*

(b) *Are the language classes $\mathcal{L}(\mathsf{(s)RWW})$ and $\mathcal{L}(\mathsf{(s)RRWW})$ closed under the operations of intersection and/or complementation?*

On the other hand, it is known that none of these classes is closed under projections.

Proposition 2.1.18 ([94]) *The language classes $\mathcal{L}(\mathsf{(s)RWW})$, $\mathcal{L}(\mathsf{(s)RRWW})$, and $\mathcal{L}(\mathsf{(s)RLWW})$ are not closed under projections.*

Proof. The class GCSL of growing context-sensitive languages is a *basis* for the class RE of recursively enumerable languages, that is, for each recursively enumerable language $L \subseteq \Sigma^*$, there exists a growing context-sensitive language B on some alphabet Δ strictly containing Σ such that $\pi_\Sigma(B) = L$, where π_Σ denotes the projection from Δ^* onto Σ^*. Hence, Theorem 1.9.28 implies that, for each recursively enumerable language L over Σ, there exist an alphabet Γ containing Σ and a language L' over Γ that is accepted by some RWW-automaton such that $L = \Pi_\Sigma(L')$. As $\mathcal{L}(\mathsf{(s)RLWW})$ only contains context-sensitive languages (see Theorem 1.9.29), we see that the above classes are not closed under projections. □

From the definitions, it is obvious that $\mathcal{L}(\mathsf{RWW})$ is contained in $\mathcal{L}(\mathsf{RRWW})$, but the following question is still open.

Problem 2.1.19 *Is $\mathcal{L}(\mathsf{RWW}) \subseteq \mathcal{L}(\mathsf{RRWW})$ a proper inclusion, or do these two language classes coincide?*

In fact, also the following question is still open.

Problem 2.1.20 *Is the language class $\mathcal{L}(\mathsf{RRW})$ contained in the class $\mathcal{L}(\mathsf{RWW})$?*

Actually, these two problems are equivalent.

Proposition 2.1.21 *The language class $\mathcal{L}(\mathsf{RRW})$ is contained in the class $\mathcal{L}(\mathsf{RWW})$ if and only if the classes $\mathcal{L}(\mathsf{RWW})$ and $\mathcal{L}(\mathsf{RRWW})$ coincide.*

Proof. If $\mathcal{L}(\mathsf{RWW}) = \mathcal{L}(\mathsf{RRWW})$, then $\mathcal{L}(\mathsf{RRW}) \subseteq \mathcal{L}(\mathsf{RWW})$ follows from the fact that $\mathcal{L}(\mathsf{RRW}) \subseteq \mathcal{L}(\mathsf{RRWW})$ holds.

Conversely, assume that $\mathcal{L}(\mathsf{RRW}) \subseteq \mathcal{L}(\mathsf{RWW})$, and let $L \in \mathcal{L}(\mathsf{RRWW})$. Then there exists an RRW-automaton M_1 and a regular language R such that $L = L(M_1) \cap R$. As $\mathcal{L}(\mathsf{RRW}) \subseteq \mathcal{L}(\mathsf{RWW})$, there exists an RWW-automaton M_2 such that $L(M_2) = L(M_1)$. Thus, $L(M_2) \cap R = L$. By Corollary 2.1.12, $\mathcal{L}(\mathsf{RWW})$ is closed under intersection with regular languages, which implies that $L = L(M_2) \cap R \in \mathcal{L}(\mathsf{RWW})$. Hence, $\mathcal{L}(\mathsf{RRWW})$ is contained in $\mathcal{L}(\mathsf{RWW})$, and so, these two classes coincide. □

Although it is still open whether the two classes $\mathcal{L}(\mathsf{RWW})$ and $\mathcal{L}(\mathsf{RRWW})$ coincide, at least the following reduction from the latter to the former is known.

Theorem 2.1.22 ([94]) *Let L be a language over Σ, let $f, \triangle, c \notin \Sigma$ be three additional letters, let $r_3 : \Sigma^* \to (\Sigma \cup \{\triangle\})^*$ be the morphism defined through $r_3(a) = a\triangle^2$ for all $a \in \Sigma$, and let the mapping $\varphi : \Sigma^* \to (\Sigma \cup \{f, \triangle, c\})^*$ be defined by taking*

$$\varphi(x) = f^{3\cdot|x|} \cdot r_3(x) \cdot c^{3\cdot|x|}$$

for all $x \in \Sigma^*$. If $L \in \mathcal{L}(\mathsf{RRWW})$, then the language $\varphi(L) = \{\, \varphi(x) \mid x \in L \,\}$ belongs to $\mathcal{L}(\mathsf{RWW})$.

Proof outline. After executing a rewrite step, the RRWW-automaton M for the language L can scan the suffix of its tape contents that is to the right of the position where the rewrite step was executed, while an RWW-automaton M' restarts immediately after executing a rewrite step. Thus, while M may halt and reject, M' may continue the computation and halt and even accept after executing some additional cycles. It follows that it does not suffice for M' to simply simulate the first phase of each cycle of M, that is, the part up to and including the corresponding rewrite step.

In the encoding $\varphi(x) = f^{3\cdot|x|} \cdot r_3(x) \cdot c^{3\cdot|x|}$, the (input) word x is interspersed with factors $\triangle^2$, which yields a word of length $3 \cdot |x|$, and a prefix $f^{3\cdot|x|}$ and a suffix $c^{3\cdot|x|}$ are added. Now an RWW-automaton M' can be designed that processes the word $\varphi(x)$ by simulating the RRWW-automaton M on the inner factor $r_3(x)$ and, simultaneously, processing the prefix $f^{3\cdot|x|}$ and the suffix $c^{3\cdot|x|}$. Each time a rewrite step is to be applied to the suffix $c^{3\cdot|x|}$, M' is forced to read the inner factor derived from $r_3(x)$ completely, and so it will detect whether M would halt in the current cycle. In this way, it is ensured that $L(M') = \varphi(L)$ holds. However, as the details of the construction of M' are technically quite involved, we omit them, referring to [94]. □

2.1.1 On Weight-Reducing Restarting Automata

Here we present several characterizations for the class $\mathcal{L}(\mathsf{sRWW})$ of languages that are accepted by weight-reducing RWW-automata. First, we observe that a weight-reducing R(R)WW-automaton can be transformed into a length-reducing R(R)WW-automaton through a simple morphism. Let $\omega : \Gamma \to \mathbb{N}$ be a weight function, let $\diamond$ be an additional letter, and let $r_\omega : \Gamma^* \to (\Gamma \cup \{\diamond\})^*$ be the morphism that is defined through $a \mapsto a\diamond^{\omega(a)-1}$ for all $a \in \Gamma$. Then r_ω maps each word $w \in \Gamma^*$ to a word $r_\omega(w) \in (\Gamma \cup \{\diamond\})^*$ such that $|r_\omega(w)| = \omega(w)$ holds.

Proposition 2.1.23 *Let M is an sR(R)WW-automaton, and let ω be a weight function that is compatible with M. Then $r_\omega(L(M)) \in \mathcal{L}(\mathsf{R(R)WW})$.*

Proof outline. We concentrate on sRRWW-automata, as the proof for sRWW-automata is completely analogous. Let $M = (Q, \Sigma, \Gamma, \rhd, \lhd, q_0, k, \delta)$ be an sRRWW-automaton that accepts the language $L \subseteq \Sigma^*$, and let $\omega : \Gamma \to \mathbb{N}$ be a weight function that is compatible with M. Thus, $\omega(v) < \omega(u)$ for each rewrite transition $(q', v) \in \delta(q, u)$. We define an RRWW-automaton M' for the language $r_\omega(L)$ as follows. For each meta-instruction $(E_1, u \to v, E_2)$ of M, M' has a meta-instruction of the form $(r_\omega(E_1), r_\omega(u) \to r_\omega(v), r_\omega(E_2))$, where the regular expression $r_\omega(E_i)$ is obtained from the regular expression E_i $(i = 1, 2)$ by replacing each letter $a \in \Gamma$ by its image $r_\omega(a)$. Similarly, for each meta-instruction of the form (E, Accept) of M, there is a corresponding meta-instruction of the form $(r_\omega(E), \mathsf{Accept})$ for M'. It follows easily that M' accepts the language $r_\omega(L)$, and that it is length-reducing. Thus, $r_\omega(L) \in \mathcal{L}(\mathsf{RRWW})$. □

Obviously, $\mathcal{L}(\mathsf{sRWW})$ is a subclass of $\mathcal{L}(\mathsf{sRRWW})$. However, in contrast to the situation for length-reducing restarting automata, the following result has been established in [99] for weight-reducing restarting automata based on Theorem 2.1.22 and Proposition 2.1.23.

Theorem 2.1.24 *Let M be an sRRWW-automaton that accepts a language $L \subseteq \Sigma^*$, and let ω be a weight function that is compatible with M. Then there exists an sRWW-automaton M' such that $L(M') = L(M)$, and M' is compatible with a weight function ω' that satisfies the equality $\omega'(a) = 46 \cdot \omega(a)$ for each input letter $a \in \Sigma$.*

Proof outline. Let $M = (Q, \Sigma, \Gamma, \rhd, \lhd, q_0, k, \delta)$ be an sRRWW-automaton that accepts a language $L \subseteq \Sigma^*$, and let ω be a weight function that is compatible with M. From Proposition 2.1.23, we see that $r_\omega(L) \in \mathcal{L}(\mathsf{RRWW})$, and Theorem 2.1.22 implies that $\varphi(r_\omega(L))$ is accepted by some RWW-automaton M_φ. As φ and r_ω are both injective mappings, it follows that $\varphi(r_\omega(x)) \neq \varphi(r_\omega(y))$ for all $x, y \in \Sigma^*$, $x \neq y$. Thus, we have the following equivalence for all $x \in \Sigma^*$:

$$x \in L \text{ if and only if } \varphi(r_\omega(x)) \in \varphi(r_\omega(L)).$$

To prove Theorem 2.1.24, we present an sRWW-automaton M' that, given a word $x \in \Sigma^*$ as input, first transforms x into the word $z = \varphi(r_\omega(x))$ and then simulates the computation of the RWW-automaton M_φ on input z. The sRWW-automaton M' will accept on input x if and only if z belongs to the language $\varphi(r_\omega(L))$, that is, if and only if x belongs to the language L.

However, the proposed method for transforming x into $\varphi(r_\omega(x))$ is nondeterministic. Thus, for a given word x, there are several different words z that can be produced, only one of them the intended result $\varphi(r_\omega(x))$. Unfortunately, we cannot possibly verify the correctness of the word z produced without destroying it, but we can at least guarantee that $z = \varphi(r_\omega(x))$ if z belongs at all to the set $\varphi(r_\omega(L))$. As the RWW-automaton M_φ accepts only inputs from this set, it follows that this property is sufficient for our purposes.

Here we only give a high-level description of the sRWW-automaton M'. The details of its implementation can be found in [99].

Let $x \in \Sigma^*$ be the given input. The automaton M' proceeds in three stages, which will be illustrated below with an example:

1. Let Δ be a new letter, and let $r_9 : \Sigma^* \to (\Sigma \cup \{\Delta\})^*$ be the morphism that is defined through $a \mapsto a\Delta^8$ for all $a \in \Sigma$. Furthermore, let $A_0 = (\Sigma \cup \{\Delta\}) \times \{\perp\}$ be a new alphabet, the letters of which are interpreted as describing two 'tracks.' The word x is now rewritten deterministically from left to right into a word from A_0^* such that the first track contains the word $y = r_9(r_\omega(x))$, while the second track is empty (we use the symbol $\perp$ to denote 'empty' content).

2. The contents of the second track is rewritten into $f^p \cdot r_3(r_\omega(x)) \cdot c^p$, where $p = |r_3(r_\omega(x))|$. This is achieved by performing the following steps that all preserve the length of the tape:

   (a) $y' = r_3(x')$ is written as a prefix of the contents of the second track for some word x' that is a supersequence of $r_\omega(x)$ (that is, $r_\omega(x)$ is a scattered subsequence of x'). Recall that the first track contains the word $r_9(r_\omega(x))$, that is, an extended version of the word $r_\omega(x)$.

   (b) The second track, containing a word of the form $y' \perp^m$ for some integer m, is rewritten into a word of the form $y'y'' \perp^p$, where $y'' = r_3(x'')$ for a scattered subsequence x'' of x', and $p = m - |y''| > 0$. In order to mark the border between y' and y'', a new subalphabet is used for y''.

Input	$b \; d$
Stage 1	$b \triangle \triangle \triangle \triangle \triangle \triangle \triangle \triangle d \triangle \triangle \triangle \triangle \triangle \triangle \triangle \triangle \diamond \triangle \triangle \triangle \triangle \triangle \triangle \triangle \triangle$
	$\bot \bot \bot \bot \bot \bot \bot \bot \bot \bot \bot \bot \bot \bot \bot \bot \bot \bot \bot \bot \bot \bot \bot \bot \bot \bot \bot$
Stage 2(a)	$b \triangle \triangle \triangle \triangle \triangle \triangle \triangle \triangle d \triangle \triangle \triangle \triangle \triangle \triangle \triangle \triangle \diamond \triangle \triangle \triangle \triangle \triangle \triangle \triangle \triangle$
	$b \triangle \triangle d \triangle \triangle \diamond \triangle \triangle \bot \bot \bot \bot \bot \bot \bot \bot \bot \bot \bot \bot \bot \bot \bot \bot \bot \bot$
Stage 2(b)	$b \triangle \triangle \triangle \triangle \triangle \triangle \triangle \triangle d \triangle \triangle \triangle \triangle \triangle \triangle \triangle \triangle \diamond \triangle \triangle \triangle \triangle \triangle \triangle \triangle \triangle$
	$b \triangle \triangle d \triangle \triangle \diamond \triangle \triangle b \triangle \triangle d \triangle \triangle \diamond \triangle \triangle \bot \bot \bot \bot \bot \bot \bot \bot \bot$
Stage 2(c)	$b \triangle \triangle \triangle \triangle \triangle \triangle \triangle \triangle d \triangle \triangle \triangle \triangle \triangle \triangle \triangle \triangle \diamond \triangle \triangle \triangle \triangle \triangle \triangle \triangle \triangle$
	$f f f f f f f f f b \triangle \triangle d \triangle \triangle \diamond \triangle \triangle c c c c c c c c c$

Figure 2.2: Stages 1 to 2(c) of the computation of M' on input bd, where $\omega(b) = 1$ and $\omega(d) = 2$. Here some extra information has been omitted that is stored by using special letters and that is needed to 'coordinate' the computation.

(c) The current contents of the second track, $y'y'' \bot^p$, is rewritten deterministically from left to right into $z = f^{|y'|}y''c^p$.

3. The computation of the RWW-automaton M_φ on input z is simulated on the second track of the tape. The automaton M' accepts if and only if this computation of M_φ is accepting.

We illustrate the above construction by giving a simple example. Assume that $\Sigma = \{b, d\}$ and that the weight function ω satisfies $\omega(b) = 1$ and $\omega(d) = 2$. In Stages 1–2(c), M' can execute the transformations displayed in Figure 2.2 for the word bd.

Step 1 is a straightforward process that rewrites the tape contents from left to right by replacing each letter a with the word $r_9(r_\omega(a))$. Step 2 (a) is executed as follows. The prefix of the second track is rewritten from left to right, where each rewrite produces a factor of the form $r_3(a)$ for some letter a. At the same time, the first track is rewritten from left to right, where, in each rewrite, a factor of the form $r_9(a)$ is replaced with marked letters. Using the technique from Example 2.1.9 of indexing the rewritten factors alternatingly with 0 or 1, it is ensured that at least one rewrite is executed on the second track between any two rewrites on the first track. As M' restarts immediately after each rewrite step, it may execute several rewrites on the second track before another rewrite on the first track is performed. In this way, we can only guarantee that the word $y' = r_3(x')$ written on the second track satisfies the property that x' is a supersequence of $r_\omega(x)$.

Next Step 2 (b) is executed on the second track by alternatingly rewriting the prefix y' and the suffix $\bot^m$ from left to right. Here we use again the technique from Example 2.1.9, which guarantees that the word produced is $y'' = r_3(x'')$ for a scattered subsequence x'' of x'.

Finally, Step 2 (c) is straightforward, and in Step 3, the RWW-automaton M_φ is simulated on the second track of the tape. For further details, see [99]. □

From Theorem 2.1.24, we immediately get the following equality.

Corollary 2.1.25 ([99]) $\mathcal{L}(\mathsf{sRWW}) = \mathcal{L}(\mathsf{sRRWW})$.

Further characterizations for the language class $\mathcal{L}(\mathsf{sRWW})$ will be presented in Sections 2.3 and 2.5.

2.1.2 On Weakly Monotone Types of Restarting Automata

Here we establish that weakly monotone (shrinking) RWW-automata provide a characterization for the class GCSL of growing context-sensitive languages, while their deterministic variants characterize the class CRL of Church-Rosser languages.

Recall the notion of *weak monotonicity* from Definition 1.9.27. A restarting automaton M is called *weakly monotone* if there exists an integer $c \geq 0$ such that, from one rewrite step to the next within any computation of M, the right distance increases by at most the value c.

While the property of being of type X for some

$$\mathsf{X} \in \{\mathsf{R}, \mathsf{RR}, \mathsf{RL}, \mathsf{RW}, \mathsf{RRW}, \mathsf{RLW}, \mathsf{RWW}, \mathsf{RRWW}, \mathsf{RLWW}\}$$

or of being deterministic are *static* properties of a restarting automaton that can easily be checked by inspecting the transition relation, the property of being weakly monotone is a *dynamic* property, that is, it is a property of the computations of the restarting automaton considered. Thus, the question arises as to how to determine whether a given restarting automaton is weakly monotone.

The next lemma shows that, for a deterministic restarting automaton, this question can always be answered in the affirmative.

Lemma 2.1.26 *Let M be an sRRWW-automaton and let $m \in \mathbb{N}_+$ such that, for each rewrite transition $(q', v) \in \delta(q, u)$ of M, $|v| \leq m$. If M is deterministic, then it is weakly monotone of degree $m - 1$.*

Proof. Let $M = (Q, \Sigma, \Gamma, \rhd, \lhd, q_0, k, \delta)$ be an sRRWW-automaton, let $m \in \mathbb{N}$ be the length of the longest word that M can write within a single rewrite step, and let

$$\rhd uqvw\lhd \vdash_M \rhd uzq'w\lhd \vdash_M^* q_0\rhd uzw\lhd \vdash_M^* \rhd u_1q_1v_1w_1\lhd \vdash_M \rhd u_1z_1q_1'w_1\lhd$$

be a part of a computation of M, where $(q', z) \in \delta(q, v)$ and $(q_1', z_1) \in \delta(q_1, v_1)$ are rewrite transitions and the sub-computation $\rhd uzq'w\lhd \vdash_M^* \rhd u_1q_1v_1w_1\lhd$ does not contain any rewrite step. Then $D_r(\rhd uqvw\lhd) = |vw| + 1$ and $D_r(\rhd u_1q_1v_1w_1\lhd) = |v_1w_1| + 1$. If M is deterministic, then the fact that, within the computation considered, M executes the rewrite step $\rhd uqvw\lhd \vdash_M \rhd uzq'w\lhd$ implies that, starting from the restart configuration $q_0\rhd uvw\lhd$, M performs MVR steps until it reaches the configuration $\rhd uqvw\lhd$. Thus, starting from the restart configuration $q_0\rhd u_1v_1w_1\lhd = q_0\rhd uzw\lhd$, M performs MVR steps until its window contains the first letter of zw. Hence, it follows that $|u_1v_1| > |u|$, and so, $|v_1w_1| < |zw| + k$. This implies that

$$D_r(\rhd u_1q_1v_1w_1\lhd) = |v_1w_1| + 1 \leq k + |zw| \leq k + m + |w| = D_r(\rhd uqvw\lhd) + (m - 1).$$

Thus, M is weakly monotone of degree $m - 1$. □

Actually, the proof above shows that, if $|v| = 0$ for each rewrite transition $(q', v) \in \delta(q, u)$ of M, then M is *strictly monotone*, that is, the right distance strictly decreases from any rewrite configuration to the next in any computation of M. Lemma 2.1.26 shows that weak monotonicity can be seen as a generalization of the notion of determinism.

For nondeterministic restarting automata, the situation is more complicated. The next lemma gives at least an upper bound for the degree of weak monotonicity of a nondeterministic restarting automaton that is weakly monotone.

Lemma 2.1.27 ([158]) *Let $M = (Q, \Gamma, \Gamma, \rhd, \lhd, q_0, k, \delta)$ be a weakly monotone RRW-automaton. Then M is weakly c-monotone for some constant $c < |Q|^2 \cdot |\Gamma|^k + 2k$.*

Proof. Let C_1 and C_2 be two successive cycles of a computation of M such that $D_r(C_2) = D_r(C_1) + c$, that is, C_1 contains a rewrite step $\rhd xq_1uy\lhd \vdash_M \rhd xvq_1'y\lhd$, and C_2 contains a rewrite step $\rhd x'q_2u'y'\lhd \vdash_M \rhd x'v'q_2'y'\lhd$, where $q_1, q_1', q_2, q_2' \in Q$, $xvy = x'u'y'$, and $|uy\lhd| + c = |u'y'\lhd|$.

Assume that $c \geq |Q|^2 \cdot |\Gamma|^k + 2k$. Then $x = x_1x_2$, where $x'u' = x_1$, $x_2vy = y'$, and $|x_2v| = c$ implying that $|x_2| > |Q|^2 \cdot |\Gamma|^k + k$. As we can assume that M scans its tape completely from left to right during each cycle, we see that, during both cycles C_1 and C_2, the automaton M

executes $|x_2|$ MVR-steps while moving its read/write window across x_2. Let $x_2 = a_1a_2\cdots a_n$, where $a_1, a_2, \ldots, a_n \in \Gamma$ and $n = |x_2|$. With each letter a_i of x_2, we now associate a pair of states (p_1^i, p_2^i) by choosing p_j^i as the state of M at the moment when a_i is the first letter in the read/write window during the cycle C_j $(j = 1, 2)$. As $|x_2| > |Q|^2 \cdot |\Gamma|^k + k$, we see that x_2 admits a factorization of the form $x_2 = z_1az_2az_3$, where $a \in \Gamma$, $z_1, z_2, z_3 \in \Gamma^*$, and $|z_3| \geq k-1$, such that both distinguished occurrences of a have the same associated pair of states (p, p'), and the read/write window has the same contents when these occurrences of the letter a are in the first position of the read/write window. Hence, for each $m \geq 0$, the following is a valid computation of M:

$$\begin{array}{llll} q_0\rhd x_1z_1(az_2)^m az_3uy\lhd & \vdash_M^* & \rhd x_1z_1p(az_2)^m az_3uy\lhd & \vdash_M^* \\ \rhd x_1z_1(az_2)^m paz_3uy\lhd & \vdash_M^* & q_0\rhd x_1z_1(az_2)^m az_3vy\lhd & = \\ q_0\rhd x'u'z_1(az_2)^m az_3vy\lhd & \vdash_M^* & \rhd x'v'z_1p'(az_2)^m az_3vy\lhd & \vdash_M^* \\ \rhd x'v'z_1(az_2)^m p'az_3vy\lhd & \vdash_M^* & q_0\rhd x'v'z_1(az_2)^m az_3vy\lhd, & \end{array}$$

where the first rewrite step has right distance $k + |y| + 1$, while the second rewrite step has right distance $k + |z_1| + (1 + |z_2|) \cdot m + |z_3vy| + 2$. As this holds for all $m \geq 0$, we conclude that M is not weakly j-monotone for any integer j, that is, M is not weakly monotone. This contradiction proves the upper bound for the degree of weak monotonicity of M. □

In addition, we have the following decidability result.

Theorem 2.1.28 ([158]) *The following problem can be solved algorithmically:*

INSTANCE :	*An RRW-automaton M, and a constant $c \in \mathbb{N}$.*
QUESTION :	*Is M weakly c-monotone?*

Proof outline. Given an RRW-automaton M and a constant $c \in \mathbb{N}$, an NFA $A_{M,c}$ can be constructed such that the language $L(A_{M,c})$ accepted by $A_{M,c}$ is non-empty if and only if M admits a computation $C_1 \vdash_M^c C_2$ satisfying $D_r(C_2) > D_r(C_1) + c$, that is, if and only if M is *not* weakly c-monotone. This construction is a slight variant of the corresponding construction used in [87] to show that monotonicity of RRW-automata is decidable (see below). □

Together with the Lemma 2.1.27, this theorem has the following consequence.

Corollary 2.1.29 ([158]) *It is decidable whether an RRW-automaton M is weakly monotone. In the affirmative, the smallest integer c can be determined for which M is weakly c-monotone.*

It remains open whether weak monotonicity is decidable for RRWW-automata in general. Here the problem stems from the fact that, for an RRWW-automaton, weak monotonicity is only required for those computations that begin with a proper initial configuration, that is, restarting configurations that cannot be reached from an initial configuration are not considered.

Problem 2.1.30

(a) *For $c \in \mathbb{N}_+$, is it decidable whether an RRWW-automaton is weakly c-monotone?*

(b) *Is it decidable whether an RRWW-automaton is weakly monotone?*

Concerning the expressive capacity of weakly monotone sRRWW-automata, the following upper bound is known, which is a generalization of a result that was established in [94].

Theorem 2.1.31 $\mathcal{L}(\mathsf{wmon\text{-}sRRWW}) \subseteq \mathsf{GCSL}$.

Proof. Let $M = (Q, \Sigma, \Gamma, \rhd, \lhd, q_0, k, \delta)$ be an sRRWW-automaton that is weakly monotone of degree $c \geq 0$, let $L = L(M)$, and let ω be a weight function that is compatible with M. It is easily seen that we can make the following assumption about M:

- After performing a rewrite step, M continues with MVR steps until the window only contains the right sentinel $\lhd$, and then M either

(1) halts and accepts, or

(2) halts and rejects, or

(3) executes a restart step.

Accordingly, we can associate two subsets $Q_+(w)$ and $Q_{\mathrm{rs}}(w)$ of Q with each word $w \in \Gamma^+$ as follows:

$Q_+(w) = \{\, q \in Q \mid$ *There is a computation of M that, starting from the configuration $\rhd qw \lhd$, performs only MVR steps until the window just contains the $\lhd$-symbol, and that halts and accepts then* $\}$,

$Q_{\mathrm{rs}}(w) = \{\, q \in Q \mid q \notin Q_+(w)$, *but there is a computation of M that, starting from the configuration $\rhd qw \lhd$, performs only MVR steps until the window just contains the $\lhd$-symbol, and that restarts then* $\}$.

After performing a rewrite step, M is in a configuration of the form $\rhd xvqw \lhd$. If the sets $Q_+(w)$ and $Q_{\mathrm{rs}}(w)$ were known, then, instead of simulating the corresponding computation step by step, we could simply accept, if $q \in Q_+(w)$, make a restart, if $q \in Q_{\mathrm{rs}}(w)$, or halt and reject, otherwise.

By Theorem 1.2.17, the class GCSL of growing context-sensitive languages coincides with the class of languages that are accepted by shrinking TPDAs. Therefore, in order to prove the intended inclusion, it suffices to present a shrinking TPDA for the language L. Accordingly, we now describe a shrinking TPDA A that simulates the sRRWW-automaton M. Given a word z as input, this TPDA will keep track of the sets $Q_+(w)$ and $Q_{\mathrm{rs}}(w)$ for each suffix w of the actual tape contents. In this way, we can combine the rewrite steps and the restart steps of M. The pushdown stores of A will have two, respectively three, tracks in order to store these sets and information on previous states of M:

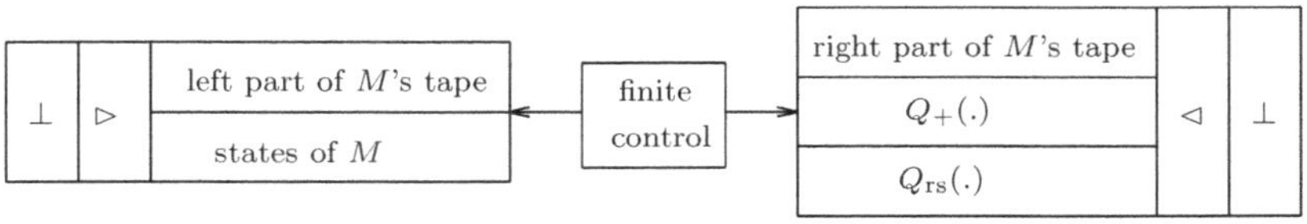

The shrinking TPDA A will work in two phases.

Phase 1 (Initialization): Proceeding from right to left, A prints encodings of the two sets $Q_+(w)$ and $Q_{\mathrm{rs}}(w)$ underneath the first letter of w for each suffix w of the given input. This process is realized in two steps:

(a) First, A shifts the tape contents z from the second pushdown onto the first pushdown (using an appropriate copy alphabet to make this process weight-reducing).

(b) Pushing z back onto the second pushdown, the corresponding sets $Q_+(.)$ and $Q_{\mathrm{rs}}(.)$ are written on tracks 2 and 3.

Phase 2 (Simulation): The TPDA A now simulates M step by step, where we assume that A sees the topmost $k+1$ symbols on each pushdown, that is, it uses pushdown windows of size $k+1$. We distinguish between the MVR steps of M and the rewrite steps of M. While performing MVR steps, the sRRWW-automaton M behaves essentially like a finite-state acceptor. Hence, the first part of each cycle of a computation of M can be simulated deterministically. Nondeterminism may come in as soon as a rewrite step is enabled. We now distinguish between the various transition steps that M may execute.

(a) Simulating a MVR step of M: Let $\rhd uq_1avw \lhd \vdash_M \rhd uaq_2vw \lhd$ be a MVR step of M, where $a \in \Gamma$ and $|v| = k-1$. The configuration of A that encodes the configuration $\rhd uq_1avw \lhd$ of M looks as follows:

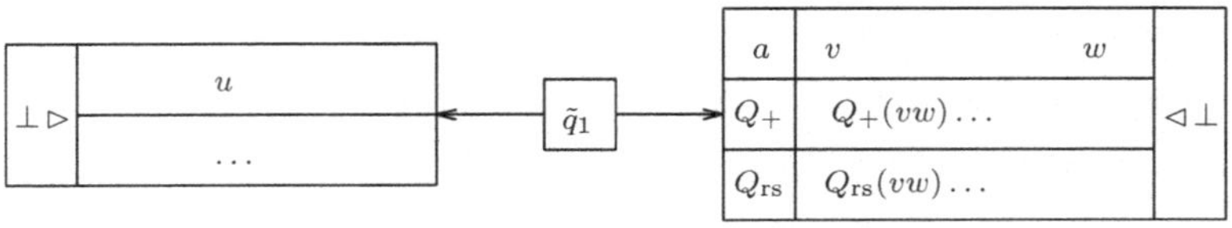

Here $Q_+ = Q_+(avw)$ and $Q_{\rm rs} = Q_{\rm rs}(avw)$. Furthermore, the state $\tilde{q}_1$ of A encodes the fact that M is in state q_1. In a single step, A transforms this configuration into the following one, thus simulating the above MVR step of M:

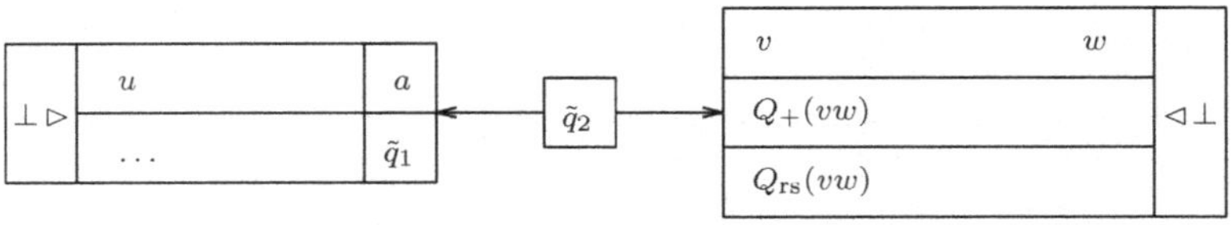

Here the state $\tilde{q}_2$ of A encodes the fact that M is now in state q_2. Observe that on the second track of its first pushdown, A stores the actual state in which it was when it pushed the letter a onto that pushdown.

(b) Simulating a rewrite step of M: Let $\rhd uq_1vw\lhd \vdash_M \rhd uyq_2w\lhd$ be a rewrite step of M, where $|v| = k$ and $\omega(v) > \omega(y)$. Then $|y| \leq \omega(y) < \omega(v) \leq c_0 \cdot |v| = c_0 \cdot k$, where $c_0 = \max\{\, \omega(a) \mid a \in \Gamma \,\}$. Observe that the right distance of the current cycle is $|w| + k + 1$. Now we distinguish between three cases:

Case 1. If $q_2 \in Q_+(w)$, then M will accept. Accordingly, A enters an ERASE-state, erases the contents of its pushdowns, and accepts.

Case 2. If q_2 is neither in $Q_+(w)$ nor in $Q_{\rm rs}(w)$, then M will reject. Accordingly, A enters an ERASE-state, erases the contents of its pushdowns, and rejects.

Case 3. If $q_2 \in Q_{\rm rs}(w)$, then the current cycle of M can be completed by

$$\rhd uyq_2w\lhd \vdash^*_{\rm MVR} \rhd uywq_3\lhd \vdash_{\rm Restart} q_0\rhd uyw\lhd$$

for some state q_3. The configuration of A that corresponds to the configuration $\rhd uq_1vw\lhd$ of M looks as follows, where $u = u_1u_2$ and $|u_2| = k + c$:

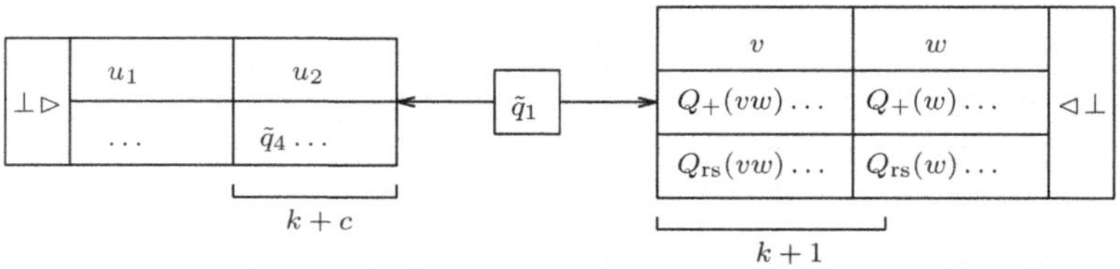

As M is weakly monotone of degree c, the next cycle of M's computation begins with some MVR steps, if $|\rhd uy| > k + c$. In fact, M will perform MVR steps until the distance of its window from the right end of the tape has decreased to $c + k + |w| + 1$. Accordingly, M's computation continues with $q_0\rhd uyw\lhd \vdash^*_{\rm MVR} \rhd u_1q_4u_2yw\lhd$, where $u = u_1u_2$ and $|u_2| = k + c$. As long as the window is inside the prefix $\rhd u$, the state transitions executed as part of these MVR steps will be the same as the ones during the previous cycle.

The TPDA A now simulates the rewrite step, the following MVR steps, the restart step, and the subsequent sequence of MVR steps by a single step, which transforms the above configuration into the following one, which corresponds to $\rhd u_1q_4u_2yw\lhd$:

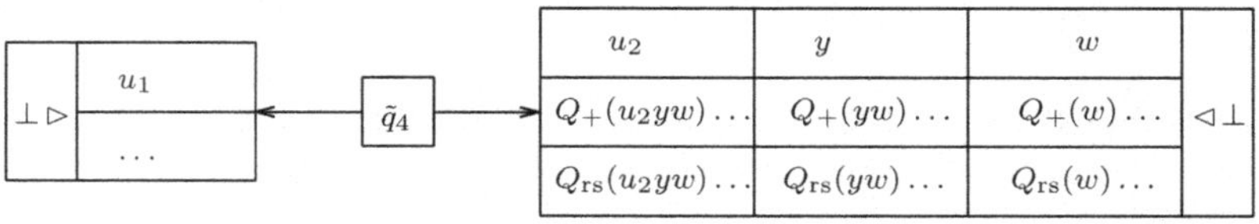

Here the sets $Q_+(.)$ and $Q_{\mathrm{rs}}(.)$ underneath the letters of u_2y on the second pushdown are computed from $Q_+(w)$ and $Q_{\mathrm{rs}}(w)$ based on the transition function of M. In case $|u| < k + c$, the first pushdown will only contain the bottom marker $\perp$, and A will be in the state that corresponds to the initial state of M.

It is easily seen that A can simulate M in this way. This shows that $L(A) = L(M) = L$ holds. Obviously steps 1 and 2(a) can be realized in a weight-reducing manner. In fact, we can choose the weight function for A in such a way that by shifting a letter from the second pushdown to the first, the weight of the configuration of A is reduced by one.

Concerning step 2(b), we see that $|u_2| = c + k$. Hence, by shifting the letters of u_2 from the first pushdown to the second, we increase the overall weight of the configuration of A by $c + k$. However, $\omega(v) \geq \omega(y) + 1$. Hence, if we choose $\omega'(a) = 2 \cdot (c + k) \cdot \omega(a)$ for all $a \in \Gamma$, then we decrease the weight of the configuration of A by at least $2 \cdot (c + k)$ when we replace the factor v with y. Thus, step 2(b) can also be realized in a weight-reducing manner. This shows that A is indeed a shrinking TPDA for L, which completes the proof of Theorem 2.1.31. □

On the other hand, we have the following lower bound result.

Theorem 2.1.32 $\mathsf{GCSL} \subseteq \mathcal{L}(\mathsf{wmon\text{-}RWW})$.

Proof. Let L be a growing context-sensitive language. By Theorem 1.2.17, there exists a length-reducing TPDA $A = (Q, \Sigma, \Gamma, \delta, k, q_0, \perp, F)$ such that $L(A) = L$. From A, we can construct an RWW-automaton $M = (Q', \Sigma, \Gamma', \rhd, \lhd, q_0', k', \delta')$ that simulates the computations of A. We choose $k' = 2k+1$, and we encode a configuration $\perp xqy \perp$ of A by the tape contents $\rhd \overline{x} qy \lhd$ of M, where $\overline{x}$ is a copy of x consisting of marked letters. The RWW-automaton M simply moves its read/write window from left to right across its tape looking for the encoded version $\overline{u}qv$ of the left-hand side of a transition $(p, u', v') \in \delta(q, u, v)$ of A. Once M discovers the factor $\overline{u}qv$, it rewrites it by $\overline{u'}pv'$ and restarts. As A is length-reducing, we have $|uv| > |u'v'|$, which shows that the above is an admissible rewrite transition of an RWW-automaton.

There is only one slight technical problem with this simulation. Given a string $w \in \Sigma^*$ as input, the length-reducing TPDA starts with the initial configuration $\perp q_0 w \perp$. The corresponding configuration of M would be $q_0' \rhd q_0 w \lhd$, but actually M starts with the initial configuration $q_0' \rhd w \lhd$. However, we can assume that A reduces the combined length of its two pushdown stores by at least two in each step (see [186]). Thus, M can print the current state symbol of A onto its tape while simulating the first step of A's computation. Thus, if the first step of A is the transition

$$\perp q_0 w \perp \; = \; \perp q_0 uz \perp \; \vdash_A \; \perp u' q_1 v' z \perp,$$

then $|u| \geq |u'| + |v'| + 2$, and M simulates this step by the cycle

$$q_0' \rhd w \lhd = q_0' \rhd uz \lhd \vdash_M^c q_0' \rhd \overline{u'} q_1 v' z \lhd .$$

The marked letters are needed to distinguish the first cycle of a computation of M from the subsequent cycles.

It is easily seen that $L(M) = L(A) = L$ holds. Furthermore, as each rewrite step of M, apart from the first one in a simulation, includes the unique state symbol of A that currently occurs in the tape inscription of M, each computation of M is weakly monotone of degree $k - 1$. □

Together with Theorem 2.1.2, Theorems 2.1.31 and 2.1.32 yield the following characterizations extending Theorem 1.9.28.

Corollary 2.1.33 $\mathsf{GCSL} = \mathcal{L}(\mathsf{wmon\text{-}(s)R(R)WW}) = \mathcal{L}(\mathsf{wmon\text{-}(s)RLWW})$.

As by Lemma 2.1.26, each deterministic sRRWW-automaton is weakly monotone, the proofs of Theorems 2.1.31 and 2.1.32 extend to the deterministic case. Together with Theorem 1.2.19, this yields the following characterization for the class CRL of Church-Rosser languages, which extends Theorem 1.9.26.

Corollary 2.1.34 $\mathsf{CRL} = \mathcal{L}(\mathsf{det\text{-}(s)R(R)WW})$.

As we saw in Example 2.1.9, the marked copy language $L'_{\text{copy}} = \{ w\#w \mid w \in \{a,b\}^* \}$ is accepted by an RWW-automaton. In fact, it is easy to extend that RWW-automaton to a deterministic RLWW-automaton for L'_{copy}. Instead of guessing which of the two factors from $\{a,b\}^*$ to rewrite next, a deterministic RLWW-automaton can first inspect the complete tape contents and decide then on the place of rewriting. As the language L'_{copy} is not growing context-sensitive, we obtain the following results.

Corollary 2.1.35

(a) $\mathcal{L}(\mathsf{det\text{-}sRRWW}) \subsetneq \mathcal{L}(\mathsf{det\text{-}RLWW}) \subseteq \mathcal{L}(\mathsf{det\text{-}sRLWW})$.

(b) $\mathcal{L}(\mathsf{det\text{-}RLWW}) \not\subseteq \mathcal{L}(\mathsf{wmon\text{-}sRLWW})$.

However, the following related problems are still open.

Problem 2.1.36

(a) *Is each growing context-sensitive language accepted by a deterministic (s)RLWW-automaton, that is, is the class of growing context-sensitive language GCSL contained in* $\mathcal{L}(\mathsf{det\text{-}(s)RLWW})$*? In fact, it is not even known whether each context-free language is accepted by a deterministic (s)RLWW-automaton.*

(b) *Is the inclusion of* $\mathcal{L}(\mathsf{det\text{-}RLWW})$ *in* $\mathcal{L}(\mathsf{det\text{-}sRLWW})$ *a proper one?*

Also it is still open whether the inclusion of $\mathcal{L}(\mathsf{det\text{-}sRLWW})$ in $\mathcal{L}(\mathsf{sRLWW})$ is proper. By Theorem 2.1.10, the class $\mathcal{L}(\mathsf{RWW})$ contains a language that is NP-complete. On the other hand, Corollary 1.9.16 shows that $\mathcal{L}(\mathsf{det\text{-}sRLWW})$ is contained in the complexity class $\mathsf{DTIMESPACE}(n^2, n)$, and therewith, it is contained in the class P. Hence, we obtain the following separation result.

Corollary 2.1.37 *If* $\mathsf{P} \neq \mathsf{NP}$, *then* $\mathcal{L}(\mathsf{RWW}) \not\subseteq \mathcal{L}(\mathsf{det\text{-}sRLWW})$ *and* $\mathcal{L}(\mathsf{det\text{-}sRLWW}) \subsetneq \mathcal{L}(\mathsf{sRLWW})$.

2.1.3 On Monotone Types of Restarting Automata

We now turn to monotone restarting automata. As monotonicity is a proper restriction of weak monotonicity, we would expect that monotone restarting automata are strictly less expressive than weakly monotone restarting automata. This is indeed the case, both for nondeterministic as well as for deterministic restarting automata. First, we establish the following upper bound, which generalizes a result from [87] on monotone RRWW-automata.

Theorem 2.1.38 $\mathcal{L}(\mathsf{mon\text{-}sRRWW}) \subseteq \mathsf{CFL}$.

Proof outline. Let $M = (Q, \Sigma, \Gamma, \rhd, \lhd, q_0, k, \delta)$ be a monotone sRRWW-automaton, let ω be a weight function that is compatible with M, and let $L = L(M)$. As M is monotone, each computation of M is monotone, that is, in each computation of M, the right distance does not increase from any rewrite step to the next. Hence, if

$$\begin{array}{llllllll} q_0\rhd xuy\lhd & \vdash^{|x|+1}_{\mathsf{MVR}} & \rhd xq_1uy\lhd & \vdash_{\mathsf{Rewrite}} & \rhd xvq_2y\lhd & \vdash^{|y|}_{\mathsf{MVR}} & \rhd xvyq_3\lhd \\ & \vdash_{\mathsf{Restart}} & q_0\rhd xvy\lhd & = & q_0\rhd x_1u_1y_1\lhd & & \\ & \vdash^{|x_1|+1}_{\mathsf{MVR}} & \rhd x_1q_4u_1y_1\lhd & \vdash_{\mathsf{Rewrite}} & \rhd x_1v_1q_5y_1\lhd, & & \end{array}$$

where $(q_2, v) \in \delta(q_1, u)$ and $(q_5, v_1) \in \delta(q_4, u_1)$ are rewrite transitions, then

$$D_r(\rhd x_1q_4u_1y_1\lhd) = |y_1| + k + 1 \leq |y| + k + 1 = D_r(\rhd xq_1uy\lhd).$$

Thus, y_1 is a suffix of y and xv is a prefix of x_1u_1, which implies that $|x_1| \geq |xv| - k$.

We simulate M with a PDA A that works as follows. For the cycle $q_0\rhd xuy\lhd \vdash^{c}_{M} q_0\rhd xvy\lhd$, the prefix $\rhd x$ of the tape contents is stored on the pushdown of A, the factor u is stored in the finite-state control of A, and the suffix $y\lhd$ is stored on the input tape of A. As in the simulation of a weakly monotone sRRWW-automaton by a weight-reducing TPDA (see the proof of Theorem 2.1.31), information on the states of M that are entered by MVR steps is stored together with the prefix $\rhd x$ on the pushdown. Now it is easily seen how the rewrite steps of M can be simulated by A.

However, there still is a problem that we need to overcome. After executing a rewrite step, the sRRWW-automaton M scans the suffix of the current tape contents, checks whether this suffix belongs to a certain regular language, and restarts (or accepts or rejects) at the end of the tape. In the aforementioned simulation of a weakly monotone sRRWW-automaton by a weight-reducing TPDA, we have precomputed the corresponding information in the form of the sets Q_+ and Q_{rs}, which were stored together with the letters of the suffix $y\lhd$. Unfortunately, here we cannot do this, as A is just a PDA. Thus, we need to store the states that M reaches by its rewrite steps in the finite-state control of A. When reading further letters from the input tape, this state information must be updated. Finally, when the right sentinel is reached, A must check that all the required restart (and accept) steps are indeed possible. The detailed description of this simulation can be found in [87]. □

As the proof of Theorem 2.1.38 carries over to the deterministic case, we obtain the following corresponding result.

Corollary 2.1.39 $\mathcal{L}(\mathsf{det\text{-}mon\text{-}sRRWW}) \subseteq \mathsf{DCFL}$.

However, also the converse inclusions hold. In fact, for the nondeterministic case, we have the following result.

Theorem 2.1.40 $\mathsf{CFL} \subseteq \mathcal{L}(\mathsf{mon\text{-}RWW})$.

Proof outline. In [182], it is shown how to construct a monotone RWW-automaton of window size three from a given context-free grammar. Here, following [163, 164], we present a modification of that construction, which yields an RWW-automaton of window size two.

Let $L \subseteq \Sigma^*$ be a context-free language, and let $G = (N, \Sigma, S, P)$ be a context-free grammar for L. Without loss of generality, we may assume that the production rules in P have the following form, which is easily obtained from the Chomsky normal form:

$$\begin{array}{lll} (1) & S \to \lambda, & \text{if } \lambda \in L, \\ (2) & S \to a, & \text{if } a \in \Sigma \cap L, \\ (3) & A \to BC, & \text{where } A \in N \text{ and } B, C \in (N \smallsetminus \{S\}) \cup \Sigma. \end{array}$$

Now we define an RWW-automaton $M = (Q, \Sigma, \Gamma, \rhd, \lhd, q_0, 2, \delta)$, where $Q = \{q_0, q, q_+\}$ and

$$\Gamma = N \cup \Sigma \cup \{\, (A, B) \mid A, B \in N \cup \Sigma \,\},$$

and we define a morphism $\pi \colon \Gamma^* \to (N \cup \Sigma)^*$ by taking

$$\pi(A) = A \text{ and } \pi((A, B)) = AB \text{ for all } A, B \in N \cup \Sigma.$$

Thus, M uses the nonterminals A of G and the pairs of the form (A, B) with $A, B \in N \cup \Sigma$ as auxiliary letters for representing the words A and AB, respectively. The transition relation δ of M is defined as follows, where $A, B, C \in N \cup \Sigma$ and $X \in N \smallsetminus \{S\}$:

$$\begin{array}{lll} (1) & \delta(q_0, \rhd \cdot \lhd) = \{\mathsf{Accept}\} & \text{if } (S \to \lambda) \in P, \\ (2) & \delta(q_0, \rhd\gamma) \ni (q_+, \mathsf{MVR}) & \text{for } \gamma \in \Gamma \text{ such that } (S \to \pi(\gamma)) \in P, \\ (3) & \delta(q_+, \gamma\lhd) = \{\mathsf{Accept}\} & \text{for } \gamma \in \Gamma \text{ such that } (S \to \pi(\gamma)) \in P, \\ (4) & \delta(q_0, \rhd\gamma) \ni (q, \mathsf{MVR}) & \text{for all } \gamma \in \Gamma, \\ (5) & \delta(q, AB) \ni (A, B) & \text{for all } A, B \in N \cup \Sigma, \\ (6) & \delta(q, AB) \ni C & \text{if } (C \to AB) \in P, \\ (7) & \delta(q, (A, B)\gamma) \ni (q, \mathsf{MVR}) & \text{for } \gamma \in \Gamma, \\ (8) & \delta(q, (A, B)C) \ni (A, X) & \text{if } (X \to BC) \in P, \\ (9) & \delta(q, (A, B)C) \ni X & \text{if } (X \to AZ), (Z \to BC) \in P \text{ for some } Z \in N. \end{array}$$

Obviously, M is an RWW-automaton of window size two. The encoding of two letters $A, B \in N \cup \Sigma$ as a single letter (A, B) is used to mark the position in the actual sentential form that has to be examined in the next step. Thus, the tape contents always consists of a sequence of pairs followed by a sequence of letters from $N \cup \Sigma$, where any of these two subsequences can be empty. Since each rewrite step is performed at the border between these two subsequences, it follows that M is monotone.

It remains to verify that M accepts the context-free language L. It is easily seen that an accepting computation of M constructs a G-derivation for the given input in reverse order. Hence, we have $L(M) \subseteq L$.

On the other hand, let $w \in L$. If $w = \lambda$, then $w \in L(M)$. So assume that $|w| \geq 1$. Then there exists a right-most G-derivation

$$S \Rightarrow_G \alpha_1 \Rightarrow_G \alpha_2 \Rightarrow_G \cdots \Rightarrow_G \alpha_n = w.$$

From the form of the productions in P, we see that, for $n = 1$, $|\alpha_1| \leq 2$, and for $n \geq 2$, $|\alpha_i| = i + 1$ for all $i = 1, 2, \ldots, n$.

If $n = 1$ or $n = 2$, then a detailed case analysis shows that $q_0 \rhd w \lhd \vdash_M^* \mathsf{Accept}$, that is, $w \in L(M)$. If $n \geq 3$, then, for all $2 \leq i \leq n - 1$, $\alpha_{i-1} \Rightarrow_G \alpha_i \Rightarrow_G \alpha_{i+1}$ is a part of the right-most derivation above. Hence, we can conclude that

$$\alpha_i = B_1 B_2 \cdots B_m A a_1 a_2 \cdots a_r \text{ and } \alpha_{i+1} = B_1 B_2 \cdots B_m C D a_1 a_2 \cdots a_r$$

for some $B_1, B_2, \ldots, B_m \in N \cup \Sigma$, $(A \to CD) \in P$, and $a_1, a_2, \ldots, a_r \in \Sigma$, where $m + r = i$. Furthermore,

$$\alpha_{i-1} = B_1 B_2 \cdots B_m X a_2 a_3 \cdots a_r \text{ for some } (X \to A a_1) \in P, \tag{2.1}$$

or

$$\alpha_{i-1} = B_1 B_2 \cdots B_{m-1} X a_1 a_2 \cdots a_r \text{ for some } (X \to B_m A) \in P, \tag{2.2}$$

or

$$\alpha_{i-1} = B_1 B_2 \cdots B_m A a_1 \cdots a_{s-1} X a_{s+2} \cdots a_r \text{ for some } s \geq 1 \text{ and } (X \to a_s a_{s+1}) \in P. \tag{2.3}$$

It can now be checked (see [164]) that, in case m is even,

$$q_0 \rhd (B_1, B_2) \cdots (B_{m-1}, B_m) C D a_1 a_2 \cdots a_r \lhd \vdash_M^* \mathsf{Accept}, \tag{2.4}$$

and in case m is odd,

$$q_0 \rhd (B_1, B_2) \cdots (B_{m-2}, B_{m-1})(B_m, C) D a_1 a_2 \cdots a_r \lhd \vdash_M^* \mathsf{Accept}, \tag{2.5}$$

where, in either case, the first rewrite step is of the form (6), (8), or (9), based on the production $(A \to CD) \in P$.

For $i = n - 1$, let $\alpha_{n-1} = a_1 a_2 \cdots a_{m-1} A a_{m+1} a_{m+2} \cdots a_{n+1}$, where $(A \to a_m a_{m+1}) \in P$ is the production that rewrites α_{n-1} into $\alpha_n = w$ and $a_1, a_2, \ldots, a_{n+1} \in \Sigma$. Then the computations (2.4) and (2.5) imply that

$$\begin{array}{rcl} q_0 \rhd w \lhd & = & q_0 \rhd a_1 a_2 \cdots a_{m-1} a_m a_{m+1} a_{m+2} \cdots a_{n+1} \lhd \\ & \vdash_M^* & q_0 \rhd (a_1, a_2) \cdots (a_{m-2}, a_{m-1}) a_m a_{m+1} a_{m+2} \cdots a_{n+1} \lhd \\ & \vdash_M^* & \mathsf{Accept} \end{array}$$

or

$$\begin{array}{rcl} q_0 \rhd w \lhd & = & q_0 \rhd a_1 a_2 \cdots a_{m-1} a_m a_{m+1} a_{m+2} \cdots {}_{n+1} \lhd \\ & \vdash_M^* & q_0 \rhd (a_1, a_2) \cdots (a_{m-3}, a_{m-2})(a_{m-1}, a_m) a_{m+1} a_{m+2} \cdots a_{n+1} \lhd \\ & \vdash_M^* & \mathsf{Accept} \end{array}$$

depending on the parity of m. It follows that $w \in L(M)$. Thus, we have $L(M) = L$. □

Together with Theorem 2.1.2, Theorems 2.1.38 and 2.1.40 yield the following characterization, which extends Theorem 1.9.24(b).

Corollary 2.1.41 $\mathsf{CFL} = \mathcal{L}(\mathsf{mon}\text{-}(\mathsf{s})\mathsf{R}(\mathsf{R})\mathsf{WW}) = \mathcal{L}(\mathsf{mon}\text{-}(\mathsf{s})\mathsf{RLWW})$.

For the deterministic case, we even have the following stronger result.

Theorem 2.1.42 ([85, 87]) $\mathsf{DCFL} \subseteq \mathcal{L}(\mathsf{det}\text{-}\mathsf{mon}\text{-}\mathsf{R})$.

Proof outline. Let $L \subseteq \Sigma^*$ be a deterministic context-free language. Then $L \cdot \{\lhd\}$ is an LR(0)-language (see [81], Section 10.7). Hence, there exists an LR(0)-parser for this language. This parser is a deterministic PDA with output. Given a word $w\lhd$ as input, this parser tries to construct a right-most derivation in reverse order. This process is successful if and only if $w \in L$. We are not interested in the right-most derivation constructed by the parser – we just want to know whether w is an element of L. Thus, we do not need the output, that is, we interpret the parser as an LR(0)-analyzer for the language $L \cdot \{\lhd\}$. This analyzer is deterministic. Therefore, for each word $w \in L$, there exists a unique derivation tree T_w for $w\lhd$ that corresponds to the analysis of $w\lhd$ found by the analyzer. Let k_L be the constant for the language $L \cdot \{\lhd\}$ from the pumping lemma for context-free languages (see Lemma 1.2.24). If $|w| \geq k_L$, then T_w contains subtrees T_1 and T_2 that satisfy all of the following conditions:

1. T_1 has at most k_L many leaves;
2. T_1 and T_2 carry the same label at their roots;
3. T_2 is subtree of T_1;
4. T_2 has strictly less leaves than T_1.

This situation can be illustrated as follows, where $w\lhd = u_1v_1u_2v_2u_3$:

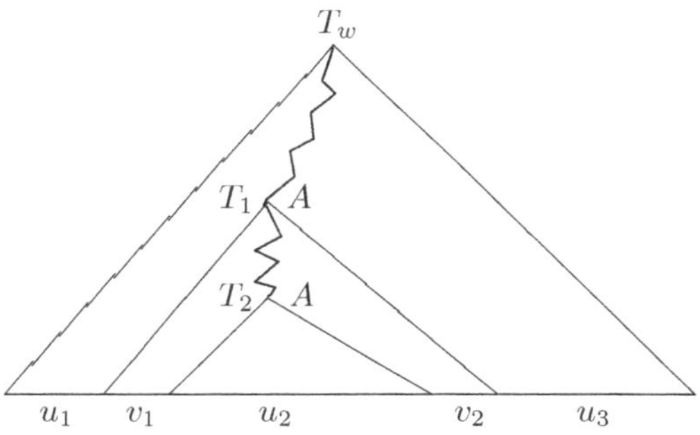

By replacing the subtree T_1 of T_w by the subtree T_2, we obtain the derivation tree $T_{w'}$ for the shorter word $w'\lhd = u_1u_2u_3$.

Now we describe a det-mon-R-automaton M for the language L. The automaton M has window size $k > k_L$. Scanning its tape from left to right, M simulates the above LR(0)-analyzer. In its finite-state control, it stores all subtrees of maximum size of the derivation tree constructed by the analyzer for which all leaves are inside the window. If one of these subtrees has the form of the tree T_1 above, then M executes a rewrite step which deletes the factors v_1 and v_2 and restarts; otherwise, M executes another MVR step. From the properties of the LR(0)-analyzer, we conclude that $w\lhd = u_1v_1u_2v_2u_3 \in L \cdot \{\lhd\}$ if and only if $w' = u_1u_2u_3\lhd \in L \cdot \{\lhd\}$. Thus, M is a deterministic R-automaton for the language L. As the LR(0)-analyzer that M simulates is deterministic, it follows that M is monotone. □

Thus, we obtain the following characterization from Corollary 2.1.39 and Theorem 2.1.42.

Corollary 2.1.43 $\mathsf{DCFL} = \mathcal{L}(\mathsf{det}\text{-}\mathsf{mon}\text{-}(\mathsf{s})\mathsf{R}(\mathsf{R})(\mathsf{W})(\mathsf{W}))$.

As weak monotonicity, also monotonicity is a dynamic property of restarting automata. Thus, it is not at all clear how to determine whether a given restarting automaton is monotone. Below we describe an algorithm for deciding this property. For doing so, we need two preliminary technical results. The first of them is a variant of Theorem 2.1.38.

Lemma 2.1.44 *There exists an algorithm that, from a given sRRWW-automaton M, computes a PDA P_M for the set of all words that are accepted by M through monotone computations.*

Proof outline. In the proof of Theorem 2.1.38, a construction is presented that turns a monotone sRRWW-automaton M into a PDA A that simulates the (monotone) computations of M. Now let M be an arbitrary sRRWW-automaton. We apply the above construction to this sRRWW-automaton, obtaining a PDA A. Of course, if M happens to be non-monotone, then A is not able to simulate all computations of M. However, from A, we can derive a PDA P_M that just simulates a computation of M until this computations ends (accepting or rejecting) or until a non-monotone rewrite step occurs. In the latter case, P_M rejects. Then $L(P_M) = \{ w \in L(M) \mid \text{There exists an accepting monotone computation of } M \text{ for input } w \}$. □

We introduce the following notion to describe those critical situations that indicate that an sRRWW-automaton is not monotone.

Definition 2.1.45 *Let $M = (Q, \Sigma, \Gamma, \rhd, \lhd, q_0, k, \delta)$ be an sRRWW-automaton. A word $w \in \Gamma^*$ is said to* enable a non-monotone rewrite step *of M, if there exist two cycles*

$$C_1 : q_0 \rhd w \lhd \vdash_M^c q_0 \rhd v \lhd \text{ and } C_2 : q_0 \rhd v \lhd \vdash_M^c q_0 \rhd z \lhd$$

such that $D_r(C_1) < D_r(C_2)$. Then $L_{\mathrm{nm}}(M)$ denotes the language

$$L_{\mathrm{nm}}(M) = \{ w \in \Gamma^* \mid w \text{ enables a non-monotone rewrite step of } M \},$$

that is, $L_{\mathrm{nm}}(M)$ consists of all those words from which a non-monotone computation of M of length two starts.

Interestingly, the language $L_{\mathrm{nm}}(M)$ of words that enable non-monotone rewrite steps is effectively regular, that is, we can actually construct an NFA for this language.

Lemma 2.1.46 *There exists an algorithm that, from a given sRRWW-automaton M, constructs an NFA for the language $L_{\mathrm{nm}}(M)$.*

Proof outline. Let $M = (Q, \Sigma, \Gamma, \rhd, \lhd, q_0, k, \delta)$ be an sRRWW-automaton. We construct an NFA A_M that, given a word $w \in \Gamma^*$ as input, simulates two cycles C_1 and C_2 of M simultaneously in order to check whether w enables a non-monotone rewrite step of M (see Definition 2.1.45 above). The NFA A_M accepts if and only if it detects a corresponding situation, that is, $L(A_M) = L_{\mathrm{nm}}(M)$.

Using its internal states, A_M realizes a buffer of size $2k+3$ for storing a word over $\Gamma \cup \{\rhd, \lhd\}$ and three internal variables Cst_1, Cst_2, Pos, which are initialized by $\mathrm{Cst}_1 = q_0$, $\mathrm{CSt}_2 = q_0$, and $\mathrm{Pos} = 0$. The variable Cst_1 (Cst_2) will be used to store the internal state of the restarting automaton M during the cycle C_1 (C_2) being simulated. During the whole simulation, the symbol at position 0 of the buffer will correspond to the first letter inside the read/write window of M during the cycle C_2, while the variable Pos will indicate the position of the read/write window of M during the cycle C_1 inside the buffer.

First, A_M fills the buffer by reading a prefix $\rhd w_1$ of $\rhd w$, where $|w_1| = 2k + 2$. Then it starts the simulation based on the following procedure:

- If $\mathrm{Pos} \leq k$, then A_M simulates the next step of C_1 inside its buffer, adjusting the contents of the buffer and the values of Cst_1 and Pos correspondingly.
- If $\mathrm{Pos} > k$, then A_M simulates the next step of C_2 inside its buffer. In addition, it moves the buffer to the right such that the first letter inside the read/write window during the cycle C_2 is again at position 0. Of course, the values of Cst_2 and Pos are adjusted accordingly.

During these steps, the buffer is always refilled from the right by reading the next letters until, at some point, the input may have been read completely.

The NFA A_M continues with the simultaneous simulation of the cycles C_1 and C_2 until one of them encounters a rewrite step or terminates. At that point, A_M behaves as follows:

– If C_1 or C_2 terminates (accepting or rejecting), then A_M halts and rejects. In this case, C_1 or C_2 is not a cycle within a computation of M.

– If a rewrite step occurs in C_2, but up to this point, no rewrite step occurred in C_1, then A_M continues with the simulation of both cycles. If both cycles lead to a restart, then A_M halts and accepts. In this case, the cycles C_1 and C_2 witness the fact that w enables a non-monotone rewrite step of M. Otherwise, A_M halts and rejects.

– If a rewrite step occurs in C_1, then A_M simulates this step inside its buffer, marking the right-most letter produced by this rewrite step (or the letter immediately to the left of the position of the rewrite step if this rewrite step erases all letters from the read/write window). Then it continues with the simultaneous simulations of C_1 and C_2. If no rewrite step occurs in C_2 before the marked letter appears inside the read/write window of M corresponding to the cycle C_2, then A_M halts and rejects. In this case, the two cycles do not witness the fact that w enables a non-monotone rewrite step of M. Otherwise, A_M completes the simulations of both cycles and halts and accepts, if both lead to a restart.

Now it is easily seen that $L(A_M) = L_{\mathrm{nm}}(M)$. Obviously, the NFA A_M can be constructed from the given sRRWW-automaton M. □

Based on these lemmas, we can now establish the following decidability result.

Theorem 2.1.47 (**[88]**) *It is decidable whether a given sRRWW-automaton is monotone.*

Proof. Let $M = (Q, \Sigma, \Gamma, \rhd, \lhd, q_0, k, \delta)$ be an sRRWW-automaton. This sRRWW-automaton is non-monotone if and only if there exists an input $w \in \Sigma^*$ and a non-monotone computation that begins with the initial configuration $q_0 \rhd w \lhd$. Hence, this computation has the following form:

$$q_0 \rhd w \lhd \vdash_M^c q_0 \rhd \alpha_1 \lhd \vdash_M^c q_0 \rhd \alpha_2 \lhd \vdash_M^c \cdots \vdash_M^c q_0 \rhd \alpha_m \lhd \vdash_M^c q_0 \rhd \alpha_{m+1} \lhd \vdash_M^c q_0 \rhd \alpha_{m+2} \lhd \vdash_M^c \cdots,$$

where

$$D_r(q_0 \rhd \alpha_m \lhd \vdash_M^c q_0 \rhd \alpha_{m+1} \lhd) < D_r(q_0 \rhd \alpha_{m+1} \lhd \vdash_M^c q_0 \rhd \alpha_{m+2} \lhd),$$

while all previous cycles are monotone. By Lemma 2.1.44, we can construct a PDA P_M for the set of all words that M accepts through monotone computations, and by Lemma 2.1.46, we can construct an NFA A_M for the language $L_{\mathrm{nm}}(M)$. We now modify the PDA P_M to get a PDA P'_M that, after simulating a number of monotone cycles of M, simply shifts the remaining part of the input onto the pushdown and halts. Then, for each input $w \in \Sigma^*$, the set of reachable pushdown contents $\mathrm{SC}_{P'_M}(w)$ of P'_M describes those restart configurations of M that M can reach through monotone computations from $q_0 \rhd w \lhd$. By Theorem 1.2.36, this is a regular language, and in addition, from P'_M (and hence, from M) one can construct an NFA AP_M for the language $\mathrm{SC}_{P'_M}(\Sigma^*)$. Now it follows that M is non-monotone if and only if the language $L(\mathrm{AP}_M) \cap L(A_M)$ is non-empty. As this is decidable, Theorem 2.1.47 follows. □

Actually, Theorem 2.1.47 extends the corresponding decidability result of [88] from RRWW-automata to sRRWW-automata.

In [88], Petr Jančar et al. also define two weaker notions of monotonicity for restarting automata. They call a restarting automaton

- *a-monotone* if *all its accepting computations* are monotone,
- *g-monotone* if, for each word $w \in L(M)$, *there exists an accepting computation* that is monotone.

They prove that, for RRWW-automata, all these types of monotonicity characterize the context-free languages, while for restarting automata without auxiliary letters, they obtain a hierarchy that is based on the type of automaton and the type of monotonicity considered. Furthermore, they show that for RRW-automata, a-monotonicity and g-monotonicity are decidable, while for RWW-automata, both a-monotonicity and g-monotonicity are undecidable.

2.1.4 On Deterministic Monotone RLWW-Automata

We finally turn to RLWW-automata and shrinking RLWW-automata that are monotone and deterministic. Example 1.9.2 presents an RR-automaton M_1 for the language $\{ a^n b^n c, a^n b^{2n} d \mid n \geq 0 \}$. This language is context-free, but not deterministic context-free. In each cycle, the RR-automaton M_1 simply deletes a factor ab or abb and checks then whether the tape contents ends with a c or a d. Thus, the automaton is obviously monotone. We can convert this RR-automaton into a monotone deterministic RL-automaton for the same language by requiring that the RL-automaton first checks the last letter and then returns to the middle of the tape by executing some MVL steps. It follows that $\mathcal{L}(\mathsf{det\text{-}mon\text{-}RR}) = \mathsf{DCFL}$ is a proper subclass of $\mathcal{L}(\mathsf{det\text{-}mon\text{-}RL})$.

On the other hand, the language $L_{\exp} = \{ a^{2^n} \mid n \geq 0 \}$ is Church-Rosser (see Example 1.2.16). However, it is not accepted by any RL-automaton, as for n sufficiently large, a single rewrite step cannot convert the word $a^{2^n} \in L_{\exp}$ into a shorter word that belongs to $L_{\exp}$. This shows that $\mathcal{L}(\mathsf{det\text{-}mon\text{-}RL})$ does not contain all Church-Rosser languages. In fact, below we shall see that $\mathcal{L}(\mathsf{det\text{-}mon\text{-}RL})$ is a proper subclass of $\mathsf{CRL} = \mathcal{L}(\mathsf{det\text{-}RRWW})$ by establishing the fact that $\mathcal{L}(\mathsf{det\text{-}mon\text{-}RL})$ coincides with the class LRR of left-to-right regular languages (see Definition 1.2.45). To derive this characterization, we need the notion of left-monotonicity and some preliminary technical results.

Definition 2.1.48 *Let $M = (Q, \Sigma, \Gamma, \rhd, \lhd, q_0, k, \delta)$ be a restarting automaton.*

(a) *For a configuration $\rhd uqvw \lhd$ of M, the number*

$$D_l(\rhd uqvw \lhd) = |\rhd uv| = |u| + k + 1$$

is called the left distance *of this configuration. It is the length of the prefix of the tape contents that ends with the factor that is currently inside the window of M, that is, it is the distance from the left end of the tape to the right end of the window.*

(b) *Let $\rhd uqvw \lhd \vdash_M \rhd uzq'w \lhd$ be a rewrite step within a computation of M in which a rewrite transition $(q', z) \in \delta(q, v)$ is applied. Then $D_l(\rhd uqvw \lhd)$ is also called the* left distance of this rewrite step.

(c) *A computation of M is called* left-monotone *if the sequence of left distances of the rewrite steps within this computation is non-increasing, that is, whenever*

$$\rhd uqvw \lhd \vdash_M \rhd uzq'w \lhd \vdash_M^* \rhd u_1 q_1 v_1 w_1 \lhd \vdash_M \rhd u_1 z_1 q_1' w_1 \lhd$$

is part of this computation, where $(q', z) \in \delta(q, v)$ and $(q_1', z_1) \in \delta(q_1, v_1)$ are rewrite transitions, then

$$D_l(\rhd uqvw \lhd) \geq D_l(\rhd u_1 q_1 v_1 w_1 \lhd).$$

(d) *The restarting automaton M is called* left-monotone *if each of its computations that begins with an initial configuration is left-monotone.*

We use the prefix left-mon- to denote left-monotone types of restarting automata. Recall that the notation w^R is used for the reversal of a word w. For a language $L \subseteq \Sigma^*$, we take L^R to denote the reversal $L^R = \{ w^R \mid w \in L \}$ of L, and for a class of languages $\mathcal{L}$, we take $\mathcal{L}^R$ to denote the class of languages $\mathcal{L}^R = \{ L^R \mid L \in \mathcal{L} \}$.

Let $M = (Q, \Sigma, \Gamma, \rhd, \lhd, q_0, k, \delta)$ be a restarting automaton and let $\rhd uqvw \lhd$ be a configuration of M, where $|v| = k$. Then $D_r(\rhd uqvw \lhd) = |w| + k + 1$ and $D_l(\rhd uqvw \lhd) = |u| + k + 1$. Consider the configuration $\rhd w^R q v^R u^R \lhd$, which corresponds to the reversal $(uvw)^R = w^R v^R u^R$ of the tape contents uvw. Then

$$D_r(\rhd w^R q v^R u^R \lhd) = |u| + k + 1 = D_l(\rhd uqvw \lhd)$$

and

$$D_l(\rhd w^R q v^R u^R \lhd) = |w| + k + 1 = D_r(\rhd uvw \lhd).$$

From a deterministic (s)RL(W)(W)-automaton M for a language L, we can easily construct a deterministic (s)RL(W)(W)-automaton M_r for the language L^R. Actually, for each rewrite transition $(q', z) \in \delta(q, v)$ of M, M_r will have the rewrite transition $(q', z^R) \in \delta_r(q, v^R)$. In particular, M is monotone if and only if M_r is left-monotone. Thus, we have the following equivalence.

Proposition 2.1.49 *For each* $\mathsf{X} \in \{\mathsf{WW}, \mathsf{W}, \lambda\}$, $\mathcal{L}(\textsf{det-left-mon-(s)RLX}) = (\mathcal{L}(\textsf{det-mon-(s)RLX}))^R$.

For deterministic left-monotone types of sRLWW-automata, the following strong result has been obtained, which shows that already det-left-mon-RL-automata are quite expressive.

Theorem 2.1.50 ([95, 96])

$$\mathcal{L}(\textsf{det-left-mon-RL}) = \mathcal{L}(\textsf{det-left-mon-(s)RLW(W)}) = \mathcal{L}(\textsf{det-left-mon-(s)R(R)WW}).$$

Thus, deterministic left-monotone RL-automata are equivalent to det-left-mon-sRLWW-automata, that is, auxiliary letters are not needed and, instead of weight-reducing rewrite transitions, deletions suffice. In addition, if auxiliary letters are provided, then MVL steps are not needed. Here it should be pointed out that det-left-mon-sRRW-automata are strictly less expressive than det-left-mon-RL-automata. In fact, while the language $\{ a^n b^n c, a^n b^{2n} d \mid n \geq 0 \}$ is accepted by a det-left-mon-RL-automaton (see above), it can be shown that this language is not accepted by any sRRW-automaton. Indeed, if no auxiliary letters are available, a single cycle can just convert a word of the form $a^n b^{2n} d$ into a word of the form $a^{n-i} b^{2n-2i} d$ for some $i \geq 1$ because of the Correctness Preserving Property for deterministic restarting automata (Proposition 1.9.8). However, a det-left-mon-sRRW-automaton cannot check whether the actual tape contents ends with a c or with a d before it deletes the factor $a^i b^{2i}$. Thus, for the word $a^n b^n c$, it would execute the same deletion, reducing this word to the word $a^{n-i} b^{n-2i} c$, which it would then have to reject eventually on detecting the letter c.

To prove the equivalences in Theorem 2.1.50, several intermediate steps are required. The first one shows that, if auxiliary letters are available, MVL transitions are superfluous.

Proposition 2.1.51 ([96]) $\mathcal{L}(\textsf{det-left-mon-sRLWW}) \subseteq \mathcal{L}(\textsf{det-left-mon-sRWW})$.

Proof outline. Let $M = (Q, \Sigma, \Gamma, \rhd, \lhd, q_0, k, \delta)$ be a deterministic sRLWW-automaton that is left-monotone and let φ be a weight function compatible with M. We construct a deterministic left-monotone sRWW-automaton M' such that M' accepts the same language as M. In fact, given an input $w \in \Sigma^*$, M' will simulate the computation of M on input w. To define M', we need to analyze the behavior of M in detail.

Each cycle of a computation of M consists of three phases:

(1) M scans its tape by repeatedly performing MVR and MVL steps.

(2) M executes a rewrite step, replacing a factor u of the current tape contents with a word v satisfying $\varphi(v) < \varphi(u)$.

(3) M rescans its tape by repeatedly performing MVR and MVL steps until it eventually accepts, rejects, or restarts.

To simplify the discussion, we may assume, without loss of generality, that in phase (1), M first scans its tape completely from left to right by performing a sequence of MVR steps.

In contrast to the behavior of M described above, M' simply scans its tape from left to right by performing a number of MVR steps until it executes a combined rewrite-restart step, thus ending the current cycle. Hence, if M' is to simulate a cycle of M, then it needs to determine the information that M collects during phases (1) and (3) *before* it can execute the corresponding rewrite step. However, M' cannot do this within a single cycle, as it does not see the contents of the tape that is to the right of the position where the rewrite step is to be performed. Thus, M' will have to perform some preparatory cycles before it can actually execute the simulation of the rewrite step of the current cycle of M.

Assume that the actual configuration of M at the start of the current cycle is $q_0 \rhd xuy \lhd$, where $x, u, y \in \Gamma^*$, $|u| = k$, and u is the factor that M is about to replace with the word v in this cycle. In order to simulate this cycle, M' will first encode information on the behavior of M on the suffix y by performing a number of cycles that replace this suffix letter by letter from right to left with an encoding of y.

This encoding is defined as follows. Let the set of states of M be $Q = \{q_0, q_1, \ldots, q_m\}$, and let

$$\Gamma_s = \{\, (a, \langle (q_0, p_0), (q_1, p_1), \ldots, (q_m, p_m) \rangle) \mid a \in \Gamma, p_i \in Q \cup \{+, -, R, \uparrow\}, 0 \le i \le m \,\}.$$

Then each letter of y is replaced with a letter from Γ_s. The replacement of a letter a is determined based on its position within y. Let $y = y_1 a y_2$. Then this particular occurrence of the letter a is replaced with the symbol

$$\psi_{ay_2}(a) = (a, \langle (q_0, p_0), (q_1, p_1), \ldots, (q_m, p_m) \rangle) \in \Gamma_s,$$

where, for each $i = 0, 1, \ldots, m$, p_i is chosen according to the following definition:

$p_i = q_j$, if, starting from the configuration $\rhd q_i a y_2 \lhd$, M first makes a MVR step, then it executes a (possibly empty) sequence consisting entirely of MVR and MVL steps during which it stays with its read/write window on the suffix $y_2 \lhd$, and finally it performs a MVL step taking it to the configuration $\rhd q_j a y_2 \lhd$;

$p_i = +$, if, starting from the configuration $\rhd q_i a y_2 \lhd$, M either accepts immediately, or it makes a MVR step, followed by a (possibly empty) sequence of MVR and MVL steps during which it stays with its read/write window on the suffix $y_2 \lhd$, and accepts then;

$p_i = -$, if, starting from the configuration $\rhd q_i a y_2 \lhd$, M either rejects immediately, or it makes a MVR step, followed by a (possibly empty) sequence of MVR and MVL steps during which it stays with its read/write window on the suffix $y_2 \lhd$, and rejects then;

$p_i = R$, if, starting from the configuration $\rhd q_i a y_2 \lhd$, M either restarts immediately, or it makes a MVR step, followed by a (possibly empty) sequence of MVR and MVL steps during which it stays with its read/write window on the suffix $y_2 \lhd$, and restarts then;

$p_i = \uparrow$, if, starting from the configuration $\rhd q_i a y_2 \lhd$, M either immediately performs a rewrite step, or it makes a MVR step, followed by a (possibly empty) sequence of MVR and MVL steps during which it stays with its read/write window on the suffix $y_2 \lhd$, and makes a rewrite step then;

$p_i = q_i$, if, starting from the configuration $\rhd q_i a y_2 \lhd$, M immediately performs a MVL-step.

It is obvious that M' can compute this encoding of the suffix y by simply replacing the letters of y from right to left. In addition, it is clear that this computation is left-monotone, and that it is compatible with an appropriately chosen weight function.

In the following, we use the notation $\psi_{gh}(g)$, where g, h are words, to denote the encoding of the word g that we obtain according to the above definition from the suffix $gh\lhd$ of a tape contents of M. Observe that, for all words f, g, h, $\psi_{fgh}(fg) = \psi_{fgh}(f)\psi_{gh}(g)$.

The sRWW-automaton M' is now defined as $M' = (Q', \Sigma, \Gamma', \rhd, \lhd, q_0', 2k, \delta')$, where $\Gamma' = \Gamma \cup \Gamma_s$ and

$$Q' = \{\, (q, \langle (q_0, s_0), (q_1, s_1), \ldots, (q_m, s_m) \rangle) \mid q \in Q, s_i \in Q \cup \{+, -, R, \uparrow\}, 0 \le i \le m \,\},$$

and the transition function δ' is defined in such a way that a rewrite step

$$\rhd x_1 x_2 q_i u b y \lhd \vdash_M \rhd x_1 x_2 v q_j b y \lhd \quad (|x_2| = k-1, |u| = k, b \in \Gamma) \tag{2.6}$$

of M is simulated through a rewrite step of the form

$$\rhd x_1 q_i' x_2 \psi_{uby}(u) \psi_{by}(b) \psi_y(y) \lhd \vdash_{M'} q_0' \rhd x_1 x_2 \psi_{vby}(v) \psi_{by}(b) \psi_y(y) \lhd . \tag{2.7}$$

Observe that the actual simulation of the rewrite step of M, which replaces the factor u with the word v, is performed by M' on the border between the prefix of the tape contents that is still unencoded and the suffix of the tape contents that has already been encoded. Furthermore, we see that the read/write window of M' contains one encoded letter (the letter $\psi_{by}(b)$ in (2.7)) to the right of the factor $\psi_{uby}(u)$ that is to be rewritten, and that it contains $k-1$ still unencoded letters to the left of this factor (the word x_2 in (2.7)).

It is clear that M' can immediately determine the encoding $\psi_{vby}(v)$ from the transition function δ of M and the information stored in $\psi_{by}(b)$. In addition, as M is shrinking, so is M', if the weight function is chosen appropriately.

As M is left-monotone, the next cycle of M has left distance at most $1+|x_1x_2|+k$, and so the next rewrite transition of M' is to be performed on a prefix of $x_4x_2\psi_{vby}(vb)\psi_y(y)\lhd$, where $x_1 = x_3x_4$ and $|x_4| \geq 0$. Hence, M' may first have to execute some cycles computing the encoding $\psi_{x_6vby}(x_6)$ of a suffix x_6 of x_1x_2 before it can simulate the next rewrite step of M. Anyway, we see that with M, also M' is left-monotone.

For a detailed description of the transition function of M' and a proof that $L(M') = L(M)$, we refer to [96]. □

The next result states that we can do away with weight-reducing rewrite transitions.

Proposition 2.1.52 ([96]) $\mathcal{L}(\text{det-left-mon-sRWW}) \subseteq \mathcal{L}(\text{det-left-mon-RWW})$.

Proof outline. The proof follows a simulation technique presented in [186], where it is used to show that length-reducing DTPDAs can simulate shrinking DTPDAs. However, if one applies this technique directly to RWW-automata, then the resulting automaton is not left-monotone, even if the simulated automaton is. Thus, this technique must be adjusted carefully in order to preserve the property of left-monotonicity. We like to stress that an essential property for this simulation technique to work is the fact that two consecutive rewrites must 'overlap,' which is the case for all deterministic left-monotone sRWW-automata.

Here we only give a high-level description of the simulation of a deterministic left-monotone sRWW-automaton $M = (Q, \Sigma, \Gamma, \rhd, \lhd, q_0, k, \delta)$ (with weight function φ) by a deterministic left-monotone RWW-automaton. This simulation consists of three major steps, which are outlined below. For the technically involved details, we refer to [96].

(1) For the deterministic sRWW-automaton M, we first construct a deterministic sRWW-automaton M' such that $L(M') = L(M)$ and each rewrite transition of M' reduces the weight of the actual tape contents exactly by one (using a method similar to Lemma 4 of [186]). Here the main difference is that we do not assign weights to states. Instead of using intermediate states to reduce the weight by one in each step, we simply use additional letters in order to perform these 'intermediate' rewrite steps. As these additional rewrite steps have the same left distance as the rewrite step of M being simulated, it follows that M' is left-monotone, if M is. Thus, we can assume in the following that each rewrite transition of M reduces the weight exactly by one.

(2) Let $\#$ be a new letter, and let $h : \Gamma^* \to (\Gamma \cup \{\#\})^*$ be the morphism that is induced by mapping a to $a\#^{\varphi(a)-1}$ for each $a \in \Gamma$. Then, for each word $w \in \Gamma^*$, the word $h(w) \in (\Gamma \cup \{\#\})^*$ satisfies $|h(w)| = \varphi(w)$. From M, we obtain an RWW-automaton M_1 by replacing each rewrite transition $\delta(q, u) = v$ of M by the rewrite transition $\delta_1(q, h(u)) = h(v)$. Then M_1 simulates the computation of M on the tape contents $\rhd w\lhd$ ($w \in \Gamma^*$) step by step on the tape contents $\rhd h(w)\lhd$. It follows that $L(M_1) = h(L(M))$. Furthermore, if M is left-monotone, then so is M_1: in a left-monotone computation, if $p_1, p_2, p_3, \ldots$ are the prefixes to the left of the actual rewrite positions in a sequence of consecutive cycles of M, then p_{i+1} is necessarily a prefix of p_i (and all of them are prefixes of the input word). Hence, $|h(p_{i+1})| \leq |h(p_i)|$, and so $h(p_{i+1})$ is a prefix of $h(p_i)$. Moreover, M_1 is length-reducing, as each rewrite step of M reduces the weight by one, and so each rewrite step of M_1 reduces the length of the actual tape contents by one.

(3) To complete the construction, we would now like to simulate the automaton M_1 by an RWW-automaton that, instead of processing an input of the form $h(x)$ ($x \in \Sigma^*$), works directly with the original input x. However, it might be impossible to simulate the computation of M_1 on $h(x)$ in

a length-reducing manner on the input x itself, as already the length of $h(x)$ will, in general, be larger than the length of x. In order to overcome this problem, a strategy from [186] (Proof of Theorem 5) can be applied:

(a) First, an automaton M_2 is used to replace the input word x with a 'compressed' version of $h(x)$ using the compression ratio 2μ, where $\mu = \max\{ \varphi(a) \mid a \in \Gamma \}$.

(b) Then, an automaton M_3 is used that, in each cycle, simulates 2μ cycles of M_1.

The compression of ratio 2μ guarantees that the compressed version x_c of $h(x)$ satisfies $|x_c| \leq |x|$, and by simulating 2μ cycles of M_1 in a single cycle of M_3, we guarantee that the length of the actual tape contents of M_3 is reduced by exactly one per cycle. Thus, we see that the composition of M_2 and M_3 is length-reducing. Furthermore, M_2 can clearly be realized in a left-monotone manner, and also M_3 is left-monotone, as M_1 is.

However, the composition of M_2 and M_3 is clearly not left-monotone, as the 'compression phase' realized by M_2, in which the tape contents is completely rewritten, precedes the 'real' simulation. In order to make this part of the simulation left-monotone, the strategy of 'lazy' compression can be adopted, that is, we start on the uncompressed input and use the compression in combination with the simulation of rewrite steps (that is, we combine M_2 and M_3 into one automaton). During this computation, the tape contents will always consist of an uncompressed prefix that is followed by a compressed suffix, and each rewrite step just encodes (compresses) a suffix of the still uncompressed part or rewrites a prefix of the compressed part. □

Finally, we want to show that left-monotone deterministic RLWW-automata do not need auxiliary letters.

Proposition 2.1.53 ([95]) $\mathcal{L}(\text{det-left-mon-RLWW}) \subseteq \mathcal{L}(\text{det-left-mon-RL})$.

To prove this result, we follow the presentation in [95]. With every deterministic RWW-automaton, we can associate a UDGSM (see Definition 1.2.76) as follows.

Let $M = (Q, \Sigma, \Gamma, \rhd, \lhd, q_0, k, \delta)$ be a deterministic RWW-automaton. Without loss of generality, we can assume that during the tail of each computation, M scans its tape completely from left to right before it accepts or rejects. Given a word $w \in \Sigma^+$ as input for which M performs at least one rewrite step, M will first execute a sequence of transitions of the form

$$q_0 \rhd w \lhd = q_0 \rhd w_1 u w_2 \lhd \vdash_M^* \rhd w_1 p_1 u w_2 \lhd \vdash_M q_0 \rhd w_1 v w_2 \lhd,$$

where $p_1 \in Q$, $\delta(p_1, u) = v$ is the rewrite transition applied during this cycle, and $|u| = k$. (The case that the first rewrite step is applied to a suffix of w of length smaller than k can be treated in an analogous manner).

For $i = k-1, k, k+1, \ldots, |w_1| + k$, we associate a state q_i of M with the letter $w[i]$ as follows. For all $i \in \{k-1, k, \ldots, |w_1| + k\}$, we take q_i to denote the state of M during the above sequence at that moment when the right-most position of the read/write window contains the letter $w[i]$. Furthermore, for $i \in \{1, 2, \ldots, |w|\} \smallsetminus \{k-1, k, k+1, \ldots, |w_1| + k\}$, we take $q_i = \perp$, where $\perp \notin Q$ is a new (dummy) symbol, as, during the above cycle, the right-most position of the read/write window is never on a position $i < k-1$ or on a position $i > |w_1| + k$. The sequence $(q_1, q_2, \ldots, q_{|w|})$ will be denoted by $\text{trace}_M(w)$.

As the RWW-automaton M is deterministic, there exists a UDGSM G_M that, given a word $w \in \Sigma^n$ as input, will produce the output

$$(w[1], q_1)(w[2], q_2) \cdots (w[n], q_n) \in (\Sigma \times (Q \cup \{\perp\}))^n,$$

that is, for each language $L \subseteq \Sigma^*$,

$$G_M(L) = \{ y \in (\Sigma \times (Q \cup \{\perp\}))^* \mid \pi_1(y) \in L \text{ and } \pi_2(y) = \text{trace}_M(\pi_1(y)) \}.$$

Here π_1 and π_2 denote the projections from $(\Sigma \times (Q \cup \{\perp\}))^*$ onto Σ^* and $(Q \cup \{\perp\})^*$, respectively. Thus, $G_M(L)$ contains the words of L 'enriched' with information on the behavior of M during the first cycle of its computation on that particular input. The following result establishes a connection between left-monotone deterministic RWW-automata, UDGSMs, and the language class DCFL.

Proposition 2.1.54 ([95]) *For each left-monotone deterministic RWW-automaton M,*

$$G_M(L(M)) \in \mathsf{DCFL}^R.$$

Proof outline. Let $M = (Q, \Sigma, \Gamma, \rhd, \lhd, q_0, k, \delta)$ be a deterministic RWW-automaton that is left-monotone. By Theorem 1.9.24 (a), $\mathsf{DCFL} = \mathcal{L}(\mathsf{det\text{-}mon\text{-}RRWW})$. Hence, it suffices to construct a monotone deterministic RRWW-automaton $M' = (Q', \Omega, \Gamma', \rhd, \lhd, q_0', k', \delta')$ for the language $(G_M(L(M)))^R$, where $\Omega = \Sigma \times (Q \cup \{\perp\})$ and $k' = 2k+1$. This automaton will simulate M cycle by cycle.

Recall that each cycle of M consists of two phases:

(1) a MVR phase, in which M scans a prefix of the current tape contents from left to right using MVR steps only, and

(2) a rewrite phase, in which M applies a rewrite transition and restarts.

Let $C_1, C_2, \ldots, C_m$ be the sequence of cycles of a computation of M. As M is left-monotone, we have $D_l(C_1) \geq D_l(C_2) \geq \cdots \geq D_l(C_m)$. On the other hand, as M is deterministic, we have $D_l(C_{i+1}) > D_l(C_i) - k$, as M cannot make a rewrite step in cycle C_{i+1} while its read/write window is still completely on the prefix of the current tape contents that was scanned in phase (1) of the previous cycle, that is, for all $i = 1, 2, \ldots, m-1$, $D_l(C_i) - k + 1 \leq D_l(C_{i+1}) \leq D_l(C_i)$.

Now we describe the behavior of the monotone deterministic RRWW-automaton M'. For an input $y \in \Omega^+$, M' simulates the computation of M for the input $w = (\pi_1(y))^R$. For doing so, the automaton M' uses the part from positions 2 to $k+1$ of its read/write window to simulate the read/write window of M, while the part from positions $k+2$ to $2k+1$ serves as a kind of look-ahead, in which M' sees those letters (in reverse) that M saw in the previous k positions. Each cycle of a computation of M' consists of three phases:

(1) First, M' executes a number of MVR steps, scanning a prefix of y. This phase continues until M' detects the reversal of the left-hand side of a rewrite step of M such that the state stored with the left-most of these letters indicates that M would now execute a rewrite step, or until M' reaches the right sentinel. While making these MVR steps, M' determines the following set of states of M for the current position of its read/write window, where y_2 is the prefix that has been scanned so far (including the first letter of the current contents of the read/write window), and $w_2 = (\pi_1(y_2))^R$:

$$Q_+(w_2) \quad = \quad \{\, q \in Q \mid \rhd q w_2 \lhd \vdash_M^{\mathrm{MVR}^*} \mathsf{Accept}\,\}.$$

Here $\vdash_M^{\mathrm{MVR}^*}$ denotes a finite sequence of MVR steps of M.

If a rewrite step of M is encountered, then M' continues with (2) below. Otherwise, on reaching the right sentinel, M' checks whether the set $Q_+(y)$ that is computed for the last letter of y contains a state $q \in Q$ such that $\delta(q_0, \rhd w_1) = (q, \mathsf{MVR})$, where w_1^R is the image under π_1 of the suffix of length $k-1$ of y of M'. In the affirmative, M' accepts; otherwise, it rejects.

(2) When M' contains the reversal u^R of the left-hand side of a rewrite transition $\delta(p_1, u) = v$ of M in positions 2 to $k+1$ of its read/write window, then it can determine the actual state of M from the state stored with the second letter in its read/write window, and it can verify that M would now execute this rewrite transition. Observe that due to the fact that M is left-monotone, the prefix w_1 to the left of the current position of the read/write window of M has not yet been rewritten in any way, that is, these letters are still from the original input. Now M' simulates the rewrite step of M, replacing the factor of y corresponding to u^R by v^R. In addition, it stores those states of M with the letters of v^R that M would enter during a sequence of MVR steps on the word $w_1 v$. The automaton M' can determine these states from the states of M stored with the letters in positions $k+2$ to $2k+1$ in its window and the word v.

(3) After executing a rewrite step, M' scans the remaining suffix of its tape contents. As long as the symbols read are input letters, it checks that the states stored in the second components describe the reverse of a valid sequence of state transitions of M that is compatible with the letters from Σ stored in the first components and that correspond to a first phase of a cycle of M. If all these tests are successful, then M' restarts at the right sentinel.

It can now be verified that M' does indeed accept the language $(G_M(L(M)))^R$, and that M' is monotone. □

As a direct consequence of Propositions 2.1.51, 2.1.52, and 2.1.54, we see that, for each language $L \in \mathcal{L}(\text{det-left-mon-sRLWW})$, there exists a UDGSM G such that $(G(L))^R \in \text{DCFL}$.

In order to prove Proposition 2.1.53, we now present a technical result which may be seen as the converse of Proposition 2.1.54. However, it is stronger than that, as it applies to det-left-mon-RL-automata.

Proposition 2.1.55 *Let G be a UDGSM with input alphabet Σ that induces an injective mapping from $L(G)$ into Δ^*, and let $L \subseteq \Sigma^*$ such that $L \subseteq L(G)$. If $(G(L))^R \in \text{DCFL}$, then there exists a det-left-mon-RL-automaton for the language L.*

Observe that the UDGSM G_M associated above to a det-left-mon-RWW-automaton M induces an injective mapping from Σ^* into $(\Sigma \times \{\perp\})^*$, and that $L(M) \subseteq L(G_M)$.

Proof outline for Proposition 2.1.55. Let $G = (Q, \Sigma, \Delta, p_0, \delta, F)$ be a UDGSM such that the induced mapping from $L(G)$ into Δ^* is injective, and let $L \subseteq \Sigma^*$ such that $L \subseteq L(G)$. Thus, G can process each word from L, and therewith, $G(w)$ is defined for each word $w \in L$.

First, we extend G to a UDGSM $\tilde{G} = (Q, \Sigma, \Gamma, p_0, \tilde{\delta}, F)$ that encodes information on its input within its output. We take $\Gamma = \Sigma \times Q \times \Delta$, and we define $\tilde{\delta} : Q \times \Sigma \to Q \times \Gamma$ through

$$\tilde{\delta}(q, a) = (p, (a, p, b)), \text{ if } \delta(q, a) = (p, b).$$

Then, for $x = a_1 a_2 \cdots a_n$, if $G(x) = b_1 b_2 \cdots b_n$,

$$\tilde{G}(x) = (a_1, p_1, b_1)(a_2, p_2, b_2) \cdots (a_n, p_n, b_n),$$

where, for $i = 1, 2, \ldots, n$, p_i is the state that G reaches from p_0 by reading the prefix $a_1 a_2 \cdots a_i$ of x. As the mapping that is induced by the UDGSM G is injective, we see that, for each word $y \in L(G)$, there is just a single word $x \in \Sigma^*$ such that $G(x) = y$. Thus, there is only a single word $z \in \Gamma^*$ that is produced by $\tilde{G}$ and the third components of which yield the word y. The language $(G(L))^R$ is deterministic context-free, that is, it is accepted by a DPDA. From this DPDA, we easily obtain a DPDA for the language $(\tilde{G}(L))^R$, that is, we have $(\tilde{G}(L))^R \in \text{DCFL}$, too.

As $\text{DCFL} = \mathcal{L}(\text{det-mon-R})$ (Theorem 1.9.21), there exists a monotone det-R-automaton M_1 that accepts the language $(\tilde{G}(L))^R$. From M_1, we immediately obtain a det-RL-automaton M_2 for the language $\tilde{G}(L)$: in each cycle, M_2 first moves its window to the right sentinel, checking that the actual tape contents is of the form $\tilde{G}(x)$ for some word $x \in \Sigma^*$. In the negative, it rejects immediately, while, in the affirmative, it then simulates the current cycle of M_1, replacing MVR steps by MVL steps. We can even require that M_2 aborts this simulation and rejects when it comes upon a rewrite transition that would transform a word of the form $\tilde{G}(x)$ into a word that does not belong to the set $\tilde{G}(\Sigma^*)$. As M_1 is monotone, it follows from Proposition 2.1.49 that M_2 is left-monotone. Hence, we see that $\tilde{G}(L) \in \mathcal{L}(\text{det-left-mon-RL})$.

Finally, we present a left-monotone det-RL-automaton M_3 that, given a word $x \in \Sigma^*$ as input, simulates the computation of M_2 on $\tilde{G}(x)$. Notice that the information that is stored in the second and third coordinates of $\tilde{G}(x)$ is missing when the input x is being processed. Thus, M_3 needs to 'recover' this information from x. For doing so, the following two observations are useful.

First of all, there exists a DFA A_G that simulates the UDGSM G in such a way that, after processing the i-th symbol of an input word $x \in \Sigma^+$, where $1 \leq i \leq |x|$, the state of A_G contains the i-th symbol of the word $\tilde{G}(x)$. Accordingly, when scanning the given input x from left to right, the det-RL-automaton M_3 can easily recover that part of $\tilde{G}(x)$ that corresponds to the part of x that is currently inside the read/write window.

For 'recovering' this information also in the case that the read/write window is moving from right to left, we need Lemma 1.2.71. In fact, this lemma is crucial for our construction. It tells us that there exists a 2DFA A'_G that, starting in state $q_{A_G}(x, i)$ with tape contents x and its head on the letter $x[i]$, finishes its computation in state $q_{A_G}(x, i-1)$ with its head on $x[i-1]$. Here $q_{A,G}(x, i)$ is the state that A_G reaches after processing the prefix of length i of x, and $q_{A_G}(x, i-1)$ is the previous state of A_G. Using A'_G, the det-RL-automaton M_3 is able to recover the information on $\tilde{G}(x)$ from x while moving its read/write window from right to left.

Now we are ready to describe the restarting automaton M_3. Each cycle of M_2 on input $\tilde{G}(x)$ is simulated by a cycle of M_3 on input x as follows:

(1) First, M_3 simulates the computation of the DFA A_G until it reaches the right sentinel. In this way, it computes the k right-most positions of $\tilde{G}(x)$.

(2) Next, M_3 simulates the behavior of M_2 step by step until it reaches the configuration in which M_2 applies the rewrite step of the current cycle. Each time it must simulate a MVL step, it runs the automaton A'_G in order to recover the value of $\tilde{G}(x)$ at the new left-most position in the read/write window. Note that, at the beginning of the simulation, M_3 knows the part of $\tilde{G}(x)$ that is contained in the read/write window (see (1)). Hence, by using A'_G, it is able to satisfy this condition for each successive step.

(3) Finally, M_3 simulates the current rewrite step of M_2 (that is, it removes the appropriate letters).

Thus, given an input $x \in \Sigma^*$, M_3 simulates the computation of M_2 on $\tilde{G}(x)$ cycle by cycle. Furthermore, M_3 accepts the given input x if and only if M_2 accepts the input $\tilde{G}(x)$. It follows that $L(M_3) = L$. As M_2 is left-monotone, M_3 is left-monotone, too. This completes the proof of Proposition 2.1.55. □

Actually, Proposition 2.1.55 even extends to non-uniform DGSMs that are λ-free, that is, for which each transition produces a non-empty output [95]. Together Propositions 2.1.54 and 2.1.55 prove that $\mathcal{L}(\text{det-left-mon-RWW}) \subseteq \mathcal{L}(\text{det-left-mon-RL})$. In combination with Propositions 2.1.51 and 2.1.52, this yields Theorem 2.1.50.

From the above results on deterministic left-monotone restarting automata, we can now derive the following characterization for the class LRR of left-to-right regular languages. Recall from the paragraph following Definition 1.2.45 that, for each LRR-language $L \subseteq \Sigma^*$, there exist a DRLST G that defines a partial mapping $G : \Sigma^* \to \Delta^*$ and a DPDA P with input alphabet Δ such that $L = \{ w \in \Sigma^* \mid G(w) \in L(P) \}$, that is, a word $w \in \Sigma^*$ belongs to the language L if and only if the DPDA P accepts the transformed word $G(w)$.

Theorem 2.1.56 $\text{LRR} = \mathcal{L}(\text{det-mon-RL}) = \mathcal{L}(\text{det-mon-(s)RLW(W)})$.

Proof. By Theorem 2.1.50, $\mathcal{L}(\text{det-left-mon-RL}) = \mathcal{L}(\text{det-left-mon-sRLWW})$. Hence, Proposition 2.1.49 implies that $\mathcal{L}(\text{det-mon-RL}) = \mathcal{L}(\text{det-mon-sRLWW})$.

Now let $L \subseteq \Sigma^*$ be an LRR-language. According to the proof of Theorem 2.1 of [37], there exists a DRLST G such that $L_1 = G(L)$ is a deterministic context-free language. In fact, proceeding from right to left, G outputs a pair of the form (a, p_a) for each letter a read, where p_a is some additional information that depends on the suffix already read by G. From G, we obtain a UDGSM G^R such that $G^R(L^R)$ belongs to DCFL^R. Obviously, $L^R \subseteq L(G^R)$, and G^R is injective. Hence, by Proposition 2.1.55, L^R is accepted by a det-left-mon-RL-automaton, which implies that $L \in \mathcal{L}(\text{det-mon-RL})$ by Proposition 2.1.49. Thus, it follows that $\text{LRR} \subseteq \mathcal{L}(\text{det-mon-RL})$.

Conversely, let $L \in \mathcal{L}(\text{det-mon-RL})$. Then $L^R \in \mathcal{L}(\text{det-left-mon-RL})$ by Proposition 2.1.49. Hence, by Theorem 2.1.50, there is a det-left-mon-RWW-automaton $M = (Q, \Sigma, \Gamma, \rhd, \lhd, q_0, k, \delta)$ such that $L(M) = L^R$. This RWW-automaton can be described succinctly through a finite sequence of *rewriting meta-instructions* $I_1, I_2, \ldots, I_n$ and a single *accepting meta-instruction* I_0 (see Example 2.1.7 and the paragraph preceding it). Here each I_i is of the form $I_i = (E_i, u_i \to v_i)$, where, for each $i = 1, 2 \ldots, n$, E_i is a regular language, and u_i and v_i are words satisfying

$k \geq |u_i| > |v_i|$. By adjusting the size of the read/write window of M accordingly, we may even assume that $|v_i| \geq 2$, implying that v_i is neither empty nor that it is just a sentinel. Furthermore, $I_0 = (E_0, \mathsf{Accept})$, where E_0 is a regular language. In a restarting configuration $q_0 \triangleright w \triangleleft$, the meta-instruction I_i is applicable, if w admits a factorization of the form $w = w_1 u_i w_2$ such that $\triangleright w_1 \in E_i$ holds. In this situation $q_0 \triangleright w \triangleleft$ yields the restarting configuration $q_0 \triangleright w_1 v_i w_2 \triangleleft$ in one cycle, that is, $q_0 \triangleright w \triangleleft \vdash_M^c q_0 \triangleright w_1 v_i w_2 \triangleleft$. If $\triangleright w \triangleleft \in E_0$, then I_0 is applicable to the restarting configuration $q_0 \triangleright w \triangleleft$, and M accepts in a tail computation.

As M is deterministic, we can assume that at most a single meta-instruction is applicable to any given restarting configuration. In fact, the regular languages E_i, $1 \leq i \leq n$, can be chosen in such a way that, for each word $w \in \Gamma^*$, there exists at most one index $i \in \{1, 2, \ldots, n\}$ and at most one factorization of the form $w = w_1 u w_2$ with $\triangleright w_1 \in E_i$ and $u = u_i$.

Next, we associate a DGSM to the RWW-automaton M as follows. For $i = 1, 2, \ldots, n$, let $A_i = (Q_i, \Gamma \cup \{\triangleright, \triangleleft\}, q_0^{(i)}, \delta_i, F_i)$ be a complete DFA for the language $\triangleright \cdot E_i$. Then we can construct the product automaton $P = (Q_P, \Gamma \cup \{\triangleright, \triangleleft\}, q_0^{(P)}, \delta_P, Q_P)$ of the DFAs $A_1, A_2, \ldots, A_n$, that is, $Q_P = Q_1 \times Q_2 \times \ldots \times Q_n$, $q_0^{(P)} = (q_0^{(1)}, q_0^{(2)}, \ldots, q_0^{(n)})$, and

$$\delta_P((q_{i_1}^{(1)}, q_{i_2}^{(2)}, \ldots, q_{i_n}^{(n)}), a) = (\delta_1(q_{i_1}^{(1)}, a), \delta_2(q_{i_2}^{(2)}, a), \ldots, \delta_n(q_{i_n}^{(n)}, a))$$

for all states $q_{i_j}^{(j)} \in Q_j$, $1 \leq j \leq n$, and all $a \in \Gamma \cup \{\triangleright, \triangleleft\}$. The DGSM G is now defined as $G = (Q_G, \Gamma, \Delta, q_0^{(G)}, \delta_G, Q_G)$, where $Q_G = Q_P \cup \{q_0^{(G)}\}$, the output alphabet is $\Delta = \Gamma \times Q_P$, and the transition function δ_G is defined through $\delta_G = (\eta_G, \mu_G)$, where

$$\begin{array}{rcll} \eta_G(q_0^{(G)}, a) & = & \delta_P(q_0^{(P)}, \triangleright a) & \text{for all } a \in \Gamma, \\ \eta_G(q, a) & = & \delta_P(q, a) & \text{for all } q \in Q_P \text{ and all } a \in \Gamma, \end{array}$$

and the 'output function' μ_G is given through

$$\begin{array}{rcll} \mu_G(q_0^{(G)}, a) & = & (a, \delta_P(q_0^{(P)}, \triangleright)) & \text{for all } a \in \Gamma, \\ \mu_G(q, a) & = & (a, q) & \text{for all } q \in Q_P \text{ and all } a \in \Gamma. \end{array}$$

Let $a_1, a_2, \ldots, a_m \in \Gamma$, and let $p_i = \delta_P(q_0^{(P)}, \triangleright a_1 a_2 \cdots a_i)$ for all $i = 0, 1, \ldots, m$. Then

$$\eta_G(q_0^{(G)}, a_1 a_2 \cdots a_i) = p_i \text{ for all } i = 1, 2, \ldots, m,$$

and

$$G(a_1 a_2 \cdots a_m) = (a_1, p_0)(a_2, p_1) \cdots (a_m, p_{m-1}).$$

In analogy to the proof of Propositionn 2.1.54, it can now be shown that the language $G(L^R)$ belongs to the class DCFL^R (see Lemma 2.4 of [194]). Thus, $(G(L^R))^R \in \mathsf{DCFL}$.

For each state q of the product automaton P considered above, let

$$\pi_q = \{ w \in \Sigma^* \mid \delta_P(q_0^{(P)}, \triangleright w^R) = q \}.$$

Then $\pi = (\pi_q)_{q \in Q_P}$ is a finite regular partition of Σ^*, as all component automata $A_1, A_2, \ldots, A_n$ of P are complete DFAs. We say that two words $x, y \in \Sigma^*$ are congruent mod π, denoted as $x \equiv y \bmod(\pi)$, if x and y belong to the same set π_q. In fact, this relation is a left congruence on Σ^*. If $x, y, z \in \Sigma^*$ are any words satisfying $x \equiv y \bmod(\pi)$, then $\delta_P(q_0^{(P)}, \triangleright x^R) = \delta_P(q_0^{(P)}, \triangleright y^R)$. Hence,

$$\delta_P(q_0^{(P)}, \triangleright (zx)^R) = \delta_P(q_0^{(P)}, \triangleright x^R z^R) = \delta_P(q_0^{(P)}, \triangleright y^R z^R) = \delta_P(q_0^{(P)}, \triangleright (zy)^R),$$

which shows that $zx \equiv zy \bmod(\pi)$ holds.

Let $w = a_m \cdots a_2 a_1$, where $a_1, a_2, \ldots, a_m \in \Sigma$. Furthermore, let $p_0 = \delta_P(q_0^{(P)}, \triangleright)$, and let $p_i = \delta_P(q_0^{(P)}, \triangleright a_1 a_2 \cdots a_i)$ $(1 \leq i \leq m)$, that is, p_i is the index of the subset of π that contains the suffix $a_i \cdots a_2 a_1$ of w. Then it follows immediately from the construction of G that $G(w^R) = (a_1, p_0)(a_2, p_1) \cdots (a_m, p_{m-1})$ holds. We now define a mapping $f_\pi : \Sigma^* \to \rhd \cdot (\Sigma \times Q_P)^* \cdot \lhd$ by taking

$$f_\pi(a_m \cdots a_2 a_1) = \rhd(a_m, p_{m-1}) \cdots (a_2, p_1)(a_1, p_0)\lhd,$$

that is, $f_\pi(w) = \rhd \cdot (G(w^R))^R \cdot \lhd$. Obviously, f_π is an injective mapping. Furthermore, let $h_\pi : ((\Sigma \times Q_P) \cup \{\rhd, \lhd\})^* \to \Sigma^*$ be the morphism that is defined through $(a, q) \mapsto a$ $(a \in \Sigma,\ q \in Q_P)$, $\rhd \mapsto \lambda$, and $\lhd \mapsto \lambda$. If R_π denotes the range $R_\pi = f_\pi(\Sigma^*)$ of f_π, then f_π^{-1} is simply the restriction of h_π to R_π. Thus, h_π is one-to-one on R_π.

As the language $(G(L^R))^R$ is deterministic context-free, the language $f_\pi(L) = \rhd \cdot (G(L^R))^R \cdot \lhd$ is generated by an $\mathsf{LR}(0)$ grammar G'. By replacing each occurrence of each terminal symbol in G' with its image under h_π, we obtain a grammar G''. This grammar generates the language $h_\pi(f_\pi(L)) = L$, and according to Lemma 3.2 of [37], it is an $\mathsf{LR}(\pi)$ grammar. This implies that L is a left-to-right regular language, thus completing the proof of Theorem 2.1.56. □

Let RLR denote the class of *right-to-left regular languages*, which are the reversals of the left-to-right regular languages, that is, $\mathsf{RLR} = \mathsf{LRR}^R$ [37]. From Corollary 1.2.46, we see that $\mathsf{DCFL}^R \subsetneq \mathsf{RLR}$ and, from Theorem 1.2.48, we see that the class RLR is incomparable under inclusion to the class DCFL. Furthermore, Proposition 2.1.49, Theorem 2.1.50, and Theorem 2.1.56 yield the following characterization.

Corollary 2.1.57

$\mathsf{RLR} = \mathcal{L}(\text{det-left-mon-RL}) = \mathcal{L}(\text{det-left-mon-(s)RLW(W)}) = \mathcal{L}(\text{det-left-mon-(s)R(R)WW})$.

The notions of monotonicity and left-monotonicity seem to be symmetric to each other, and indeed, for (deterministic) (s)RL(W)(W)-automata, they are symmetric, as shown by Proposition 2.1.49. However, as shown by Corollary 2.1.43 and Theorem 2.1.50, these notions lead to completely different forms of behavior for deterministic one-way restarting automata. This stems from the fact that a restarting automaton starts each cycle of a computation at the left end of its tape. Hence, a monotone computation proceeds similarly to that of a pushdown automaton, while a left-monotone computation essentially processes the given input from right to left, rescanning the still to be processed prefix of the tape contents in each cycle.

In the diagram in Figure 2.3, which is a refined version of the diagram in Figure 1.12, we summarize the characterizations of language classes by the various types of restarting automata that we have studied above. All these characterizations have in common that they involve types of restarting automata with auxiliary letters and unrestricted window size.

All types of restarting automata considered so far accept the regular languages. In fact, even the det-mon-R-automata, which are the most restricted type of restarting automata considered up to now, accept a proper superclass of the regular languages, as $\mathcal{L}(\text{det-mon-R}) = \mathsf{DCFL}$ (Corollary 2.1.43). In Section 2.3, we shall encounter some restricted types of shrinking RRWW-automata (with auxiliary letters) that accept exactly the regular languages.

In [264, 265], Qichao Wang and Yongming Li introduce and study so-called *jumping* restarting automata. Such an automaton uses a *jump operation* instead of the move-right operation, where a jump operation comprises a (maximal) sequence of move-right steps. It is easily seen that (deterministic) jumping restarting automata of type R, RR, RW, RRW, RWW, or RRWW have exactly the same expressive capacity as the classical (deterministic) restarting automata of the same type. However, by restricting the number of jump operations that may be executed within a cycle, we obtain still another parameter for the restarting automaton. And indeed, Qichao Wang and Yongming Li show that, for those types of restarting automata that do not admit auxiliary letters, the number of jump operations admitted within a cycle induces infinite strictly ascending hierarchies of language classes.

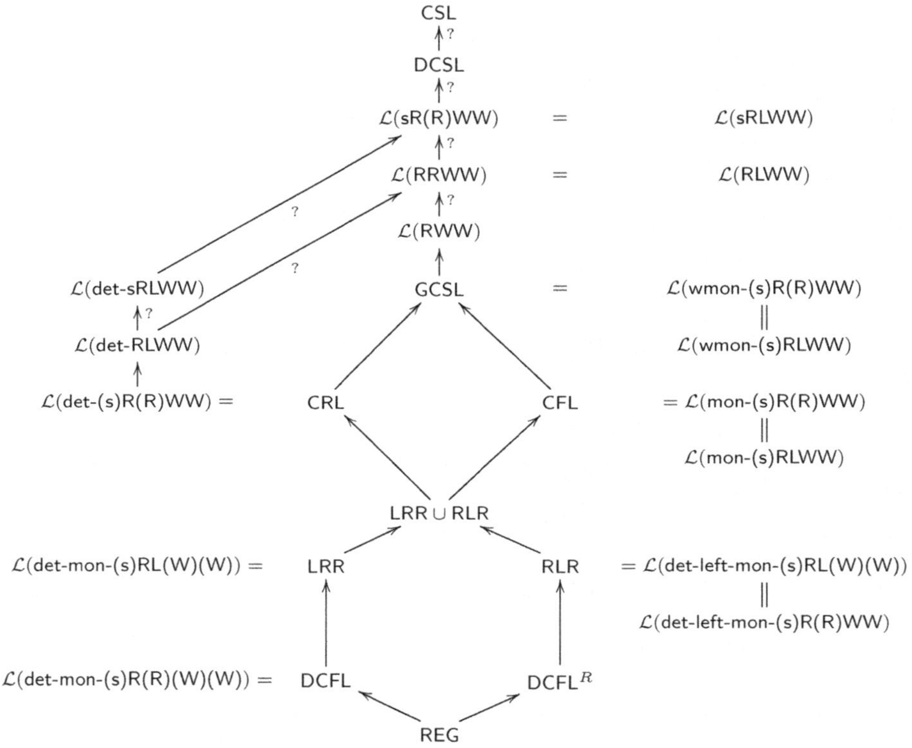

Figure 2.3: A characterization of the lower part of an extended Chomsky hierarchy by various subtypes of sRLWW-Automata. An arrow indicates a proper inclusion, while an arrow indexed by a question mark indicates an inclusion that is not known to be proper.

2.2 Restricting the Number of Auxiliary Letters

Here we look at essentially the same types of restarting automata as in the previous section, but we study various restrictions on auxiliary letters. First, in Subsection 2.2.1, we study types of restarting automata that have no auxiliary letters at all. For deterministic RRWW- and RLWW-automata that are monotone (or left-monotone), we have seen that the same language classes are obtained no matter whether or not auxiliary letters are available. Accordingly, here we concentrate on nondeterministic types of restarting automata and on deterministic non-monotone types. We shall see that, for these types of restarting automata, the absence of auxiliary letters restricts their expressive capacity considerably. In fact, we present a detailed hierarchy of language classes that are obtained from the various types of restarting automata without auxiliary letters. At the end of Subsection 2.2.1, we also discuss the so-called clearing restarting automaton, which is a rather restricted type of R-automaton. Then, in Subsection 2.2.2, we look at restarting automata that have just a single auxiliary letter at their disposal, and finally, in Subsection 2.2.3, we present some results on restarting automata that make very efficient use of their auxiliary letters.

2.2.1 Restarting Automata without Auxiliary Letters

We start this subsection with a number of example languages for which we determine upper and lower bounds. These results are then used to derive proper inclusion results and incomparability results for various types of restarting automata without auxiliary letters.

The first of these examples is the language $L_1 = \{ a^n b^n c, a^n b^{2n} d \mid n \geq 0 \}$ that we already encountered in Example 1.9.2. As shown there, L_1 is accepted by a monotone RR-automaton. On the other hand, it is shown in [87] that this language is not accepted by any RW-automaton. Actually, this result can be slightly strengthened as follows.

Lemma 2.2.1 ([200]) $L_1 \in \mathcal{L}(\mathsf{mon\text{-}RR}) \smallsetminus \mathcal{L}(\mathsf{sRW})$.

Proof. It remains to prove that L_1 is not accepted by any sRW-automaton. Assume that $M = (Q, \Sigma, \Sigma, \rhd, \lhd, q_0, k, \delta)$ is an sRW-automaton such that $L(M) = L_1$, where $\Sigma = \{a, b, c, d\}$. We consider an accepting computation of M for the word $a^n b^{2n} d \in L_1$, where n is sufficiently large. This computation cannot only consist of an accepting tail, since then, using pumping, it would follow that M also accepts a word of the form $a^{n+r} b^{2n} d$ for some $r > 0$, a contradiction. Hence, the computation considered begins with a cycle of the form $q_0 \rhd a^n b^{2n} d \lhd \vdash_M^c q_0 \rhd w \lhd$ for some word $w \in L_1$. Since M is shrinking with respect to some weight function, it follows that $w = a^{n-i} b^{2n-2i} d$ for some integer i satisfying $1 \leq i \leq k/3$. However, as M restarts immediately after executing a rewrite step, this means that, for the input word $a^n b^{n+i} c \notin L_1$, M can perform the cycle $q_0 \rhd a^n b^{n+i} c \lhd \vdash_M^c q_0 \rhd a^{n-i} b^{n-i} c \lhd$, which contradicts the Error Preserving Property (see Proposition 1.9.6), as $a^{n-i} b^{n-i} c \in L_1$. Thus, it follows that L_1 is not accepted by any sRW-automaton. □

Concerning deterministic types of restarting automata, it is easily seen that the language L_1 is accepted by a monotone det-RL-automaton. However, it is not accepted by any det-sRRW-automaton.

Lemma 2.2.2 ([200]) $L_1 \in \mathcal{L}(\mathsf{det\text{-}mon\text{-}RL}) \smallsetminus \mathcal{L}(\mathsf{det\text{-}sRRW})$.

Proof. It remains to prove that L_1 is not accepted by any det-sRRW-automaton. Assume that M is a det-sRRW-automaton for the language L_1, and let $w = a^n b^n c$. Hence, $w \in L_1$ and the computation of M on input w is accepting. If the integer n is large, then this computation cannot be an accepting tail computation, that is, it begins with a cycle of the form $q_0 \rhd w \lhd \vdash_M^c q_0 \rhd z \lhd$. By the Correctness Preserving Property (see Proposition 1.9.8), $z \in L_1$, that is, z has necessarily the form $z = a^{n-i} b^{n-i} c$ for some $i \geq 1$. Now consider the input $w' = a^n b^{2n} d$. As $w' \in L_1$, the computation of M on input w' is accepting, and as n is large, it cannot simply be an accepting tail computation. Thus, it starts with a cycle $q_0 \rhd w' \lhd \vdash_M^c q_0 \rhd z' \lhd$. As M is deterministic, and as it can read its input only from left to right, this cycle contains the same rewrite step as the computation on input w, that is, it rewrites the word $w' = a^n b^{2n} d$ into the word $z' = a^{n-i} b^{2n-i} d$. As $2(n-i) = 2n - 2i < 2n - i$, we see that $z' \notin L_1$. This, however, violates the Correctness Preserving Property. It follows that the language L_1 is not accepted by any deterministic sRRW-automaton. □

The second example language is $L_2 = \{ a^n b^n \mid n \geq 0 \} \cup \{ a^n b^m \mid m > 2n \geq 0 \}$. It is known that L_2 is a Church-Rosser language [193], and it has been shown in [87] that L_2 is not accepted by any RRW-automaton. However, we even have the following slightly stronger result.

Lemma 2.2.3 $L_2 \in \mathsf{CRL} \smallsetminus \mathcal{L}(\mathsf{sRRW})$.

Proof. Assume that $M = (Q, \{a,b\}, \{a,b\}, \rhd, \lhd, q_0, k, \delta)$ is an sRRW-automaton for L_2, let n be a sufficiently large integer, and let $a^n b^n \in L_2$ be given as input. In the first cycle of an accepting computation of M on this input, $a^n b^n$ is rewritten into a word w from L_2. In a single rewrite step, M can only rewrite a word of length k into a word of length at most $c \cdot k$, where c is a constant that depends on the underlying weight function. It follows that the word w is of the form $w = a^{n-r} b^{n-r}$, where $1 \leq r \leq k/2$.

Now let p be the constant from Proposition 2.1.8 for M, and choose the integer n such that n is a multiple of p. Then we can write the suffix b^n of $a^n b^n$ as $b^n = uzv$, where $|z| = p$, and, for all $i \geq 1$, M can execute the cycle

$$q_0 \rhd a^n u z^i v \lhd = q_0 \rhd a^n b^{n+(i-1)\cdot p} \lhd \vdash^c_M q_0 \rhd a^{n-r} b^{n-r+(i-1)\cdot p} \lhd .$$

For $i = \frac{n}{p} + 1$, we now obtain $n + (i-1) \cdot p = 2n$, which implies that $a^n b^{n+(i-1)\cdot p} = a^n b^{2n} \notin L_2$. However, $n - r + (i-1) \cdot p = 2n - r > 2(n-r)$, and hence, $a^{n-r} b^{n-r+(i-1)\cdot p} \in L_2$, which contradicts the Error Preserving Property for M (Proposition 1.9.6). It follows that $L_2 \notin \mathcal{L}(\mathsf{sRRW})$. □

The third example language is $L_3 = \{ a^n b^n, a^n c b^n \mid n \geq 0\} \cup \{ a^n b^m, a^n d b^m \mid m > 2n \geq 0 \}$. For this language, the following result holds.

Lemma 2.2.4 $L_3 \in \mathcal{L}(\mathsf{mon\text{-}RW}) \smallsetminus \mathcal{L}(\mathsf{RR})$.

Proof. An RW-automaton A_3 can proceed as follows, given a word $w \in \{a,b,c,d\}^*$ as input:

1. If $w \in \{ab, c, \lambda\} \cup \{ b^m, db^m \mid m \geq 1 \}$, then A_3 accepts immediately.
2. If $w = a^n bb\alpha$ for some $n \geq 1$ and some word α, then A_3 rewrites the factor abb into the word cb or into the word d.
3. If $w = a^n cb\alpha$ for some $n \geq 1$ and some word α, then A_3 rewrites the factor acb into c.
4. If $w = a^n dbb\alpha$ for some $n \geq 1$ and some word α, then A_3 rewrites the factor $adbb$ into d.

It is easily seen that $L(A_3) = L_3$ and that A_3 is monotone.

Now assume that B is an RR-automaton for the language L_3. Then

$$L(B) \cap \{a,b\}^* = L_3 \cap \{a,b\}^* = \{ a^n b^n, a^n b^m \mid m > 2n \geq 0 \} = L_2.$$

As all rewrite steps of B are just deletions, this means that by removing the letters c and d from the input alphabet of B, we obtain an RR-automaton for the language L_2. This contradicts the fact that L_2 is not even accepted by any sRRW-automaton by Lemma 2.2.3. It follows that L_3 is not accepted by any RR-automaton. □

The fourth example language is $L_4 = \{ ca^n b^n, ea^n b^n \mid n \geq 0 \} \cup \{ da^n b^m, ea^n b^m \mid m > 2n \geq 0 \}$. For L_4, the following result holds.

Lemma 2.2.5 ([200]) $L_4 \in \mathcal{L}(\mathsf{mon\text{-}sRW}) \smallsetminus \mathcal{L}(\mathsf{RRW})$.

Proof. An sRW-automaton A_4 can proceed as follows, given a word $w \in \{a,b,c,d,e\}^*$ as input, where we assume that the weight function ω satisfies the conditions $\omega(e) > \omega(c)$ and $\omega(e) > \omega(d)$:

1. If $w \in \{eab, cab, e, c\} \cup \{\, eb^m, db^m \mid m \geq 1\,\}$, then A_4 accepts immediately.

2. If $w = ea\alpha$ for some word α, then A_4 rewrites the letter e into c or d.

3. If $w = ca^n bb\alpha$ for some $n \geq 2$ and some word α, then A_4 rewrites the factor abb into b.

4. If $w = da^n bbb\alpha$ for some $n \geq 1$ and some word α, then A_4 rewrites the factor $abbb$ into b.

It is easily seen that $L(A_4) = L_4$ and that A_4 is monotone.

Now assume that B is an RRW-automaton for the language L_4. Let $w = ea^n b^n$ for some large integer n. Then B cannot accept w in a tail computation, that is, each accepting computation of B on input w begins with a cycle of the form $q_0 \triangleright w \triangleleft \vdash_M^c q_0 \triangleright z \triangleleft$. Because of the Correctness Preserving Property, $z \in L_4$. As each rewrite step of B is length-reducing, $z = ea^{n-i}b^{n-i}$ for some small positive value of i. Now the proof continues in the same way as the proof of Lemma 2.2.3, leading to a contradiction, which shows that L_4 is not accepted by any RRW-automaton. $\square$

The fifth example language is $L_5 = \{\, a^n b^m \mid 0 \leq n \leq m \leq 2n \,\}$. For L_5, we have the following result, which, however, requires a somewhat more involved proof.

Lemma 2.2.6 ([200]) $L_5 \in \mathcal{L}(\text{mon-R}) \smallsetminus \mathcal{L}(\text{det-sRLW})$.

Proof. It is shown in [87] that L_5 is accepted by a monotone R-automaton. Thus, it remains to prove that L_5 is not accepted by any det-sRLW-automaton.

Assume that $B = (Q, \{a,b\}, \{a,b\}, \triangleright, \triangleleft, q_0, k, \delta)$ is a det-sRLW-automaton for the language L_5, let $\omega : \{a,b\} \to \mathbb{N}_+$ be a weight function that is compatible with B, and let $\nu = \frac{\omega(a)}{\omega(b)}$. Finally, let $w = a^n b^n$ for some large integer n that is to be determined later. Then $w \in L_5$, and hence, B accepts on input w. As n is large, the accepting computation of B on input w is not a tail computation, that is, it begins with a cycle of the form $q_0 \triangleright w \triangleleft \vdash_B^c q_0 \triangleright z \triangleleft$. By the Correctness Preserving Property, $z \in L_5$.

Claim. $z = a^{n-i}b^{n+j}$ for some integers i, j such that $0 < i \leq k$ and either $-i \leq j \leq 0$ or $1 \leq j < i \cdot \nu$.

Proof of Claim. As $z \in L_5$, we see that $z = a^r b^s$ for some integers r and s such that $r \leq s \leq 2r$. Furthermore, as k is the size of the read/write window of B, only a factor u of length k of $w = a^n b^n$ is replaced with a factor v in the above cycle, that is, $w = xuy = a^n b^n$ and $z = xvy$. If $r \geq n$, then also $s \geq r \geq n$, which means that $|z|_a \geq |w|_a$ and $|z|_b \geq |w|_b$. This implies that $\omega(z) \geq \omega(w)$, a contradiction. Hence, it follows that $r < n$, which yields that $r = n - i$ for some integer i satisfying $0 < i \leq k$.

During the rewrite step from w to z, i occurrences of the letter a are deleted or replaced with some occurrences of the letter b. As $\omega(w) - \omega(z) = \omega(u) - \omega(v) > 0$ and as i occurrences of the letter a are deleted or replaced, which have a combined weight of $i \cdot \omega(a)$, we see that less than $i \cdot \nu$ many occurrences of the letter b can be generated by this rewrite step. Hence, either $s = n - j$ for some integer j satisfying $0 \leq j \leq i$, or $s = n + j$ for some integer j satisfying $1 \leq j < i \cdot \nu$. $\square$

From the above claim, it follows that the rewrite step in the cycle rewriting w into z is performed on the prefix of length $n + k - 1$ of w. Hence, this rewrite step does not touch the suffix of length $n - k + 1$ of w. However, during the above cycle, B may read across the suffix $b^{n-k+1}\triangleleft$. Hence, with each position within this suffix, we can associate two *crossing sequences*. The first one consists of the sequence of states in which B has the letter at that position in the left-most place of its window while being in the part of the cycle *before* the rewrite step is executed, and the second one consists of the corresponding sequence of states while B is in the part of the cycle *after* the rewrite step has been executed. As B is deterministic, no crossing sequence can contain any state of B twice, that is, $|Q|$ is an upper bound for the length of each of these crossing sequences. In particular, this means that there are at most

$$\rho = \sum_{m=0}^{|Q|} \binom{|Q|}{m} \cdot m!$$

many different such crossing sequences.

Now we choose the integer n by taking $n = (2k + \rho^2)!$. Then within the suffix of length $k + \rho^2$ of $w = a^n b^n$, there exist two positions such that the same crossing sequences occur at these positions. Let t be the minimal distance between two such positions. Then $t \leq \rho^2$. It now follows that B will execute a cycle that contains the same rewrite operation replacing the factor u by v for any input of the form $a^n b^{n+h\cdot t}$. Now we choose $h = \frac{n}{t} = \frac{(2k+\rho^2)!}{t}$, which means that $n + h \cdot t = n + (2k + \rho^2)! = 2n$. Then B executes the cycle $q_0 \rhd a^n b^{2n} \lhd \vdash_B^c q_0 \rhd a^{n-i} b^{2n+j} \lhd$, which contradicts the Correctness Preserving Property, as $a^n b^{2n} \in L_5$, while $a^{n-i} b^{2n+j} \notin L_5$, since $2(n - i) = 2n - 2i < 2n - i \leq 2n + j$. Thus, L_5 is not accepted by any det-sRLW-automaton. □

The sixth example language is $L_6 = L_{6,1} \cup L_{6,2} \cup L_{6,3}$, where

- $L_{6,1} = \{ (ab)^{2^n - i} c (ab)^i \mid n \geq 0, 0 \leq i \leq 2^n \}$,
- $L_{6,2} = \{ (ab)^{2^n - 2i} (abb)^i \mid n \geq 1, 0 \leq i \leq 2^{n-1} \}$, and
- $L_{6,3} = \{ (abb)^{2^n - i} (ab)^i \mid n \geq 0, 0 \leq i \leq 2^n \}$.

This language has already been considered in [193]. It is easily verified that L_6 is accepted by a det-RR-automaton. However, the following negative result holds.

Lemma 2.2.7 $L_6 \notin \mathcal{L}(\mathsf{sRW})$.

Proof. Assume that $M = (Q, \Sigma, \Sigma, \rhd, \lhd, q_0, k, \delta)$ is an sRW-automaton that accepts L_6, where $\Sigma = \{a, b, c\}$, and let $w = (ab)^{2^n} c (ab)^{2^n} \in L_{6,1}$. If n is sufficiently large, then M cannot accept w in a tail computation. Hence, an accepting computation of M on input w begins with a cycle of the form $q_0 \rhd w \lhd \vdash_M^c q_0 \rhd w_1 \lhd$. Since we consider an accepting computation, the Correctness Preserving Property for M implies that $w_1 \in L_6$. From the form of w and the structure of the words in L_6 it follows that $w_1 = (ab)^{2^{n+1}}$.

Now consider the input word $w' = (ab)^{2^n} c (ab)^{2^n} c \notin L_6$. Given w' as input, M can execute the cycle

$$q_0 \rhd w' \lhd = q_0 \rhd (ab)^{2^n} c (ab)^{2^n} c \lhd \vdash_M^c q_0 \rhd (ab)^{2^n} (ab)^{2^n} c \lhd,$$

which contradicts the Error Preserving Property for M, as $(ab)^{2^n} (ab)^{2^n} c \in L_6$. This means that L_6 is not accepted by any sRW-automaton. □

The next example language is $L_7 = L_{7,1} \cup L_{7,2}$, where

- $L_{7,1} = \{ a^{2^n - 2i} c a^i \mid n \geq 1, 0 \leq 2i < 2^n \}$ and
- $L_{7,2} = \{ a^i d a^{2^n - 2i} \mid n \geq 1, 0 \leq 2i < 2^n \}$.

This language is taken from [158], where the following result has been established.

Lemma 2.2.8 $L_7 \in \mathcal{L}(\mathsf{det\text{-}RW}) \smallsetminus \mathcal{L}(\mathsf{RR})$.

As by Theorem 2.1.2, $\mathcal{L}(\mathsf{RR}) = \mathcal{L}(\mathsf{RL})$, it follows that $L_7 \in \mathcal{L}(\mathsf{det\text{-}RW}) \smallsetminus \mathcal{L}(\mathsf{RL})$. Finally, let $L_8 = L_{8,1} \cup L_{8,2}$, where

- $L_{8,1} = \{ a^{2^n - i} c b^i \mid n \geq 1, 0 \leq i < 2^n \}$ and
- $L_{8,2} = \{ a^i d b^{2^n - 2i} \mid n \geq 1, 0 \leq 2i < 2^n \}$.

For this language, we have the following result.

Lemma 2.2.9 ([200]) $L_8 \in \mathcal{L}(\mathsf{det\text{-}sRW}) \smallsetminus \mathcal{L}(\mathsf{RLW})$.

Proof. First, we describe a det-sRW-automaton M_8 on $\Sigma = \{a, b, c, d\}$ for L_8, taking the weight function $\omega : \Sigma \to \mathbb{N}_+$ that is defined through $\omega(a) = 3$ and $\omega(b) = \omega(c) = \omega(d) = 2$. In each cycle, M_8 scans the tape from left to right and applies one of the following rewrite steps, based on the prefix of the tape contents α that it encounters:

1. If $\alpha = \rhd a^n ac\lhd$ for some $n \geq 1$, then M_8 rewrites the suffix $ac\lhd$ into $cb\lhd$. Here we need that $\omega(a) > \omega(b)$ holds.
2. If $\alpha = \rhd a^n acb\alpha_1$ for some $n \geq 1$ and some word α_1, then M_8 rewrites the factor acb into cbb. Here we need again that $\omega(a) > \omega(b)$ holds.
3. If $\alpha = \rhd acb\alpha_1$, then M_8 rewrites the prefix $\rhd acb$ into the word $\rhd dbb$. Here it suffices that $\omega(c) = \omega(d)$ and $\omega(a) > \omega(b)$.
4. If $\alpha = \rhd a^n dbbb\alpha_1$ for some $n \geq 0$ and some word α_1, then M_8 rewrites the factor $dbbb$ into adb. Here we need that $2\omega(b) > \omega(a)$ holds.
5. If $\alpha = \rhd a^n dbb\lhd$ for some $n \geq 1$, then M_8 rewrites the suffix $dbb\lhd$ into $ac\lhd$. Here it suffices that $\omega(c) = \omega(d)$ and $2\omega(b) > \omega(a)$.
6. Finally, M_8 accepts if and when $\alpha = \rhd dbb\lhd$.

It follows easily that M_8 is a det-sRW-automaton with weight function ω and that $L(M_8) = L_8$.

Now assume that there exists an RLW-automaton $M' = (Q, \Sigma, \Sigma, \rhd, \lhd, q_0, k, \delta)$ for L_8. Let $w = a^{2^n}c \in L_{8,1}$ for a sufficiently large n. Then M' cannot accept on input w without performing any rewrite/restart steps. Thus, the first cycle of an accepting computation of M' on input w yields a restart configuration of the form $q_0\rhd a^{2^n-i}cb^j\lhd$ or $q_0\rhd a^{2^n-i}db^j\lhd$ for some $0 \leq j < i \leq k$. Obviously, $a^{2^n-i}cb^j \notin L_8$, as $2^n - i + j < 2^n$ is not a power of two. On the other hand, as i and j are small in comparison to 2^n, $j + 2(2^n - i) = j + 2^{n+1} - 2i$ is only a power of two, if $j = 2i$, contradicting the fact that $j < i$. Hence, neither $a^{2^n-i}cb^j$ nor $a^{2^n-i}db^j$ belongs to L_8, which contradicts the Correctness Preserving Property for M'. It follows that $L_8 \notin \mathcal{L}(\mathsf{RLW})$. □

The last example is the language $L'_{\text{copy}} = \{\, w\#w \mid w \in \{a,b\}^* \,\}$. In Example 2.1.9, we saw that this language is accepted by an RWW-automaton. If MVL steps are provided, then L'_{copy} can even be accepted by a deterministic RLWW-automaton. On the other hand, it is easily seen that no shrinking RLW-automaton can accept this language, as such an automaton has neither auxiliary letters nor can it rewrite both $\{a,b\}$-factors of an input of the form $a^m b^n \# a^m b^n$ in the same way within a single cycle. Thus, we have the following result.

Lemma 2.2.10 $L'_{\text{copy}} \in \mathcal{L}(\mathsf{det\text{-}RLWW}) \smallsetminus \mathcal{L}(\mathsf{sRLW})$.

Based on these example languages, we obtain the following separation results for nondeterministic restarting automata without auxiliary letters.

Theorem 2.2.11 *All arrows in the diagram in Figure 2.4 denote proper inclusions, and language classes not connected by a sequence of arrows are incomparable under inclusion.*

Proof. By Lemma 2.2.10, $L'_{\text{copy}} \in \mathcal{L}(\mathsf{sRLWW}) \smallsetminus \mathcal{L}(\mathsf{sRLW})$. By Lemma 2.2.1, the language L_1 has the property that $L_1 \in \mathcal{L}(\mathsf{RR}) \smallsetminus \mathcal{L}(\mathsf{sRW})$. Furthermore, by Lemma 2.2.8, $L_7 \in \mathcal{L}(\mathsf{det\text{-}RW}) \smallsetminus \mathcal{L}(\mathsf{RL})$. Finally, by Lemma 2.2.9, $L_8 \in \mathcal{L}(\mathsf{det\text{-}sRW}) \smallsetminus \mathcal{L}(\mathsf{RLW})$. We see from these results that all arrows in the diagram in Figure 2.4 denote proper inclusions and that all classes that are not connected by a sequence of arrows are incomparable under inclusion. □

Our second theorem concerns separation results for deterministic restarting automata without auxiliary letters.

Theorem 2.2.12 *All arrows in the diagram in Figure 2.5 denote proper inclusions, and language classes not connected by a sequence of arrows are incomparable under inclusion.*

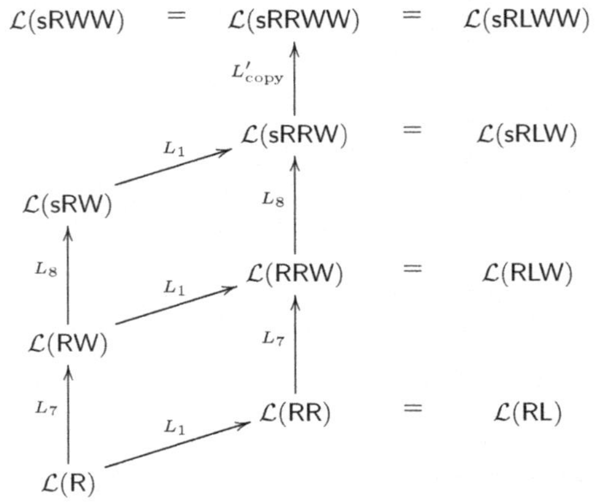

Figure 2.4: The taxonomy of nondeterministic restarting automata without auxiliary letters.

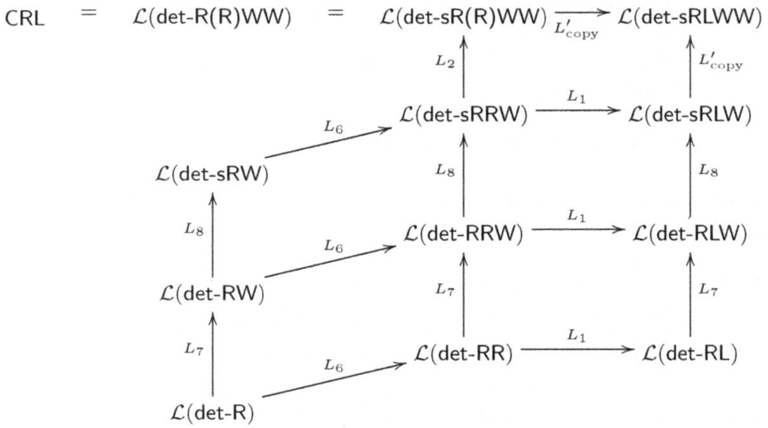

Figure 2.5: The taxonomy of deterministic restarting automata without auxiliary letters.

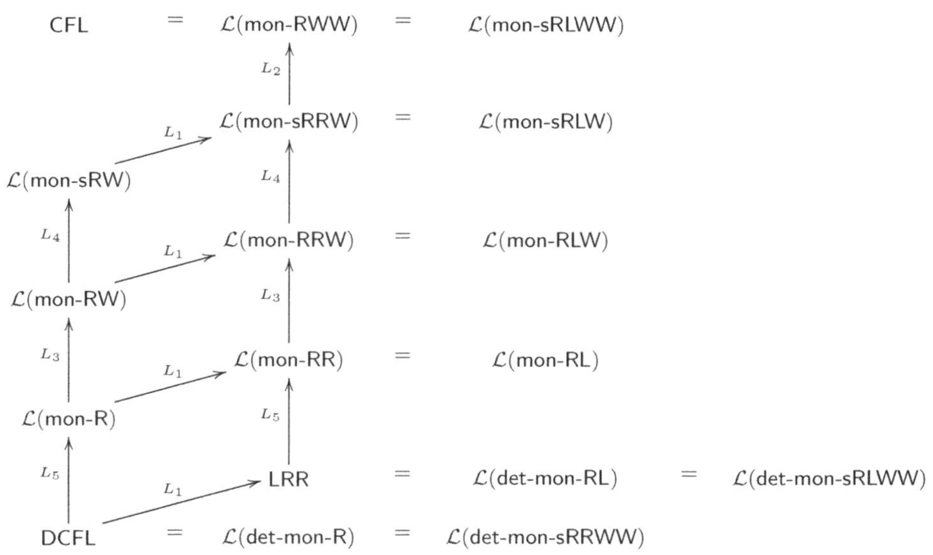

Figure 2.6: The taxonomy of monotone restarting automata without auxiliary letters.

Proof. The language L'_{copy} is accepted by a deterministic (shrinking) RLWW-automaton, but not by any sRLW-automaton, as shown in Lemma 2.2.10. It is further known that L'_{copy} is not a Church-Rosser language, and hence, it is not accepted by any det-sRRWW-automaton. By Lemma 2.2.2, the language L_1, which is accepted by a det-RL-automaton, is not accepted by any det-sRRW-automaton.

By Lemma 2.2.3, L_2 is a Church-Rosser language that is not accepted by any sRRW-automaton, by Lemma 2.2.7, $L_6 \in \mathcal{L}(\mathsf{det\text{-}RR}) \smallsetminus \mathcal{L}(\mathsf{sRW})$, and by Lemma 2.2.8, $L_7 \in \mathcal{L}(\mathsf{det\text{-}RW}) \smallsetminus \mathcal{L}(\mathsf{RL})$. Finally, by Lemma 2.2.9, $L_8 \in \mathcal{L}(\mathsf{det\text{-}sRW}) \smallsetminus \mathcal{L}(\mathsf{RLW})$. We see from these results that all arrows in the diagram in Figure 2.5 denote proper inclusions and that all classes that are not connected by a sequence of arrows are incomparable under inclusion. □

Next, we relate the various classes of monotone restarting automata to each other. As noted above, $L_1 \in \mathcal{L}(\mathsf{mon\text{-}RR}) \smallsetminus \mathcal{L}(\mathsf{sRW})$, and $L_1 \in \mathcal{L}(\mathsf{det\text{-}mon\text{-}RL}) \smallsetminus \mathcal{L}(\mathsf{det\text{-}sRRW})$. Furthermore, the language L_2 is obviously context-free, but $L_2 \notin \mathcal{L}(\mathsf{sRLW})$ by Lemma 2.2.3, and by Lemma 2.2.4, $L_3 \in \mathcal{L}(\mathsf{mon\text{-}RW}) \smallsetminus \mathcal{L}(\mathsf{RR})$. Finally, by Lemma 2.2.5, $L_4 \in \mathcal{L}(\mathsf{mon\text{-}sRW}) \smallsetminus \mathcal{L}(\mathsf{RRW})$, and by Lemma 2.2.6, $L_5 \in \mathcal{L}(\mathsf{mon\text{-}R}) \smallsetminus \mathcal{L}(\mathsf{det\text{-}sRLW})$. These properties of the languages L_1 to L_5 and Corollary 2.1.41, Corollary 2.1.43, and Theorem 2.1.56 yield the following result.

Theorem 2.2.13 *All arrows in the diagram in Figure 2.6 denote proper inclusions, and language classes not connected by a sequence of arrows are incomparable under inclusion.*

As each monotone restarting automaton is weakly monotone, the following result is obtained for weakly monotone restarting automata from Corollary 2.1.33 by again using the example languages L_1 to L_4.

Theorem 2.2.14 *All arrows in the diagram in Figure 2.7 denote proper inclusions, and language classes not connected by a sequence of arrows are incomparable under inclusion.*

It remains to relate the various monotone and weakly monotone classes and the various deterministic classes to one another and to the general (that is, nondeterministic and non-monotone) classes. Obviously, for each type $\mathsf{X} \in \{\mathsf{R}, \mathsf{RR}, \mathsf{RL}, \mathsf{RW}, \mathsf{RRW}, \mathsf{RLW}, \mathsf{sRW}, \mathsf{sRRW}, \mathsf{sRLW}\}$ of restarting automata,

$$\mathcal{L}(\mathsf{det\text{-}X}) \cup \mathcal{L}(\mathsf{mon\text{-}X}) \subseteq \mathcal{L}(\mathsf{wmon\text{-}X}) \subseteq \mathcal{L}(\mathsf{X}).$$

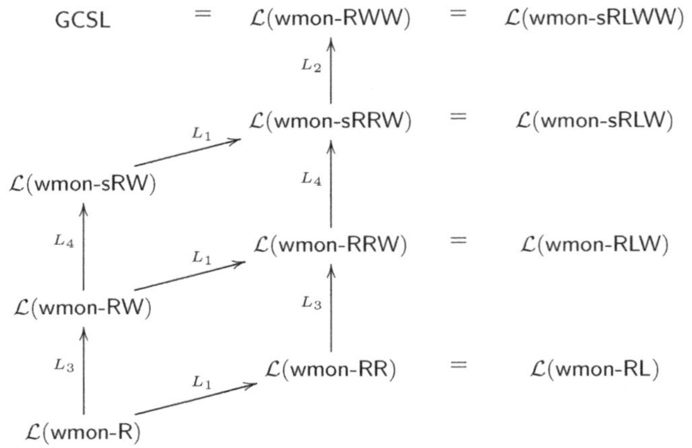

Figure 2.7: The taxonomy of weakly monotone restarting automata without auxiliary letters.

Theorem 2.2.15 ([103]) *Let* $\mathsf{X} \in \{\mathsf{R}, \mathsf{RR}, \mathsf{RL}\}$. *For each* XW*-automaton* M*, there exists an injective morphism (an encoding)* φ *such that the language* $\varphi(L(M))$ *is accepted by an* X*-automaton* M'*. If* M *is deterministic and/or monotone, then so is* M'*.*

Proof outline. Let $M = (Q, \Sigma, \Sigma, \rhd, \lhd, q_0, k, \delta)$ be an RLW-automaton, let $\Sigma = \{a_1, a_2, \ldots, a_m\}$, and let $\Gamma = \{0, 1, c, d\}$. We define an encoding $\varphi_{k,m} : \Sigma \to \Gamma^+$ as follows:

$$a_i \mapsto c1^{m+1-i}0^i(cd1^{m+1}0^{m+1})^k \quad (1 \le i \le m).$$

Then, for all $1 \le i \le m$,

$$|\varphi_{k,m}(a_i)| = (m+1) \cdot (2k+1) + 2k + 1 = (m+2) \cdot (2k+1).$$

The encoding $\varphi_{k,m}$ is naturally extended to words by taking

$$\varphi_{k,m}(x_1 x_2 \cdots x_n) = \varphi_{k,m}(x_1)\varphi_{k,m}(x_2) \cdots \varphi_{k,m}(x_n) \text{ for all } n \ge 0 \text{ and } x_1, x_2, \ldots, x_n \in \Sigma.$$

It follows that $\varphi_{k,m} : \Sigma^* \to \Gamma^*$ is an injective morphism. It has the following important property (see [103] Lemma 3.4).

Claim. For all $u \in \Sigma^k$ and $v \in \Sigma^*$, if $|v| < k$, then $\varphi_{k,m}(v)$ is a proper scattered subword of $\varphi_{k,m}(u)$.

From M, we can now construct an RL-automaton $M' = (Q', \Gamma, \Gamma, \rhd, \lhd, q_0', (m+2)\cdot(2k+1)\cdot k, \delta')$ which accepts the language $\varphi_{k,m}(L(M)) \subseteq \Gamma^*$. Essentially, each rewrite transition $(p, v) \in \delta(q, u)$ of M is replaced by a rewrite transition of the form $(p', \varphi_{k,m}(v)) \in \delta'(q', \varphi_{k,m}(u))$. As $|u| = k > |v|$, the above claim shows that $\varphi_{k,m}(v)$ is a proper scattered subword of $\varphi_{k,m}(u)$. Thus, the rewrite transition $(p', \varphi_{k,m}(v)) \in \delta'(q', \varphi_{k,m}(u))$ transforms $\varphi_{k,m}(u)$ into $\varphi_{k,m}(v)$ by deleting some letters. This shows that M' is indeed an RL-automaton.

For RRW- and RW-automata, the proof is completely analogous. □

As pointed out in Section 1.2, the language $L_{\text{pal}} = \{ ww^R \mid w \in \{a, b\}^* \}$ of palindromes of even length is not a Church-Rosser language (see [93]). Hence, by Corollary 2.1.34, this language is not accepted by any det-sRRWW-automaton. However, as L_{pal} is context-free, Corollary 2.1.41 shows that there exists a monotone RWW-automaton M_{pal} such that $L(M_{\text{pal}}) = L_{\text{pal}}$. In fact, M_{pal} can be constructed in such a way that all its computations are monotone, not just those that begin with a proper initial configuration. To that aim, we take $M_{\text{pal}} = (Q, \Sigma, \Gamma, \rhd, \lhd, q_0, 4, \delta)$, where $Q = \{q_0\}$, $\Sigma = \{a, b\}$, and $\Gamma = \Sigma \cup \{ [c, d] \mid c, d \in \Sigma \} \cup \{X\}$. The transition relation δ is defined as follows, where $c, d, e, f, g, h \in \Sigma$ and $A \in \Gamma$. As q_0 is the only state, we present the transitions without the components that refer to states:

$$
\begin{array}{rlcll}
(1) & \delta(\rhd u \lhd) & = & \{\mathsf{Accept}\} & \text{for all } u \in \{\lambda, aa, bb\},\\
(2) & \delta(\rhd cde) & = & \{\rhd[c,d]e\}, & \\
(3) & \delta(\rhd[c,d]ef) = & = & \{\rhd[c,d][e,f]\}, & \text{if } e \neq f \wedge (c \neq f \vee d \neq e),\\
(4) & \delta(\rhd[c,d]ee) & = & \{\rhd[c,d]X, \rhd[c,d][e,e]\}, & \text{if } c \neq e \vee d \neq e\\
(5) & \delta(\rhd[c,d]dc) & = & \{\rhd X, \rhd[c,d][d,c]\}, & \text{if } c \neq d,\\
(6) & \delta(\rhd[c,c]cc) & = & \{\rhd X, \rhd[c,c]X, \rhd[c,c][c,c]\}, & \\
(7) & \delta(\rhd[c,d][e,f]A) & = & \{\mathsf{MVR}\}, & \\
(8) & \delta([c,d][e,f][g,h]A) & = & \{\mathsf{MVR}\}, & \\
(9) & \delta([c,d][e,f]gh) & = & \{[c,d][e,f][g,h]\}, & \text{if } g \neq h \wedge (e \neq h \vee f \neq g),\\
(10) & \delta([c,d][e,f]gg) & = & \{[c,d][e,f]X, [c,d][e,f][g,g]\}, & \text{if } e \neq g \vee f \neq g,\\
(11) & \delta([c,d][e,f]fe) & = & \{[c,d]X, [c,d][e,f][f,e]\}, & \text{if } e \neq f,\\
(12) & \delta([c,d][e,e]ee) & = & \{[c,d]X, [c,d][e,e]X, [c,d][e,e][e,e]\}, & \\
(13) & \delta(\rhd X \lhd) & = & \{\mathsf{Accept}\}, & \\
(14) & \delta(\rhd[c,d]Xe) & = & \{\mathsf{MVR}\}, & \\
(15) & \delta([c,d][e,f]Xg) & = & \{\mathsf{MVR}\}, & \\
(16) & \delta([c,d]Xdc) & = & \{X\}. &
\end{array}
$$

The auxiliary letters of the form $[c,d]$ are used to encode factors of length two. Given a word $w \in \Sigma^*$ as input, where $|w| > 2$, M_{pal} encodes the consecutive factors of length two of w from left to right. If, at some point, an auxiliary letter $[c,d]$ is followed by the factor dc, then M_{pal} can continue by encoding the factor dc into the letter $[d,c]$, or it can guess that the middle of the input has been reached, and it can then replace the factor $[c,d]dc$ with the auxiliary letter X (see (5), (6), (11), and (12)). Furthermore, if, at some point, an auxiliary letter $[c,d]$ is followed by a factor ee, then M_{pal} can continue by encoding the factor ee into the letter $[e,e]$, or it can guess that the middle of the input has been reached, and it can then replace the factor ee with the auxiliary letter X (see (4), (6), (10), and (12)). Thereafter, M_{pal} checks whether the remaining suffix that follows after the letter X is the reversal of the encoded prefix that precedes the letter X (see (16)). It follows that M_{pal} is a monotone RWW-automaton for the language L_{pal}. In addition, if $q_0 \rhd \alpha \lhd$ is an arbitrary restarting configuration of M_{pal}, then each computation of M_{pal} that starts from this configuration is monotone.

Now let M'_{pal} be the RW-automaton that is obtained from M_{pal} by declaring all letters of Γ to input letters. Then M'_{pal} is monotone, and $L(M'_{\mathrm{pal}})$ is a context-free language that satisfies the condition $L(M'_{\mathrm{pal}}) \cap \{a,b\}^* = L_{\mathrm{pal}}$. As the class CRL of Church-Rosser languages is closed under intersection with regular sets [186], it follows that the language $L(M'_{\mathrm{pal}})$ is not Church-Rosser.

By Theorem 2.2.15, we obtain a monotone R-automaton $\tilde{M}_{\mathrm{pal}}$ from the monotone RW-automaton M'_{pal} such that $L(\tilde{M}_{\mathrm{pal}}) = \varphi(L(M'_{\mathrm{pal}}))$, where φ is an injective morphism. Then $L(\tilde{M}_{\mathrm{pal}})$ is a context-free language that is not Church-Rosser, as the language class CRL is closed under inverse morphisms [186] and $L(M'_{\mathrm{pal}}) = \varphi^{-1}(L(\tilde{M}_{\mathrm{pal}}))$. Thus, we obtain the following result.

Proposition 2.2.16 *The language $L(\tilde{M}_{\mathrm{pal}})$ that is accepted by the monotone R-automaton $\tilde{M}_{\mathrm{pal}}$ is context-free, but it is not a Church-Rosser language, and hence, it is not accepted by any det-sRRWW-automaton.*

It follows that no nondeterministic monotone class is contained in the class CRL of Church-Rosser languages, and from Lemma 2.2.6, we see that no nondeterministic monotone class is contained in $\mathcal{L}(\mathsf{det\text{-}sRLW})$. However, the following question remains open.

Problem 2.2.17 *Is the class $\mathcal{L}(\mathsf{mon\text{-}R})$ of languages that are accepted by monotone R-automata contained in the class $\mathcal{L}(\mathsf{det\text{-}sRLWW})$ of languages that are accepted by deterministic shrinking RLWW-automata?*

Observe that the language L_{pal} is accepted by a det-sRLWW-automaton, and so is the above language $L(\tilde{M}_{\mathrm{pal}})$.

It is known that the non-context-free language $L_{\text{exp}} = \{ a^{2^n} \mid n \geq 0 \}$ is a Church-Rosser language (see Example 1.2.16). Thus, there exists a det-RWW-automaton M_{exp} such that $L(M_{\text{exp}}) = L_{\text{exp}}$. Let M'_{exp} be the det-RW-automaton that is obtained from M_{exp} by declaring all letters of the tape alphabet of M_{exp} to input letters. Then $L(M'_{\text{exp}}) \cap \{a\}^* = L_{\text{exp}}$, which implies that $L(M'_{\text{exp}})$ is not context-free, either. By Theorem 2.2.15, there exists an injective morphism φ such that the language $\varphi(L(M'_{\text{exp}}))$ is accepted by a det-R-automaton $\tilde{M}_{\text{exp}}$. As $\varphi^{-1}(L(\tilde{M}_{\text{exp}})) = L(M'_{\text{exp}})$, and as the class CFL is closed under inverse morphisms, it follows that the language $L(\tilde{M}_{\text{exp}})$ is not context-free, either. Thus, we have the following result.

Proposition 2.2.18 *The language $L(\tilde{M}_{\text{exp}})$ that is accepted by the det-R-automaton $\tilde{M}_{\text{exp}}$ is a Church-Rosser language, but it is not context-free, and hence, it is not accepted by any monotone sRLWW-automaton.*

Lemma 2.2.6 and Propositions 2.2.16 and 2.2.18 imply that all nondeterministic monotone classes are incomparable under inclusion to all deterministic non-monotone classes with the only possible exception of $\mathcal{L}(\mathsf{det\text{-}(s)RLWW})$. In particular, this yields the following proper inclusions.

Corollary 2.2.19 *For each type* $\mathsf{X} \in \{\mathsf{R}, \mathsf{RR}, \mathsf{RL}, \mathsf{RW}, \mathsf{RRW}, \mathsf{RLW}, \mathsf{sRW}, \mathsf{sRRW}, \mathsf{sRLW}\}$,

$$\mathcal{L}(\mathsf{det\text{-}X}) \subsetneq \mathcal{L}(\mathsf{wmon\text{-}X}) \text{ and } \mathcal{L}(\mathsf{mon\text{-}X}) \subsetneq \mathcal{L}(\mathsf{wmon\text{-}X}).$$

As seen in Example 2.1.9, the copy language $L'_{\text{copy}} = \{ w\#w \mid w \in \{a,b\}^* \}$, which is not growing context-sensitive [25], is accepted by some RWW-automaton. Thus, there exists an RWW-automaton M_{copy} such that $L(M_{\text{copy}}) = L_{\text{copy}}$. Let M'_{copy} be the RW-automaton that is obtained from M_{copy} by declaring all letters of the tape alphabet of M_{copy} to input letters. Then $L(M'_{\text{copy}}) \cap \{a,b,\#\}^* = L_{\text{copy}}$, which implies that $L(M'_{\text{copy}})$ is not growing context-sensitive, either. By Theorem 2.2.15, there exists an injective morphism φ such that the language $\varphi(L(M'_{\text{copy}}))$ is accepted by an R-automaton $\tilde{M}_{\text{copy}}$. As $\varphi^{-1}(L(\tilde{M}_{\text{copy}})) = L(M'_{\text{copy}})$, and as the class GCSL is closed under inverse morphisms, it follows that the language $L(\tilde{M}_{\text{copy}})$ is not growing context-sensitive, either. Thus, we have the following result.

Proposition 2.2.20 *The language $L(\tilde{M}_{\text{copy}})$ that is accepted by the R-automaton $\tilde{M}_{\text{copy}}$ is not a growing context-sensitive language, and hence, it is not accepted by any weakly monotone sRLWW-automaton.*

Propositions 2.2.16, 2.2.18, and 2.2.20 imply the following separation results.

Corollary 2.2.21 *For each type* $\mathsf{X} \in \{\mathsf{R}, \mathsf{RR}, \mathsf{RL}, \mathsf{RW}, \mathsf{RRW}, \mathsf{RLW}, \mathsf{sRW}, \mathsf{sRRW}, \mathsf{sRLW}\}$,

$$\mathcal{L}(\mathsf{mon\text{-}X}) \not\subseteq \mathsf{CRL},\ \mathcal{L}(\mathsf{det\text{-}X}) \not\subseteq \mathsf{CFL},\ \text{and } \mathcal{L}(\mathsf{X}) \not\subseteq \mathsf{GCSL}.$$

In addition, we have the following non-inclusion results.

Lemma 2.2.22 (a) $\mathcal{L}(\mathsf{det\text{-}RW}) \not\subseteq \mathcal{L}(\mathsf{RL})$.

(b) $\mathcal{L}(\mathsf{det\text{-}RR}) \not\subseteq \mathcal{L}(\mathsf{sRW})$.

(c) $\mathcal{L}(\mathsf{det\text{-}sRW}) \not\subseteq \mathcal{L}(\mathsf{RRW})$.

(d) $\mathsf{CRL} \not\subseteq \mathcal{L}(\mathsf{sRLW})$.

Proof. (a) holds, as by Lemma 2.2.8, $L_7 \in \mathcal{L}(\mathsf{det\text{-}RW}) \smallsetminus \mathcal{L}(\mathsf{RL})$, (b) holds, as by Lemma 2.2.7, $L_6 \in \mathcal{L}(\mathsf{det\text{-}RR}) \smallsetminus \mathcal{L}(\mathsf{sRW})$, and (c) holds, as by Lemma 2.2.9, $L_8 \in \mathcal{L}(\mathsf{det\text{-}sRW}) \smallsetminus \mathcal{L}(\mathsf{RRW})$. Finally, (d) holds, as by Lemma 2.2.3, $L_2 \in \mathsf{CRL} \smallsetminus \mathcal{L}(\mathsf{sRLW})$. □

Lemma 2.2.23 (a) $\mathcal{L}(\mathsf{mon\text{-}RW}) \not\subseteq \mathcal{L}(\mathsf{RL})$.

(b) $\mathcal{L}(\mathsf{mon\text{-}RR}) \not\subseteq \mathcal{L}(\mathsf{sRW})$.

(c) $\mathcal{L}(\text{mon-sRW}) \not\subseteq \mathcal{L}(\text{RRW})$.

(d) $\text{CFL} \not\subseteq \mathcal{L}(\text{sRLW})$.

Proof. (a) holds, as $L_3 \in \mathcal{L}(\text{mon-RW}) \setminus \mathcal{L}(\text{RL})$ by Lemma 2.2.4, (b) holds, as $L_1 \in \mathcal{L}(\text{mon-RR}) \setminus \mathcal{L}(\text{sRW})$ by Lemma 2.2.1, and (c) holds, as $L_4 \in \mathcal{L}(\text{mon-sRW}) \setminus \mathcal{L}(\text{RRW})$ by Lemma 2.2.5. Finally, (d) holds, as $L_2 \in \text{CFL} \setminus \mathcal{L}(\text{sRLW})$. □

Furthermore, Theorem 2.1.56, Lemma 2.2.6, and Lemma 2.2.8 yield the following results.

Corollary 2.2.24 (a) $\text{LRR} \subsetneq \mathcal{L}(\text{mon-RR})$, *but* $\mathcal{L}(\text{mon-R}) \not\subseteq \text{LRR}$.

(b) $\text{LRR} \subsetneq \text{CRL}$.

Proof. (a) By Theorem 2.1.56, $\text{LRR} = \mathcal{L}(\text{det-mon-RL})$, and hence, $\text{LRR} \subseteq \mathcal{L}(\text{mon-RL}) = \mathcal{L}(\text{mon-RR})$. As by Lemma 2.2.6, $L_5 \in \mathcal{L}(\text{mon-R}) \subsetneq \mathcal{L}(\text{mon-RR})$, but $L_5 \notin \mathcal{L}(\text{det-mon-RL})$, the results follow.

(b) In [193], it is shown that $\mathcal{L}(\text{det-mon-RL}) \subseteq \text{CRL}$. Since by Lemma 2.2.8, $L_7 \in \mathcal{L}(\text{det-RW}) \subseteq \text{CRL}$, while $L_7 \notin \mathcal{L}(\text{RR})$, which includes the class LRR, we see that LRR is a proper subclass of CRL. □

By Lemma 2.2.2, the language L_1, which is accepted by a det-mon-RL-automaton, is not accepted by any det-sRRW-automaton. Thus, L_1 separates the class LRR from all deterministic classes that are contained in $\mathcal{L}(\text{det-sRRW})$. In addition, L_1 is not accepted by any sRW-automaton, that is, it separates the class LRR also from all classes contained in $\mathcal{L}(\text{sRW})$. These observations complete the proof of our final separation result.

Theorem 2.2.25 *All arrows in the diagram in Figure 2.8 denote proper inclusions, and language classes not connected by a sequence of arrows are incomparable under inclusion.*

Finally, we take a short look at those classes of languages that are accepted by the various types of deterministic left-monotone restarting automata. Recall from Corollary 2.1.57 that

$$\text{RLR} = \mathcal{L}(\text{det-left-mon-RL}) = \mathcal{L}(\text{det-left-mon-(s)RLW(W)}) = \mathcal{L}(\text{det-left-mon-(s)R(R)WW}),$$

that is, deterministic left-monotone restarting automata accept the language class RLR ($= \text{LRL}^R$) if they can use MVL steps or auxiliary letters. What can we say about those types of deterministic left-monotone restarting automata that can neither use MVL steps nor auxiliary letters? In particular, how does the class DCFL^R, which is properly contained in the class RLR, relate to these types of deterministic left-monotone restarting automata? Recall that all languages from DCFL are already accepted by deterministic monotone R-automata.

By Lemma 2.2.2, the language $L_1 = \{ a^n b^n c, a^n b^{2n} d \mid n \geq 0 \}$ is accepted by a deterministic monotone RL-automaton, but not by any deterministic shrinking RRW-automaton. As the det-mon-RL-automaton for L_1 simply cuts out factors of the form $a^i b^i$ or $a^i b^{2i}$ from the middle of the word that is currently on its tape, we see that this automaton is also left-monotone. It follows that $L_1 \in \mathcal{L}(\text{det-left-mon-RL}) \setminus \mathcal{L}(\text{det-left-mon-sRRW})$.

The language $L_1^R = \{ cb^n a^n, db^{2n} a^n \mid n \geq 0 \}$ is deterministic context-free, and so, $L_1 \in \text{DCFL}^R$. Thus, DCFL^R contains languages that cannot be accepted by deterministic left-monotone sRRW-automata.

On the other hand, the deterministic context-free language L_1^R is easily seen to be accepted by a deterministic left-monotone R-automaton. However, $L_1^R \notin \text{DCFL}^R$, as $L_1 = (L_1^R)^R$ is not deterministic context-free. Thus, already deterministic left-monotone R-automata accept languages that do not belong to the class DCFL^R. This yields the following incomparability result, which, in combination with Corollary 2.1.43, shows that the notions of monotonicity and left-monotonicity are, in general, not symmetric to each other.

Corollary 2.2.26 *The language classes* $\mathcal{L}(\text{det-left-mon-X})$ *and* DCFL^R *are incomparable under inclusion for each* $\text{X} \in \{\text{R}, \text{RR}, \text{RW}, \text{RRW}, \text{sRW}, \text{sRRW}\}$.

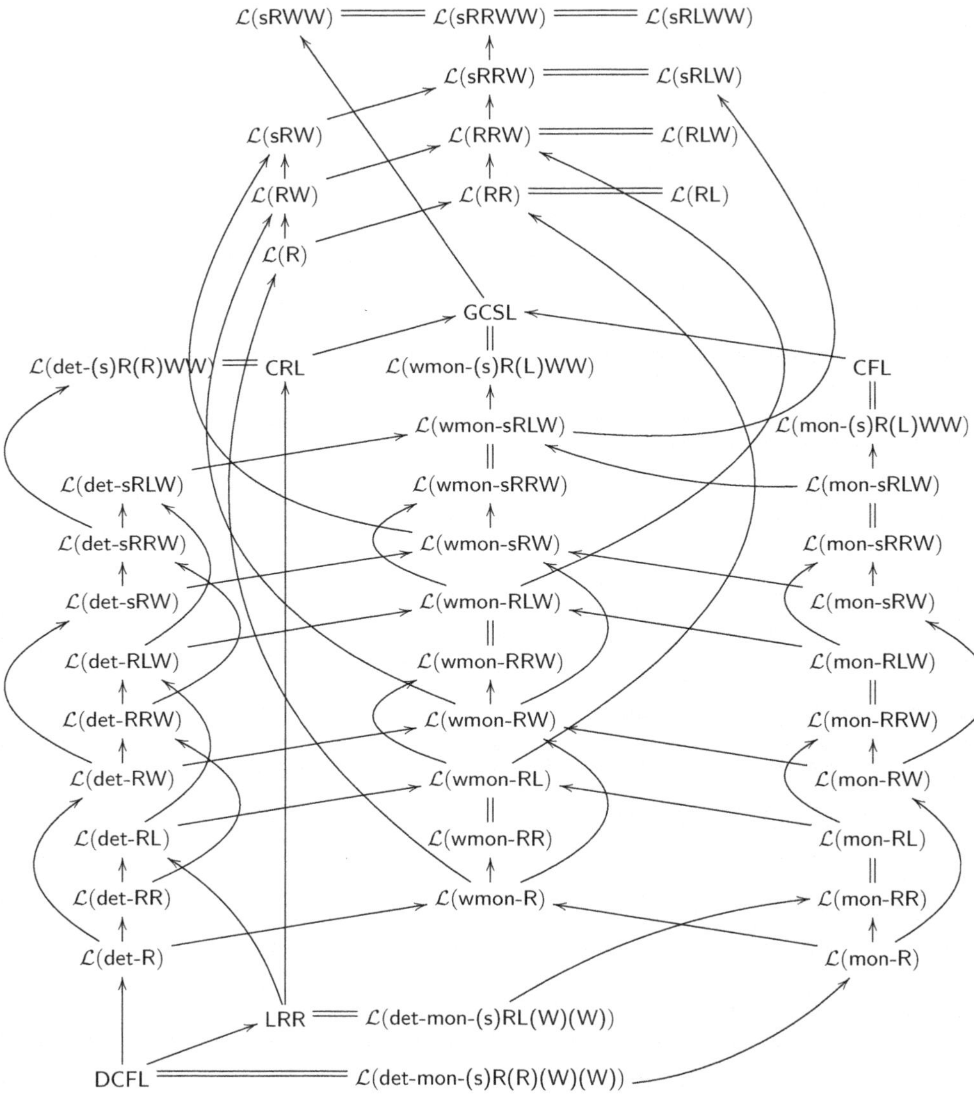

Figure 2.8: The complete taxonomy of restarting automata without auxiliary letters.

Concerning these classes of deterministic left-monotone restarting automata, the following problems have not yet been studied in detail.

Problem 2.2.27 *For all* $\mathsf{X}, \mathsf{Y} \in \{\mathsf{R}, \mathsf{RR}, \mathsf{RW}, \mathsf{RRW}, \mathsf{sRW}, \mathsf{sRRW}\}$, *if type* X *is a restriction of type* Y, *then* $\mathcal{L}(\text{det-left-mon-}\mathsf{X}) \subseteq \mathcal{L}(\text{det-left-mon-}\mathsf{Y})$. *Which of these inclusions are proper? And how do the resulting language classes relate to the classes in the diagram in Figure 2.8?*

Concerning the complexity of the membership problems for the language classes displayed in the diagram in Figure 2.8, we have the following dichotomy. The membership problem for each growing context-sensitive language is solvable in polynomial time [25]. On the other hand, by Theorem 2.1.10, there exists an RWW-automaton $M = (Q, \Sigma, \Gamma, \triangleright, \triangleleft, q_0, k, \delta)$ such that the membership problem for the language $L(M)$ is NP-complete. Hence, the membership problem for the language $L_{\mathrm{C}}(M)$ is NP-complete, too. That is, $M' = (Q, \Gamma, \Gamma, \triangleright, \triangleleft, q_0, k, \delta)$ is an RW-automaton such that the membership problem for the language $L(M')$ is NP-complete. From Theorem 2.2.15, we thus obtain an R-automaton with an NP-complete membership problem. In summary, we have the following complexity results.

Theorem 2.2.28 (a) *The membership problem for each language that is accepted by a weakly monotone shrinking restarting automaton or by any of its restricted variants is decidable in polynomial time.*

(b) *The language class* $\mathcal{L}(\mathsf{R})$, *and therewith any superclass of* $\mathcal{L}(\mathsf{R})$, *contains NP-complete languages. Thus,* $\mathcal{L}(\mathsf{R}) \not\subseteq \mathsf{P}$ *unless* $\mathsf{P} = \mathsf{NP}$.

It follows that we have a clear partition of the diagram in Figure 2.8 based on the complexity of the membership problem: all classes below (and including) GCSL have membership problems that are solvable in polynomial time, while all classes above (and including) $\mathcal{L}(\mathsf{R})$ contain NP-complete languages.

Now we turn to a proper subclass of R-automata, the so-called clearing restarting automata. This type of restarting automaton was introduced by Peter Černo and František Mráz in connection with a study on inductive inference ('automated learning') of restarting automata. We shall address this topic in Chapter 4 – here we are just interested in the expressive capacity of clearing restarting automata. Clearing restarting automata are defined through a particular class of context rewriting systems.

Definition 2.2.29 ([257, 258])

(a) *Let* k *be a positive integer. A* k-context rewriting system *is a system* $S = (\Sigma, \Gamma, I)$, *where* Σ *is a finite input alphabet,* Γ *is a finite working alphabet containing* Σ *but not the sentinels* $\triangleright$ *and* $\triangleleft$, *and* I *is a finite set of instructions of the form*

$$(x, z \to t, y),$$

where $x \in \Gamma^k \cup \triangleright \cdot \Gamma^{\leq k-1}$ *is called a* left context, $y \in \Gamma^k \cup \Gamma^{\leq k-1} \cdot \triangleleft$ *is called a* right context, *and* $z, t \in \Gamma^*$. *The integer* $|x| + |z| + |y|$ *is called the* width *of instruction* $(x, z \to t, y)$, *and the pair* $(z \to t)$ *is called a* rule.

A word $w = uzv$ *can be rewritten into* utv, *denoted as* $uzv \to_S utv$, *if there exists an instruction* $i = (x, z \to t, y) \in I$ *such that* x *is a suffix of* $\triangleright \cdot u$ *and* y *is a prefix of* $v \cdot \triangleleft$.

The reduction language *associated with* S *is defined as* $L(S) = \{ w \in \Sigma^* \mid w \to_S^* \lambda \}$, *where* $\to_S^*$ *denotes the reflexive and transitive closure of* $\to_S$.

(b) *A* k-clearing restarting automaton *is a* k-*context rewriting system* $C = (\Sigma, \Sigma, I)$ *such that, for each instruction* $i = (x, z \to t, y) \in I$, *we have* $z \in \Sigma^+$ *and* $t = \lambda$. *The* language accepted *by* C *is the reduction language* $L(C) = \{ w \in \Sigma^* \mid w \to_C^* \lambda \}$. *Then* k-CRA *denotes the class of all* k-*clearing restarting automata.*

(c) *A* clearing restarting automaton *is a k-clearing restarting automaton for some $k \geq 1$, and* CRA *denotes the class of all clearing restarting automata.*

Each instruction $(x, z \to \lambda, y)$ of a k-CRA C rewrites a factor of the form xzy into the word xy, that is, it simply deletes the inner factor z. Thus, C can be viewed as a special case of an R-automaton. It follows immediately that $\mathcal{L}(\mathsf{CRA}) \subseteq \mathcal{L}(\mathsf{R})$.

A CRA $C = (\Sigma, \Sigma, I)$ accepts the language $L(C) = \{ w \in \Sigma^* \mid w \to_C^* \lambda \}$, that is, a word w is accepted by C if w can be rewritten into the empty word λ by repeatedly using the instructions from I. This means, in particular, that $\lambda \in L(C)$. Hence, any language not containing λ as an element cannot be accepted by a clearing restarting automaton. In order to overcome this problem, we consider the equality of languages only up to the empty word, that is, two languages L and L' on Σ are considered equal, denoted by $L \doteq L'$, if $L \cap \Sigma^+ = L' \cap \Sigma^+$.

We illustrate the above definition with an example.

Example 2.2.30 *Let $C = (\Sigma, \Sigma, I)$, where $\Sigma = \{a, b\}$ and $I = \{(a, ab \to \lambda, b), (\rhd, ab \to \lambda, \lhd)\}$ is the set of instructions. Then $a^4b^4 \to_C a^3b^3 \to_C a^2b^2 \to_C ab \to_C \lambda$, which shows that a^4b^4 is accepted by C. In fact, it is easily seen that $L(C) = \{ a^nb^n \mid n \geq 0 \}$.* ■

The 1-CRA in Example 2.2.30 accepts the deterministic context-free language $\{ a^nb^n \mid n \geq 0 \}$, which is not regular. As we shall see below, not all deterministic context-free languages are accepted by clearing restarting automata, but we do have at least the following result.

Proposition 2.2.31 ([257, 258]) $\mathsf{REG} \subsetneq \mathcal{L}(\mathsf{CRA})$.

Proof. Let $L \subseteq \Sigma^*$ be a regular language. By the Pumping Lemma for regular languages (Lemma 1.2.78), there exists a constant k such that, for each word $z \in L$ of length $|z| \geq k$ and each factorization $z = wh$, where $|w| = k$, there exists a factorization of the form $w = uxy$ that satisfies the following three conditions:

$$(1)\ |x| > 0,\ (2)\ |ux| \leq k, \text{ and } (3)\ ux^iyh \in L \text{ for all } i \in \mathbb{N}.$$

For each word w of length k that is a prefix of a word from L, we choose one such factorization $w = uxv$, and we take the instruction $(\rhd u, x \to \lambda, v)$. Furthermore, for each word $z \in L$ of length $|z| < k$, we take the instruction $(\rhd, z \to \lambda, \lhd)$. Then it is easily seen that the resulting CRA C satisfies $L(C) \doteq L$, that is, it accepts the regular language L. □

Let L_c denote the non-regular language $L_c = \{ a^ncb^n \mid n \geq 0 \}$, which is obviously deterministic context-free. This language is not accepted by any clearing restarting automaton.

Lemma 2.2.32 ([258]) *The language L_c is not accepted by any clearing restarting automaton.*

Proof. Assume to the contrary that there exists a k-CRA $C = (\Sigma, \Sigma, I)$ such that $L(C) \doteq L_c$. Let m be the maximal width of the instructions of C, that is,

$$m = \max\{ |xzy| \mid (x, z \to \lambda, y) \in I \}.$$

Obviously, as $a^mcb^m \in L_c$, we have $a^mcb^m \to_C^* \lambda$. From the choice of m, we see that the word a^mcb^m cannot be reduced to λ in a single step, that is, $a^mcb^m \to_C r \to_C^* \lambda$ for some word $r \neq \lambda$. Thus, a^mcb^m can be written as $a^mcb^m = uxzyv$ for some instruction $(x, z \to \lambda, y) \in I$ and some words $u, v \in \Sigma^*$, and $r = uxyv$. Then $r \in L(C)$, but as r is obtained from a^mcb^m by deleting the non-empty proper factor z, we conclude that r is not of the form a^icb^i for any integer i, that is, $r \notin L_c$. As this contradicts our hypothesis on $L(C)$, we have a contradiction. It follows that the language L_c is in fact not accepted by any clearing restarting automaton. □

Thus, we have the following non-inclusion result.

Corollary 2.2.33 $\mathsf{DCFL} \not\subseteq \mathcal{L}(\mathsf{CRA})$.

As $\mathsf{DCFL} = \mathcal{L}(\mathsf{det\text{-}mon\text{-}R}) \subsetneq \mathcal{L}(\mathsf{R})$, we thus get the following proper inclusion.

Corollary 2.2.34 $\mathcal{L}(\mathsf{CRA}) \subsetneq \mathcal{L}(\mathsf{R})$.

Concerning language operations, the class $\mathcal{L}(\mathsf{CRA})$ has the following non-cloure properties.

Proposition 2.2.35 ([258]) *The language class $\mathcal{L}(\mathsf{CRA})$ is not closed under union, product, morphisms, or intersection with regular sets.*

Proof outline. The languages $L_a = \{ a^n b^n \mid n \geq 0 \}$ and $L_b = \{ a^n b^{2n} \mid n \geq 0 \}$ are easily seen to be accepted by 1-CRAs. However, it can be shown that neither $L_a \cup L_b$ nor $L_a \cdot L_b$ is accepted by any CRA.

The language $L = \{ a^n b^n c^m d^{2m} \mid n, m \geq 0 \}$ is accepted by 1-CRA. However, the morphism h that is defined through $a \mapsto a$, $b \mapsto b$, $c \mapsto a$, and $d \mapsto b$ yields $h(L) = L_a \cdot L_b \notin \mathcal{L}(\mathsf{CRA})$, which showns that $\mathcal{L}(\mathsf{CRA})$ is not closed under morphisms.

Finally, let $L_d = \{ a^n c b^n \mid n \geq 0 \} \cup \{ a^n b^n \mid n \geq 0 \}$, which is accepted by a 1-CRA, and let $L_e = \{ a^n c b^m \mid n, m \geq 0 \}$, which is regular. Then $L_d \cap L_e = \{ a^n c b^n \mid n \geq 0 \} = L_c$, which is not accepted by any CRA by Lemma 2.2.32. This shows non-closure under intersection with regular sets. □

By definition, the clearing restarting automata are parameterized by the length k of the contexts considered in their delete operations. As it turns out, this parameter induces an infinite strictly ascending hierarchy of language classes.

Theorem 2.2.36 ([258]) *For all $k \geq 1$, $\mathcal{L}(k\text{-}\mathsf{CRA}) \subsetneq \mathcal{L}((k+1)\text{-}\mathsf{CRA})$.*

Proof outline. For each $k \geq 1$, let $L_k = \{ (c^k a c^k)^n (c^k b c^k)^n \mid n \geq 0 \}$. Then $L_k \in \mathcal{L}((k+1)\text{-}\mathsf{CRA})$, as L_k is accepted by the $(k+1)$-CRA $C_k = (\Sigma, \Sigma, I)$ that is defined by taking $\Sigma = \{a, b, c\}$ and

$$I = \{(ac^k, c^k a c^k c^k b c^k \to \lambda, c^k b), (\rhd, c^k a c^k c^k b c^k \to \lambda, \lhd)\}.$$

However, it can be shown that L_k is not accepted by any k-CRA, that is, $L_k \in \mathcal{L}((k+1)\text{-}\mathsf{CRA}) \smallsetminus \mathcal{L}(k\text{-}\mathsf{CRA})$. On the other hand, it is easily seen that, from a k-CRA C, one can easily obtain a $(k+1)$-CRA C' by extending the left and right contexts by all possible letters such that $L(C') = L(C)$. Together, these results yield the intended proper inclusion. □

While CRA do not accept all deterministic context-free languages by Corollary 2.2.33, it still remains to determine whether all languages accepted by CRA are (deterministic) context-free. The next result shows that this is at least true for 1-CRA.

Theorem 2.2.37 ([258]) $\mathcal{L}(1\text{-}\mathsf{CRA}) \subsetneq \mathsf{CFL}$.

Proof outline. From a 1-CRA C, one can actually construct a context-free grammar for the language $L(C)$. Thus, it follows that $\mathcal{L}(1\text{-}\mathsf{CRA}) \subseteq \mathsf{CFL}$. Because of Corollary 2.2.33, this is a proper inclusion. □

This result does not extend to 2-CRA. In fact, there exist 2-CRA for which the accepted languages are not even context-free. In [258], Peter Černo and František Mráz present a rather involved construction of a 2-CRA over an alphabet of cardinality six that accepts a non-context-free language. In [263], Vojtěch Vorel improves upon this result by presenting such a 2-CRA over a binary alphabet.

Theorem 2.2.38 ([258]) $\mathcal{L}(2\text{-}\mathsf{CRA}) \not\subseteq \mathsf{CFL}$.

We shall see below that the class GCSL is an upper bound for the expressive capacity of clearing restarting automata [7]. In Chapter 4, we shall return to clearing restarting automata, when we study the notion of learnability for restarting automata.

2.2.2 Restarting Automata with a Single Auxiliary Letter

Now we turn our attention to restarting automata that have just a single auxiliary letter, that is, the tape alphabet of a restarting automaton of this type is of the form $\Gamma = \Sigma \cup \{c\}$, where Σ is the input alphabet and c is an additional (auxiliary) letter. In this context, we first consider some extensions of the clearing restarting automaton, the so-called Δ-clearing restarting automaton and the Δ^*-clearing restarting automaton, that Peter Černo and František Mráz introduced in [257, 258].

Definition 2.2.39 (a) *A k-Δ-*clearing restarting automaton *is a k-context rewriting system $R = (\Sigma, \Gamma, I)$ such that $\Gamma = \Sigma \cup \{\Delta\}$, where Δ is a new letter, and for each instruction $i = (x, z \to t, y) \in I$, we have $z \in \Gamma^+$ and $z \neq t \in \{\lambda, \Delta\}$. Then k-Δ-CRA denotes the class of k-Δ-clearing restarting automata, and Δ-CRA denotes the class of all Δ-clearing restarting automata, that is, $\Delta\text{-CRA} = \bigcup_{k\geq 1} k\text{-}\Delta\text{-CRA}$.*

(b) *A k-Δ^*-*clearing restarting automaton *is a k-context rewriting system $R = (\Sigma, \Gamma, I)$ such that $\Gamma = \Sigma \cup \{\Delta\}$, where Δ is a new letter, and for each instruction $i = (x, z \to t, y) \in I$, we have $z \in \Gamma^+$ and $z \neq t = \Delta^i$ for some i satisfying $0 \leq i \leq |z|$. Then k-Δ^*-CRA denotes the class of k-Δ^*-clearing restarting automata, and Δ^*-CRA denotes the class of all Δ^*-clearing restarting automata, that is, $\Delta^*\text{-CRA} = \bigcup_{k\geq 1} k\text{-}\Delta^*\text{-CRA}$.*

The restrictions on instructions for Δ- and Δ^*-CRA show that, for each instruction $(x, z \to t, y)$ of an automaton of one of these types, either $|z| > |t|$ or $|z| = |t|$ and $|z|_\Sigma > |t|_\Sigma = 0$. Hence, by assigning the weight 1 to the letter Δ and 2 to each input letter, we see that each Δ- or Δ^*-CRA is a weight-reducing RWW-automaton. Thus, we have the following sequence of inclusions:

$$\mathcal{L}(\mathsf{CRA}) \subseteq \mathcal{L}(\Delta\text{-}\mathsf{CRA}) \subseteq \mathcal{L}(\Delta^*\text{-}\mathsf{CRA}) \subseteq \mathcal{L}(\mathsf{sRWW}).$$

The following example already shows that the availability of a single auxiliary letter can be quite useful.

Example 2.2.40 *Let $L_c = \{ a^n cb^n \mid n \geq 0 \}$. We have seen in Lemma 2.2.32 that this language is not accepted by any clearing restarting automaton. However, it is accepted by the following 1-Δ-CRA $C_c = (\{a, b, c\}, \{a, b, c, \Delta\}, I)$, where*

$$I = \{(a, acb \to \Delta, b), (a, a\Delta b \to \Delta, b), (\rhd, acb \to \lambda, \lhd), (\rhd, a\Delta b \to \lambda, \lhd), (\rhd, c \to \lambda, \lhd)\}. \quad \blacksquare$$

This example has the following consequence.

Corollary 2.2.41 $\mathcal{L}(\mathsf{CRA}) \subsetneq \mathcal{L}(\Delta\text{-}\mathsf{CRA})$.

The next example is more interesting, but also more involved. In [58], Sheila Greibach introduced a particular context-free language H and proved that H is the *hardest context-free language*. This means that any context-free language can be parsed in the same time or space that it takes to parse the language H. In addition, any context-free language L can be obtained from H by an inverse morphism.

Definition 2.2.42 (a) *Let D_2 be the* semi-Dyck language *over the alphabet $T_2 = \{a_1, a_2, \bar{a}_1, \bar{a}_2\}$, that is, D_2 is the language that is generated by the context-free grammar*

$$G_2 = (\{S\}, T_2, S, \{(S \to \lambda), (S \to SS), (S \to a_1 S \bar{a}_1), (S \to a_2 S \bar{a}_2)\}).$$

Then D_2 is the set of correctly bracketed expressions, where a_1 and a_2 are interpreted as opening brackets and $\bar{a}_1$ and $\bar{a}_2$ are interpreted as the corresponding closing brackets.

(b) *Let $\Sigma = T_2 \cup \{c, \#\}$ and $\Sigma' = \Sigma \cup \{d\}$, where c, d and $\#$ are additional letters. The* hardest context-free language *$H \subseteq \Sigma'^*$ is defined as*

$$\begin{aligned} H = \{\lambda\} \cup \{\, & x_1 c y_1 c z_1 d x_2 c y_2 c z_2 d \cdots x_n c y_n c z_n d \mid n \geq 1, x_i, z_i \in \Sigma^* \text{ for all } i = 1, 2, \ldots, n, \\ & y_1 \in \# \cdot T_2^*, y_i \in T_2^* \text{ for all } i = 2, 3, \ldots, n, \\ & \text{and } y_1 y_2 \cdots y_n \in \# \cdot D_2 \,\}. \end{aligned}$$

Observe that the factors x_i and z_i may contain occurrences of the letters c and $\#$. The occurrences of the letter d divide a word $w \in H$ into blocks. Each block is in turn divided into segments from $(T_2 \cup \{\#\})^*$ by occurrences of the letter c. Each block must contain (at least) one segment such that the concatenation of these segments yields a word from the language $\# \cdot D_2$. It is easy to see that H is context-free. A pushdown automaton can simply guess a segment from each block and then verify that the word resulting from the concatenation of these segments is an element of $\# \cdot D_2$.

The following result on the language H has been established in [258].

Proposition 2.2.43 $H \in \mathcal{L}(\text{1-}\Delta\text{-CRA}) \setminus \mathcal{L}(\text{CRA})$.

Proof outline. Let $w = x_1cy_1cz_1dx_2cy_2cz_2d \cdots x_ncy_ncz_nd$, where $n \geq 1$, $x_i, z_i \in \Sigma^*$ for all $i = 1, 2, \ldots, n$, $y_1 \in \# \cdot T_2^*$, $y_i \in T_2^*$ for all $i = 2, 3, \ldots, n$, and $y_1y_2 \cdots y_n \in \# \cdot D_2$. A 1-$\Delta$-CRA C_H can first delete letters from the alphabet Σ from the right side of $\rhd$ and from the left and right sides of the letters d. At some point, it guesses that the word $cy_1cdcy_2cd \cdots cy_ncd$ has been obtained, and it introduces occurrences of the letter Δ, producing the word $\Delta y_1 \Delta y_2 \Delta \cdots \Delta y_n \Delta$. Thereafter it checks whether $y_1y_2 \cdots y_n$ belongs to $\{\#\} \cdot D_2$. The definition of C_H and a detailed proof for $L(C_H) = H$ can be found in [258].

The language H is not accepted by any CRA. Suppose that there exists a k-CRA $C = (\Sigma', \Sigma', I)$ such that $L(C) = H$, and let m be the maximal width of any instruction of C. Obviously, the word $w = c\#a_1^m cdc\bar{a}_1^m cd$ belongs to H. Hence, C has an accepting computation of the form $w = c\#a_1^m cdc\bar{a}_1^m cd \to_C w_1 \to_C \cdots \to_C \lambda$. In the first reduction, the factor deleted must be of the form $a_1^r cdc\bar{a}_1^r$ for some r such that $0 \leq r < m$, as otherwise, the resulting word w_1 would not be an element of H. Let i be the instruction that is applied in the first step. From the choice of m, we conclude that $i = (a_1^k, a_1^r cdc\bar{a}_1^r \to \lambda, \bar{a}_1^k)$. Now consider the word $u = c\#a_1^{m+1}a_1^r cdc\bar{a}_1^r\bar{a}_1^m c\#a_1\bar{a}_1cd$. Obviously, $u \notin H$, but $u = c\#a_1^{m+1}a_1^r cdc\bar{a}_1^r\bar{a}_1^m c\#a_1\bar{a}_1cd \to_C c\#a_1^{m+1}\bar{a}_1^m c\#a_1\bar{a}_1cd \in H$, which implies that $u \in L(C)$, a contradiction. Thus, H is not accepted by any CRA. □

As there is a Δ-CRA for the hardest context-free language H, we may speculate that actually all context-free languages are accepted by Δ-CRA. And indeed, this is the case. To establish this result, we make a detour by first showing the following weaker result.

Proposition 2.2.44 ([258, 259]) $\mathsf{CFL} \subseteq \mathcal{L}(\text{1-}\Delta^*\text{-CRA})$.

Proof outline. Let $L \subseteq \Sigma^*$ be a context-free language. Then there exists a grammar $G = (N, \Sigma, S, P)$ in Chomsky normal form that generates the language $L' = L \setminus \{\lambda\}$. Assume that $N = \{V_1, V_2, \ldots, V_m\}$, where $V_1 = S$. From G, we obtain another context-free grammar $G' = (N, \Gamma, S, P')$ by taking $\Gamma = \Sigma \cup \{\Delta\}$ and

$$P' = P \cup \{\, V_i \to a\Delta^i b \mid a, b \in \Sigma, i \in \{1, 2, \ldots, m\} \,\}.$$

Then $L(G') \cap \Sigma^* = L(G) = L'$, as the additional productions in G' cannot be used in any derivation of a word from Σ^+.

Let $c = m + 2$. For each $i \in \{1, 2, \ldots, m\}$, we take F_i to denote the finite language

$$F_i = \{\, z \in \Gamma^* \mid N_i \Rightarrow_{G'}^* z \text{ and } c < |z| \leq 2 \cdot c \,\}.$$

Now the 1-Δ^*-CRA $C = (\Sigma, \Gamma, I)$ is defined by taking $I = I_1 \cup I_2$, where

$$\begin{aligned} I_1 &= \{\, (\rhd, w \to \lambda, \lhd) \mid w \in L(G'), |w| \leq c \,\} \text{ and} \\ I_2 &= \textstyle\bigcup_{1 \leq i \leq m} \{\, (z_1, z_2z_3 \cdots z_{s-1} \to \Delta^i, z_s) \mid z_1, z_2, \ldots, z_s \in \Gamma, z_1z_2 \cdots z_{s-1}z_s \in F_i \,\}. \end{aligned}$$

It can now be shown that $L_C(C) = \{\, w \in \Gamma^* \mid w \to_C^* \lambda \} \doteq L(G')$. A detailed proof can be found in [258, 260]. It follows that $L(C) = L_C(C) \cap \Sigma^* \doteq L(G') \cap \Sigma^* = L' = L \setminus \{\lambda\}$, which yields $L(C) \doteq L$. Thus, $L \in \mathcal{L}(\text{1-}\Delta^*\text{-CRA})$ follows. □

In [259] (see also [260]), Peter Černo and František Mráz extend the above result by presenting a technically quite involved construction that turns a 1-Δ^*-CRA of the form described in the proof of Proposition 2.2.44 into a Δ-CRA for the same language. In this way, they derive the following stronger result.

Theorem 2.2.45 ([259]) $\mathsf{CFL} \subsetneq \mathcal{L}(\Delta\text{-}\mathsf{CRA})$.

Here the properness of the inclusion follows from the fact that already clearing restarting automata can accept languages that are not context-free (see Theorem 2.2.38). However, it is not clear whether there exists a general construction that turns an arbitrary Δ^*-CRA into an equivalent Δ-CRA. In fact, the following question is still open.

Problem 2.2.46 *Is the inclusion of* $\mathcal{L}(\Delta\text{-}\mathsf{CRA})$ *in* $\mathcal{L}(\Delta^*\text{-}\mathsf{CRA})$ *a proper one?*

Next we derive the announced upper bound for the expressive capacity of clearing restarting automata. To do so, we need the following notions and results.

Definition 2.2.47 *Let Σ be a finite alphabet.*

(a) *A* string-rewriting system *S on Σ consists of (finitely many) pairs of words from Σ^*, called* rewrite rules, *which are written as $(\ell \to r)$. Then* $\mathrm{dom}(S) = \{\, \ell \mid \exists r \in \Sigma^* : (\ell \to r) \in S \,\}$ *is the set of left-hand sides of rules of S. The* reduction relation $\Rightarrow_S^*$ *on Σ^* that is induced by S is the reflexive and transitive closure of the* single-step reduction relation

$$\Rightarrow_S = \{\, (u\ell v, urv) \mid (\ell \to r) \in S, u, v \in \Sigma^* \,\}.$$

For a word $u \in \Sigma^*$, if there exists a word v such that $u \Rightarrow_S v$ holds, then u is called reducible *modulo S. If such a word v does not exist, then u is called* irreducible *modulo S. The set of all* descendants *of u is denoted by $\Delta_S^*(u)$, that is, $\Delta_S^*(u) = \{\, v \mid u \Rightarrow_S^* v \,\}$, $\nabla_S^*(v) = \{\, u \mid u \Rightarrow_S^* v \,\}$ is the set of all* ancestors *of v, and* $\mathrm{IRR}(S)$ *denotes the set of all irreducible words modulo S. The* Thue congruence *on Σ^* that is induced by S is denoted by $\Leftrightarrow_S^*$. It is the smallest equivalence relation on Σ^* containing the single-step reduction relation $\Rightarrow_S$.*

(b) *A string-rewriting system S is called* terminating, *if there is no infinite sequence of reduction steps $w \Rightarrow_S w_1 \Rightarrow_S w_2 \Rightarrow_S \dots$.*

(c) *A string-rewriting system S is called* weight-reducing, *if there exists a weight function ω satisfying $\omega(\ell) > \omega(r)$ for each rule $(\ell \to r) \in S$.*

(d) *A string-rewriting system S is called* length-reducing, *if $|\ell| > |r|$ for each rule $(\ell \to r) \in S$.*

(e) *A string-rewriting systen S is called* confluent, *if, for all $u, v \in \Sigma^*$, $u \Leftrightarrow_S^* v$ implies that there exists some $z \in \Sigma^*$ such that $u \Rightarrow_S^* z$ and $v \Rightarrow_S^* z$ hold.*

(f) *A string-rewriting system S is called* convergent, *if it is both terminating and confluent.*

It is easily seen that $\mathrm{IRR}(S)$ is a regular language for each finite string-rewriting system S. Furthermore, each length-reducing string-rewriting system is weight-reducing, and each weight-reducing string-rewriting system is terminating. For a convergent system S, the set $\mathrm{IRR}(S)$ of irreducible words is a complete set of unique representatives for the Thue congruence $\Leftrightarrow_S^*$ (see, e.g., [19]). That is, each congruence class contains one and only one irreducible word. In addition, the irreducible word in the congruence class of a word w can be computed from w by simply applying reductions until the irreducible word is reached. This means, in particular, that the word problem for S ('Decide whether two words are congruent modulo S!') is decidable. Next we come to the notion of a McNaughton family of languages.

Definition 2.2.48 ([9]) *A language $L \subseteq \Sigma^*$ is called a* McNaughton language, *if there exist a finite alphabet Γ strictly containing Σ, a finite string-rewriting system S on Γ, words $t_1, t_2 \in (\Gamma \smallsetminus \Sigma)^* \cap \mathrm{IRR}(S)$, and a letter $Y \in (\Gamma \smallsetminus \Sigma) \cap \mathrm{IRR}(S)$ such that, for all $w \in \Sigma^*$,*

$$w \in L \text{ if and only if } t_1 w t_2 \Rightarrow_S^* Y.$$

Here the letters of Σ are terminals, *while those of $\Gamma \smallsetminus \Sigma$ can be seen as* nonterminals. *We say that the McNaughton language L is* specified *by the four-tuple (S, t_1, t_2, Y). This fact will be expressed as $L = L(S, t_1, t_2, Y)$.*

By placing restrictions on the finite string-rewriting systems used, special families of McNaughton languages are obtained.

Definition 2.2.49 ([9]) (a) *A McNaughton language is called* weight-reducing, *if it is defined using a finite string-rewriting system that is weight-reducing. The resulting class of languages is denoted by $\mathcal{L}(\mathsf{wr\text{-}McNL})$.*

(b) *A McNaughton language is called* length-reducing, *if it is defined using a finite string-rewriting system that is length-reducing. The resulting language class is denoted by $\mathcal{L}(\mathsf{lr\text{-}McNL})$.*

(c) *By requiring in addition that the string-rewriting system used in the definition is confluent, we obtain the McNaughton families $\mathcal{L}(\mathsf{con\text{-}wr\text{-}McNL})$ and $\mathcal{L}(\mathsf{con\text{-}lr\text{-}McNL})$ of* confluent weight-reducing *and* confluent length-reducing McNaughton languages.

The following characterizations are known for these families of McNaughton languages.

Theorem 2.2.50 ([9]) (a) $\mathsf{GCSL} = \mathcal{L}(\mathsf{lr\text{-}McNL}) = \mathcal{L}(\mathsf{wr\text{-}McNL})$.
(b) $\mathsf{CRL} = \mathcal{L}(\mathsf{con\text{-}lr\text{-}McNL}) = \mathcal{L}(\mathsf{con\text{-}wr\text{-}McNL})$.

The above characterization of the class CRL of Church-Rosser languages by confluent length-reducing string-rewriting systems is actually the original definition of this class that was given in [151]. We illustrate these definitions by presenting a simple example.

Example 2.2.51 *Let $\Sigma = \{a\}$, $\Gamma = \{a, \rhd, \lhd, F, Y\}$, and*

$$S = \{\rhd aaaa \to \rhd aaF, Faa \to aF, F\lhd \to \lhd, \rhd aa\lhd \to \rhd a\lhd, \rhd a\lhd \to Y\}.$$

Then S is a finite length-reducing string-rewriting system on Γ, and it can be shown that S is also confluent. For all $m \in \mathbb{N}$, we have

$$\rhd a^m \lhd \to_R^* Y \text{ if and only if } \exists\, n \in \mathbb{N} : m = 2^n.$$

Thus, $L_{\exp} = \{ a^{2^n} \mid n \geq 0 \}$ is the McNaughton language that is specified by the four-tuple $(S, \rhd, \lhd, Y)$. It follows that $L_{\exp}$ is a Church-Rosser language (see also Example 1.2.16). ∎

The following result establishes the class GCSL as an upper bound for all types of clearing restarting automata defined above.

Theorem 2.2.52 ([202]) $\mathcal{L}(\Delta^*\text{-}\mathsf{cl\text{-}RA}) \subseteq \mathsf{GCSL}$.

Proof. Let $C = (\Sigma, \Gamma, I)$ be a k-Δ^*-clearing restarting automaton for some $k \geq 1$. Let $\Omega = \Gamma \cup \{\rhd, \lhd, Y\}$, where Y is a new letter, let $t_1 = \rhd$, $t_2 = \lhd Y$, and let S be the string-rewriting system

$$S = \{ xzy \to xty \mid (x, z \to t, y) \in I \} \cup \{\rhd\lhd \to \lambda\}.$$

If we assign each letter $a \in \Sigma \cup \{\rhd, \lhd, Y\}$ the weight $\omega(a) = 2$ and take $\omega(\Delta) = 1$, then $\omega(\ell) > \omega(r)$ for each rule $(\ell \to r) \in S$. Thus, S is a weight-reducing system (with respect to the weight function ω).

Claim. $L(C)$ coincides with the McNaughton language specified by (S, t_1, t_2, Y).

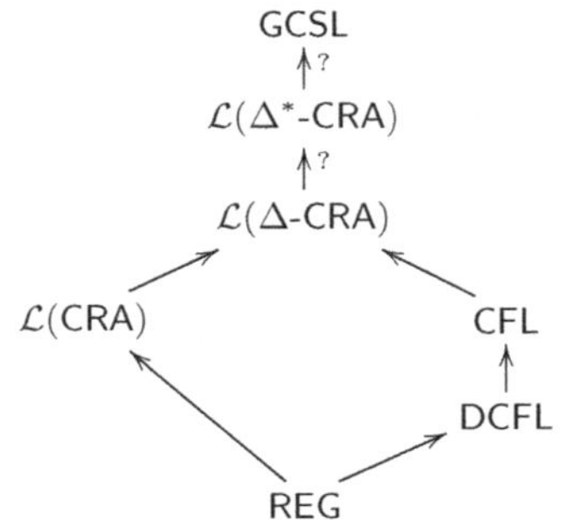

Figure 2.9: The taxonomy of clearing restarting automata.

Proof. Let $w \in \Sigma^*$. Then $w \in L(C)$ iff $w \to_C^* \lambda$ iff $\rhd w \lhd \Rightarrow_S^* \rhd\lhd \Rightarrow_S \lambda$ iff $t_1 w t_2 = \rhd w \lhd Y \Rightarrow_S^+ Y$. It follows that $L(C)$ is the McNaughton language that is specified by the 4-tuple (S, t_1, t_2, Y). □

As S is a finite weight-reducing system, Theorem 2.2.50 (a) implies that the McNaughton language specified by the 4-tuple above is a growing context-sensitive language, that is, the language $L(C)$ is growing context-sensitive. □

However, the following question remains open.

Problem 2.2.53 *Is GCSL contained in the class of languages $\mathcal{L}(\Delta^*\text{-CRA})$ that are accepted by Δ^*-clearing restarting automata, or is there a growing context-sensitive language that is not accepted by any Δ^*-CRA?*

The diagram in Figure 2.9 shows the taxonomy of those language classes that are defined by the various types of clearing restarting automata. The question marks indicate that it is not known whether the corresponding inclusions are proper.

To complete this subsection, we state some results on decision problems for clearing restarting automata. Andreas Malcher obtained the following undecidability results based on his results on insertion systems.

Theorem 2.2.54 ([146]) (a) *The problems of equivalence, inclusion, and inclusion of a regular language are undecidable for k-clearing restarting automata for all $k \geq 1$.*

(b) *The finiteness problem, the regularity problem, and the problem of inclusion in a given regular language are undecidable for k-clearing restarting automata for all $k \geq 4$.*

Actually, these undecidability results immediately extend to Δ-clearing and Δ*-clearing restarting automata.

2.2.3 Restarting Automata with Restricted Utilization of Auxiliary Letters

Here we place additional restrictions on how restarting automata make use of auxiliary letters. We focus on RLWW-automata and some of their subclasses and consider two types of restrictions simultaneously: the number of auxiliary letters in the tape alphabet, which can be seen as a measure of the *descriptional complexity* of a restarting automaton, and the number of occurrences of auxiliary letters on the tape, which can be interpreted as a *dynamic* complexity measure. These restrictions are defined as follows.

Definition 2.2.55 ([97]) *Let $\mathsf{X} \in \{\mathsf{RWW}, \mathsf{RRWW}, \mathsf{RLWW}, \text{det-}\mathsf{RWW}, \text{det-}\mathsf{RRWW}, \text{det-}\mathsf{RLWW}\}$ be a type of restarting automaton with auxiliary letters, and let $i, j \in \mathbb{N}$.*

(a) *We use* aux(j,i)-X *to denote the class of restarting automata of type* X *for which the number of auxiliary letters in the tape alphabet does not exceed the number i and the number of occurrences of auxiliary letters in* any *configuration during* any *computation of M starting from an initial configuration is not larger than j.*

(b) *The class of restarting automata of type* X *for which the number of auxiliary letters in the tape alphabet does not exceed the number i and the number of occurrences of auxiliary letters in* any *configuration during* any accepting *computation of M starting from an initial configuration is not larger than j is denoted by* a-aux(j,i)-X.

(c) *Finally, we use* g-aux(j,i)-X *to denote the class of restarting automata of type* X *for which the number of auxiliary letters in the tape alphabet does not exceed the number i and, for each $w \in L(M)$,* there exists *an accepting computation of M for input w such that the number of occurrences of auxiliary letters in* any *configuration during that computation is not larger than j.*

At times the constant j may be replaced by a non-constant function, which is used to measure the number of occurrences of auxiliary letters on the tape as a function of the length of the input.

Observe that, for each type X $\in$ {R, RR, RL, det-R, det-RR, det-RL}, the class of restarting automata aux$(0,i)$-XWW is essentially the same as the class XW.

First, we consider deterministic types of restarting automata. For each deterministic type det-X, the restrictions a-aux(j,i)-det-X and g-aux(j,i)-det-X yield the same class of automata, as a deterministic restarting automaton has only a single computation for each input word. Recall that L_{exp} denotes the language $L_{\mathrm{exp}} = \{ a^{2^n} \mid n \geq 0 \}$.

Proposition 2.2.56 $L_{\mathrm{exp}} \in \mathcal{L}(\mathsf{aux}(1,1)\text{-}\mathsf{det}\text{-}\mathsf{RWW}) \smallsetminus \mathcal{L}(\mathsf{RLW})$.

Proof. Let $M = (Q, \{a\}, \{a, A\}, \rhd, \lhd, q_0, 5, \delta)$ be the RWW-automaton that is described by the following set of meta-instructions:

$$\begin{array}{llll} (1) & (\rhd \cdot \{a, a^2, a^4\} \cdot \lhd, \mathsf{Accept}), & (3) & (\rhd \cdot a^+, a^4 A \to A a^2), \\ (2) & (\rhd \cdot a^+, a^4 \lhd \to Aaa\lhd), & (4) & (\rhd, a^4 A \to a^2). \end{array}$$

It follows easily that M is deterministic, that $L(M) = L_{\mathrm{exp}}$, and that no configuration of M that is reachable from an initial configuration ever contains more than a single occurrence of the auxiliary letter A. Hence, $L_{\mathrm{exp}} \in \mathcal{L}(\mathsf{aux}(1,1)\text{-}\mathsf{det}\text{-}\mathsf{RWW})$.

On the other hand, assume that M' is an RLW-automaton with a read-write window of size k that accepts the language L_{exp}, and let $w = a^{2^n}$. As $L(M') = L_{\mathrm{exp}}$, there exists an accepting computation of M' on input w. If n is sufficiently large, then M' cannot accept w in a tail computation. Thus, this accepting computation starts with a cycle of the form

$$q_0 \rhd w \lhd = q_0 \rhd a^{2^n} \lhd \vdash^c_{M'} q_0 \rhd a^{2^n - j} \lhd,$$

where $1 \leq j \leq k$. However, for sufficiently large values of n, the number $2^n - j$ will not be a power of two, that is, $a^{2^n - j} \notin L_{\mathrm{exp}}$. This contradicts our assumption on $L(M')$. Hence, L_{exp} is not accepted by any RLW-automaton. □

This result yields the following proper inclusions, which show that a single occurrence of a single auxiliary letter already suffices to properly increase the expressive capacity of restarting automata.

Corollary 2.2.57 *For each type* X $\in$ {det-R(R)WW, det-RLWW, R(R)WW, RLWW},

$$\mathcal{L}(\mathsf{aux}(0,1)\text{-}\mathsf{X}) \subsetneq \mathcal{L}(\mathsf{aux}(1,1)\text{-}\mathsf{X}).$$

By Lemma 2.2.10, the language $L'_{\mathrm{copy}} = \{ w\#w \mid w \in \{a,b\}^* \}$, which is not growing context-sensitive, is accepted by a det-RLWW-automaton. Hence, there exists a det-RLWW-automaton

$M_{\text{copy}} = (Q, \Sigma, \Gamma, \triangleright, \triangleleft, q_0, k, \delta)$ such that $L(M_{\text{copy}}) = L'_{\text{copy}}$. It follows that the det-RLW-automaton $M'_{\text{copy}} = (Q, \Gamma, \Gamma, \triangleright, \triangleleft, q_0, k, \delta)$ accepts the language $L(M'_{\text{copy}}) = L_C(M_{\text{copy}})$, which is not growing context-sensitive, either. Hence, we see that the language class $\mathcal{L}(\mathsf{aux}(0,1)\text{-}\mathsf{det}\text{-}\mathsf{RLWW})$ is not included in the class GCSL of growing context-sensitive languages. As GCSL includes the class of Church-Rosser languages, which coincides with $\mathcal{L}(\mathsf{det}\text{-}\mathsf{RRWW})$ (see Theorem 1.9.26), we obtain the following consequences.

Corollary 2.2.58 *For each $i \in \mathbb{N}_+$ and each function $j : \mathbb{N} \to \mathbb{N}$,*

$$\mathcal{L}(\mathsf{aux}(0,i)\text{-}\mathsf{det}\text{-}\mathsf{RLWW}) \not\subset \mathcal{L}(\mathsf{aux}(j(n),i)\text{-}\mathsf{det}\text{-}\mathsf{RRWW}) \subsetneq \mathcal{L}(\mathsf{aux}(j(n),i)\text{-}\mathsf{det}\text{-}\mathsf{RLWW}).$$

We do not know whether all context-free languages are accepted by det-RLWW-automata (see Problem 2.1.36). However, the following result shows that this is impossible if the number of occurrences of auxiliary letters is restricted too much.

Theorem 2.2.59 ([97]) *The language $L_{\text{pal2}} = \{ ww^R vv^R \mid w, v \in \{a,b\}^* \}$ is not accepted by any deterministic RLWW-automaton that uses only $o(n/\log^5 n)$ occurrences of auxiliary letters, that is, $L_{\text{pal2}} \notin \mathcal{L}(\mathsf{a}\text{-}\mathsf{aux}(o(n/\log^5 n), i)\text{-}\mathsf{det}\text{-}\mathsf{RLWW})$ for any $i \in \mathbb{N}_+$.*

Proof outline. This theorem is proved in [97] by making use of the notion of Kolmogorov complexity and its properties [140]. Let $K(x)$ denote the *Kolmogorov complexity* of a word x over a finite alphabet Σ satisfying $s = |\Sigma| > 1$. In the following, all logarithms used will be taken with respect to base s. A word $x \in \Sigma^+$ is called *random* if $K(x) > |x| - 4 \cdot \log |x|$, and it is called *incompressible* if $K(x) \geq |x|$.

The theorem claims that the language L_{pal2} is not accepted by any deterministic RLWW-automaton that uses only $o(n/\log^5 n)$ occurrences of auxiliary letters. To derive a contradiction, let us assume that there exists a det-RLWW-automaton $M = (Q, \Sigma, \Gamma, \triangleright, \triangleleft, q_0, k, \delta)$ for L_{pal2} that uses only $o(n/\log^5 n)$ occurrences of auxiliary letters.

For obtaining the intended contradiction, the (accepting) computation of M on an input of the form $w_1 w_1^R w_2^R w_2$ is studied, where $|w_1| = |w_2|$, and $w = w_1 w_2$ satisfies the conditions that $n = |w|$ is sufficiently large and that w is incompressible (that is, $K(w) \geq |w|$). It can then be shown that, as long as a long infix x of $w_1 w_1^R w_2^R w_2$ remains unchanged during this computation (that is, no rewrite operation is performed inside the factor x), each rewrite operation is executed inside the prefix or inside the suffix in which rewrite steps were already executes before, or within a distance of at most $\log^4 n$ from that prefix or that suffix.

As each rewrite step shortens the tape, the above property implies that the prefix w_1 or the suffix w_2 is shortened significantly within a certain number of cycles, while no rewrite operation is applied to the infix $w_1^R w_2^R$. On the other hand, the rewrite steps add some extra information to the prefix and to the suffix, as they introduce occurrences of auxiliary letters. Each occurrence of an auxiliary letter is uniquely determined by its position on the tape and its number in a linear ordering of Γ. Hence, it can be encoded by a word from Σ^+ of length $\log n + \log |\Gamma|$. As the number of occurrences of auxiliary letters on the tape is limited, however, they cannot make up for the loss of information that follows from the reduction in length. Thus, the suffix w_2 will finally be shortened to a word that can be encoded by less than $n/2 - \omega(\log n)$ letters without applying any rewrite step to the infix w_2^R, or the prefix w_1 will be shortened to a word that can be encoded by less than $n/2 - \omega(\log n)$ letters without applying any rewrite step to the infix w_1^R. As M accepts the language L_{pal2}, both cases yield a unique 'short' representation of w, which contradicts the incompressibility of w. The details can be found in the appendix of [97]. □

This result yields the following lower bound result.

Corollary 2.2.60 *If CFL is contained in the language class $\mathcal{L}(\mathsf{aux}(j(n),i)\text{-}\mathsf{det}\text{-}\mathsf{RLWW})$ for some function $j(n)$ and some integer i, then $j(n) \notin o(n/\log^5 n)$.*

It is currently not known whether the deterministic RLWW-automaton is at all less expressive than the nondeterministic RLWW-automaton. However, as the language L_{pal2} is 2-linear (see below), and as the class of 2-linear languages is included in $\mathcal{L}(\mathsf{aux}(1,1)\text{-}\mathsf{RLWW})$ (see Theorem 2.2.67 below), we have at least the following separation result.

Corollary 2.2.61 *For each function* $j(n) \in o(n/\log^5 n)$ *and each integer* $i > 0$,

$$\mathcal{L}(\mathsf{aux}(j(n), i)\text{-}\mathsf{det}\text{-}\mathsf{RLWW}) \subsetneq \mathcal{L}(\mathsf{aux}(j(n), i)\text{-}\mathsf{RLWW}).$$

Now we turn to the nondeterministic case. In fact, we concentrate on context-free languages and some of their subclasses. The next theorem states that all context-free languages are accepted by RWW-automata that have only a single auxiliary letter, provided the number of occurrences of that auxiliary letter is not restricted. To state this result, we use $\mathrm{id}(n)$ to denote the identity function on $\mathbb{N}$.

Theorem 2.2.62 ([97]) $\mathsf{CFL} \subseteq \mathcal{L}(\mathsf{aux}(\mathrm{id}(n), 1)\text{-}\mathsf{RWW})$.

Proof outline. Let $G = (N, T, S, P)$ be a context-free grammar in Chomsky normal form, let $m = |N|$, and let $\hat{L}$ be the set of all sentential forms that can be derived in G.

For each $\alpha \in \hat{L}$, we consider a derivation tree for α. If α is sufficiently long, then there exists a subtree with at least $4m$ (and at most $8m$) leaves. An RWW-automaton can guess a subword of α that corresponds to such a subtree and replace it with the encoding of the nonterminal appearing at the root of that subtree.

In order to use this technique when there is only one auxiliary letter in the alphabet, we encode the i-th nonterminal of G by Aa^iA, where A is the only auxiliary letter of the RWW-automaton considered and a is a fixed terminal letter. As each rewrite step shortens the sentential form by at least $4m - 1$ letters, the rewrite steps remain length-reducing even when the above encoding for nonterminals of G is being used. □

If only the accepting computations with the smallest number of occurrences of auxiliary letters are taken into account, then a technique of Lane A. Hemaspaandra et al. for space efficient computations [66] can be used to derive the following result.

Theorem 2.2.63 ([97]) $\mathsf{CFL} \subseteq \mathcal{L}(\mathsf{g}\text{-}\mathsf{aux}(\log n, 1)\text{-}\mathsf{RWW})$.

Thus, in this case, it suffices to admit a logarithmically bounded number of occurrences of the auxiliary letter. We complete this subsection by looking at a particular subclass of the context-free languages.

Definition 2.2.64 ([231]) *A language L is called* k-linear *for some $k \geq 2$, if there is a context-free grammar $G = (N, \Sigma, S, P)$ for L that contains a starting rule of the form $S \to S_1 S_2 \cdots S_k$ such that S does not occur in any other rule of G, and, for each $i \in \{1, 2, \ldots, k\}$, S_i is the start letter of a linear subgrammar $G_i = (N_i, \Sigma, S_i, P_i)$ of G. Furthermore, $N_i \cap N_j = \emptyset$ for each $i \neq j$, and S_i does not occur on the right-hand side of any rule of G_i $(1 \leq i \leq k)$. Thus, L is the concatenation $L_1 \cdot L_2 \cdot \ldots \cdot L_k$ of the linear context-free languages $L_i = L(G_i)$ $(1 \leq i \leq k)$. We use k-LIN to denote the class of all k-linear languages.*

All k-linear languages can be accepted by RLWW-automata that use only two occurrences of a single auxiliary letter.

Theorem 2.2.65 ([97]) $\bigcup_{k \in \mathbb{N}} k\text{-}\mathsf{LIN} \subsetneq \mathcal{L}(\mathsf{aux}(2, 1)\text{-}\mathsf{RLWW})$.

Proof outline. Let $k \geq 1$, L be a k-linear language, and G be a k-linear grammar that generates L. First, we describe the idea of accepting L using only two occurrences of auxiliary letters on the tape, but without restricting the number of auxiliary letters in the alphabet.

For an input word x, we first guess a G_1-derivation $S_1 \Rightarrow^* x_1$ in a bottom-up fashion for a prefix x_1 of x such that $x = x_1 x_2 \cdots x_k$, where $x_i \in L(G_i)$ for all $i \in \{1, 2, \ldots, k\}$. We start by choosing a production $(X \to \alpha)$ for $X \in N_1$ and $\alpha \in \Sigma^*$. That is, we perform a rewrite step $\alpha \to X$. Then we simulate consecutive steps of the derivation in reverse order by applying meta-instructions

$$(\rhd \cdot \Sigma^*, \alpha X \beta \to Y, \Sigma^* \cdot \lhd)$$

for $X, Y \in N_1$, $\alpha, \beta \in \Sigma^*$, corresponding to productions $(Y \to \alpha X \beta)$ of G_1.

When a tape contents of the form $S_1 y$ is reached, where $y \in \Sigma^*$, we begin to simulate a G_2-derivation for $L_2 = L(G_2)$ by first executing the last step in a derivation of $x_2 \in L_2$. Thereafter, the tape contains two auxiliary letters: $S_1 \in N_1$ and $X \in N_2$. This means that we have already found a prefix $x_1 \in L_1$ and have started to simulate a G_2-derivation for $x_2 \in L_2$. So we can remove S_1. Furthermore, we process consecutive factors analogously. In general, we can describe this behavior by the following meta-instructions, where $u, y, v \in \Sigma^*$, $i \in \{1, 2, \ldots, k\}$:

$$\begin{array}{ll}
(\rhd \cdot \Sigma^*, u \to X, \Sigma^* \cdot \lhd) & \text{for } (X \to u) \in P_1, \\
(\rhd \cdot \Sigma^*, uXy \to Y, \Sigma^* \cdot \lhd) & \text{for } X, Y \in N_i, (Y \to uXy) \in P_i, \\
(\rhd \cdot S_i \cdot \Sigma^*, u \to X, \Sigma^* \cdot \lhd) & \text{for } X \in N_{i+1}, (X \to u) \in P_{i+1}, \\
(\rhd, S_i \to \lambda, \Sigma^* \cdot X \cdot \Sigma^* \cdot \lhd) & \text{for } X \in N_{i+1}, \\
(\rhd \cdot S_k \cdot \lhd, \mathsf{Accept}). &
\end{array}$$

However, this schema does not guarantee that the automaton is length-reducing, for example, a production $X \to y$, where $|y| \leq 1$, can be applied. Furthermore, we want to use only one auxiliary letter in the alphabet.

Without loss of generality, we can assume that the grammar does neither contain any productions of the form $(X \to Y)$ for $|Y| \leq 1$ and $X \notin \{S_1, S_2, \ldots, S_k\}$ nor of the form $(S_i \to X)$ for $i \in \{1, 2, \ldots, k\}$ and $X \in N$. Furthermore, we can assume that Σ contains at least two letters, say 0 and 1 (as context-free languages over a one-letter alphabet are regular). In order to apply the above strategy using only one auxiliary letter, an occurrence of this auxiliary letter will be followed by a binary encoding (of a fixed length) of the actual nonterminal of G. In order to make the resulting rewrite operations length-reducing, 'short' factors x_i can be processed separately and for the remaining 'long' factors, several derivation steps are simulated by a single rewrite operation. In this way, there will be sufficient space for the encodings. A detailed description of the resulting RLWW-automaton can be found in [97]. It follows that $k\text{-}\mathsf{LIN} \subseteq \mathcal{L}(\mathsf{aux}(2,1)\text{-}\mathsf{RLWW})$.

As already $\mathcal{L}(\mathsf{RLW}) = \mathcal{L}(\mathsf{aux}(0,1)\text{-}\mathsf{RLWW})$ contains non-context-free languages (see, e.g., Proposition 2.2.20), the above inclusion is a proper one. □

From the proof outline above, we see that a linear language can be accepted by an RLWW-automaton that uses only a single occurrence of a single auxiliary letter, that is, we have the following inclusion.

Corollary 2.2.66 $\mathsf{LIN} \subsetneq \mathcal{L}(\mathsf{aux}(1,1)\text{-}\mathsf{RLWW})$.

This result can even be extended to two-linear languages, thus improving Theorem 2.2.65. For a proof, we refer to [97].

Theorem 2.2.67 ([97]) $2\text{-}\mathsf{LIN} \subsetneq \mathcal{L}(\mathsf{aux}(1,1)\text{-}\mathsf{RLWW})$.

We have seen, in particular, that two occurrences of a single auxiliary letter suffice to accept every k-linear language, and that for $k = 2$, already a single occurrence suffices. Observe that the language L_{pal2} considered in Theorem 2.2.59 is two-linear. On the other hand, we have seen that a bounded number of occurrences of auxiliary letters does not suffice to accept all context-free languages by deterministic RLWW-automata. Hence, we obtain, in particular, the following proper inclusion.

Corollary 2.2.68 $\mathcal{L}(\mathsf{aux}(1,1)\text{-}\mathsf{det}\text{-}\mathsf{RLWW}) \subsetneq \mathcal{L}(\mathsf{aux}(1,1)\text{-}\mathsf{RLWW})$.

However, many problems concerning these measures remain open.

Problem 2.2.69 (a) *Is there an infinite hierarchy with respect to the number of auxiliary letters in the tape alphabet of an RLWW-automaton? Or is it possible to show that a single auxiliary letter is always sufficient by using appropriate encodings?*

(b) *Is there an infinite hierarchy with respect to the number of occurrences of auxiliary letters?*

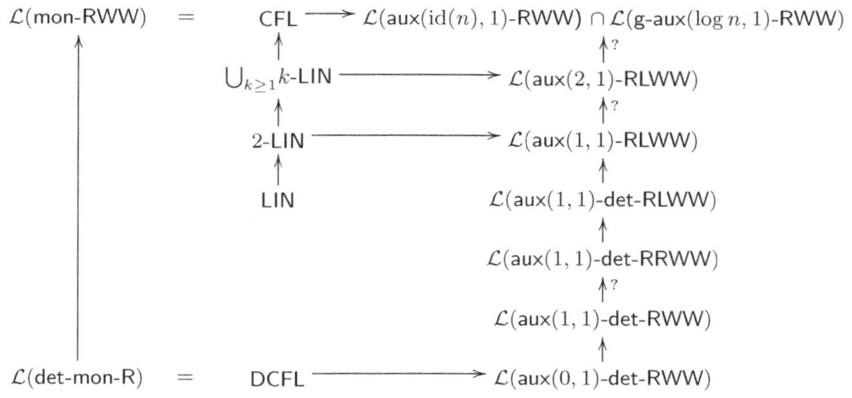

Figure 2.10: Inclusion relations concerning the utilization of auxiliary letters.

Actually, we do not even know the answer to the following question.

Problem 2.2.70 *Is* $\mathcal{L}$(aux(1, 1)-RLWW) *a proper subclass of* $\mathcal{L}$(aux(2, 1)-RLWW)*?*

Also there is another interesting question concerning the context-free languages.

Problem 2.2.71 *Is there a constant d such that each context-free language is accepted by a nondeterministic RLWW-automaton that uses at most d occurrences of auxiliary letters?*

Recall that each *deterministic context-free* language is accepted by a monotone det-R-automaton, that is, for these languages no auxiliary letters are required at all. Finally, also the following problem remains open.

Problem 2.2.72 *In Corollary 2.2.58, we saw that* $\mathcal{L}$(aux(1, 1)-det-RRWW) *is a proper subclass of* $\mathcal{L}$(aux(1, 1)-det-RLWW). *However, we do not know whether* $\mathcal{L}$(aux(1, 1)-det-RWW) *is a proper subclass of* $\mathcal{L}$(aux(1, 1)-det-RRWW).

The major inclusion results that we obtained concerning the use of auxiliary letters are summarized in the diagram in Figure 2.10, where $\rightarrow$ denotes a proper inclusion, while $\underset{?}{\rightarrow}$ denotes an inclusion, for which it is still open whether it is proper or not.

2.3 Restricting the Size of the Read/Write Window

In this section, we study the influence of the size of the read/write window on the expressive capacity of various types of restarting automata. In Subsection 2.3.1, we explore this question for restarting automata without auxiliary letters and, in Subsection 2.3.2, we analyze the situation for length-reducing restarting automata with auxiliary letters. Then, in Subsection 2.3.3, we concentrate on weight-reducing restarting automata with auxiliary letters, proving that for sRRWW-automata, window size one suffices. In Subsection 2.3.4, we consider the so-called *ordered* restarting automata. They form particular classes of shrinking restarting automata with auxiliary letters. The various types of ordered restarting automata have in common that they use a window of size three, but that, in each rewrite step, they just replace the letter in the middle of the window with another letter. Finally, in Subsection 2.3.5, we study weight-reducing RWW-automata of window size one.

2.3.1 On the Window Size for Restarting Automata without Auxiliary Letters

Here we consider sRLW-automata and their various subclasses, studying the influence that the window size has on their expressive capacity. As we shall see, for each type of restarting automaton considered, the window size induces an infinite strictly ascending hierarchy of language classes.

Definition 2.3.1 *For each type X of restarting automaton and each integer $k \geq 1$, $\mathsf{X}(k)$ denotes the class of all automata of type X that have a read/write window of size k.*

Let L_1 be the semi-Dyck language D_1 over the alphabet $T_1 = \{a_1, \bar{a}_1\}$ (see Example 1.2.22), that is, D_1 is the language that is generated by the context-free grammar

$$G_1 = (\{S\}, T_1, S, \{(S \to \lambda), (S \to SS), (S \to a_1 S \bar{a}_1)\}).$$

For $k \geq 2$, let L_k be the language $L_k = \{\, a^n c^{k-1} b^n \mid n \geq 0 \,\}$ over $\Sigma = \{a, b, c\}$. In [157], František Mráz shows that, for each $k \geq 1$, $L_k \in \mathcal{L}(\mathsf{det\text{-}mon\text{-}R}(k+1)) \smallsetminus \mathcal{L}(\mathsf{RRW}(k))$. Here we establish the following slightly stronger result.

Lemma 2.3.2 *For all $k \geq 1$, $L_k \in \mathcal{L}(\mathsf{det\text{-}mon\text{-}R}(k+1)) \smallsetminus \mathcal{L}(\mathsf{sRLW}(k))$.*

Proof. First, we consider the case $k = 1$. An R-automaton M_1 with window size two for $L_1 = D_1$ is given by the meta-instructions

$$(1) \quad (\rhd \cdot \lhd, \mathsf{Accept}) \quad \text{and} \quad (2) \quad (\rhd \cdot a_1^*, a_1\bar{a}_1 \to \lambda).$$

It is easily seen that M_1 is deterministic and monotone, and that $L(M_1) = L_1$.

Now assume that M is an sRLW-automaton with window size one, and that $L(M) = L_1$. For the word $w = a_1^n \bar{a}_1^n \in L_1$, M has an accepting computation, which, however, cannot just consist of an accepting tail, if n is large. Thus, this accepting computation begins with a cycle of the form $q_0 \rhd a_1^n \bar{a}_1^n \lhd \vdash_M^c q_0 \rhd z \lhd$. As we consider an accepting computation, $z \in L_1$. The word z is obtained from $a_1^n \bar{a}_1^n$ by replacing a single letter with a word of less weight. This implies the following. If the letter replaced is an occurrence of a_1, then the word it is replaced with is a power of $\bar{a}_1$, and conversely, if the letter replaced is an occurrence of $\bar{a}_1$, then the word it is replaced with is a power of a_1. In either case, it follows that $|z|_{a_1} \neq |z|_{\bar{a}_1}$. Hence, $z \notin L_1$, a contradiction. Thus, L_1 is not accepted by any sRLW-automaton of window size one.

Now we consider the case $k \geq 2$. An R-automaton M_k with window size $k+1$ for L_k is given by the following meta-instructions:

$$(1) \quad (\rhd \cdot c^{k-1} \cdot \lhd, \mathsf{Accept}) \quad \text{and} \quad (2) \quad (\rhd \cdot a^*, ac^{k-1}b \to c^{k-1}).$$

It is easily seen that M_k is deterministic and monotone, and that $L(M_k) = L_k$.

Now assume that M is an sRLW-automaton with window size k, and that $L(M) = L_k$. For the word $w = a^n c^{k-1} b^n \in L_k$, M has an accepting computation, which cannot be an accepting tail computation, if n is large. Thus, this accepting computation begins with a cycle of the form $q_0 \triangleright w \triangleleft = q_0 \triangleright a^n c^{k-1} b^n \triangleleft \vdash_M^c q_0 \triangleright z \triangleleft$. As we consider an accepting computation, $z \in L_k$, that is, $z = a^m c^{k-1} b^m$ for some m. The automaton M is weight-reducing, that is, it replaces a factor of length k with a word of smaller weight. This implies that the weight of z is strictly smaller than the weight of w, which means that $m < n$, that is, $m = n - i$ for some $i \geq 1$. However, there is no way to transform the word $w = a^n c^{k-1} b^n$ into $z = a^{n-i} c^{k-1} b^{n-i}$ by replacing a factor of length k of w with a shorter word. Thus, L_k is not accepted by any sRLW-automaton of window size k. □

This lemma has the following consequences, extending the corresponding results of [157].

Corollary 2.3.3 *For all* $k \geq 1$, *for all* $\mathsf{X} \in \{\mathsf{R}, \mathsf{RR}, \mathsf{RL}, \mathsf{RW}, \mathsf{RRW}, \mathsf{RLW}, \mathsf{sRW}, \mathsf{sRRW}, \mathsf{sRLW}\}$, *and for all prefixes* $\mathsf{pref}_1, \mathsf{pref}_2 \in \{\mathsf{det\text{-}mon\text{-}}, \mathsf{det\text{-}}, \mathsf{mon\text{-}}, \lambda\}$,

(a) $\mathcal{L}(\mathsf{pref}_1\text{-}\mathsf{X}(k)) \subsetneq \mathcal{L}(\mathsf{pref}_1\text{-}\mathsf{X}(k+1))$ *and*
(b) $\mathcal{L}(\mathsf{pref}_1\text{-}\mathsf{X}(k+1)) \smallsetminus \mathcal{L}(\mathsf{pref}_2\text{-}\mathsf{X}(k)) \neq \emptyset$.

For all $\mathsf{X} \in \{\mathsf{R}, \mathsf{RR}, \mathsf{RL}, \mathsf{RW}, \mathsf{RRW}, \mathsf{RLW}, \mathsf{sRW}, \mathsf{sRRW}, \mathsf{sRLW}\}$ and $\mathsf{pref} \in \{\mathsf{det\text{-}mon\text{-}}, \mathsf{det\text{-}}, \mathsf{mon\text{-}}, \lambda\}$, $\bigcup_{k\geq 1} \mathcal{L}(\mathsf{pref\text{-}X}(k)) = \mathcal{L}(\mathsf{pref\text{-}X})$. As $\mathcal{L}(\mathsf{det\text{-}mon\text{-}R}) = \mathcal{L}(\mathsf{det\text{-}mon\text{-}sRRW}) = \mathsf{DCFL}$ by Corollary 2.1.43, we see that, for all types of restarting automata $\mathsf{X} \in \{\mathsf{R}, \mathsf{RR}, \mathsf{RW}, \mathsf{RRW}, \mathsf{sRW}, \mathsf{sRRW}\}$, the family of language classes $(\mathcal{L}(\mathsf{det\text{-}mon\text{-}X}(k)))_{k\geq 1}$ forms an infinite ascending hierarchy inside DCFL such that

$$\bigcup_{k\geq 1} \mathcal{L}(\mathsf{det\text{-}mon\text{-}X}(k)) = \mathsf{DCFL}.$$

Analogously, as $\mathcal{L}(\mathsf{det\text{-}mon\text{-}RL}) = \mathcal{L}(\mathsf{det\text{-}mon\text{-}sRLW}) = \mathsf{LRR}$ (see Theorem 2.1.56), it follows that, for all types of restarting automata $\mathsf{X} \in \{\mathsf{RL}, \mathsf{RLW}, \mathsf{sRLW}\}$, $(\mathcal{L}(\mathsf{det\text{-}mon\text{-}X}(k)))_{k\geq 1}$ is an infinite ascending hierarchy inside LRR satisfying

$$\bigcup_{k\geq 1} \mathcal{L}(\mathsf{det\text{-}mon\text{-}X}(k)) = \mathsf{LRR}.$$

If a length-reducing restarting automaton has window size one, then all its rewrite transitions are deletions that erase single letters. Hence, for each type of restarting automaton $\mathsf{X} \in \{\mathsf{R}, \mathsf{RR}, \mathsf{RL}\}$ and each prefix $\mathsf{pref} \in \{\mathsf{det\text{-}mon\text{-}}, \mathsf{det\text{-}}, \mathsf{mon\text{-}}, \lambda\}$, the automata of type $\mathsf{pref\text{-}X}(1)$ coincide with those of type $\mathsf{pref\text{-}XW}(1)$. In addition, an RLWW(1)-automaton cannot use its auxiliary letters in any computation that begins with an initial configuration. Thus, $\mathcal{L}(\mathsf{pref\text{-}X}(1)) = \mathcal{L}(\mathsf{pref\text{-}XWW}(1))$ for each type of restarting automaton $\mathsf{X} \in \{\mathsf{R}, \mathsf{RR}, \mathsf{RL}\}$ and each prefix $\mathsf{pref} \in \{\mathsf{det\text{-}mon\text{-}}, \mathsf{det\text{-}}, \mathsf{mon\text{-}}, \lambda\}$. In fact, length-reducing restarting automata of window size one are fairly weak.

Theorem 2.3.4 ([157]) $\mathcal{L}(\mathsf{pref\text{-}RWW}(1)) = \mathsf{REG}$ *for all* $\mathsf{pref} \in \{\mathsf{det\text{-}mon\text{-}}, \mathsf{det\text{-}}, \mathsf{mon\text{-}}, \lambda\}$.

Thus, all the various types of R(W)(W)-automata of window size one accept exactly the regular languages.

Proof outline. Obviously, a det-mon-R(1)-automaton can simulate a DFA without using any rewrite/restart steps. Hence, $\mathsf{REG} \subseteq \mathcal{L}(\mathsf{det\text{-}mon\text{-}R}(1)) = \mathcal{L}(\mathsf{det\text{-}mon\text{-}RWW}(1))$.

To prove that R(1)-automata only accept regular languages, let $M = (Q, \Sigma, \Sigma, \triangleright, \triangleleft, q_0, 1, \delta)$ be an R(1)-automaton. We construct an NFA $A = (P, \Sigma, p_0, \eta, F)$ for the language $L(M) \cdot \triangleleft$. The set of states P of A is defined as

$$P = \mathcal{P}(Q) \cup \{X, X_+\},$$

where X and X_+ are two additional states,

$$p_0 = \{\, q' \in Q \mid (q', \mathsf{MVR}) \in \delta(q_0, \triangleright) \,\}$$

is the initial state of A, and $F = \{X_+\}$. Thus, p_0 consists of all states of M that M can reach from its initial state by reading the left sentinel $\rhd$. The transition relation η is defined as follows for each set $S \subseteq Q$ and each input letter $x \in \Sigma$:

$$\begin{array}{rcl} \eta(S,x) &=& S_1 \cup S_2 \cup S_3, \text{ where} \\ S_1 &=& \{ q' \in Q \mid \exists q \in S : (q', \mathsf{MVR}) \in \delta(q,x) \}, \\ S_2 &=& \begin{cases} S, & \text{if } \exists q \in S : \lambda \in \delta(q,x), \\ \emptyset, & \text{otherwise,} \end{cases} \\ S_3 &=& \begin{cases} \{X\}, & \text{if } \exists q \in S : \mathsf{Accept} \in \delta(q,x), \\ \emptyset, & \text{otherwise.} \end{cases} \end{array}$$

In addition, we take

$$\begin{array}{rcl} \eta(S,\lhd) &=& \begin{cases} \{X_+\}, & \text{if } \exists q \in S : \mathsf{Accept} \in \delta(q,\lhd), \\ \emptyset, & \text{otherwise,} \end{cases} \\ \eta(X,x) &=& \{X\}, \text{ and} \\ \eta(X,\lhd) &=& \{X_+\}. \end{array}$$

Thus, $\eta(S,x)$ contains all states that M can reach from a state in S by performing a MVR step reading the letter x and all states in S, if there exists a state in S such that M can execute a delete step for the letter x. In addition, $\eta(S,x)$ contains the state X, if there exists a state in S such that M can accept on reading the letter x. Then, for each prefix u of an input word w, it can be shown that $\eta(p_0,u)$ contains all those states q of M in which M can be after executing several (possibly none) cycles on w and being in a phase in which M leaves the part of the tape that originally contained the prefix u. In state X, A reads across the remaining input and it enters the final state X_+ on seeing the right sentinel $\lhd$. It follows that $L(A) = L(M) \cdot \lhd$, which implies that $L(M)$ is a regular language. □

This result does not extend to RR-automata. The next example shows that already monotone RR(1)-automata can accept non-regular languages.

Example 2.3.5 ([162]) *Let L'_2 be the following non-regular language:*

$$L'_2 = \{ a^m b^n \mid m \in \{n, n+1\}, n \geq 0 \}.$$

We present a monotone RR(1)-automaton for this language. Let

$$M = (Q, \{a,b\}, \{a,b\}, \rhd, \lhd, q_0, 1, \delta)$$

be the RR(1)-automaton that is defined by taking $Q = \{q_0, q_1, q_2, p_0, p_1, p_2\}$ and by defining the transition relation δ as follows:

$$\begin{array}{llcl} (1) & \delta(q_0,\rhd) &=& \{(q_0,\mathsf{MVR})\}, \\ (2) & \delta(q_0,\lhd) &=& \{\mathsf{Accept}\}, \\ (3) & \delta(q_0,a) &=& \{(p_0,\lambda),(q_2,\mathsf{MVR})\}, \\ (4) & \delta(q_1,a) &=& \{(p_2,\lambda),(q_2,\mathsf{MVR})\}, \\ (5) & \delta(q_2,a) &=& \{(p_1,\lambda),(q_1,\mathsf{MVR})\}, \\ (6) & \delta(p_0,\lhd) &=& \{\mathsf{Accept}\}, \end{array} \qquad \begin{array}{llcl} (7) & \delta(q_1,b) &=& \{(p_1,\lambda)\}, \\ (8) & \delta(q_2,b) &=& \{(p_2,\lambda)\}, \\ (9) & \delta(p_1,b) &=& \{(p_2,\mathsf{MVR})\}, \\ (10) & \delta(p_2,b) &=& \{(p_1,\mathsf{MVR})\}, \\ (11) & \delta(p_2,\lhd) &=& \{\mathsf{Restart}\}. \end{array}$$

Obviously, M accepts the empty word λ and the word a. Furthermore, it is easily seen that M only accepts words from the regular language $\{a\}^* \cdot \{b\}^*$. Now let $w = a^m b^n$ be given as input, that is, we have the initial configuration $q_0 \rhd a^m b^n \lhd$. If M deletes one of the first $m-1$ occurrences of the letter a, then it gets stuck immediately thereafter. Hence, we see that M either deletes the last occurrence of the letter a or the first occurrence of the letter b, which implies that M is monotone. From the indices of the states used, we see that to complete a cycle through the restart operation (11), M must delete the last occurrence of the letter a, if m and n do not have the same *parity mod 2, and it must delete the first occurrence of the letter b, if m and n have the same parity mod 2. Indeed, depending on the parities of m and n, we have the following cycles:*

$$
\begin{array}{llclclc}
(o,e) & q_0 \rhd a^{2r+1} b^{2s} \lhd & \vdash_M^{2r+1} & \rhd a^{2r} q_1 a b^{2s} \lhd & \vdash_M & \rhd a^{2r} p_2 b^{2s} \lhd \\
 & & \vdash_M^{2s} & \rhd a^{2r} b^{2s} p_2 \lhd & \vdash_M & q_0 \rhd a^{2r} b^{2s} \lhd, \\
(e,o) & q_0 \rhd a^{2r} b^{2s+1} \lhd & \vdash_M^{2r} & \rhd a^{2r-1} q_2 a b^{2s+1} \lhd & \vdash_M & \rhd a^{2r-1} p_1 b^{2s+1} \lhd \\
 & & \vdash_M^{2s+1} & \rhd a^{2r-1} b^{2s+1} p_2 \lhd & \vdash_M & q_0 \rhd a^{2r-1} b^{2s+1} \lhd, \\
(e,e) & q_0 \rhd a^{2r} b^{2s} \lhd & \vdash_M^{2r+1} & \rhd a^{2r} q_1 b^{2s} \lhd & \vdash_M & \rhd a^{2r} p_1 b^{2s-1} \lhd \\
 & & \vdash_M^{2s-1} & \rhd a^{2r} b^{2s-1} p_2 \lhd & \vdash_M & q_0 \rhd a^{2r} b^{2s-1} \lhd, \\
(o,o) & q_0 \rhd a^{2r+1} b^{2s+1} \lhd & \vdash_M^{2r+2} & \rhd a^{2r+1} q_2 b^{2s+1} \lhd & \vdash_M & \rhd a^{2r+1} p_2 b^{2s} \lhd \\
 & & \vdash_M^{2s} & \rhd a^{2r+1} b^{2s} p_2 \lhd & \vdash_M & q_0 \rhd a^{2r+1} b^{2s} \lhd .
\end{array}
$$

Furthermore, in each of these cases, if another occurrence of the letter b is added, in this way changing the relative parities of a's and b's, then M reaches the right sentinel while being in state p_1, and hence, it gets stuck. It follows that $L(M) = L'_2$. ■

In fact, by counting mod 4 while scanning the suffix of b's, the above RR(1)-automaton can be extended to a monotone RR(1)-automaton for the language

$$L' = \{\, a^m b^n c \mid n \in \{m, m+1\}, m \geq 0 \,\} \cup \{\, a^m b^n d \mid n \in \{2m, 2m+1, 2m+2\}, m \geq 0 \,\}.$$

Lemma 2.3.6 $L' \in \mathcal{L}(\mathsf{mon\text{-}RR}(1)) \smallsetminus \mathsf{DCFL}$.

Proof. We describe an RR(1)-automaton M' for L' through a sequence of meta-instructions:

$$
\begin{array}{rl}
(1) & (\rhd \cdot \{c, d\} \cdot \lhd, \mathsf{Accept}), \\
(2) & (\rhd \cdot (aa)^*, b \to \lambda, (bb)^* \cdot c \cdot \lhd), \\
(3) & (\rhd \cdot (aa)^* \cdot a, b \to \lambda, b \cdot (bb)^* \cdot c \cdot \lhd), \\
(4) & (\rhd \cdot (aa)^* \cdot a, a \to \lambda, (bb)^* \cdot c \cdot \lhd), \\
(5) & (\rhd \cdot (aa)^*, a \to \lambda, b \cdot (bb)^* \cdot c \cdot \lhd), \\
(6) & (\rhd \cdot (aa)^*, b \to \lambda, b \cdot (b^4)^* \cdot d \cdot \lhd), \\
(7) & (\rhd \cdot (aa)^*, b \to \lambda, (b^4)^* \cdot d \cdot \lhd), \\
(8) & (\rhd \cdot (aa)^* \cdot a, b \to \lambda, b^3 \cdot (b^4)^* \cdot d \cdot \lhd), \\
(9) & (\rhd \cdot (aa)^* \cdot a, b \to \lambda, b^2 \cdot (b^4)^* \cdot d \cdot \lhd), \\
(10) & (\rhd \cdot (aa)^*, a \to \lambda, b^2 \cdot (b^4)^* \cdot d \cdot \lhd), \\
(11) & (\rhd \cdot (aa)^* \cdot a, a \to \lambda, (b^4)^* \cdot d \cdot \lhd).
\end{array}
$$

Using instruction (1), M' accepts the words $c = a^0 b^0 c$ and $d = a^0 b^0 d$ in tail computations. For a word of the form $a^m b^n c$, M' uses the instructions (2) to (5). If $m = n \mod 2$, then the last occurrence of the letter a is deleted (by (4) or (5)), and if $m \neq n \mod 2$, then the first occurrence of the letter b is deleted (by (2) or (3)). Hence, M' accepts the word $a^m b^n c$ if and only if $n \in \{m, m+1\}$.

For a word of the form $a^m b^n d$, M' uses instructions (6) to (11). If $m = 0 \mod 2$, then the first occurrence of b is deleted in case $n = 2 \mod 4$ or $n = 1 \mod 4$ (by (6) or (7)), and the last occurrence of a is deleted in case $n = 0 \mod 4$ (by (11)). If $m = 1 \mod 2$, then the first occurrence of b is deleted in case $n = 0 \mod 4$ or $n = 3 \mod 4$ (by (8) or (9)), and the last occurrence of a is deleted in case $n = 2 \mod 4$ (by (10)). Hence, M' accepts the word $a^m b^n d$ if and only if $n \in \{2m, 2m+1, 2m+2\}$. It follows that M' is monotone and that $L(M') = L'$.

It remains to prove that the language L' is not deterministic context-free. For doing so, we use the Iteration Theorem for DCFL (Theorem 1.2.42). Assume that L' is deterministic context-free, and let k be the constant for L' from the Iteration Theorem. Let $z = a^r b^r c \in L'$, where $r > k$, and assume that the first k occurrences of the letter b are marked. Then z admits a factorization $z = uvwxy$ that satisfies all of the following conditions:

(1) $v \neq \lambda$,

(2) $uv^iwx^iy \in L'$ for all $i \geq 0$,

(3) u, v and w or w, x and y contain marked positions,

(4) the number of marked positions in vwx is at most k,

(5) and finally, if $y \neq \lambda$, then for each $m, n \geq 0$ and each $\alpha \in \Sigma^*$: $uv^{m+n}wx^n\alpha \in L'$ iff $uv^mw\alpha \in L'$.

If the prefix u contains marked positions, then v and x are both factors of the suffix b^rc, which implies immediately that the word $uv^0wx^0y = uwy$ cannot be an element of L'. Thus, it follows from (3) that w, x, and y contain marked positions, that is, $u = a^i$, $v = a^j$, $w = a^{r-i-j}b^s$, $x = b^t$, and $y = b^{r-s-t}c$ for some integers $i, j \geq 0$ and $s, t \geq 1$ such that $i + j \leq r$ and $s + t < k$. Then $uwy = a^ia^{r-i-j}b^sb^{r-s-t}c = a^{r-j}b^{r-t}c$, which implies that $t = j$ or $t = j - 1$.

Furthermore, as $y = b^{r-s-t}c$, $y \neq \lambda$. Hence, by (5), for each $m, n \geq 0$ and each $\alpha \in \Sigma^*$: $uv^{m+n}wx^n\alpha \in L'$ iff $uv^mw\alpha \in L'$. We choose $m = 1$ and $\alpha = b^{2r-s}d$. Then $uv^mw\alpha = a^ia^ja^{r-i-j}b^sb^{2r-s}d = a^rb^{2r}d \in L'$. Hence, for $n = 1$, $uv^{1+n}wx^n\alpha = a^ia^ja^ja^{r-i-j}b^sb^tb^{2r-s}d = a^{r+j}b^{2r+t}d \in L'$. However, as $2(r+j) = 2r + 2j \geq 2r + 2t > 2r + t$, we see that $uv^{1+n}wx^n\alpha \notin L'$, a contradiction. Thus, L' is not deterministic context-free. □

From Lemma 2.3.6, we obtain the following consequence.

Proposition 2.3.7 $\mathsf{REG} \subsetneq \mathcal{L}(\mathsf{mon\text{-}RR}(1)) = \mathcal{L}(\mathsf{mon\text{-}RL}(1)) \subsetneq \mathsf{CFL}$, *but* $\mathcal{L}(\mathsf{mon\text{-}RR}(1))$ *is incomparable to the class DCFL with respect to inclusion.*

Proof. It is easily verified that the deterministic context-free language $\{ a^nb^n \mid n \geq 0 \}$ is not accepted by any RR(1)-automaton. Furthermore, as Theorem 2.1.2 extends to RL(1)-automata, we have $\mathcal{L}(\mathsf{mon\text{-}RR}(1)) = \mathcal{L}(\mathsf{mon\text{-}RL}(1))$. Together with the fact that L' is accepted by a monotone RR(1)-automaton and the inclusion of $\mathcal{L}(\mathsf{mon\text{-}RR})$ in CFL, this yields the above results. □

Without the restriction of monotonicity, RR(1)-automata are even more expressive.

Proposition 2.3.8 *The language class* $\mathcal{L}(\mathsf{RR}(1)) = \mathcal{L}(\mathsf{RL}(1))$ *is incomparable to the classes DCFL, CFL, and GCSL with respect to inclusion.*

Proof. By Theorem 2.1.2, $\mathcal{L}(\mathsf{RR}(1)) = \mathcal{L}(\mathsf{RL}(1))$. As the deterministic context-free language $\{ a^nb^n \mid n \geq 0 \}$ is not accepted by any RR(1)-automaton, it remains to prove that there exists a language in $\mathcal{L}(\mathsf{RR}(1))$ that is not even growing context-sensitive. We have seen in Section 1.2 that the marked copy language $L'_{\text{copy}} = \{ w\#w \mid w \in \{a, b\}^* \}$ is not growing context-sensitive. Here we present an RR(1)-automaton that accepts a superset of this language.

Let $\Sigma = \{a, b\}$ and let $M' = (Q, \Sigma \cup \{\#\}, \Sigma \cup \{\#\}, \rhd, \lhd, q_0, 1, \delta)$ be the RR(1)-automaton that is defined through the following meta-instructions:

$$\begin{array}{lll} (1) & (\rhd \cdot \# \cdot \lhd, \mathsf{Accept}), & \\ (2) & (\rhd \cdot d \cdot (\Sigma \cdot \Sigma)^* \cdot \Sigma \cdot \#, d \to \lambda, \Sigma \cdot (\Sigma \cdot \Sigma)^* \cdot \lhd) & \text{for all } d \in \Sigma, \\ (3) & (\rhd \cdot d \cdot (\Sigma \cdot \Sigma)^* \cdot \#, d \to \lambda, (\Sigma \cdot \Sigma)^* \cdot \lhd) & \text{for all } d \in \Sigma, \\ (4) & (\rhd, d \to \lambda, (\Sigma \cdot \Sigma)^* \cdot \Sigma \cdot \# \cdot \Sigma \cdot (\Sigma \cdot \Sigma)^* \cdot \lhd) & \text{for all } d \in \Sigma, \\ (5) & (\rhd, d \to \lambda, (\Sigma \cdot \Sigma)^* \cdot \# \cdot (\Sigma \cdot \Sigma)^* \cdot \lhd) & \text{for all } d \in \Sigma. \end{array}$$

Let $z = w\#w'$ for some $w, w' \in \Sigma^*$. If $w = \lambda = w'$, then M' accepts on input z by using instruction (1). Assume now that $w \neq \lambda$ or $w' \neq \lambda$. If $|w| = |w'| \mod 2$, then M' compares the first letter of w to the first letter of w' (by (2) or (3)). If these letters coincide, then the first letter of w' is deleted; otherwise, M' gets stuck. If $|w| \neq |w'| \mod 2$, then M' simply deletes the first letter of w (by (4) or (5)). Hence, we conclude that $L'_{\text{copy}} = L(M') \cap R$, where R is the regular language that is given though the regular expression

$$((\Sigma \cdot \Sigma)^* \cdot \# \cdot (\Sigma \cdot \Sigma)^*) \cup ((\Sigma \cdot \Sigma)^* \cdot \Sigma \cdot \# \cdot \Sigma \cdot (\Sigma \cdot \Sigma)^*).$$

As the class GCSL of growing context-sensitive languages is closed under intersection with regular languages, it follows that with L'_{copy}, also the language $L(M')$ is not growing context-sensitive. This completes the proof of Proposition 2.3.8. □

In [157], František Mráz considers the language

$$L = \{ a^i b^j c^m \mid 0 \leq i \leq j \leq m \text{ and } m - i \leq 1 \}.$$

By using the technique of counting modulo two, he proves that L is accepted by an RR-automaton of window size one. On the other hand, he shows that L is not accepted by any RW-automaton. In fact, his proof can easily be extended to show that L is not even accepted by any sRW-automaton. As $\mathcal{L}(\mathsf{RW})$ is not contained in $\mathcal{L}(\mathsf{RR})$ (see Lemma 2.2.4), this yields the following separation result.

Proposition 2.3.9 *The language class $\mathcal{L}(\mathsf{RR}(1))$ is incomparable to the classes $\mathcal{L}(\mathsf{RW})$ and $\mathcal{L}(\mathsf{sRW})$ with respect to inclusion.*

However, by requiring that the RR(1)-automata considered are deterministic, we constrain the expressive capacity of RR(1)-automata considerably. In fact, deterministic RR(1)-automata just yield another characterization for the class of regular languages.

Theorem 2.3.10 ([128]) $\mathcal{L}(\mathsf{det\text{-}RR}(1)) = \mathsf{REG}$.

Proof outline. As $\mathsf{REG} = \mathcal{L}(\mathsf{det\text{-}R}(1)) \subseteq \mathcal{L}(\mathsf{det\text{-}RR}(1))$, it remains to prove that all languages accepted by deterministic RR(1)-automata are regular. So let $M = (Q, \Sigma, \Sigma, \rhd, \lhd, q_0, 1, \delta)$ be a det-RR(1)-automaton. Without loss of generality, we may assume that M performs restart, accept, and reject transitions only on seeing the right sentinel $\lhd$. Furthermore, we can partition the set Q of states of M into two disjoint subsets Q_1 and Q_2, where Q_1 contains those states that M can use during a cycle or a tail computation *before* executing a rewrite transition, and Q_2 contains those states that M can only use *after* executing a rewrite transition. Thus, each cycle consists of a phase during which M scans a prefix of the current tape contents, using states from Q_1, then a rewrite step is executed by which M deletes a letter and enters a state from Q_2, and finally, M scans the suffix of the current tape contents, using states from Q_2, until it reaches the right sentinel and restarts. A tail computation is either of the same form, ending with an accept or a reject step at the right sentinel, or it consists of just the first phase, that is, M scans the current tape contents completely, using states from Q_1, and it accepts or rejects at the right sentinel.

We now define an NFA $A = (P, \Sigma \cup \{\lhd\}, p_0, \eta, F)$ that simulates the RR(1)-automaton. Let $P = (Q \times \mathcal{P}(Q_2)) \cup \{p_+\}$, $p_0 = (q_1, \emptyset)$, where $q_1 \in Q_1$ is the unique state such that $\delta(q_0, \rhd) = (q_1, \mathsf{MVR})$, and $F = \{p_+\}$. The transition relation η is defined as follows, where $q \in Q$, $N \subseteq Q_2$, $a \in \Sigma$, and $N'_a = \{ p' \in Q_2 \mid \exists p \in N : \delta(p, a) = (p', \mathsf{MVR}) \}$:

$$\begin{array}{llll}
(1) & \eta((q, N), a) & = & \{(q', N'_a)\}, & \text{if } \delta(q, a) = (q', \mathsf{MVR}),\\
(2) & \eta((q, N), a) & = & \{(q', N'_a), (q, N'_a \cup \{q'\})\}, & \text{if } \delta(q, a) = (q', \lambda),\\
(3) & \eta((q, N), \lhd) & = & \{p_+\}, & \text{if } \delta(q, \lhd) = \mathsf{Accept} \text{ and}\\
 & & & & \delta(p, \lhd) = \mathsf{Restart} \text{ for all } p \in N.
\end{array}$$

Using the first components of its states, A simulates the current cycle (using (1)) until a rewrite step is enabled. In this situation, there are two possibilities (see (2)): either M is in a tail computation, and then A just needs to carry on with the simulation (see the first option in (2)), or M is in a cycle. In the latter case, A needs to do two things: simulate the next cycle and verify that the current cycle really ends with a restart step. As M is deterministic, the next cycle begins with the same MVR steps as the current cycle. Hence, M will reach the same position on its tape being in the same state q.

Furthermore, to verify that the current cycle really ends with a restart step, the new state q' is added to the second state component (see the second option in (2)). The NFA A uses the second components of its states to remember those states of M, which were entered after executions of rewrite steps during the simulation of cycles of M. Accordingly, this set is updated whenever A reads the next letter. Finally, on reaching the right sentinel, A accepts if the computation of M

modelled by the first state component accepts at the right sentinel and if, for all states stored in the second state component, M executes a restart step at the right sentinel. It follows that $L(A) = L(M) \cdot \lhd$. Hence, $L(M) \cdot \lhd$ is a regular language, and so is $L(M)$. □

From Theorem 2.3.10, we see immediately that $\mathcal{L}(\mathsf{det\text{-}mon\text{-}RR}(1)) = \mathcal{L}(\mathsf{det\text{-}RR}(1)) = \mathsf{REG}$. However, it is actually not just the language classes that are identical – the classes of restarting automata themselves are identical.

Proposition 2.3.11 ([163]) *Each deterministic RWW- or RRWW-automaton of window size one or two is monotone.*

Proof. Let $M = (Q, \Sigma, \Gamma, \rhd, \lhd, q_0, k, \delta)$ be a deterministic RRWW-automaton of window size $k = 2$. Each rewrite step of M replaces a factor of length two of the tape contents with the empty word λ or with a single letter. Thus, if M executes a cycle of the form

$$q_0 \rhd a_1 a_2 \cdots a_{i-1} a_i a_{i+1} a_{i+2} \cdots a_n \lhd \vdash_M^c q_0 \rhd a_1 a_2 \cdots a_{i-1} a_{i+2} \cdots a_n \lhd,$$

by deleting the factor $a_i a_{i+1}$, where $a_1, a_2, \ldots, a_n \in \Gamma$, then this cycle begins with a sequence of i MVR steps that shift the window to the factor $a_i a_{i+1}$ and a subsequent rewrite step that deletes this factor. As M is deterministic, the next cycle begins with a sequence of $i-1$ MVR steps that shift the window to the factor $a_{i-1} a_{i+2}$, which implies that the latter cycle has a smaller right distance than the former.

If M executes a cycle of the form

$$q_0 \rhd a_1 a_2 \cdots a_{i-1} a_i a_{i+1} a_{i+2} \cdots a_n \lhd \vdash_M^c q_0 \rhd a_1 a_2 \cdots a_{i-1} b a_{i+2} \cdots a_n \lhd,$$

by replacing the factor $a_i a_{i+1}$ with the letter b, where $a_1, a_2, \ldots, a_n, b \in \Gamma$, then this cycle begins with a sequence of i MVR steps that shift the window to the factor $a_i a_{i+1}$ and the subsequent rewrite step. As M is deterministic, the next cycle begins with a sequence of $i-1$ MVR steps that shift the window to the factor $a_{i-1} b$, implying that the latter cycle has at most the same right distance as the former.

Together these two cases show that M is indeed monotone. Obviously, the same arguments apply if M is a deterministic RWW-automaton of window size two. Furthermore, if M has window size one only, then in each cycle, it just deletes a single letter. Monotonicity now follows as in the first case above. □

In the proof of Lemma 2.3.6 above, we defined the transition relation of a monotone RR(1)-automaton M' for the language

$$L' = \{ a^m b^n c \mid n \in \{m, m+1\}, m \geq 0 \} \cup \{ a^m b^n d \mid n \in \{2m, 2m+1, 2m+2\}, m \geq 0 \}$$

through a set of eleven meta-instructions. From the regular constraints of these meta-instructions, we see that, for each tape contents $\rhd z \lhd$, there is at most a single meta-instruction of M' that is applicable to this tape contents. Thus, a deterministic monotone RL(1)-automaton can first scan its tape in order to determine which of the meta-instructions applies, and then it can execute the corresponding delete operation and restart. Hence, $L' \in \mathcal{L}(\mathsf{det\text{-}mon\text{-}RL}(1))$, which yields the following results. Recall that $\mathcal{L}(\mathsf{det\text{-}mon\text{-}RL}(1)) \subsetneq \mathcal{L}(\mathsf{det\text{-}mon\text{-}RL}(2)) \subsetneq \mathsf{LRR}$ by Corollary 2.3.3.

Proposition 2.3.12 $\mathsf{REG} \subsetneq \mathcal{L}(\mathsf{det\text{-}mon\text{-}RL}(1)) \subsetneq \mathsf{LRR}$, *but* $\mathcal{L}(\mathsf{det\text{-}mon\text{-}RL}(1))$ *is incomparable to the class DCFL with respect to inclusion.*

In the proof of Proposition 2.3.8 above, we defined the transition relation of an RR(1)-automaton M' for a superset of the language $L'_{\mathrm{copy}} = \{ w\#w \mid w \in \{a, b\}^* \}$ through a set of five meta-instructions that are pairwise disjoint. Thus, a deterministic RL(1)-automaton can first scan its tape in order to determine which of the meta-instructions applies, and then it can execute the corresponding delete operation and restart. Hence, $L(M') \in \mathcal{L}(\mathsf{det\text{-}RL}(1))$, which yields the following result.

Proposition 2.3.13 *The language class $\mathcal{L}(\text{det-RL}(1))$ is incomparable to the classes DCFL, CFL, and GCSL with respect to inclusion.*

It remains to determine the expressive capacity of weight-reducing RW-, RRW-, and RLW-automata of window size one. We shall address this problem in Subsection 2.3.3, where we investigate the expressive capacity of weight-reducing RWW- and RRWW-automata of window size one. Here we turn to the problem of determining the relationship between the various types of restarting automata of a given window size $k \geq 2$. First, we consider the case $k = 2$.

From Corollary 2.3.3, we know that $\mathcal{L}(\text{det-mon-R}(2)) \smallsetminus \mathcal{L}(\text{sRLW}(1)) \neq \emptyset$. Thus, no language class defined by any type of restarting automaton of window size two is contained in any class defined by a type of restarting automaton of window size one. We continue with some more example languages and their properties.

Lemma 2.3.14 $L = \{\, a^n b^n \mid n \geq 0 \,\} \in \mathcal{L}(\text{det-mon-RR}(2)) \smallsetminus \mathcal{L}(\text{sRW}(2))$.

Proof. An RR(2)-automaton M for $L = \{\, a^n b^n \mid n \geq 0 \,\}$ is given through the meta-instructions

$$\begin{array}{ll} (1) & (\rhd \cdot \lhd, \mathsf{Accept}), \\ (2) & (\rhd \cdot a^*, ab \to \lambda, b^* \cdot \lhd). \end{array}$$

Obviously, this RR-automaton is deterministic and monotone.

Assume that M' is an sRW(2)-automaton such that $L(M') = L$, and let $w = a^n b^n \in L$. Then M' has an accepting computation for input w. If n is sufficiently large, then this computation cannot just consist of an accepting tail. Thus, it begins with a cycle

$$q_0 \rhd w \lhd = q_0 \rhd a^n b^n \lhd \vdash^c_{M'} q_0 \rhd z \lhd$$

for some word $z \in L$. As M' is weight-reducing, $z = a^{n-i} b^{n-i}$ for some $i \geq 1$. Furthermore, M' has window size two, which implies that $i = 1$. Now let $w' = a^n bab^n \notin L$. On input w', M' can execute the cycle

$$q_0 \rhd w' \lhd = q_0 \rhd a^n bab^n \lhd \vdash^c_{M'} q_0 \rhd a^{n-1} ab^n \lhd = q_0 \rhd w \lhd,$$

which contradicts the Error Preserving Property for M', as $w \in L$. It follows that L is not accepted by any sRW-automaton of window size two. □

Hence, the language class $\mathcal{L}(\text{det-mon-RR}(2)) = \mathcal{L}(\text{det-RR}(2))$ is not contained in $\mathcal{L}(\text{pref-sRW}(2))$ for any prefix $\text{pref} \in \{\text{det-mon-}, \text{det-}, \text{mon-}, \lambda\}$.

Lemma 2.3.15 $L = \{\, a^n b^{2n}, a^{n-1} cb^{2n-1}, a^{n-1} db^{2n-2} \mid n \geq 1 \,\} \in \mathcal{L}(\text{det-mon-RW}(2)) \smallsetminus \mathcal{L}(\text{RR}(2))$.

Proof. An RW(2)-automaton M for $L = \{\, a^n b^{2n}, a^{n-1} cb^{2n-1}, a^{n-1} db^{2n-2} \mid n \geq 1 \,\}$ is given through the following meta-instructions:

$$\begin{array}{ll} (1) & (\rhd \cdot d \cdot \lhd, \mathsf{Accept}), \\ (2) & (\rhd \cdot a^*, ab \to c), \\ (3) & (\rhd \cdot a^*, cb \to d), \\ (4) & (\rhd \cdot a^*, db \to b). \end{array}$$

Then

$$q_0 \rhd a^n b^{2n} \lhd \vdash^c_M q_0 \rhd a^{n-1} cb^{2n-1} \lhd \vdash^c_M q_0 \rhd a^{n-1} db^{2n-2} \lhd \vdash^c_M q_0 \rhd a^{n-1} b^{2n-2} \lhd,$$

and $L(M) = L$ follows. Also it is easily seen that M is deterministic and monotone.

Assume that M' is an RR-automaton of window size two that accepts the language L, and let $w = a^n b^{2n} \in L$. Then M' has an accepting computation for input w, which cannot just consist of an accepting tail, if n is large. Thus, this computation begins with a cycle

$$q_0 \rhd w \lhd = q_0 \rhd a^n b^{2n} \lhd \vdash^c_{M'} q_0 \rhd z \lhd$$

for some word $z \in L$. As M' is an RR(2)-automaton, z is obtained from w by simply deleting a factor of length one or two. However, no word that is obtained from $w = a^n b^{2n}$ by deleting a factor of length one or two belongs to L. This contradicts our assumption on M'. It follows that L is not accepted by any RR-automaton of window size two. $\square$

Hence, the language class $\mathcal{L}(\mathsf{det\text{-}mon\text{-}RW}(2)) = \mathcal{L}(\mathsf{det\text{-}RW}(2))$ is not contained in $\mathcal{L}(\mathsf{pref\text{-}RR}(2))$ for any prefix $\mathsf{pref} \in \{\mathsf{det\text{-}mon\text{-}}, \mathsf{det\text{-}}, \mathsf{mon\text{-}}, \lambda\}$.

Next we consider a variant of the language L_8 from Lemma 2.2.9. Let $L_8' = L_{8,1}' \cup L_{8,2}' \cup L_{8,3}'$, where

- $L_{8,1}' = \{ a^{2^n-i} c b^i \mid n \geq 0, 0 \leq i < 2^n \}$,
- $L_{8,2}' = \{ a^i d b^{2^n-2i} \mid n \geq 1, 0 \leq 2i \leq 2^n \} \cup \{db\}$, and
- $L_{8,3}' = \{ a^i e b^{2^n-2i+1} \mid n \geq 1, 0 \leq 2i \leq 2^n \} \cup \{ae\}$.

For this language, we have the following result.

Lemma 2.3.16 $L_8' \in \mathcal{L}(\mathsf{det\text{-}sRW}(2)) \smallsetminus \mathcal{L}(\mathsf{RLW})$.

Proof. Let M be the sRW(2)-automaton that is given through the following meta-instructions:

$$\begin{array}{ll}
(1) & (\rhd \cdot ae \cdot \lhd, \mathsf{Accept}),\\
(2) & (\rhd \cdot a^+, ac \to cb),\\
(3) & (\rhd, ac \to db),\\
(4) & (\rhd \cdot a^*, db \to ae),\\
(5) & (\rhd \cdot a^*, eb \to d),\\
(6) & (\rhd \cdot a^*, d\lhd \to c\lhd).
\end{array}$$

Then, for all $n \geq 1$,

$$\begin{array}{llllll}
q_0 \rhd a^{2^n} c \lhd & \vdash_M^{c^*} & q_0 \rhd acb^{2^n-1} \lhd & \vdash_M^c & q_0 \rhd db^{2^n} \lhd \\
 & \vdash_M^c & q_0 \rhd aeb^{2^n-1} \lhd & \vdash_M^c & q_0 \rhd adb^{2^n-2} \lhd \\
 & \vdash_M^{c^*} & q_0 \rhd a^{2^{n-1}} d \lhd & \vdash_M^c & q_0 \rhd a^{2^{n-1}} c \lhd
\end{array}$$

and

$$q_0 \rhd ac \lhd \vdash_M^c q_0 \rhd db \lhd \vdash_M^c q_0 \rhd ae \lhd \vdash_M \mathsf{Accept}.$$

It follows that $L(M) = L_8'$. Furthermore, it is easily seen that M is deterministic. Finally, the weight function ω that is defined by taking $\omega(a) = 6$, $\omega(b) = 4$, $\omega(c) = 3$, $\omega(d) = 4$, and $\omega(e) = 1$ is compatible with M. Hence, M is a deterministic sRW-automaton with a window of size two that accepts the language L_8'.

In analogy to the corresponding proof of Lemma 2.2.9, it can be shown that the language L_8' is not accepted by any RLW-automaton. $\square$

From Lemmas 2.3.14, 2.3.15, and 2.3.16, we obtain the following incomparability and proper inclusion results.

Corollary 2.3.17 (a) *The language classes* $\mathcal{L}(\mathsf{pref_1\text{-}RR}(2))$ *and* $\mathcal{L}(\mathsf{pref_2\text{-}(s)RW}(2))$ *are incomparable with respect to inclusion for all prefixes* $\mathsf{pref}_1, \mathsf{pref}_2 \in \{\mathsf{det\text{-}mon\text{-}}, \mathsf{det\text{-}}, \mathsf{mon\text{-}}, \lambda\}$.

(b) $\mathcal{L}(\mathsf{pref\text{-}RR}(2)) \subsetneq \mathcal{L}(\mathsf{pref\text{-}RRW}(2))$ *and* $\mathcal{L}(\mathsf{pref\text{-}RW}(2)) \subsetneq \mathcal{L}(\mathsf{pref\text{-}RRW}(2))$ *for any prefix* $\mathsf{pref} \in \{\mathsf{det\text{-}mon\text{-}}, \mathsf{det\text{-}}, \mathsf{mon\text{-}}, \lambda\}$.

(c) $\mathcal{L}(\mathsf{pref\text{-}R}(2)) \subsetneq \mathcal{L}(\mathsf{pref\text{-}RR}(2))$ *and* $\mathcal{L}(\mathsf{pref\text{-}R}(2)) \subsetneq \mathcal{L}(\mathsf{pref\text{-}RW}(2))$ *for any prefix* $\mathsf{pref} \in \{\mathsf{det\text{-}mon\text{-}}, \mathsf{det\text{-}}, \mathsf{mon\text{-}}, \lambda\}$.

(d) $\mathcal{L}(\mathsf{det\text{-}R(R)W}(2)) \subsetneq \mathcal{L}(\mathsf{det\text{-}sR(R)W}(2))$ *and* $\mathcal{L}(\mathsf{R(R)W}(2)) \subsetneq \mathcal{L}(\mathsf{sR(R)W}(2))$.

Here it remains open whether the properness of the second inclusion in (d) also extends to monotone R(R)W(2)-automata.

Problem 2.3.18 *Is the inclusion* $\mathcal{L}(\mathsf{mon\text{-}R(R)W(2)}) \subseteq \mathcal{L}(\mathsf{mon\text{-}sR(R)W(2)})$ *a proper one?*

Concerning restarting automata with window size two, we still need to determine whether the following inclusions are proper for all types X of restarting automata without auxiliary letters:

$$\mathcal{L}(\mathsf{det\text{-}mon\text{-}X(2)}) \subseteq \mathcal{L}(\mathsf{mon\text{-}X(2)}) \subseteq \mathcal{L}(\mathsf{X(2)}).$$

From Proposition 2.3.8, we recall that the class $\mathcal{L}(\mathsf{RR(1)})$ contains a language that is not even growing context-sensitive. As RR(1)-automata are a restricted class of RR(W)(2)-automata, and as all types of monotone sRRWW-automata just accept certain context-free languages (see Theorem 2.1.38), we immediately obtain the following proper inclusions.

Corollary 2.3.19 $\mathcal{L}(\mathsf{mon\text{-}RR(2)}) \subsetneq \mathcal{L}(\mathsf{RR(2)})$ *and* $\mathcal{L}(\mathsf{mon\text{-}RRW(2)}) \subsetneq \mathcal{L}(\mathsf{RRW(2)})$.

Lemma 2.3.16 states that the language L_8' is accepted by a det-sRW(2)-automaton. As

$$L_8' \cap (\{a\}^* \cdot \{c\}) = \{\, a^{2^n} c \mid n \geq 0 \,\},$$

it is clear that L_8' is not context-free. Therefore, we also have the following proper inclusions.

Corollary 2.3.20 *For all types of restarting automata* $\mathsf{X} \in \{\mathsf{sRW}, \mathsf{sRRW}\}$,

$$\mathcal{L}(\mathsf{det\text{-}mon\text{-}X(2)}) \subsetneq \mathcal{L}(\mathsf{det\text{-}X(2)}) \text{ and } \mathcal{L}(\mathsf{mon\text{-}X(2)}) \subsetneq \mathcal{L}(\mathsf{X(2)}).$$

To separate the monotone R- and RW-automata of window size two from their non-monotone variants, we consider the following language $L_{a,c}$. This language is generated by the context-free grammar

$$G_{a,c} = (\{S\}, \{a,b,c\}, S, \{S \to \lambda), (S \to SS), (S \to aSb), (S \to bSc)\}).$$

For example, $L_{a,c}$ contains the words $a^m b^{m+n} c^n$ and $a^m b^n c^n b^m$ for all $m, n \geq 0$. For this language, we have the following result.

Lemma 2.3.21 $L_{a,c} \in \mathcal{L}(\mathsf{R(2)}) \smallsetminus \mathcal{L}(\mathsf{mon\text{-}RW(2)})$.

Proof. The R(2)-automaton that is given by the meta-instructions

$$(1) \quad (\rhd \cdot \lhd, \mathsf{Accept}), \quad (2) \quad (\rhd \cdot \{a,b,c\}^*, ab \to \lambda), \quad (3) \quad (\rhd \cdot \{a,b,c\}^*, bc \to \lambda)$$

accepts the language $L_{a,c}$. This is easily verified by induction on the length of a word $w \in L_{a,c}$ on the one hand and by induction on the number of cycles in an accepting computation of the R(2)-automaton on the other hand.

However, $L_{a,c}$ is not accepted by any RW(2)-automaton that is monotone. Assume that M is an RW(2)-automaton such that $L(M) = L_{a,c}$. We claim that M is not monotone. The word $w = a^m b^m$ belongs to $L_{a,c}$. Hence, M has an accepting computation for input w. This computation is not just an accepting tail, if m is large. Thus, it begins with a cycle

$$q_0 \rhd w \lhd = q_0 \rhd a^m b^m \lhd \vdash_M^c q_0 \rhd z \lhd$$

for some word $z \in L_{a,c}$. From the definition of $L_{a,c}$, it is easily seen that $|z|_b = |z|_a + |z|_c$. It follows that M must delete the factor ab from the middle of the word w, which yields $z = a^{m-1} b^{m-1}$.

Also the word $u = a^m b^m c^m b^m$ belongs to the language $L_{a,c}$. Thus, M also has an accepting computation for input u, which cannot just be an accepting tail, if m is large. Hence, this computation begins with a cycle

$$q_0 \rhd u \lhd = q_0 \rhd a^m b^m c^m b^m \lhd \vdash_M^c q_0 \rhd y \lhd$$

for some word $y \in L_{a,c}$. As $a^{m-1} b^{m-1} c^m b^m \notin L_{a,c}$ (there are not sufficiently many occurrences of the letter b to the left of the factor c^m), M can either delete a factor bc or a factor cb, that is,

$y = a^m b^{m-1} c^{m-1} b^m$ or $y = a^m b^m c^{m-1} b^{m-1}$. In either case, $y = a^m b^{m-1} v$ for some word v, and hence, M can execute the cycle

$$q_0 \rhd y \lhd = q_0 \rhd a^m b^{m-1} v \lhd \vdash^c_M q_0 \rhd a^{m-1} b^{m-2} v \lhd .$$

This yields the sequence of two cycles

$$q_0 \rhd u \lhd = q_0 \rhd a^m b^m c^m b^m \lhd \vdash_M q_0 \rhd a^m b^{m-1} v \lhd \vdash^c_M q_0 \rhd a^{m-1} b^{m-2} v \lhd .$$

The first cycle has the right distance $D_1 = 2m+2$ (if bc is deleted) or $D_1 = m+2$ (if cb is deleted), while the second cycle has the right distance $D_2 = 3m$. As m is large, $D_2 = 3m > 2m+2 \geq D_1$, which shows that M is not monotone. □

This result has the following consequences.

Corollary 2.3.22 $\mathcal{L}(\textsf{mon-R(2)}) \subsetneq \mathcal{L}(\textsf{R(2)})$ *and* $\mathcal{L}(\textsf{mon-RW(2)}) \subsetneq \mathcal{L}(\textsf{RW(2)})$.

For deriving further separation results, we consider the language $\hat{L}_{\text{pal}}$ on $\Sigma = \{a, b, c, c_a, c_b, d, e\}$, which is an extension of the language $L_{\text{pal}} = \{ ww^R \mid w \in \{a,b\}^+ \}$ (see Example 1.2.50):

$$\begin{aligned}
\hat{L}_{\text{pal}} &= L^{(1)}_{\text{pal}} \cup L^{(2)}_{\text{pal}} \cup L^{(3)}_{\text{pal}} \cup L^{(4)}_{\text{pal}} \cup L^{(5)}_{\text{pal}}, \text{ where}\\
L^{(1)}_{\text{pal}} &= \{ b_1 d^{i_1} b_2 d^{i_2} \cdots d^{i_{m-1}} b_m d^{j_n} a_n d^{j_{n-1}} a_{n-1} d^{j_{n-2}} \cdots d^{j_1} a_1 d^{j_0} \mid n \geq m \geq 1, i_1, i_2, \ldots, i_{m-1} \geq 0,\\
&\qquad j_0, j_1, \ldots, j_n \geq 1, b_1, b_2, \ldots, b_m, a_1, a_2, \ldots, a_n \in \{a,b\}, \text{ and}\\
&\qquad \exists w \in \{a,b\}^+ : b_1 b_2 \cdots b_m a_n a_{n-1} \cdots a_1 = ww^R \},\\
L^{(2)}_{\text{pal}} &= \{ a_1 a_2 \cdots a_n e d^{j_n} a_n d^{j_{n-1}} \cdots d^{j_1} a_1 d^{j_0} \mid n \geq 0, j_0, j_1, \ldots, j_n \geq 1, a_1, a_2, \ldots, a_n \in \{a,b\} \},\\
L^{(3)}_{\text{pal}} &= \{ a_1 a_2 \cdots a_n c a_n d^{j_{n-1}} \cdots d^{j_1} a_1 d^{j_0} \mid n \geq 1, j_0, j_1, \ldots, j_{n-1} \geq 1, a_1, a_2, \ldots, a_n \in \{a,b\} \} \cup \{c\},\\
L^{(4)}_{\text{pal}} &= \{ a_1 a_2 \cdots a_n a c_a d^{j_n} a_n d^{j_{n-1}} \cdots d^{j_1} a_1 d^{j_0} \mid n \geq 0, j_0 j_1, \ldots, j_n \geq 1, a_1, a_2, \ldots, a_n \in \{a,b\} \},\\
L^{(5)}_{\text{pal}} &= \{ a_1 a_2 \cdots a_n b c_b d^{j_n} a_n d^{j_{n-1}} \cdots d^{j_1} a_1 d^{j_0} \mid n \geq 0, j_0, j_1, \ldots, j_n \geq 1, a_1, a_2, \ldots, a_n \in \{a,b\} \}.
\end{aligned}$$

For the language $\hat{L}_{\text{pal}}$, we have the following result.

Lemma 2.3.23 $\hat{L}_{\text{pal}} \in \mathcal{L}(\textsf{mon-RW(2)}) \smallsetminus \textsf{CRL}$.

Proof. First, we present an RW(2)-automaton $\hat{M}_{\text{pal}}$ for the language $\hat{L}_{\text{pal}}$. This automaton is specified by the following meta-instructions:

$$\begin{array}{lll}
(1) & (\rhd \cdot c \cdot \lhd, \textsf{Accept}), & \\
(2) & (\rhd \cdot \{a,b\}^*, xd \to x) & \text{for all } x \in \{a,b\},\\
(3) & (\rhd \cdot \{a,b\}^+, dx \to c_x) & \text{for all } x \in \{a,b\},\\
(4) & (\rhd \cdot \{a,b\}^*, xc_x \to e) & \text{for all } x \in \{a,b\},\\
(5) & (\rhd \cdot \{a,b\}^*, ed \to e), & \\
(6) & (\rhd \cdot \{a,b\}^*, ed \to c), & \\
(7) & (\rhd \cdot \{a,b\}^*, cx \to c_x) & \text{for all } x \in \{a,b\}.
\end{array}$$

Meta-instruction (2) is used to delete occurrences of the letter d proceeding from left to right. Using meta-instruction (3), $\hat{M}_{\text{pal}}$ can guess the middle of the palindrome by replacing the first letter $x \in \{a,b\}$ of the suffix w^R with the letter c_x. By meta-instruction (4), it is verified that the previous letter is also the letter x. Then the subsequent occurrences of the letter d are removed (by (5) and (6)), and the comparison of the next letters is initiated (by (7)). For example,

$$\begin{array}{llllll}
q_0 \rhd addabddbdaddadd \lhd & \vdash^{c^2}_{\hat{M}_{\text{pal}}} & q_0 \rhd aabddbdaddadd \lhd & \vdash^{c^2}_{\hat{M}_{\text{pal}}} & q_0 \rhd aabc_b daddadd \lhd\\
& \vdash^{c}_{\hat{M}_{\text{pal}}} & q_0 \rhd aaedaddadd \lhd & \vdash^{c}_{\hat{M}_{\text{pal}}} & q_0 \rhd aacaddadd \lhd\\
& \vdash^{c}_{\hat{M}_{\text{pal}}} & q_0 \rhd aac_a ddadd \lhd & \vdash^{c}_{\hat{M}_{\text{pal}}} & q_0 \rhd aeddadd \lhd\\
& \vdash^{c^2}_{\hat{M}_{\text{pal}}} & q_0 \rhd acadd \lhd & \vdash^{c}_{\hat{M}_{\text{pal}}} & q_0 \rhd ac_a dd \lhd\\
& \vdash^{c}_{\hat{M}_{\text{pal}}} & q_0 \rhd edd \lhd & \vdash^{c^2}_{\hat{M}_{\text{pal}}} & q_0 \rhd c \lhd\\
& \vdash_{\hat{M}_{\text{pal}}} & \textsf{Accept}. & &
\end{array}$$

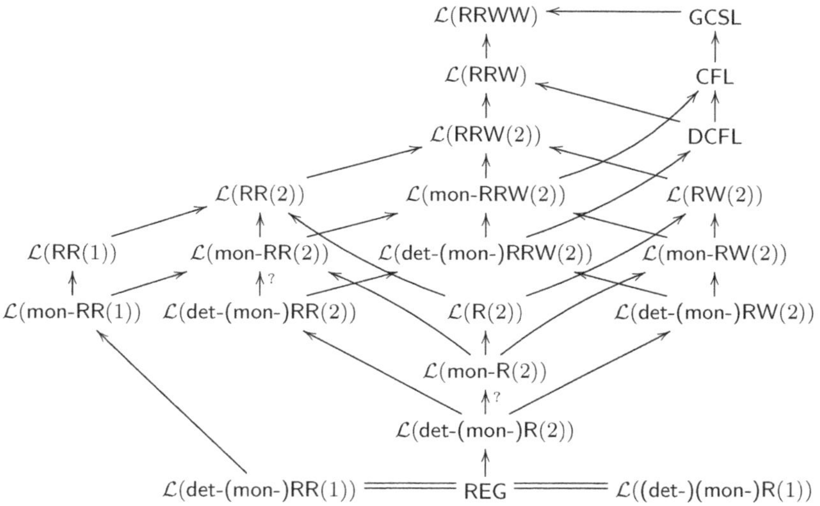

Figure 2.11: The taxonomy of restarting automata without auxiliary letters and window size one or two.

It follows that the RW(2)-automaton is monotone and that it accepts the language $\hat{L}_{\text{pal}}$.

Assume that $\hat{L}_{\text{pal}}$ is a Church-Rosser language. As the class of Church-Rosser languages is closed under intersections with regular sets, this implies that the language

$$L' = \hat{L}_{\text{pal}} \cap \{ad, bd\}^* = \{\, a_1da_2d \cdots a_nda_nd \cdots a_2da_1d \mid n \geq 1, a_1, a_2, \ldots, a_n \in \{a,b\}\,\}$$

is a Church-Rosser language. Thus, by Theorem 1.2.19, there exists a shrinking DTPDA A that accepts the language L'. From A, we can construct a shrinking DTPDA B that, given a word $w = a'_1a'_2 \cdots a'_n \in \{a', b'\}^*$ as input, first produces the word $z = a_1da_2d \cdots a_nd$ by replacing each letter a'_i with a_id and then checks whether the word z belongs to the language L' by simply running the DTPDA A. Then $L(B) = \varphi(L_{\text{pal}})$ is a Church-Rosser language, where φ is the isomorphism that is defined by sending a to a' and b to b'. However, as L_{pal} is not a Church-Rosser language by [93], we see that $\varphi(L_{\text{pal}})$ is not a Church-Rosser language, either. This contradiction shows that the language $\hat{L}_{\text{pal}}$ does not belong to the class CRL of Church-Rosser languages. □

It follows, in particular, that the language $\hat{L}_{\text{pal}}$ is not accepted by any deterministic sRRWW-automaton (see Corollary 2.1.34). Thus, we obtain the following proper inclusions and non-inclusions.

Corollary 2.3.24 *For all types of restarting automata* $\mathsf{X} \in \{\mathsf{RW}, \mathsf{RRW}, \mathsf{sRW}, \mathsf{sRRW}\}$,

$$\mathcal{L}(\text{det-mon-X}(2)) \subsetneq \mathcal{L}(\text{mon-X}(2)) \not\subseteq \mathcal{L}(\text{det-X}(2)).$$

However, currently the following question remains unanswered.

Problem 2.3.25 *Are the inclusions* $\mathcal{L}(\text{det-mon-R}(2)) \subseteq \mathcal{L}(\text{mon-R}(2))$ *and* $\mathcal{L}(\text{det-mon-RR}(2)) \subseteq \mathcal{L}(\text{mon-RR}(2))$ *proper inclusions?*

The diagram in Figure 2.11 illustrates the relationships between the language classes that are accepted by the various types of restarting automata of window sizes one and two. As before, an arrow indicates a proper inclusion, while an arrow indexed with a question mark represents an inclusion that is currently not known to be proper.

Next, we scrutinize the language classes that are accepted by restarting automata of window size $k \geq 3$. In order to separate those language classes from one another that are accepted by different types of deterministic monotone/deterministic/monotone/nondeterministic restarting automata of window size k, we present three more groups of example languages.

Lemma 2.3.26 *For all* $k \geq 3$, $L_9^{(k)} = \{ a^n b^{n\cdot(k-1)} \mid n \geq 0 \} \in \mathcal{L}(\mathsf{det\text{-}mon\text{-}RR}(k)) \smallsetminus \mathcal{L}(\mathsf{sRW}(k))$.

Proof. A monotone deterministic RR(k)-automaton for the language $L_9^{(k)}$ is simply given through the meta-instructions $(\rhd \cdot \lhd, \mathsf{Accept})$ and $(\rhd \cdot a^*, ab^{k-1} \to \lambda, b^* \cdot \lhd)$.

On the other hand, let M be an sRW(k)-automaton for $L_9^{(k)}$, and let $w = a^n b^{n\cdot(k-1)} \in L_9^{(k)}$. Then M has an accepting computation for input w, which cannot just consist of an accepting tail, if n is large. Thus, this computation begins with a cycle

$$q_0 \rhd w \lhd = q_0 \rhd a^n b^{n\cdot(k-1)} \lhd \vdash_M^c q_0 \rhd z \lhd$$

for some word $z \in L_9^{(k)}$. From the form of the words in $L_9^{(k)}$ and the fact that M has window size k, we can conclude that $z = a^{n-1} b^{(n-1)\cdot(k-1)}$, that is, M executes the rewrite step $ab^{k-1} \to \lambda$. Hence, for the word $u = a^n b^{k-1} ab^{n\cdot(k-1)} \notin L_9^{(k)}$, M can execute the cycle

$$q_0 \rhd u \lhd = q_0 \rhd a^n b^{k-1} ab^{n\cdot(k-1)} \lhd \vdash_M^c q_0 \rhd a^{n-1} ab^{n\cdot(k-1)} \lhd = q_0 \rhd a^n b^{n\cdot(k-1)} \lhd .$$

This, however, contradicts the Error Preserving Property for M, as $a^n b^{n\cdot(k-1)} \in L_9^{(k)}$. It follows that $L_9^{(k)}$ is not accepted by any sRW-automaton of window size k. □

Thus, the language $L_9^{(k)}$ separates the language class $\mathcal{L}(\mathsf{det\text{-}mon\text{-}RR}(k))$ and all its superclasses from all classes contained in $\mathcal{L}(\mathsf{sRW}(k))$.

Lemma 2.3.27 *For all* $k \geq 3$,
$L_{10}^{(k)} = \{ a^n b^{n\cdot(2k-3)}, a^n c b^{n\cdot(2k-3)+(k-2)} \mid n \geq 0 \} \in \mathcal{L}(\mathsf{det\text{-}mon\text{-}RW}(k)) \smallsetminus \mathcal{L}(\mathsf{RR}(k))$.

Proof. The language $L_{10}^{(k)}$ is accepted by the deterministic monotone RW(k)-automaton $M_{10}^{(k)}$ that is defined through the following meta-instructions:

$$(\rhd \cdot \lhd, \mathsf{Accept}), (\rhd \cdot a^*, ab^{k-1} \to c), (\rhd \cdot a^*, cb^{k-1} \to b), (\rhd, cb^{k-2} \lhd \to \lhd).$$

Obviously, the automaton $M_{10}^{(k)}$ accepts the empty word. For $w = a^n b^{n\cdot(2k-3)}$ $(n \geq 1)$, it executes the following sequence of cycles:

$$q_0 \rhd a^n b^{n\cdot(2k-3)} \lhd \vdash_{M_{10}^{(k)}}^c q_0 \rhd a^{n-1} c b^{(n-1)\cdot(2k-3)+(k-2)} \lhd \vdash_{M_{10}^{(k)}}^c q_0 \rhd a^{n-1} b^{(n-1)\cdot(2k-3)} \lhd .$$

It now follows by induction on n that $L(M_{10}^{(k)}) = L_{10}^{(k)}$.

Assume that M is an RR(k)-automaton that accepts the language $L_{10}^{(k)}$. Then M has an accepting computation for each word $w = a^n b^{n\cdot(2k-3)}$. If n is large, then the corresponding accepting computation begins with a cycle of the form

$$q_0 \rhd w \lhd = q_0 \rhd a^n b^{n\cdot(2k-3)} \lhd \vdash_M^c q_0 \rhd z \lhd$$

for some word $z \in L_{10}^{(k)}$. All rewrite transitions of M are deletions that erase at most k letters. However, by deleting k or fewer letters from $w = a^n b^{n\cdot(2k-3)}$, it is not possible to obtain an element of the language $L_{10}^{(k)}$, as $k \geq 3$. Hence, $L_{10}^{(k)}$ is not accepted by any RR(k)-automaton. □

The language $L_{10}^{(k)}$ separates the language class $\mathcal{L}(\mathsf{det\text{-}mon\text{-}RW}(k))$ and all its superclasses from all classes contained in $\mathcal{L}(\mathsf{RR}(k))$.

Lemma 2.3.28 *For* $k \geq 3$, *let* $L_{11}^{(k)} = \{ a^{2n} b^{n\cdot(k-1)}, a^{2n+1} c d^{k-1} b^{n\cdot(k-1)}, a^{2n} e d b^{n\cdot(k-1)} \mid n \geq 0 \}$. *Then* $L_{11}^{(k)} \in \mathcal{L}(\mathsf{det\text{-}mon\text{-}sRW}(k)) \smallsetminus \mathcal{L}(\mathsf{RRW}(k))$.

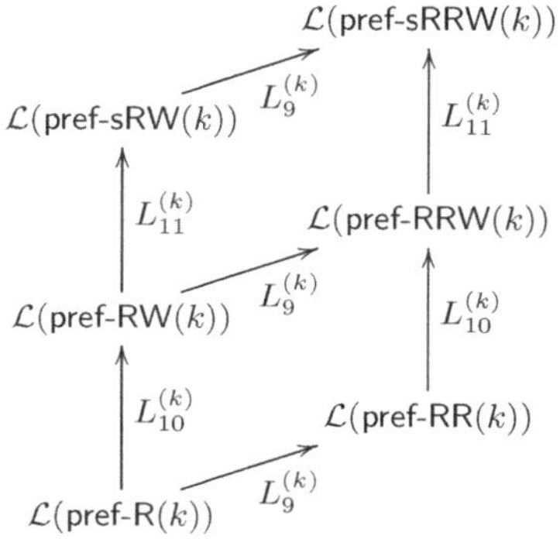

Figure 2.12: The taxonomy of restarting automata with window size $k \geq 3$ and identical prefixes. The index of each arrow shows the separating example language.

Proof. The language $L_{11}^{(k)}$ is accepted by the deterministic monotone sRW(k)-automaton $M_{11}^{(k)}$ that is defined through the following meta-instructions:

$$(\rhd \cdot \lhd, \mathsf{Accept}), (\rhd \cdot a^*, ab^{k-1} \to cd^{k-1}), (\rhd \cdot a^*, acd^{k-2} \to e), (\rhd \cdot a^*, edb \to b), (\rhd, ed\lhd \to \lhd).$$

For $w = a^{2n+2}b^{(n+1)\cdot(k-1)}$, $M_{11}^{(k)}$ can execute the following sequence of cycles:

$$\begin{array}{rcl} q_0 \rhd w \lhd & = & q_0 \rhd a^{2n+2}b^{(n+1)\cdot(k-1)} \lhd \ \vdash^c_{M_{11}^{(k)}} \ q_0 \rhd a^{2n+1}cd^{k-1}b^{n\cdot(k-1)} \lhd \\ & \vdash^c_{M_{11}^{(k)}} & q_0 \rhd a^{2n}edb^{n\cdot(k-1)} \lhd \ \vdash^c_{M_{11}^{(k)}} \ q_0 \rhd a^{2n}b^{n\cdot(k-1)} \lhd . \end{array}$$

Thus, it follows by induction on n that $L(M_{11}^{(k)}) = L_{11}^{(k)}$.

Assume now that M is an RRW(k)-automaton for $L_{11}^{(k)}$. For the word $a^{2n+2}b^{(n+1)\cdot(k-1)} \in L_{11}^{(k)}$, the automaton M has an accepting computation, which begins with a cycle of the form

$$q_0 \rhd a^{2n+2}b^{(n+1)\cdot(k-1)} \lhd \vdash^c_M q_0 \rhd z \lhd$$

for some word $z \in L_{11}^{(k)}$, if n is large. As M can only execute length-reducing rewrite steps, and as M has window size k, we have

$$n \cdot (k+1) < (n+1) \cdot (k+1) - k \leq |z| < (n+1) \cdot (k+1).$$

The only element of $L_{11}^{(k)}$ that satisfies this restriction is the word $z = a^{2n}edb^{n\cdot(k-1)}$, which has length $n \cdot (k+1) + 2$. However, in order to rewrite the word $a^{2n+2}b^{(n+1)\cdot(k-1)}$ into the word $a^{2n}edb^{n\cdot(k-1)}$, the inner factor a^2b^{k-1} must be rewritten into the word ed. This, however, is not possible with a window of size k. Thus, $L_{11}^{(k)}$ is not accepted by any RRW(k)-automaton. □

The language $L_{11}^{(k)}$ separates the language class $\mathcal{L}$(det-mon-sRW(k)) and all its superclasses from all classes contained in $\mathcal{L}$(RRW(k)). Based on the example languages $L_9^{(k)}$, $L_{10}^{(k)}$, and $L_{11}^{(k)}$, we obtain the following separation result.

Theorem 2.3.29 *For all $k \geq 3$ and all prefixes* pref- $\in$ {det-mon-, det-, mon-, λ}*, all arrows in the diagram in Figure 2.12 denote proper inclusions, and language classes not connected by a sequence of arrows are incomparable under inclusion.*

Finally, it remains to compare those language classes that are specified by (deterministic) monotone restarting automata of window size $k \geq 3$ of a given type to those classes that are specified by (deterministic) non-monotone automata of the same type.

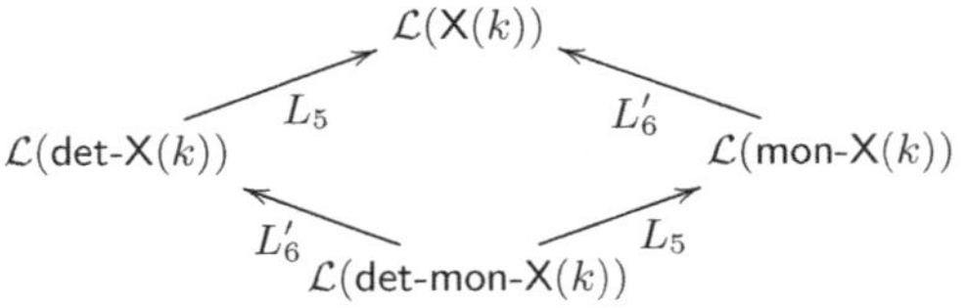

Figure 2.13: The taxonomy of restarting automata of type X with window size $k \geq 5$. The index of each arrow shows the separating example language.

In Subsection 2.2.1, we introduced and studied a number of example languages. These languages were then employed to separate the language classes from one another that are accepted by the various types of restarting automata without auxiliary letters. Here we are particularly interested in the language $L_5 = \{ a^n b^m \mid 0 \leq n \leq m \leq 2n \}$, which, according to Lemma 2.2.6, belongs to the set $\mathcal{L}(\mathsf{mon\text{-}R}) \smallsetminus \mathcal{L}(\mathsf{det\text{-}sRLW})$. In fact, it is easily seen that L_5 is accepted by a monotone R-automaton of window size four, that is, $L_5 \in \mathcal{L}(\mathsf{mon\text{-}R(4)}) \smallsetminus \mathcal{L}(\mathsf{det\text{-}sRLW})$. Thus, for $k \geq 4$, the language L_5 separates all monotone classes from all deterministic classes.

Furthermore, in [86], it is shown that there exists a non-context-free language L'_6 that is accepted by a deterministic R-automaton. In fact, we have the following result.

Lemma 2.3.30 ([86]) *There exists a deterministic R-automaton M'_6 such that*

$$L'_6 = L(M'_6) \in \mathcal{L}(\mathsf{det\text{-}R(5)}) \smallsetminus \mathcal{L}(\mathsf{mon\text{-}sRRW}).$$

Proof. First of all, the deterministic R-automaton M'_6 is given through the following meta-instructions:

$$\begin{array}{ll}
(1) & (\rhd \cdot ab \cdot \lhd, \mathsf{Accept}),\\
(2) & (\rhd \cdot (abab)^*, abab\lhd \to abb\lhd),\\
(3) & (\rhd \cdot (abab)^* \cdot ab, ababb \to babb),\\
(4) & (\rhd \cdot (abb)^*, abb\lhd \to ab\lhd),\\
(5) & (\rhd \cdot (abb)^* \cdot a, bbab\lhd \to bab\lhd),\\
(6) & (\rhd \cdot (abb)^* \cdot a, bbaba \to baba).
\end{array}$$

It follows that $L'_6 = L(M'_6) \in \mathcal{L}(\mathsf{det\text{-}R(5)})$. Given a word $w = (ab)^{2^n}$ $(n \geq 1)$ as input, M'_6 executes the following accepting computation:

$$\begin{array}{llllll}
q_0 \rhd (ab)^{2^n} \lhd & \vdash^c_{M'_6} & q_0 \rhd (ab)^{2^n-2} abb\lhd & \vdash^{c^{2^{n-1}-1}}_{M'_6} & q_0 \rhd (abb)^{2^{n-1}} \lhd\\
& \vdash^c_{M'_6} & q_0 \rhd (abb)^{2^{n-1}-1} ab\lhd & \vdash^{c^{2^{n-1}-1}}_{M'_6} & q_0 \rhd (ab)^{2^{n-1}} \lhd\\
& \vdash^{c^*}_{M'_6} & q_0 \rhd abab\lhd & \vdash^c_{M'_6} & q_0 \rhd abb\lhd\\
& \vdash^c_{M'_6} & q_0 \rhd ab\lhd & \vdash_{M'_6} & \mathsf{Accept}.
\end{array}$$

It follows that $L'_6 \cap \{ab\}^* = \{ (ab)^{2^n} \mid n \geq 0 \}$. As this language is not context-free, we conclude that L'_6 is not context-free, either. Hence, we can conclude that L'_6 is not accepted by any monotone sRRW-automaton. □

Thus, for $k \geq 5$, the language L'_6 separates all deterministic classes from all monotone classes. Together the languages L_5 and L'_6 yield the following separation results.

Theorem 2.3.31 *For all $k \geq 5$ and all types $\mathsf{X} \in \{\mathsf{R}, \mathsf{RR}, \mathsf{RW}, \mathsf{RRW}, \mathsf{sRW}, \mathsf{sRRW}\}$ of restarting automata, all arrows in the diagram in Figure 2.13 denote proper inclusions, and language classes not connected by a sequence of arrows are incomparable under inclusion.*

The diagram in Figure 2.14 summarizes all the results for window size $k \geq 5$. All arrows in this diagram denote inclusions that are proper, and language classes that are not connected by a sequence of arrows are incomparable under inclusion.

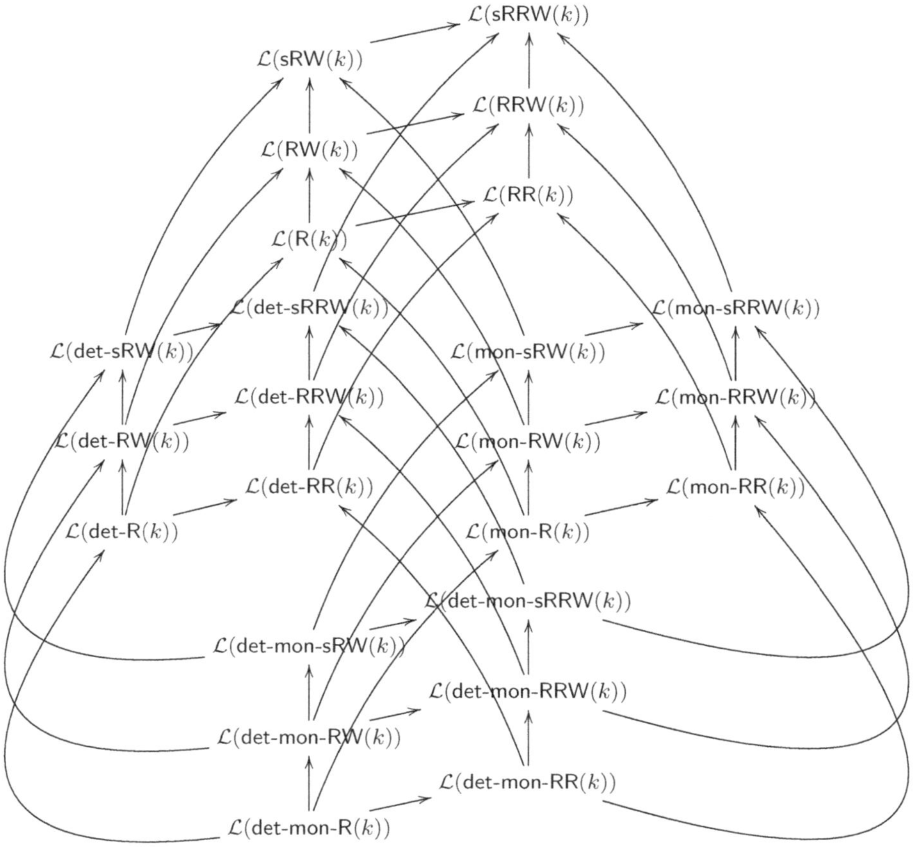

Figure 2.14: The taxonomy of restarting automata with window size $k \geq 5$.

For window sizes 3 and 4, some of the relationships between the monotone classes and the deterministic classes remain open due to the fact that the separating example languages above can only be employed for window size 4 or even window size 5.

Problem 2.3.32 *What is the exact relationship between those language classes that are defined by the various types of restarting automata without auxiliary letters that have window size $k = 3$ or $k = 4$?*

In Lemma 2.1.26, we saw that each deterministic sRRWW-automaton is weakly monotone. In fact, if M is a deterministic RRWW-automaton with window size k for some $k \geq 2$, then M is weakly monotone of degree $k-2$. Thus, for deterministic restarting automata, the degree of weak monotonicity is closely related to the window size. This raises the question of whether the degree of weak monotonicity induces an infinite strictly ascending hierarchy of language classes for the various types of restarting automata. This question has been studied in [158]. In the following, we restate the corresponding results from that paper.

For each integer $i \geq 1$, let $L_c^{(i)} \subseteq \{a,b,c,d,e\}^*$ be the language $L_c^{(i)} = L_{c,1}^{(i)} \cup L_{c,2}^{(i)}$, where

$$\begin{aligned} L_{c,1}^{(i)} &= \{\, a^n(b^ic^i)^{n-k}(b^i)^k d \mid n \geq k \geq 0 \,\} \text{ and} \\ L_{c,2}^{(i)} &= \{\, a^n(b^ic^i)^{m-k}(c^i)^k e \mid n \geq 0,\ m > 2n \text{ and } m \geq k \geq 0 \,\}. \end{aligned}$$

Notice that, for each $w \in L_c^{(i)}$, if w contains a factor b^{i+1}, then $w \in L_{c,1}^{(i)}$. Similarly, if w contains a factor c^{i+1} or ac, then $w \in L_{c,2}^{(i)}$. Obviously, for each $i \geq 1$, $L_c^{(i)}$ is a context-free language.

The idea behind the languages $L_c^{(i)}$ is the following: the words of each of these languages can be cut in the middle by two types of operations depending on whether w belongs to $L_{c,1}^{(i)}$ or to $L_{c,2}^{(i)}$. If w starts with $a^n(b^ic^i)^m$ for some $m > 0$, then the information of whether w contains b^{i+1} as a factor or ends in d, or whether it contains c^{i+1} as a factor or ends in e, tells the type of w. This information can be passed from the right end of w to the right-most occurrence of the letter a by a deterministic computation that is weakly monotone of degree i. In the following, we use the prefix wmon(i)- to denote types of restarting automata that are weakly monotone of degree i.

Lemma 2.3.33 ([158]) *For each $i \geq 1$, $L_c^{(i)} \in \mathcal{L}(\mathsf{det\text{-}wmon}(i)\text{-}\mathsf{R})$.*

In the corresponding proof in [158], a deterministic R-automaton of window size $k = 3i+2$ is defined for $L_c^{(i)}$ that is weakly monotone of degree i. On the other hand, the following negative result is established, which states that the degree i of weak monotonicity is also necessary for any deterministic RRW-automaton accepting $L_c^{(i)}$.

Lemma 2.3.34 ([158]) *For each $i \geq 1$, $L_c^{(i)} \notin \mathcal{L}(\mathsf{det\text{-}wmon}(i-1)\text{-}\mathsf{RRW})$.*

Thus, for each $i \geq 1$, $L_c^{(i)} \in \mathcal{L}(\mathsf{det\text{-}wmon}(i)\text{-}\mathsf{R}) \smallsetminus \mathcal{L}(\mathsf{det\text{-}wmon}(i-1)\text{-}\mathsf{RRW})$. This yields the following result.

Corollary 2.3.35 ([158]) *For all $i \geq 0$ and all types $\mathsf{X} \in \{\mathsf{R}, \mathsf{RR}, \mathsf{RW}, \mathsf{RRW}\}$ of restarting automata,*

$$\mathcal{L}(\mathsf{det\text{-}wmon}(i)\text{-}\mathsf{X}) \subsetneq \mathcal{L}(\mathsf{det\text{-}wmon}(i+1)\text{-}\mathsf{X}).$$

Hence, for deterministic R(R)(W)-automata, we have an infinite ascending hierarchy of language classes that is based on the degree of weak monotonicity. However, it is quite easily seen that $L_c^{(i)}$ is accepted by a monotone RR-automaton. Therefore, in order to derive a corresponding result for nondeterministic restarting automata, different example languages are needed.

For each $i \geq 1$, let $L_d^{(i)} = L_c^{(i)} \cup L_{a1}^{(i)} \cdot L_{de1} \cup L_{a2}^{(i)} \cdot L_{de2}$, where

$$\begin{aligned} L_{a1}^{(i)} &= \{\, a^n(b^ic^i)^n \mid n \geq 0 \,\}, & L_{de1} &= \{\, d^re^s \mid r > s \geq 0, r+s > 1 \,\}, \\ L_{a2}^{(i)} &= \{\, a^n(b^ic^i)^m \mid m > 2n \geq 0 \,\}, & L_{de2} &= \{\, d^re^s \mid 0 \leq r < s, r+s > 1 \,\}. \end{aligned}$$

Clearly, for each $i \geq 1$, the language $L_d^{(i)}$ is context-free. Notice further that, for any $w = uv \in L_d^{(i)}$, where $u \in \{a,b,c\}^*$ and $v \in \{d,e\}^*$, an occurrence of the factor b^{i+1} in u implies $w \in L_{c,1}^{(i)}$. Similarly, an occurrence of the factor c^{i+1} or ac implies $w \in L_{c,2}^{(i)}$. Moreover, $L_{a1}^{(i)} \cdot \{d\} \subset L_{c,1}^{(i)}$ and $L_{a2}^{(i)} \cdot \{e\} \subset L_{c,2}^{(i)}$. For the language $L_d^{(i)}$, the following result holds.

Theorem 2.3.36 ([158]) *For each* $i \geq 1$, $L_d^{(i)} \in \mathcal{L}(\mathsf{det\text{-}wmon}(i)\text{-}\mathsf{R}) \smallsetminus \mathcal{L}(\mathsf{wmon}(i-1)\text{-}\mathsf{RRW})$.

Hence, we also have the following hierarchies.

Corollary 2.3.37 ([158]) *For all* $i \geq 0$ *and all types* $\mathsf{X} \in \{\mathsf{R}, \mathsf{RR}, \mathsf{RW}, \mathsf{RRW}\}$ *of restarting automata,*

$$\mathcal{L}(\mathsf{wmon}(i)\text{-}\mathsf{X}) \subsetneq \mathcal{L}(\mathsf{wmon}(i+1)\text{-}\mathsf{X}).$$

In addition, it is shown in [158] that $\mathcal{L}(\mathsf{wmon}(i)\text{-}\mathsf{X})$ and $\mathcal{L}(\mathsf{wmon}(i)\text{-}\mathsf{Y})$ are incomparable under inclusion whenever the corresponding types X and Y of restarting automata are incomparable under inclusion. It remains, however, to extend these results on the degree of weak monotonicity to shrinking RW- and RRW-automata.

2.3.2 On the Window Size for Length-Reducing Restarting Automata with Auxiliary Letters

Here we study the influence that the window size has on the expressive capacity of RWW- and RRWW-automata. The first results on this topic are due to Natalie Schluter. In [236], she established the following results on the window size for monotone restarting automata, which were already announced in [234] and [235].

Theorem 2.3.38 ([236]) *For all* $k \geq 2$,

(a) $\mathcal{L}(\mathsf{mon\text{-}RWW}(k)) = \mathcal{L}(\mathsf{mon\text{-}RRWW}(k))$.
(b) $\mathcal{L}(\mathsf{det\text{-}mon\text{-}RWW}(k)) = \mathcal{L}(\mathsf{det\text{-}mon\text{-}RRWW}(k))$.

Proof outline. Let $M_1 = (Q, \Sigma, \Gamma, \rhd, \lhd, q_0, k, \delta)$ be a monotone (deterministic) RRWW-automaton of window size $k \geq 2$. Without loss of generality, we may assume that M_1 executes restart, accept, and reject steps only at the right end of its tape. Hence, each cycle of each computation of M_1 can be split into two parts: the first part consists of those MVR steps that are performed *before* a rewrite step is executed and the rewrite step, while the second part consists of those MVR steps that are performed *after* the rewrite step and the final restart step at the right sentinel. The idea of the proof is to construct a monotone (deterministic) RWW-automaton M_2 of window size k that, in each cycle, simulates the first part of the corresponding cycle of M_1 and encodes the information on the position of the rewrite step and the state reached by that rewrite step in the letters written during that rewrite step.

Accordingly, the tape alphabet Γ_2 of M_2 contains the tape alphabet Γ of M_1 together with marked copies $\bar{a}$ ($a \in \Gamma$) of these letters and so-called 'compound letters' of the form $[a, \mathsf{RC}]$, where $a \in \Gamma$ and RC is an ordered subset of Q. The letters of the form $\bar{a}$ are used to mark the first letter of v when M_2 simulates a rewrite step $u \to v$ of M_1. Furthermore, the compound letters are used to store the state that M_1 enters after executing a rewrite step. From these compound letters, M_2 can later extract the state information for the simulation of the second parts of the previous cycles of M_1 and simulate the next steps of these cycles whenever it moves its window further to the right. Of course, after some time, there may be several compound letters on the tape of M_2, but as the automaton M_1 is monotone, it is clear that the right-most compound letter is always the one that contains the correct information. Accordingly, M_2 has to abandon the current simulation of the second parts of the cycles of M_1 and restart these simulations anew whenever it encounters the next compound letter. The details of the construction of M_2 can be found in [236]. □

A corresponding result also holds for (deterministic) left-monotone RWW-automata. The construction of the simulating (deterministic) left-monotone RWW(k)-automaton from the given (deterministic) left-monotone RRWW(k)-automaton is essentially the same as for monotone RWW-automata. However, left-monotonicity implies that the latest compound letter is encountered before the previously written ones, which means that the information stored in these compound letters cannot be ignored. Thus, the simulating RWW-automaton must collect the information from all compound letters it encounters and simulate the corresponding MVR steps whenever it moves its window further to the right [236].

Thus, for monotone (and left-monotone) restarting automata of window size $k \geq 2$, RWW-automata are as expressive as RRWW-automata. The next theorem establishes a somewhat weaker result for deterministic automata that are not monotone.

Theorem 2.3.39 ([236]) *For all* $k \geq 2$, $\mathcal{L}(\text{det-RRWW}(k)) \subseteq \mathcal{L}(\text{det-RWW}(2k-2))$.

Proof outline. The idea of the proof is an extension of the one used to prove Theorem 2.3.38. From Lemma 2.1.26, we know that each deterministic RRWW-automaton M_1 of window size k is weakly monotone of degree $k-2$. Hence, by extending the window size of the simulating deterministic RWW-automaton M_2 by $k-2$ and by rewriting the first k letters contained in the window just as M_1 would rewrite them, while keeping (or marking) the other $k-2$ letters, we obtain an automaton that, in the current cycle, will only rewrite when it has completely seen the result of the previous rewrite step. Now monotone segments of computations can be simulated similarly to the simulation in the proof of Theorem 2.3.38: M_2 abandons the information from former compound letters whenever it encounters a new compound letter. For non-monotone segments, that is, when M_1 executes a rewrite step at a position that is up to $k-2$ letters further to the left than the previous one, M_2 needs to merge all information collected in the corresponding compound letters similarly to the situation in the proof for left-monotone automata. The detailed construction can be found in [236]. □

It is still open whether the bound given in Theorem 2.3.39 is the best possible. In fact, the following question remains open.

Problem 2.3.40 *For* $k \geq 2$, *is* $\mathcal{L}(\text{det-RWW}(k))$ *a proper subclass of* $\mathcal{L}(\text{det-RRWW}(k))$, *or are deterministic RWW-automata of window size k as expressive as deterministic RRWW-automata of window size k?*

Concerning the influence of the window size on the expressive capacity of nondeterministic restarting automata, Natalie Schluter established the following important results.

Theorem 2.3.41 ([236]) *For all* $k \geq 2$,

(a) $\mathcal{L}(\text{RRWW}(k+1)) = \mathcal{L}(\text{RRWW}(k))$.

(b) $\mathcal{L}(\text{mon-RRWW}(k+1)) = \mathcal{L}(\text{mon-RRWW}(k))$.

Thus, for nondeterministic RRWW-automata, the window size does not matter as long as it is at least two.

Proof outline. Let $M_1 = (Q_1, \Sigma, \Gamma_1, \triangleright, \triangleleft, q_0, k+1, \delta_1)$ be an RRWW-automaton of window size $k+1$. From this automaton, an RRWW-automaton $M_2 = (Q_2, \Sigma, \Gamma_2, \triangleright, \triangleleft, q_0, k, \delta_2)$ of window size k is constructed such that $L(M_2) = L(M_1)$. For this construction, the nondeterminism of M_2 and the fact that it has separate rewrite and restart steps are essential. The window size of M_2 is one less than that of M_1, and so, M_2 does not see the complete window contents of M_1. Accordingly, M_2 will simulate a rewrite step $u \to v$ of M_1 by guessing the contents a_r of the right-most letter in M_1's window, which is the last letter of u, by replacing the prefix u_1 of length k of u by an encoding of v together with the information that the subsequent letter a_r has to be interpreted as the right-most letter of v. As after a rewrite step, M_2 continues reading its tape, it can verify the correctness of its guess about the letter a_r immediately after executing the simulation of M_1's rewrite step.

If, in a later cycle, there is a rewrite step, the first letter of which is the last letter of v, then M_2 will record on its tape that the information on a_r stored in the last letter of the encoding of v should be ignored in all later cycles – that is, the information on a_r is up-to-date as long as there is no subsequent rewrite step the first letter of which is this particular letter. In order to guarantee that the information on the letter a_r is up-to-date, M_2 uses particular compound letters that encode the various possibilities about the status of a_r. The important point is that, at any time, the actual tape contents of M_1 can be derived from the current tape contents of M_2. The technically quite involved details of this construction and the proof of its correctness can be found in [236]. □

Also this theorem carries over to left-monotone RRWW-automata [236]. As an immediate consequence of Theorems 2.3.38 and 2.3.41, we obtain the following characterization.

Corollary 2.3.42 ([236]) *For all* $k \geq 2$, $\mathsf{CFL} = \mathcal{L}(\text{mon-RWW}(k)) = \mathcal{L}(\text{mon-RRWW}(k))$.

Based on the constructive proofs of Theorems 2.3.38 and 2.3.41, a monotone RWW-automaton M_k of window size $k \geq 3$ can be converted into a monotone RWW-automaton M_2 of window size two that accepts the same language as M_k. Obviously, M_k can be viewed as a monotone RRWW(k)-automaton. Hence, by iterating the construction from the proof of Theorem 2.3.41 $k-2$ times, we obtain a monotone RRWW-automaton M_2' of window size two for the language $L(M_k)$. Then the construction from the proof of Theorem 2.3.38 yields the intended monotone RWW(2)-automaton. As these constructions are technically very involved, the resulting RWW(2)-automaton is quite complicated. However, in the proof of Theorem 2.1.40, we constructed a monotone RWW-automaton M from a context-free grammar G such that $L(M) = L(G)$. In fact, this RWW-automaton M has a read/write window of size two only. Accordingly, we can restate Theorem 2.1.40 as follows.

Theorem 2.3.43 ([163, 164]) *From a context-free grammar G, one can construct a monotone RWW-automaton of window size two for the language $L(G)$.*

From a given monotone RWW-automaton M_k of window size $k \geq 3$, we can now construct an equivalent monotone RWW-automaton of window size two as follows. First, from M_k, we can construct a pushdown automaton P for the language $L(M_k)$ as shown in the proof of Theorem 1.9.23 (b) in [87]. From this PDA, we can derive a context-free grammar G in Chomsky normal form for $L(M_k)$, and then, using the construction from the proof of Theorem 2.1.40, we obtain a monotone RWW-automaton of window size two for $L(M_k)$.

Next, we prove that Corollary 2.3.42 carries over to the deterministic case. Our proof consists of two major steps. First, we show that each deterministic context-free language is accepted by a monotone deterministic RWW-automaton of window size three, and then we present a simulation of a monotone deterministic RWW-automaton of window size three by a monotone deterministic RWW-automaton of window size two.

Let $L \subseteq \Sigma^*$ be a deterministic context-free language. Then there exists a DPDA $A = (Q_A, \Sigma, \Delta_A, \#, p_0, \delta_A, F_A)$ that accepts L by final state. Here Q_A is a finite set of states, Σ is the input alphabet, Δ_A is the pushdown alphabet, $\# \notin \Delta_A$ is the bottom marker of the pushdown, $p_0 \in Q_A$ is the initial state,

$$\delta_A : (Q_A \times (\Sigma \cup \{\lambda\}) \times (\Delta_A \cup \{\#\})) \to Q_A \times (\{\#, \lambda\} \cdot \Delta_A^*)$$

is the (partial) transition function, and $F_A \subseteq Q_A$ is the set of final states. Without loss of generality, we can assume that the bottom marker $\#$ occurs only as the bottommost letter on the pushdown and that this letter is never popped from the pushdown.

A configuration of A is written as $(p, u, \#\alpha)$, where $p \in Q_A$ is the current state, $u \in \Sigma^*$ is the suffix of the input that has not yet been processed, and $\#\alpha \in \{\#\} \cdot \Delta_A^*$ is the current contents of the pushdown. A word $w \in \Sigma^*$ is accepted by A if the computation of A that starts from the initial configuration $(p_0, w, \#)$ reaches a configuration of the form $(p, \lambda, \#\alpha)$ for some final state $p \in F_A$ and some word $\alpha \in \Delta_A^*$.

We now establish the following technical result.

Theorem 2.3.44 ([163, 164]) *From a DPDA A, one can construct a deterministic monotone RWW-automaton of window size three for the language $L(A)$.*

Proof outline. Let $A = (Q_A, \Sigma, \Delta_A, \#, p_0, \delta_A, F_A)$ be a DPDA and let $L = L(A) \subseteq \Sigma^*$ be the language accepted by A. Without loss of generality, we may assume that each λ-step of A pops a letter from the pushdown, that is, if $\delta_A(p, \lambda, x) = (p', y)$ for some $p, p' \in Q_A$, $x \in \Delta_A \cup \{\#\}$, and $y \in \{\#, \lambda\} \cdot \Delta_A^*$, then $x \in \Delta_A$ and $y = \lambda$ (see, e.g., [3] Prop. 5.4). Thus, given a word $w = a_1 a_2 \cdots a_n \in L(A)$ as input, the computation of A begins with a reading step that reads the first letter a_1, and then there is a sequence of $n-1$ phases that each consists of a (possibly empty) sequence of λ-steps during which some letters are popped from the pushdown that is followed by a reading step. Finally, after the last reading step, which reads the letter a_n, another sequence of λ-steps that pop some letters from the pushdown may follow taking A into a final state.

For constructing an RWW-automaton $M = (Q, \Sigma, \Gamma, \rhd, \lhd, q_0, 3, \delta)$ of window size three that simulates the computations of A, we need the constant

$$c_A = \max\{\, |\gamma| \mid \exists\, p, p' \in Q_A, a \in \Sigma, x \in \Delta_A \cup \{\#\} : \delta_A(p, a, x) = (p', \gamma) \,\},$$

that is, c_A is the length of the longest word that A can push onto its pushdown in a single step. Furthermore, let $c = 2c_A - 1$.

The idea for the construction of M is as follows. Using code letters of the form $[\alpha]$ and $[\alpha, p]$, the contents $\#\alpha_1\alpha_2 \cdots \alpha_m$ of the pushdown of A and the actual state p of A are encoded by a word of the form $[\#\alpha_1][\alpha_2] \cdots [\alpha_m, p]$, where $|\#\alpha_1| = |\alpha_2| = \cdots = |\alpha_{m-1}| = c$ and $1 \leq |\alpha_m| \leq c$. Thus, the contents of the pushdown is compressed by the factor c, and its topmost part is stored together with the current state of A. Processing the input $w = a_1 a_2 \cdots a_n$ from left to right, M tries to simulate a (possibly empty) sequence of λ-steps together with the next reading step. This sequence of steps causes a change in the contents of the pushdown, that is, some letters may be popped from the pushdown and a new word may be pushed onto the pushdown. If the corresponding change of the pushdown contents can be stored in the right-most code letter, then M can simulate these steps by removing the input letter read and by replacing the right-most code letter. However, if the right-most code letter does not have sufficient storage space left, then an additional code letter must be used. This causes a problem as each rewrite step of M must be length-reducing. To overcome this problem, M combines the above steps with the next sequence of λ-steps. If these λ-steps decrease the size of the contents of the pushdown sufficiently much, then the simulation can continue by just manipulating the right-most code letter. Finally, if that is not the case, either, then M moves its window one more step to the right and simulates another reading step, reading the next input letter as well.

To realize this strategy, the RWW(3)-automaton M is now defined by taking

– $Q = \{q_0\}$,

– $\Gamma = \Sigma \cup \{\, [\nu_\#] \mid \nu_\# \in \{\#, \lambda\} \cdot \Delta_A^*, |\nu_\#| = c \}$
$\quad\quad \cup \{\, [\alpha_\#, p] \mid \alpha_\# \in \{\#, \lambda\} \cdot \Delta_A^*, 1 \leq |\alpha_\#| \leq c, p \in Q_A \,\}$,

and the transition function δ is defined by the following table, where $a, b \in \Sigma$, $p, p_1, p_2, p_3, p_4 \in Q_A$, $x, y \in \Delta_A$, $\alpha, \beta, \gamma, \eta, \eta_1, \eta_2, \mu, \nu \in \Delta_A^*$, $\alpha_\#, \nu_\# \in \{\#, \lambda\} \cdot \Delta_A^*$, $1 \leq |\alpha_\#| \leq c$, and $|\nu_\#| = c$:

(1) $\delta(q_0, \rhd a \lhd) = \mathsf{Accept}$ for all $a \in (\Sigma \cup \{\lambda\}) \cap L$,
by using this rule, M accepts inputs of length at most one,

(2) $\delta(q_0, \rhd ab) = \rhd[\#\alpha\gamma, p_3]$, if $\delta_A(p_0, a, \#) = (p_1, \#\alpha x \beta)$,
$(p_1, \lambda, x\beta) \vdash_A^{|\beta|} (p_2, \lambda, x)$,
and $\delta_A(p_2, b, x) = (p_3, \gamma)$,

(3) $\delta(q_0, \rhd ab) = \rhd[\#\gamma, p_3]$, if $\delta_A(p_0, a, \#) = (p_1, \#\alpha)$,
$(p_1, \lambda, \#\alpha) \vdash_A^{|\alpha|} (p_2, \lambda, \#)$,
and $\delta_A(p_2, b, \#) = (p_3, \#\gamma)$,

rules (2) and (3) create the first code letter on the tape,

(4) $\delta(q_0, \triangleright[\#\alpha x\beta, p]a) = \triangleright[\#\alpha\gamma, p_2]$, if $(p, \lambda, x\beta) \vdash_A^{|\beta|} (p_1, \lambda, x)$,
$\delta_A(p_1, a, x) = (p_2, \gamma)$,
and $|\#\alpha\gamma| \leq c$,

(5) $\delta(q_0, \triangleright[\#\alpha x\beta, p]a) = \triangleright[\#\alpha\gamma, p_3]$, if $(p, \lambda, x\beta) \vdash_A^{|\beta|} (p_1, \lambda, x)$,
$\delta_A(p_1, a, x) = (p_2, \gamma\eta)$,
$|\#\alpha\gamma| = c, |\eta| > 0$, and
$(p_2, \lambda, \eta) \vdash_A^{|\eta|} (p_3, \lambda, \lambda)$,

(6) $\delta(q_0, \triangleright[\#\alpha, p]a) = \triangleright[\#\gamma, p_2]$, if $(p, \lambda, \#\alpha) \vdash_A^{|\alpha|} (p_1, \lambda, \#)$,
and $\delta_A(p_1, a, \#) = (p_2, \#\gamma)$,

rules (4)–(6) read the next input letter if the whole new pushdown contents fits into a single code letter,

(7) $\delta(q_0, \triangleright[\#\alpha x\beta, p]a) = (q_0, \mathsf{MVR})$, if $(p, \lambda, x\beta) \vdash_A^{|\beta|} (p_1, \lambda, x)$,
$\delta_A(p_1, a, x) = (p_2, \gamma\eta)$,
$|\#\alpha\gamma| = c, |\eta| > 0$, but
$(p_2, \lambda, \eta) \not\vdash_A^{|\eta|} (p_3, \lambda, \lambda)$,

(8) $\delta(q_0, [\alpha_{\#} x\beta, p]ab) = [\alpha_{\#}\gamma][\eta_1\mu, p_4]$, if $(p, \lambda, x\beta) \vdash_A^{|\beta|} (p_1, \lambda, x)$,
$\delta_A(p_1, a, x) = (p_2, \gamma\eta)$,
$|\alpha_{\#}\gamma| = c, |\eta| > 0, \eta = \eta_1 y \eta_2$,
$(p_2, \lambda, y\eta_2) \vdash_A^{|\eta_2|} (p_3, \lambda, y)$,
and $\delta_A(p_3, b, y) = (p_4, \mu)$,

rule (8) preceded by (7) or (17) reads the next two input letters if, after reading the first letter, another code letter is needed,

(9) $\delta(q_0, \triangleright[\#\alpha][\beta, p]) = (q_0, \mathsf{MVR})$,
(10) $\delta(q_0, \triangleright[\#\alpha][\beta]) = (q_0, \mathsf{MVR})$,
(11) $\delta(q_0, [\nu_{\#}][\beta][\gamma, p]) = (q_0, \mathsf{MVR})$,
(12) $\delta(q_0, [\nu_{\#}][\beta][\gamma]) = (q_0, \mathsf{MVR})$,
rules (9)–(12) move the window over a sequence of code letters,

(13) $\delta(q_0, [\nu_{\#}][\alpha, p]a) = [\nu_{\#}, p_1]a$, if $(p, \lambda, \alpha) \vdash_A^{|\alpha|} (p_1, \lambda, \lambda)$,
rule (13) removes the last code letter by a sequence of λ-steps,

(14) $\delta(q_0, [\nu_{\#}][x\beta, p]a) = [\nu_{\#}, p_2]$, if $(p, \lambda, x\beta) \vdash_A^{|\beta|} (p_1, \lambda, x)$,
and $\delta_A(p_1, a, x) = (p_2, \lambda)$,

rule (14) removes the last code letter by a sequence of λ-steps and reads the next input letter,

(15) $\delta(q_0, [\nu_{\#}][\alpha x\beta, p]a) = [\nu_{\#}][\alpha\gamma, p_2]$, if $(p, \lambda, x\beta) \vdash_A^{|\beta|} (p_1, \lambda, x)$,
$\delta_A(p_1, a, x) = (p_2, \gamma)$,
and $|\alpha\gamma| \leq c$,

rule (15) reads the next input letter if no additional code letter is needed,

(16) $\delta(q_0, [\nu_{\#}][\alpha x\beta, p]a) = [\nu_{\#}][\alpha\gamma, p_3]$, if $(p, \lambda, x\beta) \vdash_A^{|\beta|} (p_1, \lambda, x)$,
$\delta_A(p_1, a, x) = (p_2, \gamma\eta)$,
$|\alpha\gamma| = c, |\eta| > 0$, and
$(p_2, \lambda, \eta) \vdash_A^{|\eta|} (p_3, \lambda, \lambda)$,

rule (16) reads the next input letter if no additional code letter is needed because of a subsequent sequence of λ-steps,

(17) $\delta(q_0, [\nu_{\#}][\alpha x\beta, p]a) = (q_0, \mathsf{MVR})$, if $(p, \lambda, x\beta) \vdash_A^{|\beta|} (p_1, \lambda, x)$,
$\delta_A(p_1, a, x) = (p_2, \gamma\eta)$,
$|\alpha\gamma| = c, |\eta| > 0$, but
$(p_2, \lambda, \eta) \not\vdash_A^{|\eta|} (p_3, \lambda, \lambda)$,

rule (17) realizes a move to the right as reading the next input letter would require an additional code letter – this rule can be followed by (8) or (21),

(18) $\delta(q_0, \rhd[\#\alpha\beta, p]\lhd) = \mathsf{Accept},$ if $(p, \lambda, \beta) \vdash_A^{|\beta|} (p_1, \lambda, \lambda)$ and $p_1 \in F_A$,

(19) $\delta(q_0, [\nu_\#][\alpha\beta, p]\lhd) = \mathsf{Accept},$ if $(p, \lambda, \beta) \vdash_A^{|\beta|} (p_1, \lambda, \lambda)$ and $p_1 \in F_A$,

rules (18) and (19) accept when the whole input has been read,

(20) $\delta(q_0, [\nu_\#][\alpha, p]\lhd) = [\nu_\#, p_1]\lhd,$ if $(p, \lambda, \alpha) \vdash_A^{|\alpha|} (p_1, \lambda, \lambda)$ without entering a final state,

rule (20) removes the last code letter by a sequence of λ-steps after the whole input has been read,

(21) $\delta(q_0, [\alpha_\# x\beta, p]a\lhd) = \mathsf{Accept},$ if $(p, \lambda, x\beta) \vdash_A^{|\beta|} (p_1, \lambda, x)$, $\delta_A(p_1, a, x) = (p_2, \gamma\eta)$, $|\alpha_\#\gamma| = c, |\eta| > 0, \eta = \eta_1 y \eta_2$, $(p_2, \lambda, y\eta_2) \vdash_A^{|\eta_2|} (p_3, \lambda, y)$, and $p_3 \in F_A$,

rule (21) accepts if reading the last input letter would require an additional code letter, but a subsequent sequence of λ-steps leads to an accepting state.

As each accepting computation of M obviously simulates an accepting computation of the DPDA A, it follows that $L(M) \subseteq L = L(A)$ holds. On the other hand, we have the following claim, which can be proved by induction on the length of the input word w (see [164]).

Claim. For all $p \in Q_A$, $w \in \Sigma^*$, and $\alpha \in \Delta_A^*$, if $(p, w, \#\alpha) \vdash_A^* (p_f, \lambda, \#\gamma)$ for some $p_f \in F_A$ and $\gamma \in \Delta_A^*$, then

$$q_0 \rhd [\#\alpha_1][\alpha_2] \cdots [\alpha_{m-1}][\alpha_m, p]w\lhd \vdash_M^* \mathsf{Accept},$$

where $\alpha = \alpha_1\alpha_2 \cdots \alpha_m$, $|\#\alpha_1| = |\alpha_2| = \cdots = |\alpha_{m-1}| = c$, and $1 \le |\alpha_m| \le c$.

Now let $w \in L(A)$. If $|w| \le 1$, then M accepts on input w by (1). So assume that $|w| \ge 2$, and let $w = abw'$ for some $a, b \in \Sigma$. Then

$$(p_0, abw', \#) \vdash_A (p, bw', \#\alpha) \vdash_A^* (p', w', \#\alpha') \vdash_A^* (p_f, \lambda, \#\gamma)$$

for some $p, p' \in Q_A$, $p_f \in F_A$, and words $\alpha, \alpha', \gamma \in \Delta_A^*$. It is easily seen that $|\#\alpha'| \le c$, and hence, M can execute the following computation:

$$\begin{array}{rll} q_0 \rhd w \lhd & = & q_0 \rhd abw' \lhd \\ & \vdash_M^c & q_0 \rhd [\#\alpha', p']w' \lhd \quad \text{(by (2) or (3))} \\ & \vdash_M^* & \mathsf{Accept} \quad \text{(by the claim above).} \end{array}$$

It follows that $L = L(A) \subseteq L(M)$, and hence, $L(M) = L = L(A)$.

During a computation, the tape contents of M is always of the form

$$\rhd [\#\alpha_1][\alpha_2] \cdots [\alpha_{m-1}][\alpha_m, p]a_r a_{r+1} \cdots a_n \lhd,$$

where $\alpha_1, \alpha_2, \ldots, \alpha_m \in \Delta_A^*$, $p \in Q_A$, and $a_r, a_{r+1}, \ldots, a_n \in \Sigma$. As each rewrite step involves the right-most code letter on the tape, and as it processes the left-most input letter (or the two left-most input letters), it follows that M is monotone. Thus, M is a deterministic monotone RWW(3)-automaton for the language $L(A)$. □

From Theorem 2.3.44, we conclude that $\mathcal{L}(\mathsf{det\text{-}mon\text{-}RWW}(3)) = \mathsf{DCFL}$. The following technical result allows us to lower the window size even further.

Theorem 2.3.45 ([163, 164]) *Each deterministic monotone RWW-automaton of window size three can be simulated by a deterministic RWW-automaton of window size two.*

Proof outline. Let $M = (Q, \Sigma, \Gamma, \rhd, \lhd, q_0, 3, \delta)$ be a deterministic monotone RWW-automaton, and let $F(M)$ be the set of all words $x \in \Gamma^*$ such that, after starting from the restarting configuration $q_0 \rhd x \lhd$, M will accept eventually, but the first rewrite/restart step within this computation is performed at the right end of the tape (that is, with the right sentinel $\lhd$ inside the read/write window). Then $F(M)$ is a regular language.

In fact, if $x \in F(M)$, then all rewrite/restart steps within the computation of M that starts from the configuration $q_0 \rhd x \lhd$ occur at the right sentinel $\lhd$, as M is monotone. In addition, we can assume, without loss of generality, that the accept step is also performed at the right sentinel. Furthermore, observe that the move-right steps of M can be simulated by a DFA A_{MVR}. Based on Lemma 1.2.71, we obtain a 2DFA A'_{MVR} that can simulate the reverse transitions of A_{MVR}.

Now we construct a 2DFA A_1 for the set $F(M)$. The acceptor A_1 simulates the RWW-automaton M while scanning the tape from left to right. If M is to execute a rewrite/restart step before reaching the right sentinel, then A_1 halts in a non-final state. When M reaches the right end of its tape (that is, when the right sentinel $\lhd$ appears in the read/write window), then, instead of executing the rewrite/restart step of M, the acceptor A_1 simulates the rewrite step within its finite-state control and

(a) it remembers the contents of the rewritten tape between the left-most letter in the window of M and the right sentinel, and

(b) by using the 2DFA A'_{MVR}, it computes the state that M enters within the previous cycle when it reaches the first letter that is produced by the rewrite step. Then it continues the simulation of the computation of M from this point onwards. When M halts accepting or rejecting, then A_1 accepts or rejects as well. Otherwise, A_1 simulates the next rewrite step in its finite-state control and continues.

Obviously, the computation of A_1 is finite for each input word x. Thus, it follows that $F(M)$ is a regular language. In addition, from A_1, we can construct a (one-way) DFA $A = (Q_A, \Gamma, \delta_A, q_{A,0}, F_A)$ for the language $F(M)$.

We now show how to construct a deterministic RWW-automaton $M' = (Q', \Sigma, \Gamma', \rhd, \lhd, q'_0, 2, \delta')$ of window size two that accepts the same language as M.

The read/write window of M' is smaller than the read/write window of M. Hence, in order to simulate a cycle of M, the automaton M' may have to perform more than one cycle. Accordingly, its state will be used to represent not only the current state of M, but also the letter immediately to the left of its current window position and the corresponding state of the DFA A. Hence, the set of states of M' will be

$$Q' = \{\, [q, x, p] \mid q \in Q, x \in \Gamma \cup \{\rhd, \lambda\}, p \in Q_A \,\}.$$

The initial state of M' is $q'_0 = [q_0, \lambda, q_{A,0}]$, and the first step performed by M' from a restarting configuration with a word x on its tape is

$$[q_0, \lambda, q_{A,0}] \rhd x \lhd \vdash_{M'} \rhd [q_0, \rhd, q_{A,0}] x \lhd .$$

A series of move-right steps of M can be simulated easily. For each move-right step $\delta(q, u_1u_2u_3) = (q', \mathsf{MVR})$ of M, the automaton M' has the move-right step

$$\delta'([q, u_1, p], u_2u_3) = ([q', u_2, p'], \mathsf{MVR})$$

for all states $p, p' \in Q_A$ such that $\delta_A(p, u_2) = p'$.

However, the simulation of the rewrite steps of M is more complicated. First of all, no rewrite at the right end of the tape of M needs to be simulated, as all the remaining rewrite steps by M must then also occur at the right end of the tape. Instead, M' can inspect the state of A after scanning the last letter of the current contents of the tape and accept or reject immediately. Thus, M' will only simulate a rewrite step of M if the corresponding contents of the window of M does not contain the right sentinel $\lhd$. Any combined rewrite/restart step of M according to

$$\delta(q, u_1u_2u_3) = v, \text{ where } u_1, u_2, u_3 \in \Gamma \text{ and } v \in \Gamma^{\leq 2}, \tag{2.8}$$

will be simulated as follows:

(i) If $v = \lambda$, the automaton M' rewrites u_2u_3 with a special letter $\Delta \notin \Gamma$ and restarts. In a subsequent cycle, when the letter Δ appears in the read/write window of M', the automaton deletes Δ and the letter immediately to the left of Δ. This completes the simulation of (2.8) by M'.

(ii) If $v = v_1$ for some $v_1 \in \Gamma$, the automaton M' rewrites u_2u_3 by the pair $[\Delta, v_1]$ and restarts. When $[\Delta, v_1]$ appears as the second letter within the read/write window of M', the automaton rewrites the contents of its read/write window by v_1, in this way completing the simulation of (2.8).

(iii) If $v = v_1v_2$ for some $v_1, v_2 \in \Gamma$, the automaton M' cannot simulate this rewrite step in two cycles, as two cycles would shorten the tape by at least two letters. The automaton M' must first read the tape until it sees u_2u_3 (preceded by u_1). If $v_1 = u_1$, the automaton simply rewrites u_2u_3 into v_2 and the simulation of (2.8) is complete. Otherwise, M' rewrites u_2u_3 into the letter $[v_1, v_2]$ with the meaning that the contents of the corresponding tape field is v_2 and its left neighbour should be v_1. Because of the monotonicity of M, after performing the combined rewrite/restart step using (2.8), M cannot perform another rewrite within the next cycle before its window contains the whole factor $v = v_1v_2$ (otherwise the right distance of the latter cycle would be larger than that of the former). Therefore, the simulating automaton M' will scan the tape until it sees $u_1[v_1, v_2]$. It can then interpret the contents of both fields containing u_1 and $[v_1, v_2]$ properly as fields containing v_1 and v_2. Of course, the transition relation δ' of M' must also include move-right instructions over fields containing pairs of letters, as the next rewrite after using (2.8) can occur to the right of v_1, and in addition, all rewrite instructions of M' must preserve the information within the first element of a pair letter on its tape.

In general, the tape of M' will contain letters from Γ and pairs of letters from $\Gamma \times \Gamma$:

- The automaton M' interprets a letter $x \in \Gamma$ on its tape as x on the tape of M, if it is not followed by a pair, and as v_1 on the tape of M, if it is followed by a pair $[v_1, v_2]$.
- The automaton M' interprets a letter $[x, y] \in \Gamma \times \Gamma$ on its tape as y on the tape of M, if it is not followed by a pair, and as v_1 on the tape of M, if it is followed by a pair $[v_1, v_2]$.

As M is deterministic and monotone, all pair letters on the tape of M' will be scanned by M' prior to simulating any further rewrites by M. Hence, all letters on the tape of M' will be interpreted correctly and the automaton M' is deterministic. Moreover, as all computations of deterministic RWW(2)-automata are monotone by Proposition 2.3.11, it follows that M' is monotone. Thus, M' is a deterministic monotone RWW(2)-automaton for the language $L(M)$. □

Because of Theorem 2.3.44, the above simulation has the following consequence.

Corollary 2.3.46 *For all* $k \geq 2$,
$$\begin{aligned}\mathsf{DCFL} &= \mathcal{L}(\mathsf{det\text{-}mon\text{-}RWW}(k)) = \mathcal{L}(\mathsf{det\text{-}mon\text{-}RRWW}(k))\\ &= \mathcal{L}(\mathsf{det\text{-}RWW}(2)) = \mathcal{L}(\mathsf{det\text{-}RRWW}(2)).\end{aligned}$$

In combination, our results yield the following construction of a deterministic monotone RWW-automaton of window size two from a deterministic monotone RWW-automaton of window size $k \geq 4$. Let M be a deterministic monotone RWW-automaton of window size $k \geq 4$. From M, we can first construct a DPDA P for the language $L(M)$, as shown in the proof of Corollary 2.1.39 (see [87]). From this DPDA, we can derive a deterministic monotone RWW-automaton of window size three for $L(M)$ as in the proof of Theorem 2.3.44, and then, using the construction above, we obtain a deterministic (monotone) RWW-automaton of window size two for $L(M)$.

Finally, we turn to deterministic RWW-automata that are not (necessarily) monotone. We have seen before that deterministic RWW- and RRWW-automata of window size two are necessarily monotone, which implies that they yield a characterization for the class DCFL of deterministic context-free languages. What can we say about deterministic RWW- and RRWW-automata of window size larger than two?

We recall the example language $L_{\exp} = \{ a^{2^n} \mid n \geq 0 \}$, which is a Church-Rosser language that is not context-free (see Example 1.2.16). Hence, by Corollary 2.1.34, this language is accepted by a deterministic RWW-automaton. In fact, it is even accepted by a deterministic RWW-automaton of window size three.

Example 2.3.47 *Let $M = (Q, \{a\}, \Gamma, \rhd, \lhd, q_0, 3, \delta)$ be the deterministic RWW-automaton of window size three that is defined by taking $Q = \{q_0\}$, $\Gamma = \{a, b\}$, and by defining the transition function δ as follows:*

$$\begin{array}{llcl@{\qquad}llcl}
(1) & \delta(q_0, \rhd a \lhd) & = & \mathsf{Accept}, & (6) & \delta(q_0, \rhd b \lhd) & = & \mathsf{Accept}, \\
(2) & \delta(q_0, \rhd aa) & = & (q_0, \mathsf{MVR}), & (7) & \delta(q_0, \rhd bb) & = & (q_0, \mathsf{MVR}), \\
(3) & \delta(q_0, aaa) & = & (q_0, \mathsf{MVR}), & (8) & \delta(q_0, bbb) & = & (q_0, \mathsf{MVR}), \\
(4) & \delta(q_0, aa \lhd) & = & b \lhd, & (9) & \delta(q_0, bb \lhd) & = & a \lhd, \\
(5) & \delta(q_0, aab) & = & bb, & (10) & \delta(q_0, bba) & = & aa.
\end{array}$$

It is easily seen that M accepts the language $L_{\exp}$. Also observe that M is non-monotone, as, for example,

$$q_0 \rhd aaaaaaaa \lhd \vdash^c_M q_0 \rhd aaaaaab \lhd \vdash^c_M q_0 \rhd aaaabb \lhd \vdash^c_M q_0 \rhd aabbb \lhd \vdash^{c^*}_M \mathsf{Accept}$$

is a non-monotone accepting computation. ■

As $L_{\exp} \in \mathcal{L}(\mathsf{det\text{-}RWW}(3))$, we have the following chain of inclusions:

$$\begin{array}{lcl}
\mathsf{REG} & = & \mathcal{L}(\mathsf{det\text{-}R(R)WW}(1)) \\
 & \subsetneq & \mathcal{L}(\mathsf{det\text{-}R(R)WW}(2)) \quad = \quad \mathsf{DCFL} \\
 & \subsetneq & \mathcal{L}(\mathsf{det\text{-}RWW}(3)) \\
 & \subseteq & \mathcal{L}(\mathsf{det\text{-}RRWW}(3)) \quad \subseteq \quad \mathcal{L}(\mathsf{det\text{-}R(R)WW}) \quad = \quad \mathsf{CRL},
\end{array}$$

but it remains open whether the latter inclusions are proper. In fact, we have the following open problems.

Problem 2.3.48 (a) *Is there an integer $k \geq 3$ such that*

$$\mathcal{L}(\mathsf{det\text{-}RWW}(k)) = \mathcal{L}(\mathsf{det\text{-}RWW}) = \mathsf{CRL},$$

or do the language classes $(\mathcal{L}(\mathsf{det\text{-}RWW}(k))_{k \geq 3}$ (and $(\mathcal{L}(\mathsf{det\text{-}RRWW}(k))_{k \geq 3})$ yield an infinite strictly ascending hierarchy within the class CRL of Church-Rosser languages?

(b) *For which values of $k \geq 3$ do the language classes $\mathcal{L}(\mathsf{det\text{-}RWW}(k))$ and $\mathcal{L}(\mathsf{det\text{-}RRWW}(k))$ coincide? Recall from Theorem 2.3.39 that Natalie Schluter has only shown that, for all $k \geq 2$, $\mathcal{L}(\mathsf{det\text{-}RRWW}(k)) \subseteq \mathcal{L}(\mathsf{det\text{-}RWW}(2k-2))$.*

Thus, for deterministic RWW- and RRWW-automata that are non-monotone, the influence of the window size on the expressive capacity of these automata is still unsolved.

2.3.3 For sRRWW-Automata Window Size One Suffices

According to Theorem 2.3.41, the expressive capacity of RRWW-automata is not diminished by limiting their window size to two, while by Proposition 2.3.8, RRWW-automata of window size one are strictly less expressive than unrestricted RRWW-automata. Here we present a characterization of the language class $\mathcal{L}(\mathsf{sRRWW})$ in terms of a restricted type of Turing machine. Based on this characterization, we obtain some new relationships between the language classes accepted by shrinking RRWW-automata and some time and space complexity classes. In addition, it turns out that window size one suffices for sRRWW-automata.

In [262], Burchard von Braunmühl and Rutger Verbeek introduced a model of the Turing machine that they called 'finite-change automaton.'

Definition 2.3.49 *A* finite-change automaton *is a nondeterministic single-tape Turing machine A that is parametrized by a function $f : \mathbb{N} \to \mathbb{N}$ satisfying $f(n) \geq n$ for all $n \in \mathbb{N}$ and a constant $k \in \mathbb{N}_+$. Given an input of length n (as the initial inscription of its tape), A must not visit more than $f(n)$ tape cells, and it must not change the contents of any cell more than k times during any accepting computation on the given input.*

Then $k\mathsf{C}(f)$ denotes the class of finite-change automata meeting these restrictions, and $\mathsf{FC}(f)$ denotes the union

$$\mathsf{FC}(f) = \bigcup_{k>0} k\mathsf{C}(f).$$

For the special case of the identity function $f(n) = n$, the corresponding classes of finite-change automata are denoted by $k\mathsf{C}$ and FC, respectively.

In order to enable the finite-change automaton to recognize the left end and the right end of the given input, we assume here that the initial tape contents for a given input $x \in \Sigma^*$ is of the form $\rhd x \lhd$, where $\rhd$ and $\lhd$ are special markers not contained in Σ. Hence, the length of the initial tape inscription is $n = |x| + 2$. Another option would be to use particularly marked letters for the first and the last letter of the input word. The following technical result shows that these approaches are equivalent.

Lemma 2.3.50 ([262]) *Let $f : \mathbb{N} \to \mathbb{N}$ be a function satisfying $f(n) \geq n$ for each $n \in \mathbb{N}$. Then $\mathcal{L}(\mathsf{FC}(f(n))) = \mathcal{L}(\mathsf{FC}(c \cdot f(n)))$ for each constant $c \geq 1$.*

The following proposition expresses an easy observation.

Proposition 2.3.51 $\mathcal{L}(\mathsf{RR}) \subseteq \mathcal{L}(1\mathsf{C})$.

Proof. Let M be an RR-automaton, that is, in each rewrite step, M only deletes some letters from the current contents of its read/write window. A one-change automaton A can simulate the computations of M cycle by cycle as follows. If there are only input letters on the tape between the sentinels $\rhd$ and $\lhd$, then A simulates the first cycle of a computation of M, starting at the left sentinel $\rhd$. After finding those positions on the tape that contain the letters that M deletes in the first cycle of the current computation, A simply replaces each of them with the special 'erase letter' E. Thereafter, A moves its head back to the left sentinel $\rhd$ and starts the simulation of the next cycle of M. If there are occurrences of the letter E on its tape, A just ignores all occurrences of this special letter, determining those positions on the tape that contain the input letters that M deletes in the current cycle. Again, A replaces each of these letters with the letter E. It follows that A changes the contents of each tape cell at most once. Hence, $\mathcal{L}(\mathsf{RR}) \subseteq \mathcal{L}(1\mathsf{C})$. □

By using a more sophisticated simulation, we obtain the following result.

Theorem 2.3.52 ([99]) $\mathcal{L}(\mathsf{sRRWW}) \subseteq \mathcal{L}(\mathsf{FC})$.

Proof outline. Let M be an sRRWW-automaton accepting a language $L \subseteq \Sigma^*$. By Proposition 2.1.23, there exist an injective morphism r_ω and a (length-reducing) RRWW-automaton M' with input alphabet $\Sigma \cup \{\diamond\}$ such that, for each word $x \in \Sigma^*$, $x \in L$ if and only if $r_\omega(x) \in L(M')$. Furthermore, by Theorem 2.2.15, there exist an injective morphism φ and an RR-automaton M'' such that, for all words $x' \in (\Sigma \cup \{\diamond\})^*$, $x' \in L(M')$ if and only if $\varphi(x') \in L(M'')$. Thus, we see that, for all words $x \in \Sigma^*$, $x \in L$ if and only if $\varphi'(x) \in L(M'')$, where φ' is the morphism obtained by the composition of r_ω and φ.

Based on the observations above, we construct a finite-change automaton A that proceeds as follows:

1. First, the image $\varphi'(x)$ of the input word x is written onto the part of the tape immediately to the right of the given input.

2. Then the computation of the RR-automaton M'' on $\varphi'(x)$ is simulated.

Obviously, A accepts the language L. Furthermore, this simulation requires at most space $(c+1) \cdot n$, where $c = \max\{\, |\varphi'(a)| \mid a \in \Sigma \,\}$. During the first part of the computation, the contents of each tape cell is changed at most once. During the second part of the computation, the contents of each cell is again changed at most once (see Proposition 2.3.51). Hence, A is a two-change automaton for the language L that uses only linear space. Now, it follows from Lemma 2.3.50 that $L = L(A) \in \mathcal{L}(\mathsf{FC})$. □

Thus, each shrinking RRWW-automaton can be simulated by a finite-change automaton. Interestingly, also the converse holds.

Theorem 2.3.53 ([99]) $\mathcal{L}(\mathsf{FC}) \subseteq \mathcal{L}(\mathsf{sRRWW}(1))$.

Proof outline. Let $A \in \mathsf{FC}$ be a finite-change automaton. Notice that, in an accepting computation, A can only visit the cells containing the original input word x and the cells located directly to the left and to the right of the input word. Recall that we assume that the input is given in the form $\rhd x \lhd$, where $\rhd$ and $\lhd$ are special markers not contained in the input alphabet.

By a simple modification, we can convert A into a finite-change automaton A' such that $L(A') = L(A)$, and A' meets the following restrictions during accepting computations:

- A' only visits the cells containing the input $\rhd x \lhd$;
- A' changes each cell at most j times, where $j \in \mathbb{N}_+$ is a constant;
- each step of A' which changes the contents of a cell leaves the head of A' stationary, that is, rewrite operations and head movements are performed by different steps;
- the working alphabet Γ of A' consists of $j+1$ disjoint subalphabets $\Gamma_0, \Gamma_1, \ldots, \Gamma_j$, where Γ_0 is the input alphabet, and the i-th change of the contents of a cell produces an element of Γ_i for all $i = 1, 2, \ldots, j$.

We now present a simulation of the finite-change automaton A' by an sRLWW-automaton M. If Q is the set of states of A', then we take $\Lambda = \Gamma \cup (\Gamma \times Q \times \{0,1\})$ to be the tape alphabet of M. Recall that $\Gamma_0 \subseteq \Gamma$ is the input alphabet of A', and therewith of M. The automaton M works according to the following description:

1. If there are no auxiliary letters on the tape, M simulates that part of a computation of A' that starts with an initial configuration and that ends when A' changes the contents of a tape cell for the first time, or that ends with A' accepting or rejecting without changing the contents of any tape cell. In the latter case, M also accepts or rejects, respectively, in a tail computation. In the former case, assume that A' changes the contents of a tape cell by executing the instruction $(q', b) \in \delta(q, a)$, that is, A' replaces an occurrence of the letter $a \in \Gamma_0$ with an occurrence of the letter $b \in \Gamma_1$ and changes its state from q to q'. Then M determines the corresponding tape cell, and it replaces the letter a with the letter $(b, q', 0)$.

2. If the tape contents is of the form $wa'z$ for some words $w, z \in \Gamma^*$ and a letter $a' = (a, q, 0) \in \Gamma \times Q \times \{0\}$, then M simulates that part of a computation of A' on waz that starts in state q at the position of the letter a' and that ends when A' changes the contents of the next tape cell, or that ends with A' accepting or rejecting, if no more tape cells are changed. Assume that this operation replaces an occurrence of the letter b with an occurrence of the letter c, and that A' enters state q' after executing this operation. Then M replaces the contents of the tape cell corresponding to the letter b with the letter $c' = (c, q', 1)$. Should the positions of the letters b and a' coincide, which means, in particular, that $b = a$, then M replaces the letter a' with c'.

3. If the tape contents is of the form $wa'y$ for a letter $a' = (a, q, 0) \in \Gamma \times Q \times \{0\}$ and some words w, y satisfying $wy \in \Gamma^* \cdot (\Gamma \times Q \times \{1\}) \cdot \Gamma^*$, then M simply rewrites the letter a' into the letter a.

4. If the tape contents is of the form $wa'z$ for some words $w, z \in \Gamma^*$ and a letter $a' = (a, q, 1) \in \Gamma \times Q \times \{1\}$, then M replaces the letter a' with the letter $(a, q, 0) \in \Gamma \times Q \times \{0\}$.

Note that the third coordinate of the letters from $\Gamma \times Q \times \{0, 1\}$ is used to distinguish between the positions of the last and the last but one change operation of A' in the current computation. One can easily verify that each accepting computation of M corresponds to an accepting computation of A'. Furthermore, for each accepting computation of A', there exists an accepting computation of M. Thus, we conclude that $L(M) = L(A') = L(A)$ holds.

Finally, it remains to show that M is shrinking. For doing so, we define a weight function ω by taking $\omega(a) = 3 \cdot (j + 1 - s)$ and $\omega((a, q, i)) = 3 \cdot (j + 1 - s) + i + 1$ for each $a \in \Gamma_s$, $s = 0, 1, \ldots, j$, $i \in \{0, 1\}$, and $q \in Q$. Note that each rewrite operation of M satisfies one of the following conditions:

- it replaces an element of Γ_s with an element of $\Gamma_{s+1} \times Q \times \{0, 1\}$ for some $s < j$ (in steps 1 and 2);
- it replaces an element of $\Gamma_s \times Q \times \{1\}$ with the corresponding element of $\Gamma_s \times Q \times \{0\}$ for some $s \leq j$ (in step 4);
- it replaces an element of $\Gamma_s \times Q \times \{0\}$ with an element of $\Gamma_{s+1} \times Q \times \{1\}$ for some $s < j$ (in step 2);
- it replaces an element of $\Gamma_s \times Q \times \{0\}$ with the corresponding element of Γ_s for some $s \leq j$ (in step 3).

Each of these rewrite steps is weight-reducing with respect to ω. Hence, M is indeed an sRLWW-automaton for the language $L(A)$. In addition, we see that the sRLWW-automaton M just needs a window of size one, as in each cycle, it just replaces a single letter. Finally, Corollary 2.1.4(a) implies that we can turn the sRLWW(1)-automaton M into an sRRWW(1)-automaton for the language $L(M) = L(A)$. □

As a consequence of Theorems 2.3.52 and 2.3.53, we obtain the following characterization, which states, in particular, that sRRWW-automata just need read/write windows of size one.

Corollary 2.3.54 ([99]) $\mathcal{L}(\mathsf{FC}) = \mathcal{L}(\mathsf{sRRWW}) = \mathcal{L}(\mathsf{sRRWW}(1))$.

This characterization allows us to establish some new relationships between (shrinking) restarting automata on the one hand and some more classical classes of languages on the other hand. Recall from Section 1.2 that CSL and DCSL denote the class of context-sensitive languages and the class of deterministic context-sensitive languages, respectively. It is known that (D)CSL contains some languages that are PSPACE-complete with respect to polynomial-time reductions (see Theorem 1.4.10). In fact, the derivations of a context-sensitive grammar can be of exponential length in relation to the length of the terminal word generated. Accordingly, the class $\mathsf{CSL}_{\mathsf{lin}}$ of *linear-time bounded context-sensitive languages* has been introduced and studied by Ronald V. Book [17]. A language L belongs to the class $\mathsf{CSL}_{\mathsf{lin}}$, if there exist a context-sensitive grammar $G = (N, T, S, P)$ that generates L and a constant $c \geq 1$ such that, for all $n \in \mathbb{N}_+$, each word of length n in L has a derivation in G of length at most $c \cdot n$. Finally, Q denotes the class of *quasi-realtime languages*. This is the class of languages that are accepted by nondeterministic multi-tape Turing machines in realtime, that is, $\mathsf{Q} = \mathsf{NTIME}(n)$. In fact, in [78], the class Q is characterized as the class of languages that are accepted by *shrinking 3-pushdown automata*. Concerning these classes, the following results are known.

Proposition 2.3.55 ([17, 18, 23]) $\mathsf{GCSL} \subsetneq \mathsf{CSL}_{\mathsf{lin}} \subsetneq \mathsf{Q} = \bigcup_{c \geq 1} \mathsf{NTIME}(c \cdot n)$.

From Theorems 2 and 3 of [262], the inclusions $\mathsf{Q} \subseteq \mathcal{L}(\mathsf{FC}) \subseteq \mathsf{DCSL}$ follow (see also [83]). Together with the above characterization of the class $\mathcal{L}(\mathsf{sRRWW})$, this yields the following upper and lower bounds for the language class $\mathcal{L}(\mathsf{sRRWW})$.

Corollary 2.3.56 ([99]) $\mathsf{Q} \subseteq \mathcal{L}(\mathsf{sRRWW}) \subseteq \mathsf{DCSL}$.

We have seen above that sRRWW-automata of window size one are equivalent in expressive capacity to finite-change automata and, therewith, to sRRWW-automata of any window size. This raises the question about the expressive capacity of sRWW-automata of bounded window size. The simulation of an sRRWW-automaton by an sRWW-automaton given in [99] (see the proof outline of Theorem 2.1.24) yields that the latter has window size $\max\{2k, 9\}$, if the former has window size k. This yields the following result.

Corollary 2.3.57 $\mathcal{L}(\mathsf{FA}) = \mathcal{L}(\mathsf{sRWW}(9))$.

Below we shall see that sRWW-automata of window size one are less expressive than finite-change automata. However, the following problem is still unsolved.

Problem 2.3.58 *For $k \in \{2, 3, \ldots, 8\}$, what is the expressive capacity of sRWW-automata of window size k? Are these automata really less expressive than finite-change automata?*

Concerning this problem, we have at least the following result on sRWW-automata of window size two.

Theorem 2.3.59 ([162, 164]) $\mathsf{GCSL} \subsetneq \mathcal{L}(\mathsf{sRWW}(2))$.

Proof outline. From Proposition 2.3.8, we recall that the class $\mathcal{L}(\mathsf{RR}(1))$ already contains a language that is not even growing context-sensitive. So it remains to prove that each growing context-sensitive language is accepted by some sRWW(2)-automaton.

Let $L \subseteq \Sigma^*$ be a growing context-sensitive language. By Theorem 1.2.17, there exists an sTPDA $A = (P, \Sigma, \Gamma, \delta, p_0, \bot, t_1, t_2, \{p_f\})$ that accepts the language L. In fact, we can even assume that $t_1 = \lambda = t_2$ holds. Let $\varphi : P \cup \Gamma \to \mathbb{N}_+$ be a weight function such that A is shrinking with respect to this weight function. Without loss of generality, we may assume that $\varphi(aqb) - \varphi(upv) \geq 2$ for each transition $(p, u, v) \in \delta(q, a, b)$. We now present an sRWW(2)-automaton M that simulates the computations of A.

First, we choose $\Sigma' = \{\, a' \mid a \in \Sigma \,\}$ as a new input alphabet that is disjoint from Γ, but that is in one-to-one correspondence to Σ. Let $M = (Q, \Sigma', \Omega, \rhd, \lhd, q_0, 2, \delta_M)$ be defined by taking $Q = \{q_0\}$, $\Omega = \Sigma' \cup P \cup \Gamma \cup (\Gamma \times P)$ and by defining the transition relation δ_M as follows, where we ignore the state components as M has only a single state, and $p, p_1 \in P$, $a \in \Sigma$, $x, y, z \in \Gamma$, and $u, v \in \Gamma^*$:

$$\begin{array}{rlcll}
(1) & \delta_M(\rhd \cdot \lhd) & = & \{\mathsf{Accept}\}, & \text{if } \delta(p_0, \bot, \bot) = \{(p_f, \lambda, \lambda)\},\\
(2) & \delta_M(\rhd a') & \ni & \rhd[\bot, p_0]a, & \\
(3) & \delta_M(\rhd \bot) & = & \{\mathsf{MVR}\}, & \\
(4) & \delta_M(\rhd [\bot, p]) & = & \{\mathsf{MVR}\}, & \\
(5) & \delta_M([\bot, p]\lhd) & = & \{\mathsf{Accept}\}, & \text{if } (p_f, \lambda, \lambda) \in \delta(p, \bot, \bot),\\
(6) & \delta_M(xy) & = & \{\mathsf{MVR}\}, & \\
(7) & \delta_M(x[y, p]) & = & \{\mathsf{MVR}\}, & \\
(8) & \delta_M(xp) & = & \{[x, p]\}, & \\
(9) & \delta_M([x, p]a') & = & \{[x, p]a\}, & \\
(10) & \delta_M([x, p]\lhd) & \ni & u[z, p_1]v\lhd, & \text{if } (p_1, uz, v\bot) \in \delta(p, x, \bot),\\
(11) & \delta_M([x, p]\lhd) & \ni & p_1 v\lhd, & \text{if } (p_1, \lambda, v\bot) \in \delta(p, x, \bot),\\
(12) & \delta_M([x, p]y) & \ni & u[z, p_1]v, & \text{if } (p_1, uz, v) \in \delta(p, x, y),\\
(13) & \delta_M([x, p]y) & \ni & p_1 v, & \text{if } (p_1, \lambda, v) \in \delta(p, x, y).
\end{array}$$

Furthermore, we define a weight function $\omega : \Omega \to \mathbb{N}_+$ as follows:

- $\omega(a') = \varphi(a) + \varphi(\bot) + \varphi(p_0) + 1$ for all $a \in \Sigma$,
- $\omega(x) = \varphi(x)$ for all $x \in \Gamma$,
- $\omega(p) = \varphi(p) + 1$ for all $p \in P$,
- $\omega([x, p]) = \varphi(x) + \varphi(p)$ for all $x \in \Gamma$ and $p \in P$.

Using this weight function, it is easily verified that the RWW-automaton M is shrinking. Indeed, instructions of types (2) and (9) are weight-reducing because of the weight associated with the letters from Σ', instructions of type (8) are weight-reducing because of the weight associated with the letters from the subalphabet P of Ω, instructions of types (10) and (12) are weight-reducing, as the corresponding instructions of A are weight-reducing with respect to φ, and the instructions of types (11) and (13) are weight-reducing because of our assumption that each instruction of A reduces the weight of the corresponding configuration by at least two.

It remains to show that $L(M) = h(L(A))$, where $h : \Sigma^* \to \Sigma'^*$ is the morphism induced by mapping a to a' for all $a \in \Sigma$. A configuration of the form $\bot uxpv\bot$ of A, where $u, v \in \Gamma^*$, $x \in \Gamma$, and $p \in P$, is encoded by the tape contents $\rhd\bot u[x,p]v\lhd$ of M, or by the tape contents $\rhd\bot uxpv\lhd$. The latter type of encoding is used whenever a step of A is being simulated that only pops from the left-hand pushdown (see instructions (11) and (13)). However, as soon as such an encoding is detected, it is immediately transformed into an encoding of the former type by instruction (8). Now, using this encoding of the configurations of A, the sRWW-automaton M simulates the computations of A step by step. Hence, it follows that $L(M) = h(L(A))$.

By renaming the letters of Ω accordingly, an sRWW(2)-automaton is obtained that accepts the language $L(A)$. This completes the proof of Theorem 2.3.59. □

Actually, the sRWW(2)-automaton M in the above proof is weakly monotone. Hence, we even obtain the following characterization.

Corollary 2.3.60 GCSL = $\mathcal{L}$(wmon-sRWW(2)) = $\mathcal{L}$(wmon-sRRWW(2)).

Concerning monotone sRWW- and sRRWW-automata of window size two, we immediately obtain the following result from Theorem 2.1.38 and Corollary 2.3.42.

Corollary 2.3.61 CFL = $\mathcal{L}$(mon-sRWW(2)) = $\mathcal{L}$(mon-sRRWW(2)).

Finally, we turn to deterministic sRWW- and sRRWW-automata of window size two. The simulation of an sTPDA by an sRWW(2)-automaton in the proof of Theorem 2.3.59 carries over to the deterministic case. As deterministic sTPDAs characterize the class CRL of Church-Rosser languages (see Corollary 2.1.34), this yields the following result.

Corollary 2.3.62 ([162, 164]) CRL = $\mathcal{L}$(det-sRWW(2)) = $\mathcal{L}$(det-sRRWW(2)).

Thus, we see that for deterministic shrinking RWW- and RRWW-automata, the hierarchy based on window size consists of at most two levels: window size one and window size two. Recall from Problem 2.3.48 that the corresponding question for deterministic RWW- and RRWW-automata is still open.

Finally, concerning monotone deterministic sRWW- and sRRWW-automata of window size two, we obtain the following characterization from Corollaries 2.1.39 and 2.3.46.

Corollary 2.3.63 DCFL = $\mathcal{L}$(det-mon-sRWW(2)) = $\mathcal{L}$(det-mon-sRRWW(2)).

In summary, we have seen that for deterministic and for monotone sRWW- and sRRWW-automata, window size two suffices, while for nondeterministic sRRWW-automata in general, already window size one suffices. It remains to investigate the expressive capacity of sRWW- and of deterministic or monotone sRRWW-automata of window size one. We shall return to this topic in Subsection 2.3.5.

2.3.4 Ordered Restarting Automata

Here we introduce and study some types of restarting automata that are known as 'ordered restarting automata.' These types of restarting automata, which have been studied in detail by Kent Kwee in his doctoral dissertation [129], are shrinking restarting automata with a window of size three that, however, in each rewrite step, just replace the letter in the middle of the window with another, smaller, letter. This means, in particular, that the length of the tape remains unchanged during a computation. In addition, the actual weights of the various letters are not of interest – rather their relative weights are important. Therefore, instead of providing a weight function, a partial ordering on the tape alphabet is given for an ordered restarting automaton.

Definition 2.3.64 ([131]) *An* ordered RRWW-automaton (*ORRWW-automaton*) *is an sRRWW-automaton of window size three that is described by an 8-tuple* $M = (Q, \Sigma, \Gamma, \rhd, \lhd, q_0, \delta, >)$, *where* $>$ *is a strict* partial ordering *on* Γ *and*

$$\delta : (Q \times ((\Gamma \cup \{\rhd\})^{\leq 1} \cdot \Gamma \cdot (\Gamma \cup \{\lhd\}))) \cup \{(q_0, \rhd\lhd)\} \to \mathcal{P}((Q \times (\{\mathsf{MVR}\} \cup \Gamma)) \cup \{\mathsf{Restart}, \mathsf{Accept}\})$$

is the transition relation. *While the move-right, restart, and accept steps are defined as usual, the rewrite steps are restricted as follows:*

- *A* rewrite step *has the form* $(q', b) \in \delta(q, a_1a_2a_3)$, *where* $q, q' \in Q$, $a_1 \in \Gamma \cup \{\rhd\}$, $a_2, b \in \Gamma$, *and* $a_3 \in \Gamma \cup \{\lhd\}$ *such that* $a_2 > b$ *holds. It causes* M *to replace the letter* a_2 *in the middle of its window with the letter* b, *to move the window one position to the right, and to change to state* q'.

If $|\delta(q, u)| \leq 1$ *for all pairs* (q, u), *then* M *is a* deterministic *ORRWW-automaton* (*det-ORRWW-automaton*).

In the proof of Theorem 2.3.53, a finite-change automaton A is simulated by an sRRWW-automaton M of window size one. In fact, the sRRWW(1)-automaton M just performs rewrite steps that replace a single letter with another letter of smaller weight. Hence, by extending the window to size three, we can convert M into an ORRWW-automaton for the language $L(A)$. This yields the following consequence, which answers the question about the expressive capacity of ORRWW-automata that was left open in [131].

Corollary 2.3.65 $\mathcal{L}(\mathsf{FC}) = \mathcal{L}(\mathsf{sRRWW}(1)) = \mathcal{L}(\mathsf{ORRWW})$.

Next we turn to ordered RWW-automata, which are a restricted class of sRWW-automata of window size three.

Definition 2.3.66 ([132]) *An* ordered RWW-automaton (*ORWW-automaton*) *is an sRWW-automaton of window size three that is described by an 8-tuple* $M = (Q, \Sigma, \Gamma, \rhd, \lhd, q_0, \delta, >)$, *where* $>$ *is a strict* partial ordering *on* Γ *and*

$$\delta : (Q \times ((\Gamma \cup \{\rhd\}) \cdot \Gamma \cdot (\Gamma \cup \{\lhd\}) \cup \{\rhd\lhd\})) \to \mathcal{P}((Q \times \mathsf{MVR}) \cup \Gamma \cup \{\mathsf{Accept}\})$$

is the transition relation. *While the move-right and accept steps are defined as usual, the combined rewrite/restart steps are restricted as follows:*

- *A* rewrite/restart step *has the form* $b \in \delta(q, a_1a_2a_3)$, *where* $q \in Q$, $a_1 \in \Gamma \cup \{\rhd\}$, $a_2, b \in \Gamma$, *and* $a_3 \in \Gamma \cup \{\lhd\}$ *such that* $a_2 > b$. *It causes* M *to replace the letter* a_2 *in the middle of its window with the letter* b *and to restart, that is, the window is moved back to the left end of the tape, and* M *reenters its initial state* q_0.

If $|\delta(q, u)| \leq 1$ *for all* q *and* u, *then* M *is a* deterministic ORWW-automaton (*det-ORWW-automaton*), *and if* $Q = \{q_0\}$, *that is, if the initial state is the only state of* M, *then we call* M *a* stateless *ORWW-automaton* (*stl-ORWW-automaton*) *or a* stateless deterministic ORWW-automaton (*stl-det-ORWW-automaton*), *as in this case the state is actually not needed. Accordingly, for stateless ORWW-automata, we drop the components that refer to states to simplify the notation.*

The following example illustrates the way in which a stateless det-ORWW-automaton works.

Example 2.3.67 *Let $n \geq 2$ be a fixed integer, and let $M = (\Sigma, \Gamma, \rhd, \lhd, \delta, >)$ be defined by taking $\Sigma = \{a, b\}$ and $\Gamma = \Sigma \cup \{a_i, b_i, x_i \mid 1 \leq i \leq n-1\}$, by choosing the ordering $>$ such that $a > a_i > x_j$ and $b > b_i > x_j$ for all $1 \leq i, j \leq n-1$, and by defining the transition function δ in such a way that M proceeds as follows: On input $w = w_1 w_2 \cdots w_m$, $w_1, w_2, \ldots, w_m \in \Sigma$, M numbers the first $n-1$ letters of w from left to right, by replacing $w_i = a$ (b) by a_i (b_i) for $i = 1, 2, \ldots, n-1$. If $w_n \neq a$, then the computation fails, but if $w_n = a$, then M continues by replacing the last $n-1$ letters of w from right to left using the letters x_1 to x_{n-1}. If the n-th last letter is b or some b_i, then M accepts, otherwise, the computation fails again. Then $L(M) = \{ w \in \{a, b\}^m \mid m > n,\ w_n = a, \text{ and } w_{m+1-n} = b \}$.* ■

Let $\Sigma = \{a, b, \#\}$, and let

$$\hat{L}'_{\text{copy}} = \{ w\#u \mid w, u \in \{a, b\}^*, |w|, |u| \geq 2, \text{ and } u \text{ is a scattered subword of } w \}.$$

Lemma 2.3.68 ([132]) *The language $\hat{L}'_{\text{copy}}$ is not growing context-sensitive, but there exists an ORWW-automaton M such that $L(M) = \hat{L}'_{\text{copy}}$.*

Proof outline. Let M be the ORWW-automaton on $\Sigma = \{a, b, \#\}$ and $\Gamma = \{a, a_1, a_2, b, b_1, b_2, \#\}$ that is given by the following meta-instructions using the ordering $\# > a > b > a_1 > b_1 > a_2 > b_2$, where $c, d, e \in \{a, b\}$:

$$
\begin{array}{rl}
(1) & (\lambda, \rhd cd \to \rhd c_1 d),\\
(2) & (\lambda, \rhd c_1 d \to \rhd c_2 d),\\
(3) & (\rhd \cdot \{a_2, b_2\}^*, c_2 de \to c_2 d_1 e),\\
(4) & (\rhd \cdot \{a_2, b_2\}^*, c_2 d_1 e \to c_2 d_2 e),\\
(5) & (\rhd \cdot \{a_2, b_2\}^*, c_2 d\# \to c_2 d_1 \#),\\
(6) & (\rhd \cdot \{a_2, b_2\}^*, c_2 d_1 \# \to c_2 d_2 \#),\\
(7) & (\rhd \cdot \{a_2, b_2\}^* \cdot c_1 \cdot \{a, b\}^+, \#cd \to \#c_1 d),\\
(8) & (\rhd \cdot \{a_2, b_2\}^* \cdot c_2 \cdot \{a, b\}^+, \#c_1 d \to \#c_2 d),\\
(9) & (\rhd \cdot \{a_2, b_2\}^* \cdot c_1 \cdot \{a, b\}^+ \cdot \# \cdot \{a_2, b_2\}^*, d_2 ce \to d_2 c_1 e),\\
(10) & (\rhd \cdot \{a_2, b_2\}^* \cdot c_2 \cdot \{a, b\}^+ \cdot \# \cdot \{a_2, b_2\}^*, d_2 c_1 e \to d_2 c_2 e),\\
(11) & (\rhd \cdot \{a_2, b_2\}^* \cdot c_1 \cdot \{a, b\}^+ \cdot \# \cdot \{a_2, b_2\}^*, d_2 c\lhd \to d_2 c_1 \lhd),\\
(12) & (\rhd \cdot \{a_2, b_2\}^* \cdot c_2 \cdot \{a, b\}^+ \cdot \# \cdot \{a_2, b_2\}^*, d_2 c_1 \lhd \to d_2 c_2 \lhd),\\
(13) & (\rhd \cdot \{a_2, b_2\}^+ \cdot c_1 \cdot \# \cdot \{a_2, b_2\}^*, d_2 c\lhd \to d_2 c_1 \lhd),\\
(14) & (\rhd \cdot \{a_2, b_2\}^+ \cdot c_2 \cdot \# \cdot \{a_2, b_2\}^*, d_2 c_1 \lhd \to d_2 c_2 \lhd),\\
(15) & (\rhd \cdot \{a_2, b_2\}^+ \cdot \# \cdot \{a_2, b_2\}^+ \cdot \lhd, \mathsf{Accept}).
\end{array}
$$

For a word of the form $w\#u$, where $w, u \in \{a, b\}^*$, it is easily seen from rules (15), (1), and (7) that $|w|, |u| \geq 2$, if M is to accept on input $w\#u$. By rules (1) to (6), the prefix w is rewritten from left to right, where each letter is first replaced with its copy with index 1, and then this is replaced with the corresponding letter with index 2. Also the suffix u is rewritten in this way by rules (7) to (14); however, here the first letter from $\{a, b\}$ from the left, say c, can only be rewritten into c_1, if, at that moment, the right-most already rewritten letter in w happens to be the letter c_1, and analogously, c_1 can further be rewritten into c_2 only if, at that moment, the right-most already rewritten letter in w happens to be the letter c_2. Thus, it follows that u is a scattered subword of w, that is, $L(M) = \hat{L}'_{\text{copy}}$.

In [25], it is shown that each growing context-sensitive language is accepted by a one-way auxiliary pushdown automaton with a logarithmic space bound, that is, the class GCSL of growing context-sensitive languages is contained in $\mathcal{L}(\mathsf{OW\text{-}auxPDA(log)})$. On the other hand, Clemens Lautemann has shown in [138] that the language $L_{\text{copy}} = \{ ww \mid w \in \{a, b\}^* \}$ is not accepted by any OW-auxPDA with a logarithmic space bound, and his argument immediately extends to the language $L'_{\text{copy}} = \{ w\#w \mid w \in \{a, b\}^* \}$.

Now assume that the language $\hat{L}'_{\text{copy}}$ is growing context-sensitive. Then there is a OW-auxPDA A that accepts this language with a logarithmic space bound. By using an extra track of the auxiliary tape to implement a binary counter, we can extend A into a OW-auxPDA B for the language L'_{copy}, which contradicts the statement above. Hence, the language $\hat{L}'_{\text{copy}}$ is not growing context-sensitive. □

Thus, we already see that ORWW-automata are quite expressive. In fact, the following additional result has been established in [134].

Theorem 2.3.69 *There exists an ORWW-automaton M such that the language $L(M)$ is NP-complete with respect to log-space reductions.*

Proof outline. Let $\Sigma_0 = \{\wedge, \vee\}$, $V = \{ v_n \mid n \in \mathbb{N}_+ \}$, $\bar{V} = \{ \bar{v}_n \mid n \in \mathbb{N}_+ \}$, and let 3SAT be the set of satisfiable propositional formulas in conjunctive normal form of degree 3 over $V \cup \bar{V} \cup \Sigma_0$, that is, each $\alpha \in$ 3SAT is of the form

$$\alpha = v_{1,1}^{\mu_{1,1}} \vee v_{1,2}^{\mu_{1,2}} \vee v_{1,3}^{\mu_{1,3}} \wedge v_{2,1}^{\mu_{2,1}} \vee v_{2,2}^{\mu_{2,2}} \vee v_{2,3}^{\mu_{2,3}} \wedge \cdots \wedge v_{m,1}^{\mu_{m,1}} \vee v_{m,2}^{\mu_{m,2}} \vee v_{m,3}^{\mu_{m,3}}$$

for some $m \geq 1$, where $v_{i,j} \in V$ and $\mu_{i,j} \in \{1, -1\}$. Here $v_{i,j}^1 = v_{i,j}$ and $v_{i,j}^{-1} = \bar{v}_{i,j}$. In addition, there exists an assignment $\varphi : V \to \{0,1\}$ such that, for each $j \in \{1, 2, \ldots, m\}$, there is an index $s_j \in \{1,2,3\}$ such that $\varphi(v_{j,s_j}^{\mu_{j,s_j}}) = 1$ holds. It is well-known that the language 3SAT is NP-complete with respect to log-space reductions (see, e.g., [49]). By renaming the variables if necessary, we can assume that α is *normalized*, that is, it contains the variables $v_1, v_2, \ldots, v_k$ for some $k \geq 1$.

Now let $\Sigma = \{x, \#, \circ, +, \neg, \wedge, \vee\}$. We define the function $\Psi : \left(V \cup \bar{V} \cup \Sigma_0\right)^* \to \Sigma^*$ by taking $\Psi(\alpha) = x^k \# c_k(\alpha) \#$, where k is the number of different variables occurring in α, and the encoding function c_k is the morphism that is defined as follows:

$$c_k(a) = \begin{cases} \circ^{i-1} + \circ^{k-i}, & \text{if } a = v_i \in V \text{ and } 1 \leq i \leq k, \\ \circ^{i-1} \neg \circ^{k-i}, & \text{if } a = \bar{v}_i \in \bar{V} \text{ and } 1 \leq i \leq k, \\ \lambda, & \text{if } a = v_i \text{ or } a = \bar{v}_i \text{ for some } i > k, \\ a, & \text{if } a \in \Sigma_0. \end{cases}$$

Using Ψ, we obtain the language $L_{3SAT} = \{ \Psi(\alpha) \mid \alpha \in \text{3SAT} \}$ from 3SAT.

In [134], an ORWW-automaton $M = (Q, \Sigma, \Gamma, \rhd, \lhd, q_0, \delta, >)$ is presented such that the language $L(M)$ contains L_{3SAT}. In addition, for a normalized propositional formula α that is in the conjunctive normal form of degree 3, α is satisfiable, that is, $\alpha \in$ 3SAT, if and only if $\Psi(\alpha) \in L(M)$. This shows that Ψ is a reduction from 3SAT to $L(M)$. As Ψ is obviously computable in logarithmically bounded space, this proves that $L(M)$ is NP-complete with respect to log-space reductions. □

In the following, we present a 'Cut-and-Paste Lemma' for ORWW-automata that can be used to prove that certain languages are not accepted by ORWW-automata. First, however, we need the following technical lemma.

Lemma 2.3.70 *For each ORWW-automaton $M = (Q, \Sigma, \Gamma, \rhd, \lhd, q_0, \delta, >)$, there exists an ORWW-automaton $M' = (Q, \Sigma, \Gamma', \rhd, \lhd, q_0, \delta', >')$ such that $L(M') = L(M)$, but M' only halts (accepting or non-accepting) with the left sentinel $\rhd$ in its window.*

Proof. Let $M = (Q, \Sigma, \Gamma, \rhd, \lhd, q_0, \delta, >)$ be an ORWW-automaton. Each computation of M consists of a finite sequence of cycles that is followed by a tail computation, which either ends with an accept instruction or by reaching a configuration in which M gets stuck. We now modify M into an ORWW-automaton $M' = (Q, \Sigma, \Gamma', \rhd, \lhd, q_0, \delta', >')$ by taking $\Gamma' = \Gamma \cup \{@, \circledR\}$, by extending the partial ordering $>$ to $>'$ by taking $x >' @$ and $x >' \circledR$ for all $x \in \Gamma$, and by defining the transition relation δ' as follows:

(1) We replace each accept instruction $\mathsf{Accept} \in \delta(q, abc)$ with the rewrite/restart instruction $@ \in \delta'(q, abc)$.

(2) For each $q \in Q$, $a \in \Gamma \cup \{\rhd\}, b \in \Gamma$, and $c \in \Gamma \cup \{\lhd\}$, if $\delta(q, abc) = \emptyset$, then we take $\delta'(q, abc) = \{\circledR\}$.

(3) We introduce the transitions $\delta'(q, ab@) = \{@\}$ and $\delta'(q, ab\text{®}) = \{\text{®}\}$ for all $q \in Q$ and all $a \in \Gamma \cup \{\rhd\}$ and all $b \in \Gamma$.

(4) Finally, we introduce the transitions $\delta'(q_0, \rhd @ b) = \{\mathsf{Accept}\}$ for all $b \in \Gamma \cup \{@, \lhd\}$.

Given an input $w \in \Sigma^+$, each computation of M ends by either an accept step or by reaching a configuration in which M has no applicable transition. In the former case, M' will produce an occurrence of the letter @ by (1), in the latter, it will produce an occurrence of the letter ® by (2). Observe that in the next cycle, M' can move its window all the way to the right until it detects the letter @ or ®, and then it can rewrite all the letters to the left of this newly written letter into the same letter, proceeding from right to left by (3). It follows that M' only halts with the left sentinel in its window. Finally, if and when the first letter to the right of the left sentinel has been rewritten into the letter @, then M' halts and accepts by (4). Hence, it is immediate that $L(M) \subseteq L(M')$ holds.

Notice that even after producing an occurrence of the letter @ or ® on the tape, M' may still apply a rewrite operation of M within the prefix of the tape contents that ends with the letter @ or ®. This, however, means that M could also have executed this rewrite step instead of performing the tail computation that was simulated by M'. Hence, if this additional rewrite step leads to an accepting computation, then this corresponds to an accepting computation of M. Thus, it follows that $L(M') = L(M)$. □

Whenever the marker @ or ® appears as the first letter to the right of the left sentinel $\rhd$, then, proceeding from left to right, M could copy this letter to all other tape cells and then halt at the right sentinel $\lhd$. Thus, instead of requiring that M always halts at the left sentinel, we can also require that M always halts at the right sentinel, if that fits our purpose. We are now ready to state and prove the following result.

Theorem 2.3.71 (Cut-and-Paste Lemma [134])
For each ORWW-automaton M, there exists a computable constant $N(M) > 0$ such that each word $w \in L(M)$, $|w| \geq N(M)$, has a factorization $w = xyz$ satisfying all of the following conditions:

$$(1)\ |yz| \leq N(M),\ (2)\ |y| > 0,\ \textit{and}\ (3)\ xz \in L(M).$$

Proof outline. Let $M = (Q, \Sigma, \Gamma, \rhd, \lhd, q_0, \delta, >)$ be an ORWW-automaton, let $Q = \{q_0, q_1, \ldots, q_k\}$, and let $\Gamma = \{s_1, s_2, \ldots, s_n\}$. By Lemma 2.3.70, we may assume that M accepts at the left end of its tape, that is, it accepts in state q_0 with its window containing the left sentinel $\rhd$ and the first two letters of the proper tape inscription. The transition relation δ of M can be represented by a finite set of five-tuples of the form (q, a, b, c, r), where $q \in Q$, $a \in \Gamma \cup \{\rhd\}$, $b \in \Gamma$, $c \in \Gamma \cup \{\lhd\}$, and $r \in Q \cup \Gamma \cup \{\mathsf{Accept}\}$. Here a five-tuple (q, a, b, c, q') with $q' \in Q$ represents the move-right operation $(q', \mathsf{MVR}) \in \delta(q, abc)$, and a five-tuple (q, a, b, c, d) with $d \in \Gamma$ represents the rewrite/restart operation $d \in \delta(q, abc)$, and analogously for $(q, a, b, c, \mathsf{Accept})$. As $|Q| = k + 1$ and $|\Gamma| = n$, we see that this set consists of $K \leq (k+1) \cdot n \cdot (n+1)^2 \cdot (k+n+2)$ many five-tuples. Accordingly, we can introduce a new alphabet $\Omega = \{t_1, t_2, \ldots, t_K\}$ the letters of which are in 1-to-1 correspondence to these five-tuples.

We now consider a shortest accepting computation C of M on an input $w_m \in \Sigma^m$, where m is sufficiently large. To each number $j = 0, 1, \ldots, m-2$, we associate a word $x_j \in \Omega^*$ such that x_j describes the sequence of operations that are performed within the computation C at position $m-j$, that is, when the $(m-j)$-th letter of w_m is in the middle of the window of M. This means that x_0 is the sequence of operations that are performed within C on the last letter of w_m, x_1 is the sequence of operations that are performed within C on the last but one letter of w_m, and so forth. Thus, we obtain a sequence of words $X_C = (x_0, x_1, \ldots, x_{m-2})$ over Ω.

Claim. $|x_0| \leq n - 1$, and for all $j = 1, 2, \ldots, m-2$, $|x_{j-1}| \leq |x_j| \leq (j+1) \cdot (n-1)$.

Proof. We proceed by induction on j. For $j = 0$, x_j is the sequence of operations that are performed within C at the right-most position. Hence, x_0 only consists of rewrite/restart operations, and as $|\Gamma| = n$, it follows that $|x_0| \leq (n-1)$.

Now assume that $|x_{j-1}| \leq j \cdot (n-1)$ has been established for some $j \geq 1$. We consider the sequence of operations that is described by the word x_j. This word describes all the rewrite/restart operations and all the move-right operations that are performed within C at position $m - j$. Each move-right operation executed at this position leads to an operation at its right-hand neighbour, that is, at position $m - j + 1$. Hence, the number of these move-right operations is exactly $|x_{j-1}|$, which implies that $|x_{j-1}| \leq |x_j| \leq |x_{j-1}| + (n-1) \leq (j+1) \cdot (n-1)$, which completes the proof of the claim. □

Finally, we extend each word x_j into $a_j x_j s_j$, where a_j is the input letter at position $m - j$ and s_j is the letter from Γ into which the input letter a_j is being rewritten by the sequence of operations x_j. Now we consider the sequence $(a_0 x_0 s_0, a_1 x_1 s_1, \ldots, a_{m-2} x_{m-2} s_{m-2})$ over $\Omega \cup \Gamma$.

To determine the constant $N(M)$, we use Higman's theorem [68] (see also [34]). Let $g : \mathbb{N} \to \mathbb{N}$ denote the function $g(x) = x + n - 1$. Then we see from Claim 1 that

$$|a_j x_j s_j| = |x_j| + 2 \leq (j+1) \cdot (n-1) + 2 = j \cdot (n-1) + n + 1 = g^j(n+1),$$

that is, the sequence $(a_j x_j s_j)_{j \geq 0}$ is controlled by $(g, n+1)$. Finally, let $\mathrm{Hig}(\omega^{K+n}, 2, g)(n+1)$ be the least positive integer N such that, for each $(g, n+1)$-controlled sequence $\sigma_0, \sigma_1, \ldots, \sigma_N$ of words over $\Omega \cup \Gamma$, there exist indices $0 \leq j_1 < j_2 \leq N$ such that σ_{j_1} is a scattered subword of σ_{j_2}. The function Hig is called the *Higman function* in [34], and Higman's theorem says that Hig is a total function.

Now, we choose $N(M) = \mathrm{Hig}(\omega^{K+n}, 2, g)(n+1) + 2$. If $m \geq N(M)$, then we see from the definition of the function Hig that there are indices $0 \leq j_1 < j_2 \leq m - 2$ such that $a_{j_1} x_{j_1} s_{j_1}$ is a scattered subword of $a_{j_2} x_{j_2} s_{j_2}$. Thus, $a_{j_1} = a_{j_2}$, $s_{j_1} = s_{j_2}$, and if $x_{j_1} = t_1 t_2 \cdots t_r$ for some $r \geq 1$ and $t_1, t_2, \ldots, t_r \in \Omega$, then x_{j_2} can be written as $x_{j_2} = y_0 t_1 y_1 t_2 y_2 \cdots y_{r-1} t_r y_r$ for some words $y_0, y_1, y_2, \ldots, y_r \in \Omega^*$.

The subsequence of rewrite operations of x_{j_1} rewrites the input letter a_{j_1} into the letter s_{j_1}, and the subsequence of rewrite operations of x_{j_2} rewrites the input letter $a_{j_2} = a_{j_1}$ into the letter $s_{j_2} = s_{j_1}$. Hence, as the former is a scattered subsequence of the latter, it follows that actually the same rewrite operations occur in x_{j_2} and in x_{j_1}, and they occur in the same order. In particular, this means that the factors $y_0, y_1, \ldots, y_r$ only consist of move-right operations.

Next, we take x as the prefix of w_m up to position $m - j_2$, y as the factor of w_m from positions $m - j_2 + 1$ to $m - j_1$, and z as the remaining suffix of w_m. Then $w_m = xyz$, $|yz| \leq N(M)$ and $|y| = j_2 - j_1 > 0$. Finally, let $w' = xz$. Then M has an accepting computation C' for input w'. This computation is obtained from the computation C as follows.

Let $(C_1, C_2, \ldots, C_\mu)$ be the sequence of cycles of the computation C. We consider these cycles in turn, proceeding from C_1 to C_μ. Let $j \in \{1, 2, \ldots, \mu\}$, and let C_j be the cycle currently considered.

1. If the rewrite step in C_j is performed on the prefix of length $m - j_2$ of the current tape, then we append C_j to C'. This includes, in particular, all those cycles that include a rewrite operation at position $m - j_2$, that is, the rewrite operations encoded within the word x_{j_2}.

2. If C_j includes a move-right step at position $m - j_2$ that contributes a letter to one of the factors $y_0, y_1, \ldots, y_r$ of x_{j_2}, then C_j is not appended to C'.

3. Finally, if C_j includes a move-right operation at position $m - j_2$ that corresponds to a letter t_l of the word x_{j_2} for some $1 \leq l \leq r$, then we combine the initial part of this cycle, up to the point where the operation t_l is executed at position $m - j_2$, with the final part of the cycle which starts with this very operation at position $m - j_1$. The resulting cycle C'_j is appended to C'. Observe that due to the fact that $x_{j_1} = t_1 t_2 \cdots t_r$ is a scattered subword of x_{j_2}, C'_j is indeed a valid cycle of M.

The computation C' is completed by appending the accepting tail of C to it. Then it can be checked that C' is an accepting computation of M on input w'. □

It follows from the Cut-and-Paste Lemma that the emptiness problem for ORWW-automata is decidable.

Theorem 2.3.72 ([134]) *The following emptiness problem is decidable:*

INSTANCE	:	*An ORWW-automaton M.*
QUESTION	:	*Is $L(M) \neq \emptyset$?*

Proof. Let $M = (Q, \Sigma, \Gamma, \triangleright, \triangleleft, q_0, \delta, >)$ be an ORWW-automaton, and let $N(M)$ be the corresponding constant from the Cut-and-Paste Lemma. As shown in the proof above, $N(M) = \text{Hig}(\omega^{K+n}, 2, g)(n+1) + 2$, where Hig is the so-called Higman function, which is recursive. It now follows that $L(M) \neq \emptyset$ if and only if $L(M)$ contains a word of length at most $N(M)$. As the membership problem for $L(M)$ is decidable, this means that we can enumerate all input words up to length $N(M)$ and check each of them for membership in $L(M)$. Thus, emptiness of $L(M)$ is decidable. □

Notice that the Higman function grows very fast, which means that the algorithm for the emptiness problem described above is by no means practical.

Problem 2.3.73 *Can the emptiness problem for ORWW-automata be solved in a more efficient way?*

Let M be an ORWW-automaton. The Cut-and-Paste Lemma tells us that a factor of the *suffix* of a sufficiently long word from $L(M)$ can be deleted in such a way that the resulting word still belongs to $L(M)$. In a sense, this corresponds to the exponent $i = 0$ in the Pumping Lemma for regular languages (Lemma 1.2.78). However, there is also a Pumping Lemma for ORWW-automata that corresponds to the positive exponents of the Pumping Lemma for regular languages.

Theorem 2.3.74 (Pumping Lemma [133])
For each ORWW-automaton M, there exists a computable constant $N_p(M) > 0$ such that each word $w \in L(M)$, $|w| \geq N_p(M)$, has a factorization $w = xyz$ satisfying all of the following conditions:

$$(1)\ |xy| \leq N_p(M),\ (2)\ |y| > 0,\ \textit{and}\ (3)\ xy^m z \in L(M)\ \textit{for all}\ m \geq 1.$$

Thus, this Pumping Lemma tells us that a non-empty factor of the *prefix* of a sufficiently long word from $L(M)$ can be iterated such that all resulting words belong to $L(M)$.

Proof outline. Let $M = (Q, \Sigma, \Gamma, \triangleright, \triangleleft, q_0, \delta, >)$ be an ORWW-automaton. By Lemma 2.3.70, we can assume that M accepts at the left sentinel. As seen in the proof of the Cut-and-Paste Lemma, the transition relation of M can be represented by a set of five-tuples of the form (q, a, b, c, r), where $q \in Q$, $a \in \Gamma \cup \{\triangleright\}$, $b \in \Gamma$, $c \in \Gamma \cup \{\triangleleft\}$, and $r \in Q \cup \Gamma \cup \{\mathsf{Accept}\}$. Let Ω be a new alphabet, the letters of which are in 1-to-1 correspondence to these five-tuples.

Let $w \in L(M)$ and let C be an accepting computation of M on input w. With each integer i, $1 \leq i \leq |w|$, we associate a word $\sigma_i^C \in \Omega^*$ that corresponds to the sequence of operations that M executes within the computation C at position i, that is, when the i-th letter is in the middle of the window. Let $\sigma_i^C = t_{j_1} t_{j_2} \cdots t_{j_s}$, where $t_{j_r} \in \Omega$ for all $1 \leq r \leq s$. If $t_{j_r} = (q_1, a_1, a_2, a_3, o_1)$ and $t_{j_{r+1}} = (q_2, b_1, b_2, b_3, o_2)$, then $a_1 \geq b_1$, $a_2 \geq b_2$, and $a_3 \geq b_3$. In addition, if $o_1 = q' \in Q$, that is, it represents a move-right operation, then $a_2 = b_2$, and if $o_1 = b \in \Gamma$, that is, it represents a rewrite/restart operation, then $a_2 > b = b_2$. Now the *pattern* $\tau_i^C \in \Omega^*$ is the word that is obtained from σ_i^C by condensing consecutive identical letters into a single letter. Observe that only sequences of MVR operations are condensed.

For two patterns τ_1^C and τ_2^C, we write $\tau_1^C \sqsubseteq \tau_2^C$ if τ_1^C is a *scattered subword* of τ_2^C, that is, if $\tau_1^C = \omega_1 \omega_2 \cdots \omega_m$ for some $\omega_1, \omega_2, \ldots, \omega_m \in \Omega$, then there are words $y_0, y_1, \ldots, y_m \in \Omega^*$ such that $\tau_2^C = y_0 \omega_1 y_1 \omega_2 y_2 \cdots y_{m-1} \omega_m y_m$. Concerning these patterns, the following results can be proved (see [133]).

Claim 1. Let C be an accepting computation of M for the input w, and let $1 \leq i < j \leq |w|$ be indices such that $\tau_i^C(w) \sqsubseteq \tau_j^C(w)$ and these two patterns contain the same rewrite operations. Then w can be written as $w = xyz$, where $|x| = i$ and $|y| = j - i$, such that $xyyz \in L(M)$. In fact, there exists an accepting computation C' for $xyyz$ satisfying $\tau_i^{C'}(xyyz) = \tau_j^{C'}(xyyz)$.

The ORWW-automaton $M = (Q, \Sigma, \Gamma, \rhd, \lhd, q_0, \delta, >)$ is said to have *deterministic MVR operations* if, for all $q \in Q$ and all $a, b, c \in \Gamma \cup \{\rhd, \lhd\}$, $\delta(q, abc)$ contains at most a single MVR operation. This notion was introduced in [173] for general restarting automata under the name of *det-MVR$_1$-form*. Using the well-known powerset construction, it can be shown that, for each ORWW-automaton M, there exists an ORWW-automaton M' with deterministic MVR operations that accepts the same language as M. If M accepts at the left sentinel, then so does M'. Hence, we may assume, without loss of generality, that the ORWW-automaton M has deterministic MVR operations.

Claim 2. From M, a constant $N_p(M) > 0$ can be computed such that, for each $w \in L(M)$ with $|w| \geq N_p(M)$ and each accepting computation C of M on input w, there are indices $1 \leq i < j \leq N_p(M)$ such that $\tau_i^C(w) \sqsubseteq \tau_j^C(w)$ and these patterns contain the same rewrite operations.

Now we can complete the proof as follows. By Claim 2, a constant $N_p(M)$ can be computed such that, for each $w \in L(M)$ satisfying $|w| \geq N_p(M)$, and each accepting computation C of M on input w, there are indices $1 \leq i < j \leq N_p(M)$ such that $\tau_i^C(w) \sqsubseteq \tau_j^C(w)$ and these patterns contain the same rewrite operations. Hence, by Claim 1, w can be factored as $w = xyz$ such that $|xy| \leq N_p(M)$, $|y| > 0$, $xyyz \in L(M)$, and $\tau_{|x|}^{C'}(xyyz) = \tau_{|xy|}^{C'}(xyyz)$, where C' is the accepting computation of M for input $xyyz$ that is obtained from the computation C. Using Claim 1 repeatedly, we obtain that $xy^mz \in L(M)$ holds for all $m \geq 1$. □

Above we used the Cut-and-Paste Lemma to prove that emptiness is decidable for ORWW-automata. Based on the Pumping Lemma, we can now show that finiteness is also decidable for ORWW-automata.

Theorem 2.3.75 ([133]) *The following* finiteness problem *is decidable:*

INSTANCE: *An ORWW-automaton M.*

QUESTION: *Is the language L(M) finite?*

Proof. Let $M = (Q, \Sigma, \Gamma, \rhd, \lhd, q_0, \delta, >)$ be an ORWW-automaton, let $N_c(M)$ be the corresponding constant from the Cut-and-Paste Lemma for M, and $N_p(M)$ be the corresponding constant from the Pumping Lemma for M. We claim that $L(M)$ is finite iff it does not contain any word w such that $N_p(M) \leq |w| \leq N_p(M) + N_c(M)$.

Indeed, if $L(M)$ contains a word w such that $N_p(M) \leq |w| \leq N_p(M) + N_c(M)$, then the Pumping Lemma tells us that $L(M)$ is infinite. Conversely, if $L(M)$ is infinite, then it contains a word w of length at least $N_p(M)$. Assume that w is the shortest word with these properties. If $|w| \leq N_p(M)+N_c(M)$, then there is nothing to prove. On the other hand, if $|w| > N_p(M)+N_c(M)$, then we can apply the Cut-and-Paste Lemma to w, which yields a factorization $w = xyz$ such that $|yz| \leq N_c(M)$, $|y| > 0$, and $xz \in L(M)$. Thus, $|w| > |xz| = |w| - |y| \geq |w| - N_c(M) > N_p(M)$, which contradicts our choice of w. Hence, we see that $L(M)$ is infinite iff it contains a word w such that $N_p(M) \leq |w| \leq N_p(M) + N_c(M)$. Therefore, in order to check whether the language $L(M)$ is finite, we just check membership in $L(M)$ for all words w satisfying $N_p(M) \leq |w| \leq N_p(M) + N_c(M)$. □

Again we notice that the above algorithm for solving the finiteness problem for ORWW-automata is by no means practical.

Problem 2.3.76 *Can the finiteness problem for ORWW-automata be solved in a more efficient way?*

As seen above, ORWW-automata are quite powerful. In addition, the language class $\mathcal{L}(\mathsf{ORWW})$ is an Abstract Family of Languages. In fact, this class has the following closure properties.

Theorem 2.3.77 ([134]) *The language class $\mathcal{L}(\mathsf{ORWW})$ is closed under union, intersection, product, Kleene star, inverse morphisms, and non-erasing morphisms.*

Proof outline. For $i = 1, 2$, let $M_i = (Q_i, \Sigma, \Gamma_i, \rhd, \lhd, q_0^{(i)}, \delta_i, >_i)$ be an ORWW-automaton such that $L(M_i) = L_i$. By Lemma 2.3.70, we can assume that M_i only halts (accepting or non-accepting) with the left sentinel $\rhd$ in its window.

Closure under intersection and union: From M_1 and M_2, we can construct an ORWW-automaton M for $L = L_1 \cap L_2$ on the alphabet $\Delta = \Sigma \cup \{ [a, b] \mid a \in \Gamma_1, b \in \Gamma_2 \}$ that works as follows:

(1) From right to left, M rewrites each input letter a into the pair $[a, a]$.

(2) Then M simulates M_1 using the first component of each letter.

(3) If and when M_1 accepts, which happens at the left sentinel $\rhd$, then M simulates M_2 using the second component of each letter. If M_2 accepts, then so does M.

Obviously, $L(M) = L_1 \cap L_2$ follows.

To obtain an ORWW-automaton M' such that $L(M') = L(M_1) \cup L(M_2)$, we modify the above construction of M in that, in step (3), M' halts and accepts, if M_1 accepts. On the other hand, if the computation of M_1 simulated by M' is non-accepting, then it still ends at the left sentinel, and then M' can continue in the same way as M. It follows that $L(M') = L(M_1) \cup L(M_2)$.

Closure under product: An ORWW-automaton $M = (Q, \Sigma, \Gamma, \rhd, \lhd, q_0, \delta, >)$ for the language $L(M_1) \cdot L(M_2)$ works as follows:

1. Given a word $w \in \Sigma^*$ as input, M rewrites w from right to left, letter by letter, such that each letter of a suffix v of w is marked by an index 2, and then each letter of the corresponding prefix u is marked by an index 1. In this way, $w \in \Sigma^*$ is (nondeterministically) split into $w = uv$ with the idea that $u \in L(M_1)$ and $v \in L(M_2)$ are to be checked.

2. After the first letter of w has been marked by an index 1, M simulates the automaton M_1 on the prefix u. During this process, M interprets the left-most occurrence of a letter with index 2 as the right sentinel $\lhd$.

3. If and when the simulated computation of M_1 on u accepts, then M simulates M_2 on the suffix v. During this process, M simply ignores the prefix of letters with index 1. Now M accepts if this computation of M_2 accepts.

Closure under Kleene star: Here the idea is essentially the same as for the operation of product. Given a word $w \in \Sigma^*$ as input, M rewrites the word from right to left, letter by letter, attaching indices 1 or 2 to these letters. In this way, a factorization $w = u_1 u_2 \cdots u_m$ is chosen nondeterministically, and it remains to check that $u_1, u_2, \ldots, u_m \in L(M_1)$. This can be done as above, using two copies of the automaton M_1, where the one works on an alphabet in which all letters have index 1, and the other one works on an alphabet in which all letters have index 2.

Closure under inverse morphisms: Let $f : \Sigma'^* \to \Sigma^*$ be a morphism. We describe an ORWW-automaton $M' = (Q', \Sigma', \Gamma', \rhd, \lhd, q_0', \delta', >')$ such that

$$L(M') = f^{-1}(L(M_1)) = \{ w \in \Sigma'^* \mid f(w) \in L(M_1) \}.$$

Here we assume that the automaton M_1 always halts at the right sentinel (see the remark following Lemma 2.3.70).

Basically, the automaton M' proceeds as follows. Given an input $w = a_1 a_2 \cdots a_n \in \Sigma'^*$, it rewrites each letter $a_i \in \Sigma'$, proceeding from right to left, by its image $f(a_i) \in \Sigma^*$, and then it simulates a computation of M_1 on input $f(w)$. However, there are two problems that we need to overcome. First, the length of a word $f(a_i)$ may be larger than one. Accordingly, Γ' will contain block letters of the form $[u]$ that represent a word from $u \in \Sigma^+$ of length up to $\mu = \max\{ |f(a)| \mid a \in \Sigma' \}$. Secondly, it may happen that $f(a) = \lambda$ for some letters $a \in \Sigma^*$. In this situation, a will be rewritten into a letter $[u]^c \in \Gamma'$ representing a copy of its right-hand neighbour $[u]$. Of course, there can be several of these copy letters in a row. In the course of a computation, they will always be updated from right to left. As these copy letters may separate the block letters on the tape from each other, M' must carry information on the last block letter it has seen when moving to the right. For the details, we refer to [134].

Closure under non-erasing morphisms: Let $f : \Sigma^* \to \Omega^*$ be a non-erasing morphism, that is, $f(a) \neq \lambda$ for each letter $a \in \Sigma$. We describe an ORWW-automaton $M' = (Q', \Omega, \Gamma', \triangleright, \triangleleft, q_0', \Delta, >')$ such that $L(M') = f(L(M_1))$. Basically, M' proceeds as follows.

Given a word $w \in \Omega^*$ as input, M' first guesses a factorization $u_1 u_2 \cdots u_m$ of w such that, for each $i = 1, 2, \ldots, m$, $|u_i| \leq \mu = \max\{\, |f(a)| \mid a \in \Sigma\,\}$. This is done by marking the letters of w, one by one, from right to left, by indices 1 and 2 (see above). Each factor u_i is a candidate for an image of a letter under the morphism f. Then, processing the factors u_i from right to left, M' checks whether $u_i = f(a)$ for some letter $a \in \Sigma$. In the negative, it halts immediately without accepting, while in the affirmative, it nondeterministically chooses a letter $a_i \in \Sigma$ satisfying $f(a_i) = u_i$ and rewrites u_i into the word $[a_i]^c \ldots [a_i]^c[a_i]$, that is, the last letter of u_i is rewritten into a block letter that encodes the letter $a_i \in \Sigma$, and all the other letters of u_i (if any) are rewritten into corresponding copy letters. Thereafter, M' simulates a computation of M_1 on the input $a_1 a_2 \cdots a_m$. It follows that M' accepts on input $w \in \Omega^*$ if and only if there exists a word $u \in \Sigma^*$ such that $f(u) = w$ and $u \in L(M_1)$, that is, if and only if $w \in f(L(M_1))$. □

On the other hand, the following lemma shows that the linear language

$$L_{\leq} = \{\, a^m b^n \mid 1 \leq m \leq n \,\}$$

is not accepted by any ORWW-automaton.

Lemma 2.3.78 $L_{\leq} \notin \mathcal{L}(\mathsf{ORWW})$.

Proof. Assume to the contrary that there is an ORWW-automaton $M = (Q, \Sigma, \Gamma, \triangleright, \triangleleft, q_0, \delta, >)$ such that $L(M) = L_{\leq}$, and let $N(M)$ be the corresponding constant from the Cut-and-Paste Lemma (Theorem 2.3.71). We consider the word $w = a^{N(M)} b^{N(M)} \in L_{\leq}$. Then w admits a factorization $w = xyz$ such that $|yz| \leq N(M)$, $|y| > 0$, and $w' = xz \in L_{\leq}$. From the two factorizations of w, we see that $y = b^i$ for some $i > 0$, which implies that $w' = a^{N(M)} b^{N(M)-i} \notin L_{\leq}$, a contradiction. It follows that $L_{\leq}$ is not accepted by any ORWW-automaton. □

Thus, we obtain the following incomparability results. Recall that DLIN denotes the class of deterministic linear languages, that is, those languages that are accepted by deterministic one-turn pushdown automata (see Definition 1.2.55).

Theorem 2.3.79 ([134]) *The language class $\mathcal{L}(\mathsf{ORWW})$ is an Abstract Family of Languages that is incomparable to the language classes DLIN, LIN, DCFL, CFL, CRL, and GCSL with respect to inclusion.*

Finally, Lemma 2.3.78 also allows us to derive the following non-closure properties.

Theorem 2.3.80 *The language class $\mathcal{L}(\mathsf{ORWW})$ is neither closed under the operation of reversal nor under complementation.*

Proof outline. Using the technique from the proof of Lemma 2.3.68, it can be shown that the language $L_{\geq} = \{\, b^m a^n \mid m \geq n \geq 1\,\}$ is accepted by some ORWW-automaton. As $L_{\leq} = L_{\geq}^R$, Lemma 2.3.78 implies that the language class $\mathcal{L}(\mathsf{ORWW})$ is not closed under the operation of reversal.

Obviously, also the language $L'_{\geq} = \{\, a^m b^n \mid m \geq n \geq 1\,\}$ is accepted by some ORWW-automaton. Assume that its complement $(L'_{\geq})^c$ is accepted by some ORWW-automaton. Then also the language $(L'_{\geq})^c \cap (\{a\}^+ \cdot \{b\}^+)$ is accepted by some ORWW-automaton, since all regular languages are accepted by these automata and $\mathcal{L}(\mathsf{ORWW})$ is closed under intersection. However,

$$(L'_{\geq})^c \cap (\{a\}^+ \cdot \{b\}^+) = \{\, a^m b^n \mid 1 \leq m < n \,\},$$

and in analogy to the proof of Lemma 2.3.78, it can be shown that this language is not accepted by any ORWW-automaton, either. Thus, it follows that $\mathcal{L}(\mathsf{ORWW})$ is not closed under complementation. □

Now that we have studied the language classes $\mathcal{L}(\mathsf{ORRWW})$ and $\mathcal{L}(\mathsf{ORWW})$ in detail, we turn to the corresponding deterministic classes. It is clear that a DFA can be simulated by a det-ORWW-automaton that does not execute any rewrite/restart steps at all, and so,

$$\mathsf{REG} \subseteq \mathcal{L}(\mathsf{det\text{-}ORWW}) \subseteq \mathcal{L}(\mathsf{det\text{-}ORRWW}).$$

Actually, the stateless det-ORWW-automata are already as expressive as the variants with states.

Proposition 2.3.81 ([195]) *For each det-ORWW-automaton $M = (Q, \Sigma, \Gamma, \rhd, \lhd, q_0, \delta, >)$, there exists a stateless det-ORWW-automaton $M' = (\Sigma, \Theta, \rhd, \lhd, \delta', >')$ such that $L(M') = L(M)$.*

Proof outline. The stl-det-ORWW-automaton M' needs to store the actual state of M on its tape. Accordingly, we construct M' from M as follows:

- $\Theta = \Gamma \cup \{\, [a, q, b] \mid q \in Q, a, b \in \Gamma \,\} \cup \{\, [\rhd, q_0, a] \mid a \in \Gamma \,\}$,
- for all $a, b \in \Gamma$, $c \in \Gamma \cup \{\rhd\}$, and $q \in Q$, if $a > b$, then $a >' [c, q, a] >' b$,
- δ' is defined as follows, where $a, b, c, A, B, C \in \Gamma$, $d \in \Gamma \cup \{\lhd\}$, and $p, q, r \in Q$:

$$\begin{array}{rlcll}
(1) & \delta'(\rhd u \lhd) & = & \mathsf{Accept} & \text{for all } u \in (\Sigma \cup \{\lambda\}) \cap L(M),\\
(2) & \delta'(\rhd ab) & = & [\rhd, q_0, a], & \\
(3) & \delta'(\rhd [\rhd, q_0, a] b) & = & A, & \text{if } \delta(q_0, \rhd ab) = A,\\
(4) & \delta'(\rhd [\rhd, q_0, a] b) & = & \mathsf{MVR}, & \text{if } \delta(q_0, \rhd ab) = (p, \mathsf{MVR}),\\
(5) & \delta'([\rhd, q_0, a] bd) & = & [a, p, b], & \text{if } \delta(q_0, \rhd ab) = (p, \mathsf{MVR}),\\
(6) & \delta'(\rhd [\rhd, q_0, a] b) & = & \mathsf{Accept}, & \text{if } \delta(q_0, \rhd ab) = \mathsf{Accept},\\
(7) & \delta'([\rhd, q_0, a][a, p, b] d) & = & B, & \text{if } \delta(p, abd) = B,\\
(8) & \delta'([\rhd, q_0, a][a, p, b] c) & = & \mathsf{MVR}, & \text{if } \delta(p, abc) = (q, \mathsf{MVR}),\\
(9) & \delta'([a, p, b] cd) & = & [b, q, c], & \text{if } \delta(p, abc) = (q, \mathsf{MVR}),\\
(10) & \delta'([\rhd, q_0, a][a, p, b] d) & = & \mathsf{Accept}, & \text{if } \delta(p, abd) = \mathsf{Accept},\\
(11) & \delta'(\rhd [\rhd, q_0, a][a, p, b]) & = & \mathsf{MVR}, & \\
(12) & \delta'([a, p, b][b, q, A][A, r, B]) & = & \mathsf{MVR}, & \\
(13) & \delta'([a, p, b][b, q, A] d) & = & C, & \text{if } \delta(q, bAd) = C,\\
(14) & \delta'([a, p, b][b, q, A] B) & = & \mathsf{MVR}, & \text{if } \delta(q, bAB) = (r, \mathsf{MVR}),\\
(15) & \delta'([b, q, A] Bd) & = & [A, r, B], & \text{if } \delta(q, bAB) = (r, \mathsf{MVR}),\\
(16) & \delta'([a, p, b][b, q, A] d) & = & \mathsf{Accept}, & \text{if } \delta(q, bAd) = \mathsf{Accept}.
\end{array}$$

For an input $u \in \Sigma \cup \{\lambda\}$, M' will accept immediately if and when $u \in L(M)$ holds. So let us consider an input $w = a_1 a_2 \cdots a_n$, where $n \geq 2$ and $a_1, a_2, \ldots, a_n \in \Sigma$. The ORWW-automaton M will scan the input from left to right until it detects the first letter, say a_i, that is to be rewritten into b, that is, M executes the following cycle:

$$q_0 \rhd a_1 a_2 \cdots a_n \lhd \vdash_M^{i-1} \rhd a_1 \cdots a_{i-2} q_{i-1} a_{i-1} a_i a_{i+1} \cdots a_n \lhd \vdash_M q_0 \rhd a_1 a_2 \cdots a_{i-1} b a_{i+1} \cdots a_n \lhd .$$

Now M' will simulate this cycle as follows:

$$\begin{array}{rl}
\rhd a_1 a_2 \cdots a_n \lhd \ \vdash_{M'}^{c} & \rhd [\rhd, q_0, a_1]\, a_2 \cdots a_n \lhd\\
\vdash_{M'}^{c} & \rhd [\rhd, q_0, a_1][a_1, q_1, a_2]\, a_3 \cdots a_n \lhd\\
\vdash_{M'}^{c^*} & \rhd [\rhd, q_0, a_1] \cdots [a_{i-2}, q_{i-2}, a_{i-1}]\, a_i a_{i+1} \cdots a_n \lhd\\
\vdash_{M'}^{c} & \rhd [\rhd, q_0, a_1] \cdots [a_{i-2}, q_{i-2}, a_{i-1}][a_{i-1}, q_{i-1}, a_i]\, a_{i+1} \cdots a_n \lhd\\
\vdash_{M'}^{c} & \rhd [\rhd, q_0, a_1] \cdots [a_{i-2}, q_{i-2}, a_{i-1}]\, b a_{i+1} \cdots a_n \lhd,
\end{array}$$

that is, scanning the tape from left to right, M' replaces the letter a_j $(1 \leq j \leq i)$ with the triple $[a_{j-1}, q_{j-1}, a_j]$, where $a_0 = \rhd$ and q_{j-1} is the state in which M reaches the window contents

$a_{j-1}a_ja_{j+1}$. When M reaches the letter a_{i+1}, it realizes that it must simulate a rewrite/restart step of M, and accordingly it replaces the triple $[a_{i-1}, q_{i-1}, a_i]$ with the letter b. By induction on the number of cycles that M executes, it can now be shown that $L(M') = L(M)$ holds. □

The next result shows that deterministic ORRWW-automata are not more expressive than deterministic ORWW-automata.

Proposition 2.3.82 ([131]) $\mathcal{L}(\text{det-ORRWW}) \subseteq \mathcal{L}(\text{det-ORWW})$.

Proof outline. Let $M = (Q, \Sigma, \Gamma, \rhd, \lhd, q_0, \delta, >)$ be a det-ORRWW-automaton, and let $L = L(M)$. Without loss of generality, we may assume that M performs restart and accept operations only at the right sentinel $\lhd$. We present a det-ORWW-automaton $M' = (Q', \Sigma, \Gamma', \rhd, \lhd, q_0, \delta', >')$ that simulates M. Each cycle of a computation of M is of the following form, where $u, v \in \Gamma^*$, $a, b, b', c, d, e \in \Gamma$, and $q_1, q_2, q_3 \in Q$:

$$\begin{array}{llllll} q_0 \rhd uabcvde \lhd & \vdash^{1+|u|}_{\text{MVR}} & \rhd uq_1abcvde \lhd & \vdash_{\text{Rewrite}} & \rhd uaq_2b'cvde \lhd \\ & \vdash^{|v|+2}_{\text{MVR}} & \rhd uab'cvq_3de \lhd & \vdash_{\text{Restart}} & q_0 \rhd uab'cvde \lhd, \end{array}$$

and, in the next cycle, M moves its window at least until it contains the newly written letter b' before the next rewrite step can be executed. In order for the det-ORWW-automaton M' to be able to correctly simulate the above cycle, M' must ensure (or verify) in some way that M will indeed perform a restart after the above rewrite operation. Therefore, we let M' perform some kind of preprocessing during which it encodes certain additional information on its tape.

For each word $w \in \Gamma^+$, $|w| \geq 2$, and each letter $a \in \Gamma$, we define two sets $Q^{(a)}_{\text{rs}}(w)$ and $Q^{(a)}_{+}(w)$ of states of M as follows, where $w = w_1bc$ for some $b, c \in \Gamma$:

$$\begin{array}{lll} Q^{(a)}_{\text{rs}}(w) & = & \{ p \in Q \mid \rhd paw \lhd \vdash^{|w|-1}_{\text{MVR}} \rhd aw_1p'bc \lhd \vdash_{\text{Restart}} q_0 \rhd aw \lhd \} \text{ and} \\ Q^{(a)}_{+}(w) & = & \{ p \in Q \mid \rhd paw \lhd \vdash^{|w|-1}_{\text{MVR}} \rhd aw_1p'bc \lhd \vdash_{\text{Accept}} \mathsf{Accept} \}. \end{array}$$

If the det-ORWW-automaton M' is to simulate the above cycle of M, then it sees that M will actually restart at the right end of the tape from the fact that $q_2 \in Q^{(b')}_{\text{rs}}(cvde)$, and hence, it can safely perform the same rewrite operation and restart. Accordingly, we define a precomputation for M' that assigns, from right to left, the collection of sets $(Q^{(a)}_{\text{rs}}(z), Q^{(a)}_{+}(z))_{a\in\Gamma}$ to the first letter z_1 of each suffix z of the given input w. Thus, we define

$$\Gamma' = \Sigma \cup \{ (A, (Q^{(a)}_1, Q^{(a)}_2)_{a\in\Gamma}) \mid A \in \Gamma, Q^{(a)}_1, Q^{(a)}_2 \subseteq Q \},$$

take $Q' = Q \cup \{q_C\}$, define $>'$ by taking $A >' (A, (Q^{(a)}_1, Q^{(a)}_2)_{a\in\Gamma})$ for all $A \in \Gamma$ and $Q^{(a)}_1, Q^{(a)}_2 \subseteq Q$ and $(A, (Q^{(a)}_1, Q^{(a)}_2)_{a\in\Gamma}) >' (B, (P^{(a)}_1, P^{(a)}_2)_{a\in\Gamma})$ if $A > B$ and $Q^{(a)}_1, Q^{(a)}_2, P^{(a)}_1, P^{(a)}_2 \subseteq Q$.

The transition function can now be defined in such a way that M' first encodes the information on the sets $(Q^{(a)}_{\text{rs}}(z), Q^{(a)}_{+}(z))_{a\in\Gamma}$ proceeding from right to left until it detects the position, say i, at which the next rewrite operation of M is to be simulated. Based on the information from the encoded sets of states, it then simulates this rewrite step, updating also the information on the stored sets of states of M at the current position. For this, it can extract the information on the corresponding sets from the letter stored at position $i + 1$. Observe that in the next cycle, M cannot execute a rewrite step until it has the newly written letter in its window, that is, not to the left of position $i - 1$. It can be verified that, in this way, M' can simulate M correctly, implying that $L(M') = L(M)$. It follows that $\mathcal{L}(\text{det-ORRWW}) \subseteq \mathcal{L}(\text{det-ORWW})$, □

Thus, we have the following inclusion and equalities.

Corollary 2.3.83 $\text{REG} \subsetneq \mathcal{L}(\text{stl-det-ORWW}) = \mathcal{L}(\text{det-ORWW}) = \mathcal{L}(\text{det-ORRWW})$.

Next, we introduce the stateless variants of (deterministic) ORRWW-automata. For restarting automata in general, each RR-variant is at least as expressive as the corresponding R-variant, but the situation is not that obvious for stateless automata. The feature of continuing to read the tape after a rewrite step has been executed is problematic for these automata, as they cannot distinguish between the phase of a cycle *before* the rewrite step and the phase *after* the rewrite step. Clearly, this distinction is important, since no rewrite steps may appear in the latter phase. For general restarting automata, this is avoided by using states, but how to deal with this situation for stateless RR-automata?

In [122], this problem has been addressed, and two options for dealing with it have been proposed. First, one can interpret any additional rewrite step within a cycle as a reject. However, this approach amounts to an *external* supervisor that aborts the computation in an unwanted situation. Here, we rather follow the second option presented in [122] in which two *phases* of each cycle are distinguished: the first phase, which ends with the execution of a rewrite operation, and the second phase, which starts after the execution of a rewrite operation and ends with either a restart or an accept step. These two phases are realized by providing two separate transition functions. In [122], the corresponding stateless restarting automata are called *two-phase* restarting automata, but as we only deal with this type of stateless (deterministic) ORRWW-automata, we just call them *stateless (deterministic) ORRWW-automata* (stl-(det-)ORRWW-automata). Formally, these automata are defined as follows.

Definition 2.3.84 *A* stl-ORRWW-automaton *is described by a 7-tuple* $M = (\Sigma, \Gamma, \rhd, \lhd, \delta_1, \delta_2, >)$, *where* Σ, Γ, $\rhd$, $\lhd$, *and* $>$ *are defined as for ORRWW-automata, and*

$$\delta_1 : ((\Gamma \cup \{\rhd\}) \cdot \Gamma \cdot (\Gamma \cup \{\lhd\})) \cup \{\rhd\lhd\} \to \mathcal{P}(\Gamma \cup \{\mathsf{MVR}, \mathsf{Accept}\})$$

and

$$\delta_2 : (\Gamma^{\leq 2} \cdot (\Gamma \cup \{\lhd\})) \to \mathcal{P}(\{\mathsf{MVR}, \mathsf{Restart}, \mathsf{Accept}\})$$

are the transition relations. *Here it is required that* $b > b'$ *holds for each rewrite instruction* $b' \in \delta_1(abc)$.

As it turns out, stateless (deterministic) ORRWW-automata only accept regular languages.

Theorem 2.3.85 ([131]) $\mathcal{L}(\mathsf{stl\text{-}det\text{-}ORRWW}) \subseteq \mathcal{L}(\mathsf{stl\text{-}ORRWW}) \subseteq \mathsf{REG}$.

Proof outline. Let $M = (\Sigma, \Gamma, \rhd, \lhd, \delta_1, \delta_2, >)$ be a stl-ORRWW-automaton. We show that $L(M)$ is a regular language by verifying that the Nerode relation $\sim$ of $L(M)$ has a finite index (see, e.g., [81]). To do so, we proceed as follows.

Let $w \in L(M)$, let m be an integer such that $1 \leq m \leq |w|$, and let C be an accepting computation of M on input w. During this computation, M executes certain operations at position m, that is, when position m is in the middle of the window of M. These operations may include rewrite steps $b' \in \delta_1(abc)$, move-right steps $\mathsf{MVR} \in \delta_1(abc)$ or $\mathsf{MVR} \in \delta_2(abc)$, restart steps $\mathsf{Restart} \in \delta_2(abc)$, and accept steps $\mathsf{Accept} \in \delta_1(abc)$ or $\mathsf{Accept} \in \delta_2(abc)$. As by a rewrite step, the letter in the middle of the window is replaced with a smaller letter with respect to $>$, the rewrite steps that occur at position m are obviously ordered. Before the first rewrite step, and between two successive rewrite steps, a sequence of move-right steps may occur at position m. Here again an ordering is induced by $>$, if one of the letters at position $m-1$ or $m+1$ is rewritten during this part of the computation. It remains the case that a sequence of move-right steps occurs at position m that are all applied to the same window contents abc. Some of them may be δ_1-steps, while others may be δ_2-steps. By associating the number 1 with a positive number of δ_1-steps and the number 2 with a positive number of δ_2-steps, we can assign a *type*

$$t \in (1 \cdot (2 \cdot 1)^* \cdot \{2, \lambda\}) \cup (2 \cdot (1 \cdot 2)^* \cdot \{1, \lambda\})$$

to this sequence. By rearranging the corresponding cycles of the computation C, this computation can be transformed into an equivalent computation C' for which the type of any sequence of move-right steps with the same window contents at position m is from the set

$$T = \{1, 2, 1 \cdot 2, 2 \cdot 1, 1 \cdot 2 \cdot 1, 2 \cdot 1 \cdot 2\}.$$

Additionally, we require that all cycles associated with the same number 1 appear uninterrupted within the computation. We call such a computation *normalized.*

Now let Ω be the following extended set of operations of M, where $a \in \Gamma \cup \{\triangleright\}$, $b, b' \in \Gamma$, and $c \in \Gamma \cup \{\triangleleft\}$:

$$\begin{array}{rcl}\Omega & = & \{\,(a,b,c,b') \mid b' \in \delta_1(abc)\,\} \cup \{\,(a,b,c,t) \mid t \in T\,\} \cup \\ & & \{\,(a,b,c,-) \mid \mathsf{Restart} \in \delta_2(abc)\,\} \cup \{\,(a,b,c,+_i) \mid i = 1,2,\ \mathsf{Accept} \in \delta_i(abc)\,\}.\end{array}$$

Then the sequence of operations that M executes during the computation C' at position m can be described by a word $A_m^{C'}(w) \in \Omega^*$. In fact, as at most $|\Gamma| - 1$ rewrite steps can occur in this sequence, $A_m^{C'}(w)$ is of length $\mathcal{O}(|\Gamma|)$.

With each word $w \in \Sigma^+$, we now associate two sets $S_1(w)$ and $S_2(w)$:

$$\begin{array}{rl} S_1(w) = \{\,A_{|w|}^{C}(wz) \mid & z \in \Sigma^* \text{ and } C \text{ is a normalized computation of } M \text{ for } wz \\ & \text{that accepts at a position} \leq |w|\,\}, \\ S_2(w) = \{\,A_{|w|}^{C}(wz) \mid & z \in \Sigma^* \text{ and } C \text{ is a normalized computation of } M \text{ for } wz \\ & \text{that accepts at a position} > |w|\,\}. \end{array}$$

It can be shown that there are no distinguishing extensions for $x, y \in \Sigma^+$ if $S_i(x) = S_i(y)$ for $i = 1, 2$, that is, if $S_1(x) = S_1(y)$ and $S_2(x) = S_2(y)$, then, for all words $z \in \Sigma^*$, $xz \in L(M)$ if and only if $yz \in L(M)$. Hence, if $S_1(x) = S_1(y)$ and $S_2(x) = S_2(y)$, then $x \sim y$ holds. As there are only finitely many words $A_m^{C'}(w) \in \Omega^*$ that can occur as descriptions of sequences of operations of M, there are only finitely many different sets $S_1(x)$ and $S_2(x)$. Hence, the Nerode relation $\sim$ of $L(M)$ has a finite index, which means that $L(M)$ is indeed a regular language. □

As each stateless ORWW-automaton can easily be interpreted as a stateless ORRWW-automaton, we obtain the following characterizations for the class of regular languages.

Corollary 2.3.86 ([131, 132, 195])

$$\begin{array}{rcccccl}\mathsf{REG} & = & \mathcal{L}(\mathsf{stl\text{-}det\text{-}ORWW}) & = & \mathcal{L}(\mathsf{det\text{-}ORWW}) & = & \mathcal{L}(\mathsf{stl\text{-}ORWW}) \\ & = & \mathcal{L}(\mathsf{stl\text{-}det\text{-}ORRWW}) & = & \mathcal{L}(\mathsf{det\text{-}ORRWW}) & = & \mathcal{L}(\mathsf{stl\text{-}ORRWW}).\end{array}$$

We complete this subsection by presenting an extension of the det-ORWW-automaton, the deterministic ORD-automaton, that has been introduced in [197] and studied in detail in [198].

Definition 2.3.87 *The* deterministic ORD-automaton *(det-ORD-automaton) is obtained from the det-ORWW-automaton by admitting additional delete/restart steps of the form $\delta(q, abc) = \lambda$. Such a delete/restart step erases the letter b from the tape, removes the corresponding tape cell, in this way shortening the tape, and performs a restart. A det-ORD-automaton is called* stateless *(or a* stl-det-ORD-automaton) *if it has just a single state.*

We illustrate this definition by presenting a stateless det-ORD-automaton for the language $L = \{\,a^m b^n \mid m \geq 0, n \in \{m, m+1\}\,\}$.

Example 2.3.88 *Let $M = (\Sigma, \Gamma, \triangleright, \triangleleft, \delta, >)$ be defined by taking $\Sigma = \{a, b\}$, $\Gamma = \Sigma \cup \{a_1, a_2, b_1, b_2\}$, $a > a_1 > a_2$, $b > b_1 > b_2$, and by defining the transition function δ by the following meta-*

instructions, where $c \in \{a,b\}$*:*

(1) $(\rhd \cdot \{\lambda, b, b_1\} \cdot \lhd, \mathsf{Accept})$,
(2) $(\lambda, \rhd ac \to \rhd a_1 c)$,
(3) $(\rhd \cdot \{a_1a_2\}^*, a_1ac \to a_1a_2c)$,
(4) $(\rhd \cdot \{a_1a_2\}^* \cdot a_1, a_2ac \to a_2a_1c)$,
(5) $(\rhd \cdot \{a_1a_2\}^* \cdot b^*, bb\lhd \to bb_1\lhd)$,
(6) $(\rhd \cdot \{a_1a_2\}^* \cdot a_1 \cdot b^*, bb\lhd \to bb_1\lhd)$,
(7) $(\rhd \cdot \{a_1a_2\}^* \cdot b^*, bbb_1 \to bb_2b_1)$,
(8) $(\rhd \cdot \{a_1a_2\}^* \cdot a_1 \cdot b^*, bbb_1 \to bb_2b_1)$,
(9) $(\rhd \cdot \{a_1a_2\}^* \cdot b^*, bbb_2 \to bb_1b_2)$,
(10) $(\rhd \cdot \{a_1a_2\}^* \cdot a_1 \cdot b^*, bbb_2 \to bb_1b_2)$,
(11) $(\rhd \cdot \{a_1a_2\}^* \cdot a_1, a_2bb_1 \to a_2b_2b_1)$,
(12) $(\rhd \cdot \{a_1a_2\}^*, a_1bb_1 \to a_1b_2b_1)$,
(13) $(\rhd \cdot \{a_1a_2\}^* \cdot a_1, a_2bb_2 \to a_2b_1b_2)$,
(14) $(\rhd \cdot \{a_1a_2\}^*, a_1bb_2 \to a_1b_1b_2)$,
(15) $(\rhd \cdot \{a_1a_2\}^* \cdot a_1, a_2a_1b_1 \to a_2b_1)$,
(16) $(\lambda, \rhd a_1b_1 \to \rhd b_1)$,
(17) $(\rhd \cdot \{a_1a_2\}^*, a_1a_2b_2 \to a_1b_2)$,
(18) $(\rhd \cdot \{a_1a_2\}^*, a_1b_2b_1 \to a_1b_1)$,
(19) $(\rhd \cdot \{a_1a_2\}^* \cdot a_1, a_2b_1b_2 \to a_2b_2)$.

Using rules (2) to (4), M marks the letters a from left to right alternatingly with indices 1 and 2, and then, using rules (5) to (14), it marks the letters b from right to left in the same way. Finally, using rules (15) to (19), it deletes the last occurrence of the letter a, if the prefix of a's and the suffix of b's have the same parity mod 2, and it deletes the first occurrence of the letter b, if the parity of the prefix of a's differs from the parity of the suffix of b's. Hence, we see from rule (1) that M accepts on input a^mb^n *if and only if* $m \le n \le m+1$*, that is,* $L(M) = L$*.* ■

From the Pumping Lemma for ORWW-automata (Theorem 2.3.74), it is easily seen that the above language L is not accepted by any ORWW-automaton. In analogy to Proposition 2.3.81, it can be shown that each det-ORD-automaton is equivalent to a stateless det-ORD-automaton. Furthermore, it turns out that det-ORD-automata accept all deterministic context-free languages. This is proved in [198] by providing a simulation of a DPDA by a det-ORD-automaton. In fact, the following inclusion holds.

Theorem 2.3.89 ([198]) $\mathsf{LRR} \cup \mathsf{RLR} \subsetneq \mathcal{L}(\mathsf{stl\text{-}det\text{-}ORD}) = \mathcal{L}(\mathsf{det\text{-}ORD})$.

Proof outline. Let L be generated by an $\mathsf{LR}(\pi)$ grammar. Then according to the proof of Theorem 2.1 of [37], there exists a particular deterministic length-preserving transducer G such that the language $L' = (G(L^R))^R$ is deterministic context-free. Thus, we just need to run this transducer from right to left across a given input w, replacing w letter by letter with the corresponding output, and then check whether the resulting word w' belongs to the language L'. As this simulation of G can easily be performed by a det-ORD-automaton, and as, by the observation above, there exists a det-ORD-automaton for L', we obtain a det-ORD-automaton for the language L. Thus, $\mathsf{LRR} \subseteq \mathcal{L}(\mathsf{det\text{-}ORD}) = \mathcal{L}(\mathsf{stl\text{-}det\text{-}ORD})$ follows.

It can be shown that the language class $\mathcal{L}(\mathsf{stl\text{-}det\text{-}ORD})$ is closed under the operation of reversal. Hence, as $\mathsf{LRR}^R = \mathsf{RLR}$, we see that $\mathsf{RLR} \subseteq \mathcal{L}(\mathsf{stl\text{-}det\text{-}ORD})$, too. Finally, the language

$$L_{\text{3blocks}} = \{\, a^mb^ma^nb^na^pb^p, a^mb^{2m}a^{n+k}b^na^pb^{2p} \mid m,n,k,p \ge 1 \,\},$$

which, according to [37], does not belong to the union $\mathsf{LRR} \cup \mathsf{RLR}$, is accepted by a det-ORD-automaton [198]. This completes the proof. □

Actually, the language class $\mathcal{L}(\mathsf{det\text{-}ORD})$ is closed under quite a few operations. Let $L_1, L_2 \subseteq \Sigma^*$ be two languages, and let $c, d \notin \Sigma$ be two additional letters. Then $\{c\} \cdot L_1 \cup \{d\} \cdot L_2$ is the *marked union* of L_1 and L_2, $L_1 \cdot \{c\} \cdot L_2$ is the *marked product* of L_1 and L_2, and $(\{c\}L_1)^*$ is the *marked iteration* of L_1. Furthermore, let $G = (Q, \Sigma, \Delta, \$, p_0, \delta, \iota, F)$ be a *marked DGSM*, where Q is a finite set of states, Σ is the finite input alphabet, Δ is the finite output alphabet, $\$$ is a special end-of-tape marker for the input, $p_0 \in Q$ is the initial state, $\delta : (Q \times (\Sigma \cup \{\$\})) \to Q$ is the state transition function, and $\iota : Q \times (\Sigma \cup \{\$\}) \to (\Delta^* \cup \Delta^* \cdot \{\$\})$ is the output function, where $\iota(q,a) \in \Delta^*$ for all $q \in Q$ and all $a \in \Sigma$ and $\iota(q,\$) \in \Delta^* \cdot \$$ for all $q \in Q$. Then G defines a transformation from $\Sigma^* \cdot \{\$\}$ to $\Delta^* \cdot \{\$\}$, which is called a *marked GSM-mapping*, and $G^{-1}(L) = \{\, w \in \Sigma^* \mid \iota(p_0, w\$) \in L \cdot \{\$\} \,\}$ is an *inverse marked GSM-mapping*. Following [37], a family of languages that is closed under marked union, marked iteration, and inverse marked GSM mappings is called an *abstract family of deterministic languages*, or an *AFDL*.

Proposition 2.3.90 ([198]) *The language class $\mathcal{L}(\mathsf{det\text{-}ORD})$ is an AFDL that, in addition, is closed under complementation, intersection with regular sets, and reversal.*

However, it can be shown that the class $\mathcal{L}(\mathsf{det\text{-}ORD})$ is not closed under union, intersection, product, iteration (Kleene star), or erasing morphisms. On the other hand, each stl-det-ORD-automaton can be simulated by a PDA. In fact, the PDA simulates the accepting computations of the given stl-det-ORD-automaton. Thus, for each input accepted, the PDA has only a single accepting computation. This means that the language accepted is unambiguously context-free. As the language class $\mathcal{L}(\mathsf{det\text{-}ORD})$ is closed under complementation, this yields the following inclusion, where UCFL denotes the class of *unambiguous context-free languages* and $\mathsf{co\text{-}UCFL}$ denotes the class of complements of the unambiguous context-free languages.

Theorem 2.3.91 ([198]) $\mathcal{L}(\mathsf{det\text{-}ORD}) \subseteq \mathsf{CRL} \cap \mathsf{UCFL} \cap \mathsf{co\text{-}UCFL}$.

It remains open whether this inclusion is proper. In fact, consider the linear language $L_{\text{lin}} = \{ a^n b^n, a^n b^{2n} \mid n \geq 1 \}$. This language is Church-Rosser (see, e.g., [193]), and it is unambiguous context-free. On the other hand, its complement L_{lin}^c can be written as

$$\begin{array}{rcll} L_{\text{lin}}^c & = & (\{a,b\}^* \smallsetminus (\{a\}^+ \cdot \{b\}^+)) & \cup \ \{ a^m b^n \mid m \geq 1, n \notin \{m, 2m\} \} \\ & = & (\{a,b\}^* \smallsetminus (\{a\}^+ \cdot \{b\}^+)) & \cup \ \{ a^m b^n \mid m \geq 1, n < m \} \\ & & & \cup \ \{ a^m b^n \mid m \geq 1, m < n < 2m \} \\ & & & \cup \ \{ a^m b^n \mid m \geq 1, n > 2m \}, \end{array}$$

from which it can be seen that L_{lin}^c is also Church-Rosser and unambiguous context-free. Thus, $L_{\text{lin}} \in \mathsf{CRL} \cap \mathsf{UCFL} \cap \mathsf{Co\text{-}UCFL}$.

Problem 2.3.92 *Is the language L_{lin} accepted by any det-ORD-automaton?*

Also nondeterministic ORD-automata have been studied to some extent. This type of automaton is obtained from the ORWW-automaton by admitting additional delete/restart steps of the form $\lambda \in \delta(q, abc)$. Obviously, the ORD-automaton is an sRWW-automaton that extends the ORWW-automaton. From Example 2.3.88, we see that $\mathcal{L}(\mathsf{ORWW}) \subsetneq \mathcal{L}(\mathsf{ORD}) \subseteq \mathcal{L}(\mathsf{sRWW}) = \mathcal{L}(\mathsf{FC})$, but it is open whether the ORD-automaton is actually less expressive than the sRWW-automaton.

Problem 2.3.93 *Does there exist a language L that is accepted by an sRWW-automaton (or a finite-change automaton) but that is not accepted by any ORD-automaton?*

It remains to consider the *stateless ORD-automaton*, abbreviated as *stl-ORD-automaton*. It is shown in [199] that a PDA can be simulated by a stateless ORD-automaton, which implies that $\mathsf{CFL} \subseteq \mathcal{L}(\mathsf{stl\text{-}ORD})$. In fact, this result can be strengthened as follows, based on the notion of a *swift* ORD-automaton.

Definition 2.3.94 *A stl-ORD-automaton $M = (\Sigma, \Gamma, \rhd, \lhd, \delta, >)$ is called* swift *(or a* swift-ORD-automaton*) if* $\mathsf{MVR} \in \delta(a_1 a_2 a_3)$ *for all $a_1 \in \Gamma \cup \{\rhd\}$ and all $a_2, a_3 \in \Gamma$.*

Thus, from a restarting configuration $\rhd w \lhd$, a swift-ORD-automaton M can move its window to any position on the tape. This means that a computation of M cannot be blocked by a factor across which M cannot move its window. It can be shown that the language considered in Example 2.3.88 is actually accepted by a swift-ORD-automaton. Instead of first rewriting all a's from left to right and only then all b's from right to left, it does not matter in which order the a's and the b's are rewritten. What is important is the observation that the meta-instructions that compare the parity of the length of the prefix of a's to the parity of the length of the suffix of b's (that is, meta-instructions (15) to (19)) can only be applied *after* all a's and all b's have been rewritten. Now the following characterization has been obtained.

Theorem 2.3.95 ([199]) $\mathsf{CFL} = \mathcal{L}(\mathsf{swift\text{-}ORD})$.

A detailed proof, which is technically quite involved, can be found in [201]. However, it remains open whether stl-ORD-automata that are not swift are actually more expressive than swift-ORD-automata.

Problem 2.3.96 *Is there any non-context-free language that is accepted by a stl-ORD-automaton? In fact, is the stl-ORD-automaton at all less expressive than the ORD-automaton with states?*

Also the ORRWW-automaton and its deterministic and/or stateless variants can be extended by introducing delete operations of the form $(q', \lambda) \in \delta(q, abc)$, which would just delete the letter in the middle of the window, remove the corresponding tape cell, move the window one position to the right, and change to state q'. In this way, we obtain the ORRD-automaton and its variants det-ORRD, stl-det-ORRD, and stl-ORRD. As the ORRD-automaton extends the ORRWW-automaton, Corollary 2.3.65 immediately implies that $\mathcal{L}(\mathsf{ORRD}) = \mathcal{L}(\mathsf{ORRWW}) = \mathcal{L}(\mathsf{FC})$. On the other hand, the proof of Proposition 2.3.82 easily extends to ORRD-automata, which yields $\mathcal{L}(\text{det-ORRD}) = \mathcal{L}(\mathsf{det\text{-}ORD})$. Thus, the only case of interest is that of stateless nondeterministic ORRD-automata.

Problem 2.3.97 *What is the expressive capacity of stateless ORRD-automata?*

A diagram showing the relationships between the language classes accepted by the various types of ordered restarting automata can be found at the end of Subsection 2.3.5.

2.3.5 On Shrinking RWW-Automata of Window Size One

Finally, we turn to sRWW-automata of window size one. The first result states that sRWW-automata of window size one can be simulated by ORWW-automata. By Lemma 2.3.78, this implies, in particular, that the linear language $L_{\leq} = \{ a^m b^n \mid 1 \leq m \leq n \}$ is not accepted by any sRWW-automaton of window size one.

Proposition 2.3.98 ([162, 164]) $\mathcal{L}(\mathsf{sRWW}(1)) \subseteq \mathcal{L}(\mathsf{ORWW})$.

Proof outline. Let $M = (Q, \Sigma, \Gamma, \rhd, \lhd, q_0, 1, \delta)$ be a shrinking RWW(1)-automaton that is compatible with the weight function $\varphi : \Gamma \to \mathbb{N}_+$, and let $c = \max\{ \varphi(a) \mid a \in \Sigma \}$ be the maximal weight of an input letter. Without loss of generality, we can assume that M only accepts with its read/write window on the right sentinel $\lhd$.

We define an ORWW-automaton $M_o = (Q, \Sigma, \Delta, \rhd, \lhd, q_0, \delta_o, >)$. First, we take

$$\Delta = \Sigma \cup \{ [\alpha] \mid \alpha \in \Gamma^*, \varphi(\alpha) \leq c \}.$$

Here the letter $[\alpha]$ encodes the word $\alpha \in \Gamma^*$, where the weight $\varphi(\alpha)$ is bounded from above by the constant c. As the weight of each letter $a \in \Gamma$ is positive, we see that there are only finitely many words from Γ^* with weight bounded from above by c. Hence, Δ is indeed a finite alphabet. We define a morphism $\psi : \Delta^* \to \Gamma^*$ through $\psi(a) = a$ for all $a \in \Sigma$ and $\psi([\alpha]) = \alpha$ for all $[\alpha] \in \Delta \smallsetminus \Sigma$, and we define the partial ordering $>$ on Δ by taking, for all $a, b \in \Sigma$, $a > [a]$, and for all $x, y \in \Delta \smallsetminus \Sigma$,

$$x > y \text{ if } \varphi(\psi(x)) > \varphi(\psi(y)).$$

Finally, we specify the transition relation δ_o as follows, where $\vdash_{\mathsf{MVR}}$ denotes the single-step computation relation that is induced by the MVR steps of M, $a, b \in \Sigma$, $u, v, z, \alpha \in \Gamma^*$, $\omega \in \Delta$, $X \in \Gamma$, and $q_1, q_2 \in Q$:

$$\begin{array}{rlcll}
(1) & \delta_o(q_0, \rhd \cdot \lhd) & = & \{\mathsf{Accept}\}, & \text{if } q_0 \rhd \lhd \vdash_{\mathrm{MVR}} \rhd q_1 \lhd \text{ and } \delta(q_1, \lhd) = \{\mathsf{Accept}\},\\
(2) & \delta_o(q_0, \rhd a \lhd) & = & \{[a]\}, & \\
(3) & \delta_o(q_0, \rhd [u] \lhd) & = & \{\mathsf{Accept}\}, & \text{if } q_0 \rhd u \lhd \vdash^{|u|+1}_{\mathrm{MVR}} \rhd u q_1 \lhd \text{ and } \delta(q_1, \lhd) = \{\mathsf{Accept}\},\\
(4) & \delta_o(q_0, \rhd [uXv] \lhd) & \ni & [uzv], & \text{if } q_0 \rhd uXv \lhd \vdash^{|u|+1}_{\mathrm{MVR}} \rhd u q_1 X v \lhd \text{ and } \delta(q_1, X) \ni z,\\
(5) & \delta_o(q_0, \rhd ab) & = & \{[a]\}, & \\
(6) & \delta_o(q_0, \rhd [u] \omega) & \ni & (q_1, \mathsf{MVR}), & \text{if } q_0 \rhd u \psi(\omega) \vdash^{|u|+1}_{\mathrm{MVR}} \rhd u q_1 \psi(\omega),\\
(7) & \delta_o(q_0, \rhd [uXv] \omega) & \ni & [uzv], & \text{if } q_0 \rhd uXv \vdash^{|u|+1}_{\mathrm{MVR}} \rhd u q_1 X v \text{ and } \delta(q_1, X) \ni z,\\
(8) & \delta_o(q_1, [\alpha] ab) & = & \{[a]\}, & \\
(9) & \delta_o(q_1, [\alpha][u] \omega) & \ni & (q_2, \mathsf{MVR}), & \text{if } q_1 u \psi(\omega) \vdash^{|u|}_{\mathrm{MVR}} u q_2 \psi(\omega),\\
(10) & \delta_o(q_1, [\alpha][uXv] \omega) & \ni & [uzv], & \text{if } q_1 uXv \vdash^{|u|}_{\mathrm{MVR}} u q_2 X v \text{ and } \delta(q_2, X) \ni z,\\
(11) & \delta_o(q_1, [\alpha] a \lhd) & = & \{[a]\}, & \\
(12) & \delta_o(q_1, [\alpha][u] \lhd) & = & \{\mathsf{Accept}\}, & \text{if } q_1 u \lhd \vdash^{|u|}_{\mathrm{MVR}} u q_2 \lhd \text{ and } \delta(q_2, \lhd) = \{\mathsf{Accept}\},\\
(13) & \delta_o(q_1, [\alpha][uXv] \lhd) & \ni & [uzv], & \text{if } q_1 uXv \vdash^{|u|}_{\mathrm{MVR}} u q_2 X v \text{ and } \delta(q_2, X) \ni z.
\end{array}$$

Note that instruction (9) also simulates the process of moving over a deleted part of the tape of M, as $\delta_o(q_1, [\alpha][\lambda]\omega) \ni (q_1, \mathsf{MVR})$ for all states $q_1 \in Q$. Each rewrite step of M_o either replaces an input letter a with the corresponding auxiliary letter $[a]$ or it simulates a rewrite step of M on some auxiliary letter. Hence, each rewrite step of M_o replaces the letter in the middle of its window with a smaller one with respect to the partial ordering $>$. Thus, we see that M_o is indeed an ORWW-automaton.

It remains to prove that M_o accepts the same (input) language as M. It is easily seen from the definition of δ_o that M_o accepts on input λ iff M accepts on input λ. So let $w = a_1 a_2 \cdots a_n$ be given as input, where $n \geq 1$ and $a_1, a_2, \ldots, a_n \in \Sigma$. Assume that $w \in L(M)$, that is, M has an accepting computation on input w. As M only accepts with its read/write window on the right sentinel $\lhd$, this computation looks as follows:

$$\begin{array}{rcccccc}
q_0 \rhd w \lhd & = & q_0 \rhd a_1 a_2 \cdots a_n \lhd & \vdash^c_M & q_0 \rhd w_1 \lhd & \vdash^c_M & q_0 \rhd w_2 \lhd\\
\vdash^c_M & & \cdots & \vdash^c_M & q_0 \rhd w_m \lhd & \vdash^+_{\mathrm{MVR}} & \rhd w_m q_+ \lhd\\
\vdash_M & & \mathsf{Accept}, & & & &
\end{array}$$

where $q_+ \in Q$, $\delta(q_+, \lhd) = \{\mathsf{Accept}\}$, and $w_1, w_2, \ldots, w_m \in \Gamma^*$. As M is shrinking with window size one, each word w_i can be factored as $w_i = u_{i,1} u_{i,2} \cdots u_{i,n}$, where $u_{i,j}$ is the factor of w_i that is obtained from the input letter a_i by those rewrite steps in the above computation that have been applied to a_i and to the i-th factors of $w_2, w_3, \ldots, w_{i-1}$.

Now the ORWW-automaton M_o proceeds as follows. On input $w = a_1 a_2 \cdots a_n$, it replaces each letter a_i with the auxiliary letter $[a_i]$ using instructions (2), (5), (8), and (11). Then it simulates the cycles of M by performing the rewrite steps from M's computation within the corresponding auxiliary letters, that is, if in a cycle

$$\begin{array}{rcl}
q_0 \rhd w_i \lhd & = & q_0 \rhd u_{i,1} u_{i,2} \cdots u_{i,j-1} u_{i,j} u_{i,j+1} \cdots u_{i,n} \lhd\\
& \vdash^c_M & q_0 \rhd u_{i,1} u_{i,2} \cdots u_{i,j-1} u_{i+1,j} u_{i,j+1} \cdots u_{i,n} \lhd\\
& = & q_0 \rhd w_{i+1} \lhd
\end{array}$$

the factor $u_{i,j}$ is rewritten into the factor $u_{i+1,j}$, then M_o executes the cycle

$$\begin{array}{rcl}
q_0 \rhd w'_i \lhd & = & q_0 \rhd [u_{i,1}][u_{i,2}] \cdots [u_{i,j-1}][u_{i,j}][u_{i,j+1}] \cdots [u_{i,n}] \lhd\\
& \vdash^c_M & q_0 \rhd [u_{i,1}][u_{i,2}] \cdots [u_{i,j-1}][u_{i+1,j}][u_{i,j+1}] \cdots [u_{i,n}] \lhd\\
& = & q_0 \rhd w'_{i+1} \lhd
\end{array}$$

by rewriting the letter $[u_{i,j}]$ into the letter $[u_{i+1,j}]$ using instruction (4), (7), (10), or (13). Here it is possible that some of the factors $u_{i,j+1}$ to $u_{i,n}$ are just input letters that have not yet been rewritten into auxiliary letters by M_o. Finally, as

$$q_0 \rhd w_m \lhd = q_0 \rhd u_{m,1} u_{m,2} \cdots u_{m,n} \lhd \vdash^*_{\mathrm{MVR}} \rhd u_{m,1} u_{m,2} \cdots u_{m,n} q_+ \lhd$$

and $\delta(q_+, \lhd) = \{\mathsf{Accept}\}$, M_o can execute an accepting tail computation starting from the configuration

$$q_0 \rhd w'_m \lhd = q_0 \rhd [u_{m,1}][u_{m,2}] \cdots [u_{m,n}] \lhd$$

using instructions (3), (6), (9), and (12).

Conversely, it is easily seen that each accepting computation of M_o is just the simulation of an accepting computation of M. Thus, $L(M_0) = L(M)$ follows. □

It is verified easily that each ORD-automaton can be simulated by an sRWW-automaton of window size two. Thus, we have the following chain of inclusions.

Corollary 2.3.99 $\mathsf{REG} \subsetneq \mathcal{L}(\mathsf{sRWW}(1)) \subseteq \mathcal{L}(\mathsf{ORWW}) \subsetneq \mathcal{L}(\mathsf{ORD}) \subseteq \mathcal{L}(\mathsf{sRWW}(2))$.

However, the following questions remain open.

Problem 2.3.100 (a) *Is the inclusion of $\mathcal{L}(\mathsf{sRWW}(1))$ in $\mathcal{L}(\mathsf{ORWW})$ proper?*

(b) *Is the inclusion of $\mathcal{L}(\mathsf{ORD})$ in $\mathcal{L}(\mathsf{sRWW}(2))$ proper?*

(c) *Is the class GCSL contained in $\mathcal{L}(\mathsf{ORD})$?*

For monotone sRWW-automata of window size one, we even have the following result.

Proposition 2.3.101 ([162, 164]) *For each monotone sRWW(1)-automaton M, there exists a stateless ORWW-automaton M_s such that $L(M_s) = L(M)$.*

A detailed proof is given in [164]. This proof, which is technically quite involved, extends the technique used in the proof of Proposition 2.3.98. As a consequence of the above results, we obtain the following inclusions.

Theorem 2.3.102 ([162, 164])

$$\mathsf{REG} = \mathcal{L}(\mathsf{mon\text{-}sRWW}(1)) \subsetneq \mathcal{L}(\mathsf{mon\text{-}RRWW}(1)) \subsetneq \mathcal{L}(\mathsf{mon\text{-}sRRWW}(1)).$$

Proof. Obviously, each regular language is accepted by some monotone sRWW(1)-automaton that does not execute any rewrite step. On the other hand, from Example 2.3.5, we know that the non-regular language

$$L'_2 = \{\, a^m b^n \mid m \in \{n, n+1\}, n \geq 0 \,\}$$

is accepted by a monotone RR(1)-automaton.

Let us extend the RR(1)-automaton M from Example 2.3.5 into a shrinking RRWW(1)-automaton M' as follows: during the first cycle, M' replaces the first occurrence of the letter a on its tape with an auxiliary letter a' and it verifies that the number of a's has the same parity mod 2 as the number of b's. In the affirmative, it then simulates M step by step, interpreting the letter a' in the same way as M would interpret the letter a, while in the negative, it just halts without accepting. Then M' is a monotone sRRWW(1)-automaton for the language $L_2 = \{\, a^m b^m \mid m \geq 0 \,\}$, which is obviously not accepted by any RRWW(1)-automaton.

By Proposition 2.3.101, each monotone sRWW(1)-automaton can be simulated by a stateless ORWW-automaton. As $\mathcal{L}(\mathsf{stl\text{-}ORWW}) = \mathsf{REG}$ according to Corollary 2.3.86, this yields the equality $\mathsf{REG} = \mathcal{L}(\mathsf{mon\text{-}sRWW}(1))$. □

From Corollary 2.1.41, we know that monotone sRRWW-automata accept context-free languages only. Thus, $\mathcal{L}(\mathsf{mon\text{-}sRRWW}(1)) \subseteq \mathsf{CFL}$. However, the following problem remains currently open.

Problem 2.3.103 *Does there exist a context-free language that is not accepted by any monotone sRRWW(1)-automaton?*

It has been conjectured that the context-free language $L_{\text{pal}} = \{ ww^R \mid w \in \{a,b\}^* \}$ is not accepted by any monotone sRRWW(1)-automaton, but currently we do not yet have an idea of how to prove this. Finally, we consider deterministic sRWW- and sRRWW-automata. The construction in the proof of Proposition 2.3.98 carries over to the deterministic case, and it can easily be extended to simulate a det-sRRWW(1)-automaton by a det-ORRWW-automaton. As det-ORWW-automata and det-ORRWW-automata only accept regular languages (see Corollary 2.3.86), we obtain the following results.

Corollary 2.3.104 $\mathsf{REG} = \mathcal{L}(\mathsf{det\text{-}sRWW}(1)) = \mathcal{L}(\mathsf{det\text{-}sRRWW}(1))$.

Of course, these equalities extend to monotone deterministic sRWW(1)- and sRRWW(1)-automata. The diagram in Figure 2.15 summarizes the inclusion results that we presented in this subsection.

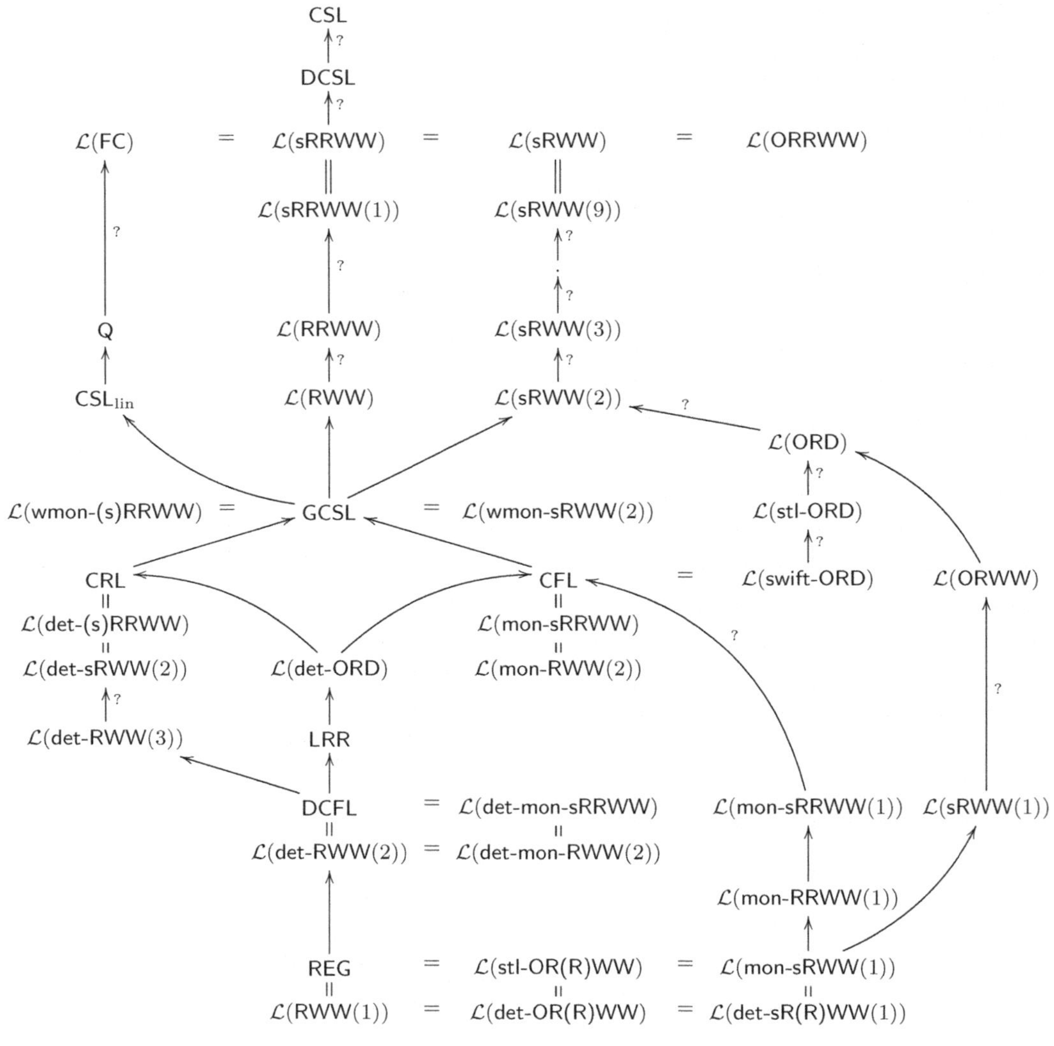

Figure 2.15: The taxonomy of (shrinking) restarting automata with small window size. An arrow $\rightarrow$ denotes a proper inclusion, while $\rightarrow^?$ denotes an inclusion which is not known to be proper.

2.4 Stateless Restarting Automata

Almost all classical types of automata like Turing machines, pushdown automata, or stack automata can be seen as extensions of finite-state acceptors, that is, one of their main ingredients is a finite-state control (see, e.g., [60, 81]). On the other hand, the so-called P systems introduced by Gheorghe Păun as an unconventional computing model realizing membrane computing are stateless [215], because it is unrealistic to maintain a global state for a massively parallel group of objects appearing in natural phenomena of cell evolution and chemical reactions. Accordingly, it is of interest to study stateless variants of classical models of automata to obtain insight into the real importance of the finite-state control for these devices.

An NFA without states (or rather, with a single state only) accepts all words that it can read completely. Thus, the language it accepts is either empty or of the form Σ_0^*, where Σ_0 is a subset of the input alphabet. For stateless pushdown automata accepting by empty pushdown, it is well-known (see, e.g., [81]) that the class of languages they accept coincides with the class CFL of context-free languages. Thus, in this case, the resource 'pushdown store' can compensate for the absence of states. On the other hand, for deterministic pushdown automata accepting by empty pushdown, the expressive capacity is known to increase strictly with the number of states [60]. In particular, a language is accepted by a stateless deterministic pushdown automaton if and only if it is a *simple* language, that is, it is generated by a context-free grammar of a very restricted form. So in this case, the resource 'pushdown store' cannot compensate for the absence of states.

Here we investigate the expressive capacity of stateless restarting automata. In particular, we study which other resources given to a restarting automaton can compensate for the absence of states. In Subsection 2.3.4, we saw that deterministic ORWW-, ORRWW-, and ORD-automata are equivalent to their stateless variants. When we examine the proof of Proposition 2.3.81, we see that it is the presence of auxiliary letters together with the fact that the read/write window has size three and the fact that deterministic ORWW-automata are weakly monotone of degree one that enable stateless deterministic ORWW-automata to encode the state information in such a way that they can simulate deterministic ORWW-automata with states. On the other hand, the ORWW-automaton M for the language $\hat{L}'_{\text{copy}}$ given in the proof of Lemma 2.3.68 shows that the rewrite steps executed in an accepting computation of a nondeterministic ORWW-automaton do, in general, not satisfy any principle of locality. Accordingly, it is impossible for a stateless nondeterministic ORWW-automaton to encode the state information in such a way that it can simulate the computations of M. And indeed, as shown by Corollary 2.3.86, stateless ORWW-automata are strictly less expressive than ORWW-automata, and the same is true for ORRWW-automata. Thus, it is only natural to also study the influence that the absence of states has on the expressive capacity of other types of restarting automata.

2.4.1 On Stateless sRWW-Automata and Their Subclasses

First, we consider the stateless variants of those types of restarting automata that have a combined rewrite/restart step.

Definition 2.4.1 *An sRWW-automaton* $M = (Q, \Sigma, \Gamma, \rhd, \lhd, q_0, k, \delta)$ *is called* stateless *if* $Q = \{q_0\}$, *that is, the initial state* q_0 *is the only state of* M. *In this case,* M *can simply be described by the 6-tuple* $M = (\Sigma, \Gamma, \rhd, \lhd, k, \delta)$. *We can assume that* δ *assigns the operation* Accept *to certain words from the set* $\rhd \cdot \Gamma^{\leq k-2} \cdot \lhd$, *and that, otherwise, it is a partial mapping from* $\mathcal{D}^{(k)} = \rhd \cdot \Gamma^{k-1} \cup \Gamma^k \cup \Gamma^{k-1} \cdot \lhd$ *to the set of operations* $\{\mathsf{MVR}, \mathsf{Accept}\} \cup \{ w \mid w \in \Gamma^* \}$. *As in Subsection 2.3.4, we use the prefix stl- to denote stateless types of restarting automata.*

The following example presents a stateless R-automaton.

Example 2.4.2 *Let* M *be the stateless R-automaton on* $\Sigma = \{a, b\}$ *that is given through the following transition function* δ:

$$\begin{array}{llllllll} \delta(\rhd \cdot \lhd) & = \mathsf{Accept}, & \delta(\rhd aaa) & = \mathsf{MVR}, & \delta(aaaa) & = \mathsf{MVR}, & \delta(aabb) & = ab, \\ \delta(\rhd ab \lhd) & = \mathsf{Accept}, & \delta(\rhd aab) & = \mathsf{MVR}, & \delta(aaab) & = \mathsf{MVR}. & & \end{array}$$

Then M is deterministic and monotone, and it is easily seen that $L(M) = \{ a^n b^n \mid n \geq 0 \}$. ■

Thus, already stateless deterministic R-automata that are monotone accept some non-regular languages. On the other hand, all regular languages are accepted by stateless R-automata that are deterministic and monotone. Thus, we have the following proper inclusion.

Proposition 2.4.3 $\mathsf{REG} \subsetneq \mathcal{L}(\mathsf{stl\text{-}det\text{-}mon\text{-}R})$.

Proof. Let $L \subseteq \Sigma^*$ be a regular language, let $A = (Q, \Sigma, q_0, \delta_A, F)$ be a complete DFA for L, and let $k = |Q|$. Then, for each word $z \in \Sigma^k$, there exists a factorization $z = uvw$ such that $|v| > 0$ and $\delta_A(q_0, uw) = \delta_A(q_0, uvw) = \delta_A(q_0, z)$. Actually, if, for a given word z, there exist several such factorizations, then we just choose one. Then, for all words $y \in \Sigma^*$, $zy = uvwy \in L$ if and only if $uwy \in L$.

Now we define the stateless deterministic R-automaton M_L through the following transition function:

$$\begin{array}{llcll} (1) & \delta(\rhd z \lhd) & = & \mathsf{Accept} & \text{for all } z \in L \cap \Sigma^{\leq k-1}, \\ (2) & \delta(\rhd z) & = & \rhd uw & \text{for all } z \in \Sigma^k, \text{ where } z = uvw, |v| > 0, \text{ and } \delta_A(q_0, uw) = \delta_A(q_0, z). \end{array}$$

By (1), M_L accepts all words from L of length at most $k-1$ immediately, and for a word y of length at least k, it executes a delete operation at the left sentinel. This shows that M_L is monotone. Furthermore, from the choice of the chosen factorizations of the words of length k, it follows that, for any words $z \in \Sigma^k$ and $y \in \Sigma^*$, if $\rhd zy \lhd = \rhd uvwy \lhd \vdash^c_{M_L} \rhd uwy \lhd$, then $zy \in L$ if and only if $uwy \in L$. It follows that $L(M_L) = L$. □

The following proposition shows that we may require that a stateless sRWW-automaton executes accept instructions only at the right end of its tape.

Proposition 2.4.4 ([123]) *From a stateless sRWW-automaton $M = (\Sigma, \Gamma, \rhd, \lhd, k, \delta)$, one can construct a stateless sRWW-automaton $M' = (\Sigma, \Gamma, \rhd, \lhd, k+1, \delta')$ that executes accept instructions only at the right end of the tape, and that accepts the same characteristic language as M. If M is a stateless RWW-, RW-, or R-automaton, then so is M', and if M is deterministic, then so is M'.*

Proof. Let $M = (\Sigma, \Gamma, \rhd, \lhd, k, \delta)$ be a stateless sRWW-automaton and let ω be a weight function that is compatible with M. Assume that M executes accept instructions also in the middle of the tape, that is, $\mathsf{Accept} \in \delta(u)$ for some words $u \in \rhd \cdot \Gamma^{k-1} \cup \Gamma^k$. Observe that we can make the following assumption without loss of generality: whenever $\mathsf{Accept} \in \delta(u)$ for some $u \in \rhd \cdot \Gamma^{k-1} \cup \Gamma^k$, then $\delta(u) = \{\mathsf{Accept}\}$. Now we define a stateless sRWW-automaton $M' = (\Sigma, \Gamma, \rhd, \lhd, k+1, \delta')$ as follows:

$$\begin{array}{llcll} (1) & \delta'(\rhd u \lhd) & = & \{\mathsf{Accept}\} & \text{for all } u \in \Gamma^{\leq k-1} \cap L_C(M), \\ (2) & \delta'(ua) & = & \{\mathsf{MVR}, v_1 a, v_2 a, \ldots, v_r a\} & \text{for all } a \in \Gamma \text{ and all } u \in \rhd \cdot \Gamma^{k-1} \cup \Gamma^k \\ & & & & \text{satisfying } \delta(u) = \{\mathsf{MVR}, v_1, v_2, \ldots, v_r\}, \\ (3) & \delta'(ua) & = & \{v_1 a, v_2 a, \ldots, v_r a\} & \text{for all } a \in \Gamma \text{ and all } u \in \rhd \cdot \Gamma^{k-1} \cup \Gamma^k \\ & & & & \text{satisfying } \delta(u) = \{v_1, v_2, \ldots, v_r\}, \\ (4) & \delta'(ua) & = & \{u\} & \text{for all } a \in \Gamma \text{ and all } u \in \rhd \cdot \Gamma^{k-1} \cup \Gamma^k \\ & & & & \text{satisfying } \delta(u) = \{\mathsf{Accept}\}, \\ (5) & \delta'(u \lhd) & = & \{v_1 \lhd, v_2 \lhd, \ldots, v_r \lhd\} & \text{for all } u \in \Gamma^k \text{ satisfying } \delta(u) = \{v_1, v_2, \ldots, v_r\}, \\ (6) & \delta'(au \lhd) & = & \{av_1 \lhd, av_2 \lhd, \ldots, av_r \lhd\} & \text{for all } a \in \Gamma \text{ and all } u \in \Gamma^{k-1} \text{ satisfying} \\ & & & & \mathsf{MVR} \in \delta(au) \text{ and } \delta(u \lhd) = \{v_1 \lhd, v_2 \lhd, \ldots, v_r \lhd\}, \\ (7) & \delta'(au \lhd) & = & \{\mathsf{Accept}\} & \text{for all } a \in \Gamma \text{ and all } u \in \Gamma^{k-1} \text{ satisfying} \\ & & & & \delta(au) = \{\mathsf{Accept}\} \text{ or } (\mathsf{MVR} \in \delta(au) \text{ and} \\ & & & & \delta(u \lhd) = \{\mathsf{Accept}\}). \end{array}$$

Then M' is a stateless sRWW-automaton that is also compatible with the weight function ω. Furthermore, M' executes accept instructions only at the right end of its tape. In addition, if all rewrite instructions of M are length-reducing or even deletions, then the same is also true for M', and if M is deterministic, then so is M'. It remains to show that $L_C(M') = L_C(M)$ holds.

If $w \in L_C(M)$, then there exists a sequence of cycles of the form

$$\rhd w \lhd \vdash_M^c \rhd w_1 \lhd \vdash_M^c \cdots \vdash_M^c \rhd w_n \lhd = \rhd xuy \lhd$$

such that $\delta(u) = \{\mathsf{Accept}\}$. If $y = \lambda$ and $|u| = k - 1$, then M' can execute this sequence as well, implying that $w \in L_C(M')$. If, however, $|u| = k$ and $y = y_1 y_2 \cdots y_m \in \Gamma^m$ for some $m \geq 0$, then M' can execute the following sequence of cycles:

$$\rhd w \lhd \vdash_{M'}^c \rhd w_1 \lhd \vdash_{M'}^c \cdots \vdash_{M'}^c \rhd w_n \lhd = \rhd xuy_1 y_2 \cdots y_m \lhd \vdash_{M'}^{c^*} \rhd xu \lhd,$$

where the last part follows from rule (4). Since $\delta(u) = \{\mathsf{Accept}\}$ implies $\delta'(u\lhd) = \{\mathsf{Accept}\}$ (by rule (7)), this shows that $w \in L_C(M')$ also holds in this case. It follows that $L_C(M) \subseteq L_C(M')$.

On the other hand, if $w \in L_C(M')$, then it follows easily from the construction of M' that $w \in L_C(M)$ holds. Thus, we have $L_C(M) = L_C(M')$. □

For an sRWW-automaton M with tape alphabet Γ, $S_C(M)$ denotes the *simple characteristic language* of M, which is the set of words $w \in \Gamma^*$ that M accepts in tail computations. If M is stateless, and if M executes accept instructions only at the right end of its tape, then a word $w \in \Gamma^*$, $|w| \geq k - 1$, is a member of $S_C(M)$ if and only if, when starting from the restarting configuration $q_0 \rhd w \lhd$, M performs move-right operations until its read/write window sees the suffix $w_2 \lhd$ of length k of the tape contents, at which point M accepts. Thus, M executes move-right operations for the prefix of length k of $\rhd w$ and for each factor of length k of w. Hence, $S_C(M)$ can be characterized using the notion of a strictly locally testable language [149, 273].

For a word $w \in \Gamma^*$, $|w| \geq j$, let $P_j(w)$ and $S_j(w)$ be the prefix and the suffix of w of length j, respectively. Furthermore, let $I_j(w)$ be the set of all inner factors of w of length j, that is,

$$I_j(w) = \{\, u \mid |u| = j \text{ and } \exists\, x, y \in \Gamma^+ : w = xuy \,\}.$$

These are defined only for $|w| \geq j$. If $|w| = j$, then $P_j(w) = S_j(w) = w$, while $I_j(w)$ is empty, whenever $j \leq |w| \leq j + 1$. For example, $P_2(aababab) = aa$, $S_2(aababab) = ab$, and $I_2(aababab) = \{ab, ba\}$.

A language $L \subseteq \Gamma^*$ is called *strictly j-testable* if there exist finite sets $A, B, C \subseteq \Gamma^j$ such that, for all $w \in \Gamma^*$ satisfying $|w| \geq j$, we have

$$w \in L \text{ if and only if } P_j(w) \in A,\ I_j(w) \subseteq B, \text{ and } S_j(w) \in C.$$

In this case, (A, B, C) is called a *triple* for L. Finally, L is called *strictly locally testable* if it is strictly j-testable for some $j > 0$. Note that the definition of 'strictly j-testable' says nothing about the words of length $j - 1$ or less.

The family of strictly j-testable languages is denoted by j-SLT and the class of strictly locally testable languages is denoted by SLT. It is easy to see that $\mathsf{SLT} \subsetneq \mathsf{REG}$ (for example, the regular language $\{aa\}^*$ is not strictly locally testable). It is also known that j-$\mathsf{SLT} \subsetneq (j+1)$-$\mathsf{SLT}$ holds.

From the observation above, we can derive the following characterization.

Proposition 2.4.5 ([120, 123]) *If M is a stateless sRWW-automaton with a window of size k (for any $k \geq 1$) that executes accept instructions only at the right end of its tape, then the language $S_C(M)$ is strictly k-testable.*

Proof. Let $M = (\Sigma, \Gamma, \rhd, \lhd, k, \delta)$ be a stateless sRWW-automaton. Define the sets $A, B, C \subseteq \Gamma^k$ as follows:

$$\begin{aligned} A &= \{\, x \in \Gamma^k \mid \mathsf{MVR} \in \delta(x) \text{ and } \exists\, a \in \Gamma : x = x_1 a \text{ and } \mathsf{MVR} \in \delta(\rhd x_1) \,\}, \\ B &= \{\, x \in \Gamma^k \mid \mathsf{MVR} \in \delta(x) \,\}, \\ C &= \{\, x \in \Gamma^k \mid \mathsf{MVR} \in \delta(x) \text{ and } \exists\, a \in \Gamma : x = a x_1 \text{ and } \mathsf{Accept} \in \delta(x_1 \lhd) \,\}. \end{aligned}$$

Then $S_C(M)$ is the strictly k-testable language that is specified by the triple (A, B, C). □

Conversely, we have the following result.

Proposition 2.4.6 ([123]) *For each strictly k-testable language $L \subseteq \Gamma^*$, there exists a stateless deterministic R-automaton M with tape alphabet Γ and a read/write window of size $k+2$ such that $S_C(M) = L$.*

Proof. Let $L \subseteq \Gamma^*$ be the strictly k-testable language that is specified by the triple (A, B, C), where $A, B, C \subseteq \Gamma^k$. We define a stateless deterministic R-automaton $M = (\Gamma, \Gamma, \rhd, \lhd, k+2, \delta)$ as follows:

(1)	$\delta(\rhd x \lhd)$	=	Accept	for all $x \in L, \lvert x\rvert \leq k$,	
(2)	$\delta(\rhd x)$	=	MVR	for all $x = a_1 a_2 \cdots a_{k+1} \in \Gamma^{k+1}$	satisfying $a_1 a_2 \cdots a_k \in A$,
(3)	$\delta(x)$	=	MVR	for all $x = a_1 a_2 \cdots a_{k+2} \in \Gamma^{k+2}$	satisfying $a_2 a_3 \cdots a_{k+1} \in B$,
(4)	$\delta(x \lhd)$	=	Accept	for all $x = a_1 a_2 \cdots a_{k+1} \in \Gamma^{k+1}$	satisfying $a_2 a_3 \cdots a_{k+1} \in C$.

Then it can be checked easily that $S_C(M) = L$ holds. □

Notice that the stateless R-automaton constructed in the proof above executes all its accept instructions at the right end of its tape. Thus, we see that the class of simple characteristic languages of stateless (deterministic) (s)R(W)(W)-automata that execute accept steps only at the right end of the tape coincides with the class of strictly locally testable languages.

Now we investigate the expressive capacity of the stateless variants of various subtypes of sRWW-automata. For this, we first reconsider the language $L_1^R = \{ cb^n a^n, db^{2n} a^n \mid n \geq 0 \}$, which belongs to the class DLIN of deterministic linear languages.

Lemma 2.4.7 *The language L_1^R is not accepted by any stateless sRW-automaton.*

Proof. Assume that $M = (\Sigma, \Sigma, \rhd, \lhd, k, \delta)$ is a stateless sRW-automaton such that $L(M) = L_1^R$ holds, where $\Sigma = \{a, b, c, d\}$. Then M has an accepting computation on input $w = db^{2n}a^n$, where $n > k$. Obviously, this computation cannot be an accepting tail, that is, it begins with a cycle of the form $\rhd w \lhd \vdash_M^c \rhd w' \lhd$ for some word $w' \in L_1^R$. By rewriting the prefix db^{k-1}, even when using a weight-reducing rewrite transition, the word $w = db^{2n}a^n$ cannot be transformed into a word of the form $cb^m a^m$, as $k < n$. Thus, it follows that $w' = db^{2n-2i}a^{n-i}$ for some i, $0 < i \leq k/3$. This means that M contains the rewrite operation $b^{k-l-2i}a^{l-i} \in \delta(b^{k-l}a^l)$ for some $l \geq i$. Next, M also has an accepting computation for the word $z = cb^{n+i}a^{n+i}$. Finally, consider the word $v = cb^{n+i}a^n$, which does not belong to L_1^R. Starting with input v, M cannot simply reject, as it cannot distinguish between v and z before it has seen the tape contents completely. Thus, the computation of M on input v begins by moving the read/write window of M to the border between the factors b^{n+i} and a^n. However, at that place, M can apply the above rewrite operation, which yields the cycle $\rhd v \lhd = \rhd cb^{n+i}a^n \lhd \vdash_M^c \rhd cb^{n-i}a^{n-i} \lhd$. This contradicts the Error Preserving Property for M, as $cb^{n-i}a^{n-i} \in L_1^R$. Hence, L_1^R is not accepted by any stateless sRW-automaton. □

As the language L_1^R is easily seen to be accepted by a det-mon-R-automaton, the above result shows that stateless (det-)(mon-)(s)R(W)-automata are strictly less expressive than their corresponding counterparts with states. As $\mathcal{L}(\text{det-mon-sRWW}) = \text{DCFL}$ and $\mathcal{L}(\text{mon-sRWW}) = \text{CFL}$, Lemma 2.4.7 has the following consequences.

Corollary 2.4.8 $\mathcal{L}(\text{stl-det-mon-sRW}) \subsetneq \text{DCFL}$ *and* $\mathcal{L}(\text{stl-mon-sRW}) \subsetneq \text{CFL}$.

However, the language L_1^R is accepted by a stateless RWW-automaton that is monotone and deterministic. In fact, we have the following characterizations.

Theorem 2.4.9 ([120]) (a) $\mathcal{L}(\text{stl-mon-(s)RWW}) = \text{CFL}$.
(b) $\mathcal{L}(\text{stl-det-mon-(s)RWW}) = \text{DCFL}$.

Proof. It remains to prove the inclusions from right to left.

(a) In the proof of Theorem 2.1.40, we constructed a mon-RWW-automaton M of window size two from a context-free grammar. The automaton M has three states, but it is easily seen that we can do away with two of these states if we enlarge the read/write window to size three. This implies that $\mathsf{CFL} \subseteq \mathcal{L}(\mathsf{stl\text{-}mon\text{-}RWW}(3))$.

(b) In the proof of Theorem 2.3.44, we constructed a det-mon-RWW-automaton M of window size three for simulating a given DPDA. As the automaton M has just a single state, this yields $\mathsf{DCFL} \subseteq \mathcal{L}(\mathsf{stl\text{-}det\text{-}mon\text{-}RWW}(3))$. □

The following result shows that states are not needed for weakly monotone RWW-automata.

Theorem 2.4.10 ([120]) (a) $\mathcal{L}(\mathsf{stl\text{-}wmon\text{-}(s)RWW}) = \mathsf{GCSL}$.
(b) $\mathcal{L}(\mathsf{stl\text{-}det\text{-}(s)RWW}) = \mathsf{CRL}$.

Proof. Again, we just need to verify the inclusions from right to left.

(a) In the proof of Theorem 2.3.59, we constructed an sRWW-automaton M of window size two from a given sTPDA. The resulting automaton M is weakly monotone, and it has only a single state. Thus, $\mathsf{GCSL} \subseteq \mathcal{L}(\mathsf{stl\text{-}wmon\text{-}sRWW}(2))$ follows. As the growing context-sensitive languages are characterized by length-reducing TPDAs (see Theorem 1.2.17), we can apply the same construction to a length-reducing TPDA. In this way, we obtain a stateless weakly monotone RWW-automaton for the growing context-sensitive language accepted by the given length-reducing TPDA. It follows that $\mathsf{GCSL} \subseteq \mathcal{L}(\mathsf{stl\text{-}wmon\text{-}RWW})$. Notice, however, that there is no known constant $c > 1$ such that the window size of the length-reducing TPDA can be restricted to size $k \leq c$, and hence, there is no a priori bound for the window size of the RWW-automaton constructed.

(b) This follows completely analogously by using the characterization of the class CRL by length-reducing DTPDAs. □

The language $L_{\text{pal}} = \{ ww^R \mid w \in \{a,b\}^* \}$ is not Church-Rosser [93, 188], but as it is context-free, it is accepted by a stl-mon-RWW-automaton M by Theorem 2.4.9(a). Now, let M' be the stl-mon-RW-automaton obtained from M by declaring all tape symbols to be input letters, and let $L'_{\text{pal}} = L(M')$ be the resulting language. Finally, let $\hat{L}_{\text{pal}} = \varphi_{k,m}(L'_{\text{pal}})$, where $\varphi_{k,m}$ is the corresponding morphism from Theorem 2.2.15. Then $\hat{L}_{\text{pal}}$ is accepted by a stl-mon-R-automaton. However, as the class CRL is closed under intersection with regular sets and inverse morphisms, and as $L_{\text{pal}} = \varphi^{-1}_{m,k}(\hat{L}_{\text{pal}}) \cap \{a,b\}^*$, it follows that $\hat{L}_{\text{pal}}$ is not Church-Rosser. This observation yields the following non-inclusion result.

Corollary 2.4.11 $\mathcal{L}(\mathsf{stl\text{-}mon\text{-}R}) \not\subseteq \mathsf{CRL}$.

For the following considerations, we need a number of additional example languages.

Definition 2.4.12

(a) $L_e = \{ c(ac)^m(aee)^{n-m}b^n, d(ad)^m(aee)^{n-m}b^{2n} \mid 0 \leq m \leq n \}$.

(b) $L_g = \{ a^ncb^n, a^neeb^n, a^ndb^{2n}, a^neeb^{2n} \mid n \geq 0 \}$.

(c) $L_h = \{ a^nb^m \mid 0 \leq n \leq m \leq 2n \}$.

(d) $L_{\text{expo}} = \{ a^{i_0}ba^{i_1}b\cdots a^{i_{n-1}}ba^{i_n} \mid n \geq 0,\ i_0, i_1, \ldots, i_n \geq 0,\ \textit{and}\ \exists m \geq 0 : \sum_{j=0}^{n} 2^j \cdot i_j = 2^m \} \cup \{b\}^*$.

(e) $L^{(\varphi)}_{\text{expo}} = \varphi(L_{\text{expo}})$, *where* φ *is the morphism induced by* $a \mapsto ab$ *and* $b \mapsto b$.

Concerning these languages, we have the following results.

Lemma 2.4.13

(a) $L_e \in \mathcal{L}(\mathsf{stl\text{-}det\text{-}mon\text{-}RW}) \smallsetminus \mathcal{L}(\mathsf{stl\text{-}det\text{-}R})$.

(b) $L_g \in \mathcal{L}(\mathsf{stl\text{-}mon\text{-}RW}) \smallsetminus \mathcal{L}(\mathsf{R})$.

(c) $L_h \in \mathcal{L}(\mathsf{stl\text{-}mon\text{-}R}) \smallsetminus \mathcal{L}(\mathsf{det\text{-}RW})$.

(d) $L_{\text{expo}} \in \mathcal{L}(\mathsf{stl\text{-}det\text{-}RW}) \smallsetminus \mathcal{L}(\mathsf{R})$.

(e) $L^{(\varphi)}_{\text{expo}} \in \mathcal{L}(\mathsf{stl\text{-}det\text{-}R}) \smallsetminus \mathsf{CFL}$.

Proof. (a) Let $M = (\Sigma, \Sigma, \rhd, \lhd, k, \delta)$, where $\Sigma = \{a,b,c,d,e\}$, $k = 7$, and δ is defined as follows:

(1)	$\delta(\rhd x \lhd)$	=	Accept	for all $x \in \{c, d, cacb, dadbb, caeeb\}$,			
(2)	$\delta(\rhd x)$	=	MVR	for all $x \in \Sigma^6$,			
(3)	$\delta(x)$	=	MVR	for all $x \in \{aca, ada, cac, dad\} \cdot \Sigma^4$,			
(4)	$\delta(caeeae)$	=	$cacae$,	(7)	$\delta(daeeae)$	=	$dadae$,
(5)	$\delta(caeebb)$	=	$cacbb$,	(8)	$\delta(daeebb)$	=	$dadbb$,
(6)	$\delta(acbb)$	=	b,	(9)	$\delta(adbbb)$	=	b.

Then M is a stateless deterministic RW-automaton. For an input $w = c(ac)^m(aee)^{n-m}b^n$, where $n \geq 1$ and $0 \leq m \leq n$, M first transforms this word into $c(ac)^n b^n$ using rules (4) and (5), and then it reduces this word to $cacb$ by rule (6). Analogously, a word of the form $d(ad)^m(aee)^{n-m}b^{2n}$, $n \geq 1$ and $0 \leq m \leq n$, is first rewritten into $d(ad)^n b^{2n}$ using rules (7) and (8), and then this word is reduced to $dadbb$ by rule (9). It follows that $L(M) = L_e$, and that M is also monotone. Thus, M witnesses the fact that $L_e \in \mathcal{L}(\textsf{stl-det-mon-RW})$ holds.

Finally assume that L_e is accepted by a stateless deterministic R-automaton M', and let $w = d(aee)^n b^{2n}$ for a sufficiently large value of n. As M' can only apply deletions, it must execute a cycle of the form

$$\rhd d(aee)^n b^{2n} \lhd \vdash^c_{M'} \rhd d(aee)^{n-i} b^{2n-2i} \lhd$$

for an integer $i \leq k/3$, where k denotes the size of the read/write window of M'. However, as M' is deterministic and stateless, it will execute the same rewrite operation given the input $z = c(aee)^n b^{n+i}$, which yields the cycle

$$\rhd c(aee)^n b^{n+i} \lhd \vdash^c_{M'} \rhd c(aee)^{n-i} b^{n-i} \lhd .$$

However, the latter word belongs to L_e, while z does not belong to L_e. This contradicts the Error Preserving Property for M'. Hence, it follows that L_e is not accepted by any stateless deterministic R-automaton.

(b) Let $M = (\Sigma, \Sigma, \rhd, \lhd, k, \delta)$, where $\Sigma = \{a, b, c, d, e\}$, $k = 6$, and δ is defined as follows:

(1)	$\delta(\rhd x \lhd)$	=	Accept	for all $x \in \{c, d, ee, acb, aeeb, adbb\}$,			
(2)	$\delta(\rhd x)$	=	MVR	for all $x \in \{a^4, a^3c, a^3d, a^3e, a^2cb, a^2db, a^2ee, aeeb\} \cdot \Sigma$,			
(3)	$\delta(x)$	=	MVR	for all $x \in \{a^5, a^4c, a^4d, a^4e, a^3cb, a^3db, a^3ee, a^2cb^2, a^2db^2, a^2eeb\} \cdot \Sigma$,			
(4)	$\delta(acb^3)$	=	cb^2,	(7)	$\delta(acb^2\lhd)$	=	$cb\lhd$,
(5)	$\delta(adb^3)$	=	db,	(8)	$\delta(adbb\lhd)$	=	$d\lhd$.
(6)	$\delta(aeeb^2)$	=	$\{acb^2, adb^2\}$,				

Then M is a stateless RW-automaton that is easily seen to be monotone, and $L(M) = L_g$. On the other hand, it can be shown that L_g is not accepted by any R-automaton M'. Indeed, given an input of the form $a^n eeb^n$ for a large enough value of n, M' cannot accept in a tail computation, and hence, an accepting computation of M' will start with a cycle of the form

$$\rhd a^n eeb^n \lhd \vdash^c_{M'} \rhd a^{n-i} eeb^{n-i} \lhd,$$

where $1 \leq i \leq k'/2$. Thus, given the input $a^n eeb^{2n-i} \notin L_g$, M' will execute the cycle

$$\rhd a^n eeb^{2n-i} \lhd \vdash^c_{M'} \rhd a^{n-i} eeb^{2n-2i} \lhd .$$

As $a^{n-i}eeb^{2n-2i} \in L_g$, this contradicts the Error Preserving Property for M'. Thus, it follows in particular that L_g is not accepted by any R-automaton.

(c) It is well known that the language L_h is not accepted by any deterministic RW-automaton (see Lemma 2.2.6). On the other hand, the following stateless R-automaton $M = (\Sigma, \Sigma, \rhd, \lhd, k, \delta)$ is monotone, and it accepts the language L_h. Here $\Sigma = \{a, b\}$, $k = 4$, and δ is defined as follows:

(1)	$\delta(\rhd x \lhd)$	=	Accept	for all $x \in \{\lambda, ab\}$,	(4)	$\delta(ab^3)$	=	$\{b^2, b\}$,
(2)	$\delta(\rhd x)$	=	MVR	for all $x \in \{a^3, a^2b, ab^2\}$,	(5)	$\delta(ab^2\lhd)$	=	$\{b\lhd, \lhd\}$.
(3)	$\delta(x)$	=	MVR	for all $x \in \{a^4, a^3b, a^2b^2\}$,				

(d) Let M be the stateless deterministic RW-automaton on $\Sigma = \{a, b\}$ that is given through the following transition function:

$$\begin{array}{llllll} (1) & \delta(\rhd x \lhd) & = & \mathsf{Accept} & \text{for all } x \in \{\lambda, a, aa\}, \\ (2) & \delta(\rhd x) & = & \mathsf{MVR} & \text{for all } x \in a \cdot \Sigma^3, \\ (3) & \delta(x) & = & \mathsf{MVR} & \text{for all } x \in a^3 \cdot \Sigma, \end{array} \quad \begin{array}{llll} (4) & \delta(\rhd b) & = & \rhd, \\ (5) & \delta(aab) & = & ba, \\ (6) & \delta(a^4 \lhd) & = & baa \lhd . \end{array}$$

If $w = b^m$ for some $m \geq 0$, then obviously w is accepted by M. If $w = a^{i_0} b a^{i_1} b \cdots a^{i_{n-1}} b a^{i_n}$ is given as input to M, where $n, i_0, i_1, \ldots, i_n \geq 0$, and $\sum_{j=0}^{n} 2^j \cdot i_j = 2^m$ for some $m \geq 0$, then the first occurrence of b is first shifted to the left end of the word. As $\sum_{j=0}^{n} 2^j \cdot i_j = 2^m$, we see that i_0 is an even number. Thus, the first occurrence of b is moved to the left and then deleted. This results in the word $w_1 = a^{i_0/2+i_1} b \cdots a^{i_{n-1}} b a^{i_n}$. As

$$i_0/2 + i_1 + \sum_{j=2}^{n} 2^{j-1} \cdot i_j = (\sum_{j=0}^{n} 2^j \cdot i_j)/2 = 2^{m-1},$$

we see that this word belongs to the language L_{expo}. Thus, we can iterate the above process until all occurrences of the letter b have been deleted. The resulting word is of the form a^{2^l} for some $l \geq 0$. If $l \leq 1$, then the word is accepted, otherwise, an occurrence of b is generated at the right end of the word and shifted through the word as described above, which results in the word $a^{2^{l-1}}$. It follows that $L(M) = L_{\text{expo}}$ implying that $L_{\text{expo}} \in \mathcal{L}(\mathsf{stl\text{-}det\text{-}RW})$ holds.

On the other hand, it is easily seen that there exists no R-automaton that accepts the language L_{expo}. Just consider an input of the form $w = a^{2^n}$ for a sufficiently large value of n. Thus, $L_{\text{expo}} \notin \mathcal{L}(\mathsf{R})$.

(e) The morphism φ is an encoding, and therewith it is injective. Hence, it follows that

$$L_{\text{expo}}^{(\varphi)} \cap \{ab\}^* = \varphi(L_{\text{expo}} \cap \{a\}^*) = \{\, (ab)^{2^n} \mid n \geq 0 \,\},$$

which shows that $L_{\text{expo}}^{(\varphi)}$ is not a context-free language. On the other hand, we see that $\varphi(aab) = ababb$, which contains $\varphi(ba) = bab$ as a factor, and that $\varphi(a^4) = abababab$, which contains $\varphi(baa) = babab$ as a factor. Thus, by applying the morphism φ to all instructions of the stateless deterministic RW-automaton M given in the proof of part (d) above, we obtain a stateless deterministic R-automaton for the language $L_{\text{expo}}^{(\varphi)}$. □

Together with Lemma 2.4.7, these results yield the following consequences.

Corollary 2.4.14

(a)	$\mathcal{L}(\mathsf{stl\text{-}det\text{-}mon\text{-}R})$	$\subsetneq$	$\mathcal{L}(\mathsf{stl\text{-}det\text{-}mon\text{-}RW})$.	(e)	$\mathcal{L}(\mathsf{stl\text{-}det\text{-}mon\text{-}R})$	$\subsetneq$	$\mathcal{L}(\mathsf{stl\text{-}det\text{-}R})$.
(b)	$\mathcal{L}(\mathsf{stl\text{-}mon\text{-}R})$	$\subsetneq$	$\mathcal{L}(\mathsf{stl\text{-}mon\text{-}RW})$.	(f)	$\mathcal{L}(\mathsf{stl\text{-}det\text{-}R})$	$\not\subseteq$	CFL.
(c)	$\mathcal{L}(\mathsf{stl\text{-}det\text{-}R})$	$\subsetneq$	$\mathcal{L}(\mathsf{stl\text{-}det\text{-}RW})$.	(g)	DCFL	$\not\subseteq$	$\mathcal{L}(\mathsf{stl\text{-}RW})$.
(d)	$\mathcal{L}(\mathsf{stl\text{-}det\text{-}mon\text{-}R})$	$\subsetneq$	$\mathcal{L}(\mathsf{stl\text{-}mon\text{-}R})$.				

The above results on stateless sRWW-automata and their subclasses are summarized in the diagram in Figure 2.16.

Finally, we study the stateless deterministic R-automata in more detail. First, we derive a characterization for the class of languages that are accepted by stateless deterministic R-automata of window size one.

Definition 2.4.15 *Assume that $M = (\Sigma, \Sigma, \rhd, \lhd, 1, \delta)$ is a stateless deterministic R-automaton of window size one. We partition the alphabet Σ into four disjoint subalphabets:*

$$\begin{array}{llll} (1) & \Sigma_1 & = & \{\, a \in \Sigma \mid \delta(a) = \mathsf{MVR} \,\}, \\ (2) & \Sigma_2 & = & \{\, a \in \Sigma \mid \delta(a) = \lambda \,\}, \end{array} \quad \begin{array}{llll} (3) & \Sigma_3 & = & \{\, a \in \Sigma \mid \delta(a) = \mathsf{Accept} \,\}, \\ (4) & \Sigma_4 & = & \{\, a \in \Sigma \mid \delta(a) = \emptyset \,\}. \end{array}$$

Thus, Σ_1 is the set of letters that M just moves across, Σ_2 is the set of letters that M deletes, Σ_3 is the set of letters which cause M to accept, and Σ_4 is the set of letters on which M gets stuck.

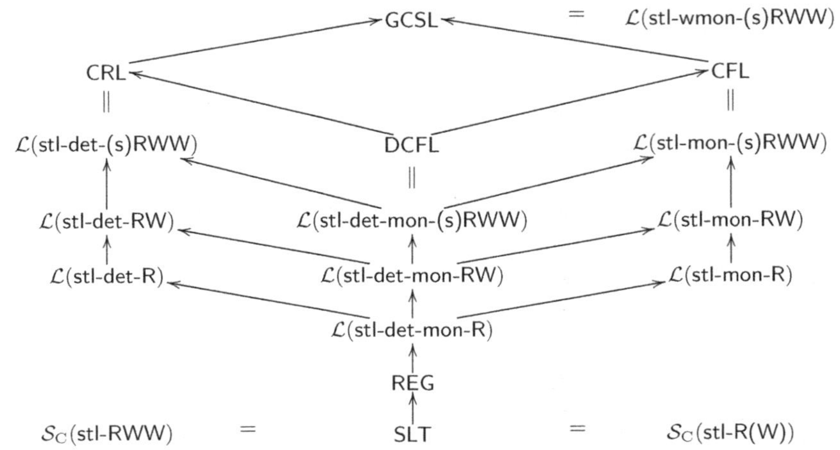

Figure 2.16: Inclusion relations between language classes defined by various types of stateless sRWW-automata. Classes that are not (directly or indirectly) connected are incomparable under inclusion. Here $\mathcal{S}_C$(stl-R(W)(W)) denotes the class of simple characteristic languages of stateless R(W)(W)-automata that execute accept steps only at the right end of the tape.

The following characterization holds.

Proposition 2.4.16 ([178, 179]) *Let $M = (\Sigma, \Sigma, \rhd, \lhd, 1, \delta)$ be a stateless deterministic R(1)-automaton, and assume that the subalphabets $\Sigma_1, \Sigma_2, \Sigma_3, \Sigma_4$ are defined as above. Then the simple language $S(M)$ of words accepted by M in tail computations can be characterized as*

$$S(M) \quad = \quad \begin{cases} \emptyset, & \text{if } \delta(\rhd) = \emptyset, \\ \Sigma^*, & \text{if } \delta(\rhd) = \mathsf{Accept}, \\ \Sigma_1^* \cdot \Sigma_3 \cdot \Sigma^*, & \text{if } \delta(\rhd) = \mathsf{MVR} \text{ and } \delta(\lhd) \neq \mathsf{Accept}, \\ \Sigma_1^* \cdot ((\Sigma_3 \cdot \Sigma^*) \cup \{\lambda\}), & \text{if } \delta(\rhd) = \mathsf{MVR} \text{ and } \delta(\lhd) = \mathsf{Accept}, \end{cases}$$

and the language $L(M)$ can be characterized as

$$L(M) \quad = \quad \begin{cases} \emptyset, & \text{if } \delta(\rhd) = \emptyset, \\ \Sigma^*, & \text{if } \delta(\rhd) = \mathsf{Accept}, \\ (\Sigma_1 \cup \Sigma_2)^* \cdot \Sigma_3 \cdot \Sigma^*, & \text{if } \delta(\rhd) = \mathsf{MVR} \text{ and } \delta(\lhd) \neq \mathsf{Accept}, \\ (\Sigma_1 \cup \Sigma_2)^* \cdot ((\Sigma_3 \cdot \Sigma^*) \cup \{\lambda\}), & \text{if } \delta(\rhd) = \mathsf{MVR} \text{ and } \delta(\lhd) = \mathsf{Accept}. \end{cases}$$

Proof. If $\delta(\rhd) = \emptyset$, then M gets immediately stuck for each word $w \in \Sigma^*$, and if $\delta(\rhd) = \mathsf{Accept}$, then M accepts each word $w \in \Sigma^*$ in a tail computation. Thus, we can concentrate on the case that $\delta(\rhd) = \mathsf{MVR}$ holds. Obviously, M will then accept each word from $\Sigma_1^* \cdot \Sigma_3 \cdot \Sigma^*$ in a tail computation, and if $\delta(\lhd) = \mathsf{Accept}$, it will also accept each word from Σ_1^* in a tail computation. Furthermore, each word $w = uav$, where $u \in \Sigma_1^*$, $a \in \Sigma_2$, and $v \in \Sigma^*$ will cause a cycle of the form $\rhd w \lhd = \rhd uav \lhd \vdash_M^c \rhd uv \lhd$. Hence, one by one those letters from Σ_2 are removed from w that in w are only preceded by letters from $\Sigma_1 \cup \Sigma_2$. This yields the above description for the language $L(M)$. □

It is easily seen that a stateless finite-state acceptor with input alphabet Σ accepts a language of the form Σ_0^*, where Σ_0 is a subalphabet of Σ. Thus, we easily obtain the following consequence.

Corollary 2.4.17 *A language L is accepted by a stateless deterministic R(1)-automaton that only accepts on reaching the right sentinel $\lhd$, if and only if L is the simple language of a stateless deterministic R(1)-automaton that only accepts on reaching the right sentinel $\lhd$, if and only if L is accepted by a stateless finite-state acceptor.*

Thus, stateless deterministic R(1)-automata can be seen as stateless deterministic finite-state acceptors that are enabled to accept without having read their input completely. Next we turn to stateless deterministic R-automata of window size 2.

Lemma 2.4.18 *For each integer $n \geq 1$, the semi-Dyck language D_n is accepted by a stateless deterministic R(2)-automaton.*

Proof. The semi-Dyck language D_1 is defined over the alphabet $T_1 = \{a, b\}$. It is generated by the context-free grammar $G_1 = (\{S\}, T_1, S, P_1)$, where P_1 contains the productions $(S \to \lambda)$, $(S \to SS)$, and $(S \to aSb)$ (see Example 1.2.22). In fact, a word $w \in T_1^*$ belongs to D_1 if and only if $|w|_a = |w|_b$, and for each proper prefix x of w, we have $|x|_a \geq |x|_b$. Thus, it is easily seen that D_1 is accepted by the stateless deterministic $\mathsf{R}(2)$-automaton M_1 that is defined by the following transition function:

$$\begin{array}{llcllcl} (1) & \delta(\rhd \cdot \lhd) & = & \mathsf{Accept}, & (3) & \delta(aa) & = \mathsf{MVR}, \\ (2) & \delta(\rhd a) & = & \mathsf{MVR}, & (4) & \delta(ab) & = \lambda. \end{array}$$

Here we assume that $\delta(u) = \emptyset$ for all other cases. Thus, we see that $D_1 \in \mathcal{L}(\mathsf{stl\text{-}det\text{-}R(2)})$ holds. It can be shown analogously that each semi-Dyck language D_n, $n \geq 2$, is accepted by a stateless deterministic $\mathsf{R}(2)$-automaton. □

By Proposition 2.3.11, each stateless deterministic R(2)-automaton is necessarily monotone. As monotone deterministic R-automata accept deterministic context-free languages only (see Corollary 2.1.43), this observation has the following consequence.

Lemma 2.4.19 $\mathcal{L}(\mathsf{stl\text{-}det\text{-}R(2)}) \subseteq \mathsf{DCFL}$.

Actually, this inclusion is strict. This follows immediately from the following result.

Lemma 2.4.20 *For each integer $k \geq 1$, there exists a regular language $L_k \subseteq \{a, b\}^*$ such that $L_k \in \mathcal{L}(\mathsf{stl\text{-}det\text{-}mon\text{-}R}(k+1)) \smallsetminus \mathcal{L}(\mathsf{stl\text{-}sRW}(k))$, that is, L_k is accepted by a stateless deterministic and monotone R-automaton of window size $k+1$, but it is not accepted by any stateless shrinking RW-automaton of window size k.*

Proof. For $k \geq 1$, let $L_k = \{ (ab^k)^i \mid i \geq 0 \}$. Then L_k is obviously regular. Furthermore, let M_k be the stateless deterministic R-automaton of window size $k+1$ that is defined by the following transition function δ_{k+1}:

$$(1)\ \delta_{k+1}(\rhd \cdot \lhd) = \mathsf{Accept}, \quad (2)\ \delta_{k+1}(\rhd ab^{k-1}) = \mathsf{MVR}, \quad (3)\ \delta_{k+1}(ab^k) = \lambda.$$

Here we again use the convention that $\delta_{k+1}(u) = \emptyset$ for all other cases. It is obvious that the R-automaton M_k is monotone and that it accepts the language L_k.

On the other hand, assume that $M = (\Sigma, \Sigma, \rhd, \lhd, k, \delta)$ is a stateless sRW-automaton of window size k only that accepts the language L_k, and let $\omega : \Sigma \to \mathbb{N}_+$ be a weight function that is compatible with M. For the input ab^k, M will have an accepting computation. If $\mathsf{Accept} \in \delta(\rhd ab^{k-2})$, then M would accept on input $ab^{k-2} \notin L_k$, a contradiction. If $\rhd v \in \delta(\rhd ab^{k-2})$ is the first step in this accepting computation, then this computation begins with the cycle $\rhd ab^k \lhd \vdash_M^c \rhd vb^2 \lhd$. As we consider an accepting computation, $vb^2 \in L_k$. Hence, $v \in \{ (ab^k)^i ab^{k-2} \mid i \geq 0 \}$. However, $\omega(v) < \omega(ab^{k-2})$, which is impossible. Hence, it follows that the above computation begins with a MVR step, that is, M reaches the configuration $\rhd qab^k \lhd$, where q symbolizes the unique state of M. Now a transition from $\delta(ab^{k-1})$ has to be applied. Again it can neither be an accept nor a rewrite operation, that is, a MVR step is used, and so M reaches the configuration $\rhd aqb^k \lhd$. Continuing in this way, we see that M will reach the configuration $\rhd abqb^{k-1} \lhd$, and it will have to accept. However, it will then also accept the word ab^{k+1} that does not belong to the language L_k. Hence, L_k is not accepted by any stateless sRW-automaton of window size k. □

Together with Lemma 2.4.18, this yields the following result.

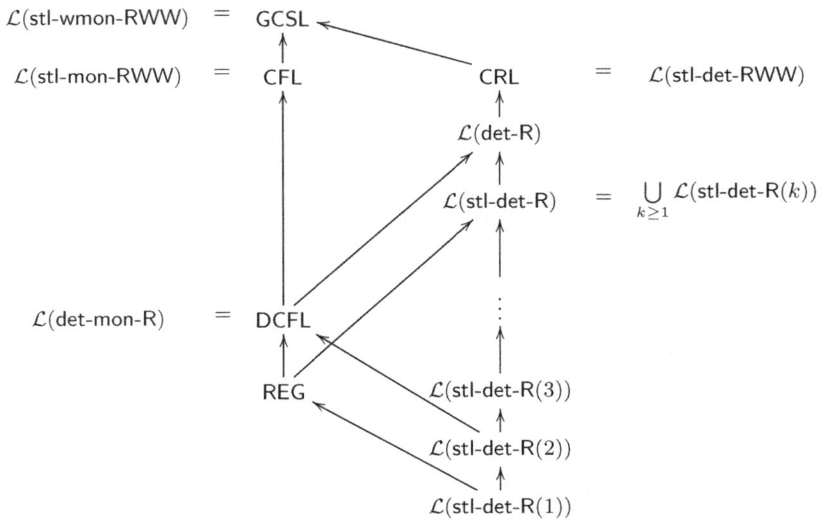

Figure 2.17: Taxonomy of language classes accepted by stateless deterministic R-automata. Here an arrow indicates a proper inclusion.

Corollary 2.4.21 ([179]) *The language classes* $(\mathcal{L}(\textsf{stl-det-R}(k)))_{k\geq 1}$ *form an infinite strictly ascending hierarchy. For all* $k \geq 2$, *the class* $\mathcal{L}(\textsf{stl-det-R}(k))$ *is incomparable under inclusion to the class* REG *of regular languages.*

In fact, we see that the same result also holds for the restarting automata of type stl-pref-X, where X is any of the types from $\{\textsf{R}, \textsf{RW}, \textsf{sRW}\}$ and $\textsf{pref} \in \{\textsf{det-mon-}, \textsf{det-}, \textsf{mon-}, \lambda\}$.

As noticed above, stateless deterministic R-automata of window size two only accept certain deterministic context-free languages. With window size larger than two, these automata accept some languages that are not even context-free. In the proof of Lemma 2.4.13(e), a stateless deterministic R-automaton of window size 9 is given for the non-context-free language $L_{\text{expo}}^{(\varphi)} = \varphi(L_{\text{expo}})$, where

$$L_{\text{expo}} = \{\, a^{i_0}ba^{i_1}b\cdots a^{i_{n-1}}ba^{i_n} \mid n \geq 0,\ i_0, i_1, \ldots, i_n \geq 0, \text{ and } \exists m \geq 0 : \sum_{j=0}^{n} 2^j \cdot i_j = 2^m \,\} \cup \{b\}^*.$$

Together with Corollary 2.4.21, this yields the following consequence.

Corollary 2.4.22 ([179]) *For all* $k \geq 9$, *the class* $\mathcal{L}(\textsf{stl-det-R}(k))$ *is incomparable under inclusion to the class CFL of context-free languages.*

It remains open whether the integer nine is the smallest number with the above property.

Problem 2.4.23 *What is the smallest integer* k *such that the language class* $\mathcal{L}(\textsf{stl-det-R}(k))$ *contains a non-context-free language? We know that* $3 \leq k \leq 9$ *holds, but it is open whether already the class* $\mathcal{L}(\textsf{stl-det-R}(3))$ *contains a non-context-free language.*

The diagram in Figure 2.17 summarizes the inclusion relations between the language classes that are accepted by the various types of stateless deterministic R-automata and some classical language families.

2.4.2 On Stateless sRRWW-Automata and Their Subclasses

Here we study the effect of the restriction to a single state on those restarting automata that, after executing a rewrite step, may continue to read before performing a restart. These are the so-called stateless sRRWW-automata and their variants. Thus, even after executing a rewrite step, such an automaton still has the option of accepting or rejecting instead of performing a restart. Actually, there are two variants of stateless sRRWW-automata. The first variant cannot distinguish between the part of a cycle *before* a rewrite step and the part *after* a rewrite step. Hence, such an automaton may try to execute a second rewrite step within a cycle. As this is not a legal move, it will be interpreted as a reject operation. This type of stateless sRRWW-automaton has been studied in [121, 122]. Here, however, we only consider the second variant, which can distinguish between the two parts of a cycle. This corresponds to the way in which stateless ORRWW-automata are defined in Subsection 2.3.4. It will turn out that, in the presence of auxiliary letters, the stateless restarting automata that are deterministic and/or monotone have the same expressive capacity as the corresponding types of restarting automata with states.

Definition 2.4.24 ([121, 122]) *A* stateless *sRRWW*-automaton, *or a* stl-sRRWW*-automaton for short, is described by a 7-tuple* $M = (\Sigma, \Gamma, \triangleright, \triangleleft, k, \delta_1, \delta_2)$, *where* δ_1 *is the transition relation that specifies the behavior of* M *during the first phase of each cycle, which ends with the execution of a rewrite step, while* δ_2 *is the transition relation that specifies the behavior of* M *after executing a rewrite step. Accept instructions can occur in both* δ_1 *and* δ_2. *In the former case, they correspond to accepting tail computations that do not contain rewrite steps, while, in the latter case, they correspond to accepting tail computations that contain rewrite steps.*

Let $M = (\Sigma, \Gamma, \triangleright, \triangleleft, k, \delta)$ be a stateless sRWW-automaton. We can convert M into an equivalent stateless sRRWW-automaton $M' = (\Sigma, \Gamma, \triangleright, \triangleleft, k, \delta_1, \delta_2)$ by simply taking $\delta_1 = \delta$ and by defining $\delta_2(w) = \{\mathsf{Restart}\}$ for each possible window contents w. Then M' executes the same cycles and tails as M. In particular, M' is deterministic and/or monotone if M is. Thus, we immediately get the following results.

Proposition 2.4.25 *For each* $\mathsf{X} \in \{\mathsf{WW}, \mathsf{W}, \lambda\}$ *and each* pref $\in$ {det-, mon-, wmon-, det-mon-, λ}, $\mathcal{L}$(stl-pref-(s)RX) $\subseteq$ $\mathcal{L}$(stl-pref-(s)RRX).

This yields the following characterizations from Theorems 2.4.9 and 2.4.10.

Corollary 2.4.26 ([121, 122])

(a) $\mathcal{L}$(stl-det-mon-(s)RRWW) = DCFL.
(b) $\mathcal{L}$(stl-mon-(s)RRWW) = CFL.
(c) $\mathcal{L}$(stl-det-(s)RRWW) = CRL.
(d) $\mathcal{L}$(stl-wmon-(s)RRWW) = GCSL.

Using again the language L_1^R, the next result states that stateless sRRWW-automata without auxiliary letters are quite weak.

Lemma 2.4.27 *The deterministic linear context-free language*

$$L_1^R = \{ cb^n a^n, db^{2n} a^n \mid n \geq 0 \}$$

is not accepted by any stateless sRRW-automaton.

Proof. Assume that $M = (\Sigma, \Sigma, \triangleright, \triangleleft, k, \delta_1, \delta_2)$ is a stateless sRRW-automaton such that $L(M) = L_1^R$ holds, where $\Sigma = \{a, b, c, d\}$. Then M has an accepting computation for the word $w = db^{2n}a^n$, where $n > k$. Obviously, this computation cannot be an accepting tail, that is, it begins with a cycle of the form $\triangleright w \triangleleft \vdash_M^c \triangleright w' \triangleleft$ for some word $w' \in L_1^R$. As in the proof of Lemma 2.4.7 above, it follows that $w' = db^{2n-2i}a^{n-i}$ for some $i \leq k/3$. Thus, M contains the rewrite transition $b^{k-l-2i}a^{l-i} \in \delta_1(b^{k-l}a^l)$ for some $l \geq i$ and, after executing this rewrite transition, M performs a restart on the suffix $a^{n-l}\triangleleft$ of the tape contents. Next, M also has an accepting computation for the word $z = cb^{n+i}a^{n+i}$. Finally, consider the word $v = cb^{n+i}a^n$, which does not belong to L_1^R.

Starting with input v, M cannot simply reject as it cannot distinguish between v and z before it has seen the tape contents completely. Thus, the computation of M on input v begins by moving the read/write window of M to the border between the factors b^{n+i} and a^n. However, at that place, M can apply the above rewrite transition, which yields the configuration $\triangleright cb^{n-i}a^{l-i}q_0a^{n-l}\triangleleft$, where q_0 denotes the unique state of M. As above, M will then perform a restart on this suffix, thus completing the cycle $\triangleright v\triangleleft = \triangleright cb^{n+i}a^n\triangleleft \vdash_M^c \triangleright cb^{n-i}a^{n-i}\triangleleft$. This, however, means that together with the word $cb^{n-i}a^{n-i} \in L_1^R$, M will also accept the word $v \notin L_1^R$, contradicting our assumption that $L(M) = L_1^R$ holds. Thus, L_1^R is not accepted by any stateless sRRW-automaton. □

Observe that the language L_1^R is already accepted by a det-mon-RR-automaton. It follows that without auxiliary letters, stateless sRRWW-automata are strictly less expressive than their counterparts with states, that is, $\mathcal{L}(\mathsf{stl\text{-}(det)\text{-}(mon)\text{-}(s)RRX}) \subsetneq \mathcal{L}(\mathsf{(det)\text{-}(mon)\text{-}(s)RRX})$ holds for all $\mathsf{X} \in \{\mathsf{W}, \lambda\}$. Below, we shall repeatedly utilize the witness language $L_{\text{expo}}^{(1)}$:

$$L_{\text{expo}}^{(1)} = \{\, a^{2^n} \mid n \geq 0 \,\} \cup \{\, a^iba^j \mid i,j \geq 0, \text{ and } \exists m \geq 1 : i + 2\cdot j = 2^m \,\}.$$

Lemma 2.4.28 $L_{\text{expo}}^{(1)} \in \mathcal{L}(\mathsf{stl\text{-}det\text{-}RRW})$.

Proof. Let $M = (\{a,b\}, \{a,b\}, \triangleright, \triangleleft, 5, \delta_1, \delta_2)$ be the stateless deterministic RRW-automaton that is specified through the following transition functions:

$$\begin{array}{llcllllcl}
(1) & \delta_1(\triangleright \cdot x \cdot \triangleleft) & = & \multicolumn{6}{l}{\mathsf{Accept}, \text{ for all } x \in \{a, a^2, ba, a^2b, ba^2\},} \\
(2) & \delta_1(\triangleright a^4) & = & \mathsf{MVR}, & (6) & \delta_1(a^4b) & = & ba^2, \\
(3) & \delta_1(\triangleright a^2ba) & = & \triangleright a^2, & (7) & \delta_1(a^4\triangleleft) & = & ba^2\triangleleft, \\
(4) & \delta_1(\triangleright ba^3) & = & \triangleright a^3, & (8) & \delta_2(a^5) & = & \mathsf{MVR}, \\
(5) & \delta_1(a^5) & = & \mathsf{MVR}, & (9) & \delta_2(a^i\triangleleft) & = & \mathsf{Restart}, \text{ for all } 0 \leq i \leq 4.
\end{array}$$

Let $w \in \{a,b\}^*$. If $|w| \leq 4$, then it is easily seen that M will accept input w if and only if $w \in L_{\text{expo}}^{(1)}$ holds. Thus, assume that $|w| \geq 5$. If $|w|_b \geq 2$, then M will get stuck on reading w. If $w = a^iba^j$, then M rejects immediately if $i = 1$ or if $i = 3$. If $i = 0$ or $i = 2$, then M immediately executes a rewrite operation that transforms w into the word $w_1 = a^{i/2+j}$ and restarts, and if $i \geq 4$, then it rewrites w into the word $w_1 = a^{i-4}ba^{j+2}$ and restarts. Finally, if $w = a^m$, then w is rewritten into $w_1 = a^{m-4}ba^2$. Thus, in each case, w_1 belongs to $L_{\text{expo}}^{(1)}$ if and only if w does. It follows that $L(M) = L_{\text{expo}}^{(1)}$. □

The next result states that stateless sRW-automata are less expressive.

Lemma 2.4.29 $L_{\text{expo}}^{(1)} \notin \mathcal{L}(\mathsf{stl\text{-}sRW})$.

Proof. Assume that $M = (\{a,b\}, \{a,b\}, \triangleright, \triangleleft, k, \delta)$ is a stateless sRW-automaton such that $L(M) = L_{\text{expo}}^{(1)}$. Consider the word $w = ba^{2^n} \in L_{\text{expo}}^{(1)}$, where n is sufficiently large. If M accepts w in a tail computation, then it will also accept the word $wa = ba^{2^n+1} \notin L_{\text{expo}}^{(1)}$, as M is stateless. On the other hand, if an accepting computation of M on input w begins with a cycle of the form $\triangleright w\triangleleft \vdash_M^c \triangleright w_1\triangleleft$, then w_1 must be an element of $L_{\text{expo}}^{(1)}$. As each rewrite step of M is weight-reducing, it follows that $w_1 = a^{2^n}$, that is, M rewrites the prefix $\triangleright ba^{k-1}$ into the word $\triangleright a^{k-1}$. Now consider the word $z = ba^{2^n}ba^{2^{n-1}} \notin L_{\text{expo}}^{(1)}$. On input z, M can execute the cycle $\triangleright z\triangleleft = \triangleright ba^{2^n}ba^{2^{n-1}}\triangleleft \vdash_M^c \triangleright a^{2^n}ba^{2^{n-1}}\triangleleft$. As $a^{2^n}ba^{2^{n-1}} \in L_{\text{expo}}^{(1)}$, this implies that $z \in L(M)$. It follows that $L(M) \neq L_{\text{expo}}^{(1)}$. □

Together with Proposition 2.4.25, Lemmas 2.4.28 and 2.4.29 yield the following proper inclusions.

Corollary 2.4.30 (a) $\mathcal{L}(\mathsf{stl\text{-}det\text{-}(s)RW}) \subsetneq \mathcal{L}(\mathsf{stl\text{-}det\text{-}(s)RRW})$.
(b) $\mathcal{L}(\mathsf{stl\text{-}(s)RW}) \subsetneq \mathcal{L}(\mathsf{stl\text{-}(s)RRW})$.

In order to derive corresponding results for stl-det-RR-automata, we consider the following example language.

Definition 2.4.31 *Let $\varphi : \{a,b\}^* \to \{a,b\}^*$ be the morphism that is induced by mapping $a \mapsto ab$ and $b \mapsto b$. Then φ is an injective mapping, that is, it is an encoding. Now let $L_\varphi^{(1)}$ be the language $L_\varphi^{(1)} = \varphi(L_{\text{expo}}^{(1)})$, that is,*

$$L_\varphi^{(1)} = \{\, (ab)^{2^n} \mid n \geq 0 \,\} \cup \{\, (ab)^i b (ab)^j \mid i,j \geq 0, \text{ and } \exists m \geq 1 : i + 2 \cdot j = 2^m \,\}.$$

The following result holds for this language.

Lemma 2.4.32 $L_\varphi^{(1)} \in \mathcal{L}(\text{stl-det-RR})$.

Proof. Let $M = (\{a,b\},\{a,b\},\rhd,\lhd,9,\delta_1,\delta_2)$ be the stateless deterministic RR-automaton that is specified through the following transition functions:

$$\begin{array}{lllllll}
(1) & \delta_1(\rhd \cdot x \cdot \lhd) & = & \multicolumn{4}{l}{\mathsf{Accept} \text{ for all } x \in \{ab, (ab)^2, b(ab), b(ab)^2, (ab)^2 b, (ab)^2 b(ab)\},} \\
(2) & \delta_1(\rhd (ab)^4) & = & \mathsf{MVR}, & (9) & \delta_1(\rhd b(ab)^3 a) & = \rhd (ab)^3 a, \\
(3) & \delta_1((ab)^3 b(ab)) & = & \mathsf{MVR}, & (10) & \delta_1(\rhd (ab)^2 b(ab)a) & = \rhd (ab)^2 a, \\
(4) & \delta_1((ab)^4 a) & = & \mathsf{MVR}, & (11) & \delta_1(b(ab)^2 b(ab)a) & = bb(ab)^2 a, \\
(5) & \delta_1(b(ab)^4) & = & \mathsf{MVR}, & (12) & \delta_2((ab)^4 a) & = \mathsf{MVR}, \\
(6) & \delta_1((ab)^4 b) & = & \mathsf{MVR}, & (13) & \delta_2(b(ab)^4) & = \mathsf{MVR}, \\
(7) & \delta_1(b(ab)^3 ba) & = & \mathsf{MVR}, & (14) & \delta_2(b(ab)^i \lhd) & = \mathsf{Restart},\ 0 \leq i \leq 3, \\
(8) & \delta_1((ab)^4 \lhd) & = & b(ab)^2 \lhd, & (15) & \delta_2((ab)^4 \lhd) & = \mathsf{Restart}.
\end{array}$$

Essentially, M just simulates the stateless deterministic RRW-automaton from the proof of Lemma 2.4.28. Observe that the rewritten factors in rules (9), (10), and (11) all end with the letter a. This implies that M will never accept a word that contains the factor aa, as such a factor is not contained in any word accepted in a tail computation (rule (1)), nor can M ever remove such a factor from the tape. Thus, whenever one of the rules (9) to (11) is applied within an accepting computation, then the first letter to the right of the place where the rewrite step is executed is necessarily a b. Together with the fact that the rewritten factors always end with the letter a, this ensures that M will detect the occurrence of a second copy of $\varphi(b)$ in the actual tape contents from $\varphi(\{a,b\}^*)$. Based on this observation, it can now be verified that $L(M) = L_\varphi^{(1)}$. □

By using essentially the same arguments as in the proof of Lemma 2.4.29, it can be shown that $L_\varphi^{(1)}$ is not accepted by any stateless R-automaton, which yields the following separation results.

Corollary 2.4.33 (a) $\mathcal{L}(\text{stl-det-R}) \subsetneq \mathcal{L}(\text{stl-det-RR})$.
(b) $\mathcal{L}(\text{stl-R}) \subsetneq \mathcal{L}(\text{stl-RR})$.

Finally, we consider the complement $\bar{L}_{\text{expo}}^{(1)} = \{a,b\}^* \smallsetminus L_{\text{expo}}^{(1)}$ of the language $L_{\text{expo}}^{(1)}$. Obviously,

$$\begin{array}{rcl}
\bar{L}_{\text{expo}}^{(1)} & = & \{\, w \in \{a,b\}^* \mid |w|_b \geq 2 \,\} \cup \{\, a^m \mid m \text{ is not a power of } 2 \,\} \cup \\
& & \{\, a^i b a^j \mid i,j \geq 0, \text{ and } i + 2 \cdot j \text{ is not a power of } 2 \,\}.
\end{array}$$

It is not hard to construct a stl-det-RRW-automaton $\overline{M}$ for this language. On words of the form a^m or $a^i b a^j$, $\overline{M}$ behaves essentially just like the stateless deterministic RRW-automaton M for the language $L_{\text{expo}}^{(1)}$ from the proof of Lemma 2.4.28, only that it accepts on other words of length at most 3, while it simply accepts on encountering two b's that are close together in the first phase of a cycle or on encountering a b in the second phase of a cycle. On the other hand, we have the following result.

Lemma 2.4.34 *$\bar{L}_{\text{expo}}^{(1)}$ is not accepted by any stateless deterministic sRRW-automaton that executes accept instructions only at the right end of the tape.*

Proof. Assume that there is a stl-det-sRRW-automaton $M = (\{a,b\},\{a,b\},\rhd,\lhd,k,\delta_1,\delta_2)$ that executes accept instructions only at the right end of the tape and that accepts the language $\bar{L}_{\text{expo}}^{(1)}$.

First, we consider the input $w_1 = ba^{2^m+1} \in \bar{L}^{(1)}_{\text{expo}}$, where $m > 0$ is a large integer. Given w_1 as input, M will accept, but it cannot accept in a tail computation, since then it would also accept the word ba^{2^m}, which does not belong to the language $\bar{L}^{(1)}_{\text{expo}}$. Hence, the accepting computation of M on input w_1 begins with a cycle of the form $\triangleright w_1 \triangleleft \vdash^c_M \triangleright w_2 \triangleleft$ for some word $w_2 \in \bar{L}^{(1)}_{\text{expo}}$. In this cycle, M executes a rewrite step $\delta_1(u) = v$ such that either $u = \triangleright ba^{k-2}$, $u = ba^{k-1}$, $u = a^k$, or $u = a^j \triangleleft$ for some $1 \leq j \leq k-1$. Accordingly, $\triangleright w_2 = va^{2^m+3-k}$, $w_2 = va^{2^m+2-k}$, $w_2 = bva^{2^m+1-k}$, or $w_2 \triangleleft = ba^{2^m+1-j}v$. As M is stateless, it will execute a corresponding cycle for the input word $w_1 a^{2^m-1} = ba^{2^{m+1}} \in L^{(1)}_{\text{expo}}$, resulting in the word $\triangleright w_3 = va^{2^{m+1}+2-k}$, $w_3 = va^{2^{m+1}+1-k}$, $w_3 = bva^{2^{m+1}-k}$, or $w_3 \triangleleft = ba^{2^{m+1}-j}v$. The fact that $w_1 a^{2^m-1} \in L^{(1)}_{\text{expo}}$ implies that $w_3 \in L^{(1)}_{\text{expo}}$.

If $|u|_b = 0 = |v|_b$, then the above rewrite operation simply removes $j \geq 1$ occurrences of the letter a, where $j \leq k$. As m is large, this implies that $w_3 \in \bar{L}^{(1)}_{\text{expo}}$, a contradiction. If $|v|_b \geq 2$, or if $|u|_b = 0$ and $|v|_b = 1$, we obtain the same contradiction.

Next consider the case that $|u|_b = 1$ and $|v|_b = 1$. Then the above rewrite transition is of the form $\delta_1(\triangleright ba^{k-2}) = \triangleright a^i ba^{k-2-r}$ or $\delta_1(ba^{k-1}) = a^i ba^{k-1-r}$ for some $i, r \geq 0$ satisfying $i < r \leq k-2$ (respectively, $i < r \leq k-1$). However, this implies that $w_3 = a^i ba^{2^{m+1}-r} \in \bar{L}^{(1)}_{\text{expo}}$, again giving the same contradiction.

Finally, assume that $|u|_b = 1$ and $|v|_b = 0$, that is, the rewrite transition above is of the form $\delta_1(\triangleright ba^{k-2}) = \triangleright a^{k-2+j}$ or $\delta_1(ba^{k-1}) = a^{k-1+j}$ for some integer j. Then $w_3 = a^{2^{m+1}+j}$, which again yields the same contradiction as above if $j \neq 0$. It follows that $j = 0$. Now consider the input $w_4 = ba^{2^{m+1}}ba^{2^m} \in \bar{L}^{(1)}_{\text{expo}}$. On input w_4, M will accept, but the corresponding accepting computation begins with an application of the above rewrite transition. Thus, $w_4 = ba^{2^{m+1}}ba^{2^m}$ is rewritten into the word $a^{2^{m+1}}ba^{2^m} \in L^{(1)}_{\text{expo}}$. After executing this rewrite step, M will scan the remaining tape. On encountering the second occurrence of the letter b, it 'knows' that the given input w_4 belongs to the language $\bar{L}^{(1)}_{\text{expo}}$, but, by our assumption, M cannot accept at that point. Instead, it has to scan the remaining suffix a^{2^m}. Now, on encountering the right sentinel $\triangleleft$, M does not remember that it has seen two occurrences of the letter b, that is, it cannot distinguish between w_4 and the input $w_5 = ba^{2^m} \notin \bar{L}^{(1)}_{\text{expo}}$. Thus, M either accepts, that is, it accepts both w_4 and w_5, a contradiction, or it makes a restart, which means that it executes the cycle $\triangleright w_4 \triangleleft \vdash^c_M \triangleright a^{2^{m+1}}ba^{2^m} \triangleleft$. However, as $a^{2^{m+1}}ba^{2^m} \in L^{(1)}_{\text{expo}}$, M will have to reject eventually, which means that it also rejects the input $w_4 \in \bar{L}^{(1)}_{\text{expo}}$, which is again a contradiction. As this covers all cases, it follows that $L(M) \neq \bar{L}^{(1)}_{\text{expo}}$. □

In an analogous manner, it can also be shown that the language $\bar{L}^{(1)}_{\varphi} = \{a, b\}^* \smallsetminus L^{(1)}_{\varphi}$ is not accepted by any stl-det-RR-automaton that executes all its accept instructions at the right end of the tape, but that an (unrestricted) stl-det-RR-automaton can accept this language. Thus, by restricting stl-det-(s)RR(W)-automata to execute accept instructions only at the right end of the tape, the expressive capacity of these types of automata is properly diminished. This contrasts the situation for stateless RW-automata.

Finally, we turn to the closure properties of those language classes that are specified by the various types of stateless deterministic restarting automata without auxiliary letters. Closure under certain operations indicates a certain robustness of the language classes considered, while non-closure properties may serve, for example, as a valuable basis for extensions.

As we shall see, almost all language families considered here form *anti-AFLs*, that is, they are not closed under any of the AFL operations. Anti-AFLs are sometimes referred to as 'unfortunate families of languages,' but there is linguistical evidence that such language families might be of crucial importance, since the family of natural languages is an anti-AFL, too [38]. Hence, the quest for uncommon automata models that induce anti-AFLs seems to be worthwhile. Our results are summarized in Corollary 2.4.44 at the end of this section.

First, we explore the closure properties under the Boolean operations union, intersection, and complementation. The languages $L_{d,1} = \{ cb^n a^n \mid n \geq 0 \}$ and $L_{d,2} = \{ db^{2n} a^n \mid n \geq 0 \}$ are easily seen to be accepted by stl-det-R-automata. As shown in Lemma 2.4.27, their union $L^R_1 = L_{d,1} \cup L_{d,2}$

is not accepted by any stl-det-sRRW-automaton. This yields the following non-closure results.

Theorem 2.4.35 *The language classes* $\mathcal{L}(\mathsf{stl\text{-}det\text{-}R(R)})$ *and* $\mathcal{L}(\mathsf{stl\text{-}det\text{-}(s)R(R)W})$ *are not closed under union.*

Let M be a stateless deterministic R(R)-automaton or a stateless deterministic (s)R(R)W-automaton accepting a language $L \subseteq \Sigma^*$. By switching accepting and rejecting (that is, undefined) transition steps, we obtain an automaton of the same type as M that accepts the language $L^c = \Sigma^* \smallsetminus L$. This gives our only closure properties.

Theorem 2.4.36 *The language classes* $\mathcal{L}(\mathsf{stl\text{-}det\text{-}R(R)})$ *and* $\mathcal{L}(\mathsf{stl\text{-}det\text{-}(s)R(R)W})$ *are closed under complementation.*

From Lemmas 2.4.28, 2.4.32, and 2.4.34, we see that the language classes $\mathcal{L}(\mathsf{stl\text{-}det\text{-}(s)RR(W)})$ would not be closed under complementation, if stateless (s)RR(W)-automata were required to execute accept steps only at the right end of the tape. For the stateless deterministic R(R)- and (s)R(R)W-automata, non-closure under intersection is now immediate. However, we even have the following stronger result.

Theorem 2.4.37 *The language classes* $\mathcal{L}(\mathsf{stl\text{-}det\text{-}R(R)})$ *and* $\mathcal{L}(\mathsf{stl\text{-}det\text{-}(s)R(R)W})$ *are not closed under intersection with regular languages.*

Proof. By Lemma 2.4.13, the language

$$L_{\text{expo}} = \{\, a^{i_0}ba^{i_1}b\cdots a^{i_{n-1}}ba^{i_n} \mid n \geq 0,\ i_0, i_1, \ldots, i_n \geq 0, \text{ and } \exists\, m \geq 0 : \sum_{j=0}^{n} 2^j \cdot i_j = 2^m \,\} \cup \{b\}^*$$

is accepted by a stl-det-RW-automaton, while $L_{\text{expo}} \cap \{a\}^* = \{\, a^{2^m} \mid m \geq 0 \,\}$ is not accepted by any sRRW-automaton. Analogously, the language $L_{\text{expo}}^{(\varphi)} = \varphi(L_{\text{expo}})$ is accepted by a stl-det-R-automaton, while $L_{\text{expo}}^{(\varphi)} \cap \{ab\}^* = \{\, (ab)^{2^n} \mid n \geq 0 \,\}$ is not accepted by any sRRW-automaton. Thus, none of the language classes considered here is closed under intersection with regular languages. □

Next we consider the closure under reversal. Here we have the following negative result, which extends a result from [122], as the proof given in [122] easily generalizes to the corresponding types of shrinking restarting automata.

Theorem 2.4.38 ([122]) *None of the language classes* $\mathcal{L}(\mathsf{stl\text{-}det\text{-}R(R)})$ *or* $\mathcal{L}(\mathsf{stl\text{-}det\text{-}(s)R(R)W})$ *is closed under reversal.*

Proof outline. First, we consider the case of stateless deterministic (s)R(W)-automata. It is quite easy to design a stl-det-R-automaton M for the language

$$L_{acab} = \{\, a^m c^n a^{n+r} b^{m+r} \mid m, n \geq 1, r \geq 0 \,\}.$$

For deriving a contradiction, assume that $M_R = (\Sigma, \Sigma, \rhd, \lhd, k, \delta)$ is a stateless deterministic sRW-automaton accepting the reversal of L_{acab}. Let $b^{m+r}a^{n+r}c^n a^m$ be a word with large m, n, r. The automaton M_R cannot accept this word in a tail computation. Furthermore, it cannot rewrite just one type of letters without producing a word that does not belong to L_{acab}^R. Now assume that M_R contains a rewrite step of the form $\delta(b^i a^j) = v$, where $i + j = k$. Then M_R can execute the cycle $\rhd b^{m+r}a^{n+r}c^n a^m \lhd \vdash_{M_R}^{c} \rhd b^{m+r-i} v a^{n+r-j} c^n a^m \lhd$, and as M_R is deterministic, $b^{m+r-i} v a^{n+r-j} c^n a^m \in L_{acab}^R$ by the Correctness Preserving Property for M_R. This implies that $v = b^s a^t$ for some $s, t \geq 0$. As M_R is weight-reducing, this means that $s < i$ or $t < j$. The conditions on the exponents of the various letters require that

$$m + r - i + s - (n + r - j + t) + n = m,$$

which yields $i - s = j - t$. Thus, $v = b^{i-l}a^{j-l}$ for some $l \geq 1$. Hence, after at most $r+1$ cycles, we obtain a word of the form $b^{m-s}a^{n-s}c^n a^m \notin L_{acab}^R$ for some $s \geq 1$, which contradicts the Correctness Preserving Property for M_R. Therefore, M_R cannot rewrite in this situation, which means that M_R can never delete one of the leading b's and, thus, cannot check the correct suffix length m. We obtain a contradiction, showing that the reversal of the language L_{acab} is not accepted by any stl-det-sRW-automaton.

Finally, we give the proof for stl-det-(s)RR(W)-automata. By Lemma 2.4.28, the language $L_{\text{expo}}^{(1)}$ is accepted by a stl-det-RRW-automaton. However, its reversal

$$(L_{\text{expo}}^{(1)})^R = \{\, a^{2^n} \mid n \geq 0 \,\} \cup \{\, a^i b a^j \mid i, j \geq 0, \text{ and } \exists\, m \geq 0 : 2 \cdot i + j = 2^m \,\}$$

cannot even be accepted by a deterministic sRRW-automaton with states. Assume that $M = (Q, \{a,b\}, \{a,b\}, \rhd, \lhd, q_0, k, \delta)$ is a det-sRRW-automaton such that $(L_{\text{expo}}^{(1)})^R = L(M)$ holds. Consider the word $w = a^{2^n} \in (L_{\text{expo}}^{(1)})^R$, where $n > 0$ is sufficiently large. As M cannot accept w in a tail computation, the accepting computation of M on input w starts with a cycle $q_0 \rhd w \lhd \vdash_M^c q_0 \rhd w_1 \lhd$. Then $w_1 \in (L_{\text{expo}}^{(1)})^R$, and it follows from the fact that each rewrite step of M is weight-reducing that $w_1 = a^i b a^{2^n - 2i}$ for some i satisfying $2 \leq i < k/2$. Hence, M transforms a prefix a^m of w into the word $a^i b a^{m-2i}$, where $m \leq 2k$.

Now consider the input $z = a^{2^n} b \in (L_{\text{expo}}^{(1)})^R$. Again M cannot accept z in a tail computation. Thus, the accepting computation of M on input z begins with a cycle $q_0 \rhd z \lhd \vdash_M^c q_0 \rhd z_1 \lhd$. As M is deterministic, this computation begins with the transformation above, which implies that $z_1 = a^i b a^{2^n - 2i} b$. As $z_1 \notin (L_{\text{expo}}^{(1)})^R$, this contradicts our assumption that $(L_{\text{expo}}^{(1)})^R = L(M)$ holds. It follows that $(L_{\text{expo}}^{(1)})^R$ is not accepted by any deterministic sRRW-automaton.

By Lemma 2.4.32, $L_{\varphi}^{(1)}$ is accepted by a stl-det-RR-automaton, but by using essentially the same reasoning as above, it can be shown that $(L_{\varphi}^{(1)})^R$ is not accepted by any det-RR-automaton with states. □

The proof above even shows that the language classes $\mathcal{L}(\mathsf{det\text{-}RR(W)})$ are not closed under reversal, either. Next we disprove the closure of the language families under consideration with respect to morphisms, even non-erasing morphisms, and with respect to inverse morphisms.

Theorem 2.4.39 *None of the language classes $\mathcal{L}(\mathsf{stl\text{-}det\text{-}R(R)})$ or $\mathcal{L}(\mathsf{stl\text{-}det\text{-}(s)R(R)W})$ is closed under non-erasing morphisms.*

Proof. We consider the language $L_{dm} = \{\, cb^n \bar{c} a^n \mid n \geq 0 \,\} \cup \{\, db^{2n} \bar{d} a^n \mid n \geq 0 \,\}$, which is easily seen to be accepted by a stl-det-R-automaton. Now let h be the non-erasing morphism that is defined by taking $h(a) = a$, $h(b) = b$, $h(c) = c$, $h(d) = d$, $h(\bar{c}) = ba$, and $h(\bar{d}) = bba$. Then $h(L_{dm}) = \{\, cb^n a^n \mid n \geq 1 \,\} \cup \{\, db^{2n} a^n \mid n \geq 1 \,\}$, which equals the language L_1^R except for the case $n = 0$. As in the proof of Lemma 2.4.27, it can be shown that this language is not accepted by any stateless sRRW-automaton, either, and, therewith, not by an automaton of any of the types considered here. □

The language L_{expo} (see Definition 2.4.12) is not accepted by any RR-automaton, while by Lemma 2.4.13(e), its morphic image $L_{\text{expo}}^{(\varphi)} = \varphi(L_{\text{expo}})$ even belongs to $\mathcal{L}(\mathsf{stl\text{-}det\text{-}R})$, where $\varphi : \{a,b\}^* \to \{a,b\}^*$ is the morphism defined through $a \mapsto ab$ and $b \mapsto b$. Since this morphism is injective, we obtain the following corollary.

Corollary 2.4.40 *The language classes $\mathcal{L}(\mathsf{stl\text{-}det\text{-}R})$ and $\mathcal{L}(\mathsf{stl\text{-}det\text{-}RR})$ are not closed under inverse morphisms.*

In fact, also the following language classes are not closed under inverse morphisms.

Lemma 2.4.41 ([122]) *The language classes $\mathcal{L}(\mathsf{stl\text{-}det\text{-}RW})$ and $\mathcal{L}(\mathsf{stl\text{-}det\text{-}RRW})$ are not closed under inverse morphisms.*

For a proof, we refer to [122]. However, it remains open whether this result extends to shrinking stl-det-R(R)W-automata.

Problem 2.4.42 *Are the language classes* $\mathcal{L}(\mathsf{stl\text{-}det\text{-}sR(R)W})$ *closed under inverse morphisms?*

We conclude this section by showing that none of the language families considered here is closed under product or Kleene plus.

Lemma 2.4.43 *The language classes* $\mathcal{L}(\mathsf{stl\text{-}det\text{-}R(R)})$ *and* $\mathcal{L}(\mathsf{stl\text{-}det\text{-}(s)R(R)W})$ *are neither closed under product nor under Kleene plus.*

Proof. We consider the language

$$L_f = \{\, a^n b^n \mid n \geq 0 \,\} \cup \{a\}^* \cup \{\, b^n c^n \mid n \geq 0 \,\},$$

which is accepted by the stateless deterministic R-automaton that is defined by the following transition function:

$$\begin{array}{rlcl rlcl}
(1) & \delta(\rhd \cdot \lhd) & = & \mathsf{Accept}, & (9) & \delta(\rhd bbc) & = & \mathsf{MVR},\\
(2) & \delta(\rhd ab\lhd) & = & \mathsf{Accept}, & (10) & \delta(aaaa) & = & \mathsf{MVR},\\
(3) & \delta(\rhd a\lhd) & = & \mathsf{Accept}, & (11) & \delta(aaab) & = & \mathsf{MVR},\\
(4) & \delta(\rhd aa\lhd) & = & \mathsf{Accept}, & (12) & \delta(bbbb) & = & \mathsf{MVR},\\
(5) & \delta(\rhd bc\lhd) & = & \mathsf{Accept}, & (13) & \delta(bbbc) & = & \mathsf{MVR},\\
(6) & \delta(\rhd aaa) & = & \mathsf{MVR}, & (14) & \delta(aabb) & = & ab,\\
(7) & \delta(\rhd aab) & = & \mathsf{MVR}, & (15) & \delta(aaa\lhd) & = & aa\lhd,\\
(8) & \delta(\rhd bbb) & = & \mathsf{MVR}, & (16) & \delta(bbcc) & = & bc.
\end{array}$$

A word of the form $w(m,n,r) = a^m b^n c^r$, where $m,n,r \geq 1$, is an element of $L_f \cdot L_f$ if and only if $n = r$ or $n = m + r$, and $w(m,n,r)$ is an element of $(L_f)^+$ if and only if $r \leq n \leq m + r$.

Assume that M' is a stateless determinininistic sRRW-automaton of window size k for the language $L_f \cdot L_f$. An input of the form $a^n b^n \in L_f \cdot L_f$ with large n cannot be accepted by M' in a tail computation, that is, it has to be rewritten. Because of the Correctness Preserving Property, the word obtained by this rewrite operation must belong to $L_f \cdot L_f$.

Case 1. Assume that a^i is rewritten into some factor u. Then $|u|_a < i$. Hence, the word $a^n b^{2n} c^n \in L_f \cdot L_f$ is rewritten into the word $w' = ua^{n-i}b^{2n}c^n$. As $|u|_a + n - i < n$ and $2n > (|u|_a + n - i) + n$, it follows from the observation above that $w' \notin (L_f)^+$, which contradicts the Correctness Preserving Property for M'.

Case 2. Assume that $a^i b^j$ is rewritten into a word u for some $i, j > 0$. If $|u|_b < j$, then the word $a^n b^n c^n \in L_f \cdot L_f$ is rewritten into the word $a^{n-i}ub^{n-j}c^n$, which does not belong to $(L_f)^+$, as $|u|_b + n - j < n$. Thus, $|u|_b \geq j$ and therefore, $|u|_a < i$. Then the word $a^n b^{2n} c^n \in L_f \cdot L_f$ is rewritten into the word $a^{n-i}ub^{2n-j}c^n$, which does not belong to $(L_f)^+$, as

$$|a^{n-i}u|_a = n - i + |u|_a < n \leq |u|_b + n - j.$$

Again, this contradicts the Correctness Preserving Property for M'.

Case 3. If b^i is replaced with some word u, then $|u|_b < i$. Then the word $a^n b^n c^n \in L_f \cdot L_f$ is rewritten into $a^n u b^{n-i} c^n$, which does not belong to $(L_f)^+$, as $|u|_b + n - i < n$. Again, this contradicts the Correctness Preserving Property for M'.

Case 4. Finally, assume that $b^i\lhd$ is replaced with $u\lhd$ for some $i \geq 1$. Then $|u|_b < i$, and we can assume without loss of generality that u does not begin with a b. Thus, $u = c^j v$ for some $j \geq 0$, where v does not begin with a c. Then $a^n b^n \in L_f \cdot L_f$ is rewritten into the word

$$a^n b^{n-i} c^j v = (a^{i+j})(a^{n-i-j} b^{n-i-j})(b^j c^j) v.$$

If $j > 0$ or $v \neq \lambda$, then this word does not belong to $L_f \cdot L_f$, which contradicts the Correctness Preserving Property for M'. Hence, $u = \lambda$, which implies that the word $a^n b^{n+i} \notin (L_f)^+$ is rewritten into the word $a^n b^n \in L_f \cdot L_f$. This, however, contradicts the Error Preserving Property for M'.

As this covers all possible cases, we see that the language $L_f \cdot L_f$ is not accepted by any stateless deterministic sRRW-automaton. It follows that the language classes $\mathcal{L}(\mathsf{stl\text{-}det\text{-}R(R)})$ and $\mathcal{L}(\mathsf{stl\text{-}det\text{-}(s)R(R)W})$ are not closed under product.

Actually, the above proof easily extends to show that the language $(L_f)^+$ is not accepted by any stateless deterministic sRRW-automaton. Assume that M' is a stateless deterministic sRRW-automaton for the language $(L_f)^+$. Cases 1 to 3 apply directly to $(L_f)^+$, while in Case 4, we obtain the following. If $b^i \lhd$ is rewritten into $c^j v \lhd$ for some $j \geq 0$, then the word $a^n b^n \in L_f \cdot L_f$ is rewritten into the word

$$a^n b^{n-i} c^j v = (a^{i+j})(a^{n-i-j} b^{n-i-j})(b^j c^j)v.$$

This word belongs to $(L_f)^+$, if $v \in (L_f)^+$. But then the word $a^n b^{n+i+j} \notin (L_f)^+$ is rewritten into the word $a^n b^{n+j} c^j v = (a^n b^n)(b^j c^j)v \in (L_f)^+$, which contradicts the Error Preserving Property for M'. Hence, the classes $\mathcal{L}(\mathsf{stl\text{-}det\text{-}R(R)})$ and $\mathcal{L}(\mathsf{stl\text{-}det\text{-}(s)R(R)W})$ are not closed under Kleene plus, either. □

In summary, we have derived the following results.

Corollary 2.4.44 ([122]) (a) *The language classes* $\mathcal{L}(\mathsf{stl\text{-}det\text{-}R(R)})$ *and* $\mathcal{L}(\mathsf{stl\text{-}det\text{-}(s)R(R)W})$ *are closed under complementation, but not under reversal.*

(b) *The language classes* $\mathcal{L}(\mathsf{stl\text{-}det\text{-}R(R)})$ *and* $\mathcal{L}(\mathsf{stl\text{-}det\text{-}R(R)W})$ *are anti-AFLs, that is, they are not closed under union, intersection with regular sets, product, Kleene plus, non-erasing morphisms, and inverse morphisms.*

(c) *The language classes* $\mathcal{L}(\mathsf{stl\text{-}det\text{-}sR(R)W})$ *are anti-AFLs if they are not closed under inverse morphisms.*

For the various types of restarting automata considered in this section, auxiliary letters can compensate for the absence of states, but without them, the stateless deterministic variants are strictly weaker than those with states. In particular, for (almost) all types of stateless deterministic restarting automata without auxiliary letters considered, the corresponding language class is an anti-AFL. We expect that many of these results carry over to the nondeterministic case.

2.5 Increasing the Number of Rewrites Per Cycle

Here we study the influence of the number of rewrite steps executed within a single cycle on the expressive capacity of the various types of restarting automata. First, we study this question for sRWW-automata. We shall see that, for this type of automaton, the number of allowed rewrites per cycle does not influence their expressive capacity. In fact, for sRWW-automata, even admitting an unbounded number of rewrites per cycle does not affect their expressive capacity.

In the second subsection, we focus on constrained computations of restarting automata. In natural languages with a high degree of word order freedom, syntactic phenomena like dependencies (subordinations) or valences do not depend on the word order (that is, on the individual positions of the individual words). This means that some permutations of sentences of these languages are in some (important) sense syntactically equivalent. Here we consider this phenomenon in a formal way. Various types of j-monotonicity are studied for restarting automata that can serve as parameters for the degree of word order freedom and for the complexity of the word order in sentences (languages). We combine two types of parameters on computations of restarting automata: the degree of j-monotonicity and the number of rewrites per cycle. By studying these notions formally, we obtain an adequate tool for modelling and comparing formal descriptions of (natural) languages with different degrees of word order freedom and word order complexity. Accordingly, we first discuss the notion of j-monotonicity, presenting a number of important results from the literature. Then we combine this notion with multiple rewrites per cycle, which leads to the notion of j-constrained computations. For us, the degree of constrainability serves as a synonym for the degree of word order complexity of a language. We concentrate on characteristic languages as the full analysis by reduction is applied to tagged sentences (see Section 1.8).

In Subsection 2.5.3, we relate RR-automata that execute up to t delete steps per cycle to t-contextual languages with regular selection (see Section 1.3). Then we introduce an additional locality restriction for the latter, which yields a correspondence to RR-automata that execute a single delete step of cut-index t within each cycle. Such a delete step removes exactly t factors from the current contents of the window. As it turns out, the cut-index induces strict infinite hierarchies of language classes for deterministic and nondeterministic R- and RR-automata.

In the forth subsection, we turn to a restricted class of restarting automata that have two windows. This model is motivated by the phenomenon of *long-distance scrambling*, which induces a dependency of items across a large distance (see, e.g., [227]). Certainly, the use of two independent heads or windows can help in this matter. In fact, in [55], an ad-hoc variant of the restarting automaton is defined that has two windows: one window can only delete a single letter in a rewrite step, while the other window may rewrite a non-empty word into a word of length at most one. It is shown in [55] that a certain restricted type of these restarting automata corresponds to *sorted dependency insertion grammars with regular selectors* that work in a top-down derivation style. Here we present a rather restricted type of restarting automaton with two windows, called *det-2-RR-automaton*. Such an automaton is deterministic, and the rewrite operations that it can perform are only deletions. In addition, we require that each of the two windows executes at most one such operation within a cycle.

2.5.1 On sRWW-Automata with Multiple Rewrites per Cycle

A (shrinking) restarting automaton with *multiple rewrites* is a (shrinking) restarting automaton that may perform more than one rewrite step in a cycle or a tail. Observe that, by definition, each rewrite operation of a (length-reducing) restarting automaton reduces the length of the tape contents, and that each rewrite operation of a shrinking restarting automaton reduces the overall weight of the tape contents with respect to a compatible weight function. In fact, we distinguish between several variants of restarting automata with multiple rewrites.

Definition 2.5.1 *Let* $\mathsf{X} \in \{\mathsf{R}, \mathsf{RR}, \mathsf{RW}, \mathsf{RRW}, \mathsf{sRW}, \mathsf{sRRW}, \mathsf{RWW}, \mathsf{RRWW}, \mathsf{sRWW}, \mathsf{sRRWW}\}$ *be a type of restarting automaton, and let* $c \in \mathbb{N}_+$ *be a positive integer. Then* c-r-X *denotes the class of* c-rewriting *restarting automata of type X. An automaton of this form executes between one and* c

rewrite steps in each cycle, and it may execute up to c rewrite steps in each tail computation. Furthermore, $\mathsf{MX} = \bigcup_{c \geq 1} c\text{-}\mathsf{r}\text{-}\mathsf{X}$ *is the class of restarting automata of type X with a* bounded number of rewrites, *and* FX *is the class of* freely rewriting *restarting automata of type X, which are allowed to execute an arbitrary positive number of rewrite steps in each cycle.*

We illustrate this definition with a simple example.

Example 2.5.2 *For each* $c \geq 2$, *let* $L_{c-r} = \{ (a^n \# b^n)^c \mid n \geq 0 \}$. *We claim that*

$$L_{c-r} \in \mathcal{L}(\text{det-}c\text{-r-R}) \setminus \mathcal{L}((c-1)\text{-r-sRRW}),$$

that is, the language L_{c-r} *is accepted by a deterministic c-rewriting R-automaton, but it is not accepted by any sRRW-automaton that can only execute up to* $c - 1$ *rewrite steps in a cycle. Indeed, scanning its tape from left to right, a deterministic c-r-R-automaton M can execute the rewrite transitions* $\delta(q_i, a\#b) = (q_{i+1}, \#)$, $i = 1, 2, \ldots, c-1$, *and* $\delta(q_c, a\#b) = \#$, *which turns a word of the form* $(a^n \# b^n)^c$ *into the word* $(a^{n-1} \# b^{n-1})^c$. *Finally, M accepts the word* $\#^c$ *in a tail computation.*

On the other hand, an MsRRW-automaton M' *that can execute at most* $c - 1$ *rewrite steps in a cycle cannot possibly rewrite a word of the form* $(a^n \# b^n)^c$ *into a word from the language* L_{c-r} *within a single cycle, if n is large.*

The same arguments show that the language $L_{\infty-r} = \{ (a^n \# b^n)^m \# a^n \mid m, n \geq 0 \}$ *is accepted by a freely rewriting det-R-automaton, but it is not accepted by any sRRW-automaton with a bounded number of rewrites per cycle.* ■

Hence, we immediately obtain the following hierarchies.

Proposition 2.5.3 *For each type* $\mathsf{X} \in \{\mathsf{R}, \mathsf{RR}, \mathsf{RW}, \mathsf{RRW}, \mathsf{sRW}, \mathsf{sRRW}\}$ *of restarting automaton and each* $c \geq 1$,

(a) $\mathcal{L}(\text{det-}c\text{-r-X}) \subsetneq \mathcal{L}(\text{det-}(c+1)\text{-r-X}) \subsetneq \mathcal{L}(\text{det-MX}) \subsetneq \mathcal{L}(\text{det-FX})$.
(b) $\mathcal{L}(c\text{-r-X}) \subsetneq \mathcal{L}((c+1)\text{-r-X}) \subsetneq \mathcal{L}(\text{MX}) \subsetneq \mathcal{L}(\text{FX})$.

Thus, for each type of restarting automaton without auxiliary letters, the number of allowed rewrites per cycle yields an infinite ascending hierarchy of language classes. Hence, for each of these types of restarting automata, the generalization to multiple rewrites per cycle increases the expressive capacity considerably. It is not known whether this is also true for (length-reducing) restarting automata with auxiliary letters.

Problem 2.5.4 *Are* $(c+1)$*-rewriting RWW- or RRWW-automata more expressive than c-rewriting RWW- or RRWW-automata?*

However, we can at least show that, for shrinking restarting automata with auxiliary letters, the generalization to multiple rewrites does not increase their expressive capacity.

Theorem 2.5.5 ([99]) *For each sRRWW-automaton with multiple rewrites, there is an sRRWW-automaton that accepts the same language.*

Proof. Let $M = (Q, \Sigma, \Gamma, \rhd, \lhd, q_0, k, \delta)$ be a c-r-sRRWW-automaton for some $c \geq 2$. Without loss of generality, we may assume that each rewrite step of M is of the form $u \to y$ for some word $y \notin \{\rhd, \lhd, \lambda\}$. By Corollary 2.1.4, it suffices to describe a simulation of M by an sRLWW-automaton M'.

First, we assume that M performs exactly c rewrite steps in each cycle. The case that a cycle contains less than c rewrite steps will be discussed later. The automaton M' simulates each cycle of M by $2c$ cycles. At the beginning and at the end of such a simulation, the tape contents of M' will be identical to the corresponding tape contents of M, while M' will use some new auxiliary letters during the simulation process.

During the first c cycles of such a simulation, M' simulates the c rewrite steps of M from left to right, one at a time. However, each letter $a \in \Gamma$ that is written by M during the i-th rewrite step is encoded by M' by the letter (a, q, i), where q is the state of M after performing this rewrite step. In the next c cycles, M' replaces the factors from $(\Gamma \times Q \times \{1, 2, \ldots, c\})^+$ with the appropriate factors from Γ^+, again from left to right, one at a time.

Let $\Gamma_i = \Gamma \times Q \times \{i\}$ $(1 \leq i \leq c)$. Each time the tape contains occurrences of letters from $\Gamma_1, \Gamma_2, \ldots, \Gamma_i$ for some $i < c$, the automaton M' should simulate the $(i+1)$-st rewrite step of the current cycle of M. On the other hand, each time the tape contains occurrences of letters from $\Gamma_i, \Gamma_{i+1}, \ldots, \Gamma_c$ for some $i > 0$, M' has to replace a factor from Γ_i^+ with the appropriate factor from Γ^+.

Finally, assume that during the current cycle, M only performs c' rewrite steps for some $c' < c$. Then M' uses essentially the technique described above for the case c'. However, during each of the first c' rewrite steps, M' encodes the additional information that it is currently simulating a cycle of M that contains only c' rewrite steps into the letters written. Of course, M' does not know this fact at the beginning of the simulation, so it has to guess the value of c', and in case the guess is not correct, it will realize this and reject.

One can easily verify that M' accepts the same language as M. It remains to show that M' is shrinking. Let ω be a weight function that is compatible with M, and let

$$\mu = \max\{\, |y| \mid \exists q, q' \in Q, u \in \Gamma^k : (q', y) \in \delta(q, u) \,\}$$

be the maximal length of a word that is written by M in a single step. We define a new weight function $\omega' : \Gamma \to \mathbb{N}_+$ for M by taking $\omega'(a) = (c+1) \cdot \mu \cdot \omega(a)$ for each $a \in \Gamma$. With respect to the weight function ω', each rewrite step of M reduces the weight of the tape contents by at least $(c+1) \cdot \mu$. Now, we extend the function ω' to elements of Γ_i by taking $\omega'((a, q, i)) = \omega'(a) + i$ for each $a \in \Gamma$, $q \in Q$, and $1 \leq i \leq c$. Then the sRLWW-automaton M' is compatible with this weight function ω'. Indeed, if M' applies the simulation of a rewrite transition of the automaton M, then the overall weight of the tape contents is reduced with respect to ω', as each rewrite step of M decreases the overall weight of the tape contents by at least $(c+1) \cdot \mu$. On the other hand, the replacement of the letters from Γ with those from Γ_i in the corresponding rewrite step of M' increases the overall weight of the resulting tape contents by at most $i \cdot \mu$. Of course, the overall weight of the tape contents of M' is properly reduced, whenever a letter $(a, p, i) \in \Gamma_i$ is replaced with the letter a. This completes the proof of Theorem 2.5.5. □

By adjusting the technique from the proof of Theorem 2.3.53 accordingly, even the following stronger result can be derived.

Theorem 2.5.6 ([99]) *For each freely rewriting sRRWW-automaton, there is an sRRWW-automaton that accepts the same language.*

Together with Corollary 2.1.25, this yields the following equalities.

Corollary 2.5.7
For all $c \geq 1$, $\mathcal{L}(\mathsf{sRWW}) = \mathcal{L}(c\text{-}\mathsf{r}\text{-}\mathsf{sR(R)WW}) = \mathcal{L}(\mathsf{MsR(R)WW}) = \mathcal{L}(\mathsf{FsR(R)WW})$.

2.5.2 On Constrained Computations

In order to limit the expressive capacity of restarting automata, the notion of monotonicity was introduced. This notion is based on the idea that, from one cycle to the next in a computation, the actual place where a rewrite step is performed must not increase its distance from the *right* end of the tape (see Definition 1.9.19). Monotone restarting automata essentially model bottom-up one-pass parsers. Accordingly, it turned out that monotone R(R)WW-automata accept the context-free languages (see Theorem 1.9.24).

Also a generalization of the notion of monotonicity, called *j-monotonicity*, has been introduced, which models the generalization from bottom-up one-pass parsers to bottom-up multi-pass parsers [218, 220]. Here we present this notion and some of the basic results that have been obtained for it. However, before studying the notion of j-monotonicity itself, we consider the restricted variant of sequential j-monotonicity that has been introduced in [98].

Definition 2.5.8 *Let M be a restarting automaton and let j be a positive integer. A sequence of cycles $S = (C_1, C_2, \ldots, C_n)$ of the restarting automaton M is called* sequentially j-monotone *if there exist indices $0 = p_0 < p_1 < \cdots < p_j = n$ such that the subsequence $(C_{p_{i-1}+1}, C_{p_{i-1}+2}, \ldots, C_{p_i})$ is monotone for each $i = 1, 2, \ldots, j$. Thus, the sequence of cycles S is cut into j consecutive subsequences, each of which is monotone, that is, the j monotone subsequences follow* sequentially *one after the other. The restarting automaton M is called* sequentially j-monotone *if each of its computations that starts with an initial configuration is sequentially j'-monotone for some $j' \leq j$. We use the prefix j-s-mon- to denote classes of sequentially j-monotone restarting automata.*

Obviously, monotonicity corresponds to sequential 1-monotonicity. Hence, it follows that $\mathcal{L}(\text{mon-X}) \subseteq \mathcal{L}(j\text{-s-mon-X})$ for each type X of restarting automaton and each integer $j \geq 1$.

We begin our study of sequential j-monotonicity by investigating its influence on nondeterministic restarting automata without auxiliary letters. We shall see that sequential $(j+1)$-monotonicity is strictly more expressive than sequential j-monotonicity for these types of restarting automata. Hence, the degree of sequential monotonicity induces infinite strictly ascending hierarchies of language classes for these automata. To obtain this result, we present a family of example languages L_j $(j \geq 1)$. To define these languages, we introduce the function $\vartheta : (\bigcup_{p \geq 1} \mathbb{N}_+^{2p}) \to \{0, 1\}$ that is defined inductively as follows:

- For all $n, m \in \mathbb{N}_+$, $\vartheta(n, m) = \left\{ \begin{array}{ll} 1, & \text{if } n = m, \\ 0, & \text{if } n \neq m, \end{array} \right\}$ and,

- for all $p \geq 1$ and all $n, m, r_1, r_2, \ldots, r_{2p} \in \mathbb{N}_+$,

$$\vartheta(n, m, r_1, r_2, \ldots, r_{2p}) = \left\{ \begin{array}{ll} 1, & \text{if } n = m \text{ and } \vartheta(r_1, r_2, \ldots, r_{2p}) = 1 \\ & \text{or } n > 2m \text{ and } \vartheta(r_1, r_2, \ldots, r_{2p}) = 0, \\ 0, & \text{otherwise.} \end{array} \right.$$

The following observations on ϑ are useful. They follow easily from the above definition.

Lemma 2.5.9 *Let $j \geq 2$ and $n_1, m_1, n_2, m_2, \ldots, n_j, m_j \in \mathbb{N}_+$.*

(a) *For $0 < i < j$, if $n_i \neq m_i$ and $n_i \leq 2m_i$, then $\vartheta(n_i, m_i, \ldots, n_j, m_j) = 0$.*

(b) *If $\vartheta(n_i, m_i, \ldots, n_j, m_j) = 0$ for some i satisfying $0 < i \leq j$, and if $n_l \leq 2m_l$ for each $l < i$, then $\vartheta(n_1, m_1, n_2, m_2, \ldots, n_j, m_j) = 0$.*

Now, for each integer $j \geq 2$, the language L_j on $\Sigma = \{a, b\}$ is defined as

$$L_j = \{\, a^{n_1} b^{m_1} a^{n_2} b^{m_2} \cdots a^{n_j} b^{m_j} \mid \vartheta(n_1, m_1, n_2, m_2, \ldots, n_j, m_j) = 1 \,\}.$$

For each $1 \leq i < j$, the value of $\vartheta(n_{i+1}, m_{i+1}, \ldots, n_j, m_j)$ determines which comparison between a^{n_i} and b^{m_i} is to be made. We shall see below that this forces the degree of sequential monotonicity for an RLW-automaton for L_j to be at least j. First, however, we show that the language L_j is accepted by a deterministic RL-automaton that is sequentially j-monotone.

Proposition 2.5.10 ([98]) *For each $j \geq 2$, $L_j \in \mathcal{L}(\text{det-}j\text{-s-mon-RL})$.*

Proof. The language L_j is accepted by a deterministic j-s-mon-RL-automaton M that works as follows. If the word on the tape does not belong to $(a^+ \cdot b^+)^j$, it is rejected immediately. For a word of the form $(a^+ \cdot b^+)^j$, we call the factors from $a^+ \cdot b^+$ *blocks*. Let $a^{n_1} b^{m_1} a^{n_2} b^{m_2} \cdots a^{n_j} b^{m_j}$ be the given input. First, M determines the last block $a^{n_i} b^{m_i}$ for which $m_i > 1$ and $n_i > 2$ hold. The automaton M can do this by first moving its read/write window all the way to the right sentinel $\lhd$, and by then moving it back across all those blocks $a^{n_l} b^{m_l}$ for which $m_l = 1$ or $n_l \leq 2$ holds. If $i = j$, then M removes a factor ab from this block and restarts. Otherwise, M can obviously compute the value of $\vartheta(n_{i+1}, m_{i+1}, \ldots, n_j, m_j)$ in its finite-state control while moving its read/write window to the left.

If $\vartheta(n_{i+1}, m_{i+1}, \ldots, n_j, m_j) = 1$, then M removes a factor ab from the i-th block, otherwise, M removes a factor a^2b from that block. In each case, M restarts after performing this rewrite step.

In this way, the tape contents is reduced until all blocks satisfy $m_i = 1$ or $n_i \leq 2$. Now M accepts if and only if $\vartheta(n_1, m_1, n_2, m_2, \ldots, n_j, m_j) = 1$ holds. It follows easily that $L(M) = L_j$. As M processes the input block by block from right to left, each computation of M consists of (at most) j monotone subsequences that follow one after the other. Hence, M is sequentially j-monotone. □

By Theorem 2.1.2, there exists an RR-automaton that accepts the same language and that executes exactly the same rewrite steps as the above RL-automaton. Hence, Proposition 2.5.10 has the following consequence.

Corollary 2.5.11 *For each $j \geq 2$, $L_j \in \mathcal{L}(j\text{-s-mon-RR})$.*

Next, we show that, for $j \geq 2$, the language L_j is not accepted by any sequentially $(j-1)$-monotone sRLW-automaton.

Proposition 2.5.12 ([98]) *For each $j \geq 2$, $L_j \notin \mathcal{L}((j-1)\text{-s-mon-sRLW})$.*

Proof outline. Let $M = (Q, \Sigma, \Sigma, \rhd, \lhd, q_0, k, \delta)$ be an sRLW-automaton for L_j, let p be the constant from the Pumping Lemma for M (see Proposition 2.1.8), and let $r = p!$. We say that the i-th block of a word of the form $a^{n_1}b^{m_1}a^{n_2}b^{m_2}\cdots a^{n_j}b^{m_j}$ is *short* if $n_i < 3r$ or $m_i < 3r$.

Claim 1. Let $q_0 \rhd a^{n_1}b^{m_1}a^{n_2}b^{m_2}\cdots a^{n_j}b^{m_j} \lhd \vdash_M^c q_0 \rhd a^{n'_1}b^{m'_1}a^{n'_2}b^{m'_2}\cdots a^{n'_j}b^{m'_j} \lhd$ be a cycle of a computation of the sRLW-automaton M. Then, for each $\alpha_1, \alpha_2, \ldots, \alpha_j, \beta_1, \beta_2, \ldots, \beta_j \in \mathbb{N}$, the cycle

$$q_0 \rhd a^{n_1+\alpha_1 r}b^{m_1+\beta_1 r}\cdots a^{n_j+\alpha_j r}b^{m_j+\beta_j r} \lhd \vdash_M^c q_0 \rhd a^{n'_1+\alpha_1 r}b^{m'_1+\beta_1 r}\cdots a^{n'_j+\alpha_j r}b^{m'_j+\beta_j r} \lhd$$

is also part of a computation of M, provided that $\alpha_i = \beta_i = 0$ for each i for which the i-th block in $a^{n_1}b^{m_1}a^{n_2}b^{m_2}\cdots a^{n_j}b^{m_j}$ is short.

Proof of Claim 1. We can apply pumping to each a-factor and each b-factor longer than $2r$. As r is divisible by the length of any resulting pumping factor, the result follows. □

A word $(a^nb^n)^j$ is called a *basic input* if n is a multiple of r and $n \geq 3r$. Note that each basic input belongs to L_j, and that none of its blocks is short.

Claim 2. Let $q_0 \rhd a^nb^n\cdots a^nb^n \lhd \vdash_M^{c^*} q_0 \rhd a^{n'_1}b^{m'_1}\cdots a^{n'_j}b^{m'_j} \lhd$ be an initial segment of an accepting computation of M on the basic input $w = (a^nb^n)^j \in L_j$, and let $i \in \{1, 2, \ldots, j\}$. If the i-th block is not short in any of the configurations during the above computation, then

(a) during this computation, no rewrite step is applied to any of the first $i-1$ blocks, that is, $n'_t = m'_t = n$ for each $t < i$;

(b) $n'_i = m'_i \geq 3r$, and each rewrite step that is applied during this computation to the i-th block is of the form $a^sb^s \to a^{s-t}b^{s-t}$ for some $k > s \geq t > 0$.

Proof of Claim 2. This claim can be proved by contradiction, using a technically quite involved case analysis. See [98] for details. □

Using these two claims, we now complete the proof of Proposition 2.5.12. Let $w = (a^nb^n)^j \in L_j$ be a basic input. We analyze the accepting computations on this input. From Claim 1, we see that w cannot be accepted by M as long as the first block is not short, since, otherwise, also the input $v \notin L_j$ would be accepted that is obtained from w by replacing the first block with a^nb^{n+r}.

On the other hand, Claim 2 implies that the first rewrite step that changes the i-th block is not applied before a configuration has been reached in which the $(i+1)$-st block is short. Thus, each accepting computation first reduces the j-th block into a short block, then the $(j-1)$-st block and so on. Furthermore, the first rewrite step that changes the i-th block is performed in the center of that block (see Claim 2). Hence, its right distance is larger than the right distance of the previous rewrite step that was applied within the blocks $i+1,\ldots,j$ by (at least) the number $n-k$. Thus, this rewrite step starts a new monotone subsequence. By applying this observation to all blocks, we obtain at least j monotone subsequences that follow sequentially one after the other. Thus, M is not sequentially $(j-1)$-monotone. □

Together, Corollary 2.5.11 and Proposition 2.5.12 yield hierarchy results with respect to the degree of sequential monotonicity for (s)RR(W)- and for (s)RL(W)-automata. In order to also obtain corresponding hierarchies for (s)R(W)-automata, we need a somewhat more involved variant of the language L_j.

Let $\Sigma = \{a,b,c,d\}$ be the new input alphabet. For a subset $\Delta \subseteq \Sigma$, the projection from Σ^* onto Δ^* is denoted by π_Δ, that is, for $x \in \Sigma^*$, $\pi_\Delta(x)$ is obtained from x by removing all occurrences of letters from $\Sigma \smallsetminus \Delta$. For $j \geq 1$, the language $L'_j \subseteq \Sigma^*$ is defined as follows:

$$\begin{array}{lll} L'_j = \{\, xy \mid & \exists i \in \{0,1,\ldots,j\}\, \exists n_1, m_1, \ldots, n_j, m_j \in \mathbb{N}_+\, \exists y_{i+1}, \ldots, y_j \in \{c,d\} : & \\ & x = a^{n_1} b^{m_1} \cdots a^{n_i} b^{m_i} \text{ and } y = a^{n_{i+1}} y_{i+1} b^{m_{i+1}} \cdots a^{n_j} y_j b^{m_j} & \\ & \text{such that } \ (i) \quad \pi_{\{a,b\}}(xy) \in L_j, & \\ & \qquad (ii) \quad n_l < 3 \text{ or } m_l < 2 \text{ for each } l > i+1, & \\ & \qquad (iii) \quad n_l \geq 3 \text{ and } m_l \geq 2 \text{ for each } l \leq i, \text{ and} & \\ & \qquad (iv) \quad \text{for all } l \in \{i+1, i+2, \ldots, j\},\ y_l = c \text{ if and only if} & \\ & \qquad\qquad l = j \text{ or } \vartheta(n_{l+1}, m_{l+1}, \ldots, n_j, m_j) = 1 \,\}. & \end{array}$$

The idea is that the letter c is used to 'mark' those blocks for which it should be checked whether $n_l = m_l$ holds, and the letter d is used to 'mark' those blocks for which it should be checked whether $n_l > 2m_l$ holds. Furthermore, c and d only occur in a number of 'suffix blocks,' which will force the restarting automaton to process the blocks from right to left. For the language L'_j, the following positive result has been derived.

Proposition 2.5.13 ([98]) *For each $j \geq 2$, $L'_j \in \mathcal{L}(j\text{-s-mon-RW})$.*

For the description of the sequentially j-monotone RW-automaton accepting the language L'_j, we refer to [98]. Contrasting the above result, the following negative result has been established.

Proposition 2.5.14 ([98]) *For each $j \geq 2$, $L'_j \notin \mathcal{L}((j-1)\text{-s-mon-sRLW})$.*

Actually, in [98], it is only shown that $L'_j \notin \mathcal{L}((j-1)\text{-s-mon-RLW})$, but the given proof easily extends to shrinking RLW-automata.. Propositions 2.5.13 and 2.5.14 establish a hierarchy result for (s)RW-automata. In order to also obtain the corresponding result for R-automata, the following technical result will be used.

Let M be a sequentially j-monotone RW-automaton for the language L'_j, let k be the size of its read/write window, and let m be the cardinality of its tape alphabet (that is, $m = 4$). Finally, let $L''_j = \varphi_{k,m}(L'_j)$, where $\varphi_{k,j}$ is the encoding defined in Theorem 2.2.15.

Proposition 2.5.15 ([98]) *For each $j \geq 2$, $L''_j \in \mathcal{L}(j\text{-s-mon-R}) \smallsetminus \mathcal{L}((j-1)\text{-s-mon-sRLW})$.*

Proof outline. It follows from Theorem 2.2.15 and Proposition 2.5.13 that $L''_j \in \mathcal{L}(j\text{-s-mon-R})$.

In order to prove by contradiction that $L''_j \notin \mathcal{L}((j-1)\text{-s-mon-sRLW})$, we assume that there exists a sequentially $(j-1)$-monotone sRLW-automaton M that accepts the language L''_j. From M, a sequentially $(j-1)$-monotone sRLW-automaton M' can be constructed such that $L(M') = L'_j$, which contradicts Proposition 2.5.14.

On a tape contents $x \in \Sigma^*$, M' simulates a computation of M on the tape contents $\varphi_{k,m}(x)$. Whenever M intends to perform a rewrite step that converts the tape contents into a word that is not of the form $\varphi_{k,m}(y)$ for any $y \in \Sigma^*$, M' rejects, as this rewrite step clearly indicates that the computation of M being simulated is not accepting. In all other cases, M' is able to 'mimic' the corresponding steps of M. It is easily verified that, in this way, M' recognizes the language L'_j, and that M' is sequentially $(j-1)$-monotone if M is sequentially $(j-1)$-monotone. □

As a consequence of all the results above, we obtain the following theorem.

Theorem 2.5.16 ([98]) *For each $j \in \mathbb{N}_+$ and each $X \in \{\mathsf{R}, \mathsf{(s)RW}, \mathsf{RR}, \mathsf{(s)RRW}, \mathsf{RL}, \mathsf{(s)RLW}\}$,*

(a) $\mathcal{L}(j\text{-s-mon-X}) \subsetneq \mathcal{L}((j+1)\text{-s-mon-X})$;

(b) $\mathcal{L}((j+1)\text{-s-mon-R}) \smallsetminus \mathcal{L}(j\text{-s-mon-sRLW}) \neq \emptyset$.

Observe, however, that by Lemma 2.2.4, the language

$$L_3 = \{\, a^n b^n, a^n c b^n \mid n \geq 0 \} \cup \{\, a^n b^m, a^n d b^m \mid m > 2n \geq 0 \,\}$$

is not accepted by any RR-automaton, although it is accepted by a monotone RW-automaton. Thus, $\mathcal{L}(\text{mon-RW}) \not\subseteq \bigcup_{j\geq 1} \mathcal{L}(j\text{-s-mon-RR})$, which implies that $\mathcal{L}(j\text{-s-mon-sRLW})$ is not contained in $\mathcal{L}((j+1)\text{-s-mon-R})$. In particular, the language classes $\mathcal{L}(j\text{-s-mon-sRLW})$ and $\mathcal{L}((j+1)\text{-s-mon-R})$ are incomparable under inclusion.

While the degree of sequential monotonicity induces infinite strictly ascending hierarchies of language classes for restarting automata without auxiliary letters, we now show that, in the presence of auxiliary letters, sequentially j-monotone restarting automata are equivalent to monotone restarting automata. We recall from Corollary 2.1.41 that the classes of languages $\mathcal{L}(\text{mon-(s)R(R)WW})$ and $\mathcal{L}(\text{mon-(s)RLWW})$ coincide with the class CFL of context-free languages. Here we demonstrate that this characterization extends to sequentially j-monotone (s)R(R)WW- and (s)RLWW-automata for all $j \geq 2$.

With an (s)RRWW-automaton M with tape alphabet Γ, we can associate the set $L_{\text{mon}}(M)$ of words over Γ that M accepts by monotone computations. In addition, we can define a mapping f_M that maps each word $w \in \Gamma^*$ to the set of words that M can reach from w by performing a monotone computation. The set $L_{\text{mon}}(M)$ is context-free, and from M, we can construct a pushdown automaton P_M and an alphabetic morphism h such that, for each $w \in \Gamma^*$, the set $f_M(w)$ coincides with the image under h of the set of final stack contents that P_M can generate on input w (see Lemma 2.1.44). Based on this characterization, we derive the fact that, for each $j \geq 2$, the language $L^{(j)}_{\text{mon}}(M)$ of words $w \in \Gamma^*$ that M accepts by sequentially j-monotone computations is also context-free (Theorem 2.5.19). If M is sequentially j-monotone, then $L(M) = L^{(j)}_{\text{mon}}(M) \cap \Sigma^*$, where Σ is the input alphabet of M, which then yields the intended result. We begin our investigation with the following technical result on pushdown automata. Recall from Section 1.2 that, for a PDA $P = (Q, \Sigma, \Gamma \cup \{\#\}, \delta, q_0, \#, F)$ and an input word $w \in \Sigma^*$,

$$\text{SC}_P(w) = \{\, \alpha \in (\Gamma \smallsetminus \{\#\})^* \mid \exists q \in F : (q_0, w, \#) \vdash_P^* (q, \lambda, \#\alpha) \,\}$$

is the set of *possible pushdown contents of* P *on input* w.

Lemma 2.5.17 ([98]) *Let P be a pushdown automaton with input alphabet Σ and pushdown alphabet $\Gamma \cup \{\#\}$, and let S be a subset of $\text{SC}_P(\Sigma^*)$. If S is context-free, then so is the language $\text{SC}_P^{-1}(S) = \{\, u \in \Sigma^* \mid \text{SC}_P(u) \cap S \neq \emptyset \,\}$.*

Proof. Let $P = (Q, \Sigma, \Gamma \cup \{\#\}, \delta, q_0, \#, F)$, let $\overline{\Gamma}$ be a new alphabet in one-to-one correspondence to Γ such that Γ and $\overline{\Gamma}$ are disjoint, and let $\overline{\#}$ be another new symbol. Furthermore, let R be the finite string-rewriting system

$$R = \{\, b\bar{b} \to \lambda \mid b \in \Gamma \cup \{\#\} \,\}$$

on $\Omega = \Gamma \cup \overline{\Gamma} \cup \{\#, \overline{\#}\}$. Then R is a special system that is confluent (see, e.g., [19]). For $w \in \Omega^*$, $\Delta_R^*(w)$ is the set of all descendants of w with respect to the reduction relation induced by R, that is, $\Delta_R^*(w) = \{\, z \in \Omega^* \mid w \Rightarrow_R^* z \,\}$, and $\Delta_R^*(T) = \bigcup_{w\in T} \Delta_R^*(w)$ for each subset $T \subseteq \Omega^*$. It is well-known that the set $\Delta_R^*(T)$ is regular, whenever T is a regular language.

From the PDA P, one easily obtains a finite-state transducer B with λ-transitions, input alphabet Σ, and output alphabet Ω that imitates the behavior of P step by step as follows. Whenever P performs a transition $(q', \alpha) \in \delta(q, a, b)$, where q, q' are states of P, $a \in \Sigma \cup \{\lambda\}$ is the input letter read, $b \in \Gamma$ is the topmost letter on P's pushdown store, and $\alpha \in \Gamma^*$ is the pushdown word with which the letter b is replaced, then B executes the transition $(q,a) \to (q', \bar{b}\alpha)$, that is, B reads the same input letter and performs the same change-of-state as P, but it simulates the pushdown operation $b \mapsto \alpha$ by producing the output $\bar{b}\alpha$. This means that B just guesses the topmost letter on the pushdown store of P. The string-rewriting system R is then used to verify that this guess is correct by matching the output letter $\bar{b}$ to the last output letter produced previously. It can be shown that the following equality holds for each word $w \in \Sigma^*$ [36]:

$$\Delta_R^*(B(w)) \cap \overline{\#}\# \cdot \Gamma^* = \overline{\#}\# \cdot \mathrm{SC}_P(w).$$

Now let S be a subset of $\mathrm{SC}_P(\Sigma^*)$. Then a word $w \in \Sigma^*$ belongs to the set $\mathrm{SC}_P^{-1}(S)$ if and only if $\Delta_R^*(B(w)) \cap \overline{\#}\# \cdot S \neq \emptyset$ holds.

Let $\nabla_R^*(w)$ denote the set of ancestors of w with respect to the reduction relation induced by R, that is, $\nabla_R^*(w) = \{\, x \in \Omega^* \mid x \Rightarrow_R^* w \,\}$, and for $T \subseteq \Omega^*$, $\nabla_R^*(T) = \bigcup_{w \in T} \nabla_R^*(w)$. Then we obtain the following equality:

$$\mathrm{SC}_P^{-1}(S) = B^{-1}(\nabla_R^*(\overline{\#}\# \cdot S)).$$

Now, if S is a context-free language, then so is the language $\overline{\#}\# \cdot S$. From the form of the rules of R, we see immediately that $\nabla_R^*(\overline{\#}\# \cdot S)$ is context-free, too, which implies that $B^{-1}(\nabla_R^*(\overline{\#}\# \cdot S))$ is context-free, as the class of context-free languages is closed under (inverse) finite transductions [11]. Thus, it follows that $\mathrm{SC}_P^{-1}(S)$ is context-free. □

Let $M = (Q, \Sigma, \Gamma, \rhd, \lhd, q_0, k, \delta)$ be an sRRWW-automaton. With M, we associate the language

$$L_{\mathrm{mon}}(M) = \{\, w \in \Gamma^* \mid M \text{ accepts } w \text{ by a monotone computation} \,\}$$

and the mapping $f_M : \Gamma^* \to \mathcal{P}(\Gamma^*)$ that is defined as follows:

$$\begin{array}{rcll} f_M(w) & = & \{\, y \in \Gamma^* \mid & \text{There exists a monotone sequence of cycles of } M \\ & & & \text{that starts from the restarting configuration } q_0 \rhd w \lhd \\ & & & \text{and ends with the restarting configuration } q_0 \rhd y \lhd \,\}. \end{array}$$

By Lemma 2.1.44, there exists a PDA P_M' for the language $L_{\mathrm{mon}}(M)$. Accordingly, this language is context-free. Observe that the language $f_M(\Gamma^*)$ is simply the set Γ^*, as from each restarting configuration, a monotone computation of M originates, which, however, may consist of a single cycle only, or which may even consist of no cycle at all.

Lemma 2.5.18 *Let $M = (Q, \Sigma, \Gamma, \rhd, \lhd, q_0, k, \delta)$ be an sRRWW-automaton. Then there exist a pushdown automaton P_M with input alphabet Σ and pushdown alphabet Θ and an alphabetic morphism $h : \Theta^* \to \Gamma^*$ such that, for each word $w \in \Gamma^*$, $h(\mathrm{SC}_{P_M}(w)) = f_M(w)$ holds.*

Proof. The PDA P_M' for the language $L_{\mathrm{mon}}(M)$ simulates the monotone initial parts of all computations of M. It has input alphabet Σ and pushdown alphabet $\Theta' = \Gamma \times \mathcal{P}(Q)$, as it uses its pushdown to store a prefix u of the tape contents of M together with information on the subset of states of M that M can reach from its initial state q_0 by reading the prefix u. We modify P_M' in such a way that, each time it starts the simulation of a cycle of M, it may decide (nondeterministically) to abort the simulation process. In this case, it pushes the remaining suffix of the input onto the pushdown store, and halts and accepts. Hence, the resulting PDA P_M has input alphabet Σ and pushdown alphabet $\Theta = \Theta' \cup \Gamma$. We define an alphabetic morphism $h : \Theta^* \to \Gamma^*$ through $a \mapsto a$ and $(a, Q') \mapsto a$ for each $a \in \Gamma$ and $Q' \subseteq Q$. Then $f_M(w) = h(\mathrm{SC}_{P_M}(w))$ holds for each word $w \in \Gamma^*$. □

Let M be an sRRWW-automaton with tape alphabet Γ. For each integer $j \geq 1$, let $L_{\mathrm{mon}}^{(j)}(M)$ denote the language

$$L_{\mathrm{mon}}^{(j)}(M) = \{\, y \in \Gamma^* \mid M \text{ accepts } y \text{ by a sequentially } j\text{-monotone computation} \,\}.$$

Then, for each word $w \in \Gamma^*$ and each number $j \geq 2$,

$$w \in L_{\mathrm{mon}}^{(j)}(M) \text{ if and only if } f_M(w) \cap L_{\mathrm{mon}}^{(j-1)}(M) \neq \emptyset.$$

Now, the following result on the language $L_{\mathrm{mon}}^{(j)}(M)$ can be proved by induction on the integer j.

Theorem 2.5.19 ([98]) *$L^{(j)}_{\text{mon}}(M)$ is a context-free language for each sRRWW-automaton M and each integer $j \geq 1$.*

Proof. For $j = 1$, this is an immediate consequence of Lemma 2.1.44, as sequential 1-monotonicity coincides with monotonicity. So assume that $j > 1$. By the induction hypothesis, we know that $L^{(j-1)}_{\text{mon}}(M)$ is a context-free language.

As observed above, $w \in L^{(j)}_{\text{mon}}(M)$ if and only if $f_M(w) \cap L^{(j-1)}_{\text{mon}}(M) \neq \emptyset$ if and only if $h(\text{SC}_{P_M}(w)) \cap L^{(j-1)}_{\text{mon}}(M) \neq \emptyset$, where P_M is the PDA and h is the alphabetic morphism from Lemma 2.5.18. Thus,

$$\begin{aligned} L^{(j)}_{\text{mon}}(M) &= \{ w \in \Gamma^* \mid f_M(w) \cap L^{(j-1)}_{\text{mon}}(M) \neq \emptyset \} \\ &= \{ w \in \Gamma^* \mid h(\text{SC}_{P_M}(w)) \cap L^{(j-1)}_{\text{mon}}(M) \neq \emptyset \} \\ &= \text{SC}^{-1}_{P_M}(h^{-1}(L^{(j-1)}_{\text{mon}}(M))), \end{aligned}$$

implying that the language $L^{(j)}_{\text{mon}}(M)$ is context-free by Lemma 2.5.17. □

If the sRRWW-automaton $M = (Q, \Sigma, \Gamma, \rhd, \lhd, q_0, k, \delta)$ is sequentially j-monotone, then

$$L(M) = \bigcup_{i=1}^{j} L^{(i)}_{\text{mon}}(M) \cap \Sigma^*.$$

By the result above, this yields that $L(M)$ is context-free. As each context-free language is accepted by a monotone RWW-automaton, we obtain the following characterization.

Corollary 2.5.20 ([98]) $\mathsf{CFL} = \mathcal{L}(j\text{-s-mon-(s)RRWW}) = \mathcal{L}(j\text{-s-mon-(s)R(L)WW})$ *for all* $j \geq 1$.

Thus, for all types of nondeterministic restarting automata with auxiliary letters, the degree of sequential monotonicity does not yield a hierarchy in contrast to the situation for restarting automata without auxiliary letters. Finally, we recall from Lemma 2.2.3 that the context-free language

$$L = \{ a^n b^n \mid n \geq 0 \} \cup \{ a^n b^m \mid m > 2n \geq 0 \}$$

is not accepted by any sRLW-automaton. This implies the following proper inclusion.

Corollary 2.5.21 $\bigcup_{j\geq 1} \mathcal{L}(j\text{-s-mon-sRLW}) \subsetneq \mathsf{CFL}$.

Now we turn to the general form of j-monotonicity as defined in [96].

Definition 2.5.22 *Let M be a restarting automaton, and let $j \geq 1$ be a positive integer. We say that a sequence of cycles $S = (C_1, C_2, \ldots, C_n)$ of M is* j-monotone *if there is a partition of S into j (scattered) subsequences that are monotone. Formally, we say that the sequence of cycles S is* j-monotone *if there is a partition of S into j subsequences*

$$\begin{aligned} S_1 &= (C_{1,1}, C_{1,2}, \ldots, C_{1,p_1}), \\ S_2 &= (C_{2,1}, C_{2,2}, \ldots, C_{2,p_2}), \\ &\ldots \\ S_j &= (C_{j,1}, C_{j,2}, \ldots, C_{j,p_j}), \end{aligned}$$

such that each S_i, $1 \leq i \leq j$, is monotone.

Obviously, a sequence of cycles $(C_1, C_2, \ldots, C_n)$ is *not* j-monotone if and only if there exist indices $1 \leq i_1 < i_2 < \cdots < i_{j+1} \leq n$ such that

$$D_r(C_{i_1}) < D_r(C_{i_2}) < \cdots < D_r(C_{i_{j+1}}). \tag{2.9}$$

Thus, in contrast to the situation for sequential j-monotonicity, the j monotone subsequences $S_1, S_2, \ldots, S_j$ do not necessarily follow sequentially one after the other. Instead, they will, in general, be interspersed.

Definition 2.5.22 (cont.) *A* computation *of the restarting automaton M is called j-*monotone *if the corresponding sequence of cycles is j-monotone. Again the tail of the computation does not play any role here. Finally, the restarting automaton M is called j-*monotone *if all its computations that start with an initial configuration are j-monotone. We use the prefix j-mon- to denote the corresponding classes of restarting automata.*

Observe that 1-monotonicity coincides with monotonicity. The next result shows that the degree of monotonicity does not influence the expressive capacity of deterministic (one-way) restarting automata.

Theorem 2.5.23 ([96]) *For each $j \in \mathbb{N}_+$ and $\mathsf{X} \in \{\mathsf{R}, \mathsf{RR}, \mathsf{(s)RW}, \mathsf{(s)RRW}, \mathsf{(s)RWW}, \mathsf{(s)RRWW}\}$,*

$$\mathsf{DCFL} = \mathcal{L}(\mathsf{det\text{-}mon\text{-}X}) = \mathcal{L}(\mathsf{det\text{-}}j\mathsf{\text{-}mon\text{-}X}).$$

Proof. Let $j > 1$, and let $M = (Q, \Sigma, \Gamma, \rhd, \lhd, q_0, k, \delta)$ be a j-monotone deterministic sRRWW-automaton that is compatible with the weight function ω. In each cycle, M scans at least one letter which was written in the previous cycle, that is, from one cycle to the next, the right distance can increase by at most $m - 1$, where $m \in \mathbb{N}_+$ is the length of the longest word that M can write in a single rewrite step. As M has window size k, we see that $m \leq k \cdot \mu - 1$, where $\mu = \max\{\, \omega(x) \mid x \in \Gamma\,\}$. Together with condition (2.9), this implies that, for each sequence of cycles $C_1, C_2, \ldots, C_n$ that is part of a j-monotone computation of M, and for each pair of indices i, l satisfying $1 \leq i < l \leq n$,

$$D_r(C_l) \leq D_r(C_i) + (j-1) \cdot (k \cdot \mu - 2) < D_r(C_i) + (j-1) \cdot k \cdot \mu. \tag{2.10}$$

We now construct a monotone sRRWW-automaton $M_j = (Q', \Sigma, \Gamma', \rhd, \lhd, q_0', k', \delta')$ that accepts the same language as M, where $\Gamma' = \Gamma \cup \overline{\Gamma}$ and $k' = (j+1) \cdot k \cdot \mu$. Here $\overline{\Gamma} = \{\, \bar{a} \mid a \in \Gamma\,\}$ is a new alphabet in one-to-one correspondence to Γ. The automaton M_j will use the letters from $\overline{\Gamma}$ to mark those tape positions at which M has executed a rewrite step (see below).

The automaton M_j works as follows. The right-most $k \cdot \mu + 1$ positions of its read/write window are used as a kind of 'look-ahead,' while the remaining part will be used to simulate the rewrite steps of M. The automaton M_j simulates M cycle by cycle. Performing MVR-steps, it scans its tape from left to right, looking for the position at which M would now apply the next rewrite transition, say $u \to v$. Having found that position, M_j keeps moving its read/write window to the right for $k \cdot \mu + 1$ more steps.

(i) If the look-ahead does not contain a letter from $\overline{\Gamma}$ in one of its right-most $k \cdot \mu$ positions, then M_j executes a rewrite step that consists of the following two parts:

  (a) the actual rewrite transition $u \to v$ of M is being simulated;

  (b) if the letter a that is immediately to the right of the replaced factor u belongs to Γ, then it is replaced with the corresponding letter $\bar{a} \in \overline{\Gamma}$, in this way marking the position of the current rewrite for the next cycles.

  Thereafter, M_j scans the remaining part of the tape and restarts, accepts, or rejects just like M.

(ii) If there is a letter from $\overline{\Gamma}$ in one of the right-most $k \cdot \mu$ positions of the look-ahead, thus indicating that, in a previous cycle, a rewrite step was performed to the right of the position of the current rewrite, then M_j moves its read/write window to the right until either the right sentinel is reached or until the $k \cdot \mu$ right-most positions of the look-ahead do not contain any letters from $\overline{\Gamma}$ anymore. As M is j-monotone, the place where the actual rewrite step is to be performed is less than $(j-1) \cdot k \cdot \mu$ positions to the left of the right-most position at which M has executed a rewrite step in a previous cycle (see (2.10)). Hence, the place where the actual rewrite step is to be performed is still inside the read/write window of M_j. From the considerations above, it follows that the suffix of the tape contents that has not yet been scanned in this cycle does not contain any letters from $\overline{\Gamma}$. Now M_j continues by executing the rewrite step in the same way as in (i).

It follows that M_j accepts the language $L(M)$. As observed above, M scans the right-most 'marked' letter in each cycle. Hence, M_j is necessarily monotone. Thus, we see that, for each $j > 1$, $\mathcal{L}(\text{det-}j\text{-mon-sRRWW}) = \mathcal{L}(\text{det-mon-sRRWW})$. As, by Corollary 2.1.43, $\mathcal{L}(\text{det-mon-X}) = \text{DCFL}$ for each $\text{X} \in \{\text{R}, \text{RR}, \text{(s)RW}, \text{(s)RRW}, \text{(s)RWW}, \text{(s)RRWW}\}$, the theorem follows. □

Below we show that, based on the degree of monotonicity, we obtain infinite strictly ascending hierarchies for restarting automata without auxiliary letters. Accordingly, we now present a sequence of languages that will be used as witness languages to establish corresponding separation results.

For $j \in \mathbb{N}_+$, let

$$\bar{L}_j = \{ a^{n_1}b^{n_1}a^{n_2}b^{n_2}\cdots a^{n_j}b^{n_j} \mid n_1 \geq n_2 \geq \cdots \geq n_j \geq 1 \}.$$

The next lemma states that, for each $j \geq 2$, $\bar{L}_j$ is accepted by certain j-monotone restarting automata.

Lemma 2.5.24 *For each $j \geq 2$, $\bar{L}_j \in \mathcal{L}(j\text{-mon-R}) \cap \mathcal{L}(\text{det-}j\text{-mon-RL})$.*

Proof. For a word of the form $(a^+ \cdot b^+)^j$, we call the factors from $a^+ \cdot b^+$ 'blocks.' An R-automaton M can accept the language $\bar{L}_j$ by proceeding as follows. In each cycle, M guesses in which of the blocks a rewrite step is to be executed, and it removes a factor ab from that block, provided the block is of length at least four. However, M is allowed to execute this operation in the t-th block only if the parity of the number of a's (and b's) in all previous blocks is equal to the parity of the number of a's (and b's) in the block t. In this way, we ensure that two consecutive rewrite steps in the t-th block are not possible without applying any rewrite step in the $(t-1)$-st block. The automaton M accepts if and when the tape contents is $(ab)^j$. It is easily verified that, in this way, M accepts the language $\bar{L}_j$. In addition, we see that M is j-monotone, as its computations consist of j monotone sequences of cycles, one for each of the j blocks.

A deterministic RL-automaton can realize the same strategy. In each cycle, it simply removes a factor ab from the last block for which the parity of the number of a's (and b's) is equal to the parity of the number of a's (and b's) in all previous blocks. Thus, it is j-monotone just as the R-automaton described above. □

On the other hand, the following negative result can be derived for the language $\bar{L}_j$.

Proposition 2.5.25 ([96]) *For each $j \geq 2$, $\bar{L}_j \notin \mathcal{L}((j-1)\text{-mon-sRLW})$.*

Proof outline. Let M be an sRLW-automaton for the language $\bar{L}_j$, and let p be the constant from the Pumping Lemma for M (see Proposition 2.1.8). We consider a particular family of inputs

$$F = \{ a^{n+i_1\cdot r}b^{n+l_1\cdot r}a^{n+i_2\cdot r}b^{n+l_2\cdot r}\cdots a^{n+i_j\cdot r}b^{n+l_j\cdot r} \mid i_1, i_2, \ldots, i_j, l_1, l_2, \ldots, l_j \geq 0 \},$$

where $r = p!$ and n is a sufficiently large integer. The word $w_0 = (a^n b^n)^j \in F$ is called the *basic input* from F. As w_0 belongs to $\bar{L}_j$, M has at least one accepting computation for this input. By exploiting the Pumping Lemma, it can now be proved that each accepting computation of M for the basic input $(a^n b^n)^j$ must reduce all j blocks in an almost synchronous manner (for details, see [96]). Hence, M is not $(j-1)$-monotone. □

From the above results, we immediately obtain the following proper inclusion results.

Theorem 2.5.26 ([96]) *For each $j \in \mathbb{N}_+$,*

(a) *for each $\text{X} \in \{\text{R}, \text{(s)RW}, \text{RR}, \text{(s)RRW}, \text{RL}, \text{(s)RLW}\}$, $\mathcal{L}(j\text{-mon-X}) \subsetneq \mathcal{L}((j+1)\text{-mon-X})$, and*

(b) *for each $\text{X} \in \{\text{RL}, \text{(s)RLW}\}$, $\mathcal{L}(\text{det-}j\text{-mon-X}) \subsetneq \mathcal{L}(\text{det-}(j+1)\text{-mon-X})$.*

It remains to compare the various types of restarting automata at the same level of j-monotonicity to each other. By Lemma 2.2.2, the language $L = \{ b^n a^n c \mid n \geq 0 \} \cup \{ b^n a^{2n} d \mid n \geq 0 \}$, which is not deterministic context-free, is accepted by a det-mon-RL-automaton, but not by any deterministic sRRW-automaton. Together with Theorem 2.5.23, this yields the following proper inclusions.

Corollary 2.5.27
For each $j \in \mathbb{N}_+$, $\mathsf{X} \in \{\mathsf{WW}, \mathsf{W}, \lambda\}$, $\mathcal{L}(\text{det-}j\text{-mon-(s)RRX}) \subsetneq \mathcal{L}(\text{det-}j\text{-mon-(s)RLX})$.

From Lemma 2.2.1, we know that $L \in \mathcal{L}(\text{mon-RR}) \smallsetminus \mathcal{L}(\text{sRW})$, which has the following consequences.

Corollary 2.5.28 *For each* $j \geq 1$,

(a) $\mathcal{L}(j\text{-mon-R}) \subsetneq \mathcal{L}(j\text{-mon-RR})$.
(b) $\mathcal{L}(j\text{-mon-(s)RW}) \subsetneq \mathcal{L}(j\text{-mon-(s)RRW})$.

According to Lemma 2.2.4, the language

$$L_3 = \{\, a^n b^n, a^n c b^n \mid n \geq 0 \,\} \cup \{\, a^n b^m, a^n d b^m \mid m > 2n \geq 0 \,\}$$

is accepted by a monotone RW-automaton, but not by any RL-automaton. This yields the following result showing that, for all types of monotone restarting automata without auxiliary letters, the deleting model is strictly weaker than the rewriting model.

Corollary 2.5.29 *For each* $j \in \mathbb{N}_+$ *and* $\mathsf{X} \in \{\mathsf{R}, \mathsf{RR}, \mathsf{RL}\}$, $\mathcal{L}(j\text{-mon-X}) \subsetneq \mathcal{L}(j\text{-mon-XW})$.

By Lemma 2.2.3, $L_2 = \{\, a^n b^n \mid n \geq 0 \,\} \cup \{\, a^n b^m \mid m > 2n \geq 0 \,\} \in \mathsf{CRL} \smallsetminus \mathcal{L}(\text{sRLW})$. In addition, it is easily seen that L_2 is accepted by a monotone RWW-automaton. Hence, we obtain the following result.

Corollary 2.5.30 *For each* $j \geq 1$,

(a) $\mathcal{L}(j\text{-mon-(s)RLW}) \subsetneq \mathcal{L}(j\text{-mon-(s)RLWW})$,
(b) $\mathcal{L}(j\text{-mon-(s)RRW}) \subsetneq \mathcal{L}(j\text{-mon-(s)RRWW})$,
(c) $\mathcal{L}(j\text{-mon-(s)RW}) \subsetneq \mathcal{L}(j\text{-mon-(s)RWW})$.

Let $L_d = \{\, cwcw \mid w \in \{a,b\}^* \text{ and } |w| = 2n \text{ for some } n \geq 0 \,\}$. Concerning this language, we have the following result.

Proposition 2.5.31 ([96]) $L_d \in \mathcal{L}(\text{det-2-mon-RLWW}) \smallsetminus \mathcal{L}(\text{sRLW})$.

Proof outline. It is straightforward to see that L_d is not accepted by any sRLW-automaton. This follows from the fact that, without the use of auxiliary letters, a single rewrite step is, in general, not sufficient to transform a word from L_d into another word from L_d.

It remains to prove that L_d belongs to the class $\mathcal{L}(\text{det-2-mon-RLWW})$. Below we sketch a det-2-mon-RLWW-automaton M_d for L_d. This automaton has one auxiliary letter D and it works as follows:

- M_d accepts cc and DD without a restart.
- On words of length at least 6, M_d works according to the following table, where $x, y \in \{a,b\}$, and $w, w' \in \{aa, bb, ab, ba\}^*$:

word of the form	rewrites into
$cxywcxyw'$	$Dwcxyw'$
$Dwcxyw'$	$DwDw'$
$DxywDxyw'$	$cwDxyw'$
$cwDxyw'$	$cwcw'$

- If the contents of its tape has any other form, then M_d rejects.

Clearly, as an RLWW-automaton, M_d can first read its tape completely and can then perform the corresponding rewrite step deterministically. As all rewrite steps are done either at the beginning or in the middle of the current tape contents, M_d is 2-monotone.

By induction on the length of w, it can easily be checked that the computation of M_d is accepting on all words of the form $cwcw$ or $DwDw$, where $w \in \{a,b\}^*$ and $|w| = 2n$ for some $n \geq 0$. On the other hand, any word from $\{a,b,c\}^* \smallsetminus L_d$ is rejected by M_d. Thus, $L(M_d) = L_d$, that is, $L_d \in \mathcal{L}(\mathsf{det\text{-}2\text{-}mon\text{-}RLWW})$. □

Furthermore, let M'_d be the RLW-automaton that is obtained from M_d by including the letter D into its input alphabet, and let $L'_d = L(M'_d)$. By using similar arguments as in the proof of Proposition 2.5.31, the following result can be derived.

Proposition 2.5.32 ([96]) $L'_d \in \mathcal{L}(\mathsf{det\text{-}2\text{-}mon\text{-}RLW}) \smallsetminus \mathcal{L}(\mathsf{RL})$.

Together, these technical results yield the following consequences.

Theorem 2.5.33 ([96]) *For each* $j \geq 2$,

(a) $\mathcal{L}(\mathsf{det}\text{-}j\text{-}\mathsf{mon\text{-}RLW}) \subsetneq \mathcal{L}(\mathsf{det}\text{-}j\text{-}\mathsf{mon\text{-}RLWW})$, *and*
(b) $\mathcal{L}(\mathsf{det}\text{-}j\text{-}\mathsf{mon\text{-}RL}) \subsetneq \mathcal{L}(\mathsf{det}\text{-}j\text{-}\mathsf{mon\text{-}RLW})$.

By employing the technique that we already used in Example 2.1.9 for constructing an RWW-automaton for the marked copy language, the following result can also be established on the language L_d.

Lemma 2.5.34 ([96]) $L_d \in \mathcal{L}(\mathsf{2\text{-}mon\text{-}RWW})$.

As the language L_d is not context-free, Proposition 2.5.31 and Lemma 2.5.34 yield the following results.

Corollary 2.5.35 ([96])
(a) $\mathcal{L}(\mathsf{det\text{-}mon\text{-}(s)RLWW}) \subsetneq \mathcal{L}(\mathsf{det\text{-}2\text{-}mon\text{-}(s)RLWW})$.
(b) $\mathcal{L}(\mathsf{mon\text{-}(s)RWW}) \subsetneq \mathcal{L}(\mathsf{2\text{-}mon\text{-}(s)RWW})$.
(c) $\mathcal{L}(\mathsf{mon\text{-}(s)RRWW}) \subsetneq \mathcal{L}(\mathsf{2\text{-}mon\text{-}(s)RRWW})$.
(d) $\mathcal{L}(\mathsf{mon\text{-}(s)RLWW}) \subsetneq \mathcal{L}(\mathsf{2\text{-}mon\text{-}(s)RLWW})$.

Thus, even in the presence of auxiliary letters, 2-monotone restarting automata are more expressive than monotone restarting automata.

In Corollary 2.5.27, we have seen that the j-monotone deterministic RL-automata are more expressive than the corresponding deterministic RR-automata. Here we finally study the relationship between the deterministic types of RR- and RL-automata and the nondeterministic j-monotone variants. For that, we consider the language $L_7 = L_{7,1} \cup L_{7,2}$, where

– $L_{7,1} = \{ a^{2^n-2i}ca^i \mid n \geq 1, 0 \leq 2i < 2^n \}$ and
– $L_{7,2} = \{ a^i da^{2^n-2i} \mid n \geq 1, 0 \leq 2i < 2^n \}$.

We recall from Lemma 2.2.8 that $L_7 \in \mathcal{L}(\mathsf{det\text{-}RW}) \smallsetminus \mathcal{L}(\mathsf{RL})$. The next proposition states that the language L_7 is essentially non-monotone.

Proposition 2.5.36 ([96]) *Let* $j \in \mathbb{N}_+$. *Then* $L_7 \notin \mathcal{L}(j\text{-}\mathsf{mon\text{-}RLW})$.

Proof. Assume that there is an integer i_0 such that some i_0-mon-RLW-automaton M with a read/write window of size k accepts the language L_7. Let $2^n > p \cdot (k \cdot i_0 + 1)$, where p is the constant from the Pumping Lemma for M (Proposition 2.1.8), and let $w = a^{2^n}c \in L_7$. Obviously, the word w cannot be accepted directly by a tail computation. After the first cycle C_1 of an accepting computation of M on w, we obtain a word w_1 of the form $w_1 = a^{2^n-2j_1}ca^{j_1}$, where $j_1 > 0$. Through the next cycle C_2, a word w_2 of the form $w_2 = a^{2^n-2j_2}ca^{j_2}$ is obtained, where $j_1 < j_2$. We can continue in this way for $k \cdot i_0 + 1$ cycles. For each cycle C_i, $1 \leq i \leq k \cdot i_0 + 1$, we obtain a word $w_i = a^{2^n-2j_i}la^{j_i}$, where $j_1 < \cdots < j_i < \cdots < j_{k \cdot i_0+1}$. For each $i \geq 1$, the rewrite step performed in cycle C_i increases the distance of the position of the symbol c from the right sentinel from j_{i-1} to j_i, where we take $j_0 = 0$. Hence,

$$D_r(C_i) \geq |ca^{j_{i-1}} \lhd| = j_{i-1} + 2$$

and

$$D_r(C_i) \leq |a^{k-1}ca^{j_{i-1}} \lhd| = j_{i-1} + k + 1.$$

As $j_{i+k-1} > j_{i+k-2} > \cdots > j_{i-1}$, we obtain that

$$D_r(C_{i+k}) \geq j_{i+k-1} + 2 \geq j_{i-1} + k + 2 > D_r(C_i).$$

Thus,

$$D_r(C_1) < D_r(C_{k+1}) < D_r(C_{2k+1}) < \cdots < D_r(C_{i_0 \cdot k+1}).$$

By (2.9), this contradicts our assumption that M is i_0-monotone. □

Thus, we obtain the following incomparability results.

Corollary 2.5.37 ([96]) *For all $j \in \mathbb{N}_+$ and all $X \in \{\mathsf{R}, \mathsf{RR}, \mathsf{RL}\}$, $\mathcal{L}(\mathsf{det\text{-}XW}) \not\subseteq \mathcal{L}(j\text{-}\mathsf{mon\text{-}RLW})$.*

As seen above, 2-monotone nondeterministic restarting automata are more expressive than the corresponding monotone restarting automata. However, it remains open whether this result extends to higher degrees of j-monotonicity.

Problem 2.5.38 *For the various types of nondeterministic restarting automata with auxiliary letters, does the degree j of monotonicity yield infinite strictly ascending hierarchies of language classes?*

Lemma 2.5.24 and Proposition 2.5.25 show that, for each $j \geq 2$, the language

$$\bar{L}_j = \{\, a^{n_1}b^{n_1}a^{n_2}b^{n_2} \cdots a^{n_j}b^{n_j} \mid n_1 \geq n_2 \geq \cdots n_j \geq 1 \,\}$$

belongs to the difference $\mathcal{L}(j\text{-}\mathsf{mon\text{-}R}) \smallsetminus \mathcal{L}((j-1)\text{-}\mathsf{mon\text{-}sRLW})$. In fact, in the proof of Proposition 2.5.25, it is shown that an sRLW-automaton M for the language $\bar{L}_j$ must reduce all blocks from $\{a\}^+ \cdot \{b\}^+$ in an almost synchronous manner. Accordingly, M cannot possibly be sequentially i-monotone for any $i \geq 1$, that is, $\bar{L}_j \in \mathcal{L}(j\text{-}\mathsf{mon\text{-}R}) \smallsetminus \bigcup_{i \geq 1} \mathcal{L}(i\text{-}\mathsf{s\text{-}mon\text{-}sRLW})$.

On the other hand, the proof of Proposition 2.5.15 shows that the language L''_j is not accepted by any sRLW-automaton that is $(j-1)$-monotone. Thus,

$$L''_{j+1} \in \mathcal{L}((j+1)\text{-}\mathsf{s\text{-}mon\text{-}R}) \smallsetminus \mathcal{L}(j\text{-}\mathsf{mon\text{-}sRLW}).$$

Together with the above result on the language $\bar{L}_j$, this yields the following results.

Corollary 2.5.39 ([98]) *For each $j \geq 1$ and each $\mathsf{X} \in \{\mathsf{R}, \mathsf{(s)RW}, \mathsf{RR}, \mathsf{(s)RRW}, \mathsf{RL}, \mathsf{(s)RLW}\}$, the language classes $\mathcal{L}((j+1)\text{-}\mathsf{s\text{-}mon\text{-}X})$ and $\mathcal{L}(j\text{-}\mathsf{mon\text{-}X})$ are incomparable under inclusion. In particular, $\mathcal{L}(j\text{-}\mathsf{s\text{-}mon\text{-}X}) \subsetneq \mathcal{L}(j\text{-}\mathsf{mon\text{-}X})$.*

Finally, while the membership problem for a language that is accepted by a monotone restarting automaton is decidable in polynomial time, as such a language is necessarily context-free, it has been proved that there exist 2-monotone restarting automata for which the membership problem is quite complex.

Theorem 2.5.40 ([103]) *The language class $\mathcal{L}(2\text{-}\mathsf{mon\text{-}R})$ contains NP-complete languages.*

Hence, already 2-monotone R-automata are too expressive to admit efficient implementations. In addition, it is proved in [103] that j-monotonicity is undecidable for R-automata.

Theorem 2.5.41 ([103]) *The following problem is undecidable in general:*

INSTANCE	:	*An R-automaton M and an integer $j \geq 2$.*
QUESTION	:	*Is M j-monotone?*

Recall from Theorem 2.1.47 that monotonicity is decidable even for sRRWW-automata. In [96], the notion of left-monotonicity (see Definition 2.1.48) is also generalized to that of j-left-monotonicity, and results similar to those for j-monotonicity are established. In addition, *right-left-monotone* restarting automata are considered, which are restarting automata that are simultaneously monotone and left-monotone. Also for right-left-monotonicity, degrees are defined and corresponding results are derived. Here we do not consider this notion – instead, we refer the interested reader to the original paper [96].

Finally, we introduce those constraints, which we want to use to characterize word order complexity and word order freedom. Here we restrict our attention mainly to characteristic languages.

Definition 2.5.42 ([168]) *Let $M = (Q, \Sigma, \Gamma, \triangleright, \triangleleft, q_0, k, \delta)$ be an FsRRWW-automaton and let $j \in \mathbb{N}_+$ be a positive integer. A computation of M is called* j-constrained *if it is both j-rewriting and j-monotone. The restarting automaton M itself is called* j-constrained *if all its computations are j-constrained.*

Thus, each cycle of each computation of a j-constrained FsRRWW-automaton contains at least one but at most j applications of rewrite steps and, in addition, the sequence of all rewrite configurations of a computation can be partitioned into at most j monotone subsequences.

Definition 2.5.43 *Let M be an FsRRWW-automaton with input alphabet Σ and working alphabet Γ, and let $j \in \mathbb{N}_+$. Then*

$$L_C(M, j) = \{\, w \in L_C(M) \mid M \text{ accepts } w \text{ by a } j\text{-constrained computation}\}$$

and

$$L(M, j) = \{\, w \in L(M) \mid M \text{ accepts } w \text{ by a } j\text{-constrained computation}\},$$

that is, $L_C(M, j)$ $(L(M, j))$ is the subset of the characteristic (input) language of M that consists of all those words that M accepts through j-constrained computations. Furthermore,

$$\mathcal{L}_C(j, \mathsf{FsRRWW}) = \bigcup_{M \text{ is an FsRRWW-automaton}} L_C(M, j)$$

and

$$\mathcal{L}(j, \mathsf{FsRRWW}) = \bigcup_{M \text{ is an FsRRWW-automaton}} L(M, j),$$

denote the resulting classes of languages.

As j-monotonicity is a restriction of $(j+1)$-monotonicity, and as j-rewriting computations are a special case of $(j+1)$-rewriting computations, we see that j-constrained computations are a special class of $(j+1)$-constrained computations. Hence, it follows that, for each FsRRWW-automaton M and each $j \geq 1$, $L_C(M, j) \subseteq L_C(M, j+1)$ and $L(M, j) \subseteq L(M, j+1)$. In addition,

$$\mathcal{L}_C(j, \mathsf{FsRRWW}) \subseteq \mathcal{L}_C(j+1, \mathsf{FsRRWW}) \text{ and } \mathcal{L}(j, \mathsf{FsRRWW}) \subseteq \mathcal{L}(j+1, \mathsf{FsRRWW}).$$

Also $\mathcal{L}_C(j, \mathsf{FsRRWW}) \subseteq \mathcal{L}(j, \mathsf{FsRRWW})$, as each FsRRWW-automaton $M = (Q, \Sigma, \Gamma, \triangleright, \triangleleft, q_0, k, \delta)$ can be transformed into an FsRRWW-automaton $M' = (Q, \Gamma, \Gamma, \triangleright, \triangleleft, q_0, k, \delta)$ with input alphabet Γ, which yields $L(M', j) = L_C(M, j)$.

As each context-free language is the (input) language of a monotone sRRWW-automaton, we obtain the following characterization from Corollary 2.1.41.

Corollary 2.5.44 $\mathcal{L}(1, \mathsf{FsRRWW}) = \mathcal{L}(\mathsf{mon\text{-}sRRWW}) = \mathcal{L}(\mathsf{mon\text{-}RRWW}) = \mathsf{CFL}$.

Obviously, $\mathcal{L}_C(1, \mathsf{FsRRWW}) = \mathcal{L}_C(\mathsf{mon\text{-}sRRWW}) = \mathcal{L}(\mathsf{mon\text{-}sRRW})$. From this observation, the following proper inclusions follow (see Theorem 2.2.13).

Corollary 2.5.45 $\mathsf{DCFL} \subsetneq \mathcal{L}_C(1, \mathsf{FsRRWW}) \subsetneq \mathsf{CFL}$.

We recall from Lemma 2.2.3 that the context-free language

$$L_2 = \{ a^n b^n \mid n \geq 0 \} \cup \{ a^n b^m \mid m > 2n \geq 0 \}$$

is not accepted by any sRRW-automaton, and hence, $L_2 \notin \mathcal{L}_C(1, \mathsf{FsRRWW})$. On the other hand, the language $L_1 = \{ a^n b^n c, a^n b^{2n} d \mid n \geq 0 \}$ is accepted by a mon-RR-automaton by Lemma 2.2.1, but L_1 is not deterministic context-free.

While an FsRRWW-automaton can execute an arbitrary number of rewrite steps within a single cycle, an MsRRWW-automaton can only perform a bounded number of rewrite steps (see Definition 2.5.1). In fact, for each MsRRWW-automaton M, there exists a number $j_M \geq 1$ such that no cycle of any computation of M contains more than j_M applications of rewrite steps, that is, each computation of M is j_M-rewriting. Accordingly, the transition relation of an MsRRWW-automaton M can be described through a finite sequence of *meta-instructions* (see Section 2.1) of the form

$$(E_1, u_1 \to v_1, E_2, u_2 \to v_2, E_3, \ldots, E_i, u_i \to v_i, E_{i+1}),$$

where $E_1, E_2, \ldots, E_{i+1}$ are regular expressions, and for each $j = 1, 2, \ldots, i$, $u_j, v_j \in \Gamma^*$ are words satisfying $\omega(v_j) < \omega(u_j)$. Here $\omega : \Gamma \to \mathbb{N}_+$ is a weight function that is compatible with M, the rules $u_1 \to v_1$, $u_2 \to v_2$, $\ldots$, $u_i \to v_i$ embody rewrite transitions of M, and $i \leq j_M$. On trying to execute this meta-instruction, M will get stuck (and so reject) starting from the configuration $q_0 \rhd w \lhd$, if w does not admit a factorization of the form $w = w_1 u_1 w_2 u_2 \cdots w_i u_i w_{i+1}$ such that $\rhd w_1 \in L(E_1)$, $w_2 \in L(E_2)$, $\ldots$, $w_{i+1} \lhd \in L(E_{i+1})$, where $L(E_j)$ denotes the language described by the regular expression E_j. On the other hand, if w does have factorizations of this form, then one such factorization is chosen nondeterministically, and $q_0 \rhd w \lhd$ is transformed into the configuration $q_0 \rhd w_1 v_1 w_2 v_2 w_3 \cdots w_i v_i w_{i+1} \lhd$. In order to describe the tails of accepting computations of M, we use meta-instructions of the form $(\rhd \cdot E \cdot \lhd, \mathsf{Accept})$, which accept the words from the regular language $L(E)$.

As MsRRWW-automata only have a bounded number of rewrites per cycle, they are intuitively weaker than FsRRWW-automata. To illustrate this fact, we consider the following example.

Example 2.5.46 ([168]) *Let $L_\infty = \{ (a^n b^n)^m \mid n, m \geq 0 \}$, and let M_∞ be the deterministic FRRWW-automaton M_∞ with initial state q_0 and tape alphabet $\Gamma = \{a, b\}$ that is defined through the following transition function:*

$$\begin{array}{lcllcl}
\delta(q_0, \rhd \cdot \lhd) & = & \mathsf{Accept}, & \delta(q_1, aab) & = & (q_0, \mathsf{MVR}), \\
\delta(q_0, \rhd aa) & = & (q_0, \mathsf{MVR}), & \delta(q_1, bb\lhd) & = & \mathsf{Restart}, \\
\delta(q_0, aaa) & = & (q_0, \mathsf{MVR}), & \delta(q_1, b\lhd) & = & \mathsf{Restart}, \\
\delta(q_0, aab) & = & (q_0, \mathsf{MVR}), & \delta(q_1, \lhd) & = & \mathsf{Restart}, \\
\delta(q_0, abb) & = & (q_1, b), & \delta(q_0, \rhd ab) & = & (q_2, \rhd), \\
\delta(q_1, bbb) & = & (q_1, \mathsf{MVR}), & \delta(q_2, ab) & = & (q_2, \lambda), \\
\delta(q_1, bba) & = & (q_1, \mathsf{MVR}), & \delta(q_2, \lhd) & = & \mathsf{Accept}. \\
\delta(q_1, baa) & = & (q_0, \mathsf{MVR}), & & &
\end{array}$$

In each rewrite step, M_∞ simply deletes a factor of the form ab. Given the word $w = (a^3b^3)^4$ as input, M_∞ executes the following computation:

$$\begin{array}{lcllcl}
q_0 \rhd a^3 b^3 (a^3 b^3)^3 \lhd & \vdash^3_{M_\infty} & \rhd a^2 q_0 abbb (a^3 b^3)^3 \lhd & \vdash_{M_\infty} & \rhd a^2 b q_1 b (a^3 b^3)^3 \lhd \\
& \vdash^3_{M_\infty} & \rhd a^2 b^2 a^2 q_0 abbb (a^3 b^3)^2 \lhd & \vdash_{M_\infty} & \rhd a^2 b^2 a^2 b q_1 b (a^3 b^3)^2 \lhd \\
& \vdash^3_{M_\infty} & \rhd (a^2 b^2)^2 a^2 q_0 abbba^3 b^3 \lhd & \vdash_{M_\infty} & \rhd (a^2 b^2)^2 a^2 b q_1 ba^3 b^3 \lhd \\
& \vdash^3_{M_\infty} & \rhd (a^2 b^2)^3 a^2 q_0 abbb \lhd & \vdash_{M_\infty} & \rhd (a^2 b^2)^3 a^2 b q_1 b \lhd
\end{array}$$

$$\begin{array}{llll}
\vdash_{M_\infty} & q_0 \rhd aabb(a^2b^2)^3 \lhd & \vdash^2_{M_\infty} & \rhd aq_0abb(a^2b^2)^3 \lhd \\
\vdash_{M_\infty} & \rhd abq_1aabb(a^2b^2)^2 \lhd & \vdash_{M_\infty} & \rhd abaq_0abb(a^2b^2)^2 \lhd \\
\vdash_{M_\infty} & \rhd ababq_1aabba^2b^2 \lhd & \vdash_{M_\infty} & \rhd ababaq_0abba^2b^2 \lhd \\
\vdash_{M_\infty} & \rhd abababq_1aabb \lhd & \vdash_{M_\infty} & \rhd abababaq_0abb \lhd \\
\vdash_{M_\infty} & \rhd ababababq_1 \lhd & \vdash_{M_\infty} & q_0 \rhd abababab \lhd \\
\vdash_{M_\infty} & \rhd q_2abababab \lhd & \vdash^3_{M_\infty} & \rhd q_2 \lhd \; \vdash_{M_\infty} \; \mathsf{Accept}.
\end{array}$$

In fact, it is easily verified that $L_C(M_\infty) = L(M_\infty) = L_\infty$. ■

On the other hand, L_∞ is not the characteristic language of any MsRRWW-automaton.

Lemma 2.5.47 ([168]) $L_\infty \notin \mathcal{L}_C(\mathsf{MsRRWW})$.

Proof. Assume to the contrary that M' is an MsRRWW-automaton with tape alphabet $\Gamma = \{a, b\}$ such that $L_C(M') = L_\infty$. We consider an input of the form $w = (a^nb^n)^{j_{M'}+1}$, where n is sufficiently large, and $j_{M'}$ is the maximal number of rewrite steps that M' can execute within a single cycle. As $w \in L_\infty$, M' has an accepting computation for input w, but as M' can execute at most $j_{M'}$ rewrite steps per cycle, the first cycle of M' in this computation will transform the word w into a word that does not belong to the language L_∞. Thus, $L_C(M') \neq L_\infty$, that is, L_∞ is not the characteristic language of any MsRRWW-automaton. □

This example has the following consequence.

Corollary 2.5.48 ([168]) $\mathcal{L}_C(\mathsf{MsRRWW}) \subsetneq \mathcal{L}_C(\mathsf{FsRRWW})$.

For the FRRWW-automaton M_∞ of Example 2.5.46, we see that

$$L_C(M_\infty, j) = \{\, (a^nb^n)^m \mid n \geq 0,\ j \geq m \geq 0 \,\},$$

which shows that the languages $L_C(M_\infty, j)$ $(j \geq 1)$ form an infinite strictly ascending sequence that approximates the language $L_C(M_\infty) = L_\infty$. In analogy to the arguments in the proof of Lemma 2.5.47, it can be shown that the language $\{\, (a^nb^n)^m \mid n \geq 0,\ j \geq m \geq 0 \,\}$ does not coincide with the language $L_C(M', j-1)$ for any FsRRWW-automaton M'. Hence, we have the following strictly ascending infinite hierarchy.

Corollary 2.5.49 ([168]) *For all* $j \geq 1$, $\mathcal{L}_C(j, \mathsf{FsRRWW}) \subsetneq \mathcal{L}_C(j+1, \mathsf{FsRRWW})$.

We continue with further examples.

Example 2.5.50 *Let* M_1 *be the MRRWW-automaton with tape alphabet* $\{a, b\}$ *that is given through the following meta-instructions:*

$$\begin{array}{ll}
(1) & (\rhd \cdot a^+, abb \to b, b^* \cdot \lhd), \\
(2) & (\rhd \cdot a^+, abb \to b, b^* \cdot a^+, abb \to b, b^* \cdot \lhd), \\
(3) & (\rhd \cdot (ab + abab) \cdot \lhd, \ \mathsf{Accept}).
\end{array}$$

It is easy to see that $L_C(M_1, 1) = \{\, a^nb^n \mid n > 0 \,\} \cup \{abab\}$, *as in a 1-constrained computation,* M_1 *can only use meta-instructions* (1) *and* (3), *while* $L_C(M_1, 2) = L_C(M_1, 1) \cup \{\, a^nb^na^nb^n \mid n > 0 \,\}$. *Hence,* $L_C(M_1) = L_C(M_1, 2) \supsetneq L_C(M_1, 1)$. ■

Observe that $L_C(M_1) = L_C(M_1, 2) = \{\, a^nb^n, a^nb^na^nb^n \mid n > 0 \,\}$ is not context-free, and so $L_C(M_1) \notin \mathcal{L}_C(1, \mathsf{FsRRWW})$ by Corollary 2.5.45.

Example 2.5.51 *Let* M_2 *be the MRRWW-automaton that is given through the meta-instructions* (1) *to* (3) *of* M_1 *and the following two meta-instructions:*

$$\begin{array}{ll}
(4) & (\rhd \cdot a^+, abb \to b, b^* \cdot ab \lhd), \\
(5) & (\rhd ab \cdot a^+, abb \to b, b^* \cdot \lhd).
\end{array}$$

In a 1-constrained computation, M_2 can use meta-instructions (1) and (3) to (5). It follows that $L_C(M_2, 1) = \{ a^n b^n, aba^n b^n, a^n b^n ab \mid n > 0 \}$, while $L_C(M_2, 2) = \{ a^n b^n a^m b^m \mid n > 0,\ m \geq 0 \} = L_C(M_2)$.

In contrast to $L_C(M_1)$, the language $L_C(M_2)$ is context-free, and $L_C(M_2)$ is even accepted by an MRRWW-automaton M' that executes only 1-constrained computations, that is, $L_C(M_2) \in \mathcal{L}_C(1, \mathsf{FsRRWW})$. The automaton M' is given through the following meta-instructions:

$$\begin{array}{llll} (1) & (\rhd \cdot a^+, abb \to b, b^* \cdot \lhd), & (3) & (\rhd \cdot a^+, abb \to b, b^* \cdot a^+ \cdot b^+ \cdot \lhd), \\ (2) & (\rhd, ab \to \lambda, a^+ \cdot b^+ \cdot \lhd), & (4) & (\rhd ab \lhd, \mathsf{Accept}). \end{array}$$

■

Below we use the following families of example languages from [168].

Definition 2.5.52 *Let $j \in \mathbb{N}_+$, let $\Gamma_j = \{a, b, c_0, c_1, \ldots, c_{j-1}\}$, and let $\Delta_j = \{a_1, a_2, \ldots, a_j\}$. The languages LC_j and LE_j are defined as follows:*

$$\begin{array}{lcll} LC_j & = & \{ c_0 w c_1 w c_2 w \cdots c_{j-2} w c_{j-1} w \mid w \in \{a, b\}^* \} & \subseteq \Gamma_j^* \text{ and} \\ LE_j & = & \{ w \in \{a_1, a_2, \ldots, a_j\}^* \mid |w|_{a_1} = |w|_{a_2} = \cdots = |w|_{a_j} \} & \subseteq \Delta_j^*. \end{array}$$

We remark that the languages LC_j $(j \geq 1)$ represent those languages in which valences are modelled through fixed reduction positions (with an increasing number of such positions), and the languages LE_j $(j \geq 1)$ represent those languages in which valences are modelled by j-tuples of letters in varying positions, independent of the word order. For the languages LC_j $(j \geq 1)$, we have the following results.

Proposition 2.5.53 ([168]) (a) *For each $j \geq 1$, $LC_j \in \mathcal{L}_C(j, \mathsf{FsRRWW})$.*

(b) *For each $j \geq 1$, $LC_{j+1} \notin \mathcal{L}_C(j, \mathsf{FsRRWW})$.*

(c) *For all $j \geq 1$, $LC_j \in \mathcal{L}(2, \mathsf{FsRRWW})$.*

Proof. As (a) and (b) are easily proved, we concentrate on (c). For $j \geq 1$, let $\overline{M}_j$ be the MsRRWW-automaton with input alphabet Γ_j and tape alphabet $\Omega_j = \Gamma_j \cup D$, where $D = \{d_a, d_b\}$, that is given through the following meta-instructions, where $u \in \Sigma_0 = \{a, b\}$:

$$\begin{array}{ll} (1) & (\rhd c_0, u \to \lambda, \Sigma_0^* \cdot c_1 \cdot D^*, u \to d_u, \Sigma_0^* \cdot c_2 \cdots c_{j-1} \cdot \Sigma_0^* \cdot \lhd), \\ (2) & (\rhd c_0 c_1, d_u \to \lambda, D^* \cdot c_2 \cdot D^*, u \to d_u, \Sigma_0^* \cdot c_3 \cdots c_{j-1} \cdot \Sigma_0^* \cdot \lhd), \\ \ldots & \ldots \\ (j-2) & (\rhd c_0 c_1 \cdots c_{j-3}, d_u \to \lambda, D^* \cdot c_{j-2} \cdot D^*, u \to d_u, \Sigma_0^* \cdot c_{j-1} \cdot \Sigma_0^* \cdot \lhd), \\ (j-1) & (\rhd c_0 c_1 \cdots c_{j-2}, d_u \to \lambda, D^* \cdot c_{j-1}, u \to \lambda, \Sigma_0^* \cdot \lhd), \\ (j) & (\rhd c_0 c_1 \cdots c_{j-1} \lhd, \mathsf{Accept}). \end{array}$$

Here we take the weight function $\omega(x) = 2$ $(x \in \Gamma_j)$ and $\omega(d) = 1$ $(d \in D)$.

Given an input $c_0 w_1 c_1 w_2 \cdots c_{j-2} w_{j-1} c_{j-1} w_j$ with $w_1, w_2, \ldots, w_j \in \Sigma_0^*$, $\overline{M}_j$ gradually compares the neighbouring factors w_i and w_{i+1} $(1 \leq i \leq j-1)$ from left to right. First, meta-instructions of type (1) are used repeatedly to compare w_1 to w_2, thereby deleting w_1 letter by letter from left to right, and encoding each letter u of w_2 by the letter d_u. Then, meta-instructions of type (2) are used to compare w_2 to w_3, thereby deleting (the encoded version of) w_2 letter by letter from left to right, and encoding each letter u of w_3 by the letter d_u. This continues for indices $3, 4, \ldots, j-2$ until finally meta-instructions of type $(j-1)$ are used repeatedly to compare (the encoded version of) w_{j-1} and w_j, thereby deleting both factors from left to right. It follows that each computation of $\overline{M}_j$ is 2-constrained, that is, $LC_j \in \mathcal{L}(2, \mathsf{FsRRWW})$. □

Thus, we see that the hierarchy of classes of input languages and the hierarchy of classes of characteristic languages of FsRRWW-automata significantly differ from each other. As shown by Proposition 2.5.53, a language may be of a lower degree of constrainability when it is interpreted as the input language of an FsRRWW-automaton, as when it is considered as the language of sentential forms of an FsRRWW-automaton. The reason for this phenomenon is the fact that, even in an accepting computation of an FsRRWW-automaton, a word from the input language may be converted into a word that does not belong to the input language. The following theorem summarizes these observations.

Theorem 2.5.54 ([168])

(a) $\mathcal{L}_C(\mathsf{FsRRWW}) \subsetneq \mathcal{L}(\mathsf{FsRRWW})$, *and*
(b) $\mathcal{L}_C(i, \mathsf{FsRRWW}) \subsetneq \mathcal{L}(i, \mathsf{FsRRWW})$ *for all* $i \in \mathbb{N}_+$.

Proof outline. For $i \geq 2$, the proper inclusion in (b) is an immediate consequence of Proposition 2.5.53, while, for $i = 1$, this is simply a part of the statement of Corollary 2.5.45. For proving the statement in (a), we consider the language $L'_\infty = \{ (a^n b^n)^n \mid n \geq 1 \}$. On the one hand, it can be shown that $L'_\infty \in \mathcal{L}(\mathsf{FsRRWW})$, while, on the other hand, $L'_\infty \notin \mathcal{L}_C(\mathsf{FsRRWW})$. For the details, we refer to [168]. □

Next, we introduce some notions that will be used to formalize the notion of *word order freedom* of languages.

Definition 2.5.55 ([168]) (a) *Two words* $u, v \in \Gamma^*$ *are called* letter-equivalent, *denoted by* $u \equiv v$, *if* $|u|_a = |v|_a$ *holds for each* $a \in \Gamma$.

(b) *Let* M *be an FsRRWW-automaton, and let* $u, v \in L_C(M)$. *The word* u *is* M-transformable *into* v, *denoted by* $u \Rrightarrow_M v$, *if* $u \equiv v$ *holds, and for each word* u_1 *satisfying* $|u| > |u_1|$ *and* $q_0 \rhd u \lhd \vdash^c_M q_0 \rhd u_1 \lhd$, *there exists a word* v_1 *such that* $q_0 \rhd v \lhd \vdash^{c^*}_M q_0 \rhd v_1 \lhd$ *and* $u_1 \equiv v_1$.

(c) *An FsRRWW-automaton* M *is called* reduction-preserving *if, for each* $j > 0$ *and each* $w \in L_C(M, j+1)$, *there exists a word* $v \in L_C(M, j)$ *such that* $w \Rrightarrow_M v$.

If M is reduction-preserving, then, for each $j > 0$ and each word w accepted by M through a $(j+1)$-constrained computation, there exists a word v that is accepted by M through a j-constrained computation such that w and v are letter-equivalent. In addition, each word that is shorter than w and that can be reached from w by a reduction mod M is also letter-equivalent to some word that can be reached from v by a sequence of reductions mod M. Intuitively, this means that, by commutating w, we obtain a word v that is of a lower degree of word order complexity, but that admits essentially the same reductions (modulo commutation).

Example 2.5.56 *The MRRWW-automaton* M_1 *of Example 2.5.50 is reduction-preserving. Indeed, let* $n \geq 2$ *and* $u = a^n b^n a^n b^n \in L_C(M_1, 2) \smallsetminus L_C(M_1, 1)$. *We take* $v = a^{2n} b^{2n} \in L_C(M_1, 1)$. *Then* $u \Rrightarrow_{M_1} v$, *as* $u \equiv v$ *and* $q_0 \rhd u \lhd \vdash^c_{M_1} q_0 \rhd u_1 \lhd$ *implies that* $u_1 = a^{n-1} b^{n-1} a^{n-1} b^{n-1}$, *and so* $v_1 = a^{2n-2} b^{2n-2} \in L_C(M_1, 1)$ *satisfies the conditions that* $q_0 \rhd v \lhd \vdash^{c^*}_{M_1} q_0 \rhd v_1 \lhd$ *and* $v_1 \equiv u_1$. ■

For an FsRRWW-automaton M, if $L_C(M, j) = L_C(M, 1)$ holds for all $j \geq 1$, then M is trivially reduction-preserving. The following notion will be used for reduction-preserving FsRRWW-automata to measure their distance from this trivial case.

Definition 2.5.57 ([168]) *An FsRRWW-automaton* M *is called* 1-scalable *if it is reduction-preserving. It is called* j-scalable *for some* $j \geq 2$, *if it is reduction-preserving and if* $L_C(M, i+1) \notin \mathcal{L}_C(i, \mathsf{FsRRWW})$ *for all* $i = 1, 2, \ldots, j-1$. *A language* L *of sentential forms is called* j-scalable, *if there exists a* j-*scalable FsRRWW-automaton* M *such that* $L = L_C(M)$.

If an FsRRWW-automaton M is j-scalable for some $j \geq 2$, then, for all i, $1 \leq i \leq j-1$, the language $L_C(M, i+1)$ of sentential forms that M accepts through $(i+1)$-constrained computations does not coincide with the language of sentential forms that are accepted by any FsRRWW-automaton by performing only i-constrained computations.

In the following, the notion of scalability is seen as a synonym for the degree of word order complexity for languages with free word order. The following proposition is an immediate consequence of the above definition.

Proposition 2.5.58 ([168]) *If an FsRRWW-automaton M is j-scalable for some integer $j \geq 2$, then M is $(j-1)$-scalable as well.*

We now illustrate the above concepts with some examples.

Example 2.5.59 *As seen above, the MRRWW-automaton M_1 of Example 2.5.50 is reduction-preserving. Furthermore, the language $L_C(M_1, 2) = \{ a^n b^n, a^n b^n a^n b^n \mid n > 0 \}$ does not coincide with the characteristic language that any FsRRWW-automaton can accept by 1-constrained computations. Thus, M_1 is 2-scalable. However, it is not 3-scalable, as $L_C(M_1) = L_C(M_1, 2)$. On the other hand, the MRRWW-automaton M_2 of Example 2.5.51 is only 1-scalable, but it is not 2-scalable, as the language $L_C(M_2, 2)$ is also accepted by the MRRWW-automaton M' performing only 1-constrained computations.* ■

Example 2.5.60 *The language LC_2 (see Definition 2.5.52) is not accepted by any reduction-preserving FsRRWW-automaton. Indeed, assume that M is an FsRRWW-automaton for LC_2 with a read/write window of size k. We consider the word $w_n = c_0 a^n b^{k \cdot n} c_1 a^n b^{k \cdot n} \in LC_2$, where n is sufficiently large. If w_n is letter-equivalent to a word of the form $c_0 u^m c_1 u^m \in LC_2$, then u must contain at least one occurrence of the letter a. This implies that $m \leq n$, which in turn means that $|u| \geq k+1$. M can delete at most k letters in any rewrite step, and so it cannot delete a complete copy of u from both factors in a single rewrite step. Hence, we see that M cannot accept $c_0 u^m c_1 u^m$ through a 1-constrained computation. Thus, LC_2 is not accepted by any reduction-preserving FsRRWW-automaton, and therewith LC_2 is not j-scalable for any $j \geq 1$. The same argument applies to each language LC_j $(j \geq 3)$.* ■

This observation supports the claim that reduction-preserving FsRRWW-automata are an adequate tool for describing free word order languages. Finally, we turn to the family of languages LE_j $(j \geq 2)$.

The language $LE_2 = \{ w \in \{a_1, a_2\}^* \mid |w|_{a_1} = |w|_{a_2} \}$ coincides with the characteristic language of the MRRWW-automaton M_2 that is given by the following meta-instructions:

$$(\rhd \cdot a_1^*, a_1 a_2 \to \lambda, \{a_1, a_2\}^* \cdot \lhd), \ (\rhd \cdot a_2^*, a_2 a_1 \to \lambda, \{a_1, a_2\}^* \cdot \lhd), \ (\rhd \cdot \lhd, \mathsf{Accept}).$$

It is easily seen that all computations of M_2 are 1-constrained, which means that $L_C(M_2) = L_C(M, j)$ holds for all $j \geq 1$. Hence, M_2 is reduction-preserving and therewith 1-scalable. Thus, the language LE_2 is 1-scalable, but obviously not 2-scalable, as it is the characteristic language of the 1-constrained MRRWW-automaton M_2. This statement generalizes to all languages LE_j $(j \geq 2)$.

Proposition 2.5.61 ([168]) *For all $j \geq 2$, LE_j is $(j-1)$-scalable, but it is not j-scalable.*

Proof outline. As LE_2 has been considered above, it remains the case $j \geq 3$. So let $j \geq 3$, and let M_j be the MRRWW-automaton with tape alphabet $\Delta_j = \{a_1, a_2, \ldots, a_j\}$ that is defined by the following meta-instructions, where π ranges over the set of permutations of the index set $\{1, 2, \ldots, j\}$:

$$\begin{array}{ll} (\pi) & (\rhd \cdot a_{\pi(1)}^*, a_{\pi(1)} a_{\pi(2)} \to \lambda, \{a_{\pi(1)}, a_{\pi(2)}\}^*, a_{\pi(3)} \to \lambda, \{a_{\pi(1)}, a_{\pi(2)}, a_{\pi(3)}\}^*, \\ & \qquad a_{\pi(4)} \to \lambda, \ldots, (\Delta_j \smallsetminus \{a_{\pi(j)}\})^*, a_{\pi(j)} \to \lambda, \Delta_j^* \cdot \lhd), \\ (1) & (\rhd, a_1 a_2 \cdots a_j \to \lambda, (a_1 a_2 \cdots a_j)^* \cdot \lhd), \\ (2) & (\rhd \cdot a_2^*, a_2 a_1 \to \lambda, a_1^*, a_3 a_4 \cdots a_j \to \lambda, (a_3 a_4 \cdots a_j)^* \cdot \lhd) \text{ for } j \geq 4, \\ (+) & (\rhd \cdot \lhd, \mathsf{Accept}). \end{array}$$

Observe that each meta-instruction (π) is $(j-1)$-rewriting, while meta-instruction (1) is 1-rewriting, and meta-instruction (2) is 2-rewriting.

For $j \geq 5$, the following meta-instructions are used in addition to the above, where i ranges over the set of integers $\{3, 4, \ldots, j-2\}$:

$$\begin{array}{ll}(i.2) & (\rhd \cdot a_2^*, a_2a_1 \to \lambda, a_1^*, a_3 \to \lambda, a_3^* \cdot a_1^*, a_4 \to \lambda, a_4^* \cdot a_1^*, \ldots, a_i \to \lambda, \\ & \qquad a_i^* \cdot a_1^*, a_{i+1}a_{i+2}\cdots a_j \to \lambda, (a_{i+1}a_{i+2}\cdots a_j)^* \cdot \lhd), \\ (i.3) & (\rhd \cdot a_2^*, a_2 \to \lambda, a_3^*, a_3a_1 \to \lambda, a_1^*, a_4 \to \lambda, a_4^* \cdot a_1^*, \ldots, a_i \to \lambda, \\ & \qquad a_i^* \cdot a_1^*, a_{i+1}a_{i+2}\cdots a_j \to \lambda, (a_{i+1}a_{i+2}\cdots a_j)^* \cdot \lhd), \\ \ldots & \ldots\ldots \\ (i.i) & (\rhd \cdot a_2^*, a_2 \to \lambda, a_3^*, a_3 \to \lambda, a_4^*, a_4 \to \lambda, a_5^*, \ldots, a_{i-1} \to \lambda, \\ & \qquad a_i^*, a_ia_1 \to \lambda, a_1^*, a_{i+1}a_{i+2}\cdots a_j \to \lambda, (a_{i+1}a_{i+2}\cdots a_j)^* \cdot \lhd).\end{array}$$

Observe that, for all $i = 3, 4, \ldots, j-2$ and all $s = 2, 3, \ldots, i$, meta-instruction $(i.s)$ is i-rewriting.

Claim. $L_{\mathrm{C}}(M_3) = LE_3$, and M_3 is 2-scalable.

Proof. If the tape contents is of the form $(a_1a_2a_3)^m$ for some integer $m \geq 1$, then it is reduced to the empty word by m applications of meta-instruction (1). The resulting computation is 1-constrained. If the tape contents $x \in LE_3$ is not of the form above, then there exists a permutation π such that meta-instruction (π) is applicable. Repeated applications of meta-instructions of this form reduce x to the empty word or to a word of the form $(a_1a_2a_3)^m$ for some $m \geq 1$, which is then reduced as described above. The resulting computation is 2-constrained, and it follows easily that $L_{\mathrm{C}}(M_3) = LE_3$ holds.

If $w \in LE_3 = L_{\mathrm{C}}(M_3) = L_{\mathrm{C}}(M_3, 2)$, then $|w|_{a_1} = |w|_{a_2} = |w|_{a_3} = m$ for some $m \geq 0$. The word $v = (a_1a_2a_3)^m \in L_{\mathrm{C}}(M_3, 1)$ is letter-equivalent to w, and actually, $w \Rrightarrow_{M_3} v$ holds. Thus, M_3 is reduction-preserving. Finally, it remains to show that $L_{\mathrm{C}}(M_3, 2) = LE_3 \notin \mathcal{L}_{\mathrm{C}}(1, \mathsf{FsRRWW})$. Assume to the contrary that there is an FsRRWW-automaton M for which LE_3 coincides with the language that is accepted by the 1-constrained computations of M. Consider the word $w = a_1^na_2^na_3^n$ for a sufficiently large $n > 0$. Then $w \in LE_3$, but the first cycle of a 1-constrained computation of M can only rewrite one or two types of letters. Thus, it will transform w into a word that does not belong to LE_3, which implies that the 1-constrained computation considered is not accepting. It follows that M_3 is 2-scalable. □

Analogously, it can be shown for all $j \geq 4$ that $L_{\mathrm{C}}(M_j) = LE_j$ and that M_j is $(j-1)$-scalable. The details can be found in [168]. □

The next theorem, which completes these considerations, is a consequence of the above proposition. It shows that there exists an infinite sequence of classes of free word order languages with an increasing degree of word order complexity. Here we use the notation r-scal- to denote types of FsRRWW-automata that are r-scalable.

Theorem 2.5.62 ([168]) *For all $i, j \in \mathbb{N}_+$, $i < j$:*

(a) $\mathcal{L}_{\mathrm{C}}((j+1)\text{-scal-FsRRWW}) \subsetneq \mathcal{L}_{\mathrm{C}}(j\text{-scal-FsRRWW})$,
(b) $\mathcal{L}_{\mathrm{C}}(i, j\text{-scal-FsRRWW}) \subsetneq \mathcal{L}_{\mathrm{C}}(i+1, j\text{-scal-FsRRWW})$.

We interpret the notion of j-constrainability as a measure for the complexity of the word order of (individual syntactic phenomena of) natural languages. Furthermore, we propose to use reduction-preserving FsRRWW-automata to model free word order languages, where the notion of j-scalability serves as a measure for the complexity of the word order for languages with free word order. From the languages LC_j $(j \geq 1)$ and LE_j $(j \geq 1)$, we see that the word order complexity can be caused by phenomena that are based on fixed syntactic positions as well as by phenomena that are based on flexible (free) syntactic positions.

Each context-free language is the (input) language that is accepted by the 1-constrained computations of an FsRRWW-automaton, while the characteristic languages that are accepted by 1-constrained computations of FsRRWW-automata form a proper subclass of CFL (Corollary 2.5.45). On the other hand, the classes of characteristic languages that are accepted by i-constrained computations of FsRRWW-automata form an infinite strictly ascending hierarchy with respect to the parameter i (Corollary 2.5.49). However, the following problem is still open.

Problem 2.5.63 *Does there exist a corresponding hierarchy within CFL? Or is there an upper bound for the degree of constrainability for context-free languages that occur as characteristic languages of FsRRWW-automata?*

For example, it is easily seen that the context-free language $L_{\text{pal}} = \{ ww^R \mid w \in \{a,b\}^* \}$ is accepted by the 2-constrained computations of an FsRRWW-automaton that, in each cycle, simply compares and removes the first letter and the last letter from the actual tape contents. On the other hand, it appears highly unlikely that the language L_{pal} coincides with the characteristic language of an FsRRWW-automaton that performs only 1-constrained computations. Hence, the context-free language L_{pal} seems to belong to $\mathcal{L}_{\text{C}}(2, \mathsf{FsRRWW}) \smallsetminus \mathcal{L}_{\text{C}}(1, \mathsf{FsRRWW})$. Are there any context-free languages in the set $\mathcal{L}_{\text{C}}(j+1, \mathsf{FsRRWW}) \smallsetminus \mathcal{L}_{\text{C}}(j, \mathsf{FsRRWW})$ for larger values of j? Are there at all context-free languages that are not accepted as characteristic languages by any FsRRWW-automata?

2.5.3 Cut Hierarchies and Contextual Languages

The motivation for Marcus contextual grammars [147] as well as for restarting automata comes mainly from linguistics. A *contextual grammar* is a generative device that describes a language through the process of inserting contexts into words and that works completely without nonterminals. Starting with a word from a finite set of *axioms*, a contextual grammar allows to insert two words (called *contexts*) in two places of the current word in each derivation step (see Definition 1.3.1). Which words are inserted at which places is controlled by the so-called *choice mapping*. Contextual grammars are rather universal in the sense that their choice mappings can be very general. Accordingly, various restrictions have been considered in the literature (see, e.g., [214]).

An RR-automaton, on the other hand, is a particular type of restarting automaton which does not distinguish between input letters and categories (working letters). Obviously, RR-automata can be used as recognizers for certain languages that are generated by contextual grammars with regular selection [84, 102, 174]. It turned out, however, that, in some respect, RR-automata are more general than contextual grammars with regular selection, as such an automaton may delete more than two factors simultaneously during a cycle. This corresponds to the notion of *t-contextual grammar* (see Definition 1.3.36), which is a contextual grammar that inserts t factors in each derivation step [214], where t is any positive integer. It is known that the expressive capacity of t-contextual grammars increases with the number t. This remains true even in the case of t-contextual grammars with regular selection (see Definition 1.3.37), that is, for t-contextual grammars for which the choice mapping can be described through regular expressions.

However, an RR-automaton executes just a single delete step in each cycle, which removes one or more non-empty factors from the current contents of the window. Thus, all factors deleted are in close proximity. Accordingly, to relate t-contextual grammars to RR-automata, we need a more general model of the RR-automaton, an RR-automaton that may perform more than a single delete step during a cycle. This leads to the t-r-RR-automaton (see Definition 2.5.1).

Definition 2.5.64 ([170, 208]) *Let $M = (Q, \Sigma, \Sigma, \rhd, \lhd, q_0, k, \delta)$ be a t-r-RR-automaton for some integer $t \geq 1$. We say that M has* cut-index i *if, in each delete operation of M, at most i separate factors are deleted from the actual window contents. The class of all t-r-RR-automata with cut-index i is denoted by t-$\mathsf{cut}(i)$-RR.*

If M is a t-r-RR-automaton with window size k and cut-index i, then $1 \leq i \leq \lfloor (k+1)/2 \rfloor$, as any two neighbouring non-empty factors that are deleted within a single delete step are separated by a non-empty factor. The transition relation of a t-$\mathsf{cut}(i)$-RR-automaton M can be described by a finite sequence of so-called *meta-instructions* (see Section 2.1) of the form

$$(E_0, u_1, E_1, u_2, E_2, \ldots, E_{s-1}, u_s, E_s),$$

where $1 \leq s \leq i{\cdot}t$, $E_0, E_1, \ldots, E_s$ are regular languages (usually represented by regular expressions), called the *regular constraints* of this instruction, and $u_1, u_2, \ldots, u_s$ are words such that $1 \leq |u_j| \leq k$

$(1 \leq j \leq s)$, which correspond to factors that M deletes during one cycle. On trying to execute this meta-instruction, the t-cut(i)-RR-automaton M will get stuck (and so reject) starting from the configuration $q_0 \rhd w \lhd$, if w does not admit a factorization of the form $w = v_0 u_1 v_1 u_2 \cdots v_{s-1} u_s v_s$ such that $\rhd \cdot v_0 \in E_0$, $v_i \in E_i$ for all $i = 1, 2, \ldots, s-1$, and $v_s \cdot \lhd \in E_s$. On the other hand, if w does have a factorization of this form, then one such factorization is chosen nondeterministically, and $q_0 \rhd w \lhd$ is transformed into $q_0 \rhd v_0 v_1 \cdots v_{s-1} v_s \lhd$ by deleting all the factors u_j, $1 \leq j \leq s$. In order to be able to describe the tails of accepting computations, we use meta-instructions of the form $(\rhd \cdot E \cdot \lhd, \mathsf{Accept})$, expressing the fact that the words from the regular language E are accepted by M in tail computations.

Example 2.5.65 *Let $t \geq 1$, and let $LC_t = \{ c_0 w c_1 w c_2 \cdots c_{t-1} w \mid w \in \{a,b\}^* \}$, where $\Sigma_0 = \{a, b\}$ and $\Sigma_t = \Sigma_0 \cup \{c_0, c_1, \ldots, c_{t-1}\}$. We obtain a t-cut(1)-RR-automaton M_t for the language LC_t through the following sequence of meta-instructions:*

$$\begin{array}{ll} (1) & (\rhd \cdot c_0, a, \Sigma_0^* \cdot c_1, a, \Sigma_0^* \cdot c_2, \ldots, \Sigma_0^* \cdot c_{t-1}, a, \Sigma_0^* \cdot \lhd), \\ (2) & (\rhd \cdot c_0, b, \Sigma_0^* \cdot c_1, b, \Sigma_0^* \cdot c_2, \ldots, \Sigma_0^* \cdot c_{t-1}, b, \Sigma_0^* \cdot \lhd), \\ (3) & (\rhd \cdot c_0 c_1 \cdots c_{t-1} \cdot \lhd, \mathsf{Accept}). \end{array}$$

Given the word $w = c_0 abac_1 abac_2 \cdots c_{t-1} aba$ as input, M_t can execute the following accepting computation, where the letters that are deleted in a cycle are underlined:

$$\begin{array}{rcl} q_0 \rhd w \lhd & = & q_0 \rhd c_0 \underline{a} bac_1 \underline{a} bac_2 \cdots c_{t-1} \underline{a} ba \lhd \\ & \vdash_{M_t}^c & q_0 \rhd c_0 \underline{b} ac_1 \underline{b} ac_2 \cdots c_{t-1} \underline{b} a \lhd \\ & \vdash_{M_t}^c & q_0 \rhd c_0 \underline{a} c_1 \underline{a} c_2 \cdots c_{t-1} \underline{a} \lhd \\ & \vdash_{M_t}^c & q_0 \rhd c_0 c_1 c_2 \cdots c_{t-1} \lhd \\ & \vdash_{M_t}^* & \mathsf{Accept}. \end{array}$$

It follows easily that $L(M_t) = LC_t$. ■

On the other hand, we have the following negative result, which is obtained by observing that, by executing at most $t-1$ delete steps, the word $c_0 a^m b^m c_1 a^m b^m c_2 \cdots c_{t-1} a^m b^m \in LC_t$ can neither be converted into a shorter word that belongs to the language LC_t, nor can it be accepted in a tail computation, if m is a sufficiently large integer that depends on the RR-automaton considered.

Proposition 2.5.66 *For each $t \geq 2$, $LC_t \notin \mathcal{L}((t-1)\text{-r-RR})$.*

This yields the following hierarchy results.

Corollary 2.5.67 ([170, 208]) *For each $t \geq 2$ and each $i \geq 1$:*

$$\begin{array}{lrcl} (a) & \mathcal{L}((t-1)\text{-cut}(i)\text{-RR}) & \subsetneq & \mathcal{L}(t\text{-cut}(i)\text{-RR}), \\ (b) & \mathcal{L}((t-1)\text{-r-RR}) & \subsetneq & \mathcal{L}(t\text{-r-RR}). \end{array}$$

Let $G = (\Sigma, A, C, \mathcal{L}_1, \mathcal{L}_2, \ldots, \mathcal{L}_{t+1}, f)$ be a t-contextual grammar with regular selection, that is, Σ is a finite alphabet, A is a finite language over Σ, C is a finite subset of $(\Sigma^*)^t$, $\mathcal{L}_1, \mathcal{L}_2, \ldots, \mathcal{L}_{t+1}$ are finite sets of regular languages over Σ, and

$$f : \mathcal{L}_1 \times \mathcal{L}_2 \times \cdots \times \mathcal{L}_{t+1} \to \mathcal{P}(C)$$

is the (regular) t-selection mapping (see Definition 1.3.37). Then $L(G) = \{ v \mid \exists u \in A : u \Rightarrow_G^* v \}$, where $x \Rightarrow_G y$ iff there exist sets $P_1 \in \mathcal{L}_1, P_2 \in \mathcal{L}_2, \ldots, P_{t+1} \in \mathcal{L}_{t+1}$ and words $x_1 \in P_1, x_2 \in P_2, \ldots, x_{t+1} \in P_{t+1}$ such that

$$x = x_1 x_2 x_3 \cdots x_t x_{t+1} \text{ and } y = x_1 u_1 x_2 u_2 x_3 \cdots x_t u_t x_{t+1}$$

for some context $(u_1, u_2, \ldots, u_t) \in f(P_1, P_2, \ldots, P_{t+1})$. We now define a t-cut(1)-RR-automaton M_G by taking the following set of meta-instructions:

$$\begin{array}{lll} (1) & (\rhd \cdot P_1, u_1, P_2, u_2, \ldots, P_t, u_t, P_{t+1} \cdot \lhd) & \text{for all } P_j \in \mathcal{L}_j, 1 \leq j \leq t+1, \\ & & \text{and all } (u_1, u_2, \ldots, u_t) \in f(P_1, P_2, \ldots, P_{t+1}), \\ (2) & (\rhd \cdot A \cdot \lhd, \mathsf{Accept}). & \end{array}$$

Then $q_0\rhd y\lhd \vdash^c_{M_G} q_0\rhd x\lhd$ iff $x \Rightarrow_G y$, and it follows that $L(M_G) = L(G)$.

Conversely, let M be a t-cut(1)-RR-automaton, and assume that M is defined through a set of meta-instructions

$$\begin{array}{ll}
(0) & (\rhd \cdot E_0^{(0)} \cdot \lhd, \mathsf{Accept}),\\
(1) & (\rhd \cdot E_0^{(1)}, u_1^{(1)}, E_1^{(1)}, u_2^{(1)}, E_2^{(1)}, \ldots, E_{t-1}^{(1)}, u_t^{(1)}, E_t^{(1)} \cdot \lhd),\\
(2) & (\rhd \cdot E_0^{(2)}, u_1^{(2)}, E_1^{(2)}, u_2^{(2)}, E_2^{(2)}, \ldots, E_{t-1}^{(2)}, u_t^{(2)}, E_t^{(2)} \cdot \lhd),\\
\ldots & \ldots\\
(n) & (\rhd \cdot E_0^{(n)}, u_1^{(n)}, E_1^{(n)}, u_2^{(n)}, E_2^{(n)}, \ldots, E_{t-1}^{(n)}, u_t^{(n)}, E_t^{(n)} \cdot \lhd),
\end{array}$$

where the set $E_0^{(0)}$ is finite, that is, there are only finitely many words that M accepts in tail computations. From M, we construct a t-contextual grammar with regular selection $G_M = (\Sigma, A, C, \mathcal{L}_1, \mathcal{L}_2, \ldots, \mathcal{L}_{t+1}, f)$ as follows:

$$\begin{array}{lll}
- \ A & = & E_0^{(0)},\\
- \ C & = & \{ (u_1^{(j)}, u_2^{(j)}, \ldots, u_t^{(j)}) \mid j = 1, 2, \ldots, n \},\\
- \ \mathcal{L}_i & = & \{ E_{i-1}^{(j)} \mid j = 1, 2, \ldots, n \} \text{ for all } i = 1, 2, \ldots, t+1,\\
- \ f(F_1, F_2, \ldots, F_{t+1}) & = & \{ (u_1^{(j)}, u_2^{(j)}, \ldots, u_t^{(j)}) \mid F_i = E_{i-1}^{(j)} \text{ for all } 1 \le i \le t+1 \}.
\end{array}$$

Then $x \Rightarrow_{G_M} y$ iff $q_0\rhd y\lhd \vdash^c_M q_0\rhd x\lhd$, and it follows that $L(G_M) = L(M)$. In summary, we have the following equivalence.

Theorem 2.5.68 ([170, 208])

(a) *For each t-contextual grammar with regular selection G, there exists a t-*cut(1)-RR*-automaton M such that $L(M) = L(G)$.*

(b) *For each t-*cut(1)-RR*-automaton M that only accepts a finite set of words in tail computations, there exists a t-contextual grammar with regular selection G such that $L(G) = L(M)$.*

In both cases, the derivation relation $\Rightarrow_G$ of G is essentially just the converse of the cycle reduction relation $\vdash^c_M$ of M.

The next example illustrates that, for all values of t, the expressive capacity of t-r-RR-automata increases substantially, when the cut-index is raised from one to two.

Example 2.5.69 *Let $LR_t^{(2)} = \{ c_0wc_1w^Rc_2 \cdots c_{2t-2}wc_{2t-1}w^R \mid w \in \{a,b\}^* \}$, where $t \ge 1$, $\Sigma_0 = \{a,b\}$, and $\Sigma_t = \Sigma_0 \cup \{c_0, c_1, \ldots, c_{2t-1}\}$. The language $LR_t^{(2)}$ is accepted by the deterministic t-*cut(2)-RR*-automaton $M_t^{(2)}$ that has window size 3 and that is given through the following sequence of meta-instructions:*

$$\begin{array}{ll}
(1) & (\rhd c_0 \cdot \Sigma_0^*, ac_1a \to c_1, \Sigma_0^* \cdot c_2 \cdot \Sigma_0^*, ac_3a \to c_3, \ldots, ac_{2t-1}a \to c_{2t-1}, \Sigma_0^* \cdot \lhd),\\
(2) & (\rhd c_0 \cdot \Sigma_0^*, bc_1b \to c_1, \Sigma_0^* \cdot c_2 \cdot \Sigma_0^*, bc_3b \to c_3, \ldots, bc_{2t-1}b \to c_{2t-1}, \Sigma_0^* \cdot \lhd),\\
(3) & (\rhd \cdot c_0c_1 \cdots c_{2t-1} \cdot \lhd, \mathsf{Accept}).
\end{array}$$

It is easily verified that $L(M_t^{(2)}) = LR_t^{(2)}$ holds. However, with less than t delete operations per cycle, or with t delete operations with cut-index one, the language $LR_t^{(2)}$ cannot be accepted, that is, for each $t \ge 2$, $LR_t^{(2)} \notin \mathcal{L}((t-1)\text{-r-RR}) \cup \mathcal{L}(t\text{-cut(1)-RR})$. ■

This yields the following results.

Corollary 2.5.70 ([170, 208]) *For each $t \ge 2$,*

(a) $\mathcal{L}(t\text{-cut(1)-RR}) \subsetneq \mathcal{L}(t\text{-cut(2)-RR})$.

(b) *The class of languages generated by t-contextual grammars with regular selection is a proper subclass of $\mathcal{L}(t\text{-r-RR})$.*

(c) *For each t-*r-RR*-automaton with cut-index i that only accepts a finite set of words in tail computations, there is an equivalent s-contextual grammar with regular selection for some* $s \leq i \cdot t$.

It remains open whether the cut-index yields an infinite ascending hierarchy of language classes for t-r-RR-automata.

Problem 2.5.71 *For each* $t \geq 2$*, is there a language that is accepted by a* t-cut(3)-RR*-automaton, but not by any* t-cut(2)-RR*-automaton? In general, for each* $t \geq 2$ *and each* $j \geq 2$*, is there a language that is accepted by a* t-cut$(j+1)$-RR*-automaton, but not by any* t-cut(j)-RR*-automaton?*

According to Definition 2.5.42, an FsRRWW-automaton is called j-constrained for an integer $j \in \mathbb{N}_+$, if all its computations are j-rewriting and j-monotone, that is, in each cycle of each computation, at most j rewrite steps are executed, and the sequence of all rewrite configurations can be partitioned into j (interspersed) subsequences that are monotone. Obviously, this notion carries over to t-r-RR-automata.

Definition 2.5.72 *Let* $t \in \mathbb{N}_+$ *be an integer and let* M *be a* t*-r-RR-automaton.*

(a) *A configuration* $C = \alpha q \beta$ *of* M *in which a delete operation is to be applied is called a* delete configuration. *The number* $|\beta|$ *is called the* right distance *of* C*, denoted by* $D_r(C)$*, and the number* $|\alpha|$ *is the* left distance *of* C*, denoted by* $D_l(C)$.

(b) *A* sequence of delete configurations $S = (C_1, C_2, \ldots, C_n)$ *is called* monotone *(or* right-monotone*) if*

$$D_r(C_1) \geq D_r(C_2) \geq \cdots \geq D_r(C_n),$$

it is called left-monotone *if*

$$D_l(C_1) \geq D_l(C_2) \geq \cdots \geq D_l(C_n),$$

and it is called right-left-monotone *if it is simultaneously right- and left-monotone.*

(c) *A computation of* M *is called* t-right-monotone, t-left-monotone, *or* t-right-left-monotone *if the corresponding sequence of delete configurations can be partitioned into at most* t *subsequences* $S_1, S_2, \ldots, S_t$ *such that each of these subsequences is right-monotone, left-monotone, or right-left-monotone, respectively.*

(d) *The* t*-r-RR-automaton* M *is called* right-monotone, left-monotone, *or* right-left-monotone *if each of its computations is* t*-right-monotone,* t*-left-monotone, or* t*-right-left-monotone, respectively.*

Obviously, the 1-constrained FsRRWW-automata are just the monotone sRRWW-automata, and hence, they characterize the class CFL of context-free languages (Corollary 2.5.44). Analogously, the right-monotone 1-r-RR-automata are just the monotone RR-automata, which means that they just accept a proper subclass of the context-free languages that contains the deterministic context-free languages as a proper subclass (see the diagram in Figure 2.6). On the other hand, for $t \geq 2$, the language $LC_t = \{\, c_0wc_1wc_2 \cdots c_{t-1}w \mid w \in \{a,b\}^* \,\}$ is not context-free, but the t-cut(1)-RR-automaton M_t for the language LC_t presented in Example 2.5.65 is obviously t-right-monotone and t-left-monotone. Moreover, the language $L_2 = \{\, a^nb^n \mid n \geq 0 \,\} \cup \{\, a^nb^m \mid m > 2n \geq 0 \,\}$ is obviously context-free, but in analogy to the proof of Lemma 2.2.3, it can be verified that this language is not accepted by any t-r-RR-automaton. Thus, we obtain the following.

Theorem 2.5.73 ([170]) DCFL $\subsetneq \mathcal{L}$(right-mon-1-r-RR) $\subsetneq$ CFL, *and* $\mathcal{L}$(X-t-r-RR) *is incomparable to* CFL *with respect to inclusion for all* $t \geq 2$ *and all types* X *of monotonicity.*

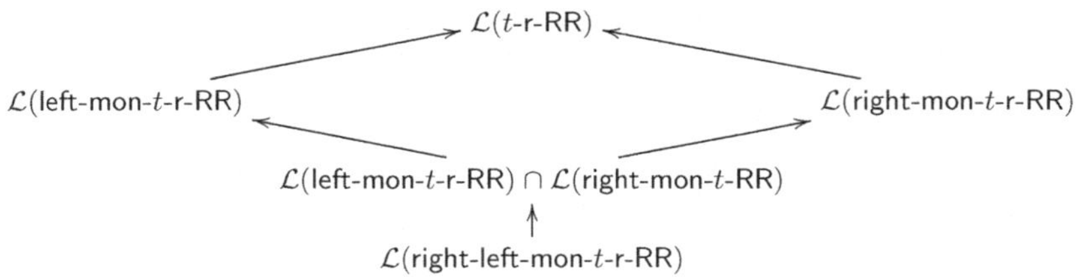

Figure 2.18: Proper inclusion relations between the various types of t-r-RR-automata.

In [170, 208], the various notions of monotonicity are explored in detail for t-r-RR-automata. Using particular example languages, the proper inclusions in the diagram in Figure 2.18 are established. Here it is of special importance to observe that the class of languages accepted by right-left-monotone t-r-RR-automata is only a proper subclass of the intersection of the class of languages that are accepted by right-monotone t-r-RR-automata with the class of languages that are accepted by left-monotone t-r-RR-automata.

Let $G = (\Sigma, A, C, \mathcal{L}_1, \mathcal{L}_2, \ldots, \mathcal{L}_{t+1}, f)$ be a t-contextual grammar with regular selection. If the finite sets $\mathcal{L}_2, \mathcal{L}_3, \ldots, \mathcal{L}_t$ of regular languages only contain finite languages, then G belongs to the class of contextual grammars $\mathsf{CGR}[t](\mathsf{REG}, \mathsf{FIN}, \ldots, \mathsf{FIN}, \mathsf{REG})$. Assume that $x \Rightarrow_G y$. Then there are sets $P_i \in \mathcal{L}_i$ and words $x_i \in P_i$, $1 \leq i \leq t+1$, and a t-context $(u_1, u_2, \ldots, u_t) \in f(P_1, P_2, \ldots, P_{t+1})$ such that $x = x_1 x_2 \cdots x_t x_{t+1}$ and $y = x_1 u_1 x_2 u_2 x_3 \cdots x_t u_t x_{t+1}$. As observed above, the language $L(G)$ is accepted by a t-$\mathsf{cut}(1)$-RR-automaton that just reverses the derivation steps of G. However, as each of the sets $\mathcal{L}_2, \mathcal{L}_3, \ldots, \mathcal{L}_t$ only contains finitely many finite sets, we see that the factor $u_1 x_2 u_2 x_3 \cdots x_t u_t$ of y is bounded in length from above by the value $k = k_1 + k_2$, where

$$k_1 = \max\{\, |u_1| + |u_2| + \cdots + |u_k| \mid (u_1, u_2, \ldots, u_t) \in C \,\}$$

and

$$k_2 = \sum_{i=2}^{t} \max\{\, |v| \mid \exists P_i \in \mathcal{L}_i : v \in P_i \,\}.$$

Thus, there is actually an RR-automaton M with window size k such that $L(M) = L(G)$. As in each delete step, M erases up to t factors of the current window contents, M has cut-index t, that is, M is actually a $\mathsf{cut}(t)$-RR-automaton.

Conversely, it is easily seen that, for each $\mathsf{cut}(t)$-RR-automaton that only accepts a finite set of words in tail computations, there exists a t-contextual grammar of the above form. Thus, we have the following consequence.

Theorem 2.5.74 ([102, 170])

(a) *For each t-contextual grammar G from* $\mathsf{CGR}[t](\mathsf{REG}, \mathsf{FIN}, \ldots, \mathsf{FIN}, \mathsf{REG})$, *there exists a* $\mathsf{cut}(t)$-RR-*automaton M such that $L(M) = L(G)$.*

(b) *For each* $\mathsf{cut}(t)$-RR-*automaton M that only accepts a finite set of words in tail computations, there exists a t-contextual grammar G in* $\mathsf{CGR}[t](\mathsf{REG}, \mathsf{FIN}, \ldots, \mathsf{FIN}, \mathsf{REG})$ *such that $L(G) = L(M)$.*

In both cases, the derivation relation $\Rightarrow_G$ of G is essentially just the converse of the cycle reduction relation $\vdash^{c}_{M}$ of M.

If M is an RR-automaton with window size k and cut-index t, then $k \geq 2t - 1$, as neighbouring non-empty factors that are deleted within a single delete step are separated by a non-empty factor. As observed in Corollary 2.3.3, the window size induces an infinite strictly ascending hierarchy of language classes for RR-automata. A corresponding result also holds for the cut-index. For deriving this fact, we consider the following example language

$$L^{(2)}_{\text{expo}} = \{\, x^{i_0}y^{i_1}x^{i_2}y^{i_3}\cdots x^{i_{m-1}}y^{i_m} \mid x,y \in \{a,b\}, x \neq y, m > 0, i_0 > 0, i_1 > 0, \ldots, i_{m-1} > 0, \\ i_m \geq 0, \exists p \geq 0 : 2^p = i_0 + 2\cdot i_1 + 4\cdot i_2 + \cdots + 2^m \cdot i_m \,\}.$$

This language is accepted by a deterministic RW-automaton.

Lemma 2.5.75 ([170]) *The language $L^{(2)}_{\text{expo}}$ is accepted by a deterministic RW-automaton that has a read/write window of size 3.*

Proof outline. Let $M = (Q, \{a,b\}, \{a,b\}, \rhd, \lhd, q_0, 3, \delta)$ be the RW-automaton that is given by the following meta-instructions:

$$\begin{array}{llll} (1) & (\rhd \cdot a^*, aa \cdot \lhd \to b \cdot \lhd), & (4) & (\rhd \cdot b^*, bba \to aa), \\ (2) & (\rhd \cdot b^*, bb \cdot \lhd \to a \cdot \lhd), & (5) & (\rhd \cdot \{a,b\} \cdot \lhd, \mathsf{Accept}). \\ (3) & (\rhd \cdot a^*, aab \to bb), & & \end{array}$$

Obviously, the RW-automaton M is deterministic, and it has window size 3. In addition, it can be checked that $L(M) = L^{(2)}_{\text{expo}}$. □

Now let t be any positive integer. For t, we define a morphism $\varphi_t : \{a,b\}^* \to \{0,1\}^*$ by taking $\varphi_t(a) = (001)^t$ and $\varphi_t(b) = (01)^t$, and we define the language L_t as $L_t = \varphi_t(L^{(2)}_{\text{expo}})$. Based on M and φ_t, a deterministic R-automaton M_t can easily be constructed that accepts the language L_t. The delete instructions of M_t correspond to the rewrite instructions of M, which rewrite aa into b and bb into a. In order to rewrite $\varphi_t(aa) = (001)^{2t}$ into $\varphi_t(b) = (01)^t$, we can delete the prefix $(001)^t0$ and delete one occurrence of the letter 0 from each of the remaining $t-1$ factors 001. Similarly, to rewrite $\varphi_t(bb) = (01)^{2t}$ into $\varphi_t(a) = (001)^t$, we simply delete every odd-numbered occurrence of the letter 1 from $(01)^t$. Hence, M_t has cut-index t. Thus, we see that $L_t \in \mathcal{L}(\mathsf{cut}(t)\text{-}\mathsf{det}\text{-}\mathsf{R})$. However, this language is not accepted by any RR-automaton of cut-index $t-1$, that is, we have the following result.

Proposition 2.5.76 ([170]) *For each $t \geq 2$, $L_t \in \mathcal{L}(\mathsf{cut}(t)\text{-}\mathsf{det}\text{-}\mathsf{R}) \smallsetminus \mathcal{L}(\mathsf{cut}(t-1)\text{-}\mathsf{RR})$.*

Proof. It remains to prove that L_t is not accepted by any RR-automaton with cut-index $t-1$. Assume that L_t is accepted by some RR-automaton M'_t with a window of size k'. For a sufficiently large integer $n > k'$, the word $w = \varphi_t(a^{2^n}) = (001)^{2^n \cdot t} \in L_t$ is not accepted by M'_t in a tail computation, as otherwise, using pumping techniques, we can easily construct a word outside L_t which is also accepted by M'_t. Thus, each accepting computation of M'_t on input w starts with a cycle $q_0 \rhd w \lhd \vdash^c_{M'_t} q_0 \rhd w' \lhd$ for some word $w' \in L_t$. As each word in $L_t \cap \varphi_t(a^+)$ that is shorter than the word $\varphi_t(a^{2^n})$ is of length at most $|\varphi_t(a^{2^{n-1}})| = |\varphi_t(a^{2^n})| - 2^{n-1}\cdot 3t < |\varphi_t(a^{2^n})| - k'$, the word w' must contain at least one factor of the form $\varphi_t(b)$. The first such factor of w' is either preceded by $\rhd$, if it is a prefix of w', or it is preceded by a factor of the form $\varphi_t(a) = (001)^t$ that ends with an occurrence of the letter 1. Hence, $\rhd w' \lhd$ either contains the factor $\rhd(01)^t$ or the factor $1(01)^t$. In either case, this factor cannot be obtained from $\rhd(001)^{2^n \cdot t}\lhd$ by deleting less than t separate factors. Hence, M'_t must have a cut-index larger than or equal to t, which completes the proof. □

As an immediate consequence, we obtain the following hierarchies.

Corollary 2.5.77 ([170]) *For each $t \geq 1$ and each $\mathsf{X} \in \{\mathsf{R}, \mathsf{RR}\}$,*

(a) $\mathcal{L}(\mathsf{cut}(t)\text{-}\mathsf{det}\text{-}\mathsf{X}) \subsetneq \mathcal{L}(\mathsf{cut}(t+1)\text{-}\mathsf{det}\text{-}\mathsf{X})$ *and*
(b) $\mathcal{L}(\mathsf{cut}(t)\text{-}\mathsf{X}) \subsetneq \mathcal{L}(\mathsf{cut}(t+1)\text{-}\mathsf{X})$.

Thus, it follows from Theorem 2.5.74 that the parameter t induces a strictly ascending infinite hierarchy of classes of languages that are generated by t-contextual grammars with regular selection from the class $\mathsf{CGR}[t](\mathsf{REG}, \mathsf{FIN}, \ldots, \mathsf{FIN}, \mathsf{REG})$.

In [100, 103], a log-space reduction is presented that, for any NP-complete language L, yields an NP-complete language L' which is accepted by a shrinking RWW-automaton M (see also Theorem 2.1.10). By modifying this shrinking RWW-automaton in an appropriate way, an R-automaton with cut-index 1 can be constructed that still accepts an NP-complete language. In fact, first M can be transformed into a shrinking RWW-automaton M' such that $L(M') = L(M)$ and all rewrite instructions of M' replace a nonempty factor with a single letter or the empty word. Then, by introducing a morphism φ such that $\varphi(L(M'))$ is still an NP-complete language, an R-automaton M'' can be constructed such that $L(M'') \cap \varphi(\Sigma^*) = \varphi(L(M'))$, which implies that $L(M'')$ is NP-complete, too. Because of the restricted form of the rewrite instructions of M', M'' has cut-index 1.

Theorem 2.5.78 ([170]) *The language class $\mathcal{L}(\mathsf{cut}(1)\text{-}\mathsf{R})$ contains NP-complete languages.*

Thus, already $\mathsf{cut}(1)$-R-automata are quite powerful. Therefore, in [103], the influence of the cut-index on certain restricted variants of RR-automata is studied, where the restrictions considered concern determinism on the one hand and various notions of monotonicity on the other hand. First of all, based on the Pumping Lemma for regular languages (see Lemma 1.2.78), it is easily seen that each regular language is accepted by a deterministic $\mathsf{cut}(1)$-R-automaton that is right-left-monotone. As the non-regular language $\{ a^n b^n \mid n \geq 1 \}$ is accepted by the deterministic R-automaton that is defined through the meta-instructions $(\triangleright \cdot a^+, abb \to b)$ and $(\triangleright \cdot \{ab\} \cdot \triangleleft, \mathsf{Accept})$, we have the following proper inclusion.

Proposition 2.5.79 ([170]) $\mathsf{REG} \subsetneq \mathcal{L}(\mathsf{det\text{-}right\text{-}left\text{-}mon\text{-}cut}(1)\text{-}\mathsf{R})$.

By Theorem 2.2.13, $\mathcal{L}(\mathsf{mon\text{-}RR})$ is a proper subclass of the context-free languages. In fact, according to Lemma 2.2.3, the context-free language $L_2 = \{ a^n b^n \mid n \geq 0 \} \cup \{ a^n b^m \mid m > 2n \geq 0 \}$ is not accepted by any (shrinking) RLW-automaton, while it is easily seen from the proof of Corollary 2.1.41 that $\mathcal{L}(\mathsf{left\text{-}mon\text{-}RWW}) = \mathsf{CFL}$ [96]. Thus, we have the following consequence.

Corollary 2.5.80 ([170]) *For all $t \geq 1$, $\mathcal{L}(\mathsf{mon\text{-}cut}(t)\text{-}\mathsf{RR}) \cup \mathcal{L}(\mathsf{left\text{-}mon\text{-}cut}(t)\text{-}\mathsf{RR}) \subsetneq \mathsf{CFL}$.*

From the proof of Theorem 2.1.42, we see that each deterministic context-free language is accepted by a deterministic monotone R-automaton of cut-index 2. As deterministic monotone RR-automata only accept deterministic context-free languages (see Corollary 2.1.39), we obtain the following characterization.

Corollary 2.5.81 ([170]) *For all $t \geq 2$, $\mathcal{L}(\mathsf{det\text{-}mon\text{-}cut}(t)\text{-}\mathsf{R}) = \mathcal{L}(\mathsf{det\text{-}mon\text{-}cut}(t)\text{-}\mathsf{RR}) = \mathsf{DCFL}$.*

Finally, by using appropriate example languages, the following hierarchies based on the cut-index have been established for the various types of monotone R- and RR-automata.

Theorem 2.5.82 ([170]) *For each $t \geq 1$, each type of restarting automaton $\mathsf{X} \in \{\mathsf{R}, \mathsf{RR}\}$, and each type of monotonicity $\mathsf{pre} \in \{\mathsf{mon}, \mathsf{left\text{-}mon}, \mathsf{right\text{-}left\text{-}mon}\}$, the following proper inclusions hold:*

(a) $\mathcal{L}(\mathsf{pre\text{-}cut}(t)\text{-}\mathsf{X}) \subsetneq \mathcal{L}(\mathsf{pre\text{-}cut}(t+1)\text{-}\mathsf{X})$.
(b) $\mathcal{L}(\mathsf{pre\text{-}cut}(t)\text{-}\mathsf{R}) \subsetneq \mathcal{L}(\mathsf{pre\text{-}cut}(t)\text{-}\mathsf{RR})$.
(c) $\mathcal{L}(\mathsf{det\text{-}pre\text{-}cut}(t)\text{-}\mathsf{X}) \subsetneq \mathcal{L}(\mathsf{pre\text{-}cut}(t)\text{-}\mathsf{X})$.
(d) $\mathcal{L}(\mathsf{det\text{-}pre\text{-}cut}(1)\text{-}\mathsf{X}) \subsetneq \mathcal{L}(\mathsf{det\text{-}pre\text{-}cut}(2)\text{-}\mathsf{X})$.
(e) $\mathcal{L}(\mathsf{det\text{-}pre\text{-}cut}(1)\text{-}\mathsf{R}) \subsetneq \mathcal{L}(\mathsf{det\text{-}pre\text{-}cut}(1)\text{-}\mathsf{RR})$.
(f) $\mathcal{L}(\mathsf{det\text{-}left\text{-}mon\text{-}cut}(t)\text{-}\mathsf{X}) \subsetneq \mathcal{L}(\mathsf{det\text{-}left\text{-}mon\text{-}cut}(t+1)\text{-}\mathsf{X})$.
(g) $\mathcal{L}(\mathsf{det\text{-}left\text{-}mon\text{-}cut}(t)\text{-}\mathsf{R}) \subsetneq \mathcal{L}(\mathsf{det\text{-}left\text{-}mon\text{-}cut}(t)\text{-}\mathsf{RR})$.

Thus, in the nondeterministic case, the cut-index induces strictly ascending infinite hierarchies for R- as well as for RR-automata and for all types of monotonicity. Because of Proposition 2.5.79 and Corollary 2.5.80, these hierarchies are located strictly between the regular languages on the one hand and the context-free languages on the other hand. Actually, the above results remain valid also when we restrict our attention to restarting automata that only accept finite sets of words in accepting tail computations. Because of the correspondence between restarting automata of this form and t-contextual grammars with regular selection that satisfy an additional locality condition (the places of insertion are required to be close to each other), as expressed in Theorem 2.5.74, the notion of determinism and the various notions of monotonicity considered for restarting automata translate into corresponding notions for t-contextual grammars, and our hierarchy results induce corresponding results for these classes of t-contextual grammars.

2.5.4 Restarting Automata with Two Windows

A serious problem in (some) free word order languages is caused by *long-distance scrambling*, which induces a dependency of items across a large distance (see, e.g., [227]). Certainly, the use of two independent heads or windows can help in this matter. And indeed, in [55], an ad-hoc variant of the restarting automaton is defined that has two windows: one window can only delete a single letter in a rewrite step and the other window may rewrite a non-empty word into a word of length at most one. It is shown in [55] that a certain restricted type of these restarting automata corresponds to *sorted dependency insertion grammars with regular selectors* that work in top-down derivation style. However, it is only in [160, 161] that a restricted type of deterministic restarting automaton with two windows, denoted as det-2-RR-automaton, has been studied systematically. In each cycle of a computation, a det-2-RR-automaton can perform up to two delete operations, one with each of its two windows. Here we present the det-2-RR-automaton and the main results derived in [160, 161].

Definition 2.5.83 ([161]) *A* det-2-RR-automaton *consists of a finite-state control, a flexible tape with end-of-tape markers, and two windows of a fixed finite size. Formally, it is defined by a 7-tuple* $M = (Q, \Sigma, \rhd, \lhd, \delta, q_0, k)$, *where* Q *is a finite set of states,* Σ *is a finite input alphabet,* $\rhd$ *and* $\lhd$ *are special letters that mark the left and right border of the tape (these letters are not elements of* Σ*),* $q_0 \in Q$ *is the initial state,* $k \geq 1$ *is the size of the windows, and* $\delta : Q \times \mathcal{PC}^k \times \mathcal{PC}^k \to \mathcal{OP}$ *is the (partial) transition function. Here* $\mathcal{PC}^k$ *denotes the set of all possible words that can occur in a window of* M*, and* $\mathcal{OP}$ *is the set of possible operations, which are defined as follows:*

- *An operation of the form* $(q', \mathsf{MVR}_i) \in \delta(q, u_1, u_2)$, $i \in \{1, 2\}$, *moves window* i *one position to the right and changes the state to* q'. *However, such an operation is only applicable if* $u_i \neq \lhd$.
- *An operation of the form* $(q', \mathsf{DEL}_i(v)) \in \delta(q, u_1, u_2)$, $i \in \{1, 2\}$, *replaces the factor* u_i *contained in window* i *with the word* v, *where* v *is a proper scattered subword of* u_i, *moves this window by* $|u_i| - |v|$ *steps to the right (which means that window* i *is refilled from the right), and changes the state to* q'. *Here some restrictions apply in that the sentinels* $\rhd$ *and* $\lhd$ *must not be deleted and that a window cannot be moved across the right sentinel* $\lhd$. *In addition, if one or more of the letters deleted are currently also contained in the other window, then this window is also refilled from the right.*
- *An operation of the form* $\mathsf{Restart} \in \delta(q, u_1, u_2)$ *moves both windows to the left end of the tape such that the first letter they contain is the left sentinel* $\rhd$, *and resets the state to the initial state* q_0.
- *An operation of the form* $\mathsf{Accept} \in \delta(q, u_1, u_2)$ *causes* M *to halt and accept.*

If $\delta(q, u_1, u_2)$ *is undefined, then* M *halts without accepting. It is required that, before the first restart operation and between any two successive restart operations in a computation of* M*, each window can execute at most one delete operation, that at least one delete operation is indeed executed, and that after the last restart operation in a computation, none, one, or two delete operations (of different windows) can be performed. For each* $k \geq 1$, *det-2-RR*(k) *denotes the class of deterministic 2-RR-automata with windows of size* k.

The notions of configuration, cycle, and tail computations carry over from RR-automata (see Section 1.9). However, as a det-2-RR-automaton has two windows, we use the additional letters H_1, H_2, and $H_{1,2}$ to denote the positions of these windows, where H_1 (H_2) is placed immediately to the left of the first letter that is currently inside window one (two), and $H_{1,2}$ is used if both windows are at the same position. Accordingly, a *configuration* of a det-2-RR-automaton $M = (Q, \Sigma, \rhd, \lhd, \delta, q_0, k)$ is written as a pair $(q, \rhd u H_i v H_{3-i} w \lhd)$ or $(q, \rhd u H_{1,2} v \lhd)$, where $q \in Q$ is the current state, $\rhd uvw \lhd$ or $\rhd uv \lhd$ is the current tape contents, and H_i and H_{3-i}, $i \in \{1,2\}$, or $H_{1,2}$ mark the positions of window i and $3-i$ or the common position of both windows. For a word $w \in \Sigma^*$, the configuration $(q_0, H_{1,2} \rhd w \lhd)$ is the *initial configuration* for input w. As in the general case, we use Accept to denote those configurations that M reaches by executing an accept step.

Each computation of the det-2-RR-automaton M consists of a sequence of cycles and a tail computation. Here a *cycle* is a part of a computation that starts with an initial configuration $(q_0, H_{1,2} \rhd w \lhd)$, that consists of a sequence of move-right and (one or two) delete operations, and that ends with a restart operation that takes M into a new initial configuration $(q_0, H_{1,2} \rhd w' \lhd)$. Then $\vdash_M^c$ denotes the binary relation on the set of initial configurations that is induced by the execution of a cycle, and $\vdash_M^{c^*}$ is the reflexive and transitive closure of this relation. Finally, a *tail* computation is defined like a cycle but instead of a restart, it ends with either an accept step or with M getting stuck. In the former case, we talk about an *accepting tail computation*, while in the latter case, we have a *rejecting tail computation*.

The language accepted by M is the set

$$L(M) = \{ w \in \Sigma^* \mid (q_0, H_{1,2} \rhd w \lhd) \vdash_M^* \mathsf{Accept} \},$$

where $\vdash_M$ denotes the single-step computation relation that M induces on its set of configurations, and $\vdash_M^*$ denotes its reflexive and transitive closure. Then $\mathcal{L}(\mathsf{det\text{-}2\text{-}RR}(k))$ is the class of languages that are accepted by det-2-RR-automata with windows of size k. Finally,

$$\mathcal{L}(\mathsf{det\text{-}2\text{-}RR}) = \bigcup_{k \geq 1} \mathcal{L}(\mathsf{det\text{-}2\text{-}RR}(k))$$

is the class of languages that are accepted by det-2-RR-automata.

It is easily seen that the Error Preserving Property (see Definition 1.9.5) and the Correctness Preserving Property (see Definition 1.9.7) also hold for det-2-RR-automata. The following examples illustrate how det-2-RR-automata work.

Example 2.5.84 ([161]) *A det-2-RR(1)-automaton M for the marked copy language*

$$L'_{\text{copy}} = \{ wcw \mid w \in \{a,b\}^* \}$$

is given through the following transition function, where $x, x' \in \{a,b\}$, $y \in \{a,b,c\}$, and $z \in \{a,b,\lhd\}$:

$$\begin{array}{rclrcl}
\delta(q_0, \rhd, \rhd) &=& (q_1, \mathsf{MVR}_1), & \delta(q_1, y, \rhd) &=& (q_2, \mathsf{MVR}_2),\\
\delta(q_2, c, c) &=& (q_3, \mathsf{MVR}_1), & \delta(q_3, \lhd, c) &=& \mathsf{Accept},\\
\delta(q_2, x, x') &=& (q_2, \mathsf{MVR}_2), & \delta(q_2, x, c) &=& (q_4, \mathsf{MVR}_2),\\
\delta(q_4, x, x) &=& (q_5, \mathsf{DEL}_1(\lambda)), & \delta(q_5, y, x) &=& (q_6, \mathsf{DEL}_2(\lambda)),\\
\delta(q_6, y, z) &=& \mathsf{Restart}. & & &
\end{array}$$

On input $w = abcab$, M executes the following computation:

$$\begin{array}{rcccc}
(q_0, H_{1,2} \rhd abcab \lhd) & \vdash_M & (q_1, H_2 \rhd H_1 abcab \lhd) & \vdash_M & (q_2, \rhd H_{1,2} abcab \lhd)\\
& \vdash_M & (q_2, \rhd H_1 a H_2 bcab \lhd) & \vdash_M & (q_2, \rhd H_1 ab H_2 cab \lhd)\\
& \vdash_M & (q_4, \rhd H_1 abc H_2 ab \lhd) & \vdash_M & (q_5, \rhd H_1 bc H_2 ab \lhd)\\
& \vdash_M & (q_6, \rhd H_1 bc H_2 b \lhd) & \vdash_M & (q_0, H_{1,2} \rhd bcb \lhd)\\
& \vdash_M & (q_1, H_2 \rhd H_1 bcb \lhd) & \vdash_M & (q_2, \rhd H_{1,2} bcb \lhd)\\
& \vdash_M & (q_2, \rhd H_1 b H_2 cb \lhd) & \vdash_M & (q_4, \rhd H_1 bc H_2 b \lhd)\\
& \vdash_M & (q_5, \rhd H_1 c H_2 b \lhd) & \vdash_M & (q_6, \rhd H_1 c H_2 \lhd)
\end{array}$$

$$\begin{array}{llll} \vdash_M & (q_0, H_{1,2}\rhd c\lhd) & \vdash_M & (q_1, H_2\rhd H_1 c\lhd) \\ \vdash_M & (q_2, \rhd H_{1,2}c\lhd) & \vdash_M & (q_3, \rhd H_2 c H_1\lhd) \\ \vdash_M & \mathsf{Accept}. & & \end{array}$$

Thus, it follows that abcab $\in L(M)$. *Actually, it is easy to see that* $L(M) = L'_{\text{copy}}$. ■

Example 2.5.85 ([161]) *For* $n \geq 2$, *let* L_n *denote the following language on* $\Sigma = \{a, b, \#, \&\}$:

$$L_n = \{\, w_1\#w_2\#\cdots\#w_n\&w_n\#\cdots\#w_2\#w_1 \mid w_1, w_2, \ldots, w_n \in \{a,b\}^* \,\}.$$

It is known that the language L_n *is accepted by a k-head pushdown automaton (k-head PDA) if and only if* $n \leq \binom{k}{2}$ *[32, 33]. This implies that the language*

$$L_\infty = \{\, w_1\#w_2\#\cdots\#w_n\&w_n\#\cdots\#w_2\#w_1 \mid n \geq 1, w_1, w_2, \ldots, w_n \in \{a,b\}^* \,\}$$

is not accepted by any multi-head PDA. However, based on Example 2.5.84, it can be shown that the language L_∞ *is accepted by a det-2-RR(1)-automaton.* ■

It is easily seen that the language of marked palindromes $L'_{\text{pal}} = \{\, wcw^R \mid w \in \{a,b\}^* \,\}$ is accepted by a det-2-RR(1)-automaton. However, as shown in [249], this language is not accepted by any one-way two-head writing finite automaton and, as pointed out in [76], this language is not even accepted by any multi-head nondeterministic finite automaton. In fact, also the language $L_{\text{pal}} = \{\, ww^R \mid w \in \{a,b\}^* \,\}$ of palindromes of even length without a middle marker is accepted by a det-2-RR(2)-automaton M_{pal} that, in each cycle, deletes the first and the last letter, if they coincide.

Example 2.5.86 ([161]) *A det-2-RR(2)-automaton* M_{copy} *for the copy language* $L_{\text{copy}} = \{\, ww \mid w \in \{a,b\}^* \,\}$ *is given through the following transition function, where* $d, e, f, g \in \{a,b\}$:

$$\begin{array}{rlcl rlcl}
(1) & \delta(q_0, \rhd d, \rhd d) & = & (q_1, \mathsf{MVR}_2), & (9) & \delta(q_2, de, fg) & = & (q_0, \mathsf{MVR}_1), \\
(2) & \delta(q_0, de, fg) & = & (q_1, \mathsf{MVR}_2), & (10) & \delta(q_2, de, f\lhd) & = & (q_3, \mathsf{MVR}_1), \\
(3) & \delta(q_1, \rhd d, de) & = & (q_2, \mathsf{MVR}_2), & (11) & \delta(q_3, de, d\lhd) & = & (q_4, \mathsf{DEL}_1(e)), \\
(4) & \delta(q_1, de, fg) & = & (q_2, \mathsf{MVR}_2), & (12) & \delta(q_4, de, f\lhd) & = & (q_5, \mathsf{DEL}_2(\lhd)), \\
(5) & \delta(q_2, \rhd d, ef) & = & (q_0, \mathsf{MVR}_1), & (13) & \delta(q_5, de, \lhd) & = & \mathsf{Restart}, \\
(6) & \delta(q_2, \rhd d, e\lhd) & = & (q_3, \mathsf{MVR}_1), & (14) & \delta(q_0, \rhd\lhd, \rhd\lhd) & = & \mathsf{Accept}, \\
(7) & \delta(q_5, \lhd, \lhd) & = & \mathsf{Restart}, & (15) & \delta(q_5, d\lhd, \lhd) & = & \mathsf{Restart}. \\
(8) & \delta(q_4, d\lhd, d\lhd) & = & (q_5, \mathsf{DEL}_2(\lhd)), & & & &
\end{array}$$

Given an input of the form $w = a_1a_2\cdots a_nb_1b_2\cdots b_n$ *of length* $2n$, M_{copy} *cycles through the states* q_0, q_1, *and* q_2, *in each round moving window 2 two letters to the right and window 1 only one letter to the right. Hence, when window 2 reaches the suffix* $b_n\lhd$, *then window 1 contains the factor* a_nb_1. *Now* M_{copy} *enters state* q_3 *and checks whether* $a_n = b_n$ *holds. In the affirmative, the letters* a_n *and* b_n *are deleted and* M_{copy} *restarts; otherwise,* M_{copy} *gets stuck and therewith rejects. It follows that indeed* $L(M_{\text{copy}}) = L_{\text{copy}}$. ■

Recall that the languages L_{copy} and L'_{copy} are not even growing context-sensitive (see the remark following Theorem 1.2.17), and so they are not accepted by any weakly monotone sRRWW-automata by Corollary 2.1.33.

Example 2.5.87 *By adjusting the det-2-RR(2)-automaton* M_{copy} *appropriately, we can even design a det-2-RR(2)-automaton for the following language*

$$L_{\text{pal,copy}} = \{\, ww^Rd \mid w \in \{a,b\}^* \,\} \cup \{\, wwe \mid w \in \{a,b\}^* \,\},$$

which is neither growing context-sensitive nor accepted by any multihead NFA. ■

On the other hand, it is obvious that the language $L_{abc} = \{ a^n b^n c^n \mid n \geq 0 \}$ is accepted by a det-2-RR(1)-automaton that only performs tail computations. The same is true for the languages $L_{\text{copy3}} = \{ wcwcw \mid w \in \{a,b\}^* \}$ and $L_{\text{copy}*} = \{ (wc)^n cw \mid w \in \{a,b\}^*, n \geq 1 \}$. In fact, each language that is accepted by a 2-head deterministic finite automaton (DFA(2)) can be accepted by a det-2-RR(1)-automaton that only executes tail computations. Thus, the det-2-RR-automaton is strictly more expressive than the 2-head DFA.

For future reference, we restate in short the definition of the one-way multi-head writing finite automaton from [249].

Definition 2.5.88 *For $n \geq 1$, a (nondeterministic)* one-way n-head writing finite automaton, *a wNFA(n), is given through an 8-tuple $A = (Q, \Sigma, \Gamma, \delta, h, q_0, \$, F)$, where*

(a) *Q is a finite non-empty set of states,*

(b) *Σ is a finite input alphabet,*

(c) *Γ is a finite tape alphabet containing Σ,*

(d) *$\$ \in \Gamma \smallsetminus \Sigma$ is the end-of-tape marker,*

(e) *$\delta : Q \times \Gamma \to \mathcal{P}(Q \times \Gamma \times \{0,1\})$ is the transition relation,*

(f) *$h : Q \to \{1, 2, \ldots, n\}$ is the head selector function,*

(g) *$q_0 \in Q$ is the initial state, and*

(h) *$F \subseteq Q$ is the set of final states.*

For $q \in Q$ and $a \in \Gamma$, a triple $(q', b, \mu) \in \delta(q, a)$ means that the wNFA A in state q scanning the letter a with head $h(q)$ may change to state q', replace the letter a with b, and move head $h(q)$ by μ fields to the right.

If $|\delta(q,a)| \leq 1$ for all $q \in Q$ and all $a \in \Gamma$, then A is a deterministic *one-way n-head writing finite automaton (wDFA(n)). Furthermore, A is called* non-writing *if, for each $q \in Q$, each $a \in \Gamma$, and each transition $(q', b, \mu) \in \delta(q, a)$, $a = b$ holds.*

Observe that the non-writing wNFA(n) (wDFA(n)) corresponds to the n-head NFA (DFA).

A *configuration* of a wNFA(n) A is given through a triple (q, w, f), where $q \in Q$ is the current state, $w \in \Gamma^*$ is the current tape contents, and $f : \{1, 2, \ldots, n\} \to \{1, 2, \ldots, |w| + 1\}$ describes the current head positions, where, for $1 \leq i \leq n$, head i is currently scanning field $f(i)$. As usual, the transition relation δ induces a computation relation $\vdash_A^*$ on the set of configurations. Finally, the language $L(A)$ accepted by A is defined as

$$L(A) = \{ x \in \Sigma^* \mid (q_0, x\$, f_0) \vdash_M^* (q, w, f_e) \text{ for some } q \in F \text{ and } w \in \Gamma^* \},$$

where $f_0(i) = 1$ and $f_e(i) = |x| + 1$ for all $i = 1, 2, \ldots, n$.

It is known that the language class $\mathcal{L}(\mathsf{wNFA(2)})$ is closed under the operations of union, product, Kleene star, intersection with regular languages, λ-free morphisms, and inverse morphisms, but that the language of marked palindromes $L'_{\text{pal}} = \{ wcw^R \mid w \in \{a,b\}^* \}$ is not accepted by any wNFA(2) [249]. Here we are interested in wNFA(2)-automata because of their ability to simulate tail computations of det-2-RR-automata.

Definition 2.5.89 *Let $M = (Q, \Sigma, \rhd, \lhd, \delta, q_0, k)$ be a det-2-RR-automaton. The* simple (characteristic) language *$S_C(M)$ of M is the sublanguage of $L(M)$ that consists of all those words $w \in \Sigma^*$ that M accepts through tail computations, that is,*

$$S_C(M) = \{ w \in \Sigma^* \mid (q_0, H_{1,2} \rhd w \lhd) \vdash_M^* \mathsf{Accept} \textit{ without using a restart} \}.$$

Proposition 2.5.90 ([161]) *For each det-2-RR(1)-automaton M, $S_C(M) \in \mathcal{L}(\mathsf{wDFA(2)})$.*

Proof. Let $M = (Q, \Sigma, \triangleright, \triangleleft, \delta, q_0, 1)$ be a det-2-RR-automaton with window size 1. A wDFA(2)-automaton A can simulate the tail computations of M by using its two heads to simulate the two windows of size 1 of M. In addition, a delete operation $a \mapsto \lambda$ of M is simulated by the rewrite operation $a \to \#_a$, where $\{ \#_a \mid a \in \Sigma \}$ are new auxiliary letters. When a head of A reaches one of these auxiliary letters, then it just moves on to the next letter without changing the state. It now follows easily that $L(A) = S_{\mathrm{C}}(M)$. □

However, the situation is more complicated for det-2-RR-automata M with window size $k \geq 2$. First of all, a wDFA(2) A has only two heads that each see a single letter only. Hence, each head must make k move-right steps until it has seen the current contents of the corresponding window of M. Next, A may have to simulate a delete operation of M, which deletes between 1 and k letters from the k letters inside one of the windows. To simulate these deletions, A would have to move back to the left, which it cannot do. Thus, we need a different way of simulating the tail computations of a det-2-RR(k)-automaton.

Proposition 2.5.91 ([161]) *For each $k \geq 2$ and each det-2-RR(k)-automaton M,*

$$S_{\mathrm{C}}(M) \in \mathcal{L}(\mathsf{wNFA}(2)).$$

Proof. Let $M = (Q, \Sigma, \triangleright, \triangleleft, \delta, q_0, k)$ be a det-2-RR(k)-automaton for some integer $k \geq 2$. A wNFA(2)-automaton A can simulate the tail computations of M as follows, using its two heads to simulate the two windows of M. Instead of first reading all the k letters inside the corresponding window of M, A guesses the next $k-1$ letters when it sees only the first letter. This means that the simulating wNFA(2)-automaton A is necessarily nondeterministic. After guessing the next $k-1$ letters (for each of its heads), A simulates the next operation of M, realizing deletions of the form $a \mapsto \lambda$ by rewrites of the form $a \mapsto \#_a$. Here, the information on the deleted letters is important for the following reason. A window of M may delete some letters that are also contained in the other window. For the det-2-RR(k)-automaton M, that does not cause any problems, since M has seen both window contents before executing these deletions, but for the simulating wNFA(2) A, this would cause a problem as it must still verify the correctness of the letters guessed. However, by simulating a delete operation $a \mapsto \lambda$ by the rewrite operation $a \mapsto \#_a$, this information is saved, allowing A to perform the required verification. It now follows that A has an accepting computation for an input $w \in \Sigma^*$ if and only if M accepts w through a tail computation, that is, $L(A) = S_{\mathrm{C}}(M)$. □

Actually, it can be shown that the simple language of a det-2-RR-automaton is even accepted by a deterministic one-way writing 2-head finite automaton. Next we show that the simple language of a det-2-RR-automaton is accepted by a sensing deterministic one-way 6-head finite automaton, as we shall need this result later.

Definition 2.5.92 *For $n \geq 2$, a* sensing deterministic one-way n-head finite automaton, *an sDFA(n), is a non-writing wDFA(n) for which a head i $(1 \leq i \leq n)$ can sense when it is at the same position as another head j. This can be realized by a function $S : \{1, 2, \ldots, n\} \to \mathcal{P}(\{1, 2, \ldots, n\})$ such that $S(i) = \{ j \in \{1, 2, \ldots, n\} \mid$ Head j is currently at the same position as head $i \}$ for all $i = 1, 2, \ldots, n$.*

As in an initial configuration of an sDFA(n), all heads are on the first letter of the input, we have $S(i) = \{1, 2, \ldots, n\}$ for all i at that moment. The configurations of an sDFA(n) are described by the same triples of the form (q, w, f) as the configurations of a wDFA(n), as the current value of the function S can be inferred from the function f describing the current head positions.

Proposition 2.5.93 ([161]) *For each $k \geq 1$ and each det-2-RR(k)-automaton M,*

$$S_{\mathrm{C}}(M) \in \mathcal{L}(\mathsf{sDFA}(6)).$$

Proof. Let $M = (Q, \Sigma, \triangleright, \triangleleft, \delta, q_0, k)$ be a det-2-RR-automaton with window size $k \geq 1$. An sDFA A with six heads can simulate the tail computations of M as follows. For each of the two windows of M, the sDFA A uses three of its heads, where two heads are used for pointing to the right-most and the left-most letter inside the corresponding window of M, and the third head is carried along with the second head until a delete operation is executed by this window. In addition, during the simulation, the actual contents of the windows of M is stored in the finite-state control of A.

When a delete operation is carried out by one of the windows of M, then the information on the effects of this delete operation is stored in the finite-state control of A, and the third head of A that is assigned to this particular window becomes stationary at the left-most letter that was inside the window when the delete operation was executed. If, at this point, the two windows of M overlap, which A can detect based on its sensing heads, then the effect of the above delete operation on the contents of the other window of M is easily determined by A, and it can carry on with the simulation accordingly. If the two windows do not overlap at this point, but the other window will only later reach the point where the above delete operation was performed, then A will detect this through the sensing ability of the head pointing to the right-most letter in this other window and the head that marks the position of the above delete operation. Then, when this other window is moved across the rewritten factor, A simulates those actions of this window that M would execute on the rewritten tape. This is possible as the corresponding information is contained in the finite-state control of A. As there are at most two delete operations in a tail computation of M, one by each of the windows, it follows that the sDFA(6)-automaton A can correctly simulate the tail computations of M. □

Next we show that the det-2-RR-automaton induces a strictly ascending infinite hierarchy of language classes based on the size of the windows.

Let $\varphi : \{a, b, c\}^* \to \{a', b', c\}^*$ be the morphism that is defined through $a \mapsto a'$, $b \mapsto b'$, and $c \mapsto c$, and let $L_{\mathrm{pal},\varphi} = \{ wc(\varphi(w))^R \mid w \in \{a, b\}^* \}$ be a variant of the language of marked palindromes, that is, a word $w \in \{a, b, c, a', b'\}^*$ belongs to $L_{\mathrm{pal},\varphi}$ if and only if $w = ucv$ for some words $u \in \{a, b\}^*$ and $v \in \{a', b'\}^*$ such that v is the mirror image of the word $\varphi(u)$. The language $L'_{\mathrm{pal}} = \{ wcw^R \mid w \in \{a, b\}^* \}$ is not accepted by any 2-head writing NFA. As the class of languages accepted by 2-head writing NFAs is closed under λ-free morphisms, it follows that $L_{\mathrm{pal},\varphi}$ is not accepted by any 2-head writing NFA, either, although it is easily seen that this language is accepted by a det-2-RR(1)-automaton.

For an integer $k \geq 2$, let $\psi_k : \{a, b, c, a', b'\}^* \to \{a_1, a_2, b_1, b_2, c\}^*$ be the morphism that is defined through $a \mapsto a_1 a_2^{k-1}$, $b \mapsto b_1 b_2^{k-1}$, $c \mapsto c$, $a' \mapsto a_2^{k-1} a_1$, and $b' \mapsto b_2^{k-1} b_1$. Then

$$\begin{aligned} L^{(k)}_{\mathrm{pal},\varphi} = \psi_k(L_{\mathrm{pal},\varphi}) &= \{ \psi_k(w) c \psi_k((\varphi(w))^R) \mid w \in \{a, b\}^* \} \\ &= \{ \psi_k(w) c (\psi_k(w))^R \mid w \in \{a, b\}^* \}. \end{aligned}$$

Proposition 2.5.94 ([161]) *For all $k \geq 2$, $L^{(k)}_{\mathrm{pal},\varphi} \in \mathcal{L}(\text{det-2-RR}(k)) \smallsetminus \mathcal{L}(\text{det-2-RR}(k-1))$.*

Proof. The language $L^{(k)}_{\mathrm{pal},\varphi}$ is obtained from the language of marked palindromes $L_{\mathrm{pal},\varphi} = \{ wc(\varphi(w))^R \mid w \in \{a, b\}^* \}$ by replacing each letter a or b by the block $a_1 a_2^{k-1}$ or $b_1 b_2^{k-1}$ and by replacing each letter a' or b' by the block $a_2^{k-1} a_1$ or $b_2^{k-1} b_1$. Thus, from the det-2-RR(1)-automaton for $L_{\mathrm{pal},\varphi}$, we easily obtain a det-2-RR(k)-automaton for $L^{(k)}_{\mathrm{pal},\varphi}$.

Assume now that M is a det-2-RR-automaton with windows of size $k-1$ such that $L(M) = L^{(k)}_{\mathrm{pal},\varphi}$, and let $x = \psi_k(u) c (\psi_k(u))^R \in L^{(k)}_{\mathrm{pal},\varphi}$. Then M has an accepting computation on input x. Assume that this computation begins with a cycle that rewrites x into the word y. In the corresponding rewrite steps, M deletes between 1 and $2k-2$ letters, that is, $1 \leq |x| - |y| \leq 2k - 2$. From the form of the words in the language $L^{(k)}_{\mathrm{pal},\varphi}$, it then follows that $y \notin L^{(k)}_{\mathrm{pal},\varphi}$, contradicting the Correctness Preserving Property for M. Therefore, the accepting computation of M on input x must be a tail computation. By Proposition 2.5.91, this implies that the language $L^{(k)}_{\mathrm{pal},\varphi}$ is accepted by a 2-head writing NFA. However, $\psi_k^{-1}(L^{(k)}_{\mathrm{pal},\varphi}) = L_{\mathrm{pal},\varphi}$, and as the class of languages accepted by 2-head writing NFAs is closed under inverse morphisms (see above), it follows that the

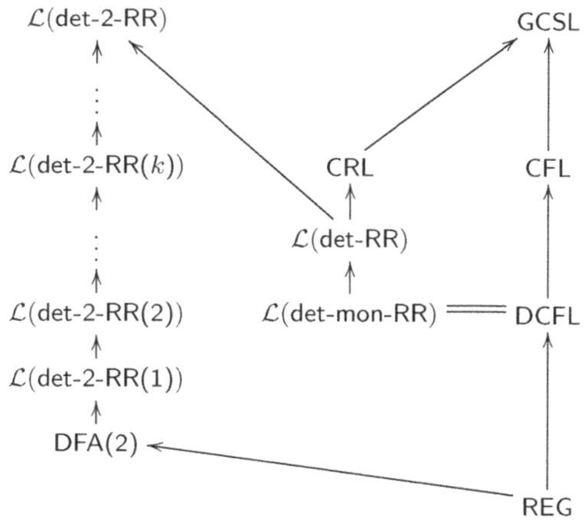

Figure 2.19: Relating det-2-RR-automata to the Chomsky hierarchy.

language $L_{\text{pal},\varphi}$ is accepted by a 2-head writing NFA, a contradiction. Thus, we see that $L^{(k)}_{\text{pal},\varphi}$ is not accepted by any det-2-RR$(k-1)$-automaton. □

This result yields the following infinite hierarchy.

Corollary 2.5.95 ([161]) *For all $k \geq 1$, $\mathcal{L}(\text{det-2-RR}(k)) \subsetneq \mathcal{L}(\text{det-2-RR}(k+1))$.*

As, for all $k \geq 1$, $L^{(k)}_{\text{pal},\varphi}$ is a deterministic linear language, we obtain the following incomparability results from Example 2.5.84 and Proposition 2.5.94.

Corollary 2.5.96 ([161]) *For all $k \geq 1$, the language class $\mathcal{L}(\text{det-2-RR}(k))$ is incomparable to the classes DLIN, LIN, DCFL, CFL, CRL, and GCSL with respect to inclusion.*

Concerning the det-2-RR-automata with windows of arbitrary size, however, we have the following result.

Corollary 2.5.97 ([161]) $\text{DCFL} = \mathcal{L}(\text{det-mon-RR}) \subsetneq \mathcal{L}(\text{det-RR}) \subsetneq \mathcal{L}(\text{det-2-RR})$.

The equality $\text{DCFL} = \mathcal{L}(\text{det-mon-RR})$ follows from Corollary 2.1.43, the non-context-free language L_6 is accepted a det-RR-automaton (see Lemma 2.2.7), and the properness of the last inclusion follows from Example 2.5.84, as the marked copy language L'_{copy} is not even growing context-sensitive, while each language that is accepted by a det-RR-automaton is a Church-Rosser language. Furthermore, the following negative result can be established for the language $L_{\text{exp}} = \{\, a^{2^n} \mid n \geq 0 \,\}$.

Proposition 2.5.98 ([161]) *The language L_{exp} is not accepted by any det-2-RR-automaton.*

Thus, we also have the following incomparability results.

Corollary 2.5.99 ([161]) *The language class $\mathcal{L}(\text{det-2-RR})$ is incomparable to the classes CRL and GCSL with respect to inclusion.*

The diagram in Figure 2.19 summarizes the inclusion relations derived above. However, the following question remains open.

Problem 2.5.100 *Is the class CFL of context-free languages included in the class $\mathcal{L}(\text{det-2-RR})$, that is, is every context-free language accepted by some det-2-RR-automaton?*

By interchanging the accept transitions with the undefined transitions, a det-2-RR(k)-automaton for a language L is turned into a det-2-RR(k)-automaton for the complement L^c. Hence, the following closure property follows.

Proposition 2.5.101 *The language classes* $\mathcal{L}(\text{det-2-RR}(k))$, $k \geq 1$, *and* $\mathcal{L}(\text{det-2-RR})$ *are closed under complementation.*

However, these language classes are not closed with respect to many other classical language operations. The language $L^{(k)}_{\text{pal},\varphi}$ is obtained as the image of the language $L_{\text{pal},\varphi}$ under the λ-free morphism ψ_k. From Proposition 2.5.94, we know that, for all $k \geq 1$, $\psi_{k+1}(L_{\text{pal},\varphi}) \notin \mathcal{L}(\text{det-2-RR}(k))$, while $L_{\text{pal},\varphi} \in \mathcal{L}(\text{det-2-RR}(1)) \subsetneq \mathcal{L}(\text{det-2-RR}(k))$. Hence, for all $k \geq 1$, the language class $\mathcal{L}(\text{det-2-RR}(k))$ is not closed under λ-free morphisms.

Let $\psi_* : \{a, b, a', b', c\}^* \to \mathcal{P}(\{a_1, a_2, b_1, b_2, c\}^*)$ be the regular substitution that is defined through $a \mapsto a_1 \cdot a_2^*$, $b \mapsto b_1 \cdot b_2^*$, $a' \mapsto a_2^* \cdot a_1$, $b' \mapsto b_2^* \cdot b_1$, and $c \mapsto c$. Then the language $L^{(*)}_{\text{pal},\varphi} = \psi_*(L_{\text{pal},\varphi})$ is accepted by a det-2-RR-automaton with windows of size one [161]. For each $k \geq 1$, if R_k is the regular language that is given through the regular expression

$$R_k = \left((a_1 \cdot a_2^k) \cup (b_1 \cdot b_2^k)\right)^* \cdot c \cdot \left((a_2^k \cdot a_1) \cup (b_2^k \cdot b_1)\right)^*,$$

then $L^{(k+1)}_{\text{pal},\varphi} = L^{(*)}_{\text{pal},\varphi} \cap R_k$. Hence, it follows from Proposition 2.5.94 that the language class $\mathcal{L}(\text{det-2-RR}(k))$ is not closed under intersection with regular languages. As each regular language is accepted by a det-2-RR(1)-automaton, Proposition 2.5.101 yields that the language class $\mathcal{L}(\text{det-2-RR}(k))$ is not closed under union and intersection, either.

Finally, let $\Sigma = \{a, b, c, d, e\}$, and let L_{rev} be the following language over Σ:

$$L_{\text{rev}} = \{\, dwcwcw^R, ewcw^Rcw^R \mid w \in \{a, b\}^+ \,\}.$$

It can be seen quite easily that $L_{\text{rev}} \in \mathcal{L}(\text{det-2-RR}(3))$. However, it can be proved that the mirror image L^R_{rev} of this language is not accepted by any det-2-RR(k)-automaton. Although this result is not that surprising, the proof given in [161] is unexpectedly difficult and quite interesting. It is a proof by contradiction that proceeds in three main steps.

Assume that L^R_{rev} is accepted by a det-2-RR(k)-automaton M for some $k \geq 1$. First, it is shown that a certain sublanguage L'_{rev} of L^R_{rev} is contained in the simple language $S_C(M)$ of M. In the next step, a det-2-RR(k)-automaton M' is constructed such that $L(M') = S_C(M') = L''_{\text{rev}}$, where L''_{rev} is obtained from L'_{rev} by deleting the trailing symbols d and e from all words in L'_{rev}. By Proposition 2.5.93, this means that L''_{rev} is accepted by a sensing deterministic 6-head finite automaton. From this observation, a contradiction is then derived by reusing a technique developed in [268] for multi-head finite automata. For the detailed proof, we refer to [161].

Lemma 2.5.102 ([161]) $L^R_{\text{rev}} \notin \mathcal{L}(\text{det-2-RR}(k))$ *for any* $k \geq 1$.

It follows that, for all $k \geq 3$, the language class $\mathcal{L}(\text{det-2-RR}(k))$ is not closed under reversal, and neither is the class $\mathcal{L}(\text{det-2-RR})$. However, the following question remains open.

Problem 2.5.103 *Are the language classes* $\mathcal{L}(\text{det-2-RR}(1))$ *and* $\mathcal{L}(\text{det-2-RR}(2))$ *not closed under reversal, either?*

Let $\psi : \{a, b, c, d, e\}^* \to \{a, b, c, d\}^*$ be the morphism that is given through $a \mapsto a$, $b \mapsto b$, $c \mapsto c$, $d \mapsto d$, and $e \mapsto d$. Then $\psi(L_{\text{rev}}) = \{\, dwcwcw^R, dwcw^Rcw^R \mid w \in \{a, b\}^+ \,\}$, and in analogy to the proof of Lemma 2.5.102, it can be shown that this language is not accepted by any det-2-RR(k)-automaton, either. Hence, we see that the language class $\mathcal{L}(\text{det-2-RR})$ is not closed under λ-free morphisms. Furthermore, this class is not closed under intersection with regular sets and, therewith it is not closed under union and intersection. Finally, it is proved in [161] that, for each $k \geq 1$, the language class $\mathcal{L}(\text{det-2-RR}(k))$ is not closed under inverse morphisms, but the following problems have not been solved yet.

Problem 2.5.104 *Is any of the language classes* $\mathcal{L}(\mathsf{det\text{-}2\text{-}RR}(k))$, $k \geq 1$, *or* $\mathcal{L}(\mathsf{det\text{-}2\text{-}RR})$ *closed under product and/or Kleene star?*

Finally, we take a look at the algorithmic properties of det-2-RR(k)-automata.

Proposition 2.5.105 $\mathcal{L}(\mathsf{det\text{-}2\text{-}RR}) \subseteq \mathsf{DTIME}(n^2)$, *that is, the membership problem for each language that is accepted by a det-2-RR-automaton is decidable deterministically in time* $\mathcal{O}(n^2)$.

Proof. Let $L = L(M)$ for a det-2-RR-automaton M and let w be an input word of length n. We consider the computation of M for input w. This computation consists of at most n cycles and a tail. Each cycle is executed in $\mathcal{O}(n)$ many steps, as in each step, one of the two heads is moved at least one position to the right. This also holds for the tail computation. Hence, M can be simulated by a deterministic multi-tape Turing machine in time $\mathcal{O}(n^2)$. □

From the decidability of the membership problem, it follows that the non-emptiness problem for det-2-RR-automata is recursively enumerable. However, this is the best one can do as shown by the following proposition, which can be proved by a reduction from the emptiness problem for Turing machines.

Proposition 2.5.106 ([161]) *For all* $k \geq 1$, *emptiness, finiteness, regularity, context-freeness, universality, inclusion, and equivalence are undecidable for det-2-RR(*k*)-automata.*

In fact, the problems above are not even recursively enumerable for det-2-RR(k)-automata. Thus, there is no Turing machine that, given an appropriate encoding of a det-2-RR(k)-automaton M as input, halts eventually if and only if the language $L(M)$ is empty (finite, regular, etc.).

In summary, we have seen that the quite restricted model of the det-2-RR-automaton already has a rather large expressive capacity and that the resulting language classes form an infinite strictly ascending hierarchy with respect to the size of the windows. Unfortunately, these language classes are again anti-AFLs, that is, they are not closed under any of the AFL operations, if they are not closed under product and Kleene star.

Of course, one can easily define more general types of restarting automata with multiple windows. On the one hand, the det-2-RR-automaton can be extended by admitting more general rewrite steps or by considering its nondeterministic variant. On the other hand, automata with three or more windows can be introduced. However, it should be clear from the results above that these types of restarting automata will be even more expressive than the det-2-RR-automaton.

2.6 Relating Auxiliary Letters To Input Letters

Analysis by reduction, in general, facilitates the development and testing of categories for syntactic and semantic disambiguation of sentences of natural languages. It is often used (implicitly) for developing formal descriptions of natural languages based on the notion of *dependency* [144, 243]. In particular, the Functional Generative Description (FGD) for the Czech language that has been developed in Prague since the 1960s (see, e.g., [145]) is based on this method.

FGD is a dependency-based system. It does not only specify the surface structures of given sentences, but it also translates them into their underlying tectogrammatical representations, which are (at least in principle) disambiguated. Analysis by reduction then allows to obtain (in)dependencies through correct reductions of Czech sentences. It consists in stepwise simplifications (reductions) of a given (disambiguated) input word, that is, a sequence of tokens (word forms and punctuation marks) that is enriched with syntactical and semantical categories. This enriched sequence is simplified until the so-called core predicative structure of the sentence is reached. Each simplification replaces a small part of the sentence with an even shorter phrase.

The original motivation for introducing the restarting automaton was the desire to model this process. In fact, many aspects of the work on restarting automata are motivated by the basic tasks of computational linguistics (e.g., devising multilevel language descriptions, see [145]) as well as by applied tasks (e.g., constructing grammar checkers for free word order languages [114]).

We have already considered various restricted versions of restarting automata and various constraints for them. In particular, monotone restarting automata, which essentially model bottom-up context-free analyzers, have received much attention as they characterize the class of context-free languages. However, in our studies so far, auxiliary letters have been used quite freely to encode information without much regard for their linguistic motivation. Here we consider two extensions of the notions studied that yield a closer relationship between auxiliary letters and characteristic languages on the one hand and input letters and languages on the other hand.

In Subsection 2.6.1, we formalize analysis by reduction by using deterministic restarting automata for *proper languages*. These automata work on *characteristic languages*, that is, on languages that include auxiliary letters (categories) in addition to the input letters. The *proper language* is obtained from a characteristic language by removing all auxiliary letters from its words (sentences). By requiring that the automata considered are *lexicalized*, we then restrict the lengths of the blocks of auxiliary letters that are allowed on the tape by a constant. This restriction is quite natural from a linguistic point of view, as these blocks of auxiliary letters model the meta-language categories from individual linguistic layers with which a given input is being enriched when its disambiguated form is being produced. We use deterministic restarting automata in order to ensure the *correctness preserving property* for the analysis. In fact, we also concentrate on *strongly lexicalized* restarting automata. This additional restriction requires that all rewrite operations must be deletions. For example, this type of automaton can be used for modelling the surface (syntactic) level(s) of the Functional Generative Description. In addition, we study proper languages of deterministic FRRWW-automata that are (strongly) lexicalized, where we focus on two types of constraints: the number of rewrites per cycle, which models the degree of valences within sentences, and the number of occurrences of auxiliary letters in the words of the corresponding characteristic language, which models the use of categories during the process of syntactic disambiguation.

In Subsection 2.2.3, we already studied restarting automata with restricted utilization of auxiliary letters, where we placed two restrictions on restarting automata by limiting the number of auxiliary letters in the tape alphabet and by bounding the number of occurrences of auxiliary letters within the configurations of a computation. However, in Subsection 2.2.3, we were concerned with the influence of these restrictions on the *input languages* of restarting automata, while here we study *proper languages*. A proper language is much more closely related to the characteristic language of a restarting automaton than the input language, as it contains the projections of all words from the characteristic language, that is, each word from the characteristic language contributes to the proper language.

In Subsection 2.6.2, we introduce and study *h-lexicalized* restarting automata. While, in general, the auxiliary letters of a restarting automaton can be used quite freely to encode information on the current input or the current computation of a restarting automaton on its tape, this is not the case in a linguistic setting, where auxiliary letters model tags or categories. Accordingly, for an h-lexicalized restarting automaton, each auxiliary letter is closely connected to an input letter by a morphism that maps each auxiliary letter to an input letter. In fact, each auxiliary letter can be interpreted as a pair that consists of an input letter and some additional information (tags). Now the *h-proper language* of an h-lexicalized restarting automaton is obtained from the characteristic language by replacing each occurrence of an auxiliary letter with an occurrence of its associated input letter. This implies that all words from the characteristic language that occur within an accepting computation of an h-lexicalized restarting automaton contribute to the h-proper language of that automaton.

Additionally, the constraint of *strong cyclic form* is introduced for h-lexicalized restarting automata, which requires that acceptance and rejection are only possible for short words. This constraint necessitates a restarting automaton to first reduce a given word into a short word by executing a sequence of cycles before it can accept or reject. Finally, we also introduce a constraint that bounds the number of cycles in accepting computations of restarting automata. Based on this constraint and the strong cyclic form, it is possible to extend the complexity results that are obtained for classes of infinite languages even to classes of finite languages. This is quite useful for the formulation of techniques for the localization of syntactic errors. Recall that formal language theory is mainly concerned with the structure of infinite languages. In fact, finite languages are mainly considered to be trivial in formal language theory, as they can (at least in principle) simply be described by enumerating their elements. In fact, the class of finite languages is already a proper subclass of the regular languages. In traditional and corpus linguistics, however, only finite language phenomena can be directly observed. Accordingly, it is quite difficult to directly apply techniques and results from formal language theory in a linguistic setting. Now, in combination with the strong cyclic form, the restriction on the number of cycles in accepting computations allows us to carry results on restarting automata over to classes of finite languages.

2.6.1 On Proper Languages and Lexicalized Restarting Automata

Here we study proper languages of restarting automata with auxiliary letters. These proper languages are obtained from characteristic languages by removing all occurrences of auxiliary letters.

Definition 2.6.1 ([167, 172]) *Let* $M = (Q, \Sigma, \Gamma, \rhd, \lhd, q_0, k, \delta)$ *be a restarting automaton, and let* $\pi_\Sigma : \Gamma^* \to \Sigma^*$ *be the projection that is given through* $a \mapsto a$ *for all* $a \in \Sigma$ *and* $B \mapsto \lambda$ *for all* $B \in \Gamma \smallsetminus \Sigma$. *For words* $w \in \Gamma^*$ *and* $v \in \Sigma^*$, *if* $v = \pi_\Sigma(w)$, *then* v *is the* Σ-projection *of* w, *and* w *is an* expanded version *of* v. *The* proper language *of* M *is defined as* $L_\mathrm{P}(M) = \pi_\Sigma(L_\mathrm{C}(M))$, *that is, a word* v *belongs to the proper language* $L_\mathrm{P}(M)$ *of* M *if and only if there exists an expanded version* w *of* v *in the characteristic language of* M. *For each type* X *of restarting automaton, we use the notation* $\mathcal{L}_\mathrm{P}(\mathsf{X})$ *to denote the class of proper languages of automata of type* X.

We recall from the proof of Proposition 2.2.56 that the deterministic RWW-automaton $M = (Q, \{a\}, \{a, A\}, \rhd, \lhd, q_0, 5, \delta)$, which is defined by the set of meta-instructions

$$\begin{array}{llll} (1) & (\rhd \cdot \{a, a^2, a^4\} \cdot \lhd, \mathsf{Accept}), & (3) & (\rhd \cdot a^+, a^4 A \to Aa^2), \\ (2) & (\rhd \cdot a^+, a^4 \lhd \to Aaa\lhd), & (4) & (\rhd, a^4 A \to a^2). \end{array}$$

accepts the (input) language $L_\mathrm{exp} = \{ a^{2^n} \mid n \geq 0 \}$. In addition, it is easily checked that its characteristic language is

$$L_\mathrm{C}(M) = \{ a^{2^n} \mid n \geq 0 \} \cup \{ a^i A a^j \mid i \geq 4, j \geq 2, i, j \equiv 0 \bmod 2, \text{ and } \exists n \geq 3 : i + 2j = 2^n \}.$$

Thus, it follows that the proper language of M is

$$L_\mathrm{P}(M) = \{ a^{2^n} \mid n \geq 0 \} \cup \{ a^{i+j} \mid i \geq 4, j \geq 2, i, j \equiv 0 \bmod 2, \text{ and } \exists n \geq 3 : i + 2j = 2^n \}.$$

Obviously, the proper language $L_P(M)$ contains the (input) language $L(M) = L_{\text{exp}}$, but $L_P(M)$ also contains the word $a^{12} = a^{8+4} \notin L_{\text{exp}}$, as $8 + 2 \cdot 4 = 16 = 2^4$. In fact, the following observation is easily verified.

Proposition 2.6.2 *For each restarting automaton $M = (Q, \Sigma, \Gamma, \triangleright, \triangleleft, q_0, k, \delta)$, $L(M) \subseteq L_P(M)$. If M does not have any auxiliary letters, that is, if $\Sigma = \Gamma$, then $L(M) = L_P(M) = L_C(M)$.*

For a restarting automaton with auxiliary letters, the proper language will, in general, be a proper superset of the input language. As each language accepted by a deterministic sRRWW-automaton M is a Church-Rosser language (see Corollary 2.1.34), we know that the membership problem for the language $L_C(M)$ is decidable in linear time. In contrast to this result, it has been shown that the class $\mathcal{L}_P(\mathsf{det\text{-}RRWW})$ of proper languages of deterministic RRWW-automata is 'almost' universal.

In [204], it has been established that the class CRL of Church-Rosser languages is a *basis* for the class RE of recursively enumerable languages, that is, for each recursively enumerable language $L \subseteq \Sigma^*$, there exists a Church-Rosser language B on some alphabet Δ strictly containing Σ such that $\pi_\Sigma(B) = L$. As CRL coincides with the class of input languages of deterministic RRWW-automata, there exists a deterministic RRWW-automaton M' with input alphabet Δ and tape alphabet Γ such that $L(M') = B$. Hence, $L = \pi_\Sigma(B) \subseteq \pi_\Sigma(L_C(M'))$. However, the language $L_C(M')$ will, in general, also contain words for which the projection onto Σ does not belong to the language L, that is, the above inclusion is, in general, proper. Accordingly, in order to derive the intended universality result, a somewhat more sophisticated construction is provided in [167].

For the following considerations, we restrict our attention to recursively enumerable languages over the fixed two-letter alphabet $\Sigma_0 = \{a, b\}$. Let $\Sigma_1 = \Sigma_0 \cup \{c\}$, let $\varphi_0 : \Sigma_0^* \to \Sigma_0^*$ be the injective morphism that is defined by $a \mapsto aa$ and $b \mapsto bb$, and let $\varphi : \Sigma_0^* \to \Sigma_1^*$ denote the mapping that is defined by $\varphi(w) = \varphi_0(w) \cdot c$. Then φ is an encoding that can be computed by a finite-state transducer. The following result expresses the universality of $\mathcal{L}_P(\mathsf{det\text{-}RRWW})$ announced above.

Proposition 2.6.3 ([167]) *For each recursively enumerable language $L \subseteq \Sigma_0^+$, there exists a deterministic RRWW-automaton M such that $L_P(M) \cap \Sigma_0^* \cdot \{c\} = \varphi(L)$.*

Proof outline. Let $L \subseteq \Sigma_0^+$ be a recursively enumerable language. In the proof of Theorem 7.1 of [204], a Church-Rosser language of the form $B = \{\, wde^{m(w)} \mid w \in L \,\}$ is constructed from a Turing machine accepting the language L, where d and e are two new letters, and $m(w)$ is a unique integer associated with the word w.

Let $\Sigma_0' = \{a', b'\}$, let $\Delta' = \Sigma_0' \cup \{d, e\}$, and let $\varphi' : \Sigma_0^* \to \{a', b'\}^*$ denote the morphism that is induced by $a \mapsto a'$ and $b \mapsto b'$. Then B' denotes the Church-Rosser language $B' = \{\, \varphi'(w)de^{m(w)} \mid w \in L \,\}$. As noted above, there exists a deterministic RRWW-automaton $M' = (Q', \Delta', \Gamma', \triangleright, \triangleleft, q_0', k', \delta')$ satisfying $L(M') = B'$.

From M', a deterministic RRWW-automaton M with input alphabet Σ_1 can be constructed such that

$$L_P(M) \cap \Sigma_0^* \cdot \{c\} = \varphi(L).$$

Given a word of the form $xcde^m$ as input, where $x \in \Sigma_0^*$ and $m \geq 0$, this automaton works in two phases. In the first phase, M checks that the prefix xc is a word of the form $\varphi(w)$ for some word $w \in \Sigma_0^*$. In the negative, M halts and rejects, while in the affirmative, it replaces $\varphi(w)$ with the word $\varphi'(w)$, which yields the word $\varphi'(w)de^m$. Then M simulates the automaton M' step by step on $\varphi'(w)de^m$. It follows that M is a deterministic RRWW-automaton and that $L_P(M) \cap \Sigma_0^* \cdot \{c\} = \varphi(L)$. □

Thus, a word $w \in \Sigma_0^*$ belongs to the recursively enumerable language L if and only if its image $\varphi(w)$ belongs to the proper language $L_P(M)$. This yields the following consequence.

Corollary 2.6.4 ([167]) *There exists a deterministic RRWW-automaton M such that the language $L_P(M)$ is non-recursive.*

From Corollary 2.6.4, we see that proper languages of deterministic RRWW-automata are in general far more complex than the corresponding input and characteristic languages. Therefore, we turn our attention to deterministic RRWW-automata for which the use of auxiliary letters is somehow restricted.

Definition 2.6.5 *Let* $M = (Q, \Sigma, \Gamma, \rhd, \lhd, q_0, k, \delta)$ *be a deterministic RRWW-automaton.*

(a) *A word* $w \in \Gamma^*$ *is* not immediately rejected *by* M *if there exists a meta-instruction of* M *that is applicable to the restarting configuration* $q_0 \rhd w \lhd$, *that is,* M *can either perform a cycle of the form* $q_0 \rhd w \lhd \vdash^c_M q_0 \rhd z \lhd$ *for some word* $z \in \Gamma^*$, *or* M *accepts* w *in a tail computation. We use* $\mathrm{NIR}(M)$ *to denote the set of all words that are not immediately rejected by* M.

(b) *The deterministic RRWW-automaton* M *is called* lexicalized *if there exists a constant* $j \in \mathbb{N}_+$ *such that, whenever* $v \in (\Gamma \setminus \Sigma)^*$ *is a factor of a word* $w \in \mathrm{NIR}(M)$, *then* $|v| \leq j$. *We use the prefix lex- to denote classes of lexicalized RRWW-automata.*

(c) *The deterministic RRWW-automaton* M *is called* strongly lexicalized *if it is lexicalized, and if each of its rewrite steps only deletes letters. We use the prefix slex- to denote classes of strongly lexicalized RRWW-automata.*

Observe that a strongly lexicalized deterministic RRWW-automaton is not necessarily an RR-automaton, as it may have auxiliary letters. In [171], the notion of a 'reasonably constructed' RRWW-automaton is introduced, which is equivalent to the above notion of lexicalization. Note that, according to the above definition, a lexicalized RRWW-automaton is necessarily deterministic. Strong lexicalization is a technique that is used in dependency (or categorially) based formal descriptions of natural languages [145]. If M is a lexicalized RRWW-automaton, and if $w \in \Gamma^*$ is an extended version of an input word $v = \pi_\Sigma(w)$ such that w is not immediately rejected by M, then $|w| \leq (j+1) \cdot |v| + j$ for some constant $j > 0$. Thus, $L_{\mathrm{P}}(M)$ is context-sensitive, contrasting Corollary 2.6.4. Actually, we even have the following stronger result.

Proposition 2.6.6 ([167]) *If* M *is a lexicalized RRWW-automaton, then the proper language* $L_{\mathrm{P}}(M)$ *is growing context-sensitive.*

Proof. Let M be a deterministic RRWW-automaton with input alphabet Σ and tape alphabet Γ, and assume that M is lexicalized with constant $j \in \mathbb{N}_+$. Then no word $w \in L_{\mathrm{C}}(M)$ contains any factor from $(\Gamma \setminus \Sigma)^*$ of length exceeding j. Thus, the morphism $\pi_\Sigma : \Gamma^* \to \Sigma^*$ has j*-limited erasing* (see, e.g, [81]) on $L_{\mathrm{C}}(M)$. As M is a deterministic RRWW-automaton, $L_{\mathrm{C}}(M)$ is a Church-Rosser language, which means that it belongs to the class GCSL of growing context-sensitive languages. This, in turn, implies that $L_{\mathrm{P}}(M) = \pi_\Sigma(L_{\mathrm{C}}(M))$ is also growing context-sensitive, as this class is closed under limited erasing [23]. □

However, not every growing context-sensitive language is the proper language of a lexicalized RRWW-automaton.

Proposition 2.6.7 ([167]) *The Church-Rosser language* $L_{\mathrm{exp}} = \{ a^{2^n} \mid n \geq 0 \}$ *is not the proper language of any lexicalized RRWW-automaton.*

Proof. Assume to the contrary that $L_{\mathrm{exp}} = L_{\mathrm{P}}(M)$ for a lexicalized RRWW-automaton $M = (Q, \{a\}, \Gamma, \rhd, \lhd, q_0, k, \delta)$, and let $z = a^{2^n} \in L_{\mathrm{exp}}$, where n is a large integer. Then there exists an expanded version $w \in \Gamma^*$ of z such that $w \in L_{\mathrm{C}}(M)$. Thus, the computation of M on input w is accepting. From the Pumping Lemma for restarting automata (Proposition 2.1.8), we see that this computation cannot just consist of an accepting tail, that is, it begins with a cycle of the form $q_0 \rhd w \lhd \vdash^c_M q_0 \rhd w' \lhd$ for some word $w' \in L_{\mathrm{C}}(M)$. This implies that $\pi_{\{a\}}(w') \in L_{\mathrm{P}}(M) = L_{\mathrm{exp}}$. Thus, $\pi_{\{a\}}(w') = a^m$ for some integer m satisfying $2^n - k \leq m < 2^n + k$, as the rewrite step in the above cycle replaces a factor of length k with a shorter word. From the choice of z, it follows that $m = 2^n$, that is, w' is obtained from w by rewriting some auxiliary letters only. We can repeat this argument until eventually M either rewrites some occurrences of the letter a, which then yields a word $\hat{w} \in L_C(M)$ for which the projection $\pi_{\{a\}}(\hat{w})$ does not belong to the language L_{exp} anymore, or until M accepts a word $\tilde{w}$ in a tail computation for which $\pi_{\{a\}}(\tilde{w}) = a^{2^n}$ holds. In the latter case, the Pumping Lemma shows that $L_P(M)$ also contains words that do not belong to the language L_{exp}. In either case, it follows that L_{exp} is not the proper language of any lexicalized RRWW-automaton. □

Next, we study the expressive capacity of lexicalized RRWW-automata that are monotone. In contrast to the definition of monotonicity in Section 1.9 (see Definition 1.9.19(d)), we follow the usage in [167, 172] and call a lexicalized RRWW-automaton *monotone* if *all* its computations are monotone, not just those that begin with an initial configuration. Thus, a lexicalized RRWW-automaton $M = (Q, \Sigma, \Gamma, \rhd, \lhd, q_0, k, \delta)$ is called monotone if the det-RRW-automaton $(Q, \Gamma, \Gamma, \rhd, \lhd, q_0, k, \delta)$ is monotone. This is reasonable as we are concerned with the proper language of M, which is obtained from the characteristic language through a projection. Concerning the expressive capacity of lexicalized RRWW-automata that are monotone, we have the following result.

Theorem 2.6.8 ([167]) *The class CFL of context-free languages coincides with the class of proper languages of monotone (strongly) lexicalized RRWW-automata, that is,*

$$\mathsf{CFL} = \mathcal{L}_P(\text{lex-mon-RRWW}) = \mathcal{L}_P(\text{slex-mon-RRWW}).$$

Proof. If M is a monotone RRWW-automaton, then its characteristic language $L_C(M)$ is context-free by Corollary 2.1.41. As $L_P(M) = \pi_\Sigma(L_C(M))$, and as the class CFL is closed under morphisms, it follows that $L_P(M)$ is context-free.

Conversely, assume that $L \subseteq \Sigma^*$ is a context-free language. Without loss of generality, we may assume that L does not contain the empty word. Thus, there exists a context-free grammar $G = (N, \Sigma, S, P)$ for L that is in *Greibach normal form*, that is, each rule of P has the form $(A \to \alpha)$ for some word $\alpha \in \Sigma \cdot N^*$ (see Theorem 1.2.28). For the following construction, we assume that the rules of G are numbered from 1 to m.

From G, we construct a new grammar $G' = (N, \Sigma \cup B, S, P')$, where $B = \{ \nabla_i \mid 1 \leq i \leq m \}$ is a set of new terminal symbols that are in one-to-one correspondence to the rules of G, and

$$P' = \{ A \to \nabla_i \alpha \mid (A \to \alpha) \text{ is the } i\text{-th rule of } G,\ 1 \leq i \leq m \}.$$

Obviously, a word $\omega \in (\Sigma \cup B)^*$ belongs to $L(G')$ if and only if $\omega = \nabla_{i_1} a_1 \nabla_{i_2} a_2 \cdots \nabla_{i_n} a_n$ for some integer $n > 0$, where $a_1, a_2, \ldots, a_n \in \Sigma$, $i_1, i_2, \ldots, i_n \in \{1, 2, \ldots, m\}$, and the sequence of these indices describes a (left-most) derivation of $w = a_1 a_2 \cdots a_n$ from S in G. Thus, $\pi_\Sigma(L(G')) = L(G) = L$. From ω, this derivation can be reconstructed deterministically. In fact, the language $L(G')$ is deterministic context-free. Hence, by Corollary 2.1.43, there exists a monotone deterministic RR-automaton M for this language. By interpreting the letters in B as auxiliary letters, we obtain a monotone deterministic RRWW-automaton M' such that $\pi_\Sigma(L_C(M')) = \pi_\Sigma(L(M)) = \pi_\Sigma(L(G')) = L$.

It remains to verify that M' is lexicalized. From the observation above, we see that, within each word $\omega \in L(G')$, symbols from B and letters from Σ occur alternatingly. As the RR-automaton M is correctness preserving, each restarting configuration of M within an accepting computation is of the form $q_0 \rhd \gamma \lhd$ for some $\gamma \in L(G')$. Thus, it only contains factors from B^+ of length one. It follows that M' is lexicalized with constant 1. As M is an RR-automaton, all rewrite operations of M' are deletions. Hence, M' is even strongly lexicalized. □

Together with Propositions 2.6.6 and 2.6.7, this yields the following consequence, as the class CRL is incomparable to the class CFL with respect to inclusion.

Corollary 2.6.9 ([167]) $\mathcal{L}_P(\text{lex-RRWW})$ *is a proper subclass of GCSL that is incomparable under inclusion to the class CRL of Church-Rosser languages.*

In the next step, we introduce a static complexity measure for lexicalized RRWW-automata by restricting the number of occurrences of auxiliary letters on the tape.

Definition 2.6.10 *Let* $M = (Q, \Sigma, \Gamma, \rhd, \lhd, q_0, k, \delta)$ *be a lexicalized RRWW-automaton, and let* $m \in \mathbb{N}$. *The automaton* M *is said to have* word-expansion *(of degree)* m*, denoted by* $\mathsf{W}(M) = m$*, if each word from the set* $\mathrm{NIR}(M)$ *contains at most* m *occurrences of auxiliary letters, that is, if* $w \in \mathrm{NIR}(M)$*, then* $|\pi_{\Gamma \smallsetminus \Sigma}(w)| \leq m$.

Essentially, the notion of word expansion corresponds to the notion of 'degree of disambiguation' defined in [171]. We use $\mathrm{W}(m)$-lex-RRWW, to denote the class of lexicalized RRWW-automata with word-expansion m, and the strongly lexicalized variant of this class is denoted by the prefix $\mathrm{W}(m)$-slex-. For lexicalized RRWW-automata with bounded word expansion, we have the following result on the complexity of the membership problem that should be compared to Corollary 2.6.4.

Theorem 2.6.11 ([167]) *For all* $m \in \mathbb{N}$*, if* M *is a* $W(m)$*-lex-RRWW-automaton, then the membership problem for the language* $L_{\mathrm{P}}(M)$ *is solvable deterministically in time* $\mathcal{O}(n^{m+1})$.

This result follows from the observation that the number of possible expanded versions of a word w from the proper language of a lexicalized RRWW-automaton M with word expansion m is bounded from above by the expression $\binom{|w|+m}{m} \cdot (j+1)^m$, where j is the number of auxiliary letters in the tape alphabet of M.

We are interested in the classes $\mathcal{L}_{\mathrm{P}}(\mathsf{W}(m)\text{-(s)lex-(mon)-RRWW})$ of proper languages of (monotone) (strongly) lexicalized RRWW-automata with bounded word expansion. As monotone deterministic RR-automata accept the deterministic context-free languages, the following result follows immediately.

Proposition 2.6.12 ([167]) $\mathsf{DCFL} = \mathcal{L}_{\mathrm{P}}(\mathsf{W}(0)\text{-slex-mon-RRWW}) = \mathcal{L}_{\mathrm{P}}(\mathsf{W}(0)\text{-lex-mon-RRWW})$.

Actually, the correspondence between monotone strongly lexicalized RRWW-automata and monotone lexicalized RRWW-automata carries over to all finite degrees of word-expansion.

Proposition 2.6.13 ([167]) *For all* $m \in \mathbb{N}$,

$$\mathcal{L}_{\mathrm{P}}(\mathsf{W}(m)\text{-slex-mon-RRWW}) = \mathcal{L}_{\mathrm{P}}(\mathsf{W}(m)\text{-lex-mon-RRWW}).$$

Proof. Let $m \in \mathbb{N}$, and let $L = L_{\mathrm{P}}(M)$ for some monotone lexicalized RRWW-automaton $M = (Q, \Sigma, \Gamma, \rhd, \lhd, q_0, k, \delta)$. Thus, $L = \pi_\Sigma(L_{\mathrm{C}}(M))$. Consider the deterministic RRW-automaton $M' = (Q, \Gamma, \Gamma, \rhd, \lhd, q_0, k, \delta)$ that is obtained from M by simply interpreting all letters of Γ as input letters. Then M' is also monotone, and $L(M') = L_{\mathrm{C}}(M') = L_{\mathrm{C}}(M)$. It follows that $L(M')$ is a deterministic context-free language, which in turn implies that there exists a monotone deterministic RR-automaton $\hat{M} = (\hat{Q}, \Gamma, \Gamma, \rhd, \lhd, \hat{q}_0, \hat{k}, \hat{\delta})$ satisfying $L(\hat{M}) = L(M') = L_{\mathrm{C}}(M)$. Thus, $\hat{M}_\Sigma = (\hat{Q}, \Sigma, \Gamma, \rhd, \lhd, \hat{q}_0, \hat{k}, \hat{\delta})$ is a monotone deterministic RRWW-automaton satisfying $L_{\mathrm{P}}(\hat{M}_\Sigma) = L$. In fact, $\hat{M}$ can be designed in such a way that $\hat{M}_\Sigma$ is lexicalized with the same constant as the original automaton M. Here we simply have to guarantee that no rewriting meta-instruction of $\hat{M}$ can be applied to any word that contains a factor from $(\Gamma \smallsetminus \Sigma)^*$ of length exceeding j, where j is the corresponding constant for M. Hence, $\hat{M}_\Sigma$ is strongly lexicalized. Actually, if M has word-expansion m, then so does $\hat{M}_\Sigma$. This completes the proof. □

The proper languages of monotone (strongly) lexicalized RRWW-automata with word-expansion 0 are exactly the deterministic context-free languages, while the proper languages of monotone (strongly) lexicalized RRWW-automata with unbounded word-expansion cover all context-free languages (Theorem 2.6.8). Hence, the degree of word-expansion of monotone (strongly) lexicalized RRWW-automata can be interpreted as a measure for the degree of nondeterminism of context-free languages. It remains to show that the resulting classes of proper languages form an infinite hierarchy. To do so, we consider a number of example languages. For the following considerations, we fix the alphabet $\Sigma_0 = \{a, b\}$.

It is easily checked that the language $L_{\mathrm{pal}} = \{\, ww^R \mid w \in \Sigma_0^* \,\}$ is the proper language of a strongly lexicalized monotone RRWW-automaton with word expansion one. However, as this language is not the input language of any deterministic RRWW-automaton (see the remark following Theorem 1.2.19), it is not the proper language of any lexicalized RRWW-automaton with word expansion zero, that is, we have the following result.

Proposition 2.6.14 ([167, 172]) *The language* $L_{\rm pal} = \{ ww^R \mid w \in \Sigma_0^* \}$ *of palindromes of even length belongs to the class* $\mathcal{L}_{\rm P}(\textsf{W(1)-slex-mon-RRWW})$*, but it is not contained in the class* $\mathcal{L}_{\rm P}(\textsf{W(0)-lex-RRWW})$.

Next, we define an infinite family of example languages $L_p(m)$ $(m \geq 2)$, which are iterations of the language $L_{\rm pal}$.

Definition 2.6.15 *For all* $m \geq 2$, $L_p(m) = L_{\rm pal} \cdot (\{\#\} \cdot L_{\rm pal})^{m-1}$.

For these languages, the following result holds.

Proposition 2.6.16 ([167]) *For all* $m \geq 2$,

$$L_p(m) \in \mathcal{L}_{\rm P}(\textsf{W}(m)\textsf{-slex-mon-RRWW}) \smallsetminus \mathcal{L}_{\rm P}(\textsf{W}(m-1)\textsf{-lex-RRWW}).$$

Proof outline. It is easily seen that, for each $m \geq 2$, the language $L_p(m)$ is the proper language of a strongly lexicalized monotone RRWW-automaton with word expansion m. On the other hand, let $m \geq 2$ and assume that M is a lexicalized RRWW-automaton with word-expansion $m-1$ such that $L_{\rm P}(M) = L_p(m)$ holds, let $\Sigma = \Sigma_0 \cup \{\#\}$, and let Γ be the tape alphabet of M. For a word of the form $z = w_1 w_1^R \# w_2 w_2^R \# \cdots \# w_m w_m^R \in L_p(m)$, where $w_1, w_2, \ldots, w_m \in \Sigma_0^*$ are words of sufficient length, there exists a word $\alpha \in L_{\rm C}(M)$ such that $\pi_\Sigma(\alpha) = z$ and $|\alpha|_{\Gamma \smallsetminus \Sigma} \leq m-1$. Thus, the middle of at least one of the palindromes $w_i w_i^R$, $1 \leq i \leq m$, is not marked by an occurrence of an auxiliary letter. This means that M will not be able to correctly process this particular palindrome, as M is deterministic, and as it must satisfy the Correctness Preserving Property. It follows that $L_{\rm P}(M) \neq L_p(m)$ holds, implying that $L_p(m) \notin \mathcal{L}_{\rm P}(\textsf{W}(m-1)\textsf{-lex-RRWW})$. □

The propositions above immediately yield the following proper hierarchy results.

Theorem 2.6.17 ([167]) *For each* $m \geq 1$*, the following relations hold:*

(a)	$\mathcal{L}_{\rm P}(\textsf{W}(m)\textsf{-lex-mon-RRWW})$	$\subsetneq$	$\mathcal{L}_{\rm P}(\textsf{W}(m+1)\textsf{-lex-mon-RRWW})$.
(b)	$\mathcal{L}_{\rm P}(\textsf{W}(m)\textsf{-slex-RRWW})$	$\subsetneq$	$\mathcal{L}_{\rm P}(\textsf{W}(m+1)\textsf{-slex-RRWW})$.
(c)	$\mathcal{L}_{\rm P}(\textsf{W}(m)\textsf{-lex-RRWW})$	$\subsetneq$	$\mathcal{L}_{\rm P}(\textsf{W}(m+1)\textsf{-lex-RRWW})$.
(d)	$\mathcal{L}_{\rm P}(\textsf{W}(m+1)\textsf{-slex-mon-RRWW})$	$\not\subseteq$	$\mathcal{L}_{\rm P}(\textsf{W}(m)\textsf{-lex-RRWW})$.

Finally, let $L_{\rm pal^+} = \bigcup_{i \geq 1} (\{\#\} \cdot L_{\rm pal})^i$. In analogy to the proof of Proposition 2.6.16, the following result can be derived.

Proposition 2.6.18 ([167]) $L_{\rm pal^+} \notin \mathcal{L}_{\rm P}(\textsf{W}(m)\textsf{-lex-RRWW})$ *for any* $m \geq 0$.

On the other hand, it is easily seen that $L_{\rm pal^+}$ is the proper language of the strongly lexicalized RRWW-automaton $M_{\rm pal^+}$ on $\Gamma = \{a, b, \#, C\}$ that is given through the following meta-instructions, where $x \in \Sigma_0$:

$$\begin{array}{ll} (1) & (\rhd \cdot (\#C)^* \cdot \# \cdot \Sigma_0^*, xCx \to C, \Sigma_0^* \cdot (\# \cdot \Sigma_0^* \cdot C \cdot \Sigma_0^*)^* \cdot \lhd), \\ (2) & (\rhd \cdot (\#C)^+ \cdot \lhd, \textsf{Accept}). \end{array}$$

Obviously, $M_{\rm pal^+}$ is monotone, but it has unbounded word expansion. Thus, we obtain the following proper inclusions.

Corollary 2.6.19 ([167])

(a)	$\bigcup_{m \geq 0} \mathcal{L}_{\rm P}(\textsf{W}(m)\textsf{-lex-mon-RRWW})$	$\subsetneq$	$\mathcal{L}_{\rm P}(\textsf{lex-mon-RRWW})$.
(b)	$\bigcup_{m \geq 0} \mathcal{L}_{\rm P}(\textsf{W}(m)\textsf{-slex-RRWW})$	$\subsetneq$	$\mathcal{L}_{\rm P}(\textsf{slex-RRWW})$.
(c)	$\bigcup_{m \geq 0} \mathcal{L}_{\rm P}(\textsf{W}(m)\textsf{-lex-RRWW})$	$\subsetneq$	$\mathcal{L}_{\rm P}(\textsf{lex-RRWW})$.

By Theorem 2.6.17, we have three hierarchies of classes of proper languages that are based on the degree of word-expansion of lexicalized RRWW-automata. It remains to separate these hierarchies from each other.

First, we show that the classes of the monotone hierarchy are strictly contained in the corresponding classes of the non-monotone hierarchies. For this, it suffices to realize that there exists a deterministic RR-automaton M such that the input language $L = L(M)$ is not context-free (see, e.g., the language L_6 of Lemma 2.2.7). As a deterministic RR-automaton, M can also be seen as a strongly lexicalized RRWW-automaton with word-expansion 0. Since $L = L_C(M) = L_P(M)$, it follows that $L \in \mathcal{L}_P(\mathsf{W(0)\text{-}slex\text{-}RRWW})$. However, L is not the proper language of any monotone lexicalized RRWW-automaton by Theorem 2.6.8. Thus, we obtain the following separation result.

Corollary 2.6.20 ([167]) *For all* $m \geq 0$, $\mathcal{L}_P(\mathsf{W}(m)\text{-}\mathsf{lex\text{-}mon\text{-}RRWW}) \subsetneq \mathcal{L}_P(\mathsf{W}(m)\text{-}\mathsf{slex\text{-}RRWW})$.

Finally, we want to separate the hierarchy of proper languages of strongly lexicalized RRWW-automata from the corresponding hierarchy for lexicalized RRWW-automata. To this end, we consider the example language

$$L_{\text{expo}} = \{\, a^{i_0}ba^{i_1}b \cdots a^{i_{n-1}}ba^{i_n} \mid n \geq 0,\ i_0, i_1, \ldots, i_n \geq 0, \text{ and } \exists m \geq 0 : \sum_{j=0}^{n} 2^j \cdot i_j = 2^m \,\} \cup \{b\}^*$$

from Definition 2.4.12 (d), for which we have the following result.

Proposition 2.6.21 ([167]) $L_{\text{expo}} \in \mathcal{L}_P(\mathsf{W(0)\text{-}lex\text{-}RRWW}) \smallsetminus \mathcal{L}_P(\mathsf{slex\text{-}RRWW})$.

Proof. By Lemma 2.4.13 (d), L_{expo} is accepted by a deterministic RW-automaton. It follows that L_{expo} is the proper language of a lexicalized RRWW-automaton with word expansion 0.

On the other hand, assume that M' is a strongly lexicalized RRWW-automaton with input alphabet Σ_0 and tape alphabet Γ such that $L_{\text{expo}} = L_P(M')$ holds. Then a contradiction can be derived in the same way as in the proof of Proposition 2.6.7. Thus, it follows that L_{expo} is not the proper language of any strongly lexicalized RRWW-automaton. □

The inclusion results on the classes of proper languages of the various types of lexicalized RRWW-automata are summarized in the diagram in Figure 2.20.

It is known that it is decidable whether a given RRWW-automaton is monotone (see Theorem 2.1.47). In fact, the properties of being lexicalized and of having word-expansion of finite degree are also decidable.

Proposition 2.6.22 ([167]) *The following problems are decidable:*

(a)	*INSTANCE:*	*A deterministic RRWW-automaton M and an integer $j \geq 1$.*
	QUESTION:	*Is M lexicalized with constant j?*
(b)	*INSTANCE:*	*A deterministic RRWW-automaton M.*
	QUESTION:	*Is M lexicalized?*
(c)	*INSTANCE:*	*A lexicalized RRWW-automaton M and an integer $m \geq 0$.*
	QUESTION:	*Does M have word-expansion m?*
(d)	*INSTANCE:*	*A lexicalized RRWW-automaton M.*
	QUESTION:	*Does M have word-expansion of finite degree?*

Proof. Let $M = (Q, \Sigma, \Gamma, \rhd, \lhd, q_0, k, \delta)$ be a deterministic RRWW-automaton that is given through a sequence of rewriting meta-instructions $(E_{i,1}, u_i \to v_i, E_{i,2})_{1 \leq i \leq r}$ and an accepting meta-instruction (E_0, Accept). Then LEFT is used to denote the language that is described by the regular expression $\text{LEFT} = E_0 \cup \bigcup_{i=1}^{r}(E_{i,1} \cdot u_i \cdot E_{i,2})$. It consists of those words to which some meta-instruction of M applies. Thus, $\text{LEFT} = \text{NIR}(M)$. Then M is lexicalized with constant j if and only if $\text{LEFT} \subseteq \Delta^{\leq j} \cdot (\Sigma \cdot \Delta^{\leq j})^*$, where $\Delta = \Gamma \smallsetminus \Sigma$. Hence, it is decidable whether M is lexicalized with constant j.

Furthermore, for the set LEFT, we can effectively construct a deterministic finite-state acceptor A. Then the number p of states of A can serve as the constant in the pumping lemma for the regular language LEFT. Now, M is not lexicalized if and only if there exists a word in the

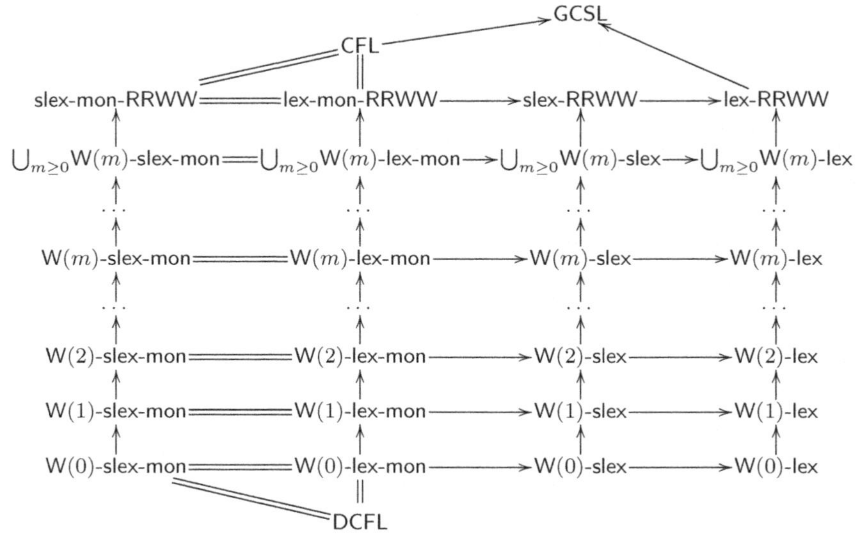

Figure 2.20: Inclusion relations between the classes of proper languages that are defined by various types of lexicalized RRWW-automata. Here W(m)-slex-mon denotes the language class $\mathcal{L}_P$(W(m)-slex-mon-RRWW), and similarly for the other classes. Classes that are not connected by a sequence of arrows are incomparable under inclusion.

language LEFT that contains a factor from Δ^* of length p. Thus, M is lexicalized if and only if it is lexicalized with constant $p-1$. This, however, is decidable, as seen above.

Next, observe that M has word expansion m if and only if the regular language $\text{LEFT}_\Delta = \pi_\Delta(\text{LEFT})$ satisfies the condition $\text{LEFT}_\Delta \subseteq \Delta^{\leq m}$. Finally, M has word-expansion of finite degree if and only if it has word expansion of degree $p'-1$, where p' is the pumping constant for the language LEFT_Δ. As above, this constant can be determined from LEFT_Δ. □

Based on the above results, the minimal constant j of lexicalization can be determined for a given lexicalized RRWW-automaton. Also the minimal degree of word-expansion can be computed, in case it is finite. In contrast to the above results, we have the following undecidability result for languages.

Proposition 2.6.23 ([167]) *The following property of languages is undecidable:*

INSTANCE:	*A context-free language L and a constant $m \in \mathbb{N}$.*
QUESTION:	*Is $L \in \mathcal{L}_P$(W(m)-lex-mon-RRWW)?*

Proof. For $m = 0$, this is simply the problem of deciding whether a given context-free language is deterministic context-free, which is known to be undecidable (see, e.g., [81]). For $m \geq 1$, consider the language $L_m = L \cdot \# \cdot L_p(m)$, where we assume that $\#$ is not contained in the alphabet of L. To accept the suffix $L_p(m)$, we need m occurrences of auxiliary letters according to Proposition 2.6.16. As we only consider RRWW-automata that are deterministic and monotone, this implies that $L_m \in \mathcal{L}_P(\text{W}(m)\text{-lex-mon-RRWW})$ if and only if $L \in$ DCFL. This means that the problem of deciding whether or not L_m is accepted by a monotone lexicalized RRWW-automaton with word-expansion m is undecidable. □

For each lexicalized RRWW-automaton, the word-expansion is bounded from above by a linear function.

Problem 2.6.24 *Is there a language that is not the proper language of any lexicalized RRWW-automata with a constant degree of word-expansion, but that is the proper language of a lexicalized*

RRWW-automaton for which the degree of word-expansion is bounded from above by a slowly growing sublinear function?

Next, we turn to the extension of the above study of proper languages to the freely rewriting restarting automata presented in [209] and [222]. In Section 2.5, we introduced some constraints for freely rewriting restarting automata that we then used to characterize word order complexity and word order freedom. Recall that we used the prefix j-constr- to denote the subclasses of restarting automata that execute only j-constrained computations, which means that these automata are j-monotone and j-rewriting. While, in Section 2.5, we concentrated on characteristic languages of FsRRWW-automata, we now study proper languages of (lexicalized) FRRWW-automata.

Obviously, Definition 2.6.5 extends to FRRWW-automata. Thus, a *lexicalized* FRRWW-automaton M is a deterministic FRRWW-automaton such that no word from the set $\mathrm{NIR}(M)$ contains a factor of length larger than j that only consists of auxiliary letters, where j is a positive integer depending on M. In addition, if all rewrite steps of M are deletions, then M is a strongly lexicalized FRRWW-automaton.

Proposition 2.6.6 states that the proper language of a lexicalized RRWW-automaton is necessarily growing context-sensitive. For lexicalized FRRWW-automata, however, we only have the following weaker result, as one can easily design a two-rewriting RRW-automaton for the marked copy language $L'_{\mathrm{copy}} = \{\, wcw \mid w \in \{a,b\}^* \,\} \notin \mathsf{GCSL}$.

Proposition 2.6.25 ([209, 222]) *If M is a lexicalized FRRWW-automaton, then the proper language $L_{\mathrm{P}}(M)$ of M is context-sensitive.*

Also the notion of *word expansion m* from Definition 2.6.10 extends to lexicalized FRRWW-automata. The following result gives an upper bound for the complexity of the membership problem for the proper language $L_{\mathrm{P}}(M)$ of a lexicalized FRRWW-automaton with word expansion m.

Theorem 2.6.26 ([222]) *For all $m \in \mathbb{N}$, if M is a $W(m)$-lex-FRRWW-automaton, then the membership problem for the language $L_{\mathrm{P}}(M)$ is solvable deterministically in time $\mathcal{O}(n^{m+2})$.*

This result is proved in the same way as the corresponding result for lexicalized RRWW-automata (Theorem 2.6.11) by using the fact that, for a deterministic FRRWW-automaton M, the membership problem for the language $L_{\mathrm{C}}(M)$ is decidable in quadratic time (Corollary 1.9.16).

By employing the following example languages, two-dimensional hierarchies of classes of proper languages of (strongly) lexicalized FRRWW-automata are derived in [222]. Let $\Sigma_0 = \{a,b\}$, let c and d be two additional letters, and let L_{rp}, $L_{\mathrm{d}}(j)$, and $L_{\mathrm{dp}}(i,j)$ be the following languages:

- $L_{\mathrm{rp}} = \{\, wwc \mid w \in \Sigma_0^* \,\}$,
- $L_{\mathrm{d}}(j) = \{\, (wc)^j dw^R \mid w \in \Sigma_0^* \,\}$ for all $j \in \mathbb{N}_+$,
- $L_{\mathrm{dp}}(i,j) = (L_{\mathrm{rp}})^i \cdot \{d\} \cdot L_{\mathrm{d}}(j)$ for all $i \geq 1$ and $j \geq 2$.

For processing the language $L_{\mathrm{d}}(j)$, no auxiliary letters are needed, but at least j rewrite steps per cycle are required, that is, for each $j \geq 1$, the language $L_{\mathrm{d}}(j)$ is the proper language of a j-constrained strongly lexicalized RRWW-automaton of word expansion 0. On the other hand, for each $j \geq 2$, $L_{\mathrm{d}}(j)$ is not the proper language of any $(j-1)$-rewriting RRWW-automaton [222]. In contrast to the situation for $L_{\mathrm{d}}(j)$, the language $L^i_{\mathrm{rp}} = (L_{\mathrm{rp}})^i$ is the proper language of a 2-constrained strongly lexicalized RRWW-automaton with word expansion i, that is, it only requires two rewrite steps per cycle, but, in that case, it needs word expansion i. However, for all $i,j \geq 1$, L^i_{rp} is not the proper language of any (1-rewriting) RRWW-automaton nor the proper language of any j-rewriting lexicalized RRWW-automaton with word expansion $(i-1)$ [222]. By combining these results, we see that, for all $i \geq 1$ and all $j \geq 2$, $L_{\mathrm{dp}}(i,j)$ is the proper language of a j-constrained strongly lexicalized RRWW-automaton with word expansion i, but it is neither the proper language of any $(j-1)$-rewriting RRWW-automaton nor the proper language of any lexicalized MRRWW-automaton with word expansion $(i-1)$. This yields the following hierarchy results.

Theorem 2.6.27 ([222]) *For all $i \geq 0$, and for all $j \geq 1$, we have the following proper inclusions:*

(a) $\mathcal{L}_P(\mathsf{W}(i)\text{-}j\text{-}\mathsf{constr}\text{-}(\mathsf{s})\mathsf{lex}\text{-}\mathsf{RRWW}) \subsetneq \mathcal{L}_P(\mathsf{W}(i+1)\text{-}j\text{-}\mathsf{constr}\text{-}(\mathsf{s})\mathsf{lex}\text{-}\mathsf{RRWW})$.
(b) $\mathcal{L}_P(\mathsf{W}(i)\text{-}j\text{-}\mathsf{r}\text{-}(\mathsf{s})\mathsf{lex}\text{-}\mathsf{RRWW}) \subsetneq \mathcal{L}_P(\mathsf{W}(i+1)\text{-}j\text{-}\mathsf{r}\text{-}(\mathsf{s})\mathsf{lex}\text{-}\mathsf{RRWW})$.
(c) $\mathcal{L}_P(\mathsf{W}(i)\text{-}j\text{-}\mathsf{constr}\text{-}(\mathsf{s})\mathsf{lex}\text{-}\mathsf{RRWW}) \subsetneq \mathcal{L}_P(\mathsf{W}(i)\text{-}(j+1)\text{-}\mathsf{constr}\text{-}(\mathsf{s})\mathsf{lex}\text{-}\mathsf{RRWW})$.
(d) $\mathcal{L}_P(\mathsf{W}(i)\text{-}j\text{-}\mathsf{r}\text{-}(\mathsf{s})\mathsf{lex}\text{-}\mathsf{RRWW}) \subsetneq \mathcal{L}_P(\mathsf{W}(i)\text{-}(j+1)\text{-}\mathsf{r}\text{-}(\mathsf{s})\mathsf{lex}\text{-}\mathsf{RRWW})$.
(e) $\mathcal{L}_P(j\text{-}\mathsf{constr}\text{-}(\mathsf{s})\mathsf{lex}\text{-}\mathsf{RRWW}) \subsetneq \mathcal{L}_P((j+1)\text{-}\mathsf{constr}\text{-}(\mathsf{s})\mathsf{lex}\text{-}\mathsf{RRWW})$.
(f) $\mathcal{L}_P(j\text{-}\mathsf{r}\text{-}(\mathsf{s})\mathsf{lex}\text{-}\mathsf{RRWW}) \subsetneq \mathcal{L}_P((j+1)\text{-}\mathsf{r}\text{-}(\mathsf{s})\mathsf{lex}\text{-}\mathsf{RRWW})$.

Observe that the inclusions in (a) and (b) contain Theorem 2.6.17 as the special case $j = 1$, while the inclusions in (c) and (d) contain Corollary 2.5.49 as the special case $i = 0$.

As 1-r-lex-RRWW-automata coincide with lexicalized RRWW-automata, we recall from above that the class of proper languages of 1-r-lex-RRWW-automata is a proper subclass of the class of growing context-sensitive languages, while each class $\mathcal{L}_P$(W(i)-j-constr-(s)lex-RRWW), $j \geq 2$, contains languages that are not growing context-sensitive.

In order to separate the classes of proper languages of (strongly) lexicalized FRRWW-automata with unbounded degree of word expansion or unbounded number of rewrites per cycle from those with bounded degree of word expansion or bounded number of rewrites per cycle, the additional example languages

$$L_{\mathrm{d}^+} = \bigcup_{j\geq 1} L_{\mathrm{d}}(j) \text{ and } L_{\mathrm{rp}^+} = \bigcup_{j\geq 1} (L_{\mathrm{rp}})^j$$

are considered in [222]. It is established there that L_{d^+} is the proper language of a strongly lexicalized FRRWW-automaton of word expansion 0, but that this language is not the proper language of any lexicalized MRRWW-automaton. Moreover, L_{rp^+} is the proper language of a 2-constrained strongly lexicalized RRWW-automaton, but it is not the proper language of any lexicalized MRRWW-automaton with finitely bounded word expansion. Thus, we have the following proper inclusions, where the case $j = 1$ in (a) and (b) corresponds to Corollary 2.6.19.

Corollary 2.6.28 ([222])

(a) $\bigcup_{i\geq 0} \mathcal{L}_P(\mathsf{W}(i)\text{-}j\text{-}\mathsf{constr}\text{-}(\mathsf{s})\mathsf{lex}\text{-}\mathsf{RRWW}) \subsetneq \mathcal{L}_P(j\text{-}\mathsf{constr}\text{-}(\mathsf{s})\mathsf{lex}\text{-}\mathsf{RRWW})$ *for all* $j \geq 1$.
(b) $\bigcup_{i\geq 0} \mathcal{L}_P(\mathsf{W}(i)\text{-}j\text{-}\mathsf{r}\text{-}(\mathsf{s})\mathsf{lex}\text{-}\mathsf{RRWW}) \subsetneq \mathcal{L}_P(j\text{-}\mathsf{r}\text{-}(\mathsf{s})\mathsf{lex}\text{-}\mathsf{RRWW})$ *for all* $j \geq 1$.
(c) $\bigcup_{j\geq 1} \mathcal{L}_P(j\text{-}\mathsf{r}\text{-}(\mathsf{s})\mathsf{lex}\text{-}\mathsf{RRWW}) \subsetneq \mathcal{L}_P((\mathsf{s})\mathsf{lex}\text{-}\mathsf{FRRWW})$.

Finally, to separate the hierarchy of proper languages of strongly lexicalized FRRWW-automata from the corresponding hierarchy for lexicalized FRRWW-automata, the example language

$$L^{(1)}_{\mathrm{expo}} = \{\, a^{2^n} \mid n \geq 0 \,\} \cup \{\, a^i b a^j \mid i, j \geq 0, \text{ and } \exists m \geq 1 : i + 2 \cdot j = 2^m \,\}$$

is considered in [222]. This language, which is accepted by a (stateless) det-RRW-automaton by Lemma 2.4.28, is the proper language of a lexicalized RRWW-automaton of word expansion 0, but it is not the proper language of any strongly lexicalized MRRWW-automaton. Analogously, it can be shown that the language $L_{\mathrm{exp}} = \{\, a^{2^n} \mid n \geq 0 \,\}$ is not the proper language of any lexicalized MRRWW-automaton. This yields the following consequence (see also Proposition 2.6.7).

Corollary 2.6.29 ([222]) $\mathsf{CRL} \not\subseteq \bigcup_{j\geq 1} \mathcal{L}_P(j\text{-}\mathsf{r}\text{-}\mathsf{lex}\text{-}\mathsf{RRWW})$.

As $L^{(1)}_{\mathrm{expo}}$ is not context-free, we see from Theorem 2.6.8 that $L^{(1)}_{\mathrm{expo}} \notin \mathcal{L}_P(\mathsf{1}\text{-}\mathsf{constr}\text{-}\mathsf{lex}\text{-}\mathsf{RRWW})$. In fact, even the following stronger result holds.

Proposition 2.6.30 ([222]) $L^{(1)}_{\mathrm{expo}} \notin \mathcal{L}_P(j\text{-}\mathsf{constr}\text{-}\mathsf{lex}\text{-}\mathsf{RRWW})$ *for any* $j \in \mathbb{N}_+$.

In summary, we obtain the following proper inclusions.

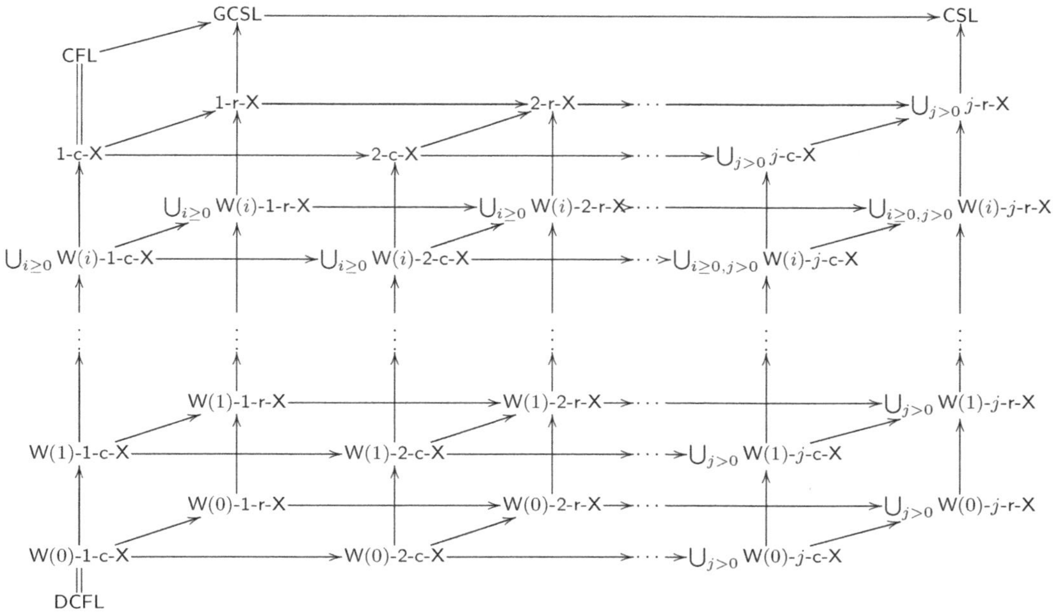

Figure 2.21: Inclusion relations between classes of proper language defined by various types of lexicalized RRWW-automata. Here W(i)-j-r-X denotes the language class $\mathcal{L}_{\mathrm{P}}$(W(i)-j-r-X) and W(i)-j-c-X denotes the language class $\mathcal{L}_{\mathrm{P}}$(W(i)-j-constr-X), where X stands for the type of restarting automaton lex-RRWW or slex-RRWW. Classes that are not connected by a sequence of arrows are incomparable under inclusion (but see Problem 2.6.34).

Corollary 2.6.31 ([222]) *For all $j \geq 1$,*

(a) $\mathcal{L}_{\mathrm{P}}$(W(i)-j-constr-lex-RRWW) $\subsetneq$ $\mathcal{L}_{\mathrm{P}}$(W(i)-j-r-lex-RRWW) *for all $i \in \mathbb{N}$.*
(b) $\mathcal{L}_{\mathrm{P}}$(j-constr-lex-RRWW) $\subsetneq$ $\mathcal{L}_{\mathrm{P}}$(j-r-lex-RRWW).

Using the encoding $\varphi : \{a,b\}^* \to \{a,b\}^*$ defined by $a \mapsto ab$ and $b \mapsto b$, we obtain the language $\hat{L}^{(1)}_{\mathrm{expo}} = \varphi(L^{(1)}_{\mathrm{expo}})$. By Lemma 2.4.13 (e), $L^{(\varphi)}_{\mathrm{expo}} \in \mathcal{L}$(stl-det-R), and hence, $\hat{L}^{(1)}_{\mathrm{expo}} \in \mathcal{L}_{\mathrm{P}}$(W(0)-1-r-slex-RRWW). On the other hand, we have the following negative result.

Proposition 2.6.32 ([222]) $\hat{L}^{(1)}_{\mathrm{expo}} \notin \mathcal{L}_{\mathrm{P}}$($j$-constr-slex-RRWW) *for any $j \in \mathbb{N}_+$.*

Thus, we also have the following proper inclusions.

Corollary 2.6.33 ([222]) *For all $j \geq 1$,*

(a) $\mathcal{L}_{\mathrm{P}}$(W(i)-j-constr-slex-RRWW) $\subsetneq$ $\mathcal{L}_{\mathrm{P}}$(W(i)-j-r-slex-RRWW) *for all $i \in \mathbb{N}$.*
(b) $\mathcal{L}_{\mathrm{P}}$(j-constr-slex-RRWW) $\subsetneq$ $\mathcal{L}_{\mathrm{P}}$(j-r-slex-RRWW).

The above results on the influence that the number of rewrites per cycle and the number of auxiliary letters that may appear concurently on the tape have on the expressive capacity of (strongly) lexicalized RRWW-automata yield two-dimensional hierarchies of classes of proper languages. These hierarchies are shown in the diagram in Figure 2.21. In this diagram, language classes which are not connected (by an oriented path) are incomparable under inclusion. The only possible exception concerns the following problem, which remains open.

Problem 2.6.34 *Is the class CFL of context-free languages contained in the class of proper languages $\bigcup_{i\geq 0,j>0} \mathcal{L}_{\mathrm{P}}$(W($i$)-$j$-r-lex-RRWW)?*

It has been conjectured in [222] that the context-free language

$$L^{+}_{\text{pal}} = \{ w_1 w_1^R w_2 w_2^R \cdots w_n w_n^R \mid n \geq 1, w_1, w_2, \ldots, w_n \in \Sigma_0^* \}$$

is not the proper language of any W(i)-j-lex-RRWW-automaton, as it appears that in order to accept an expanded version of a word of the form $w_1 w_1^R w_2 w_2^R \cdots w_n w_n^R$, a lexicalized RRWW-automaton needs n occurrences of auxiliary letters, one for each factor $w_i w_i^R$.

2.6.2 On H-Proper Languages and H-Lexicalized Restarting Automata

Here we study h-lexicalized restarting automata and h-proper languages. In this setting, auxiliary letters cannot be used freely to encode information on the tape of a restarting automaton, as each auxiliary letter will be closely related to an input letter. However, in this subsection, we use a slight modification of the definition of the RRWW- and RLWW-automaton (see Definitions 1.9.1 and 2.1.1) in that

(∗) we require that by a length-reducing rewrite transition, the read/write window of the automaton is not moved but just refilled from the left, and

(∗∗) M does not execute any rewrite steps in tail computations.

Requirement (∗) means that, when an RLWW-automaton M executes a rewrite transition $(q', v) \in \delta(q, u)$ in a configuration $\rhd xquy\lhd$, then this step yields the configuration $\rhd x_1 q' x_2 vq\lhd$, where $x = x_1 x_2$ and $|x_2| = |u| - |v|$. It is easily seen, however, that these changes do not influence the expressive capacity of RRWW- and RLWW-automata.

We begin with defining the central notion of this subsection.

Definition 2.6.35 ([224, 221]) *An* h-lexicalized FRLWW-automaton, *or* hFRLWW-automaton, *is a pair $\hat{M} = (M, h)$, where $M = (Q, \Sigma, \Gamma, \rhd, \lhd, q_0, k, \delta)$ is an FRLWW-automaton and $h : \Gamma \to \Sigma$ is a letter-to-letter morphism such that $h(a) = a$ for all input letters $a \in \Sigma$. The* input language *$L(\hat{M})$ of $\hat{M}$ is simply the language $L(M)$ and the* characteristic language *$L_C(\hat{M})$ of $\hat{M}$ is the language $L_C(M)$. Furthermore, we take $L_{hP}(\hat{M}) = h(L_C(M))$, and we say that $\hat{M}$* accepts the *h-proper language $L_{hP}(\hat{M})$. In addition, the relation*

$$L_A(\hat{M}) = \{ (h(w), w) \mid w \in L_C(M) \}$$

is called the h-lexicalized syntactic analysis *(hLSA) by $\hat{M}$.*

Clearly, this definition extends to all types of restarting automata. If X is a type of restarting automaton, then $\mathcal{L}_{hP}(\mathsf{X})$ is used to denote the class of h-proper languages of restarting automata of type X, and $\mathcal{L}_A(\mathsf{X})$ denotes the corresponding class of h-lexicalized syntactic analyses.

Obviously, for each h-lexicalized restarting automaton $\hat{M} = (M, h)$, we have

$$L(\hat{M}) \subseteq L_{hP}(\hat{M}) = h(L_C(\hat{M})),$$

as $L(\hat{M}) \subseteq L_C(\hat{M})$ and $h(w) = w$ for all input words w. Moreover, if M is an FRLW-automaton, that is, it does not have auxiliary letters, then $L(\hat{M}) = L_{hP}(\hat{M}) = L_C(\hat{M})$.

We point out that the h-syntactic analysis defined above formalizes the linguistic notion of *lexical sentence disambiguation.* Each auxiliary letter $x \in \Gamma \smallsetminus \Sigma$ occurring in a word from $L_C(\hat{M})$ can be considered as a disambiguated form of the input letter $h(x)$. For an input word (or a sentence of a natural language) w_{inp}, the h-lexicalized syntactic analysis $L_A(\hat{M})$ represents all disambiguated versions of the word w_{inp} in the form of pairs $(w_{\text{inp}}, w) \in L_A(\hat{M})$, where $w \in L_C(\hat{M})$ is one of the syntactically correct lexical disambiguations of the input word w_{inp}.

To illustrate the restriction placed on h-proper languages, we return to the example language $L_{\text{exp}} = \{ a^{2^n} \mid n \geq 0 \}$. From Example 1.2.16 and Theorem 1.2.19, we know that L_{exp} is the input language of a deterministic RWW-automaton, but recall from Proposition 2.6.7 that L_{exp} is not the proper language of any lexicalized RRWW-automaton. In fact, L_{exp} is not the h-proper language of any hRLWW-automaton, either.

Proposition 2.6.36 ([224, 221]) $L_{\exp} \notin \mathcal{L}_{\mathrm{hP}}(\mathsf{hRLWW})$.

Proof. Assume that $\hat{M} = (M, h)$ is an hRLWW-automaton, where $M = (Q, \{a\}, \Gamma, \triangleright, \triangleleft, q_0, k, \delta)$, such that $L_{\mathrm{hP}}(\hat{M}) = h(L_{\mathrm{C}}(M)) = L_{\exp}$. Let $z = a^{2^n} \in L_{\exp}$, where n is a sufficiently large integer satisfying $2^n - k > 2^{n-1}$ such that the accepting computation of M for some input word $w \in L_{\mathrm{C}}(M)$ satisfying $h(w) = z$ contains at least one cycle. It is easily seen that such a word w exists, since, otherwise, the characteristic language $L_{\mathrm{C}}(M)$ of M would be a regular set, and then so would be the language $L_{\mathrm{hP}}(\hat{M})$. The accepting computation on w begins with a cycle of the form $q_0 \triangleright w \triangleleft \vdash^{c}_{M} q_0 \triangleright w' \triangleleft$. As this cycle is a part of an accepting computation, it follows that $w' \in L_{\mathrm{C}}(M)$, which in turn implies that $h(w') \in L_{\exp}$. Thus, $h(w') = a^m$ for some integer m satisfying $2^n - k \leq m < 2^n$. As $2^{n-1} < 2^n - k \leq m < 2^n$, this is a contradiction. Hence, $L_{\exp}$ is not the h-proper language of any hRLWW-automaton. □

Below, we need some constrained types of rewrite steps motivated by different types of linguistic reductions.

Definition 2.6.37 ([221]) *Let $\hat{M} = (M, h)$ be an h-lexicalized restarting automaton.*

(a) *A* delete-left step *is a length-reducing rewrite step $(q', \mathsf{DL}(v)) \in \delta(q, u)$, where v is a proper scattered subword of u, containing all the sentinels from u (if any). It causes M to replace u with v (by deleting excessive letters), to enter state q', and to refill the window from the left.*

(b) *A* contextual-left step *is a delete-left step $(q', \mathsf{CL}(v)) \in \delta(q, u)$, where $u = v_1 u_1 v_2 u_2 v_3$, $u_1, u_2 \in \Gamma^*$, $|u_1 u_2| \geq 1$, and $v = v_1 v_2 v_3$, such that v contains all the sentinels from u (if any). It causes M to replace u with v (by deleting the factors u_1 and u_2 of u), to enter state q', and to refill the window from the left.*

An RLW-automaton all rewrite steps of which are DL-steps is an RL-automaton. It is called an *RLC*-automaton if all its rewrite steps are CL-steps. Furthermore, an (h)RLWW-automaton is called an *(h)RLWWD-automaton* or an *(h)RLWWC-automaton*, if all its rewrite steps are DL-steps or CL-steps. Observe that, when concentrating on input languages, DL- and CL-steps ensure that no auxiliary letters can ever occur on the tape; if, however, we are interested in characteristic or h-proper languages, then auxiliary letters can play an important role even though a given (h)RLWW-automaton only uses DL- or CL-steps. Therefore, we distinguish between (h)RLWWD- and (h)RL-automata and between (h)RLWWC- and (h)RLC-automata.

A restriction of the form of restarting automata called *strong cyclic form* (see [85]) can also be transferred to hFRLWW-automata. An hFRLWW-automaton $\hat{M} = (M, h)$ is said to be in *strong cyclic form* if $|uv| \leq k$ for each final configuration $\triangleright uqv \triangleleft$ of M, where k is the size of the read/write window of M. Thus, before M can halt, it must erase sufficiently many letters from its tape. The prefix scf- will be used to denote restarting automata that are in the strong cyclic form. The concept of strong cyclic form is useful for techniques of grammar-checking (localization of syntactic errors) by hFRLWW-automata. Lemma 2.6.38 below shows that every hFRLWW-automaton can be transformed into an equivalent hFRLWW-automaton in strong cyclic form. Its proof follows the one for the corresponding result for the input languages of RLWW-automata given in [85] – it can be found in [165].

Lemma 2.6.38 ([165]) *Let $\hat{M} = (M, h)$ be an hFRLWW-automaton. Then there exists an FRLWW-automaton M_{scf} in the strong cyclic form such that $L_{\mathrm{C}}(M) = L_{\mathrm{C}}(M_{\mathrm{scf}})$ and, for all words u, v, $q_0 \triangleright u \triangleleft \vdash^{c^*}_{M} q_0 \triangleright v \triangleleft$ implies that $q_0 \triangleright u \triangleleft \vdash^{c^*}_{M_{\mathrm{scf}}} q_0 \triangleright v \triangleleft$. Moreover, all rewrite steps of M_{scf} that are not possible for M are in contextual form. If M is deterministic and/or j-monotone for some $j \geq 1$, then M_{scf} is deterministic and/or j-monotone as well.*

The class DCFL of deterministic context-free languages is characterized as the class of characteristic languages of monotone deterministic RRWW- and RRWWD-automata (see Corollary 2.1.43). In fact, from the proof outline of Theorem 2.1.42, even $\mathsf{DCFL} = \mathcal{L}_{\mathrm{C}}(\mathsf{det\text{-}mon\text{-}RRWWC})$ follows. Moreover, the class LRR of left-to-right regular languages has been characterized as $\mathsf{LRR} =$

$\mathcal{L}(\mathsf{det\text{-}mon\text{-}RL}) = \mathcal{L}(\mathsf{det\text{-}mon\text{-}(s)RLW(W)})$ (see Theorem 2.1.56), which implies that LRR coincides with the class of characteristic languages of monotone deterministic RLWW- and RLWWD-automata. In fact, using the above characterization of DCFL by det-mon-RLWWC-automata, the proof of Theorem 2.1.56 can easily be extended to yield $\mathsf{LRR} = \mathcal{L}_{\mathrm{C}}(\mathsf{det\text{-}mon\text{-}RLWWC})$. Interestingly, the h-proper languages of det-mon-hRRWW(C)- and det-mon-hRLWW(C)-automata correspond to the context-free languages.

Theorem 2.6.39 ([223]) $\mathsf{CFL} = \mathcal{L}_{\mathrm{hP}}(\mathsf{det\text{-}mon\text{-}hRRWW(C)}) = \mathcal{L}_{\mathrm{hP}}(\mathsf{det\text{-}mon\text{-}hRLWW(C)})$
$= \mathcal{L}_{\mathrm{hP}}(\mathsf{mon\text{-}hRRWW(C)}) = \mathcal{L}_{\mathrm{hP}}(\mathsf{mon\text{-}hRLWW(C)})$.

This characterization is proved in [223] by exploiting the same strategy as in the proof of Theorem 2.6.8.

A restarting automaton M is in the *weak cyclic form* if $|uv| \leq k$ for each accepting final configuration $\triangleright uqv \triangleleft$ of M, where k is the size of the read/write window of M. Thus, in contrast to the strong cyclic form, here the length restriction applies only to final configurations that are accepting. We use the prefix wcf- to denote types of restarting automata that are in weak cyclic form. From the above characterizations of the language classes DCFL, LRR, and CFL, we obtain the following consequence by Lemma 2.6.38 and its extension to one-way restarting automata.

Corollary 2.6.40 ([165, 169, 221])

(a) $\mathsf{DCFL} = \mathcal{L}_{\mathrm{C}}(\mathsf{wcf\text{-}det\text{-}mon\text{-}RRWW}) = \mathcal{L}_{\mathrm{C}}(\mathsf{wcf\text{-}det\text{-}mon\text{-}RRWWC})$.

(b) $\mathsf{LRR} = \mathcal{L}_{\mathrm{C}}(\mathsf{scf\text{-}det\text{-}mon\text{-}RLWW}) = \mathcal{L}_{\mathrm{C}}(\mathsf{scf\text{-}det\text{-}mon\text{-}RLWWC})$.

(c) $\mathsf{CFL} = \mathcal{L}_{\mathrm{hP}}(\mathsf{wcf\text{-}det\text{-}mon\text{-}hRRWW(C)}) = \mathcal{L}_{\mathrm{hP}}(\mathsf{scf\text{-}det\text{-}mon\text{-}hRLWW(C)})$
$= \mathcal{L}_{\mathrm{hP}}(\mathsf{wcf\text{-}mon\text{-}hRRWW(C)}) = \mathcal{L}_{\mathrm{hP}}(\mathsf{scf\text{-}mon\text{-}hRLWW(C)})$.

Thus, while the characteristic languages of monotone deterministic RRWW- and RLWW-automata are the deterministic context-free and left-to-right regular languages, respectively, the h-proper languages of these types of automata yield all context-free languages, even if we require that the automata considered are in weak, respectively strong, cyclic form.

Let $\mathsf{CFL}_{\mathrm{A}}$ denote the class of *lexicalized syntactic analyses* of det-mon-hRLWW-automata that are in the strong cyclic form, that is, $\mathsf{CFL}_{\mathrm{A}} = \mathcal{L}_{\mathrm{A}}(\mathsf{scf\text{-}det\text{-}mon\text{-}hRLWW})$. Using this notion, we can extend the concept of context-freeness from languages to lexicalized syntactic analyses.

Corollary 2.6.41 ([165]) *For all* $X \in \{\mathsf{hRLWW}, \mathsf{hRLWWD}, \mathsf{hRLWWC}\}$,

$$\mathsf{CFL}_{\mathrm{A}} = \mathcal{L}_{\mathrm{A}}(\mathsf{scf\text{-}det\text{-}mon\text{-}}X).$$

Proof. We first recall the definition of $\mathcal{L}_{\mathrm{A}}(X)$. For a class of restarting automata X, a set of pairs P belongs to the class $\mathcal{L}_{\mathrm{A}}(X)$ if there are a restarting automaton M of type X and a letter-to-letter homomorphism h such that

$$P = \{\, (h(w), w) \mid w \in L_{\mathrm{C}}(M) \,\}.$$

The above result now follows from Corollary 2.6.40. □

In the following, we study the characteristic and h-proper languages and hLSAs of hRLWW-automata in strong cyclic form. As it will turn out, these automata (and their variants) are sensitive to several types of constraints as, e.g., the window size, the number of rewrites per cycle, and the degree of monotonicity. Through these constraints, we essentially refine the Chomsky hierarchy, and we do so in two phases. In phase one, we refine the context-sensitive languages by the number of rewrites per cycle and the degree of monotonicity. Then, by using the window size, we refine the individual areas that are given by the number of rewrites per cycle and the degree of monotonicity. We have seen in Subsection 2.3.1 that, for various subclasses of RLW-automata, the window size induces an infinite ascending hierarchy of classes of (input) languages. Also, for the number of rewrites per cycle and the degree of monotonicity, corresponding results were presented in Subsections 2.5.1 and 2.5.2.

Recall that, for any type X of restarting automaton and $k, j \in \mathbb{N}_+$, $\mathsf{X(k)}$ denotes those restarting automata of type X that have a read/write window of size k, j-r-X denotes the class of automata of type X that execute up to j rewrite steps in each cycle (see Definition 2.5.1), and j-mon-X denotes the class of automata of type X that are j-monotone (see Definition 2.5.22). Finally, we use $\mathsf{fin}(j)$-X to denote the class of automata of type X that execute at most j cycles in any accepting computation, and $\mathsf{fin\text{-}X} = \bigcup_{j \geq 0} \mathsf{fin}(j)\text{-}\mathsf{X}$.

In traditional and corpus linguistics, only finite language phenomena can be observed directly. Accordingly, it is quite difficult to apply techniques and results from formal language theory in a linguistic setting. Now in combination with the strong cyclic form, the restriction on the number of allowed cycles in accepting computations allows us to carry results on restarting automata over to classes of finite languages.

Lemma 2.6.42 *Let $i, j, k \geq 1$, and let M be an i-rewriting fin(j)-RLWW-automaton of window size k that is in weak cyclic form. Then $|w| \leq (i \cdot j + 1) \cdot k$ for all words $w \in L_C(M)$.*

Proof. Let M be a fin(j)-i-r-RLWW(k)-automaton in weak cyclic form, where $i, j, k \geq 1$, and let $w \in L_C(M)$. Then $q_0 \rhd w \lhd \vdash_M^{c^*} q_0 \rhd z \lhd$ for some word $z \in L_C(M)$ satisfying $|z| \leq k$, as M is in weak cyclic form. This computation consists of at most j cycles, and during each cycle of this computation, at most i length-reducing rewrite steps are executed that each reduce the length of the tape contents by at most k letters. It follows that $|w| \leq k + i \cdot j \cdot k$. □

Thus, $L_C(M)$ and $L_{hP}(M)$ are finite languages for all wcf-fin(i)-j-r-hRLWW-automata. The following examples establish the sensitivity of characteristic and h-proper languages of scf-hRLWW-automata to the size of their windows, the number of rewrite operations within a cycle, and the degree of monotonicity. This is achieved by providing finite witness languages, which are as small as possible. In this way, it is shown that these sensitivities rely on small syntactic observations.

Proposition 2.6.43 ([165]) *Let $k \geq 2$, let a be a letter, and let $L_1(k) = \{a^k\}$. Then the following statements hold for the language $L_1(k)$:*

(a) $L_1(k) \in \mathcal{L}_C(\mathsf{scf\text{-}fin(0)\text{-}1\text{-}r\text{-}det\text{-}mon\text{-}RLWWC}(k))$.

(b) $L_1(k) \notin \mathcal{L}_C(\mathsf{scf}\text{-}j\text{-}\mathsf{r\text{-}hRLWW}(k-1)) \cup \mathcal{L}_{hP}(\mathsf{scf}\text{-}j\text{-}\mathsf{r\text{-}hRLWW}(k-1))$ *for any $j \geq 1$.*

This proposition shows that, for the separation of language classes based on the size of the read/write window, it suffices to consider witness languages of cardinality one.

Proof. (a) Let $M_1(k)$ be the deterministic RLWWC-automaton with window size k that proceeds as follows given a word $w = a^n$ as input:

1. If $n < k$, then $M_1(k)$ rejects in a tail computation.
2. If $n = k$, then $M_1(k)$ accepts in a tail computation after moving its window to the right sentinel.
3. If $n = i \cdot k$ for some $i \geq 2$, then $M_1(k)$ deletes the last occurrence of the letter a and restarts.
4. If $n = i \cdot k + j$ for some $i \geq 1$ and some $j \in \{1, 2, \ldots, k-1\}$, then $M_1(k)$ deletes the suffix a^k and restarts.

Observe that the rewrite operations in (3) and (4) can be realized by CL-steps. It is now easily seen that $L(M_1(k)) = L_C(M_1(k)) = L_1(k)$, that $M_1(k)$ is in strong cyclic form, and that it is monotone (of degree 1). Furthermore, as the only accepting computation of $M_1(k)$ consists of just a tail, $M_1(k)$ is a fin(0)-RLWWC(k)-automaton.

(b) For any scf-j-r-hRLWW($k-1$)-automaton M, the language $L_C(M)$ (and therewith the language $L_{hP}(M)$) is either empty or it contains at least one word of length at most $k-1$. As $L_1(k)$ only contains a word of length $k > k-1$, we see that $L_1(k)$ is neither the characteristic language nor the h-proper language of any scf-j-r-hRLWW-automaton of window size $k-1$. □

Obviously, no language the shortest word of which has length at least k can be the characteristic or h-proper language of any hRLWW$(k-1)$-automaton that is in strong cyclic form.

Proposition 2.6.44 ([165]) *Let $k, j \geq 1$, let a be a letter, and let $L_2(j,k) = \{a^{k\cdot(j+1)}, a^k\}$. Then the following statements hold for $L_2(j,k)$:*

(a) $L_2(j,k) \in \mathcal{L}_C(\textsf{scf-fin(1)-}j\textsf{-r-det-mon-RLWWC}(k))$.

(b) $L_2(j,k) \notin \mathcal{L}_C(\textsf{scf-}j'\textsf{-r-hRLWW}(k)) \cup \mathcal{L}_{hP}(\textsf{scf-}j'\textsf{-r-hRLWW}(k))$ *for any* $j' < j$.

This proposition shows that, for the separation of classes of characteristic or h-proper languages based on the number of rewrites that can be executed during a cycle, it suffices to consider witness languages of cardinality two.

Proof. (a) Let $M_2(j,k)$ be the deterministic j-rewriting RLWWC-automaton with window size k that proceeds as follows given the word a^n as input:

1. If $n < k$, then $M_2(j,k)$ rejects in a tail computation.
2. If $n = k$, then $M_2(j,k)$ accepts in a tail computation.
3. If $n = i \cdot k$ for some $2 \leq i \leq j$, then $M_2(j,k)$ rewrites the word a^n into the empty word by executing i rewrite steps, each of which deletes a suffix of the form a^k.
4. If $n = (j+1)\cdot k$, then $M_2(j,k)$ rewrites the word a^n into the word a^k by executing j rewrite steps, each of which deletes a suffix of the form a^k.
5. If $n = i \cdot k$ for some $i \geq j+3$, then $M_2(j,k)$ simply deletes the last occurrence of the letter a and restarts.
6. If $n = (j+2)\cdot k$, then $M_2(j,k)$ simply deletes the last occurrence of the letter a, if $k \geq 2$, or the suffix a^2, if $k = 1$, and restarts.
7. If $n = i \cdot k + \ell$ for some $i \geq 1$ and $\ell \in \{1, 2, \ldots, k-1\}$, then $M_2(j,k)$ simply deletes the suffix a^k and restarts.

Observe that all the rewrite operations above can be realized by CL-steps. It is easily seen that $L(M_2(j,k)) = L_C(M_2(j,k)) = L_2(j,k)$ and that $M_2(j,k)$ is in strong cyclic form. Due to our assumption that, during a rewrite step, the window is not moved but refilled from the left, all the rewrite steps in (3) and in (4) can be executed with the right distance $k+1$. It follows that $M_2(j,k)$ is monotone (of degree 1). Furthermore, each accepting computation of $M_2(j,k)$ consists of at most a single cycle and a tail, that is, $M_2(j,k)$ is an scf-fin(1)-j-r-det-mon-RLWWC(k)-automaton.

(b) Assume that M is a j'-r-hRLWW(k)-automaton in strong cyclic form such that $L_C(M) = L_2(j,k)$, where $j' < j$. As $a^{k\cdot(j+1)} \in L_2(j,k)$ and $|a^{k\cdot(j+1)}| = k\cdot(j+1) > k$, and as M is in strong cyclic form, each accepting computation of M on input $a^{k\cdot(j+1)}$ begins with a cycle. As a^k is the only other word in $L_2(j,k)$, this cycle must rewrite $a^{k\cdot(j+1)}$ into the word a^k, for which $j \cdot k$ letters must be deleted. However, as M has window size k and can only execute $j' < j$ many rewrite steps per cycle, we see that it can delete at most $j' \cdot k < j \cdot k$ many letters in a single cycle. This implies that $L_C(M) \neq L_2(j,k)$. Finally, as each word $w \in L_{hP}(M)$ corresponds to a word of the same length from $L_C(M)$, the argument above also shows that $L_{hP}(M) \neq L_2(j,k)$. □

The arguments above show that assertion (b) of Proposition 2.6.44 holds for any language for which the minimal difference between the lengths of its words is at least $j \cdot k$. Also it is easily seen that there is no language of cardinality one that has the same properties as the language $L_2(j,k)$.

Proposition 2.6.45 ([165]) *Let $k, j \geq 2$, $\Sigma = \{a, b, c\}$, $u_i = a^k$ for even i, and $u_i = b^k$ for odd i. Finally, let*

$$L_3(j,k) = \{\, (u_i u_{i+1} \cdots u_j c^{k\cdot j^2})^j \mid i = 1, 2, \ldots, j \,\} \cup \{\, c^{k\cdot j\cdot r} \mid 0 \leq r \leq j^2 \,\}.$$

Then the following statements hold for $L_3(j,k)$:

(a) $L_3(j,k) \in \mathcal{L}_C(\textsf{scf-fin}(j+j^2)\textsf{-}j\textsf{-r-}j\textsf{-mon-det-RLWWC}(k))$.

(b) $L_3(j,k) \notin \mathcal{L}_C(\textsf{scf-}j\textsf{-r-}j'\textsf{-mon-hRLWW}(k)) \cup \mathcal{L}_{hP}(\textsf{scf-}j\textsf{-r-}j'\textsf{-mon-hRLWW}(k))$ *for any* $j' < j$.

(c) $L_3(j,k) \notin \mathcal{L}_C(\textsf{scf-}j'\textsf{-r-hRLWW}(k)) \cup \mathcal{L}_{hP}(\textsf{scf-}j'\textsf{-r-hRLWW}(k)))$ *for any* $j' < j$.

This proposition shows that, for the separation of classes of characteristic or h-proper languages based on the degree of monotonicity, it suffices to consider finite witness languages.

Proof outline. To simplify the notation, we introduce, for each $i = 1, 2, \ldots, j$, the word

$$w_i = (u_i u_{i+1} \cdots u_j c^{k \cdot j^2})^j$$

and the word $w_{j+1} = c^{k \cdot j^3}$.

(a) Let $M_3(j,k)$ be the j-rewriting deterministic RLWWC(k)-automaton that proceeds as follows given a word w as input. If $|w| \leq k$, then $M_3(j,k)$ performs a tail computation in which it accepts if $w = \lambda$ and rejects otherwise. If $|w| > k$, then $M_3(j,k)$ performs a cycle as follows:

1. If $w = w_i$ for some $i \in \{1, 2, \ldots, j\}$, then $M_3(j,k)$ executes j rewrite steps that each delete a factor u_i. In this way, w_i is rewritten into w_{i+1}.

2. If $w = c^{k \cdot j \cdot r}$ for some $r \in \{1, 2, \ldots, j^2\}$, then $M_3(j,k)$ deletes the suffix $c^{k \cdot j}$ by executing j rewrite steps that each delete a suffix c^k.

3. If w is not of any of the forms considered above, then $M_3(j,k)$ executes a rewrite step which either

   - deletes the last symbol of w and restarts, if $|w| = k \cdot \ell$, for some $\ell > 1$, or
   - deletes a k-letter suffix of w and restarts, if the length of w is not divisible by k.

Now it is easily seen that $L(M_3(j,k)) = L_C(M_3(j,k)) = L_3(j,k)$, that $M_3(j,k)$ is in strong cyclic form, and that each of its accepting computations consists of at most $j + j^2$ cycles and a tail. In addition, it can be checked that $M_3(j,k)$ is j-monotone.

(b) Now let $j \geq 2$ and let $\hat{M} = (M, h)$ be a j-rewriting scf-hRLWW(k)-automaton such that $L_C(M) = L_3(j,k)$. We claim that M is not j'-monotone for any $j' < j$. Assume to the contrary that M is j'-monotone for some $j' < j$. As $w_1 \in L_3(j,k)$, M has an accepting computation for w_1 that is j'-monotone. In addition, as M is in strong cyclic form, this accepting computation must rewrite w_1 into a word of length at most k before it accepts. From the definition of $L_3(j,k)$, we see that this computation must start with the following sequence of cycles, as in each cycle M can delete at most $k \cdot j$ letters:

$$q_0 \triangleright w_1 \triangleleft \ \vdash_M^c \ q_0 \triangleright w_2 \triangleleft \ \vdash_M^c \ \cdots \ \vdash_M^c \ q_0 \triangleright w_j \triangleleft \ \vdash_M^c \ q_0 \triangleright w_{j+1} \triangleleft .$$

Thus, for all $i = 1, 2, \ldots, j$, in the i-th cycle, M deletes the j occurrences of the factor u_i by using j CL-steps. As M can use move-right and move-left steps, we do not know in which order these factors are deleted. Accordingly, we cannot determine the exact right distance of these rewrite steps, but at least lower and upper bounds can be given for them (see [165]). Based on these bounds, it can be inferred that the $(i+1)$-st rewrite step from the right in cycle $(i+1)$ has a larger right distance than the i-th rewrite step from the right in cycle i. As all rewrite steps in cycle i are executed before the first rewrite step in cycle $(i+1)$ is executed, this shows that the $(i+1)$-st rewrite step from the right in cycle $(i+1)$ must belong to a different monotone subsequence than the i-th rewrite step from the right in cycle i. Hence, in order to arrange the j^2-many rewrite steps in the above computation into monotone subsequences, we need at least j such subsequences. This implies that the above computation is not j'-monotone for any $j' < j$. Thus, $L_3(j,k)$ is not the characteristic language of a scf-j-r-j'-mon-hRLWW(k)-automaton for any $j' < j$. The same arguments show that $L_3(j,k)$ is not the h-proper language of such an automaton.

(c) Let M be a scf-j'-r-hRLWW(k)-automaton for some $j' < j$. We first show that $L_C(M)$ cannot be the language $L_3(j,k)$. Assume to the contrary that $L_C(M) = L_3(j,k)$. As $w_1 \in L_3(j,k)$, M has an accepting computation for w_1. In addition, as M is in strong cyclic form, this accepting computation must reduce w_1 into a word $v \in L_3(j,k)$. But this is impossible with window size k and less than j rewrites in a cycle. Analogously, it follows that $L_3(j,k)$ is not the h-proper language of such an automaton. □

The properties of these witness languages imply that scf-hRLWW-automata are sensitive to the size of the window, the number of rewrites per cycle, and the degree of monotonicity.

Corollary 2.6.46 ([165]) *For all $j, k \geq 1$, the following hold:*

(a) $\mathcal{L}_C(\textsf{scf-fin}(1)\text{-}(j+1)\text{-r-det-mon-RLWWC}(k)) \smallsetminus (\mathcal{L}_C(\textsf{scf-}j\text{-r-hRLWW}(k)) \cup \mathcal{L}_{hP}(\textsf{scf-}j\text{-r-hRLWW}(k))) \neq \emptyset$.

(b) $\mathcal{L}_C(\textsf{scf-fin}(0)\text{-}j\text{-r-det-mon-RLWWC}(k+1)) \smallsetminus (\mathcal{L}_C(\textsf{scf-}j\text{-r-hRLWW}(k)) \cup \mathcal{L}_{hP}(\textsf{scf-}j\text{-r-hRLWW}(k))) \neq \emptyset$.

The statement in (a) follows from Proposition 2.6.44, and the statement in (b) follows from Proposition 2.6.43. Finally, we have a similar hierarchy with respect to the degree of monotonicity, which is related to the number of rewrites in a cycle. This result follows from Proposition 2.6.45 by considering the witness language $L_3(j+1,k)$.

Corollary 2.6.47 ([165]) *For all $j, k \geq 1$, the following hold:*

$\mathcal{L}_C(\textsf{scf-fin-}(j+1)\text{-r-}(j+1)\text{-mon-det-RLWWC}(k)) \smallsetminus (\mathcal{L}_C(\textsf{scf-}(j+1)\text{-r-}j\text{-mon-hRLWW}(k)) \cup \mathcal{L}_{hP}(\textsf{scf-}(j+1)\text{-r-}j\text{-mon-hRLWW}(k))) \neq \emptyset$.

When concentrating on RLWW-automata, that is, on automata that are only allowed to execute a single rewrite step in a cycle, then the results above yield an infinite strictly ascending hierarchy of language classes within the class of context-free languages. For $k \geq 1$, let $\textsf{CFL}(k)$ denote the class of h-proper languages of det-mon-RLWWC-automata in strong cyclic form that have a window of size k, that is, $\textsf{CFL}(k) = \mathcal{L}_{hP}(\textsf{scf-det-mon-hRLWWC}(k))$. From Corollary 2.6.40(c), we see that $\textsf{CFL}(k) \subseteq \textsf{CFL}$ and that $\bigcup_{k\geq 1} \textsf{CFL}(k) = \textsf{CFL}$. Furthermore, let $\textsf{CFL}_A(k)$ denote the class of lexicalized syntactic analyses $\mathcal{L}_A(\textsf{scf-det-mon-hRLWWC}(k))$. Using these notions, the concept of context-free languages and lexicalized syntactic analyses can be refined as follows.

Corollary 2.6.48 ([165]) *For all $k \geq 1$, $\textsf{CFL}(k) \subsetneq \textsf{CFL}(k+1)$ and $\textsf{CFL}_A(k) \subsetneq \textsf{CFL}_A(k+1)$.*

The inclusions above are obvious, and the example languages $L_1(k+1)$ $(k \geq 1)$ from Proposition 2.6.43 serve as witnesses that these inclusions are proper.

Finally, we look at certain classes of contextually transparent (lexicalized language) constructions, which are composed of infinitely many subclasses given by degrees of monotonicity and the number of rewrites per cycle. For these classes, the allowed number of rewrites per cycle coincides with the degree of monotonicity. Recall Definition 2.5.42, where this property was introduced under the name of j-constrainability.

Definition 2.6.49 ([165]) *For each $i \geq 1$, let $\textsf{CTL}_{hP}(i)$ denote the class of h-proper languages of deterministic i-constrained hRLWWC-automata that are in strong cyclic form, that is,*

$$\textsf{CTL}_{hP}(i) = \mathcal{L}_{hP}(\textsf{scf-}i\text{-r-}i\text{-mon-det-hRLWWC}),$$

let $\textsf{CTL}_C(i)$ be the corresponding class of characteristic languages, that is,

$$\textsf{CTL}_C(i) = \mathcal{L}_C(\textsf{scf-}i\text{-r-}i\text{-mon-det-hRLWWC}),$$

and let $\textsf{CTL}_A(i)$ be the corresponding class of lexicalized syntactic analyses, that is,

$$\textsf{CTL}_A(i) = \mathcal{L}_A(\textsf{scf-}i\text{-r-}i\text{-mon-det-hRLWWC}).$$

By taking the union over all positive integers, we obtain the classes

$$\mathsf{CTL}_{\mathrm{hP}} = \bigcup_{i \geq 1} \mathsf{CTL}_{\mathrm{hP}}(i) \text{ and } \mathsf{CTL}_{\mathrm{A}} = \bigcup_{i \geq 1} \mathsf{CTL}_{\mathrm{A}}(i).$$

We say that $\mathsf{CTL}_{\mathrm{hP}}$ *is the class of* contextually transparent languages *and that* $\mathsf{CTL}_{\mathrm{A}}$ *is the class of* contextually transparent lexicalized analyses.

With respect to the degree i of constrainability, we have the following results.

Corollary 2.6.50 ([165]) *For all* $i \geq 1$*, the following inclusions hold:*

(a) $\mathsf{CFL} = \mathsf{CTL}_{\mathrm{hP}}(1)$ *and* $\mathsf{CFL}_{\mathrm{A}} = \mathsf{CTL}_{\mathrm{A}}(1)$.
(b) $\mathsf{CTL}_{\mathrm{hP}}(i) \subsetneq \mathsf{CTL}_{\mathrm{hP}}(i+1) \subsetneq \mathsf{CTL}_{\mathrm{hP}}$ *and* $\mathsf{CTL}_{\mathrm{A}}(i) \subsetneq \mathsf{CTL}_{\mathrm{A}}(i+1) \subsetneq \mathsf{CTL}_{\mathrm{A}}$.
(c) $\mathsf{CTL}_{\mathrm{hP}} \subsetneq \mathsf{CSL}$.

Proof. The equalities in (a) follow immediately from Corollary 2.6.40(c) and Corollary 2.6.41. The inclusions in (b) are obvious, and it follows from Corollary 2.6.47 that they are proper.

Finally, the inclusion in (c) follows immediately from the definition of the hRLWWC-automaton. Furthermore, the separation in (c) can be shown by using the context-sensitive language $L_{\mathrm{exp}} = \{ a^{2^n} \mid n \geq 0 \}$. It is easily seen that the languages in $\mathsf{CTL}_{\mathrm{hP}}$ have the constant growth property (see Definition 1.5.3(b)). In fact, let Σ be an alphabet and let $L \subseteq \Sigma^*$. If $L \in \mathsf{CTL}_{\mathrm{hP}}(i)$ for some $i \geq 1$, then $L = L_{\mathrm{hP}}(M)$ for some scf-i-r-i-mon-det-hRLWWC-automaton M. Let $k \geq 1$ be the size of the window of M. Then, for all words $z, z' \in \Gamma^*$ (where Γ is the working alphabet of M), $q_0 \rhd z \lhd \vdash^c_M q_0 \rhd z' \lhd$ implies that $|z| - |z'| \leq i \cdot k$. Now assume that $w \in L$. If $|w| > k$, then because of the fact that M is in strong cyclic form, there are words $z, z' \in \Gamma^*$ such that $h(z) = w$, $q_0 \rhd z \lhd \vdash^c_M q_0 \rhd z' \lhd$, and $h(z') = w' \in L$. It follows that $|w| - |w'| = |z| - |z'| \leq i \cdot k$. Thus, we see that L has indeed the constant growth property. On the other hand, the language L_{exp} does not have this property, and so, it does not belong to the class $\mathsf{CTL}_{\mathrm{hP}}$. □

The sensitivity of i-rewriting hRLWWC-automata to the size of their windows can be used to refine the hierarchies $(\mathsf{CTL}_{\mathrm{hP}}(i))_{i \geq 1}$ and $(\mathsf{CTL}_{\mathrm{A}}(i))_{i \geq 1}$. This yields a fine classification of syntactic phenomena in lexicalized syntaxes of natural languages.

Recall that an hRLWWC(k)-automaton is an hRLWWC-automaton with a window of size k.

Definition 2.6.51 ([165]) *For* $k \geq 1$ *and* $i \geq 1$*, let* $\mathsf{CTL}_{\mathrm{hP}}(i,k)$ *denote the class*

$$\mathsf{CTL}_{\mathrm{hP}}(i,k) = \mathcal{L}_{\mathrm{hP}}(\mathsf{scf}\text{-}i\text{-}\mathsf{r}\text{-}i\text{-}\mathsf{mon}\text{-}\mathsf{det}\text{-}\mathsf{hRLWWC}(k)),$$

and analogously for $\mathsf{CTL}_{\mathrm{A}}(i,k)$*. Furthermore, let*

$$\mathsf{CTL}_{\mathrm{hP}}(*,k) = \bigcup_{i \geq 1} \mathsf{CTL}_{\mathrm{hP}}(i,k) \text{ and } \mathsf{CTL}_{\mathrm{A}}(*,k) = \bigcup_{i \geq 1} \mathsf{CTL}_{\mathrm{A}}(i,k).$$

We say that the class $\mathsf{CTL}_{\mathrm{hP}}(i,k)$ *is the set of* k-transparent context-sensitive languages of degree i, $\mathsf{CTL}_{\mathrm{A}}(i,k)$ *is the set of* k-transparent context-sensitive lexicalized (sentence) analyses of degree i, $\mathsf{CTL}_{\mathrm{hP}}(*,k)$ *is the set of* k-contextually transparent languages, *and* $\mathsf{CTL}_{\mathrm{A}}(*,k)$ *is the set of* k-contextually transparent lexicalized analyses.

Now the following inclusions follow from Corollary 2.6.46, Corollary 2.6.40(c), Corollary 2.6.41, and Proposition 2.6.43.

Corollary 2.6.52 ([165]) *For all* $i, k \geq 1$*, the following inclusions hold:*

(a) $\mathsf{CFL}(k) = \mathsf{CTL}_{\mathrm{hP}}(1,k)$ *and* $\mathsf{CFL}_{\mathrm{A}}(k) = \mathsf{CTL}_{\mathrm{A}}(1,k)$.
(b) $\mathsf{CTL}_{\mathrm{hP}}(i,k) \subsetneq \mathsf{CTL}_{\mathrm{hP}}(i,k+1)$ *and* $\mathsf{CTL}_{\mathrm{A}}(i,k) \subsetneq \mathsf{CTL}_{\mathrm{A}}(i,k+1)$.
(c) $\mathsf{CTL}_{\mathrm{hP}}(i,k) \subsetneq \mathsf{CTL}_{\mathrm{hP}}(i+1,k) \subsetneq \mathsf{CTL}_{\mathrm{hP}}(*,k)$ *and* $\mathsf{CTL}_{\mathrm{A}}(i,k) \subsetneq \mathsf{CTL}_{\mathrm{A}}(i+1,k) \subsetneq \mathsf{CTL}_{\mathrm{A}}(*,k)$.
(d) $\mathsf{CTL}_{\mathrm{hP}}(*,k) \subsetneq \mathsf{CTL}_{\mathrm{hP}}(*,k+1)$ *and* $\mathsf{CTL}_{\mathrm{A}}(*,k) \subsetneq \mathsf{CTL}_{\mathrm{A}}(*,k+1)$.

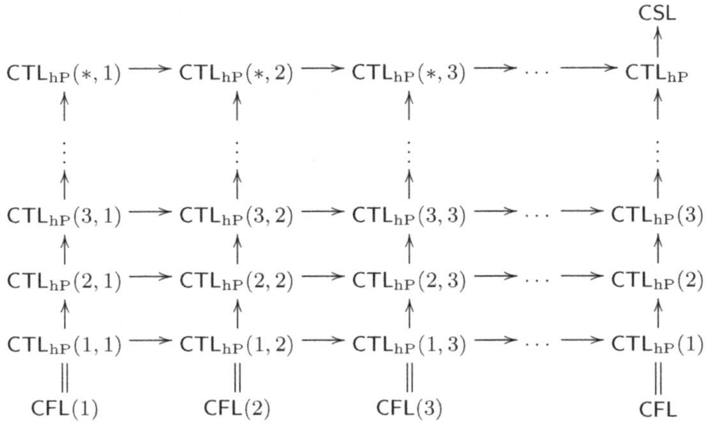

Figure 2.22: The two-dimensional hierarchy of k-transparent context-sensitive languages.

The diagram in Figure 2.22 depicts the resulting two-dimensional hierarchy of language classes. In this diagram, each arrow expresses a proper inclusion. In addition, if two language classes are not connected by a sequence of arrows, then these classes are incomparable under inclusion. An analogous hierarchy exists for the corresponding classes of lexicalized analyses.

By requiring that the RLWWC-automata considered are only allowed to execute a bounded number of cycles in each accepting computation, corresponding two-dimensional hierarchies are obtained for the resulting classes of h-proper languages and lexicalized analyses [165]. It follows from Lemma 2.6.42 that the h-proper language of an scf-fin(j)-i-r-hRLWW(k)-automaton is finite. Thus, the characteristic and the h-proper languages of hRLWWC-automata in strong cyclic form allow common classifications of finite phenomena as well as classifications of their infinite relaxations. As for restarting automata, monotonicity is a synonym for context-freeness, we are able to distinguish degrees of monotonicity not only for infinite languages, but also for finite languages (syntactic phenomena).

As pointed out in Section 1.5, context-free languages are neither sufficient nor well-suited for modelling natural languages. Therefore, other, more expressive, formalizations have been proposed in the literature. Among these are the so-called 'mildly context-sensitive languages' (see Definition 1.5.3) that have received much attention. The following result relates the language class $\mathsf{CTL}_{\mathrm{hP}} = \bigcup_{i\geq 1} \mathsf{CTL}_{\mathrm{hP}}(i)$ to the concept of mildly context-sensitive languages. In the statement below, the class $\mathsf{CTL}_{\mathrm{C}} = \bigcup_{i\geq 1} \mathsf{CTL}_{\mathrm{C}}(i)$ is used, which is called the class of *contextually transparent characteristic languages.* Moreover, for any $i \geq 2$ and any finite alphabet T, let $L_\omega(i,T)$ be the language $L_\omega(i,T) = \{ w^i \mid w \in T^* \}$.

Theorem 2.6.53 ([165]) *The following four statements hold:*

(a) $\mathsf{CFL} \subseteq \mathsf{CTL}_{\mathrm{hP}}(i)$ *for all* $i \geq 1$.

(b) *For each* $i \geq 2$ *and each finite alphabet* T *of cardinality* $|T| \geq 2$,

$$L_\omega(i,T) \in \mathsf{CTL}_{\mathrm{hP}}(i) \smallsetminus \mathsf{CTL}_{\mathrm{hP}}(i-1).$$

(c) *The languages in* $\mathsf{CTL}_{\mathrm{hP}}$ *have the constant growth property.*

(d) *The membership problem for the languages in* $\mathsf{CTL}_{\mathrm{C}}$ *is decidable in polynomial time.*

We are interested in the interplay between the number of rewrites per cycle and the degree of monotonicity for hRLWW-automata. For each $i \geq 1$, the class $\mathsf{CTL}_{\mathrm{hP}}(i)$ of contextually transparent languages of degree i has been defined as the h-proper languages of i-rewriting deterministic hRLWWC-automata that are in strong cyclic form and that are i-monotone. Thus, here the number of rewrites per cycle and the degree of monotonicity coincide. However, for each $i \geq 2$, there are deterministic RLW-automata that are i-monotone, but not $(i-1)$-monotone (see, e.g., Theorem 2.5.26). On the other hand, there are i-rewriting deterministic RLWW-automata that are monotone. In fact, by admitting i rewrites per cycle for an automaton with a window of size 1, we can simulate an RLWWD-automaton with a window of size i. Thus, in general, the number of rewrites per cycle and the degree of monotonicity are quite unrelated.

Problem 2.6.54 *Is it possible to establish a closer correspondence between the number of rewrites per cycle and the degree of monotonicity for (h)RLWW-automata?*

Preferably, this correspondence should be supported by a motivation from linguistics and by examples from natural languages.

Chapter 3

Descriptional Complexity

Here we study the descriptional complexity of several types of restarting automata. First, we investigate this topic for some types of restarting automata that characterize the class of regular languages. In Section 3.1, nondeterministic R-automata and deterministic RR-automata with window size one are considered. We know from Theorems 2.3.4 and 2.3.10 that $\mathcal{L}(\mathsf{R}(1)) = \mathcal{L}(\mathsf{det\text{-}RR}(1)) = \mathsf{REG}$. Accordingly, we can compare the size of a description of an R(1)-automaton or a deterministic RR(1)-automaton to the size of a description of an NFA or a DFA of minimal size that accepts the same (regular) language. We stress the fact that, in this setting, only DFAs are considered that are complete, that is, the transition functions of these DFAs are defined for all pairs consisting of a state and an input letter. For NFAs and DFAs, the number of states is usually taken as the measure for their size (see, e.g., [75]).

It is well known that each NFA with n states can be simulated by a complete DFA with 2^n states and that there are n-state NFAs such that an equivalent DFA needs indeed 2^n states. On the other hand, as each DFA is also an NFA, there exists an NFA with n states for each DFA with n states. In fact, also this bound is sharp, as there exist DFAs with n states such that each equivalent NFA has at least n states. An example is the cyclic DFA for the language $\{a^n\}^*$.

As R(1)- and deterministic RR(1)-automata do not have auxiliary letters, the number of states is also a reasonable measure for the size of such an automaton. Following Martin Kutrib's and Jens Reimann's studies in [126, 127, 128] (see also [228]), we show in Section 3.1 that there is an exponential trade-off when converting an R(1)-automaton or a deterministic RR(1)-automaton into an NFA or a DFA for the same language. In fact, rather exact upper and lower bounds have been obtained for these conversions.

In Section 3.2, we turn to stateless ordered restarting automata. As we know from Corollary 2.3.86, $\mathcal{L}(\mathsf{stl\text{-}det\text{-}ORWW}) = \mathcal{L}(\mathsf{stl\text{-}ORWW}) = \mathsf{REG}$. Hence, for each stateless (deterministic) ORWW-automaton, there exists an NFA (and a DFA) that accepts the same language. Obviously, for stateless types of automata, we need a different size measure. Following [195, 205], we use the cardinality of the tape alphabet as a measure for the size of a stateless ORWW-automaton. This is reasonable as, because of its window of size three, a stateless ORWW-automaton with a tape alphabet of cardinality n can have up to $\mathcal{O}(n^4)$ transitions, while a DFA with k states over an alphabet of cardinality n has $k \cdot n$ transitions and an NFA with k states over an alphabet of cardinality n has at most $n \cdot k^2$ transitions. Thus, for all these types of automata, the size of an encoding of the transition relation is polynomially related to the respective measure.

We show that stateless deterministic ORWW-automata are exponentially more succinct than NFAs and doubly exponentially more succinct than DFAs. Actually, this fact remains valid even for stateless deterministic ORWW-automata that are reversible. Moreover, we also consider stateless deterministic ORRWW-automata that are reversible. Finally, we take a look at the descriptional complexity of stateless ORD-automata. As they accept a class of languages that includes the context-free languages by Theorem 2.3.95, it is not surprising that the trade-off for turning a stateless ORD-automaton accepting a regular language into an equivalent stateless ORWW-automaton is non-recursive, that is, it cannot be bounded from above by any recursive function.

F. Otto, *Restarting Automata*, Theory and Applications of Computability,
https://doi.org/10.1007/978-3-031-70094-1_3

Then, in Section 3.3, we study the trade-offs for the conversion of a restarting automaton of window size k into an equivalent automaton of the same type that has window size $k-1$ only. For deterministic and nondeterministic RW- and RRW-automata, we prove that the corresponding trade-offs are non-recursive for all $k \geq 3$ by applying a general result of Markus Holzer and Martin Kutrib [74]. Here the main idea is a construction of a deterministic RW-automaton of window size k for a language that encodes the computation of a given deterministic Turing machine on empty input. This language is accepted by an RW-automaton of window size $k-1$ if and only if it is finite. Hence, the halting problem for Turing machines on empty input, which is known to be undecidable, is reduced to the problem considered. By following the same strategy, but using a technically somewhat more involved construction, corresponding non-recursive trade-offs are then derived for deterministic and nondeterministic R(R)-automata for all $k \geq 5$. On the other hand, for converting a deterministic R(R)(W)-automaton of window size two into an equivalent automaton of window size one, we obtain a recursive upper bound. The results presented in this section are taken from [124, 125].

Finally, in Section 3.4, we consider trade-offs between monotone RWW- and RRWW-automata on the one hand and deterministic RWW- and RRWW-automata and some of their subclasses on the other hand. Following [77, 228], we show that many trade-offs for the conversions between these types of restarting automata are non-recursive, too. In addition to the halting problem for Turing machines on empty input, an encoding of the computations of a Turing machine as a set of *valid computations* and its complement, the set of *invalid computations*, are used to prove these non-recursive trade-offs. These results emphasize the incomparability results from Subsection 2.2.1, which show that the language classes accepted by the various types of nondeterministic monotone restarting automata are incomparable under inclusion to those language classes that are accepted by the various types of non-monotone deterministic restarting automata (see the diagram in Figure 2.8).

3.1 On R(1)- and Deterministic RR(1)-Automata

From Theorem 2.3.4, we recall that (deterministic) R-automata of window size one accept the regular languages only. Thus, (deterministic) R(1)-automata have exactly the same expressive capacity as DFAs and NFAs. While a DFA or an NFA just scans its input once from left to right and accepts after having seen the last letter, an R(1)-automaton may execute several cycles. During each cycle, it scans its input from left to right until it decides to delete a letter and to restart. Thus, an accepting computation of an R(1)-automaton is, in general, more involved than an accepting computation of a DFA or an NFA. This raises the question of whether there is at all an advantage in using R(1)-automata instead of DFAs or NFAs for representing (accepting) regular languages. For example, such an advantage could be the fact that some regular languages are accepted by (deterministic) R(1)-automata that are much smaller than the smallest DFAs or NFAs for these languages. So we are interested in the descriptional complexity of R(1)-automata.

In what follows, we use the number of states as a complexity measure for the size of an R(1)-automaton. As this same complexity measure is used for NFAs and DFAs, too, we can easily compare the size of an R(1)-automaton to the size of an NFA or a DFA that accepts the same language. Before turning to nondeterministic R(1)-automata, however, we consider deterministic R(1)-automata. Obviously, a DFA can be viewed as a det-R(1)-automaton that does not execute any rewrite steps at all. On the other hand, a det-R(1)-automaton can easily be converted into a DFA.

Proposition 3.1.1 *Let M be a deterministic $R(1)$-automata with n states. Then a complete DFA with at most $n+2$ states can be constructed for the language $L(M)$.*

Proof. Let $M = (Q, \Sigma, \Sigma, \rhd, \lhd, q_0, 1, \delta)$ be a deterministic R(1)-automaton. From Proposition 2.3.11, we recall that M is strictly monotone, that is, the right distance from one cycle to the next decreases properly. In fact, if M executes a cycle of the form

$$q_0 \rhd uav \lhd \vdash_M^* \rhd uqav \lhd \vdash_M q_0 \rhd uv \lhd,$$

in which the displayed occurrence of the letter a is deleted by the rewrite/restart transition $\lambda \in \delta(q, a)$, then the next cycle (or tail) begins with a sequence of MVR steps that reaches the configuration $\rhd uqv \lhd$, as M is deterministic. Thus, instead of performing the above rewrite/restart operation and the subsequent MVR steps, M could just execute a MVR step while staying in state q. Accordingly, we can construct a DFA $A = (Q_A, \Sigma, q_s, F_A, \delta_A)$ by taking $Q_A = Q \cup \{q_+, q_-\}$, where q_+ and q_- are two new states, $q_s \in Q$ is the unique state of M that M reaches from its initial state on seeing the left sentinel $\rhd$, that is, $\delta(q_0, \rhd) = (q_s, \mathsf{MVR})$, $F_A = \{ q \in Q \mid \delta(q, \lhd) = \mathsf{Accept} \} \cup \{q_+\}$, and by defining the transition function δ_A as follows, where $q \in Q$ and $a \in \Sigma$:

$$\begin{array}{llll} (1) & \delta_A(q,a) & = & \begin{cases} q', & \text{if } \delta(q,a) = (q', \mathsf{MVR}), \\ q, & \text{if } \delta(q,a) = \lambda, \\ q_+, & \text{if } \delta(q,a) = \mathsf{Accept}, \\ q_-, & \text{if } \delta(q,a) \text{ is undefined}, \end{cases} \\ (2) & \delta_A(q_+,a) & = & q_+, \\ (3) & \delta_A(q_-,a) & = & q_-. \end{array}$$

Then it is easily seen that $L(A) = L(M)$. □

Thus, det-R(1)-automata have essentially the same descriptional complexity as DFAs. Furthermore, we have the following result for the nondeterministic case.

Proposition 3.1.2 *Let A be an NFA with n states. Then an $R(1)$-automaton M with n states can be constructed for the language $L(A)$.*

Proof. Let $A = (Q, \Sigma, I_A, F_A, \delta_A)$ be an NFA with n states. From A, we construct an R(1)-automaton $M = (Q, \Sigma, \Sigma, \rhd, \lhd, q_0, 1, \delta)$ by taking q_0 to be an arbitrary initial state from the set I_A

and by defining the transition relation δ as follows, where $q \in Q$ and $a \in \Sigma$:

$$\begin{array}{lll} (1) & \delta(q_0, \rhd) & = & \{ (q', \mathsf{MVR}) \mid q' \in I_0 \}, \\ (2) & \delta(q, a) & = & \{ (q', \mathsf{MVR}) \mid q' \in \delta_A(q, a) \}, \\ (3) & \delta(q, \lhd) & = & \begin{cases} \mathsf{Accept}, & \text{if } q \in F_A, \\ \emptyset, & \text{otherwise.} \end{cases} \end{array}$$

Then it is easily seen that M only executes tail computations, and that each of these tail computations just simulates a computation of the NFA A. It follows that $L(M) = L(A)$. □

For each $n \geq 2$, there exists an NFA for the language $\{a^n\}^*$ that has n states. Thus, there exists an R(1)-automaton M_n with n states that accepts the language $\{a^n\}^*$. For a word of the form $a^{n \cdot m}$, the automaton M_n has an accepting computation. However, this computation cannot possibly involve a delete/restart step, which implies that M_n accepts the language $\{a^n\}^*$ by only executing tail computations. Hence, M_n behaves just like an NFA, which implies that it has at least n states. This gives the following lower bound.

Corollary 3.1.3 *For each $n \geq 2$, there exists an NFA A with n states such that each $R(1)$-automaton for the language $L(A)$ has at least n states.*

Based on these observations, one could expect that (nondeterministic) R(1)-automata have the same descriptional complexity as NFAs. However, this is not the case.

In the proof of Theorem 2.3.4, a powerset construction is used to turn a given R(1)-automaton M with n states into an NFA with $2^n + 2$ states for the language $L(M) \cdot \lhd$. In fact, by slightly adjusting the definition of the transition relation of the NFA, we obtain a complete DFA with $2^n + 1$ states for the language $L(M)$ [228]. Moreover, by removing the state $\emptyset$ from this DFA, we obtain an NFA with only 2^n states for the language $L(M)$. This yields the following result.

Corollary 3.1.4 *Let M be an $R(1)$-automata with n states. Then a complete DFA with at most $2^n + 1$ states and an NFA with at most 2^n states can be constructed for the language $L(M)$.*

This result implies that R(1)-automata can at best be exponentially more succinct than NFAs and DFAs. It remains to provide matching lower bounds. This is done by presenting, for each $n \geq 2$, an example of a regular language L_n that is accepted by an R(1)-automaton with n states such that each NFA (or DFA) for L_n has at least 2^n (or $2^n + 1$) states.

Proposition 3.1.5 ([128, 228]) *For each $n \geq 2$, there exists an $R(1)$-automaton M with n states such that each NFA for the language $L(M)$ has at least 2^n states.*

Proof outline. Let $M = (Q, \Sigma, \Sigma, \rhd, \lhd, q_0, 1, \delta)$ be the R(1)-automaton on $\Sigma = \{a, b, c, d\}$ that is defined by the following transition relation, where $Q = \{q_0, q_1, \ldots, q_{n-1}\}$ and $i \in \{1, 2, \ldots, n-1\}$:

$$\begin{array}{llllllll} (1) & \delta(q_0, \rhd) & = & \{(q_0, \mathsf{MVR})\}, & (4) & \delta(q_i, a) & = & \{(q_{(i+1) \bmod n}, \mathsf{MVR}\}), \\ (2) & \delta(q_0, a) & = & \{(q_0, \mathsf{MVR}), (q_1, \mathsf{MVR})\}, & (5) & \delta(q_i, b) & = & \{(q_i, \mathsf{MVR})\}, \\ (3) & \delta(q_0, c) & = & \{\lambda\}, & (6) & \delta(q_{n-1}, d) & = & \{\mathsf{Accept}\}. \end{array}$$

Next, we present a fooling set for the language $L(M)$. Here a set of pairs of words $P = \{ (u_j, v_j) \mid 1 \leq j \leq m \}$ is called a *fooling set* for a language L, if the following two conditions hold for all $j, k \in \{1, 2, \ldots, m\}$:

1. $u_j v_j \in L$ and
2. for $j \neq k$, $u_j v_k \notin L$ or $u_k v_j \notin L$.

Whenever a regular language L has a fooling set P, then each NFA accepting L has at least $|P|$ states [14]. Thus, a fooling set yields a lower bound for the size of a minimal NFA for L. For example, the set of pairs $\{ (a^i, a^{n-i}) \mid i \in \{0, 1, \ldots, n-1\} \}$ is a fooling set for the language $\{a^n\}^*$.

The fooling set P for the language $L(M)$ contains a pair $(u_j, v_j w_j)$ for each non-empty subset Q_j of Q. Let $Q_j = \{q_{i_1}, q_{i_2}, \ldots, q_{i_r}\}$ such that $i_k < i_{k+1}$ for all $1 \leq k \leq r-1$. In the following, configurations of the R(1)-automaton M are written in the form

$$\rhd \Sigma^* S \, \Sigma^* \lhd \text{ or } \{q_0\} \rhd \Sigma^* \lhd,$$

where the position of the read-write window is on the letter following S, and S itself denotes the set of possible states. The words u_j, v_j, and w_j are chosen in such a way that M displays the following behavior:

(i) The word u_j is taken from $\{a,b\}^*$ such that M has a computation (that only consists of MVR steps) of the form $q_0 \rhd u_j \lhd \vdash_M^* \rhd u_j q \lhd$ iff $q \in Q_j$, that is, $\{q_0\} \rhd u_j \lhd \vdash_M^* \rhd u_j Q_j \lhd$.

(ii) The word v_j is taken from $\{a,b,c\}^*$ such that, for all $q \in Q_j$, M has a computation of the form $\rhd u_j q v_j \lhd \vdash_M^* \rhd u_j v'_j q_0 \lhd$ for some word v'_j and, in addition, if $\rhd u_j q v_j \lhd \vdash_M^* \rhd u_j v''_j q' \lhd$ for some word v''_j, then $q' = q_0$. Moreover, if there exists a state in Q_j that does not belong to the set Q_s, then all computations of M starting with a configuration of the form $\rhd u_s q v_j \lhd$ with $q \in Q_s$ are rejecting.

(iii) The word w_j is chosen from $\{a,b\}^* \cdot d$ such that M has a computation (that does not contain any rewrite steps) of the form $\rhd q w_j \lhd \vdash_M^*$ Accept iff $q = q_0$.

(iv) There exists a word v' such that, for all $q \in Q$ and all $x \in \{a,b\}^*$, the computation starting from the configuration $\rhd x q v' \lhd$ is rejecting.

We define the word $u_j \in \{a,b\}^*$ as follows:

$$u_j = a^{n-1}(ba)^{n-1-i_r} a(ba)^{i_r-1-i_{r-1}} a(ba)^{i_{r-1}-1-i_{r-2}} \cdots a(ba)^{i_2-1-i_1}(ab)^{i_1}.$$

Then it can be checked that $\{q_0\} \rhd u_j \lhd \vdash_M^* \rhd u_j Q_j \lhd$ holds, this is, the requirement in (i) is satisfied. Next we define the word $v_j \in \{a,b,c\}^*$ as follows:

$$v_j = \begin{cases} cba^{n-i_r} cba^{i_r-i_{r-1}} cba^{i_{r-1}-i_{r-2}} \cdots cba^{i_3-i_2} c, & \text{if } i_1 = 0, \\ a^{n-i_r} cba^{i_r-i_{r-1}} cba^{i_{r-1}-i_{r-2}} \cdots cba^{i_2-i_1} c, & \text{if } i_1 \neq 0, \end{cases}$$

and we choose the word $w_j \in \{a,b\}^* \cdot d$ by taking $w_j = (ab)^{n-1} d$. It can now be verified that all requirements in (ii) and (iii) are satisfied.

To complete the construction, we finally take $u' = (ab)^{n-1} d$ and $v' = (cba)^n c$. Then $u'x$ is accepted by M for all words $x \in \Sigma^*$. On the other hand, let $q \in Q$ and $x \in \{a,b\}^*$. Then the computation starting from the configuration $\rhd x q v' \lhd$ leads to rejection.

Now we take the set of pairs $P = \{\, (u_j, v_j w_j) \mid \emptyset \neq Q_j \subseteq Q \,\} \cup \{(u', v')\}$. Then, for each j,

$$q_0 \rhd u_j v_j w_j \lhd \;\; \vdash_M^* \rhd u_j Q_j v_j w_j \lhd \;\; \vdash_M^* \rhd u_j v'_j \{q_0\} w_j \lhd \;\; \vdash_M^* \text{Accept},$$

and for each $s \neq j$, if there is a state $q \in Q_j \smallsetminus Q_s$, then

$$q_0 \rhd u_s v_j w_j \lhd \;\; \vdash_M^* \rhd u_s Q_s v_j w_j \lhd \;\; \vdash_M^* \;\; \text{Reject}.$$

Furthermore, $u'v' \in L(M)$, but $u_j v' \notin L(M)$ for all j. Thus, P is indeed a fooling set for $L(M)$. As $|P| = 2^n$, we conclude that each NFA for the language $L(M)$ has at least 2^n states. □

As we only consider DFAs that are complete, that is, the transition function must be defined for all possible pairs consisting of a state and an input letter, it follows that each DFA for the above language $L(M)$ needs at least $2^n + 1$ states. This yields the following consequence.

Corollary 3.1.6 ([128, 228]) *For each $n \geq 2$, there exists an $R(1)$-automaton M with n states such that each complete DFA for the language $L(M)$ has at least $2^n + 1$ states.*

Together with Corollary 3.1.4, Proposition 3.1.5 and Corollary 3.1.6 show that the upper and lower bounds for converting an R(1)-automaton into an equivalent NFA (or DFA) coincide.

Theorem 3.1.7 ([128, 228]) *For each $n \geq 2$, when converting an $R(1)$-automaton M with n states into an NFA (or DFA) for the language $L(M)$, then 2^n (or $2^n + 1$) states are sufficient and also necessary in the worst case.*

Interestingly, the bound for the conversion of an R(1)-automaton into a DFA is almost identical to the bound for the conversion into an NFA. The R(1)-automaton constructed in the proof of Proposition 3.1.5 is actually monotone, as in each cycle it simply deletes the left-most occurrence of the letter c. Thus, Theorem 3.1.7 also holds for monotone R(1)-automata.

Now we turn to deterministic RR(1)-automata. In analogy to Proposition 3.1.2, the following result can be shown.

Proposition 3.1.8 *Let A be a DFA with n states. Then a det-$RR(1)$-automaton M with n states can be constructed for the language $L(A)$.*

In fact, this upper bound is also a lower bound.

Proposition 3.1.9 *For each $n \geq 2$, there exists a DFA A with n states such that each det-$RR(1)$-automaton for the language $L(A)$ has at least n states.*

Proof. Let $n \geq 2$, and let $L_n = \{a^n\}^*$. Then the minimal complete DFA for L_n has n states - it is the cyclic DFA counting mod n. Now let M be a det-RR(1)-automaton for the language L_n. For a word of the form $a^{n \cdot m}$, the computation of M is accepting. In a cycle, M can only delete a single letter, which implies that the accepting computation for $a^{n \cdot m}$ consists of just an accepting tail. Thus, M must be able to count mod n, for which it needs at least n states. □

By combining Proposition 3.1.8 with Corollary 3.1.4, we obtain the following bound for converting an R(1)-automaton into an equivalent det-RR(1)-automaton. Observe that, when combining the transformation of an R(1)-automaton into a complete DFA with the transformation of a DFA into a det-RR(1)-automaton, we can ignore the rejecting trap state of the DFA as well as the state of the DFA that it uses to read the remaining suffix once the R(1)-automaton has accepted.

Corollary 3.1.10 *Let M be an $R(1)$-automaton with n states. Then a det-$RR(1)$-automaton M with $2^n - 1$ states can be constructed for the language $L(M)$.*

In the proof of Theorem 2.3.10, an NFA A is constructed from a det-RR(1)-automaton M such that $L(A) = L(M) \cdot \lhd$. If M has n states, and if the subset of states of M that can be reached within a cycle of M after a rewrite step has been executed has cardinality r, then A has $n \cdot 2^r + 1$ states. However, some of the states of A are useless, as they cannot occur in any accepting computation. A detailed analysis shows that an NFA A' can be constructed for the language $L(M)$ such that A' has only $(2n - r + 2) \cdot 2^{r-1}$ states [128]. Thus, we have the following result.

Corollary 3.1.11 ([128, 228]) *Let M be a deterministic $RR(1)$-automata with n states such that r of these states are reachable after a rewrite step has been executed. Then an NFA with at most $(2n - r + 2) \cdot 2^{r-1}$ states can be constructed for the language $L(M)$.*

A matching lower bound for the conversion of a det-RR(1)-automaton into an equivalent NFA has also been derived.

Proposition 3.1.12 ([128, 228]) *For each $n \geq 2$ and each $r \in \{1, 2, \ldots, n-1\}$, there exists a det-$RR(1)$-automaton M with n states, r of which can be reached after a rewrite step has been executed, such that each NFA for the language $L(M)$ has at least $(2n - r + 2) \cdot 2^{r-1}$ states.*

Proof outline. Let $n \geq 2$ and let $r \in \{1, 2, \ldots, n-1\}$. We construct a det-RR(1)-automaton $M = (Q, \Sigma, \Sigma, \rhd, \lhd, q_0, 1, \delta)$ as follows.

Let $m = n - r$, let $Q_1 = \{q_0, q_1, \ldots, q_{m-1}\}$ be the set of states that can be used before a rewrite step is executed, let $Q_2 = \{q'_0, q'_1, \ldots, q'_{r-1}\}$ be the set of states that can be used after a rewrite step has been executed, and let $Q = Q_1 \cup Q_2$, that is, $|Q| = |Q_1| + |Q_2| = m + r = n$. We take $\Sigma = \{a, b, c, d, e, f, g\}$, and we define the transition function δ as follows, where $i \in \{0, 1, \ldots, m-1\}$, $j \in \{1, 2, \ldots, m-1\}$, $k \in \{0, 1, \ldots, r-1\}$, and $l \in \{1, 2, \ldots, r-1\}$:

$$
\begin{array}{llcllcl}
(1) & \delta(q_0, \rhd) & = & (q_0, \mathsf{MVR}), & & & \\
(2) & \delta(q_i, a) & = & (q_{(i+1) \bmod m}, \mathsf{MVR}) & \text{and} \ \ \delta(q'_k, a) & = & (q'_k, \mathsf{MVR}), \\
(3) & \delta(q_0, b) & = & \mathsf{Accept}, & & & \\
 & \delta(q_j, b) & = & (q_j, \mathsf{MVR}) & \text{and} \ \ \delta(q'_k, b) & = & (q'_k, \mathsf{MVR}), \\
(4) & \delta(q_i, c) & = & - & \text{and} \ \ \delta(q'_k, c) & = & -, \\
 & \multicolumn{6}{l}{\text{that is, } M \text{ gets stuck on seeing the letter } c,} \\
(5) & \delta(q_0, d) & = & (q'_0, \lambda), & & & \\
 & \delta(q_j, d) & = & (q_j, \mathsf{MVR}) & \text{and} \ \ \delta(q'_k, d) & = & (q'_k, \mathsf{MVR}), \\
(6) & \delta(q_i, e) & = & (q_i, \mathsf{MVR}) & \text{and} \ \ \delta(q'_k, e) & = & (q'_{(k+1) \bmod r}, \mathsf{MVR}), \\
(7) & \delta(q_i, f) & = & (q_i, \mathsf{MVR}) & \text{and} \ \ \delta(q'_0, f) & = & \mathsf{Accept}, \\
 & & & & \delta(q'_l, f) & = & (q'_l, \mathsf{MVR}), \\
(8) & \delta(q_i, g) & = & (q_i, \mathsf{MVR}) & \text{and} \ \ \delta(q'_0, g) & = & \mathsf{Restart}, \\
 & & & & \delta(q'_l, g) & = & (q'_l, \mathsf{MVR}).
\end{array}
$$

By Theorem 2.3.10, there exists an NFA A for the language $L(M)$. We claim that A has at least $(2n - r + 2) \cdot 2^{r-1}$ states. To prove this claim, a fooling set P of cardinality $(2n - r + 2) \cdot 2^{r-1}$ is constructed in [128] for the language $L(M)$. This completes the proof of Proposition 3.1.12. □

In combination, Corollary 3.1.11 and Proposition 3.1.12 yield the following result.

Theorem 3.1.13 ([128, 228]) *For each $n \geq 2$ and each $r \in \{1, 2, \ldots, n-1\}$, when converting a det-RR(1)-automaton M with n states, r of which are reachable after a rewrite step has been executed, into an NFA for the language $L(M)$, then $(2n - r + 2) \cdot 2^{r-1}$ states are sufficient and also necessary in the worst case.*

By combining Proposition 3.1.2 with Corollary 3.1.11, we see that a deterministic RR(1)-automata with n states, r of which are reachable after a rewrite step has been executed, can be converted into an R(1)-automaton with at most $(2n - r + 2) \cdot 2^{r-1}$ states for the language $L(M)$. As it turns out, this upper bound is sharp, too.

Proposition 3.1.14 ([228]) *For each $n \geq 2$ and each $r \in \{1, 2, \ldots, n-1\}$, there exists a det-RR(1)-automaton M with n states, r of which can be reached in a cycle after a rewrite step has been executed, such that each R(1)-automaton for the language $L(M)$ has at least $(2n - r + 2) \cdot 2^{r-1}$ states.*

Proof outline. Let $n \geq 2$, let $r \in \{1, 2, \ldots, n-1\}$, and let M be the det-RR(1)-automaton from the proof of Proposition 3.1.12. It can be verified that each R(1)-automaton for the language $L(M)$ has at least $(2n - r + 2) \cdot 2^{r-1}$ states (see [228]). □

This yields the following consequence.

Corollary 3.1.15 ([228]) *For each $n \geq 2$ and each $r \in \{1, 2, \ldots, n-1\}$, when converting a det-RR(1)-automaton M with n states, r of which are reachable after a rewrite step has been executed, into an R(1)-automaton for the language $L(M)$, then $(2n - r + 2) \cdot 2^{r-1}$ states are sufficient and also necessary in the worst case.*

We have an exponential trade-off for converting an R(1)-automaton or a det-RR(1)-automaton into an equivalent NFA. Conversely, by Proposition 3.1.2, an NFA can be converted into an equivalent R(1)-automaton of the same size. What can be said about the conversion of an NFA into an equivalent det-RR(1)-automaton? Obviously, an n-state NFA can first be converted into a DFA with 2^n states, which can then be turned into a det-RR(1)-automaton M that does not execute any rewrite steps. As in the latter conversion, the rejecting sink state of the DFA can be ignored, it follows that M has at most $2^n - 1$ states. Surprisingly, this is a tight bound, that is, the rewrite capability of det-RR(1)-automata cannot make up for the nondeterminism of NFAs.

Proposition 3.1.16 ([126, 127, 228]) *For each $n \geq 2$, there exists an NFA A with n states such that each det-RR(1)-automaton for the language $L(A)$ has at least $2^n - 1$ states.*

Proof outline. Let $n \geq 2$, and let $A = (Q, \Sigma, q_0, F, \delta)$ be the NFA that is obtained by taking $Q = \{q_0, q_1, \dots, q_{n-1}\}$, $\Sigma = \{a, b, c\}$, $F = \{q_0\}$, and by defining the transition relation δ as follows:

$$\begin{array}{llll}(1) & \delta(q_i, a) = & \{q_0, q_i\} & \text{for all } i \in \{1, 2, \dots, n-1\},\\ (2) & \delta(q_i, b) = & \{q_{(i+1) \bmod n}\} & \text{for all } i \in \{0, 1, \dots, n-1\},\\ (3) & \delta(q_0, c) = & \{q_0\}. & \end{array}$$

In [232], it is shown that the restriction of this NFA to the subalphabet $\{a, b\}$ is not equivalent to any complete DFA that has less than 2^n states. The way in which the letter c is processed by A implies that the language $L(A)$ has the following property.

Claim. For all $v \in L(A)$ and all $w \in \Sigma^*$, $vcw \in L(A)$ if and only if $w \in L(A)$.

Proof. As $v \in L(A)$ and $F = \{q_0\}$, we see that $q_0 v \vdash_A^* q_0$ holds. Hence, $vcw \in L(A)$ if and only if $q_0 vcw \vdash_A^* q_0 cw \vdash_A q_0 w \vdash_A^* q_0$ if and only if $w \in L(A)$. □

Let $j \in \{1, 2, \dots, n\}$ and let $i_1, i_2, \dots, i_j \in \{0, 1, \dots, n-1\}$ such that $i_1 < i_2 < \cdots < i_j$. We define a word $u_{(i_1, i_2, \dots, i_j)}$ as follows:

$$u_{(i_1,i_2,\dots,i_j)} = \begin{cases} b^{i_1}, & \text{if } j = 1,\\ b^{i_j - i_{j-1}} a b^{i_{j-1} - i_{j-2}} a \cdots a b^{i_2 - i_1} a b^{i_1}, & \text{if } j \geq 2.\end{cases}$$

Now assume that $M = (Q_M, \Sigma, \Sigma, \rhd, \lhd, q_0', 1, \delta_M)$ is a det-RR(1)-automaton for the language $L(A)$. We first show that M has at least $2^n - 1$ states if it performs a delete operation on any of the words $u_{(i_1, i_2, \dots, i_j)}$. Each prefix of the word $u_{(i_1, i_2, \dots, i_j)}$ is itself a word of this form. Hence, this statement can be proved by induction on the length of the word considered.

If the word has length one only, then it is the letter b. Assume that M deletes the letter b, that is, $\delta_M(q_0', \rhd) = (q', \mathsf{MVR})$ and $\delta_M(q', b) = (q'', \lambda)$. As $ba \in L(A)$, we have $bacw \in L(A)$ for each word $w \in L(A)$, that is, the computation of M on input $bacw$ is accepting. It begins with the following two steps:

$$q_0' \rhd bacw \lhd \vdash_M \rhd q' bacw \lhd \vdash_M \rhd q'' acw \lhd .$$

However, $acw \notin L(A)$, as $\delta(q_0, a)$ is undefined. Hence, the above computation of M on input $bacw$ cannot possibly contain a restart step, that is, this computation continues as $\rhd q'' acw \lhd \vdash_M^* \mathsf{Accept}$ by only MVR steps and an accept step. This means that M accepts the word $w \in L(A)$ by behaving like a DFA. As each DFA for the language $L(A)$ has at least 2^n states, and as w is an arbitrary word from $L(A)$, we see that M needs at least $2^n - 1$ states to realize this part of the above computation.

For the induction step, we have two cases:

(1) $u_{(i_1, i_2, \dots, i_j)} = ub$, where $i_1 \geq 1$ and $u = b^{i_j - i_{j-1}} a \cdots a b^{i_2 - i_1} a b^{i_1 - 1}$ or $u = b^{i_1 - 1}$.

(2) $u_{(i_1, i_2, \dots, u_j)} = ua$ for some $u = b^{i_j - i_{j-1}} a \cdots a b^{i_3 - i_2} a b^{i_2}$, that is, $j > 1$ and $i_1 = 0$.

It is shown in [126] that, in each case, the det-RR(1)-automaton M needs $2^n - 1$ states.

In summary, we see that M either performs a delete step on one of the words $u_{(i_1, i_2, \dots, i_j)}$, and then it has at least $2^n - 1$ states, or it does not perform any delete steps on any of these words.

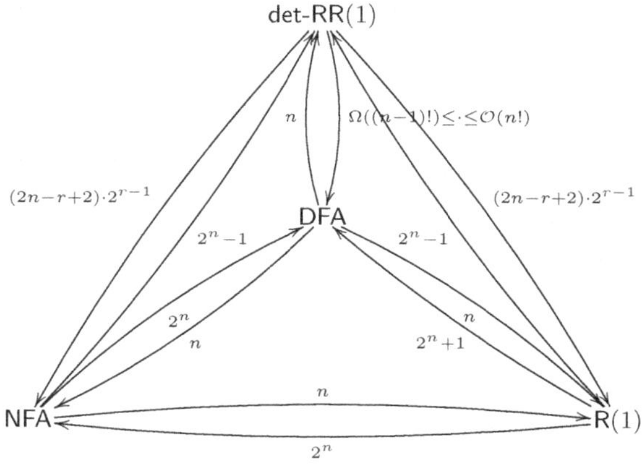

Figure 3.1: The trade-offs between DFAs, NFAs, and restarting automata of window size one.

The latter means that M behaves like a DFA on these words. After reading the prefix $u_{(i_1,i_2,\ldots,i_j)}$, the NFA A is in any of the states from the set $\{q_{i_1}, q_{i_2}, \ldots, q_{i_j}\}$. Accordingly, M needs $2^n - 1$ states to simulate A on these words as there are $2^n - 1$ subsets of Q of this form. □

From Proposition 3.1.16 and its preceding remarks, we obtain the following tight bound for the conversion of an NFA into an equivalent det-RR(1)-automaton.

Corollary 3.1.17 ([126, 127, 228]) *For each $n \geq 2$, when converting an NFA A with n states into a det-RR(1)-automaton for the language $L(A)$, then $2^n - 1$ states are sufficient and also necessary in the worst case.*

An R(1)-automaton M with n states can be converted into an equivalent det-RR(1)-automaton with $2^n - 1$ states (see Corollary 3.1.10). On the other hand, there are cases in which the det-RR(1)-automaton needs this many states. This yields the following result.

Theorem 3.1.18 ([126, 127, 228]) *For each $n \geq 2$, when converting an R(1)-automaton M with n states into a det-RR(1)-automaton for the language $L(M)$, then $2^n - 1$ states are sufficient and also necessary in the worst case.*

Proof. It remains to establish the lower bound. From Proposition 3.1.16, we have an NFA A with n states such that each equivalent det-RR(1)-automaton needs at least $2^n - 1$ states. By Proposition 3.1.2, the NFA A can be turned into an equivalent R(1)-automaton with n states. This proves the lower bound. □

Finally, we deal with the trade-off for turning a det-RR(1)-automaton into a DFA. By combining Theorem 3.1.7 with Proposition 3.1.14, we obtain a double exponential bound for this conversion. However, one can do better. By using alternating finite-state acceptors as an intermediate device, the following upper and lower bounds have been established by Martin Kutrib and Jens Reimann. As the proofs are technically rather involved, we skip them, just referring to the original papers.

Theorem 3.1.19 ([126, 127, 228])

(a) *For each $n \geq 2$, if M is a det-RR(1)-automaton with n states, then there exists a DFA with $\mathcal{O}(n!)$ states for the language $L(M)$.*

(b) *For each $n \geq 2$, there exists a det-RR(1)-automaton M with n states such that each DFA for the language $L(M)$ has at least $\Omega((n-1)!)$ states.*

We summarize the trade-offs obtained for the various conversions in the diagram in Figure 3.1, where the annotation of an arrow from a type $\mathcal{A}$ of automaton to a type $\mathcal{B}$ indicates the trade-off for converting an automaton of type $\mathcal{A}$ into an equivalent automaton of type $\mathcal{B}$. If only a single function $f(n)$ is given, then this expresses the fact that each n-state automaton of type $\mathcal{A}$ can be converted into an equivalent automaton of type $\mathcal{B}$ that has $f(n)$ states, and that this upper bound is also a lower bound in that there exist n-state automata of type $\mathcal{A}$ such that each equivalent automaton of type $\mathcal{B}$ has at least $f(n)$ states. Only for the conversion of a det-RR(1)-automaton into an equivalent DFA, the upper bound differs from the lower bound by a factor of size $\mathcal{O}(n)$.

From Theorem 2.3.102 and Corollary 2.3.104, we recall that monotone weight-reducing RWW-automata of window size one and deterministic weight-reducing RRWW-automata of window size one just accept regular languages. Obviously, weight-reducing automata with window size one can make use of auxiliary letters, in fact, an input letter may even be rewritten into a word of length larger than one. Accordingly, a measure for the size of these automata should involve the number of auxiliary letters as well as the number of states. However, the descriptional complexity of mon-sRWW(1)- and of det-sR(R)WW(1)-automata has not yet been studied.

Problem 3.1.20 (a) *What is the trade-off for turning a monotone sRWW*(1)*-automaton or a det-sR(R)WW*(1)*-automaton into an equivalent NFA or DFA?*

(b) *What is the trade-off for turning a monotone sRWW*(1)*-automaton or a det-sR(R)WW*(1)*-automaton into an equivalent R*(1)*- or det-RR*(1)*-automaton?*

3.2 On Stateless Ordered Restarting Automata

An ORWW-automaton is a weight-reducing RWW-automaton with a window of size 3 that, in each rewrite step, just replaces the letter in the middle of its window with another letter (of smaller weight). Hence, the actual weights of these letters are not important – just the relative weights are used. Accordingly, the weight function is replaced with a partial ordering on the tape alphabet (see Definition 2.3.66). As seen in Theorem 2.3.79, the class of languages accepted by ORWW-automata is quite expressive, but it is incomparable to the deterministic linear languages and the growing context-sensitive languages with respect to inclusion. On the other hand, the deterministic ORWW-automaton is a rather weak type of restarting automaton. In fact, it is shown in Proposition 2.3.81 that each det-ORWW-automaton can be converted into an equivalent det-ORWW-automaton that is stateless. Inspecting the proof of Proposition 2.3.81, we see that the tape alphabet of the simulating stateless det-ORWW-automaton has cardinality $|Q| \cdot |\Gamma|^2 + 2 \cdot |\Gamma|$, where Q is the set of states and Γ is the tape alphabet of the given det-ORWW-automaton. As it turned out, (stateless) det-ORWW-automata just accept the regular languages and, in addition, the stateless (nondeterministic) ORWW-automata are just as expressive (Corollary 2.3.86).

Here we study the descriptional complexity of stateless deterministic and nondeterministic ORWW-automata in relation to NFAs and DFAs. As mentioned before, we take the cardinality of the tape alphabet as the complexity measure for the size of a stateless ORWW-automaton. We start with the conversion of an NFA into a stateless ORWW-automaton which is in complete analogy to the corresponding result for the deterministic case presented in [195].

Proposition 3.2.1 *For each NFA $A = (Q, \Sigma, S, \varphi, F)$, there exists a stl-ORWW-automaton $M = (\Sigma, \Gamma, \rhd, \lhd, \delta, >)$ such that $L(M) = L(A)$ and $|\Gamma| = |Q| + |\Sigma|$.*

Proof. We take $\Gamma = \Sigma \cup Q$, define $a > q$ for all $a \in \Sigma$ and all $q \in Q$, and specify the transition relation δ as follows, where $a, b \in \Sigma$ and $p, q, q' \in Q$:

$$
\begin{array}{rlcll}
(1) & \delta(\rhd\lhd) & = & \{\mathsf{Accept}\}, & \text{if } \lambda \in L(A),\\
(2) & \delta(\rhd a\lhd) & = & \{\mathsf{Accept}\}, & \text{if } a \in L(A),\\
(3) & \delta(\rhd ab) & = & \{\, p \in Q \mid \exists q_0 \in S : p \in \varphi(q_0, a) \,\}, & \\
(4) & \delta(\rhd qb) & = & \{\mathsf{MVR}\}, & \\
(5) & \delta(qab) & = & \{\, p \in Q \mid p \in \varphi(q, a) \,\}, & \\
(6) & \delta(\rhd pq) & = & \{\mathsf{MVR}\}, & \\
(7) & \delta(pqq') & = & \{\mathsf{MVR}\}, & \\
(8) & \delta(pqa) & = & \{\mathsf{MVR}\}, & \\
(9) & \delta(qa\lhd) & = & \{\, p \in Q \mid p \in \varphi(q, a) \,\}, & \\
(10) & \delta(pq\lhd) & = & \{\mathsf{Accept}\}, & \text{if } q \in F.
\end{array}
$$

When a word $w = a_1 a_2 \cdots a_n$ is given as input, where $n \geq 1$ and $a_1, a_2, \ldots, a_n \in \Sigma$, then the stl-ORWW-automaton M simply replaces each letter a_i with a state from the set

$$\varphi(S, a_1 a_2 \cdots a_i) = \bigcup_{q \in S} \varphi(q, a_1 a_2 \cdots a_i),$$

proceeding from left to right. It accepts if and when the last letter a_n has been replaced with a final state of A. Hence, $L(M) = L(A)$ follows. □

If A is a DFA, then the construction in the above proof yields a stl-det-ORWW-automaton, that is, we have the following result.

Corollary 3.2.2 ([195, 205]) *For each DFA $A = (Q, \Sigma, q_0, \varphi, F)$, there exists a stl-det-ORWW-automaton $M = (\Sigma, \Gamma, \rhd, \lhd, \delta, >)$ such that $L(M) = L(A)$ and $|\Gamma| = |Q| + |\Sigma|$.*

We are interested in the reverse conversions. First, we derive an upper bound for the conversion of a stateless ORWW-automaton into an equivalent NFA by presenting a corresponding construction.

Let $M = (\Sigma, \Gamma, \rhd, \lhd, \delta, >)$ be a stateless ORWW-automaton. In analogy to Lemma 2.3.70 and the subsequent remark, we can assume without loss of generality that M only accepts with its window over the right sentinel $\lhd$. The transition relation δ of M can be represented by a set of four-tuples of the form (a, b, c, op), where $a \in \Gamma \cup \{\rhd\}$, $b \in \Gamma$, $c \in \Gamma \cup \{\lhd\}$, and $\mathrm{op} \in \Gamma \cup \{\mathsf{MVR}, \mathsf{Accept}\}$, where the operation $\mathrm{op} = \mathsf{Accept}$ occurs only in four-tuples of the form $(a, b, \lhd, \mathsf{Accept})$. The given partial order $>$ on Γ induces a partial order on these four-tuples, which we also denote by $>$:

$$\begin{array}{lcl} (a,b,c,\mathrm{op}) & > & (a',b',c',\mathrm{op}') \text{ if } a \geq a', b \geq b', c \geq c', \text{ and } (a,b,c) \neq (a',b',c'),\\ (a,b,c,\mathsf{MVR}) & > & (a,b,c,d) \;\; > \;\; (a,b,c,\mathsf{Accept}) \text{ for all } d \in \Gamma. \end{array}$$

To describe the construction of the intended NFA, we use the notion of a *pattern* (see the proof of Theorem 2.3.74). A pattern encodes the sequence of operations that M executes within an accepting computation at a particular cell of its tape. However, while the same move-right step may occur within a real computation repeatedly at a given position, a pattern will contain the corresponding move-right operation just once.

Definition 3.2.3 ([134]) *A pattern*

$$\Pi = \begin{bmatrix} a_{1,1} & a_{1,2} & a_{1,3} & \mathrm{op}_1 \\ a_{2,1} & a_{2,2} & a_{2,3} & \mathrm{op}_2 \\ \vdots & \vdots & \vdots & \vdots \\ a_{m,1} & a_{m,2} & a_{m,3} & \mathrm{op}_m \end{bmatrix}$$

is a sequence of four-tuples that satisfy all of the following conditions:

(1) $(a_{i,1}, a_{i,2}, a_{i,3}, \mathrm{op}_i) \in \delta$ *for all* $1 \leq i \leq m$.

(2) $(a_{i,1}, a_{i,2}, a_{i,3}, \mathrm{op}_i) > (a_{i+1,1}, a_{i+1,2}, a_{i+1,3}, \mathrm{op}_{i+1})$ *for all* $1 \leq i \leq m-1$.

(3) *If* $a_{1,1} = \rhd$, *then* $a_{i,1} = \rhd$ *for all* $1 \leq i \leq m$.

(4) *If* $a_{1,3} = \lhd$, *then* $a_{i,3} = \lhd$ *for all* $1 \leq i \leq m$, $\mathrm{op}_i \in \Gamma$ *for all* $1 \leq i \leq m-1$, *and* $\mathrm{op}_m = \mathsf{Accept}$.

(5) *If* $a_{1,3} \neq \lhd$, *then no accept operation occurs in* Π *and* $\mathrm{op}_m = \mathsf{MVR}$.

(6) *If* $\mathrm{op}_i = \mathsf{MVR}$ *for some* $1 \leq i \leq m-1$, *then* $a_{i+1,2} = a_{i,2}$.

(7) *If* $\mathrm{op}_i = d \in \Gamma$ *for some* $1 \leq i \leq m-1$, *then* $d < a_{i,2}$, $a_{i+1,2} = d$, *and* $a_{i+1,3} = a_{i,3}$.

(8) *If* $a_{i+1,3} < a_{i,3}$ *for some* $1 \leq i \leq m-1$, *then* $\mathrm{op}_i = \mathsf{MVR}$.

The automaton M can execute at most $n-1$ rewrite operations at each position, where $n = |\Gamma|$. Hence, a pattern can contain only up to $3n$ different three-tuples (a, b, c). Accordingly, a pattern can contain up to $3n$ move-right operations and up to $n-1$ rewrite operations, that is, we have $m \leq 4n$.

We want to relate two pattern Π_1 and Π_2 to each other, the idea being that they describe the sequences of operations of M at two neighbouring tape cells within an accepting computation. To do so, we partition Π_1 and Π_2 into blocks.

Definition 3.2.4 ([134]) *Let* $\Pi = \begin{bmatrix} a_{1,1} & a_{1,2} & a_{1,3} & \mathrm{op}_1 \\ a_{2,1} & a_{2,2} & a_{2,3} & \mathrm{op}_2 \\ \vdots & \vdots & \vdots & \vdots \\ a_{m,1} & a_{m,2} & a_{m,3} & \mathrm{op}_m \end{bmatrix}$ *be a pattern of* M.

(a) *A* right block (R-block)

$$RB = \begin{bmatrix} a_{i_1,1} & a_{i_1,2} & a_{i_1,3} & \mathrm{op}_{i_1} \\ a_{i_1+1,1} & a_{i_1+1,2} & a_{i_1+1,3} & \mathrm{op}_{i_1+1} \\ \vdots & \vdots & \vdots & \vdots \\ a_{i_1+s_1,1} & a_{i_1+s_1,2} & a_{i_1+s_1,3} & \mathrm{op}_{i_1+s_1} \end{bmatrix}$$

of Π *is a vertical section of maximal height such that*

$$a_{i_1,2} = a_{i_1+1,2} = \cdots = a_{i_1+s_1,2} \text{ and } a_{i_1,3} = a_{i_1+1,3} = \cdots = a_{i_1+s_1,3}.$$

(b) *A* left block (L-block)

$$LB = \begin{bmatrix} a_{j_1,1} & a_{j_1,2} & a_{j_1,3} & \mathrm{op}_{j_1} \\ a_{j_1+1,1} & a_{j_1+1,2} & a_{j_1+1,3} & \mathrm{op}_{j_1+1} \\ \vdots & \vdots & \vdots & \vdots \\ a_{j_1+t_1,1} & a_{j_1+t_1,2} & a_{j_1+t_1,3} & \mathrm{op}_{j_1+t_1} \end{bmatrix}$$

of Π *is a vertical section of maximal height such that*

$$a_{j_1,1} = a_{j_1+1,1} = \cdots = a_{j_1+t_1,1} \text{ and } a_{j_1,2} = a_{j_1+1,2} = \cdots = a_{j_1+t_1,2}.$$

In an R-block, the entries in the second and the third columns remain constant, while, in an L-block, the entries in the first and the second columns remain constant. As these blocks are of maximal height, we see that the row above an R-block (L-block) contains a different entry in column two or three (one or two) than the rows inside the block, and the same holds for the row below an R-block (L-block). Accordingly, the row immediately above an R-block (L-block) contains a rewrite step at the current position or at its right-hand (left-hand) neighbour, and the same holds for the last row of the R-block (L-block). The following properties are an immediate consequence of the above definitions.

Lemma 3.2.5 (a) *If* RB *is an R-block of the pattern* Π, *then*

1. $a_{i_1,1} > a_{i_1+1,1} > \cdots > a_{i_1+s_1-1,1} \geq a_{i_1+s_1,1}$,
2. $\mathrm{op}_{i_1} = \cdots = \mathrm{op}_{i_1+s_1-1} = \mathsf{MVR}$,
3. $\mathrm{op}_{i_1+s_1} \in \Gamma \cup \{\mathsf{MVR}\}$, *and*
4. *if* $\mathrm{op}_{i_1+s_1} = \mathsf{MVR}$, *then* $a_{i_1+s_1-1,1} > a_{i_1+s_1,1}$.

(b) *If* LB *is an L-block of the pattern* Π *such that* $a_{j_1,3} \in \Gamma$, *then*

1. $a_{j_1,3} > a_{j_1+1,3} > \cdots > a_{j_1+t_1-1,3} \geq a_{j_1+t_1,3}$,
2. $\mathrm{op}_{j_1} = \cdots = \mathrm{op}_{j_1+t_1-1} = \mathsf{MVR}$,
3. $\mathrm{op}_{j_1+t_1} \in \Gamma \cup \{\mathsf{MVR}\}$, *and*
4. *if* $\mathrm{op}_{j_1+t_1} = \mathsf{MVR}$, *then* $a_{j_1+t_1-1,3} > a_{j_1+t_1,3}$.

A pattern is meant to describe the sequence of operations that a stl-ORWW-automaton performs in a particular cell during an accepting computation. As it also contains the letters in the cells immediately to the left and to the right, the patterns that correspond to these cells must be compatible. This notion of compatibility is detailed in the next definition.

Definition 3.2.6 *Let* Π_1 *and* Π_2 *be two patterns of the stl-ORWW-automaton* M:

$$\Pi_1 = \begin{bmatrix} a_{1,1} & a_{1,2} & a_{1,3} & \mathrm{op}_1 \\ a_{2,1} & a_{2,2} & a_{2,3} & \mathrm{op}_2 \\ \vdots & \vdots & \vdots & \vdots \\ a_{m,1} & a_{m,2} & a_{m,3} & \mathrm{op}_m \end{bmatrix} = \begin{bmatrix} RB_1 \\ RB_2 \\ \vdots \\ RB_u \end{bmatrix} \text{ and } \Pi_2 = \begin{bmatrix} b_{1,1} & b_{1,2} & b_{1,3} & \mathrm{op}'_1 \\ b_{2,1} & b_{2,2} & b_{2,3} & \mathrm{op}'_2 \\ \vdots & \vdots & \vdots & \vdots \\ b_{r,1} & b_{r,2} & b_{r,3} & \mathrm{op}'_r \end{bmatrix} = \begin{bmatrix} LB_1 \\ LB_2 \\ \vdots \\ LB_v \end{bmatrix},$$

where $RB_1, RB_2, \ldots, RB_u$ *are the R-blocks of* Π_1, *and* $LB_1, LB_2, \ldots, LB_v$ *are the L-blocks of* Π_2. *The pattern* Π_1 *is* right-compatible *with the pattern* Π_2, *if the following conditions are satisfied:*

(1) v *is the number of R-blocks of* Π_1 *that contain move-right operations, and so,* $v \leq u$.

(2) *For* $1 \leq j \leq v$, *let* RB_{i_j} *be the* j*-th R-block of* Π_1 *that contains move-right operations. Then the second and third components of each row of* RB_{i_j} *coincide with the first and second components of each row of* LB_j.

(3) *If* RB_{i_j} *ends with a rewrite operation, then* LB_j *does not contain a rewrite operation.*

(4) *If LB_j ends with a rewrite operation, then RB_{i_j} does not contain a rewrite operation.*

(5) *Neither RB_{i_j} nor LB_j contains a rewrite operation if and only if $j = v$ and $i_v = u$.*

For each word w from the characteristic language $L_C(M)$, we have the following result.

Lemma 3.2.7 *Let $w \in L_C(M)$, let C be an accepting computation of M for w, and let Π_1 and Π_2 be patterns that are obtained from C for two neighbouring cells, where Π_1 is to the left of Π_2. Then Π_1 is right-compatible with Π_2.*

Our next result states that a sequence of right-compatible patterns satisfying certain technical conditions describes an accepting computation of the stl-ORWW-automaton M.

Theorem 3.2.8 ([134]) *Let $w = w_1 w_2 \cdots w_n \in \Gamma^+$, $w_1, w_2, \ldots, w_n \in \Gamma$, and let $(\Pi_1, \Pi_2, \ldots, \Pi_n)$ be a sequence of patterns such that*

- *Π_1 is a pattern with symbols $\rhd$ and w_1 in positions 1 and 2 of row 1,*
- *Π_n is a pattern with symbols w_n and $\lhd$ at positions 2 and 3 of row 1,*
- *for all $2 \le i \le n-1$, w_i is the letter in position 2 of row 1 of Π_i,*
- *and, for all $1 \le i \le n-1$, Π_i is right-compatible with Π_{i+1}.*

Then $w \in L_C(M)$. In fact, an accepting computation of M for w can be extracted from the sequence of patterns $(\Pi_1, \Pi_2, \ldots, \Pi_n)$.

Proof outline. We claim that the sequence of patterns $(\Pi_1, \Pi_2, \ldots, \Pi_n)$ yields an accepting computation for M on input w.

If $n = 1$, then $w = w_1 \in \Gamma$ and $\Pi_1 = \begin{bmatrix} \rhd & w_1 & \lhd & \mathrm{op}_1 \\ a_2 & b_2 & c_2 & \mathrm{op}_2 \\ \vdots & \vdots & \vdots & \vdots \\ a_{m-1} & b_{m-1} & c_{m-1} & \mathrm{op}_{m-1} \\ a_m & b_m & c_m & \mathrm{op}_m \end{bmatrix}$.

From Definition 3.2.3, it follows that $a_i = \rhd$ and $c_i = \lhd$ for all $i = 2, 3, \ldots, m$, that $\mathrm{op}_m = \mathsf{Accept}$, that $\mathrm{op}_i = b_{i+1} < b_i$ holds for all $i = 1, 2, \ldots, m-1$, where $b_1 = w_1$ is taken, and that $(\rhd, w_1, \lhd, b_2), (\rhd, b_2, \lhd, b_3), \ldots, (\rhd, b_{m-1}, \lhd, b_m), (\rhd, b_m, \lhd, \mathsf{Accept}) \in \delta$. Thus, Π_1 describes the following accepting computation of M on $w = w_1$:

$$\rhd w \lhd = \rhd w_1 \lhd \vdash_M^c \rhd b_2 \lhd \vdash_M^c \cdots \vdash_M^c \rhd b_m \lhd \vdash_M \mathsf{Accept},$$

which consists of $m-1$ cycles and an accepting tail.

If $n \ge 2$, then

$$\Pi_1 = \begin{bmatrix} \rhd & w_1 & c_{1,1} & \mathrm{op}_1^{(1)} \\ \rhd & b_{1,2} & c_{1,2} & \mathrm{op}_2^{(1)} \\ \vdots & \vdots & \vdots & \vdots \\ \rhd & b_{1,m_1-1} & c_{1,m_1-1} & \mathrm{op}_{m_1-1}^{(1)} \\ \rhd & b_{1,m_1} & c_{1,m_1} & \mathsf{MVR} \end{bmatrix}, \quad \Pi_n = \begin{bmatrix} a_{n,1} & w_n & \lhd & b_{n,2} \\ a_{n,2} & b_{n,2} & \lhd & b_{n,3} \\ \vdots & \vdots & \vdots & \vdots \\ a_{n,m_n-1} & b_{n,m_n-1} & \lhd & b_{n,m_n} \\ a_{n,m_n} & b_{n,m_n} & \lhd & \mathsf{Accept} \end{bmatrix},$$

and, for all $2 \le i \le n-1$,

$$\Pi_i = \begin{bmatrix} a_{i,1} & w_i & c_{i,1} & \mathrm{op}_1^{(i)} \\ a_{i,2} & b_{i,2} & c_{i,2} & \mathrm{op}_2^{(i)} \\ \vdots & \vdots & \vdots & \vdots \\ a_{i,m_i-1} & b_{i,m_i-1} & c_{i,m_i-1} & \mathrm{op}_{m_i-1}^{(i)} \\ a_{i,m_i} & b_{i,m_i} & c_{i,m_i} & \mathsf{MVR} \end{bmatrix}.$$

Observe that all Π_i, $1 \leq i \leq n-1$, contain at least one move-right operation. As by our hypothesis, Π_i is right-compatible with Π_{i+1}, we see that $c_{i,1} = w_{i+1}$ for all $1 \leq i \leq n-1$.

Let N be the combined number of rewrite operations contained in $\Pi_1, \Pi_2, \ldots, \Pi_n$. By induction on this number N, an accepting computation of M for the word w can now be constructed, which shows that $w \in L_C(M)$ holds. For the details of this construction, we refer to [134]. □

Based on this technical result, an NFA for the language $L_C(M)$ can be obtained from M. Thus, $L_C(M)$ is regular, and as $L(M) = L_C(M) \cap \Sigma^*$, it follows that $L(M)$ is regular, too, and that an NFA for $L(M)$ can be constructed from M.

Theorem 3.2.9 ([134]) *From a stl-ORWW-automaton M with a tape alphabet of cardinality n, an NFA $A = (Q, \Sigma, S, \delta_A, F)$ can be constructed such that $|Q| \leq 2^{13 \cdot n}$ and $L(A) = L(M)$.*

Proof outline. Let $M = (\Sigma, \Gamma, \triangleright, \triangleleft, \delta, >)$ be a stl-ORWW-automaton, where $n = |\Gamma|$. Without loss of generality, we may assume that M only accepts at the right sentinel. The NFA $A = (Q, \Sigma, S, \delta_A, F)$ is to simulate an accepting computation of M by guessing a corresponding sequence of patterns and verifying the conditions stated in Theorem 3.2.8. Accordingly, A is constructed as follows:

- The set Q contains a state for each pattern of M that only has a letter from Σ in the second position and a letter from $\Sigma \cup \{\triangleleft\}$ in the third position of its topmost row (see Definition 3.2.3) and an additional state q_+.
- The set S of initial states contains all states corresponding to patterns that contain the left sentinel $\triangleright$ in the first position of their topmost row and the state q_+, if $\lambda \in L(M)$.
- The set F of final states contains the state q_+ only.
- The transition relation δ is defined by the following rules, where Π and Π' denote patterns and $a \in \Sigma$:

$$\begin{aligned}
\delta_A(\Pi, a) &= \{\, \Pi' \mid \Pi \text{ has } a \text{ in position 2 and a letter from } \Sigma \text{ in position 3 of} \\
&\qquad \text{its topmost row and } \Pi \text{ is right-compatible with } \Pi' \,\}, \\
\delta_A(\Pi, a) &= \{\, q_+ \mid \Pi \text{ has } a \text{ in position 2 and } \triangleleft \text{ in position 3 of its topmost row} \,\}.
\end{aligned}$$

Then it can be checked that $L(A) = L(M)$. It remains to show that the number of states of the NFA A is restricted by the number $2^{13 \cdot n}$, where $n = |\Gamma|$. Obviously, it suffices to show that $2^{13 \cdot n}$ is an upper bound for the number of patterns that can occur within accepting computations of the stl-ORWW-automaton M. Let

$$\Pi = \begin{bmatrix} a_{1,1} & a_{1,2} & a_{1,3} & \mathrm{op}_1 \\ a_{2,1} & a_{2,2} & a_{2,3} & \mathrm{op}_2 \\ \vdots & \vdots & \vdots & \vdots \\ a_{m,1} & a_{m,2} & a_{m,3} & \mathrm{op}_m \end{bmatrix}$$

be such a pattern. Let us assume that there are v different letters in the first column, r different letters in the second, and s different letters in the third column, where $v, r, s \in \{1, 2, \ldots, n\}$. As $a_{i+1,j} \leq a_{i,j}$ for all $1 \leq i \leq m-1$ and $1 \leq j \leq 3$, each of these columns can be represented by a subset of Γ, which yields $\binom{n}{v}$, $\binom{n}{r}$, and $\binom{n}{s}$ choices for the first, second, and third column, respectively.

Next, we need to encode the information on the letter $a_{j,3}$ that is used in the rewriting of $a_{j,2}$ into $a_{j+1,2}$. This we can do by giving a multiset of cardinality $r-1$ with elements from the set of integers $\{1, 2, \ldots, s\}$, where the j-th integer k_j tells us that, for executing the j-th rewrite step, the k_j-th letter from the s letters occurring in the third column is used. This yields another $\binom{s+r-1-1}{r-1}$ choices, as there are $\binom{s+r-1-1}{r-1}$ such multisets. As from one row of Π to the next, at most one of the letters in column 2 and column 3 can change, it follows that all letters $a_{j,3}$ that are not chosen in this multiset are only used for move-right operations. However, some of the letters that are used for rewrite operations may also be used for move-right operations before the rewrite operation is actually executed. Let us assume that this happens t times, where $0 \leq t \leq r-1$. This gives us another $\binom{r-1}{t}$ choices. Furthermore, in the last row we either have a move-right operation, if $a_{1,3} \neq \lhd$, or we have an accept step, if $a_{1,3} = \lhd$.

So far we have described the last three columns of Π, which contain up to $r+s+t$ different triples and for which we have $\binom{n}{r} \cdot \binom{n}{s} \cdot \binom{s+r-2}{r-1} \cdot \binom{r-1}{t}$ choices. It remains to combine these triples with the information on the v letters in the first column, which can change from any row to the next. To each triple $(a_{j,2}, a_{j,3}, \mathsf{MVR})$, we add the index ℓ_j of the last letter from the first column such that $(a_{\ell_j,1}, a_{j,2}, a_{j,3}, \mathsf{MVR})$ is a row in Π. This yields $\binom{v+r+s+t-1}{r+s+t}$ choices, as there are these many corresponding multisets. In addition, we add to each of the triples the information of whether the last letter from the first column that is used with the previous triple is also used with the current triple, that is, whether the entry in the first column stays the same when going from the previous triple to the current one. This yields another 2^{r+s+t} choices. Thus, altogether this yields

$$\binom{n}{r} \cdot \binom{n}{s} \cdot \binom{s+r-2}{r-1} \cdot \binom{r-1}{t} \cdot \binom{n}{v} \cdot \binom{v+r+s+t-1}{r+s+t} \cdot 2^{r+s+t}$$

choices.

As v, r, s can range from 1 to n, we obtain the following upper bound for $|Q|$:

$$\begin{array}{rcl} |Q| & \leq & 1 + \sum_{r,s,v \in \{1,2,\ldots,n\}} \sum_{t=0}^{r-1} \binom{n}{r} \cdot \left(\binom{n}{s} \cdot \binom{s+r-2}{r-1} \cdot \binom{r-1}{t} + 1 \right) \cdot \\ & & \left(\binom{n}{v} \cdot \binom{v+r+s+t-1}{r+s+t} \cdot 2^{r+s+t} + 1 \right) \\ & \leq & 1 + \sum_{r,s,v \in \{1,2,\ldots,n\}} \sum_{t=0}^{r-1} \binom{n}{r} \cdot \binom{n}{s} \cdot \binom{2n}{r-1} \cdot \binom{n}{t} \cdot \binom{n}{v} \cdot \binom{4n}{r+s+t} \cdot 2^{r+s+t} \\ & = & 2^n \cdot 2^n \cdot 2^{2n} \cdot 2^n \cdot 2^n \cdot 2^{4n} \cdot 2^{3n} = 2^{13 \cdot n}. \end{array}$$

□

A better (that is, lower) upper bound can be obtained if M is a stateless deterministic ORWW-automaton. Again, we have $r \leq n$ different letters in the second column and $s \leq n$ different letters in the third column. However, as M is deterministic, we see that, whenever a row $(a_{j,1}, a_{j,2}, a_{j,3}, \mathsf{MVR})$ contains a move-right step, then the next rewrite operation in column 2 can occur only after the letter in row 3 has been rewritten. Thus, a pair $(a_{j,2}, a_{j,3})$ can only occur in a move-right step or in a rewrite step. Hence, we need a multiset of $r-1$ integers from the set $\{1, 2, \ldots, s\}$ to indicate the letters from column 3 that are used in the various rewrite steps. Furthermore, the letter in the first column can change, that is, it can be rewritten, only after the letter in the second column has been rewritten, and so we need only a multiset of cardinality r from Γ that indicates the letters in column 1 that occur together with a given letter from the second column. In fact, in this case, we get the upper bound of $2^{6 \cdot n}$ for the size of the resulting NFA. Accordingly, the construction in the proof of Theorem 3.2.9 yields the following result, which improves the original bound given in [130]. Observe that for turning a stl-det-ORWW-automaton into an equivalent stl-det-ORWW-automaton that only accepts at the right sentinel, an additional auxiliary letter may have to be introduced (see the proof of Lemma 2.3.70).

Corollary 3.2.10 ([134]) *From a stl-det-ORWW-automaton M with a tape alphabet of cardinality n, an NFA $A = (Q, \Sigma, S, \delta_A, F)$ can be constructed such that $|Q| \leq 2^{6 \cdot (n+1)}$ and $L(A) = L(M)$.*

Thus, $2^{\mathcal{O}(n)}$ is an upper bound for the size increase of the conversion of a stateless (deterministic or nondeterministic) ORWW-automaton into an equivalent NFA. Based on a family of example languages, it can be shown that this upper bound is also a lower bound.

Definition 3.2.11 *Let $\Sigma = \{a, b, \#, \$\}$ be an input alphabet, let $n \geq 3$ be a positive integer, and let B_n be the following language over Σ:*

$$B_n = \{ v_1 \# v_2 \# \cdots \# v_m \$ u \mid m \geq 1, v_1, v_2, \ldots, v_m, u \in \{a, b\}^n, \exists 1 \leq i \leq m : v_i = u \}.$$

Hence, if $w \in B_n$, then $w = v_1\#v_2\#\cdots\#v_m\$u$, where $v_1, v_2, \ldots, v_m, u$ are words of length n over $\{a, b\}$, and at least one of the first m words coincides with the last word u. It follows that $|w| = (m+1)\cdot n + m$ for some positive integer m, and it is easily seen that B_n is a regular language over Σ.

Proposition 3.2.12 ([195, 205]) *The language B_n is accepted by a stl-det-ORWW-automaton $M_n = (\Sigma, \Gamma_n, \rhd, \lhd, \delta_n, >)$ with an alphabet Γ_n of cardinality $18 \cdot n$.*

Proof outline. The stl-det-ORWW-automaton $M_n = (\Sigma, \Gamma_n, \rhd, \lhd, \delta_n, >)$ works in n phases. Let

$$w = v_1\#v_2\#\cdots\#v_m\$u$$

be given as input, where $m \geq 1$ and $v_1, v_2, \ldots, v_m, u \in \{a, b\}^n$,

$$v_j = v_{j,1}v_{j,2}\cdots v_{j,n},\ 1 \leq j \leq m, \text{ and } u = u_1u_2\cdots u_n.$$

In phase i, $1 \leq i \leq n$, M_n shifts the information on the letter u_{n+1-i} to the left until this information reaches the first letter of w. While doing so, it compares this letter to the letter $v_{j,n+1-i}$ of v_j for all $1 \leq j \leq m$, and it stores the result of this comparison on the tape by replacing the letter $v_{j,n+1-i}$ by some appropriate auxiliary letter. Finally, after phase n has been completed, M_n moves across the current tape contents and checks whether there is a factor from $\{a, b\}^*$ such that all letters of this factor have been matched successfully. In the affirmative, M_n accepts.

A detailed description of the stl-det-ORWW-automaton M_n can be found in [205]. It uses the tape alphabet

$$\begin{array}{rcl}\Gamma_n & = & \{a, b, \#, \$\} \cup \{\, [a, i], [b, i] \mid 1 \leq i \leq n \,\} \\ & & \cup \{\, \underline{[c, i, d]}, \mid c \in \{a, b, +, -, \#, \$\},\ 1 \leq i \leq n,\ d \in \{a, b\} \,\} \\ & & \cup \{\, \overline{[+, i, d]}, \overline{[-, i, d]} \mid 2 \leq i \leq n,\ d \in \{a, b\} \,\}.\end{array}$$

that is, we see that $|\Gamma_n| = 18 \cdot n$. Here $a, b, \#$ and $\$$ are the input letters, the letters of the form $[a, i]$ are used to indicate those letters of the factor u that have already been handled, the letters of the form $\underline{[c, i, d]}$ are used for shifting the information that the i-th letter of u is the letter d to the left, the letters of the form $\overline{[+, i, d]}$ and $\overline{[-, i, d]}$ are used to ensure that the processing of the $(i-1)$-st letter of u can start only after the processing of the i-th letter is complete. □

On the other hand, we have the following lower bound results on B_n.

Lemma 3.2.13

(a) *If $A = (Q, \Sigma, S, \delta, F)$ is an NFA such that $L(A) = B_n$, then $|Q| \geq 2^n$.*

(b) *If $A = (Q, \Sigma, q_0, \delta, F)$ is a DFA such that $L(A) = B_n$, then $|Q| \geq 2^{2^n}$.*

Proof. (a) We use the technique of *fooling set* from [13, 14]. Let $X = \{a, b\}^n$, and for each $x \in X$, let $u_x = x\$$ and $v_x = x$. Then, for all $x \in X$, we have $u_xv_x = x\$x \in B_n$, but for all $x, y \in X$, if $x \neq y$, then $u_xv_y = x\$y \notin B_n$. It follows that the set of pairs $P = \{\, (u_x, v_x) \mid x \in X \,\}$ is a fooling set for the language B_n. As $|P| = |X| = 2^n$, we see that $|Q| \geq |X| = 2^n$ for each NFA $A = (Q, \Sigma, S, \delta, F)$ satisfying $L(A) = B_n$.

(b) Assume that $A = (Q, \Sigma, q_0, \delta, F)$ is a DFA such that $L(A) = B_n$. Let $V = \{v_1, v_2, \ldots, v_m\}$ be a non-empty subset of $\{a, b\}^n$. Without loss of generality, we may assume that $v_1 \leq v_2 \leq \cdots \leq v_m$ holds, where $\leq$ is the lexicographical ordering on $\{a, b\}^n$. With V, we associate the word $w_V = v_1\#v_2\#\cdots\#v_m\$$, and furthermore, we take $q_V = \delta(q_0, w_V)$, that is, q_V is the state that A reaches from its initial state q_0 after reading the word w_V. As the word $w_Vv_1 \in B_n$, the state q_V exists, and obviously, $q_V \neq q_0$.

Now, let V_1 and V_2 be two non-empty subsets of $\{a, b\}^n$ such that $V_1 \neq V_2$. Then there exists a word $u \in \{a, b\}^n$ that belongs to the symmetric difference of V_1 and V_2. Without loss of generality, we assume that $u \in V_1$, and hence, $u \notin V_2$. Then $w_{V_1}u \in B_n$, but $w_{V_2}u \notin B_n$. Hence, it follows that the states q_{V_1} and q_{V_2} must not be identical. As there are $2^{2^n} - 1$ different non-empty subsets of $\{a,b\}^n$, we see that the set $\{ q_V \mid \emptyset \neq V \subseteq \{a,b\}^n \} \subseteq Q \setminus \{q_0\}$ contains $2^{2^n} - 1$ many different states. Thus, $|Q| \geq 2^{2^n}$ follows. □

In combination with Theorem 3.2.9, the above results on B_n yield the following consequence.

Corollary 3.2.14 ([195, 205]) *For converting a stl-ORWW-automaton or a stl-det-ORWW-automaton with a tape alphabet of cardinality n into an equivalent NFA, $2^{\mathcal{O}(n)}$ states are sufficient, and there are cases in which these many states are also necessary.*

For the conversion into DFAs, we have the following result.

Corollary 3.2.15 ([195, 205]) *For converting a stl-ORWW-automaton or a stl-det-ORWW-automaton with a tape alphabet of cardinality n into an equivalent DFA, $2^{2^{\mathcal{O}(n)}}$ states are sufficient, and there are cases in which these many states are also necessary.*

By Proposition 3.1.2, an NFA with n states can be converted into an equivalent R(1)-automaton with n states. Thus, we see from Theorem 3.2.9 that we can convert a stl-ORWW-automaton or a stl-det-ORWW-automaton into an equivalent R(1)-automaton with $\mathcal{O}(2^n)$ states. On the other hand, an R(1)-automaton (or a det-RR(1)-automaton) M for the language B_n cannot possibly execute any restart steps in any of its accepting computations, that is, M behaves essentially like an NFA (DFA). Now Lemma 3.2.13 implies that M has $\Omega(2^n)$ ($\Omega(2^{2^n})$) states. This yields the following consequences.

Corollary 3.2.16 (a) *For converting a stl-ORWW-automaton or a stl-det-ORWW-automaton with a tape alphabet of cardinality n into an equivalent R(1)-automaton, $2^{\mathcal{O}(n)}$ states are sufficient, and there are cases in which these many states are also necessary.*

(b) *For converting a stl-ORWW-automaton or a stl-det-ORWW-automaton with a tape alphabet of cardinality n into an equivalent det-RR(1)-automaton, $2^{2^{\mathcal{O}(n)}}$ states are sufficient, and there are cases in which these many states are also necessary.*

The converse transformations have not yet been studied in detail. However, from our results presented so far, we can at least derive the following upper bound.

Proposition 3.2.17 *Each R(1)-automaton with n states can be converted into an equivalent stl-ORWW-automaton (stl-det-ORWW-automaton) with a tape alphabet of cardinality $\mathcal{O}(2^n)$.*

Proof. By Corollary 3.1.4, an R(1)-automaton with n states can be converted into an equivalent NFA with 2^n states and into an equivalent DFA with $2^n + 1$ states. From the NFA, we obtain an equivalent stl-ORWW-automaton with a tape alphabet of cardinality $2^n + |\Sigma|$, where Σ is the input alphabet (by Proposition 3.2.1), and from the DFA, we obtain an equivalent stl-det-ORWW-automaton with a tape alphabet of cardinality $2^n + 1 + |\Sigma|$ (by Corollary 3.2.2). Thus, $\mathcal{O}(2^n)$ is an upper bound for the conversion of an R(1)-automaton into an equivalent stl-ORWW- or stl-det-ORWW-automaton. □

How good is this upper bound?

Problem 3.2.18 *What is the real trade-off for converting an R(1)-automaton into an equivalent stl-ORWW- or stl-det-ORWW-automaton? Can the upper bound of $\mathcal{O}(2^n)$ be improved, or are there matching lower bounds for these conversions?*

Concerning the conversion of a det-RR(1)-automaton into a stl-det-ORWW-automaton, we have the following upper bound.

Proposition 3.2.19 *Each det-RR(1)-automaton with n states can be converted into an equivalent stl-det-ORWW-automaton with a tape alphabet of cardinality $2^{\mathcal{O}(n)}$.*

Proof. Let $M = (Q, \Sigma, \Sigma, \rhd, \lhd, q_0, 1, \delta)$ be a det-RR(1)-automaton, where $|Q| = n$ and $|\Sigma| = m$. By introducing an auxiliary letter #, by defining a partial ordering $>$ on $\Gamma = \Sigma \cup \{\#\}$ by taking $a > \#$ for all $a \in \Sigma$, by replacing each delete step $\delta(q, b) = (q', \lambda)$ of M by the rewrite steps $\delta'(q, abc) = (q', \#)$ for all $a \in \Sigma \cup \{\rhd, \#\}$ and all $c \in \Sigma \cup \{\lhd, \#\}$, and by adding the move-right steps $\delta'(q, a\#c) = (q, \mathsf{MVR})$ for all $a \in \Sigma \cup \{\rhd, \#\}$ and all $c \in \Sigma \cup \{\#\}$, we obtain a det-ORRWW-automaton $M' = (Q, \Sigma, \Gamma, \rhd, \lhd, q_0, \delta', >)$ that accepts the same language as M. In addition, M' has n states and a tape alphabet of cardinality $m + 1$.

By Proposition 2.3.82, we can convert the det-ORRWW-automaton M' into an equivalent det-ORWW-automaton M''. From the proof of that proposition, we can conclude that M'' has $\mathcal{O}(n)$ states and a tape alphabet of cardinality $\mathcal{O}((m+1)^2 \cdot 2^{\mathcal{O}(n)})$. Finally, by Proposition 2.3.81, we can convert the det-ORWW-automaton M'' into an equivalent stl-det-ORWW-automaton $\tilde{M}$, which has a tape alphabet of cardinality $\mathcal{O}((m+1)^4 \cdot n \cdot 2^{\mathcal{O}(n)}) = 2^{\mathcal{O}(n)}$. Thus, $2^{\mathcal{O}(n)}$ is an upper bound for the conversion of a det-RR(1)-automaton into an equivalent stl-det-ORWW-automaton. □

Again the question of the quality of this upper bound remains open.

Problem 3.2.20 *What is the real trade-off for converting a det-RR(1)-automaton into an equivalent stl-ORWW- or stl-det-ORWW-automaton? How good is the upper bound in Proposition 3.2.19? Is there a better upper bound, or is there a matching lower bound?*

To establish one more trade-off, still another group of example languages is considered in [205].

Definition 3.2.21 *For each $n \geq 1$, let U_n be the singleton language $U_n = \{a^{2^n}\}$.*

Obviously, an NFA for the language U_n needs at least $2^n + 1$ states. In fact, according to [15], even every two-way NFA for U_n has at least $2^n + 1$ states. However, there exists a stl-det-ORWW-automaton with only $\mathcal{O}(n)$ letters that accepts this language.

Proposition 3.2.22 ([205]) *For each $n \geq 3$, the language U_n is accepted by a stl-det-ORWW-automaton M_n that has a tape alphabet of cardinality $3n - 1$.*

Proof outline. For $n \geq 3$, let

$$\begin{aligned}\Gamma_n &= \{a, [1,+,-], [1,-,+], [n,-,-], [n,-,+]\} \\ &\quad \cup \{\, [i,+,-], [i,-,+], [i,-,-] \mid i = 2, 3, \ldots, n-1 \,\},\end{aligned}$$

that is, $|\Gamma_n| = 3n - 1$. The stl-det-ORWW-automaton M_n processes a given input in n phases. In phase i, the letters of the form $[i, r, s]$ are used to rewrite the current tape contents from right to left, letter by letter. The index r indicates whether the current position corresponds to an input letter that has already been marked as deleted ($r = -$) or not ($r = +$), and the index s indicates whether the next undeleted letter to the left must be deleted ($s = -$) or whether it is to be maintained as undeleted ($s = +$). These indices are used in such a way that in each phase, every second undeleted position is kept, and the other previously undeleted positions are marked as 'deleted'. Finally, in phase n, exactly one previously undeleted position is marked as 'deleted', and M_n accepts if the first position is the second previously undeleted position from the right in phase n. For a detailed description of M_n, we refer to [205]. For example, for $n = 3$, M_3 executes the following computation on input $w = a^8$:

$$\begin{aligned}&\rhd aaaaaaaa\lhd \vdash^c \rhd aaaaaaa[1,-,+]\lhd \vdash^{c^7} \\ &\rhd[1,+,-][1,-,+][1,+,-][1,-,+][1,+,-][1,-,+][1,+,-][1,-,+]\lhd \ \vdash^{c^8} \\ &\rhd[2,+,-][2,-,+][2,-,+][2,-,-][2,+,-][2,-,+][2,-,+][2,-,-]\lhd \ \vdash^{c^7} \\ &\rhd[2,+,-][3,-,+][3,-,+][3,-,+][3,-,+][3,-,-][3,-,-][3,-,-]\lhd \ \vdash \ \ \mathsf{Accept}.\end{aligned}$$

It follows that $L(M_n) = U_n$. □

As an NFA can be seen as a 2NFA, we have the following trade-off.

Corollary 3.2.23 ([205]) *For converting a stl-ORWW-automaton or a stl-det-ORWW-automaton with a tape alphabet of cardinality n into an equivalent 2NFA, $2^{\mathcal{O}(n)}$ states are sufficient, and there are cases in which these many states are also necessary.*

It remains to study the descriptional complexity of stl-ORWW-automata in relation to that of stl-det-ORWW-automata. Of course, a stl-ORWW-automaton M with a tape alphabet of cardinality n can first be converted into an NFA with $2^{\mathcal{O}(n)}$ states. This NFA can then be turned into an equivalent DFA with $2^{2^{\mathcal{O}(n)}}$ states, which in turn yields an equivalent stl-det-ORWW-automaton with a tape alphabet of cardinality $2^{2^{\mathcal{O}(n)}}$.

Problem 3.2.24 *Is there a better upper bound for the conversion of a stl-ORWW-automaton into an equivalent stl-det-ORWW-automaton? Is there a matching lower bound?*

Although we do not know whether a double exponential lower bound exists, we can at least provide an exponential lower bound. To establish this lower bound, the following family of languages is considered in [132].

Definition 3.2.25 *Let $\Sigma = \{a, b, \#\}$, and, for $n \geq 1$, let C_n denote the following language over Σ:*

$$C_n = \{\, u_1\#u_2\#\cdots\#u_m \mid m \geq 2, u_1, u_2, \ldots, u_m \in \{a,b\}^n, \exists i < j : u_i = u_j \,\}.$$

For these languages, we have the following upper bound, which is a slight improvement over the bound given in [132].

Proposition 3.2.26 *The language C_n is accepted by a stl-ORWW-automaton M'_n with a tape alphabet of cardinality $20 \cdot n + 1$.*

Proof. By Proposition 3.2.12, there exists a stl-det-ORWW-automaton M_n with $18 \cdot n$ letters that accepts the language

$$B_n = \{\, v_1\#v_2\#\cdots\#v_m\$u \mid m \geq 1, v_1, v_2, \ldots, v_m, u \in \{a,b\}^n, \exists 1 \leq i \leq m : v_i = u \,\}.$$

The stl-ORWW-automaton M'_n is obtained from M_n by adding the $2n+1$ letters

$$a'_1, a'_2, \ldots, a'_n, b'_1, b'_2, \ldots, b'_n, \text{ and } \#'.$$

It proceeds as follows.

It first marks the letters from right to left. In a factor $v = v^{(1)}v^{(2)}\cdots v^{(n)}$, the last letter is replaced with $v_n^{(n)'}$, $v^{(n-1)}$ is replaced with $v_{n-1}^{(n-1)'}$, and so forth until finally $v^{(1)}$ is replaced with $v_1^{(1)'}$, and then the preceding letter # is replaced with #′. In this way, it is ensured that this $\{a,b\}$-factor has length n. This continues until M'_n nondeterministically chooses to replace a letter # with the letter \$. Thus, the input of the form $u_1\#u_2\#\cdots\#u_k\#u_{k+1}\#\cdots\#u_m$ is transformed into a word of the form $u_1\#u_2\#\cdots\#u_k\$\hat{u}_{k+1}\#'\cdots\#'\hat{u}_m$, where $\hat{u}_i$ $(k+1 \leq i \leq m)$ denotes the word that is obtained from $u_i \in \{a,b\}^n$ by the above marking process. Then, on the prefix $u_1\#u_2\#\cdots\#u_k\$\hat{u}_{k+1}$, M'_n simulates the stl-det-ORWW-automaton M_n, and it accepts if the computation of M_n being simulated accepts. It is obvious now that $L(M'_n) = C_n$. □

On the other hand, every stl-det-ORWW-automaton for C_n needs at least $2^{\mathcal{O}(n)}$ letters, that is, the above presentation by a stl-ORWW-automaton is exponentially more succinct than any presentation by a stl-det-ORWW-automaton.

Proposition 3.2.27 ([132]) *Let $s : \mathbb{N} \to \mathbb{N}$ be a function such that, for each $n \geq 1$, there exists a stl-det-ORWW-automaton $D_n = (\Sigma, \Gamma_n, \rhd, \lhd, \delta_n, >)$ such that $L(D_n) = C_n$ and $|\Gamma_n| \leq s(n)$. Then $s(n) \notin o(2^n)$.*

Proof. Let $n \geq 1$, and let $D_n = (\Sigma, \Gamma_n, \triangleright, \triangleleft, \delta_n, >)$ be a stl-det-ORWW-automaton such that $L(D_n) = C_n$ and $|\Gamma_n| \leq s(n)$. As D_n is deterministic, we obtain a stl-det-ORWW-automaton $E_n = (\Sigma, \Gamma_n, \triangleright, \triangleleft, \eta_n, >)$ such that $L(E_n) = C_n^c = \Sigma^* \smallsetminus D_n$ simply by interchanging accept steps with undefined steps (see, e.g., [195] Theorem 10). From E_n, we can construct an NFA F_n of size $2^{r \cdot s(n)}$ for C_n^c by Corollary 3.2.10, where r is a constant.

We now present a large fooling set for C_n^c. Let A be a subset of $\{a,b\}^n$ of cardinality 2^{n-1}. Then also the set $\bar{A} = \{a,b\}^n \smallsetminus A$ has cardinality 2^{n-1}. With these sets we associate the following languages:

$$\begin{array}{rcll} P_A & = & \{\, u_1\#u_2\#\cdots\#u_{2^{n-1}} & \mid A = \{u_1, u_2, \ldots, u_{2^{n-1}}\}\,\} \text{ and} \\ Q_A & = & \{\, \#v_1\#v_2\#\cdots\#v_{2^{n-1}} & \mid \bar{A} = \{v_1, v_2, \ldots, v_{2^{n-1}}\}\,\}. \end{array}$$

Then $uv \in C_n^c$ for all $u \in P_A$ and all $v \in Q_A$. On the other hand, if B is a subset of $\{a,b\}^n$ of cardinality 2^{n-1} such that $A \neq B$, then $uv \in C_n$ for all $u \in P_A$ and all $v \in Q_B$, because there is a word $x \in \{a,b\}^n$ such that $x \in A$ and $x \in \bar{B}$. Hence, by choosing a pair $(u_A, v_A) \in P_A \times Q_A$ for all subsets A of $\{a,b\}^n$ of cardinality 2^{n-1}, we obtain a fooling set for C_n^c of cardinality

$$\binom{2^n}{2^{n-1}} \quad = \quad \frac{(2^n)!}{(2^{n-1})! \cdot (2^{n-1})!} > \quad 2^{2^{n-1}}.$$

This implies by [13] that the number $2^{r \cdot s(n)}$ of states of the NFA F_n satisfies the inequality $2^{r \cdot s(n)} \geq 2^{2^{n-1}}$, that is, $r \cdot s(n) \geq 2^{n-1}$. Hence, $\frac{s(n)}{2^n} \geq \frac{1}{2r}$, which clearly shows that $\liminf_{n \to \infty} \frac{s(n)}{2^n} \geq \frac{1}{2r} > 0$, that is, $s(n) \notin o(2^n)$. □

Together with Proposition 3.2.26, this result provides the announced exponential lower bound for the conversion of a stl-ORWW-automaton into an equivalent stl-det-ORWW-automaton. In addition, we can also derive the following complexity result from the proof of Proposition 3.2.27.

Corollary 3.2.28 ([132]) *Let $s : \mathbb{N} \to \mathbb{N}$ be a function such that, for each $n \geq 1$, there exists a stl-ORWW-automaton $E_n = (\Sigma, \Gamma_n, \triangleright, \triangleleft, \delta_n, >)$ such that $L(E_n) = C_n^c$ and $|\Gamma_n| \leq s(n)$. Then $s(n) \notin o(2^n)$.*

Proof. By Theorem 3.2.9, we can construct an NFA F_n of size $2^{r \cdot s(n)}$ for C_n^c from E_n. Now the proof of Proposition 3.2.27 shows that $s(n) \notin o(2^n)$. □

As by Proposition 3.2.26, the language C_n is accepted by a stl-ORWW-automaton M_n' with a tape alphabet of cardinality $20 \cdot n + 1$, Corollary 3.2.28 shows that the conversion of a stl-ORWW-automaton of size n into a stl-ORWW-automaton for the complement of $L(M)$ can actually increase the alphabet size exponentially.

For future reference, we now consider the problem of constructing a small stl-det-ORWW-automaton for the intersection or union of languages that are given through DFAs.

Theorem 3.2.29 ([195, 205]) *If the languages L_1 and L_2 over an alphabet of cardinality k are accepted by DFAs with m and n states, respectively, then their intersection $L_1 \cap L_2$ is accepted by a stl-det-ORWW-automaton with a tape alphabet of cardinality $k \cdot (\min\{m,n\} + 1) + \max\{m,n\}$.*

Proof. Let $A_1 = (Q_1, \Sigma, q_0, \delta_1, F_1)$ be a DFA such that $L(A_1) = L_1$, where $|Q_1| = m$ and $|\Sigma| = k$, and let $A_2 = (Q_2, \Sigma, p_0, \delta_2, F_2)$ be a DFA such that $L(A_2) = L_2$, where $|Q_2| = n$. Without loss of generality, we may assume that $m \leq n$. From A_1 and A_2, we construct a stl-det-ORWW-automaton $M = (\Sigma, \Gamma, \triangleright, \triangleleft, \delta, >)$ for $L = L_1 \cap L_2$:

- $\Gamma = \Sigma \cup \{\, [q,a] \mid q \in Q_1 \text{ and } a \in \Sigma \,\} \cup Q_2$, that is,

$$|\Gamma| = k + k \cdot m + n = k \cdot (\min\{m,n\} + 1) + \max\{m,n\},$$

- the ordering $>$ is defined by taking $a > [q,b] > p$ for all $a, b \in \Sigma$, $q \in Q_1$, and $p \in Q_2$,

- and the transition function δ is defined as follows, where $a, b, c \in \Sigma$, $q, q' \in Q_1$, and $p, p', p_1, p_2 \in Q_2$:

$$\begin{array}{rlcll}
(1) & \delta(\rhd a \lhd) & = & \mathsf{Accept}, & \text{if } a \in (\Sigma \cup \{\lambda\}) \cap L_1 \cap L_2, \\
(2) & \delta(\rhd ab) & = & [q, a], & \text{where } q = \delta_1(q_0, a), \\
(3) & \delta(\rhd [q, a] b) & = & \mathsf{MVR}, & \\
(4) & \delta([q, a] bc) & = & [q', b], & \text{where } q' = \delta_1(q, b), \\
(5) & \delta(\rhd [q, a][q', b]) & = & p, & \text{where } p = \delta_2(p_0, a), \\
(6) & \delta(\rhd p[q, a]) & = & \mathsf{MVR}, & \\
(7) & \delta(p[q, a] b) & = & \mathsf{MVR}, & \\
(8) & \delta(p[q, a][q', b]) & = & p', & \text{where } p' = \delta_2(p, a), \\
(9) & \delta(\rhd pp') & = & \mathsf{MVR}, & \\
(10) & \delta(pp_1p_2) & = & \mathsf{MVR}, & \\
(11) & \delta(pp_1[q, a]) & = & \mathsf{MVR}, & \\
(12) & \delta([q, a] b \lhd) & = & [q', b], & \text{where } q' = \delta_1(q, b), \\
(13) & \delta(p[q, a] \lhd) & = & \mathsf{Accept}, & \text{if } q \in F_1 \text{ and } \delta_2(p, a) \in F_2.
\end{array}$$

The automaton M works as follows:

1. First, M simulates two steps of A_1 by turning the first two input letters ab into the pairs $[q, a][q', b]$, where $q = \delta_1(q_0, a)$ and $q' = \delta_1(q, b)$.

2. On the prefix $[q, a][q', b]$, the first step of A_2 can already be simulated by rewriting $[q, a]$ into p, where $p = \delta_2(p_0, a)$.

3. Now M alternates between simulating a step of A_1 and a step of A_2.

4. If the last two letters are of the form $p[q, a]$ for some $p \in Q_2$ and $q \in F_1$, and if $\delta_2(p, a) \in F_2$, then M accepts.

It is easily seen that $L(M) = L(A_1) \cap L(A_2)$. □

Observe that, by first building the product DFA of A_1 and A_2 and by then turning this into an equivalent stl-det-ORWW-automaton, we obtain a stl-det-ORWW-automaton for the language $L = L(A_1) \cap L(A_2)$ with a tape alphabet of cardinality $k + m \cdot n$ by Corollary 3.2.2. As typically m and n are large, while k is small (e.g., often binary languages are considered, that is, $k = 2$), Theorem 3.2.29 gives a much better bound. Obviously, the above construction can be adopted to the operation of union. Also, it can easily be extended to the intersection or union of more than two DFAs.

Corollary 3.2.30 ([195, 205]) *For $t \geq 3$, if A_i is a DFA with n_i states over an alphabet of cardinality k for all $1 \leq i \leq t$, then there exists a stl-det-ORWW-automaton M with a tape alphabet of cardinality $k \cdot (1 + n_1 + \cdots + n_{t-1}) + n_t$ such that $L(M) = \bigcap_{i=1}^{t} L(A_i)$ (or $L(M) = \bigcup_{i=1}^{t} L(A_i)$).*

We have seen that stl-det-ORWW-automata provide very concise presentations of (some) regular languages when compared to many other types of automata. However, this comes at a price. The emptiness problem and many other decision problems that are easily decidable for DFAs and NFAs are hard for stl-det-ORWW-automata. More specifically, it has been shown that the emptiness problem for stl-det-ORWW-automata is PSPACE-complete, that is, it is one of the hardest problems that can be solved in polynomial space.

The *emptiness problem* for NFAs is the problem of deciding whether the language accepted by a given NFA is empty. If $A = (Q, \Sigma, S, \delta, F)$ is an NFA with m states, then the emptiness of $L(A)$ can be decided nondeterministically using space $\mathcal{O}(\log m)$ [89] by checking whether there is a path in the state graph $G(A)$ of A that leads from a node corresponding to an initial state to a node corresponding to an accepting state. This result can be used to show that the emptiness problem for stl-det-ORWW-automata is decidable in polynomial space.

Theorem 3.2.31 ([130, 205]) *The emptiness problem for stl-det-ORWW-automata is PSPACE-complete.*

Proof outline. Let $M = (\Sigma, \Gamma, \rhd, \lhd, \delta, >)$ be a stl-det-ORWW-automaton such that $|\Gamma| = n$. By Corollary 3.2.10, there exists an NFA $A = (Q, \Sigma, S, \delta_A, \{q_F\})$ of size at most $2^{6\cdot(n+1)}$ such that $L(A) = L(M)$. A nondeterministic Turing machine T can now check whether $L(A)$ is empty by trying to guess an accepting computation of A, that is, a path in the state graph of A from an initial state to a final state. It is clear that each shortest path of this form has at most length $|Q| \leq 2^{6\cdot(n+1)}$, and so, if no final state is reached, then T halts without accepting after these many steps.

Obviously, T accepts if and only if $L(M) = L(A)$ is non-empty. For performing the above computation, T needs to store two states of A and a counter that it uses to count the number of steps of A it has already simulated. Thus, we see that T just needs space $6 \cdot (n + 1)$ for the counter and space $\mathcal{O}(n)$ for the two states of A. Hence, the emptiness problem for stl-det-ORWW-automata is decidable nondeterministically within polynomial space, and therewith, by Savitch's Theorem [233], it is decidable deterministically within polynomial space, that is, stl-det-ORWW-Emptiness $\in$ PSPACE.

To prove PSPACE-hardness, let $A_1, A_2, \ldots, A_t$ be DFAs over a common input alphabet Σ of cardinality k such that A_i has n_i states, $1 \leq i \leq t$. From these DFAs, we can construct a stl-det-ORWW-automaton M with a tape aphabet of cardinality $k \cdot (1 + n_1 + \cdots + n_{t-1}) + n_t$ such that $L(M) = \bigcap_{i_1}^{t} L(A_i)$ by Corollary 3.2.30. Hence, M has at most

$$\mathcal{O}((k \cdot (1 + n_1 + \cdots + n_{t-1}) + n_t)^3) = \mathcal{O}((k \cdot \sum_{i=1}^{t} n_i)^3)$$

many transitions, and so it can be computed from $A_1, A_2, \ldots, A_t$ in polynomial time.

Now $L(M) \neq \emptyset$ iff $L(A_1) \cap L(A_2) \cap \ldots \cap L(A_t) \neq \emptyset$, which shows that the above construction yields a polynomial-time reduction from the 'DFA-Intersection-Emptiness Problem' to the emptiness problem for stl-det-ORWW-automata. As the former is PSPACE-complete (see, e.g., [49]), PSPACE-completeness of the latter follows. □

Also many other decision problems are PSPACE-complete for stl-det-ORWW-automata, e.g., the universality problem, the finiteness problem, the inclusion problem, and the equivalence problem (see [130, 205]).

3.2.1 Reversible ORWW- and ORRWW-Automata

Reversibility is a property of deterministic types of automata. It requires that every configuration has not only a unique successor configuration, but also a unique predecessor configuration. This means that a reversible automaton is forward and backward deterministic. Thus, in addition to the transition function, a reversible automaton has a 'reverse' transition function that undoes computational steps. The main motivation for studying this notion is the observation that information is lost in computations that are not reversible. Each Turing machine can be simulated by a reversible Turing machine [10], which shows that reversible Turing machines are just as expressive as standard Turing machines. On the other hand, reversible DFAs are strictly less expressive than DFAs [217]. The notion of reversibility has also been studied for other types of automata, e.g., pushdown automata [118] and queue automata [119].

In [211], a notion of reversibility has been introduced for stateless deterministic ORWW-automata. However, there is a serious problem with the combined rewrite/restart steps of ORWW-automata. Such a step replaces a letter at some position on the tape with a smaller letter and then it moves the window to the beginning of the tape. So it is rather inconceivable that a reverse transition function could be designed that undoes these steps. Accordingly, the notion of reversibility defined in [211] for stl-det-ORWW-automata is specifically tuned to the spirit of restarting automata. A stl-det-ORWW-automaton is called *reversible* if there exists a reverse transition function by which reverse cycles are executed, that is, if the tape contents $\triangleright x \triangleleft$ is transformed into the tape contents $\triangleright y \triangleleft$ by a cycle of a reversible stl-det-ORWW-automaton M, then by the reverse transition function, a reverse cycle can be executed that transforms the tape contents $\triangleright y \triangleleft$ back into the tape contents $\triangleright x \triangleleft$. Thus, it is not the step-by-step computation of M that is reversible, but instead, it is the sequence of cycles that make up a computation of M that is reversible. Accordingly, the following definition is used.

Definition 3.2.32 ([211]) *A stl-det-ORWW-automaton $M = (\Sigma, \Gamma, \triangleright, \triangleleft, \delta, >)$ is called* reversible, *if there exists a (partial) reverse transition function*

$$\delta^R : ((\Gamma \cup \{\triangleright\}) \cdot \Gamma \cdot (\Gamma \cup \{\triangleleft\})) \to (\{\mathsf{MVR}\} \cup \Gamma)$$

such that, for all restarting configurations $\triangleright w \triangleleft$ and $\triangleright w' \triangleleft$ that occur in computations of M, the following equivalence holds:

$$\triangleright w \triangleleft \vdash_M^c \triangleright w' \triangleleft \ \text{ iff } \ \triangleright w' \triangleleft \vdash_M^{c^R} \triangleright w \triangleleft,$$

where $\vdash_M^{c^R}$ denotes a cycle that is realized by using the reverse transition function δ^R. We describe the above reversible stl-det-ORWW-automaton as $M = (\Sigma, \Gamma, \triangleright, \triangleleft, \delta, \delta^R, >)$, and we use the prefix rev- to denote reversible automata.

Observe that in the definition above, it is required that a cycle must be reversible by δ^R only for the case that the corresponding restarting configurations occur in a valid computation of M, that is, there exists an input $x \in \Sigma^*$ such that $\triangleright w \triangleleft$ is reached from the initial configuration $\triangleright x \triangleleft$ of M. This corresponds to the way reversibility is defined for queue automata in [119].

Obviously, reversible stl-det-ORWW-automata can only accept certain regular languages. However, in contrast to the situation for DFAs, they actually accept all regular languages, as we have the following result.

Theorem 3.2.33 ([211]) *For each DFA $A = (Q, \Sigma, q_0, \varphi, F)$, there exists a rev-stl-det-ORWW-automaton $M = (\Sigma, \Gamma, \triangleright, \triangleleft, \delta, \delta^R, >)$ such that $L(M) = L(A)$ and $|\Gamma| = |\Sigma| \cdot (|Q| + 1)$.*

Proof. Let $A = (Q, \Sigma, q_0, \varphi, F)$ be a DFA that accepts a language $L \subseteq \Sigma^*$. We take $\Gamma = \Sigma \cup (Q \times \Sigma)$, which shows that $|\Gamma| = |\Sigma| \cdot (|Q| + 1)$, and define a partial ordering on Γ through $a > (q, a)$ for all $a \in \Sigma$ and all $q \in Q$. Finally, we define the transition functions δ and δ^R as follows, where $a, b, c \in \Sigma$ and $p, q, q' \in Q$:

$$\begin{array}{lcll@{\quad}lcll}
\delta(\triangleright\triangleleft) & = & \mathsf{Accept}, & \text{if } \lambda \in L(A), & \delta(\triangleright(q,a)b) & = & \mathsf{MVR}, & \\
\delta(\triangleright a\triangleleft) & = & \mathsf{Accept}, & \text{if } a \in L(A), & \delta(\triangleright(q,a)(p,b)) & = & \mathsf{MVR}, & \\
\delta(\triangleright ab) & = & (q,a), & \text{if } \varphi(q_0,a) = q, & \delta((p,a)(q,b)(q',c)) & = & \mathsf{MVR}, & \\
\delta((q,a)bc) & = & (p,b), & \text{if } \varphi(q,b) = p, & \delta((p,a)(q,b)c) & = & \mathsf{MVR}, & \\
\delta((q,a)b\triangleleft) & = & (p,b), & \text{if } \varphi(q,b) = p, & \delta((q,a)(p,b)\triangleleft) & = & \mathsf{Accept}, & \text{if } p \in F, \\
\delta^R(\triangleright(q,a)b) & = & a, & \text{if } \varphi(q_0,a) = q, & \delta^R(\triangleright(p,a)(q,b)) & = & \mathsf{MVR}, & \\
\delta^R((p,a)(q,b)c) & = & b, & \text{if } \varphi(p,b) = q, & \delta^R((p,a)(q,b)(q',c)) & = & \mathsf{MVR}. & \\
\delta^R((p,a)(q,b)\triangleleft) & = & b, & \text{if } \varphi(p,b) = q, & & & &
\end{array}$$

Thus, given $w = a_1 a_2 \cdots a_n$ as input, where $n \geq 2$ and $a_1, a_2, \ldots, a_n \in \Sigma$, M rewrites w from left to right into the word $(q_1, a_1)(q_2, a_2) \cdots (q_{n-1}, a_{n-1})(q_n, a_n)$, where $q_i = \varphi(q_0, a_1 a_2 \cdots a_i)$, $1 \leq i \leq n$, and this word is then accepted in a tail computation if $q_n \in F$. Hence, M accepts on input w iff

$$\varphi(q_0, a_1 a_2 \cdots a_n) = \varphi(\varphi(q_0, a_1 a_2 \cdots a_{n-1}), a_n) = \varphi(q_{n-1}, a_n) = q_n \in F,$$

that is, iff A accepts on input w. It follows that $L(M) = L$.

From the definition of δ^R, we see immediately that by δ^R, a restarting configuration of the form $\triangleright(q_1, a_1)(q_2, a_2) \cdots (q_{i-1}, a_{i-1})(q_i, a_i)a_{i+1} \cdots a_n \triangleleft$ is transformed back into the restarting configuration $\triangleright(q_1, a_1)(q_2, a_2) \cdots (q_{i-1}, a_{i-1})a_i a_{i+1} \cdots a_n \triangleleft$. Thus, M is indeed reversible in the sense of the above definition. □

Hence, we obtain the following characterization.

Corollary 3.2.34 ([211]) REG = $\mathcal{L}$(stl-det-ORWW) = $\mathcal{L}$(rev-stl-det-ORWW).

Actually, each stl-det-ORWW-automaton can be converted directly into an equivalent stl-det-ORWW-automaton that is reversible. A corresponding construction can be found in the proof of the following theorem in [211].

Theorem 3.2.35 ([211]) *For each stl-det-ORWW-automaton M working on an alphabet with n letters, there exists a rev-stl-det-ORWW-automaton R with a tape alphabet of cardinality $2^{\mathcal{O}(n)}$ such that $L(R) = L(M)$ holds.*

As Corollary 3.2.10 also applies to reversible stl-det-ORWW-automata, we know that each rev-stl-det-ORWW-automaton with a tape alphabet of cardinality n can be converted into an equivalent NFA with $2^{\mathcal{O}(n)}$ states. Interestingly, this upper bound is also a lower bound. From Proposition 3.2.12, we recall that the language

$$B_n = \{ v_1\#v_2\#\cdots\#v_m\$u \mid m \geq 1,\ v_1, v_2, \ldots, v_m, u \in \{a,b\}^n,\ \exists 1 \leq i \leq m : v_i = u \}$$

is accepted by a stl-det-ORWW-automaton that has a tape alphabet of cardinality $18 \cdot n$. The following proposition shows that this result carries over to reversible stl-det-ORWW-automata, just requiring a larger multiplicative constant for the alphabet size.

Proposition 3.2.36 ([211]) *The language B_n is accepted by a rev-stl-det-ORWW-automaton that has a working alphabet of cardinality $68 \cdot n - 22$.*

Proof outline. The rev-stl-det-ORWW-automaton for B_n works essentially in the same way as the stl-det-ORWW-automaton that is given in the proof of Proposition 3.2.12. However, in order to enable the reverse transition function to undo cycles, information on those letters that are rewritten during a computation must be stored within the newly written letters. This requires a larger tape alphabet. For the details, we refer to the proof in the original paper [211]. □

This yields the following results that carry Corollaries 3.2.14 and 3.2.15 over to the setting of reversible stl-det-ORWW-automata.

Corollary 3.2.37 ([211]) (a) *For converting a reversible stl-det-ORWW-automaton with a tape alphabet of cardinality n into an equivalent NFA, $2^{\mathcal{O}(n)}$ states are sufficient, and there are cases in which these many states are also necessary.*

(b) *For converting a reversible stl-det-ORWW-automaton with a tape alphabet of cardinality n into an equivalent DFA, $2^{2^{\mathcal{O}(n)}}$ states are sufficient, and there are cases in which these many states are also necessary.*

From Theorem 3.2.33, we know that a DFA with n states and an input alphabet of cardinality k can be converted into an equivalent rev-stl-det-ORWW-automaton that has an alphabet of cardinality $k \cdot (n+1)$. For an NFA with n states, we thus obtain an equivalent rev-stl-det-ORWW-automaton with an alphabet of cardinality $k \cdot (2^n + 1)$. However, in the unary case, that is, if $k = 1$, we can do better.

Theorem 3.2.38 ([211]) *From an NFA A with n states that accepts a unary language $L(A)$, an equivalent rev-stl-det-ORWW-automaton M with an alphabet of cardinality $\mathcal{O}(n^2)$ can be constructed.*

Proof outline. In [31], it is shown that each NFA with n states can be converted into an equivalent NFA with $\mathcal{O}(n^2)$ states that is in *Chrobak normal form*, which means that the latter NFA consists of a chain of states of length at most n^2 which leads to a finite number of disjoint loops that have combined at most n states.

So, from A, we first construct an NFA $B = (S, \{a\}, s_0, \delta_B, F)$ in Chrobak normal form, where $S = C \cup P$. Here $C = \{s_0, c_1, \ldots, c_k\}$ is a chain of length $k \leq n^2$ and $P = \bigcup_{i=1}^{l} P_i$, where, for $i = 1, 2, \ldots, l$, $P_i = \{(0, p_i), (1, p_i), \ldots, (p_i - 1, p_i)\}$ is a loop of length p_i such that $\sum_{i=1}^{l} p_i \leq n$.

The tape alphabet of the rev-stl-det-ORWW-automaton $M = (\{a\}, \Gamma, \triangleright, \triangleleft, \delta, \delta^R, >)$ is

$$\Gamma = \{a\} \cup C \cup (P \times \{<, >, \perp\}),$$

where the components $\{<, >\}$ are used to locate the tape cell where the last rewrite operation has been performed, and the triples $(i, p_j, \perp) \in P \times \{\perp\}$ are used to indicate non-acceptance for the cycle P_j. We see that Γ contains $\mathcal{O}(n^2)$ letters.

The automaton M works as follows. As long as B is still within the chain C, M processes the input letter by letter from left to right by replacing each letter a with the state, which B reaches by reading the current input letter. If the length of the input a^m exceeds the length k of the chain C, M simulates the computations of B for all loops P_i, $1 \leq i \leq l$, simultaneously. For that, l subsequent symbols $(i_l, p_l, z_l), (i_{l-1}, p_{l-1}, z_{l-1}), \ldots, (i_1, p_1, z_1)$, where $z_l, z_{l-1}, \ldots, z_1 \in \{<, >\}$, are used to represent the states within the different loops that B could be in. For an input a^{k+l+r}, M will thus reach the tape contents

$$\triangleright c_1 c_2 \cdots c_k (i_l, p_l, z_l)(i_{l-1}, p_{l-1}, z_{l-1}) \cdots (i_1, p_1, z_1) a^r \triangleleft$$

after $k + l$ cycles. This is interpreted as follows: B is in the state (i_1, p_1) after reading a^{k+l} and using the first loop P_1, it is in state (i_{l-1}, p_{l-1}) after reading a^{k+2} and using the loop P_{l-1}, and it is in state (i_l, p_l) after reading a^{k+1} and using the loop P_l. The computation continues by shifting the information on the various loops to the right step by step, beginning with the state of loop P_1. Here the third components $z_j \in \{<, >\}$ are used to indicate the position at which the next rewrite must be performed. Finally, when the rewrites of M reach the right end of the tape, then it must be checked whether at least one of these cycles accepts. For this, M sends a signal to the left that tests, for one loop after another, whether this loop would lead to acceptance at the right end of the input. If the input is not in $L(M)$, then none of these tests is successful. A detailed description of the transition function of M can be found in [211]. □

The main idea of the construction in the proof of Theorem 3.2.38 can also be used to get an exponential lower bound for the conversion of a rev-stl-det-ORWW-automaton into a DFA or an NFA. In [31], the simulation costs between DFAs and NFAs and two-way DFAs (2DFAs) are investigated. In many cases, an upper bound for the simulation costs is given by Landau's function [136, 137]

$$F(n) = \max\{\, \mathrm{lcm}(p_1, p_2 \ldots, p_l) \mid p_1, p_2, \ldots, p_l \geq 1 \text{ and } p_1 + p_2 + \cdots + p_l = n \,\},$$

which gives the maximal order of the cyclic subgroups of the symmetric group of n elements, where lcm denotes the least common multiple. It is well known that the p_i can always be chosen to be relatively prime. Moreover, an easy consequence of the definition is that the p_i can always be chosen such that $p_1, p_2, \ldots, p_l \geq 2$, $p_1 + p_2 + \cdots + p_l \leq n$, and $\mathrm{lcm}(p_1, p_2, \ldots, p_l) = F(n)$.

In [136, 137], Edmund Landau proves that the asymptotic growth rate of $F(n)$ can be expressed as

$$\lim_{n \to \infty} \frac{\ln(F(n))}{\sqrt{n \cdot \ln(n)}} = 1.$$

In fact, the equality

$$F(n) = e^{\sqrt{n \cdot \ln(n)}(1+o(1))}$$

has been obtained by William Miller in [155] (see [44]). It can be concluded from the results of [31] that a DFA as well as an NFA needs at least $F(n)$ states to accept the language

$$L_n = \{\, a^m \mid m \bmod p_i \equiv 0 \text{ for all } 1 \leq i \leq l \,\},$$

where $p_1, p_2, \ldots, p_l \geq 2$, $p_1 + p_2 + \cdots + p_l \leq n$, and $\mathrm{lcm}(p_1, p_2, \ldots, p_l) = F(n)$.

Now the behavior of the rev-stl-det-ORWW-automaton M from the proof of Theorem 3.2.38 can be modified in such a way that it accepts the above language L_n with $\mathcal{O}(n)$ letters. Again, M

simulates the computation of all loops $P_1, P_2, \ldots, P_l$, working in the same way as above, but after having read the input completely, the modified M checks whether *all* of the l possible loops fit the input. This can be achieved easily by modifying the accepting transitions. Thus, we obtain the following lower bound result.

Corollary 3.2.39 ([211]) *For each $n \in \mathbb{N}$, there is a rev-stl-det-ORWW-automaton with a tape alphabet of cardinality $\mathcal{O}(n)$ that accepts a unary language L such that each DFA or NFA for L needs at least $F(n)$ states.*

The above results indicate that reversible stl-det-ORWW-automata are not only as expressive as stl-det-ORWW-automata in general, but they also have essentially the same descriptional complexity. Unfortunately, the notion of reversibility as introduced for stl-det-ORWW-automata in Definition 3.2.32 differs fundamentally from the classical notion of reversibility as it is defined for Turing machines and finite-state acceptors (see, e.g., [10, 217]). While, for the latter, the single-step computation relation is required to be backward deterministic, the notion of reversibility for stl-det-ORWW-automata only demands that the reduction relation induced by executing a single cycle is reversible. This weakened requirement is a consequence of the fact that it is not at all clear how to invert a combined rewrite/restart step of a stl-det-ORWW-automaton.

Accordingly, the notion of reversibility has also been studied for a more general type of restarting automaton, the stateless det-ORRWW-automaton (see Definitions 2.3.64 and 2.3.84). This type of automaton differs from the det-ORWW-automaton in that the combined rewrite/restart step of the latter is split into two separate operations. Thus, after performing a rewrite step, a det-ORRWW-automaton can continue to scan the rest of its tape contents and restart at the right sentinel. We recall from Theorem 2.3.85 that the det-ORRWW-automaton still characterizes the class of regular languages and that its stateless variant, which just distinguishes between the two parts of a cycle of a computation, that is, the part before (and including the rewrite step) and the part after the rewrite step, is equivalent to the variant with states.

For stl-det-ORRWW-automata, a notion of reversibility has been defined in [210] that is more in the spirit of the notion of reversibility for Turing and other classical machines. Obviously, the restart operations of a stl-det-ORRWW-automaton yield the same problem for realizing reversibility as the combined rewrite/restart steps of a stl-det-ORWW-automaton. However, a sort of normal form for stl-det-ORRWW-automata can be derived that includes the requirement that restart steps are only executed at the right end of the tape. This implies that a reverse transition function can undone restart steps. As it turns out, each stl-det-ORRWW-automaton can be converted into an equivalent stl-det-ORRWW-automaton that is in normal form. Based on this normal form, reversible stl-det-ORRWW-automata can be defined. However, to do so, a slightly revised definition of the stl-det-ORRWW-automaton is needed.

Definition 3.2.40 ([210]) *A* stl-det-ORRWW-automaton *is a one-tape machine that is described by a 7-tuple $M = (\Sigma, \Gamma, \triangleright, \triangleleft, \delta_1, \delta_2, >)$, where Σ, Γ, $\triangleright$, $\triangleleft$ and $>$ are defined as for a stl-det-ORWW-automaton,*

$$\delta_1 : ((\Gamma \cup \{\triangleright\}) \cdot \Gamma \cdot (\Gamma \cup \{\triangleleft\})) \cup \{\triangleright\triangleleft\} \to \Gamma \cup \{\mathsf{MVR}, \mathsf{Accept}, \mathsf{Reject}\}$$

and

$$\delta_2 : ((\Gamma \cup \{\triangleright\}) \cdot \Gamma \cdot (\Gamma \cup \{\triangleleft\})) \to \{\mathsf{MVR}, \mathsf{Restart}, \mathsf{Accept}, \mathsf{Reject}\}$$

are the transition functions, *which describe five different types of transition steps:*

(1) *A* move-right step *has the form $\delta_1(a_1a_2a_3) = \mathsf{MVR}$ or $\delta_2(a_1a_2a_3) = \mathsf{MVR}$, where $a_1 \in \Gamma \cup \{\triangleright\}$ and $a_2, a_3 \in \Gamma$. It causes M to shift the window one position to the right. Observe that no move-right step is possible, if the window contains the right sentinel $\triangleleft$.*

(2) *A* rewrite step *has the form $\delta_1(a_1a_2a_3) = b$, where $a_1 \in \Gamma \cup \{\triangleright\}$, $a_2, b \in \Gamma$, and $a_3 \in \Gamma \cup \{\triangleleft\}$ such that $a_2 > b$ holds. It causes M to replace the letter a_2 in the middle of its window with the letter b* without moving *the window. In addition, M switches from the transition function δ_1 to the transition function δ_2.*

(3) *A* restart step *has the form* $\delta_2(a_1a_2a_3) = \mathsf{Restart}$, *where* $a_1 \in \Gamma \cup \{\rhd\}$, $a_2 \in \Gamma$, *and* $a_3 \in \Gamma \cup \{\lhd\}$. *It causes* M *to restart, that is, the window is moved back to the left end of the tape. In addition,* M *switches back from the transition function* δ_2 *to the transition function* δ_1.

(4) *An* accept step *has the form* $\delta_1(a_1a_2a_3) = \mathsf{Accept}$ *or* $\delta_2(a_1a_2a_3) = \mathsf{Accept}$, *where* $a_1 \in \Gamma \cup \{\rhd\}$, $a_2 \in \Gamma$, *and* $a_3 \in \Gamma \cup \{\lhd\}$. *It causes* M *to halt and accept. In addition, we allow an accept step of the form* $\delta_1(\rhd\lhd) = \mathsf{Accept}$.

(5) *A* reject step *has the form* $\delta_1(a_1a_2a_3) = \mathsf{Reject}$ *or* $\delta_2(a_1a_2a_3) = \mathsf{Reject}$, *where* $a_1 \in \Gamma \cup \{\rhd\}$, $a_2 \in \Gamma$, *and* $a_3 \in \Gamma \cup \{\lhd\}$. *It causes* M *to halt without accepting. In addition, we allow a reject step of the form* $\delta_1(\rhd\lhd) = \mathsf{Reject}$.

The version of the stl-det-ORRWW-automaton defined here differs from the one considered in Section 2.3 in that here we have an explicit reject instruction, which was not used in the previous model, and secondly, in the new model, the window remains stationary during a rewrite step, while the previous model was required to move its window one step to the right whenever it executes a rewrite step. However, it is easily verified that the proof of Proposition 2.3.82 carries over to the new variant, which implies that $\mathcal{L}(\mathsf{stl\text{-}det\text{-}ORRWW}) = \mathsf{REG}$ also holds for this variant.

As a first step towards introducing the notion of reversibility for stl-det-ORRWW-automata, a restricted type of these automata is specified in [210].

Definition 3.2.41 ([210]) *A stl-det-ORRWW-automaton* $M = (\Sigma, \Gamma, \rhd, \lhd, \delta_1, \delta_2, >)$ *is said to be in* normal form, *if it satisfies the following conditions:*

(1) $\delta_2 : ((\Gamma \cup \{\rhd\}) \cdot \Gamma \cdot (\Gamma \cup \{\lhd\})) \to \{\mathsf{MVR}, \mathsf{Restart}\}$, *that is, during the second phase of a cycle (that is, after the rewrite operation)* M *can neither accept nor reject, and*

(2) *the automaton* M *only executes a restart, accept, or reject step when the right sentinel* $\lhd$ *is inside its window.*

Thus, if M is a stl-det-ORRWW-automaton in normal form, then in each cycle, the tape contents is read completely, as the corresponding restart step is not executed before the right sentinel appears inside the window, and a tail computation consists of a sequence of move-right steps and an accept or reject step at the right end of the tape. This means that, for an input of length $n \geq 1$, each cycle consists of exactly $n-1$ move-right steps, a single rewrite step, and a single restart step, and each tail consists of exactly $n-1$ move-right steps and an accept or reject step.

The next result relates stl-det-ORWW-automata to stl-det-ORRWW-automata in normal form.

Proposition 3.2.42 ([210]) *From a given stl-det-ORWW-automaton* M *with a tape alphabet of cardinality* n, *one can construct a stl-det-ORRWW-automaton* M' *in normal form such that* M' *has a tape alphabet of cardinality* $n+2$ *and* $L(M') = L(M)$.

Proof. Let $M = (\Sigma, \Gamma, \rhd, \lhd, \delta, >)$ be a stl-det-ORWW-automaton. We obtain a stl-det-ORRWW-automaton $M' = (\Sigma, \Delta, \rhd, \lhd, \delta_1, \delta_2, >')$ from M by taking $\Delta = \Gamma \cup \{+, -\}$, where $+$ and $-$ are two new letters, by defining $>'$ as follows, where $A, B \in \Gamma$:

$$A >' B \text{ iff } A > B, \text{ and } A >' + >' -,$$

and by defining δ_1 and δ_2 as follows, where $A \in \Gamma \cup \{\rhd\}$, $B, B_1 \in \Gamma$, $C \in \Gamma \cup \{\lhd\}$, and $o \in \{+, -\}$:

$$\begin{array}{llcll}
(1.1) & \delta_1(\rhd\lhd) & = & \mathsf{Accept}, & \text{if } \delta(\rhd\lhd) = \mathsf{Accept}, \\
(1.2) & \delta_1(\rhd\lhd) & = & \mathsf{Reject}, & \text{if } \delta(\rhd\lhd) = \emptyset, \\
(1.3) & \delta_1(ABC) & = & \delta(ABC), & \text{if } \delta(ABC) \in \Gamma \cup \{\mathsf{MVR}\}, \\
(1.4) & \delta_1(ABC) & = & +, & \text{if } \delta(ABC) = \mathsf{Accept}, \\
(1.5) & \delta_1(ABC) & = & -, & \text{if } \delta(ABC) = \emptyset,
\end{array}$$

(1.6)	$\delta_1(ABo)$	= MVR,		(1.11)	$\delta_1(ooo)$	= MVR,
(1.7)	$\delta_1(AoB)$	= MVR,		(1.12)	$\delta_1(A+\lhd)$	= Accept,
(1.8)	$\delta_1(oBC)$	= o,		(1.13)	$\delta_1(++\lhd)$	= Accept,
(1.9)	$\delta_1(Aoo)$	= MVR,		(1.14)	$\delta_1(A-\lhd)$	= Reject,
(1.10)	$\delta_1(ooB)$	= MVR,		(1.15)	$\delta_1(--\lhd)$	= Reject,

(2.1) $\delta_2(XYZ)$ = MVR for all $X \in \Delta \cup \{\rhd\}$ and $Y, Z \in \Delta$,
(2.2) $\delta_2(XY\lhd)$ = Restart for all $X \in \Delta \cup \{\rhd\}$ and $Y \in \Delta$.

It is easily seen that $|\Delta| = |\Gamma| + 2$ and that M' simulates the computations of M cycle by cycle, where in each cycle, after executing a rewrite step, δ_2 is used to move the window to the right end of the tape, where a restart step completes the cycle. Furthermore, whenever M executes an accept step or rejects, as there is no applicable step, then M' performs a rewrite step that replaces the current letter in the middle of its window with the new letter $+$ or $-$. Finally, the transitions of type (1.6) to (1.15) imply that, once an occurrence of the letter $+$ or $-$ has been written onto the tape, then all letters to the right of that occurrence are rewritten by the same letter, and once the last letter (the one to the left of the sentinel $\lhd$) has been rewritten, the automaton M' accepts or rejects at the right end of the tape. It follows that $L(M') = L(M)$ and that M' is a stl-det-ORRWW-automaton in normal form. □

Actually, by using a more sophisticated construction, it can be shown that each stl-det-ORRWW-automaton can be converted into an equivalent stl-det-ORRWW-automaton that is in normal form.

Proposition 3.2.43 ([210]) *From a stl-det-ORRWW-automaton M with an input alphabet of cardinality k and a tape alphabet of cardinality n, one can construct an equivalent stl-det-ORRWW-automaton M' in normal form such that M' has a tape alphabet of cardinality $k + 3n^2 + n + 2$.*

The complete construction, which is technically quite involved, can be found in [210]. If $M = (\Sigma, \Gamma, \rhd, \lhd, \delta_1, \delta_2, >)$ is a stl-det-ORRWW-automaton that is in normal form, then from M, we obtain the stl-det-ORWW-automaton $M_1 = (\Sigma, \Gamma, \rhd, \lhd, \delta_1, >)$, where each rewrite step of δ_1 is simply interpreted as a combined rewrite/restart step. It is immediate that M and M_1 accept the same language. Thus, from Proposition 3.2.43, we get the following consequence, which can be interpreted as a converse of Proposition 3.2.42.

Corollary 3.2.44 ([210]) *From a stl-det-ORRWW-automaton M with an input alphabet of cardinality k and a tape alphabet of cardinality n, one can construct an equivalent stl-det-ORWW-automaton M' that has a tape alphabet of cardinality $k + 3n^2 + n + 2$.*

These results show that stl-det-ORWW-automata and stl-det-ORRWW-automata in normal form correspond to each other. The advantage of the latter is obvious: a stl-det-ORRWW-automaton in normal form is more predictable in its behavior than a stl-det-ORWW-automaton, as in each cycle and tail of a computation, it scans its tape completely from left to right. In particular, this means that a restart step of a stl-det-ORRWW-automaton in normal form can simply be undone by moving the window to the right end of the tape. This is very important for establishing the notion of (step-by-step) reversibility for these automata. To define this notion, some additional transition steps are needed that undo the transition steps of a stl-det-ORRWW-automaton.

Definition 3.2.45 *Let $M = (\Sigma, \Gamma, \rhd, \lhd, \delta_1, \delta_2, >)$ be a stl-det-ORRWW-automaton. The* reverse transition steps *for a stl-det-ORRWW-automaton are the operations* MVL, InvRewrite, InvRestart, *and* HALT *defined as follows:*

(1) *A* move-left step *has the form $a_1a_2a_3 \mapsto$* MVL, *where $a_1, a_2 \in \Gamma$ and $a_3 \in \Gamma \cup \{\lhd\}$. It causes the automaton to shift its window one position to the left. Observe that no move-left step is possible, if the window contains the left sentinel $\rhd$.*

(2) *An* inverse rewrite step *has the form $a_1a_2a_3 \mapsto b$, where $a_1 \in \Gamma \cup \{\rhd\}$, $a_2, b \in \Gamma$, and $a_3 \in \Gamma \cup \{\lhd\}$ such that $b > a_2$ holds. It causes M to replace the letter a_2 in the middle of its window with the letter b without moving the window.*

(3) *An* inverse restart step *has the form* $\triangleright a_1 a_2 \mapsto \mathsf{InvRestart}$, *where* $a_1 \in \Gamma$ *and* $a_2 \in \Gamma \cup \{\triangleleft\}$. *It causes* M *to perform an inverse restart, that is, the window is moved to the right end of the tape. Observe that this operation is only possible when the window is at the left end of the tape.*

(4) *A* halt step *has the form* $\triangleright a_1 a_2 \mapsto \mathsf{Halt}$, *where* $a_1 \in \Gamma$ *and* $a_2 \in \Gamma \cup \{\triangleleft\}$. *It causes* M *to halt. In addition, we allow a halt step of the form* $\triangleright\triangleleft \mapsto \mathsf{Halt}$. *Again, this operation is only possible when the window is at the left end of the tape.*

Using these new operations, the notion of a reversible stl-det-ORRWW-automaton is defined as follows.

Definition 3.2.46 ([210]) (a) *A* reversible stl-det-ORRWW-automaton *is defined by a 9-tuple* $M_r = (\Sigma, \Gamma, \triangleright, \triangleleft, \delta_1, \delta_2, \delta_3, \delta_4, >)$, *where* $M = (\Sigma, \Gamma, \triangleright, \triangleleft, \delta_1, \delta_2, >)$ *is a stl-det-ORRWW-automaton that is in normal form and*

$$\delta_3 : ((\Gamma \cup \{\triangleright\}) \cdot \Gamma \cdot (\Gamma \cup \{\triangleleft\})) \to \Gamma \cup \{\mathsf{MVL}, \mathsf{Halt}\}$$

and

$$\delta_4 : ((\Gamma \cup \{\triangleright\}) \cdot \Gamma \cdot (\Gamma \cup \{\triangleleft\})) \to \{\mathsf{MVL}, \mathsf{InvRestart}\}$$

are the reverse transition functions. *Here, in* δ_3, *the symbols from* Γ *represent inverse rewrite steps.*

(b) *Using the reverse transition functions,* M_r *can execute* reverse computations, *which consist of sequences of reverse cycles. A* reverse cycle *starts in a configuration of the form* $\triangleright W\underline{AB\triangleleft}$, *where* $W \in \Gamma^*$ *and* $A, B \in \Gamma$. *It begins with a sequence of transition steps that are based on the function* δ_3, *that is, some move-left steps followed by an inverse rewrite step or a halt step. After an inverse rewrite step,* M_r *continues by executing transition steps based on the function* δ_4. *A reverse cycle ends with the execution of an inverse restart step, which leads to the next reverse cycle. A reverse computation ends when a halt step is executed.*

(c) *The transition functions* δ_1 *and* δ_2 *induce a* single step forward computation relation $\vdash_{M_r}$ *on the set of configurations of* M_r, *and the reverse transition functions* δ_3 *and* δ_4 *induce a* single step reverse computation relation $\vdash_{M_r}^{-1}$ *on the set of configurations of* M_r. *The forward computations of* M_r *and the reverse computations of* M_r *are related to each other as follows: for each* $a, b \in \Sigma$, *each* $w \in \Sigma^*$, *and each accepting or rejecting (forward) computation*

$$(*)\ \underline{\triangleright ab}w\triangleleft = \alpha_0 \vdash_{M_r} \alpha_1 \vdash_{M_r} \cdots \vdash_{M_r} \alpha_m = \triangleright W\underline{AB\triangleleft} \vdash_{M_r} \mathsf{Accept}\ (\mathsf{Reject}),$$

M_r *can execute the halting reverse computation*

$$(**)\ \triangleright W\underline{AB\triangleleft} = \alpha_m \vdash_{M_r}^{-1} \alpha_{m-1} \vdash_{M_r}^{-1} \cdots \vdash_{M_r}^{-1} \alpha_1 \vdash_{M_r}^{-1} \alpha_0 = \underline{\triangleright ab}w\triangleleft \vdash_{M_r}^{-1} \mathsf{HALT},$$

and conversely, for each reverse computation of M_r *of the form* $(**)$, M_r *has a corresponding computation of the form* $(*)$.

(d) *The class of all reversible stl-det-ORRWW-automata is denoted by* rev-stl-det-ORRWW.

The above definition shows that each computation of a reversible stl-det-ORRWW-automaton is reversible step-by-step. This is a much stronger property than the notion of reversibility for stl-det-ORWW-automata considered in Definition 3.2.32. The next result states that reversible stl-det-ORRWW-automata are as expressive as stl-det-ORRWW-automata. In addition, the proof of this result gives an important upper bound for the cardinality of the tape alphabet of a reversible stl-det-ORRWW-automaton that accepts a given regular language.

Theorem 3.2.47 ([210]) *From a DFA* A *with* n *states and an input alphabet of cardinality* k, *one can construct a reversible stl-det-ORRWW-automaton* M *with a tape alphabet of cardinality* $k \cdot (n^2 + 1)$ *such that* $L(M) = L(A)$.

Proof. Let $A = (Q, \Sigma, q_0, F, \varphi)$ be a DFA that accepts a language $L \subseteq \Sigma^*$. We take

$$\Gamma = \Sigma \cup \{\, [p, a, q] \mid p, q \in Q, a \in \Sigma \,\},$$

which shows that $|\Gamma| = k \cdot (n^2 + 1)$, and we take $a > [p, a, q]$ for all $a \in \Sigma$ and all $p, q \in Q$. Finally, we define the transition functions δ_1, δ_2, δ_3, and δ_4 as follows, where $a, b, b' \in \Sigma$, $c \in \Sigma \cup \{\lhd\}$, and $p, q, q', r \in Q$:

δ_1 :	(1.1)	$\delta_1(\rhd\lhd)$	=	Accept,	if $\lambda \in L(A)$,
	(1.2)	$\delta_1(\rhd\lhd)$	=	Reject,	if $\lambda \notin L(A)$,
	(1.3)	$\delta_1(\rhd a\lhd)$	=	Accept,	if $a \in L(A)$,
	(1.4)	$\delta_1(\rhd a\lhd)$	=	Reject,	if $a \notin L(A)$,
	(1.5)	$\delta_1(\rhd ab)$	=	$[q_0, a, q]$,	if $\varphi(q_0, a) = q$,
	(1.6)	$\delta_1(\rhd[q_0, a, q]b)$	=	MVR,	
	(1.7)	$\delta_1(\rhd[p, a, q][q, b, q'])$	=	MVR,	
	(1.8)	$\delta_1([p, a, q][q, b, q'][q', b', r])$	=	MVR,	
	(1.9)	$\delta_1([p, a, q][q, b, q']b')$	=	MVR,	
	(1.10)	$\delta_1([p, a, q]bc)$	=	$[q, b, q']$,	if $\varphi(q, b) = q'$,
	(1.11)	$\delta_1([p, a, q][q, b, q']\lhd)$	=	Accept,	if $q' \in F$,
	(1.12)	$\delta_1([p, a, q][q, b, q']\lhd)$	=	Reject,	if $q' \notin F$,
δ_2 :	(2.1)	$\delta_2(\rhd[q_0, a, q]b)$	=	MVR,	
	(2.2)	$\delta_2([p, a, q][q, b, q']b')$	=	MVR,	
	(2.3)	$\delta_2([p, a, q]bb')$	=	MVR,	
	(2.4)	$\delta_2(abb')$	=	MVR,	
	(2.5)	$\delta_2(ab\lhd)$	=	Restart,	
	(2.6)	$\delta_2([p, a, q]b\lhd)$	=	Restart,	
	(2.7)	$\delta_2([p, a, q][q, b, q']\lhd)$	=	Restart,	
δ_3 :	(3.1)	$\delta_3(\rhd\lhd)$	=	Halt,	
	(3.2)	$\delta_3(\rhd a\lhd)$	=	Halt,	
	(3.3)	$\delta_3(\rhd[q_0, a, q]b)$	=	a,	if $\varphi(q_0, a) = q$,
	(3.4)	$\delta_3([p, a, q][q, b, q']c)$	=	b,	if $\varphi(q, b) = q'$,
	(3.5)	$\delta_3([p, a, q]bc)$	=	MVL,	
	(3.6)	$\delta_3(abc)$	=	MVL,	
	(3.7)	$\delta_3(\rhd ab)$	=	Halt,	
δ_4 :	(4.1)	$\delta_4(\rhd ab)$	=	InvRestart,	
	(4.2)	$\delta_4([p, a, q]bc)$	=	MVL,	
	(4.3)	$\delta_4([p, a, q][q, b, q']b)$	=	MVL,	
	(4.4)	$\delta_4([p, a, q][q, b, q'][q', b', r])$	=	MVL,	
	(4.5)	$\delta_4(\rhd[q_0, a, q]b)$	=	InvRestart,	
	(4.6)	$\delta_4(\rhd[q_0, a, q][q, b, q'])$	=	InvRestart.	

If a word $w = a_1 a_2 \cdots a_n$ is given as input, where $n \geq 2$ and $a_1, a_2, \ldots, a_n \in \Sigma$, then, using δ_1, M rewrites w from left to right into the word

$$[q_0, a_1, q_1][q_1, a_2, q_2] \cdots [q_{n-2}, a_{n-1}, q_{n-1}][q_{n-1}, a_n, q_n],$$

where $q_i = \varphi(q_0, a_1 a_2 \cdots a_i)$, $1 \leq i \leq n$, and this word is then accepted (rejected) in a tail computation if $q_n \in F$ ($q_n \notin F$), that is, M accepts on input w iff

$$\varphi(q_0, a_1 a_2 \cdots a_n) = \varphi(\varphi(q_0, a_1 a_2 \cdots a_{n-1}), a_n) = \varphi(q_{n-1}, a_n) = q_n \in F,$$

that is, iff A accepts on input w. Hence, we see that $L(M) = L$ holds. Furthermore, from the definitions of δ_1 and δ_2, we see that M is in normal form.

Finally, using the reverse transition functions δ_3 and δ_4, M can reverse the above computation step by step. Thus, M is indeed reversible in the sense of the above definition. □

Together with Theorem 2.3.85, Theorem 3.2.47 yields the following result.

Corollary 3.2.48 ([210]) REG = $\mathcal{L}$(stl-det-ORRWW) = $\mathcal{L}$(rev-stl-det-ORRWW).

Actually, we can obtain a reversible stl-det-ORRWW-automaton M' from a given stl-det-ORRWW-automaton M that is in normal form as follows. Assume that M has a tape alphabet of cardinality n. By the remark following the proof of Proposition 3.2.43, we can interpret M as a stl-det-ORWW-automaton. According to Corollary 3.2.15, we can convert M into a DFA A such that A has $2^{2^{\mathcal{O}(n)}}$ states and $L(A) = L(M)$. Now from Theorem 3.2.47, we obtain a reversible stl-det-ORRWW-automaton M' such that $L(M') = L(A) = L(M)$ holds, where M' has a tape alphabet of cardinality $2^{2^{\mathcal{O}(n)}}$. However, a more efficient transformation exists.

Theorem 3.2.49 ([210]) *From a stl-det-ORRWW-automaton M in normal form with a tape alphabet of cardinality n, one can construct an equivalent reversible stl-det-ORRWW-automaton M' that has a tape alphabet of cardinality at most 2^{3n+1}.*

For the proof, we refer to [210]. By combining Proposition 3.2.43 and Theorem 3.2.49, the following result is obtained.

Corollary 3.2.50 ([210]) *From a stl-det-ORRWW-automaton M with a tape alphabet of cardinality n, one can construct an equivalent reversible stl-det-ORRWW-automaton M' that has a tape alphabet of cardinality at most 2^{9n^2+6n+7}.*

This corollary yields an exponential upper bound for converting a stl-det-ORRWW-automaton into an equivalent automaton of the same type that is reversible. How good is this bound?

Problem 3.2.51 *Is there a better upper bound for the above conversion, or is there a matching lower bound?*

From Theorem 3.2.47, we have an upper bound for the conversion of a DFA into a reversible stl-det-ORRWW-automaton. The following corollary provides an upper bound for the reverse conversion.

Corollary 3.2.52 ([210]) *For each reversible stl-det-ORRWW-automaton M with a tape alphabet of cardinality n, there exists an NFA A with $2^{\mathcal{O}(n)}$ states such that $L(A) = L(M)$ holds.*

Proof. Let M be a reversible stl-det-ORRWW-automaton with a tape alphabet of cardinality n. Then M is, in particular, in normal form, and hence, it can be interpreted as a stl-det-ORWW-automaton. From this stl-det-ORWW-automaton, we obtain an NFA A with $2^{\mathcal{O}(n)}$ states such that $L(A) = L(M)$ by Corollary 3.2.10. □

It follows that, for each reversible stl-det-ORRWW-automaton M with a tape alphabet of cardinality n, there exists an equivalent DFA B with $2^{2^{\mathcal{O}(n)}}$ states. This upper bound is met by a corresponding lower bound, as, for each $n \geq 2$, there exists a reversible stl-det-ORRWW-automaton with a tape alphabet of cardinality $48 \cdot n + 52$ that accepts the language B_n [210]. This yields the following trade-offs.

Corollary 3.2.53 ([210]) (a) *For converting a reversible stl-det-ORRWW-automaton with a tape alphabet of cardinality n into an equivalent NFA, $2^{\mathcal{O}(n)}$ states are sufficient, and there are cases in which these many states are also necessary.*

(b) *For converting a reversible stl-det-ORRWW-automaton with a tape alphabet of cardinality n into an equivalent DFA, $2^{2^{\mathcal{O}(n)}}$ states are sufficient, and there are cases in which these many states are also necessary.*

This is in complete analogy to the situation for reversible stl-det-ORWW-automata (see Corollary 3.2.37). In addition, also Theorem 3.2.38 and Corollary 3.2.39 extend to reversible stl-det-ORRWW-automata.

Theorem 3.2.54 ([210]) (a) *From an NFA A with n states that accepts a unary language $L(A)$, an equivalent rev-stl-det-ORRWW-automaton M with an alphabet of cardinality $\mathcal{O}(n^2)$ can be constructed.*

(b) *For each $n \in \mathbb{N}$, there is a rev-stl-det-ORRWW-automaton with a tape alphabet of cardinality $\mathcal{O}(n)$ that accepts a unary language L such that each DFA or NFA for L needs at least $F(n)$ states.*

These results show that, in the case of stl-det-ORWW-automata as well as in the case of stl-det-ORRWW-automata, the additional requirement of reversibility does not restrict the expressive capacity of these types of automata. Moreover, the descriptional complexity of the reversible types of automata is the same as that of the non-reversible types (up to a constant). This is in stark contrast to the situation for DFAs, as reversible DFAs are strictly less expressive than DFAs [217].

3.2.2 Stateless ORD-Automata

The stateless ORD-automaton is obtained from the stateless ORWW-automaton by admitting additional delete/restart steps of the form $\lambda \in \delta(q, abc)$. Such a step erases the letter b from the tape, shortens the tape by removing the corresponding tape cell, and performs a restart. We recall from Theorem 2.3.95 that all context-free languages are accepted by stl-ORD-automata. In fact, the subclass of *swift* stl-ORD-automata yields a characterization for the class of context-free languages. Here a stl-ORD-automaton is called swift, if it can always perform move-right steps (see Definition 2.3.94) unless its window is already at the right end of the tape.

We now take a look at the descriptional complexity of stl-ORD-automata, relating it to the descriptional complexity of stl-ORWW-automata. As for stl-ORWW-automata, we use the size of the tape alphabet as the complexity measure for stl-ORD-automata. Here the following result has been obtained, which shows that for some regular languages, swift-ORD-automata yield a much more concise description than corresponding stl-ORWW-automata.

Theorem 3.2.55 ([199, 201]) *There is no recursive function f such that, whenever M is a swift-ORD-automaton with a tape alphabet of cardinality n that accepts a regular language, then there exists a stl-ORWW-automaton M' for the language $L(M)$ such that M' has a tape alphabet of cardinality $m \leq f(n)$.*

Thus, the size increase that occurs when converting a swift-ORD-automaton that accepts a regular language into a stl-ORWW-automaton for the same language cannot be bounded from above by any recursive function.

Proof. According to a result by Albert Meyer and Michael Fischer [154], the increase in size when turning a context-free grammar into an equivalent NFA cannot be restricted by any recursive function. Now let G be a context-free grammar that generates a regular language. From G, we can construct an equivalent grammar G_1 that is in quadratic Greibach normal form. The grammar G_1 is, in general, much larger than the grammar G, but the size increase is bounded from above by an exponential function (see [230]). Thus, $\text{size}(G_1) \leq c^{\text{size}(G)}$, where we use $\text{size}(G)$ (or $\text{size}(A)$) to denote the size of a grammar G or an automaton A. From the latter grammar, we immediately obtain a PDA A that accepts the language $L(G) = L(G_1)$ by empty pushdown. Then $\text{size}(A) = \text{size}(G_1) \leq c^{\text{size}(G)}$. Following the construction given in the proof of Theorem 2.3.95 (see [201]), we obtain a swift-ORD-automaton M for the language $L(G)$. As is easily seen from that construction, the number of letters n in the tape alphabet of M is bounded from above by an exponential function in the size of the PDA A. Thus, $\text{size}(M) \leq c^{\text{size}(A)} \leq c^{c^{\text{size}(G)}}$.

Now assume that f is a recursive function such that, for each swift-ORD-automaton P, there exists an equivalent stl-ORWW-automaton P' such that the number of letters in the tape alphabet of P' is bounded from above by the value $f(\text{size}(P))$. Then there exists a stl-ORWW-automaton M' for the language $L(M) = L(G)$ such that $\text{size}(M') \leq f(\text{size}(M)) \leq f(c^{c^{\text{size}(G)}})$. Finally, by Theorem 3.2.9, we can convert M' into an NFA B for the language $L(G)$ that is of size $2^{\mathcal{O}(\text{size}(M'))}$.

Thus, we see that $\text{size}(B) \leq 2^{\mathcal{O}(f(c^{c^{\text{size}(G)}}))}$, which is a recursive bound for the conversion of the context-free grammar G into the equivalent NFA B. As this contradicts the aforementioned result of Albert Meyer and Michael Fischer, we see that there is no recursive bound for the conversion of a swift-ORD-automaton into an equivalent stl-ORWW-automaton. □

As the swift-ORD-automaton is just a restricted variant of the stl-ORD-automaton, Theorem 3.2.55 also holds for stl-ORD-automata in general. Notice that this result implies, in particular, that there is no effective (that is, recursive) construction that transforms a stl-ORD-automaton accepting a regular language into a stl-ORWW-automaton for that language.

Theorems 2.3.89 and 2.3.91 show that stateless deterministic ORD-automata accept a proper superset of the class of deterministic context-free languages that is properly contained in the intersection of the context-free and the Church-Rosser languages. Can the above result be extended to this type of automaton?

Problem 3.2.56 *What is the descriptional complexity of stateless det-ORD-automata? Is there a recursive bound for the size increase of the conversion of a stl-det-ORD-automaton that accepts a regular language into a stl-det-ORWW-automaton for the same language?*

3.3 Reducing the Window Size of R(R)(W)-Automata

One of the most obvious parameters for restarting automata is the size of the read/write window. In fact, for all types of restarting automata without auxiliary letters, the size of the read/write window induces infinite strictly ascending hierarchies of language classes (Corollary 2.3.3). Thus, it is natural to ask for the impact of this parameter on the size of the descriptions of these automata. What is the saving in the economy of description when changing from a restarting automaton of window size $k-1$ to an equivalent automaton of the same type of window size k? Or, to phrase it differently, what is the size increase when converting a restarting automaton of window size k into an equivalent automaton of window size $k-1$?

We study this problem for R-, RR-, RW-, and RRW-automata, showing that, in all these cases, the size increase for the conversion of an automaton of window size k into an equivalent automaton of window size $k-1$ cannot be bounded from above by a recursive function. This even remains true when the automata considered are deterministic and/or stateless. Here we follow the presentation in the papers [124, 125].

We first recall some notation for descriptional complexity. Following [74], we say that a *descriptional system* $\mathcal{S}$ is a set of finite descriptors such that each $D \in \mathcal{S}$ describes a formal language $L(D)$, and the underlying alphabet alph(D) over which D represents a language can be read off from D. The *family of languages represented* (or *described*) by $\mathcal{S}$ is

$$\mathcal{L}(\mathcal{S}) = \{\, L(D) \mid D \in \mathcal{S}\,\}.$$

For every language L, the set $\mathcal{S}(L) = \{\, D \in \mathcal{S} \mid L(D) = L\,\}$ is the set of its descriptors in $\mathcal{S}$. A *complexity measure* for a descriptional system $\mathcal{S}$ is a total recursive mapping $c : \mathcal{S} \to \mathbb{N}$.

Example 3.3.1 *Monotone det-RRW-automata can be encoded over some fixed alphabet such that their input alphabets can be extracted from the encodings. The set of these encodings is a descriptional system $\mathcal{S}$, and $\mathcal{L}(\mathcal{S})$ is the family of deterministic context-free languages* DCFL *by Corollary 2.1.43.*

Examples of complexity measures for deterministic restarting automata are the total number of symbols, that is, the length of the encoding, *denoted as* length, *or the product of the number of states and the number of possible window contents, that is, the* number of transitions, *denoted as* trans. ■

Here we use complexity measures c that are recursively related to the measure length. If there is a total recursive function $g : \mathbb{N}\times\mathbb{N} \to \mathbb{N}$ such that, for all $D \in \mathcal{S}$, $\text{length}(D) \leq g(c(D), |\text{alph}(D)|)$, then c is said to be an *s-measure*. If, in addition, for any alphabet Σ, the set of descriptors in $\mathcal{S}$ that describe languages over Σ is recursively enumerable in order of increasing size, then c is said to be an *sn-measure*. Clearly, length and trans are sn-measures for restarting automata. In addition, the cardinality of the tape alphabet is an sn-measure for stl-ORWW-automata.

Whenever we consider the relative succinctness of two descriptional systems $\mathcal{S}_1$ and $\mathcal{S}_2$, we assume that the intersection $\mathcal{L}(\mathcal{S}_1) \cap \mathcal{L}(\mathcal{S}_2)$ is non-empty, that is, there are languages that can be described by the descriptional system $\mathcal{S}_1$ as well as by the descriptional system $\mathcal{S}_2$.

Let $\mathcal{S}_1$ and $\mathcal{S}_2$ be descriptional systems with complexity measures c_1 and c_2, respectively. A total function $f : \mathbb{N} \to \mathbb{N}$ is an *upper bound* for the increase in complexity when changing from a descriptor in $\mathcal{S}_1$ to an equivalent descriptor in $\mathcal{S}_2$, if, for all $D_1 \in \mathcal{S}_1$ with $L(D_1) \in \mathcal{L}(\mathcal{S}_2)$, there exists a descriptor $D_2 \in \mathcal{S}_2(L(D_1))$ such that $c_2(D_2) \leq f(c_1(D_1))$.

If there is no recursive upper bound, then the *trade-off is said to be non-recursive.* Non-recursive trade-offs are independent of particular sn-measures. Theorem 3.2.55 shows that the trade-off between (swift) stl-ORD-automata and stl-ORWW-automata is non-recursive. To establish non-recursive trade-offs, one can either make use of a known non-recursive trade-off, as we did in the proof of Theorem 3.2.55, or one can employ the following general result that is a slightly generalized and unified form of a result of Hartmanis [61].

Theorem 3.3.2 **([74])** *Let $\mathcal{S}_1$ and $\mathcal{S}_2$ be two descriptional systems for recursive languages such that any descriptor D in $\mathcal{S}_1$ and $\mathcal{S}_2$ can effectively be converted into a Turing machine that decides membership in the language $L(D)$, and let c_1 be a measure for $\mathcal{S}_1$ and c_2 be an sn-measure for $\mathcal{S}_2$. If there exist a descriptional system $\mathcal{S}_3$ and a property P that is not semi-decidable (that is, not recursively enumerable) for descriptors from $\mathcal{S}_3$ such that, given an arbitrary $D_3 \in \mathcal{S}_3$,*

(1) *there exists an effective procedure to construct a descriptor D_1 in $\mathcal{S}_1$ for some language $L(D_1)$, and*

(2) *$L(D_1)$ has a descriptor in $\mathcal{S}_2$ if and only if D_3 does not have property P,*

then the trade-off between S_1 and S_2 is non-recursive.

In the following, we present non-recursive trade-offs between restarting automata with window sizes k and $k-1$ by using a reduction of the halting problem for Turing machines on empty tape. In order to apply Theorem 3.3.2, we use the family of deterministic one-tape Turing machines as descriptional system $\mathcal{S}_3$ and for the property P, we take the property of *not halting on empty input*. Recall that this property is indeed not semi-decidable (that is, not recursively enumerable) for deterministic one-tape Turing machines. Then, for an arbitrary deterministic one-tape Turing machine T, that is, a descriptor $D_3 \in \mathcal{S}_3$, we construct a restarting automaton with window size k, that is, a descriptor D_1 in $\mathcal{S}_1$, that has an equivalent automaton with window size $k-1$, that is, a descriptor in $\mathcal{S}_2$, if and only if T halts on empty input.

Any deterministic one-tape Turing machine can be transformed into an equivalent one that never reenters its initial state, cannot print the blank symbol, halts only in a particular halting state, and halts if and only if it accepts. So, we may assume without loss of generality that $M = (Q, \Gamma, \delta, q_0, \Box, \{q_F\})$ is such a machine. Here Q is the set of states of M, where q_0 is the initial state and q_F is the only halting state, and Γ is the tape alphabet disjoint from Q containing the blank symbol $\Box$. We assume that the transition function δ maps from $(Q \setminus \{q_F\}) \times \Gamma$ to $Q \times \Gamma \times \{\mathrm{L}, \mathrm{R}\}$ only, that is, M moves its head in each step. A configuration of M is represented by a word from $\Gamma^* \cdot Q \cdot \Gamma^*$, where $x_1 x_2 \cdots x_i q x_{i+1} \cdots x_n$ is used to express the situation in which M is in state q, scanning tape symbol x_{i+1}, and $x_1 x_2 \cdots x_n$ is the support of the tape inscription, that is, there are only blank symbols to the left and to the right of this word. So, the initial configuration on empty input is just the symbol q_0.

First, we construct a string-rewriting system which generates words that encode the complete history of a computation of M on empty input. Similar simulations of Turing machines by string-rewriting systems or Thue systems have also been used, for example, in [117, 180, 225]. Here, however, as we want to construct a det-RW(3)-automaton from the string-rewriting system that accepts these words, we use a somewhat more involved encoding for the simulation. Afterwards, we present the announced det-RW(3)-automaton.

The string-rewriting system T is a finite subset of $S^* \times S^*$, where S is the underlying alphabet. The pairs $(u, v) \in T$ are called *rules*, and they are written as $(u \to v)$. The string-rewriting system T induces a reduction relation $\Rightarrow_T^*$ on S^*, which is the reflexive and transitive closure of the following single-step reduction relation (see Definition 2.2.47):

$$s \Rightarrow_T t \text{ iff } \exists x, y \in S^* \, \exists (u \to v) \in T : s = xuy \text{ and } t = xvy.$$

The string-rewriting system T will be used to encode the history of a computation of the Turing machine M on empty input in a single word. Such a word z will consist of the encoding of a configuration xqy of M together with additional information that records the history of the computation of M, which led to this very configuration. In particular, this additional information uniquely identifies the rule of T that was used to derive the word z. This means that we can uniquely reverse the computation of M that led to the configuration xqy.

In order to satisfy all the properties we demand of the string-rewriting system T, the encoding will be quite involved. In fact, to avoid ambiguity, the letters to the left of the state symbol are distinguished from those to the right of the state symbol, and the state symbol itself carries additional information about whether the letter on the tape currently being scanned is to the left or to the right of the state symbol. Accordingly, the alphabet S of T is defined as follows:

$$\begin{array}{lcl} S & = & \{\rhd, \lhd\} \cup \overrightarrow{Q} \cup \overleftarrow{Q} \cup \overrightarrow{\Gamma} \cup \overleftarrow{\Gamma} \cup D_L \cup D_R \cup H, \text{ where} \\ D_L & = & \{\, L_z \mid z \in (\overrightarrow{Q} \times (\{\lhd\} \cup \overleftarrow{\Gamma})) \cup ((\{\rhd\} \cup \overrightarrow{\Gamma}) \times \overleftarrow{Q}) \,\}, \\ D_R & = & \{\, R_z \mid z \in (\overrightarrow{Q} \times (\{\lhd\} \cup \overleftarrow{\Gamma})) \cup ((\{\rhd\} \cup \overrightarrow{\Gamma}) \times \overleftarrow{Q}) \,\}, \text{ and} \\ H & = & \{\, I_z \mid z \in (\overrightarrow{Q} \times \{\lhd\}) \cup (\{\rhd\} \times \overleftarrow{Q}) \,\}. \end{array}$$

Here $\rhd$ and $\lhd$ are the left and right end-of-tape markers, $\overrightarrow{Q}$ and $\overleftarrow{Q}$ are disjoint copies of Q, where $\overrightarrow{q} \in \overrightarrow{Q}$ and $\overleftarrow{q} \in \overleftarrow{Q}$ mean state q such that the currently scanned letter is the one to the right or the one to the left, and $\overrightarrow{\Gamma}$ and $\overleftarrow{\Gamma}$ are disjoint copies of Γ such that $\overrightarrow{\Gamma}$ and $\overleftarrow{\Gamma}$ indicate letters such that the state symbol is to their right or to their left, respectively. The letters L_z and R_z are dummies to the left or to the right of the symbol representing the state, and the letters I_z are intermediate symbols.

Next, we define the rules of T. The histories of the computations of M are of the form

$$\rhd(\overrightarrow{\Gamma} \cup D_L)^* \cdot (\overrightarrow{Q} \cup \overleftarrow{Q}) \cdot (\overleftarrow{\Gamma} \cup D_R)^* \lhd .$$

For each letter L_z and R_z and each state $q_i \in Q \setminus \{q_F\}$, we define the rules

$$(\overrightarrow{q_i} R_z \to L_z L_z \overrightarrow{q_i}) \quad \text{and} \quad (L_z \overleftarrow{q_i} \to \overleftarrow{q_i} R_z R_z),$$

which are used to move the state symbol towards the currently scanned letter on the tape. If the currently scanned letter is non-blank, a transition $\delta(q_i, x_i) = (q_j, x_j, \mathrm{R})$ of M is simulated by the rules

$$(\overrightarrow{q_i}\overleftarrow{x_i} \to L_{(\overrightarrow{q_i}, \overleftarrow{x_i})} \overrightarrow{x_j}\overrightarrow{q_j}) \quad \text{and} \quad (\overrightarrow{x_i}\overleftarrow{q_i} \to L_{(\overrightarrow{x_i}, \overleftarrow{q_i})} \overrightarrow{x_j}\overrightarrow{q_j}).$$

If x_i is the blank symbol, then this letter is represented by an end-of-tape marker. So, we include the rules

$$\begin{array}{lclcrcl} (\overrightarrow{q_i}\lhd & \to & L_{(\overrightarrow{q_i},\lhd)} I_{(\overrightarrow{q_i},\lhd)} \lhd) & \text{and} & (L_{(\overrightarrow{q_i},\lhd)} I_{(\overrightarrow{q_i},\lhd)} & \to & L_{(\overrightarrow{q_i},\lhd)} \overrightarrow{x_j}\overrightarrow{q_j}), \quad \text{and} \\ (\rhd\overleftarrow{q_i} & \to & \rhd L_{(\rhd,\overleftarrow{q_i})} I_{(\rhd,\overleftarrow{q_i})}) & \text{and} & (L_{(\rhd,\overleftarrow{q_i})} I_{(\rhd,\overleftarrow{q_i})} & \to & L_{(\rhd,\overleftarrow{q_i})} \overrightarrow{x_j}\overrightarrow{q_j}). \end{array}$$

Observe that the rules are uniquely determined by the letters L_z and I_z on their right-hand sides.

Symmetrically, a transition $\delta(q_i, x_i) = (q_j, x_j, \mathrm{L})$ of M is simulated by the rules

$$\begin{array}{lclcrcl} (\overrightarrow{q_i}\overleftarrow{x_i} & \to & \overleftarrow{q_j}\overleftarrow{x_j} R_{(\overrightarrow{q_i},\overleftarrow{x_i})}) & \text{and} & (\overrightarrow{x_i}\overleftarrow{q_i} & \to & \overleftarrow{q_j}\overleftarrow{x_j} R_{(\overrightarrow{x_i},\overleftarrow{q_i})}), \\ (\overrightarrow{q_i}\lhd & \to & I_{(\overrightarrow{q_i},\lhd)} R_{(\overrightarrow{q_i},\lhd)} \lhd) & \text{and} & (I_{(\overrightarrow{q_i},\lhd)} R_{(\overrightarrow{q_i},\lhd)} & \to & \overleftarrow{q_j}\overleftarrow{x_j} R_{(\overrightarrow{q_i},\lhd)}), \quad \text{and} \\ (\rhd\overleftarrow{q_i} & \to & \rhd I_{(\rhd,\overleftarrow{q_i})} R_{(\rhd,\overleftarrow{q_i})}) & \text{and} & (I_{(\rhd,\overleftarrow{q_i})} R_{(\rhd,\overleftarrow{q_i})} & \to & \overleftarrow{q_j}\overleftarrow{x_j} R_{(\rhd,\overleftarrow{q_i})}). \end{array}$$

Also these rules are uniquely determined by the letters R_z and I_z on their right-hand sides.

The string-rewriting system T can simulate computations of M. As on the left-hand side of each rule, there is a state symbol for which δ is defined, or there is a corresponding symbol from the set H, and as δ is undefined for the halting state q_F, no further derivation step is possible for any encoding of a halting configuration of M. In the following, we consider the computation of M on empty input. So, the language

$$L_h(M) = \{\, w \in (S \setminus \{\rhd, \lhd\})^+ \mid \rhd\overrightarrow{q_0}\lhd \Rightarrow_T^* \rhd w \lhd \,\}$$

is the set of histories that can be derived from the unique initial configuration of M on empty input in an arbitrary number of steps. It is worth mentioning that $L_h(M)$ is finite if and only if M halts on empty input.

We illustrate the above construction with a simple example.

Example 3.3.3 *Let $M = (Q, \Gamma, \delta, q_0, \Box, \{q_F\})$ be the deterministic single-tape Turing machine that is specified by $Q = \{q_0, q_1, q_2, q_F\}$, $\Gamma = \{b, \Box\}$, and*

$$\begin{array}{rclrcl} \delta(q_0, \Box) & = & (q_1, b, R), & \delta(q_0, b) & = & (q_1, b, R), \\ \delta(q_1, \Box) & = & (q_1, b, L), & \delta(q_1, b) & = & (q_2, b, L), \\ \delta(q_2, \Box) & = & (q_F, b, R), & \delta(q_2, b) & = & (q_2, b, R). \end{array}$$

On empty input, M performs the following computation:

$$q_0 \vdash_M bq_1 \vdash_M q_1 bb \vdash_M q_2 \Box bb \vdash_M bq_F bb,$$

that is, M halts after four steps.

Following the above description, we now define a string-rewriting system T that simulates the Turing machine M. For the alphabet S, we take

$$\begin{array}{rcl} S & = & \{\rhd, \lhd, \overrightarrow{q_0}, \overrightarrow{q_1}, \overrightarrow{q_2}, \overrightarrow{q_F}, \overleftarrow{q_0}, \overleftarrow{q_1}, \overleftarrow{q_2}, \overleftarrow{q_F}, \overrightarrow{b}, \overleftarrow{b}\} \cup D_L \cup D_R \cup H, \text{ where} \\ D_L & = & \{ L_z \mid z \in \{ (\overrightarrow{q}, \lhd), (\overrightarrow{q}, \overleftarrow{b}), (\rhd, \overleftarrow{q}), (\overrightarrow{b}, \overleftarrow{q}) \mid q \in Q \} \}, \\ D_R & = & \{ R_z \mid z \in \{ (\overrightarrow{q}, \lhd), (\overrightarrow{q}, \overleftarrow{b}), (\rhd, \overleftarrow{q}), (\overrightarrow{b}, \overleftarrow{q}) \mid q \in Q \} \}, \text{ and} \\ H & = & \{ I_z \mid z \in \{ (\overrightarrow{q}, \lhd), (\rhd, \overleftarrow{q}) \mid q \in Q \} \}, \end{array}$$

and the string-rewriting system T consists of the following rules:

$$\begin{array}{lll} (0) & (\overrightarrow{q} R_z \to L_z L_z \overrightarrow{q}) \text{ and } (L_z \overleftarrow{q} \to \overleftarrow{q} R_z R_z) \text{ for all } q \in \{q_0, q_1, q_2\} \text{ and} & \\ & \qquad z \in \{ (\overrightarrow{q}, \lhd), (\overrightarrow{q}, \overleftarrow{b}), (\rhd, \overleftarrow{q}), (\overrightarrow{b}, \overleftarrow{q}) \mid q \in Q \} \}, & \\ (1) & (\overrightarrow{q_0} \lhd \to L_{(\overrightarrow{q_0},\lhd)} I_{(\overrightarrow{q_0},\lhd)} \lhd) \quad \text{and} & (L_{(\overrightarrow{q_0},\lhd)} I_{(\overrightarrow{q_0},\lhd)} \to L_{(\overrightarrow{q_0},\lhd)} \overrightarrow{b} \overrightarrow{q_1}), \\ (2) & (\rhd \overleftarrow{q_0} \to \rhd L_{(\rhd,\overleftarrow{q_0})} I_{(\rhd,\overleftarrow{q_0})}) \quad \text{and} & (L_{(\rhd,\overleftarrow{q_0})} I_{(\rhd,\overleftarrow{q_0})} \to L_{(\rhd,\overleftarrow{q_0})} \overrightarrow{b} \overrightarrow{q_1}), \\ (3) & (\overrightarrow{q_0} \overleftarrow{b} \to L_{(\overrightarrow{q_0},\overleftarrow{b})} \overrightarrow{b} \overrightarrow{q_1}) \quad \text{and} & (\overrightarrow{b} \overleftarrow{q_0} \to L_{(\overrightarrow{b},\overleftarrow{q_0})} \overrightarrow{b} \overrightarrow{q_1}), \\ (4) & (\overrightarrow{q_1} \lhd \to I_{(\overrightarrow{q_1},\lhd)} R_{(\overrightarrow{q_1},\lhd)} \lhd) \quad \text{and} & (I_{(\overrightarrow{q_1},\lhd)} R_{(\overrightarrow{q_1},\lhd)} \to \overleftarrow{q_1} \overleftarrow{b} R_{(\overrightarrow{q_1},\lhd)}), \\ (5) & (\rhd \overleftarrow{q_1} \to \rhd I_{(\rhd,\overleftarrow{q_1})} R_{(\rhd,\overleftarrow{q_1})}) \quad \text{and} & (I_{(\rhd,\overleftarrow{q_1})} R_{(\rhd,\overleftarrow{q_1})} \to \overleftarrow{q_1} \overleftarrow{b} R_{(\rhd,\overleftarrow{q_1})}), \\ (6) & (\overrightarrow{q_1} \overleftarrow{b} \to \overleftarrow{q_2} \overleftarrow{b} R_{(\overrightarrow{q_1},\overleftarrow{b})}) \quad \text{and} & (\overrightarrow{b} \overleftarrow{q_1} \to \overleftarrow{q_2} \overleftarrow{b} R_{(\overrightarrow{b},\overleftarrow{q_1})}), \\ (7) & (\overrightarrow{q_2} \lhd \to L_{(\overrightarrow{q_2},\lhd)} I_{(\overrightarrow{q_2},\lhd)} \lhd) \quad \text{and} & (L_{(\overrightarrow{q_2},\lhd)} I_{(\overrightarrow{q_2},\lhd)} \to L_{(\overrightarrow{q_2},\lhd)} \overrightarrow{b} \overrightarrow{q_F}), \\ (8) & (\rhd \overleftarrow{q_2} \to \rhd L_{(\rhd,\overleftarrow{q_2})} I_{(\rhd,\overleftarrow{q_2})}) \quad \text{and} & (L_{(\rhd,\overleftarrow{q_2})} I_{(\rhd,\overleftarrow{q_2})} \to L_{(\rhd,\overleftarrow{q_2})} \overrightarrow{b} \overrightarrow{q_F}), \\ (9) & (\overrightarrow{q_2} \overleftarrow{b} \to L_{(\overrightarrow{q_2},\overleftarrow{b})} \overrightarrow{b} \overrightarrow{q_2}) \quad \text{and} & (\overrightarrow{b} \overleftarrow{q_2} \to L_{(\overrightarrow{b},\overleftarrow{q_2})} \overrightarrow{b} \overrightarrow{q_2}). \end{array}$$

For the word $\rhd \overrightarrow{q_0} \lhd$, the system T yields the following finite derivation, where we use indices to indicate the rule that is applied in each step:

$$\begin{array}{rl} \rhd \underline{\overrightarrow{q_0} \lhd} & \Rightarrow_{(1)} \rhd \underline{L_{(\overrightarrow{q_0},\lhd)} I_{(\overrightarrow{q_0},\lhd)}} \lhd \\ & \Rightarrow_{(1)} \rhd L_{(\overrightarrow{q_0},\lhd)} \overrightarrow{b} \underline{\overrightarrow{q_1} \lhd} \\ & \Rightarrow_{(4)} \rhd L_{(\overrightarrow{q_0},\lhd)} \overrightarrow{b} \underline{I_{(\overrightarrow{q_1},\lhd)} R_{(\overrightarrow{q_1},\lhd)}} \lhd \\ & \Rightarrow_{(4)} \rhd L_{(\overrightarrow{q_0},\lhd)} \underline{\overrightarrow{b} \overleftarrow{q_1}} \overleftarrow{b} R_{(\overrightarrow{q_1},\lhd)} \lhd \\ & \Rightarrow_{(6)} \rhd \underline{L_{(\overrightarrow{q_0},\lhd)} \overleftarrow{q_2}} \overleftarrow{b} R_{(\overrightarrow{b},\overleftarrow{q_1})} \overleftarrow{b} R_{(\overrightarrow{q_1},\lhd)} \lhd \\ & \Rightarrow_{(0)} \underline{\rhd \overleftarrow{q_2}} R_{(\overrightarrow{q_0},\lhd)} R_{(\overrightarrow{q_0},\lhd)} \overleftarrow{b} R_{(\overrightarrow{b},\overleftarrow{q_1})} \overleftarrow{b} R_{(\overrightarrow{q_1},\lhd)} \lhd \\ & \Rightarrow_{(8)} \rhd \underline{L_{(\rhd,\overleftarrow{q_2})} I_{(\rhd,\overleftarrow{q_2})}} R_{(\overrightarrow{q_0},\lhd)} R_{(\overrightarrow{q_0},\lhd)} \overleftarrow{b} R_{(\overrightarrow{b},\overleftarrow{q_1})} \overleftarrow{b} R_{(\overrightarrow{q_1},\lhd)} \lhd \\ & \Rightarrow_{(8)} \rhd L_{(\rhd,\overleftarrow{q_2})} \overrightarrow{b} \overrightarrow{q_F} R_{(\overrightarrow{q_0},\lhd)} R_{(\overrightarrow{q_0},\lhd)} \overleftarrow{b} R_{(\overrightarrow{b},\overleftarrow{q_1})} \overleftarrow{b} R_{(\overrightarrow{q_1},\lhd)} \lhd. \end{array}$$

Hence, we see that $L_{(\rhd,\overleftarrow{q_2})} \overrightarrow{b} \overrightarrow{q_F} R_{(\overrightarrow{q_0},\lhd)} R_{(\overrightarrow{q_0},\lhd)} \overleftarrow{b} R_{(\overrightarrow{b},\overleftarrow{q_1})} \overleftarrow{b} R_{(\overrightarrow{q_1},\lhd)} \in L_h(M)$. ■

Next, we construct a deterministic RW(3)-automaton $M' = (Q', \Sigma, \Sigma, \rhd, \lhd, q_0', 3, \delta')$ that accepts exactly the words of $L_h(M)$. To this end, let $Q' = \{q_0'\}$, and let $\Sigma = S \setminus \{\rhd, \lhd\}$. Basically, the idea is to let M' apply the rewrite steps of T in a reversed manner, that is, whenever T applies a rule $(s \to t)$ to expand a word, M' reduces the resulting word by rewriting the factor t into s. Whenever an end-of-tape marker is involved in a rule, M' can apply the same rule, where the end-of-tape markers are replaced with its sentinels. So, let K be the set of all right-hand sides of the rules of T. Observe that $K \subseteq S^3$. Then we define

$$\begin{array}{lcll} \delta'(q_0', z) & = & (q_0', \mathsf{MVR}), & \text{if } z \notin K, \text{ and} \\ \delta'(q_0', t) & = & s, & \text{if } t \in K \text{ and } (s \to t) \in T. \end{array}$$

Finally, M' accepts if and only if an input can be reduced to the encoding of the initial configuration of M on empty input, that is,

$$\delta'(q_0', \rhd \overrightarrow{q_0} \lhd) = \mathsf{Accept}.$$

We illustrate this definition by continuing with the above example.

Example 3.3.3 (cont.) *The det-RW(3)-automaton M' that we obtain from the string-rewriting system T yields the following sequence of cycles, if $L_{(\rhd,\overleftarrow{q_2})}\, \overrightarrow{b}\, \overrightarrow{q_F} R_{(\overrightarrow{q_0},\lhd)} R_{(\overrightarrow{q_0},\lhd)}\, \overleftarrow{b}\, R_{(\overrightarrow{b},\overleftarrow{q_1})}\, \overleftarrow{b}\, R_{(\overrightarrow{q_1},\lhd)}$ is given as input. Here, in each restarting configuration, we underline the factor that is replaced in the next cycle:*

$$\begin{array}{ll} q_0' \rhd \underline{L_{(\rhd,\overleftarrow{q_2})}\, \overrightarrow{b}\, \overrightarrow{q_F}} R_{(\overrightarrow{q_0},\lhd)} R_{(\overrightarrow{q_0},\lhd)}\, \overleftarrow{b}\, R_{(\overrightarrow{b},\overleftarrow{q_1})}\, \overleftarrow{b}\, R_{(\overrightarrow{q_1},\lhd)} \lhd & \\ \vdash^c_{M'} & q_0' \underline{\rhd L_{(\rhd,\overleftarrow{q_2})} I_{(\rhd,\overleftarrow{q_2})}} R_{(\overrightarrow{q_0},\lhd)} R_{(\overrightarrow{q_0},\lhd)}\, \overleftarrow{b}\, R_{(\overrightarrow{b},\overleftarrow{q_1})}\, \overleftarrow{b}\, R_{(\overrightarrow{q_1},\lhd)} \lhd \\ \vdash^c_{M'} & q_0' \rhd \underline{\overleftarrow{q_2} R_{(\overrightarrow{q_0},\lhd)} R_{(\overrightarrow{q_0},\lhd)}}\, \overleftarrow{b}\, R_{(\overrightarrow{b},\overleftarrow{q_1})}\, \overleftarrow{b}\, R_{(\overrightarrow{q_1},\lhd)} \lhd \\ \vdash^c_{M'} & q_0' \rhd L_{(\overrightarrow{q_0},\lhd)} \underline{\overleftarrow{q_2}\, \overleftarrow{b}\, R_{(\overrightarrow{b},\overleftarrow{q_1})}}\, \overleftarrow{b}\, R_{(\overrightarrow{q_1},\lhd)} \lhd \\ \vdash^c_{M'} & q_0' \rhd L_{(\overrightarrow{q_0},\lhd)}\, \overrightarrow{b}\, \underline{\overleftarrow{q_1}\, \overleftarrow{b}\, R_{(\overrightarrow{q_1},\lhd)}} \lhd \\ \vdash^c_{M'} & q_0' \rhd L_{(\overrightarrow{q_0},\lhd)}\, \overrightarrow{b}\, \underline{I_{(\overrightarrow{q_1},\lhd)} R_{(\overrightarrow{q_1},\lhd)} \lhd} \\ \vdash^c_{M'} & q_0' \rhd \underline{L_{(\overrightarrow{q_0},\lhd)}\, \overrightarrow{b}\, \overrightarrow{q_1}} \lhd \\ \vdash^c_{M'} & q_0' \rhd \underline{L_{(\overrightarrow{q_0},\lhd)} I_{(\overrightarrow{q_0},\lhd)} \lhd} \\ \vdash^c_{M'} & q_0' \rhd \overrightarrow{q_0} \lhd \vdash_{M'} \mathsf{Accept}, \end{array}$$

that is, M' just reverses the derivation generated by the string-rewriting system T. ■

All rules of T are strictly length-increasing. Therefore, each rewrite step of M' shortens the tape. Moreover, any rewrite step occurs with a state symbol or a symbol from H in the read/write window. Whenever a state symbol that is labeled by a right (left) arrow occurs, then the two letters to the left (to the right) of it uniquely determine the rule to be applied. Furthermore, if a symbol from H occurs, then this symbol uniquely determines the rule to be applied. Thus, M' is deterministic. As M' only executes an accept step on the encoding of the initial configuration of M on empty input, it follows that M' accepts exactly the words of $L_h(M)$. So, we obtain the following proposition.

Proposition 3.3.4 ([124]) *From a deterministic one-tape Turing machine M, one can effectively construct a deterministic* RW(3)*-automaton for the language $L_h(M)$.*

In order to generalize the above result to an arbitrary window size larger than three, let $\tilde{\Sigma} = \{\, \tilde{x} \mid x \in \Sigma \,\}$ be a disjoint copy of Σ, and let $\varphi_k : \Sigma^* \to \mathcal{P}((\Sigma \cup \tilde{\Sigma})^*)$ be the finite substitution defined by $\varphi_k(x) = \{x, \tilde{x}^k\}$ $(x \in \Sigma)$.

Proposition 3.3.5 ([124]) *Let $k \geq 3$. From a deterministic one-tape Turing machine M, one can construct a deterministic* RW(k)*-automaton for the language $\varphi_k(L_h(M))$.*

Proof. Each word $w \in \varphi_k(L_h(M))$ is obtained from a word $w' \in L_h(M)$ by replacing $s \geq 0$ letters, where a letter is replaced with k consecutive marked copies of itself. A det-RW(k)-automaton M'' accepting $\varphi_k(L_h(M))$ simulates the det-RW(3)-automaton for $L_h(M)$ as long as no letter $\tilde{x}$ from $\tilde{\Sigma}$ appears in its window. Whenever this happens, M'' moves the window to the right until it contains k copies of the letter $\tilde{x}$. If this is not possible, M'' halts and rejects. Otherwise, it rewrites $\tilde{x}^k$ into x and restarts. This construction is effective. □

In order to complete the proof of the non-recursive trade-offs, we modify the Turing machines as follows. First, a deterministic one-tape Turing machine M is transformed into a machine $\hat{M}$ having three tracks on its single tape. The first track is used to simulate M on empty input. On the second track, a unary counter is maintained, which is initially set to one. Then $\hat{M}$ starts to simulate M on empty input. After every step of the simulation, $\hat{M}$ marks the current tape square, remembers the current state, moves to the counter, and increases it by one. Afterwards, it computes n^2 in unary on the third track, where n is the value of the counter. Now, $\hat{M}$ changes to a special *test state* for one time step, and then it moves across the n^2 tape squares marked on the third track. The set of test states can simply be implemented as a disjoint copy of the state set. Finally, $\hat{M}$ changes again to a *test state* for one time step, then clears the third track, returns to the tape position at which the simulation of M has been interrupted, and changes to the state remembered. It then simulates the next step of M and so on. Clearly, the language $L(\hat{M})$ accepted by $\hat{M}$ is finite if and only if the language $L(M)$ is finite.

Theorem 3.3.6 ([124]) *For all* $\mathsf{X} \in \{\mathsf{det\text{-}RW}, \mathsf{det\text{-}RRW}\}$ *and all* $k \geq 3$*, the trade-off from* $\mathsf{X}(k)$*-automata to* $\mathsf{X}(k-1)$*-automata is non-recursive.*

Proof. This theorem is proved by applying Theorem 3.3.2. Given a deterministic one-tape Turing machine M, we first construct the Turing machine $\hat{M}$ as explained above. Then, a det-RW(k)-automaton M'' for the language $\varphi_k(L_h(\hat{M}))$ is obtained according to Proposition 3.3.5. Clearly, the automaton M'' can also be seen as a det-RRW(k)-automaton. It remains to show that the language $\varphi_k(L_h(\hat{M}))$ is accepted by an X-automaton of window size $k-1$ iff M halts on empty input.

If M halts on empty input, then so does $\hat{M}$. Hence, $L_h(\hat{M})$ and $\varphi_k(L_h(\hat{M}))$ are finite. Thus, $\varphi_k(L_h(\hat{M}))$ is regular, and so it is accepted by some X-automaton of window size $k-1$. On the other hand, let M' be an X-automaton of window size $k-1$, and let $w \in \varphi_k(L_h(\hat{M}))$ such that w only contains letters from $\tilde{\Sigma}$. If $w \vdash^c_{M'} w'$, then $w' \notin \varphi_k(L_h(\hat{M}))$, as, in a single cycle, M' shortens its tape contents by at least one letter, rewriting a factor of length at most $k-1$. Therefore, if M' accepts the language $\varphi_k(L_h(\hat{M}))$, then it can do so only by accepting tail computations, which means that $\varphi_k(L_h(\hat{M}))$ is regular.

Let $R \subseteq \Sigma^*$ be the regular language of all words over Σ that contain an occurrence of a test state symbol (see above). Then $\varphi_k(L_h(\hat{M})) \cap R$ is also regular. However, since, in every step during the simulation of $\hat{M}$ by the string-rewriting system T, a dummy symbol is inserted, the lengths of the words in $\varphi_k(L_h(\hat{M})) \cap \Sigma^*$ increase with every step of $\hat{M}$. In particular, the lengths increase at least by n^2 when $\hat{M}$ moves across the n^2 marked squares on its third track after having simulated the n-th step of M. Before $\hat{M}$ starts these moves, it has changed to a test state and, at the end of these moves, it again changes to a test state. Therefore, all words in $\varphi_k(L_h(\hat{M})) \cap \Sigma^*$ that are encodings of the configurations during these moves are filtered out by the intersection with R. So, there are gaps of arbitrary sizes in the sequence of the lengths of the words in $\varphi_k(L_h(\hat{M})) \cap R$. It follows that $\varphi_k(L_h(\hat{M}))$ is not context-free if it is infinite. Since we know already that it is regular, it must be finite. As $\varphi_k(L_h(\hat{M}))$ is finite if and only if M halts on empty input, the theorem follows. □

The computational capacity of stateless restarting automata has been studied in [122, 123] (see Subsections 2.4.1 and 2.4.2). The construction of a det-RW(3)-automaton for the language $L_h(M)$ preceding Proposition 3.3.4 provides, in fact, a stateless automaton. Moreover, the generalization to $\varphi_k(L_h(M))$ shown in Proposition 3.3.5 does not require additional states. Furthermore, the proof of Theorem 3.3.6 reveals that nondeterminism cannot help to accept $\varphi_k(L_h(\hat{M}))$ by an RW-

or RRW-automaton of window size $k-1$. This implies the following theorem, where the prefix stl- denotes stateless types of restarting automata.

Theorem 3.3.7 ([124]) *For all* $\mathsf{X} \in \{\mathsf{stl\text{-}det\text{-}R(R)W}, \mathsf{det\text{-}R(R)W}, \mathsf{stl\text{-}R(R)W}, \mathsf{R(R)W}\}$ *and all* $k \geq 3$, *the trade-off from* $\mathsf{X}(k)$*-automata to* $\mathsf{X}(k-1)$*-automata is non-recursive.*

Theorem 3.3.7 establishes a non-recursive trade-off for converting an R(R)W-automaton of window size k into an equivalent automaton of window size $k-1$. In the proof, we made use of the ability of the restarting automata considered to execute proper rewrite steps as, in this way, the derivations of the string-rewriting system T could be simulated in reverse order. In [125], corresponding non-recursive trade-offs are established for R- and RR-automata, that is, for types of restarting automata the rewrite steps of which are restricted to deletions. The strategy for proving these results is the same as the one used above – however, the encoding of the configurations of the Turing machine M and the simulation of the computations of this Turing machine by a finite string-rewriting system T are technically more involved. Again, we let

$$L_h(M) = \{\, w \in (S \setminus \{\rhd, \lhd\})^+ \mid \rhd\overrightarrow{q_0}\lhd \Rightarrow_T^* \rhd w \lhd \,\}$$

denote the resulting set of histories that can be derived from the unique initial configuration of M on empty input in an arbitrary number of steps. In analogy to Proposition 3.3.4, the following technical result can be derived.

Proposition 3.3.8 ([125]) *From a deterministic one-tape Turing machine M, one can effectively construct a stateless deterministic* R(6)*-automaton for the language* $L_h(M)$.

Actually, the window size can be reduced to 5, if an additional state is provided for the det-R-automaton (see [125]). This yields the following result.

Proposition 3.3.9 ([125]) *From a deterministic one-tape Turing machine M, one can effectively construct a deterministic* R(5)*-automaton for the language* $L_h(M)$.

As in Proposition 3.3.5, these results extend to an arbitrary window size $k \geq 6$ or $k \geq 5$, respectively. From these results, the intended non-recursive trade-offs now follow as in the proof of Theorem 3.3.6.

Corollary 3.3.10 ([125]) *For all* $\mathsf{X} \in \{\mathsf{det\text{-}R}, \mathsf{det\text{-}RR}, \mathsf{R}, \mathsf{RR}\}$ *and all* $k \geq 5$, *the trade-off from* $\mathsf{X}(k)$*-automata to* $\mathsf{X}(k-1)$*-automata is non-recursive. For the stateless variants of these automata, the non-recursive trade-off holds for all* $k \geq 6$.

From the reduction of the halting problem on empty tape, we obtain some additional undecidability results for R(R)(W)-automata.

Theorem 3.3.11 ([124, 125]) (a) *For all* $\mathsf{X} \in \{\mathsf{stl\text{-}det\text{-}R(R)W}, \mathsf{det\text{-}R(R)W}, \mathsf{stl\text{-}R(R)W}, \mathsf{R(R)W}\}$ *and all* $k \geq 3$, *infiniteness is not even recursively enumerable, and finiteness, regularity, and context-freeness are undecidable for* $\mathsf{X}(k)$*-automata.*

(b) *For all* $\mathsf{X} \in \{\mathsf{det\text{-}R}, \mathsf{det\text{-}RR}, \mathsf{R}, \mathsf{RR}\}$ *and all* $k \geq 5$, *infiniteness is not even semi-decidable, and finiteness, regularity, and context-freeness are undecidable for* $\mathsf{X}(k)$*-automata. For the stateless variants of these automata, these results hold for all* $k \geq 6$.

Proof. We just prove the statements in (a), as the proof of (b) is completely analogous. Given an arbitrary deterministic one-tape Turing machine M, an $\mathsf{X}(k)$-automaton accepting the language $\varphi_k(L_h(M))$ or $\varphi_k(L_h(\hat{M}))$ can effectively be constructed by Proposition 3.3.5. Since $\varphi_k(L_h(M))$ is finite if and only if M halts on empty input, it follows immediately that infiniteness is not recursively enumerable and finiteness is undecidable for $\mathsf{X}(k)$-automata.

The proof of Theorem 3.3.6 shows that the language $\varphi_k(L_h(\hat{M}))$ is context-free if and only if M halts on empty input. This implies the undecidability of regularity and context-freeness. □

Based on his results on insertion systems, Andreas Malcher shows in [146] that, for all $k \geq 6$, the inclusion and equivalence problems are undecidable for stateless R(k)-automata. Also the problem of deciding whether the language $L(M)$ contains a given regular language is undecidable for all stateless R(k)-automata M and all $k \geq 5$, and the problem of deciding whether $L(M)$ is contained in a given regular language is undecidable for all stateless R(k)-automata M and all $k \geq 11$.

For R(R)W-automata, (non-recursive) trade-offs between window size k and window size $k-1$ have been obtained for all $k \geq 3$, while for R(R)-automata, the corresponding non-recursive trade-offs have only been established for $k \geq 5$. Accordingly, the following problem remains to be studied.

Problem 3.3.12 *What is the trade-off for converting a (deterministic)* R(R)*-automaton of window size $k \in \{3, 4\}$ into an equivalent automaton of the same type that has window size $k-1$? Is it still non-recursive? In addition, for the case of stateless (deterministic)* R(R)*-automata, what is the trade-off between window size 5 and window size 4?*

Finally, it remains to investigate the trade-offs between window size two and window size one for all the types of restarting automata considered above. Recall from Theorems 2.3.4 and 2.3.10 that

$$\mathcal{L}(\mathsf{R(W)(1)}) = \mathcal{L}(\mathsf{det\text{-}RR(W)(1)}) = \mathsf{REG},$$

while, by Propositions 2.3.7 and 2.3.8, $\mathsf{REG} \subsetneq \mathcal{L}(\mathsf{mon\text{-}RR(1)}) \subsetneq \mathcal{L}(\mathsf{RR})$. In addition, we know from Proposition 2.3.11 that every deterministic restarting automaton of window size two is monotone. Based on these results, it can be shown that the trade-off between window size two and window size one is recursive for deterministic types of restarting automata.

Theorem 3.3.13 ([124, 125]) *For* $\mathsf{X} \in \{\mathsf{det\text{-}R}, \mathsf{det\text{-}RR}, \mathsf{det\text{-}RW}, \mathsf{det\text{-}RRW}\}$*, the trade-off from* $\mathsf{X}(2)$*-automata to* $\mathsf{X}(1)$*-automata is recursive.*

Proof. We recall from Corollary 2.1.43 that monotone det-R- and monotone det-RRW-automata accept exactly the class DCFL of deterministic context-free languages. In particular, in the proof of these results, a construction is given that transforms a monotone deterministic restarting automaton into an equivalent deterministic pushdown automaton. According to a fundamental result of [248, 253], it is decidable whether the language accepted by a given deterministic pushdown automaton is regular. The corresponding algorithm reveals a recursive upper bound for the number of states of an equivalent deterministic finite-state acceptor. Together these results yield a recursive trade-off for the conversion of a deterministic R(R)(W)-automaton of window size two into an equivalent deterministic R(R)(W)-automaton of window size one. □

The precise trade-off for the conversion of deterministic restarting automata with window size two to ones with window size one is a challenging task for further studies. One aspect is to determine a good upper bound. Deterministic restarting automata of window size one just accept the regular languages, while those of window size two accept the deterministic context-free languages, if they can use auxiliary letters (see Corollary 2.3.46). Accordingly, this question is related to the problem of converting a DPDA into an equivalent DFA.

The upper bound for the latter conversion given in [253] reads as follows: Let M be a deterministic pushdown automaton with n states, t pushdown symbols, and let h be the length of the longest word that can be pushed in a single transition. If $L(M)$ is regular, then $2^{2^{\mathcal{O}(n^2 \log n + \log t + \log h)}}$ states are sufficient for a DFA that accepts $L(M)$.

The second point is to determine matching or at least good lower bounds. The following lower bound for the conversion of a DPDA to an equivalent DFA can be found in [74, 154]. Let $n \geq 1$ be an integer. Then there is a language L_n that is accepted by a deterministic pushdown automaton of size $\mathcal{O}(n^3)$ such that each equivalent DFA has at least 2^{2^n} states.

Problem 3.3.14 *Determine the exact trade-off for converting a deterministic* R(R)(W)*-automaton of window size two into an equivalent automaton of the same type of window size one!*

For the case of nondeterministic restarting automata, a result in analogy to Theorem 3.3.13 is not known, that is, also the following task remains unfinished.

Problem 3.3.15 *Determine the trade-off between nondeterministic* R(R)(W)*-automata of window size two and window size one!*

We complete this section by taking a look at the situation for restarting automata with auxiliary letters. For RRWW-automata, it has been shown in [236] that, for all $k \geq 2$, $\mathcal{L}(\mathsf{RRWW}(k+1)) = \mathcal{L}(\mathsf{RRWW}(k))$ (see Theorem 2.3.41). In fact, one can effectively construct an RRWW(k)-automaton

$$R_2 = (Q_2, \Sigma, \Gamma_2, \rhd, \lhd, q_0, k, \delta_2)$$

from a given RRWW($k+1$)-automaton

$$R_1 = (Q_1, \Sigma, \Gamma_1, \rhd, \lhd, q_0, k+1, \delta_1)$$

such that $L(R_1) = L(R_2)$ holds. Actually, the construction presented in [236] reveals that

$$|Q_2| \in \mathcal{O}(|Q_1|^3 \cdot |\Gamma_1|^{2k+2}) \quad \text{and} \quad |\Gamma_2| \in \mathcal{O}(|Q_1|^2 \cdot |\Gamma_1|^{2k+3}).$$

When taking the complexity sn-measure trans, that is, the product of the number of states and the number of possible window contents, then we obtain $|Q_2| \in \mathcal{O}(\text{trans}(R_1)^3)$ and $|\Gamma_2| \in \mathcal{O}(\text{trans}(R_1)^3)$ and, hence, $\text{trans}(R_2) \in \mathcal{O}(\text{trans}(R_1)^3 \cdot \text{trans}(R_1)^{3k}) = \mathcal{O}(\text{trans}(R_1)^{3k+3})$.

Corollary 3.3.16 *For all $k \geq 2$, the trade-off between* RRWW($k+1$)*-automata and* RRWW(k)*-automata is at most polynomial, where the degree of the polynomial depends on the window size k.*

For deterministic RRWW-automata, we do not have a corresponding construction. In fact, for all $k \geq 3$, it is open whether deterministic RRWW-automata of window size $k+1$ are at all more expressive than those of window size k (see Problem 2.3.48 (a)). In addition, we have no results concerning the corresponding trade-offs.

Problem 3.3.17 *For all $k \geq 2$, what is the trade-off for turning a deterministic* R(R)WW*-automaton of window size $k+1$ into an equivalent deterministic* R(R)WW*-automaton of window size k?*

For monotone (deterministic and nondeterministic) R(R)WW-automata, it is known that window size two suffices (see Corollaries 2.3.42 and 2.3.46). In fact, the constructions that produce an R(R)WW-automaton of window size two from a given automaton of window size $k \geq 3$ yield exponential upper bounds for the corresponding trade-offs. However, the exact trade-offs for these conversions remain to be determined.

Problem 3.3.18 *For all $k \geq 2$, determine the exact trade-off for converting a monotone (deterministic)* R(R)WW*-automaton of window size $k+1$ into an equivalent automaton of the same type that has window size k!*

3.4 On Monotone and Deterministic R(R)WW-Automata

The monotone R(R)WW-automata characterize the class CFL of context-free languages (Corollary 2.1.41), while the deterministic R(R)WW-automata specify the class CRL of Church-Rosser languages (Corollary 2.1.34). It is well-known that these two language classes are incomparable with respect to inclusion, but that their intersection is a proper superset of the class of deterministic context-free languages. In fact, this intersection includes the class $\mathcal{L}(\mathsf{det\text{-}ORD})$ of languages that are accepted by deterministic ORD-automata (see Theorem 2.3.91). Concerning the descriptional complexity of restarting automata, it is therefore of interest to study the trade-offs from monotone R(R)WW-automata to deterministic R(R)WW-automata and, conversely, from deterministic R(R)WW-automata to monotone R(R)WW-automata. As it turns out, we obtain non-recursive trade-offs for both directions.

First, by making use of the encoding of the computation of a Turing machine on empty input presented in the previous section, the following result is easily derived.

Theorem 3.4.1 **([77])** *The trade-off for the conversion of a deterministic RRWW-automaton into an equivalent monotone RRWW-automaton is non-recursive.*

Proof outline. We follow the proof of Theorem 3.3.6. Given a deterministic one-tape Turing machine M, we first construct the Turing machine $\hat{M}$ (see the paragraph following Proposition 3.3.5). Then, a stateless det-R(6)-automaton M'' for the language $L_h(\hat{M})$ is obtained according to Proposition 3.3.8. Clearly, M'' can also be seen as a det-RRWW-automaton. It remains to prove that $L_h(\hat{M})$ is accepted by a monotone RRWW-automaton iff M halts on empty input.

If M halts on empty input, then so does $\hat{M}$. Hence, $L_h(\hat{M})$ is finite, and so it is accepted by some monotone R(R)WW-automaton. Conversely, assume that M does not halt on empty input, which implies that $L_h(\hat{M})$ is infinite. Let $R \subseteq \Sigma^*$ be the regular language of all words that contain an occurrence of a test state symbol (see the definition of $\hat{M}$). Then there are gaps of arbitrary sizes in the sequence of the lengths of the words in $L_h(\hat{M}) \cap R$. It follows that $L_h(\hat{M}) \cap R$ is not context-free, and hence, neither is the language $L_h(\hat{M})$. Hence, $L_h(\hat{M})$ is not accepted by any monotone RRWW-automaton. Thus, $L_h(\hat{M})$ is accepted by a monotone RRWW-automaton if and only if M halts on empty input, which yields the stated non-recursive trade-off. □

As the language $L_h(M)$ is accepted by a deterministic R-automaton, and as all subtypes of the monotone RRWW-automaton only accept (certain) context-free languages, the above proof actually shows the following stronger result.

Corollary 3.4.2 **([77])** *Let* $\mathsf{X}, \mathsf{Y} \in \{\mathsf{R}, \mathsf{RR}, \mathsf{RW}, \mathsf{RRW}, \mathsf{RWW}, \mathsf{RRWW}\}$. *Then the trade-off for the conversion of a restarting automaton of type* X *or* det-X *into an equivalent monotone restarting automaton of type* Y *is non-recursive.*

Theorem 2.3.95 shows that swift ORD-automata, that is, stateless nondeterministic ORD-automata that can freely apply move-right steps, accept exactly the context-free languages. The proof of the inclusion of $\mathcal{L}(\mathsf{swift\text{-}ORD})$ in CFL given in [199] is constructive, that is, it is based on an algorithm that converts a swift ORD-automaton into an equivalent PDA. Accordingly, Theorem 3.4.1 can be rephrased as follows.

Corollary 3.4.3 *The trade-off for the conversion of a deterministic RRWW-automaton into an equivalent swift ORD-automaton is non-recursive.*

Actually, this result even extends to (stateless) deterministic ORD-automata. We recall from Theorem 2.3.91 that (stateless) deterministic ORD-automata accept a class of languages that is contained in the intersection of CRL with CFL.

Corollary 3.4.4 *The trade-off for the conversion of a deterministic RRWW-automaton into an equivalent (stateless) deterministic ORD-automaton is non-recursive.*

Each monotone deterministic RRWW-automaton accepts a deterministic context-free language (see Corollary 2.1.43). Hence, the language $L_h(M)$ above is accepted by a monotone deterministic RRWW-automaton if and only if the Turing machine M halts on empty input. Hence, we also obtain the following consequence.

Corollary 3.4.5 ([77]) *The trade-off for the conversion of a deterministic RRWW-automaton into an equivalent monotone deterministic RRWW-automaton is non-recursive.*

Of course, Corollaries 3.4.3 to 3.4.5 also hold for all subtypes of the deterministic RRWW-automaton. Using a different proof strategy, the following additional result is established in [77].

Theorem 3.4.6 ([77]) *The trade-off for the conversion of a deterministic* RWW*-automaton into an equivalent deterministic* R(R)W*-automaton is non-recursive.*

Now we turn to the converse direction of Theorem 3.4.1. Here we follow the presentation by Markus Holzer, Martin Kutrib, and Jens Reimann in [77]. As above, we use particular encodings of Turing machine computations. However, in contrast to the situation above, we consider the sets of *valid computations* of a Turing machine M, which is an encoding of *all* accepting computations of M.

Definition 3.4.7 *Let $M = (Q, \Gamma, \delta, q_0, \Box, \{q_F\})$ be a deterministic single-tape Turing machine. Here, in order to avoid some trivial cases, we assume that M cannot print the blank symbol, that it halts only when it accepts, and that each accepting computation of M consists of an odd number of steps larger than two. The latter means that each accepting computation of M consists of a sequence of configurations that has an even length.*

Let $\Omega = Q \cup \Gamma \cup \{\#\}$, where # is a new symbol. For $m \geq 2$, a word

$$w = w_1 \# w_2^R \# w_3 \# w_4^R \# \cdots \# w_{2m-1} \# w_{2m}^R$$

is called a valid computation *of M, if it satisfies the following conditions:*

(1) *For all $i = 1, 2, \ldots, 2m$, $w_i \in \Gamma^* \cdot Q \cdot \Gamma^*$ is a configuration of M,*

(2) *$w_1 = q_0 u$, that is, w_1 is an initial configuration,*

(3) *$w_{2m} \in \Gamma^* \cdot q_F \cdot \Gamma^*$, that is, w_{2m} is an accepting configuration, and*

(4) *for all $i = 1, 2, \ldots, 2m-1$, $w_i \vdash_M w_{i+1}$, that is, $w_1 \vdash_M w_2 \vdash_M \cdots \vdash_M w_{2m}$ is an accepting computation of M on input u.*

We use VALC(M) *to denote the language that consists of all words w of the above form, and*

$$\text{INVALC}(M) = \Omega^* \smallsetminus \text{VALC}(M)$$

is the language of invalid computations *of M.*

It is easily seen that the language VALC(M) is decidable. In addition, this language is finite if and only if the language $L(M)$ accepted by the Turing machine M is finite. In fact, the following statements hold.

Proposition 3.4.8

(a) *The language* VALC(M) *is the intersection of two deterministic context-free languages.*

(b) *The language* INVALC(M) *is a linear context-free language.*

Proof. (a) Let $\text{VALC}_1(M)$ consist of all words $w = w_1\#w_2^R\#w_3\#w_4^R\#\cdots\#w_{2m-1}\#w_{2m}^R$ that satisfy conditions (1) to (3) of Definition 3.4.7 and $w_{2i-1} \vdash_M w_{2i}$ for all $i = 1, 2, \ldots, m$, and let $\text{VALC}_2(M)$ consist of all words $w = w_1\#w_2^R\#w_3\#w_4^R\#\cdots\#w_{2m-1}\#w_{2m}^R$ that satisfy conditions (1) to (3) of Definition 3.4.7 and $w_{2i} \vdash_M w_{2i+1}$ for all $i = 1, 2, \ldots, m-1$. Then $\text{VALC}(M) = \text{VALC}_1(M) \cap \text{VALC}_2(M)$. From M, one can construct DPDAs for the languages $\text{VALC}_1(M)$ and $\text{VALC}_2(M)$ (see, e.g. [81]), which shows that these languages are deterministic context-free.

(b) A word $w \in \Omega^*$ belongs to the language $\text{INVALC}(M)$ if it does not satisfy one (or more) of the conditions given in Definition 3.4.7. For $i = 1, 2, 3, 4$, let $\text{INVALC}_i(M)$ denote the set of all words over Ω that do not satisfy condition (i). Then $\text{INVALC}_1(M)$, $\text{INVALC}_2(M)$, and $\text{INVALC}_3(M)$ are regular languages. Moreover, a word $w = w_1\#w_2^R\#w_3\#w_4^R\#\cdots\#w_{2m-1}\#w_{2m}^R$ belongs to $\text{INVALC}_4(M)$ if and only if there exists an index $j \in \{1, 2, \ldots, 2m-1\}$ such that w_{j+1} is not the immediate successor configuration of w_j. As w contains the factor $w_j\#w_{j+1}^R$, this condition can be checked by a one-turn PDA. In fact, from M, a corresponding one-turn PDA can be constructed effectively. As all regular languages are linear context-free, and as the class LIN of linear context-free languages is closed under union, it follows that $\text{INVALC}(M) = \bigcup_{i=1}^{4} \text{INVALC}_i(M)$ is a linear context-free language. □

Next, we define a particular type of example languages that are related to certain ternary relations.

Definition 3.4.9 *Let A and B be two alphabets that do not contain the letter c, and let $\psi \subseteq A^* \times A^* \times B^*$ be a relation. With this relation, we associate the language*

$$L_\psi = \{\, w_1cw_2cw_1^Rcw_2^Rcw_3 \mid w_1, w_2 \in A^* \text{ and } w_3 \in B^* \text{ such that } (w_1, w_2, w_3) \in \psi \,\}.$$

Concerning the languages of this type, the following important result is proved in [77].

Theorem 3.4.10 ([77, 228]) *Let A and B be two alphabets that do not contain the letter c, where $|A| \geq 2$, let $\psi \subseteq A^* \times A^* \times B^*$ be a ternary relation, and let ψ' be the binary relation*

$$\psi' = \{\, (w_1, w_2) \in A^* \times A^* \mid |w_1| = |w_2| \text{ and } \exists w_3 \in B^* : (|w_3| = |w_1| \text{ and } (w_1, w_2, w_3) \in \psi) \,\}.$$

If $A^n \times A^n \subset \psi'$ holds for infinitely many $n \in \mathbb{N}$, then the language L_ψ is not growing context-sensitive.

For the proof, which is rather long and technically involved, we refer to the paper [77] or the dissertation [228]. Based on this result, we can now apply Theorem 3.3.2 to establish the following non-recursive trade-off.

Theorem 3.4.11 ([77]) *The trade-off for the conversion of a monotone* R(R)WW*-automaton into an equivalent deterministic* R(R)WW*-automaton is non-recursive.*

Proof. Let M be a deterministic single-tape Turing machine, let $A = \{a, b\}$, and let B be the alphabet over which the language $\text{VALC}(M)$ is defined. We define a ternary relation $\psi \subseteq A^* \times A^* \times B^*$ as follows:

$$\psi = \{\, (w_1, w_2, w_3) \mid |w_1| = |w_2| = |w_3| \text{ and } w_3 \in \text{VALC}(M) \,\}.$$

Finally, let $L = L_\psi^c = \Sigma^* \smallsetminus L_\psi$, where $\Sigma = A \cup B \cup \{c\}$. A word $w \in \Sigma^*$ belongs to the language L if it satisfies one of the following conditions:

- $w \neq w_1cw_2cw_3cw_4cw_5$ for any $w_1, w_2, w_3, w_4 \in A^*$ and $w_5 \in B^*$, or
- $w = w_1cw_2cw_3cw_4cw_5$ for some $w_1, w_2, w_3, w_4 \in A^*$ and $w_5 \in B^*$, but
  - $w_3 \in \text{INVALC}(M)$, or
  - w_1, w_2, w_3, w_4, and w_5 do not all have the same length, or

- $w_1 \neq w_3^R$, or
- $w_2 \neq w_4^R$.

The first condition can be specified by a regular expression. By Proposition 3.4.8(b), INVALC(M) is a linear language for which a linear context-free grammar can effectively be constructed from the Turing machine M. Finally, the languages defined by the other conditions can also be specified by linear context-free grammars. Hence, it follows that L is a linear context-free language for which we can effectively construct a linear context-free grammar. Accordingly, L is accepted by a monotone R(R)WW-automaton, and we can even obtain such an automaton from the linear context-free grammar (see, e.g., the proof of Theorem 2.1.40).

Next, we claim that the language L is accepted by a deterministic R(R)WW-automaton if and only if the language $L(M)$ is finite. If $L(M)$ is finite, then the language VALC(M) is finite, too, implying that the language L_ψ is finite. Thus, in this case, the language $L = L_\psi^c$ is co-finite, and therewith, it is a regular language, which means that there exists a det-R(R)WW-automaton for L. Conversely, assume that $L(M)$ is infinite and that $L = L(R)$ for some deterministic R(R)WW-automaton R. Then also $L^c = L_\psi$ is accepted by some deterministic R(R)WW-automaton, which shows that L_ψ is a Church-Rosser language by Corollary 2.1.34. However, as $L(M)$ is infinite, so is the language VALC(M), which shows that the relation ψ satisfies all of the preconditions of Theorem 3.4.10. Hence, this theorem implies that L_ψ is not growing context-sensitive, a contradiction. It follows that the language L is accepted by a det-R(R)WW-automaton if and only if the language $L(M)$ is finite.

Now we can apply Theorem 3.3.2 as follows. Let $\mathcal{S}_1$ be the monotone R(R)WW-automata, let $\mathcal{S}_2$ be the deterministic R(R)WW-automata, let $\mathcal{S}_3$ be the deterministic single-tape Turing machines, and let P be the property of accepting an infinite language. This property is not recursively enumerable for Turing machines [81]. From a Turing machine M, we can effectively construct a monotone R(R)WW-automaton for the language L_ψ^c. Then there exists an equivalent det-R(R)WW-automaton if and only if the language $L(M)$ is finite. It follows that the trade-off from monotone R(R)WW-automata to deterministic R(R)WW-automata is non-recursive. □

The above proof also works if, instead of deterministic R(R)WW-automata, we take deterministic R(R)W- or R(R)-automata. In addition, it extends to (stateless) deterministic ORD-automata. Hence, we have the following non-recursive trade-offs.

Corollary 3.4.12 ([77]) *The trade-off for the conversion of a monotone* R(R)WW*-automaton into an equivalent deterministic* R(R)W-, R(R)-, *or (stateless) deterministic* ORD*-automaton is non-recursive.*

From the proof of Theorem 3.4.11, we see that we have even established a non-recursive trade-off from linear context-free languages to deterministic R(R)WW-automata. Theorems 3.4.1 and 3.4.11 show that monotone and deterministic R(R)WW-automata do not only accept language classes that are incomparable with respect to inclusion, but that, in addition, the trade-off for the conversion from either one of them to the other is non-recursive. This implies, in particular, that there is no effective construction that converts a monotone (or deterministic) R(R)WW-automaton M_1 into a deterministic (or monotone) R(R)WW-automaton M_2 such that $L(M_1) = L(M_2)$ holds, provided this language belongs to the intersection of CFL with CRL.

In Jens Reimann's doctoral dissertation [228], non-recursive trade-offs are presented for further types of restarting automata. Using a slightly more involved encoding for the set of invalid computations of a Turing machine M, he proves that the resulting set INVALC(M) is accepted by an R(R)W-automaton if and only if the language $L(M)$ is finite. Based on this technical result, he then establishes the following non-recursive trade-offs.

Theorem 3.4.13 ([228]) *The trade-off for the conversion of a (monotone)* R(R)WW*-automaton into an equivalent* R(R)W- *or* R(R)*-automaton is non-recursive.*

In addition, he proves that the trade-off from RRWW-automata to monotone R(R)WW-automata or to any subclass of the latter is non-recursive. These results are derived from the technical result that (a suitable encoding of) the set of valid computations of a Turing machine is accepted by an RRWW-automaton of window size two. To complete the study of trade-offs between the various types of restarting automata, the following problem remains to be solved.

Problem 3.4.14 *Does Corollary 3.4.12 extend to monotone* R(R)W- *and* R(R)*-automata? That is, is the trade-off for the conversion of a monotone* R(R)W- *or* R(R)*-automaton into an equivalent deterministic* R(R)W-, R(R)-*, or (stateless) deterministic* ORD*-automaton non-recursive, too?*

Chapter 4

Learnability for Restarting Automata

Restarting automata are a formal model for the linguistic technique of 'analysis by reduction.' Accordingly, these automata can be used to study the language-theoretical foundations of this linguistic technique, establishing theoretical results or refuting conjectures. Unfortunately, it is quite a difficult task to design a restarting automaton for a comprehensive language like, e.g., a substantial subset of a natural language. So far, only a few tools have been developed that support the design of restarting automata. In this chapter, we present several methods that have been proposed in the literature for inferring or learning restarting automata (that is, analysis by reduction) from examples and counterexamples.

Let $\mathcal{M}$ be a type of grammar (or automaton) that describes a class $\mathcal{L}$ of languages, for example, $\mathcal{M}$ can be the class of context-free grammars and $\mathcal{L}$ is the class of context-free languages. In many situations, we have a grammar G and need to verify that this grammar generates a given language L, or we have a description of a language L (for example, through a PDA) and need to define a grammar for that language. There are known techniques that can be used to prove that $L(G) = L$ or that allow to convert the PDA into an equivalent grammar. However, what happens if we do not have a formal description of the language L, but just a sequence of words from that language, or a sequence of words together with information on which of them belong to the language and which do not? This leads to the problem of inferring (or learning) a formal specification of a language (like a grammar or an automaton) from positive data (that is, from text) or from positive and negative data (that is, from an informant).

The topic of grammatical inference (or 'learning') was first described in a formal way by E. Mark Gold in [54]. In [270], Takashi Yokomori presents a survey on grammatical inference and learning. If it is possible to infer a descriptor from a class $\mathcal{M}$ of formal specifications (like grammars or automata) for a language from an enumeration of its elements (possibly with repetitions), then we say that this language can be inferred (or learnt) in the limit from positive data (or from text). A class of languages $\mathcal{L}$ is said to be inferable in the limit from positive data if, for each enumeration of a language L from the class $\mathcal{L}$, a descriptor G from $\mathcal{M}$ can be inferred that describes that language. As shown by E. Mark Gold, a class of languages that contains all finite languages and at least one infinite language is not inferable in the limit from positive data [54]. Thus, the class of regular languages and the class of context-free languages cannot be learnt this way. However, several subclasses of the class of regular languages are inferable in the limit from positive data, for example, the class of strictly locally j-testable languages [271] and the class of k-reversible languages [2].

Here, we consider the problem of learning restarting automata. As a restarting automaton realizes the process of analysis by reduction, we do not simply want to learn the language that is accepted by this restarting automaton, but moreover, we also want to learn the reduction relation that this automaton induces on the corresponding set of characteristic words. Hence, this task is

F. Otto, *Restarting Automata*, Theory and Applications of Computability,
https://doi.org/10.1007/978-3-031-70094-1_4

similar to the task of learning a rewriting system. In [176], Yasuhito Makouchi, Ikuyo Yamaue, and Masako Sato present an inference method for rewriting systems describing L systems [143], and in [45], Rémi Eyraud, Colin de la Higuera, and Jean-Christophe Janodet describe a method for learning certain string-rewriting systems from positive and negative samples.

In Sections 4.1 and 4.2, we describe some results that have been obtained on learning certain restricted types of restarting automata from positive data. Here the task of learning a restarting automaton is subdivided into the task of learning the single-step reduction relation $\vdash^{c}_{M}$ of a restarting automaton M and of learning the set of simple sentential forms $S_{\mathrm{C}}(M)$. In Section 4.1, restarting automata are considered that are defined by meta-instructions for which the (regular) context conditions are strictly j-testable languages. In this setting, the learner is given a sequence of individual reductions and positive samples of simple words. The task of learning a restarting automaton that is compatible with the given positive data is split into the task of learning individual meta-instructions by a helpful teacher, who, in addition, also provides information on the rewrite steps of the reductions given.

In Section 4.2, we present Petr Hoffmann's Omega* method of inferring a restarting automaton from fully positive analysis by reduction samples [71]. These samples are complete sequences of reductions that transform a word into a simple word. Here no helpful teacher is assumed, but the rewrite steps are extracted from the given reductions by using a simple heuristics. For this approach to succeed, the restarting automata considered are fairly restricted. First of all, the context conditions of all meta-instructions are restricted to be k-reversible languages (see, e.g., [2]), and it is required that the restarting automata considered are single automata, that is, they have only a single accepting meta-instruction and, for each rewrite step $l \to r$, there is only a single rewriting meta-instruction containing this rewrite step (see Section 4.2 for the definition). In addition to presenting the Omega* method, we also restate the results from [73] on the expressive capacity of these types of restarting automata.

Finally, in Section 4.3, we concentrate on the problem of learning clearing (and subword clearing) restarting automata from an informant, that is, we are given positive and negative samples. These results are taken from [254, 256], and they extend to all types of limited context restarting automata. Unfortunately, the problem of deciding of whether there exists a clearing retarting automaton M that is consistent with a given finite set S^+ of positive samples and a given finite set S^- of negative samples such that the width of each instruction of M is bounded by a given constant l is already NP-hard (see Theorems 4.3.16 and 4.3.17).

Also other approaches have been taken to learn certain types of restarting automata. In [8], Stanislav Basovník and František Mráz propose genetic algorithms to learn limited context restarting automata. They claim that their method works well in comparison to the methods RPNI [190] and LARS [45], but as genetic algorithms are beyond the topic of this monograph, we just refer to their work.

4.1 Learning Strictly Locally Testable Restarting Automata

A restarting automaton $M = (Q, \Sigma, \Gamma, \rhd, \lhd, q_0, k, \delta)$ of type RRWW transforms a given input word $w \in \Sigma^*$ into a simple sentential word $z \in \Gamma^*$ by executing a sequence of cycles. In each cycle, the current word is rewritten into a simpler word by replacing a factor of length k with a shorter word. Hence, the task of learning a restarting automaton (that is, analysis by reduction) consists in learning the single-step reduction relation $\vdash_M^c$ that is induced by M on its set of restarting configurations and the simple characteristic language $S_C(M)$. As the restarting automaton M can be described through a finite set of meta-instructions of the forms

$$(\rhd \cdot R_1, u \to v, R_2 \cdot \lhd) \text{ and } (\rhd \cdot R \cdot \lhd, \mathsf{Accept}),$$

this task can be split into learning individual meta-instructions. However, from just knowing that

$$q_0 \rhd abababa \lhd \vdash_M^c q_0 \rhd ababa \lhd$$

is a valid cycle of M, we cannot decide whether a factor ab was deleted, whether a factor ba was deleted, whether a factor aba was rewritten into b, or whether some other rewrite step was executed by M. Therefore, in [166], a helpful teacher is assumed, who marks the rewritten factor in such a sample reduction. In this way, the problem of learning a meta-instruction is reduced to the problem of learning the regular constraints of the meta-instruction. For this task, known techniques and results on learning regular languages can be used. In this section, we use the technique of learning languages from text, that is, from positive data only.

For a language L, a *positive presentation* of L is an infinite sequence $\{w_i\}_{i=1}^{\infty}$ of words from L such that every word $w \in L$ occurs at least once in this sequence. Let $\mathcal{M}$ be a class of grammars or automata, and let $\mathcal{A}$ be an algorithm which, on input $\{w_1, w_2, \ldots, w_i\}$ (for any $i \geq 1$), returns a conjecture grammar or automaton $M_i \in \mathcal{M}$. The algorithm $\mathcal{A}$ is said to *learn* (or *identify*) *a language L in the limit from positive data using* $\mathcal{M}$ if, for any positive presentation of L,

(1) there exists a grammar or an automaton M in $\mathcal{M}$ such that $L(M) = L$, and

(2) the infinite sequence of grammars or automata $\{M_i\}_{i=1}^{\infty}$ in $\mathcal{M}$ produced by $\mathcal{A}$ satisfies the property that, for all sufficiently large values of i, M_i is identical to M.

A class of languages $\mathcal{L}$ is *learnable in the limit from positive data* (using $\mathcal{M}$) if there exists an algorithm $\mathcal{A}$ that, for each $L \in \mathcal{L}$, learns L in the limit from positive data using $\mathcal{M}$.

In [54], E. Mark Gold proved that any class of languages containing all finite sets and at least one infinite set is not learnable in the limit from positive data only. This fact implies that even the class of regular languages is not learnable in the limit from positive data. However, there are interesting subclasses of the regular languages which are learnable in this way. One of them is the class of strictly locally testable languages [149, 273].

Recall from Subsection 2.4.1 that a language $L \subseteq \Sigma^*$ is called *strictly j-testable* if there exist finite sets $A, B, C \subseteq \Sigma^j$ such that, for all $w \in \Sigma^*$ satisfying $|w| \geq j$, we have

$$w \in L \text{ if and only if } P_j(w) \in A,\ I_j(w) \subseteq B, \text{ and } S_j(w) \in C.$$

Here $P_j(w)$ and $S_j(w)$ denote the prefix and the suffix of length j of w, and $I_j(w)$ is the set of inner factors of length j of w. Finally, L is called *strictly locally testable* if it is strictly j-testable for some $j > 0$. The family of strictly j-testable languages is denoted by j-SLT and the class of strictly locally testable languages is denoted by SLT. It is easy to see that $\mathsf{SLT} \subsetneq \mathsf{REG}$ (for example, the regular language $(aa)^*$ is not strictly locally testable). It is also known that $j\text{-}\mathsf{SLT} \subsetneq (j+1)\text{-}\mathsf{SLT}$ holds.

We briefly recall a learning algorithm for strictly j-testable languages from [271]. For a triple $S = (A, B, C)$, where $A, B, C \subseteq \Sigma^j$, we use the notation $L(A, B, C)$ to denote the strictly j-testable language that is specified by the triple S and the notation $L'(A, B, C)$ as a shorthand for the set

$L'(A,B,C) = A \cap C \cap (\Sigma^j \setminus B)$. Observe that the words in $L'(A,B,C)$ belong to the language $L(A,B,C)$, but they do not occur as proper factors within other words of $L(A,B,C)$.

First, we present a construction which, for a given triple $S = (A,B,C)$, where $A, B, C \subseteq \Sigma^j$, constructs a deterministic finite-state acceptor (DFA) $M_S = (Q, \Sigma, \delta, q_0, F)$ such that $L(M_S) = (A \cdot \Sigma^* \cap \Sigma^* \cdot C) \setminus (\Sigma^+ \cdot (\Sigma^j \setminus B) \cdot \Sigma^+) = L(A,B,C)$:

$$Q = \begin{cases} Q_I \cup \{\, [\widehat{x}] \mid x \in L'(A,B,C) \,\}, & \text{if } L'(A,B,C) \neq \emptyset, \\ Q_I, & \text{otherwise}, \end{cases}$$

where

$$Q_I = \{\, [\lambda], [a_1], [a_1a_2], \ldots, [a_1a_2\cdots a_{j-1}] \mid a_1a_2\cdots a_j \in A, a_1, a_2, \ldots, a_j \in \Sigma \,\} \cup \{\, [x] \mid x \in A \cup B \cup C \,\}.$$

Thus, the states of M_S correspond to the proper prefixes of the set A and to the words contained in $A \cup B \cup C$, and there are additional states for the words in $L'(A,B,C)$. Furthermore,

$$q_0 = [\lambda],$$
$$F = \begin{cases} \{\, [\beta] \mid \beta \in C \,\} \cup \{\, [\widehat{x}] \mid x \in L'(A,B,C) \,\}, & \text{if } L'(A,B,C) \neq \emptyset, \\ \{\, [\beta] \mid \beta \in C \,\}, & \text{otherwise}, \end{cases}$$

and δ is defined as follows:

(i) for each $\alpha = a_1a_2\cdots a_j \in A$ $(a_1, a_2, \ldots, a_j \in \Sigma)$:

$$\delta(q_0, a_1) = [a_1],$$
$$\delta([a_1\cdots a_i], a_{i+1}) = [a_1\cdots a_ia_{i+1}] \quad (1 \leq i \leq j-2),$$
$$\delta([a_1a_2\cdots a_{j-1}], a_j) = \begin{cases} [\widehat{\alpha}], & \text{if } \alpha \in C \cap (\Sigma^j \setminus B), \\ [\alpha], & \text{otherwise}; \end{cases}$$

(ii) for each $[ax], [xb] \in Q$ such that $|x| = j-1$, $ax \in A$, $xb \in B \cup C$:

$$\delta([\widehat{ax}], b) = [xb], \quad \text{if } ax \in C \cap (\Sigma^j \setminus B),$$
$$\delta([ax], b) = [xb], \quad \text{otherwise};$$

(iii) for each $[ax], [xb] \in Q$ such that $|x| = j-1$, $ax \in B$, $xb \in B \cup C$:

$$\delta([ax], b) = [xb].$$

We say that the constructed automaton M_S is *associated* to the triple $S = (A,B,C)$. This DFA is, in general, not the minimal DFA for the language $L(M_S) = L(A,B,C)$.

Now we present the learning algorithm LA (adapted from [271]).

Algorithm 4.1.1 LA: *Learning a strictly j-testable language:*

Input: *An integer $j > 0$ and a positive presentation $\{w_i\}_{i=1}^{\infty}$ of a strictly j-testable target language U.*

Output: *A sequence of DFAs accepting strictly j-testable languages.*

Procedure:

begin

$i := 0$;

initialize $E_0 := \emptyset$;

let $S_{E_0} = (A_0, B_0, C_0) := (\emptyset, \emptyset, \emptyset)$ be the initial triple;

construct DFA M_{E_0} accepting $E_0\ (= \emptyset)$;

repeat *(forever)*
begin
  let $M_{E_i} = (Q_{E_i}, \Sigma, \delta_{E_i}, q_0, F_{E_i})$ *be the current DFA;*
  read the next positive sample w_{i+1}*;*
  if $w_{i+1} \in L(M_{E_i})$ **then**
  begin $E_{i+1} := E_i$; $M_{E_{i+1}} := M_{E_i}$ **end**
  else
  begin
    $E_{i+1} := E_i \cup \{w_{i+1}\}$;
    $A_{E_{i+1}} := A_{E_i} \cup \{P_j(w_{i+1})\}$;
    $B_{E_{i+1}} := B_{E_i} \cup I_j(w_{i+1})$;
    $C_{E_{i+1}} := C_{E_i} \cup \{S_j(w_{i+1})\}$;
    $S_{E_{i+1}} := (A_{E_{i+1}}, B_{E_{i+1}}, C_{E_{i+1}})$;
    construct the DFA $M_{E_{i+1}}$ *associated with the triple* $S_{E_{i+1}}$
  end;
  output M_{i+1};
  $i := i + 1$;
end
end.

Takashi Yokomori and Satoshi Kobayashi established the following result on this algorithm.

Theorem 4.1.2 ([271]) *Let* $j > 0$ *and let* $\{w_i\}_{i=1}^{\infty}$ *be a positive presentation of a strictly* j*-testable language* U*. If* $M_{E_0}, M_{E_1}, \ldots, M_{E_i}, \ldots$ *is the sequence of DFAs that is produced by algorithm* LA *on input* j *and* $\{w_i\}_{i=1}^{\infty}$*, then*

(1) *for each* $i \geq 0$, $L(M_{E_i}) \subseteq L(M_{E_{i+1}}) \subseteq U$*, and*

(2) *there exists an index* $r > 0$ *such that* $L(M_{E_r}) = U$ *and* $M_{E_{r+i}} = M_{E_r}$ *for all* $i \geq 0$.

The algorithm LA succeeds for all positive presentations of a strictly j-testable language U as, once sufficiently many words w_i have been seen, all possible prefixes, infixes, and suffices of length j that occur in the words of the language have been encountered, and hence, a correct triple (A, B, C) representing U is found. Thus, algorithm LA shows that DFAs for strictly j-testable languages are learnable in the limit from text. In order to use this result for learning certain restricted restarting automata, we define a class of restarting automata that is based on strictly j-testable languages.

Definition 4.1.3 ([166]) *Let* j *be a positive integer and let* Γ *be an alphabet.*

(a) *A rewriting meta-instruction* $(\rhd \cdot R_1, u \to v, R_2 \cdot \lhd)$*, where* $R_1, R_2 \subseteq \Gamma^*$ *and* $u, v \in \Gamma^*$*, is called* strictly j-testable*, if the languages* R_1 *and* R_2 *are strictly* j*-testable and* $|v| < |u| \leq j$.

(b) *An accepting meta-instruction* $(\rhd \cdot R \cdot \lhd, \mathsf{Accept})$*, where* $R \subseteq \Gamma^*$*, is* strictly j-testable *if the language* R *is strictly* j*-testable.*

(c) *A restarting automaton* M *is called* strictly j-testable *if all its meta-instructions are strictly* j*-testable. We use* j*-SLT-RRWW to denote the class of all strictly* j*-testable restarting automata.*

(d) *A restarting automaton is* strictly locally testable*, if it is strictly* j*-testable for some* $j \geq 1$*. Then SLT-RRWW denotes the class of all strictly locally testable restarting automata.*

Of course, we can also consider j-SLT-RR(W)- and SLT-RR(W)-automata. The following example presents an SLT-RRW-automaton, that is, an SLT-RRWW-automaton that does not use any auxiliary letters.

Example 4.1.4 *Let* $M = (Q, \{a,b\}, \{a,b\}, \rhd, \lhd, q_0, 2, \delta)$ *be the restarting automaton that is defined by the following three meta-instructions:*

$$\begin{array}{ll} (1) & (\rhd \cdot \{a,b\} \cdot \lhd, \mathsf{Accept}), \\ (2) & (\rhd \cdot a^*, aa \to b, b^* \cdot \lhd), \\ (3) & (\rhd \cdot b^*, bb \to a, a^* \cdot \lhd). \end{array}$$

This automaton accepts the language

$$\begin{array}{rl} L(M) = & \{\, a^{2i}b^j \mid i,j \geq 0, i+j = 2^n \text{ for some } n \geq 0 \,\} \cup \\ & \{\, b^{2i}a^j \mid i,j \geq 0, i+j = 2^n \text{ for some } n \geq 0 \,\}. \end{array}$$

It is easy to check that all the constraints in the above instructions are strictly 2-testable languages. Hence, M *is a strictly 2-testable restarting automaton. In fact, it is a 2-SLT-RRW-automaton.* ■

We now illustrate our approach with an example in which we try to learn an unknown target language together with its analysis by reduction from given samples of reductions and samples of words from the target language.

Example 4.1.5 *We assume that we already know that the target language contains the words abc, aabbc, aaabbbc, aabbbbd, abbd, and that the following reductions are possible, where the words occurring are not necessarily elements of the target language. As before, the factors that are rewritten are underlined, and in order to simplify the notation, the sentinels are not displayed:*

$$\begin{array}{rcl} aaa\underline{ab}bbbc & \vdash & aaabbbc, \\ aaaa\underline{ab}bbbbbc & \vdash & aaaabbbbbc, \\ aaaa\underline{abb}bbbbd & \vdash & aaaabbbbd, \\ aa\underline{abb}bbbbd & \vdash & aabbbbd. \end{array}$$

In this extremely simple example, we see that the two types of rewritings $ab \to \lambda$ *and* $abb \to \lambda$ *are used. We may decide that we want to learn two meta-instructions. The first meta-instruction should enable the first two reductions, and the second meta-instruction should enable the remaining two reductions. In general, the partition of the set of sample reductions into groups which should be realized by different meta-instructions must be done by a helpful teacher.*

The first meta-instruction will be of the form

$$(\rhd \cdot E_{L,1}, ab \to \lambda, E_{R,1} \cdot \lhd),$$

where the language $E_{L,1}$ *contains the words aaa and aaaa, and the second language* $E_{R,1}$ *contains the words bbbc and bbbbbc. This meta-instruction can be learnt as a strictly* j*-testable meta-instruction, for* $j \geq 2$*, as the rewritten part is of length 2. Using the words aaa and aaaa as the first two positive samples for the strictly locally testable language* $E_{L,1}$*, the algorithm* LA *with* $j = 2$ *produces the triple* $(\{aa\}, \{aa\}, \{aa\})$*. This triple represents the language* aaa^**. Next, using the words bbbc and bbbbbc as input for* LA *with* $j = 2$*, we get the triple* $(\{bb\}, \{bb\}, \{bc\})$*, which represents the language* bbb^*c*. Hence, we get the first meta-instruction*

$$\text{(a)} \qquad (\rhd \cdot aaa^*, ab \to \lambda, bbb^*c \cdot \lhd).$$

In an analogous way, the second rewriting meta-instruction can be learnt from the last two samples of reductions:

$$aaaa\underline{abb}bbbbd \vdash aaaabbbbd \qquad \text{and} \qquad aa\underline{abb}bbbbd \vdash aabbbbd.$$

As there are 3 letters that are deleted in a single reduction, we take $j = 3$ *and obtain the strictly 3-testable meta-instruction*

$$\text{(b)} \qquad (\rhd \cdot aaa^*, abb \to \lambda, bbbb^*d \cdot \lhd).$$

We see that the meta-instruction (a) *can describe reductions of words of length at least 7 and the meta-instruction* (b) *can describe reductions of words of length at least 9. Let us now suppose that we know all 'short words' of the target language of length at most 7. Hence, we can use the set of words* $S = \{abc, aabbc, aaabbbc, aabbbbd, abbd\}$ *as an input for* LA *in order to learn the language of simple sentential forms. For each* $j < 6$, *the algorithm* LA *with input* S *learns also at least one word of length at most 7 which does not belong to* S. *For* $j = 6$, LA *learns the strictly 6-testable language* $\{aabbbbd, aaabbbc\}$.

Thus, we have learnt a 6-SLT-RR-automaton $M = (Q, \{a, b, c, d\}, \{a, b, c, d\}, \triangleright, \triangleleft, q_0, 6, \delta)$ *that is given by the following three meta-instructions:*

$$\begin{array}{ll} \text{(a)} & (\triangleright \cdot aaa^*, ab \to \lambda, bbb^*c \cdot \triangleleft), \\ \text{(b)} & (\triangleright \cdot aaa^*, abb \to \lambda, bbbb^*d \cdot \triangleleft), \\ \text{(c)} & (\triangleright \cdot \{aaabbbc, aabbbbd\} \cdot \triangleleft, \mathsf{Accept}). \end{array}$$

The automaton M *accepts the language* $L = \{ a^n b^n c \mid n \geq 3 \} \cup \{ a^n b^{2n} d \mid n \geq 2 \}$. *This is a fairly good approximation for the language* $L_0 = \{ a^n b^n c \mid n \geq 1 \} \cup \{ a^n b^{2n} d \mid n \geq 1 \}$, *which is known to be context-free, but not deterministic context-free.*

Actually, we have learnt analysis by reduction with two reduction rules and one accepting rule:

(a) *If a word is a sequence of a's followed by a sequence of b's that ends with the letter c (of overall length at least 7), then it can be simplified by deleting the subword ab.*

(b) *If a word is a sequence of a's followed by a sequence of b's that ends with the letter d (of overall length at least 9), then it can be simplified by deleting the subword abb.*

(c) *The words aaabbbc and aabbbbd belong to the language.* ■

By providing more and more sample reductions and sample words, we will eventually have seen all prefixes, infixes, and suffixes of length j of the strictly j-testable context sets of the meta-instructions of the automaton M to be learnt. From that point onwards, the above method will always return a strictly j-testable restarting automaton that is equivalent to the automaton M. It follows that j-SLT-RRWW-automata can be learnt in the limit from positive data. Below we study the class of languages, which are accepted by the automata of this form.

Note that, according to [54], the class of strictly locally testable languages (SLT) as a whole is not learnable in the limit from only positive data. However, the inference algorithm can be used to effectively identify any language from this class in the limit through a complete (both positive and negative) presentation sequence of the language [48]. This can be accomplished by starting with $j = 2$ and using successive positive samples to infer progressively larger (less restricted) 2-SLT's until a negative sample appears, which is incompatible with the current language. Then the value j is increased by one, and the process continues in the same way with the successive samples. Eventually, the correct value of j will be reached and then no further negative sample will ever be incompatible. The inferred language will then grow progressively with the successive positive samples until the target j-SLT is identified.

The above learning protocol can also be used for learning strictly locally testable rewriting meta-instructions, but it requires a helpful teacher as follows. Suppose a learner is being taught a rewriting meta-instruction of the form $(\triangleright \cdot E_l, aba \to b, E_r \cdot \triangleleft)$. Knowing that aba cannot be rewritten into b in the word $aabaaaa$, it is possible that:

- either $a \notin E_l$ and $aaa \in E_r$, or
- $a \in E_l$ and $aaa \notin E_r$, or
- $a \notin E_l$ and $aaa \notin E_r$.

Hence, this information must be supplied by a teacher.

It remains to determine the class of languages that are accepted by SLT-RRWW-automata. Actually, SLT-RRWW-automata are quite powerful. They can accept all growing context-sensitive languages. Recall from Definition 1.2.12 that a growing context-sensitive language is generated by a strictly monotone phrase-structure grammar, that is, by a grammar $G = (N, T, S, P)$, where the start symbol S does not appear on the right-hand side of any production, and $|\ell| < |r|$ holds for all productions $(\ell \to r) \in P$ satisfying $\ell \neq S$.

Theorem 4.1.6 ([166]) $\mathsf{GCSL} \subsetneq \mathcal{L}(\mathsf{SLT\text{-}RRWW}) \subseteq \mathsf{CSL}$.

Proof. Let $G = (N, T, S, P)$ be a strictly monotone grammar. We construct an SLT-RRWW-automaton $M = (Q, \Sigma, \Gamma, \rhd, \lhd, q_0, k, \delta)$ accepting the language $L(M) = L(G)$. To this end, we take $\Sigma = T$, $\Gamma = (N \smallsetminus \{S\}) \cup T$, and we define the following set of meta-instructions

$$I = \{\, (\rhd \cdot r \cdot \lhd, \mathsf{Accept}) \mid (S \to r) \in P \,\} \cup \{\, (\rhd \cdot \Gamma^*, r \to \ell, \Gamma^* \cdot \lhd) \mid \ell \neq S, \text{ and } (\ell \to r) \in P \,\}.$$

Trivially, M works as an analytical version of the grammar G without the rules with the initial nonterminal S, but M directly accepts (without any reduction) all right-hand sides of productions with left-hand side S. Hence $L(M) = L(G)$. As the language Γ^* is strictly 1-testable, and as the language $\{\, r \mid (S \to r) \in P \,\}$ is strictly m-testable, where $m = 1 + \max\{\, |r| \mid (S \to r) \in P \,\}$, we see that M is a strictly m-testable restarting automaton. This implies that $\mathsf{GCSL} \subseteq \mathcal{L}(\mathsf{SLT\text{-}RRWW})$.

Moreover, the marked copy language $L'_{\text{copy}} = \{\, wcw \mid w \in \{a, b\}^* \,\}$, which is not growing context-sensitive (see the remark following Theorem 1.2.17), is accepted by the SLT-RRWW-automaton M_{copy} that is given through the following set I_{copy} of meta-instructions, where $\Sigma = \{a, b, c\}$, $\Gamma = \Sigma \cup \{A_{xy} \mid x, y \in \{a, b\}\}$:

(1)	$(\rhd \cdot xy(a+b)^*c, xy$	$\to A_{xy}, (a+b)^* \cdot \lhd)$,	for each $x, y \in \{a, b\}$;
(2)	$(\rhd, xy$	$\to A_{xy}, (a+b+cA_{xy})^* \cdot \lhd)$,	for each $x, y \in \{a, b\}$;
(3)	$(\rhd \cdot A_{xy}(a+b)^*c, A_{xy}$	$\to \lambda, (a+b)^* \cdot \lhd)$,	for each $x, y \in \{a, b\}$;
(4)	$(\rhd, A_{xy}$	$\to \lambda, (a+b+c)^* \cdot \lhd)$,	for each $x, y \in \{a, b\}$;
(5)	$(\rhd \cdot \{c, aca, bcb\} \cdot \lhd,$	$\mathsf{Accept})$.	

Each meta-instruction of M_{copy} preserves the number of occurrences of the letter c in the current word. All words accepted by M_{copy} using the single accepting meta-instruction (5) contain exactly one occurrence of c. Hence, each word accepted by M_{copy} contains exactly one occurrence of c. For an input word w of length at least 4 and of the form $(a+b)^*c(a+b)^*$, the only applicable meta-instruction is a meta-instruction of type (1). In the resulting word, the letter c is followed by the working symbol A_{xy}, where $x, y \in \{a, b\}$ are the first two letters of the word. Such a word can be reduced only by a meta-instruction of type (2). Subsequently, M_{copy} must use appropriate meta-instructions of types (3) and (4). This is possible only if the word is of the form $w = xyucxyv$ for some $x, y \in \{a, b\}$ and $u, v \in \{a, b\}^*$. After executing four meta-instructions, M_{copy} obtains the word ucv. Now it is easy to see that M_{copy} accepts exactly the language L'_{copy}. Moreover, all rewriting meta-instructions in I_{copy} are strictly 2-testable, while the accepting meta-instruction is strictly 3-testable. Thus, $\mathsf{GCSL} \subsetneq \mathcal{L}(\mathsf{SLT\text{-}RRWW})$.

Finally, each restarting automaton can be simulated by a linear bounded automaton, from which it follows that $\mathcal{L}(\mathsf{SLT\text{-}RRWW}) \subseteq \mathsf{CSL}$. □

From a practical point of view, analysis by reduction without auxiliary letters enables the most transparent analysis with the best error localization. For SLT-RRWW-automata without auxiliary letters, we have the following result.

Theorem 4.1.7 ([166]) *The regular languages are properly contained in* $\mathcal{L}(\mathsf{SLT\text{-}RR})$.

Proof. For each regular language $L \subseteq \Sigma^*$, there exists a DFA A that accepts L. Let m be the number of states of A. Reading a prefix of a word from Σ^* of length at least m, the DFA A must pass some state at least twice. Hence, for each word z of length m, there exist words $u, v, w \in \Sigma^*$ such that $z = uvw$, $v \neq \lambda$, and the DFA A is in the same state after reading both prefixes u and uv. It follows that, for each word $x \in \Sigma^*$, we have $uvwx \in L$ if and only if $uwx \in L$. Thus, we can construct an m-SLT-RR-automaton $M = (Q, \Sigma, \Sigma, \rhd, \lhd, q_0, k, \delta)$ accepting L in the following way. The automaton M has a single accepting meta-instruction

$$(\rhd \cdot (L \cap \Sigma^{<m}) \cdot \lhd, \mathsf{Accept}),$$

which is strictly m-testable. For each $z \in \Sigma^m$, the automaton M has a rewriting meta-instruction

$$(\rhd, z \to uw, \Sigma^* \cdot \lhd), \text{ where } z = uvw \text{ and } u, v, w \text{ are the words from above,}$$

which is also strictly m-testable. It is easy to see that

- if $|x| < m$, then $x \in L$ if and only if $x \in L(M)$,
- if $|x| \geq m$, then there exists a word $x' \in \Sigma^*$, $|x'| < |x|$, such that $q_0 \rhd x \lhd \vdash_M^c q_0 \rhd x' \lhd$, and $x \in L$ if and only if $x' \in L$.

It follows that $L(M) = L$. Thus, we have $\mathsf{REG} \subseteq \mathcal{L}(\mathsf{SLT\text{-}RR})$.

On the other hand, the RR-automaton $M_= = (Q, \{a, b\}, \{a, b\}, \rhd, \lhd, q_0, 2, \delta)$ that is specified by the meta-instructions

$$(\rhd \cdot \lhd, \mathsf{Accept}) \text{ and } (\rhd \cdot a^*, ab \to \lambda, b^* \cdot \lhd)$$

accepts the non-regular language $\{ a^n b^n \mid n \geq 0 \}$. Obviously, the RR-automaton $M_=$ is strictly 2-testable, as the languages of constraints $\{\lambda\}$, a^*, and b^* are strictly 1-testable and $|\lambda| = 0 < 2 = |ab|$. Thus, we see that already $\mathcal{L}(\mathsf{2\text{-}SLT\text{-}RR})$ contains a non-regular language. □

Below we shall see that there is even a non-context-free language that is accepted by an SLT-RR-automaton. Note that the SLT-RR-automaton M constructed in the above proof only uses a finite language in its single accepting meta-instruction, and that all its rewriting instructions have the language $\{\lambda\}$ as their left constraint.

From Example 4.1.4, we see that SLT-RRW-automata accept some non-context-free languages. Theorem 4.1.6 implies that each context-free language is accepted by an SLT-RRWW-automaton. Unfortunately, restarting automata without auxiliary letters are not sufficiently expressive to accept all context-free languages. Lemma 2.2.3 shows that the context-free language

$$L_2 = \{ a^n b^n \mid n \geq 0 \} \cup \{ a^n b^m \mid m > 2n \geq 0 \}$$

cannot be accepted by any restarting automaton without auxiliary letters. Hence, we obtain the following consequence.

Corollary 4.1.8 ([166]) $\mathsf{CFL} \subsetneq \mathcal{L}(\mathsf{SLT\text{-}RRWW})$, *but there exist context-free languages which cannot be accepted by any SLT-RRW-automaton.*

It is known that the strictly j-testable languages form an infinite strictly ascending hierarchy of language classes based on the parameter j, that is,

$$\mathsf{1\text{-}SLT} \subsetneq \mathsf{2\text{-}SLT} \subseteq \cdots \subsetneq j\text{-}\mathsf{SLT} \subsetneq (j+1)\text{-}\mathsf{SLT} \subsetneq \cdots \subsetneq \bigcup_{j=1}^{\infty} j\text{-}\mathsf{SLT} = \mathsf{SLT}.$$

This observation leads to the question of whether the strictly j-testable restarting automata also yield infinite strictly ascending hierarchies of language classes based on this parameter. Lemma 2.3.2 shows that the window size induces such a hierarchy for each type of restarting automaton without auxiliary letters. In fact, in the proof of that lemma, it is shown that the semi-Dyck language D_1 is accepted by the R-automaton M_1 with window size two that is given by the meta-instructions

$$(1) \quad (\rhd \cdot \lhd, \mathsf{Accept}) \quad \text{and} \quad (2) \quad (\rhd \cdot a_1^*, a_1\bar{a}_1 \to \lambda).$$

This R-automaton can be seen as an RR(2)-automaton that is given by the meta-instructions

$$(1') \quad (\rhd \cdot \lhd, \mathsf{Accept}) \quad \text{and} \quad (2') \quad (\rhd \cdot a_1^*, a_1\bar{a}_1 \to \lambda, \{a_1, \bar{a}_1\}^* \cdot \lhd).$$

As the languages a_1^*, $\{a_1, \bar{a}_1\}^*$, and $\{\lambda\}$ are strictly 1-testable, and as $|\lambda| < |a_1\bar{a}_1| = 2$, these meta-instructions show that this RR(2)-automaton is strictly 2-testable, that is, $D_1 \in \mathcal{L}(\text{2-}\mathsf{SLT}\text{-}\mathsf{RR})$. The proof of Lemma 2.3.2 establishes that D_1 is not accepted by any RRW-automaton of window size one, which implies that this language is not accepted by any strictly 1-testable RRW-automaton, that is, $D_1 \notin \mathcal{L}(\text{1-}\mathsf{SLT}\text{-}\mathsf{RR})$.

For $j \geq 2$, let L_j be the language $L_j = \{\, a^n c^{j-1} b^n \mid n \geq 0 \,\}$ over $\Sigma = \{a, b, c\}$. This language is accepted by the R-automaton M_j with window size $j + 1$ that is given by the following meta-instructions:

$$(1) \quad (\rhd \cdot c^{j-1} \cdot \lhd, \mathsf{Accept}) \quad \text{and} \quad (2) \quad (\rhd \cdot a^*, ac^{j-1}b \to c^{j-1}).$$

This R-automaton can obviously be seen as an RR$(j + 1)$-automaton that is given by the meta-instructions

$$(1') \quad (\rhd \cdot c^{j-1} \cdot \lhd, \mathsf{Accept}) \quad \text{and} \quad (2') \quad (\rhd \cdot a^*, ac^{j-1}b \to c^{j-1}, b^* \cdot \lhd).$$

The languages a^* and b^* are strictly 1-testable, the language $\{c^{j-1}\}$ is strictly j-testable, and $j - 1 = |c^{j-1}| < |ac^{j-1}b| = j + 1$. Hence, this RR-automaton is strictly $(j + 1)$-testable, that is, $L_j \in \mathcal{L}((j+1)\text{-}\mathsf{SLT}\text{-}\mathsf{RR})$. On the other hand, the proof of Lemma 2.3.2 shows that the language L_j is not accepted by any RRW-automaton of window size j, which implies that $L_j \notin \mathcal{L}(j\text{-}\mathsf{SLT}\text{-}\mathsf{RRW})$. Together these results yield the following hierarchies.

Theorem 4.1.9 *For all* $j \geq 1$, $\mathcal{L}(j\text{-}\mathsf{SLT}\text{-}\mathsf{RR}) \subsetneq \mathcal{L}((j+1)\text{-}\mathsf{SLT}\text{-}\mathsf{RR})$ *and* $\mathcal{L}(j\text{-}\mathsf{SLT}\text{-}\mathsf{RRW}) \subsetneq \mathcal{L}((j+1)\text{-}\mathsf{SLT}\text{-}\mathsf{RRW})$.

It remains to study the corresponding question for strictly locally testable RRWW-automata.

Problem 4.1.10 *Does the degree j of strict testability induce an infinite strictly ascending hierarchy of language classes for SLT-RRWW-automata?*

There are many possible approaches for learning analysis by reduction (restarting automata). The method presented above reduces this task to learning a corresponding set of meta-instructions. This approach has several advantages:

1. The whole task of learning a restarting automaton can be split into smaller tasks of learning one meta-instruction at a time. Learning several simpler meta-instructions should be computationally simpler than learning the whole language at once.

2. For learning different meta-instructions, we can use different models and algorithms to learn regular languages.

3. The learning can be done in an incremental way. First, we can learn some basic meta-instructions which define only a subset of the target language. Then, we can continue to learn new meta-instructions to improve our approximation of the target language.

4. A rewriting meta-instruction of a restarting automaton M is called *correctness preserving* if, for each cycle $q_0 \rhd u \lhd \vdash_M^c q_0 \rhd v \lhd$ that is obtained by applying that meta-instruction, it holds that $u \in L_C(M)$ iff $v \in L_C(M)$. If we succeed in learning correctness preserving meta-instructions, then the target language can be learnt in parallel. That is, two or more (correctness preserving) meta-instructions can be learned separately and finally put together to yield a single restarting automaton.

In Subsection 2.2.1, we encountered the so-called *clearing restarting automaton*. A *k-clearing restarting automaton* is given through a triple $C = (\Sigma, \Sigma, I)$, where I is a finite set of instructions of the form $i = (x, z \to \lambda, y)$. Here $x \in \Sigma^k \cup \rhd \cdot \Sigma^{\leq k-1}$ is called a *left context*, $y \in \Sigma^k \cup \Sigma^{\leq k-1} \cdot \lhd$ is called a *right context*, and $z \in \Sigma^+$ (see Definition 2.2.29). The *language accepted by C* is the reduction language $L(C) = \{ w \in \Sigma^* \mid w \to_C^* \lambda \}$, that is, $w \in L(C)$ if and only if $\rhd w \lhd \vdash_C^{c^*} \rhd \cdot \lhd$. Then k-CRA is used to denote the class of all k-clearing restarting automata, and CRA denotes the class of all clearing restarting automata, that is, $\mathsf{CRA} = \bigcup_{k \geq 1} k\text{-}\mathsf{CRA}$.

If $C = (\Sigma, \Sigma, I)$ is a k-clearing restarting automaton, then C can be described by the following set of meta-instructions:

$$
\begin{array}{ll}
(\rhd \cdot \lhd, \mathsf{Accept}), & \\
(\rhd \cdot \Sigma^* \cdot x, z \to \lambda, y \cdot \Sigma^* \cdot \lhd) & \text{for } (x, z \to \lambda, y) \in I \text{ and } x, y \in \Sigma^k, \\
(x, z \to \lambda, y \cdot \Sigma^* \cdot \lhd) & \text{for } (x, z \to \lambda, y) \in I, x \in \rhd \cdot \Sigma^{\leq k-1}, \text{ and } y \in \Sigma^k, \\
(\rhd \cdot \Sigma^* \cdot x, z \to \lambda, y) & \text{for } (x, z \to \lambda, y) \in I, x \in \Sigma^k, \text{ and } y \in \Sigma^{k-1} \cdot \lhd \\
(x, z \to \lambda, y) & \text{for } (x, z \to \lambda, y) \in I, x \in \rhd \cdot \Sigma^{k-1}, \text{ and } y \in \Sigma^{k-1} \cdot \lhd.
\end{array}
$$

As the language $\{\lambda\}$ is strictly 1-testable and the languages $\{x'\}$, $\{y'\}$, $\Sigma^* \cdot x$, and $y \cdot \Sigma^*$ are strictly k-testable for all $x', y' \in \Sigma^{k-1}$ and all $x, y \in \Sigma^k$, we see that the clearing restarting automaton C is strictly j testable, where $j = \max(\{ |z| \mid (x, z \to \lambda, y) \in I \} \cup \{k\})$. Thus, each clearing restarting automaton is a strictly locally testable RR-automaton, that is, we have the following inclusion.

Theorem 4.1.11 $\mathcal{L}(\mathsf{CRA}) \subsetneq \mathcal{L}(\mathsf{SLT\text{-}RR})$.

The above inclusion is proper as, for example, the languages $L_j = \{ a^n c^{j-1} b^n \mid n \geq 0 \}$ $(j \geq 2)$ are not accepted by any clearing restarting automaton. Theorem 4.1.11 implies that we can apply the method of learning strictly locally testable restarting automata proposed above to learn clearing restarting automata from samples of reductions. However, in [258], Peter Černo and František Mráz propose another, simpler learning method for clearing restarting automata. We shall consider their method in Section 4.3. It does not need a helpful teacher, but in addition to samples of correct reductions, it needs samples of words from the language accepted as well as samples of words that do not belong to the language accepted.

4.2 Learning Single k-Reversible Restarting Automata

In [71], Petr Hoffmann presents a learning algorithm for a type of restarting automaton that is obtained by restricting the context conditions of meta-instructions to k-reversible languages. Here we first recall the necessary definitions and results on these languages, before we present the particular type of restarting automaton, survey its expressive capacity, and introduce the learning algorithm. Instead of a helpful teacher who points out the particular rewrite steps in the samples of reductions provided, this learning algorithm uses a heuristics that allows it to extract the rewrite steps and partition them into rewriting meta-instructions from so-called FPABR samples (see below).

If $A = (Q, \Sigma, S, \delta, F)$ is an NFA, then A^R denotes the NFA that is defined through $A^R = (Q, \Sigma, F, \delta^R, S)$, where $\delta^R(q, a) = \{ q' \in Q \mid q \in \delta(q', a) \}$, that is, A^R is obtained from A by interchanging initial states and final states and by reversing all transitions.

Definition 4.2.1 ([2]) *An NFA A is called* zero-reversible *(or a* zero-reversible DFA*) if A and A^R are both DFAs. A language $L \subseteq \Sigma^*$ is called* zero-reversible *if there exists a zero-reversible DFA A such that $L = L(A)$. We use* $\mathsf{REV}(0)$ *to denote the class of all zero-reversible languages.*

For example, the language $L = \{ w \in \{a, b\}^* \mid |w|_a = 0 \bmod 2 \text{ and } |w|_b = 0 \bmod 2 \}$ is zero-reversible, as it is accepted by the zero-reversible DFA $A = (\{q_{0,0}, q_{1,0}, q_{0,1}, q_{1,1}\}, \{a, b\}, q_{0,0}, \delta, \{q_{0,0}\})$ that is defined through the transition function

$$\begin{array}{rclrcl} \delta(q_{0,0}, a) & = & q_{1,0}, & \delta(q_{0,0}, b) & = & q_{0,1}, \\ \delta(q_{1,0}, a) & = & q_{0,0}, & \delta(q_{1,0}, b) & = & q_{1,1}, \\ \delta(q_{0,1}, a) & = & q_{1,1}, & \delta(q_{0,1}, b) & = & q_{0,0}, \\ \delta(q_{1,1}, a) & = & q_{0,1}, & \delta(q_{1,1}, b) & = & q_{1,0}. \end{array}$$

Observe that the language L is not strictly locally testable, as, for each $j \geq 1$, $P_j(L) = S_j(L) = I_j(L) = \{a, b\}^j$, where $P_j(L) = \{ P_j(w) \mid w \in L \}$ and, analogously, for $S_j(L)$ and $I_j(L)$.

The notion of k-reversibility is a generalization of zero-reversibility.

Definition 4.2.2 ([2]) *Let $k \geq 1$ and let $A = (Q, \Sigma, S, \delta, F)$ be an NFA.*

(a) *A word $u \in \Sigma^k$ is a* k-follower *of a state $q \in Q$, if $\delta(q, u) \neq \emptyset$, that is, starting in state q, A can read the word u completely.*

(b) *A word $v \in \Sigma^k$ is a* k-leader *of a state $q \in Q$, if $\delta^R(q, v^R) \neq \emptyset$, that is, there is a state $q' \in Q$ such that $q \in \delta(q', v)$.*

(c) *The NFA A is said to be* deterministic with look-ahead k *if, for any pair of states $p, q \in Q$, $p \neq q$, if $p, q \in S$ or $p, q \in \delta(q', a)$ for some $q' \in Q$ and $a \in \Sigma$, then there does not exist a word u that is a k-follower of both, p and q. Thus, if p and q are both initial states, or if there is a state q' such that, by reading a letter a, A can change to state p or state q, then, for each word u of length k, A cannot read this word completely when starting from state p or when starting from state q. This means that A can distinguish between these two states using a look-ahead of size k.*

(d) *The NFA A is called* k-reversible *if A is deterministic and A^R is deterministic with look-ahead k.*

(e) *A language $L \subseteq \Sigma^*$ is* k-reversible *if there exists a k-reversible NFA A such that $L = L(A)$. Then* $\mathsf{REV}(k)$ *is used to denote the class of k-reversible languages, and* $\mathsf{REV} = \bigcup_{k \geq 0} \mathsf{REV}(k)$.

We illustrate this definition by providing some examples.

Example 4.2.3 (a) *The language* $L_1 = \{a\}^* \cdot \{b\}^*$ *is 1-reversible, as it is accepted by the DFA* $A_1 = (\{q_0, q_1\}, \{a, b\}, q_0, \delta, \{q_0, q_1\})$ *that is specified through*

$$\delta(q_0, a) = q_0, \delta(q_0, b) = q_1, \delta(q_1, b) = q_1,$$

which is 1-reversible. Indeed, A is a DFA, and $A_1^R = (\{q_0, q_1\}, \{a, b\}, \{q_0, q_1\}, \delta^R, \{q_0\})$, *which is defined by the transition relation* $\delta^R(q_1, b) = \{q_0, q_1\}$ *and* $\delta^R(q_0, a) = \{q_0\}$, *is deterministic with look-ahead 1. However, it is easily seen that the language* L_1 *is not zero-reversible.*

(b) *Let* $k \geq 2$, *and let* $L_k = \{a^k\} \cdot \{a\}^*$. *Then* L_k *is accepted by the DFA*

$$A_k = (\{q_0, q_1, \ldots, q_k\}, \{a\}, q_0, \delta, \{q_k\})$$

that is defined by taking $\delta(q_i, a) = q_{i+1}$ *for all* $0 \leq i \leq k-1$ *and* $\delta(q_k, a) = q_k$. *Then*

$$A_k^R = (\{q_0, q_1, \ldots, q_k\}, \{a\}, \{q_k\}, \delta^R, \{q_0\}),$$

where $\delta^R(q_i, a) = \{q_{i-1}\}$ *for all* $1 \leq i \leq k-1$ *and* $\delta^R(q_k, a) = \{q_{k-1}, q_k\}$. *Then* A_k^R *is deterministic with look-ahead k, and hence, the language* L_k *is k-reversible. However, it is not* $(k-1)$*-reversible.* ■

We already obtain the following inclusions from the above examples.

Theorem 4.2.4 ([2]) *For all* $k \in \mathbb{N}$, $\mathsf{REV}(k) \subsetneq \mathsf{REV}(k+1) \subsetneq \mathsf{REV}$.

Furthermore, the following inclusion has been established by Satoshi Kobayashi and Takashi Yokomore in [113].

Theorem 4.2.5 $\mathsf{SLT} \subsetneq \mathsf{REV}$, *that is, the strictly locally testable languages are a proper subclass of the reversible languages.*

In [2], Dana Angluin presents a learning algorithm for inferring a k-reversible DFA from a finite set of positive samples. When it is given a finite set S of positive samples as input, this algorithm first constructs the prefix tree acceptor for S and then, through repeated merges, it derives a k-reversible DFA A. The language $L(A)$ is then shown to be the smallest k-reversible language that contains all words from S. For any k-reversible language L, there exists a finite set $S_0 \subseteq L$ such that L itself is the smallest k-reversible language containing S_0 [2]. Such a set S_0 is called a *characteristic sample* of L. If we are given a positive presentation $\{w_i\}_{i=1}^{\infty}$ of L, then by applying the above learning algorithm to $S_i = \{w_1, w_2, \ldots, w_i\}$, $i = 1, 2, \ldots$, we obtain a sequence of k-reversible DFAs $A_1, A_2, \ldots, A_i, A_{i+1}, \ldots$ such that, for all $j \geq 1$, $L(A_j) \subseteq L(A_{j+1})$. In addition, if i is sufficiently large, then the sample S_i contains a characteristic sample of L, and hence, $L(A_i) = L$ follows. Thus, k-reversible languages can be identified in the limit from positive data.

Now a type of restarting automaton can be defined by restricting the meta-instructions specifying an automaton to admit only k-reversible context conditions.

Definition 4.2.6 ([71, 72, 73]) *Let k be a non-negative integer.*

(a) *A rewriting meta-instruction* $(\rhd \cdot R_1, u \to v, R_2 \cdot \lhd)$, *where* $R_1, R_2 \subseteq \Gamma^*$ *and* $u, v \in \Gamma^*$, *is called k-*reversible, *if the languages* R_1 *and* R_2 *are k-reversible and* $|v| < |u|$.

(b) *An accepting meta-instruction* $(\rhd \cdot R \cdot \lhd, \mathsf{Accept})$, *where* $R \subseteq \Gamma^*$, *is k-*reversible *if the language R is k-reversible.*

(c) *A restarting automaton is called k-*reversible *if all its meta-instructions are k-reversible.*

(d) *An RRWW-automaton M is called* single *or an* S-RRWW-automaton *if all of the following conditions are satisfied:*

(S1) *M has at most one accepting meta-instruction.*

(S2) *For each pair* $u, v \in \Gamma^*$, *M has at most one rewriting meta-instruction of the form* $(\triangleright \cdot R_1, u \to v, R_2 \cdot \triangleleft)$.

(S3) *For each rewriting meta-instruction* $(\triangleright \cdot R_1, u \to v, R_2 \cdot \triangleleft)$, *u and v have neither a common non-empty prefix nor a common non-empty suffix.*

(e) *A restarting automaton M is called a* single k-reversible automaton *or an* S-k-rev-RRWW-automaton *if it is both single and k-reversible.*

The S-k-rev-RRWW-automaton differs from the strictly locally testable RRWW-automaton not only through the use of k-reversible languages in context conditions as opposed to strictly locally testable languages, but also through the restrictions on the number of different meta-instructions that contain the same rewrite step and through the fact that no bound is given for the length of the left-hand side of a rewrite step. Obviously, each S-k-rev-RRWW-automaton can be simulated by a nondeterministic Turing machine using linear space, that is, $\mathcal{L}(\mathsf{S}\text{-}k\text{-}\mathsf{rev}\text{-}\mathsf{RRWW}) \subseteq \mathsf{CSL}$ holds. On the other hand, already single zero-reversible RRWW-automata are sufficiently expressive to accept all growing context-sensitive languages.

Theorem 4.2.7 ([73]) $\mathsf{GCSL} \subseteq \mathcal{L}(\mathsf{S\text{-}0\text{-}rev\text{-}RRWW})$.

This result is proved in essentially the same way as Theorem 4.1.6 by constructing an S-0-rev-RRWW-automaton from a given strictly monotone grammar.

By requiring that the restarting automata considered are *single*, the sets of meta-instructions that can be used for specifying these automata are seriously restricted. This, however, does not decrease the expressive capacity of k-reversible RRWW-automata.

Theorem 4.2.8 ([73]) *For each* $k \geq 0$ *and each k-reversible RRWW-automaton M, there exists an S-k-rev-RRWW-automaton* M' *such that* $L(M') = L(M)$.

Proof outline. Let $k \geq 0$ and let M be a k-reversible RRWW-automaton that is not single. Hence, M violates at least one of the three conditions of being single, that is,

(1) M has at least two accepting meta-instructions, or

(2) M has at least two rewriting meta-instructions that contain the same rewrite step, or

(3) M has a rewriting meta-instruction $(\triangleright \cdot R_1, u \to v, R_2 \cdot \triangleleft)$ such that the words u and v have a common non-empty prefix or suffix.

As the class of k-reversible languages is not closed under union (see, e.g., [2]), we cannot simply join two accepting meta-instructions into a single accepting meta-instruction by taking the union of the corresponding k-reversible conditions. However, this problem can be overcome by introducing additional auxiliary letters and rewriting meta-instructions. In this way, M is converted into a k-reversible RRWW-automaton M_1 with only a single accepting meta-instruction.

In a similar way, the automaton M_1 is then converted into an equivalent k-reversible RRWW-automaton M_2 such that no two rewriting meta-instructions contain the same rewrite step. Finally, from M_2, a single k-reversible RRWW-automaton M' can be constructed that accepts the same language as M. □

Thus, we see that in the presence of auxiliary letters, the technical restriction of requiring that the k-reversible automata considered are single is just a convenience. As auxiliary letters play an essential role in the above proof, the following question remains open.

Problem 4.2.9 *For* $k \geq 0$, *are single k-reversible RRW-automata (RR-automata) strictly less expressive than k-reversible RRW-automata (RR-automata) that are not single?*

The next result shows that the type of rewrite steps allowed significantly influences the expressive capacity of single k-reversible restarting automata.

Theorem 4.2.10 ([73]) *For all $k \geq 0$, $\mathcal{L}(\mathsf{S}\text{-}k\text{-}\mathsf{rev}\text{-}\mathsf{RR}) \subsetneq \mathcal{L}(\mathsf{S}\text{-}k\text{-}\mathsf{rev}\text{-}\mathsf{RRW}) \subsetneq \mathcal{L}(\mathsf{S}\text{-}k\text{-}\mathsf{rev}\text{-}\mathsf{RRWW})$.*

Proof outline. The stated inclusions are obvious. It remains to show that they are proper.

In order to show that, for each $k \geq 0$, the language class $\mathcal{L}(\mathsf{S}\text{-}k\text{-}\mathsf{rev}\text{-}\mathsf{RR})$ is a proper subclass of $\mathcal{L}(\mathsf{S}\text{-}k\text{-}\mathsf{rev}\text{-}\mathsf{RRW})$, we consider the language

$$L_4' = \{\, ca^nb^n, eea^nb^n \mid n \geq 0 \,\} \cup \{\, da^nb^m, eea^nb^m \mid m > 2n \geq 0 \,\}.$$

In analogy to Lemma 2.2.5, it can be shown that the language L_4' is not accepted by any RR-automaton. Hence, it follows that $L_4' \notin \mathcal{L}(\mathsf{S}\text{-}k\text{-}\mathsf{rev}\text{-}\mathsf{RR})$ for any $k \geq 0$. On the other hand, let $M_4' = (Q, \Sigma, \Sigma, \rhd, \lhd, q_0, 3, \delta)$ be the RRW-automaton that is defined through the following meta-instructions, where $\Sigma = \{a, b, c, d, e\}$:

$$\begin{array}{llll} (1) & (\rhd, ee \to c, \{a,b\}^* \cdot \lhd), & (4) & (\rhd \cdot d \cdot a^*, abb \to \lambda, b^* \cdot \lhd), \\ (2) & (\rhd, ee \to d, \{a,b\}^* \cdot \lhd), & (5) & (\rhd \cdot db, b \to \lambda, b^* \cdot \lhd), \\ (3) & (\rhd \cdot c \cdot a^*, ab \to \lambda, b^* \cdot \lhd), & (6) & (\rhd \cdot \{c, db\} \cdot \lhd, \mathsf{Accept}). \end{array}$$

It is easily checked that $L(M_4') = L_4'$ holds. Moreover, the RRW-automaton M_4' is single and it is zero-reversible, as the languages $\{\lambda\}$, $\{a,b\}^*$, $\{c\} \cdot \{a\}^*$, $\{b\}^*$, $\{d\} \cdot \{a\}^*$, $\{db\}$, and $\{c, db\}$ are all zero-reversible. It follows that $L_4' \in \mathcal{L}(\mathsf{S}\text{-}k\text{-}\mathsf{rev}\text{-}\mathsf{RRW})$ for all $k \in \mathbb{N}$. Thus, $\mathcal{L}(\mathsf{S}\text{-}k\text{-}\mathsf{rev}\text{-}\mathsf{RR})$ is a proper subclass of $\mathcal{L}(\mathsf{S}\text{-}k\text{-}\mathsf{rev}\text{-}\mathsf{RRW})$.

By Theorem 4.2.7, each context-free language is accepted by an S-0-rev-RRWW-automaton. On the other hand, we know from Lemma 2.2.5 that the context-free language

$$L_4 = \{\, ca^nb^n, ea^nb^n \mid n \geq 0 \,\} \cup \{\, da^nb^m, ea^nb^m \mid m > 2n \geq 0 \,\}$$

is not accepted by any RRW-automaton. This implies, in particular, that this language is not accepted by any single k-reversible RRW-automaton. Hence, $\mathcal{L}(\mathsf{S}\text{-}k\text{-}\mathsf{rev}\text{-}\mathsf{RRW})$ is a proper subclass of $\mathcal{L}(\mathsf{S}\text{-}k\text{-}\mathsf{rev}\text{-}\mathsf{RRWW})$. □

Finally, we study the influence of the degree of reversibility on the expressive capacity of single restarting automata. For all $k \in \mathbb{N}$, $\mathsf{REV}(k)$ is contained in $\mathsf{REV}(k+1)$, and hence, by increasing the degree of reversibility, the expressive capacity of single restarting automata cannot be diminished. In fact, for restarting automata without auxiliary letters, that is, for RRW- and RR-automata, the expressive capacity increases with the degree of reversibility.

Theorem 4.2.11 ([73]) *For all $k \geq 0$,*

(a) $\mathcal{L}(\mathsf{S}\text{-}k\text{-}\mathsf{rev}\text{-}\mathsf{RR}) \subsetneq \mathcal{L}(\mathsf{S}\text{-}(k+1)\text{-}\mathsf{rev}\text{-}\mathsf{RR})$.
(b) $\mathcal{L}(\mathsf{S}\text{-}k\text{-}\mathsf{rev}\text{-}\mathsf{RRW}) \subsetneq \mathcal{L}(\mathsf{S}\text{-}(k+1)\text{-}\mathsf{rev}\text{-}\mathsf{RRW})$.
(c) $\mathcal{L}(\mathsf{S}\text{-}k\text{-}\mathsf{rev}\text{-}\mathsf{RRWW}) \subseteq \mathcal{L}(\mathsf{S}\text{-}(k+1)\text{-}\mathsf{rev}\text{-}\mathsf{RRWW})$.

Proof outline. The inclusions are obvious. Therefore, it remains to prove the properness of the inclusions in (a) and in (b).

For $k \in \mathbb{N}$, let $L_{\mathrm{sep},k} = L_{1,k} \cup L_{2,k}$, where

$$L_{1,k} = \{\, a^rb^sa^r \mid r > k, s > 0 \,\} \text{ and } L_{2,k} = \{\, a^rb^sa^t \mid 0 \leq r \leq k, s > k, \text{ and } t > s \,\}.$$

Let M_k be the RR-automaton that is given through the following meta-instructions:

$$\begin{array}{ll} (1) & (\rhd \cdot \{\, a^i \mid i > k \,\}, b \to \lambda, b \cdot \{a,b\}^* \cdot \lhd), \\ (2) & (\rhd \cdot \{\, a^i \mid i > k \,\}, aba \to b, a^* \cdot \lhd), \\ (3) & (\rhd \cdot \{\, a^mb^i \mid 0 \leq m \leq k, i > k \,\}, ba \to \lambda, a^* \cdot \lhd), \\ (4) & (\rhd \cdot \{\, a^mb^{k+1}a^{k+2} \mid 0 \leq m \leq k \,\}, a \to \lambda, a^* \cdot \lhd), \\ (5) & (\rhd \cdot (\{a^{k+1}ba^{k+1}\} \cup \{\, a^mb^{k+1}a^{k+2} \mid 0 \leq m \leq k \,\}) \cdot \lhd, \mathsf{Accept}). \end{array}$$

It can now be checked that $L(M_k) = L_{\mathrm{sep},k}$. Moreover, M_k is a single RR-automaton, and it is $(k+1)$-reversible. Recall from Example 4.2.3(b) that the language $\{\, a^i \mid i > k \,\}$ is $(k+1)$-reversible, but not k-reversible. It follows that $L_{\mathrm{sep},k} \in \mathcal{L}(\mathsf{S}\text{-}(k+1)\text{-}\mathsf{rev}\text{-}\mathsf{RR})$.

It remains to show that the language $L_{\text{sep},k}$ is not accepted by any single k-reversible RRW-automaton. This is the hard part of the proof. Assume that M is an S-k-rev-RRW-automaton such that $L(M) = L_{\text{sep},k}$. Through a series of technical lemmas analyzing the possible computations of M, it is shown in [73] that, for some input of the form $a^k b^n a^n$, where $n > k$, the automaton M performs a computation that reduces this word to a word of the form $a^k b^m a^n$, where $k < m < n$. As $a^k b^n a^n \notin L_{\text{sep},k}$, while $a^k b^m a^n \in L_{\text{sep},k}$, this contradicts the Error Preserving Property for the restarting automaton M. It thus follows that the language $L_{\text{sep},k}$ is not accepted by any S-k-rev-RRW-automaton. □

For restarting automata with auxiliary letters, however, it remains open whether an increase in the degree of reversibility yields an increased expressive capacity.

Problem 4.2.12 *For $k \geq 0$, is $\mathcal{L}(\text{S-}k\text{-rev-RRWW})$ a proper subclass of $\mathcal{L}(\text{S-}(k+1)\text{-rev-RRWW})$?*

We complete our survey on the expressive capacity of single k-reversible restarting automata by comparing them to the strictly locally testable restarting automata. For restarting automata without auxiliary letters, Petr Hoffmann has obtained the following incomparability result.

Theorem 4.2.13 ([73]) *The class of languages accepted by single reversible RRW-automata and the class of languages accepted by SLT-RRW-automata are incomparable with respect to inclusion.*

As $\mathsf{SLT} \subsetneq \mathsf{REV}$ (see Theorem 4.2.5), the incomparability result above states essentially that, for restarting automata without auxiliary letters, the property of being single cannot be compensated for by relaxing the property of strictly local testability to k-reversibility.

In Section 4.1, we have seen how to obtain an SLT-RRWW-automaton from a set of sample words and sample reductions. Here we present Petr Hoffmann's method Omega^* of inferring an S-k-rev-RRWW-automaton from a set of fully positive analysis by reduction samples.

Definition 4.2.14 ([71]) *A* fully positive analysis by reduction sample, *or an* FPABR sample *for short, for a language $L \subseteq \Sigma^*$ is a finite sequence $(w_i)_{i=0}^n$ of words $w_0, w_1, \ldots, w_n \in L$ satisfying $|w_i| > |w_{i+1}|$ for all $i = 0, 1, \ldots, n-1$.*

The idea underlying this definition is the assumption that an FPABR sample $(w_i)_{i=0}^n$ corresponds to a sequence of cycles $q_0 \rhd w_0 \lhd \vdash_M^c q_0 \rhd w_1 \lhd \vdash_M^c \cdots \vdash_M^c q_0 \rhd w_n \lhd$ of an unknown S-k-rev-RRWW-automaton, where w_n is accepted through a tail computation. This means that this unknown automaton has rewriting meta-instructions that can be used to transform the restarting configuration $q_0 \rhd w_i \lhd$ into the restarting configuration $q_0 \rhd w_{i+1} \lhd$ for all $i = 0, 1, \ldots, n-1$, and its accepting meta-instruction applies to the restarting configuration $q_0 \rhd w_n \lhd$. Hence, the task of learning this S-k-rev-RRWW-automaton can be formulated as follows.

Definition 4.2.15 ([71]) *An* inference algorithm for S-k-rev-RRWW-automata from FPABR samples *is an algorithm that solves the following task:*

INSTANCE: *A finite set S of FPABR samples, an input alphabet Σ, and a working alphabet Γ.*

TASK: *Find an S-k-rev-RRWW-automaton M with input alphabet Σ and working alphabet Γ such that M is consistent with S, that is, for each FPABR sample $(w_i)_{i=0}^n \in S$, $q_0 \rhd w_0 \lhd \vdash_M^c q_0 \rhd w_1 \lhd \vdash_M^c \cdots \vdash_M^c q_0 \rhd w_n \lhd$, and $w_n \in R$ for the accepting meta-instruction $(\rhd \cdot R \cdot \lhd, \mathsf{Accept})$ of M.*

For his inference algorithm, Petr Hoffmann does not presuppose the existence of a helpful teacher as opposed to the inference method for SLT-RRWW-automata considered in Section 4.1. First of all, instead of having a teacher who partitions the given reductions into groups that are to be realized by the same rewriting meta-instructions, Petr Hoffmann uses the simple heuristics of assuming that all reductions containing the same rewrite step are handled by the same rewriting meta-instruction. Assume that we have a reduction $w \Rightarrow z$, that is, the unknown RRWW-automaton M can execute the cycle $q_0 \rhd w \lhd \vdash_M^c q_0 \rhd z \lhd$. Then M executes a rewrite step $l \to r$

that replaces a factor l of w with the word r. In order to express this particular rewrite step, the reduction $w \Rightarrow z$ is denoted by the triple $(u, l \to r, v)$, where $w = ulv$ and $z = urv$, that is, u is the *left context* and v is the *right context* of the rewrite step $l \to r$ within this reduction. Now a set of reductions $\{ (u_i, l_i \to r_i, v_i) \mid i \in I \}$ is called *compatible* if all these reductions contain the same rewrite step, that is, $l_i = l_j$ and $r_i = r_j$ for all $i, j \in I$.

Secondly, instead of having a teacher point out the location where a rewrite step is to be applied, Petr Hoffmann simply takes the shortest possible rewrite step and, if there are several of them, then he takes the left-most of them. Now his Omega* method can be formulated as follows.

Algorithm 4.2.16 ([71]) Omega*: *Learning an S-k-rev-RRWW-automaton:*

Input: *A finite set S of FPABR samples, an input alphabet Σ, and a working alphabet $\Gamma \supseteq \Sigma$.*

Output: *An S-k-rev-RRWW-automaton M that is compatible with S.*

Procedure:

begin
  $M := (\{q_0\}, \Sigma, \Gamma, \rhd, \lhd, q_0, 1, \emptyset)$; (* *$M$ is initialized as the trivial automaton* *)
  if $S = \emptyset$ **then**
  begin Return M; **Halt end**;
  Transform the set S into a set of reductions $\text{Red} = \{ (u_i, l_i \to r_i, v_i) \mid i \in I \}$
    always taking the shortest left-most option;
  Partition the set Red *into maximal groups* Red_j $(j \in J)$ *of compatible reductions;*
  for each $j \in J$ **do**
  begin
    Let $\text{Red}_j = \{ (u_i, l_j \to r_j, v_i) \mid i \in I_j \}$;
    Determine the smallest k-reversible set L_j compatible with the set $\{ u_i \mid i \in I_j \}$;
    Determine the smallest k-reversible set R_j compatible with the set $\{ v_i \mid i \in I_j \}$;
    Add the rewriting meta-instruction $(\rhd \cdot L_j, l_j \to r_j, R_j \cdot \lhd)$ *to* M;
  end;
  Determine a k-reversible set E compatible with the simple words from the set of samples S;
  Add the accepting meta-instruction $(\rhd \cdot E \cdot \lhd, \text{Accept})$ *to* M;
  Return M;
end.

To determine the k-reversible sets in the above algorithm, we can use Dana Angluin's learning algorithm [2], which is known to always return the smallest k-reversible language that is compatible with the given samples. Thus, we have the following result.

Theorem 4.2.17 ([71]) *When it is given a finite set S of FPABR samples and alphabets Σ and Γ as input, algorithm* Omega* *returns an S-k-rev-RRWW-automaton M with input alphabet Σ and working alphabet Γ such that M is consistent with S.*

Let M_0 be an S-k-rev-RRWW-automaton for which all rewrite steps happen to be the left-most shortest possible ones. Furthermore, let $(S_i)_{i \geq 1}$ be a positive presentation of all FPABR samples of M_0. Then by feeding these FPABR samples to the algorithm Omega*, we will obtain a sequence of S-k-rev-RRWW-automata $(M_i)_{i \geq 1}$ such that, for all $i \geq 1$, M_i is consistent with the FPABR samples $S_1, S_2, \ldots, S_i$. In particular, as soon as the FPABR samples considered contain characteristic samples for all the k-reversible context sets of the meta-instructions of M_0, it follows that the resulting S-k-rev-RRWW-automaton M_i is equivalent to M_0. Hence, based on algorithm Omega*, S-k-rev-RRWW-automata can be learnt in the limit from FPABR samples. We close this section by considering some examples.

Example 4.2.18 *Let $k = 0$, and let D_1 be the semi-Dyck language over $\Sigma = \{a, b\}$, that is, D_1 is the language that is generated by the grammar*

$$G_1 = (\{S\}, \{a, b\}, S, \{(S \to \lambda), (S \to SS), (S \to aSb)\}).$$

We take the set of FPABR samples $S = \{(aababbab, aabbab, abab, ab, \lambda)\}$. *As always the shortest left-most possible rewrite step is chosen, we obtain the following set of reductions*

$$\text{Red} = \{(a, ab \to \lambda, abbab), (a, ab \to \lambda, bab), (\lambda, ab \to \lambda, ab), (\lambda, ab \to \lambda, \lambda)\}.$$

As all these reductions contain the rewrite step $ab \to \lambda$, *they are all compatible, that is, the set* Red *itself is the only class of the resulting partition. The set of left factors is* $\{a, \lambda\}$ *and the set of right factors is* $\{abbab, bab, ab, \lambda\}$. *Then* L *is the smallest zero-reversible language that contains the left factors* $\{a, \lambda\}$, *which is* $L = \{a\}^*$, *and* R *is the smallest zero-reversible language that contains the right factors* $\{abbab, bab, ab, \lambda\}$, *which is* $R = \Sigma^*$. *Thus, we obtain the rewriting meta-instruction*

$$i_r = (\triangleright \cdot a^*, ab \to \lambda, \{a, b\}^* \cdot \triangleleft)$$

and the accepting meta-instruction

$$i_a = (\triangleright \cdot \triangleleft, \mathsf{Accept}).$$

Hence, the resulting S-0-rev-RRWW-automaton M *that is specified by these two meta-intructions always deletes the left-most factor* ab, *provided it is only preceded by* a*'s, and it accepts the empty word. It follows that* M *is an S-0-rev-RR-automaton, and it is immediate that* $L(M) = D_1$. ■

The next example is somewhat more involved.

Example 4.2.19 *Let* $k = 0$, *and let* $L_= = \{\, w \in \{a, b\}^* \mid |w|_a = |w|_b \,\}$. *We take the following set* S *consisting of four FPABR samples:*

$$\begin{aligned} S \;=\; & \{(aaabbb, aabb, ab, \lambda), (bbbaaa, bbaa, ba, \lambda), \\ & (aabbabab, ababab, abab, ab, \lambda), (bbaababa, bababa, baba, ba, \lambda)\}. \end{aligned}$$

By taking the shortest possible left-most rewrite steps, we obtain the following set of reductions:

$$\begin{aligned} \text{Red} \;=\; & \{(aa, ab \to \lambda, bb), (a, ab \to \lambda, b), (\lambda, ab \to \lambda, \lambda)\} \cup \\ & \{(bb, ba \to \lambda, aa), (b, ba \to \lambda, a), (\lambda, ba \to \lambda, \lambda)\} \cup \\ & \{(a, ab \to \lambda, babab), (\lambda, ab \to \lambda, abab), (\lambda, ab \to \lambda, ab), (\lambda, ab \to \lambda, \lambda)\} \cup \\ & \{(b, ba \to \lambda, ababa), (\lambda, ba \to \lambda, baba), (\lambda, ba \to \lambda, ba), (\lambda, ba \to \lambda, \lambda)\}. \end{aligned}$$

Here we have the two rewrite steps $ab \to \lambda$ *and* $ba \to \lambda$, *that is, we need two rewriting meta-instructions. These are*

$$i_1 = (\triangleright \cdot L_1, ab \to \lambda, R_1 \cdot \triangleleft) \text{ and } i_2 = (\triangleright \cdot L_2, ba \to \lambda, R_2 \cdot \triangleleft),$$

where L_1 *is the smallest zero-reversible language containing the set* $\{aa, a, \lambda\}$, R_1 *is the smallest zero-reversible language containing the set* $\{babab, abab, ab, bb, b, \lambda\}$, L_2 *is the smallest zero-reversible language containing the set* $\{bb, b, \lambda\}$, *and* R_2 *is the smallest zero-reversible language containing the set* $\{ababa, baba, ba, aa, a, \lambda\}$. *Then* $L_1 = \{a\}^*$, $L_2 = \{b\}^*$, *and* $R_1 = \{a, b\}^* = R_2$. *Thus,* M *is the S-0-rev-RR-automaton that is specified by the following meta-instructions*

$$i_1 = (\triangleright \cdot a^*, ab \to \lambda, \{a, b\}^* \cdot \triangleleft),\; i_2 = (\triangleright \cdot b^*, ba \to \lambda, \{a, b\}^* \cdot \triangleleft),\; \text{and } i_a = (\triangleright \cdot \triangleleft, \mathsf{Accept}).$$

It is easily checked that $L(M) = L_=$. ■

We complete this section with an example that illustrates the use of auxiliary letters.

Example 4.2.20 *Let* $k = 0$, *and let* $L_{\text{pal}} = \{\, w \in \{a, b\}^* \mid w = w^R \,\}$, *the language of palindromes over* $\{a, b\}$. *The following set of 24 FPABR samples is provided as input, where* X *is an additional auxiliary letter:*

$$\begin{aligned} S \;=\; & \{(aaaa, aXa, X, \lambda), (baab, bXb, X, \lambda), (aaaaaa, aaXaa, aXa, X, \lambda)\} \cup \\ & \{(bbaabb, bbXbb, bXb, X, \lambda), (aaa, X, \lambda), (aaaaa, aXa, X, \lambda), (baaab, bXb, X, \lambda)\} \cup \\ & \{(aba, X, \lambda), (aabaa, aXa, X, \lambda), (babab, bXb, X, \lambda), (bbbb, bXb, X, \lambda), (abba, aXa, X, \lambda)\} \cup \\ & \{(bbbbbb, bbXbb, bXb, X, \lambda), (aabbaa, aaXaa, aXa, X, \lambda), (bbb, X, \lambda), (bbbbb, bXb, X, \lambda)\} \cup \\ & \{(abbba, aXa, X, \lambda), (bab, X, \lambda), (bbabb, bXb, X, \lambda), (ababa, aXa, X, \lambda)\} \cup \\ & \{(abbbba, abXba, aXa, X, \lambda), (aabbbbaa, aabXbaa, aaXaa, aXa, X, \lambda)\} \cup \\ & \{(baaaab, baXab, bXb, X, \lambda), (bbaaaabb, bbaXabb, bbXbb, bXb, X, \lambda)\}. \end{aligned}$$

The resulting reductions contain 9 different rewrite steps, and accordingly, we obtain the S-0-rev-RRWW-automaton M that is specified by the following 9 rewriting meta-instructions

$$\begin{array}{rcl} i_1 & = & (\triangleright \cdot \{a,b\}^*, aa \to X, \{a,b\}^* \cdot \triangleleft), \\ i_2 & = & (\triangleright \cdot \{a,b\}^*, bb \to X, \{a,b\}^* \cdot \triangleleft), \\ i_3 & = & (\triangleright \cdot \{a,b\}^*, aaa \to X, \{a,b\}^* \cdot \triangleleft), \\ i_4 & = & (\triangleright \cdot \{a,b\}^*, bbb \to X, \{a,b\}^* \cdot \triangleleft), \\ i_5 & = & (\triangleright \cdot \{a,b\}^*, aba \to X, \{a,b\}^* \cdot \triangleleft), \\ i_6 & = & (\triangleright \cdot \{a,b\}^*, bab \to X, \{a,b\}^* \cdot \triangleleft), \\ i_7 & = & (\triangleright \cdot \{a,b\}^*, aXa \to X, \{a,b\}^* \cdot \triangleleft), \\ i_8 & = & (\triangleright \cdot \{a,b\}^*, bXb \to X, \{a,b\}^* \cdot \triangleleft), \\ i_9 & = & (\triangleright, X \to \lambda, \triangleleft), \end{array}$$

and the accepting meta-instruction $i_a = (\triangleright \cdot \triangleleft, \mathsf{Accept})$. *It is immediate that* $L(M) = L_{\mathrm{pal}}$. ∎

In case the above learning algorithm does not succeed, there are at least two options to remedy the situation. On the one hand, the degree k of reversibilitity can be increased to $k+1$, and then, instead of trying to infer an S-k-rev-RRWW-automaton that is consistent with the given set of FPABR samples, one tries to infer a corresponding S-$(k+1)$-rev-RRWW-automaton. Alternatively, one can choose the rewrite steps in a different way, that is, instead of always choosing the left-most shortest rewrite step, one can choose a different occurrence of a shortest rewrite step or not a shortest rewrite step at all. All these choices lead to different versions of the Omega^* method for learning single k-reversible RRWW-automata from FPABR samples.

4.3 Learning Analysis by Reduction from an Informant

Theorem 4.1.11 implies that we can apply the method of learning strictly locally testable restarting automata from a helpful teacher, as considered in Section 4.1, to learn clearing restarting automata from samples of reductions. However, in [258], Peter Černo and František Mráz propose another, simpler learning method for clearing restarting automata. This method does not need a helpful teacher. However, in addition to samples of correct reductions, it needs positive and negative samples of words, that is, samples of words that belong to the language accepted as well as samples of words that do not belong to the language accepted. This means that we need an *informant* to tell us which of the sample words belong to the language to be accepted and which do not.

Algorithm 4.3.1 ([258])
$\mathrm{LA}_{\mathrm{CRA}}$: *Learning a clearing restarting automaton from an informant:*

Input:
- *A finite sequence* $\{w_i \vdash w_i'\}_{i=1}^{n}$ *of reductions of an unknown CRA* U,
- *some samples* $\{u_i\}_{i=1}^{m}$ *of words from* $L(U)$, *and*
- *some samples* $\{v_i\}_{i=1}^{r}$ *of words that do not belong to* $L(U)$.

Output: *A CRA* M *such that* $q_0\rhd w_i\lhd \vdash_M^c q_0\rhd w_i'\lhd$ *holds for all* $i = 1, 2, \ldots, n$, $u_i \in L(M)$ *for all* $i = 1, 2, \ldots, m$, *and* $v_i \notin L(M)$ *for all* $i = 1, 2, \ldots, r$.

Procedure:

begin
  $j := 1$;
Loop: **for** $i = 1\,(1)\,n$ **do**
    nondeterministically choose a factorization $w_i = x_i z_i y_i$ *such that* $w_i' = x_i y_i$;
  construct the CRA M *that is specified by the set of instructions*
    $I = \bigcup_{i=1}^{n}\{\,(S_j(\rhd x_i), z_i \to \lambda, P_j(y_i\lhd))\,\}$;
  for $i = 1\,(1)\,m$ **do**
   if u_i *is not accepted by* M **then**
   begin $j := j + 1$; **goto** *Loop* **end**;
  for $i = 1\,(1)\,r$ **do**
   if v_i *is accepted by* M **then**
   begin $j := j + 1$; **goto** *Loop* **end**;
  return M; (* $u_1, u_2, \ldots, u_m \in L(M)$ *and* $v_1, v_2, \ldots v_r \notin L(M)$ *)
end.

We illustrate this algorithm by giving a simple example.

Example 4.3.2 *Assume that we have the sample reductions* $aabb \vdash ab$ *and* $ab \vdash \lambda$. *Then we get the (unique) factorizations* $aabb = a \cdot ab \cdot b$ *and* $ab = \lambda \cdot ab \cdot \lambda$. *Hence, for* $j = 1$, *the set of instructions* $I = \{(a, ab \to \lambda, b), (\rhd, ab \to \lambda, \lhd)\}$ *is obtained, which is the set of instructions of a CRA for the language* $\{\,a^n b^n \mid n \geq 0\,\}$. ■

The algorithm $\mathrm{LA}_{\mathrm{CRA}}$ is very simple. Nevertheless, Peter Černo and František Mráz illustrate that it can be used successfully to infer non-trivial clearing restarting automata. In fact, they use it to generate a CRA M such that the language $L(M)$ accepted by M is not context-free.

Example 4.3.3 ([258]) *The goal consists in constructing a CRA* M *on* $\Sigma = \{a, b\}$ *such that* $L(M) \cap \{\,(ab)^n \mid n \geq 1\,\} = \{\,(ab)^{2^m} \mid m \geq 0\,\}$. *As the class of context-free languages is closed under intersection with regular languages, the above equality implies that the language* $L(M)$ *is not context-free. In addition, the above equality shows that all words of the form* $(ab)^{2^n}$ *are to be accepted by* M *(that is, these are our positive samples), while all words of the form* $(ab)^m$ *for* m *not a power of two are not to be accepted by* M *(that is, these are our negative samples).*

Assume that we are given the following sample of an accepting sequence of reductions for the input $w = (ab)^8$:

$$
\begin{array}{rlllll}
(ab)^8 & = & ababababababab\underline{a}b & \vdash & ababababab\underline{a}babb & \vdash & ababab\underline{a}babbabb \\
& \vdash & ab\underline{a}babbabbabb & \vdash & abbabbabba\underline{b}b & \vdash & abbabbab\underline{b}bab \\
& \vdash & abba\underline{b}babab & \vdash & a\underline{b}bababab & \vdash & ababab\underline{a}b \\
& \vdash & ab\underline{a}babb & \vdash & abba\underline{b}b & \vdash & a\underline{b}bab \\
& \vdash & ab\underline{a}b & \vdash & a\underline{b}b & \vdash & \underline{ab} \\
& \vdash & \lambda & \vdash & \text{Accept.} & &
\end{array}
$$

$j = 1$: *From the above reductions, we obtain the instructions $(b, a \to \lambda, b)$, $(a, b \to \lambda, b)$, and $(\rhd, ab \to \lambda, \lhd)$. However, as $(ab)^3 = abab\underline{a}b \vdash ab\underline{a}bb \vdash a\underline{b}bb \vdash a\underline{b}b \vdash \underline{ab} \vdash \lambda$, a negative sample is accepted.*

$j = 2$: *In this situation, we obtain the instructions*

$$(ab, a \to \lambda, \{b\lhd, ba\}), (\{\rhd a, ba\}, b \to \lambda, \{b\lhd, ba\}), (\rhd, ab \to \lambda, \lhd).$$

However, in this case $(ab)^3 = abab\underline{a}b \vdash aba\underline{b}b \vdash ab\underline{a}b \vdash a\underline{b}b \vdash \underline{ab} \vdash \lambda$, that is, again a negative sample is accepted.

$j = 3$: *Here we obtain the instructions*

$$(\{\rhd ab, bab\}, a \to \lambda, \{b\lhd, bab\}), (\{\rhd a, bba\}, b \to \lambda, \{b\lhd, bab\}, (\rhd, ab \to \lambda, \lhd).$$

Then $(ab)^3 = ab\underline{a}bab \vdash a\underline{b}bab \vdash ab\underline{a}b \vdash a\underline{b}b \vdash \underline{ab} \vdash \lambda$.

$j = 4$: *Finally, we get the following instructions:*

$$(\{\rhd ab, abab\}, a \to \lambda, \{b\lhd, babb\}), (\{\rhd a, abba\}, b \to \lambda, \{b\lhd, bab\lhd, baba\}), (\rhd, ab \to \lambda, \lhd).$$

In the proof of Theorem 3.6 in [258], it is shown that the CRA M that is given through these instructions accepts a language that satisfies the above requirements.

Thus, we have been able to infer a 4-CRA that accepts a non-context-free language by using the above simple algorithm $\mathrm{LA_{CRA}}$. ■

As formulated above, the algorithm $\mathrm{LA_{CRA}}$ may not always terminate. However, as soon as the size j of the chosen contexts reaches the value $j = \max\{\, |w_i| \mid i = 1, 2, \ldots, n \,\}$, all instructions will have the form $(\rhd x, \ell \to \lambda, y\lhd)$ for some $x, y, \ell \in \Sigma^*$, which means that the set of instructions will not change anymore. Thus, in this situation, the algorithm should be terminated. Moreover, if there is a positive sample $u_i \in L(U)$ that cannot be rewritten with any of the instructions that are obtained in the first round (that is, with $j = 1$), then this word will not become reducible later (that is, for any $j > 1$). In this case, we may add the reduction $u_i \vdash \lambda$ (or the instruction $(\rhd, u_i \to \lambda, \lhd)$). These modifications guarantee that algorithm $\mathrm{LA_{CRA}}$ always terminates returning a CRA that is compatible with the given reductions and the given positive and negative samples.

In [254], Peter Černo improves the above algorithm and extends it to a more general model, the subword-clearing restarting automaton.

Definition 4.3.4 (a) *Let $k \in \mathbb{N}$. A* k-subword-clearing restarting automaton *is a k-context rewriting system $C = (\Sigma, \Sigma, I)$ such that, for each instruction $i = (x, z \to t, y) \in I$, $z \in \Sigma^+$ and t is a proper (scattered) subword of z, that is, t is obtained from z by deleting one or more letters. The* language accepted by C *is the reduction language $L(C) = \{\, w \in \Sigma^* \mid w \to_C^* \lambda \,\}$. Then* k-SCRA *denotes the class of all k-subword-clearing restarting automata.*

(b) *A* subword-clearing restarting automaton *is a k-subword-clearing restarting automaton for some $k \geq 0$. We use* SCRA *to denote the class of all subword-clearing restarting automata.*

Obviously, subword-clearing restarting automata are more expressive than clearing restarting automata. For example, the language $\{ a^n cb^n \mid n \geq 0 \} \cup \{\lambda\}$ is accepted by the SCRA $M = (\{a,b,c\},\{a,b,c\},\{(\rhd, c \to \lambda, \lhd),(\lambda, acb \to c, \lambda)\})$, while it is not accepted by any clearing restarting automaton.

Proposition 4.3.5 ([254]) $\mathcal{L}(\mathsf{CRA}) \subsetneq \mathcal{L}(\mathsf{SCRA})$.

For learning a subword-clearing restarting automaton, Peter Černo proposes a schema for inferring the instructions of an unknown target automaton M from positive and negative samples of words. Thus, in this setting, no samples of reductions are provided – instead, possible reductions must be inferred from the given positive samples of words. So let Σ be the underlying alphabet, let $S^+ \subseteq L(M)$ be a set of positive samples, and let $S^- \subseteq \Sigma^*$ be a set of negative samples, that is, $S^- \cap L(M) = \emptyset$. Naturally, we may assume that $S^+ \cap S^- = \emptyset$ and that $\lambda \in S^+$.

Without further restrictions, the task is trivial, as we may simply take the CRA $C = (\Sigma, \Sigma, I)$ with $I = \{ (\rhd, w \to \lambda, \lhd) \mid w \in S^+ \smallsetminus \{\lambda\} \}$. Then C is a CRA satisfying $L(C) = S^+$ and $L(C) \cap S^- = \emptyset$. Hence, the following additional restrictions are imposed:

(1) An upper bound $l \geq 1$ for the width of the instructions admitted and

(2) a specific value $k \geq 0$ for the length of the contexts in these instructions.

Recall from Definition 2.2.29 that the width of an instruction $(x, z \to t, y)$ is the combined length $|x| + |z| + |y|$. Hence, we require that $|x|, |y| \leq k$ and $|x| + |z| + |y| \leq l$.

For inferring a SCRA from positive and negative samples, the following algorithm is provided the details of which will be given below.

Algorithm 4.3.6 ([254])
$\mathrm{LA}_{\mathrm{SCRA}}$: *Learning a subword-clearing restarting automaton from an informant:*

Input:
- *A set of positive samples* $S^+ \subseteq \Sigma^*$ *containing the empty word* λ,
- *a set of negative samples* $S^- \subseteq \Sigma^*$ *such that* $S^+ \cap S^- = \emptyset$,
- *a bound* $l \geq 1$ *for the maximal width of instructions, and*
- *a value* $k \geq 0$ *for the length of the contexts of instructions.*

Output: *A SCRA* C *such that* $u \in L(C)$ *for all* $u \in S^+$ *and* $v \notin L(C)$ *for all* $v \in S^-$, *or* Fail.

Procedure:

begin
(1) $\Phi :=$ Assumptions(S^+, l, k); (∗ *A finite set of possible instructions is chosen* ∗)
(2) **while** $\exists w_- \in S^-, w_+ \in S^+, \phi \in \Phi : w_- \vdash_\phi w_+$ **do**
(3) $\quad \Phi := \Phi \smallsetminus \{\phi\}$;
(4) $\Phi :=$ Simplify(Φ);
(5) **if** Consistent(Φ, S^+, S^-) **then**
(6) $\quad$ **Return** $C = (\Sigma, \Sigma, \Phi)$
(7) **else Return** Fail;
end.

In line (1), the function call Assumptions(S^+, l, k) returns a finite set Φ of instructions of maximal width l and with contexts of length k that are derived from the set S^+ of positive samples. We shall discuss specific examples of the function Assumptions below. In lines (2) and (3), all those instructions are removed from Φ that allow to reduce a negative sample to a positive sample, where $w_- \vdash_\phi w_+$ denotes the fact that the word w_- can be reduced to w_+ by an application of instruction ϕ. In line (4), redundant instructions are removed from the set Φ of instructions (see below), and then, in line (5), it is checked whether the remaining instructions are consistent with all positive and negative samples, that is, whether $w_+ \vdash^*_\Phi \lambda$ holds for all $w_+ \in S^+$ and $w_- \not\vdash^*_\Phi \lambda$ holds for all $w_- \in S^-$.

The function Simplify in line (4) can be realized by the following algorithm.

Algorithm 4.3.7 ([254]) Simplify : *Simplify a given set of instructions* Φ:

Input: *A finite set of instructions* Φ *of a subword-clearing restarting automaton.*

Output: *A simplified set of instructions* Ψ.

Procedure:

begin

(1) $\Psi := \emptyset$;

(2) **for each** $\phi = (x, z \to t, y) \in \Phi$ **do**

(3) **if** $xzy \not\vdash^*_\Psi xty$ **then**

(4) $\Psi := \Psi \cup \{(x, z \to t, y)\}$;

(5) **Return** Ψ;

end

In this version of the algorithm Simplify, the instructions from the set Φ are considered in some order. If, for an instruction $(x, z \to t, y) \in \Phi$ considered, the word xzy can be reduced to xty by using those instructions that are already contained in the new set of instructions Ψ, then this instruction is not needed, and hence, it is not added to the new set of instructions Ψ.

Obviously, the success of the algorithm $\mathrm{LA}_{\mathrm{SCRA}}$ depends on the choice of the initial set of instructions by the function Assumptions in line (1) and on the given sets of positive and negative samples. Accordingly, we now consider the function Assumptions in detail. In order to guarantee that subword-clearing restarting automata are inferred correctly, the following correctness condition is required for all realizations of this function.

Definition 4.3.8 ([254]) *A function* Assumptions *is called* correct *with respect to the model of subword-clearing restarting automata, if it satisfies the following conditions:*

(1) *For every finite set* $S^+ \subseteq \Sigma^*$ *and all* $l \geq 1$ *and* $k \geq 0$, *the set of instructions* $\Phi = \mathrm{Assumptions}(S^+, l, k)$ *is finite, and, for every instruction* $(x, z \to t, y) \in \Phi$, *we have* $x \in \Sigma^k \cup \rhd \cdot \Sigma^{\leq k-1}$, $z \in \Sigma^+$, *t is a proper scattered subword of z,* $y \in \Sigma^k \cup \Sigma^{\leq k-1} \cdot \lhd$, *and* $|x| + |z| + |y| \leq l$.

(2) *For every k-subword-clearing restarting automaton* $M = (\Sigma, \Sigma, I)$ *with maximal width of instructions at most l, there exists an equivalent k-subword-clearing restarting automaton* $N = (\Sigma, \Sigma, J)$, $J \subseteq I$, *and a finite set* $S_0^+ \subseteq L(N) = L(M)$ *such that, for every* $S^+ \supseteq S_0^+$, $J \subseteq \mathrm{Assumptions}(S^+, l, k)$.

The first of these conditions simply ensures that the function Assumptions returns a finite set of instructions that are all of the required form. The second condition is more serious. It requires that, for each k-SCRA M with maximal width of instructions l, there exists a finite set of positive samples S_0^+ such that, for all supersets S^+ of S_0^+, the function call $\mathrm{Assumptions}(S^+, l, k)$ returns a set of instructions that contains all the instructions of a k-SCRA N with maximal width of instructions l that is equivalent to M. Here the extension to an automaton N that is equivalent to M is necessary, as the automaton M may contain a number of superfluous instructions. The following examples describe possible realizations of the function Assumptions that are correct in the sense of Definition 4.3.8.

Example 4.3.9 *Given a finite set* $S^+ \subseteq \Sigma^*$ *and integers* $l \geq 1$ *and* $k \geq 0$ *as input, the function* Assumptions *could simply return the list of all possible instructions over* Σ *for k-SCRA of maximal width of instructions l. Because of the restriction on the maximal width, this is a finite set, and obviously, it will contain the subset J required by Definition 4.3.8 (2).* ■

While the function Assumptions from Example 4.3.9 does not use the given set S^+ of positive samples at all, the following two functions extract the suggested instructions from that set.

Example 4.3.10 ([254]) *Let*

$$\text{Assumptions}_2(S^+, l, k) = \{ (x, z \to t, y) \mid \begin{array}{l} (x, z \to t, y) \textit{ is an admissible instruction of a k-SCRA}, \\ |x| + |z| + |y| \leq l, \textit{ and } \exists w_1, w_2 \in S^+ : \\ xzy \textit{ is a factor of } \rhd w_1 \lhd \textit{ and} \\ xty \textit{ is a factor of } \rhd w_2 \lhd \}. \end{array}$$

Obviously, this function only returns instructions of the correct form. ■

Example 4.3.11 ([254]) *Let*

$$\text{Assumptions}_3(S^+, l, k) = \{ (x, z \to t, y) \mid \begin{array}{l} (x, z \to t, y) \textit{ is an admissible instruction of a k-SCRA}, \\ |x| + |z| + |y| \leq l, \textit{ and } \exists w_1, w_2 \in S^+ \\ \exists \alpha \in (\rhd \cdot \Sigma^*) \cup \{\lambda\} \, \exists \beta \in (\Sigma^* \cdot \lhd) \cup \{\lambda\} : \\ \rhd w_1 \lhd = \alpha xzy\beta \textit{ and } \rhd w_2 \lhd = \alpha xty\beta \}. \end{array}$$

Again, this function only returns instructions of the correct form. ■

It remains to verify that these functions satisfy condition (2) of Definition 4.3.8. In fact, as $\text{Assumptions}_3(S^+, l, k) \subseteq \text{Assumptions}_2(S^+, l, k)$ holds for all $S^+ \subseteq \Sigma^*$, $l \geq 1$, and $k \geq 0$, it suffices to consider the function Assumptions_3.

Lemma 4.3.12 ([254]) *For every k-subword-clearing restarting automaton $M = (\Sigma, \Sigma, I)$ with maximal width of instructions at most l, there exists an equivalent k-subword-clearing restarting automaton $N = (\Sigma, \Sigma, J)$, $J \subseteq I$, and a finite set $S_0^+ \subseteq L(N) = L(M)$ such that, for every $S^+ \supseteq S_0^+$, $J \subseteq \text{Assumptions}_3(S^+, l, k)$.*

Proof. Let $M = (\Sigma, \Sigma, I)$ be a k-SCRA with maximal width of instructions l. We take a k-SCRA $N = (\Sigma, \Sigma, J)$ with maximal width of instructions l such that $L(N) = L(M)$, where N has a minimal set of instructions, that is, for all instructions $\phi \in J$, we have $L((\Sigma, \Sigma, J \smallsetminus \{\phi\})) \subsetneq L(N)$. Such an automaton can be obtained from M by removing superfluous instructions. Then, for each instruction $\phi \in J$, there exists a shortest word $w_\phi \in L(N)$ such that w_ϕ cannot be reduced to λ without using the instruction ϕ. This implies that $w_\phi \vdash_\phi w'_\phi \vdash^*_{J \smallsetminus \{\phi\}} \lambda$. We fix this reduction and take $S_0^+ = \bigcup_{\phi \in J} \{w_\phi, w'_\phi\}$. Then S_0^+ is a finite subset of $L(N)$, and given any superset S_+ of S_0^+ as input, $\text{Assumptions}_3(S^+, l, k)$ contains all instructions from J. □

Thus, the above functions Assumptions_2 and Assumptions_3 are correct in the sense of Definition 4.3.8. The next theorem states that k-subword clearing restarting automata can be learnt from positive and negative samples.

Theorem 4.3.13 ([254]) *Let* Assumptions *be a function that is correct with respect to the model of subword-clearing restarting automata. Then, for every k-SCRA $M = (\Sigma, \Sigma, I)$ with maximal width of instructions $l \geq 1$, there exists a finite set S_0^+ of positive samples and a finite set S_0^- of negative samples consistent with M such that, for every finite set $S^+ \supseteq S_0^+$ and every finite set $S^- \supseteq S_0^-$ consistent with M, the algorithm LA_{SCRA} succeeds on input (S^+, S^-, l, k) and returns a k-SCRA $N = (\Sigma, \Sigma, J)$ satisfying $L(N) = L(M)$.*

Proof. Let $M = (\Sigma, \Sigma, I)$ be a k-SCRA with maximal width of instructions $l \geq 1$. As the function Assumptions is correct with respect to the model of subword-clearing restarting automata, there exists an equivalent k-SCRA $N = (\Sigma, \Sigma, J)$, $J \subseteq I$, and a finite set $S_0^+ \subseteq L(N) = L(M)$ such that, for every $S^+ \supseteq S_0^+$, $J \subseteq \text{Assumptions}(S^+, l, k)$ holds. Thus, on input (S^+, S^-, l, k), where $S^+ \supseteq S_0^+$, algorithm LA_{SCRA} produces a finite set of instructions containing J in line (1). It remains to determine the finite set S_0^- of negative samples that allows us to remove all incorrect instructions from the set $\text{Assumptions}(S^+, l, k)$.

Let ϕ be an instruction of the form $(x, z \to t, y)$, where $x \in \Sigma^k \cup \rhd \cdot \Sigma^{\leq k-1}$, $z \in \Sigma^+$, t a proper scattered subword of z, $y \in \Sigma^+ \cup \Sigma^{\leq k-1} \cdot \lhd$, and $|x| + |z| + |y| \leq l$. Such an instruction is called *bad* if there exist $w_- \notin L(N)$ and $w_+ \in L(N)$ such that $w_- \vdash_\phi w_+$ holds. Moreover, we say that the instruction ϕ is *disabled* by the pair (S_0^+, S_0^-) if there are $w_- \in S_0^-$ and $w_+ \in S_0^+$ such that $w_- \vdash_\phi w_+$ holds. We use the following procedure to prove the existence of the sets S_0^- and S_0^+:

Procedure ExtendSamples : *Extend a given finite set of positive samples :*

Input: *A finite set of positive samples* S_0^+ *and a set* Φ *of instructions.*

Output: *A pair* (S_0^+, S_0^-) *consisting of a finite set* S_0^+ *of positive samples and a finite set* S_0^- *of negative samples.*

Procedure:

begin
(1) $S_0^- := \emptyset$;
(2) **while** $\exists$ *bad instruction* $\phi \in \Phi$ *that is not disabled by* (S_0^+, S_0^-) **do**
(3) **begin**
(4) *Let* $w_- \in \Sigma^+ \smallsetminus L(N)$ *and* $w_+ \in L(N)$ *such that* $w_- \vdash_\phi w_+$;
(5) $S_0^+ := S_0^+ \cup \{w_+\}$;
(6) $S_0^- := S_0^- \cup \{w_-\}$;
(7) **end**;
(8) **Return** (S_0^+, S_0^-);
end.

No instruction of the set $J \subseteq \text{Assumptions}(S^+, l, k)$ is bad. Procedure *ExtendSamples* shows that there exists a finite set of positive samples S_0^+ extending the set S^+ and a finite set of negative samples S_0^- such that, using these sets, algorithm LA_{SCRA} removes all bad instructions from Φ in lines (2) to (3). The resulting set of instructions only contains correct instructions, including those from the set J. It follows that we obtain a k-SCRA that is equivalent to N, and therewith, to M. Observe that the procedure ExtendSamples just proves the existence of the required sets of positive and negative samples, but that it does not provide an efficient way for computing these sets. □

We illustrate the above result with two simple examples from [254].

Example 4.3.14 *We consider the 1-CRA* $M = (\{a,b\}, \{a,b\}, \{(\triangleright, ab \to \lambda, \triangleleft), (a, ab \to \lambda, b)\})$ *from Example 4.3.2, which accepts the language* $L(M) = \{a^n b^n \mid n \geq 0\}$. *Assume that the set* $S^+ = \{\lambda, ab, aabb\}$ *is given. First, we determine the instructions generated by the function* Assumptions_2 *given the set* S^+ *and the integers* $l = 6$ *and* $k = 1$. *According to the definition given in Example 4.3.10, an instruction* $\phi = (x, z \to \lambda, y)$ *is included in the set* $\text{Assumptions}_2(S^+, l, k)$ *if it is of the correct form and if there are words* $w_1, w_2 \in S^+$ *such that* xzy *is a factor of* $\triangleright w_1 \triangleleft$ *and* xy *is a factor of* $\triangleright w_2 \triangleleft$. *Here we have adjusted the definition to the special case of clearing restarting automata. The set of possible factors is*

$$SW^+ = \{\triangleright, a, b, \triangleleft, \triangleright\triangleleft, \triangleright a, aa, ab, bb, b\triangleleft, \triangleright aa, \triangleright ab, aab, abb, ab\triangleleft, bb\triangleleft, \triangleright ab\triangleleft, \triangleright aab, aabb, abb\triangleleft, \triangleright aabb, aabb\triangleleft, \triangleright aabb\triangleleft\}.$$

Thus, we get the following set of instructions:

$$\Phi_1 = \{(\triangleright, a \to \lambda, a), (a, a \to \lambda, b), (a, b \to \lambda, b), (b, b \to \lambda, \triangleleft), (\triangleright, ab \to \lambda, \triangleleft), (a, ab \to \lambda, b), (\triangleright, aabb \to \lambda, \triangleleft)\},$$

which includes the instructions of M. *However, the instructions*

$$(\triangleright, a \to \lambda, a), (a, a \to \lambda, b), (a, b \to \lambda, b), \text{ and } (b, b \to \lambda, \triangleleft)$$

are bad, as, for example, $aab \vdash ab$ *by the first instruction, where* $aab \notin L(M)$, *while* $ab \in L(M)$. *We can disable all these bad instructions by taking* $S^- = \{aab, abb\}$. *Now given* S^+, S^-, $l = 6$ *and* $k = 1$ *as input, the algorithm* LA_{SCRA} *yields the set of instructions*

$$\Phi_2 = \{(\triangleright, ab \to \lambda, \triangleleft), (a, ab \to \lambda, b)\},$$

as the instruction $(\triangleright, aabb \to \lambda, \triangleleft)$ *is removed by the call to Simplify in line (4).* ■

Example 4.3.15 *Let* $M = (\{a,b,c\}, \{a,b,c\}, \{(a, acb \to c, b), (\triangleright, acb \to \lambda, \triangleleft)\})$ *be a 1-SCRA. Then* $L(M) = \{a^n cb^n \mid n \geq 1\} \cup \{\lambda\}$. *Using the function* Assumptions$_2$ *with input* $S^+ = \{\lambda, acb, aacbb\}$, $l = 6$, *and* $k = 1$, *we obtain the following set of instructions:*

$$\begin{aligned}\Phi_1 \;=\; & \{(\triangleright, a \to \lambda, a), (a, a \to \lambda, c), (b, b \to \lambda, \triangleleft), (c, b \to \lambda, b), (\triangleright, aa \to a, c), (a, ac \to c, b), \\ & (c, bb \to b, \triangleleft), (a, cb \to c, b), (\triangleright, acb \to \lambda, \triangleleft), (a, acb \to c, b)\}.\end{aligned}$$

By taking $S^- = \{aacb, acbb\}$, *we can disable the first eight instructions, which yields the set of instructions* $\Phi_2 = \{(\triangleright, acb \to \lambda, \triangleleft), (a, acb \to c, b)\}$. ■

In [254], Peter Černo also presents another, more involved example. In that example, he shows how to infer a subword-clearing restarting automaton that accepts the language of simplified arithmetic expressions over the alphabet $\Sigma = \{a, +, (,)\}$, where the letter a is used as a placeholder for variables or numerical values. For example, $a + (a + a)$ and $(a + (a))$ are correct arithmetic expressions, while $a+$, $(a + a$, and $(a + ()$ are not. Again the numbers $l = 6$ and $k = 1$ are taken, and the set of positive samples is

$$S^+ = \{a, a + a, a + a + a, (a), ((a)), (a + a), ((a + a)), a + (a + a), (a + a) + a\},$$

while the set S^- of negative sample that he uses consists of 18 words of length one and two.

Finally, we address the complexity of the algorithm LA$_{\text{SCRA}}$ in short. Obviously, its complexity depends on the time complexity of the function Assumptions and the procedures Simplify and Consistent. The functions Assumptions$_2$ and Assumptions$_3$ can be realized in polynomial time, as the sets of instructions returned by them are determined based on the factors of length up to l of the positive samples in the given set S^+. This implies, in particular, that these sets of instructions are of polynomial size. Hence, the while-loop in lines (2) to (3) also runs in polynomial time. Furthermore, if the parameters l and k are taken as fixed constants, then the procedure Simplify can also be realized in polynomial time. Unfortunately, it is not clear how to realize the consistency check in polynomial time. The word problem for subword-clearing restarting automata can be solved nondeterministically in quadratic time, which yields an exponential deterministic time bound. However, from the point of view of identification in the limit, we can omit the simplification step and the consistency check, as they do not affect the correctness of the learning algorithm. In the limit, the algorithm will always return a correct solution.

In fact, the following negative result on the complexity of the learning algorithm LA$_{\text{SCRA}}$ has been obtained.

Theorem 4.3.16 ([254]) *Let* $l \geq 2$ *be a fixed integer. Then the following problem is NP-complete:*

INSTANCE:	*A finite set* S^+ *of positive samples and a finite set* S^- *of negative samples such that* $S^+ \cap S^- = \emptyset$ *and* $\lambda \in S^+$.
QUESTION:	*Is there a 0-CRA* $M = (\Sigma, \Sigma, I)$ *that is consistent with* S^+ *and* S^- *such that the width of each instruction of* M *is at most* l?

Proof outline. The result is proved by a reduction from the problem 3-SAT of deciding whether a given logical formula in conjunctive normal form of degree 3 is satisfiable. Recall from [49] that this problem is NP-complete with respect to polynomial time reductions.

Let $\psi = \wedge_{i=1}^{n} C_i$ be a formula in conjunctive normal form of degree 3, that is, each C_i has the form $C_i = \ell_{i,1} \vee \ell_{i,2} \vee \ell_{i,3}$, where the $\ell_{i,j}$ are literals over $\Omega = \{x_1, x_2, \ldots, x_m\}$. From ψ, one can construct a finite set of positive samples S^+ and a finite set S^- of negative samples as follows.

Let $\Sigma = \Omega \cup \overline{\Omega}$, where $\overline{\Omega} = \{\bar{x}_1, \bar{x}_2, \ldots, \bar{x}_m\}$ is a copy of Ω that is disjoint from Ω. We initialize the sets S^+ and S^- as $S^+ = \{\lambda\}$ and $S^- = \emptyset$. Then, for each clause $C_i = \ell_{i,1} \vee \ell_{i,2} \vee \ell_{i,3}$, we add the word $w_{\ell_i} = \bar{\ell}_{i,1}\bar{\ell}_{i,2}\bar{\ell}_{i,3}$ to the set S^- of negative samples, where $\bar{\bar{x}}_j = x_j$ for all $j = 1, 2, \ldots, m$. Furthermore, for each variable $x_i \in \Omega$, we add the words $w_{i,0} = (x_i\bar{x}_i)^l$, $w_{i,1} = x_i^l$, and $w_{i,2} = \bar{x}_i^l$ to the set S^+ of positive samples. Finally, for each $x_i \in \Omega$, we add all words $w \in \{x_i, \bar{x}_i\}^{\leq l}$ satisfying $|w|_{x_i} \geq 1$ and $|w|_{\bar{x}_i} \geq 1$ to the set S^- of negative samples. Observe that the parameter $l \geq 2$ is fixed, which means that there is only a finite number of such words. It follows that the sets S^+ and S^- are of linear size with respect to the length of the formula ψ, and that these sets can be constructed in polynomial time from the formula ψ.

It can now be shown that there is a 0-CRA $M = (\Sigma, \Sigma, I)$ that is consistent with S^+ and S^- such that the width of each instruction of M is at most l if and only if the formula ψ is satisfiable. This proves that the above problem is NP-hard.

It remains to prove that the problem of finding a 0-CRA $M = (\Sigma, \Sigma, I)$ that is consistent with S^+ and S^- such that the width of each instruction of M is at most l is in NP. It is shown in [258] that a given 1-CRA can be converted in polynomial time into an equivalent context-free grammar. Hence, the membership problem for 0-CRA and 1-CRA is decidable in polynomial time. Furthermore, if S^+ is the given finite set of positive samples, then the 0-CRA M to be constructed needs at most $\text{size}(S^+) = \sum_{w \in S^+} |w|$ many instructions, as, for each positive sample $w \in S^+$, an accepting computation $w \vdash_M^* \lambda$ consists of at most $|w|$ many steps, and accordingly, at most these many instructions are used. Therefore, we can first guess the set of instructions in polynomial time and then verify that these instructions are consistent with the given sets S^+ and S^- of positive and negative samples. This completes the proof of the NP-completeness result. □

In fact, the above result can be generalized as follows.

Theorem 4.3.17 ([254]) *Let $k \geq 1$ and $l \geq 4k + 4$ be fixed integers. Then the following problem is NP-complete for $k = 1$ and NP-hard for all $k \geq 2$:*

INSTANCE:	*A finite set S^+ of positive samples and a finite set S^- of negative samples such that $S^+ \cap S^- = \emptyset$ and $\lambda \in S^+$.*
QUESTION:	*Is there a k-CRA $M = (\Sigma, \Sigma, I)$ that is consistent with S^+ and S^- such that the width of each instruction of M is at most l?*

A detailed proof can be found in the technical report [255]. NP-hardness is again proved by a reduction from 3-SAT, while for $k = 1$, membership in NP follows from the fact that the membership problem is decidable in polynomial time for 1-CRA. For $k \geq 2$, the membership problem for a k-CRA is decidable nondeterministically in quadratic time (see, e.g., Corollary 1.9.15), but it is not clear whether non-membership in $L(M)$ is in NP for each k-CRA M. Therefore, the following question remains open.

Problem 4.3.18 *For $k \geq 2$, is the problem of deciding whether there exists a k-CRA that is consistent with given finite sets S^+ and S^- of positive and negative samples and that has maximal width of instructions bounded by a given constant $l \geq 4k + 4$ in NP?*

The above method of inferring a subword-clearing restarting automaton from finite sets of positive and negative samples can easily be extended to other types of restarting automata defined through context conditions. In [8], Stanislav Basovník and František Mráz define various types of limited context restarting automata as extensions of the clearing restarting automaton. Also these automata apply rewrite steps only based on context information, but their rewrite rules are more general. In [203] (see also [202]), several additional types of limited context restarting automata are presented and the expressive capacity of all the different types of limited context restarting automata is studied systematically. In the following, we restate the corresponding definitions and main results.

Definition 4.3.19 ([203]) *A* limited context restarting automaton *M is defined through a triple $M = (\Sigma, \Gamma, I)$, where Σ is an input alphabet, Γ is a working alphabet containing Σ, and I is a finite set of* instructions *of the form $(u, x \to y, v)$, where $x, y \in \Gamma^*$ such that $g(x) > g(y)$ for some weight function $g : \Gamma^* \to \mathbb{N}$, $u \in \{\rhd, \lambda\} \cdot \Gamma^*$, and $v \in \Gamma^* \cdot \{\lambda, \lhd\}$. Here $\rhd$ and $\lhd$ are the left and right sentinels, which are not elements of Γ.*

The limited context restarting automaton (or LCRA *for short) $M = (\Sigma, \Gamma, I)$ induces a reduction relation $\vdash_M^c$ on Γ^* that is defined as follows: for each $w, z \in \Gamma^*$, $w \vdash_M^c z$, if there exist words*

$w_1, w_2 \in \Gamma^*$ and an instruction $(u, x \to y, v)$ in I such that $w = w_1xw_2$, $z = w_1yw_2$, u is a suffix of $\rhd w_1$ and v is a prefix of $w_2\lhd$. Thus, the factor x is rewritten into y, if it appears within the context uxv. The reflexive and transitive closure of $\vdash_M^c$ is written as $\vdash_M^{c^*}$. The language accepted by the LCRA M is $L(M) = \{ w \in \Sigma^* \mid w \vdash_M^{c^*} \lambda \}$.

An LCRA M accepts exactly the set of input words that can be reduced to λ. Obviously, λ is in $L(M)$ for each LCRA M. Accordingly, if L is a language that does not contain λ as an element, then L is not accepted by any LCRA. Therefore, as in the case of clearing restarting automata, we consider equality of languages only up to the empty word, that is, two languages L and L' on Σ are considered to be equal, denoted as $L \doteq L'$, if $L \cap \Sigma^+ = L' \cap \Sigma^+$ holds.

Example 4.3.20 *Let $M = (\{a,b,c\}, \{a,b,c\}, I)$ be the LCRA that is defined by the set of instructions $I = \{(\lambda, acbb \to c, \lambda), (\rhd, c \to \lambda, \lhd)\}$. Then*

$$aaacbbbbbb \vdash_M^c aacbbbb \vdash_M^c acbb \vdash_M^c c \vdash_M^c \lambda,$$

and so the word a^3cb^6 belongs to $L(M)$. It is easily seen that $L(M) = \{ a^n cb^{2n} \mid n \geq 0 \}$. ■

Recall from Definition 4.3.19 that all instructions of an LCRA are necessarily weight-reducing. These most general LCRA are said to be of type $\mathcal{R}_0'$. We now define some restricted types of LCRA by putting additional restrictions on the form of their instructions.

Definition 4.3.21 ([203]) *We say that an LCRA $M = (\Sigma, \Gamma, I)$ is of type*

- *$\mathcal{R}_0$, if I only contains instructions of the form $(u, x \to y, v)$, where $|x| > |y|$;*
- *$\mathcal{R}_1'$, if I only contains instructions of the form $(u, x \to y, v)$, where $|y| \leq 1$, and $x \in \Gamma^+$;*
- *$\mathcal{R}_1$, if I only contains instructions of the form $(u, x \to y, v)$, where $|y| \leq 1$, and $x \in \Gamma^+$ such that $|x| > |y|$;*
- *$\mathcal{R}_2'$, if I only contains instructions of the form $(u, x \to y, v)$, where $|y| \leq 1$, $u \in \{\lambda, \rhd\}$, $v \in \{\lambda, \lhd\}$, and $x \in \Gamma^+$;*
- *$\mathcal{R}_2$, if I only contains instructions of the form $(u, x \to y, v)$, where $|y| \leq 1$, $u \in \{\lambda, \rhd\}$, $v \in \{\lambda, \lhd\}$, and $x \in \Gamma^+$ such that $|x| > |y|$;*
- *$\mathcal{R}_3'$, if I only contains instructions of the form $(u, x \to y, \lhd)$, where $|y| \leq 1$, $u \in \{\lambda, \rhd\}$, and $x \in \Gamma^+$;*
- *$\mathcal{R}_3$, if I only contains instructions of the form $(u, x \to y, \lhd)$, where $|y| \leq 1$, $u \in \{\lambda, \rhd\}$, and $x \in \Gamma^+$ such that $|x| > |y|$.*

For any $\mathcal{R} \in \{\mathcal{R}_0, \mathcal{R}_0', \mathcal{R}_1, \mathcal{R}_1', \mathcal{R}_2, \mathcal{R}_2', \mathcal{R}_3, \mathcal{R}_3'\}$, we use LCRA[$\mathcal{R}$] to denote the class of limited context restarting automata of type $\mathcal{R}$.

For an instruction $i = (u, x \to y, v)$ of an LCRA (Σ, Γ, I), the number $|u| + |x| + |v|$ is called the *width* of this instruction. For a given alphabet Γ, there are only finitely many possible instructions of width $l \geq 1$ over Γ. Hence, by adjusting the requirements for the function Assumptions in Definition 4.3.8 correspondingly, we can extend the learning algorithm $\mathrm{LA}_{\mathrm{SCRA}}$ (see Algorithm 4.3.6) to any type of limited context restarting automaton.

Obviously, the subword-clearing restarting automaton is a special case of the limited context restarting automaton of type $\mathcal{R}_0$. Moreover, each subword-clearing restarting automaton can be interpreted as an RR-automaton. It follows that there are context-free languages that are not accepted by any subword-clearing restarting automaton (see, e.g., Lemma 2.2.4). On the other hand, as the subword-clearing restarting automata extend the clearing restarting automata, they accept some languages that are not even context-free (see Theorem 2.2.38). Thus, we see that the class $\mathcal{L}(\mathsf{SCRA})$ of languages that are accepted by subword-clearing restarting automata is incomparable under inclusion to the class of context-free languages.

Concerning the various classes of limited context restarting automata, the following characterizations and inclusion relations are known. In [7], Stanislav Basovník studies length-reducing LCRA. He obtains the following characterizations.

Theorem 4.3.22 ([7]) (a) $\mathcal{L}(\mathrm{LCRA}[\mathcal{R}_0]) = \mathsf{GCSL}$.
(b) $\mathcal{L}(\mathrm{LCRA}[\mathcal{R}_2]) = \mathsf{CFL}$.
(c) $\mathcal{L}(\mathrm{LCRA}[\mathcal{R}_3]) = \mathsf{REG}$.

Let $M = (\Sigma, \Gamma, I)$ be an LCRA. With M, we can associate the finite string-rewriting system

$$R(M) = \{\, uxv \to uyv \mid (u, x \to y, v) \in I \,\}.$$

Then $R(M)$ induces a reduction relation $\Rightarrow^*_{R(M)}$ on the set of bordered words $\rhd \cdot \Gamma^* \cdot \lhd$, which is the reflexive and transitive closure of the *single-step reduction relation* $\Rightarrow_{R(M)}$ (see Definition 2.2.47). Thus, for all $w, z \in \Gamma^*$, we have $\rhd w \lhd \Rightarrow_{R(M)} \rhd z \lhd$ iff $w \vdash^{\mathsf{c}}_M z$ holds. Accordingly, we see that

$$L(M) = \{\, w \in \Sigma^* \mid w \vdash^{\mathsf{c}^*}_M \lambda \,\} = \{\, w \in \Sigma^* \mid \rhd w \lhd \Rightarrow^*_{R(M)} \rhd \cdot \lhd \,\}.$$

By taking $S(M) = R(M) \cup \{\rhd\lhd \to Y\}$, where Y is a new letter, we obtain a finite string-rewriting system on $\Gamma' = \Gamma \cup \{\rhd, \lhd, Y\}$ such that $L(M) = \{\, w \in \Sigma^* \mid \rhd w \lhd \Rightarrow^*_{S(M)} Y \,\}$ holds. It follows that $L(M)$ is the *McNaughton language* that is specified by the four-tuple $(S(M), \rhd, \lhd, Y)$ (see Definition 2.2.48).

If M is of type $\mathcal{R}'_0$, then the string-rewriting system $S(M)$ is weight-reducing. Hence, it follows from Theorem 2.2.50(a) that $L(M) \in \mathsf{GCSL}$. Together with Theorem 4.3.22(a), this yields the following characterization, as each LCRA of type $\mathcal{R}_0$ is obviously also of type $\mathcal{R}'_0$.

Theorem 4.3.23 ([203]) $\mathcal{L}(\mathrm{LCRA}[\mathcal{R}'_0]) = \mathcal{L}(\mathrm{LCRA}[\mathcal{R}_0]) = \mathsf{GCSL}$.

In the proof of Theorem 4.3.22(a) in [7], the author constructs an LCRA M of type $\mathcal{R}_0$ for the language $L(G)$ from a given growing context-sensitive grammar G. As Stanislav Basovník's thesis [7] is difficult to access, a full proof for Theorem 4.3.23 using a construction that is based on the two-pushdown automaton is given in [203].

Let $G = (N, T, S, P)$ be a weight-increasing context-sensitive grammar, that is, there exists a weight function g such that $g(\ell) < g(r)$ for each rule $(\ell \to r)$ of P, and in addition, each rule $(\ell \to r)$ has the form $\ell = uAv$ and $r = uxv$ for some $A \in N$, $u, v \in (N \cup T)^*$, and $x \in (N \cup T)^+$. By taking

$$I(G) = \{\, (u, x \to A, v) \mid (uAv \to uxv) \in P \,\} \cup \{\, (\rhd, r \to \lambda, \lhd) \mid (S \to r) \in P \,\},$$

we obtain an LCRA $M(G) = (T, N \cup T, I(G))$. It is easily seen that $M(G)$ is of type $\mathcal{R}'_1$, and that $L(M(G)) = L(G) \cup \{\lambda\}$ holds. Thus, ignoring the special case of the empty word, we see that all languages that are generated by weight-increasing context-sensitive languages are accepted by LCRAs of type $\mathcal{R}'_1$. However, the class of languages generated by weight-increasing context-sensitive grammars, known as the class ACSL of *acyclic context-sensitive languages*, coincides with the class GCSL of growing context-sensitive languages [187]. Hence, we obtain the following characterization.

Theorem 4.3.24 ([203]) $\mathcal{L}(\mathrm{LCRA}[\mathcal{R}'_1]) = \mathsf{GCSL}$.

If $M = (\Sigma, \Gamma, I)$ is an LCRA of type $\mathcal{R}_1$, then the rules of $R(M)$ have the form $(uxv \to uyv)$, where $|x| > |y|$ and $|y| \leq 1$. The following technical result can be derived by replacing each instruction of the form $(u, x \to \lambda, v) \in I$ by finitely many rules with a revised context.

Lemma 4.3.25 ([203]) *If $M = (\Sigma, \Gamma, I)$ is an LCRA of type $\mathcal{R}_1$, then there exists an equivalent LCRA $M' = (\Sigma, \Gamma, I')$ of type $\mathcal{R}_1$ such that $|y| = 1$ for all instructions $(u, x \to y, v) \in I'$ satisfying $u \neq \rhd$ or $v \neq \lhd$. In fact, for all $w, z \in \Gamma^*$, $w \vdash^{\mathsf{c}}_M z$ if and only if $w \vdash^{\mathsf{c}}_{M'} z$.*

Proof. To obtain M' from M, we simply replace each instruction of the form $i = (u, x \to \lambda, v) \in I$. If $u = u_1 A$ for some $A \in \Gamma$, then we replace i with the instruction $i' = (u_1, Ax \to A, v)$; if $u = \lambda$ or $u = \rhd$ and $v = Bv_1$ for some $B \in \Gamma$, then we replace i with the instruction $i' = (u, xB \to B, v_1)$; if $u = \rhd$ and $v = \lambda$, then we replace i with the set of instructions

$$I'(i) = \{ (\rhd, xA \to A, \lambda) \mid A \in \Gamma \} \cup \{(\rhd, x \to \lambda, \lhd)\};$$

if $u = \lambda$ and $v = \lhd$, then we replace i with the set of instructions

$$I'(i) = \{ (\lambda, Ax \to A, \lhd) \mid A \in \Gamma \} \cup \{(\rhd, x \to \lambda, \lhd)\};$$

and if $u = \lambda = v$, then we replace i with the set of instructions

$$I'(i) = \{ (\lambda, xA \to A, \lambda), (\lambda, Ax \to A, \lambda) \mid A \in \Gamma \} \cup \{(\rhd, x \to \lambda, \lhd)\}.$$

Then, for all $w, z \in \Gamma^*$, if $w \vdash_M^c z$ using instruction i, then $w \vdash_{M'}^c z$ by instruction i' or by one of the instructions of $I'(i)$, and conversely, if $w \vdash_{M'}^c z$ by instruction i' or by one of the instructions of $I'(i)$, then $w \vdash_M^c z$ by instruction i. □

Now let $M = (\Sigma, \Gamma, I)$ be an LCRA of type $\mathcal{R}_1$ that satisfies the properties of Lemma 4.3.25, let $R(M)$ be the corresponding string-rewriting system, and let $R(M)^{-1}$ denote the system

$$R(M)^{-1} = \{ (v \to u) \mid (u \to v) \in R(M) \}.$$

From $R(M)^{-1}$, we obtain a length-increasing context-sensitive grammar $G(M) = (\Gamma', \Sigma', S, R')$ that generates the language $L(G(M)) = \rhd \cdot L(M) \cdot \lhd$. Thus, the language $\rhd \cdot L(M) \cdot \lhd$ is a growing acyclic context-sensitive language (see, e.g., [187]). It is known from [23] that the class GACSL of *growing acyclic context-sensitive languages* is closed under the operations of removing left and right end-of-tape markers. Hence, the language $L(M)$ is growing acyclic context-sensitive, too. Conversely, if $G = (N, T, S, P)$ is a length-increasing context-sensitive grammar, then by taking

$$I(G) = \{ (u, x \to A, v) \mid (uAv \to uxv) \in P \} \cup \{ (\rhd, r \to \lambda, \lhd) \mid (S \to r) \in P \},$$

we obtain an LCRA $M(G) = (T, N \cup T, I(G))$ of type $\mathcal{R}_1$ such that $L(M(G)) = L(G) \cup \{\lambda\}$ holds. Thus, we have the following characterization.

Theorem 4.3.26 ([203]) $\mathcal{L}(\text{LCRA}[\mathcal{R}_1]) = \mathsf{GACSL}$.

It is known that the class GACSL properly contains the class CFL of context-free languages, and it is obviously contained in $\mathsf{ACSL} = \mathsf{GCSL}$. However, it is open whether or not this containment is strict.

Problem 4.3.27 *Is the class GACSL of growing acyclic context-sensitive languages a proper subclass of the growing context-sensitive languages?*

To continue with the study of the expressive capacity of the various types of LCRA, let $M = (\Sigma, \Gamma, I)$ be an LCRA of type $\mathcal{R}_2'$. Then, for each instruction $(u, x \to y, v) \in I$, we have $u \in \{\lambda, \rhd\}$, $v \in \{\lambda, \lhd\}$, $|x| \geq 1$, $|y| \leq 1$, and $g(x) > g(y)$ for a fixed weight function g. Hence, the corresponding string-rewriting system $R(M)$ can be split into four disjoint subsystems:

(a)	R_{bif}	$=$	$\{ (\rhd x \lhd \to \rhd y \lhd) \mid (\rhd, x \to y, \lhd) \in I \}$,	the *bifix rules* of $R(M)$,
(b)	R_{pre}	$=$	$\{ (\rhd x \to \rhd y) \mid (\rhd, x \to y, \lambda) \in I \}$,	the *prefix rules* of $R(M)$,
(c)	R_{suf}	$=$	$\{ (x \lhd \to y \lhd) \mid (\lambda, x \to y, \lhd) \in I \}$,	the *suffix rules* of $R(M)$,
(d)	R_{inf}	$=$	$\{ (x \to y) \mid (\lambda, x \to y, \lambda) \in I \}$,	the *infix rules* of $R(M)$.

Let $B(M) = \{ \alpha \in \Gamma^* \mid \rhd\alpha\lhd \in \text{dom}(R_{\text{bif}}) \text{ and } \rhd\alpha\lhd \Rightarrow_{R(M)}^* \rhd\lhd \} \cup \{\lambda\}$. As $R(M)$ is finite, so is the set $B(M)$. Let $R' = R_{\text{pre}} \cup R_{\text{suf}} \cup R_{\text{inf}}$. Then

$$L(M) = \{ w \in \Sigma^* \mid \rhd w \lhd \Rightarrow_{R(M)}^* \rhd \cdot \lhd \} = \{ w \in \Sigma^* \mid \exists \alpha \in B(M) : \rhd w \lhd \Rightarrow_{R'}^* \rhd\alpha\lhd \},$$

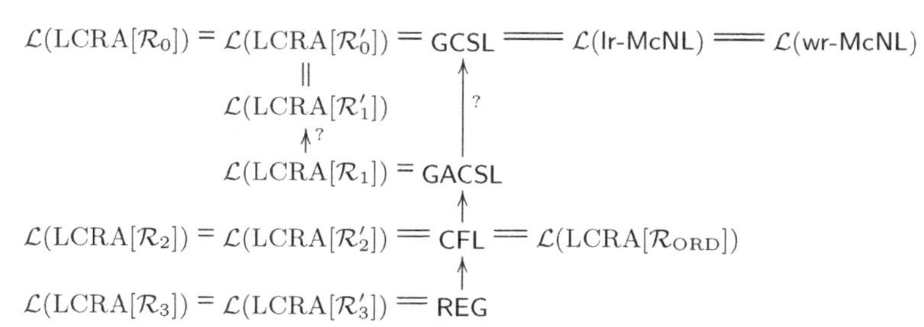

Figure 4.1: Hierarchy of language classes that are accepted by the various types of limited context restarting automata. Question marks indicate inclusions, not known to be proper.

that is, $\rhd \cdot L(M) \cdot \lhd = \nabla^*_{R'}(\rhd \cdot B(M) \cdot \lhd) \cap (\rhd \cdot \Sigma^* \cdot \lhd)$. Recall that $\nabla^*_{R'}(\alpha)$ denotes the *set of ancestors* of α mod R', and $\nabla^*_{R'}(B) = \bigcup_{\alpha \in B} \nabla^*_{R'}(\alpha)$ for any set B. Now we define a mixed rewriting system (see, e.g., [70]) $P(M) = P_{\text{pre}} \cup P_{\text{suf}} \cup P_{\text{inf}}$ by taking the *prefix-rewriting system*[1]

$$P_{\text{pre}} = \{\, (x \to y) \mid (\rhd x \to \rhd y) \in R_{\text{pre}} \,\},$$

the *suffix-rewriting system*[2]

$$P_{\text{suf}} = \{\, (x \to y) \mid (x\lhd \to y\lhd) \in R_{\text{suf}} \,\},$$

and the *string-rewriting system* $P_{\text{inf}} = R_{\text{inf}}$. Then $L(M) = \nabla^*_{P(M)}(B(M)) \cap \Sigma^*$. As $P(M)$ only contains *generalized monadic rules* (see, e.g., [139]), it follows that the set $\nabla^*_{P(M)}(B(M))$ is context-free, which in turn implies that $L(M)$ is a context-free language.

Conversely, if $L \subseteq \Sigma^*$ is a context-free language, then there exists a context-free grammar $G = (N, \Sigma, S, P)$ for $L \cap \Sigma^{\geq 2}$ such that, for each rule $(\ell \to r)$ of P, we have $|\ell| = 1$ and $|r| = 2$. We now obtain an LCRA $M(G) = (\Sigma, N \cup \Sigma, I)$ by taking

$$I = \{\, (\lambda, r \to \ell, \lambda) \mid (\ell \to r) \in P \,\} \cup \{\, (\rhd, a \to \lambda, \lhd) \mid a \in (\Sigma \cap L) \cup \{S\} \,\}.$$

Then $M(G)$ is of type $\mathcal{R}_2$, and $L(M(G)) \doteq L$. Thus, we have the following characterization.

Theorem 4.3.28 ([203]) $\mathcal{L}(\text{LCRA}[\mathcal{R}'_2]) = \mathcal{L}(\text{LCRA}[\mathcal{R}_2]) = \mathsf{CFL}$.

Finally, let $M = (\Sigma, \Gamma, I)$ be an LCRA of type $\mathcal{R}'_3$, that is, for all instructions $(u, x \to y, v) \in I$, we have $u \in \{\lambda, \rhd\}$, $v = \lhd$, $|x| \geq 1$, $|y| \leq 1$, and $g(x) > g(y)$ for a fixed weight function g. Hence, the corresponding string-rewriting system $R(M)$ can be split into two disjoint subsystems:

$$\begin{array}{llll} \text{(a)} & R_{\text{bif}} = \{\, (\rhd x\lhd \to \rhd y\lhd) \mid (\rhd, x \to y, \lhd) \in I \,\}, & \text{the } \textit{bifix rules} \text{ of } R(M), \\ \text{(b)} & R_{\text{suf}} = \{\, (x\lhd \to y\lhd) \mid (\lambda, x \to y, \lhd) \in I \,\}, & \text{the } \textit{suffix rules} \text{ of } R(M). \end{array}$$

As above, the set $B(M) = \{\, \alpha \in \Gamma^* \mid \rhd\alpha\lhd \in \text{dom}(R_{\text{bif}}) \text{ and } \rhd\alpha\lhd \Rightarrow^*_{R(M)} \rhd\lhd \,\} \cup \{\lambda\}$ is finite, and

$$L(M) = \{\, w \in \Sigma^* \mid \rhd w\lhd \Rightarrow^*_{R(M)} \rhd \cdot \lhd \,\} = \{\, w \in \Sigma^* \mid \exists \alpha \in B(M) : \rhd w\lhd \Rightarrow^*_{R_{\text{suf}}} \rhd\alpha\lhd \,\},$$

that is, $\rhd \cdot L(M) \cdot \lhd = \nabla^*_{R_{\text{suf}}}(\rhd \cdot B(M) \cdot \lhd) \cap (\rhd \cdot \Sigma^* \cdot \lhd)$. For the suffix-rewriting system $P(M) = \{\, (y \to x) \mid (x\lhd \to y\lhd) \in R_{\text{suf}} \,\}$, we obtain $L(M) = \Delta^*_{P(M)}(B(M)) \cap \Sigma^*$. As $B(M)$ is finite, and, hence, regular, it follows that the set of descendants $\Delta^*_{P(M)}(B(M))$ of this set with respect to the suffix rewriting system $P(M)$ is regular [22], which in turn implies that $L(M)$ is regular.

[1] The rules of a prefix-rewriting system can only be applied to the prefix of a word.

[2] The rules of a suffix-rewriting system can only be applied to the suffix of a word.

Conversely, if $L \subseteq \Sigma^*$ is a regular language, then there exists a regular grammar $G = (N, \Sigma, S, P)$ for $L \cap \Sigma^{\geq 2}$ such that, for each rule $(\ell \to r)$ of P, we have $\ell \in N$ and $r \in \Sigma \cdot N \cup \Sigma^2$. We now obtain an LCRA $M(G) = (\Sigma, N \cup \Sigma, I)$ by taking

$$I = \{ (\lambda, r \to \ell, \lhd) \mid (\ell \to r) \in P \} \cup \{ (\rhd, a \to \lambda, \lhd) \mid a \in (L \cap \Sigma) \cup \{S\} \}.$$

Then $M(G)$ is of type $\mathcal{R}_3$, and $L(M(G)) \doteq L$. Thus, we have the following characterization.

Theorem 4.3.29 ([203]) $\mathcal{L}(\text{LCRA}[\mathcal{R}_3']) = \mathcal{L}(\text{LCRA}[\mathcal{R}_3]) = \mathsf{REG}$.

Finally, we introduce still another type of limited context restarting automaton in order to describe swift-ORD-automata (see Section 2.3). We recall from Definition 2.3.94 that a stl-ORD-automaton $M = (\Sigma, \Gamma, \rhd, \lhd, \delta, >)$ is called *swift* if $\mathsf{MVR} \in \delta(a_1a_2a_3)$ for all $a_1 \in \Gamma \cup \{\rhd\}$ and all $a_2, a_3 \in \Gamma$. Thus, from a restarting configuration $\rhd w \lhd$, a swift-ORD-automaton M can move its window to any position on the tape before it executes a rewrite/restart, delete/restart, or accept step. Accordingly, it can be interpreted as a particular type of limited context restarting automaton.

Definition 4.3.30 ([201]) *A limited context restarting automaton $M = (\Sigma, \Gamma, I)$ is of* type $\mathcal{R}_{\text{ORD}}$ *if each instruction $(u, x \to y, v) \in I$ satisfies the restrictions $|u| = |x| = |v| = 1$ and $|y| \leq 1$. Observe that the weight function associated with M induces a partial ordering $>$ on Γ such that $x > y$ holds for each instruction $(u, x \to y, v) \in I$ for which $|y| = 1$. Thus, $\mathcal{R}_{\text{ORD}}$ is obtained from the type $\mathcal{R}_1'$ by restricting the left context, the right context, and the left-hand side of the rewrite instruction to be of length one. The class of limited context restarting automata of type $\mathcal{R}_{\text{ORD}}$ will be denoted as* $\text{LCRA}[\mathcal{R}_{\text{ORD}}]$.

The following results show that swift-ORD-automata and limited context restarting automata of type $\mathcal{R}_{\text{ORD}}$ correspond to each other.

Lemma 4.3.31 $\mathcal{L}(\text{LCRA}[\mathcal{R}_{\text{ORD}}]) \subseteq \mathcal{L}(\mathsf{swift\text{-}ORD})$.

Proof. Let $M = (\Sigma, \Gamma, I)$ be an LCRA of type $\mathcal{R}_{\text{ORD}}$. We define an ordering on Γ by taking $A > B$ if $g(A) > g(B)$, where $g : \Gamma^* \to \mathbb{N}$ is the weight function for M. We obtain the swift-ORD-automaton $M' = (\Sigma, \Gamma, \rhd, \lhd, \delta, >)$ by defining the transition relation δ as follows:

(1)	$\delta(abc)$	$\ni$	MVR	for all $a \in \Gamma \cup \{\rhd\}$ and $b, c \in \Gamma$,
(2)	$\delta(abc)$	$\ni$	y	if $(a, b \to y, c) \in I$,
(3)	$\delta(\rhd\lhd)$	$=$	Accept.	

Then $L(M') = \{ w \in \Sigma^* \mid w \vdash_M^{c^*} \lambda \} = L(M)$, which proves the above inclusion. □

In fact, we have the following characterization.

Theorem 4.3.32 ([201]) $\mathcal{L}(\text{LCRA}[\mathcal{R}_{\text{ORD}}]) = \mathcal{L}(\mathsf{swift\text{-}ORD})$.

Proof. Let $M = (\Sigma, \Gamma, \rhd, \lhd, \delta, >)$ be a swift-ORD. As shown in [201], Proposition 2, we may assume that there is a special auxiliary letter $\# \in \Gamma$ such that $\delta(\rhd\#\lhd) = \mathsf{Accept}$ is the only accept transition of M. Now we define an LCRA $S = (\Sigma, \Gamma, I)$ of type $\mathcal{R}_{\text{ORD}}$ by taking

$$I = \{ (a, b \to d, c) \mid d \in \delta(abc) \} \cup \{(\rhd, \# \to \lambda, \lhd)\}.$$

Then $L(S) = \{ w \in \Sigma^* \mid w \vdash_S^{c^*} \lambda \} \doteq L(M)$. Thus, we also have $\mathcal{L}(\mathsf{swift\text{-}ORD}) \subseteq \mathcal{L}(\text{LCRA}[\mathcal{R}_{\text{ORD}}])$, which, together with Lemma 4.3.31, yields the intended equality. □

Hence, we conclude the following from Theorem 2.3.95.

Corollary 4.3.33 ([201]) $\mathcal{L}(\text{LCRA}[\mathcal{R}_{\text{ORD}}]) = \mathsf{CFL}$.

Thus, the limited context restarting automata of type $\mathcal{R}_{\mathrm{ORD}}$ are just as expressive as those of type $\mathcal{R}'_2$. However, type $\mathcal{R}_{\mathrm{ORD}}$ is a restricted variant of type $\mathcal{R}'_1$ that is incomparable to type $\mathcal{R}'_2$. Indeed, an LCRA of type $\mathcal{R}_{\mathrm{ORD}}$ admits arbitrary left and right contexts of length one, while the only non-empty contexts that an LCRA of type $\mathcal{R}'_2$ admits are the sentinels $\rhd$ and $\lhd$. On the other hand, an LCRA of type $\mathcal{R}'_2$ may rewrite factors of arbitrary positive length, while an LCRA of type $\mathcal{R}_{\mathrm{ORD}}$ can rewrite factors of length one only. The results on the various types of LCRA are summarized in the diagram in Figure 4.1.

As defined above, an LCRA $M = (\Sigma, \Gamma, I)$ is a nondeterministic device. A word $w \in \Sigma^*$ belongs to the language $L(M)$ accepted by M if and only if there exists a computation of M that transforms the initial configuration $\rhd w \lhd$ into the accepting configuration $\rhd \cdot \lhd$. In general, many different computations of M start from the configuration with tape contents $\rhd w \lhd$, and only some of them will lead to the tape contents $\rhd \cdot \lhd$. As this phenomenon complicates the solution of the membership problem for $L(M)$, one is interested in limited context restarting automata for which all computations from $\rhd w \lhd$ lead to $\rhd \cdot \lhd$, if $w \in L(M)$. The reduction relation $\vdash^c_M$ corresponds to the single-step reduction relation $\Rightarrow_{R(M)}$ that is induced by the string-rewriting system $R(M)$ on the set of bordered words $\rhd \cdot \Gamma^* \cdot \lhd$. This leads to the study of LCRAs M for which the string-rewriting system $R(M)$ is *confluent on the congruence class* $[\rhd \cdot \lhd]_{R(M)}$.

Indeed, in [256], Peter Černo extends his learning algorithm to limited context restarting automata that are λ-confluent, which means that the corresponding string-rewriting system is confluent on the congruence class of the empty word. A word w belongs to the language $L(M)$ accepted by a λ-confluent LCRA if and only if the left-most reduction of $\rhd w \lhd$ ends with $\rhd \cdot \lhd$. It follows that the membership problem for the language $L(M)$ is decidable in linear time. Unfortunately, it is undecidable, in general, whether a finite string-rewriting system is confluent on a given congruence class, even if the given finite system only contains length-reducing rules [191]. In fact, even the following stronger negative result holds.

Proposition 4.3.34 ([159, 206]) *It is undecidable, in general, whether a given context clearing restarting automaton is λ-confluent.*

Therefore, in [203], types of LCRA are considered that satisfy an even stronger restriction than confluence on a particular congruence class.

Definition 4.3.35 *A limited context restarting automaton $M = (\Sigma, \Gamma, I)$ is called* confluent *if the corresponding string-rewriting system $R(M) = \{ (uxv \to uyv) \mid (u, x \to y, v) \in I \}$ is confluent.*

As for each LCRA M, the resulting string-rewriting system $R(M)$ is finite and terminating, confluence is a decidable property of limited context restarting automata (see, e.g., [19]). We illustrate the above definition with a simple example.

Example 4.3.36 *Let $\Sigma = \{a\}$, let $\Gamma = \{a, F\}$, and let*

$$I = \{(\rhd, aaaa \to aaF, \lambda), (\lambda, Faa \to aF, \lambda), (\lambda, F \to \lambda, \lhd), (\rhd, aa \to \lambda, \lhd), (\rhd, a \to \lambda, \lhd)\}.$$

Then $M = (\Sigma, \Gamma, I)$ is an LCRA of type $\mathcal{R}_0$ that accepts the language $L_{\mathrm{expo}} = \{ a^{2^n} \mid n \geq 0 \}$, and it is easily checked that M is confluent. ■

We use the prefix con- to denote types of LCRA that are confluent. Furthermore, for each type $\mathcal{R} \in \{ \mathcal{R}'_i, \mathcal{R}_i \mid i \in \{0, 1, 2, 3\} \}$, LCRA[con-$\mathcal{R}$] is used to denote the class of LCRA of type $\mathcal{R}$ that are confluent.

In the following, we summarize the results from [203] on the expressive capacity of the various types of LCRA that are confluent. As above, we proceed from the most general type to the most restricted one.

If $M = (\Sigma, \Gamma, I)$ is a confluent LCRA of type $\mathcal{R}'_0$, then $S(M) = R(M) \cup \{\rhd\lhd \to Y\}$ is a finite weight-reducing string-rewriting system that is confluent, and $L(M)$ is simply the McNaughton language that is specified by $(S(M), \rhd, \lhd, Y)$. Thus, $L(M)$ is a *Church-Rosser language* by Theorem 2.2.50(b). On the other hand, if $L \subseteq \Sigma^*$ is a Church-Rosser language, then it is accepted by a length-reducing deterministic two-pushdown automaton by Theorem 1.2.19. Following the proof of Theorem 4.3.23, a confluent LCRA of type $\mathcal{R}_0$ can be constructed for L. Hence, we obtain the following characterization.

Theorem 4.3.37 ([203]) $\mathcal{L}(\text{LCRA}[\text{con-}\mathcal{R}_0]) = \mathcal{L}(\text{LCRA}[\text{con-}\mathcal{R}_0']) = \mathsf{CRL}$.

In [267], Jens Woinowski introduced a normal form for presentations of Church-Rosser languages, called *context-splittable Church-Rosser language systems.* Such a presentation is of the form $(S, \rhd, \lhd, Y)$, where S is a finite, weight-reducing, and confluent string-rewriting system that consists of rules of the form $(uxv \to uyv)$, where $u, v \in \Gamma^*$, $x \in \Gamma^+$, and $|y| \leq 1$, and rules of the form $(\rhd x \lhd \to Y)$, where $x \in \Gamma^+$. As each Church-Rosser language admits a presentation of this form [267], and as a presentation of this form can immediately be translated into a confluent LCRA of type $\mathcal{R}_1'$, this gives the following characterization.

Theorem 4.3.38 ([203]) $\mathcal{L}(\text{LCRA}[\text{con-}\mathcal{R}_1']) = \mathsf{CRL}$.

For the class of languages that are accepted by confluent LCRA of type $\mathcal{R}_1$, no characterization of a similar form is currently known. On the one hand, these automata can only accept (certain) Church-Rosser languages, and hence, they do not accept all context-free languages. On the other hand, it is shown in [202] that the language $L_{\text{expo5}} = \{ a^{5^n} \mid n \geq 0 \}$ is accepted by a confluent LCRA of type $\mathcal{R}_1$. As this language is not context-free, the following incomparability result follows.

Corollary 4.3.39 ([202]) *The language class* $\mathcal{L}(\text{LCRA}[\text{con-}\mathcal{R}_1])$ *is incomparable to the class CFL with respect to inclusion.*

Concerning confluent LCRA of type $\mathcal{R}_1$, the following question remains open.

Problem 4.3.40 *Do confluent limited context restarting automata of type $\mathcal{R}_1$ accept all Church-Rosser languages? In fact, it is even open whether they accept at least all deterministic context-free languages.*

For confluent LCRA of type $\mathcal{R}_2'$, the class of languages accepted can be characterized as a specific class of McNaughton languages [203]. As a consequence of this characterization, the following sequence of inclusions follows:

$$\mathsf{REG} \subsetneq \mathcal{L}(\text{LCRA}[\text{con-}\mathcal{R}_2]) \subseteq \mathcal{L}(\text{LCRA}[\text{con-}\mathcal{R}_2']) \subsetneq \mathsf{DCFL}.$$

However, it remains open whether confluent LCRAs of type $\mathcal{R}_2$ are equivalent to those of type $\mathcal{R}_2'$.

Problem 4.3.41 *Is the inclusion of* $\mathcal{L}(\text{LCRA}[\text{con-}\mathcal{R}_2])$ *in* $\mathcal{L}(\text{LCRA}[\text{con-}\mathcal{R}_2'])$ *a proper inclusion?*

Finally, we turn to the confluent LCRAs of types $\mathcal{R}_3'$ and $\mathcal{R}_3$. If M is a confluent LCRA of type $\mathcal{R}_3'$, then $L(M)$ is a regular language by Theorem 4.3.29. Conversely, if $L \subseteq \Sigma^*$ is a regular language, then there exists a DFA $A = (Q, \Sigma, q_0, \delta, F)$ that accepts the language L^R. We define an LCRA $M = (\Sigma, Q \cup \Sigma, I)$ as follows, where $a, b \in \Sigma$ and $q, q' \in Q$:

$$\begin{array}{rcl} I & = & \{ (\rhd, ab \to q, \lambda) \mid \delta(q_0, ab) = q \} \cup \{ (\rhd, qa \to q', \lambda) \mid \delta(q, a) = q' \} \cup \\ & & \{ (\rhd, q \to \lambda, \lhd) \mid q \in F \} \cup \{ (\rhd, a \to \lambda, \lhd) \mid a \in \Sigma \cap L^R \}. \end{array}$$

It is easily seen that $L(M) \doteq L^R$, and that the string-rewriting system $R(M)$ is confluent. By taking $M' = (\Sigma, Q \cup \Sigma, I')$, where

$$I' = \{ (\lambda, u^R \to v^R, \lhd) \mid (\rhd, u \to v, \lambda) \in I \} \cup \{ (\rhd, u^R \to v^R, \lhd) \mid (\rhd, u \to v, \lhd) \in I \},$$

we obtain a confluent LCRA of type $\mathcal{R}_3$ that accepts the language L. Thus, we have the following characterization.

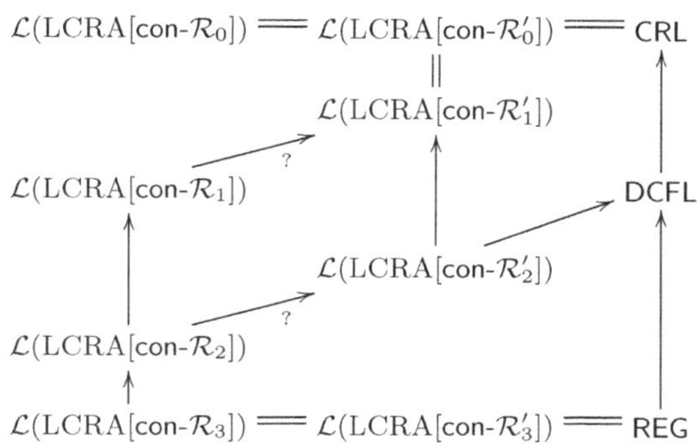

Figure 4.2: Hierarchy of language classes that are accepted by the various types of confluent limited context restarting automata. Question marks indicate inclusions, not known to be proper.

Theorem 4.3.42 ([203]) $\mathcal{L}(\text{LCRA}[\text{con-}\mathcal{R}_3]) = \mathcal{L}(\text{LCRA}[\text{con-}\mathcal{R}'_3]) = \mathsf{REG}$.

The diagram in Figure 4.2 summarizes the above results on confluent limited context restarting automata.

In contrast to the situation for λ-confluence, confluence is decidable for a limited context restarting automaton M, as the corresponding string-rewriting system $R(M)$ is finite and weight-reducing. In order to carry the learning algorithm LA_{SCRA} over to confluent types of limited context restarting automata, the function Assumptions must be extended to deliver always a set of instructions for which the corresponding string-rewriting system is confluent. Essentially, this amounts to incorporating a *completion procedure* into this function. Here a completion procedure is a process that, given a finite string-rewriting system R on some alphabet Σ and a weight function on Σ^*, tries to compute a finite confluent string-rewriting system $\hat{R}$ on Σ that is compatible with the given weight function and that is equivalent to R (see, e.g., [19]). Unfortunately, this process may not terminate, as there may not exist a finite confluent system with all these properties, or it may fail altogether, as there may not even exist an infinite system with the required properties.

To complete this section, we mention in passing that, in [207], some further extensions of limited context restarting automata have been introduced and studied. In order to get some additional control over the derivation process, various forms of regulated rewriting have been studied in formal language theory (see, e.g., [40]). In [207], two of these control mechanisms are carried over to limited context restarting automata. First, *regulated limited context restarting automata* are studied, for which the sequence of reductions is governed by a given regular language of labels. To each rewrite rule, a letter from a new alphabet is attached as a label, and it is then required that the sequence of labels that corresponds to a sequence of rule applications is an element of a given control language.

Furthermore, *random context limited context restarting automata* are considered, where a set of permitting letters and a set of forbidding letters are associated with each rewrite rule. Now a rule can be applied to a word u only if all permitting letters of that rule occur in u and none of the forbidding letters occurs in u. In both cases, the LCRAs of types $\mathcal{R}_3$ and $\mathcal{R}'_3$ still characterize the regular languages, but also, in both cases, already the LCRAs of type $\mathcal{R}_2$ are sufficiently expressive to accept languages that are beyond the growing context-sensitive languages. However, many questions regarding the expressive capacity of regulated and random context LCRAs are still open.

Appendix A

List of Open Problems

Chapter 2: The Restarting Automaton and Its Parameters

Section 2.1: Restricting the Operations

Problem 2.1.17

(a) *Is the language class* $\mathcal{L}((\mathsf{s})\mathsf{RWW})$ *closed under the operation of reversal, that is, for* $L \in \mathcal{L}((\mathsf{s})\mathsf{RWW})$, *is the language* L^R *necessarily in* $\mathcal{L}((\mathsf{s})\mathsf{RWW})$, *too?*

(b) *Are the language classes* $\mathcal{L}((\mathsf{s})\mathsf{RWW})$ *and* $\mathcal{L}((\mathsf{s})\mathsf{RRWW})$ *closed under the operations of intersection and/or complementation?*

Problem 2.1.19 *Is* $\mathcal{L}(\mathsf{RWW}) \subseteq \mathcal{L}(\mathsf{RRWW})$ *a proper inclusion, or do these two language classes coincide?*

Problem 2.1.20 *Is the language class* $\mathcal{L}(\mathsf{RRW})$ *contained in the class* $\mathcal{L}(\mathsf{RWW})$*?*

Problem 2.1.30

(a) *For* $c \in \mathbb{N}_+$, *is it decidable whether an RRWW-automaton is weakly c-monotone?*

(b) *Is it decidable whether an RRWW-automaton is weakly monotone?*

Problem 2.1.36

(a) *Is each growing context-sensitive language accepted by a deterministic (s)RLWW-automaton, that is, is the class of growing context-sensitive language GCSL contained in* $\mathcal{L}(\mathsf{det}\text{-}(\mathsf{s})\mathsf{RLWW})$*? In fact, it is not even known whether each context-free language is accepted by a deterministic (s)RLWW-automaton.*

(b) *Is the inclusion of* $\mathcal{L}(\mathsf{det}\text{-}\mathsf{RLWW})$ *in* $\mathcal{L}(\mathsf{det}\text{-}\mathsf{sRLWW})$ *a proper one?*

Section 2.2: Restricting the Number of Auxiliary Letters

Problem 2.2.17 *Is the class* $\mathcal{L}(\mathsf{mon}\text{-}\mathsf{R})$ *of languages that are accepted by monotone R-automata contained in the class* $\mathcal{L}(\mathsf{det}\text{-}\mathsf{sRLWW})$ *of languages that are accepted by deterministic shrinking RLWW-automata?*

Problem 2.2.27 *For all* $\mathsf{X}, \mathsf{Y} \in \{\mathsf{R}, \mathsf{RR}, \mathsf{RW}, \mathsf{RRW}, \mathsf{sRW}, \mathsf{sRRW}\}$, *if type* X *is a restriction of type* Y, *then* $\mathcal{L}(\mathsf{det}\text{-}\mathsf{left}\text{-}\mathsf{mon}\text{-}\mathsf{X}) \subseteq \mathcal{L}(\mathsf{det}\text{-}\mathsf{left}\text{-}\mathsf{mon}\text{-}\mathsf{Y})$. *Which of these inclusions are proper? And how do the resulting language classes relate to the classes in the diagram in Figure 2.8?*

Problem 2.2.46 *Is the inclusion of* $\mathcal{L}(\Delta\text{-}\mathsf{CRA})$ *in* $\mathcal{L}(\Delta^*\text{-}\mathsf{CRA})$ *a proper one?*

F. Otto, *Restarting Automata*, Theory and Applications of Computability,
https://doi.org/10.1007/978-3-031-70094-1

Problem 2.2.53 *Is GCSL contained in the class of languages $\mathcal{L}(\Delta^*\text{-}\mathsf{CRA})$ that are accepted by Δ^*-clearing restarting automata, or is there a growing context-sensitive language that is not accepted by any Δ^*-CRA?*

Problem 2.2.69

(a) *Is there an infinite hierarchy with respect to the number of auxiliary letters in the tape alphabet of an RLWW-automaton? Or is it possible to show that a single auxiliary letter is always sufficient by using appropriate encodings?*

(b) *Is there an infinite hierarchy with respect to the number of occurrences of auxiliary letters?*

Problem 2.2.70 *Is $\mathcal{L}(\mathsf{aux}(1,1)\text{-}\mathsf{RLWW})$ a proper subclass of $\mathcal{L}(\mathsf{aux}(2,1)\text{-}\mathsf{RLWW})$?*

Problem 2.2.71 *Is there a constant d such that each context-free language is accepted by a nondeterministic RLWW-automaton that uses at most d occurrences of auxiliary letters?*

Problem 2.2.72 *In Corollary 2.2.58, we saw that $\mathcal{L}(\mathsf{aux}(1,1)\text{-}\mathsf{det}\text{-}\mathsf{RRWW})$ is a proper subclass of $\mathcal{L}(\mathsf{aux}(1,1)\text{-}\mathsf{det}\text{-}\mathsf{RLWW})$. However, we do not know whether $\mathcal{L}(\mathsf{aux}(1,1)\text{-}\mathsf{det}\text{-}\mathsf{RWW})$ is a proper subclass of $\mathcal{L}(\mathsf{aux}(1,1)\text{-}\mathsf{det}\text{-}\mathsf{RRWW})$.*

Section 2.3: Restricting the Size of the Read/Write Window

Problem 2.3.18 *Is the inclusion $\mathcal{L}(\mathsf{mon}\text{-}\mathsf{R(R)W}(2)) \subseteq \mathcal{L}(\mathsf{mon}\text{-}\mathsf{sR(R)W}(2))$ a proper one?*

Problem 2.3.25 *Are the inclusions $\mathcal{L}(\mathsf{det}\text{-}\mathsf{mon}\text{-}\mathsf{R}(2)) \subseteq \mathcal{L}(\mathsf{mon}\text{-}\mathsf{R}(2))$ and $\mathcal{L}(\mathsf{det}\text{-}\mathsf{mon}\text{-}\mathsf{RR}(2)) \subseteq \mathcal{L}(\mathsf{mon}\text{-}\mathsf{RR}(2))$ proper inclusions?*

Problem 2.3.32 *What is the exact relationship between those language classes that are defined by the various types of restarting automata without auxiliary letters that have window size $k = 3$ or $k = 4$?*

Problem 2.3.40 *For $k \geq 2$, is $\mathcal{L}(\mathsf{det}\text{-}\mathsf{RWW}(k))$ a proper subclass of $\mathcal{L}(\mathsf{det}\text{-}\mathsf{RRWW}(k))$, or are deterministic RWW-automata of window size k as expressive as deterministic RRWW-automata of window size k?*

Problem 2.3.48

(a) *Is there an integer $k \geq 3$ such that*

$$\mathcal{L}(\mathsf{det}\text{-}\mathsf{RWW}(k)) = \mathcal{L}(\mathsf{det}\text{-}\mathsf{RWW}) = \mathsf{CRL},$$

or do the language classes $(\mathcal{L}(\mathsf{det}\text{-}\mathsf{RWW}(k)))_{k\geq 3}$ (and $(\mathcal{L}(\mathsf{det}\text{-}\mathsf{RRWW}(k)))_{k\geq 3}$) yield an infinite strictly ascending hierarchy within the class CRL of Church-Rosser languages?

(b) *For which values of $k \geq 3$ do the language classes $\mathcal{L}(\mathsf{det}\text{-}\mathsf{RWW}(k))$ and $\mathcal{L}(\mathsf{det}\text{-}\mathsf{RRWW}(k))$ coincide? Recall from Theorem 2.3.39 that Natalie Schluter has only shown that, for all $k \geq 2$, $\mathcal{L}(\mathsf{det}\text{-}\mathsf{RRWW}(k)) \subseteq \mathcal{L}(\mathsf{det}\text{-}\mathsf{RWW}(2k-2))$.*

Problem 2.3.58 *For $k \in \{2, 3, \ldots, 8\}$, what is the expressive capacity of sRWW-automata of window size k? Are these automata really less expressive than finite-change automata?*

Problem 2.3.73 *Can the emptiness problem for ORWW-automata be solved in a more efficient way than outlined in the proof of Theorem 2.3.72?*

Problem 2.3.76 *Can the finiteness problem for ORWW-automata be solved in a more efficient way than outlined in the proof of Theorem 2.3.75?*

Problem 2.3.92 *Is the language $L_{\mathrm{lin}} = \{\, a^n b^n, a^n b^{2n} \mid n \geq 1 \,\}$ accepted by any det-ORD-automaton?*

Problem 2.3.93 *Does there exist a language L that is accepted by an sRWW-automaton (or a finite-change automaton) but that is not accepted by any ORD-automaton?*

Problem 2.3.96 *Is there any non-context-free language that is accepted by a stl-ORD-automaton? In fact, is the stl-ORD-automaton at all less expressive than the ORD-automaton with states?*

Problem 2.3.97 *What is the expressive capacity of stateless ORRD-automata?*

Problem 2.3.100

(a) *Is the inclusion of* $\mathcal{L}(\mathsf{sRWW}(1))$ *in* $\mathcal{L}(\mathsf{ORWW})$ *proper?*

(b) *Is the inclusion of* $\mathcal{L}(\mathsf{ORD})$ *in* $\mathcal{L}(\mathsf{sRWW}(2))$ *proper?*

(c) *Is the class GCSL contained in* $\mathcal{L}(\mathsf{ORD})$*?*

Problem 2.3.103 *Does there exist a context-free language that is not accepted by any monotone sRRWW(1)-automaton?*

Section 2.4: Stateless Restarting Automata

Problem 2.4.23 *What is the smallest integer* k *such that the language class* $\mathcal{L}(\mathsf{stl\text{-}det\text{-}R}(k))$ *contains a non-context-free language? We know that* $3 \leq k \leq 9$ *holds, but it is open whether already the class* $\mathcal{L}(\mathsf{stl\text{-}det\text{-}R}(3))$ *contains a non-context-free language.*

Problem 2.4.42 *Are the language classes* $\mathcal{L}(\mathsf{stl\text{-}det\text{-}sR(R)W})$ *closed under inverse morphisms?*

Section 2.5: Increasing the Number of Rewrites Per Cycle

Problem 2.5.4 *Are* $(c+1)$*-rewriting RWW- or RRWW-automata more expressive than c-rewriting RWW- or RRWW-automata?*

Problem 2.5.38 *For the various types of nondeterministic restarting automata with auxiliary letters, does the degree* j *of monotonicity yield infinite strictly ascending hierarchies of language classes?*

Problem 2.5.63 *Is there an upper bound for the degree of constrainability for context-free languages that occur as characteristic languages of FsRRWW-automata? Are there any context-free languages in the set* $\mathcal{L}_{\mathrm{C}}(j+1, \mathsf{FsRRWW}) \smallsetminus \mathcal{L}_{\mathrm{C}}(j, \mathsf{FsRRWW})$ *for values of* $j \geq 2$*? Are there at all context-free languages that are not accepted as characteristic languages by any FsRRWW-automata?*

Problem 2.5.71 *For each* $t \geq 2$*, is there a language that is accepted by a* t-$\mathsf{cut}(3)$-RR*-automaton, but not by any* t-$\mathsf{cut}(2)$-RR*-automaton? In general, for each* $t \geq 2$ *and each* $j \geq 2$*, is there a language that is accepted by a* t-$\mathsf{cut}(j+1)$-RR*-automaton, but not by any* t-$\mathsf{cut}(j)$-RR*-automaton?*

Problem 2.5.100 *Is the class CFL of context-free languages included in the class* $\mathcal{L}(\mathsf{det\text{-}2\text{-}RR})$*, that is, is every context-free language accepted by some det-2-RR-automaton?*

Problem 2.5.103 *Are the language classes* $\mathcal{L}(\mathsf{det\text{-}2\text{-}RR}(1))$ *and* $\mathcal{L}(\mathsf{det\text{-}2\text{-}RR}(2))$ *not closed under reversal, either?*

Problem 2.5.104 *Is any of the language classes* $\mathcal{L}(\mathsf{det\text{-}2\text{-}RR}(k))$*,* $k \geq 1$*, or* $\mathcal{L}(\mathsf{det\text{-}2\text{-}RR})$ *closed under product and/or Kleene star?*

Section 2.6: Relating Auxiliary Letters To Input Letters

Problem 2.6.24 *Is there a language that is not the proper language of any lexicalized RRWW-automata with a constant degree of word-expansion, but that is the proper language of a lexicalized RRWW-automaton for which the degree of word-expansion is bounded from above by a slowly growing sublinear function?*

Problem 2.6.34 *Is the class CFL of context-free languages contained in the class of proper languages* $\bigcup_{i\geq 0, j>0} \mathcal{L}_{\mathrm{P}}(\mathsf{W}(i)\text{-}j\text{-}\mathsf{r\text{-}lex\text{-}RRWW})$*?*

Problem 2.6.54 *Is it possible to establish a closer correspondence between the number of rewrites per cycle and the degree of monotonicity for (h)RLWW-automata?*

Chapter 3: Descriptional Complexity

Section 3.1: On R(1)- and Deterministic RR(1)-Automata

Problem 3.1.20

(a) *What is the trade-off for turning a monotone sRWW(1)-automaton or a det-sR(R)WW(1)-automaton into an equivalent NFA or DFA?*

(b) *What is the trade-off for turning a monotone sRWW(1)-automaton or a det-sR(R)WW(1)-automaton into an equivalent R(1)- or det-RR(1)-automaton?*

Section 3.2: On Stateless Ordered Restarting Automata

Problem 3.2.18 *What is the real trade-off for converting an R(1)-automaton into an equivalent stl-ORWW- or stl-det-ORWW-automaton? Can the upper bound of $\mathcal{O}(2^n)$ be improved, or are there matching lower bounds for these conversions?*

Problem 3.2.20 *What is the real trade-off for converting a det-RR(1)-automaton into an equivalent stl-ORWW- or stl-det-ORWW-automaton? How good is the upper bound in Proposition 3.2.19? Is there a better upper bound, or is there a matching lower bound?*

Problem 3.2.24 *Is there a better than double exponential upper bound for the conversion of a stl-ORWW-automaton into an equivalent stl-det-ORWW-automaton, or is there a matching double exponential lower bound?*

Problem 3.2.51 *Is there a better upper bound for the conversion of a stl-det-ORRWW-automaton into an equivalent reversible stl-det-ORRWW-automaton than the one given in Corollary 3.2.50 or is there a matching lower bound?*

Problem 3.2.56 *What is the descriptional complexity of stateless det-ORD-automata? Is there a recursive bound for the size increase of the conversion of a stl-det-ORD-automaton that accepts a regular language into a stl-det-ORWW-automaton for the same language?*

Section 3.3: Reducing the Window Size of R(R)(W)-Automata

Problem 3.3.12 *What is the trade-off for converting a (deterministic)* R(R)*-automaton of window size $k \in \{3, 4\}$ into an equivalent automaton of the same type that has window size $k - 1$? Is it still non-recursive? In addition, for the case of stateless (deterministic)* R(R)*-automata, what is the trade-off between window size 5 and window size 4?*

Problem 3.3.14 *Determine the exact trade-off for converting a deterministic* R(R)(W)*-automaton of window size two into an equivalent automaton of the same type of window size one!*

Problem 3.3.15 *Determine the trade-off between nondeterministic* R(R)(W)*-automata of window size two and window size one!*

Problem 3.3.17 *For all $k \geq 2$, what is the trade-off for turning a deterministic* R(R)WW*-automaton of window size $k + 1$ into an equivalent deterministic* R(R)WW*-automaton of window size k?*

Problem 3.3.18 *For all $k \geq 2$, determine the exact trade-off for converting a monotone (deterministic)* R(R)WW*-automaton of window size $k+1$ into an equivalent automaton of the same type that has window size k!*

Section 3.4: On Monotone and Deterministic R(R)WW-Automata

Problem 3.4.14 *Does Corollary 3.4.12 extend to monotone* R(R)W- *and* R(R)*-automata? That is, is the trade-off for the conversion of a monotone* R(R)W- *or* R(R)*-automaton into an equivalent deterministic* R(R)W-, R(R)-, *or (stateless) deterministic* ORD*-automaton non-recursive, too?*

Chapter 4: Learnability for Restarting Automata

Section 4.1: Learning Strictly Locally Testable Restarting Automata

Problem 4.1.10 *Does the degree j of strict testability induce an infinite strictly ascending hierarchy of language classes for SLT-RRWW-automata?*

Section 4.2: Learning Single k-Reversible Restarting Automata

Problem 4.2.9 *For $k \geq 0$, are single k-reversible RRW-automata (RR-automata) strictly less expressive than k-reversible RRW-automata (RR-automata) that are not single?*

Problem 4.2.12 *For $k \geq 0$, is $\mathcal{L}(\mathsf{S}\text{-}k\text{-}\mathsf{rev}\text{-}\mathsf{RRWW})$ a proper subclass of $\mathcal{L}(\mathsf{S}\text{-}(k+1)\text{-}\mathsf{rev}\text{-}\mathsf{RRWW})$?*

Section 4.3: Learning Analysis by Reduction from an Informant

Problem 4.3.18 *For $k \geq 2$, is the problem of deciding whether there exists a k-CRA that is consistent with given finite sets S^+ and S^- of positive and negative samples and that has maximal width of instructions bounded by a given constant $l \geq 4k + 4$ in NP?*

Problem 4.3.27 *Is the class GACSL of growing acyclic context-sensitive languages a proper subclass of the growing context-sensitive languages?*

Problem 4.3.40 *Do confluent limited context restarting automata of type $\mathcal{R}_1$ accept all Church-Rosser languages? In fact, it is even open whether they accept at least all deterministic context-free languages.*

Problem 4.3.41 *Is the inclusion of* $\mathcal{L}(\text{con-LCRA}[\mathcal{R}_2])$ *in* $\mathcal{L}(\text{con-LCRA}[\mathcal{R}_2'])$ *a proper inclusion?*

Appendix B

List of Example Languages

Here we present a list of example languages that we use throughout the monograph and their main properties, together with the corresponding references.

(1) The *language of multiple agreements* $L_{\text{mul}} = \{ a^n b^n c^n \mid n \geq 0 \} \in \mathsf{CSL}$ (Example 1.2.8) is not context-free (see the remark following Corollary 1.2.25).

(2) $L_{\text{exp}} = \{ a^{2^n} \mid n \geq 0 \} \in \mathsf{GCSL}$ (Example 1.2.13). Actually, $L_{\text{exp}} \in \mathsf{CRL}$ by Example 1.2.16 and Theorem 1.2.19. In addition, $L_{\text{exp}} \in \mathcal{L}(\mathsf{aux}(1,1)\text{-}\mathsf{det}\text{-}\mathsf{RWW}) \smallsetminus \mathcal{L}(\mathsf{RLW})$ by Proposition 2.2.56. Finally, $L_{\text{exp}} \notin \mathcal{L}_{\text{P}}(\mathsf{lex}\text{-}\mathsf{RRWW})$ by Proposition 2.6.7, and $L_{\text{exp}} \notin \mathcal{L}_{\text{hP}}(\text{hRLWW})$ by Proposition 2.6.36.

(3) The *Gladkij language* $L_{\text{Glad}} = \{ wcw^Rcw \mid w \in \{a,b\}^* \notin \mathsf{GCSL}$ (see the remark following Theorem 1.2.17).

(4) The *copy language* $L_{\text{copy}} = \{ ww \mid w \in \{a,b\}^* \} \notin \mathsf{GCSL}$ (see the remark following Theorem 1.2.17).

(5) The *marked copy language* $L'_{\text{copy}} = \{ wcw \mid w \in \{a,b\}^* \} \notin \mathsf{GCSL}$ (see the remark following Theorem 1.2.17), but $L'_{\text{copy}} \in \mathcal{L}(\mathsf{RWW})$ by Example 2.1.9 and $L'_{\text{copy}} \in \mathcal{L}(\mathsf{det}\text{-}\mathsf{RLWW}) \smallsetminus \mathcal{L}(\mathsf{sRLW})$ by Lemma 2.2.10.

(6) An extension of the marked copy language

$$\hat{L}'_{\text{copy}} = \{ w\#u \mid w,u \in \{a,b\}^*, |w|, |u| \geq 2, \text{ and } u \text{ is a scattered subword of } w \}.$$

Then $\hat{L}'_{\text{copy}} \in \mathcal{L}(\mathsf{ORWW}) \smallsetminus \mathsf{GCSL}$ by Lemma 2.3.68.

(7) The *language of palindromes of even length* $L_{\text{pal}} = \{ ww^R \mid w \in \{a,b\}^* \} \in \mathsf{CFL}$ (Example 1.2.23), but $L_{\text{pal}} \notin \mathsf{CRL}$ (see the remark following Theorem 1.2.19). In fact, $L_{\text{pal}} \in \mathsf{LIN}$ by Example 1.2.50.

(8) The *language of cross-serial dependencies* $L_{\text{cd}} = \{ a^m b^n a^m b^n \mid m,n \geq 0 \}$ is not context-free (see the remark following Corollary 1.2.25).

(9) $L = \{ ca^nb^n, da^{2n}b^n \mid n \geq 0 \} \in \mathsf{DCFL}$ (see the remark following Definition 1.2.41), but $L \notin \mathcal{L}(\mathsf{stl}\text{-}\mathsf{sRW})$ by Lemma 2.4.7. Also $L \notin \mathcal{L}(\mathsf{stl}\text{-}\mathsf{sRRW})$ by Lemma 2.4.27.

(10) $L^R = \{ b^na^nc, b^na^{2n}d \mid n \geq 0 \} \in \mathsf{CFL} \smallsetminus \mathsf{DCFL}$ (see the remark following Definition 1.2.41). However, $L^R \in \mathsf{LRR}$ (see the remark following Definition 1.2.45). In addition, $L^R \in \mathsf{LIN}$ by Example 1.2.51. Also $L^R \in \mathcal{L}(\mathsf{mon}\text{-}\mathsf{RR}) \cap \mathcal{L}(\mathsf{det}\text{-}\mathsf{sRWW})$ by Example 1.9.2 and Example 1.9.9. By Lemma 2.2.1, $L^R \in \mathcal{L}(\mathsf{mon}\text{-}\mathsf{RR}) \smallsetminus \mathcal{L}(\mathsf{sRW})$ and by Lemma 2.2.2, $L^R \in \mathcal{L}(\mathsf{det}\text{-}\mathsf{mon}\text{-}\mathsf{RL}) \smallsetminus \mathcal{L}(\mathsf{det}\text{-}\mathsf{sRRW})$.

F. Otto, *Restarting Automata*, Theory and Applications of Computability,
https://doi.org/10.1007/978-3-031-70094-1

(11) $L = \{ a^m b^{2m} a^n b^n, a^m b^m a^{n+k} b^n \mid k, m, n \geq 1 \} \in \mathsf{CFL}$ is not an LRR-language (see the remark following Corollary 1.2.46).

(12) $L_2 = \{ a^n b^n \mid n \geq 0 \} \cup \{ a^n b^m \mid m > 2n \geq 0 \} \in \mathsf{CRL} \smallsetminus \mathcal{L}(\mathsf{sRRW})$ by Lemma 2.2.3.

(13) $L_3 = \{ a^n b^n, a^n c b^n \mid n \geq 0\} \cup \{ a^n b^m, a^n d b^m \mid m > 2n \geq 0 \} \in \mathcal{L}(\mathsf{mon\text{-}RW}) \smallsetminus \mathcal{L}(\mathsf{RR})$ by Lemma 2.2.4.

(14) $L_4 = \{ c a^n b^n, e a^n b^n \mid n \geq 0 \} \cup \{ d a^n b^m, e a^n b^m \mid m > 2n \geq 0 \} \in \mathcal{L}(\mathsf{mon\text{-}sRW}) \smallsetminus \mathcal{L}(\mathsf{RRW})$ by Lemma 2.2.5.

(15) $L_5 = \{ a^n b^m \mid 0 \leq n \leq m \leq 2n \} \in \mathcal{L}(\mathsf{mon\text{-}R}) \smallsetminus \mathcal{L}(\mathsf{det\text{-}sRLW})$ by Lemma 2.2.6.

(16) $L_6 = L_{6,1} \cup L_{6,2} \cup L_{6,3} \in \mathcal{L}(\mathsf{det\text{-}RR}) \smallsetminus \mathcal{L}(\mathsf{sRW})$ by Lemma 2.2.7, where

- $L_{6,1} = \{ (ab)^{2^n - i} c (ab)^i \mid n \geq 0, 0 \leq i \leq 2^n \}$,
- $L_{6,2} = \{ (ab)^{2^n - 2i} (abb)^i \mid n \geq 1, 0 \leq i \leq 2^{n-1} \}$, and
- $L_{6,3} = \{ (abb)^{2^n - i} (ab)^i \mid n \geq 0, 0 \leq i \leq 2^n \}$.

(17) $L_7 = L_{7,1} \cup L_{7,2} \in \mathcal{L}(\mathsf{det\text{-}RW}) \smallsetminus \mathcal{L}(\mathsf{RL})$ by Lemma 2.2.8, where

- $L_{7,1} = \{ a^{2^n - 2i} c a^i \mid n \geq 1, 0 \leq 2i < 2^n \}$ and
- $L_{7,2} = \{ a^i d a^{2^n - 2i} \mid n \geq 1, 0 \leq 2i < 2^n \}$.

Furthermore, by Proposition 2.5.36, $L_7 \notin \mathcal{L}(j\text{-}\mathsf{mon\text{-}RLW})$ for any $j \in \mathbb{N}_+$.

(18) $L_8 = L_{8,1} \cup L_{8,2} \in \mathcal{L}(\mathsf{det\text{-}sRW}) \smallsetminus \mathcal{L}(\mathsf{RLW})$ by Lemma 2.2.9, where

- $L_{8,1} = \{ a^{2^n - i} c b^i \mid n \geq 1, 0 \leq i < 2^n \}$ and
- $L_{8,2} = \{ a^i d b^{2^n - 2i} \mid n \geq 1, 0 \leq 2i < 2^n \}$.

(19) The language $L_{ab} = \{ a^n b^n \mid n \geq 0 \} \in \mathcal{L}(\mathsf{1\text{-}CRA})$ by Example 2.2.30. In addition, $L_{ab} \in \mathcal{L}(\mathsf{det\text{-}mon\text{-}RR(2)}) \smallsetminus \mathcal{L}(\mathsf{sRW(2)})$ by Lemma 2.3.14. Also $L_{ab} \in \mathcal{L}(\mathsf{stl\text{-}det\text{-}mon\text{-}R})$ (Example 2.4.2).

(20) $L_c = \{ a^n c b^n \mid n \geq 0 \} \in \mathcal{L}(\mathsf{1\text{-}\Delta\text{-}CRA}) \smallsetminus \mathcal{L}(\mathsf{CRA})$ by Lemma 2.2.32 and Example 2.2.40.

(21) Let D_2 be the *semi-Dyck language* over $T_2 = \{a_1, a_2, \bar{a}_1, \bar{a}_2\}$. Then $D_2 \in \mathcal{L}(\mathsf{stl\text{-}det\text{-}mon\text{-}R(2)})$ by Lemma 2.4.18.

(22) Let H be Greibach's *hardest context-free language.* Then $H \in \mathcal{L}(\mathsf{1\text{-}\Delta\text{-}CRA}) \smallsetminus \mathcal{L}(\mathsf{CRA})$ by Proposition 2.2.43.

(23) $L_{\text{pal2}} = \{ w w^R v v^R \mid w, v \in \{a, b\}^* \} \notin \mathcal{L}(\mathsf{a\text{-}aux}(o(n/\log^5 n), i)\text{-}\mathsf{det\text{-}RLWW})$ for any $i \in \mathbb{N}_+$ (Theorem 2.2.59).

(24) For all $k \geq 1$, $L_k = \{ a^n c^{k-1} b^n \mid n \geq 0 \} \in \mathcal{L}(\mathsf{det\text{-}mon\text{-}R}(k+1)) \smallsetminus \mathcal{L}(\mathsf{sRLW}(k))$ by Lemma 2.3.2.

(25) $L'_2 = \{ a^m b^n \mid m \in \{n, n+1\}, n \geq 0 \} \in \mathcal{L}(\mathsf{mon\text{-}RR(1)})$ (Example 2.3.5). Also $L'_2 \in \mathcal{L}(\mathsf{stl\text{-}det\text{-}ORD})$ analogously to Example 2.3.88.

(26) $L' = \{ a^m b^n c \mid n \in \{m, m+1\}, m \geq 0 \} \cup \{ a^m b^n d \mid n \in \{2m, 2m+1, 2m+2\}, m \geq 0 \} \in \mathcal{L}(\mathsf{mon\text{-}RR(1)}) \smallsetminus \mathsf{DCFL}$ by Lemma 2.3.6. Also $L' \in \mathcal{L}(\mathsf{det\text{-}mon\text{-}RL(1)})$ (see the remark following Proposition 2.3.11).

(27) $L = \{ a^i b^j c^m \mid 0 \leq i \leq j \leq m \text{ and } m - i \leq 1 \} \in \mathcal{L}(\mathsf{RR(1)}) \smallsetminus \mathcal{L}(\mathsf{RW})$ (see the remark following Proposition 2.3.8).

(28) $L = \{ a^n b^{2n}, a^{n-1} c b^{2n-1}, a^{n-1} d b^{2n-2} \mid n \geq 1 \} \in \mathcal{L}(\mathsf{det\text{-}mon\text{-}RW(2)}) \smallsetminus \mathcal{L}(\mathsf{RR(2)})$ by Lemma 2.3.15.

(29) $L'_8 = L'_{8,1} \cup L'_{8,2} \cup L'_{8,3} \in \mathcal{L}(\mathsf{det\text{-}sRW}(2)) \smallsetminus \mathcal{L}(\mathsf{RLW})$ by Lemma 2.3.16, where

$$\begin{array}{lll} - & L'_{8,1} & = & \{ a^{2^n-i}cb^i \mid n \geq 0, 0 \leq i < 2^n \}, \\ - & L'_{8,2} & = & \{ a^i db^{2^n-2i} \mid n \geq 1, 0 \leq 2i \leq 2^n \} \cup \{db\}, \text{ and} \\ - & L'_{8,3} & = & \{ a^i eb^{2^n-2i+1} \mid n \geq 1, 0 \leq 2i \leq 2^n \} \cup \{ae\}. \end{array}$$

(30) Let $L_{a,c}$ be the language that is generated by the context-free grammar

$$G_{a,c} = (\{S\}, \{a,b,c\}, S, \{S \to \lambda), (S \to SS), (S \to aSb), (S \to bSc)\}).$$

Then $L_{a,c} \in \mathcal{L}(\mathsf{R}(2)) \smallsetminus \mathcal{L}(\mathsf{mon\text{-}RW}(2))$ by Lemma 2.3.21.

(31) Let $\hat{L}_{\mathrm{pal}} = L^{(1)}_{\mathrm{pal}} \cup L^{(2)}_{\mathrm{pal}} \cup L^{(3)}_{\mathrm{pal}} \cup L^{(4)}_{\mathrm{pal}} \cup L^{(5)}_{\mathrm{pal}}$, where

$$\begin{aligned} L^{(1)}_{\mathrm{pal}} = \{ & b_1 d^{i_1} b_2 d^{i_2} \cdots d^{i_{m-1}} b_m d^{j_n} a_n d^{j_{n-1}} a_{n-1} d^{j_{n-2}} \cdots d^{j_1} a_1 d^{j_0} \mid n \geq m \geq 1, \\ & i_1, \ldots, i_{m-1} \geq 0, j_0, \ldots, j_n \geq 1, b_1, \ldots, b_m, a_1, \ldots, a_n \in \{a,b\}, \text{ and} \\ & \exists w \in \{a,b\}^+ : b_1 b_2 \cdots b_m a_n a_{n-1} \cdots a_1 = ww^R \}, \\ L^{(2)}_{\mathrm{pal}} = \{ & a_1 a_2 \cdots a_n e d^{j_n} a_n d^{j_{n-1}} \cdots d^{j_1} a_1 d^{j_0} \mid n \geq 0, j_0, \ldots, j_n \geq 1, a_1, a_2, \ldots, a_n \in \{a,b\} \}, \\ L^{(3)}_{\mathrm{pal}} = \{ & a_1 a_2 \cdots a_n c a_n d^{j_{n-1}} \cdots d^{j_1} a_1 d^{j_0} \mid n \geq 0, j_0, \ldots, j_{n-1} \geq 1, a_1, \ldots, a_n \in \{a,b\} \} \cup \{c\}, \\ L^{(4)}_{\mathrm{pal}} = \{ & a_1 a_2 \cdots a_n a c_a d^{j_n} a_n d^{j_{n-1}} \cdots d^{j_1} a_1 d^{j_0} \mid n \geq 0, j_0, \ldots, j_n \geq 1, a_1, a_2, \ldots, a_n \in \{a,b\} \}, \\ L^{(5)}_{\mathrm{pal}} = \{ & a_1 a_2 \cdots a_n b c_b d^{j_n} a_n d^{j_{n-1}} \cdots d^{j_1} a_1 d^{j_0} \mid n \geq 0, j_0, \ldots, j_n \geq 1, a_1, a_2, \ldots, a_n \in \{a,b\} \}. \end{aligned}$$

Then $\hat{L}_{\mathrm{pal}} \in \mathcal{L}(\mathsf{mon\text{-}RW}(2)) \smallsetminus \mathsf{CRL}$ by Lemma 2.3.23.

(32) For all $k \geq 3$, $L^{(k)}_9 = \{ a^n b^{n \cdot (k-1)} \mid n \geq 0 \} \in \mathcal{L}(\mathsf{det\text{-}mon\text{-}RR}(k)) \smallsetminus \mathcal{L}(\mathsf{sRW}(k))$ by Lemma 2.3.26.

(33) For all $k \geq 3$, $L^{(k)}_{10} = \{ a^n b^{n \cdot (2k-3)}, a^n c b^{n \cdot (2k-3)+(k-2)} \mid n \geq 0 \} \in \mathcal{L}(\mathsf{det\text{-}mon\text{-}RW}(k)) \smallsetminus \mathcal{L}(\mathsf{RR}(k))$ by Lemma 2.3.27.

(34) For $k \geq 3$, let $L^{(k)}_{11} = \{ a^{2n} b^{n \cdot (k-1)}, a^{2n+1} c d^{k-1} b^{n \cdot (k-1)}, a^{2n} e d b^{n \cdot (k-1)} \mid n \geq 0 \}$. Then $L^{(k)}_{11} \in \mathcal{L}(\mathsf{det\text{-}mon\text{-}sRW}(k)) \smallsetminus \mathcal{L}(\mathsf{RRW}(k))$ by Lemma 2.3.28.

(35) For each integer $i \geq 1$, let $L^{(i)}_c \subseteq \{a,b,c,d,e\}^*$ be the language $L^{(i)}_c = L^{(i)}_{c,1} \cup L^{(i)}_{c,2}$, where

$$\begin{array}{lll} L^{(i)}_{c,1} & = & \{ a^n (b^i c^i)^{n-k} (b^i)^k d \mid n \geq k \geq 0 \}, \text{ and} \\ L^{(i)}_{c,2} & = & \{ a^n (b^i c^i)^{m-k} (c^i)^k e \mid n \geq 0,\ m > 2n \text{ and } m \geq k \geq 0 \}. \end{array}$$

Then $L^{(i)}_c \in \mathcal{L}(\mathsf{det\text{-}wmon}(i)\text{-}\mathsf{R}) \smallsetminus \mathcal{L}(\mathsf{det\text{-}wmon}(i-1)\text{-}\mathsf{RRW})$ by Lemmas 2.3.33 and 2.3.34.

(36) For each $i \geq 1$, let $L^{(i)}_d = L^{(i)}_c \cup L^{(i)}_{a1} \cdot L_{de1} \cup L^{(i)}_{a2} \cdot L_{de2}$, where

$$\begin{array}{ll} L^{(i)}_{a1} = \{ a^n (b^i c^i)^n \mid n \geq 0 \}, & L_{de1} = \{ d^r e^s \mid r > s \geq 0, r+s > 1 \}, \\ L^{(i)}_{a2} = \{ a^n (b^i c^i)^m \mid m > 2n \geq 0 \}, & L_{de2} = \{ d^r e^s \mid 0 \leq r < s, r+s > 1 \}. \end{array}$$

For each $i \geq 1$, $L^{(i)}_d \in \mathcal{L}(\mathsf{det\text{-}wmon}(i)\text{-}\mathsf{R}) \smallsetminus \mathcal{L}(\mathsf{wmon}(i-1)\text{-}\mathsf{RRW})$ by Theorem 2.3.36.

(37) $L_{\leq} = \{ a^m b^n \mid 1 \leq m \leq n \} \notin \mathcal{L}(\mathsf{ORWW})$ by Lemma 2.3.78.

(38) $L_{\mathrm{3blocks}} = \{ a^m b^m a^n b^n a^p b^p, a^m b^{2m} a^{n+k} b^n a^p b^{2p} \mid m,n,k,p \geq 1 \} \in \mathcal{L}(\mathsf{det\text{-}ORD}) \smallsetminus (\mathsf{LRR} \cup \mathsf{RLR})$ (see the proof outline of Theorem 2.3.89).

(39) $L_{\mathrm{lin}} = \{ a^n b^n, a^n b^{2n} \mid n \geq 1 \} \in \mathsf{CRL} \cap \mathsf{UCFL} \cap \mathsf{Co\text{-}UCFL}$ (see the remark following Theorem 2.3.91).

(40) $L_e = \{ c(ac)^m (aee)^{n-m} b^n, d(ad)^m (aee)^{n-m} b^{2n} \mid 0 \leq m \leq n \} \in \mathcal{L}(\mathsf{stl\text{-}det\text{-}mon\text{-}RW}) \smallsetminus \mathcal{L}(\mathsf{stl\text{-}det\text{-}R})$ (Lemma 2.4.13 (a)).

(41) $L_g = \{ a^n cb^n, a^n eeb^n, a^n db^{2n}, a^n eeb^{2n} \mid n \geq 0 \} \in \mathcal{L}(\mathsf{stl\text{-}mon\text{-}RW}) \setminus \mathcal{L}(\mathsf{R})$ (Lemma 2.4.13 (b)).

(42) $L_h = \{ a^n b^m \mid 0 \leq n \leq m \leq 2n \} \in \mathcal{L}(\mathsf{stl\text{-}mon\text{-}R}) \setminus \mathcal{L}(\mathsf{det\text{-}RW})$ (Lemma 2.4.13 (c)).

(43) $L_{\mathrm{expo}} = \{ a^{i_0} ba^{i_1} b \cdots a^{i_{n-1}} ba^{i_n} \mid n \geq 0,\, i_0, i_1, \ldots, i_n \geq 0, \exists m \geq 0 : \sum_{j=0}^{n} 2^j \cdot i_j = 2^m \} \cup \{b\}^*$. Then $L_{\mathrm{expo}} \in \mathcal{L}(\mathsf{stl\text{-}det\text{-}RW}) \setminus \mathcal{L}(\mathsf{R})$ (Lemma 2.4.13 (d)).

(44) $L^{(\varphi)}_{\mathrm{expo}} = \varphi(L_{\mathrm{expo}})$, where φ is the morphism induced by $a \mapsto ab$ and $b \mapsto b$. Then $L^{(\varphi)}_{\mathrm{expo}} \in \mathcal{L}(\mathsf{stl\text{-}det\text{-}R}) \setminus \mathsf{CFL}$ (Lemma 2.4.13 (e)).

(45) For $k \geq 1$, let $L_k = \{ (ab^k)^i \mid i \geq 0 \}$. Then $L_k \in (\mathsf{REG} \cap \mathcal{L}(\mathsf{stl\text{-}det\text{-}mon\text{-}R}(k+1))) \setminus \mathcal{L}(\mathsf{stl\text{-}sRW}(k))$ by Lemma 2.4.20.

(46) $L^{(1)}_{\mathrm{expo}} = \{ a^{2^n} \mid n \geq 0 \} \cup \{ a^i ba^j \mid i, j \geq 0, \text{ and } \exists m \geq 1 : i + 2 \cdot j = 2^m \} \in \mathcal{L}(\mathsf{stl\text{-}det\text{-}RRW})$ (Lemma 2.4.28), but $L^{(1)}_{\mathrm{expo}} \notin \mathcal{L}(\mathsf{stl\text{-}sRW})$ (Lemma 2.4.29). Also by Proposition 2.6.30, $L^{(1)}_{\mathrm{expo}} \notin \mathcal{L}_{\mathrm{P}}(j\text{-}\mathsf{constr\text{-}lex\text{-}FRRWW})$ for any $j \in \mathbb{N}_+$.

Furthermore, let $\bar{L}^{(1)}_{\mathrm{expo}} = \{a, b\}^* \setminus L^{(1)}_{\mathrm{expo}}$ be the complement of the language $L^{(1)}_{\mathrm{expo}}$. Then $\bar{L}^{(1)}_{\mathrm{expo}} \in \mathcal{L}(\mathsf{stl\text{-}det\text{-}RRW})$, but $\bar{L}^{(1)}_{\mathrm{expo}}$ is not accepted by any stateless deterministic sRRW-automaton that executes accept instructions only at the right end of the tape (Lemma 2.4.34). Finally, $(L^{(1)}_{\mathrm{expo}})^R \notin \mathcal{L}(\mathsf{det\text{-}sRRW})$ (see [122]).

(47) Let φ be defined by $a \mapsto ab$ and $b \mapsto b$, and let $L^{(1)}_{\varphi} = \varphi(L^{(1)}_{\mathrm{expo}})$. Then $L^{(1)}_{\varphi} \in \mathcal{L}(\mathsf{stl\text{-}det\text{-}RR}) \setminus \mathcal{L}(\mathsf{stl\text{-}R})$ by Lemma 2.4.32.

(48) $L_{acab} = \{ a^m c^n a^{n+r} b^{m+r} \mid m, n \geq 1, r \geq 0 \} \in \mathcal{L}(\mathsf{stl\text{-}det\text{-}R})$, but $L^R_{acab} \notin \mathcal{L}(\mathsf{stl\text{-}det\text{-}sRW})$ (see the proof of Theorem 2.4.38).

(49) $L_{dm} = \{ cb^n \bar{c}a^n \mid n \geq 0 \} \cup \{ db^{2n} \bar{d}a^n \mid n \geq 0 \} \in \mathcal{L}(\mathsf{stl\text{-}det\text{-}R})$ (see the proof of Theorem 2.4.39).

(50) $L_f = \{ a^n b^n \mid n \geq 0 \} \cup \{a\}^* \cup \{ b^n c^n \mid n \geq 0 \} \in \mathcal{L}(\mathsf{stl\text{-}det\text{-}R})$ (see the proof of Theorem 2.4.43).

(51) For each $c \geq 2$, let $L_{c-r} = \{ (a^n \# b^n)^c \mid n \geq 0 \}$. Then, by Example 2.5.2,

$$L_{c-r} \in \mathcal{L}(\mathsf{det}\text{-}c\text{-}\mathsf{r\text{-}R}) \setminus \mathcal{L}((c-1)\text{-}\mathsf{r\text{-}sRRW}).$$

(52) For each integer $j \geq 2$, let

$$L_j = \{ a^{n_1} b^{m_1} a^{n_2} b^{m_2} \cdots a^{n_j} b^{m_j} \mid \vartheta(n_1, m_1, n_2, m_2, \ldots, n_j, m_j) = 1 \},$$

where the function $\vartheta : (\bigcup_{p \geq 1} \mathbb{N}_+^{2p}) \to \{0, 1\}$ is defined inductively as follows:

For all $n, m \in \mathbb{N}_+$,

$$\vartheta(n, m) = \begin{cases} 1, & \text{if } n = m, \\ 0, & \text{if } n \neq m, \end{cases}$$

and for all $p \geq 1$ and all $n, m, r_1, r_2, \ldots, r_{2p} \in \mathbb{N}_+$,

$$\vartheta(n, m, r_1, r_2, \ldots, r_{2p}) = \begin{cases} 1, & \text{if } n = m \text{ and } \vartheta(r_1, r_2, \ldots, r_{2p}) = 1 \\ & \text{or } n > 2m \text{ and } \vartheta(r_1, r_2, \ldots, r_{2p}) = 0, \\ 0, & \text{otherwise.} \end{cases}$$

Then

$$L_j \in (\mathcal{L}(\mathsf{det}\text{-}j\text{-}\mathsf{s\text{-}mon\text{-}RL}) \cap \mathcal{L}(j\text{-}\mathsf{s\text{-}mon\text{-}RR})) \setminus \mathcal{L}((j-1)\text{-}\mathsf{s\text{-}mon\text{-}sRLW})$$

by Proposition 2.5.10, Corollary 2.5.11, and Proposition 2.5.12.

(53) For $j \geq 2$,

$$L'_j = \{\, xy \mid \begin{array}{l} \exists i \in \{0,1,\ldots,j\}\, \exists n_1, m_1, \ldots, n_j, m_j \in \mathbb{N}_+ \,\exists y_{i+1}, \ldots, y_j \in \{c,d\} : \\ x = a^{n_1}b^{m_1}\cdots a^{n_i}b^{m_i} \text{ and } y = a^{n_{i+1}}y_{i+1}b^{m_{i+1}}\cdots a^{n_j}y_jb^{m_j} \\ \text{such that } \begin{array}{ll} (i) & \pi_{\{a,b\}}(xy) \in L_j, \\ (ii) & n_l < 3 \text{ or } m_l < 2 \text{ for each } l > i+1, \\ (iii) & n_l \geq 3 \text{ and } m_l \geq 2 \text{ for each } l \leq i, \text{ and} \\ (iv) & \text{for all } l \in \{i+1, i+2, \ldots, j\},\ y_l = c \text{ if and only if} \\ & l = j \text{ or } \vartheta(n_{l+1}, m_{l+1}, \ldots, n_j, m_j) = 1 \,\}. \end{array} \end{array}$$

Then $L'_j \in \mathcal{L}(j\text{-s-mon-RW}) \smallsetminus \mathcal{L}((j-1)\text{-s-mon-sRLW})$ by Propositions 2.5.13 and 2.5.14.

(54) For $j \in \mathbb{N}_+$, let

$$\bar{L}_j = \{\, a^{n_1}b^{n_1}a^{n_2}b^{n_2}\cdots a^{n_j}b^{n_j} \mid n_1 \geq n_2 \geq \cdots \geq n_j \geq 1 \,\}.$$

Then, for $j \geq 2$,

$$\bar{L}_j \in (\mathcal{L}(j\text{-mon-R}) \cap \mathcal{L}(\text{det-}j\text{-mon-RL})) \smallsetminus \mathcal{L}((j-1)\text{-mon-sRLW})$$

by Lemma 2.5.24 and Proposition 2.5.25. In addition, $\bar{L}_j \notin \bigcup_{i\geq 1} \mathcal{L}(i\text{-s-mon-sRLW})$.

(55) Let $L_d = \{\, cwcw \mid w \in \{a,b\}^* \text{ and } |w| = 2n \text{ for some } n \geq 0 \,\}$. By Proposition 2.5.31 and Lemma 2.5.34, $L_d \in (\mathcal{L}(\text{det-2-mon-RLWW}) \cap \mathcal{L}(\text{2-mon-RWW})) \smallsetminus \mathcal{L}(\text{sRLW})$.

(56) $L_\infty = \{\, (a^nb^n)^m \mid n, m \geq 0 \,\} \in \mathcal{L}_C(\text{det-FsRRWW}) \smallsetminus \mathcal{L}_C(\text{MsRRWW})$ by Example 2.5.46 and Lemma 2.5.47.

(57) $L'_\infty = \{\, (a^nb^n)^n \mid n \geq 1 \,\} \in \mathcal{L}(\text{FsRRWW}) \smallsetminus \mathcal{L}_C(\text{FsRRWW})$ (see the proof of Theorem 2.5.54).

(58) Let $j \in \mathbb{N}_+$, let $\Gamma_j = \{a, b, c_0, c_1, \ldots, c_{j-1}\}$, and let $\Delta_j = \{a_1, a_2, \ldots, a_j\}$. In Definition 2.5.52, the languages LC_j and LE_j are defined as follows:

$$\begin{array}{lclcl} LC_j & = & \{\, c_0wc_1wc_2w\cdots c_{j-2}wc_{j-1}w \mid w \in \{a,b\}^* \,\} & \subseteq & \Gamma_j^* \text{ and} \\ LE_j & = & \{\, w \in \{a_1, a_2, \ldots, a_j\}^* \mid |w|_{a_1} = |w|_{a_2} = \ldots = |w|_{a_j} \,\} & \subseteq & \Delta_j^*. \end{array}$$

By Proposition 2.5.53, for all $j \geq 2$,

$$LC_j \in (\mathcal{L}_C(j, \text{FsRRWW}) \cap \mathcal{L}(2, \text{FsRRWW})) \smallsetminus \mathcal{L}_C(j-1, \text{FsRRWW}).$$

On the other hand, by Proposition 2.5.61, for each $j \geq 2$, the language LE_j is $(j-1)$-scalable, but it is not j-scalable.

(59) Let $\Sigma_0 = \{a, b\}$, let c, d be two additional letters, and let L_{rp}, $L_{\text{d}}(j)$, and $L_{\text{dp}}(i,j)$ be the following languages:

$$\begin{array}{llcll} (1) & L_{\text{rp}} & = & \{\, wwc \mid w \in \Sigma_0^* \,\}, & \\ (2) & L_{\text{d}}(j) & = & \{\, (wc)^j dw^R \mid w \in \Sigma_0^* \,\} & \text{for all } j \in \mathbb{N}_+, \\ (3) & L_{\text{dp}}(i,j) & = & (L_{\text{rp}})^i \cdot \{d\} \cdot L_{\text{d}}(j) & \text{for all } i \geq 1 \text{ and } j \geq 2. \end{array}$$

By [222], for all $j \geq 2$,

$$L_{\text{d}}(j) \in \mathcal{L}_P(\text{W(0)-}j\text{-constr-slex-FRRWW}) \smallsetminus \mathcal{L}_P((j-1)\text{-r-FRRWW}),$$

and, for all $i \geq 1$ and all $j \geq 1$,

$$L_{\text{rp}}^i \in \mathcal{L}_P(\text{W}(i)\text{-2-constr-slex-FRRWW}) \smallsetminus \mathcal{L}_P(\text{W}(i-1)\text{-}j\text{-r-lex-FRRWW}).$$

Finally, for all $i \geq 1$ and all $j \geq 2$, the following results hold:

(a) $L_{\text{dp}}(i,j) \in \mathcal{L}_P(\text{W}(i)\text{-}j\text{-constr-slex-FRRWW})$.

(b) $L_{\text{dp}}(i,j) \notin \mathcal{L}_P((j-1)\text{-r-FRRWW})$.

(c) $L_{\text{dp}}(i,j) \notin \mathcal{L}_P(\text{W}(i-1)\text{-}m\text{-r-lex-FRRWW})$ for any $m \in \mathbb{N}_+$.

(60) Let $L_{\mathrm{d}^+} = \bigcup_{j\geq 1} L_{\mathrm{d}}(j)$ and $L_{\mathrm{rp}^+} = \bigcup_{j\geq 1}(L_{\mathrm{rp}})^j$. Then

$$L_{\mathrm{d}^+} \in \mathcal{L}_{\mathrm{P}}(\mathsf{W(0)\text{-}slex\text{-}FRRWW}) \smallsetminus \mathcal{L}_{\mathrm{P}}(j\text{-}\mathsf{r\text{-}FRRWW})$$

for all $j \in \mathbb{N}_+$ and

$$L_{\mathrm{rp}^+} \in \mathcal{L}_{\mathrm{P}}(\mathsf{2\text{-}constr\text{-}slex\text{-}FRRWW}) \smallsetminus \mathcal{L}_{\mathrm{P}}(\mathsf{W}(i)\text{-}j\text{-}\mathsf{r\text{-}lex\text{-}FRRWW})$$

for all $i \in \mathbb{N}$ and $j \in \mathbb{N}_+$ [222].

(61) The language

$$L_{\mathrm{expo}}^{(2)} = \{\, x^{i_0}y^{i_1}x^{i_2}y^{i_3}\cdots x^{i_{m-1}}y^{i_m} \mid x,y \in \{a,b\}, x \neq y, m > 0, i_0 > 0, i_1 > 0, \ldots, i_{m-1} > 0,\\ i_m \geq 0, \exists p \geq 0 : 2^p = i_0 + 2\cdot i_1 + 4\cdot i_2 + \cdots + 2^m \cdot i_m \,\}$$

is accepted by a deterministic RW-automaton of window size 3 (Lemma 2.5.75).

(62) For $t \geq 2$, let $\varphi_t : \{a,b\}^* \to \{0,1\}^*$ be the morphism that is defined by taking $\varphi_t(a) = (001)^t$ and $\varphi_t(b) = (01)^t$, and let $L_t = \varphi_t(L_{\mathrm{expo}}^{(2)})$. Then, by Proposition 2.5.76, $L_t \in \mathcal{L}(\mathsf{cut}(t)\text{-}\mathsf{det\text{-}R}) \smallsetminus \mathcal{L}(\mathsf{cut}(t-1)\text{-}\mathsf{RR})$.

(63) For $n \geq 3$,

$$B_n = \{\, v_1\#v_2\#\ldots\#v_m\$u \mid m \geq 1,\ v_1, v_2, \ldots, v_m, u \in \{a,b\}^n,\ \exists 1 \leq i \leq m : v_i = u \,\}.$$

Then B_n is accepted by a stl-det-ORWW-automaton that has a tape alphabet of cardinality $18 \cdot n$ (Proposition 3.2.12) and by a reversible stl-det-ORWW-automaton that has a tape alphabet of cardinality $68 \cdot n - 22$ (Proposition 3.2.36).

Bibliography

[1] Alfred V. Aho, John E. Hopcroft, and Jeffrey D. Ullman. A general theory of translation. *Mathematical Systems Theory*, 3:193–221, 1969.

[2] Dana Angluin. Inference of reversible languages. *Journal of the Association for Computing Machinery*, 29:741–765, 1982.

[3] Jean-Michel Autebert, Jean Berstel, and Luc Boasson. Context-free languages and push-down automata. In Grzegorz Rozenberg and Arto Salomaa, editors, *Handbook of Formal Languages*, volume 1, pages 111–174. Springer, Berlin, Heidelberg, 1997.

[4] John W. Backus, Friedrich L. Bauer, Julien Green, Charles Katz, John McCarthy, Alan J. Perlis, Heinz Rutishauser, Klaus Samelson, Bernard Vauquois, Joseph Henry Wegstein, A. van Wijngaarden, and M. Woodger. Report on the algorithmic language ALGOL 60. *Communications of the ACM*, 3:299–311, 1960.

[5] José L. Balcázar, Josep Díaz, and Joaquím Gabarró. *Structural Complexity*, volume I of *EATCS Monographs on Theoretical Computer Science*. Springer, Berlin, 1988.

[6] Yehoshua Bar-Hillel, Micha A. Perles, and Eli Shamir. On formal properties of simple phrase structure grammars. *Zeitschrift für Phonetik, Sprachwissenschaft und Kommunikationsforschung*, 14:143–172, 1961.

[7] Stanislav Basovník. Learning Restricted Restarting Automata Using Genetic Algorithm (in Czech). Master's thesis, Charles University, Faculty of Mathematics and Physics, Prague, 2010.

[8] Stanislav Basovník and František Mráz. Learning limited context restarting automata by genetic algorithms. In Jürgen Dassow and Bianca Truthe, editors, *Theoretag 2011, Proc.*, Technical report, pages 25–28. Otto-von-Guericke-Universität, Magdeburg, 2011.

[9] Martin Beaudry, Markus Holzer, Gundula Niemann, and Friedrich Otto. McNaughton families of languages. *Theoretical Computer Science*, 290:1581–1628, 2003.

[10] Charles H. Bennett. Logical reversibility of computation. *IBM Journal of Research and Development*, 17:525–532, 1973.

[11] Jean Berstel. *Transductions and Context-Free Languages*. Teubner, Stuttgart, 1979.

[12] Eberhard Bertsch and Mark-Jan Nederhof. On the complexity of some extensions of RCG parsing. In H. Bunt, editor, *7th IWPT, Proc.*, pages 66–77. Tsinghua University Press, Beijing, China, 2001.

[13] Jean-Camille Birget. Intersection and union of regular languages and state complexity. *Information Processing Letters*, 43:185–190, 1992.

[14] Jean-Camille Birget. Partial orders on words, minimal elements of regular languages, and state complexity. *Theoretical Computer Science*, 119:267–291, 1993.

F. Otto, *Restarting Automata*, Theory and Applications of Computability,
https://doi.org/10.1007/978-3-031-70094-1

[15] Jean-Camille Birget. State-complexity of finite-state devices, state compressibility and incompressibility. *Mathematical Systems Theory*, 26:237–269, 1993.

[16] Ronald V. Book. *Grammars with Time Functions*. PhD thesis, Harvard University, Cambridge, Massachusetts, February 1969.

[17] Ronald V. Book. Time-bounded grammars and their languages. *Journal of Computer and System Sciences*, 5:397–429, 1971.

[18] Ronald V. Book and Sheila Greibach. Quasi-realtime languages. *Mathematical Systems Theory*, 4:97–111, 1970.

[19] Ronald V. Book and Friedrich Otto. *String-Rewriting Systems*. Springer, New York, 1993.

[20] Henning Bordihn, Markus Holzer, and Martin Kutrib. Input reversals and interated pushdown automata: A new characterization of Khabbaz geometric hierarchy of languages. In Cristian S. Calude, Elena Calude, and Michael J. Dinneen, editors, *DLT 2004, Proc.*, volume 3340 of *Lecture Notes in Computer Science*, pages 102–113. Springer, Heidelberg, 2004.

[21] Joan Bresnan, Ronald M. Kaplan, Stanley Peters, and Annie Zaenen. Cross-serial dependencies in Dutch. *Linguistic Inquiry*, 13:613–635, 1982.

[22] J. Richard Büchi. Regular canonical systems. *Archiv für mathematische Logik und Grundlagenforschung*, 6:91–111, 1964.

[23] Gerhard Buntrock. Wachsende kontext-sensitive Sprachen. Habilitationsschrift, Fakultät für Mathematik und Informatik, Universität Würzburg, July 1996.

[24] Gerhard Buntrock and Krzysztof Loryś. On growing context-sensitive languages. In Werner Kuich, editor, *ICALP 92, Proc.*, volume 623 of *Lecture Notes in Computer Science*, pages 77–88. Springer, Heidelberg, 1992.

[25] Gerhard Buntrock and Friedrich Otto. Growing context-sensitive languages and Church-Rosser languages. *Information and Computation*, 141:1–36, 1998.

[26] Cristian S. Calude and Gheorghe Păun. *Computing with Cells and Atoms. An Introduction to Quantum, DNA and Membrane Computing*. Taylor and Francis, London and New York, 2001.

[27] Noam Chomsky. Three models for the description of language. *IRE Transactions on Information Theory*, 2:113–124, 1956.

[28] Noam Chomsky. A note on phrase structure grammars. *Information and Control*, 2:393–395, 1959.

[29] Noam Chomsky. On certain formal properties of grammars. *Information and Control*, 2:137–167, 1959.

[30] Noam Chomsky. Context-free grammars and push-down storage. *Quarterly Progress Report No. 65, Research Laboratory of Electronics, M.I.T.*, 1962.

[31] Marek Chrobak. Finite automata and unary languages. *Theoretical Computer Science*, 47:149–158, 1986.

[32] Marek Chrobak. Hierarchies of one-way multihead automata languages. *Theoretical Computer Science*, 48:153–181, 1986.

[33] Marek Chrobak and Ming Li. $k+1$ heads are better than k for PDAs. *Journal of Computer and System Sciences*, 37:144–155, 1988.

[34] E.A. Cichon and Elias Tahhan Bittar. Ordinal recursive bounds for Higman's theorem. *Theoretical Computer Science*, 201:63–84, 1998.

[35] John Cocke and Jacob T. Schwartz. Programming Languages and Their Compilers, Preliminary Notes. Technical report, Courant Institute of Mathematical Sciences, New York, NY, 1970.

[36] Robert Cremanns and Friedrich Otto. The language of final stack contents of a pushdown automaton is effectively regular. Mathematische Schriften Kassel 11/93, Fachbereich Mathematik/Informatik, Universität Kassel, 1993.

[37] Karel Čulik II and Rina Cohen. LR-regular grammars – an extension of LR(k) grammars. *Journal of Computer and System Sciences*, 7:66–96, 1973.

[38] Christopher Culy. Formal properties of natural language and linguistic theories. *Linguistics and Philosophy*, 19:599–617, 1996.

[39] Elias Dahlhaus and Manfred K. Warmuth. Membership for growing context-sensitive grammars is polynomial. *Journal of Computer and System Sciences*, 33:456–472, 1986.

[40] Jürgen Dassow and Gheorghe Păun. *Regulated Rewriting in Formal Language Theory*, volume 18 of *EATCS Monographs on Theoretical Computer Science*. Springer, Berlin, 1989.

[41] Alexander Dikovsky and Larissa Modina. Dependencies on the other side of the curtain. *Traitement Automatique des Langues*, 41:67–96, 2000.

[42] Jay Earley. An efficient context-free parsing algorithm. *Communications of the Association for Computing Machinery*, 13:94–102, 1970.

[43] Andrzej Ehrenfeucht, Gheorghe Păun, and Grzegorz Rozenberg. Contextual grammars and formal languages. In Grzegorz Rozenberg and Arto Salomaa, editors, *Handbook of Formal Languages*, volume 2, pages 237–293. Springer, Berlin, Heidelberg, 1997.

[44] Keith Ellul, Bryan Krawetz, Jeffrey Shallit, and Ming-Wei Wang. Regular expressions: New results and open problems. *Journal of Automata, Languages and Combinatorics*, 10:407–437, 2005.

[45] Rémi Eyraud, Colin de la Higuera, and Jean-Christophe Janodet. Representing languages by learnable rewriting systems. In Georgios Paliouras and Yasubumi Sakakibara, editors, *ICGI 2004, Proc.*, volume 3264 of *Lecture Notes in Artificial Intelligence*, pages 139–150. Springer, Heidelberg, 2004.

[46] Robert W. Floyd. On the nonexistence of a phrase structure grammar for ALGOL 60. *Communications of the Association for Computing Machinery*, 5:483–484, 1962.

[47] Haim Gaifman. Dependency systems and phrase-structure systems. *Information and Control*, 8:304–337, 1965.

[48] Pedro García and Enrique Vidal. Inference of k-testable languages in the strict sense and application to syntactic pattern recognition. *IEEE Transactions on Pattern Analysis and Machine Intelligence*, 12:920–925, 1990.

[49] Michael R. Garey and David S. Johnson. *Computers and Intractability. A Guide to the Theory of NP-Completeness.* Freeman, San Francisco, 1979.

[50] Daniel Genkin, Nissim Francez, and Michael Kaminski. Mildly context-sensitive languages via buffer augmented pregroup grammars. In Zohar Manna and Doron A. Peled, editors, *Time for Verification, Essays in Memory of Amir Pnueli*, volume 6200 of *Lecture Notes in Computer Science*, pages 144–166. Springer, heidelberg, 2010.

[51] Seymour Ginsburg and Edwin H. Spanier. Finite-turn pushdown automata. *SIAM Journal on Control and Optimization*, 4:429–453, 1966.

[52] A.V. Gladkij. Algorithmic nature of invariant properties of context-sensitive grammars. *Algebra i Logika*, 3(5-6):17–32, 1964. In Russian.

[53] Kurt Gödel. Über formal unentscheidbare Sätze der Principia Mathematica und verwandter Systeme I. *Monatshefte für Mathematik und Physik*, 38:173–198, 1931.

[54] E. Mark Gold. Language identification in the limit. *Information and Control*, 10:447–474, 1967.

[55] Radu Gramatovici and Carlos Martín-Vide. Sorted dependency insertion grammars. *Theoretical Computer Science*, 354:142–152, 2006.

[56] Sheila A. Greibach. A new normal form theorem for context-free phrase structure grammars. *Journal of the Association for Computing Machinery*, 12:42–52, 1965.

[57] Sheila A. Greibach. A note on pushdown store automata and regular systems. *Proceedings of the American Mathematical Society*, 18:263–268, 1967.

[58] Sheila A. Greibach. The hardest context-free language. *SIAM Journal on Computing*, 2:304–310, 1973.

[59] Thomas V. Griffiths. Some remarks on derivations in general rewriting systems. *Information and Control*, 12:27–54, 1968.

[60] Michael A. Harrison. *Introduction to Formal Language Theory*. Addison-Wesley, Reading, M.A., 1978.

[61] Juris Hartmanis. On Gödel speed-up and succinctness of language representations. *Theoretical Computer Science*, 26:335–342, 1983.

[62] Juris Hartmanis and Harry B. Hunt III. The LBA problem and its importance in the theory of computing. In Richard M. Karp, editor, *Complexity of Computation*, volume 7 of *SIAM-AMS Proceedings*, pages 1–26. American Mathematical Society, Providence, R.I., 1974.

[63] Juris Hartmanis and Richard E. Stearns. On the computational complexity of algorithms. *Transactions of the American Mathematical Society*, 117:285–306, 1965.

[64] David G. Hays. Dependency theory: A formalism and some observations. *Language*, 40:511–525, 1964.

[65] Tom Head. Formal language theory and DNA: An analysis of the generative capability of specific recombinant behaviors. *Bulletin of Mathematical Biology*, 49:737–759, 1987.

[66] Lane A. Hemaspaandra, Proshanto Mukherji, and Till Tantau. Context-free languages can be accepted with absolutely no space overhead. *Information and Computation*, 203:163–180, 2005.

[67] Rudolf Herschel and Friedrich Pieper. *PASCAL – Systematische Darstellung von PASCAL und CONCURRENT PASCAL für den Anwender*. Oldenbourg, München, 1979.

[68] Graham Higman. Ordering by divisibility in abstract algebras. *Proceedings of the London Mathematical Society*, 2:326–336, 1952.

[69] David Hilbert. Mathematische Probleme. Vortrag, gehalten auf dem internationalen Mathematiker-Kongreß zu Paris, 1900. *Nachrichten der Königlichen Gesellschaft der Wissenschaften zu Göttingen, mathematisch-physikalische Klasse*, 3:253–297, 1900.

[70] Dieter Hofbauer and Johannes Waldmann. Deleting string rewriting systems preserve regularity. *Theoretical Computer Science*, 327:301–317, 2004.

[71] Petr Hoffmann. *Machine Learning of Analysis by Reduction.* PhD thesis, Department of Software and Computer Science Education, Charles University in Prague, 2013.

[72] Petr Hoffmann. Power of S-kR-RRWW-automata. In Suna Bensch, Frank Drewes, Rudolf Freund, and Friedrich Otto, editors, *NCMA 2013, Proc.*, volume 294 of *books@ocg.at*, pages 163–178. Österreichische Computer Gesellschaft, Wien, 2013.

[73] Petr Hoffmann. Power of S-kR-RRWW-automata. *Fundamenta Informaticae*, 136:85–112, 2015.

[74] Markus Holzer and Martin Kutrib. Descriptional complexity – An introductory survey. In Carlos Martín-Vide, editor, *Scientific Applications of Language Methods*, volume 2 of *Mathematics, Computing, Language, and Life: Frontiers in Mathematical Linguistics and Language Theory*, pages 1–58. World Scientific/Imperial College Press, 2010.

[75] Markus Holzer and Martin Kutrib. Descriptional and computational complexity of finite automata: A survey. *Information and Computation*, 209:456–470, 2011.

[76] Markus Holzer, Martin Kutrib, and Andreas Malcher. Complexity of multi-head finite automata: Origins and directions. *Theoretical Computer Science*, 412:83–96, 2011.

[77] Markus Holzer, Martin Kutrib, and Jens Reimann. Non-recursive trade-offs for deterministic restarting automata. *Journal of Automata, Languages and Combinatorics*, 12:195–213, 2007.

[78] Markus Holzer and Friedrich Otto. Shrinking multi-pushdown automata. In Maciej Liśkiewicz and Rüdiger Reischuk, editors, *Fundamentals of Computation Theory, FCT 2005, Proc.*, volume 3623 of *Lecture Notes in Computer Science*, pages 305–316. Springer, Heidelberg, 2005.

[79] John E. Hopcroft, Rajeev Motwani, and Jeffrey D. Ullman. *Introduction to Automata Theory, Languages, and Computation.* Pearson, Boston, M.A., 3rd edition, 2007.

[80] John E. Hopcroft and Jeffrey D. Ullman. An approach to a unified theory of automata. *Bell System Technical Journal*, 46:1793–1829, 1967.

[81] John E. Hopcroft and Jeffrey D. Ullman. *Introduction to Automata Theory, Languages, and Computation.* Addison-Wesley, Reading, M.A., 1979.

[82] Neil Immerman. Languages that capture complexity classes. *SIAM Journal on Computing*, 16:760–778, 1987.

[83] Petr Jančar. Nondeterministic forgetting automata are less powerful than deterministic linear bounded automata. *Acta Mathematica et Informatica Universitatis Ostraviensis*, 1:67–73, 1993.

[84] Petr Jančar, František Mráz, Martin Plátek, Martin Procházka, and Jörg Vogel. Restarting automata, Marcus grammars and context-free languages. In Jürgen Dassow, Grzegorz Rozenberg, and Arto Salomaa, editors, *Developments in Language Theory II, Proc.*, pages 102–111. World Scientific, Singapore, 1996.

[85] Petr Jančar, František Mráz, Martin Plátek, and Jörg Vogel. Restarting automata. In Horst Reichel, editor, *FCT'95, Proc.*, volume 965 of *Lecture Notes in Computer Science*, pages 283–292. Springer, Heidelberg, 1995.

[86] Petr Jančar, František Mráz, Martin Plátek, and Jörg Vogel. On restarting automata with rewriting. In Gheorghe Păun and Arto Salomaa, editors, *New Trends in Formal Languages*, volume 1218 of *Lecture Notes in Computer Science*, pages 119–136. Springer, Heidelberg, 1997.

[87] Petr Jančar, František Mráz, Martin Plátek, and Jörg Vogel. On monotonic automata with a restart operation. *Journal of Automata, Languages and Combinatorics*, 4:287–311, 1999.

[88] Petr Jančar, František Mráz, Martin Plátek, and Jörg Vogel. Monotonicity of restarting automata. *Journal of Automata, Languages and Combinatorics*, 12:355–371, 2007.

[89] Neil D. Jones. Space-bounded reducibility among combinatorial problems. *Journal of Computer and System Sciences*, 11:68–85, 1975.

[90] Aravind K. Joshi. Tree adjoining grammars: How much context-sensitivity is required to provide reasonable structural descriptions. In David R. Dowdy, Lauri Karttuhen, and Arnold M. Zwicky, editors, *Natural Language Parsing*, pages 206–250. Cambridge University Press, 1985.

[91] Aravind K. Joshi, Leon S. Levy, and Masako Takahashi. Tree adjunct grammars. *Journal of Computer and System Sciences*, 10:136–163, 1975.

[92] Aravind K. Joshi, K. Vijay-Shanker, and David J. Weir. The Convergence of Mildly Context-Sensitive Grammar Formalisms. Technical Report MS-CIS-90-01, University of Pennsylvania, Philadelphia, Pa, 1990.

[93] Tomasz Jurdziński and Krzysztof Loryś. Lower bound technique for length-reducing automata. *Information and Computation*, 205:1387–1412, 2007.

[94] Tomasz Jurdziński, Krzysztof Loryś, Gundula Niemann, and Friedrich Otto. Some results on RWW- and RRWW-automata and their relation to the class of growing context-sensitive languages. *Journal on Automata, Languages and Combinatorics*, 9:407–437, 2004.

[95] Tomasz Jurdziński, František Mráz, Friedrich Otto, and Martin Plátek. Monotone deterministic RL-automata don't need auxiliary symbols. In Clelio De Felice and Antonio Restivo, editors, *Developments in Language Theory, DLT 2005, Proc.*, volume 3572 of *Lecture Notes in Computer Science*, pages 284–295. Springer, Heidelberg, 2005.

[96] Tomasz Jurdziński, František Mráz, Friedrich Otto, and Martin Plátek. Degrees of non-monotonicity for restarting automata. *Theoretical Computer Science*, 369:1–34, 2006.

[97] Tomasz Jurdziński and Friedrich Otto. Restarting automata with restricted utilization of auxiliary symbols. *Theoretical Computer Science*, 363:162–181, 2006.

[98] Tomasz Jurdziński and Friedrich Otto. Sequential monotonicity for restarting automata. *RAIRO Theoretical Informatics and Applications*, 41:157–175, 2007.

[99] Tomasz Jurdziński and Friedrich Otto. Shrinking restarting automata. *International Journal of Foundations of Computer Science*, 18:361–385, 2007.

[100] Tomasz Jurdziński, Friedrich Otto, František Mráz, and Martin Plátek. On the complexity of 2-monotone restarting automata. In Cristian S. Calude, Elena Calude, and Michael J. Dinneen, editors, *DLT 2004, Proc.*, volume 3340 of *Lecture Notes in Computer Science*, pages 237–248. Springer, Heidelberg, 2004.

[101] Tomasz Jurdziński, Friedrich Otto, František Mráz, and Martin Plátek. Cut hierarchies for restarting automata and Marcus t-contextual grammars. In Symeon Bozapalidis, Antonios Kalampakas, and George Rahonis, editors, *Conference on Algebraic Informatics, CAI 2005, Proc.*, pages 157–171. Aristotle University, Thessaloniki, 2005.

[102] Tomasz Jurdziński, Friedrich Otto, František Mráz, and Martin Plátek. Deterministic two-way restarting automata and Marcus contextual grammars. *Fundamenta Informaticae*, 64:217–228, 2005.

[103] Tomasz Jurdziński, Friedrich Otto, František Mráz, and Martin Plátek. On the complexity of 2-monotone restarting automata. *Theory of Computing Systems*, 42:488–518, 2008.

[104] Laura Kallmeyer. *Parsing Beyond Context-Free Grammars.* Cognitive Technologies. Springer, Berlin, 2010.

[105] Lila Kari, Grzegorz Rozenberg, and Arto Salomaa. L-systems. In Grzegorz Rozenberg and Arto Salomaa, editors, *Handbook of Formal Languages*, volume 1, pages 253–328. Springer, Berlin, Heidelberg, 1997.

[106] Richard M. Karp. Reducibility among combinatorial problems. In Raymond E. Miller, James W. Thatcher, and Jean D. Bohlinger, editors, *Complexity of Computer Computations*, The IBM Research Symposia Series, pages 85–103. Springer, Boston, MA, 1972.

[107] Tadao Kasami. An efficient recognition and syntax algorithm for context-free languages. Scientific Report AFCRL-65-758, Air Force Cambridge Research Lab., Bedford, Mass., 1965.

[108] Stephen C. Kleene. General recursive functions of natural numbers. *Mathematische Annalen*, 112:727–742, 1936.

[109] Stephen C. Kleene. Representation of events in nerve nets and finite automata. Technical report, RAND Corporation, Santa Monica, CA, 1951.

[110] Stephen C. Kleene. Representation of events in nerve nets and finite automata. In Claude Shannon and John McCarthy, editors, *Automata Studies*, volume 34 of *Annals of Mathematical Studies*, pages 3–41. Princeton University Press, San Diego, CA, 1956.

[111] Donald E. Knuth. On the translation of languages from left to right. *Information and Control*, 8:607–639, 1965.

[112] Donald E. Knuth. Semantics of context-free languages. *Mathematical Systems Theory*, 2:127–145, 1968.

[113] Satoshi Kobayashi and Takashi Yokomori. Learning concatenations of locally testable languages from positive data. In Setsuo Arikawa and Klaus P. Jantke, editors, *ALT'94, Proc.*, volume 872 of *Lecture Notes in Computer Science*, pages 407–422. Springer, Heidelberg, 1994.

[114] Vladislav Kuboň and Martin Plátek. A grammar based approach to a grammar checking of free word order languages. In Yorick Wilks, editor, *COLING'94, Proc., Vol. II*, pages 906–910. Association for Computational Linguistics, Stroudsburg, PA, 1994.

[115] Jürgen Kunze. *Abhängigkeitsgrammatik*, volume XII of *studia grammatica*. Akademie-Verlag, Berlin, 1975.

[116] Shigeyuki Kuroda. Classes of languages and linear-bounded automata. *Information and Control*, 7:207–223, 1964.

[117] Martin Kutrib and Andreas Malcher. When Church-Rosser becomes context-free. *International Journal of Foundations of Computer Science*, 18:1293–1302, 2007.

[118] Martin Kutrib and Andreas Malcher. Reversible pushdown automata. *Journal of Computer and System Sciences*, 78:1814–1827, 2012.

[119] Martin Kutrib, Andreas Malcher, and Matthias Wendlandt. Reversible queue automata. In Suna Bensch, Rudolf Freund, and Friedrich Otto, editors, *Sixth Workshop on Non-Classical Models of Automata and Applications (NCMA 2014), Proc.*, volume 304 of *books@ocg.at*, pages 163–178. Österreichische Computer Gesellschaft, Wien, 2014.

[120] Martin Kutrib, Hartmut Messerschmidt, and Friedrich Otto. On stateless two-pushdown automata and restarting automata. In Erzsébet Csuhaj-Varjú and Zoltán Ésik, editors, *Automata and Formal Languages, AFL 2008, Proc.*, pages 257–268. Computer and Automation Research Institute, Hungarian Academy of Sciences, 2008.

[121] Martin Kutrib, Hartmut Messerschmidt, and Friedrich Otto. On stateless deterministic restarting automata. In Mogens Nielsen, Antonín Kučera, Peter Bro Miltersen, Catuscia Palamidessi, Petr Tůma, and Frank Valencia, editors, *SOFSEM 2009: Theory and Practice of Computer Science, Proc.*, volume 5404 of *Lecture Notes in Computer Science*, pages 353–364. Springer, Heidelberg, 2009.

[122] Martin Kutrib, Hartmut Messerschmidt, and Friedrich Otto. On stateless deterministic restarting automata. *Acta Informatica*, 47:391–412, 2010.

[123] Martin Kutrib, Hartmut Messerschmidt, and Friedrich Otto. On stateless two-pushdown automata and restarting automata. *International Journal of Foundations of Computer Science*, 21:781–798, 2010.

[124] Martin Kutrib and Friedrich Otto. On the descriptional complexity of the window size for deterministic restarting automata. In Nelma Moreira and Rogério Reis, editors, *CIAA 2012*, volume 7381 of *Lecture Notes in Computer Science*, pages 253–264. Springer, Heidelberg, 2012.

[125] Martin Kutrib and Friedrich Otto. On the descriptional complexity of the window size for deleting restarting automata. *International Journal of Foundations of Computer Science*, 24:831–846, 2013.

[126] Martin Kutrib and Jens Reimann. Optimal simulations of weak restarting automata. In Viliam Geffert and Giovanni Pighizzini, editors, *9th International Workshop on Descriptional Complexity of Formal Systems - DCFS 2007, High Tatras, Slovakia, July 20 – 22, 2007*, pages 81–92. University of Kosice, Slovakia, 2007.

[127] Martin Kutrib and Jens Reimann. Optimal simulations of weak restarting automata. *International Journal of Foundations of Computer Science*, 19:795–811, 2008.

[128] Martin Kutrib and Jens Reimann. Succinct description of regular languages by weak restarting automata. *Information and Computation*, 206:1152–1160, 2008.

[129] Kent Kwee. Ordered Restarting Automata. Doctoral dissertation, Fachbereich Elektrotechnik/Informatik, Universität Kassel, 2018.

[130] Kent Kwee and Friedrich Otto. On some decision problems for stateless deterministic ordered restarting automata. In Jeffrey Shallit and Alexander Okhotin, editors, *DCFS 2015, Proc.*, volume 9118 of *Lecture Notes in Computer Science*, pages 165–176. Springer, Heidelberg, 2015.

[131] Kent Kwee and Friedrich Otto. On ordered RRWW-automata. In Srečko Brlek and Christophe Reutenauer, editors, *DLT 2016, Proc.*, volume 9840 of *Lecture Notes in Computer Science*, pages 268–279. Springer, Heidelberg, 2016.

[132] Kent Kwee and Friedrich Otto. On the effects of nondeterminism on ordered restarting automata. In Rūsiņš Mārtiņš Freivalds, Gregor Engels, and Barbara Catania, editors, *SOFSEM 2016, Proc.*, volume 9587 of *Lecture Notes in Computer Science*, pages 369–380. Springer, Heidelberg, 2016.

[133] Kent Kwee and Friedrich Otto. A pumping lemma for ordered restarting automata. In Giovanni Pighizzini and Cezar Câmpeanu, editors, *DCFS 2017, Proc.*, volume 10316 of *Lecture Notes in Computer Science*, pages 226–237. Springer, Heidelberg, 2017.

[134] Kent Kwee and Friedrich Otto. Nondeterministic ordered restarting automata. *International Journal of Foundations of Computer Science*, 29:663–685, 2018.

[135] Gerhard Lallement. *Semigroups and Combinatorial Applications.* Wiley-Interscience, New York, 1979.

[136] Edmund Landau. Über die Maximalordnung der Permutationen gegebenen Grades. *Archiv der Mathematik und Physik*, 3:92–103, 1903.

[137] Edmund Landau. *Handbuch der Lehre von der Verteilung der Primzahlen*, volume I. Teubner, Leipzig, 1909.

[138] Clemens Lautemann. One pushdown and a small tape. In Klaus W. Wagner, editor, *Dirk Siefkes zum 50. Geburtstag*, pages 42–47. Technische Universität Berlin and Universität Augsburg, 1988.

[139] Peter Leupold and Friedrich Otto. On McNaughton families of languages that are specified by some variants of monadic string-rewriting systems. *Fundamenta Informaticae*, 112:219–238, 2011.

[140] Ming Li and Paul Vitányi. *An Introduction to Kolmogorov Complexity and Its Applications.* Springer, New York, 1997.

[141] Aristid Lindenmayer. Mathematical models for cellular interactions in development I. Filaments with one-sided inputs. *Journal of Theoretical Biology*, 18:280–299, 1968.

[142] Aristid Lindenmayer. Mathematical models for cellular interactions in development II. Simple and branching filaments with two-sided inputs. *Journal of Theoretical Biology*, 18:300–315, 1968.

[143] Aristid Lindenmayer. Developmental systems without cellular interactions, their languages and grammars. *Journal of Theoretical Biology*, 30:455–484, 1971.

[144] Markéta Lopatková, Martin Plátek, and Vladislav Kuboň. Modeling syntax of free word-order languages: Dependency analysis by reduction. In Václav Matoušek, Pavel Mautner, and Tomáš Pavelka, editors, *Text, Speech and Dialogue (TSD 2005), Proc.*, volume 3658 of *Lecture Notes in Artificial Intelligence*, pages 140–147. Springer, Heidelberg, 2005.

[145] Markéta Lopatková, Martin Plátek, and Petr Sgall. Towards a formal model for Functional Generative Description. *Prague Bulletin of Mathematical Linguistics*, 87:1–20, 2007.

[146] Andreas Malcher. Decidability questions for insertion systems and related models. *Fundamenta Informaticae*, 180:53–76, 2021.

[147] Solomon Marcus. Contextual grammars. *Revue Roumaine de Mathématiques Pures et Appliquées*, 14:1525–1534, 1969.

[148] Solomon Marcus. Contextual grammars and natural languages. In Grzegorz Rozenberg and Arto Salomaa, editors, *Handbook of Formal Languages*, volume 2, pages 215–235. Springer, Berlin, Heidelberg, 1997.

[149] Robert F. McNaughton. Algebraic decision procedures for local testability. *Mathematical Systems Theory*, 8:60–76, 1974.

[150] Robert F. McNaughton. An insertion into the Chomsky hierarchy? In Juhani Karhumäki, Hermann Maurer, Gheorghe Păun, and Grzegorz Rozenberg, editors, *Jewels are Forever, Contributions on Theoretical Computer Science in Honor of Arto Salomaa*, pages 204–212. Springer, Berlin, 1999.

[151] Robert F. McNaughton, Paliath Narendran, and Friedrich Otto. Church-Rosser Thue systems and formal languages. *Journal of the Association for Computing Machinery*, 35:324–344, 1988.

[152] Robert F. McNaughton and H. Yamada. Regular expressions and state graphs for automata. *IEEE Transactions on Electronic Computers*, 9:39–47, 1960.

[153] Hartmut Messerschmidt and Heiko Stamer. Restart-Automaten mit mehreren Restart-Zuständen. In Henning Bordihn, editor, *Workshop 'Formale Methoden in der Linguistik' und 14. Theorietag 'Automaten und Formale Sprachen,' Proc.*, pages 111–116. Institut für Informatik, Universität Potsdam, Potsdam, 2004.

[154] Albert R. Meyer and Michael J. Fischer. Economy of description by automata, grammars, and formal systems. In *IEEE Symposium on Switching and Automata Theory (SWAT 1971)*, pages 188–191. IEEE Press, 1971.

[155] William Miller. The maximum order of an element of a finite symmetric group. *The American Mathematics Monthly*, 94:497–506, 1987.

[156] František Mráz. Forgetting and Restarting Automata. Phd thesis (Kandidátska dizertačná práca), Faculty of Mathematics and Physics, Charles University, Prague, 2001.

[157] František Mráz. Lookahead hierarchies of restarting automata. *Journal of Automata, Languages and Combinatorics*, 6:493–506, 2001.

[158] František Mráz and Friedrich Otto. Hierarchies of weakly monotone restarting automata. *RAIRO Theoretical Informatics and Applications*, 39:325–342, 2005.

[159] František Mráz and Friedrich Otto. Lambda-confluence is undecidable for clearing restarting automata. In Stavros Konstantinidis, editor, *CIAA 2013, Proc.*, volume 7982 of *Lecture Notes in Computer Science*, pages 256–267. Springer, Heidelberg, 2013.

[160] František Mráz and Friedrich Otto. Deleting deterministic restarting automata with two windows. In Émilie Charlier, Julien Leroy, and Michel Rigo, editors, *DLT 2017, Proc.*, volume 10396 of *Lecture Notes in Computer Science*, pages 272–283. Springer, Heidelberg, 2017.

[161] František Mráz and Friedrich Otto. On deleting deterministic restarting automata that have two windows. *Journal of Automata, Languages and Combinatorics*, 23:387–417, 2018.

[162] František Mráz and Friedrich Otto. On shrinking restarting automata of window size one and two. In Piotrek Hofman and Michał Skrzypczak, editors, *DLT 2019, Proc.*, volume 11647 of *Lecture Notes in Computer Science*, pages 140–153. Springer, Heidelberg, 2019.

[163] František Mráz and Friedrich Otto. Window size two suffices for deterministic monotone RWW-automata. In Rudolf Freund, Markus Holzer, and José M. Sempere, editors, *Eleventh Workshop on Non-Classical Models of Automata and Applications (NCMA 2019), Proc.*, volume 336 of *books@ocg.at*, pages 139–154. Österreichische Computer Gesellschaft, Wien, 2019.

[164] František Mráz and Friedrich Otto. On restarting automata with auxiliary symbols and small window size. *RAIRO Theoretical Informatics and Applications*, 55:pp. 31, 2021.

[165] František Mráz, Friedrich Otto, Dana Pardubská, and Martin Plátek. Lexicalized syntactic analysis by two-way restarting automata. *Journal of Automata, Languages and Combinatorics*, 26:145–171, 2021.

[166] František Mráz, Friedrich Otto, and Martin Plátek. Learning analysis by reduction from positive data. In Yasubumi Sakakibara, Satoshi Kobayashi, Kengo Sato, Tetsuro Nishino, and Etsuji Tomita, editors, *ICGI 2006, Proc.*, volume 4201 of *Lecture Notes in Artificial Intelligence*, pages 125–136. Springer, Heidelberg, 2006.

[167] František Mráz, Friedrich Otto, and Martin Plátek. The degree of word-expansion of lexicalized RRWW-automata – a new measure for the degree of nondeterminism of (context-free) languages. *Theoretical Computer Science*, 410:3530–3538, 2009.

[168] František Mráz, Friedrich Otto, and Martin Plátek. Free word order and restarting automata. *Fundamenta Informaticae*, 133:399–419, 2014.

[169] František Mráz, Friedrich Otto, and Martin Plátek. Characterizations of LRR-languages by correctness-preserving computations. In Rudolf Freund, Michal Hospodár, Galina Jirásková, and Giovanni Pighizzini, editors, *Tenth Workshop on Non-Classical Models of Automata and Applications (NCMA 2018), Proc.*, volume 332 of *books@ocg.at*, pages 149–164. Österreichische Computer Gesellschaft, Wien, 2018.

[170] František Mráz, Friedrich Otto, Martin Plátek, and Tomasz Jurdziński. Marcus t-contextual grammars and cut hierarchies and monotonicity for restarting automata. *Theoretical Computer Science*, 366:272–296, 2006.

[171] František Mráz, Martin Plátek, and Tomasz Jurdziński. Ambiguity by restarting automata. *International Journal of Foundations of Computer Science*, 18:1343–1352, 2007.

[172] František Mráz, Martin Plátek, and Friedrich Otto. A measure for the degree of nondeterminism of context-free languages. In Jan Holub and Jan Žďárek, editors, *CIAA 2007, Proc.*, volume 4783 of *Lecture Notes in Computer Science*, pages 192–202. Springer, Heidelberg, 2007.

[173] František Mráz, Martin Plátek, and Martin Procházka. On special forms of restarting automata. *Grammars*, 2:223–233, 1999.

[174] František Mráz, Martin Plátek, and Martin Procházka. Restarting automata, deleting, and Marcus grammars. In *Recent Topics in Mathematical and Computational Linguistics*, pages 218–233. The Publishing House of the Romanian Academy, Bucharest, 2000.

[175] František Mráz, Martin Plátek, and Jörg Vogel. Restarting automata with rewriting. In Keith G. Jeffery, Jaroslav Král, and Miroslav Bartošek, editors, *SOFSEM'96: Theory and Practise of Informatics*, volume 1175 of *Lecture Notes in Computer Science*, pages 401–408. Springer, Heidelberg, 1996.

[176] Yasuhito Mukouchi, Ikuyo Yamaue, and Masako Sato. Inferring a rewriting system from examples. In Setsuo Arikawa and Hiroshi Motoda, editors, *Discovery Science, Proc.*, volume 1532 of *Lecture Notes in Artificial Intelligence*, pages 93–104. Springer, Heidelberg, 1998.

[177] Benedek Nagy. A family of two-head pushdown automata. In Rudolf Freund, Markus Holzer, Nelma Moreira, and Rogério Reis, editors, *Seventh Workshop on Non-Classical Models of Automata and Applications (NCMA 2015), Proc.*, volume 318 of *books@ocg.at*, pages 177–191. Österreichische Computer Gesellschaft, Wien, 2015.

[178] Benedek Nagy and Friedrich Otto. Globally deterministic CD-systems of stateless R(1)-automata. In Adrian-Horia Dediu, Shunsuke Inenaga, and Carlos Martín-Vide, editors, *Language and Automata Theory and Applications, LATA 2011, Proc.*, volume 6638 of *Lecture Notes in Computer Science*, pages 390–401. Springer, Heidelberg, 2011.

[179] Benedek Nagy and Friedrich Otto. On CD-systems of stateless deterministic R-automata with window size one. *Journal of Computer and System Sciences*, 78:780–806, 2012.

[180] Paliath Narendran, Colm Ó'Dúnlaing, and Heinrich Rolletschek. Complexity of certain decision problems about congruential languages. *Journal of Computer and System Sciences*, 30:343–358, 1985.

[181] Gundula Niemann. Church-Rosser Languages and Related Classes. Doctoral dissertation, Fachbereich Mathematik/Informatik, Universität Kassel, 2002.

[182] Gundula Niemann and Friedrich Otto. Restarting automata, Church-Rosser languages, and confluent internal contextual languages. Mathematische Schriften Kassel 4/99, Universität Kassel, March 1999.

[183] Gundula Niemann and Friedrich Otto. Restarting automata, Church-Rosser languages, and representations of r.e. languages. In Grzegorz Rozenberg and Wolfgang Thomas, editors, *Developments in Language Theory – Foundations, Applications, and Perspectives, DLT 1999, Proc.*, pages 103–114. World Scientific, Singapore, 2000.

[184] Gundula Niemann and Friedrich Otto. On the power of RRWW-automata. In Masami Ito, Gheorghe Păun, and Sheng Yu, editors, *Words, Semigroups, and Transductions. Essays in Honour of Gabriel Thierrin, On the Occasion of His 80th Birthday*, pages 341–355. World Scientific, Singapore, 2001.

[185] Gundula Niemann and Friedrich Otto. Further results on restarting automata. In Masami Ito and Teruo Imaoka, editors, *Words, Languages and Combinatorics III, Proc.*, pages 352–369, Singapore, 2003. World Scientific.

[186] Gundula Niemann and Friedrich Otto. The Church-Rosser languages are the deterministic variants of the growing context-sensitive languages. *Information and Computation*, 197:1–21, 2005.

[187] Gundula Niemann and Jens Woinowski. The growing context-sensitive languages are the acyclic context-sensitive languages. In Werner Kuich, Grzegorz Rozenberg, and Arto Salomaa, editors, *DLT 2001, Proc.*, volume 2295 of *Lecture Notes in Computer Science*, pages 197–205. Springer, Heidelberg, 2002.

[188] Colm Ó'Dúnlaing and Natalie Schluter. A shorter proof that palindromes are not a Church-Rosser language, with extensions to almost-confluent and preperfect Thue systems. *Theoretical Computer Science*, 411:677–690, 2010.

[189] Karel Oliva and Martin Plátek. Formal word order complexity of Czech. In Gerhild Zybatow, Uwe Junghanns, Grit Mehlhorn, and Luka Szucsich, editors, *Current Issues in Formal Slavic Linguistics*, volume 5 of *Linguistik International*, pages 306–313. P. Lang, Frankfurt/Main, 2001.

[190] José Oncina and Pedro García. Inferring regular languages in polynomial update time. In Nicolás Pérez de la Blanca, Alberto Sanfeliu, and Enrique Vidal, editors, *Pattern Recognition and Image Analysis*, volume 1 of *Machine Perception and Artificial Intelligence*, pages 49–61. World Scientific, Singapore, 1992.

[191] Friedrich Otto. On deciding the confluence of a finite string-rewriting system on a given congruence class. *Journal of Computer and System Sciences*, 35:285–310, 1987.

[192] Friedrich Otto. Restarting automata and their relations to the Chomsky hierarchy. In Zoltán Ésik and Zoltán Fülöp, editors, *DLT 2003, Proc.*, volume 2710 of *Lecture Notes in Computer Science*, pages 55–74. Springer, Heidelberg, 2003.

[193] Friedrich Otto. Restarting automata. In Zoltán Ésik, Carlos Martín-Vide, and Victor Mitrana, editors, *Recent Advances in Formal Languages and Applications*, volume 25 of *Studies in Computational Intelligence*, pages 269–303. Springer, Heidelberg, 2006.

[194] Friedrich Otto. Left-to-right regular languages and two-way restarting automata. *RAIRO Theoretical Informatics and Applications*, 43:653–665, 2009.

[195] Friedrich Otto. On the descriptional complexity of deterministic ordered restarting automata. In Helmut Jürgensen, Juhani Karhumäki, and Alexander Okhotin, editors, *DCFS 2014, Proc.*, volume 8614 of *Lecture Notes in Computer Science*, pages 318–329. Springer, Heidelberg, 2014.

[196] Friedrich Otto. Restarting automata for picture languages: A survey on recent developments. In Markus Holzer and Martin Kutrib, editors, *CIAA 2014, Proc.*, volume 8587 of *Lecture Notes in Computer Science*, pages 16–41. Springer, Heidelberg, 2014.

[197] Friedrich Otto. On deterministic ordered restart-delete automata. In Mizuho Hoshi and Shinnosuke Seki, editors, *DLT 2018, Proc.*, volume 11088 of *Lecture Notes in Computer Science*, pages 529–540. Springer, Heidelberg, 2018.

[198] Friedrich Otto. On deterministic ordered restart-delete automata. *Theoretical Computer Science*, 795:257–274, 2019.

[199] Friedrich Otto. A characterization of the context-free languages by stateless ordered restart-delete automata. In Alexander Chatzigeorgiou, Riccardo Dondi, Herodotos Herodotou, Christos Kapoutsis, Yannis Manolopoulos, George A. Papadopoulos, and Florian Sikora, editors, *SOFSEM 2020, Proc.*, volume 12011 of *Lecture Notes in Computer Science*, pages 39–50. Springer, Heidelberg, 2020.

[200] Friedrich Otto. A complete taxonomy of restarting automata without auxiliary symbols. *Fundamenta Informaticae*, 180:77–101, 2021.

[201] Friedrich Otto. On the expressive power of stateless ordered restart-delete automata. *Theory of Computing Systems*, 65:1033–1068, 2021.

[202] Friedrich Otto, Peter Černo, and František Mráz. Limited context restarting automata and McNaughton families of languages. In Rudolf Freund, Markus Holzer, Bianca Truthe, and Ulrich Ultes-Nitsche, editors, *Fourth Workshop on Non-Classical Models for Automata and Applications (NCMA 2012), Proc.*, volume 290 of *books@ocg.at*, pages 165–180. Österreichische Computer Gesellschaft, Wien, 2012.

[203] Friedrich Otto, Peter Černo, and František Mráz. On the classes of languages accepted by limited context restarting automata. *RAIRO Theoretical Informatics and Applications*, 48:61–84, 2014.

[204] Friedrich Otto, Masashi Katsura, and Yuji Kobayashi. Infinite convergent string-rewriting systems and cross-sections for finitely presented monoids. *Journal of Symbolic Computation*, 26:621–648, 1998.

[205] Friedrich Otto and Kent Kwee. On the descriptional complexity of stateless ordered restarting automata. *Information and Computation*, 259:277–302, 2018.

[206] Friedrich Otto and František Mráz. Lambda-confluence for context rewriting systems. *Theoretical Computer Science*, 578:88–99, 2015.

[207] Friedrich Otto and František Mráz. Regulated variants of limited context restarting automata. *Theoretical Computer Science*, 682:190–207, 2017.

[208] Friedrich Otto, František Mráz, and Martin Plátek. Degrees of monotonicity and Marcus t-contextual grammars. In Zoltán Ésik and Zoltán Fülöp, editors, *Automata and Formal Languages, AFL 2005, Proc.*, pages 249–262. Institute of Informatics, University of Szeged, 2005.

[209] Friedrich Otto and Martin Plátek. A two-dimensional taxonomy of proper languages of lexicalized FRR-automata. In Carlos Martín-Vide, Friedrich Otto, and Henning Fernau, editors, *Language and Automata Theory and Applications, LATA 2008, Proc.*, volume 5196 of *Lecture Notes in Computer Science*, pages 409–420. Springer, Heidelberg, 2008.

[210] Friedrich Otto and Matthias Wendlandt. Reversibility for stateless ordered RRWW-automata. *Acta Informatica*, 58:397–425, 2021.

[211] Friedrich Otto, Matthias Wendlandt, and Kent Kwee. Reversible ordered restarting automata. In Jean Krivine and Jean-Bernard Stefani, editors, *RC 2015, Proc.*, volume 9138 of *Lecture Notes in Computer Science*, pages 60–75. Springer, Heidelberg, 2015.

[212] Jukka Paakki. Attribute grammar paradigms – A high-level methodology in language implementation. *ACM Computing Surveys*, 27:196–255, 1995.

[213] Rohit J. Parikh. On context-free languages. *Journal of the Association for Computing Machinery*, 13:570–581, 1966.

[214] Gheorghe Păun. *Marcus Contextual Grammars*, volume 67 of *Studies in Linguistics and Philosophy*. Kluwer, Dordrecht/Boston/London, 1997.

[215] Gheorghe Păun. Computing with membranes. *Journal of Computer and System Sciences*, 61:108–143, 2000.

[216] Gheorghe Păun, Grzegorz Rozenberg, and Arto Salomaa. Computing by slicing. *Theoretical Computer Science*, 168:321–336, 1996.

[217] Jean-Eric Pin. On reversible automata. In Imre Simon, editor, *LATIN'92, Proc.*, volume 583 of *Lecture Notes in Computer Science*, pages 401–416. Springer, Heidelberg, 1992.

[218] Martin Plátek. Two-way restarting automata and j-monotonicity. In Leszek Pacholski and Peter Ružička, editors, *SOFSEM 2001: Theory and Practice of Informatics, Proc*, volume 2234 of *Lecture Notes in Computer Science*, pages 316–325. Springer, Heidelberg, 2001.

[219] Martin Plátek, Tomáš Holan, and Vladislav Kuboň. On relax-ability of word-order by D-grammars. In Cristian S. Calude, Michael J. Dinneen, and Silviu Sburlan, editors, *Combinatorics, Computability and Logic, Proceedings of the Third International Conference on Combinatorics, Computability and Logic, DMTCS 2001, Constanta, Romania*, Discrete Mathematics and Theoretical Computer Science, pages 159–173. Springer, Heidelberg, 2001.

[220] Martin Plátek and František Mráz. Degrees of (non)monotonicity of RRW-automata. In Jürgen Dassow and Detlef Wotschke, editors, *Preproceedings of the 3rd Workshop on Descriptional Complexity of Automata, Grammars and Related Structures*, Technical Report No. 16, pages 159–165. Fakultät für Informatik, Universität Magdeburg, Magdeburg, Germany, 2001.

[221] Martin Plátek and Friedrich Otto. On h-lexicalized restarting automata. In Erzsébet Csuhaj-Varjú, Pál Dömösi, and György Vaszil, editors, *15th International Conference on Automata and Languages (AFL 2017)*, volume 252 of *EPTCS*, pages 219–233. Open Publishing Association, 2017.

[222] Martin Plátek, Friedrich Otto, and František Mráz. Two-dimensional hierarchies of proper languages of lexicalized FRR-automata. *Information and Computation*, 207:1300–1314, 2009.

[223] Martin Plátek, Friedrich Otto, and František Mráz. On h-lexicalized restarting list automata. *Journal of Automata, Languages, and Combinatorics*, 25:201–234, 2020.

[224] Martin Plátek, Friedrich Otto, and František Mráz. One-way restarting automata and their sensitivity. *International Journal of Foundations of Computer Science*, 33:371–387, 2022.

[225] Emil L. Post. Recursive unsolvability of a problem of Thue. *The Journal of Symbolic Logic*, 12:1–11, 1947.

[226] Michael O. Rabin and Dana Scott. Finite automata and their decision problems. *IBM Journal of Research and Development*, 3:115–125, 1959.

[227] Owen Rambow and Aravind K. Joshi. A preprocessing model for free word order languages. In Charles Clifton Jr., Lyn Frazier, Keith Rayner, and Charles Clifton, editors, *Perspectives on Sentence Processing*, pages 267–301. Lawrence Erlbaum Associates, Mahwah, N.J., 1994.

[228] Jens Reimann. Beschreibungskomplexität von Restart-Automaten. Doctoral dissertation, University of Giessen, Gießen, Germany, 2007.

[229] Arnold L. Rosenberg. A machine realization of the linear context-free languages. *Information and Control*, 10:175–188, 1967.

[230] Daniel J. Rosenkrantz. Matrix equations and normal forms for context-free grammars. *Journal of the Association for Computing Machinery*, 14:501–507, 1967.

[231] Arto Salomaa. *Formal Languages*. Academic Press, London, 1973.

[232] Kai Salomaa and Sheng Yu. NFA to DFA transformation for finite languages over arbitrary alphabets. *Journal of Automata, Languages and Combinatorics*, 2:177–186, 1997.

[233] Walter J. Savitch. Relationships between nondeterministic and deterministic tape complexities. *Journal of Computer and System Sciences*, 4:177–192, 1970.

[234] Natalie Schluter. On lookahead hierarchies for monotone and deterministic restarting automata with auxiliary symbols (Extended abstract). In Yuan Gao, Hanlin Lu, Shinnosuke Seki, and Sheng Yu, editors, *DLT 2010, Proc.*, volume 6224 of *Lecture Notes in Computer Science*, pages 440–441. Springer, Heidelberg, 2010.

[235] Natalie Schluter. Restarting automata with auxiliary symbols and small lookahead. In Adrian-Horia Dediu, Shunsuke Inenaga, and Carlos Martín-Vide, editors, *LATA 2011, Proc.*, volume 6638 of *Lecture Notes in Computer Science*, pages 499–510. Springer, Heidelberg, 2011.

[236] Natalie Schluter. Restarting automata with auxiliary symbols restricted by lookahead size. *International Journal of Computer Mathematics*, 92:908–938, 2015.

[237] Marcel-Paul Schützenberger. On context-free languages and pushdown automata. *Information and Control*, 6:246–264, 1963.

[238] Hiroyuke Seki, Takashi Matsumura, Mamori Fujii, and Tadao Kasami. On multiple context-free grammars. *Theoretical Computer Science*, 88:191–229, 1991.

[239] Géraud Sénizergues. The equivalence problem for deterministic pushdown automata is decidable. In Pierpaolo Degano, Roberto Gorrieri, and Alberto Marchetti-Spaccamela, editors, *Automata, Languages and Programming*, volume 1256 of *Lecture Notes in Computer Science*, pages 671–681. Springer, Heidelberg, 1997.

[240] Géraud Sénizergues. Complete formal systems for equivalence problems. *Theoretical Computer Science*, 231:309–334, 2000.

[241] Géraud Sénizergues. $L(A) = L(B)$? decidability results from complete formal systems. *Theoretical Computer Science*, 251:1–166, 2001.

[242] Géraud Sénizergues. $L(A) = L(B)$? A simplified decidability proof. *Theoretical Computer Science*, 281:555–608, 2002.

[243] Petr Sgall, Eva Hajičová, and Jarmila Panevová. *The Meaning of the Sentence in Its Semantic and Pragmatic Aspects*. Reidel Publishing Company, Dordrecht, 1986.

[244] John C. Sheperdson. The reduction of two-way automata to one-way automata. *IBM Journal of Research and Development*, 3:198–200, 1959.

[245] Stuart M. Shieber. Evidence against the context-freeness of natural languages. *Linguistics and Philosophy*, 8:333–343, 1985.

[246] Stefan Sokolowski. A method for proving programming languages non context-free. *Information Processing Letters*, 7:151–153, 1978.

[247] Heiko Stamer. Restarting Tree Automata. Doctoral dissertation, Fachbereich Elektrotechnik/Informatik, Universität Kassel, 2008.

[248] Richard E. Stearns. A regularity test for pushdown machines. *Information and Control*, 11:323–340, 1967.

[249] Ivan Hal Sudborough. One-way multihead writing finite automata. *Information and Control*, 30:1–20, 1976.

[250] Róbert Szelepczényi. The method of forced enumeration for nondeterministic automata. *Acta Informatica*, 26:279–284, 1988.

[251] Alan Turing. On computable numbers, with an application to the Entscheidungsproblem. *Proceedings of the London Mathematical Society*, 2:230–265, 1937.

[252] Leslie G. Valiant. General context-free recognition in less than cubic time. *Journal Computer System Sciences*, 10:308–315, 1975.

[253] Leslie G. Valiant. Regularity and related problems for deterministic pushdown automata. *Journal of the Association for Computing Machinery*, 22:1–10, 1975.

[254] Peter Černo. Clearing restarting automata and grammatical inference. In Jeffrey Heinz, Colin de la Higuera, and Tim Oates, editors, *Eleventh International Conference on Grammatical Inference*, volume 21 of *JMLR Workshop and Conference Proc.*, pages 54–68. ML Research Press, Copenhagen, 2012.

[255] Peter Černo. Clearing restarting automata and grammatical inference. Technical Report 1/2012, Charles University, Faculty of Mathematics and Physics, Prague, 2012.

[256] Peter Černo. Grammatical inference of lambda-confluent context rewriting systems. In Suna Bensch, Frank Drewes, Rudolf Freund, and Friedrich Otto, editors, *NCMA 2013, Proc.*, volume 294 of *books@ocg.at*, pages 85–100. Österreichische Computer Gesellschaft, Wien, 2013.

[257] Peter Černo and František Mráz. Clearing restarting automata. In Henning Bordihn, Rudolf Freund, Markus Holzer, Martin Kutrib, and Friedrich Otto, editors, *NCMA 2009, Proc.*, volume 256 of *books@ocg.at*, pages 77–90. Österreichische Computer Gesellschaft, Wien, 2009.

[258] Peter Černo and František Mráz. Clearing restarting automata. *Fundamenta Informaticae*, 104:17–54, 2010.

[259] Peter Černo and František Mráz. Δ-clearing restarting automata and CFL. In Giancarlo Mauri and Alberto Leporati, editors, *DLT 2011, Proc.*, volume 6795 of *Lecture Notes in Computer Science*, pages 153–164. Springer, Heidelberg, 2011.

[260] Peter Černo and František Mráz. Delta-clearing restarting automata and CFL. Technical report, Faculty of Mathematics and Physics, Charles University, Prague, 2011.

[261] K. Vijay-Shanker, David J. Weir, and Aravind K. Joshi. Characterizing structural descriptions produced by various grammatical formalisms. In *25th ACL, Proc.*, pages 104–111, 1987.

[262] Burchard von Braunmühl and Rutger Verbeek. Finite-change automata. In Klaus Weihrauch, editor, *Theoretical Computer Science, 4th GI Conference, Proc*, volume 67 of *Lecture Notes in Computer Science*, pages 91–100. Springer, Heidelberg, 1979.

[263] Vojtěch Vorel. *Synchronization and Discontinuous Input Processing in Transition Systems.* PhD thesis, Faculty of Mathematics and Physics, Charles University, Prague, 2018.

[264] Qichao Wang and Yongming Li. Jumping restarting automata. In Rudolf Freund, Michal Hospodár, Galina Jirásková, and Giovanni Pighizzini, editors, *Tenth Workshop on Non-Classical Models of Automata and Applications (NCMA 2018), Proc.*, volume 332 of *books@ocg.at*, pages 181–196, Wien, 2018. Österreichische Computer Gesellschaft.

[265] Qichao Wang and Yongming Li. A hierarchy of jumping restarting automata. *Information Sciences*, 657:14, 2024.

[266] Niklaus Wirth. The programming language Pascal. *Acta Informatica*, 1:35–63, 1971.

[267] Jens Woinowski. The context-splittable normal form for Church-Rosser language systems. *Information and Computation*, 183:245–274, 2003.

[268] Andrew Chi-Chih Yao and Ronald L. Rivest. $k+1$ heads are better than k. *Journal of the Association for Computing Machinery*, 25:337–340, 1978.

[269] Anssi Yli-Jyrä. Approximating dependency grammars through intersection of star-free regular languages. *International Journal of Foundations of Computer Science*, 16:565–579, 2005.

[270] Takashi Yokomori. Grammatical inference and learning. In Carlos Martín-Vide, Victor Mitrana, and Gheorghe Păun, editors, *Formal Languages and Applications*, volume 148 of *Studies in Fuzziness and Soft Computing*, pages 507–528. Springer, Berlin, 2004.

[271] Takashi Yokomori and Satoshi Kobayashi. Learning local languages and their application to DNA sequence analysis. *IEEE Transactions on Pattern Analysis and Machine Intelligence*, 20:1067–1079, 1998.

[272] Daniel H. Younger. Recognition and parsing of context-free languages in time n^3. *Information and Control*, 10:189–208, 1967.

[273] Yechezkel Zalcstein. Locally testable languages. *Journal of Computer and System Sciences*, 6:151–167, 1972.

Index

F. Otto, *Restarting Automata*, Theory and Applications of Computability,
https://doi.org/10.1007/978-3-031-70094-1

SPRINGER NATURE

GPSR Compliance

The European Union's (EU) General Product Safety Regulation (GPSR) is a set of rules that requires consumer products to be safe and our obligations to ensure this.

If you have any concerns about our products, you can contact us on ProductSafety@springernature.com

In case Publisher is established outside the EU, the EU authorized representative is:

Springer Nature Customer Service Center GmbH
Europaplatz 3
69115 Heidelberg, Germany

The manufacturer's authorised representative in the EU is Springer Nature Customer Service Centre GmbH, Europaplatz 3, 69115 Heidelberg, Germany. If you have any concerns regarding our products, please contact ProductSafety@springernature.com

Printed and bound by CPI Group (UK) Ltd, Croydon, CR0 4YY

01/10/2026

02225915-0020